MAIN CITIES OF EUROPE

2002

- Selection of hotels and restaurants
- *Sélection d'hôtels et de restaurants*
- Auswahl an Hotels und Restaurants
- 厳選されたホテルおよびレストラン

MICHELIN

CITIES
OF
EUROPE

From 1 January 2002 the euro has replaced the national currency of twelve European countries : Austria, Belgium, Finland, France, Germany, Greece, Italy, Ireland, Luxemburg, the Netherlands, Portugal and Spain.

With this in mind, the hotels and restaurants in these countries now have their prices listed in euro, which you will find here in this fully revised 2002 edition of The Red Guide Europe.

Establishments in those countries which have not entered the euro will continue to publish their prices in the local currency. In this guide you will therefore find local currency prices for the Czech Republic, Denmark, Great Britain, Hungary, Norway, Poland, Sweden and Switzerland.

In total this guide covers 67 towns and cities in 20 European countries from which the Michelin inspectors have selected the best hotels and restaurants.

The complete selection is also available online at *www.ViaMichelin.com*, and you can e-mail us with your comments to *theredguide-europe@uk.michelin.com*. In this time of monetary transition, your thoughts are more important to us than ever, so don't forget to write to The Red Guide !

Contents

*In addition to those situated in the main cities,
restaurants renowned for their excellent cuisine
will be found in the towns printed
in light type in the list above.*

How the Guide Works

With the aim of giving the maximum amount
of information in a limited number of pages
Michelin has adopted a system of symbols.
which is renowned the world over.
Failing this system the present publication would run
to six volumes.
Judge for yourselves by comparing the descriptive text below
with the equivalent extract from the Guide in symbol form.
In the following example prices are quoted in euro (€).

La Résidence (Paul) ⌖, ℰ 09 18 21 32 43,
laresidence@wanadoo.fr
Fax 09 18 21 32 49, ≤ lake, ⌖ « Flowered garden »,
▢ ℀ – ⇆ ⇐, ⓂⓄ ☎ ᴊᴄʙ   BX a
March-November – **Meals** *(closed Sunday)* 53.50/99 –
⚏ 11.60 – **25 rm** 76/122.
Spec. Goujonnettes de sole. Poulet aux écrevisses. Profiteroles.
Wines. Vouvray, Bourgueil.

This demonstration
clearly shows that each
entry contains a great
deal of information.
The symbols are easily
learnt and knowing
them will enable
you to understand
the Guide and to choose
those establishments
that you require.

A very comfortable hotel where you will enjoy
a pleasant stay and be tempted to prolong your visit.
The excellence of the cuisine, which is personally supervised
by the proprietor Mr Paul, is worth a detour on your journey.
The hotel is in a quiet secluded setting, away
from built-up areas.
To reserve phone 09 18 21 32 43
or e-mail laresidence@wanadoo.fr ; the Fax number
is 09 18 21 32 49.
The hotel affords a fine view of the lake,
in good weather it is possible to eat outdoors.
The hotel is enhanced by an attractive flowered garden
and has an indoor swimming pool and a private tennis
court. Smoking is not allowed in certain areas
of the hotel.
Parking facilities, under cover, are available to hotel guests.
The hotel accepts payment by MasterCard, American Express,
and Japan Credit Bureau credit cards.
Letters giving the location of the hotel
on the town plan : BX a
The hotel is open from March to November
but the restaurant closes every Sunday.
The set meal prices range from 53.50 € for the lowest
to 99 € for the highest.
The cost of continental breakfast served in the bedroom is 11.60 €.
25 bedroomed hotel. The high season charges vary from
76 € for a single to 122 € for the best double or twin
bedded room. Included for the gourmet are some culinary
specialities, recommended by the hotelier : Strips of
deep-fried sole fillets, Chicken with crayfish, Choux
pastry balls filled with ice cream and covered with
chocolate sauce.
In addition to the best quality wines you will find many
of the local wines worth sampling : Vouvray, Bourgueil.

Hotels, Restaurants

Categories, standard of comfort

▲▲▲▲	XXXXX	*Luxury in the traditional style*
▲▲▲	XXXX	*Top class comfort*
▲▲	XXX	*Very comfortable*
▲▲	XX	*Comfortable*
▲	X	*Quite comfortable*
↑		*Other recommended accommodation*
	🍺	*Traditional pubs serving food*
	♈/	*Tapas bars*
M		*In its class, hotel with modern amenities*

Atmosphere and setting

▲▲▲ ... ▲	*Pleasant hotels*
XXXXX ... X, ♈/	*Pleasant restaurants*
« Park »	*Particularly attractive feature*
⟫	*Very quiet or quiet secluded hotel*
⟫	*Quiet hotel*
⩽ sea, ⁕	*Exceptional view, Panoramic view*
⩽	*Interesting or extensive view*

Cuisine

✿✿✿	*Exceptional cuisine in the country, worth a special journey*
✿✿	*Excellent cooking : worth a detour*
✿	*A very good restaurant in its category*
🅐 Meals	*The* **"Bib Gourmand"** *: Good food at moderate prices*

Hotel facilities

30 rm	*Number of rooms*
🛗 TV	*Lift (elevator) – Television in room*
⇝	*Non-smoking areas*
▤	*Air conditioning*
📞	*Minitel – modem point in the bedrooms*
✕ ⊿ ▣	*Tennis court(s) – Outdoor or indoor swimming pool*
≋s ⅙	*Sauna – Exercise room*
�/ 🦆 ⛱ₛ	*Garden – Park – Beach with bathing facilities*
⛱	*Meals served in garden or on terrace*
⚓	*Landing stage*
🚗 P P	*Garage – Car park, enclosed parking*
♿	*Bedrooms accessible to disabled people*
🏛 150	*Equipped conference room : maximum capacity*
🐕̸	*Dogs are not allowed*
without rest.	*The hotel has no restaurant*

Prices

These prices are given in the currency of the country in question. Valid for 2002 the rates shown should only vary if the cost of living changes to any great extent.

Meals

Meals 40/56	*Set meal prices*
Meals a la carte 48/64	*"a la carte" meal prices*
b.i.	*House wine included*
🍶	*Table wine available by the carafe*
🍾 24	*Price of a bottle of house wine*

Hotels

30 rm 120/239	*Lowest price for a comfortable single and highest price for the best double room.*
30 rm ⊇ 155/270	*Price includes breakfast*

Breakfast

⊇ 16	*Price of breakfast*

Credit cards

MO AE GB S ⑩ JCB VISA	*Credit cards accepted*

Service and Taxes

*Except in Finland, Greece, Hungary, Poland and Spain, prices shown are inclusive, that is to say service and V.A.T. included. In the U.K. and Ireland, **s** = service only included, **t** = V.A.T. only included. In Italy, when not included, a percentage for service is shown after the meal prices, eg. (16 %).*

Town Plans

Main conventional signs

🚩	*Tourist Information Centre*
☐ @ ● ● a	*Hotel, restaurant – Reference letter on the town plan*
■ ▪ ☐ ▨	*Place of interest and its main entrance* ⎱ *Reference letter*
🛉 ♦ 🛉 ♦ ♦ B	*Interesting church or chapel* ⎰ *on the town plan*
Thiers (R.) 🅿 🅟	*Shopping street – Public car park – Park and Ride*
——·——	*Tram*
⊡ ●	*Underground station*
→ ►	*One-way street*
🛉 ♦	*Church or chapel*
▨ ⊗ ☏	*Poste restante, telegraph – Telephone*
☐ ▨	*Public buildings located by letters :*
POL T M	*Police (in large towns police headquaters) – Theatre – Museum*
🚌 ✈ ⊞ ▭	*Coach station – Airport – Hospital – Covered market*
⁖ ■ ⊙	*Ruins – Monument, statue – Fountain*
▭ ▨ ♰♰ ⊡	*Garden, park, wood – Cemetery, Jewish cemetery*
≋ ⊾ ▨ ▨ 🏇	*Outdoor or indoor swimming pool – Racecourse*
🏴₁₈	*Golf course*
▢▪▢▪▢ ▢++++++▢	*Cable-car – Funicular*
○ ≺ ✳	*Sports ground, stadium – View – Panorama*

Names shown on the street plans are in the language of the country to conform to local signposting.

Sights

★★★	*Highly recommended*
★★	*Recommended*
★	*Interesting*

Le 1er janvier 2002 l'euro a remplacé la monnaie nationale dans douze pays européens : l'Allemagne, l'Autriche, la Belgique, l'Espagne, la Finlande, la France, la Grèce, l'Irlande, l'Italie, le Luxembourg, les Pays-Bas et le Portugal.

Les hôteliers et les restaurateurs de ces pays établissent désormais tous leurs prix en euros et vous les trouverez ainsi dans cette édition 2002 du Guide Rouge Europe entièrement mise à jour.

Les établissements des pays n'ayant pas adopté l'euro continuent quant à eux d'appliquer des tarifs en monnaie nationale. Il en est ainsi, dans ce guide, pour la République tchèque, le Danemark, la Hongrie, la Norvège, la Pologne, la Suède, la Suisse et le Royaume-Uni.

Au total, ce sont 67 villes réparties dans 20 pays que les inspecteurs Michelin vous proposent de découvrir à travers leur sélection européenne des meilleurs hôtels et restaurants.

Vous pouvez retrouver l'ensemble de cette sélection sur *www.ViaMichelin.com*, et nous faire part de vos commentaires à *theredguide-europe@uk.michelin.com*. Car plus que jamais en cette période de transition monétaire, Le Guide Rouge a besoin de vous : écrivez-nous !

Hôtels, Restaurants

Classe et confort

🏨	XXXXX	*Grand luxe et tradition*
🏨	XXXX	*Grand confort*
🏨	XXX	*Très confortable*
🏨	XX	*Bon confort*
🏨	X	*Assez confortable*
⌂		*Autres formes d'hébergement conseillées*
	🍺	*Traditionnel "pub" anglais servant des repas*
	♈/	*Bars à tapas*
M		*Dans sa catégorie, hôtel d'équipement moderne*

L'agrément

🏨 ... 🏨	*Hôtels agréables*
XXXXX ... X, ♈/	*Restaurants agréables*
« Park »	*Élément particulièrement agréable*
🐾	*Hôtel très tranquille, ou isolé et tranquille*
🐾	*Hôtel tranquille*
≤ sea, ❄	*Vue exceptionnelle, panorama*
≤	*Vue intéressante ou étendue*

La table

❁❁❁	*Une des meilleures tables du pays, vaut le voyage*
❁❁	*Table excellente, mérite un détour*
❁	*Une très bonne table dans sa catégorie*
🍝 Meals	*Le "Bib Gourmand" :*
	Repas soignés à prix modérés

L'installation

30 rm	*Nombre de chambres*
🛗 📺	*Ascenseur – Télévision dans la chambre*
🚭	*Non-fumeurs*
▭	*Air conditionné*
✆	*Prise Modem – Minitel dans la chambre*
✗ 🏊 🏊	*Tennis – Piscine : de plein air ou couverte*
⊆s 🏋	*Sauna – Salle de remise en forme*
🎠 🐾 🏖	*Jardin – Parc – Plage aménagée*
🍽	*Repas servis au jardin ou en terrasse*
⚓	*Ponton d'amarrage*
🚗 🅿 🅿	*Garage – Parc à voitures, parking clos*
🦽	*Chambres accessibles aux handicapés physiques*
🔔 150	*Salles de conférences : capacité maximum*
🐕	*Accès interdit aux chiens*
without rest.	*L'hôtel n'a pas de restaurant*

Les prix

Les prix sont indiqués dans la monnaie du pays. Établis pour l'année 2002, ils ne doivent être modifiés que si le coût de la vie subit des variations importantes.

Au restaurant

Meals 40/56	*Prix des repas à prix fixes*
Meals à la carte 48/64	*Prix des repas à la carte*
b.i.	*Boisson comprise*
🍶	*Vin de table en carafe*
🍾 24	*Prix pour une bouteille de vin de la maison*

A l'hôtel

30 rm 120/239	*Prix minimum pour une chambre d'une personne et maximum pour la plus belle chambre occupée par deux personnes*
30 rm � 135/270	*Prix des chambres petit déjeuner compris*

Petit déjeuner

⊆ 16	*Prix du petit déjeuner*

Cartes de crédit

🏧 AE GB 🅂
🅾 JCB VISA

Cartes de crédit acceptées

Service et taxes

*A l'exception de la Finlande, de la Grèce, de la Hongrie, de la Pologne et de l'Espagne, les prix indiqués sont nets. Au Royaume Uni et en Irlande, **s** = service compris, **t** = T.V.A. comprise. En Italie, le service est parfois compté en supplément aux prix des repas. Ex. : (16 %).*

Les Plans

Principaux signes conventionnels

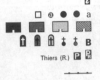

Information touristique

Hôtel, restaurant – Lettre les repérant sur le plan

Monument intéressant et entrée principale ⎱ *Lettre les repérant*
Église ou chapelle intéressante ⎰ *sur le plan*

Thiers (R.) *Rue commerçante – Parking – Parking Relais*

Tramway

Station de métro

Sens unique

Église ou chapelle

Poste restante, télégraphe – Téléphone

Édifices publics repérés par des lettres :

POL T M *Police (dans les grandes villes commissariat central) –*
Théâtre – Musée

Gare routière – Aéroport – Hôpital – Marché couvert

Ruines – Monument, statue – Fontaine

Jardin, parc, bois – Cimetière, Cimetière israélite

Piscine de plein air, couverte – Hippodrome –

Golf

Téléphérique – Funiculaire

Stade – Vue – Panorama

Les indications portées sur les plans
sont dans la langue du pays,
en conformité avec la dénomination locale.

Les curiosités

★★★ *Vaut le voyage*
★★ *Mérite un détour*
★ *Intéressante*

Der Euro hat am 1. Januar 2002 die nationale Währung in 12 europäischen Ländern ersetzt : Belgien, Deutschland, Finnland, Frankreich, Griechenland, Italien, Irland, Luxemburg, Niederlande, Österreich, Portugal und Spanien.

Die von den Hotel und Restaurantbesitzern uns übermittelten Preise, alle in Euro, finden sie nach völliger Überarbeitung im Guide Rouge Europe.

Für die Betriebe in den Ländern, welche den Euro noch nicht anwenden, geben wir weiterhin die Preise in der jeweiligen nationalen Währung an. In diesem Führer betrifft dies die: Tschechische Republik, Dänemark, Ungarn, Norwegen, Schweden, Schweiz und Groß Britannien.

Insgesamt werden Ihnen von den Michelin-Inspektoren in dieser Europäischen Auswahl, in 67 Städten und 20 Ländern, Hotels und Restaurants empfohlen.
Die gesamte Auswahl dieser Ausgabe finden Sie auch im Internet unter www.ViaMichelin.com. Besonders in diesem Jahr, sind wir durch die Währungsumstellung, auf Ihre Hinweise, mehr den je, angewiesen, Ihre Kommentare sind uns sehr wichtig.

Sie erreichen den Guide Rouge auch unter seiner E-Mail *theredguide-europe@uk.michelin.com* -Bitte Schreiben Sie uns !

Hotels, Restaurants

Klasseneinteilung und Komfort

🏨	XXXXX	*Großer Luxus und Tradition*
🏨	XXXX	*Großer Komfort*
🏨	XXX	*Sehr komfortabel*
🏨	XX	*Mit gutem Komfort*
🏨	X	*Mit Standard-Komfort*
↑		*Andere empfohlene Übernachtungsmöglichkeiten*
	🍺	*Traditionelle Pubs die Spiesen anbieten*
	🍷	*Tapas bars*
Ⓜ		*Moderne Einrichtung*

Annehmlichkeiten

🏨 ... 🏨	*Angenehme Hotels*
XXXXX ... X, 🍷	*Angenehme Restaurants*
« Park »	*Besondere Annehmlichkeit*
🦢	*Sehr ruhiges oder abgelegenes und ruhiges Hotel*
🦢	*Ruhiges Hotel*
≤ sea, ※	*Reizvolle Aussicht, Rundblick*
≤	*Interessante oder weite Sicht*

Küche

❀❀❀	*Eine der besten Küchen des Landes : eine Reise wert*
❀❀	*Eine hervorragende Küche : verdient einen Umweg*
❀	*Eine sehr gute Küche : verdient Ihre besondere Beachtung*
🍴 Meals	*Der "Bib Gourmand" :*
	Sorgfältig zubereitete preiswerte Mahlzeiten

Einrichtung

30 rm	*Anzahl der Zimmer*
🛗 📺	*Fahrstuhl – Fernsehen im Zimmer*
⊷ 🗐	*Nichtraucher – Klimaanlage*
📞	*Minitel Anschluß im Zimmer*
🎾 🏊 🏊	*Tennis – Freibad – Hallenbad*
🧖 🏋	*Sauna – Fitneßraum*
🚲 🏕	*Garten – Park – Strandbad*
🍴	*Garten-, Terrassenrestaurant*
⚓	*Bootssteg*
🚗 P P	*Garage – Parkplatz, gesicherter Parkplatz*
♿	*Für Körperbehinderte leicht zugängliche Zimmer*
🏛 150	*Konferenzräume mit Höchstkapazität*
🐕	*Hunde sind unerwünscht*
without rest.	*Hotel ohne Restaurant*

Die Preise

Die Preise sind in der jeweiligen Landeswährung angegeben. Sie gelten für das Jahr 2002 und ändern sich nur bei starken Veränderungen der Lebenshaltungskosten.

Im Restaurant

Meals 40/56	*Feste Menupreise*
Meals à la carte 48/64	*Mahlzeiten "a la carte"*
b.i.	*Getränke inbegriffen*
🍷	*Preiswerter Wein in Karaffen*
🍾 24	*Preis für eine Flasche Hauswein*

Im Hotel

30 rm 120/239	*Mindestpreis für ein Einzelzimmer und Höchstpreis für das schönste Doppelzimmer für zwei Personen.*
30 rm ⚌ 135/270	*Zimmerpreis inkl. Frühstück*

Frühstück

⚌ 16	*Preis des Frühstücks*

Kreditkarten

🆇 AE GB 🆂
🅓 JCB *VISA*   *Akzeptierte Kreditkarten*

Bedienungsgeld und Gebühren

Mit Ausnahme von Finnland, Griechenland, Ungarn, Polen und Spanien sind die angegebenen Preise Inklusivpreise. In den Kapiteln über Großbritannien und Irland bedeutet s = Bedienungsgeld inbegriffen, t = MWSt inbegriffen. In Italien wird für die Bedienung gelegentlich ein Zuschlag zum Preis der Mahlzeit erhoben, zB (16 %).

Stadtpläne

Erklärung der wichtigsten Zeichen

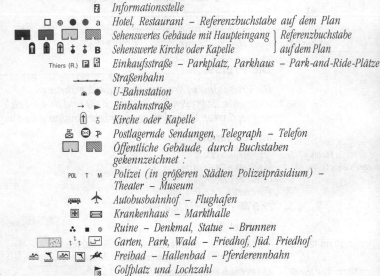

Informationsstelle	
Hotel, Restaurant – Referenzbuchstabe auf dem Plan	
Sehenswertes Gebäude mit Haupteingang ⎤ Referenzbuchstabe	
Sehenswerte Kirche oder Kapelle ⎦ auf dem Plan	
Einkaufsstraße – Parkplatz, Parkhaus – Park-and-Ride-Plätze	
Straßenbahn	
U-Bahnstation	
Einbahnstraße	
Kirche oder Kapelle	
Postlagernde Sendungen, Telegraph – Telefon	
Öffentliche Gebäude, durch Buchstaben gekennzeichnet :	
Polizei (in größeren Städten Polizeipräsidium) – Theater – Museum	
Autobusbahnhof – Flughafen	
Krankenhaus – Markthalle	
Ruine – Denkmal, Statue – Brunnen	
Garten, Park, Wald – Friedhof, Jüd. Friedhof	
Freibad – Hallenbad – Pferderennbahn	
Golfplatz und Lochzahl	
Seilschwebebahn – Standseilbahn	
Sportplatz – Aussicht – Rundblick	

Die Angaben auf den Stadtplänen erfolgen,
übereinstimmend mit der örtlichen Beschilderung,
in der Landessprache.

Sehenswürdigkeiten

★★★   Eine Reise wert
★★   Verdient einen Umweg
★   Sehenswert

2002年1月1日、ユーロが、ドイツ、オーストリア、ベルギー、スペイン、フィンランド，フランス、ギリシャ、アイルランド，イタリア、リュクセンブルグ、オランダ、ポルトガルといったヨーロッパ 12ヶ国の各国の通貨にとってかわります。
これらの国々のホテルやレストランは、これからはその料金をユーロで表示します。したがってギッド・ルージュの 2002 年版ヨーロッパ編もまったく新しくなっています。

ユーロを採用しなかった国々のホテルやレストランは、各国通貨の料金を適用し続けます。したがってこのガイドでも、チェコ、デンマーク、ハンガリー、ノルウェー、ポーランド、スエーデン、スイス、イギリスはそのようになっています。

ミシュランのインスペクターは、全部で 20 ヶ国、67 都市にわたって、ヨーロッパ最高のホテル、レストランを選りすぐってみなさまに御提案いたしております。

これらの厳選されたセレクションは www.ViaMichelin.com で御覧になれます。また、みなさまのコメントについては theredguide-europe@uk.michelin.com までお寄せください。それというのも、このような通貨移行の時期にそギッド・ルージュはみなさまを必要としているからです。どうぞお手紙をお寄せください。

ホテル　レストラン

等級と快適さ

🏨🏨🏨	XXXXX	豪華で伝統的様式
🏨🏨	XXXX	トップクラス
🏨🏨	XXX	たいへん快適
🏨	XX	快適
🏠	X	割に快適
⚑		**その他の御推薦ホテル**
	🍺	食事もできる伝統的なパブ
	⚐	タパス・バー
Ⓜ		等級内での近代的設備のホテル

居心地

🏨🏨🏨 … 🏠		居心地よいホテル
XXXXX … X, ⚐		居心地よいレストラン
« Park »		特に魅力的な特徴
🐾		大変静かなホテルまたは人里離れた静かなホテル
🐾		静かなホテル
≤ sea, ※		見晴らしがよい展望（例：海）、パノラマ
≤		素晴らしい風景

料理

✸✸✸		最上の料理、出かける価値あり
✸✸		素晴らしい、寄り道の価値あり
✸		等級内では大変おいしい料理
🍤 Meals		"Bib Gourmand"!：手頃な値段でおいしい料理

設備

30 rm	部屋数
🛗 📺	エレベーター　室内テレビ
✖	禁煙
🖭	空調設備
📞	ミニテル／モデムの回線付き
✖ 🦯 🏊	テニスコート　屋外プール　屋内プール
⚓ 🏋	サウナ　トレーニングルーム
🛶 🏖	くつろげる庭 庭園 整備された海水浴場
🍴	食事が庭またはテラスでできる
🛥	専用桟橋
🚗 🅿 🅿	駐車場　パーキング
♿	休の不自由な方のための設備あり
🏛 150	会議／研修会の出来るホテル：数字は最大収容人数
✖	犬の連れ込みおことわり
without rest.	レストランのないホテル

料金

料金は2002年のその国の貨幣単位で示してありますが、物価の変動などで変わる場合もあります。

レストラン

Meals 40/56 Meals a la carte 48/64	コース、ア・ラ・カルトそれぞれの最低料金と最高料金
b.i.	飲みもの付き
🍷	デカンター入りテーブルワインあり

ホテル

30 rm 120/239	一人部屋の最低料金と二人部屋の最高料金
30 rm 🍽 135/270	朝食込みの宿泊最低料金と最高料金

朝食

🍽 16	朝食料金

クレジット・カード

🅼 🄰🄴 🄶🄱 🅂 🅓 JCB VISA	使用可能なクレジット・カード

サービス料と税金

フィンランド、ギリシャ、ハンガリー、ポーランド、スペイン以外の国に関しては正価料金、イギリス及びアイルランドでは、s,：サービス料込み、t,：付加価値税込み、を意味する。イタリアでは、サービス料が食事料金に加算されることがある。例：(16%)

地図

主な記号

🖩	ツーリスト・インフォメーション
□ ⓐ ● ● a	ホテル・レストラン―地図上での目印番号
■ ■ ◻ ▨	興味深い歴史的建造物とその中央入口 } 地図上での
🛆 🛆 🛆 ⚑ ⚑ B	興味深い教会または聖堂 } 目印番号
Thiers (R.) 🅿 🅿	商店街　公共駐車場
—•—•—	路面電車
⬤ ●	地下鉄駅
→ ►	一方通行路
🛆 ⚐ 🛆 ✉ ☎	教会または聖堂―局留郵便、電報―電話
◻ ▨	公共建造物、記号は下記の通り
POL T M	警察(大都市では、中央警察署)―劇場―美術館、博物館
🚐 ✈ ⊞ ✉	バス・ターミナル―空港―病院―屋内市場
⁂ ■ ◉	遺跡―歴史的建造物、像―泉
▦ 🏞 ✝ ✝ ✡	庭園、公園、森林―墓地―ユダヤ教の墓地
≋ ⊿ 🏊 🏊 🏇 ⛳	屋外プール、屋内プール―競馬場―ゴルフ場
⚏⚏⚏ ⚌⚌⚌⚌	ロープウェイ―ケーブルカー
⬭ ≺ ✳	スタジアム―展望―パノラマ

地図上の名称は、地方の標識に合わせてその国の言葉で表記されていま

名所

★★★	ぜひ訪ねたいところ
★★	その次に訪ねたいところ
★	おすすめのところ

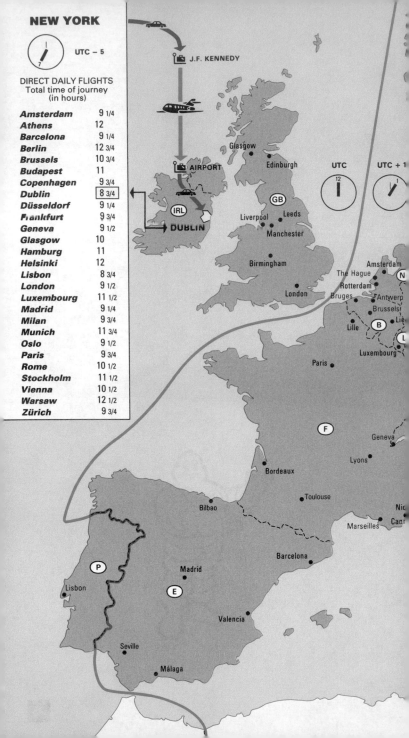

NEW YORK

UTC − 5

DIRECT DAILY FLIGHTS
Total time of journey
(in hours)

Amsterdam	9 1/4
Athens	12
Barcelona	9 1/4
Berlin	12 3/4
Brussels	10 3/4
Budapest	11
Copenhagen	9 3/4
Dublin	8 3/4
Düsseldorf	9 1/4
Frankfurt	9 3/4
Geneva	9 1/2
Glasgow	10
Hamburg	11
Helsinki	12
Lisbon	8 3/4
London	9 1/2
Luxembourg	11 1/2
Madrid	9 1/4
Milan	9 3/4
Munich	11 3/4
Oslo	9 1/2
Paris	9 3/4
Rome	10 1/2
Stockholm	11 1/2
Vienna	10 1/2
Warsaw	12 1/2
Zürich	9 3/4

J.F. KENNEDY

AIRPORT

DUBLIN

IRL

GB

Glasgow
Edinburgh
Liverpool   Leeds
Manchester
Birmingham
London

UTC

UTC + 1

Amsterdam
The Hague
Rotterdam
Bruges   Antwerp
         Brussels
Lille   B   Liè
             L
Luxembourg

N

Paris

F

Geneva
Lyons

Bordeaux

Toulouse
Bilbao
Marseilles   Nic
Can

Barcelona

P

Madrid

E

Lisbon

Valencia

Seville

Málaga

DISTANCES BY ROAD

(in kilometres)

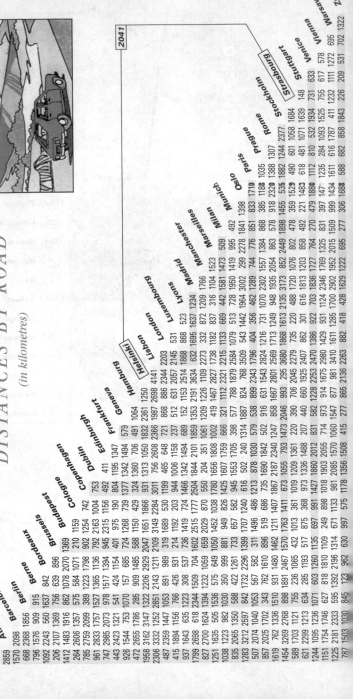

Boxed example value: **2041**

The chart is a triangular road-distance matrix. The cities (forming the diagonal headers, in order) are:

Amsterdam, Athens, Barcelona, Berlin, Berne, Bordeaux, Brussels, Budapest, Cologne, Copenhagen, Dublin, Edinburgh, Frankfurt, Geneva, Hamburg, Helsinki, Lisbon, London, Luxembourg, Lyons, Madrid, Manchester, Marseilles, Milan, Munich, Oslo, Paris, Prague, Rome, Stockholm, Strasbourg, Stuttgart, Venice, Vienna, Warsaw, Zurich.

Each row below lists the distances (km) from the named city to the preceding cities, in order (Amsterdam, Athens, Barcelona, Berlin, Berne, Bordeaux, …).

From	Distances in km (to Amsterdam, Athens, Barcelona, …)
Athens	2859
Barcelona	1570 2098
Berlin	668 2368 1856
Berne	796 1576 909 915
Bordeaux	1092 2243 560 1637 842
Brussels	206 2107 1369 756 639 896
Budapest	1412 1483 1916 862 1078 2070 1369
Cologne	264 2606 1357 575 584 1071 210 1159
Copenhagen	785 2759 2099 389 1223 1798 902 1254 742
Dublin	961 2833 1757 1527 1365 1136 792 2163 1004 753
Edinburgh	747 2985 2073 978 1517 1394 945 2315 1156 492 411
Frankfurt	443 2423 1321 541 424 1154 401 975 190 804 1195 1347
Geneva	926 1544 753 1070 157 685 724 1268 739 1377 1342 1494 579
Hamburg	472 2655 1786 285 909 1485 588 1150 429 324 1360 706 491 1064
Helsinki	1958 3162 3147 1322 2206 2929 1866 2047 1651 931 1313 1050 1832 2361 1250
Lisbon	2306 3332 1252 2851 2143 319 1211 3149 1866 3011 1756 608 987 2366 2608 4141
London	415 1894 1156 766 426 931 214 1192 203 944 1158 237 512 721 868 2145 2203
Luxembourg	937 1643 635 1223 308 537 736 1419 724 1466 1342 1494 152 689 1153 2514 1868 523

AIR LINKS *(in hours)*

31/2 not daily

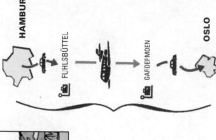

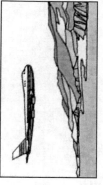

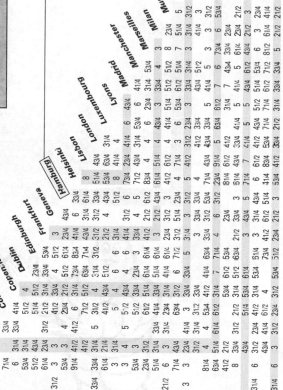

HAMBURG
FUHLSBÜTTEL
GARDERMOEN
OSLO

	Amsterdam	Athens	Barcelona	Berlin	Berne	Bordeaux	Brussels	Budapest	Cologne	Copenhagen	Dublin	Edinburgh	Frankfurt	Geneva	Hamburg	Helsinki	Lisbon	London	Luxembourg	Lyons	Madrid	Manchester	Marseilles	Milan	Munich	Oslo	Paris	Prague	Rome	Stockholm	Strasbourg	Stuttgart	Venice	Vienna	Warsaw
Athens	5																																		
Barcelona	33/4	41/2																																	
Berlin	3	8	53/4																																
Berne	31/4																																		
Bordeaux	23/4	9		81/2																															
Brussels	21/2	5	33/4	41/4	31/2	51/2																													
Budapest	4	33/4		31/2			4																												
Cologne		6	51/4	23/4		71/4		33/4																											
Copenhagen	3	5	41/2	4		6	31/4	33/4	41/4																										
Dublin	31/4	8	61/2	51/2		53/4	31/4		51/2	4																									
Edinburgh	33/4	81/2	61/4	6		51/2	43/4		51/4	51/2	23/4																								
Frankfurt	23/4	41/2	33/4	23/4		61/4	23/4	31/2	21/2	31/4	33/4	53/4																							
Geneva	3	41/2	3	41/2	31/2	3	3		41/2	33/4	4	51/2	3																						
Hamburg	23/4	61/2	51/2	21/2		53/4	3	4	23/4	21/2	51/2	61/4	23/4	43/4																					
Helsinki	51/4	91/2	71/2	5		91/4	41/2	41/2	6	31/4	73/4	83/4	41/4	6	33/4																				
Lisbon	41/2	91/2	31/4	71/2			41/2		71/2	51/2	63/4	71/4	43/4	31/4	61/4	8																			
London	23/4	53/4	41/4	7	33/4	33/4	31/4	5	31/2	4	31/4	31/2	31/2	31/2	33/4	51/4	43/4																		
Luxembourg	21/2	61/2	63/4	43/4		61/4	21/4		41/2	43/4	51/2		21/2	4	43/4	53/4	63/4	31/4																	
Lyons	31/2	71/4	3	4		3	31/4		5	4	6	6	31/4		51/2	8	41/4	4																	
Madrid	3	61/4	23/4	61/4		3	4	5	51/2	43/4	4	6	41/4	31/2	6	73/4	23/4	41/4	6	43/4															
Manchester	3	71/4	6	51/2		53/4	3		51/2	33/4	23/4	3	33/4	4	5	71/2	43/4	31/4	53/4	6	41/4														
Marseilles	41/2	53/4	23/4	71/4		23/4	31/2		61/2	51/4	61/4	61/4	41/2	21/2	61/2	83/4	4	4	6	23/4	31/4	53/4													
Milan	3	33/4	31/4	5		51/4	31/4	33/4	41/4	33/4	51/4	61/4	3	21/2	43/4	61/4	51/4	4	43/4	3	33/4	4	3												
Munich	31/4	41/4	33/4	3	21/2	6	3	31/4	23/4	31/4	41/4	61/4	23/4	31/2	3	41/2	61/2	4	41/4	51/4	51/2	51/2	8	23/4											
Oslo	3	83/4	61/4	41/4		71/4	43/4		63/4	31/2	6	71/2	31/2	51/4	23/4	4	71/4	3	6	53/4	61/2	51/4	7	51/4	5										
Paris	2	5	31/2	43/4	3	3	23/4	41/4	3	33/4	33/4	5	31/4	3	31/2	5	41/2	31/2	23/4	3	33/4	31/4	3	31/4	31/2	4									
Prague	31/2	41/2	41/4	3			31/2	31/4	31/2	33/4			3	33/4	33/4	4		41/2	33/4		43/4	51/2		41/4	3		33/4								
Rome	3	33/4	31/2	51/4		81/4	4	4	53/4	41/2	41/4	63/4	33/4	31/2	53/4	71/4	43/4	43/4	33/4	5	41/4	5	3	3	31/2	61/2	41/4	41/4							
Stockholm	4	61/4	73/4	5		63/4	51/4	61/4	61/2	31/4	7	71/4	4	6	31/2	23/4	91/4	5	63/4	61/2	7	6	73/4	6	53/4	23/4	43/4	41/4	7						
Strasbourg	21/2	71/4	63/4			41/2	21/2			53/4	61/2	53/4		23/4		81/4	61/2	41/2		31/4	7	43/4	33/4	23/4		63/4	3		43/4	81/2					
Stuttgart	33/4	8	33/4	3		8	33/4	31/2	21/2	31/4	51/2	63/4	21/2	33/4	3	61/4	43/4	33/4	41/4	5	41/4	5	61/4	23/4	21/2	5	31/4	3	51/2	51/2					
Venice	51/2	61/4	53/4	5			43/4		51/4	53/4	61/4		3	43/4	5	71/4	7	41/4	5	5	43/4	61/2	43/4	21/2	3	6	31/2		3	61/2		5			
Vienna	31/2	4	4	5	31/4	6	31/2	23/4	41/2	31/4	53/4	51/4	3	31/4	43/4	6	61/2	41/2	43/4	51/2	51/4	53/4	6	3	23/4	5	33/4	3	31/2	41/4		3	31/4		
Warsaw	43/4	51/4	73/4	41/4			43/4	41/4	61/2	4		73/4	41/2	61/2	51/4	41/4	83/4	53/4	71/4	71/4	61/2	71/2	81/2	61/4	41/4	43/4	51/4	41/4	51/2	43/4		51/4	8	4	
Zurich	3	41/2	31/4	31/4	31/4	6	3	31/2	23/4	31/2	53/4	51/2	23/4	21/2	3	53/4	41/2	33/4	21/2	31/4	33/4	33/4	5	21/2	21/2	5	33/4	33/4	31/2	41/2	21/2	21/2	33/4	3	43/4

Hamburg – Oslo: 23/4

Austria

Österreich

VIENNA

INNSBRUCK – SALZBURG

PRACTICAL INFORMATION

LOCAL CURRENCY

1 euro (€) = 0,89 USD ($) (Déc. 2001)

TOURIST INFORMATION

In Vienna: *Österreich-Information, 1040 Wien, Margaretenstr. 1, ℘ (01) 245 55, www.info.Wien.at*
Niederösterreich Touristik-Information, 1010 Wien, Fischhof 3/3, ℘ (01) 53 61 00, Fax (01) 513 80 22 30
Austrian National Holiday: *26 October*

AIRLINES

Austrian-Airlines: *1010 Wien, Kärntner Ring 18, ℘ (05) 17 89, Fax (01) 1 76 61 76 99*
Air France: *1010 Wien, Walfischgasse 1, ℘ (01) 5 02 22 21 00, Fax (01) 5 02 22 24 07*
British Airways: *1010 Wien, Kärntner Ring 10, ℘ (01) 5 06 60, Fax (01) 5 04 20 84*
Japan Airlines: *1010 Wien, Kärntner Str. 11, ℘ (01) 512 75 22, Fax (01) 512 75 54*
Lufthansa City Center: *1060 Wien, Kärntner Ring 18, ℘ (0800) 90 08 00*

FOREIGN EXCHANGE

Hotels, restaurants and shops do not always accept foreign currencies and it is wise, therefore, to change money and cheques at the banks and exchange offices which are found in the larger stations, airports and at the border.

SHOPPING and BANK HOURS

Shops are open from 9am to 6pm, but often close for a lunch break. They are closed Sunday and Bank Holidays (except the shops in railway stations).
Branch offices of banks are open from Monday to Friday between 8am and 12.30pm (in Salzburg 12am) and from 1.30pm to 3pm (in Salzburg 2pm to 4.30pm), Thursday to 5.30pm (only in Vienna).
In the index of street names, those printed in red are where the principal shops are found.

BREAKDOWN SERVICE

ÖAMTC: *See addresses in the text of each city.*
ARBÖ: *in Vienna: Mariahilfer Str. 180, ℘ (01) 89 12 10, Fax (01) 89 12 12 36 in Salzburg: Münchner Bundesstr. 9, ℘ (0662) 43 83 81, in Innsbruck: Stadlweg 7, ℘ (0512) 34 51 23*
In Austria the ÖAMTC (emergency number ℘ 120) and the ARBÖ (emergency number ℘ 123) make a special point of assisting foreign motorists. They have motor patrols covering main roads.

TIPPING

Service is generally included in hotel and restaurant bills. But in Austria, it is usual to give more than the expected tip in hotels, restaurants and cafés. Taxi-drivers, porters, barbers and theatre attendants also expect tips.

SPEED LIMITS

The speed limit in built up areas (indicated by place name signs at the beginning and end of such areas) is 50 km/h - 31 mph; on motorways 130 km/h - 80 mph and on all other roads 100 km/h - 62 mph. Driving on Austrian motorways is subject to the purchase of a road tax obtainable from border posts and ÖAMTC.

SEAT BELTS

The wearing of seat belts in Austria is compulsory for drivers and all passengers.

VIENNA
(WIEN)

Austria 🄈🄈🄖 V 4 – *pop. 1 640 000 – alt. 156 m.*

Budapest 208 ④ *– München 435* ⑦ *– Praha 292* ① *– Salzburg 292* ⑦ *– Zagreb 362* ⑥.

🛈 *Tourist-information,* ✉ *A-1010, Albertinaplatz,* 🕿 *(01) 245 55*
ÖAMTC, ✉ *A-1010, Schubertring 1,* 🕿 *(01) 71 19 90, Fax (01) 7 13 18 07*

🛅 *Freudenau 65a,* 🕿 *(01) 728 95 64,*
🛅 *Weingartenallee 22,* 🕿 *(01) 250 72*
🛈 *At Wienerherg* 🕿 *(01) 661 23 70 00*
✈ *Wien-Schwechat by* ③, 🕿 *(01) 7 00 70.*
🚗 🕿 *(01) 58 00 29 89. – Exhibition Centre (Wiener Messe), Messestr. 1,* 🕿 *(01) 727 20.*

SIGHTS

THE HOFBURG★★★ AND SOUVENIRS OF THE HABSBURGS

Around the Hofburg JR: St Michael's Square (Michaelerplatz)★ – St Michael's Gate (Michaelertor)★ – Swiss Gate (Schweizertor)★ – Josefsplatz★ – Heroe's Square (Heldenplatz)★ HJR Souvenirs of the Habsburgs; Imperial Apartments (Kaiserappartments)★ – Imperial porcelain and silver collection★. Milan centerpiece★★ – Imperial Treasury★★★; Rudolf Imperial Crown★★★; Insignia and regalia of the Holy Roman Germanic Empire★★; Reichskrone★★★ – Spanish Riding School★★ – Austrian National Library★ – Albertina Collection of Graphic Art★★ JR Other Museums in the Hofburg; Ephesos-Museum★★ (Frieze from the Parthian momument★★) Museum of Ancient Musical Instruments★★ – Collection of Arms and Armour★★ – Ethnographic Museum★ – Papyrusmuseum★

SCHÖNBRUNN★★★

Schloss Schönbrunn AZ; Tour of the Palace★★ – Carriage Museum★ – Park★★ ≤★ of the Gloriette★★ – Zoo★ – Palmenhaus★

BUILDINGS AND MONUMENTS

St. Stephen's Cathedral (Stephansdom)★★★ KR – Stephansplatz★★ – Cathedral Museum (Dom-und Diözesanmuseum)★ KR M[19] – Church of the Capucins (Kapuzinerkirche): Imperial Crypt of the Habsburg pantheon (Kaisergruft)★★ JR
Church of the Capucins (Kapuzinerkirche) : Imperial Crypt of the Habsburg pantheon (Kaisergruft)★★ JR Unters Belvedere★ CY Museum of Austrian Medieval Art (Museum für mittelalterliche Österreichische Kunst)★ – Museum of Austrian Baroque Art (Barockmuseum)★★ Oberes Belvedere★★ CY: 19 and 20C Austrian and International Art (Galerie des 19. und 20. Jahrhunderts)★★ – Staatsoper★★ JS – Church of Charles Borromero (Karlskirche)★★ CY – Burgtheater★ HR – St. Peter's Church (Peterskirche)★ JR – Church of the Jesuits (Jesuitenkirche)★ KLR – Maria am Gestade★ JP – Abbey of the Scots (Schottenstift)★, Scotsaltar★★ JPR

JUGENDSTIL AND SECESSION

Post Office Savings Bank (Postsparkasse)★ KLR – Wagner-Pavillons★ JS – Secession Pavilion (Secessionsgebäude)★★ JS – Buildings★ by Wagner on Linke Wienzeile – Wagner Villas★ (in Penzing) BYZ – St. Leopold's Church in Penzing (Kirche am Steinhof)★★ AY

STREETS, SQUARES AND PARKS

The Tour of the Ring (Rundfahrt über den Ring)★★ – Graben★ (Plague Pillar★★) JR – Donner Brunner★★ JR – Volksgarten★ HR – Spittelberg Quarter★ HS – Prater★ (Riesenrad★★) CY

MUSICAL VIENNA

Pasqualatihaus★ (Beethoven) HP 85 – Figaro-Haus★ (Mozart) KR Schubert-Museum★ BY M[5] – Haydn-Museum★ BYZ M[10] – Johann-Strauss "Gedenkstätte"★ LP – Haus der Musik★ KS

IMPORTANT MUSEUMS

Museum of Art History (Kunsthistorisches Museum)★★★ HS – Museumsquartier★★ (Leopold-Museum★) HS – Art Gallery of the Academy of Fine Arts (Gemäldegalerie der Akademie der Bildenden Künste)★★ JS – Austrian Museum of Applied and Decorative Arts (Österreichische Museum für Angewandte Kunst)★★ LR – Historical Museum of the City of Vienna (Historisches Museum der Stadt Wien)★ KS Natural History Museum (Naturhistorisches Museum)★ HS – City of Vienna Jewish Museum (Jüdisches Museum der Stadt Wien)★ JR – Museum of Military History (Heeresgeschichtliches Museum)★ CZ M[23] – Treasure Chamber of the Grand Masters (Schatzkammer des Deutschen Ordens)★ KR – Josephinum★ BY – M[24] – Sigmund Freud Museum★ BY M[25] – Tram Museum (Wiener Strassenbahnmuseum)★ CY M[3] – Clock and Watch Museum (Uhrenmuseum der Stadt Wien)★ JR M[17] – Technisches Museum★ AZ M[2]

EXCURSIONS

UNO-City★ CY – Donaupark★ CX – Donauturm ≤★★ CX – Leopoldsberg★★ ≤★★ BX – Klosterneuburg Abbey (Stift Klosterneuburg)★ (Altarpiece by Nicolas of Verdun★★); Sammlung Essl★ North: 13km – Heiligenkreuz★ South-West: 32 km by ⑥ – Grinzing★ BX – Wienerwald★ South-West by ⑥ – Heiligenstadt★ (Karl-Marx-Hof★) BX.

AUSTRIA

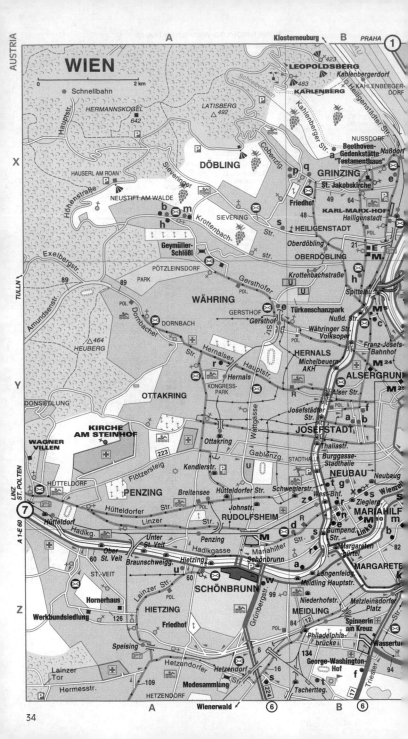

H J

ALSERGRUND

Garnisong.
Berg-gasse
Türkenstraße
Schlick-platz
Deutschmeister-Denkmal
Schotten-ring
Höf. gasse
Schwarz-spanierstr.
Wäringer Str.
Ringturm
Motivkirche
Roosevelt-platz
SIGMUND-FREUD-PARK
RING
a
POL.
b
Börse
Börse
Universitätsstr.
Garnisong.
Str. Maria- Theresien-Str.
Schotten-
Wipplingerstr.
Börsegasse
Concordiapl.
Schottentor-Universität
e h
MARIA AM GESTADE
102
f
Hohe Brücke
Gerichtsstr.
U
85
a
SCHOTTENSTIFT
95
106
Universität
PASQUALATI-HAUS
Schotten-kirche
120
Altes Rathaus
Dreimäderl-haus
Feuerwehr-museum
Römische Baureste
Felderstr.
RATHAUS
103
FREYUNG
M
Am Hof
67
105
M 17
Friedrich-Schmidt-Platz
Neues Rathaus
Rathauspl.
Luger- Ring
90
e
e
Palais Kinsky
M
13
123
Rathaus
79
Bankgasse
Herrengasse
Wallner- str.
107
PETERSKIRCHE
Lichtenfelsg.
BURG THEATER
d
Minoriten-Kirche
Herreng.
L
L
Palais Mollard-Clary
GRABEN
PESTSÄULE
Langesg.
Rathaus-park
Dr. Karl-
Minoritenplatz
70
Michaeler Kirche
15
25
116
Parlament
Theseus-Tempel
79
Bundeskanzleramt
97
c
Dr. K.- Renner-Ring
Ballhaus-pl.
MICHAELER PL.
b
JÜDISCHES MUSEUM
Auerspergstr.
VOLKSGARTEN
HOFBURG
Stallburg
92
DONNER BRUNNEN
Lerchenfelder Str.
Burgring
HELDENPLATZ
KONGRESS-ZENTRUM
JOSEFS PL.
Shlegelg.
a
Museumst.
J
Palais Trautson
NATURHISTORISCHES MUSEUM
Äußeres Burgtor
KAPUZINER-KIRCHE
87
88
Volkstheater
M
KAPUZINERGRUFT
Burg99.
Volkstheater
Neue Burg
ALBERTINA
117
b
Maria-Theresien-Platz
Glashaus
114
51
KUNSTHISTORISCHES MUSEUM
Burggarten
X 91
r
SPITTELBERG
a
Museumsquartier
Musalinplatz
Babenbergerstr.
Opern-
RING
Albertina-Platz
STAATSOPER
Siebensterng.
m
Museumsquartier
42
Nibelungeng.
ring
Kärntner
NEUBAU
Tabak-Museum
Schiller-Denkmal
Café Museum
Mariahilfer
Straße
Str
AKADEMIE DER BILDENDEN KÜNSTE
Künstler-haus
Gumpendorfer
U
SECESSIONS-GEBÄUDE
M
38
Karlsplatz
P
Theater an der Wien
42
Kunsthalle Project Center
132
WAGNER-PAVILLONS

H J

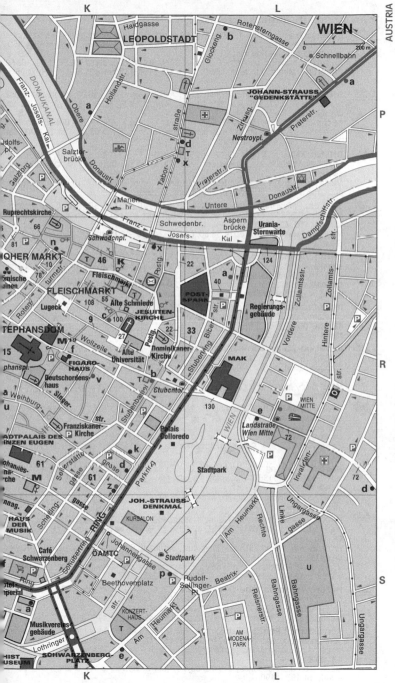

WIEN

LEOPOLDSTADT

JOHANN-STRAUSS-"GEDENKSTÄTTE"

Nestroypl.

DONAUKANAL

Franz-Josefs-Kai

Salztor-brücke

Marien-br

Ruprechtskirche

Schwedenbr.

Aspern-brücke

Urania-Sternwarte

Schwedenpl.

HOHER MARKT

FLEISCHMARKT

Fleischmarkt

Alte Schmiede

Lugeck

JESUITEN-KIRCHE

STEPHANSDOM

FIGARO-HAUS

Alte Universität

Dominikaner-Kirche

MAK

POST-SPARK.

Regierungs-gebäude

Deutschordens-haus

Franziskaner-Kirche

STADTPALAIS DES PRINZEN EUGEN

Johannes-narsche-che

HAUS DER MUSIK

Café Schwarzenberg

ÖAMTC

Palais Colloredo

Stadtpark

JOH.-STRAUSS-DENKMAL

KURSALON

Landstraße Wien Mitte

WIEN MITTE

Beethovenplatz

Rudolf-Sellinger-Pl.

Musikvereins-gebäude

KONZERT-HAUS

SCHWARZENBERG-PLATZ

HIST. MUSEUM

AM MODENA-PARK

Schnellbahn

200 m

Town Centre, city districts (Stadtbezirke) 1 - 9 :

Imperial, Kärntner Ring 16, ✉ A-1015, 𝒫 (01) 50 11 00, *hotel.imperial@luxurycollection.com, Fax (01) 50110410*, « Converted 19C palace » – |‡|, ⇔ rm, 🗏 📺 🖘 – 🏛 150.
AE ① ◯◐ VISA JCB. ❄ rest
KS a
Imperial (booking essential) (dinner only) **Meals** à la carte 58,50/76 – *Café Imperial :* **Meals** à la carte 33,80/49 – ⇆ 31 – **138 rm** 425/625 – 510/625 – 30 suites.

ANA Grand Hotel, Kärntner Ring 9, ✉ A-1010, 𝒫 (01) 51 58 00, *reservation@anagrand.com, Fax (01) 5151312*, 🍴, 𝑓ᵈ – |‡|, ⇔ rm, 🗏 📺 🖘 & 🖘 – 🏛 220. ◯◐ VISA JCB
KS f
Le ciel (closed Sunday) **Meals** 35,97 (lunch) and à la carte 51,46/59,09 – *Unkai* (Japanese) (closed Monday lunch) **Meals** 26,89 (lunch) and à la carte 17,80/63,96 – ⇆ 26 – **205 rm** 290/370 – 360/440 – 11 suites.

Bristol, Kärntner Ring 1, ✉ A-1015, 𝒫 (01) 51 51 60, *hotel.bristol@westin.com, Fax (01) 51516550* – |‡|, ⇔ rm, 🗏 📺 🖘 – 🏛 180. AE ① ◯◐ VISA JCB.
❄ rest
JS m
Meals (see also *Korso* below) *Rôtisserie Sirk :* (closed July for dinner) **Meals** à la carte 30,30/56,30 – ⇆ 28 – **140 rm** 345/450 – 10 suites.

Sacher, Philharmonikerstr. 4, ✉ A-1010, 𝒫 (01) 51 45 60, *wien@sacher.com, Fax (01) 51456810*, « Collection of valuable furniture and paintings » – |‡|, ⇔ rm, 🗏 📺 🖘 – 🏛 100. AE ① ◯◐ VISA JCB. ❄ rest
JS x
Meals 35 (lunch) and à la carte 38,50/64,50 – ⇆ 25 – **104 rm** 205/280 – 348/385 – 5 suites.

Hilton Vienna Plaza Ⓜ, Schottenring 11, ✉ A-1010, 𝒫 (01) 31 39 00, *cb_vienna-plaza@hilton.com, Fax (01) 3139022422,* Massage, 𝑓ᵈ, ⇔ – |‡|, ⇔ rm, 🗏 📺 🖘 & 🖘 – 🏛 110. AE ① ◯◐ VISA JCB. ❄ rest
JP a
La Scala (closed Saturday lunch, Sunday and Bank Holidays) **Meals** 30 (lunch) and à la carte 42/65 – ⇆ 23 – **218 rm** 276 – 312 – 31 suites.

Inter-Continental, Johannesgasse 28, ✉ A-1037, 𝒫 (01) 71 12 20, *vienna@interconti.com, Fax (01) 7134489,* ≤, 𝑓ᵈ, ⇔ – |‡|, ⇔ rm, 🗏 📺 🖘 & 🖘 – 🏛 560. AE ① ◯◐ VISA JCB
KS p
Meals à la carte 30/57 – ⇆ 22 – **453 rm** 180/228 – 220/265 – 60 suites.

Hotel im Palais Schwarzenberg, Schwarzenbergplatz 9, ✉ A-1030, 𝒫 (01) 7 98 45 15, *hotel@palais-schwarzenberg.com, Fax (01) 7984714,* « Converted 1732 baroque palace ; park », 🌳, 🍴 – |‡|, ⇔ rm, 📺 🖘 & 🖘 – 🏛 250. AE ① ◯◐ VISA JCB.
❄ rest
CY p
Meals 30,52 (lunch) à la carte 37,78/62,86 – ⇆ 27 – **44 rm** 235/380 – 265/450 – 8 suites.

Radisson SAS Palais, Parkring 16, ✉ A-1010, 𝒫 (01) 51 51 70, *sales.vienna@radissonsas.com, Fax (01) 5122216,* ⇔ – |‡|, ⇔ rm, 🗏 📺 🖘 & 🖘 – 🏛 240. AE ① ◯◐ VISA JCB. ❄ rest
KR z
Le siècle (closed Saturday, Sunday and Bank Holidays) **Meals** 31 (buffet lunch) and à la carte 43,40/52/90 – *Palais Café :* **Meals** à la carte 21/31,10 – ⇆ 22 – **247 rm** 212 – 395 – 42 suites.

Marriott, Parkring 12a, ✉ A-1010, 𝒫 (01) 51 51 80, *vienna.marriott.sales@marriott.com, Fax (01) 515186736,* Massage, 𝑓ᵈ, ⇔, ⊠ – |‡|, ⇔ rm, 🗏 📺 🖘 & 🖘 – 🏛 500. AE ① ◯◐ VISA JCB. ❄ rest
KR d
Meals (closed dinner Sunday and Monday) 26,37/45,42 and à la carte – ⇆ 21 – **313 rm** 262 – 7 suites.

Hilton, Landstraßer Hauptstr. 2 (near Stadtpark), ✉ A-1030, 𝒫 (01) 71 70 00, *do_vienna@hilton.com, Fax (01) 7128012,* ≤, 🍴 – |‡|, ⇔ rm, 🗏 📺 🖘 🖘 – 🏛 600. AE ① ◯◐ VISA JCB
LR e
Prinz Eugen (closed 29 July - 25 August, Saturday, Sunday and Bank Holidays) (dinner only) **Meals** à la carte 44,96/61/34 – *Arcadia* (Monday - Friday lunch only) **Meals** à la carte 25,64/38,46 – *Sam's* (closed 15 July - 25 August, Sunday and Monday) (dinner only) **Meals** à la carte 32,96/46,15 – ⇆ 23 – **600 rm** 205/275 – 241/311 – 19 suites.

Hilton Vienna-Danube Ⓜ, Handelskai 269, ✉ A-1020, 𝒫 (01) 7 27 77, *sales_vienna-danube@hilton.com, Fax (01) 72777199,* 🍴, 𝑓ᵈ, ⇔, ⊠ (heated), 🍴 – |‡|, ⇔ rm, 🗏 📺 🖘 🖘 – 🏛 300. AE ① ◯◐ VISA JCB. ❄ rest
CY h
Meals 27,62 (buffet lunch) and à la carte 24,88/35,71 – ⇆ 17 – **367 rm** 225 – 247.

Renaissance Penta Ⓜ, Ungargasse 60, ✉ A-1030, 𝒫 (01) 71 17 50, *rhi.viese.dom@renaissancehotels.com, Fax (01) 711758146,* 🍴, (former imperial riding school with modern hotel wing), Massage, ⇔, ⊠, 🌳 – |‡|, ⇔ rm, 🗏 📺 🖘 & 🖘 – 🏛 260. AE ① ◯◐ VISA JCB
CY a
Meals (closed dinner Sunday and Monday) 27 (buffet lunch) and à la carte 20/30 – ⇆ 17 – **342 rm** 183 – 190.

🏨 **Ambassador**, Kärntner Str. 22, ✉ A-1010, ✆ (01) 96 16 10, *office@ambassador.at*, Fax (01) 5132999 – 🛗 ⇆ 🚭 🗙 – 🚗 60. 🖭 ⓪ 🐵 𝚅𝙸𝚂𝙰 ⒿⒸⒷ 　　　JR s
Meals see also **Mörwald im Ambassador** below – ☕ 20 – **86 rm** 185/340 – 235/425.

🏨 **Das Triest** Ⓜ, Wiedner Hauptstr. 12, ✉ A-1040, ✆ (01) 58 91 80, *manager@dastri est.at*, Fax (01) 5891818, 佘, « Modern interior design », ℟, ⇔ – 🛗, ⇆ rm, 🖭 📺 🗙 – 🚗 60. 🖭 ⓪ 🐵 𝚅𝙸𝚂𝙰 ⒿⒸⒷ 　　　CY t
Meals *(closed Saturday lunch and Sunday)* (Italian rest.) à la carte 31/46 – **72 rm** ☕ 185 – 235 – 3 suites.

🏨 **Hotel de France**, Schottenring 3, ✉ A-1010, ✆ (01) 31 36 80, *defrance@austria-h otels.co.at*, Fax (01) 3195969, ⇔ – 🛗, ⇆ rm, 🖭 rest, 📺 & – 🚗 80. 🖭 ⓪ 🐵 𝚅𝙸𝚂𝙰 ⒿⒸⒷ 　　　HP b
Meals 25,64 *(buffet lunch)* and à la carte 26/40,60 – **212 rm** ☕ 149/167 – 189/240 – 8 suites.

🏨 **Arcotel Hotel Wimberger** Ⓜ, Neubaugürtel 34, ✉ A-1070, ✆ (01) 52 16 50, *wimb erger@arcotel.at*, Fax (01) 52165811, ℟, ⇔ – 🛗, ⇆ rm, 🖭 rm, 📺 🗙 & ⇐ – 🚗 60. 🖭 ⓪ 🐵 𝚅𝙸𝚂𝙰 ⒿⒸⒷ 　　　BY t
Meals 21 *(buffet lunch)* and à la carte 24,90/35,16 – **225 rm** ☕ 150 – 200 – 7 suites.

🏨 **Astron Hotel Wien Belvedere** Ⓜ without rest, Rennweg 129, ✉ 1030, ✆ (01) 2 06 11, *wien-belvedere@astron-hotels.de*, Fax (01) 2061115 – 🖭 ⓪ 🐵 𝚅𝙸𝚂𝙰 ⒿⒸⒷ ☕ 12,50 – **114 rm** 155 – 183. 　　　CY z

🏩 **Dorint Biedermeier**, Landstraßer Hauptstr. 28 (at Sünnhof), ✉ A-1030, ✆ (01) 71 67 10, *dorint.biedermeier@dorint.com*, Fax (01) 71671503, 佘, « Bedrooms furnished in the Biedermeier style » – 🛗, ⇆ rm, 🖭 📺 🗙 ⇐ – 🚗 60. 🖭 ⓪ 🐵 𝚅𝙸𝚂𝙰 ⒿⒸⒷ ⚌ rest 　　　LR d
Meals 24 *(buffet lunch)* and à la carte 31/42 – ☕ 15 – **203 rm** 149/161 – 179 – 13 suites.

🏩 **Kaiserin Elisabeth** without rest, Weihburggasse 3, ✉ A-1010, ✆ (01) 51 52 60, *info @kaiserinelisabeth.at*, Fax (01) 515267 – 🛗 📺 🖭 ⓪ 🐵 𝚅𝙸𝚂𝙰 ⒿⒸⒷ 　　　KR a
63 rm ☕ 113/160 – 193.

🏩 **Mercure Wien City** without rest, Hollandstr. 3, ✉ A-1020, ✆ (01) 21 31 30, *h1568@a ccor-hotels.com*, Fax (01) 21313230 – 🛗, ⇆ rm, 🖭 📺 & ⇐ – 🖭 ⓪ 🐵 𝚅𝙸𝚂𝙰 ⒿⒸⒷ ☕ 13 – **123 rm** 115 – 135. 　　　KP a

🏩 **König von Ungarn**, Schulerstr. 10, ✉ A-1010, ✆ (01) 51 58 40, *hotel@kvu.at*, Fax (01) 515848, 佘 – 🛗, 🖭 rm, 📺 🗙 – 🚗 15. 🖭 ⓪ 🐵 𝚅𝙸𝚂𝙰 ⒿⒸⒷ 　　　KR f
Meals *(dinner only)* à la carte 35,53/43/22 – **55 rm** ☕ 130/150 – 182 – 8 suites.

🏩 **K. u. K. Hotel Maria Theresia** without rest, Kirchberggasse 6, ✉ A-1070, ✆ (01) 5 21 23, *kk.maria.theresia@kuk.at*, Fax (01) 5212370 – 🛗, ⇆ rm, 🖭 📺 🗙 – 🚗 40. 🖭 ⓪ 🐵 𝚅𝙸𝚂𝙰 ⒿⒸⒷ 　　　HS a
123 rm ☕ 149 – 198.

🏩 **K. u. K. Palais Hotel** without rest, Rudolfsplatz 11, ✉ A-1010, ✆ (01) 5 33 13 53, *kk.palais.hotel@kuk*, Fax (01) 533135370 – 🛗, ⇆ rm, 🖭 📺 🗙. 🖭 ⓪ 🐵 𝚅𝙸𝚂𝙰 ⒿⒸⒷ 　　　JP h
66 rm ☕ 149/173 – 198.

🏩 **Starlight Suiten** Ⓜ without rest, Salzgries 12, ✉ A-1010, ✆ (01) 5 35 92 22, *rese rvation@starlighthotel.co.at*, Fax (01) 535922211, ℟, ⇔ – 🛗 ⇆ 🖭 📺 🗙 ⇐. 🖭 ⓪ 🐵 　　　JP e
☕ 12 – **49 suites** ☕ 129 – 162.

🏩 **Sofitel** Ⓜ, Am Heumarkt 35, ✉ A-1030, ✆ (01) 71 61 60, *h1276@accor-hotels.com*, Fax (01) 71616844 – 🛗, ⇆ rm, 🖭 📺 🗙 ⇐ – 🚗 120. 🖭 ⓪ 🐵 𝚅𝙸𝚂𝙰 ⒿⒸⒷ ⚌ rest 　　　KS e
Meals à la carte 23/38,50 – ☕ 17 – **211 rm** 168/195 – 183/210.

🏩 **Astron Suite Hotel** Ⓜ without rest, Mariahilfer Str. 78, ✉ A-1070, ✆ (01) 5 24 56 00, *wien-atterseehaus@astron-hotels.de*, Fax (01) 524560015, ℟, ⇔ – 🛗 ⇆ 🖭 📺 🗙 & ⇐. 🖭 ⓪ 🐵 𝚅𝙸𝚂𝙰 ⒿⒸⒷ 　　　BY x
☕ 13 – **73 suites** 122/155 – 144/181.

🏩 **Arkadenhof** Ⓜ without rest, Viriotgasse 5, ✉ A-1090, ✆ (01) 3 10 08 37, *manage ment@arkadenhof.com*, Fax (01) 3107686 – 🛗 ⇆ 🖭 📺 ⇐ – 🚗 20. 🖭 ⓪ 🐵 𝚅𝙸𝚂𝙰 　　　BY c
44 rm ☕ 115/129 – 151.

🏩 **Mercure Nestroy** Ⓜ, Rotensterngasse 12, ✉ A-1020, ✆ (01) 21 14 00, *nestroy@h otel-mercure.co.at*, Fax (01) 211407, ⇔ – 🛗 ⇆ 📺 🗙 ⇐ – 🚗 70. 🖭 ⓪ 🐵 𝚅𝙸𝚂𝙰 LP b
Meals *(closed Sunday)* à la carte 200/400 – ☕ 13 – **87 rm** 119/133 – 140/155 – 4 suites.

🏩 **Astoria**, Kärntner Str. 32, ✉ A-1015, ✆ (01) 51 57 70, *astoria@austria-trend.at*, Fax (01) 5157782, (19C house with period interior) – 🛗, ⇆ rm, 📺 🗙 – 🚗 40. 🖭 ⓪ 🐵 𝚅𝙸𝚂𝙰 ⒿⒸⒷ 　　　JR r
Meals *(closed Saturday and Sunday)* à la carte 25/36 – **118 rm** ☕ 135/164 – 190.

🏩 **Lassalle** Ⓜ without rest, Engerthstr. 173, ✉ A-1020, ✆ (01) 21 31 50, *lassalle@aus tria.trend.at*, Fax (01) 21315100, ⇔, 🌿 – 🛗 ⇆ 📺 🗙 & ⇐ – 🚗 40. 🖭 ⓪ 🐵 𝚅𝙸𝚂𝙰 ⒿⒸⒷ 　　　CY r
140 rm ☕ 113/125 – 149 – 4 suites.

🏨🏨 **Erzherzog Rainer**, Wiedner Hauptstr. 27, ✉ A-1040, ℘ (01) 50 11 10, *rainer@sch ick-hotels.com, Fax (01) 50111350* – 🛗, ✳️ rm, 🍽 rest, 📺 – 🛋 30. 🆎 ① 🐴 🆎 💳 JCB   CY g
Meals *(closed dinner Sunday and Monday)* à la carte 19/33 – **84 rm** ☐ 99/131 – 123/179.

🏨🏨 **Holiday Inn Vienna City** Ⓜ, Margaretenstr. 53, ✉ A-1050, ℘ (01) 5 88 50, *vien na.city@holiday-inn.at, Fax (01) 58850899*, 🏡 – 🛗, ✳️ rm, 📺 🗲 👌 🚗 – 🛋 40. 🆎 ① 🐴 💳 JCB. ✳️ rest   BY m
Meals à la carte 24/35 – ☐ 15 – **101 rm** 140/170 – 210.

🏨🏨 **Stefanie**, Taborstr. 12, ✉ A-1020, ℘ (01) 21 15 00, *stefanie@schick-hotels.com, Fax (01) 21150160*, 🏡 – 🛗 ✳️, 🍽 rm, 📺 🗲 🚗 – 🛋 70. 🆎 ① 🐴 💳 JCB
Meals à la carte 22,71/36,26 – **130 rm** ☐ 123/137 – 159/193.   KLP d

🏨🏨 **InterCityHotel** Ⓜ, Mariahilferstr. 122, ✉ A-1070, ℘ (01) 52 58 50, *wien@intercity hotel.at, Fax (01) 52585111*, 🏡 – 🛗, ✳️ rm, 📺 🗲 👌 – 🛋 60. 🆎 ① 🐴 💳 JCB
Meals à la carte 15,70/29,70 – ☐ 13 – **179 rm** 101/106 – 126/131.   BY r

🏨🏨 **Falkensteiner Hotel Palace**, Margaretenstr. 92, ✉ A-1050, ℘ (01) 54 68 60, *pala ce@falkensteiner.com, Fax (01) 5468686*, 🍸 – 🛗 🍽 📺 🗲 🚗 – 🛋 60. 🆎 ① 🐴 💳 ✳️ rest – **Meals** à la carte 15,10/39,20 – **117 rm** ☐ 103 – 140.   BZ b

🏨🏨 **Amadeus** without rest, Wildpretmarkt 5, ✉ A-1010, ℘ (01) 5 33 07 30, *amadeus.vi enna@mcnon.com, Fax (01) 533873838* – 🛗 🍽 📺 🗲 🗲. ① 🐴 💳 ✳️.   JR y
closed 20 to 26 December – **30 rm** ☐ 85/120 – 160.

🏨🏨 **Mercure Europaplatz** Ⓜ, Matrosengasse 6, ✉ A-1060, ℘ (01) 59 90 10, *H1707@a ccor-hotels.com, Fax (01) 5976900* – 🛗, ✳️ rm, 🍽 📺 🗲 👌 🚗 – 🛋 40. 🆎 ① 🐴 💳 JCB   BY n
Meals à la carte 20/34 – ☐ 13 – **210 rm** 105/115 – 125/135 – 5 suites.

🏨🏨 **City-Central** without rest, Taborstr. 8, ✉ A-1020, ℘ (01) 21 10 50, *city.central@sc hick-hotels.com, Fax (01) 21105140* – 🛗 ✳️ 🍽 📺 🗲 👌 🅿. 🆎 ① 🐴 💳 JCB
58 rm ☐ 131/166 – 193.   KP x

🏨🏨 **Am Parkring**, Parkring 12, ✉ A-1015, ℘ (01) 51 48 00, *parkring@schick-hotels.com, Fax (01) 5148040*, ≼ Vienna – 🛗, ✳️ rm, 🍽 📺 🚗 – 🛋 20. 🆎 ① 🐴 💳 ✳️ rest   KR k
Meals à la carte 32/43,50 – **64 rm** ☐ 130/200 – 210 – 8 suites.

🏨🏨 **Kummer**, Mariahilfer Str. 71a, ✉ A-1060, ℘ (01) 5 88 95, *kummer@austria-hotels.c o.at, Fax (01) 5878133* – 🛗, ✳️ rm, 📺 🗲. 🆎 ① 🐴 💳 JCB   BY s
Meals à la carte 19,76/37,79 – **100 rm** ☐ 140/207 – 215.

🏨🏨 **Mercure Wien Zentrum**, Fleischmarkt 1a, ✉ A-1010, ℘ (01) 53 46 00, *h0781@a ccor-hotels.com, Fax (01) 53460232* – 🛗, ✳️ rm, 🍽 📺 🗲 👌. 🆎 ① 🐴 💳 JCB
Meals à la carte 22/30 – ☐ 13 – **154 rm** ☐ 125 – 145.   KR n

🏨🏨 **Capricorno** without rest, Schwedenplatz 3, ✉ A-1010, ℘ (01) 53 33 10 40, *caprico rno@schick-hotels.com, Fax (01) 53376714* – 🛗 📺 🗲 🚗 🅿. 🆎 ① 🐴 💳 JCB
46 rm ☐ 123 – 160.   KR x

🏨🏨 **Europa**, Kärntner Str. 18, ✉ A-1010, ℘ (01) 51 59 40, *europa.wien@austria.at, Fax (01) 51594888* – 🛗 🍽 📺 ☎. 🆎 ① 🐴 💳 JCB   JS a
Meals à la carte 24/36,52 – **116 rm** ☐ 135/163 – 190.

🏨 **Ibis Messe** Ⓜ, Lassallestr. 7a, ✉ A-1020, ℘ (01) 21 77 00, *h2736@accor-hotels.com, Fax (01) 21770555* – 🛗, ✳️ rm, 🍽 📺 🗲 👌 – 🛋 170. 🆎 ① 🐴 💳 JCB   CY b
Meals 15/25 – ☐ 9 – **166 rm** 59 – 74.

🏨 **Ibis Wien Mariahilf**, Mariahilfer Gürtel 22, ✉ A-1060, ℘ (01) 5 99 98, *h0796@accor-h otels.com, Fax (01) 5979090* – 🛗, ✳️ rm, 🍽 📺 🗲 🚗 – 🛋 120. 🆎 ① 🐴 💳 JCB
Meals à la carte 13,81/21,66 – ☐ 9 – **341 rm** 64/69 – 79/84.   BY e

🍴🍴🍴🍴 **Steirereck**, Rasumofskygasse 2/corner Weißgerberlände, ✉ A-1030, ℘ (01) 7 13 31 68, *wien@steirereck.at, Fax (01) 71351682* – 🍽. 🆎 ① 🐴 💳   CY c
closed Saturday, Sunday and Bank Holidays – **Meals** (booking essential) (outstanding wine list, tour of the wine-cellar possible) 31,25 *(lunch)*/67,58 and à la carte
Spec. Gänseleber warm oder kalt. Pogusch Lamm. Variation von Eis und Sorbet.

🍴🍴🍴🍴 **Korso** - Hotel Bristol, Kärntner Ring 1, ✉ A-1010, ℘ (01) 51 51 65 46, *Fax (01) 51516550* – 🍽. 🆎 ① 🐴 💳 JCB.   JS m
closed 3 weeks August and Saturday lunch – **Meals** 37 *(lunch)* and à la carte 59/83,50
Spec. Riesling-Kalbsbeuscherl. Gefüllte Bauernente. Gebratenes Lammkarree.

🍴🍴🍴 **Mörwald im Ambassador**, Kärntner Str. 22, ✉ A-1010, ℘ (01) 96 16 10, *Fax (01) 5132999.* 🆎 ① 🐴 💳 ✳️   JR s
Meals 14,17 *(lunch)* à la carte 23,07/52,38.
Spec. Szege diner Hummerkrautfleisch. Milchferkelrücken mit Weisskrautknödeln. Feines Griesskoch.

🍴🍴🍴 **Drei Husaren**, Weihburggasse 4, ✉ A-1010, ℘ (01) 51 21 09 20, *restaurant@dreih usaren.at, Fax (01) 512109218* – 🆎 ① 🐴 💳 JCB   KR u
Meals 32,70 *(lunch)* and à la carte 53,40/74,11.

XXX **Grotta Azzurra**, Babenbergerstr. 5, ✉ A-1010, ✆ (01) 5 86 10 44, *office@grotta
-azzurra.at, Fax (01) 586104415* – **AE** ⓞ **MO** **VISA** **JCB**   HS s
closed 24 to 26 December – **Meals** (Italian) 20,88 *(lunch)* and à la carte 26,89/45,36.

XXX **Steirer Stub'n**, Wiedner Hauptstr. 111, ✉ A-1050, ✆ (01) 5 44 43 49, *steirerstube
n@chello.at, Fax (01) 5440888* – ▤. **AE** ⓞ **MO** **VISA**   BZ k
closed Sunday and Bank Holidays – **Meals** (booking essential) 23,44 and à la carte
25,34/33,69.

XX **Selina**, Laudongasse 13, ✉ A-1080, ✆ (01) 4 05 64 04, *Fax (01) 4080459* – **AE** ⓞ ● **MO**
VISA **JCB**   BY f
closed Sunday and Bank Holidays – **Meals** 26,50 *(lunch)* and à la carte 32,70/46,50.

XX **Palais Daun Kinsky**, Freyung 4, ✉ A-1010, ✆ (01) 5 32 62 71 11, *palaisdaunkinsk
y@haslauer.at, Fax (01) 532627150*, 斎 – **AE** ⓞ **MO** **VISA**   JR e
closed Sunday – **Meals** à la carte 38,50/51.

XX **Walter Bauer**, Sonnenfelsgasse 17, ✉ A-1010, ✆ (01) 5 12 98 71, *Fax (01) 5129871*
– **AE** ⓞ   KR c
*closed easter, 20 July - 18 August, 21 to 26 December, Saturday, Sunday and Monday
lunch* – **Meals** (booking essential) à la carte 33,33/49,81.

XX **Vestibül**, Dr. Karl-Lueger-Ring 2 (at Burgtheater), ✉ A-1010, ✆ (01) 5 32 49 99, *rest
aurant@vestibuel.at, Fax (01) 532499910* – **MO** **VISA**   HR d
closed Saturday lunch, Sunday and Bank Holidays – **Meals** à la carte 23,50/43.

XX **Novelli**, Bräunerstr. 11, ✉ A-1010, ✆ (01) 5 13 42 00, *novelli@haslauer.at,
Fax (01) 51342001*, 斎 – **AE** ⓞ **MO** **VISA**   JR b
closed Sunday – **Meals** (Italian) (booking essential) à la carte 33/56,50.

XX **Chrinor**, Kirchengasse 21, ✉ A-1070, ✆ (01) 5 22 32 36, *chrinor@chrinor.at,
Fax (01) 522323611* – **MO** **VISA**   BY g
closed Sunday and Bank Holidays – **Meals** *(dinner only)* à la carte 24,20/35,09.

XX **Piaristenkeller**, Piaristengasse 45, ✉ A-1080, ✆ (01) 4 06 01 93, *restaurant@piari
stenkeller.co.at, Fax (01) 4064173*, 斎, « Historical interior with Imperial hat and wine
museum » – **AE** ⓞ **MO** **VISA** **JCB**   BY a
closed Sunday – **Meals** *(dinner only)* (booking essential) à la carte 26,53/44,47.

XX **Kupferdachl**, Schottengasse 7 (first floor, entrance Mölker Bastei), ✉ A-1010, ✆ (01)
5 33 93 81 14, *office@leupold.at, Fax (01) 53393814* – **AE** ⓞ **MO** **VISA** **JCB**   HP a
closed 25 to 26 Dezember – **Meals** à la carte 16,50/37,20.

XX **Schubertstüberln**, Schreyvogelgasse 4, ✉ A-1010, ✆ (01) 5 33 71 87,
Fax (01) 5353546, 斎 – **AE** ⓞ **MO** **VISA** **JCB**   HR e
closed Sunday – **Meals** à la carte 27/43.

XX **Salut**, Wildpretmarkt 3, ✉ A-1010, ✆ (01) 5 33 13 22, *Fax (01) 5331322* – **AE** ⓞ ● **MO**
VISA   JR y
closed 1 to 21 August, Sunday, Monday and Bank Holidays – **Meals** à la carte 26,93/41,77.

XX **Plachutta**, Wollzeile 38, ✉ A-1010, ✆ (01) 5 12 15 77, *wollzeile@plachutta.at,
Fax (01) 512157720*, 斎 – ▤. **AE** ⓞ **MO** **VISA**   KR b
Meals (booking essential) à la carte 33,80/38,30.

XX **Cantinetta Antinori**, Jasomirgottstrasse 3, ✉ A-1010, ✆ (01) 5 33 77 22, *cantinc
tta.antinori@aon.at, Fax (01) 533772211* – **AE** ⓞ **MO** **VISA**   KR s
Meals (Italian) (booking essential) à la carte 30,05/42,12.

XX **Fadinger**, Wipplingerstr. 29, ✉ A-1010, ✆ (01) 5 33 43 41, *restaurant@fadinger.at,
Fax (01) 5324451* – **VISA**   JP f
closed Saturday, Sunday and Bank Holidays – **Meals** (booking essential) 15 *(lunch)* and
à la carte 22,34/46,52.

XX **Enoteca Frizzante**, Kumpfgasse 3, ✉ A-1010, ✆ (01) 5 13 07 47, *Fax (01) 5133109*,
斎 – **AE** ⓞ **MO** **VISA**   KR v
closed 24 to 30 December, Sunday and Bank Holidays – **Meals** (Italian) à la carte
25,64/34,43.

X **Tempel**, Praterstr. 56, ✉ A-1020, ✆ (01) 2 14 01 79, *tempel@i-one.at,
Fax (01) 2140179* – ⓞ **MO** **VISA**   LP a
*closed 2 weeks end December - early January, 2 weeks August - September, Saturday
lunch, Sunday and Monday* – **Meals** à la carte 24,54/37.

X **Aioli**, Stephansplatz 12 (3th floor), ✉ A-1010, ✆ (01) 532 03 73, *aioli@doco.com,
Fax (01) 5320575* – ▤. **VISA**   JR c
Meals à la carte 22,71/34,16.

X **Schnattl**, Lange Gasse 40, ✉ A-1080, ✆ (01) 4 05 34 00, *Fax (01) 4053400* – **AE** ⓞ
MO   BY b
closed 2 weeks end August, 2 weeks April, Saturday and Sunday – **Meals** à la
carte 27/35.

X **Zu ebener Erde und erster Stock**, Burggasse 13, ✉ A-1070, ✆ (01) 5 23 62 54
– ▤. 🅰🅴 𝗩𝗜𝗦𝗔   HS b
*closed 1 - 6 January, 1 to 9 February, 5 to 25 August, Saturday lunch, Sunday, Monday
and Bank Holidays* – **Meals** à la carte 25,80/31,50.

X **Hedrich**, Stubenring 2, ✉ A-1010, ✆ (01) 5 12 95 88   LR a
🍴 *closed August, Saturday, Sunday and Bank Holidays* – **Meals** à la carte 23,44/34,06.

City districts (Stadtbezirke) 10 - 15 :

🏨 **Holiday Inn Vienna South** M, Triester Str. 72, ✉ A-1100, ✆ (01) 6 05 30, *info
@ holiday-inn.co.at, Fax (01) 60530580*, ≤, 🏡 – |󰀀|, ↳≠ rm, ▤ 📺 🆚 & 🚗 – 🅰 420.
🅰🅴 ⓞ 🆚🅾 𝗩𝗜𝗦𝗔 🅹🅲🅱   BZ f
Meals 26 *(buffet lunch)* and à la carte 27,50/38 – ☕ 17 – **174 rm** 193 – 207 –
4 suites.

🏨 **Renaissance Wien**, Ullmannstr. 71, ✉ A-1150, ✆ (01) 89 10 20, *renaissance.vienn
a.viehw.@ renaissancehotels.com, Fax (01) 89102100*, 𝐼₅, ≦ₛ, ⬚ – |󰀀|, ↳≠ rm, ▤ 📺 🆚
& 🚗 – 🅰 200. 🅰🅴 ⓞ 🆚🅾 𝗩𝗜𝗦𝗔 🅹🅲🅱   BZ a
Orangerie : **Meals** à la carte 32,60/47,60 – *Allegro :* **Meals** 31/37,80 (buffet only) – ☕
19 – **309 rm** 215 – 237 – 3 suites.

🏨 **Gartenhotel Altmannsdorf** ⌂, Hoffingergasse 26, ✉ A-1120, ✆ (01) 8 01 23,
office@ gartenhotel.com, Fax (01) 8012351, 🏡, Park, ≦ₛ – |󰀀|, ↳≠ rm, 📺 🚗 – 🅰 60.
🅰🅴 ⓞ 🆚🅾 𝗩𝗜𝗦𝗔. ✂ rest   AZ s
Meals à la carte 29,30/39,92 – **95 rm** ☕ 120/127 – 152.

🏨 **Bosei** M ⌂, Gutheil-Schoder-Gasse 9, ✉ A-1100, ✆ (01) 6 61 06, *bosei@ austria-tre
nd.at, Fax (01) 6610699* – |󰀀|, ↳≠ rm, 📺 🅿. – 🅰 200. 🅰🅴 ⓞ 🆚🅾 𝗩𝗜𝗦𝗔 🅹🅲🅱   BZ t
Meals à la carte 22,90/31 – **193 rm** ☕ 108 – 134 – 8 suites.

🏨 **Favorita** M *without rest*, Laxenburger Str. 8, ✉ A-1100, ✆ (01) 60 14 60, *favorita
@ austria-trend.at, Fax (01) 60146720*, ≦ₛ – |󰀀| 📺 🚗 – 🅰 150. 🅰🅴 ⓞ 🆚🅾 𝗩𝗜𝗦𝗔 🅹🅲🅱
161 rm ☕ 108 – 134 – 3 suites.   CZ n

🏨 **Kaiserpark-Schönbrunn**, Grünbergstr. 11, ✉ A-1120, ✆ (01) 8 13 86 10, *kaiserp
ark@ co.at, Fax (01) 8138183* – |󰀀|, ↳≠ rm, ▤ 📺 – 🅰 20. 🅰🅴 ⓞ 🆚🅾 𝗩𝗜𝗦𝗔. ✂ restAZ w
Meals *(dinner only)* à la carte 16/33 – **45 rm** ☕ 65/76 – 102/130.

🏨 **Dorint Am Europaplatz**, Felberstr. 4, ✉ A-1150, ✆ (01) 98 11 10, *info.viebud@ d
orint.com, Fax (01) 98111930*, ≦ₛ – |󰀀|, ↳≠ rm, 📺 🆚 & 🚗 – 🅰 140. 🅰🅴 ⓞ 🆚🅾 𝗩𝗜𝗦𝗔.
✂ rest   BY z
Meals à la carte 20,50/33 – ☕ 15 – **253 rm** ☕ 137 – 148.

🏠 **Reither** *without rest*, Graumanngasse 16, ✉ A-1150, ✆ (01) 8 93 68 41, *hotel.reithe
r@ aon.at, Fax (01) 8936835*, ≦ₛ, ⬚ – |󰀀| ↳≠ 📺 🚗. 🅰🅴 ⓞ 🆚🅾 𝗩𝗜𝗦𝗔   BZ r
closed 22 to 27 December – **50 rm** ☕ 85/100 – 125.

XXX **Altwienerhof** *with rm*, Herklotzgasse 6, ✉ A-1150, ✆ (01) 8 92 60 00, *altwienerho
f@ netway.at, Fax (01) 89260008*, « Winter garden, courtyard-terrace » – |󰀀| 📺 🚗. 🅰🅴
ⓞ 🆚🅾 𝗩𝗜𝗦𝗔   BZ s
closed 6 to 24 January – **Meals** *(closed Saturday lunch and Sunday)* (outstanding wine list)
22 *(lunch)* and à la carte 43,70/64,40 – **22 rm** ☕ 60 – 90.

XX **Vikerl's Lokal**, Würfelgasse 4, ✉ A-1150, ✆ (01) 8 94 34 30, *Fax (01) 8924183* –
🍴 𝗩𝗜𝗦𝗔   BYZ d
closed Sunday dinner and Monday – **Meals** à la carte 23,07/37,36.

XX **Hietzinger Bräu**, Auhofstr. 1, ✉ A-1130, ✆ (01) 87 77 08 70, *hietzing@ plachutta.at,
Fax (01) 877708722*, 🏡 – ▤. 🅰🅴 ⓞ 🆚🅾 𝗩𝗜𝗦𝗔   AZ u
closed 15 July - 15 August – **Meals** *(mainly boiled beef dishes)* (booking essential) à la carte
31,70/40,70.

City districts (Stadtbezirke) 16 - 19 :

🏨 **Landhaus Fuhrgassl-Huber** ⌂ *without rest*, Rathstr. 24, ✉ A-1190, ✆ (01)
4 40 30 33, *Fax (01) 4402714*, « Country house atmosphere », 🐾 – |󰀀| 📺 🆚 🚗 🅿. 🅰🅴
🆚🅾 𝗩𝗜𝗦𝗔   AX m
closed 1 week February – **36 rm** ☕ 70/77 – 107/115.

🏠 **Jäger** *without rest*, Hernalser Hauptstr. 187, ✉ A-1170, ✆ (01) 48 66 62 00, *hotelja
eger@ aon.at, Fax (01) 48666208* – |󰀀| 📺 🆚. 🅰🅴 ⓞ 🆚🅾 𝗩𝗜𝗦𝗔   AY r
18 rm ☕ 75/99 – 105/125.

🏠 **Celtes** *without rest*, Celtesgasse 1, ✉ A-1190, ✆ (01) 4 40 41 51, *hotel.celtes@ surf
eu.at, Fax (01) 4404151116* – |󰀀| 📺 🆚. 🅰🅴 ⓞ 🆚🅾 𝗩𝗜𝗦𝗔   AX b
16 rm ☕ 70 – 109/155.

🏠 **Schild** *without rest*, Neustift am Walde 97, ✉ A-1190, ✆ (01) 44 04 04 40, *office@h
otel-schild.at, Fax (01) 4404000*, 🐾 – |󰀀| 📺 🅿. – 🅰 20. 🅰🅴 ⓞ 🆚🅾 𝗩𝗜𝗦𝗔   AX h
30 rm ☕ 69/71 – 115.

XX **Eckel**, Sieveringer Str. 46, ✉ A-1190, ☎ (01) 3 20 32 18, *restaurant.eckel@aon.at*, Fax (01) 3206660, 🏠 – 🗚 ⓞ *VISA*　　　　　　　　　　　　　　　　　AX s
closed 24 December to mid January, 2 weeks August, Sunday and Monday – **Meals** à la carte 30,76/43,95.

XX **Plachutta** with rm, Heiligenstädter Str. 179, ✉ A-1190, ☎ (01) 3 70 41 25, *nussdor f@plachutta.at*, Fax (01) 370412520, 🏠 – 📺. 🗚 ⓞ ⓜⓞ *VISA*　　　　　　　BX e
closed 2 weeks July - August – **Meals** (mainly boiled beef dishes) à la carte 32/46 – ☐ 7 – **4 rm** 43 – 72.

XX **Sailer**, Gersthofer Str. 14, ✉ A-1180, ☎ (01) 4 79 21 21, Fax (01) 479212118, 🏠 – 🗚 ⓞ ⓜⓞ *VISA*　　　　　　　　　　　　　　　　　　　　　　　　AY e
closed 24 to 25 December – **Meals** à la carte 30,67/43,46.

City district (Stadtbezirk) 22 :

🏨 **Crowne Plaza** Ⓜ, Wagramer Str. 21, ✉ A-1220, ☎ (01) 26 02 00, *crowneplazavien na@gc.com*, Fax (01) 2602020, 🍴👄, ☎ – 🛗, 🔆 rm, 🗐 📺 🌫 🔥 🚗 – 🏛 300. 🗚 ⓞ ⓜⓞ *VISA* ⒿⒸⒷ. ✂ rest　　　　　　　　　　　　　　　　　　　　CY v
Meals 18 *(lunch)* and à la carte 20,30/34,30 – ☐ 18 – **252 rm** 175 – 235 – 3 suites.

🏨 **Donauzentrum** Ⓜ without rest, Wagramer Str. 83, ✉ A-1220, ☎ (01) 20 35 54 50, *donauzentrum@austria-trend.at*, Fax (01) 2035545183, ☎ – 🛗 🔆 📺 🌫 🚗 – 🏛 60. 🗚 ⓞ ⓜⓞ *VISA* ⒿⒸⒷ　　　　　　　　　　　　　　　　　　　　　　CX b
137 rm ☐ 113 – 149.

XXXX **Mraz u. Sohn**, Wallensteinstr. 59, ✉ A-1200, ☎ (01) 3 30 45 94, Fax (01) 3501536, 🏠
❀　– 🕵. ⓞ ⓜⓞ *VISA*　　　　　　　　　　　　　　　　　　　　　　CY s
closed 3 weeks August, 24 December - 7 January, Saturday, Sunday and Bank Holidays – **Meals** (booking essential) à la carte 36,63/54,94
Spec. Gebratene Gänseleber mit Marillenmarmeladepalatschinken. Oxenfilet mit Rotwein-zwetschken und zweierlei Sellerie. Valhrona-Schokoladendessert.

XX **Sichuan**, Arbeiterstrandbadstr. 122, ✉ A-1220, ☎ (01) 2 63 57 13, *info@sichuan.at*, Fax (01) 2633714, 🏠, « Chinese garden » – ⓞ ⓜⓞ *VISA*　　　　　　　　CX a
Meals (Chinese) 8,72 *(lunch)* and à la carte 15,77/22,17.

Heurigen and Buschen-Schänken (wine gardens) – *(mostly self-service, hot and cold dishes from buffet, prices according to weight of chosen meals, therefore not shown below. Buschen-Schänken sell their own wines only)* :

X **Oppolzer**, Himmelstr. 22, ✉ A-1190, ☎ (01) 3 20 24 16, *mtoppolzer@compuserve.c om*, Fax (01) 320241621, « Garden » – *VISA*　　　　　　　　　　　　BX p
closed 1 week Christmas and Sunday – **Meals** (dinner only) (buffet only) à la carte 12,99/18,89.

X **Schübel-Auer**, Kahlenberger Str. 22, ✉ A-1190, ☎ (01) 3 70 22 22, Fax (01) 3702222, 🏠, « Courtyard-terrace » – 🗚 ⓞ ⓜⓞ *VISA*　　　　　　　　　　　　BX a
closed 22 December - 31 January and Sunday – **Meals** (dinner only) (buffet only).

X **Altes Preßhaus**, Cobenzlgasse 15, ✉ A-1190, ☎ (01) 3 20 02 03, *a.p.@aon.at*, Fax (01) 320020323, 🏠, « Old vaulted wine cellar with wine press » – 🗚 ⓞ ⓜⓞ *VISA* ⒿⒸⒷ　　　　　　　　　　　　　　　　　　　　　　　　　　BX p
closed January and February – **Meals** (dinner only) (buffet only) à la carte 15,01/38,82.

X **Wolff**, Rathstr. 44, ✉ A-1190, ☎ (01) 4 40 23 35, *wolff-heuriger@vip.at*, ☎ Fax (01) 4401403, « Terraced garden » – 🗚 ⓜⓞ *VISA*　　　　　　　　　AX m
Meals à la carte 12,93/23,40.

X **Fuhrgassl Huber**, Neustift am Walde 68, ✉ A-1190, ☎ (01) 4 40 14 05, Fax (01) 4402730, (wine-garden with Viennese Schrammelmusik), « Courtyard-terrace » – 🗚 ⓞ ⓜⓞ *VISA*　　　　　　　　　　　　　　　　　　　　　　　　AX b
open from 2pm – **Meals** (buffet only).

X **Grinzinger Hauermandl**, Cobenzlgasse 20, ✉ A-1190, ☎ (01) 3 20 89 49, *hauerm andl@grinzing.net*, Fax (01) 320571322, 🏠 – 🗚 ⓞ ⓜⓞ *VISA*　　　　BX q
closed Sunday – **Meals** (dinner only) à la carte 20,35/31,25.

at Auhof motorway station *West : 8 km by* ⑦ :

🏨 **Novotel Wien-West**, Am Auhof, ✉ A-1140, ☎ (01) 9 79 25 42, *h0521@accor-hot els.com*, Fax (01) 9794140, 🏠, ⧓ (heated), ☂ – 🛗, 🔆 rm, 🗐 📺 🔥 🕵 – 🏛 180. 🗚 ⓞ ⓜⓞ *VISA*
Meals à la carte 14,65/30 – **111 rm** ☐ 99 – 118.

at Perchtoldsdorf *Southwest : 13 km by B12 and Breitenfurter Straße AZ* :

XXXX **Jahreszeiten** (Winter), Hochstr. 17, ✉ A-2380, ☎ (01) 8 65 31 29, Fax (01) 865312973
❀　– 🗐. 🗚 ⓞ ⓜⓞ *VISA*
closed 25 March to 1 April, 29 July to 19 August, Saturday lunch, Sunday dinner, Monday and Bank Holidays – **Meals** 24 *(lunch)* and à la carte 41,60/49,20
Spec. Parfait von der Gänseleber in der Rotweinbirne. Garnelen gebraten in Thai-Sun-Sauce. Nougatknödel in Caramelsauce, Zitronensorbet.

at Vienna-Schwechat Airport by ③ : *20 km* :

🏨 **Astron Hotel Vienna Airport** Ⓜ, at the airport, ✉ A-1300, ℰ (01) 70 15 10, *vienna-airport@astron-hotels.de*, Fax (01) 7062828 – 🛗, ↻ rm, 🗏 📺 🖫 🖭 – 🔏 300. 🖭 ⓸ ⓿ 𝗩𝗜𝗦𝗔 𝗷𝗰𝗯
Meals (Italian rest.) 15,29 *(lunch)* and à la carte 29,07/46,87 – ☑ 12/17 – **328 rm** 123/269 – 142/298.

at Mayerling *Southwest* : *25 km by A 23 and A 21 CZ* :

🏕 **Kronprinz** (Hanner) 🍴 with rm, Mayerling 1, ✉ A-2534, ℰ (02258) 23 78, *kronprinz@aon.at*, Fax (02258) 237841, 🍽 – 🛗 📺 🖫 🖭 – 🔏 15. 🖭 ⓸ ⓿ 𝗩𝗜𝗦𝗔
Meals à la carte 40,50/69 – 19 rm ☑ 80/110 – 130
Spec. Nudelartischocke mit Entenleber. Holzschläger Berglamm mit Knoblauch-Rosinen und Grießkoch. Kleine Auswahl aus der Patisserie.

INNSBRUCK *Austria* 🄐🄑🄖 *G 7* – *pop. 120 000* – *alt. 580 m* – *Wintersport : 580/2300 m* ⛷ 3 7.
See : *Maria-Theresien-Strasse* ★ *CZ* ≤ ★★ *on the Nordkette, Hungerburg* ★, *Belfry (Stadtturm) CZ B* ☀ ★ *over the city* – *Little Golden Roof (Goldenes Dachl)* ★ *CZ* – *Helblinghaus* ★ *CZ* – *Dom (Inneres* ★, *Grabmal von Erzherzog Maximilian* ★ *) - Hofburg* ★ *(Riesensaal* ★ *) CZ* – *Hofkirche CZ (Maximilian's Mausoleum* ★★, *Silver Chapel* ★★*) – Tyrol Museum of Popular Art (Tiroler Volkskunstmuseum)* ★★ *CDZ* – *"Ferdinandeum" Tyrol Museum (Tiroler Landesmuseum "Ferdinandeum")* ★ *DZ M2* – *Wilten Basilica* ★ *AY*.
Envir. : *Hafelekar* ☀ ★★ – *Schloß Ambras C1e (Rüstkammern* ★, *Porträgalerie* ★, *Spanischer Saal* ★*) – Upland Tour (Mittelgebirge)* ★★ *(Hall in Tirol* ★, *Volders* ★, *Swarowski Kristallwelten Wathens* ★, *Igls* ★, – *Ellbögen road* ★★*) – The Stubaital* ★★.
🏌 *Innsbruck-Igls, Lans,* ℰ *(0512) 37 71 65* ; 🏌 *Innsbruck-Igls, Rinn,* ℰ *(05223) 7 81 77.*
🛈 *Innsbruck Information, Burggraben 3,* ✉ *A-6020,* ℰ *(0512) 53 56, Fax (0512) 535614.*
ÖAMTC, *Andechsstr. 81,* ℰ *(0512) 3 32 01 20, Fax (0512) 33206500.*
Wien 733 – München 140 – Salzburg 164.

Plans on following pages

🏨 **Europa-Tyrol**, Südtiroler Platz 2, ✉ A-6020, ℰ (0512) 59 31, *hotel@europatyrol.com*, Fax (0512) 587800, « Baroque hall », 🚬 – 🛗, ↻ rm, 🗏 rest, 📺 🖫 🚗 – 🔏 200. 🖭 ⓸ ⓿ 𝗩𝗜𝗦𝗔 𝗷𝗰𝗯   DZ a
Meals 27,75/31,40 and à la carte – **122 rm** ☑ 120/135 – 245 – 6 suites.

🏨 **Hilton**, Salurner Str. 15, ✉ A-6010, ℰ (0512) 5 93 50, *reservation@holiday-inn-innsbruck .com*, Fax (0512) 5935220, 🚬 – 🛗, ↻ rm, 🗏 📺 🖫 – 🔏 250. 🖭 ⓸ ⓿ 𝗩𝗜𝗦𝗔 𝗷𝗰𝗯. ⁕ rest *Guggeryllis* : **Meals** à la carte 27,20/37,10 – ☑ 16 – **176 rm** 115 – 160 – 4 suites. CDZ b

🏨 **Romantik Hotel Schwarzer Adler**, Kaiserjägerstr. 2, ✉ A-6020, ℰ (0512) 58 71 09, *info@deradler.com*, Fax (0512) 561697, « Elegant and individual installation, Restaurant in Tyrolean style » – 🛗, ↻ rm, 📺 🖫 – 🔏 40. 🖭 ⓸ ⓿ 𝗩𝗜𝗦𝗔   DZ e
Meals *(closed Sunday and Bank Holidays)* à la carte 21,25/35,79 – **39 rm** ☑ 117/131 – 190.

🏨 **Neue Post**, Maximilianstr. 15, ✉ A-6020, ℰ (0512) 5 94 76, *innsbruck@hotel-neue-post.at*, Fax (0512) 581818 – 🛗, ↻ rm, 📺 🖫 🖭 🖭 ⓸ ⓿ 𝗩𝗜𝗦𝗔 𝗷𝗰𝗯. ⁕   CZ v
Meals *(closed Saturday lunch, Sunday and Bank Holidays)* à la carte 18,25/35,79 – **52 rm** ☑ 98/110 – 140.

🏨 **Goldener Adler** 🍴, Herzog-Friedrich-Str. 6, ✉ A-6020, ℰ (0512) 57 11 11, *office @goldeneradler.com*, Fax (0512) 584409, 🍽, « 14C Tyrolean inn » – 🛗 📺 🖭 ⓸ ⓿ 𝗩𝗜𝗦𝗔   CZ c
Meals à la carte 23/37,98 – **35 rm** ☑ 87 – 168.

🏨 **Sporthotel Penz**, Fürstenweg 183, ✉ A-6020, ℰ (0512) 2 25 14, Fax (0512) 22514124, 🚬 – 🛗 📺 🖭 – 🔏 35. 🖭 ⓿ 𝗩𝗜𝗦𝗔. ⁕ rest   by Fürstenweg AY
Meals *(closed Sunday and Bank Holidays)* à la carte 14,29/29,94 – **77 rm** ☑ 72/93 – 137

🏨 **Grauer Bär**, Universitätsstr. 7, ✉ A-6020, ℰ (0512) 5 92 40, *grauer-baer@magnet.at*, Fax (0512) 574535, 🚬 – 🛗 📺 🖭 – 🔏 240. 🖭 ⓸ ⓿ 𝗩𝗜𝗦𝗔 𝗷𝗰𝗯   DZ k
Meals à la carte 23,50/47,50 – **189 rm** ☑ 90/105 – 125.

🏨 **Central**, Gilmstr. 5, ✉ A-6020, ℰ (0512) 5 92 00, *central@netway.at*, Fax (0512) 580310, 🖽, 🚬 – 🛗, ↻ rm, 📺 – 🔏 30. 🖭 ⓸ ⓿ 𝗩𝗜𝗦𝗔   DZ c
Meals à la carte 14,82/32,21 – **85 rm** ☑ 90/95 – 115.

🏨 **Innsbruck**, Innrain 3, ✉ A-6020, ℰ (0512) 5 98 68, *office@hotelinnsbruck.com*, Fax (0512) 572280, 🚬, 🖽 – 🛗 🗏 📺 🚗 – 🔏 50. 🖭 ⓸ ⓿ 𝗩𝗜𝗦𝗔   CZ e
Meals *(dinner for residents only)* – **114 rm** ☑ 87/94 – 123.

🏨 **Maximilian** without rest, Marktgraben 7, ✉ A-6020, ℰ (0512) 59 96 70, *hotel.maximilian@eunet.at*, Fax (0512) 577450 – 🛗 📺 ☎. 🖭 ⓸ ⓿ 𝗩𝗜𝗦𝗔   CZ a
43 rm ☑ 106/120 – 138.

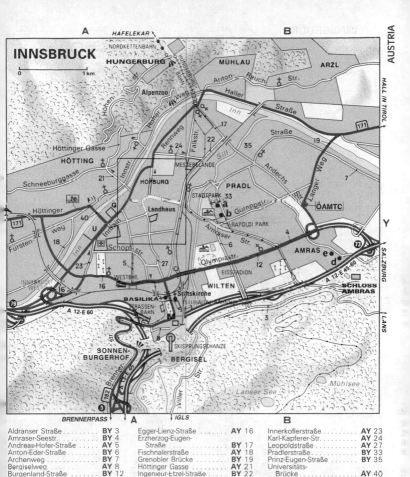

🏨 **Zach** without rest, Wilhelm-Greil-Str. 11, ⊠ A-6020, ✆ (0512) 58 96 67, *info@hotel-z ach.at, Fax (0512) 5896677* – 📶 📺 🖭 ⓞ 🅾🄾 𝘝𝘐𝘚𝘈. 🍴   DZ h
24 rm ⊇ 66/80 – 95/109.

🏨 **Mondschein** without rest, Mariahilfstr. 6, ⊠ A-6020, ✆ (0512) 2 27 84, *mondschei n@tirol.com, Fax (0512) 2278490* – 📶 📺 📞 🍴 – 🔒 30. 🅰🄴 ⓞ 🅾🄾 𝘝𝘐𝘚𝘈 𝖩𝖢𝖡. 🍴   CZ m
34 rm ⊇ 73/123 – 131/145.

🏨 **Weisses Rössl** 🍴, Kiebachgasse 8, ⊠ A-6020, ✆ (0512) 58 30 57, *weisses@roessl.at, Fax (0512) 5830575*, 🍴 – 📶 📺 🅾🄾 𝘝𝘐𝘚𝘈   CZ n
closed 2 weeks April and 2 weeks November – **Meals** *(closed Sunday and Bank Holidays)* à la carte 14,38/32,70 – **12 rm** ⊇ 69 – 109.

🏨 **Weisses Kreuz** 🍴, Herzog-Friedrich-Str. 31, ⊠ A-6020, ✆ (0512) 5 94 79, *hotel.w eisses.kreuz@eunet.at, Fax (0512) 5947990*, 🍴, « 15C Tyrolean inn » – 📶 📺 🅰🄴 🅾🄾 𝘝𝘐𝘚𝘈   CZ r
Meals à la carte 18,25/31,40 – **40 rm** ⊇ 59/67 – 106.

🏨 **Tourotel Breinössl**, Maria-Theresien-Str. 12, ⊠ A-6020, ✆ (0512) 58 41 65, *touro telinnsbruck@via.at, Fax (0512) 58416526* – 📶, 🍴 rm, 📺. 🅰🄴 ⓞ 🅾🄾 𝘝𝘐𝘚𝘈 𝖩𝖢𝖡   CZ p
Meals à la carte 15,33/21,90 – **40 rm** ⊇ 67/77 – 102/121.

INNSBRUCK

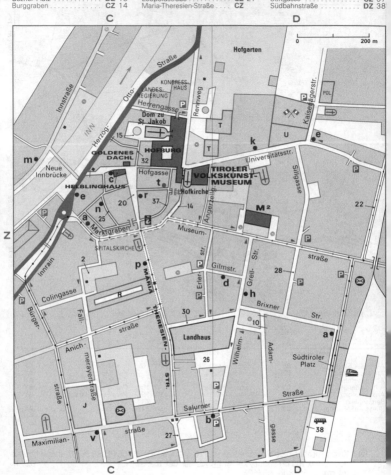

XX **Dengg**, Riesengasse 13, ⊠ A-6020, ℰ (0512) 58 23 47, *dengg. @ chello.at*,
Fax (0512) 936088 – AE ① ⓜⓒ VISA   CZ t
closed Sunday and Bank Holidays – **Meals** à la carte 15,70/33,90.

at Innsbruck-Amras :

🏠 **Kapeller**, Philippine-Welser-Str. 96, ⊠ A-6020, ℰ (0512) 34 31 06, *office@kapeller.at*,
Fax (0512) 34310668, 🏡 – 📱 TV 🄿 – 🔏 20. AE ① ⓜⓒ VISA JCB   BY e
closed July **Meals** *(closed Monday lunch, Sunday and Bank Holidays)* à la carte 19,94/39,88
– **36 rm** ⊇ 55/69 – 139.

🏠 **Bierwirt**, Bichlweg 2, ⊠ A-6020, ℰ (0512) 34 21 43, *bierwirt @ aon.at*,
Fax (0512) 3421435, 🏡, « Comfortable, rustic lounge in typical Tyrolean style », 🖛s –
📱, ⇔ rm, TV 📞 & 🄿 – 🔏 80. ⓜⓒ VISA   BY d
Meals *(closed Saturday lunch and Sunday)* à la carte 16,36/30,30 – **50 rm** ⊇ 62 – 95.

at Innsbruck-Pradl :

Alpinpark, Pradlerstr. 28, ✉ A-6020, ☎ (0512) 34 86 00, *Fax (0512) 364172*, – TV – 30. AE VISA JCB BY a
Meals à la carte 15,33/36,51 – **87 rm** 79/95 – 114.

Parkhotel Leipzigerhof, Defreggerstr. 13, ✉ A-6020, ☎ (0512) 34 35 25, *reception @ parkhotel-leipzigerhof.at, Fax (0512) 394357*, – , rm, TV P. AE VISA JCB BY b
Meals *(closed Sunday)* à la carte 15,60/30,60 – **53 rm** 60/95 – 116.

at Igls *South : 4 km by Viller Straße AB :*

Schlosshotel, Viller Steig 2, ✉ A-6080, ☎ (0512) 37 72 17, *hotel@schlosshotel -igls.com, Fax (0512) 378679*, ≤ mountains, « Mansion in garden, elegant installation », , – TV P – 15. AE VISA JCB. rest
closed April, 20 October - 20 December – **Meals** à la carte 30,70/39,20 – **21 rm** 208/311 – 387 – 5 suites.

Sporthotel Igls, Hilber Str. 17, ✉ A-6080, ☎ (0512) 37 72 41, *hotel@sporthotel-igls.com, Fax (0512) 378679*, , Massage, , , , – TV – 50. AE VISA JCB
closed 15 October - 6 December – **Meals** à la carte 28,47/43,81 – **80 rm** 90/120 – 190 – 6 suites.

Batzenhäusl, Lanserstr. 12, ✉ A-6080, ☎ (0512) 3 86 18, *hotel@batzenhaeusel.at, Fax (0512) 386187*, , , – TV P. AE VISA. rest
closed 15 October - 15 December – **Meals** à la carte 21,91/40,90 – **29 rm** 73 – 156 – 3 suites.

Römerhof, Römerstr. 62, ✉ A-6080, ☎ (0512) 37 89 02, *roemerhof@netway.at, Fax (0512) 37890220*, , , TV P. VISA JCB. rest
closed 3 weeks end April - mid May, 3 weeks mid October - early November – **Meals** à la carte 18,25/32,86 – **18 rm** 44/66 – 88.

at Lans *Southeast : 6 km by Aldranser Straße BY :*

Wilder Mann with rm, Römerstr. 12, ✉ A-6072, ☎ (0512) 37 96 96, *wildermann@tirol.com, Fax (0512) 379139*, – TV P – 40. AE VISA
Meals à la carte 20,95/40,94 – **12 rm** 51/73 – 114.

at Wattens *East : 16 km : by A 12 BY :*

Gasthof Zum Schwan, Swarovskistr. 2, ✉ A-6112, ☎ (05224) 5 21 21, *Fax (05224) 55175*, , « Tyrolean inn with convivial atmosphere » – P
closed 24 December - 10 January, Saturday, Sunday and Bank Holidays – **Meals** à la carte 23/36.

SALZBURG *Austria* 926 *L 5 – pop. 147 000 – alt. 425 m.*

See : *≤ ★★ over the town (from the Mönchsberg) X and ≤★★ (from Hettwer Bastei)Y – Hohensalzburg ★★ X, Z : ≤★★ (from the Kuenburg Bastion), ★★ (from the Reck Tower), Museum (Burgmuseum)★ – St. Peter's Churchyard (Petersfriedhof)★★ Z – St. Peter's Church (Stiftskirche St. Peter)★★ Z – Residenz★★ Z – Natural History Museum (Haus der Natur)★★ Y* **M2** *– Franciscan's Church (Franziskanerkirche)★ Z* **A** *– Getreidegasse★ Y – Mirabell Gardens (Mirabellgarten)★ V (Grand Staircase ★★ of the castle) – Baroquemuseum ★ V* **M 3** *– Dom★ Z.*

Envir. : *Road to the Gaisberg (Gaisbergstraße)★★ (≤★) by ① – Untersberg★ by ② : 10 km (with) – Castle Hellbrunn (Schloß Hellbrunn) ★ (Volkskundemuseum★) by Nonntaler Hauptstraße X.*

Salzburg-Wals, Schloß Klessheim, ☎ (0662) 85 08 51 ; Hof (by ① : 20 km), ☎ (06229) 23 90 ; St. Lorenz (by ① : 29 km), ☎ (06232) 38 35.

Innsbrucker Bundesstr. 95 (by ③), ☎ (0662) 85 12 23 - City Air Terminal(Autobus Station), Südtiroler Platz V.

Lastenstraße V.

Exhibition Centre (Messegelände), Linke Glanzeile 65, ☎ (0662) 3 45 66.

Tourist-Information, Mozartplatz 5, ✉ A-5020, ☎ (0662) 88 98 73 30, Fax (0662) 8898732.

ÖAMTC, *Alpenstr. 102 (by ②), ☎ (0662) 63 99 90, Fax (0662) 6399945.*

Wien 292 ① – Innsbruck 177 ③ – München 140 ③

Plans on following pages

Sacher, Schwarzstr. 5, ✉ A-5020, ☎ (0662) 8 89 77, *salzburg@sacher.com, Fax (0662) 88977551*, « Salzach-side setting, terrace with ≤ old town and castle », Massage, , – , rm, TV – 80. AE VISA JCB Y b
Zirbelstube **:** Meals à la carte 37,40/51,90 – ***Salzach Grill*** **:** Meals à la carte 23,80/30,30 – **118 rm** 210/320 – 335/525 – 3 suites.

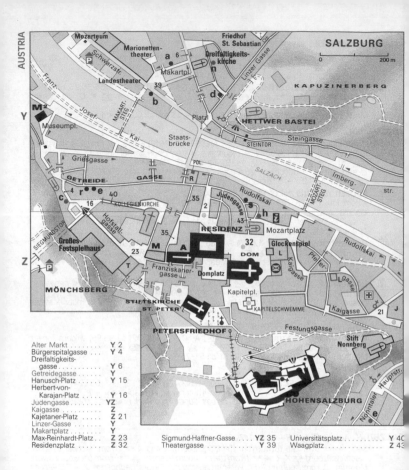

SALZBURG

0   200 m

Bristol, Makartplatz 4, ⊠ A-5020, ℰ (0662) 87 35 57, *hotel.bristol@salzburg.co.at*, Fax (0662) 8735576 – |≱|, ↮ rm, ☰ ⊺⊽ ℰ – ♨ 60. ☎ ⓪ ⓪ *VISA* JCB – Y a closed 5 February - 22 March – **Meals** see **Bei Bruno** below – **61 rm** ⊇ 207/253 - 298/392 – 9 suites.

Altstadt Radisson SAS, Judengasse 15, ⊠ A-5020, ℰ (0662) 8 48 57 10, *radisson-altstadt@austria-trend.at*, Fax (0662) 8485716, ☞, « Modernised 14C nobleman's house, antique furnishings » – |≱|, ↮ rm, ☰ rm, ⊺⊽ ℰ ☞ – ♨ 40. ☎ ⓪ ⓪ *VISA* JCB Y s **Meals** (closed Sunday, except festival period) à la carte 22,90/44,40 – **62 rm** ⊇ 145/175 - 215/375 – 13 suites.

Crowne Plaza-Pitter M, Rainerstr. 6, ⊠ A-5020, ℰ (0662) 88 97 80, *crowneplaza-pitter@salzburginfo.or.at*, Fax (0662) 878893, ☎s – |≱|, ↮ rm, ☰ ⊺⊽ ℰ ♨ – ♨ 160. ☎ ⓪ ⓪ *VISA* JCB V r **Meals** à la carte 28,12/45 – **187 rm** ⊇ 195 - 220/235 – 4 suites.

Sheraton, Auerspergstr. 4, ⊠ A-5020, ℰ (0662) 88 99 90, *sheraton.salzburg@sheraton.com*, Fax (0662) 881776, « Terrace in spa gardens », Massage, Ⅼ⊙, entrance to the spa facilities – |≱|, ↮ rm, ☰ ⊺⊽ ℰ ♨ – ♨ 50. ☎ ⓪ ⓪ *VISA* JCB V s **Mirabell** (closed Monday - Tuesday, except festival period) **Meals** à la carte 30,15/49,05 – ⊇ 20 – **163 rm** 180/216 - 230/267 – 9 suites.

Renaissance M, Fanny-von-Lehnert-Str. 7, ⊠ A-5020, ℰ (0662) 4 68 80, *rhi.szgbr.business.center@renaissancehotels.com*, Fax (0662) 4688298, ☞, Massage, Ⅼ⊙, ☎s, ☒ – |≱|, ↮ rm, ☰ ⊺⊽ ℰ ♨ ☞ – ♨ 500. ☎ ⓪ ⓪ *VISA* by Kaiserschützenstraße V **Meals** à la carte 19,62/31,25 – **257 Z** ⊇ 166/217 - 189/240.

SALZBURG

AUSTRIA

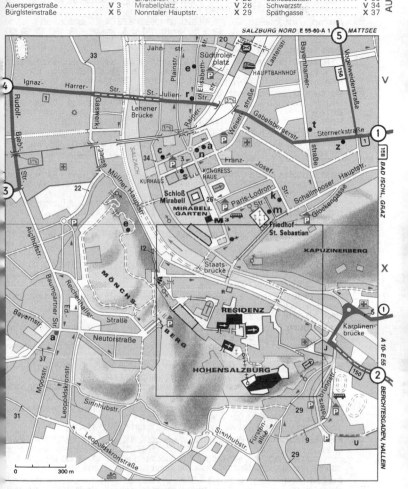

🏨🏨🏨 **Goldener Hirsch**, Getreidegasse 37, ✉ A-5020, 𝒫 (0662) 8 08 40, *welcome@ gold enerhirsch.com, Fax (0662) 843349*, « 15C nobleman's house, tastefully furnished » – 📶, ⇄ rm, 🗄 📺 🕻 – 🔬 30. 🆎 ① 🏧 VISA JCB.   Y e
Meals à la carte 40/48 – ⚏ 24 – **69 rm** 192/253 – 262/356 – 4 suites.

🏨🏨🏨 **Schloß Mönchstein** ⑤, Mönchsberg Park 26, ✉ A-5020, 𝒫 (0662) 8 48 55 50, *salz burg@ monchstein.at, Fax (0662) 848559*, ≤ Salzburg and surroundings, 😤, « Small castle with elegant furnishings ; wedding chapel ; park », 🌳, ⛳ – 📶 📺 🕻 ⟺ 🅿 – 🔬 20. 🆎 ① 🏧 VISA JCB. 🛇 rest   X e
Meals à la carte 35,61/55,76 – **16 rm** ⚏ 334 – 334/429 – 3 suites.

🏨🏨 **Dorint** 🅜, Sterneckstr. 20, ✉ A-5027, 𝒫 (0662) 8 82 03 10, *info.szgsal@dorint.com, Fax (0662) 8820319*, 😤, ⇄ – 📶, ⇄ rm, 📺 🕻 ⟺ – 🔬 160. 🆎 ① 🏧 VISA. 🛇 rest   V z
Meals à la carte 25/35 – **139 rm** ⚏ 180/188 – 197/205 – 4 suites.

🏨🏨 **Zum Hirschen**, St.-Julien-Str. 21, ✉ A-5020, 𝒫 (0662) 88 90 30, *zumhirschen@ ains.at, Fax (0662) 8890358*, Massage, ⇄ – 📶, ⇄ rm, 🗄 📺 🕻 🅿 – 🔬 30. 🆎 ① 🏧 VISA JCB. 🛇 rm – **Meals** à la carte 15,20/32,90 – **64 rm** ⚏ 74/87 – 111/133.   V r

49

🏨 **Carlton** without rest, Markus-Sittikus-Str. 3, ✉ A-5020, ℰ (0662) 8 82 19 10, *carlto n@astron-hotels.at, Fax (0662) 88219188,* ⇔s – 🛗 ✲ 📺 ✆ ⇐ 🅿 🅰🅴 ⑩ 🆚🆂🅰 🆓
⇌ 13 – **39 rm** 97/145 – 120/145 – 13 suites.   V c

🏨 **Astron**, Franz-Josef-Str. 26, ✉ A-5020, ℰ (0662) 8 82 04 10, *salzburg-city@astron -hotels.at, Fax (0662) 874240,* ⇔s – 🛗 ✲ rm, 📺 ✆ & ⇐ 🅿 – 🅰 150. 🅰🅴 ⑩ ⑩⑩ 🆚🆂🅰 🆓
Meals à la carte 16/32 – **140 rm** ⇌ 104/131 – 128/178.   V k

🏨 **CD Hotel**, Am Messezentrum 2, ✉ A-5020, ℰ (0662) 4 35 54 60, *salzburg@cdhotels.at, Fax (0662) 43951095,* ⇔s – 🛗 ✲ rm, 📺 ✆ ⇐ 🅿 – 🅰 300. 🅰🅴 ⑩ ⑩⑩ 🆚🆂🅰
Meals à la carte 15,55/28,42 – **120 rm** ⇌ 98/105 – 137/144.   by ④

🏨 **Mercure** Ⓜ, Bayerhamerstr. 14, ✉ A-5020, ℰ (0662) 8 81 43 80, *h0984@accor-ho tels.com, Fax (0662) 871111411,* ☞ – 🛗 ✲ rm, 📺 ✆ & ⇐ 🅿 – 🅰 100. 🅰🅴 ⑩ ⑩⑩ 🆚🆂🅰   V t
Meals à la carte 16,80/31,83 – **121 rm** ⇌ 101/121 – 109/145.

🏨 **Wolf-Dietrich**, Wolf-Dietrich-Str. 7, ✉ A-5020, ℰ (0662) 87 12 75, *office@salzburg -hotel.at, Fax (0662) 882320,* ☞, ⇔s, 🔲 – 🛗 📺 ✆ ⇐ 🅰🅴 ⑩ ⑩⑩ 🆚🆂🅰 🆓   V m
Ährlich *(closed 4 February - 20 March, Saturday lunch and Sunday)* **Meals** à la carte 17,50/31 – **29 rm** ⇌ 74/99 – 124/159.

🏨 **Altstadthotel Blaue Gans**, Getreidegasse 41, ✉ A-5020, ℰ (0662) 84 24 91, *offi ce@blauegans.at, Fax (0662) 8424919,* « Restored 15 C inn » – 🛗 📺 ✆ 🅰🅴 ⑩ ⑩⑩ 🆚🆂🅰 🆓   Y r
closed 10 January - 20 March (hotel) – **Meals** *(closed 6 to 20 March and Tuesday, except festival period)* à la carte 15,70/36,60 – **40 rm** ⇌ 69/95 – 138/160.

🏨 **Markus Sittikus** without rest, Markus-Sittikus-Str. 20, ✉ A-5020, ℰ (0662) 8 71 12 10, *markus-sittikus@austria.at, Fax (0662) 87112158* – 🛗 📺 ✆ – 🅰 15. 🅰🅴 ⑩ ⑩⑩ 🆚🆂🅰   V a
39 rm ⇌ 55/72 – 88/117.

🏨 **Hohenstauffen** without rest, Elisabethstr. 19, ✉ A-5020, ℰ (0662) 8 77 66 90, *hohe nstauffen@aon.at, Fax (0662) 87219351* – 🛗 ✲ 📺 ⇐ 🅿 🅰🅴 ⑩ ⑩⑩ 🆚🆂🅰 🆓
31 rm ⇌ 58/72 – 79/123.   V e

🏨 **Gablerbräu**, Linzer Gasse 9, ✉ A-5020, ℰ (0662) 8 89 65, *hotel@gablerbraeu.com, Fax (0662) 8896555,* ☞ – 🛗 📺 – 🅰 20. 🅰🅴 ⑩ ⑩⑩ 🆚🆂🅰 🆓   Y d
Meals à la carte 14,26/25,60 – **52 rm** ⇌ 65/73 – 100/116.

🍴 **Alt Salzburg**, Bürgerspitalgasse 2, ✉ A-5020, ℰ (0662) 84 14 76, *altsalzburg@aon.at, Fax (0662) 8414764* – 🅰🅴 ⑩ ⑩⑩ 🆚🆂🅰 🆓   Y c
closed 1 week mid February, Sunday and Monday lunch, except festival period – **Meals** (booking essential for dinner) à la carte 23,50/35,70.

🍴 **Bei Bruno** - Hotel Bristol, Makartplatz 4, ✉ A-5020, ℰ (0662) 87 84 17, *bruno@res taurant-austria.net, Fax (0662) 8735576* – 🅰🅴 ⑩ ⑩⑩ 🆚🆂🅰 🆓   Y a
closed 5 February - 3 March and Sunday, except festival period – **Meals** à la carte 24,50/44,20.

🍴 **Riedenburg**, Neutorstr. 31, ✉ A-5020, ℰ (0662) 83 08 15, *reservierung@riedenbu rg.at, Fax (0662) 843923,* ☞ – 🅿 🅰🅴 ⑩ ⑩⑩ 🆚🆂🅰   X a
closed Sunday, except festival period – **Meals** à la carte 25,39/45,42.

🍴 **K+K Restaurant am Waagplatz**, Waagplatz 2 (1st floor), ✉ A-5020, ℰ (0662) 84 21 56, *kk.restaurant@kuk.at, Fax (0662) 84215633,* ☞, « Medieval dinner with period performance in the Freysauff-Keller (by arrangement) » – ▤ 🅰🅴 ⑩ ⑩⑩ 🆚🆂🅰 🆓 Z h
closed 4 February - 10 March – **Meals** (booking essential) à la carte 19,50/31,11.

🍴 **Perkeo**, Priesterhausgasse 20, ✉ A-5020, ℰ (0662) 87 08 99, *Fax (0662) 870833,* ☞
closed Saturday and Sunday, during festival period only Sunday – **Meals** (booking essential) à la carte 31,70/43,40.   Y n

at Salzburg-Aigen *Southeast : 6 km, by Bürgelsteinstraße* X :

🏨 **Rosenvilla** without rest, Höfelgasse 4, ✉ A-5020, ℰ (0662) 62 17 65, *hotel.rosenvi la@salzburg-online.at, Fax (0662) 6252308,* ☞ – ✲ 📺 ✆ 🅿 🅰🅴 ⑩ ⑩⑩ 🆚🆂🅰. ✳
13 rm ⇌ 59/84 – 95/142.

🏨 **Doktorwirt**, Glaser Str. 9, ✉ A-5026, ℰ (0662) 62 29 73, *schnoell@doktorwirt.co.at Fax (0662) 62171724,* ☞, ⇔s, 🔲 (heated), ☞ – ✲ rest, 📺 ✆ ⇐ 🅿 – 🅰 25. 🅰🅴 ⑩ ⑩⑩ 🆚🆂🅰. ✳ rest
closed 2 weeks February and 16 October - 26 November – **Meals** *(closed Monday, Sep tember - Easter Sunday dinner and Monday)* à la carte 15/32 ♨ – **39 rm** ⇌ 64/72 – 99/128.

🍴 **Gasthof Schloß Aigen**, Schwarzenbergpromenade 37, ✉ A-5026, ℰ (0662) 62 12 84, *Fax (0662) 6212844,* ☞ – 🅿 🅰🅴 ⑩ ⑩⑩ 🆚🆂🅰
closed 3 weeks January - February, Wednesday and Thursday lunch, except festival period – **Meals** à la carte 26,53/42,08.

at Salzburg-Gnigl *East : 3,5 km, by ① :*

   ✗ **Pomodoro**, Eichstr. 54, ✉ A-5023, ℰ (0662) 64 04 38, 🏡 – 🄿 🄰🄴 ⬤🄾 𝗩𝗜𝗦𝗔
     closed end July - end August, Monday and Tuesday – **Meals** *(Italian) (booking essential)*
     à la carte 26,29/33,42.

In Salzburg-Itzling *North : 1,5 km, by Kaiserschützenstraße V :*

   🏠 **Auerhahn**, Bahnhofstr. 15, ✉ A-5020, ℰ (0662) 45 10 52, *auerhahn@eunet.at*,
   🐾 *Fax (0662) 4510523,* 🏡 – ✿ rest, 📺 🍴 🄿 🄰🄴 🄾 ⬤🄾 𝗩𝗜𝗦𝗔
     closed 1 week February, 2 weeks July – **Meals** *(closed Sunday dinner and Monday)* à la carte
     24,68/33,30 – **14 rm** ⇄ 41/43 – 72/80.

at Salzburg-Liefering *Northwest : 4 km, by ④ :*

   🏨 **Brandstätter**, Münchner Bundesstr. 69, ✉ A-5020, ℰ (0662) 43 45 35, *info@hote*
   ⚭ *l-brandstaetter.com, Fax (0662) 43453590,* 🏡, ⇆, 🄽, 🍴 – ⃤ ✿ 📺 🍴 🄿 – 🄰 30.
     ✿ rest
     closed 22 to 27 December – **Meals** *(closed 1 week early January, 1 week June and Sunday*
     except in season) (booking essential) à la carte 23/50.11 – **36 rm** ⇄ 65/81 – 81/108
     Spec. Lauwarmer Kalbsbrustsalat mit Gemüsevinaigrette. Bauernente im Rohr gebraten
     mit Blaukraut und Grießknödel. Grießflammerie mit marinierten Erdbeeren.

at Salzburg-Maria Plain *North : 3 km, by Plainstraße V :*

   🏨 **Maria Plain** 🐾, Plainbergweg 41, ✉ A-5101, ℰ (0662) 4 50 70 10, *info@mariaplai*
     n.com, Fax (0662) 45070119, « 17 C inn ; garden with ≤ Salzburg », 🍴 – ⃤ ✿ rest,
     📺 🍴 🄿 – 🄰 40. 🄰🄴 🄾 ⬤🄾 𝗩𝗜𝗦𝗔
     closed 1 week July – **Meals** *(closed Tuesday and Wednesday, except festival period)* à la
     carte 20.10/26,60 – **27 rm** ⇄ 55 – 95 – 5 suites.

at Salzburg-Nonntal :

   ✗✗ **Purzelbaum**, Zugallistr. 7, ✉ A-5020, ℰ (0662) 84 88 43, *Fax (0662) 8443529,* 🏡,
     (Bistro rest.) – 🄰🄴 🄾 ⬤🄾 𝗩𝗜𝗦𝗔   Z e
     closed 3 weeks June, 1 week early September, Sunday and Bank Holidays, except festival
     period – **Meals** *(booking essential for dinner)* à la carte 31,50/46.

on the Heuberg *Northeast : 3 km by ① – alt. 565 m*

   🏠 **Schöne Aussicht** 🐾, Heuberg 3, ✉ A-5023 Salzburg, ℰ (0662) 64 06 08, *sch.aus*
     sicht@salzburginfo.at, Fax (0662) 6406082, « Garden with ≤ Salzburg and Alps », ⇆,
     🏊, 🏡, ✗ – 📺 🍴 🄿 – 🄰 30. 🄰🄴 🄾 ⬤🄾 𝗩𝗜𝗦𝗔
     March - October – **Meals** *(closed Wednesday) (weekdays dinner only)* à la carte 15/31,20
     – **28 rm** ⇄ 69/87 – 101/153.

on the Gaisberg *East : 5 km, by ① :*

   🏨🏨 **Vitalhotel Kobenzl** 🐾, Gaisberg 11, alt. 730 m, ✉ A-5020 Salzburg, ℰ (0662)
     64 15 10, *info@kobenzl.at, Fax (0662) 642238,* 🏡, « Beautiful panoramic location with
     ≤ Salzburg and Alps », Massage, 🔥, ⇆, 🄽, 🍴 – ⃤ 📺 🍴 🄿 – 🄰 40. 🄰🄴 🄾 ⬤🄾 𝗩𝗜𝗦𝗔
     🄹🄲🄱 ✿ rest
     closed 7 January - 7 March – **Meals** à la carte 30,68/55,96 – **40 rm** ⇄ 120/171 – 142/269
     – 4 suites.

   🏨🏨 **Romantik Hotel Gersberg Alm** 🐾, Gersberg 37, alt. 800 m, ✉ A-5023 Salzburg-
     Gnigl, ℰ (0662) 64 12 57, *office@gersbergalm.at, Fax (0662) 644278,* 🏡, ⇆, 🏊, 🍴,
     ✗ – 📺 🍴 🄿 – 🄰 120. 🄰🄴 🄾 ⬤🄾 𝗩𝗜𝗦𝗔. ✿ rest
     Meals *(booking essential)* à la carte 23,98/37,78 – **45 rm** ⇄ 84/125 – 125/262.

near Airport *Southwest : 5 km, by ③ :*

   🏨 **Airporthotel**, Dr.-M.-Laireiter-Str. 9, ✉ A-5020 Salzburg-Loig, ℰ (0662) 85 00 20, *airp*
     orthotel@aon.at, Fax (0662) 85002044, 🏡, 🔥, ⇆, 🄽 – ⃤, ✿ rm, 📺 🍴 🚗 🄿 –
     🄰 20. 🄰🄴 🄾 ⬤🄾 𝗩𝗜𝗦𝗔 🄹🄲🄱
     Meals *(residents only) –* **39 rm** ⇄ 84/115 – 123/130.

at Anif *South : 7 km, by ② :*

   🏨🏨 **Friesacher**, Hellbrunner Str. 17, ✉ A-5081, ℰ (06246) 89 77, *first@hotelfriesacher*
     .com, Fax (06246) 897749, 🏡, Massage, 🔥, 🏡, 🍴 – ⃤ ✿ rm, 📺 🍴 🚗 🄿 – 🄰 25
     closed 2 to 24 January – **Meals** *(closed Wednesday, except festival period)* à la carte
     17,05/32,70 🍷 – **53 rm** ⇄ 58/80 – 102/131.

   🏨 **Schloßwirt zu Anif** (with guest house), Salzachtal Bundesstr. 22, ✉ A-5081,
     ℰ (06246) 7 21 75, *info@schlosswirt.com, Fax (06246) 721758,* 🏡, « 17 C inn with
     Biedermeier installation », 🍴 – ⃤ 📺 🚗 🄿 – 🄰 70. 🄰🄴 𝗩𝗜𝗦𝗔
     closed 2 weeks February and 2 weeks October – **Meals** *(closed Tuesday, except festival*
     period) à la carte 27,76/43,46 – **28 rm** ⇄ 66 – 124.

at Bergheim *North : 7 km by Plainstrasse* V :

🏠 **Gasthof Gmachl**, Dorfstr. 35, ✉ A-5101, 𝒫 (0662) 45 21 24, *info@gmachl.at*, *Fax (0662) 45212468*, 🌰, « Lounges in convivial regional style ; park », ≦s, 🛆 (heated), 🚗, ✗ – |≢|, 🔄 rm, 🆃🆅 📞 🅿 – 🅰 40. 🆎 🆖 VISA
closed 2 weeks July – **Meals** à la carte 16,56/31,96 – **58 rm** 🖙 73/100 – 124/193 – 5 suites.

at Hallwang-Söllheim *Northeast : 7 km, by ① and Linzer Bundesstraße* :

XX **Pfefferschiff**, Söllheim 3, ✉ A-5300, 𝒫 (0662) 66 12 42, *restaurant@pfefferschiff.at*, ❀ *Fax (0662) 661841*, 🌰 – 🅿. 🆎. ✗
closed end June - mid July, early - mid September, Sunday and Monday, during festival period only Monday – **Meals** (booking essential) 28 *(lunch)* and à la carte 33,80/51,50
Spec. Flußkrebsravioli mit Eierschwammerl und Kohlrabi. Blunzenguglhupf mit schwarzem Trüffel und Selleriepüree. Rehrückenfilet in der Apfelkruste mit Topfennockerl.

at Elixhausen *North : 11 km, by ⑤, direction Obertrum* :

🏠 **Romantik Hotel Gmachl**, Dorfstr. 14, ✉ A-5161, 𝒫 (0662) 4 80 21 20, *romantik hotel@gmachl.com*, *Fax (0662) 48021272*, 🌰, « 14 C inn ; former taverna of Benedictine monks », ≦s, 🛆 (heated), 🚗, ✗ (indoor) – |≢| 🆃🆅 📞 🅿 – 🅰 70. 🆎 🆔 🆖 VISA
closed mid June - mid July – **Meals** (closed Sunday dinner and Monday lunch, except festival period) à la carte 16/37 – **34 rm** 🖙 80/112 – 134/207 – 3 suites.

at Hof *East : 20 km, by ① and B 158* :

🏰 **Schloß Fuschl** 🦢 (with 🏠 guest houses), Vorderelsenwang 19, ✉ A-5322, 𝒫 (06229) 2 25 30, *schloss.fuschl@arabellasheraton.com*, *Fax (06229) 2253531*, ≤, 🌰, « 15C Former hunting lodge », Massage, 𝑓₆, ≦s, 🛆, ⛳, 🚗, ✗, |5 – |≢| 🆃🆅 📞 🚗 🅿 – 🅰 100. 🆎 🆔 🆖 VISA JCB. ✗ rest
Meals à la carte 39,61/60,12 – 🖙 22 – **84 rm** 136/451 – 147/451 – 3 suites.

at Fuschl am See *East : 26 km, by ① and B 158* :

🏠 **Ebner's Waldhof** 🦢, Seepromenade, ✉ A-5330, 𝒫 (06226) 82 64, *info@ebners -waldhof.at*, *Fax (06226) 8644*, ≤, 🌰, Massage, ≦s, 🛆, 🚣, 🚗, ✗ – |≢| 🆃🆅 🅿 – 🅰 60. 🆔 🆖 VISA ✗ rest
closed 3 to 23 March, end October - mid December – **Meals** (booking essential) à la carte 23,90/34,90 – **75 rm** 🖙 70/105 – 110/240.

on the Mondsee *East : 28 km, by ⑤ (by motorway A 1, exit Mondsee, left lakeside, direction Attersee)*

🏰 **Seehof** 🦢, ✉ A-5311 Loibichl, 𝒫 (06232) 50 31, *seehof@nextra.de*, *Fax (06232) 503151*, ≤, « Garden-terrace », Massage, ≦s, 🚣, 🚗, ✗ – ✗ rest, 🆃🆅 🚗 🅿 – 🅰 15. 🆖 VISA JCB. ✗
8 May - 16 September – **Meals** à la carte 25/41,50 – **30 rm** 🖙 255 – 322/435 – 4 suites.

at Golling *South : 25 km by ② and A 10* :

🏠 **Döllerer's Goldener Stern**, Am Marktplatz 56, ✉ A-5440, 𝒫 (06244) 4 22 00, *offi* ❀ *ce@doellerer.at*, *Fax (06244) 691242*, ≦s – 🆃🆅 📞 – 🅰 20. 🆎 🆔 🆖 VISA
closed 2 weeks January and 1 week October – **Meals** (closed 2 weeks July, Sunday and Monday lunch) (outstanding wine list) 30,50/58 and à la carte 34/50 – ***Bürgerstube*** (closed Sunday and Monday lunch) **Meals** à la carte 16,30/33,40 – **15 rm** 🖙 44/73 – 73/138
Spec. Gebratener Steinbutt mit Karfiol und schwarzer Trüffel. Taube mit Kaffeearoma und Gewürzbirne. Bitterschokoladentarte mit Sansho-Pfeffereis.

at Werfen *South : 42 km by ② and A 10* :

XXX **Karl-Rudolf Obauer** with rm, Markt 46, ✉ A-5450, 𝒫 (06468) 5 21 20, *ok@obau* ❀❀ *er.com*, *Fax (06468) 521212*, « Garden terrace » – ▤ rest, 🆃🆅 🅿 🆎
Meals (closed Monday - Tuesday, except out of season and festival period) (booking essential) 32 *(lunch)*/64 *(dinner)* and à la carte 36/63 – **8 rm** 🖙 62/95 – 120/142
Spec. Geräucherte Kalbsleber mit Trüffel. Forellenstrudel mit Veltlinersauce und Pilzpüree. Nougatbirne mit Mandelmilchschlag und Erdnußbuttereis.

Benelux

Belgium
BRUSSELS – ANTWERP – BRUGES – LIÈGE

Grand Duchy of Luxembourg
LUXEMBOURG

Netherlands
AMSTERDAM – The HAGUE – ROTTERDAM

PRACTICAL INFORMATION

LOCAL CURRENCY

1 euro (€) = 0,90 USD ($) (Déc. 2001)

TOURIST INFORMATION

Telephone numbers and addresses of Tourist Offices are given in the text of each city under 🅱.

National Holiday: *Belgium: 21 July; Netherlands: 30 April; Luxembourg: 23 June.*

AIRLINES

AIRLINES LUXAIR : *Luxembourg Airport, L-2987 Luxembourg, ℘ 4 79 81.*

KLM : *at airport, 1930 Zaventem, ℘ 0 2 717 20 70, Luxembourg Airport, L-2987 Luxembourg, ℘ 34 20 80 83 33, at Schiphol, ℘ (020) 474 77 47.*

FOREIGN EXCHANGE

In Belgium, *banks close at 4.30pm and weekends;*

in the Netherlands, *banks close at 5.00pm and weekends, Schiphol Airport exchange offices open daily from 6.30am to 11.30pm.*

TRANSPORT

Taxis: *may be hailed in the street, at taxi ranks or called by telephone.*
Bus, tramway: *practical for long and short distances and good for sightseeing.*
Brussels has a **Métro** *(subway) network. In each station complete information and plans will be found.*

POSTAL SERVICES – SHOPPING

Post offices open Monday to Friday from 9am to 5pm in Benelux.
Shops and boutiques are generally open from 9am to 7pm in Belgium and Luxembourg, and from 9am to 6pm in the Netherlands. The main shopping areas are:

in Brussels: *Rue Neuve, Porte de Namur, Avenue Louise, Avenue de la Toison d'Or, Boulevard de Waterloo, Rue de Namur - Also Brussels antique market on Saturday from 9am to 3pm, and Sunday from 9am to 1pm (around Place du Grand-Sablon) - Flower and Bird market (Grand-Place) on Sunday morning - Flea Market (Place du Jeu de Balles) – Shopping Centres: Basilix, Westland Shopping Center, Woluwé Shopping Center, City 2, Galerie Louise.*

in Luxembourg: *Grand'Rue and around Place d'Armes - Station Quarter.*

in Amsterdam: *Kalverstraat, Leidsestraat, Nieuwendijk, P.C. Hoofstraat, Beethoven-straat, Van Baerlestraat and Utrechtsestraat – Shopping Center, Magna Plaza – Second-hand goods and antiques (around Rijksmuseum and Spiegelgracht) – Flower Market – Amsterdam Flea Market (near Waterlooplein).*

BREAKDOWN SERVICE *24 hour assistance:*

Belgium: *TCB, Brussels ℘ 0 2 233 22 11 – VTB-VAB, Antwerp ℘ 0 3 253 63 63 – RACB, Brussels ℘ 0 2 287 09 00.*

Luxembourg: *ACL ℘ 45 00 451.*

Netherlands: *ANWB, The Hague ℘ (070) 314 71 47 – KNAC, The Hague ℘ (070) 383 16 12.*

TIPPING *In Benelux, prices include service and taxes.*

SPEED LIMITS – SEAT BELTS

In Belgium and Luxembourg, the maximum speed limits are 120 km/h-74 mph on motorways and dual carriageways, 90 km/h-56 mph on all other roads and 50 km/h-31 mph in built-up areas. In the Netherlands, 100/120 km/h-62/74 mph on motorways and "autowegen", 80 km/h-50 mph on other roads and 50 km/h-31 mph in built-up areas. In each country, the wearing of seat belts is compulsory for drivers and passengers.

BRUSSELS
(BRUXELLES/BRUSSEL)

1000 Région de Bruxelles-Capitale – Brussels Hoofdstedelijk Gewest 213 L 17 *and* 909 G 3 *– Pop. 959 318.*

Paris 308 – Amsterdam 204 – Düsseldorf 222 – Lille 116 – Luxembourg 219.

TOURIST OFFICES

TIB Hôtel de Ville, Grand'Place, ✉ *1000,* ☎ *0 2 513 89 40, tourism.brussels@tib.be, Fax 0 2 514 45 38.*
Office de Promotion du Tourisme (OPT), r. Marché-aux-Herbes 61, ✉ *1000,* ☎ *0 2 504 03 90, wallonie_bruxelles@yahoo.com, Fax 0 2 504 02 70.*
Toerisme Vlaanderen, Grasmarkt 61, ✉ *1000,* ☎ *0 2 504 03 00, info@toerismevlaande ren.be, Fax 0 2 513 88 03.*

For more information on tourist attractions consult our Green Guide to Brussels and our Map N° 44.

BRUXELLES
BRUSSEL

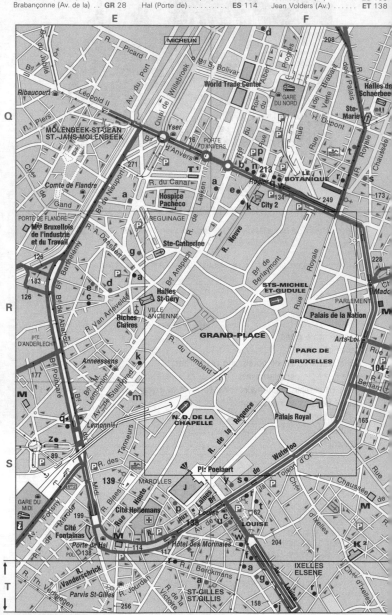

BRUXELLES
BRUSSEL

Américaine (R.) .... **FU** 8
Auguste Rodin (Av.) ..... **GU** 12
Besme (Av.) .... **EV** 18

Boondael (Drève de) ..... **GX** 22
Cambre (Bd de la) .... **GV** 33
Coccinelles (Av. des) .... **HX** 40
Congo (Av. du) .... **GV** 48
Copernic (R.) .... **FX** 51
Dodonée (R.) .... **FV** 61
Dries .... **HX** 63

Emile de Beco (Av.) ..... **GU** 79
Emile De Mot (Av.) ..... **GV** 81
Eperons d'Or
  (Av. des) .... **GU** 85
Everard (av.) .... **EV** 91
Hippodrome
  (Av. de l') .... **GU** 120

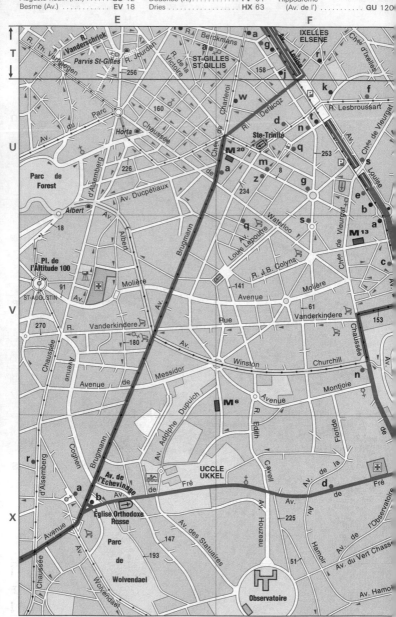

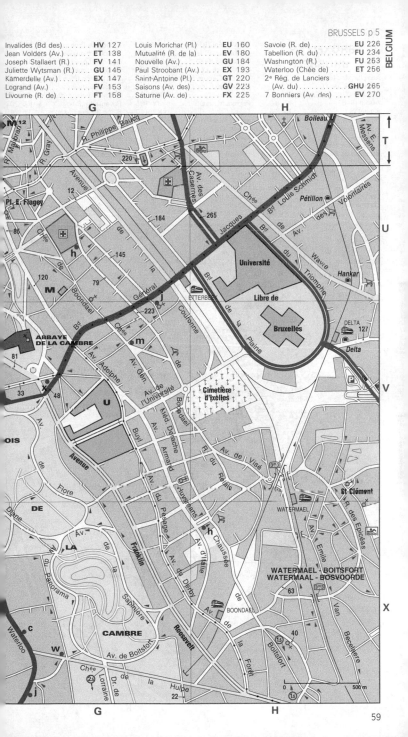

BRUXELLES
BRUSSEL

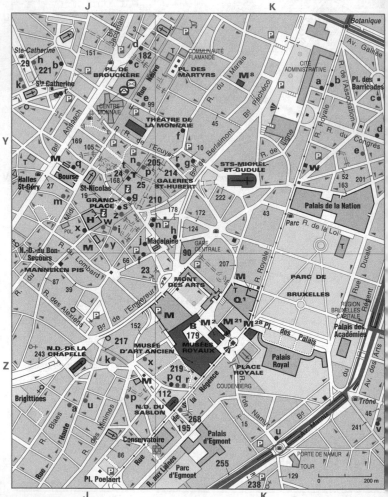

GOLF COURSES

🏌18 🏌9 *Southeast : 14 km at Tervuren, Château de Ravenstein* 📞 *0 2 767 58 01, Fax 0 2 767 28 41 –* 🏌18 *Northeast : 14 km at Melsbroek, Steenwagenstraat 11* 📞 *0 2 751 82 05, Fax 0 2 751 84 25 –* 🏌18 *at Anderlecht, Sports Area of la Pede, r. Scholle 1* 📞 *0 2 521 16 87, Fax 0 2 521 51 56 –* 🏌9 *at Watermael-Boitsfort, chaussée de la Hulpe 53a* 📞 *0 2 672 22 22, Fax 0 2 675 34 81 –* 🏌9 *Southeast : 16 km at Overijse, Gemslaan 55* 📞 *0 2 687 50 30, Fax 0 2 687 37 68 –* 🏌9 *West : 8 km at Itterbeek, J.M. Van Lierdelaan 24* 📞 *0 2 567 00 38, Fax 0 2 567 02 23 –* 🏌18 *Northeast : 20 km at Kampenhout, Wildersedreef 56* 📞 *0 16 65 12 16, Fax 0 16 65 16 80 –* 🏌9 *East : 18 km at Duisburg, Hertswegenstraat 59* 📞 *0 2 769 45 85, Fax 0 2 767 97 52.*

PLACES OF INTEREST

BRUSSELS SEEN FROM ABOVE

Atomium★ – Basilica of the Sacred Heart★ – Arcades of the Royal Museum of the Army and Military History★ HS **M25**.

FAMOUS VIEWS OF BRUSSELS

The Law Courts ES **J** *– Administrative sections of the City of Brussels* KY *– Place Royale★* KZ.

GREEN AREAS

Parks : Bruxelles, Wolvendael, Woluwé, Laeken, Cinquantenaire, Duden, Bois de la Cambre, Forêt de Soignes.

HISTORICAL MONUMENTS

Grand-Place★★★ JY *– Monnaie Theatre★* JY *– St Hubert Arcades★★* JKY *– Erasmus' House (Anderlecht)★★ – Castle and park (Gaasbeek)★★ (Southwest : 12 km) – Royal Greenhouses (Laeken)★★.*

CHURCHES

Sts-Michael's and Gudule's Cathedral★★ KY *– Church of N.-D. de la Chapelle★* JZ *– Church of N.-D. du Sablon★* KZ *– Abbey of la-Cambre (Ixelles)★★* FGV *– Church of Sts-Pierre and Guidon (Anderlecht)★.*

MUSEUMS

Museum of Ancient Art★★★ KZ *– Museum of the Cinquantenaire★★★* HS **M11** *– Museum of Modern Art★★* KZ **M2** *– Belgian Centre for Comic Strip Art★★* KY **M8** *– Autoworld★★* HS **M3** *– Natural Science Museum★★* GS **M29** *– Museum of Musical Instruments★★★* KZ **M21** *– Constantin Meunier Museum (Ixelles)★* FV **M13** *– Ixelles Community Museum (Ixelles)★★* GT **M12** *– Charlier Museum★* FR **M9** *– Bibliotheca Wittockiana (Woluwé-St-Pierre)★ – Royal Museum of Central Africa (Tervuren/ district)★★ – Horta Museum (St-Gilles)★★* EFU **M20** *– Van Buuren Museum (Uccle)★* EFV **M6** *– Bellevue★* KZ **M28**.

MODERN ARCHITECTURE

Atomium★ – Berlaymont Centre GR *– European Parliament* GS *– Arts Centre* KZ **Q1** *– Administrative sections of the City of Brussels* KY *– Garden-Cities Le Logis and Floréal (Watermael-Boitsfort) – Garden-Cities Kapelleveld (Woluwé-St-Lambert) – UCL Campus (Woluwé-St-Lambert) – Stoclet Palace (Tervuren/district)★ – Swift (La Hulpe/district) – Shop-front P. Hankar★* KY **W** *– Ixelles council building* FS **K2** *– Van Eetvelde Hotel★* GR 187 *– Old England★* KZ **N** *– Cauchie House (Etterbeek)★* HS **K1**.

SCENIC AREAS

Grand-Place★★★ JY *– Grand and Petit Sablon★★* JZ *– St-Hubert Arcades★★* JKY *– Place du Musée* KZ *– Place Ste-Catherine* JY *– The Old Town (Halles St-Géry – vault of the Senne – Church of Riches Claires)* ER *– Rue des Bouchers★* JY *– Manneken Pis★★* JZ *– The Marolles District* JZ *– Galerie Bortier* JY.

Alphabetical listing of hotels and restaurants

Starred establishments

✲ ✲ ✲

21	XXXX	Bruneau		15	XXX	Comme Chez Soi

✲ ✲

26	XXXXX	Bijgaarden (De)		14	XXXX	Sea Grill (H. Radisson SAS)
28	XXXX	Château du Mylord		21	XXX	Claude Dupont

✲

27	XXXX	Barbizon		19	XXX	Saint Guidon
17	XXXX	Maison du Bœuf		19	XXX	Truffe Noire (La)
		(H. Hilton)		19	XX	Baguettes Impériales (Les)
19	XXXX	Villa Lorraine		20	XX	Brouette (La)
17	XXX	Écailler		25	XX	Deux Maisons (les)
		du Palais Royal (L')		24	XX	Pain et le Vin (Le)
26	XXX	Michel		24	XX	Vieux Boitsfort (Au)
27	XXX	Orangerie Roland Debuyst (L')		21	X	Marie
				24	X	Passage (Le)

Establishments according to style of cuisine

Buffets

15 Atelier (L') *Q. de l'Europe*
18 Café Wiltcher's (H. Conrad) *Q. Louise*
19 Crescendo (H. Sheraton Towers) *Q. Botanique, Gare du Nord*

Grill

21 Aub. de Boendael (L') *Ixelles Q. Boondael*
25 auberg'in (l') *Woluwé-St-Pierre*
22 French Kiss *Jette*
24 Grill (Le) *Watermael-Boitsfort*
22 Vieux Pannenhuis (Rôtiss. Le) *Jette*

Pub rest – Brasseries

18 Atelier de la Truffe Noire (L') *Q. Louise*
26 Bistrot Alfons (H. Gosset) *Env. at Groot-Bijgaarden*
20 Brasserie de la Gare (La) *Berchem-Ste-Agathe*
24 Brasseries Georges *Uccle*
20 Erasme *Anderlecht*
14 Golden Tulip Grand-Place
27 Istas *Env. at Overijse*
26 Kasteel Gravenhof *Env. at Dworp*
28 Lindbergh Taverne (H. Sheraton Airport) *Env. at Zaventem*
16 Matignon *Q. Grand'Place*
21 Quincaillerie (La) *Ixelles Q. Bascule*
16 Roue d'Or (La) *Q. Grand'Place*
28 Stockmansmolen *Env. at Zaventem*
22 Vigne... à l'Assiette (De la) *Ixelles Q. Louise*

Regional

15 In 't Spinnekopke
16 Kelderke ('t) *Q. Grand'Place*

Seafood – Oyster bar

17 Belle Maraîchère (La) *Q. Ste-Catherine*
24 Brasseries Georges *Uccle*

17 Écailler du Palais Royal (L') *Q. des Sablons*
17 François *Q. Ste-Catherine*
21 Quincaillerie (La) *Ixelles Q. Bascule*
14 Sea Grill (H. Radisson SAS)
27 Stoveke ('t) *Env. at Strombeek-Bever*
17 Truite d'Argent and H. Welcome (La) *Q. Ste-Catherine*
25 Vignoble de Margot (Le) *Woluwé-St-Pierre*

Basque

21 fils de Jules (Le) *Ixelles Q. Bascule*

Chinese

24 Cité du Dragon (La) *Uccle*
19 Lychee *Q. Atomium*
19 Ming Dynasty *Q. Atomium*
20 New Asia *Auderghem*

Indian

18 Palais des Indes (Au) *Q. Louise*
18 Porte des Indes (La) *Q. Louise*

Italian

23 Amici miei *Schaerbeek Q. Meiser*
27 Arlecchino (L') (H. Aub. de Waterloo) *Env. at Sint-Genesius-Rode*
17 Castello Banfi *Q. des Sablons*
23 I Trulli *St-Gilles Q. Louise*
15 Pappa e Citti *Q. de l'Europe*
21 San Daniele *Ganshoren*
23 Senza Nome *Schaerbeek*
20 Stromboli *Berchem-Ste-Agathe*
22 Tutto Pepe *Ixelles Q. Louise*

Japanese

17 Herbe Rouge (L') *Q. des Sablons*
20 Momotaro Etterbeek *Q. Cinquantenaire*
15 Samourai
18 Tagawa *Q. Louise*
15 Take Sushi *Q. de l'Europe*

Moroccan

20 Khaïma (La) *Auderghem*

Portuguese

22 Forcado (Le) *St-Gilles*

Spanish

20 Grillange *Etterbeek*
15 Jardin d'Espagne (Le)
   Q. de l'Europe

Thai

24 Blue Elephant *Uccle*
18 Larmes du Tigre (Les)
   Q. Palais de Justice
22 Perles de Pluie (Les)
   Ixelles Q. Louise

Vietnamese

19 Baguettes Impériales (Les)
   Q. Atomium
21 Pagode d'Or (La)
   Ixelles Q. Boondael
21 Yen (Le) *Ixelles*

BRUXELLES (BRUSSEL)

🏨🏨🏨 **Radisson SAS** Ⓜ, r. Fossé-aux-Loups 47, ⊠ 1000, ℰ 0 2 219 28 28, Fax 0 2 219 62 62, « Patio with remains of 12C City enclosure wall », ↳6, ⇌ – 🕸 ⇌ 🖵 TV ₺ ↬– ⅍ 25-420. 🆎 ⑩ ⑯ VISA
KY f
Meals see *Sea Grill* below – *Atrium* Lunch 26 – a la carte approx. 45 – � 25 – **275 rm** 290, 6 suites.

🏨🏨🏨 **Astoria**, r. Royale 103, ⊠ 1000, ℰ 0 2 227 05 05, H1154@accor-hotels.com, Fax 0 2 217 11 50, « Early 20C residence, Belle Epoque style », ↳6 – 🕸 ⇌ 🖵 TV 🅿 – ⅍ 25-180. 🆎 ⑩ ⑯ VISA JCB
KY b
Meals *Le Palais Royal* (closed 15 July-15 August and weekends) 40 – � 23 – **106 rm** 170/250, 12 suites.

🏨🏨🏨 **Le Plaza**, bd. A. Max 118, ⊠ 1000, ℰ 0 2 227 67 00 , reservations@leplaza-brussels.be, Fax 0 2 227 67 20, « Lobby-bar underneath cupola » – 🕸 ⇌ 🖵 TV ↬– ⅍ 25-800.
🆎 ⑩ ⑯ VISA JCB
FQ e
Meals (closed Saturday and Sunday) Lunch 30 – a la carte 40/53 – � 25 – **187 rm** 350/400, 6 suites.

🏨🏨🏨 **Métropole**, pl. de Brouckère 31, ⊠ 1000, ℰ 0 2 217 23 00 , info@metropolehotel.be, Fax 0 2 218 02 20, « Late 19C hall and lounges », ↳6, ⇌ – 🕸 ⇌ 🖵 TV ↬– ⅍ 25-400.
🆎 ⑩ ⑯ VISA JCB ⁂ rest
JY c
Meals see *L'Alban Chambon* below – **296 rm** ⊠ 304/425, 5 suites.

🏨🏨 **Bedford**, r. Midi 135, ⊠ 1000, ℰ 0 2 507 00 00, hotelbedfordb@pophost.eunet.be, Fax 0 2 507 00 10, ↳6 – 🕸 ⇌ 🖵 TV ↬– ⅍ 25-250. 🆎 ⑩ ⑯ VISA JCB ⁂
ER k
Meals Lunch 22 – a la carte 56/71 ☂ – **309 rm** ⊠ 200/250, 12 suites.

🏨🏨 **Atlanta**, bd A. Max 7, ⊠ 1000, ℰ 0 2 217 01 20 , info@gtatlanta.goldentulip.be, Fax 0 2 217 37 58 – 🕸 ⇌, ⊜ rest, TV ↬– ⅍ 25-50. 🆎 ⑩ ⑯ VISA
JY d
Meals Lunch 10 – a la carte 30/48 – ⊠ 21 – **235 rm** 300/385, 6 suites.

🏨🏨 **President Centre** without rest, r. Royale 160, ⊠ 1000, ℰ 0 2 219 00 65 , hotelpr esident@arcadis.be, Fax 0 2 218 09 10 – 🕸 ⇌ 🖵 TV ↬. 🆎 ⑩ ⑯ VISA JCB. ⁂
73 rm ⊠ 170/195.
KY a

🏨🏨 **Scandic Grand'Place**, r. Arenberg 18, ⊠ 1000, ℰ 0 2 548 18 11 , info@scandicg randplacebrussels.be, Fax 0 2 548 18 20, ⇌ – 🕸 ⇌ 🖵 ₺ – ⅍ 25-80. 🆎 ⑩ ⑯ VISA JCB. ⁂ rest
KY r
Meals (closed lunch Saturday, Sunday and Bank Holidays) Lunch 16 – a la carte 22/31 – **100 rm** ⊠ 186/225.

🏨🏨 **Golden Tulip Grand Place**, r. Assaut 15, ⊠ 1000, ℰ 0 2 501 16 16, info@gtgra ndplace.goldentulip.be, Fax 0 2 501 18 18 – 🕸 ⇌ 🖵 TV ↬– ⅍ 25-75. 🆎 ⑩ ⑯ VISA JCB
KY g
Meals (closed Saturday and Sunday lunch) (Pub rest). Lunch 8 – a la carte approx. 28 – ⊠ 20 – **155 rm** 223/249.

🏨🏨 **Agenda Midi** without rest, bd Jamar 11, ⊠ 1060, ℰ 0 2 520 00 10, midi@hotel-ag enda.com, Fax 0 2 520 00 20 – 🕸 ⇌ TV. 🆎 ⑩ ⑯ VISA JCB. ⁂
ES z
35 rm ⊠ 84/97.

🏨 **Chambord** without rest, r. Namur 82, ⊠ 1000, ℰ 0 2 548 99 10 , hotel-chambord @hotel-chambord.be, Fax 0 2 514 08 47 – 🕸 TV. 🆎 ⑩ ⑯ VISA JCB. ⁂
KZ u
⊠ 17 – **69 rm** 130/147.

🏨 **Queen Anne** without rest, bd E. Jacqmain 110, ⊠ 1000, ℰ 0 2 217 16 00, Fax 0 2 217 18 38 – 🕸 TV. 🆎 ⑩ ⑯ VISA. ⁂
EFQ a
60 rm ⊠ 112/124.

🏨 **George V** without rest, r. 't Kint 23, ⊠ 1000, ℰ 0 2 513 50 93 , reservations@geo rge5.com, Fax 0 2 513 44 93 – 🕸 TV. 🆎 ⑩ ⑯ VISA JCB
ER c
17 rm ⊠ 70.

🏨 **Sabina** without rest, r. Nord 78, ⊠ 1000, ℰ 0 2 218 26 37 , hotel.sabina@advalvas.be, Fax 0 2 219 32 39 – 🕸 TV. 🆎 ⑩ ⑯ VISA JCB
KY c
24 rm ⊠ 61/73.

XXXX ❀❀ **Sea Grill** - Hotel Radisson SAS, r. Fossé-aux-Loups 47, ⊠ 1000, ℰ 0 2 227 31 20, Fax 0 2 219 62 62, Seafood – ⊜ 🅿. 🆎 ⑩ ⑯ VISA. ⁂
KY l
closed 31 March-7 April, 21 July-18 August, Saturday lunch, Sunday and Bank Holidays – Meals Lunch 72 b.i. – 100 b.i./160 b.i., a la carte 89/105 ☂
Spec. St-Jacques à la vapeur d'algues, crème légère au cresson (15 September-15 April). Bar de ligne cuit en croûte de gros sel. Manchons de crabe de la mer de Barents tiédis au beurre de persil plat.

XXXX **L'Alban Chambon** - Hotel Métropole, pl. de Brouckère 31, ⊠ 1000, ℰ 0 2 217 23 00, info@metropolehotel.be, Fax 0 2 218 02 20, « Late 19C atmosphere » – ⊜ 🅿. 🆎 ⑩ ⑯ VISA JCB
JY c
closed 15 July-15 August, Saturday and Sunday – Meals Lunch 39 – 55 b.i./90 b.i. ☂.

Comme Chez Soi (Wynants), pl. Rouppe 23, ⊠ 1000, ℰ 0 2 512 29 21, Fax 0 2 511 80 52, « Belle Epoque atmosphere with Horta decor » – 🍴 P. 🖭 ⓪ 🐵 VISA, closed 30 June-29 July, Christmas-New Year, Sunday and Monday – **Meals** (booking essential) 62/135, a la carte 85/116   ES m
Spec. Filets de sole, mousseline au Riesling et aux crevettes grises. Alle de pigeon rôtie sur son gateau parmentier de cuisses confites au beurre de foies. Crêpe soufflée, sauce à la fenouillette au lait d'amandes et dés de bananes.

Astrid "Chez Pierrot", r. Presse 21, ⊠ 1000, ℰ 0 2 217 38 31 , astrid.brack@sky net.be, Fax 0 2 217 38 31 – 🖭 VISA   KY e
closed Easter week, 15 July-15 August and Sunday – **Meals** Lunch 19 – 26.

La Manufacture, r. Notre-Dame du Sommeil 12, ⊠ 1000, ℰ 0 2 502 25 25, manu facture@skynet.be, Fax 0 2 502 27 15, ☆, Open until 11 p.m., « Contemporary brasserie in a converted Moroccan leather factory » – P. 🖭 ⓪ 🐵 VISA   ER e
closed Saturday lunch and Sunday – **Meals** Lunch 25 b.i. – 30 b.i./65 b.i.

Samourai, r. Fossé-aux-Loups 28, ⊠ 1000, ℰ 0 2 217 56 39, Fax 0 2 771 97 61, Japanese cuisine – 🖭 ⓪ 🐵 VISA JCB. ☆   JY e
closed 15 July-16 August, Tuesday and Sunday lunch – **Meals** Lunch 18 – a la carte 41/61.

In 't Spinnekopke, pl. du Jardin aux Fleurs 1, ⊠ 1000, ℰ 0 2 511 86 95 , info@s pinnekopke.be, Fax 0 2 513 24 97, ☆, Partly regional cuisine, open until 11 p.m., « Typical ancient Brussels pub » – 🍴 🖭 ⓪ 🐵 VISA. ☆   ER d
Meals Lunch 9 – a la carte approx. 30.

Quartier de l'Europe

Dorint Ⓜ, bd Charlemagne 11, ⊠ 1000, ℰ 0 2 231 09 09 , info@dorintbru.be, Fax 0 2 230 33 71, « Contemporary photography exhibition », ℐ₅, ≦s, 🚴, – 🛗 ☆ 🖭 📺 &, ⇐⇒ – 🔏 25-150. 🖭 ⓪ 🐵 VISA   GR c
Meals L'Objectif (closed 20 July-25 August and lunch Saturday and Sunday) Lunch 32 – a la carte 42/51 ♀ – ⊡ 22 – **210 rm** 325/350, 2 suites.

Europa Inter.Continental, r. Loi 107, ⊠ 1040, ℰ 0 2 230 13 33, Fax 0 2 230 36 82, ☆, ℐ₅, 🛗 ☆ 🖭 ⇐⇒ P. – 🔏 25-350. 🖭 ⓪ 🐵 VISA. ☆ rm   GR d
Meals (closed August and Saturday lunch) 25/42 – ⊡ 22 – **236 rm** 250/450, 4 suites.

Eurovillage, bd Charlemagne 80, ⊠ 1000, ℰ 0 2 230 85 55, Fax 0 2 230 56 35, ☆, ℐ₅, ≦s – 🛗 ☆ 🖭 ⇐⇒ – 🔏 25-130. 🖭 ⓪ 🐵 VISA JCB. ☆   GR a
Meals (closed August, Saturday and Sunday lunch) Lunch 20 – a la carte approx. 32 ⊡ 16 – **80 rm** 180/200.

New Hotel Charlemagne, bd Charlemagne 25, ⊠ 1000, ℰ 0 2 230 21 35, bruss elscharlemagne@new-hotel.be, Fax 0 2 230 25 10, 🚴 – 🛗 ☆ 📺 ⇐⇒ – 🔏 30-60. 🖭 ⓪ 🐵 VISA JCB. ☆ rest   GR k
Meals (residents only) – ⊡ 17 – **66 rm** 176/191.

Libertel City Garden without rest, r. Joseph II 59, ⊠ 1000, ℰ 0 2 282 82 82, H2740@accor-hotels.com, Fax 0 2 230 64 37 – 🛗 ☆ 🖭 📺 ⇐⇒ – 🔏 25-50. 🖭 ⓪ 🐵 VISA JCB   GR v
96 rm ⊡ 175.

Pappa e Citti, r. Franklin 18, ⊠ 1000, ℰ 0 2 732 61 10, pappaecittl@skynet.be, Fax 0 2 752 57 40, ☆, Italian cuisine – 🖭 ⓪ 🐵 VISA. ☆   GR e
closed August, 22 December-6 January, Saturday, Sunday and Bank Holidays – **Meals** Lunch 26 – a la carte approx. 47.

Le Jardin d'Espagne, r. Archimède 65, ⊠ 1000, ℰ 0 2 736 34 49, Fax 0 2 735 17 45, ☆, Spanish cuisine with tapas-bar – 🖭 ⓪ 🐵 VISA   GR s
closed August, Saturday lunch and Sunday – **Meals** Lunch 9 – a la carte 22/32.

Balthazar, r. Archimède 63, ⊠ 1000, ℰ 0 2 742 06 00, Fax 0 2 735 70 07, ☆ – 🖭 🐵 VISA   GR s
closed 22 December-5 January, Saturday lunch and Sunday – **Meals** a la carte 28/38.

L'Atelier, r. Franklin 28, ⊠ 1000, ℰ 0 2 734 91 40 , info@atelier.euro, Fax 0 2 735 35 98, ☆, Partly buffets – 🖭 ⓪ 🐵 VISA   GR y
closed 2 August-2 September, 20 December-6 January, weekends and Bank Holidays – **Meals** Lunch 19 – 22 b.i./28 b.i.

Take Sushi, bd Charlemagne 21, ⊠ 1000, ℰ 0 2 230 56 27, Fax 0 2 231 10 44, ☆, Japanese cuisine with Sushi-bar – 🖭 ⓪ 🐵 VISA JCB. ☆   GR z
closed Saturday and Sunday lunch – **Meals** Lunch 14 – 22/52.

Quartier Grand'Place (Ilot Sacré)

Royal Windsor, r. Duquesnoy 5, ⊠ 1000, ℰ 0 2 505 55 55, sales.royalwindsor@wa rwickhotels.com, Fax 0 2 505 55 00, ℐ₅, ≦s – 🛗 ☆ 🖭 📺 ⇐⇒ P. – 🔏 25-350. 🖭 ⓪ 🐵 VISA JCB. ☆ rest   JYZ f
Meals Les 4 Saisons (closed 20 July-August, Saturday lunch and Sunday) Lunch 30 – a la carte 61/81 – ⊡ 25 – **232 rm** 360/446, 34 suites.

Le Méridien 🏨 ⌘, Carrefour de l'Europe 3, ⊠ 1000, ℰ 0 2 548 42 11, *info@me ridien.be*, Fax 0 2 548 40 80, ≤, 🔬 – 🛗 ⇔ ≡ 📺 ᘓ – 🔬 25-200. 🆎 ⓘ ⓶ 𝗩𝗜𝗦𝗔 𝗝𝗖𝗕 ⌘
KY h
Meals *L'Épicerie* (closed Saturday lunch) Lunch 36 – 47 – ⊐ 22 – **217 rm** 425/605, 3 suites.

Amigo, r. Amigo 1, ⊠ 1000, ℰ 0 2 547 47 47 , *hotelamigo@hotelamigo.com*, Fax 0 2 513 52 77, « Collection of works of art » – 🛗 ⇔ ≡ 📺 ᘓ – 🔬 25-200. 🆎 ⓘ ⓶ 𝗩𝗜𝗦𝗔. ⌘
JY x
Meals (Open until 11 p.m.) a la carte 33/45 ⅄ – ⊐ 25 – **152 rm** 400/430, 7 suites.

Carrefour de l'Europe, r. Marché-aux-Herbes 110, ⊠ 1000, ℰ 0 2 504 94 00 , *carr efour@sabenahotels.com*, Fax 0 2 504 95 00 – 🛗 ⇔ ≡ 📺 ᘓ – 🔬 25-200. 🆎 ⓘ ⓶ 𝗩𝗜𝗦𝗔 𝗝𝗖𝗕. ⌘ rest
JKY n
Meals (closed Saturday, Sunday and Bank Holidays) 36/46 – ⊐ 21 – **58 rm** 260/340, 5 suites.

Le Dixseptième without rest, r. Madeleine 25, ⊠ 1000, ℰ 0 2 502 17 17, *info@le dixseptieme.be*, Fax 0 2 502 64 24, « Elegant town house » – 🛗 ≡ 📺 – 🔬 25. 🆎 ⓘ ⓶ 𝗩𝗜𝗦𝗔. ⌘
JY j
18 rm ⊐ 170/240, 6 suites.

Novotel off Grand'Place, r. Marché-aux-Herbes 120, ⊠ 1000, ℰ 0 2 514 33 33 , *H1030@accor-hotels.com*, ⊠ 1030 – 🛗 ⇔ ≡ 📺 ᘓ – 🔬 25-200. 🆎 ⓘ ⓶ 𝗩𝗜𝗦𝗔 JKY n
Meals (Open until 11 p.m.) a la carte approx. 29 ⅄ – **138 rm** ⊐ 175/205.

Aris without rest, r. Marché-aux-Herbes 78, ⊠ 1000, ℰ 0 2 514 43 00, Fax 0 2 514 01 19 – 🛗 ≡ 📺 ᘓ. ⓘ ⓶ 𝗩𝗜𝗦𝗔 𝗝𝗖𝗕
JY g
55 rm ⊐ 200/225.

Matignon, r. Bourse 10, ⊠ 1000, ℰ 0 2 511 08 88, Fax 0 2 513 69 27, 🍴 – 🛗 📺. 🆎 ⓘ ⓶ 𝗩𝗜𝗦𝗔
JY q
Meals (closed 10 January-February and Monday) (Pub rest, open until 11 p.m.) Lunch 17 – 22 – **37 rm** ⊐ 85/102.

Floris without rest, r. Harengs 6, ⊠ 1000, ℰ 0 2 514 07 60, *floris.grandplace@grou ptorus.com*, Fax 0 2 548 90 39 – 🛗 📺. 🆎 ⓘ ⓶ 𝗩𝗜𝗦𝗔. ⌘
JY s
11 rm ⊐ 124/213.

La Maison du Cygne, Grand'Place 9, ⊠ 1000, ℰ 0 2 511 82 44, Fax 0 2 514 31 48, « 17C former guildhouse » – ≡ 🅿. 🆎 ⓘ ⓶ 𝗩𝗜𝗦𝗔 𝗝𝗖𝗕
JY w
closed first 3 weeks August, late December, Saturday lunch and Sunday – **Meals** Lunch 36 – 62/69.

Aux Armes de Bruxelles, r. Bouchers 13, ⊠ 1000, ℰ 0 2 511 55 98 , *arbrux@b eon.be*, Fax 0 2 514 33 81, Open until 11 p.m., « Brussels atmosphere » – ≡. 🆎 ⓘ ⓶ 𝗩𝗜𝗦𝗔 𝗝𝗖𝗕. ⌘
JY t
closed 17 June-15 July and Monday – **Meals** Lunch 23 b.i. – 29/45 ⅄.

Le Cerf, Grand'Place 20, ⊠ 1000, ℰ 0 2 511 47 91, Fax 0 2 546 09 59, Open until 11.30 p.m. – ≡. 🆎 ⓘ ⓶ 𝗩𝗜𝗦𝗔
JY z
closed 20 July-20 August, Saturday and Sunday – **Meals** Lunch 11 – 46 b.i./53 b.i. ⅄.

L'Ogenblik, Galerie des Princes 1, ⊠ 1000, ℰ 0 2 511 61 51, Fax 0 2 513 41 58, 🍴 Open until midnight, « Ancient pub interior » – 🆎 ⓘ ⓶ 𝗩𝗜𝗦𝗔
JY p
closed Sunday – **Meals** a la carte 45/60.

La Roue d'Or, r. Chapeliers 26, ⊠ 1000, ℰ 0 2 514 25 54, Fax 0 2 512 30 81, Open until midnight, « Typical ancient Brussels pub with surrealist murals » – 🆎 ⓘ ⓶ 𝗩𝗜𝗦𝗔
JY y
closed 20 July-20 August – **Meals** Lunch 10 – 43 b.i./52 b.i.

Vincent, r. Dominicains 8, ⊠ 1000, ℰ 0 2 511 26 07, *info@restaurantvincent.com*, Fax 0 2 502 36 93, 🍴, Open until 11.30 p.m., « Ancient grill room decorated with original painted ceramic frescos, Brussels atmosphere » – ≡. 🆎 ⓘ ⓶ 𝗩𝗜𝗦𝗔 𝗝𝗖𝗕
JY r
closed first 2 weeks August, 24 and 25 December and 2 to 12 January – **Meals** Lunch 1 – a la carte 26/66.

Falstaff Gourmand, r. Pierres 38, ⊠ 1000, ℰ 0 2 512 17 61, Fax 0 2 512 17 61, Open until 11 p.m. – ≡. 🆎 ⓘ ⓶ 𝗩𝗜𝗦𝗔
JY n
closed last 2 weeks July-first week August, Sunday dinner and Monday – **Meals** Lunch 1 – a la carte 24/32.

't Kelderke, Grand'Place 15, ⊠ 1000, ℰ 0 2 513 73 44, Fax 0 2 512 30 81, Regional cooking, open until 2 a.m., « Pub in a vaulted cellar, Brussels atmosphere » – 🆎 ⓘ ⓶ 𝗩𝗜𝗦𝗔
JY
closed 1 to 15 July – **Meals** Lunch 8 – a la carte 22/34.

Quartier Ste-Catherine (Marché-aux-Poissons)

Novotel Tour Noire 🏨, r. Vierge Noire 32, ⊠ 1000, ℰ 0 2 505 50 50, *H2122@ ccor-hotels.com*, Fax 0 2 505 50 00, 🔬, ≦ – 🛗 ⇔ 📺 ᘓ – 🔬 25-220. 🆎 ⓘ ⓶ 𝗩𝗜𝗦𝗔 𝗝𝗖𝗕
JY
Meals Lunch 25 – a la carte 30/41 ⅄ – ⊐ 15 – **217 rm** 180/200.

Atlas ⌕ without rest, r. Vieux Marché-aux-Grains 30, ⌑ 1000, ℰ 0 2 502 60 06 , *info @ atlas.be*, Fax 0 2 502 69 35 – 🔌 📺 ⟺ – 🛗 30. 🆎 ⓞ ⓜⓢ 𝘝𝘐𝘚𝘈 ⅏ ER a
83 rm ⌑ 145/168, 5 suites.

Astrid Centre without rest, pl. du Samedi 11, ⌑ 1000, ℰ 0 2 219 31 19, Fax 0 2 219 31 70 – 🔌 📺 ⅃ ⟺ – 🛗 25-80. ⓞ ⓜⓢ 𝘝𝘐𝘚𝘈 𝗝𝗖𝗕 JY b
100 rm ⌑ 200.

La Belle Maraîchère, pl. Ste-Catherine 11, ⌑ 1000, ℰ 0 2 512 97 59, Fax 0 2 513 76 91, Seafood – ▤ ℙ. 🆎 ⓞ ⓜⓢ 𝘝𝘐𝘚𝘈 JY k
closed 3 weeks July, 2 weeks January, Wednesday and Thursday – **Meals** Lunch 31 – 27/46.

François, quai aux Briques 2, ⌑ 1000, ℰ 0 2 511 60 89, Fax 0 2 512 06 67, 🍽, Oyster bar, seafood – ▤ 🆎 ⓞ ⓜⓢ 𝘝𝘐𝘚𝘈 𝗝𝗖𝗕 JY k
closed Sunday and Monday – **Meals** Lunch 25 – 32 ⅀.

La Truite d'Argent and H. Welcome with rm, quai au Bois-à-Brûler 23, ⌑ 1000, ℰ 0 2 219 95 46, *info@ hotelwelcome.com*, Fax 0 2 217 18 87, 🍽 – 🔌, ▤ rest, 📺. ⓞ ⓜⓢ 𝘝𝘐𝘚𝘈 JY h
Meals *(closed 31 July-16 August, 22 December-8 January, Saturday lunch and Sunday)* *(Seafood, open until 11.30 p.m.)* Lunch 22 – 36/46 – ⌑ 8 – **10 rm** 65/120.

Le Loup-Galant, quai aux Barques 4, ⌑ 1000, ℰ 0 2 219 99 98, *loupgalant@ swing.be*, Fax 0 2 219 99 98 – 🆎 ⓞ ⓜⓢ 𝘝𝘐𝘚𝘈 EQ a
closed 1 week Easter, 1 to 15 August, 1 week Christmas, Sunday and Monday – **Meals** Lunch 19 – 24/42.

Le Bistro M'Alain, r. Flandre 6, ⌑ 1000, ℰ 0 2 503 14 80, *alain.troubat@ skynet.be*, Fax 0 2 503 14 80 – 🆎 ⓞ ⓜⓢ 𝘝𝘐𝘚𝘈 ER g
closed first week February, first 3 weeks August, Sunday and Monday – **Meals** Lunch 25 – 31.

Quartier des Sablons

Jolly du Grand Sablon Ⓜ, r. Bodenbroek 2, ⌑ 1000, ℰ 0 2 518 11 00, *jollyhotel sablon@ jollyhotels.be*, Fax 0 2 512 67 66, 🍽 – 🔌 ⅀⅄ ▤ 📺 ⟺ – 🛗 25-150. 🆎 ⓞ ⓜⓢ 𝘝𝘐𝘚𝘈. ⅏ KZ p
Meals *(closed 3 to 25 August and 21 December-5 January)* Lunch 20 – 31 – **193 rm** ⌑ 289/370, 5 suites.

L'Écaillier du Palais Royal (Hahn), r. Bodenbroek 18, ⌑ 1000, ℰ 0 2 512 87 51, Fax 0 2 511 99 50, Seafood – ▤. 🆎 ⓞ ⓜⓢ 𝘝𝘐𝘚𝘈 KZ r
closed August and Sunday – **Meals** a la carte 69/96
Spec. Gratin d'étrilles au beurre de mangues. Homard rôti et beurre de sauge. Bouillabaisse parfumée au pastis.

Trente rue de la Paille, r. Paille 30, ⌑ 1000, ℰ 0 2 512 07 15, Fax 0 2 514 23 33 – ▤. 🆎 ⓞ ⓜⓢ 𝘝𝘐𝘚𝘈. ⅏ JZ x
closed mid July-mid August, Christmas-New Year, Saturday and Sunday – **Meals** Lunch 31 – a la carte 50/60.

Castello Banfi, r. Bodenbroek 12, ⌑ 1000, ℰ 0 2 512 87 94, Fax 0 2 512 87 94, Partly Italian cuisine – ▤. 🆎 ⓞ ⓜⓢ 𝘝𝘐𝘚𝘈 KZ q
closed Easter week, last 3 weeks August, late December, Sunday and Monday – **Meals** Lunch 27 – 47.

"Chez Marius" En Provence, pl. du Petit Sablon 1, ⌑ 1000, ℰ 0 2 511 12 08, Fax 0 2 512 27 89, 🍽 – 🆎 ⓞ ⓜⓢ 𝘝𝘐𝘚𝘈. ⅏ KZ s
closed 21 July-20 August, Sunday and Bank Holidays – **Meals** Lunch 22 – 39/55.

La Clef des Champs, r. Rollebeek 23, ⌑ 1000, ℰ 0 2 512 11 93, Fax 0 2 512 11 93, 🍽 – ▤. 🆎 ⓞ ⓜⓢ 𝘝𝘐𝘚𝘈 𝗝𝗖𝗕 JZ k
closed Sunday dinner, Monday and Bank Holidays – **Meals** 29/36.

L'Herbe Rouge, r. Minimes 34, ⌑ 1000, ℰ 0 2 512 48 34, Fax 0 2 511 62 88, Japanese cuisine, open until 1 p.m. – 🆎 ⓞ ⓜⓢ 𝘝𝘐𝘚𝘈 JZ p
closed 15 July-3 August and Sunday – **Meals** a la carte 29/41.

Quartier Palais de Justice

Hilton, bd de Waterloo 38, ⌑ 1000, ℰ 0 2 504 11 11 and 0 2 504 13 33 (rest), Fax 0 2 504 21 11, ← town, 🛋, ⓢ – 🔌 ⅀⅄ ▤ 📺 ⟺ – 🛗 45-650. 🆎 ⓞ ⓜⓢ 𝘝𝘐𝘚𝘈 FS s
Meals see **Maison du Bœuf** below – **Café d'Egmont** (Open until midnight) 35 – ⌑ 23 – **418 rm** 345/369, 13 suites.

Maison du Bœuf - Hotel Hilton, 1st floor, bd de Waterloo 38, ⌑ 1000, ℰ 0 2 504 13 34, Fax 0 2 504 21 11, ← – 🆎 ⓞ ⓜⓢ 𝘝𝘐𝘚𝘈. ⅏ FS s
Meals Lunch 49 – 53/63, a la carte approx. 89
Spec. Côte de bœuf rôtie en croûte de sel. Bar rôti au thym frais, crème d'échalotes. Tartare maison au caviar.

XX **J and B,** r. Grand Cerf 24, ⊠ 1000, 𝒫 0 2 512 04 84, *jb@resto.be, Fax 0 2 511 79 30*
– 🔲, 🖭 ⓐ ⓜⓔ 𝘝𝘐𝘚𝘈. ⊗   FS y
closed Saturday lunch, Sunday and Bank Holidays – Meals 17/27.

X **Les Larmes du Tigre,** r. Wynants 21, ⊠ 1000, 𝒫 0 2 512 18 77, *Fax 0 2 502 10 03*,
🏠, Thai cuisine – 🖭 ⓐ ⓜⓔ 𝘝𝘐𝘚𝘈   ES p
closed Tuesday and Saturday lunch – **Meals** Lunch 11 – a la carte 25/31.

X **L'Idiot du village,** r. Notre Seigneur 19, ⊠ 1000, 𝒫 0 2 502 55 82, Open until 11 p.m.
– 🖭 ⓐ ⓜⓔ 𝘝𝘐𝘚𝘈   JZ a
closed 15 July-15 August, 24 December-2 January, Saturday and Sunday – **Meals** Lunch 14
– a la carte 33/55.

Quartier Léopold *(see also at Ixelles)*

🏨 **Stanhope,** r. Commerce 9, ⊠ 1000, 𝒫 0 2 506 91 11, *summithotels@stanhope.be,*
Fax 0 2 512 17 08, « Town house with walled terrace », 𝄋, ⇔ – 🛗 🔲 📺 🚗. 🖭 ⓐ
ⓜⓔ 𝘝𝘐𝘚𝘈 ᴊᴄʙ. ⊗   KZ v
Meals see *Brighton* below – �}} 22 – **35 rm** 295/395, 15 suites.

XXX **Brighton** - Hotel Stanhope, r. Commerce 9, ⊠ 1000, 𝒫 0 2 506 95 55, *summithotel*
s@stanhope.be, Fax 0 2 512 17 08, 🏠 – 🔲 🖳 🖭 ⓐ ⓜⓔ 𝘝𝘐𝘚𝘈 ᴊᴄʙ. ⊗   KZ v
closed Saturday and Sunday – Meals a la carte 48/83.

Quartier Louise *(see also at Ixelles and at St-Gilles)*

🏨 **Conrad,** av. Louise 71, ⊠ 1050, 𝒫 0 2 542 42 42 and 0 2 542 48 50 (rest), *bruhc_g*
m@hilton.com, Fax 0 2 542 42 00 and 0 2 542 48 42 (rest), 🏠, « Hotel complex around
an early 20C mansion », 𝄋, ⇔, 🏊 – 🛗 🍴 🔲 📺 🚗 – 🔬 25-650. 🖭 ⓐ ⓜⓔ 𝘝𝘐𝘚𝘈
ᴊᴄʙ   FS f
Meals see *La Maison de Maître* below – *Café Wiltcher's* Lunch 31 – a la carte 46/58 ⌦
– �}} 29 – **254 rm** 495/570, 15 suites.

🏨 **Bristol Stephanie** Ⓜ, av. Louise 91, ⊠ 1050, 𝒫 0 2 543 33 11 , *hotel_bristol@br*
istol.be, Fax 0 2 538 03 07, 𝄋, ⇔, 🏊 – 🛗 🍴 🔲 📺 🚗 – 🔬 25-215. 🖭 ⓐ ⓜⓔ 𝘝𝘐𝘚𝘈
ᴊᴄʙ. ⊗ rest   FT g
Meals *(closed July-August, Saturday and Sunday)* Lunch 25 – a la carte 35/44 – ⊟ 22 –
140 rm 300/365, 2 suites.

🏨 **Barsey,** av. Louise 381, ⊠ 1050, 𝒫 0 2 649 98 00 and 0 2 649 11 11 (rest), *info@b*
arsey.com, Fax 0 2 640 17 64, 🏠, « Restaurant with a cosy neo-classical interior and
trendy ambience », 𝄋, ⇔ – 🛗 🍴 🔲 📺 🚗 – 🔬 40. 🖭 ⓐ ⓜⓔ 𝘝𝘐𝘚𝘈 ᴊᴄʙ. ⊗ rest
Meals *(closed 21 July-18 August, Saturday lunch, Sunday and Bank Holidays)* (open until
11 p.m.) a la carte 32/60 – ⊟ 22 – **95 rm** 295/345, 4 suites.   FV a

🏨 **Le Châtelain** Ⓜ, r. Châtelain 17, ⊠ 1000, 𝒫 0 2 646 00 55, *hq@le-chatelain.net,*
Fax 0 2 646 00 88, 𝄋 – 🛗 🍴 🔲 📺 🚗 – 🔬 25-250. 🖭 ⓐ ⓜⓔ 𝘝𝘐𝘚𝘈. ⊗   FU t
Meals *(closed Saturday lunch and Sunday)* Lunch 17 – a la carte approx. 38 – ⊟ 20 – **106 rm**
273/397.

🏨 **Brussels** without rest, av. Louise 315, ⊠ 1050, 𝒫 0 2 640 24 15, *brussels-hotel@sk*
ynet.be, Fax 0 2 647 34 63 – 🛗 🖳 📺 🚗 – 🔬 30. 🖭 ⓐ ⓜⓔ 𝘝𝘐𝘚𝘈 ᴊᴄʙ   FU b
66 rm ⊟ 170/210, 1 suite.

🏨 **Agenda Louise** without rest, r. Florence 6, ⊠ 1000, 𝒫 0 2 539 00 31, *louise@hot*
el-agenda.com, Fax 0 2 539 00 63 – 🛗 📺 🚗. 🖭 ⓐ ⓜⓔ 𝘝𝘐𝘚𝘈 ᴊᴄʙ   FT j
38 rm ⊟ 117.

XXX **La Maison de Maître** - Hotel Conrad, av. Louise 71, ⊠ 1050, 𝒫 0 2 542 47 16, *bruh*
c_gm@hilton.com, Fax 0 2 542 42 00 – 🔲 🍴 🖭 ⓐ ⓜⓔ 𝘝𝘐𝘚𝘈   FS f
closed August, Saturday lunch, Sunday, Monday and Bank Holidays – **Meals** Lunch 42 – a
la carte approx. 74.

XX **Au Palais des Indes,** av. Louise 263, ⊠ 1050, 𝒫 0 2 646 09 41, *Fax 0 2 646 33 05*,
Indian cuisine, « Collection of Indian guitars » – 🔲. 🖭 ⓐ ⓜⓔ 𝘝𝘐𝘚𝘈 ᴊᴄʙ   FU h
closed lunch Saturday and Sunday – **Meals** Lunch 15 – a la carte 22/35.

XX **La Porte des Indes,** av. Louise 455, ⊠ 1050, 𝒫 0 2 647 86 51, *piblx@hotmail.com,*
Fax 0 2 640 30 59, Indian cuisine, « Indian antiques collection » – 🔲. 🖭 ⓐ ⓜⓔ 𝘝𝘐𝘚𝘈
closed Sunday lunch – **Meals**. Lunch 12 – a la carte approx. 46.   FV c

XX **Tagawa,** av. Louise 279, ⊠ 1050, 𝒫 0 2 640 50 95, *Fax 0 2 648 41 36*, Japanese cuisine
– 🔲. 🖭 ⓐ ⓜⓔ 𝘝𝘐𝘚𝘈 ᴊᴄʙ. ⊗   FU e
closed 2 and 3 January, Saturday lunch, Sunday and Holidays – **Meals** Lunch 42 – a la carte
44/62.

X **L'Atelier de la Truffe Noire,** av. Louise 300, ⊠ 1050, 𝒫 0 2 640 54 55, *luigi.cio*
riello@truffenoire.com, Fax 0 2 648 11 44, Open until 11 p.m., « Modern brasserie » – 🔲
🖭 ⓐ ⓜⓔ 𝘝𝘐𝘚𝘈   FU f
closed 29 July-18 August, 1 to 7 January, Sunday and Monday lunch – **Meals** a la carte
40/73 ⌦.

BELGIUM

Quartier Bois de la Cambre

XXXX **Villa Lorraine** (Vandecasserie), av. du Vivier d'Oie 75, ✉ 1000, ✆ 0 2 374 31 63 , *info@ vill alorraine.be, Fax 0 2 372 01 95*, 🍴, « Shaded terrace » – 🅿. 🆎 ① ⑩ 🆅🆂🅰 𝐉𝐂𝐁, 🍴 *closed 3 weeks July and Sunday* – **Meals** *Lunch* 50 – 80 b.i., a la carte 75/110 **GX w**
Spec. Carpaccio de bonite et foie de canard. Noix de ris de veau argenteuil. Glace au chocolat amer et miel de fleurs d'oranger.

XXX **La Truffe Noire,** bd de la Cambre 12, ✉ 1000, ✆ 0 2 640 44 22, *luigi.ciciriello@ tr uffenoire.com, Fax 0 2 647 97 04*, « Elegant interior » – 🔳. 🆎 ① ⑩ 🆅🆂🅰 **GV x** *closed first 3 weeks August, first week January, Monday and Saturday lunch* – **Meals** *Lunch* 50 b.i. – 68/95, a la carte approx. 105
Spec. Carpaccio aux truffes. St-Pierre aux poireaux et truffes. Soufflé chaud aux noisettes grillées.

Quartier Botanique, Gare du Nord *(see also at St-Josse-ten-Noode)*

🏨 **Sheraton Towers,** pl. Rogier 3, ✉ 1210, ✆ 0 2 224 31 11, *reservations_brussels @sheraton.com, Fax 0 2 224 34 56*, 🛦, 🆕, 🔲 – 🛗 🍴 ☰ 📺 ♿ – 🏛 25-600. 🆎 ① ⑩ 🆅🆂🅰 𝐉𝐂𝐁. 🍴 **FQ n**
Meals *Crescendo* (Partly buffets, open until 11 p.m.) 38 – ☕ 24 – **486 rm** 325/400, 43 suites.

🏨 **President World Trade Center,** bd du Roi Albert II 44, ✉ 1000, ✆ 0 2 203 20 20, *wtc.info@ presidenthotels.be, Fax 0 2 203 24 40*, 🛦, 🆕, 🍴 – 🛗 🍴 📺 🚗 – 🏛 25-350. 🆎 ① ⑩ 🆅🆂🅰 🍴 rest **FQ d**
Meals *Lunch* 26 – a la carte 41/52 – ☕ 18 – **283 rm** 248/348, 19 suites.

🏨 **Le Dome** (annex Le Dome II), bd du Jardin Botanique 12, ✉ 1000, ✆ 0 2 218 06 80, *dome@ s kypro.be, Fax 0 2 218 41 12*, 🍴 – 🛗 🍴, ☰ rm, 📺 – 🏛 25-100. 🆎 ① ⑩ 🆅🆂🅰 **Meals** *Lunch* 16 – 27/35 – **125 rm** ☕ 99/112. **FQ m**

🏨 **Tulip Inn Boulevard,** av. du Boulevard 17, ✉ 1210, ✆ 0 2 205 15 11, *info.hotel @tulipinnbb.be, Fax 0 2 201 15 15*, 🛦, 🆕 – 🛗 🍴 ☰ 📺 ♿ 🚗 – 🏛 25-120. 🆎 ① ⑩ 🆅🆂🅰 𝐉𝐂𝐁. 🍴 **FQ b**
Meals *(closed lunch Saturday and Sunday)* *Lunch* 12 – 25 – **450 rm** ☕ 170/300, 4 suites.

🏨 **President Nord** without rest, bd A. Max 107, ✉ 1000, ✆ 0 2 219 00 60, *presiden tnord@ online.be, Fax 0 2 218 12 69* – 🛗 ☰ 📺. 🆎 ① ⑩ 🆅🆂🅰. 🍴 **FQ k**
63 rm ☕ 170/245.

Quartier Atomium (Centenaire - Trade Mart - Laeken)

XX **Les Baguettes Impériales** (Mrs Ma), av. J. Sobieski 70, ✉ 1020, ✆ 0 2 479 67 32, *Fax 0 2 479 67 52*, 🍴, Partly Vietnamese cuisine, « Terrace » – 🔳. 🆎 ① ⑩ 🆅🆂🅰. 🍴 *closed 2 weeks Easter, August, 1 week before Christmas, Sunday dinner, Monday and Tuesday lunch* – **Meals** *Lunch* 38 – a la carte approx. 67
Spec. Mi au homard. Supion farci au foie gras. Pigeonneau farci aux nids d'hirondelle.

XX **Ming Dynasty,** Parc des Expositions - av. de l'Esplanade BP 9, ✉ 1020, ✆ 0 2 475 23 45, *ming_dynasty@ chello.be, Fax 0 2 475 23 50*, Chinese cuisine, open until 11 p.m. – 🔳 🅿. 🆎 ① ⑩ 🆅🆂🅰
closed 16 July-August, Tuesday dinner and Saturday lunch – **Meals** *Lunch* 17 – a la carte approx. 22.

X **Lychee,** r. De Wand 118, ✉ 1020, ✆ 0 2 268 19 14, *Fax 0 2 268 19 14*, Chinese cuisine, open until 11 p.m. – 🔳. 🆎 ① ⑩ 🆅🆂🅰
closed July – **Meals** *Lunch* 9 – 22/32.

X **La Balade Gourmande,** av. Houba de Strooper 95, ✉ 1020, ✆ 0 2 478 94 34, *Fax 0 2 479 89 52*, 🍴 – ① ⑩ 🆅🆂🅰
closed 2 weeks carnival, 15 August-early September, Wednesday, Saturday lunch and Sunday dinner – **Meals** *Lunch* 14 – 24.

ANDERLECHT

🏨 **Le Prince de Liège,** chaussée de Ninove 664, ✉ 1070, ✆ 0 2 522 16 00 , *prince.de.liege @proximedia.be, Fax 0 2 520 81 85* – 🛗, ☰ rm, 📺 🚗 – 🏛 25. 🆎 ① ⑩ 🆅🆂🅰 **Meals** *(closed 8 July-8 August, Saturday lunch and Sunday dinner)* *Lunch* 14 – 29/35 – **29 rm** ☕ 69/92.

🏨 **Ustel,** Square de l'Aviation 6, ✉ 1070, ✆ 0 2 520 60 53 and 0 2 522 30 25 (rest), *Fax 0 2 520 33 28*, 🍴, « Restaurant situated in the machinery room of a lock » – 🛗 🍴 ☰ 📺 🚗 – 🏛 25-100. 🆎 ① ⑩ 🆅🆂🅰. 🍴 **ES q**
Meals *(closed Saturday lunch and Sunday)* (Open until 11 p.m.) *Lunch* 11 – 22/30 – **94 rm** ☕ 159/163.

🏨 **Erasme,** rte de Lennik 790, ✉ 1070, ✆ 0 2 523 62 82, *comfort@ skynet.be, Fax 0 2 523 62 83*, 🍴 – 🛗 🍴, ☰ rest, 📺 ♿ 🅿 – 🏛 25-80. 🆎 ① ⑩ 🆅🆂🅰 𝐉𝐂𝐁 **Meals** *(closed 1 to 15 August)* (Pub rest) *Lunch* 16 – 22 – **73 rm** ☕ 73/148, 1 suite.

73

XXX **Saint Guidon** 2nd floor, in the R.S.C. Anderlecht football stadium, av. Théo Verbeeck 2
⊠ 1070, ℰ 0 2 520 55 36, saint-guidon@skynet.be, Fax 0 2 523 38 27 – ▤ 🅿 – 🚗 25-
500. 🆎 ⑩ 🞓 𝗩𝗜𝗦𝗔. ⸝
closed 20 June-21 July, Saturday, Sunday and first league match days – **Meals** (lunch only
30/55 b.i., a la carte 55/75
Spec. Ravioles de homard aux truffes. Sole meunière à la purée de pommes de terre et
carottes au cerfeuil. Côte à l'os Blanc Bleu Belge au gros sel.

XX **Alain Cornelis,** av. Paul Janson 82, ⊠ 1070, ℰ 0 2 523 20 83, Fax 0 2 523 20 83, 😤
– 🆎 ⑩ 🞓 𝗩𝗜𝗦𝗔
*closed 1 week Easter, first 2 weeks August, 24 December-early January, Wednesday dinner
Saturday lunch and Sunday* – **Meals** 30/40 b.i..

XX **La Brouette,** bd Prince de Liège 61, ⊠ 1070, ℰ 0 2 522 51 69, Fax 0 2 522 51 69 -
🆎 ⑩ 🞓 𝗩𝗜𝗦𝗔 – *closed 14 July-12 August, Saturday lunch, Sunday dinner and Monday*
– **Meals** Lunch 21 – 36/57 b.i. ⸗
Spec. Petits-gris en raviolis à la nage de céleri. Filet de cabillaud braisé aux champignons
et thym. Salade et confit d'orange à la vanille et marmelade.

AUDERGHEM (OUDERGEM)

XX **La Grignotière,** chaussée de Wavre 2041, ⊠ 1160, ℰ 0 2 672 81 85, Fax 0 2
672 81 85 – 🆎 ⑩ 🞓 𝗩𝗜𝗦𝗔
closed August, Sunday and Monday – **Meals** 43/56.

X **New Asia,** chaussée de Wavre 1240, ⊠ 1160, ℰ 0 2 660 62 06, Fax 0 2 673 40 54
😤, Chinese cuisine – ▤. 🆎 ⑩ 🞓 𝗩𝗜𝗦𝗔. ⸝   HU
closed last 3 weeks July and Monday except Bank Holidays – **Meals** Lunch 8 – 12/23.

X **La Khaïma,** chaussée de Wavre 1390, ⊠ 1160, ℰ 0 2 675 00 04, Fax 0 2 675 12 25
Moroccan cuisine, open until 11 p.m., « Berber tent interior theme » – ▤. 🆎 🞓 𝗩𝗜𝗦𝗔. ⸝
closed August – **Meals** a la carte approx. 28.

BERCHEM-STE-AGATHE (SINT-AGATHA-BERCHEM)

XXX **Stromboli** with rm, chaussée de Gand 1202, ⊠ 1082, ℰ 0 2 465 66 51, Fax 0
465 66 51, 😤, Partly Italian cuisine, « Terrace » – 📺. 🆎 ⑩ 𝗩𝗜𝗦𝗔. ⸝
closed 21 July-21 August – **Meals** (closed Tuesday and Wednesday) Lunch 25 – 50 – 4 rr
⟳ 100.

X **La Brasserie de la Gare,** chaussée de Gand 1430, ⊠ 1082, ℰ 0 2 469 10 09, Fax 0
469 10 09 – ▤ 🅿. 🆎 ⑩ 🞓 𝗩𝗜𝗦𝗔
closed Saturday lunch and Sunday – **Meals** Lunch 12 – 25.

ETTERBEEK

XX **Stirwen,** chaussée St-Pierre 15, ⊠ 1040, ℰ 0 2 640 85 41, Fax 0 2 648 43 08 – 🆎 ⑩
🞓 𝗩𝗜𝗦𝗔   GS
closed 2 weeks August, Saturday and Sunday – **Meals** Lunch 27 – a la carte approx. 43

XX **Grillange** 1st floor, av. Eudore Pirmez 7, ⊠ 1040, ℰ 0 2 649 26 85, grillange@sky
et.be, Fax 0 2 647 43 50, Spanish cuisine – ▤. 🆎 ⑩ 🞓 𝗩𝗜𝗦𝗔. ⸝   GT
closed 15 July-27 August, Saturday lunch and Sunday – **Meals** 33/38.

Quartier Cinquantenaire (Montgomery)

🏩 **Park** without rest, av. de l'Yser 21, ⊠ 1040, ℰ 0 2 735 74 00, info@parkhotelbru.
els.be, Fax 0 2 735 19 67, 🛋, 😤, 🌱 – 🕴 ⸽ 📺 – 🚗 25-80. 🆎 ⑩ 🞓 𝗩𝗜𝗦𝗔 ⸺
51 rm ⟳ 225/320.   HS

X **Momotaro,** av. d'Auderghem 106, ⊠ 1040, ℰ 0 2 734 06 64, momotaro@chello.b
Fax 0 2 734 64 18, Japanese cuisine with Sushi-bar – 🆎 ⑩ 🞓 𝗩𝗜𝗦𝗔. ⸝   GS
closed 1 to 15 August and lunch Saturday and Sunday – **Meals** Lunch 10 – 22.

EVERE

🏩 **Belson** without rest, chaussée de Louvain 805, ⊠ 1140, ℰ 0 2 705 20 30, resa@
lson.be, Fax 0 2 705 20 43, 🛋 – 🕴 ⸽ ▤ 📺 ⸺ – 🚗 25. 🆎 ⑩ 🞓 𝗩𝗜𝗦𝗔. ⸝
⟳ 20 – 131 rm 260, 3 suites.

🏩 **Mercure,** av. J. Bordet 74, ⊠ 1140, ℰ 0 2 726 73 35, H0958@accor-hotels.co
Fax 0 2 726 82 95, 😤 – 🕴 ⸽ ▤ rest, 📺 ⸺ – 🚗 25-120. 🆎 ⑩ 🞓 𝗩𝗜𝗦𝗔. ⸝ re
Meals (closed Friday dinner, Saturday and Sunday lunch). Lunch 30 – a la carte 34/43
⟳ 15 – 113 rm 200/250, 7 suites.

FOREST (VORST)

🏛 **De Fierlant** without rest, r. De Fierlant 67, ⊠ 1190, ℰ 0 2 538 60 70, de_fierla
@skynet.be, Fax 0 2 538 91 99 – 🕴 📺. 🆎 ⑩ 🞓 𝗩𝗜𝗦𝗔. ⸝
40 rm ⟳ 79/87.

GANSHOREN

XXXX ✿✿✿ **Bruneau,** av. Broustin 75, ⌧ 1083, ℰ 0 2 421 70 70, *restaurant_bruneau@skynet.be*, Fax 0 2 425 97 26, 斧, « Terrace » – ▤, ﴾ ⑩ ⑩ 𝑉𝐼𝑆𝐴
closed 1 to 10 February, August, Bank Holiday Thursdays, Tuesday dinner and Wednesday – **Meals** Lunch 46 – 136 b.i., a la carte 65/107
Spec. Émincé de céleri et cèpes au foie de canard (September-November). Cannelloni de homard aux morilles à la mousse de langoustines. Galette de pigeon.

XXX ✿✿ **Claude Dupont,** av. Vital Riethuisen 46, ⌧ 1083, ℰ 0 2 426 00 00, *claudedupont @resto.be*, Fax 0 2 426 65 40 – ﴾ ⑩ ⑩ 𝑉𝐼𝑆𝐴
closed July, Monday and Tuesday – **Meals** Lunch 44 – 60/86, – a la carte 66/97
Spec. Timbale de homard en mousseline de jeunes poireaux. Coussinet de barbue soufflé au Champagne (October-late April). Pigeonneau en aiguillettes sur une galette de pommes de terre au foie gras poêlé et baies de genèvrier.

XXX **San Daniele,** av. Charles-Quint 6, ⌧ 1083, ℰ 0 2 426 79 23, Fax 0 2 426 92 14, Partly Italian cuisine – ▤, ﴾ ⑩ ⑩ 𝑉𝐼𝑆𝐴
closed 15 July-15 August, Sunday, Monday dinner and Bank Holidays – **Meals** a la carte 44/54.

XX ⊕ **Cambrils** 1st floor, av. Charles-Quint 365, ⌧ 1083, ℰ 0 2 465 50 70, Fax 0 2 465 76 63, 斧 – ▤, ﴾ ⑩ 𝑉𝐼𝑆𝐴
closed 15 July-15 August, dinner Monday and Thursday and Sunday – **Meals** Lunch 32 b.i. – 30/40

IXELLES (ELSENE)

XX **Le Yen,** r. Lesbroussart 49, ⌧ 1050, ℰ 0 2 649 07 47, 斧, Vietnamese cuisine – ﴾ ⑩ ⑩ 𝑉𝐼𝑆𝐴, ✻
FU f
closed Saturday lunch and Sunday – **Meals** Lunch 8 – a la carte approx. 30.

Quartier Boondael (University)

XX **L'Aub. de Boendael,** square du Vieux Tilleul 12, ⌧ 1050, ℰ 0 2 672 70 55, *auberge-de-b oendael@resto.be*, Fax 0 2 660 75 82, 斧, Grill rest, « Rustic » – ℙ, ﴾ ⑩ ⑩ 𝑉𝐼𝑆𝐴
closed first 3 weeks August, late December, Saturday, Sunday and Bank Holidays – **Meals** 39.
HX h

X ⊕ **le Prévot,** r. Victor Greyson 93, ⌧ 1050, ℰ 0 2 644 37 78, Fax 0 2 644 12 67, Open until 11 p.m. – ﴾ ⑩ 𝑉𝐼𝑆𝐴 𝐽𝐶𝐵
GU p
closed 21 July-18 August, 22 December-6 January, Saturday lunch and Sunday – **Meals** Lunch 20 – 27/37 ℒ.

X ⊕ **La Pagode d'Or,** chaussée de Boondael 332, ⌧ 1050, ℰ 0 2 649 06 56, Fax 0 2 649 09 00, 斧, Vietnamese cuisine, open until 11 p.m. – ﴾ ⑩ ⑩ 𝑉𝐼𝑆𝐴, ✻
GV m
closed Monday – **Meals** Lunch 9 – 22/34.

X ✿ **Marie,** r. Alphonse De Witte 40, ⌧ 1050, ℰ 0 2 644 30 31, Fax 0 2 644 27 37 – ▤, ﴾ ⑩ 𝑉𝐼𝑆𝐴, ✻
GU a
closed 21 July-15 August, 24 December-2 January and Sunday – **Meals** Lunch 15 – a la carte 34/46 ℒ
Spec. Foie gras farci à la queue de bœuf. Tourte de caille sauce civet. Tian d'épaule d'agneau aux aubergines.

Quartier Bascule

XX **Maison Félix** 1st floor, r. Washington 149 (square Henri Michaux), ⌧ 1050, ℰ 0 2 345 66 93 – ﴾ ⑩ ⑩ 𝑉𝐼𝑆𝐴 𝐽𝐶𝐵 – closed last 2 weeks July, first 2 weeks January, Sunday and Monday – **Meals** Lunch 32 – 37/47.
FV s

XX **Alain Bohné,** pl. Albert Leemans 10, ⌧ 1050, ℰ 0 2 544 01 30, Fax 0 2 534 14 24 – ﴾ ⑩ 𝑉𝐼𝑆𝐴
FU g
closed last 2 weeks August, late December-early January, Sunday dinner and Monday – **Meals** Lunch 21 – 31/62.

X ⊕ **La Quincaillerie,** r. Page 45, ⌧ 1050, ℰ 0 2 538 25 53, *info@quincaillerie.be*, Fax 0 2 539 40 95, Brasserie with oyster bar, open until midnight, « Ancient store in Art Deco style » – ▤ ℙ, ﴾ ⑩ ⑩ 𝑉𝐼𝑆𝐴 𝐽𝐶𝐵
FU z
closed lunch Saturday and Sunday – **Meals** Lunch 13 – 25 ℒ.

X **Le fils de Jules,** r. Page 35, ⌧ 1050, ℰ 0 2 534 00 57, *info@filsdejules.be*, Fax 0 2 534 52 00, 斧, Basque and Landes cuisine, open until 11 p.m. – ﴾ ⑩ ⑩ 𝑉𝐼𝑆𝐴
closed 12 to 16 August, 24 December-2 January and lunch Saturday and Sunday – **Meals** Lunch 10 – 35.
FU m

Quartier Léopold (see also at Bruxelles)

🏨 **Renaissance** Ⓜ, r. Parnasse 19, ⌧ 1050, ℰ 0 2 505 29 29, *renaissance.brussels@r enaissancehotels.com*, Fax 0 2 505 25 55, ♨, 🏋, 🏊 – 🛗 ✽ ▤ 📺 ♿ ⬅ – 🔒 25-360. ﴾ ⑩ ⑩ 𝑉𝐼𝑆𝐴 𝐽𝐶𝐵, ✻ rm
FS e
Meals (closed Saturday and Sunday lunch) Lunch 24 – a la carte 45/58 ℒ – ⌧ 23 – **262 rm** 372, 19 suites.

Leopold, r. Luxembourg 35, ✉ 1050, ℰ 0 2 511 18 28, *reservations@hotel-leopold.be*,
Fax 0 2 514 19 39, 🛱, 🕿 – 🛗 🖿 📺 – 🕿 25-60. ᴁᴇ ① ⓶⑨ 𝐕𝐈𝐒𝐀   FS y
Meals *Salon Les Anges* (closed Saturday lunch and Sunday) 25 – 🖙 12 – **86 rm** 149/162.

Quartier Louise (see also at Bruxelles and at St-Gilles)

Sofitel without rest, av. de la Toison d'Or 40, ✉ 1050, ℰ 0 2 514 22 00, H1071@a
ccor-hotels.com, Fax 0 2 514 57 44, 🖪 – 🛗 ❄ 📺 – 🕿 25-120. ᴁᴇ ① ⓶⑨ 𝐕𝐈𝐒𝐀
𝐉𝐂𝐁   FS r
🖙 21 – **166 rm** 250, 4 suites.

Four Points Sheraton, r. Paul Spaak 15, ✉ 1000, ℰ 0 2 645 61 11, *reservations*
brussels@sheraton.com, Fax 0 2 646 63 44, 🛱, 🕿, 🖼 – 🛗 ❄ 📺 ⅙ 🚗 – 🕿 25-
40. ᴁᴇ ① ⓶⑨ 𝐕𝐈𝐒𝐀   FU k
Meals (Open until 11 p.m.) Lunch 25 – a la carte 28/35 – 🖙 17 – **128 rm** 210.

Beau-Site without rest, r. Longue Haie 76, ✉ 1000, ℰ 0 2 640 88 89, Fax 0 2 640 16 11
– 🛗 ❄ 📺. ᴁᴇ ① ⓶⑨ 𝐕𝐈𝐒𝐀   FT
38 rm 🖙 91/145.

Argus without rest, r. Capitaine Crespel 6, ✉ 1050, ℰ 0 2 514 07 70, reception@ho
tel-argus.be, Fax 0 2 514 12 22 – 🛗 📺. ᴁᴇ ① ⓶⑨ 𝐕𝐈𝐒𝐀   FS
41 rm 🖙 89/99.

O' comme 3 Pommes, pl. du Châtelain 40, ✉ 1050, ℰ 0 2 644 03 23, resto@o
3pommes.be, Fax 0 2 644 03 23, 🛱 – ᴁᴇ ⓶⑨ 𝐕𝐈𝐒𝐀   FU c
closed Sunday and lunch Monday and Saturday – Meals Lunch 27 – 47.

De la Vigne... à l'Assiette, r. Longue Haie 51, ✉ 1000, ℰ 0 2 647 68 03, Fax 0
647 68 03, Bistro, open until 11 p.m. – ᴁᴇ ① ⓶⑨ 𝐕𝐈𝐒𝐀   FT
closed 20 July-20 August, Saturday lunch, Sunday and Monday – Meals Lunch 12 – 20/32 9

Tutto Pepe, r. Faider 123, ✉ 1050, ℰ 0 2 534 96 19, ubruno@ulb.ac.be, Italian cuisine
– 🖿. ᴁᴇ ① ⓶⑨ 𝐕𝐈𝐒𝐀. ❄   FU c
closed 20 July-20 August, 23 December-2 January, Saturday, Sunday and Bank Holiday
– Meals a la carte 42/67.

Les Perles de Pluie, r. Châtelain 25, ✉ 1050, ℰ 0 2 649 67 23, info@lesperlesd
pluie.be, Fax 0 2 644 07 60, Thai cuisine, open until 11 p.m. – ᴁᴇ ⓶⑨ 𝐕𝐈𝐒𝐀   FU
closed lunch Monday and Saturday – Meals Lunch 13 – a la carte 24/37.

JETTE

Rôtiss. Le Vieux Pannenhuis, r. Léopold Iᵉʳ 317, ✉ 1090, ℰ 0 2 425 83 73
Fax 0 2 420 21 20, 🛱, « 17C former coaching inn with rustic grill room » – 🖿. ᴁᴇ ①
⓶⑨ 𝐕𝐈𝐒𝐀
closed July, Saturday lunch and Sunday – Meals Lunch 20 – 27/46.

French Kiss, r. Léopold Iᵉʳ 470, ✉ 1090, ℰ 0 2 425 22 93, Fax 0 2 428 68 24, Part
grill rest – 🖿. ᴁᴇ ① ⓶⑨ 𝐕𝐈𝐒𝐀
closed 21 July-15 August, 25 December-2 January and Monday – Meals 16/26.

ST-GILLES (SINT-GILLIS)

Cascade Ⓜ without rest, r. Berckmans 128, ✉ 1060, ℰ 0 2 538 88 30, info@casc
dehotel.be, Fax 0 2 538 92 79 – 🛗 ❄ 🖿 📺 🚗 – 🕿 25. ᴁᴇ ① ⓶⑨ 𝐕𝐈𝐒𝐀. ❄
80 rm 🖙 204/229.   ES

Inada, r. Source 73, ✉ 1060, ℰ 0 2 538 01 13, Fax 0 2 538 01 13 – ⓶⑨ 𝐕𝐈𝐒𝐀 ET
closed 16 July-15 August, Saturday lunch, Sunday, Monday and Bank Holidays – Meals Lun
15 – a la carte 41/61.

Le Forcado, chaussée de Charleroi 192, ✉ 1060, ℰ 0 2 537 92 20, jook17@yahoo.f
Fax 0 2 537 92 20, Portuguese cuisine – 🖿. ᴁᴇ ① ⓶⑨ 𝐕𝐈𝐒𝐀   EFU
closed carnival week, August, Sunday and Monday – Meals a la carte 29/36.

Quartier Louise (see also at Bruxelles and at Ixelles)

Manos Stephanie without rest, chaussée de Charleroi 28, ✉ 1060, ℰ 0 2 539 02 5
manos@manoshotel.com, Fax 0 2 537 57 29, « Mansion with period interior », 🚲 –
🖿 📺 🚗. ᴁᴇ ① ⓶⑨ 𝐕𝐈𝐒𝐀 𝐉𝐂𝐁   FT
50 rm 🖙 234/259, 5 suites.

Manos Premier, chaussée de Charleroi 102, ✉ 1060, ℰ 0 2 537 96 82 a
0 2 533 18 30 (rest), manos@manoshotel.com, Fax 0 2 539 36 55, 🛱, « Elegant tov
house », 🖪, 🕿, 🖼, 🚲 – 🛗 🖿 📺 🚗 🖥 – 🕿 25-100. ᴁᴇ ① ⓶⑨ 𝐕𝐈
𝐉𝐂𝐁   FU
Meals *Kolya* (closed 11 to 18 August, 23 December-6 January, Saturday lunch and Sunda
(Open until 11 p.m.) Lunch 15 – 33 – **45 rm** 🖙 234/259, 5 suites.

Tulip Inn City Centre, chaussée de Charleroi 17, ✉ 1060, ☎ 0 2 539 01 60, *Fax 0 2 537 90 11* – |♦| ⇔ ▤ TV ⇔ – 🏠 25-75. AE ① ⓞ VISA JCB. ✂ rest FS w
Meals *(closed lunch Saturday and Sunday)* Lunch 9 – a la carte approx. 32 – ☕ 19 – **246 rm** 180/250.

Les Capucines, r. Jourdan 22, ✉ 1060, ☎ 0 2 538 69 24, *Fax 0 2 538 69 24,* ☂ – AE ① ⓞ VISA FS u
closed 1 week Easter, 15 to 31 August, Sunday and Monday – **Meals** Lunch 17 – 25/52.

I Trulli, r. Jourdan 18, ✉ 1060, ☎ 0 2 537 79 30, *Fax 0 2 538 98 20,* ☂, Partly Italian cuisine, open until 11 p.m. – AE ① ⓞ VISA JCB FS c
closed 11 to 31 July, 22 December-4 January and Sunday – **Meals** Lunch 15 – a la carte 48/62.

ST-JOSSE-TEN-NOODE (SINT-JOOST-TEN-NODE)

Quartier Botanique *(see also at Bruxelles)*

Gd H. Mercure Royal Crown, r. Royale 250, ✉ 1210, ☎ 0 2 220 66 11, *H1728@accor-hotels.com, Fax 0 2 217 84 44,* 🏋, ≘s – |♦| ⇔ ▤ TV ⇔ – 🏠 25-550. AE ① ⓞ VISA JCB FQ r
Meals see ***Rue Royale*** below – ☕ 19 – **310 rm** 260, 5 suites.

Crowne Plaza, r. Gineste 3, ✉ 1210, ☎ 0 2 203 62 00, *sales@crowneplaza.gth.be, Fax 0 2 203 55 55,* ☂, 🏋, ≘s – |♦| ⇔ ▤ TV – 🏠 25-500. AE ① ⓞ VISA JCB
Meals ***Brasserie du Palace*** *(closed lunch Saturday, Sunday and Bank Holidays)* a la carte approx. 40 – ☕ 22 – **357 rm** 495, 1 suite. FQ v

Hilton Brussels City, pl. Rogier 20, ✉ 1210, ☎ 0 2 203 31 25, *info_brussels-city@hilton.com, Fax 0 2 203 43 31,* 🏋, ≘s – |♦| TV – 🏠 25-60. AE ① ⓞ VISA. ✂ rest
Meals Lunch 15 – a la carte 45/55 ♀ – ☕ 24 – **280 rm** 350/385, 3 suites. FQ q

Rue Royale - Gd H. Mercure Royal Crown, r. Royale 250, ✉ 1210, ☎ 0 2 220 66 11, *H1728@accor-hotels.com, Fax 0 2 217 84 44* – ▤ P. AE ① ⓞ VISA JCB. ✂ FQ r
closed 21 July-15 August, Saturday lunch, Sunday and Bank Holidays – **Meals** Lunch 33 – a la carte 41/50.

De Ultieme hallucinatie, r. Royale 316, ✉ 1210, ☎ 0 2 217 06 14, *Fax 0 2 217 72 40,* ☂, « Art Nouveau interior » – ▤ P – 🏠 40. AE ① ⓞ VISA ✂
closed 20 July-19 August, Saturday lunch, Sunday and Bank Holidays – **Meals** Lunch 27 – 41/75 b.i.. FQ t

Les Dames Tartine, chaussée de Haecht 58, ✉ 1210, ☎ 0 2 218 45 49 – ① ⓞ VISA FQ s
closed first 3 weeks August, Saturday lunch, Sunday and Monday – **Meals** Lunch 19 – 28/37.

SCHAERBEEK (SCHAARBEEK)

Senza Nome, r. Royale Ste-Marie 22, ✉ 1030, ☎ 0 2 223 16 17, *senzanome@belgacom.net, Fax 0 2 223 16 17,* Italian cuisine – ▤. ⓞ VISA. ✂ FQ u
closed August, Saturday lunch and Sunday – **Meals** a la carte 32/42 ♀.

Quartier Meiser

Lambermont 🐎 without rest, Allée des Frésias 18, ✉ 1030, ☎ 0 2 246 02 11, *Fax 0 2 246 02 00,* 🏋, ⛱ – |♦| TV ⇔ – 🏠 25. AE ① ⓞ VISA GHQ c
55 rm ☕ 110/125.

Amici miei, bd. Gén. Wahis 248, ✉ 1030, ☎ 0 2 705 49 80, *Fax 0 2 705 29 65,* Italian cuisine – AE ① ⓞ VISA HQ k
closed Saturday lunch and Sunday – **Meals** a la carte approx. 41.

UCCLE (UKKEL)

County House, square des Héros 2, ✉ 1180, ☎ 0 2 375 44 20 , *countyhouse@skynet.be, Fax 0 2 375 31 22* – |♦| ⇔, ▤ rest, TV ⇔ – 🏠 25-150. AE ① ⓞ VISA. ✂
Meals a la carte 31/40 – **86 rm** ☕ 125/165, 16 suites. EX b

Les Frères Romano, av. de Fré 182, ✉ 1180, ☎ 0 2 374 70 98, *Fax 0 2 374 04 18* – P. AE ① ⓞ VISA FX d
closed Easter holidays, last 3 weeks August, Sunday and Monday – **Meals** Lunch 32 – a la carte 38/60.

Villa d'Este, r. Etoile 142, ✉ 1180, ☎ 0 2 376 48 48, ☂, « Terrace surrounded by palisaded vines » – P. AE ① ⓞ VISA
closed July, late December, Sunday dinner and Monday – **Meals** 27/45.

Le Chalet de la Forêt, Drêve de Lorraine 43, ✉ 1180, ☎ 0 2 374 54 16, *Fax 0 2 374 35 71,* ☂, « On the edge of Soignes forest » – P. AE ① ⓞ VISA
closed Saturday and Sunday – **Meals** Lunch 24 – a la carte 51/66 ♀.

XX **Blue Elephant,** chaussée de Waterloo 1120, ⊠ 1180, ℘ 0 2 374 49 62, bebxl@ho
tmail.com, Fax 0 2 375 44 68, Thai cuisine, « Exotic decor » – 🗏 🅿. 🗚 ⓪ 🐠 𝗩𝗜𝗦𝗔
closed Saturday lunch – **Meals** Lunch 13 – 45.   GX j

XX **Le Pain et le Vin** (Mendrowski), chaussée d'Alsemberg 812a, ⊠ 1180, ℘ 0 2 332 37 74,
☼ painvin@ glo.be, Fax 0 2 332 17 40, 🈂 – 🅿. 🗚 🐠 𝗩𝗜𝗦𝗔, ❄
closed Christmas-New Year, Saturday lunch and Sunday – **Meals** (booking essential) Lunch
12 – 27/46, a la carte 35/45 ♀
Spec. Risotto vert aux coquillages. Daurade aux aubergines. Gateau aux amandes et frangipane.

XX **Willy et Marianne,** chaussée d'Alsemberg 705, ⊠ 1180, ℘ 0 2 343 60 09 – 🗚 🐠
🍴 𝗩𝗜𝗦𝗔   EX r
closed late January-early February, mid-July-mid August, Tuesday and Wednesday – **Meals**
Lunch 12 – 27.

X **La Cité du Dragon,** chaussée de Waterloo 1024, ⊠ 1180, ℘ 0 2 375 80 80, Fax 0 2
375 69 77, 🈂, Chinese cuisine, open until 11.30 p.m., « Exotic garden with fountains »
– 🅿. 🗚 ⓪ 🐠 𝗩𝗜𝗦𝗔   GX c
Meals Lunch 12 – 20/58.

X **Brasseries Georges,** av. Winston Churchill 259, ⊠ 1180, ℘ 0 2 347 21 00, info@b
🍴 rasseriesgeorges.be, Fax 0 2 344 02 45, 🈂, Oyster bar, open until midnight – 🗏 🅿. 🗚
⓪ 🐠 𝗩𝗜𝗦𝗔   FV n
Meals Lunch 15 – a la carte 26/41 ♀.

Quartier St-Job

XX **Les Menus Plaisirs,** r. Basse 7, ⊠ 1180, ℘ 0 2 374 69 36, lesmenusplaisirs@belga
🍴 com.net, Fax 0 2 331 38 13, 🈂 – 🗚 ⓪ 🐠 𝗩𝗜𝗦𝗔
closed 2 weeks Easter, last week August, Saturday lunch and Bank Holidays – **Meals**
Lunch 12 – 29.

X **Le Passage,** av. J. et P. Carsoel 13, ⊠ 1180, ℘ 0 2 374 66 94, Fax 0 2 374 69 26, 🈂
☼ – 🅿. 🗚 ⓪ 🐠 𝗩𝗜𝗦𝗔
closed 3 weeks July, first week January, Saturday lunch and Bank Holidays – **Meals**
Lunch 17 – 36, a la carte 44/55
Spec. Carpaccio de bœuf et foie gras au vinaigre balsamique. Raviolis d'escargots à l'a
doux et thym citronné. Blanc de turbotin cuit au lait épicé et mousseline de crevettes grises

X **le pré en bulle,** av. J. et P. Carsoel 5, ⊠ 1180, ℘ 0 2 374 08 80, 🈂 – 🅿. 🗚 𝗩𝗜𝗦𝗔
🍴 closed Monday dinner and Tuesday – **Meals** Lunch 11 – 27/43 b.i. ♀.

WATERMAEL-BOITSFORT (WATERMAAL-BOSVOORDE)

XX **Au Vieux Boitsfort** (Gillet), pl. Bischoffsheim 9, ⊠ 1170, ℘ 0 2 672 23 32, Fax 0 2
☼ 660 22 94, 🈂 – 🗚 ⓪ 🐠 𝗩𝗜𝗦𝗔
closed first 3 weeks August, Saturday lunch and Sunday – **Meals** (booking essential) Lunch
44 – 77 b.i. a la carte approx. 60
Spec. Lasagne de langoustines rôties et pointes vertes. Petite lotte fumée à la minute et fleu
de courgette à la niçoise. Filets de rouget rôtis en écailles de pommes de terre à la tapenade

X **Le Grill,** r. Trois Tilleuls 1, ⊠ 1170, ℘ 0 2 672 95 13, Fax 0 2 660 22 94, Grill rest – 🗚
🍴 ⓪ 🐠 𝗩𝗜𝗦𝗔
closed first 3 weeks July, Saturday lunch and Sunday dinner – **Meals** 22.

WOLUWE-ST-LAMBERT (SINT-LAMBRECHTS-WOLUWE)

🏨 **Sodehotel La Woluwe** Ⓜ ♨, av. E. Mounier 5, ⊠ 1200, ℘ 0 2 775 21 11, soo
hotel@ sabenahotels.com, Fax 0 2 770 47 80, 🈂 – 🛗 ♨ 🗏 📺 🚿 🅿 – 🛎 25-20
🗚 ⓪ 🐠 𝗩𝗜𝗦𝗔. ❄ rest
Meals **Leonard** Lunch 22 – 35/54 – ⊇ 21 – **118 rm** 275/315, 8 suites.

🏠 **Lambeau** without rest, av. Lambeau 150, ⊠ 1200, ℘ 0 2 732 51 70, info@hotella
beau.com, Fax 0 2 732 54 90 – 🛗 📺. 🗚 ⓪ 🐠 𝗩𝗜𝗦𝗔. ❄   HR
24 rm ⊇ 71/78.

XX **Moulin Lindekemale,** av. J.-F. Debecker 6, ⊠ 1200, ℘ 0 2 770 90 57, lindekema
@ swing.be, Fax 0 2 762 94 57, 🈂, « Former watermill » – 🅿. 🗚 ⓪ 🐠 𝗩𝗜𝗦𝗔. ❄ close
Easter week, 1 to 15 August, late December, Saturday lunch, Sunday dinner and Monda
– **Meals** Lunch 45 b.i. – a la carte approx. 44.

XX **Da Mimmo,** av. du Roi Chevalier 24, ⊠ 1200, ℘ 0 2 771 58 60, Fax 0 2 771 58 60, 🈂
Italian cuisine – 🗏. 🗚 ⓪ 🐠 𝗩𝗜𝗦𝗔. ❄
closed August, 20 December-5 January, Sunday and lunch Saturday and Bank Holidays
Meals a la carte 30/44.

X **La Table de Mamy,** av. des Cerisiers 212, ⊠ 1200, ℘ 0 2 779 00 9
🍴 Fax 0 2 779 00 96, 🈂 – 🗚 ⓪ 🐠 𝗩𝗜𝗦𝗔
closed 3 weeks August, Saturday lunch and Sunday – **Meals** 32.

Les Amis du Cep, r. Th. Decuyper 136, ⊠ 1200, ℘ 0 2 762 62 95, Fax 0 2 771 20 32, 斎 – AE ⓐ VISA . ⅏ – closed 15 July-10 August, late December, Sunday and Monday – **Meals** Lunch 13 – a la carte 40/51 ⬝.

de Maurice à Olivier in the back room of a bookshop, chaussée de Roodebeek 246, ⊠ 1200, ℘ 0 2 771 33 98 – 🔳, AE ⓪ ⓐ VISA
closed 15 July-1 August and Sunday – **Meals** Lunch 16 – 32/42.

WOLUWE-ST-PIERRE (SINT-PIETERS-WOLUWE)

Montgomery 🅜 ⅙, av. de Tervuren 134, ⊠ 1150, ℘ 0 2 741 85 11, hotel@montgome ry.be, Fax 0 2 741 85 00, 🛋, ⬝s – 🛗 🖙 🔳 📺 ⬅ – 🔬 35. AE ⓪ ⓐ VISA JCB . ⅏.
Meals La Duchesse (closed Saturday and Sunday) Lunch 42 b.i. – 47 b.i. – ⬝⬝ 20 – **61 rm** 320/360, 2 suites.
HS k

Des 3 Couleurs, av. de Tervuren 453, ⊠ 1150, ℘ 0 2 770 33 21, Fax 0 2 770 80 45, 斎, « Terrace » – AE ⓐ VISA
closed 2 weeks Easter, last 2 weeks August, Saturday lunch, Sunday dinner and Monday – **Meals** a la carte approx. 55.

Le Vignoble de Margot, av. de Tervuren 368, ⊠ 1150, ℘ 0 2 779 23 23, Fax 0 2 779 05 45, ⬝, 斎, Partly oyster bar, « Surrounded by vines, overlooking park and ponds » – 🔳 🄿, AE ⓐ VISA . ⅏
closed 23 December-3 January, Saturday lunch, Sunday and Bank Holidays – **Meals** a la carte 46/56.

Les Deux Maisons (Demartin), Val des Seigneurs 81, ⊠ 1150, ℘ 0 2 771 14 47, Fax 0 2 771 14 47, 斎 – AE ⓪ ⓐ VISA
closed 31 March-8 April, 4 to 27 September, 22 December-1 January, Sunday and Monday – **Meals** 30/65 b.i., a la carte 40/97
Spec. Bar en croûte de sel (Easter-15 October). Foie gras de canard et chutney. Moelleux au chocolat, sirop chocolaté au thé.

Medicis, av. de l'Escrime 124, ⊠ 1150, ℘ 0 2 779 07 00, Fax 0 2 779 19 24, 斎 – AE ⓪ VISA
closed Saturday lunch and Sunday – **Meals** Lunch 15 – 28/50.

L'Escoffier, r. Paul Wemaere 2, ⊠ 1150, ℘ 0 2 771 88 80, lescoffier@tiscalinet.be, Fax 0 2 771 58 56, Open until 11 p.m. – 🔳. AE ⓐ VISA . ⅏
closed 1 week carnival, July, Monday and dinner Tuesday and Sunday – **Meals** Lunch 14 – 27/34 b.i.

l'auberg'in, r. au Bois 198, ⊠ 1150, ℘ 0 2 770 68 85, Fax 0 2 770 68 85, 斎, Grill rest, « Farmhouse with fire place » – 🄿. AE ⓪ ⓐ VISA
closed Saturday lunch and Sunday – **Meals** 29.

BRUSSELS ENVIRONS

at Diegem Brussels-Zaventem motorway A 201, Diegem exit ⓒ Machelen pop. 11 838 – ⊠ 1831 Diegem :

Sofitel Airport 🅜, Bessenveldstraat 15 ℘ 0 2 713 66 66, H0548@accor-hotels.com, Fax 0 2 721 43 45, 🛋, ⬝ – 🖙 🔳 📺 🄿 – 🔬 25-300. AE ⓪ ⓐ VISA JCB
Meals La Pléiade 38 – ⬝⬝ 21 – **125 rm** 255/350.

Holiday Inn Airport, Holidaystraat 7 ℘ 0 2 720 58 65, hibrusselsairport@sixcontin entshotels.com, Fax 0 2 720 41 45, 🛋, ⬝s, 🅸, 🍴, 🚲 – 🛗 🖙 🔳 📺 🄿 – 🔬 25-400. AE ⓪ ⓐ VISA JCB . ⅏ rest
Meals (Open until 11 p.m.) Lunch 31 – a la carte approx. 37 – ⬝⬝ 21 – **310 rm** 595.

Novotel Airport, Olmenstraat ℘ 0 2 725 30 50, H0467@accor-hotels.com, Fax 0 2 721 39 58, 斎, 🛋, 🅸 – 🛗 🖙 🔳 📺 🄿 – 🔬 25-100. AE ⓪ ⓐ VISA JCB . ⅏ rest
Meals (Open until midnight) Lunch 15 – a la carte 25/36 ⬝ – ⬝⬝ 14 – **207 rm** 155/160.

Rainbow Airport 🅜, Berkenlaan 4 ℘ 0 2 721 77 77, rainbowbrussels@easyacces.be, Fax 0 2 721 55 96, 斎 – 🛗 🖙 🔳 📺 🄿 – 🔬 25-80. AE ⓪ ⓐ VISA . ⅏
Meals (closed Saturday dinner and Sunday lunch) 22/31 – ⬝⬝ 17 – **100 rm** 179/219.

Express without rest, Berkenlaan 5 ℘ 0 2 725 33 80, expressbruxelles@alliance-hosp itality.com, Fax 0 2 725 38 10 – 🛗 🖙 📺 ⬝ 🄿 – 🔬 25-50. AE ⓪ ⓐ VISA JCB
85 rm ⬝⬝ 236.

at Dilbeek West : 7 km. pop. 37 722 – ⊠ 1700 Dilbeek :

Relais Delbeccha ⅙, Bodegemstraat 158 ℘ 0 2 569 44 30, relais.delbeccha@skyn et.be, Fax 0 2 569 75 30, 斎, 🌳 – 📺 🄿 – 🔬 25-120. AE ⓪ ⓐ VISA . ⅏
closed 7 to 28 July – **Meals** (closed Sunday dinner) Lunch 30 – 48 – **14 rm** ⬝⬝ 93/120.

Host. d'Arconati ⅙ with rm, d'Arconatistraat 77 ℘ 0 2 569 35 00, Fax 0 2 569 35 04, 斎, « Floral terrace », 🌳 – 📺 🄿. AE ⓐ VISA . ⅏ – closed February and 1 week July – **Meals** (closed Sunday dinner, Monday and Tuesday) 39 – **4 rm** ⬝⬝ 76/87.

BELGIUM

XX **De Kapblok,** Ninoofsesteenweg 220 ℰ 0 2 569 31 23, *reservatie@dekapblok.be*, Fax 0 2 569 67 23 – ◍◍ 𝘝𝘐𝘚𝘈
closed 2 weeks after Easter, 30 July-14 August, late December-early January, Sunday and Monday – **Meals** Lunch 18 – 41/50.

at Dworp *(Tourneppe) South : 16 km* Ⓒ *Beersel pop. 22 880* – ✉ *1653 Dworp :*

🏫 **Kasteel Gravenhof** ⌂, Alsembergsesteenweg 676 ℰ 0 2 380 44 99, *info@grave nhof.be*, Fax 0 2 380 40 60, 佘, « 17C castle and lake », ☞ – ▤ 🅣🅥 🄿 – 🏛 25-120. 🄰🄴 ◍ ◍◍ 𝘝𝘐𝘚𝘈
Meals (Pub rest) Lunch 17 – a la carte approx. 37 – ☲ 12 – **26 rm** 125/145.

at Grimbergen *North : 11 km. pop. 32 930* – ✉ *1850 Grimbergen :*

🏫 **Abbey,** Kerkeblokstraat 5 ℰ 0 2 270 08 88, *hotelabbey@pandora.be*, Fax 0 2 270 81 88, 佘, 🛏, ⛨s, ☞, ⛵ – ▤, ▦ rest, 🅣🅥 🄿 – 🏛 30-200. 🄰🄴 ◍ ◍◍ 𝘝𝘐𝘚𝘈. ✎ rm
closed July – **Meals** *'t Wit Paard (closed Saturday and Sunday)* Lunch 32 – a la carte approx. 55 – ☲ 15 – **28 rm** 112/115.

at Groot-Bijgaarden *Northwest : 7 km* Ⓒ *Dilbeek pop. 37 722* – ✉ *1702 Groot-Bijgaarden :*

🏬 **Waerboom,** Jozef Mertensstraat 140 ℰ 0 2 463 15 00, *info@waerboom.com*, Fax 0 2 463 10 30, ⛨s, ▧ – ▤ 🅣🅥 🄿 – 🏛 25-270. 🄰🄴 ◍ ◍◍ 𝘝𝘐𝘚𝘈. ✎
closed mid July-mid August – **Meals** (residents only) – **35 rm** ☲ 102/114.

🏬 **Gosset,** Gossetlaan 52 ℰ 0 2 466 21 30, *info@gosset.be*, Fax 0 2 466 18 50, 佘 – ▤ ⛨✎ 🅣🅥 🄿 – 🏛 25-200. 🄰🄴 ◍ ◍◍ 𝘝𝘐𝘚𝘈
closed 22 December-3 January – **Meals** *Bistrot Alfons* Lunch 30 – a la carte approx. 42 – **48 rm** ☲ 87/97.

XXXXX **De Bijgaarden,** I. Van Beverenstraat 20 ℰ 0 2 466 44 85, *debijgaarden@skynet.be*, ✿✿ Fax 0 2 463 08 11, ≼, 佘, « Rural setting facing the castle » – 🄿 🄰🄴 ◍ ◍◍ 𝘝𝘐𝘚𝘈 ᴊᴄʙ
closed 1 to 8 April, 12 August-2 September, Saturday lunch and Sunday – **Meals** 62/130, a la carte 101/131
Spec. Langoustines aux échalotes, mille-feuille de tomates en aigre-doux. Poularde de ferme aux morilles (April-September). Turbot rôti au four et béarnaise de homard.

XXX **Michel** (Coppens), Gossetlaan 31 ℰ 0 2 466 65 91, Fax 0 2 466 90 07, 佘 – 🄿 ◍◍ 𝘝𝘐𝘚𝘈 ✿ *closed August, 23 December-2 January, Sunday and Monday* – **Meals** 46/55
Spec. Turbot grillé et lasagne à la brunoise de légumes. Perdreau rôti à la feuille de vigne (15 September-15 October). Civet de homard au Vouvray et gingembre.

at Hoeilaart *Southeast : 13 km. pop. 9 783* – ✉ *1560 Hoeilaart :*

XX **Aloyse Kloos,** Terhulpsesteenweg 2 (at Groenendaal) ℰ 0 2 657 37 37 Fax 0 2 657 37 37, 佘, « On the edge of a forest » – 🄿 🄰🄴 ◍ ◍◍ 𝘝𝘐𝘚𝘈
closed August, Sunday dinner and Monday – **Meals** Lunch 37 – 47/55.

at Huizingen *South : 12 km* Ⓒ *Beersel pop. 22 880* – ✉ *1654 Huizingen :*

XX **Terborght,** Oud Dorp 16 (near E 19 - A 7, exit ㉑) ℰ 0 2 380 10 10, Fax 0 2 380 10 97 « Crow-stepped gable, rustic interior » – ▦ 🄿 🄰🄴 ◍ ◍◍ 𝘝𝘐𝘚𝘈
closed 15 July-15 August, Monday and dinner Sunday and Tuesday – **Meals** Lunch 29 – la carte approx. 58.

at Machelen *Northeast : 12 km. pop. 11 838* – ✉ *1830 Machelen :*

XXX **Pyramid,** Heirbaan 210 ℰ 0 2 253 54 56, Fax 0 2 253 47 65, 佘, « Modern interior terrace with landscaped English garden » – 🄿 🄰🄴 ◍ ◍◍ 𝘝𝘐𝘚𝘈 ᴊᴄʙ. ✎
closed 1 week after Easter, late July-early August, late December, Saturday and Sunda – **Meals** Lunch 36 – 56/73 b.i. ⌕.

at Meise *North : 14 km. pop. 18 347* – ✉ *1860 Meise :*

XXX **Aub. Napoléon,** Bouchoutlaan 1 ℰ 0 2 269 30 78, Fax 0 2 269 79 98, Grill rest – 🄿 🄰🄴 ◍ ◍◍ 𝘝𝘐𝘚𝘈
closed August – **Meals** Lunch 36 – 56.

XX **Koen Van Loven,** Brusselsesteenweg 11 ℰ 0 2 270 05 77, Fax 0 2 270 05 46, 佘 🏛 25-150. ✎
closed 7 to 20 April, last week July-first 2 weeks August, 28 October-3 November, Sunda dinner, Monday and Tuesday – **Meals** Lunch 29 b.i. – 40/47.

at Melsbroek *Northeast : 14 km* Ⓒ *Steenokkerzeel pop. 10 419* – ✉ *1820 Melsbroek :*

XXX **Boetfort,** Sellaerstraat 42 ℰ 0 2 751 64 00, *boetfort@proximedia.be*, Fax 0 751 62 00, 佘, « 17C mansion, park » – 🄿 🏛 25-40. 🄰🄴 ◍ ◍◍ 𝘝𝘐𝘚𝘈. ✎   DK
closed carnival week, Wednesday dinner, Saturday lunch and Sunday – **Meals** Lunch 34 37/45.

at Nossegem *East : 13 km* Ⓒ *Zaventem pop. 26 901 –* ⌧ *1930 Nossegem :*

XXX **L'Orangeraie Roland Debuyst,** Leuvensesteenweg 614 ℰ 0 2 757 05 59, *roland.*
❀ *debuyst@wanadoo.bc,* Fax 0 2 759 50 08, ☞, « Pergola covered terrace in leafy
surroundings » – 🅿 – 🛦 35. ⬛ ⬛ 🆚
closed 1 week Easter, first 2 weeks August, Saturday lunch, Sunday and Monday – **Meals**
Lunch 37 – 51/66, a la carte 63/71 ⵏ
Spec. Cuisses de grenouilles et écrevisses aux raviolis de persil. Lasagne de jarret de veau
aux tomates et foie de canard. Ravioli de crème brûlée à l'orange et gingembre.

at Overijse *Southeast : 16 km. pop. 23 738 –* ⌧ *3090 Overijse :*

🏠 **Soret** Ⓜ ☜, Kapucijnendreef 1 (at Jezus-Eik) ℰ 0 2 657 37 82, *hotel.soret.bvba@pa*
ndora.be, Fax 0 2 657 72 66 – 🕸 📺 🅿 – 🛦 40. ⬛ ⬛ 🆚   DN s
Meals see **Istas** below – ⌷ 7 – **39 rm** 72/84, 1 suite.

XXXX **Barbizon** (Deluc), Welriekendedreef 95 (at Jezus-Eik) ℰ 0 2 657 04 62, *barbizon@eur*
❀ *onet.be,* Fax 0 2 657 40 66, ☞, « Norman style villa, terrace and garden on the edge of
a forest » – 🅿 ⬛ ⬛ 🆚
closed late July-early August, January, Tuesday and Wednesday – **Meals** *Lunch 36 –*
46/72 b.i., a la carte approx. 84
Spec. Bavarois d'avocat et tartare de langoustines au foie gras et gelée de poulette. Croustillant de ris de veau aux carottes et cumun (September-January). Gibier (September-January).

XX **Lipsius,** Brusselsesteenweg 671 (at Jezus-Eik) ℰ 0 2 657 34 32, Fax 0 2 657 31 47 – ⬛
⬛ 🆚 ⬛ ⬛ ☀
closed 1 to 11 April, 29 July-29 August, Saturday lunch, Sunday dinner and Monday – **Meals**
Lunch 25 a la carte 45/61.

X **Istas** - Hotel Soret, Brusselsesteenweg 652 (at Jezus-Eik) ℰ 0 2 65/05 11, Fax 0 2
657 72 66, ☞, Pub rest – 🅿 ⬛ ⬛ 🆚
closed Wednesday and Thursday – **Meals** a la carte 22/36.

at Sint-Genesius-Rode (Rhode-St-Genèse) *South : 13 km. pop. 17 998 –* ⌧ *1640 Sint-Genesius-*
Rode :

🏠 **Aub. de Waterloo,** chaussée de Waterloo 212 ℰ 0 2 358 35 80, *aubergedewaterlo*
o@skynet.be, Fax 0 2 358 38 06, 🛁, 🍴 – 🕸 ✳ ⬛ 📺 🅿 – 🛦 25-70. ⬛ ⬛ ⬛ 🆚
closed August – **Meals** see **L'Arlecchino** below – **85 rm** ⌷ 138/191.

XX **L'Arlecchino** - Hotel Aub. de Waterloo, chaussée de Waterloo 212 ℰ 0 2 358 34 16,
Fax 0 2 358 28 96, ☞, Italian cuisine, partly trattoria – ⬛ 🅿 ⬛ ⬛ 🆚
closed August – **Meals** 33/41 b.i..

XX **Michel D,** l. Station 182 ℰ 0 2 381 20 66, Fax 0 2 380 45 80, ☞ – 🅿 ⬛ ⬛ ⬛ 🆚
closed 17 July-9 August, Wednesday, Saturday lunch and Sunday dinner – **Meals** *Lunch 25*
– 40/62 ⵏ.

at Sint-Pieters-Leeuw *Southwest : 13 km. pop. 30 013 –* ⌧ *1600 Sint-Pieters-Leeuw :*

🏠 **Green Park** Ⓜ, V. Nonnemanstraat 15 ℰ 0 2 331 19 70, *info@greenparkhotel.be,*
Fax 0 2 331 03 11, ☞, « Lakeside setting », 🛁, ☀, 🚲 – 🕸 📺 ⬛ 🅿 – 🛦 25-100.
⬛ ⬛ ⬛ 🆚
closed July – **Meals** (closed Friday) *Lunch 17* – a la carte 22/38 – **18 rm** ⌷ 99/112.

at Strombeek-Bever *North : 9 km* Ⓒ *Grimbergen pop. 32 930 –* ⌧ *1853 Strombeek-Bever :*

🏠 **Rijkendael** Ⓜ ☜, J. Van Elewijckstraat 35 ℰ 0 2 267 41 24, *info@alfarijkendael.*
gth.be, Fax 0 2 267 94 01, ☞, 🍴 – 🕸 📺 ⬛ 🅿 – 🛦 25-40. ⬛ ⬛ ⬛ 🆚
Meals *Lunch 22* – 33/41 – **49 rm** ⌷ 156/186.

XX **Val Joli,** Leestbeekstraat 16 ℰ 0 2 460 65 43, *valjoli@euronet.be,* Fax 0 2 460 04 00, ☞,
« Terrace and garden with an ornamental pond » – 🅿 – 🛦 25-40. ⬛ ⬛ ⬛ 🆚 ☀ rm
closed 2 weeks June, late October-early November, Monday and Tuesday – **Meals** *Lunch*
22 – 30/42.

XX **'t Stoveke,** Jetsestraat 52 ℰ 0 2 267 67 25, ☞, Seafood – ⬛ ⬛ ⬛ 🆚
closed 3 weeks June, Christmas-New Year, Sunday, Monday and Bank Holidays – **Meals** *Lunch*
32 – a la carte 47/59.

t Vilvoorde (Vilvorde) *North : 17 km. pop. 34 982 –* ⌧ *1800 Vilvoorde :*

XX **de Rembrandt,** Lange Molensstraat 60 ℰ 0 2 251 04 72, « In a 15C watchtower » –
⬛ ⬛ ⬛ 🆚
closed 20 July-20 August, Saturday, Sunday and dinner Monday and Wednesday – **Meals**
Lunch 41 – a la carte 47/57.

t Wemmel *North : 12 km. pop. 13 932 –* ⌧ *1780 Wemmel :*

🏠 **La Roseraie,** Limburg Stirumlaan 213 ℰ 0 2 456 99 10 and 0 2 460 51 34 (rest),
Fax 0 2 460 83 20, ☞ – ⬛ 📺 🅿 ⬛ ⬛ ⬛ 🆚 ⬛
Meals (closed Monday and Saturday lunch) *Lunch 22* – a la carte approx. 50 – **8 rm**
⌷ 123/148.

XXX **Le Gril aux herbes d'Evan,** Brusselsesteenweg 21 ℘ 0 2 460 52 39, Fax 0 2
461 19 12, 🌳 – 🆎 ① ⓂⓈ 𝐕𝐈𝐒𝐀
closed 1 to 21 July, 24 December-1 January, Tuesday, Wednesday and Saturday lunch –
Meals Lunch 25 – 43/53.

XX **Oliartes,** Parklaan 7 ℘ 0 2 460 42 89, Fax 0 2 460 25 10, 🌳, « Terrace in public park »
– 🅿. 🆎 ⓂⓈ 𝐕𝐈𝐒𝐀
closed Monday and dinner Wednesday and Sunday – **Meals** Lunch 24 – 35/55 b.i..

at Wezembeek-Oppem East : 11 km. pop. 13 622 – ✉ 1970 Wezembeek-Oppem :

XX **L'Aub. Saint-Pierre,** Sint-Pietersplein 8 ℘ 0 2 731 21 79, bf@skynet.be, Fax 0 2
731 28 28, 🌳 – ▤. 🆎 ① ⓂⓈ 𝐕𝐈𝐒𝐀. ✦
closed Saturday lunch and Sunday – **Meals** Lunch 24 – 48/66 ♈.

at Zaventem Brussels-Zaventem airport motorway A 201. pop. 26 901 – ✉ 1930 Zaventem :

🏨🏨 **Sheraton Airport,** at airport ℘ 0 2 710 80 00, reservations.brussels@sheraton.com,
Fax 0 2 710 80 80, 🍸, ⅃₆ – 🛗 ⇆ ▤ 📺 ⅚ ⇦ 🅿. – 🏋 25-600. 🆎 ① ⓂⓈ 𝐕𝐈𝐒𝐀
ⒿⒸⒷ
Meals *Concorde* (closed Saturday lunch) Lunch 45 – a la carte 60/72 ♈ – **Lindbergh
Taverne** (Open until 11.30 p.m.) Lunch 13 – a la carte 30/43 ♈ – ⇌ 25 – **297 rm** 410/515,
2 suites.

XX **Stockmansmolen** 1st floor, H. Henneaulaan 164 ℘ 0 2 725 34 34, info@stockman
smolen.be, Fax 0 2 725 75 05, Partly pub rest, « Former watermill » – ▤ 🅿. 🆎 ① ⓂⓈ
𝐕𝐈𝐒𝐀. ✦
closed last 2 weeks July-first week August, Christmas, New Year, Saturday and Sunday –
Meals Lunch 45 – 67.

ELLEZELLES (ELZELE) 7890 Hainaut 𝟮𝟭𝟯 H 18, 𝟮𝟭𝟰 H 18 et 𝟵𝟬𝟵 E 3. pop. 5 580 – 55 km.

XXXX **Château du Mylord** (Thomaes brothers), r. St-Mortier 35 ℘ 0 68 54 26 02, chateau
❀❀ udumylord@pi.be, Fax 0 68 54 29 33, 🌳, « Manor house inside a park » – 🅿. 🆎 ① ⓂⓈ
𝐕𝐈𝐒𝐀
closed 2 to 10 April, 19 to 28 August, 24 December-8 January, Monday lunch except
Bank Holidays and dinner Sunday and Monday – **Meals** Lunch 60 b.i. – 60/95, – a la carte
60/75 ♈
Spec. Toast aux escargots, compote persillée et lard seché. Daurade aux calamars et poivrons confits. Pigeonneau aux épices et miel (late March-late September).

ANTWERP (ANTWERPEN) 2000 𝟮𝟭𝟯 L 15 – ⑮ S and 𝟵𝟬𝟵 G 2 – ⑧ S. pop. 446 525.

See : Around the Market Square and the Cathedral★★★ : Market Square★ (Grote Markt) FY
Vlaaikensgang★ FY, Cathedral★★★ and its tower★★★ FY – Butchers' House★ (Vleeshuis)
Musical instruments★ FY D – Rubens' House★★ (Rubenshuis) GZ – Interior★ of St. James
Church (St-Jacobskerk) GY - Hendrik Conscience Place★ GY – St. Charles Borromeo's
Church★ (St-Carolus Borromeuskerk) GY – St. Paul's Church (St-Pauluskerk) : interior★ FY
– Zoo★★ (Dierentuin) DEU – Zurenborg Quarter★★ EV – The port (Haven) ⇌ FY.
Museums : Maritime "Steen"★ (Nationaal Scheepvaartmuseum Steen) FY – Etnographic
Museum★ FY M¹ – Plantin-Moretus★★★ FZ – Mayer Van den Bergh★★ (Dulle
Griet) GZ – Rockox House★ (Rockoxhuis) GY M² – Royal Art Gallery★★★ (Koninklijk Museum
voor Schone Kunsten) CV M⁵ – Museum of Photography★ CV M⁶ – Open-air Museum of
Sculpture Middelheim★ (Openluchtmuseum voor Beeldhouwkunst) – Provincial Museum
Sterckshof-Zilvercentrum★.
🏌 🏌 North : 15,5 km at Kapellen, G. Capiaulei 2 ℘ 0 3 666 84 56, - 🏌 South : 10 km at
Aartselaar, Kasteel Cleydael, Cleydaellaan 36 ℘ 0 3 887 00 79 - 🏌 🏌 East : 10 km at Wom-
melgem, Uilenbaan 15 ℘ 0 3 355 14 30 - 🏌 🏌 East : 13 km at Broechem, Kasteel Bos-
senstein, Moor 16 ℘ 0 3 485 64 16.
🛈 Grote Markt 15 ℘ 0 3 232 01 03, toerisme@antwerpen.be, Fax 0 3 231 19 37 – Tourist
association of the province, Koningin Elisabethlei 16, ✉ 2018, ℘ 0 3 240 63 73, info@
tpa@pandora.be, Fax 0 3 240 63 83.
Brussels 48 – Amsterdam 159 – Luxembourg 261 – Rotterdam 103.

Plans on following pages

Old Antwerp

🏨🏨 **Hilton** Ⓜ, Groenplaats ℘ 0 3 204 12 12, hiltongm@planetinternet.be, Fax 0 3
204 12 13, « Facade of an early 20C department store », 🍸, ⇌ – 🛗 ⇆ ▤ 📺
– 🏋 30-1000. 🆎 ① ⓂⓈ 𝐕𝐈𝐒𝐀 ⒿⒸⒷ   FZ
Meals see *Het Vijfde Seizoen* below – ⇌ 21 – **199 rm** 258/332, 12 suites.

🏨 **De Witte Lelie** 🌿 without rest, Keizerstraat 16 ℘ 0 3 226 19 66, hotel@dewitte
lie.be, Fax 0 3 234 00 19, « Typical 17C terraced houses, patio » – 🛗 📺 ⇦. 🆎 ① ⓂⓈ
𝐕𝐈𝐒𝐀 ⒿⒸⒷ   GY
closed 20 December-15 January – **7 rm** ⇌ 170/400, 3 suites.

ANTWERPEN

BELGIUM

Pleasant hotels and restaurants
are shown in the Guide by a red sign.

Please send us the names
of any where you have enjoyed your stay.

Your **Michelin Guide** will be even better.

ANTWERPEN

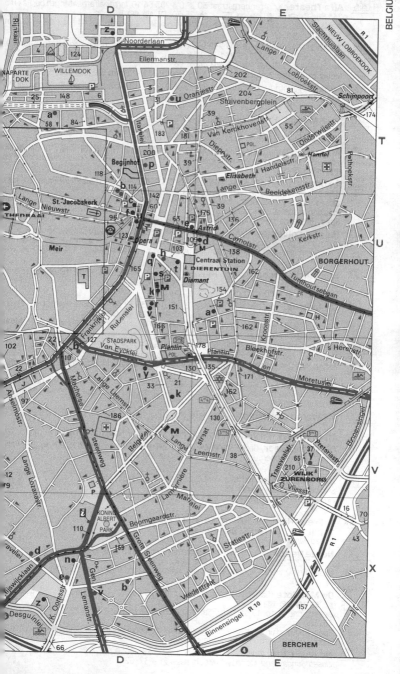

Alfa Theater Ⓜ, Arenbergstraat 30 ℰ 0 3 203 54 10, *info@alfatheater.gth.be*, Fax 0 3 233 88 58, ⓔⓢ – ⓲ ⓧ⊷ 🖭 – 🏊 25-50. 🆎 ① ⓶ 𝗩𝗜𝗦𝗔. ❀   GZ t
Meals *(closed Saturday lunch and Sunday)* Lunch 16 – a la carte 36/44 – ⏴ 19 – **122 rm** 170/220, 5 suites.

't Sandt, Het Zand 17 ℰ 0 3 232 93 90 and 0 3 231 96 91 (rest), *info@hotel-sandt.be*, Fax 0 3 232 56 13 and 0 3 231 79 01 (rest), « 19C residence in rococo style » – 🆎 ① ⓶ 𝗩𝗜𝗦𝗔 ᴊᴄʙ.   FZ w
⇔ – 🏊 25-150. 🆎 ① ⓶ 𝗩𝗜𝗦𝗔 ᴊᴄʙ.
Meals *de kleine Zavel* Lunch 15 – a la carte 33/41 – **29 rm** ⏴ 130/220, 1 suite.

Rubens ⚘ without rest, Oude Beurs 29 ℰ 0 3 222 48 48, *hotel.rubens@glo.be*, Fax 0 3 225 19 40 – ⓲ 🖭 ⇔. 🆎 ① ⓶ 𝗩𝗜𝗦𝗔 ᴊᴄʙ. ❀   FY y
35 rm ⏴ 155/230, 1 suite.

Villa Mozart, Handschoenmarkt 3 ℰ 0 3 231 30 31, *villa.mozart@village.uunet.be*, Fax 0 3 231 56 85, ⮯, ⓔⓢ – ⓲ 🖭. 🆎 ① ⓶ 𝗩𝗜𝗦𝗔 ᴊᴄʙ   FY e
Meals (Pub rest) Lunch 15 – 22 – ⏴ 13 – **25 rm** 94.

Antigone without rest, Jordaenskaai 11 ℰ 0 3 231 66 77 – ⓲ 🖭 – 🏊 30. 🆎 ① ⓶ 𝗩𝗜𝗦𝗔   ΓY ᴅ
18 rm ⏴ 77/90.

't Fornuis (Segers), Reyndersstraat 24 ℰ 0 3 233 62 70, Fax 0 3 233 99 03, « 17C residence, rustic interior » – 🆎 ① ⓶ 𝗩𝗜𝗦𝗔.   FZ c
closed last 3 weeks August, 24 December-1 January, Saturday and Sunday – **Meals** (booking essential) a la carte 56/71
Spec. Salade de tourteau. Ris de veau rôti au chou et truffes. Sabayon au Champagne.

Huis De Colvenier, St-Antoniusstraat 8 ℰ 0 3 226 65 73, *info@colvenier.be*, Fax 0 3 227 13 14, ⮯, « Late 19C residence, murals and winter garden » – 🖭 🅿. 🆎 ① ⓶ 𝗩𝗜𝗦𝗔
closed carnival week, August, Sunday and Monday – **Meals** Lunch 62 – a la carte approx 69.   FZ

Het Vijfde Seizoen - Hotel Hilton, Groenplaats ℰ 0 3 204 12 12, *hiltongm@planet.internet.be*, Fax 0 3 204 12 13 – 🖭. 🆎 ① ⓶ 𝗩𝗜𝗦𝗔 ᴊᴄʙ   FZ n
Meals Lunch 25 – 43.

La Rade 1st floor, E. Van Dijckkaai 8 ℰ 0 3 233 37 37, *larade@skynet.be*, Fax 0 3 233 49 63, « 19C former freemason's lodge » – 🆎 ① ⓶ 𝗩𝗜𝗦𝗔   FY
closed 8 to 28 July, late December, Saturday lunch, Sunday and Bank Holidays – **Meals** Lunch 37 – 62.

De Kerselaar (Michiels), Grote Pieter Potstraat 22 ℰ 0 3 233 59 69, *dekerselaar@andora.be*, Fax 0 3 233 11 49 – 🖭. 🆎 ① ⓶ 𝗩𝗜𝗦𝗔 ᴊᴄʙ.   FY
closed first 2 weeks September, Sunday and lunch Monday, Wednesday and Saturday – **Meals** Lunch 42 – a la carte approx. 68
Spec. Écrevisses, artichauts, foie d'oie et truffes en feuille croquante. Blanc de St-Pierre couvert de carottes, lard et truffes, sauce au cresson. Pain d'épice façon pain perdu au figues et poires.

't Silveren Claverblat, Grote Pieter Potstraat 16 ℰ 0 3 231 33 88, Fax 0 3 231 31 4 – 🆎 ① ⓶ 𝗩𝗜𝗦𝗔. ❀   FY
closed Tuesday and lunch Wednesday and Saturday – **Meals** 35/67 b.i..

De Gulden Beer, Grote Markt 14 ℰ 0 3 226 08 41, Fax 0 3 232 52 09, ≤, ⮯, Part Italian cuisine, open until 11 p.m. – 🖭. 🆎 ① ⓶ 𝗩𝗜𝗦𝗔. ❀   FY
Meals Lunch 25 – 35/62.

Het Nieuwe Palinghuis, Sint-Jansvliet 14 ℰ 0 3 231 74 45, Fax 0 3 231 50 5 Seafood – 🖭. 🆎 ① ⓶ 𝗩𝗜𝗦𝗔   FZ
closed June, last 2 weeks January, Monday and Tuesday – **Meals** Lunch 32 – a la car 42/64 ⏴.

P. Preud'Homme, Suikerrui 28 ℰ 0 3 233 42 00, Fax 0 3 233 42 00, ⮯, Open ur 11 p.m. – 🖭. 🆎 ① ⓶ 𝗩𝗜𝗦𝗔 ᴊᴄʙ. ❀   FY
closed January – **Meals** a la carte 46/76.

Neuze Neuze 1st floor, Wijngaardstraat 19 ℰ 0 3 232 27 97, *neuzeneuze@pandora.b* Fax 0 3 225 27 38 – 🆎 ① ⓶ 𝗩𝗜𝗦𝗔 ᴊᴄʙ   FY
closed first 2 weeks August, first week January, Saturday lunch and Sunday – **Meals** Lu 24 – 55.

De Matelote (Garnich), Haarstraat 9 ℰ 0 3 231 32 07, Fax 0 3 231 08 13, Seafood 🖭. 🆎 ① ⓶ 𝗩𝗜𝗦𝗔   FY
closed June, 1 to 15 January, Saturday lunch, Sunday and Monday – **Meals** a la car 49/68
Spec. Anguille fumée, sauce au bacon (April-October). Homard et sa mayonnaise d'homa (April-August). Barbue à l'huile de curry.

Nouveau Zirk, Zirkstraat 29 ℰ 0 3 225 25 86, Fax 0 3 226 51 77 – 🖭. ⓶ 𝗩𝗜𝗦𝗔 *closed Sunday and Monday* – **Meals** Lunch 21 – 37/62.   FY

Dock's Café, Jordaenskaai 7 📞 0 3 226 63 30, info@docks.be, Fax 0 3 226 65 72, Brasserie-Oyster bar, open until midnight, « Futuristic decorated mezzanine » – 🍽. AE 🌐 VISA JCB. ※
closed 1 January and Saturday lunch – **Meals** 21/27 ℃.
FY h

De Manie, H. Conscienceplein 3 📞 0 3 232 64 38, Fax 0 3 232 64 38 – AE 🌐 VISA JCB.
closed 9 to 17 February, 14 August-2 September, Sunday lunch school holidays, Wednesday and Sunday dinner – **Meals** Lunch 24 – 35/46.
GY u

De Reddende Engel, Torfbrug 3 📞 0 3 233 66 30, Fax 0 3 233 73 79, 🌳 – AE 🌐
🌐 VISA – closed 2 to 8 April, 11 August-9 September, Tuesday, Wednesday and Saturday lunch – **Meals** 24/31.
FY p

Café de la Gare, Haarstraat 3 📞 0 3 226 49 27, 🌳, Partly Italian cuisine, « Artistic ambience in a small cellar » – 🌐 VISA
FY u
closed last 2 weeks June, late December-early January, Tuesday and Wednesday – **Meals** (dinner only until 11 p.m.) a la carte 36/49.

Maritime, Suikerrui 4 📞 0 3 233 07 58, restaurant.maritime@pandora.be, Fax 0 3 233 18 87, 🌳 – 🍽. AE 🌐 VISA
FY f
closed June, Wednesday and Thursday – **Meals** a la carte 34/43.

Town Centre, Station and Docks

Radisson SAS Park Lane M, Van Eycklei 34, ✉ 2018, 📞 0 3 285 85 85, guest@a nrzh.rdsas.com, Fax 0 3 285 85 86, ≤, 𝄞, ≋, 🔲, 🚲 – 🛗 ↔ 🍽 📺 🚗 – 🛎 25-600. AE 🌐 🌐 VISA JCB. ※
DV y
Meals Longchamps (closed Sunday) 30 – ☑ 21 – **156 rm** 185/220, 14 suites.

Astrid Park Plaza M, Koningin Astridplein 1, ✉ 2018, 📞 0 3 203 12 34, appsales @parkplazahotels.be, Fax 0 3 203 12 51, ≤, 𝄞, ≋, 🔲 – 🛗 ↔ 🍽 📺 🚗 – 🛎 25-500. AE 🌐 🌐 VISA
DEU e
Meals a la carte approx. 30 – ☑ 20 – **225 rm** 220/275, 3 suites.

Carlton, Quinten Matsijslei 25, ✉ 2018, 📞 0 3 225 15 15, info@carltonhotel-antwer p.com, Fax 0 3 225 30 90 – 🛗 ↔ 🍽 📺 🚗 – 🛎 25-100. AE 🌐 🌐 VISA ※ rest
Meals (closed 3 weeks August and Sunday dinner) Lunch 20 – a la carte approx. 35 – **127 rm** ☑ 180/228.
DU v

Alfa De Keyser M, De Keyserlei 66, ✉ 2018, 📞 0 3 206 74 60, info@alfadekeyse r.gth.be, Fax 0 3 232 39 70, 𝄞, ≋, 🔲 – 🛗 ↔ 🍽 📺 – 🛎 25-160. AE 🌐 🌐 VISA JCB
Meals (closed Sunday) (Pub rest) Lunch 16 – a la carte 25/35 – ☑ 19 – **120 rm** 145/195, 3 suites.
DU t

Hyllit M without rest, De Keyserlei 28 (access by Appelmansstraat), ✉ 2018, 📞 0 3 202 68 00, info@hyllithotel.be, Fax 0 3 202 68 90, 𝄞, ≋, 🔲, 🚲 – 🛗 ↔ 🍽 📺 🚗
– 🛎 25-120. AE 🌐 🌐 VISA JCB. ※
DU q
☑ 16 – **117 rm** 196, 5 suites.

Plaza without rest, Charlottalei 43, ✉ 2018, 📞 0 3 287 28 70, plaza@plaza.be, Fax 0 3 287 28 71 – 🛗 ↔ 🍽 📺 🚗 – 🛎 25. AE 🌐 🌐 VISA ※
DV k
80 rm ☑ 145/195.

Eurotel without rest, Copernicuslaan 2, ✉ 2018, 📞 0 3 223 40 40, info@eurotel.be, Fax 0 3 223 40 41, 𝄞, ≋, 🔲 – 🛗 ↔ 🍽 📺 🚗 – 🛎 25-650. AE 🌐 🌐 VISA ※
145 rm ☑ 155/180, 3 suites.
EU a

Residence without rest, Molenbergstraat 9 📞 0 3 232 76 75, residence@demahotel s.net, Fax 0 3 233 73 28 – 🛗 📺 🚗 – 🛎 40. AE 🌐 🌐 VISA ※
DU c
48 rm ☑ 124/183.

Astoria without rest, Korte Herentalsestraat 5, ✉ 2018, 📞 0 3 227 31 30, info@ca rltonhotel-antwerp.com, Fax 0 3 227 31 34, 𝄞 – 🛗 ↔ 🍽 📺 🚗. AE 🌐 🌐 VISA
66 rm ☑ 140/175.
DU r

Antverpia without rest, Sint-Jacobsmarkt 85 📞 0 3 231 80 80, antverpia@skynet.be, Fax 0 3 232 43 43 – 🛗 📺 🚗. AE 🌐 🌐 VISA JCB. ※
DU f
☑ 10 – **18 rm** 99/123.

Alfa Empire without rest, Appelmansstraat 31, ✉ 2018, 📞 0 3 203 54 00, Fax 0 3 233 40 60 – 🛗 ↔ 🍽 📺. AE 🌐 🌐 VISA ※
DU s
☑ 15 – **70 rm** 90/145.

Tulip Inn Docklands M without rest, Kempisch Dok Westkaai 84 📞 0 3 231 07 26, info @tiantwerpen.goldentulip.be, Fax 0 3 231 57 49 – 🛗 ↔ 📺 – 🛎 25. AE 🌐 🌐 VISA ※
☑ 12 – **32 rm** 105/140.
DT z

Columbus without rest, Frankrijklei 4 📞 0 3 233 03 90, colombushotel@skynet.be, Fax 0 3 226 09 46, 𝄞, 🔲 – 🛗 📺 🚗. AE 🌐 🌐 VISA
DU u
32 rm ☑ 89/108.

Atlanta without rest, Koningin Astridplein 14, ✉ 2018, 📞 0 3 203 09 19, atlanta@d emahotels.be, Fax 0 3 226 37 37 – 🛗 📺 – 🛎 25. AE 🌐 🌐 VISA ※
DEU d
60 rm ☑ 94/134.

Eden without rest, Lange Herentalsestraat 25, ⊠ 2018, ℰ 0 3 233 06 08, *hotel.eden @ skynet.be, Fax 0 3 233 12 28* – ⫯ 📺 🚗. 🅰🅴 ① ⑩⑥ 𝖵𝖨𝖲𝖠 𝖩𝖢𝖡   DU k
66 rm ⊇ 99/110.

De Barbarie, Van Breestraat 4, ⊠ 2018, ℰ 0 3 232 81 98, Fax 0 3 231 26 78, 😤,
« Silverware collection » – 🗏. 🅰🅴 ① ⑩⑥ 𝖵𝖨𝖲𝖠. ✸   DV b
closed Easter, 1 to 14 September, Saturday lunch, Sunday and Monday – **Meals** Lunch 37
– a la carte approx. 68 ♀.

La Luna, Italiëlei 177 ℰ 0 3 232 23 44, *info@laluna.be, Fax 0 3 232 24 41,* Multinational
cuisines, open until 11 p.m. – 🗏. 🅰🅴 ① ⑩⑥ 𝖵𝖨𝖲𝖠   DT p
closed first 3 weeks August, Christmas-New Year, Saturday lunch, Sunday and Monday –
Meals a la carte 37/47 ♀.

de nieuwe HARMONY, Mechelsesteenweg 169, ⊠ 2018, ℰ 0 3 239 70 05, *acs.ac s@yucom.be, Fax 0 3 239 63 61* – 🗏. 🅰🅴 ① ⑩⑥ 𝖵𝖨𝖲𝖠   DV n
closed Monday and Saturday lunch – **Meals** Lunch 24 – 38/53 ♀.

De Lepeleer, Lange St-Annastraat 10 ℰ 0 3 225 19 31, *delepeleer@loyaltypartners. org, Fax 0 3 231 31 24,* 😤, « Several small houses in a 16C cul-de-sac » – 🗏 🄿 – 🏛 25-
50. 🅰🅴 ① ⑩⑥ 𝖵𝖨𝖲𝖠   DU b
closed 21 July-17 August, Saturday lunch, Sunday and Bank Holidays – **Meals** Lunch 25 –
62.

't Peerd, Paardenmarkt 53 ℰ 0 3 231 98 25, *resto_t_peerd@ yahoo.com, Fax 0 3 231 59 40,* 😤 – 🗏 🄿. 🅰🅴 ① ⑩⑥ 𝖵𝖨𝖲𝖠 𝖩𝖢𝖡   GY e
closed 2 weeks Easter, 2 weeks October, Tuesday and Wednesday – **Meals** Lunch 34 – a
la carte 40/53.

De Zeste, Lange Dijkstraat 36, ⊠ 2060, ℰ 0 3 233 45 49, *dezeste@ resto.be, Fax 0 3 232 34 18* – 🗏. 🅰🅴 ① ⑩⑥ 𝖵𝖨𝖲𝖠   DT L
closed last 2 weeks July, Wednesday dinner and Sunday – **Meals** Lunch 62 b.i. – a la carte
approx. 60.

Pazzo, Oude Leeuwenrui 12 ℰ 0 3 232 86 82, *pazzo@skynet.be, Fax 0 3 232 79 34,*
« Old warehouse converted into a modern brasserie » – 🗏. 🅰🅴 ①
⑩⑥ 𝖵𝖨𝖲𝖠   DT a
closed last week July-first 2 weeks August, Christmas-New Year, Tuesday and lunch Saturday and Sunday – **Meals** Lunch 19 – a la carte approx. 38 ♀.

Yamayu Santatsu, Ossenmarkt 19 ℰ 0 3 234 09 49, Fax 0 3 234 09 49, Japanese
cuisine with Sushi-bar – 🗏. 🅰🅴 ① ⑩⑥ 𝖵𝖨𝖲𝖠 𝖩𝖢𝖡   DTU
closed 2 weeks August, last week December, Sunday lunch and Monday – **Meals** Lunch 1
– 40/45.

South Quarter

Crowne Plaza Ⓜ, G. Legrellelaan 10, ⊠ 2020, ℰ 0 3 237 29 00, *crowneplaza.ant erp@ pi.be, Fax 0 3 216 02 96,* 🛋, ☎, 🔲 – ⫯ ✳ 🗏 📺 🚗 🄿 – 🏛 25-600. 🅰🅴 ⑥
⑩⑥ 𝖵𝖨𝖲𝖠
Meals *Nico Central* Lunch 22 – 27/30 ♀ – ⊇ 20 – 256 rm 235, 6 suites.

Mercure Diamant, Desguinlei 94, ⊠ 2018, ℰ 0 3 244 82 11, *H1277@ accor-hote .com, Fax 0 3 216 47 12,* 😤, 🛋, ☎ – ⫯ ✳ 🗏 📺 🚗 🄿 – 🏛 25-590. 🅰🅴 ① ⑩
𝖵𝖨𝖲𝖠. ✸ rest   DX
Meals *Tiffany's* (closed Saturday and Sunday lunch) Lunch 24 – a la carte approx. 38
⊇ 17 – 210 rm 129, 5 suites.

Firean ⧖, Karel Oomsstraat 6, ⊠ 2018, ℰ 0 3 237 02 60, *info@hotelfirean.con Fax 0 3 238 11 68,* « Period residence, Art Deco style with patio », 🚲 – ⫯ 🗏 📺 🚗
🅰🅴 ① ⑩⑥ 𝖵𝖨𝖲𝖠 𝖩𝖢𝖡   DX
closed 27 July-19 August and 21 December-6 January – **Meals** see *Minerva* below – 15 r
⊇ 126/150.

Industrie Ⓜ without rest, Emiel Banningstraat 52 ℰ 0 3 238 66 00, *hotelindustr @ pandora.be, Fax 0 3 238 86 88* – 📺 🚗. 🅰🅴 ① ⑩⑥ 𝖵𝖨𝖲𝖠. ✸   CV
13 rm ⊇ 75/92.

Loncin, Markgravelei 127, ⊠ 2018, ℰ 0 3 248 29 89, *info@ loncinrestaurant.be, Fax C 248 38 66,* 😤 – 🗏 🄿. 🅰🅴 ① ⑩⑥ 𝖵𝖨𝖲𝖠. ✸   DX
closed Saturday lunch and Sunday – **Meals** Lunch 35 – a la carte 60/79.

Liang's Garden, Markgravelei 141, ⊠ 2018, ℰ 0 3 237 22 22, Fax 0 3 248 38 ⧖
Chinese cuisine – 🗏. 🅰🅴 ① ⑩⑥ 𝖵𝖨𝖲𝖠   DX
closed late July-early August and Sunday – **Meals** Lunch 24 – a la carte 28/44 ♀.

De Poterne, Desguinlei 186, ⊠ 2018, ℰ 0 3 238 28 24, Fax 0 3 248 59 67 – 🅰🅴
⑩⑥ 𝖵𝖨𝖲𝖠   DX
closed 21 July-15 August, 24 December-1 January, Saturday lunch, Sunday and Bank H
days – **Meals** Lunch 39 – a la carte approx. 62.

XX **Minerva** Hotel Firean, Karel Oomsstraat 36, ⊠ 2018, ℘ 0 3 216 00 55, *info@reta urantminerva.com*, Fax 0 3 216 00 55 – ▤. 𝖠𝖤 ⓪ ⓶⓼ 𝖵𝖨𝖲𝖠 𝗝𝖢𝖡   DX e
closed 28 July-20 August, 22 December-7 January, Sunday and Monday – **Meals** a la carte 43/72.

XX **Kommilfoo**, Vlaamse Kaai 17 ℘ 0 3 237 30 00, Fax 0 3 237 30 00 – ▤. 𝖠𝖤 ⓪ ⓶⓼ 𝖵𝖨𝖲𝖠.
⫸   CV e
closed first 2 weeks July, Sunday and Monday – **Meals** Lunch 28 – 46.

Suburbs

North – ⊠ 2030 :

🏨 **Novotel**, Luithagen-haven 6 (Haven 200) ℘ 0 3 542 03 20, *H0465@accor-hotels.com*, Fax 0 3 541 70 93, 🐜, ⤢, ⫸ – ⧉ ⭢⭠ ▤ 𝖳𝖵 ℙ – 🔼 25-180. 𝖠𝖤 ⓪ ⓶⓼ 𝖵𝖨𝖲𝖠. ⫸ rest
Meals Lunch 13 – a la carte 26/38 – ⫸ 13 – **120 rm** 99.

at Berchem Ⓒ Antwerpen – ⊠ 2600 Berchem :

XXX **De Tafeljoncker**, Frederik de Merodestraat 13 ℘ 0 3 281 20 34, *de-tafeljoncker@b elgacom.be*, Fax 0 3 281 20 34, 🐜 – ▤. 𝖠𝖤 ⓪ ⓶⓼ 𝖵𝖨𝖲𝖠   DX f
closed 20 to 28 February, 4 to 19 September, Sunday dinner, Monday and Tuesday – **Meals** Lunch 47 b.i. – 73/87.

XX **Brasserie Marly**, Generaal Lemanstraat 64 ℘ 0 3 281 23 23, *info@marly.be*, Fax 0 3 281 33 10 – 𝖠𝖤 ⓪ ⓶⓼ 𝖵𝖨𝖲𝖠. ⫸   DX c
closed 22 July-18 August and Sunday – **Meals** Lunch 10 – 20/41 ⚲.

XX **Margaux**, Terlinckstraat 2 ℘ 0 3 230 55 99, Fax 0 3 230 40 71, 🐜, « Shaded terrace » – ▤. ⓶⓼ 𝖵𝖨𝖲𝖠. ⫸   DX b
closed 2 weeks Easter, 1 to 19 September, Sunday and Monday – **Meals** Lunch 29 – a la carte 36/62.

XX **De Troubadour**, Driekoningenstraat 72 ℘ 0 3 239 39 16, Fax 0 3 230 82 71 – ▤ ℙ. 𝖠𝖤 ⓪ ⓶⓼ 𝖵𝖨𝖲𝖠   DX a
closed first 3 weeks July, Sunday and Monday – **Meals** Lunch 23 – 30 ⚲.

at Borgerhout East : 3 km Ⓒ Antwerpen – ⊠ 2140 Borgerhout :

🏨 **Holiday Inn**, Luitenant Lippenslaan 66 ℘ 0 3 235 91 91, *info@holiday-inn-antwerp.com*, Fax 0 3 235 08 96, ⭢⭠, ⬚, – ⧉ ⭢⭠ ▤ 𝖳𝖵 🔼 ℙ – 🔼 25-230. 𝖠𝖤 ⓪ ⓶⓼ 𝖵𝖨𝖲𝖠. ⫸
Meals *(closed Saturday lunch)* Lunch 25 – a la carte approx. 44 – ⫸ 18 – **201 rm** 200/250, 3 suites.

at Deurne Northeast : 3 km Ⓒ Antwerpen – ⊠ 2100 Deurne :

XX **De Violin**, Bosuil 1 ℘ 0 3 324 34 04, Fax 0 3 326 33 20, 🐜, « Small farmhouse, Asian style terrace » – ℙ. 𝖠𝖤 ⓪ ⓶⓼ 𝖵𝖨𝖲𝖠. ⫸
closed 21 August-12 September, Sunday and Monday dinner – **Meals** Lunch 37 b.i. – a la carte approx. 50.

at Ekeren North : 11 km Ⓒ Antwerpen – ⊠ 2180 Ekeren :

X **De Mangerie**, Kapelsesteenweg 4/1 (par ②) ℘ 0 3 605 26 26, Fax 0 3 605 24 16, 🐜, « Nautical inspired interior » – 𝖠𝖤 ⓪ ⓶⓼ 𝖵𝖨𝖲𝖠
closed Saturday lunch – **Meals** 25 ⚲.

Environs

at Aartselaar South : 10 km. pop. 14 438 – ⊠ 2630 Aartselaar :

🏨 **Kasteel Solhof** ⫸ without rest, Baron Van Ertbornstraat 116 ℘ 0 3 877 30 00, Fax 0 3 877 31 31, « Terrace in public park », 🐜 – ⧉ 𝖳𝖵 ℙ – 🔼 25-50. 𝖠𝖤 ⓪ ⓶⓼ 𝖵𝖨𝖲𝖠. ⫸
closed Christmas-New Year – ⫸ 14 – **24 rm** 136/198.

at Boechout Southeast : 9 km. pop. 11 919 – ⊠ 2530 Boechout :

XXX **De Schone van Boskoop** (Keersmaekers), Appelkantstraat 10 ℘ 0 3 454 19 31, ⊛ Fax 0 3 454 02 10, 🐜, « Interior design, ornamental pool and statues in garden » – ℙ. 𝖠𝖤 ⓶⓼ 𝖵𝖨𝖲𝖠. ⫸
closed 2 to 6 April, 13 August-2 September, 25 December-2 January, Sunday and Monday – **Meals** Lunch 37 – a la carte approx. 87
Spec. Boudin de canard sauvage au foie gras sauce à la bière Kriek (15 August-January). Cabillaud en brandade, tempura de calamar. Dessert tout chocolat.

at Edegem Southeast : 5 km. pop. 22 253 – ⊠ 2650 Edegem :

🏨 **Ter Elst**, Terelststraat 310 (by Prins Boudewijnlaan) ℘ 0 3 450 90 00, Fax 0 3 450 90 90, 🐜, 🔳, ⭢⭠, – ⧉ ⭢⭠ ▤ 𝖳𝖵 ℙ – 🔼 25-500. 𝖠𝖤 ⓪ ⓶⓼ 𝖵𝖨𝖲𝖠. ⫸
Meals *Couvert Classique* *(closed 2 July-10 August, 24 and 31 December and 1 January)* Lunch 35 – 33/50 – **53 rm** ⫸ 99/110.

XX **La Cabane,** Mechelsesteenweg 11 ✆ 0 3 454 58 98, *restaurantlacabane@skynet.be*, Fax 0 3 455 34 26 – 🅾🅾 🆅🅸🆂🅰 . closed 23 July-7 August, All Saints' week, last week December, Saturday lunch, Sunday dinner and Monday – **Meals** Lunch 31 – 46/55.

at Kapellen North : 15,5 km. pop. 25 671 – ✉ 2950 Kapellen :

XXX **De Bellefleur** (Buytaert), Antwerpsesteenweg 253 ✆ 0 3 664 67 19, Fax 0 3 665 02 01, 🈺🈺 🍴 , « Veranda with pergola surrounded by floral garden » – 🅿 🅰🅴 🅾 🅾🅾 🆅🅸🆂🅰
closed July, Saturday lunch, Sunday and Monday – **Meals** Lunch 46 – 96 b.i., a la carte approx. 108 ♀
Spec. Navarin de sole aux chanterelles et aux truffes d'été (April-October). Homard de Zélande rôti au four, sauce mousseline au limon. Lièvre des neiges au Malt Whisky.

at Schoten Northeast : 10 km. pop. 32 733 – ✉ 2900 Schoten :

XXX **Kleine Barreel,** Bredabaan 1147 ✆ 0 3 645 85 84, *info@kleine-barreel.be*, Fax 0 3 645 85 03 – 📻 🅿 – 🅰 25-60. 🅰🅴 🅾 🅾🅾 🆅🅸🆂🅰 🅹🅲🅱
Meals Lunch 32 – 44.

XX **Uilenspiegel,** Brechtsebaan 277 (3 km on N 115) ✆ 0 3 651 61 45, Fax 0 3 652 08 08, 🍴 , « Terrace and garden » – 🅿 – 🅰 25. 🅰🅴 🅾🅾 🆅🅸🆂🅰
closed carnival week, 3 weeks July, Tuesday and Wednesday – **Meals** 27/37 ♀.

at Wijnegem East : 10 km. pop. 8 660 – ✉ 2110 Wijnegem :

XXX **Ter Vennen,** Merksemsebaan 278 ✆ 0 3 326 20 60, *tervennen@skynet.be*, Fax 0 3 326 38 47, 🍴 , « Terrace » – 🅿 – 🅰 50. 🅰🅴 🅾 🅾🅾 🆅🅸🆂🅰
closed 12 to 17 February, 30 July-11 August, 29 and 30 December, Sunday dinner and Monday – **Meals** Lunch 42 b.i. – 32/57 b.i..

Kruiningen Zeeland (Netherlands) Ⓒ Reimerswaal pop. 20 524 🄟🄟🄟 J 14 and 🄟🄟🄟 D 7 – 56 km.

🏛 **Le Manoir** 🦢 , Zandweg 2 (West : 1 km), ✉ 4416 NA, ✆ (0 113) 38 17 53, Fax (0 113) 38 17 63, 🍴 , 🦿 , 🚲 – 📺 🅿 🅰🅴 🅾 🅾🅾 🆅🅸🆂🅰
closed first week October and first 2 weeks January – **Meals** see **Inter Scaldes** below – ☕ 20 – **10 rm** 161, 2 suites.

XXXX **Inter Scaldes** (Brevet) - Hotel Le Manoir, Zandweg 2 (West : 1 km), ✉ 4416 NA ✆ (0 113) 38 17 53, Fax (0 113) 38 17 63, 🍴 , « Terrace-veranda overlooking an English style garden » – 🅿 🅰🅴 🅾 🅾🅾 🆅🅸🆂🅰
closed first week October, first 2 weeks January, Monday and Tuesday – **Meals** Lunch 4 – 57, a la carte 76/113
Spec. Foie gras mariné aux huîtres et mousse de tomate. Pigeon fermier en croûte de sel à l'ail. Turbot grillé, sauce aux anchois, câpres et tomates.

The hotels have entered into certain undertakings towards the readers of this Guide.
Make it plain that you have the most recent Guide.

BRUGES (BRUGGE) 8000 West-Vlaanderen 🄟🄟🄟 E 15 and 🄟🄟🄟 C 2. pop. 116 246.

See : Procession of the Holy Blood★★★ (De Heilig Bloedprocessie) – Historic centre an canals★★★ (Historisch centrum en grachten) – Market square★★ (Markt) AU, Belfry an Halles★★★ (Belfort en Hallen) ≤★★ from the top AU – Market-town★★ (Burg) AU – Basilic of the Holy Blood★ (Basiliek van het Heilig Bloed) : low Chapel★ or St. Basiles Chapel (bene den- of Basiliuskapel) AU B – Chimney of the "Brugse Vrije"★ in the Palace of the "Brugs Vrije" AU S – Rosery quay (Rozenhoedkaai) ≤★★ AU 63 – Dijver ≤★★ AU – St. Bonifac bridge (Bonifatiusbrug) : site★★ AU – Beguinage★★ (Begijnhof) AV – Trips on th canals★★ (Boottocht) AU – Church of Our Lady★ (O.-L.-Vrouwekerk) : tower★, statu of the Madonna★★, tombstone★★ of Mary of Burgundy★★ AV N.

Museums : Groeninge★★★ (Stedelijk Museum voor Schone Kunsten) AU – Mem ling★★★ (St. John's Hospital) AU – Gruuthuse★ (Gruuthuse) AU M¹ – Arentshuis★ AU M⁴ – Folklore★ (Museum voor Volk kunde) DY M².

Envir : Southwest : 10,5 km at Zedelgem : baptismal font★ in the St. Lawrence's churc – Northeast : 7 km : Damme★.

🏌 Northeast : 7 km at Sijsele, Doornstraat 16 ✆ 0 50 35 35 72, Fax 0 50 35 89 25.

🄱 Burg 11 ✆ 0 50 44 86 86, *toerisme@brugge.be*, Fax 0 50 44 86 00 and at railway st tion, Stationsplein – Tourist association of the province, Kasteel Tillegem ✉ 8200 Sir Michiels, ✆ 0 50 38 02 96, *westtoer@westtoerisme.be*, Fax 0 50 38 02 92.

Brussels 96 – Ghent 45 – Lille 72 – Ostend 28.

Plans on following pages

Town Centre

Crowne Plaza M 🕭, Burg 10 ℰ 0 50 44 68 44, *hotel@ crowne-plaza-brugge.com*, Fax 0 50 44 68 68, ≤, 🛒, « Interesting medieval remains and objects in basement », ₤ᴃ, ⇋, ⬛ – 🛗 ✦ ⬛ TV ⅃ 🔇 P – 🏛 25-400. ᴀᴇ ⓘ 🔞 VISA ᴊᴄʙ. ✦
AU a
Meals *'t Kapittel (closed Wednesday dinner, Saturday lunch and Sunday) Lunch* 19 – 30/46
– **De Linde** *Lunch* 9 – a la carte 26/40 – ⬚ 18 – **93 rm** 204/246, 3 suites.

de tuilerieën without rest, Dijver 7 ℰ 0 50 34 36 91, *info@hoteltuilerieen.com*, Fax 0 50 34 04 00, ≤, ₤ᴃ, ⬛, 🚲 – 🛗 ✦ ⬛ TV – 🏛 25-45. ᴀᴇ ⓘ 🔞 VISA ᴊᴄʙ
⬚ 19 – **43 rm** 173/247, 2 suites.
AU c

Relais Oud Huis Amsterdam 🕭 without rest, Spiegelrei 3 ℰ 0 50 34 18 10, *info @oha.be*, Fax 0 50 33 88 91, ≤, « 17C residence, former Dutch trading post », 🌼 – 🛗 ✦ ⬛ TV 🔇 – 🏛 25. ᴀᴇ ⓘ 🔞 VISA ᴊᴄʙ
AT d
32 rm ⬚ 174/250, 2 suites.

de orangerie 🕭 without rest, Kartuizerinnenstraat 10 ℰ 0 50 34 16 49, *info@ hotelorangerie.com*, Fax 0 50 33 30 16, « Period canalside residence », 🚲 – 🛗 ✦ ⬛ TV 🚺 🔇 P ᴀᴇ ⓘ 🔞 VISA ᴊᴄʙ
AU e
⬚ 19 – **20 rm** 173/247.

Die Swaene 🕭, Steenhouwersdijk 1 ℰ 0 50 34 27 98, *info@dieswaene-hotel.com*, Fax 0 50 33 66 74, ≤, « Stylish furnishings », ₤ᴃ, ⬛ – 🛗 ⬛ rm, TV 🔇 – 🏛 30. ᴀᴇ ⓘ 🔞 VISA ᴊᴄʙ
AU p
Meals *(closed 2 weeks July, 2 weeks January, Wednesday and Thursday lunch) Lunch* 35 – 52/70 – **22 rm** ⬚ 170/245.

Sofitel, Boeverlestraat 2 ℰ 0 50 44 97 11, *H1278@ accor-hotels.com*, Fax 0 50 44 97 99, ₤ᴃ, ⬛, 🌼 – 🛗 ✦ ⬛ TV 🔇 – 🏛 25-150. ᴀᴇ ⓘ 🔞 VISA ᴊᴄʙ
CZ b
Meals *Ter Boeverie* 25/48 – ⬚ 18 – **155 rm** 161/190.

Pandhotel without rest, Pandreitje 16 ℰ 0 50 34 06 66, *info@ pandhotel.be*, Fax 0 50 34 05 56, « Homely character and opulent interior » – 🛗 ⬛ TV. ᴀᴇ ⓘ 🔞 VISA ᴊᴄʙ
AU q
24 rm ⬚ 120/300.

Prinsenhof 🕭 without rest, Ontvangersstraat 9 ℰ 0 50 34 26 90, *info@ prinsenhof.com*, Fax 0 50 34 23 21, « Opulent interior » – 🛗 ⬛ TV 🔇 🚺 P. ᴀᴇ ⓘ 🔞 VISA ᴊᴄʙ. ✦
CY s
16 rm ⬚ 118/263.

Acacia 🕭 without rest, Korte Zilverstraat 3a ℰ 0 50 34 44 11, *info@hotel-acacia.com*, Fax 0 50 33 88 17, « Cosy interior, patio », ₤ᴃ, ⬛ – 🛗 ⬛ TV 🔇 P – 🏛 25-40. ᴀᴇ ⓘ 🔞 VISA ᴊᴄʙ. ✦
AU n
closed 6 to 24 January – **46 rm** ⬚ 113/163, 2 suites.

de' Medici 🕭, Potterierei 15 ℰ 0 50 33 98 33, *info@hoteldemedici.com*, Fax 0 50 33 07 64, « Modern style », ₤ᴃ, ₤ᴃ, 🌼 – 🛗 ✦ TV 🔇 🔇 – 🏛 25-170. ᴀᴇ ⓘ 🔞 VISA ᴊᴄʙ. ✦ rest
CX g
Meals *see rest **Koto** below* – **79 rm** ⬚ 162/196.

Hansa M 🕭 without rest, N. Desparsstraat 11 ℰ 0 50 44 44 44, *information@ hansa.be*, Fax 0 50 44 44 40, « Late 19C residence », ₤ᴃ, ₤ᴃ, 🚲 – 🛗 ✦ ⬛ TV 🔇. ᴀᴇ ⓘ 🔞 VISA ᴊᴄʙ. ✦
AT k
24 rm ⬚ 125/205.

Walburg sans rest, Boomgaardstraat 13 ℰ 0 50 34 94 14, Fax 0 50 33 68 84 – 🛗 TV – 🏛 30. ᴀᴇ ⓘ 🔞 VISA ᴊᴄʙ. ✦
AT f
closed 2 to 26 January – **12 rm** ⬚ 130/200, 1 suite.

Novotel Centrum 🕭, Katelijnestraat 65b ℰ 0 50 33 75 33, *H1033@ accor-hotels.com*, Fax 0 50 33 65 56, 🛒, ⬛, 🌼 – 🛗 ✦ ⬛ TV – 🏛 50-400. ᴀᴇ ⓘ 🔞 VISA ᴊᴄʙ
AV h
Meals *(dinner only)* 23 – **126 rm** ⬚ 118/165.

Jan Brito without rest, Freren Fonteinstraat 1 ℰ 0 50 33 06 01, *info@ janbrito.com*, Fax 0 50 33 06 52, « Gabled façade, 16, 17 and 18C interior », 🌼 – 🛗 ⬛ TV 🚺 – 🏛 25-40. ᴀᴇ ⓘ 🔞 VISA ᴊᴄʙ
AU j
18 rm ⬚ 109/159.

Navarra without rest, St-Jakobsstraat 41 ℰ 0 50 34 05 61, *reservations@ hotelnavarra.com*, Fax 0 50 34 05 61, ₤ᴃ, ₤ᴃ, ⬛, 🌼 – 🛗 ⬛ TV 🚺 – 🏛 25-110. ᴀᴇ ⓘ 🔞 VISA ᴊᴄʙ
AT n
87 rm ⬚ 120/140.

Montanus 🕭 without rest, Nieuwe Gentweg 78 ℰ 0 50 33 11 76, *info@ montanus.be*, Fax 0 50 34 09 38, 🌼, 🚲 – 🛗 ✦ TV 🔇 🚺 – 🏛 25-40. ᴀᴇ ⓘ 🔞 VISA ᴊᴄʙ
AV e
22 rm ⬚ 140/235, 2 suites.

De Castillion (annexe Het Gheestelic Hof - 14 ch), Heilige Geeststraat 1 ℰ 0 50 34 30 01, *info@castillion.be*, Fax 0 50 33 94 75, 🛒, ₤ᴃ – ⬛ TV 🚺 – 🏛 25-50. ᴀᴇ ⓘ 🔞 VISA ᴊᴄʙ. ✦ rest
AU r
Meals *(closed Sunday dinner and lunch Monday and Tuesday except Bank Holidays) Lunch* 42 – 62 – **20 rm** ⬚ 175/325.

A
0 ___ 100 m

B
BRUGGE
0 ___ 300 m

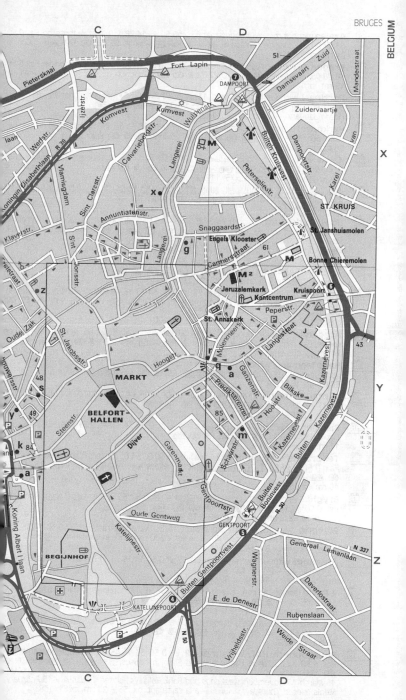

C
D

Pieterskaai
Fort Lapin
51
Damsevaart Zuid
Manderstraat

DAMPOORT 7

Komvest
Komvest
Wulpenstr.
Zuidervaartje

Calvariebergstr.
Langerei
Buiten Kruisvest
Dampoortstr.
Van
Karel

Koningin Elisabethlaan
R 30
Vlamingdam
M

Iaan
Werfstr.

Peterseliestr.

X
ST. KRUIS

Klaverstr.
Sint Clarestr.
Annuntiatenstr.
St. Janshuismolen

Sint Jorisstr.
Langerei
Snaggaardstr.
Engels Klooster
g
Carmersstraat
61
M
Bonne Chieremolen

Z
M 2
Kruispoort

Oude Zak
St. Jakobsstr.
Jeruzalemkerk
Kantcentrum
Peperstr.

St. Annakerk

Hoogstr.
Molenmeers
Langestraat
J
43

48
S
MARKT
q
a
Ganzenstr.
Bilkske

y
49
Predikherenrei
Hoogstr.
Kazernevest
Buiten Kazernevest

k
84
Steenstr.
BELFORT-HALLEN
85
m

a
Dijver
Garenmarkt
Schaarstr.

P
Gentpoortstr.
Buiten Boninvest
R 30

Koning Albert I laan
Oude Gentweg

BEGIJNHOF
Katelijnestr.
GENTPOORT 5
Generaal Lemanlaan
N 337

Buiten Gentpoortvest
Wagnerstr.
Daverlostraat

KATELIJNEPOORT 4
N 50
E. de Denestr.
Rubenslaan

Vrijheidsstr.
Weide Straat

C
D

Azalea without rest, Wulfhagestraat 43 ℰ 0 50 33 14 78, info@azaleahotel.be, Fax 0 50 33 97 00, « Canalside terrace », ⬿ – ☝ ⇆ TV ⟸ P. AE ⓪ ⓶⬤ VISA JCB   CY y
24 rm ⟷ 99/120.

Aragon M without rest, Naaldenstraat 22 ℰ 0 50 33 35 33, info@aragon.be, Fax 0 50 34 28 05 – ☝ ▤ TV P. – ⚒ 25. AE ⓪ ⓶⬤ VISA   AT v
42 rm ⟷ 105/155.

Portinari without rest, 't Zand 15 ℰ 0 50 34 10 34, info@portinari.be, Fax 0 50 34 41 80 – ☝ ⇆ ▤ TV ⟸ – ⚒ 25-80. AE ⓪ ⓶⬤ VISA JCB   CY k
closed January – **40 rm** ⟷ 120/135.

Parkhotel without rest, Vrijdagmarkt 5 ℰ 0 50 33 33 64, info@parkhotel-brugge.be, Fax 0 50 33 47 63 – ☝ ▤ TV ⟸ – ⚒ 25-250. AE ⓪ ⓶⬤ VISA   CY j
86 rm ⟷ 112/142.

Karos without rest, Hoefijzerlaan 37 ℰ 0 50 34 14 48, hotel.karos@compagnet.be, Fax 0 50 34 00 91, ⇆, ⬿ – ☒, ☝ ▤ TV P. AE ⓪ ⓶⬤ VISA   BY f
closed January – **60 rm** ⟷ 75/112.

Ter Duinen ⬙ without rest, Langerei 52 ℰ 0 50 33 04 37, info@terduinenhotel.be, Fax 0 50 34 42 16, ⇐ – ☝ ▤ TV ⟸. AE ⓪ ⓶⬤ VISA. ⬥   CX x
20 rm ⟷ 93/130.

Gd H. Oude Burg, Oude Burg 5 ℰ 0 50 44 51 11, grandhotel.oudebrug@skynet.be, Fax 0 50 44 51 00, ⇆, ⬿ – ☝ ⇆, ▤ rest, TV ⟸ – ⚒ 25-160. AE ⓪ ⓶⬤ VISA.
⬥ rest   AU i
Meals (Open until 11 p.m.) Lunch 12 – 24/26 – **138 rm** ⟷ 136/161.

Flanders without rest, Langestraat 38 ℰ 0 50 33 88 89, info@flandershotel.be, Fax 0 50 33 93 45, ☒, ⬿ – ☝ ⇆ TV P. AE ⓪ ⓶⬤ VISA. ⬥   DY a
closed 7 January-7 February – **25 rm** ⟷ 110/155.

Adornes without rest, St-Annarei 26 ℰ 0 50 34 13 36, hotel.adornes@proximedia.be, Fax 0 50 34 20 85, ⇐, « Period vaulted cellars », ⬿ – ☝ TV ⟸ P. AE ⓶⬤
VISA JCB   AT u
closed January-12 February – **20 rm** ⟷ 75/100.

Academie ⬙ without rest, Wijngaardstraat 7 ℰ 0 50 33 22 66, hotel.academie@on line.be, Fax 0 50 33 21 66, « Patio » – ☝ ⇆ ▤ TV ⟸. AE ⓪ ⓶⬤ VISA JCB. ⬥
74 rm ⟷ 106/160.   AV b

Hans Memling without rest, Kuipersstraat 18 ℰ 0 50 47 12 12, hotel.memling@gro uptorus.com, Fax 0 50 47 12 10 – ☝ TV. AE ⓪ ⓶⬤ VISA. ⬥   AT b
36 rm ⟷ 161/174.

Dante without rest, Coupure 29a ℰ 0 50 34 01 94, info@hoteldante.be, Fax 0 50 34 35 39, ⇐ – ☝ ⇆ TV. AE ⓪ ⓶⬤ VISA JCB. ⬥   DY m
22 rm ⟷ 105/130.

Biskajer ⬙ without rest, Biskajersplein 4 ℰ 0 50 34 15 06, info@hotelbiskajer.com, Fax 0 50 34 39 11 – ☝ TV. AE ⓪ ⓶⬤ VISA   AT w
17 rm ⟷ 75/104.

Ter Brughe without rest, Oost-Gistelhof 2 ℰ 0 50 34 03 24, info@hotelterbrughe.com Fax 0 50 33 88 73, « Ancient vaulted cellars » – ⇆ TV ⟸ – ⚒ 25. AE ⓪
⓶⬤ VISA   AT a
46 rm ⟷ 75/171.

Bryghia without rest, Oosterlingenplein 4 ℰ 0 50 33 80 59, info@bryghiahotel.be Fax 0 50 34 14 30 – ☝ TV. AE ⓪ ⓶⬤ VISA JCB. ⬥   AT
closed 14 December-13 February – **18 rm** ⟷ 67/135.

Egmond ⬙ without rest, Minnewater 15 (by Katelijnestraat) ℰ 0 50 34 14 45, info @egmond.be, Fax 0 50 34 29 40, ⇐, « Early 20C residence in garden » – TV P. ⬥
closed January – **8 rm** ⟷ 112/120.   AV g

Anselmus without rest, Ridderstraat 15 ℰ 0 50 34 13 74, info@anselmus.be, Fax 0 50 34 19 16, ⬿ – TV. AE ⓪ ⓶⬤ VISA. ⬥   AT h
closed January – **10 rm** ⟷ 80/95.

't Putje (annex - 13 rm), 't Zand 31 ℰ 0 50 33 28 47, hotelputje@pandora.be, Fax 0 50 34 14 23, ⇆ – ☝ TV ⟸ VISA   CZ c
Meals (Pub rest) Lunch 9 – a la carte 22/39 – **24 rm** ⟷ 74/99.

ter Reien without rest, Langestraat 1 ℰ 0 50 34 91 00, hotel.ter.reien@online.be Fax 0 50 34 40 48, ⬿ – ☝ ⇆ TV. AE ⓪ ⓶⬤ VISA   DY
26 rm ⟷ 75/90.

Bourgoensch Hof, Wollestraat 39 ℰ 0 50 33 16 45, info@bourgoensch-hof.be Fax 0 50 34 63 78, ⇐ canals and old Flemish houses, ⇆, ⬿ – ☝ TV ⟸ P. ⬤
VISA. ⬥   AU
15 March-15 November, weekends and Bank Holidays ; closed 10 January-15 February
Meals (closed Thursday) Lunch 31 – a la carte approx. 35 – **23 rm** ⟷ 81/138.

Gd H. du Sablon, Noordzandstraat 21 ✆ 0 50 33 39 02, *info@sablon.be, Fax 0 50 33 39 08,* « Early 20C hall with Art Deco cupola » – |‡| ⇜ TV – 25-100. AE MC VISA. rest AU h
Meals (residents only) – **36 rm** ☕ 89/107.

Boterhuis without rest, St-Jakobsstraat 38 ✆ 0 50 34 15 11, *boterhuis@pandora.be, Fax 0 50 34 70 89* – TV. AE ⓓ MC VISA JCB AT m
closed late November-early December – **6 rm** ☕ 74/90.

Malleberg without rest, Hoogstraat 7 ✆ 0 50 34 41 11, *Fax 0 50 34 67 69* – TV. AE ⓓ MC VISA JCB ATU b
8 rm ☕ 87.

XXXX ✿✿✿ **De Karmeliet** (Van Hecke), Langestraat 19 ✆ 0 50 33 82 59, *Fax 0 50 33 10 11*, « Ancient patrician residence with modern art and walled inner terrace » – P. AE ⓓ MC VISA JCB. DY q
closed 18 August-5 September, 1 to 30 January, Tuesday lunch and Sunday dinner October-June, Sunday lunch and Monday – **Meals** *Lunch 50* 90/115, a la carte 98/167 ♀
Spec. Tuile sucrée et salée aux grosses langoustines rôties. Suprême de pigeon et saucisses de pieds de porc au risotto de champignons des bois. Ravioli à la vanille et pommes caramélisées en chaud-froid.

XXX **De Snippe** with rm, Nieuwe Gentweg 53 ✆ 0 50 33 70 70, *desnippe@pandora.be, Fax 0 50 33 76 62*, « 18C residence with murals, shaded terrace with fountain », – |‡|, ▤ rm, TV P. AE ⓓ MC VISA AV r
Meals *(closed 3 to 22 March, late November, Sunday and Monday lunch) Lunch 38* – 71 – **8 rm** *(closed 3 to 22 March, late November and Sunday in winter)* ☕ 135/150.

XXX **Den Braamberg,** Pandreitje 11 ✆ 0 50 33 73 70, *Fax 0 50 33 99 73* – AE ⓓ MC VISA AU q
closed 15 to 31 July, 1 to 15 January, Thursday and Sunday – **Meals** *Lunch 31* – 45/69.

XXX ✿ **Den Gouden Harynck** (Serruys), Groeninge 25 ✆ 0 50 33 76 37, *goud.harynck@pandora.be, Fax 0 50 34 42 70* – P. AE ⓓ MC VISA AUV w
closed 1 week Easter, last 2 weeks July-first week August, 1 week Christmas, Saturday lunch, Sunday and Monday – **Meals** *Lunch 43* – 87 b.i. a la carte approx. 70
Spec. Thon mariné au crabe. Coucou de Malines farci aux aromates. Sandre flambé au thym.

XXX **'t Pandreitje,** Pandreitje 6 ✆ 0 50 33 11 90, *info@pandreitje.be, Fax 0 50 34 00 70* – AE ⓓ MC VISA JCB AU x
closed 23 to 30 March, 7 to 21 July, 27 October-4 November, Wednesday and Sunday – **Meals** *Lunch 45* – 52/112 b.i. ♀.

XXX **Duc de Bourgogne** with rm, Huidenvettersplein 12 ✆ 0 50 33 20 38, *duc@ssi.be, Fax 0 50 34 40 37*, ≤ canals and typical houses, « Rustic décor and murals of late medieval style », – ▤ rest, TV. AE ⓓ MC VISA JCB AU t
closed 10 to 31 July and 3 to 31 January – **Meals** *(closed Monday and Tuesday lunch) Lunch 33* – 42/56 – **10 rm** ☕ 104/141.

XXX **De Witte Poorte,** Jan Van Eyckplein 6 ✆ 0 50 33 08 83, *Fax 0 50 34 55 60*, « Vaulted dining room, walled inner garden » – AE ⓓ MC VISA JCB AT x
closed carnival week, 2 weeks July, 2 weeks January, Saturday lunch, Sunday and Monday – **Meals** *Lunch 29* – a la carte 46/57.

XX **De Lotteburg,** Goezeputstraat 43 ✆ 0 50 33 75 35, *lotteburg@pi.be, Fax 0 50 33 04 04*, Seafood, « Shaded terrace » – ▤. AE ⓓ MC VISA JCB. AV d
closed 4 to 13 September, first 3 weeks January, Monday and Tuesday – **Meals** *Lunch 30* – 50 b.i./53.

XX **Patrick Devos "Zilveren Pauw",** Zilverstraat 41 ✆ 0 50 33 55 66, *info@patrickdevos.be, Fax 0 50 33 58 67*, « Belle Epoque interior, patio » – P. AE ⓓ MC VISA JCB. AU y
closed Saturday lunch and Sunday – **Meals** *Lunch 28* – 43/66.

XX **'t Bourgoensche Cruyce** with rm, Wollestraat 41 ✆ 0 50 33 79 26, *bour.cruyce@ssi.be, Fax 0 50 34 19 68*, ≤ canals and old Flemish houses – |‡|, ▤ rest, TV. AE ⓓ MC VISA AU f
Meals *(closed 25 June-4 July, 18 November-13 December, Tuesday and Wednesday)* 48/60 ♀ – **7 rm** *(closed 18 November-13 December)* ☕ 117/127.

XX **'t Stil Ende,** Scheepsdalelaan 12 ✆ 0 50 33 92 03, *Fax 0 50 33 26 22*, « Modern interior » – ▤. MC VISA BX a
closed last 2 weeks July, Saturday lunch, Sunday dinner and Monday – **Meals** 27/53.

XX **Hermitage,** Ezelstraat 18 ✆ 0 50 34 41 73, *restaurant.hermitage@planetinternet.be, Fax 0 50 34 14 75*, « Opulent interior » – AE ⓓ MC VISA JCB. CY z
closed 1 week January, Sunday dinner and Monday – **Meals** *Lunch 23* – a la carte approx. 56.

XX **Kardinaalshof**, St-Salvatorskerkhof 14 𝒫 0 50 34 16 91, Fax 0 50 34 20 62 – AE ⊙
🐵 VISA   AUV g
closed first 2 weeks July, Wednesday and Thursday lunch – **Meals** Lunch 35 – 46/53.

XX **Den Dijver**, Dijver 5 𝒫 0 50 33 60 69, Fax 0 50 34 10 64, 🏠, Beer cuisine – AE 🐵
VISA   AU c
closed Wednesday and Thursday lunch – **Meals** Lunch 22 – 42/50.

XX **Loreto** with rm, Katelijnestraat 40 𝒫 0 50 33 43 32, rocolies.bvba@skynet.be,
Fax 0 50 33 95 90 – |🛄| TV. ⊙ 🐵 VISA. 🛇 rm   AV c
closed 1 week March and 2 weeks September – **Meals** (closed Wednesday and lunch Thursday and Saturday) (Partly Italian cuisine) Lunch 25 – 39/50 – **7 rm** 🖙 125/140.

XX **Tanuki**, Oude Gentweg 1 𝒫 0 50 34 75 12, info@tanuki.be, Fax 0 50 33 82 42, Japanese
cuisine with Teppan-Yaki and Sushi-bar, « Japanese atmosphere created in an authentic
setting » – ▤. AE 🐵 VISA JCB   AV f
closed carnival week, 2 weeks July, All Saints' week, Monday and Tuesday – **Meals** Lunch
18 – 45/60.

XX **Ambrosius**, Arsenaalstraat 55 𝒫 0 50 34 41 57, Fax 0 50 34 41 57, 🏠, « Rustic » –
AE 🐵 VISA. 🛇   AV a
closed last 2 weeks March, Tuesday and Wednesday – **Meals** (dinner only until 1 a.m.) a
la carte 44/66.

XX **Spinola**, Spinolarei 1 𝒫 0 50 34 17 85, spinola@pandora.be, Fax 0 50 34 13 71,
« Rustic » – AE ⊙ 🐵 VISA   AT c
*closed last week January-first week February, last week June-first week July, Sunday and
Monday lunch* – **Meals** 40/50.

XX **Aneth**, Maria van Bourgondiëlaan 1 (behind the Graaf Visart park) 𝒫 0 50 31 11 89,
info@aneth.be, Fax 0 50 32 36 46, Seafood – AE ⊙ 🐵 VISA JCB. 🛇   BY g
closed first 2 weeks January, Saturday lunch, Sunday and Monday – **Meals** Lunch 37 – 60/74.

X **Bhavani**, Simon Stevinplein 5 𝒫 0 50 33 90 25, info@bhavani.be, Fax 0 50 34 89 52,
🏠, Indian cuisine – AE ⊙ VISA   AU z
Meals Lunch 14 – a la carte approx. 31.

X **René Van Puyenbroeck**, St-Jakobsstraat 58 𝒫 0 50 34 12 24, Fax 0 50 31 68 66 –
AE 🐵 VISA. 🛇   AT e
closed last 3 weeks July, Sunday dinner and Monday – **Meals** Lunch 32 – a la carte 36/46.

X **Koto** - Hotel de' Medici, Potterierei 15 𝒫 0 50 44 31 31, koto@hoteldemedici.com,
Fax 0 50 33 05 71, Japanese cuisine with Teppan-Yaki – AE ⊙ 🐵 VISA JCB   CX g
closed Monday – **Meals** Lunch 16 – 43/70.

X **Cafedraal**, Zilverstraat 38 𝒫 0 50 34 08 45, Fax 0 50 33 52 41, 🏠, Open until 11 p.m.,
« Historical residence with courtyard terrace » – AE ⊙ 🐵 VISA JCB   AU s
closed Sunday and Monday – **Meals** Lunch 10 – a la carte approx. 43.

X **Brasserie Raymond**, Eiermarkt 5 𝒫 0 50 33 78 48, raymond_vermast@ycom.be,
Fax 0 50 33 78 48, 🏠 – AE ⊙ 🐵 VISA JCB   AT g
closed Monday dinner and Tuesday – **Meals** Lunch 13 – a la carte approx. 38.

X **Huyze Die Maene**, Markt 17 𝒫 0 50 33 39 59, huyzediemaene@pandora.be, Fax 0 50
33 44 60, 🏠, Pub rest – ▤. AE ⊙ 🐵 VISA   AU w
Meals Lunch 12 – 15/24.

Suburbs

Northwest : 5 km – ✉ 8000 :

XXX **De gouden Korenhalm**, Oude Oostendsesteenweg 79a (Sint-Pieters) 𝒫 0 50
31 33 93, info@degoudenkorenhalm.be, Fax 0 50 31 18 96, 🏠, « Typical Flemish
farmhouse » – 🅿. AE ⊙ 🐵 VISA
*closed 28 January-8 February, 8 to 15 April, 26 August-6 September, Monday and Wed-
nesday dinner* – **Meals** Lunch 31 – a la carte 49/69.

at Sint-Andries Southwest : 4 km © Bruges – ✉ 8200 Sint-Andries :

🏠🏠 **Host. Pannenhuis** 🏖, Zandstraat 2 𝒫 0 50 31 19 07, hostellerie@pannenhuis.be,
Fax 0 50 31 77 66, ≤, 🏠, « Terrace and garden », 🚲 – TV & 🅿 – 🔏 25. AE ⊙ 🐵
VISA JCB
Meals (closed 15 January-2 February, 2 to 18 July, Tuesday dinner and Wednesday) Lunch
33 – 48 ♀ – **18 rm** (closed 15 January-2 February) 🖙 98/123.

XX **Herborist** (Hanbuckers) 🏖 with rm, De Watermolen 15 (by ⑥) : 6 km, then on the right
⚘ after E 40 - A 10) 𝒫 0 50 38 76 00, a.hanbuckers@aubergedeherborist.be, Fax 0 50
39 31 06, 🏠, « Inn with country atmosphere », 🌿, 🚲 – ▤ rest, TV 🅿. AE 🐵 VISA. 🛇
*closed 18 to 28 March, 17 to 27 June, 16 to 26 September, 19 December-3 January, Monday
and dinner Thursday and Sunday* – **Meals** (only one menu) Lunch 16 – 98 b.i. – **4 rm** 🖙 120
Spec. Foie gras poêlé aux pommes de terre écrasées, vinaigrette de soja. Magret de canard
à l'infusion de thym. Pain d'épice et glace vanille à l'ananas confit.

at Sint-Kruis *East : 6 km* 🄲 *Bruges –* ✉ *8310 Sint-Kruis :*

🏨 **Wilgenhof** 🦢 without rest, Polderstraat 151 *ℰ* 0 50 36 27 44, *Fax* 0 50 36 28 21, ≤, « An area of reclaimed land (polder) », 🍴, 🚲 – 📺 🅿. 🖭 ⑪ ⓦ *VISA* 🄹🄲🄱. ✖
closed January – **6 rm** ⇆ 74/144.

XXX **Ronnie Jonkman**, Maalsesteenweg 438 *ℰ* 0 50 36 07 67, *Fax* 0 50 35 76 96, 🍴, « Terraces » – 🅿. 🖭 ⑪ ⓦ 🄹🄲🄱
closed 2 weeks Easter, 1 to 15 July, 2 weeks October, Sunday and Monday – **Meals** *Lunch 56 –* a la carte 54/64.

at Sint-Michiels *South : 4 km* 🄲 *Bruges –* ✉ *8200 Sint-Michiels :*

XXX **Weinebrugge**, Koning Albertlaan 242 *ℰ* 0 50 38 44 40, *Fax* 0 50 39 35 63, 🍴, « Flemish style villa » – 🅿. 🖭 ⑪ ⓦ *VISA* ✖
closed carnival week, Monday dinner and Tuesday – **Meals** a la carte 45/58.

XX **Casserole** (Hotel school), Groene-Poortdreef 17 *ℰ* 0 50 40 30 30, *casserole@ivvgroe
ncpoorte.be, Fax* 0 50 40 30 35, 🍴, « Garden » – 🅿. – 🔥 25-50. 🖭 ⑪ ⓦ *VISA*
closed school holidays, Saturday and Sunday – **Meals** (lunch only with one menu) 25.

Environs

at Hertsberge *South by N 50 : 12,5 km* 🄲 *Oostkamp pop. 21 218 –* ✉ *8020 Hertsberge :*

XXX **Manderley**, Kruisstraat 13 *ℰ* 0 50 27 80 51, *Fax* 0 50 27 80 51, 🍴, « Terrace and garden » – 🅿. 🖭 ⑪ ⓦ *VISA*
closed late September-early October, January, Tuesday October-April, Sunday dinner and Monday – **Meals** *Lunch 33 –* 46/57.

at Varsenare *West : 6,5 km* 🄲 *Jabbeke pop. 13 609 –* ✉ *8490 Varsenare :*

XXX **Manoir Stuivenberg** (Scherrens brothers) with rm, Gistelsteenweg 27 *ℰ* 0 50
🕸 38 15 02, *info@manoirstuivenberg.be, Fax* 0 50 38 28 92, 🍴, 🚲 – 📶, 🍽 rest, 📺 🚗
🅿. – 🔥 25-300. 🖭 ⑪ ⓦ *VISA*. ✖
closed 15 to 31 July and 1 to 22 January – **Meals** (closed Monday and dinner Tuesday and Sunday) *Lunch 42 –* 62/77, a la carte 67/85 – **8 rm** (closed Sunday dinner and Monday) ⇆ 124/162, 1 suite
Spec. Pavé de cabillaud aux condiments, crevettes grises fraîches et petit jus aux herbes. Poitrine de pigeon en crapaudine. Gibier (en saison).

at Waardamme *South by N 50 : 11 km* 🄲 *Oostkamp pop. 21 218 –* ✉ *8020 Waardamme :*

XX **Ter Talinge**, Rooiveldstraat 46 *ℰ* 0 50 27 90 61, *Fax* 0 50 28 00 52, 🍴, « Terrace » – 🅿. 🖭 ⓦ *VISA*
closed 22 February-12 March, 23 August-6 September, Wednesday and Thursday – **Meals** *Lunch 20* 43.

at Zedelgem *Southwest : 10,5 km. pop. 22 020 –* ✉ *8210 Zedelgem :*

🏨 **Zuidwege**, Torhoutsesteenweg 128 *ℰ* 0 50 20 13 39, *angelo@zuidwege.be, Fax* 0 50
20 17 39, 🍴, 🚲 – ✖, 🍽 rm, 📺 🅿. – 🔥 25. 🖭 ⑪ ⓦ *VISA*. ✖ rm
Meals (closed first week June, Christmas holiday and Saturday)(Pub rest) *Lunch 8 –* a la carte approx. 36 – **20 rm** (closed Christmas holidays) ⇆ 54/67.

XX **Ter Leepe**, Torhoutsesteenweg 168 *ℰ* 0 50 20 01 97, *Fax* 0 50 20 88 54 – 🍽 🅿. – 🔥 220. 🖭 ⑪ ⓦ *VISA*
closed 22 July-4 August, 14 to 24 January, Wednesday dinner and Sunday – **Meals** *Lunch 35 b.i. –* 57 b.i..

Kruishoutem *9770 Oost-Vlaanderen* 🄫🄫🄫 *G 17 and* 🄎🄎🄎 *D 3. pop. 7 849 – 44 km.*

XXX **Hof van Cleve** (Goossens), Riemegemstraat 1 (near N 459, motorway E 17 - A 14, exit
🕸🕸 ⑥) *ℰ* 0 9 383 58 48, *hofvancleve@skynet.be, Fax* 0 9 383 77 25, ≤, 🍴, « Farmhouse in open fields » – 🅿. 🖭 ⑪ ⓦ *VISA*. ✖
closed 1 week Easter, 2 weeks August, All Saints' week, late December-early January, Sunday and Monday – **Meals** *Lunch 79 b.i. –* 84/119, a la carte 75/98 ⓨ
Spec. Ravioli ouvert de girolles et joue de bœuf braisée, sabayon à l'estragon. Pigeonneau au lard croustillant, parmentière aux truffes et Banyuls. Moelleux au chocolat, coulis de griottes et glace au thé vert.

Waregem *8790 West-Vlaanderen* 🄫🄫🄫 *F 17 and* 🄎🄎🄎 *D 3. pop. 35 839 – 47 km.*

XXXX **'t Oud Konijntje** (Mmes Desmedt), Bosstraat 53 (South : 2 km near E 17 - A 14) *ℰ* 0 56
🕸🕸 60 19 37, *info@oudkonijntje.be, Fax* 0 56 60 92 12, 🍴, « Terrace with fountain and floral garden » – 🅿. 🖭 ⑪ ⓦ
*closed 12 to 12 April, 18 July-9 August, 22 December-4 January, Friday and dinner Thurs-
day and Sunday –* **Meals** *Lunch 56 –* 62/87, a la carte approx. 95 ⓨ
Spec. Homard aux primeurs, vinaigrette à la purée de truffe. St-Jacques enrobées de lard sur une mousse de céleri aux truffes. Escalope de pigeonneau, foie d'oie chaud et mille-feuille au chou.

Zeebrugge West-Vlaanderen ⓒ Brugge pop. 116 246 **213** E 14 and **909** C 1 – ⊠ 8380 Zee-brugge (Brugge) – 15 km.

XX   **'t Molentje** (Horseele), Baron de Maerelaan 211 (South : 2 km on N 31) ℰ 0 50 54 61 64,
🕸🕸   molentje@pi.be, Fax 0 50 54 79 94, 🛱 , « Farmhouse with personalized decor » – 🅿. 🆎
🔘 🕼 VISA. 🛠
closed 4 to 13 March, 16 to 23 June, 9 September-3 October, 1 to 5 January and Wed-nesday and Sunday except Bank Holidays – **Meals** (booking essential) Lunch 46 b.i. – a la carte 66/95 🍷
Spec. St-Jacques aux épices orientales et étuvée de poireaux. Bar à la fleur de poivre, caviar d'aubergines et vinaigre balsamique. Mousse chaude au chocolat amer à l'huile d'olives.

Sluis Zeeland (Netherlands) ⓒ Sluis-Aardenburg pop. 6 509 **211** F 15 and **908** B 8 – 21 km.

XXX   **Oud Sluis** (Herman), Beestenmarkt 2, ⊠ 4524 EA, ℰ (0 117) 46 12 69, oudsluis@alli
🕸🕸   ance.nl, Fax (0 117) 46 30 05, 🛱 , Seafood, « Typical farmhouse » – 🆎 🔘 🕼 VISA. 🛠
closed 2 weeks June, 2 weeks October, last week December, Monday and Tuesday – **Meals**
Lunch 43 – 57/79, a la carte 75/87 🍷
Spec. Tartare de langoustines aux asperges et gelée de limon (April-June). Bar aux girolles et risotto de homard au jus de bouillabaisse. St-Jacques à la coque aux cèpes et foie gras (September-March).

LIÈGE 4000 **213** S 19, **214** S 19 – ㉕ S and **909** J 4 - ⑰ N. pop. 185 639.

See : Citadel ≤≤★★ DW – Cointe Park ≤★ CX – Old town★★ – Palace of the Prince-Bishops★ : court of honour★★ EY – The Perron★ (market cross) EY A – Baptismal font★★★ of St. Bartholomew's church FY – Treasury★ of St. Paul's Cathedral : reliquary of Charles the Bold★★ EZ – St. James church★★ : vaults of the nave★★ EZ – Altarpiece★ in the St. Denis church EY – Church of St. John : Wooden Calvary statues★ EY – Aquarium★ FZ D.
Museums : Life in Wallonia★★ EY – Religious and Roman Art Museum★ FY M⁵ – Curtius and Glass Museum★ : evangelistary of Notger★★★, collection of glassware★ FY M¹ – Arms★ FY M³ – Ansembourg★ FY M² – Modern Art and Contemporary Art★ DX M⁷.
Envir : Northeast : 20 km : Blégny-Trembleur★★ – Southwest : 27 km : Baptismal font★ in the church★ of St. Severin – North : 17 km at Visé, Reliquary of St. Hadelin★ in the collegiate church.
🏌 r. Bernalmont 2 ℰ 0 4 227 44 66, Fax 0 4 227 91 92 - 🏌 South : 8 km at Angleur, rte du Condroz 541 ℰ 0 4 336 20 21, Fax 0 4 337 20 26 - 🏌 Southeast : 18 km at Gomzé-Andoumont, Sur Counachamps, r. Gomzé 30 ℰ 0 4 360 92 07, Fax 0 4 360 92 06.
🚗 ℰ 0 4 342 52 14, Fax 0 4 229 27 33.
🚉 En Féronstrée 92 ℰ 0 4 221 92 21, office.tourisme@liège.be, Fax 0 4 221 92 22 and Gare des Guillemins ℰ (0 4) 252 44 19 – Tourist association of the province, bd de la Sauvenière 77 ℰ 0 4 232 65 10, ftpl@ftpl.be, Fax 0 4 232 65 11.
Brussels 97 – Amsterdam 242 – Antwerp 119 – Cologne 122 – Luxembourg 159 – Maastricht 32.

Plans on following pages

🏨   **Bedford** Ⓜ, quai St-Léonard 36 ℰ 0 4 228 81 11, hotelbedfordlg@pophost.eunet.be,
Fax 0 4 227 45 75, 🛱 , « Inner garden », 🗴 – 📳 🖐 ☰ 🔟 🕭 🚗 🅿. – 🔬 25-220. 🆎
🔘 🕼 VISA   DW g
Meals Lunch 22 – a la carte 22/36 – **147 rm** ⊡ 209/222, 2 suites.

XX   **Le bateau ivre**, bd Frère Orban (Meuse-side setting) ℰ 0 4 252 13 21, mercurelieg
e@alliance-hospitality.com, Fax 0 4 252 57 50, ≤, 🛱 , Oyster bar – 🅿. 🆎 🕼 VISA
closed 2 weeks February, 2 weeks November, Saturday lunch and Sunday – **Meals** a la carte
40/51.   CX e

Old town

🏨   **Mercure**, bd de la Sauvenière 100 ℰ 0 4 221 77 11, mercureliege@alliance-hospitali
y.com, Fax 0 4 221 77 01 – 📳 🖐 ☰ 🔟 🚗 – 🔬 25-100. 🆎 🔘 🕼 VISA. 🛠 rest
Meals (closed Saturday lunch and Sunday dinner) Lunch 12 – a la carte approx. 22 – **105 rm**
⊡ 174/188.   EY

XXX   **Au Vieux Liège,** quai Goffe 41 ℰ 0 4 223 77 48, Fax 0 4 223 78 60, « 16C residence »
🕸🕸🕸   – ☰. 🆎 🔘 🕼 VISA   FY a
closed mid July-mid August, Wednesday dinner, Sunday and Bank Holidays – **Meal**
25/36.

XXX   **Max,** pl. Verte 2 ℰ 0 4 222 08 59, Fax 0 4 222 90 02, 🛱 , Seafood and oyster bar, open unt
🕸🕸🕸   11 p.m., « Elegant brasserie decorated by Luc Genot » – 🅿. 🔬 25. 🆎 🔘 🕼 VISA. 🛠 EY
closed last 2 weeks July, Saturday lunch and Sunday – **Meals** Lunch 31 – a la carte 31/69

XX   **Robert Lesenne**, r. Boucherie 9 ℰ 0 4 222 07 93, Fax 0 4 222 92 33, « Ancient alms
🕸🕸   house watchtower in an atrium » – ☰. 🆎 🔘 🕼 VISA   FY r
closed 1 week carnaval, first 3 weeks August, Saturday lunch and Sunday – **Meals** Lunc
40 b.i. – a la carte 43/51.

XX **Le Shanghai** 1st floor, Galeries Cathédrale 104 ☎ 0 4 222 22 63, Fax 0 4 223 00 50, Chinese cuisine – 🍽️. 🆎 ⓪ ⓶⓪ 𝗩𝗜𝗦𝗔
EZ r
closed 2 weeks February, 3 weeks July and Tuesday – **Meals** *Lunch* 14 – 22/43 ⓨ.

XX **Septime,** r. St-Paul 12 ☎ 0 4 221 03 06, Grill room, open until 11 p.m. – 🅿️. 🆎 ⓶⓪ 𝗩𝗜𝗦𝗔
Meals a la carte approx. 32.
EZ c

XX **Folies Gourmandes,** r. Clarisses 48 ☎ 0 4 223 16 44, 🌤️, « Early 20C house with garden-terrace » – 🆎 ⓪ ⓶⓪ 𝗩𝗜𝗦𝗔
EZ q
closed 1 week Easter, last 2 weeks August, Sunday dinner and Monday – **Meals** – 31 ⓨ.

X **Enoteca,** r. Casquette 5 ☎ 0 4 222 24 64, Fax 0 4 222 24 64 – 🍽️.
🏵️ EY g
closed Saturday lunch, Sunday and Bank Holidays – **Meals** *Lunch* 19 – 32.

X **Lalo's Bar,** r. Madeleine 18 ☎ 0 4 223 22 57, Fax 0 4 223 22 57, Italian cuisine – 🍽️. 🆎 ⓪ ⓶⓪ 𝗩𝗜𝗦𝗔
EY d
closed Saturday lunch and Sunday – **Meals** *Lunch* 18 – 22/33.

X **As Ouhès,** pl. du Marché 19 ☎ 0 4 223 32 25, 🌤️, Brasserie – 🆎 ⓶⓪ 𝗩𝗜𝗦𝗔 EY e
Meals a la carte approx. 31.

Guillemins

🏨 **L'Univers** without rest, r. Guillemins 116 ☎ 0 4 254 55 55, *comfort.inn.liege@skynet.be*, Fax 0 4 254 55 00 – 📶 ✂️ 📺 🅿️ – 🔏 25-80. 🆎 ⓪ ⓶⓪ 𝗩𝗜𝗦𝗔
CX a
47 rm ⇌ 62/75.

X **Le Duc d'Anjou,** r. Guillemins 127 ☎ 0 4 252 28 58, Mussels in season, open until 11.30 p.m. – 🍽️. 🆎 ⓪ ⓶⓪ 𝗩𝗜𝗦𝗔 – **Meals** 21/31.
CX n

Right banc (Outremeuse - Palais des Congrès)

🏨 **Holiday Inn** without rest, Esplanade de l'Europe 2, ✉️ 4020, ☎ 0 4 342 20 00, *hiliege@alliance-hospitality.com*, Fax 0 4 343 48 10, <, 🌤️, 𝐿𝑎, 🏋️, ⌧ – 📶 ✂️ 🍽️ 📺 👍 🚗
🅿️ – 🔏 25-70. 🆎 ⓪ ⓶⓪ 𝗩𝗜𝗦𝗔
DX a
214 rm ⇌ 180/195, 5 suites.

🏨 **Simenon,** bd de l'Est 16, ✉️ 4020, ☎ 0 4 342 86 90, Fax 0 4 344 26 69 – 📶 📺. 🆎 ⓪ ⓶⓪ 𝗩𝗜𝗦𝗔
FZ x
closed 1 to 20 January – **Meals** *(closed Sunday, Monday and Tuesday)* (Grill rest) a la carte approx. 29 – ⇌ 6 – **11 rm** 62/87.

Suburbs

at Angleur *South : 4 km* Ⓒ *Liège* – ✉️ *4031 Angleur :*

🏨 **Le Val d'Ourthe** without rest, rte de Tilff 412 ☎ 0 4 365 91 71, Fax 0 4 365 62 89 – 🍽️ 📺 🚗 🅿️. ⓪ ⓶⓪ 𝗩𝗜𝗦𝗔
⇌ 9 – **12 rm** 82/94.

XX **L'Orchidée Blanche,** rte du Condroz 457 (N 680) ☎ 0 4 365 11 48, Fax 0 4 367 09 16, 🌤️ – 🅿️. 🆎 ⓪ ⓶⓪ 𝗩𝗜𝗦𝗔 🇯🇨🇧
closed last 3 weeks July, last week January, Tuesday dinner and Wednesday – **Meals** *Lunch* 25 b.i. – 36 b.i./45 b.i.

at Chênée *East : 7,5 km* Ⓒ *Liège* – ✉️ *4032 Chênée :*

XXX **Le Gourmet,** r. Large 91 ☎ 0 4 365 87 97, Fax 0 4 365 38 12, 🌤️, « Winter garden » – 🅿️. 🆎 ⓪ ⓶⓪ 𝗩𝗜𝗦𝗔
closed 2 weeks July, first 2 weeks January, Tuesday and Wednesday – **Meals** 24/45.

XX **Le Vieux Chênée,** r. Gravier 45 ☎ 0 4 367 00 92, Fax 0 4 367 59 15, Mussels in season – 🆎 ⓪ ⓶⓪ 𝗩𝗜𝗦𝗔
closed Thursday – **Meals** *Lunch* 22 – 24/31.

at Rocourt *North : 4 km* Ⓒ *Liège* – ✉️ *4000 Rocourt :*

X **La Petite Table** (Gillard), pl. Reine Astrid 3 ☎ 0 4 239 19 00, Fax 0 4 239 19 77 – ⓶⓪ 𝗩𝗜𝗦𝗔
🏵️ *closed 1 to 11 April, 29 July-14 August, 23 December-8 January, Monday, Tuesday and Saturday lunch* – **Meals** *Lunch* 29 – a la carte approx. 51
Spec. Mille-feuille de saumon en tartare et betterave rouge. Raviolis de St-Jacques au homard. Café liégeois de Valerie.

Environs

at Ans *Northwest : 4 km. pop. 27 528* – ✉️ *4430 Ans :*

XX **Le Marguerite,** r. Walthère Jamar 171 ☎ 0 4 226 43 46, Fax 0 4 226 38 35, 🌤️ – 🆎 ⓪ ⓶⓪ 𝗩𝗜𝗦𝗔
closed 1 week Eastern, last week July-first week August, Saturday lunch, Sunday and Monday dinner – **Meals** *Lunch* 25 – 30/37.

XX **La Fontaine de Jade,** r. Yser 321 ☎ 0 4 246 49 72, Fax 0 4 263 69 53, Chinese cuisine, open until 11 p.m. – 🍽️. 🆎 ⓪ ⓶⓪ 𝗩𝗜𝗦𝗔. ✂️
closed first 3 weeks July and Tuesday – **Meals** *Lunch* 12 – 17/35.

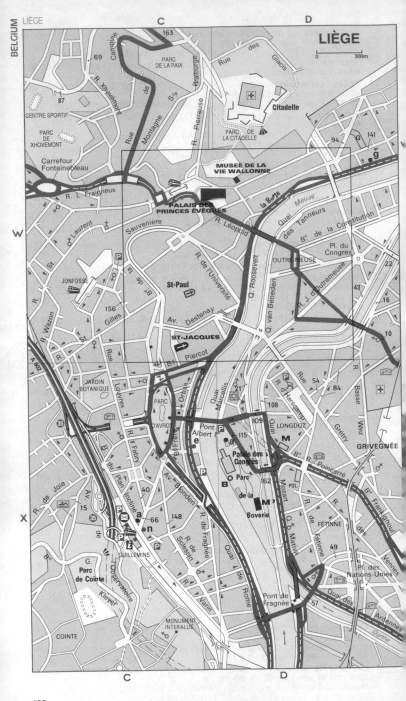

LIÈGE

0   300m

PARC
DE LA PAIX

Citadelle

PARC DE
LA CITADELLE

163

69

87

CENTRE SPORTIF

PARC
DE
XHOVEMONT

94

G

141

g

Carrefour
Fontainebleau

R. L. Fraigneux

MUSÉE DE LA
VIE WALLONNE

PALAIS DES
PRINCES ÉVÊQUES

la Batte

Quai Meuse

Quai des Tanneurs

Bd de la Constitution

W

Sauvenière

R. Léopold

OUTREMEUSE

Pl. du
Congrès

22

Laurent

St.

JONFOSSE

St-Paul

R. de l'Université

Q. Roosevelt

Q. van Beneden

R. J. d'Outremeuse

43

16

156

Gilles

Av. Destenay

ST-JACQUES

10

4m3

R. Wazon

A 602

Rue

Louvrex

Piercot

JARDIN
BOTANIQUE

Orban

R. Fabry

PARC
D'AVROY

Bd Frère

Quai
Marcellis

21

Quai d'Harscamp

Rue

54

84

Basse
Wez

108

Pont
Albert I

e

a

109

115

Quai
LONGDOZ

M

GRIVEGNÉE

Grétry

Palais des
Congrès

B

162

Bd
Poincarré

35

40

Av. Blonden

R. de Fragnée

Parc
de la
Boverie

M

Mozart

POL

R.

de Fétinne

Bd Frankignoul

15

a

66

148

R. de Selessin

Quai de Rome

Mativa

49

FÉTINNE

Pl. des
Nations-Unies

G.
Observatoire

GUILLEMINS

Parc
de Cointe

Kleyer

COINTE

MONUMENT
INTERALLIE

Pont de
Fragnée

57

Quai des

Ardennes

Ourthe

C   D

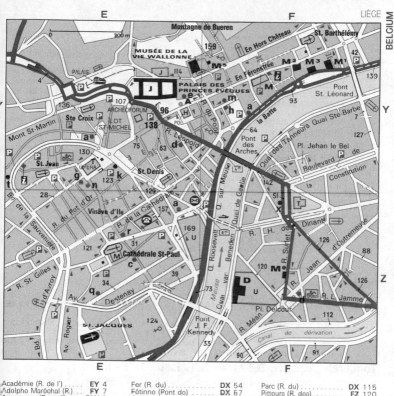

at **Flémalle** Southwest : 16 km. pop. 25 777 – ⌀ 4400 Flémalle :

XXX   **La Ciboulette,** chaussée de Chokier 96 ✆ 0 4 275 19 65, la_ciboulette@teledisnet.be,
      Fax 0 4 275 05 81, ⌂ – ▤. 🆎 ① 🅼🅲 𝗩𝗜𝗦𝗔
      closed 5 to 20 August, 1 to 15 January, Monday, Saturday lunch and dinner Sunday and
      Wednesday – **Meals** Lunch 49 b.i. – 39/67 ♈.

XX   **Le Gourmet Gourmand,** Grand-Route 411 ✆ 0 4 233 07 56, Fax 0 4 233 19 21, ⌂
      – ▤. 🆎 ① 🅼🅲 𝗩𝗜𝗦𝗔
      closed Monday, Saturday lunch and dinner Tuesday, Wednesday and Thursday – **Meals**
      Lunch 27 – 36/43.

XX   **Jacques Koulic,** chaussée de Chockier 82 ✆ 0 4 275 53 15, jacques.koulic@ciberne
      t.be, ⌂ – 🆎 ① 🅼🅲 𝗩𝗜𝗦𝗔. ✼
      closed 1 week March, first 2 weeks September, Tuesday, Wednesday and Thursday – **Meals**
      Lunch 30 – 29/58.

at Liers *North : 8 km* Ⓒ *Herstal pop. 36 292* – ⊠ *4042 Liers :*

   Ⅹ   **La Bartavelle,** r. Provinciale 138 ✆ *0 4 278 51 55, Fax 0 4 278 51 57,* �<, « Shaded
   🦐   terrace » – 🅿. ⒶⒺ ⓞ ⓜⓢ 𝘝𝘐𝘚𝘈 ⒿⒸⒷ
      closed 16 to 30 July and Saturday lunch – **Meals** (lunch only except weekends) 27/35.

at Neuville-en-Condroz *South : 18 km* Ⓒ *Neupré pop. 9 513* – ⊠ *4121 Neuville-en-Condroz :*

  ⅩⅩⅩⅩ **Le Chêne Madame** (Mrs Tilkin), av. de la Chevauchée 70 (Southeast : 2 km in Rognacs
    🕸 wood) ✆ *0 4 371 41 27, Fax 0 4 371 29 43,* 🌳, « Country inn » – 🅿. ⒶⒺ ⓞ ⓜⓢ 𝘝𝘐𝘚𝘈
      closed August, Monday and dinner Thursday and Sunday – **Meals** *Lunch 37* – 73, a la carte
      53/71
      Spec. Homard au Lillet et poivre rose. St-Pierre au beurre blanc à la coriandre. Gibier (Sep-
      tember-December).

at Tilleur *Southwest : 8 km* Ⓒ *St-Nicolas pop. 23 101* – ⊠ *4420 Tilleur :*

   Ⅹ   **Chez Massimo,** quai du Halage 78 ✆ *0 4 233 69 27, Fax 0 4 234 00 31,* 🌳, Italian
   🦐 cuisine – ⓜⓢ 𝘝𝘐𝘚𝘈
      closed Monday and lunch Saturday and Sunday – **Meals** *Lunch 25* – 33.

Namur *5000 Namur* 𝟮𝟭𝟯 *O 20,* 𝟮𝟭𝟰 *O 20 and* 𝟵𝟬𝟵 *H 4. pop. 105 419* – 61 km.

at Lives-sur-Meuse *East : 9 km* Ⓒ *Namur* – ⊠ *5101 Lives-sur-Meuse :*

  ⅩⅩⅩⅩ **La Bergerie** (Lefevere), r. Mosanville 100 ✆ *0 81 58 06 13, marc@bergerielives.be,*
   🕸🕸 *Fax 0 81 58 19 39,* « Elegant residence bordered by ornamental lakes in a luxuriant garden
      setting » – 🍽 🅿. ⒶⒺ ⓞ ⓜⓢ 𝘝𝘐𝘚𝘈
      closed last 2 weeks February, last 2 weeks August, Sunday dinner, Monday and Tuesday
      – **Meals** *Lunch 63 b.i.* – 50/70, a la carte approx. 70
      Spec. Truites de notre vivier. Agneau rôti "Bergerie". Le gâteau de crêpes soufflées.

Pepinster *4860 Liège* 𝟮𝟭𝟯 *T 19,* 𝟮𝟭𝟰 *T 19 and* 𝟵𝟬𝟵 *K 4. pop. 9 292* – 26 km.

  ⅩⅩⅩ **Host. Lafarque** 🛏 with rm, Chemin des Douys 20 (West : 4 km by N 61, locality Gof-
  🕸🕸 fontaine) ✆ *0 87 46 06 51, Fax 0 87 46 97 28,* ≼, 🌳, « Park », 🚗 – 📺 🅿. ⒶⒺ ⓞ ⓜⓢ
      𝘝𝘐𝘚𝘈. 🍽 rm
      closed 20 February-20 March, 2 to 20 September, Monday and Tuesday – **Meals** *(closed
      after 8.30 p.m.) Lunch 62* – 65/75, a la carte 73/89 – 🍽 13 – **6 rm** 87/135
      Spec. Crabe royal au jus de persil et huile de truffes blanches. Ris de veau braisé aux
      pamplemousses. Gibier en saison.

Tongeren *3700 Limburg* 𝟮𝟭𝟯 *R 18 and* 𝟵𝟬𝟵 *J 3. pop. 29 723* – 19 km.

at Vliermaal *North : 5 km* Ⓒ *Kortessem pop. 8 010* – ⊠ *3724 Vliermaal :*

  ⅩⅩⅩⅩⅩ **Clos St. Denis** (Denis), Grimmertingenstraat 24 ✆ *0 12 23 60 96, info@closstdenis.be,*
   🕸🕸 *Fax 0 12 26 32 07,* « 17C farmhouse manor, shaded terrace and garden » – 🅿. ⒶⒺ ⓞ ⓜⓢ
      𝘝𝘐𝘚𝘈. 🍽
      closed 2 to 10 April, 15 to 31 July, 29 October-6 November, 26 December-8 January,
      Tuesday and Wednesday – **Meals** *Lunch 62 b.i.* – 93/159 b.i., a la carte 86/118
      Spec. Homard haché à cru, préparé comme un tartare. Blanc de turbot, bintjes écrasées
      à l'huile d'olive, citron et câpres. Déclinaison tout chocolat.

LUXEMBOURG — LËTZEBUERG

924 V 25 and **909** L 7 – pop. 80 700.

Amsterdam 391 – Bonn 190 – Brussels 219.

Plans of Luxembourg

TOURIST OFFICE

Luxembourg City Tourist Office, pl. d'Armes, ⊠ *2011,* ✆ *22 28 09, touristinfo@luxem bourg_city.lu, Fax 46 70 70.*
Air Terminus, gare centrale ⊠ *1010,* ✆ *42 82 82 20, info@ont.lu, Fax 42 82 82 30.*
Airport at Findel ✆ *42 82 82 21, info@ont.lu, Fax 42 82 82 30.*

GOLF COURSE

⒔ *Hoehenhof (Senningerberg) near Airport, r. de Trèves 1,* ⊠ *2633,* ✆ *34 00 90, Fax 34 03 91.*

PLACES OF INTEREST

VIEWPOINTS

Place de la Constitution★★ F *– St-Esprit*★★ *Plateau* G *– Cliff Path*★★ G *– The Bock*★★ G *– Boulevard Victor Thorn*★ G 121 *– Three Acorns*★ DY.

MUSEUMS

National Museum of History and Art★ *: Gallo Roman section*★ *and Luxembourg Life section (decorative arts, folk art and traditions)*★★ G **M¹** *– Historical Museum of the City of Luxembourg*★ G **M³**.

OTHER THINGS TO SEE

Bock Casemates★★ G *– Grand Ducal Palace*★ G *– Cathedral of Our Lady*★ F *– Grand Duchess Charlotte Bridge*★ DY.

MODERN ARCHITECTURE

Plateau de Kirchberg : European Centre DEY.

LUXEMBOURG

LUXEMBOURG

0   400 m

C   D

R. F. Seimetz

Square Édouard André

LIMPERTSBERG

CIMETIÈRE ISRAÉLITE

Côte d'Eich

N 7

GR 218

Bons Malades

Konrad

Cour de Justice Européenne 22

37

21

60

N 52

Glacis

R. des Glacis

87

R. St Mathieu

Laurent

BANQUE EUROPÉENNE D'INVESTISSEMENT

42

J.

Bâtiment Tour

Av. du bois

Henri VII

Victor

Pasteur

Av. de la R.

Faïencerie

105

T

99

100

Côte d'Eich

Av. de la Foire

Avenue

Centre R. Schuman

PONT GRANDE-DUCHESSE CHARLOTTE

Les Trois Glands

TOUR MALAKOF

CHAMP DES GLACIS

P Foire

N 52

3

88

Allmaïgen

118

117

93

27

CLAUSEN

66

N 12

N 6

Bd

Pce Henri

Royal

Porte Neuve

Alzette

Vauban

de Clausen

N 1

M

Joseph II

Av. E. Reuter

PALAIS Gᴰ-DUCAL

Montée

de

Trèves

Charlotte

Grande-Duchesse

126

Av.

Monterey

Bd

CATHÉDRALE N.-DAME

Rue

Alzette

86

a

c

127

55

N 5

N 54

Av. Marie-Thérèse

p

Pétrusse

97

G

94

N 5A

106

de

Bd

la

Pétrusse

103

75

31

Viaduc

N 2

97

69

50

12

82

d'Esch

Rue

78

POL

h

x

85

40

d

69

120

81

Route E. Lavandier

Bd de la vallée

Rue

e

f

R. d'Anvers

Liberté

49

a

14

14

96

Fraternité

Strasbourg

k

14

Bd

de

Trèves

A.

124

39

45

z

b

V

14

30

HOLLERICH

N 56

63

Rue

Fischer

de

Hollerich

N 3

Pl. de la Gare

Rue

14

Y

Z

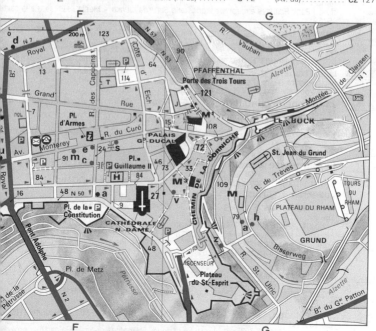

LUXEMBOURG

Luxembourg-Centre

Le Royal, bd Royal 12, ⊠ 2449, 𝒫 241 61 61, sm@hotelroyal.lu, Fax 22 59 48, 🍴, F d
🏋, ≦s, 🔲, 🏊 – 🛗 ⚒ 🔳 📺 🚗 – 🔬 25-350. 🆎 ① 🚧 𝗩𝗜𝗦𝗔
Meals see *La Pomme Cannelle* below – *Le Jardin* Lunch 27 – a la carte approx. 45 ♀ –
190 rm ⊇ 265/395, 20 suites.

Gd H. Cravat, bd Roosevelt 29, ⊠ 2450, 𝒫 22 19 75, contact@hotelcravat.lu, F a
Fax 22 67 11 – 🛗 ⚒ 🔳 📺 – 🔬 25. 🆎 ① 🚧 𝗩𝗜𝗦𝗔. ✻
Meals (Pub-rest) Lunch 12 – 31/59 ♀ – **58 rm** ⊇ 215/230.

Domus M without rest, av. Monterey 37, ⊠ 2163, 𝒫 467 87 81, info@domus.lu, F u
Fax 46 78 79 – 🛗 🔳 📺 🚗. 🚧 𝗩𝗜𝗦𝗔. ✻
⊇ 10 – **39 rm** 112/127, 1 suite.

Rix without rest, bd Royal 20, ⊠ 2449, 𝒫 47 16 66, rixhotel@cmdnet.lu, Fax 22 75 35, F b
🏊 – 🛗 📺 🅿. 🚧 𝗩𝗜𝗦𝗔. ✻
closed 20 December-4 January – **21 rm** ⊇ 141/161.

Parc-Belle-Vue 🕭, av. Marie-Thérèse 5, ⊠ 2132, 𝒫 45 61 41, bellevue@hpb.lu, CZ p
Fax 456 14 12 22, ≤, 🍴, 🏊 – 🛗 📺 🚗 🅿. – 🔬 25-400. 🆎 ① 🚧 𝗩𝗜𝗦𝗔
Meals (Partly buffet and grill rest) Lunch 25 – a la carte 23/40 – **58 rm** ⊇ 108/133.

Clairefontaine (Magnier), pl. de Clairefontaine 9, ⊠ 1341, 𝒫 46 22 11, clairefo@pt.lu, G v
Fax 47 08 21, 🍴 – 🔳. 🆎 ① 🚧 𝗩𝗜𝗦𝗔
closed 12 to 25 August, Saturday lunch, Sunday and Bank Holidays – **Meals** Lunch 46 – 66/83,
a la carte 54/78
Spec. La tranche de foie gras d'oie traditionnelle au Porto. Pavé de sandre rôti, sauce aux
échalotes confites et Syrah. Déclinaison d'agneau de lait, légumes oubliés en plusieurs cuis-
sons (November-May). **Wines** Pinot gris, Riesling.

Le Bouquet Garni Salon Saint Michel (Duhr), r. Eau 32, ⊠ 1449, 𝒫 26 20 06 20, G e
bouquetgarni@internet.lu, Fax 26 20 09 11 – 🆎 ① 🚧 𝗩𝗜𝗦𝗔
closed 15 August-10 September, Saturday lunch and Sunday – **Meals** Lunch 30 – 78, a la
carte 52/64
Spec. Mousseline de rattes aux petits-gris et champignons sauvages. St-Pierre au four dans
un bouillon d'haricots coco, tomate et basilic. Gibier (15 October-December). **Wines** Pinot
Gris, Riesling.

La Pomme Cannelle - Hotel Le Royal, bd Royal 12, ⊠ 2449, 𝒫 241 61 67 36, cate
ring@hotelroyal.lu, Fax 22 59 48, « Indian Empire style interior atmosphere » – 🔳 🅿. 🆎 F d
① 🚧 𝗩𝗜𝗦𝗔
closed Bank Holidays except weekends and Saturday lunch – **Meals** Lunch 39 – a la carte
45/69.

Speltz, r. Chimay 8, ⊠ 1333, 𝒫 47 49 50, speltz@resto.lu, Fax 47 46 77, 🍴 – 🆎 ① F c
🚧 𝗩𝗜𝗦𝗔
closed 30 March-7 April, 1 to 5 May, 9 to 11 May, 27 July-11 August, 1 to 3 November, 24
December-3 January, Saturday lunch, Sunday and Bank Holidays – **Meals** Lunch 38 – 48/63.

La Lorraine, pl. d'Armes 7, ⊠ 1136, 𝒫 47 14 36, lorraine@pt.lu, Fax 47 09 64, 🍴 F e
Partly oyster bar and seafood – 🔳. 🆎 ① 🚧 𝗩𝗜𝗦𝗔
closed Sunday and Bank Holidays – **Meals** a la carte 51/65 ♀.

Jan Schneidewind, r. Curé 20, ⊠ 1368, 𝒫 22 26 18, info@schneidewind.lu F s
Fax 46 24 40, 🍴 – 🆎 ① 🚧 𝗩𝗜𝗦𝗔. ✻
closed Monday and lunch Saturday and Sunday – **Meals** Lunch 32 – 69 ♀.

L'Océan, r. Louvigny 7, ⊠ 1946, 𝒫 22 88 66, Fax 22 88 67, Oyster bar and Seafood F
– 🆎 ① 🚧 𝗩𝗜𝗦𝗔
Meals 41.

la fourchette à droite, av. Monterey 5, ⊠ 2163, 𝒫 22 13 60, o.jolly@gms.lu F n
Fax 22 24 95, 🍴 – 🆎 ① 🚧 𝗩𝗜𝗦𝗔
closed Saturday lunch and Sunday – **Meals** Lunch 15 – a la carte 35/49 ♀.

Luxembourg-Grund

Mosconi, r. Munster 13, ⊠ 2160, 𝒫 54 69 94, Fax 54 00 43, Italian cuisine – 🆎 ① 🚧 G
𝗩𝗜𝗦𝗔
closed 1 week Easter, 11 August-2 September, 22 September, 2 January, Sunday and
Monday – **Meals** Lunch 34 – 39, a la carte 47/81
Spec. Crème de pois chiches aux cappelletti et romarin. Risotto aux truffes blanches (October-December). Tagliata manzo chianina, rucola et parmesan. **Wines** Pinot gris, Vin de
barrique.

Kamakura, r. Münster 4, ⊠ 2160, 𝒫 47 06 04, kamakura@pe.lu, Fax 46 73 30, Japa- G
nese cuisine – 🆎 ① 🚧 𝗩𝗜𝗦𝗔. ✻
closed 2 weeks August, Sunday and lunch Saturday and Bank Holidays – **Meals** Lunch 10 –
19/49.

Thai Céladon, Montée du Grund 28, ⊠ 1645, 𝒫 47 49 34, 🍴, Thai cuisine – 🆎 G
🚧 𝗩𝗜𝗦𝗔. ✻
closed 1 to 15 April, Saturday lunch and Sunday – **Meals** Lunch 17 – a la carte approx. 3

Luxembourg-Station

🏨 **Gd H. Mercure Alfa**, pl. de la Gare 16, ✉ 1616, ℰ 490 01 11, *H2058@accor-hote ls.com*, Fax 49 00 09 – 📶 ⁕ ≡ 📺 🅰️🅴 ⓸ ⓽ *VISA*. ⅏
DZ z
Meals *Lunch* 15 – 28 ♀ – ⥮ 18 – **140 rm** 135/195, 1 suite.

🏨 **President** (annexe Les Jardins du President), pl. de la Gare 32, ✉ 1024, ℰ 48 61 61, *president@pt.lu*, Fax 48 61 80 – 📶 ⁕ ≡ 📺 🄿 – 🔬 40. 🅰️🅴 ⓸ ⓽ *VISA* ᴊᴄʙ
DZ v
Meals *(closed August, Sunday and Bank Holidays)* (dinner only until 11 p.m.) a la carte approx. 38 – **42 rm** ⥮ 150/185.

🏨 **City** Ⓜ without rest, r. Strasbourg 1, ✉ 2561, ℰ 29 11 22, *mail@cityhotel.lu*, Fax 29 11 33 – 📶 📺 ⟺ – 🔬 25-100. 🅰️🅴 ⓸ ⓽ *VISA*
DZ k
35 rm ⥮ 100/140.

🏨 **Christophe Colomb** without rest, r. Anvers 10, ✉ 1130, ℰ 408 41 41, *mail@chri stophe-colomb.lu*, Fax 40 84 08 – 📶, ≡ rest, 📺 – 🔬 25. 🅰️🅴 ⓸ ⓽ *VISA*
CZ h
24 rm ⥮ 115/125.

🏨 **International**, pl. de la Gare 20, ✉ 1616, ℰ 48 59 11, *info@hotelinter.lu*, Fax 49 32 27
– 📶 ⁕ ≡ rest, 📺 – 🔬 25-50. 🅰️🅴 ⓸ ⓽ *VISA*
DZ z
Meals *(closed 20 December-10 January)* 22/36 ♀ – **49 rm** ⥮ 107/134, 1 suite.

🏨 **Central Molitor**, av. de la Liberté 28, ✉ 1930, ℰ 48 99 11, *molitor@pt.lu*, Fax 48 33 82, ⇆ – 📶, ≡ rest, 📺 ⟺ – 🔬 35. 🅰️🅴 ⓸ ⓽ *VISA*
CDZ x
Meals *(closed 19 August-15 September, 23 December-5 January, Saturday and Sunday dinner)* *Lunch* 9 – 22 ♀ – **36 rm** ⥮ 105/130.

🏨 **Marco Polo** without rest, r. Fort Neipperg 27, ✉ 2230, ℰ 406 41 41, *mail@marco -polo.lu*, Fax 40 48 84 – 📶 📺 ⟺, 🅰️🅴 ⓸ ⓽ *VISA*
DZ d
18 rm ⥮ 115/125.

🏨 **Le Châtelet** (annex 🏠 - 9 rm) without rest, bd de la Pétrusse 2, ✉ 2320, ℰ 40 21 01, *contact@chatelet.lu*, Fax 40 36 66 – 📶 📺 🄿. 🅰️🅴 ⓸ ⓽ *VISA*
CZ e
closed February – **36 rm** ⥮ 89/99.

🏨 **Nobilis**, av. de la Gare 47, ✉ 1611, ℰ 49 49 71, Fax 40 31 01 – 📶 ≡ 📺 🄿 – 🔬 50.
🅰️🅴 ⓸ ⓽ *VISA*. ⅏ rest
DZ a
Meals *Lunch* 16 – a la carte approx. 24 – ⥮ 11 – **47 rm** 97/114.

✕✕ **Italia** with rm, r. Anvers 15, ✉ 1130, ℰ 486 62 61, *italia@euro.lu*, Fax 48 08 07, ⌂,
Partly Italian cuisine – 📺, 🅰️🅴 ⓸ ⓽ *VISA*
CZ f
Meals a la carte 31/45 – **20 rm** ⥮ 65/81.

✕✕ **Au Quai de la Gare**, pl. de la Gare 13 (1st floor in the station), ✉ 1616, ℰ 40 67 67,
⌾ Fax 40 67 66 – 🅰️🅴 ⓸ ⓽ *VISA*. ⅏
DZ b
closed first 3 weeks August, 20 to 30 December, Saturday lunch and Sunday – **Meals** *Lunch* 20 – 24/31 b.i..

Suburbs

Airport *Northeast : 8 km :*

🏨 **Sheraton Aérogolf** ⌘, rte de Trèves 1, ✉ 1019, ℰ 34 05 71, *sheraton-luxembo urg@sheraton.com*, Fax 34 02 17 – 📶 ⁕ ≡ 📺 🄿 – 🔬 25-120. 🅰️🅴 ⓸ ⓽ *VISA*
Meals *Le Montgolfier* (Open until midnight) *Lunch* 34 – a la carte 31/60 ♀ – ⥮ 18 – **143 rm** 269/294, 5 suites.

🏨 **Ibis**, rte de Trèves, ✉ 2632, ℰ 43 88 01, *H0974@accor-hotels.com*, Fax 43 88 02, ≼
– 📶 ≡ 📺 🄿 🔬 25-80. 🅰️🅴 ⓸ ⓽ *VISA*
Meals *Lunch* 18 – 22 – ⥮ 10 – **120 rm** 75/85.

🏨 **Trust Inn** without rest, r. Neudorf 679 (by rte de Trèves), ✉ 2220, ℰ 423 05 11, *trustinn@pt.lu*, Fax 42 30 56, 🚲 – ≡ 📺 🄿. 🅰️🅴 ⓸ ⓽ *VISA*
7 rm ⥮ 55/79.

✕✕ **Le Grimpereau**, r. Cents 140, ✉ 1319, ℰ 43 67 87, Fax 42 60 26, ⌂ – 🄿. 🅰️🅴 ⓽
⌾ *VISA*. ⅏
closed first 3 weeks August, Sunday dinner and Monday – **Meals** 34/42.

at Belair *West : 1,5 km* Ⓒ *Luxembourg :*

🏨 **Albert Premier** ⌘ without rest, r. Albert Iᵉʳ 2a, ✉ 1117, ℰ 442 44 21, *hotel-albe rt-premier@resto.lu*, Fax 44 74 41, « English style opulent interior », 🛁, ⌘ – 📶 📺 ⟺.
🅰️🅴 ⓸ ⓽ *VISA*
CZ c
closed 20 to 27 December – ⥮ 11 – **14 rm** 198/347.

🏨 **Parc Belair** Ⓜ ⌘, av. du X Septembre 111, ✉ 2551, ℰ 44 23 23, *paribel@hpb.lu*, Fax 44 44 84, ≼, ⌂, 🛁, ⌘, 🚲 – 📶 ⁕, ≡ rest, 📺 ⟺ – 🔬 25-400. 🅰️🅴 ⓸ ⓽ *VISA*
Meals (dinner only except Sunday) a la carte 28/50 – **45 rm** ⥮ 195/235, 7 suites.

XX **Astoria**, av. du X Septembre 44, ⊠ 2550, ℰ 44 62 23, Fax 45 82 96, 佘 – ▤ – ⚓ 25.
ÆÕ ⑩ ⑩Ⓞ ᵛⁱˢᵃ
CZ a
closed 1 week carnival, Saturday and dinner Sunday and Monday – **Meals** *Lunch* 23 – a la
carte 30/51.

XX **Thailand**, av. Gaston Diderich 72, ⊠ 1420, ℰ 44 27 66, Thai cuisine – ÆÕ ⑩ ⑩Ⓞ ᵛⁱˢᵃ
缶
closed 15 August-15 September, Monday and Saturday lunch – **Meals** a la carte approx.
36.

at Dommeldange *(Dummeldéng) North : 5,5 km* ⓒ *Luxembourg :*

🏨 **Hilton** ⊱, r. Jean Engling 12, ⊠ 1466, ℰ 4 37 81, lxmhihioth@hilton.com, Fax 43 60 95,
≪, ₤₅, 龠, 🏊, ♣⅙ – ▥ 🛏 🔟 ℙ – ⚓ 25-360. ÆÕ ⑩ ⑩Ⓞ ᵛⁱˢᵃ ᴶᶜᴮ. ✀ rest
Meals See **Les Continents** below – **Café Stiffchen** *(Open until 11.30 p.m.) Lunch* 26 – a
la carte 39/53 ♀ – ⊷ 19 – **306 rm** 270, 31 suites.

🏨 **Parc**, rte d'Echternach 120, ⊠ 1453, ℰ 43 56 43, info@parc-hotel.lu, Fax 43 69 03, 佘,
₤₅, 龠, 🏊, ♣⅙, ✀, ※ – ▥ 🛏 🔟 ℙ – ⚓ 25-1500. ÆÕ ⑩ ⑩Ⓞ ᵛⁱˢᵃ
Meals *(Open until 11.30 p.m.) Lunch* 21 – a la carte 32/46 – **271 rm** ⊷ 95/139.

🏨 **Host. du Grünewald**, rte d'Echternach 10, ⊠ 1453, ℰ 43 18 82 and 42 06 46 (rest),
hostgrun@pt.lu, Fax 42 06 46, ✀ – ▥ ▤ rest, 🔟 ℙ – ⚓ 25-40. ÆÕ ⑩ ⑩Ⓞ ✀ rest
Meals *(closed 15 to 30 August, 2 to 21 January, Saturday lunch, Sunday and Bank Holidays)*
Lunch 45 – 69/87 – **26 rm** ⊷ 97/122, 2 suites.

XXXX **Les Continents** - Hotel Hilton, 1st floor, r. Jean Engling 12, ⊠ 1466, ℰ 4 37 81, lxmh
ihioth@hilton.com, Fax 43 60 95, ≪, 佘 – ▤ ℙ. ÆÕ ⑩ ⑩Ⓞ ᵛⁱˢᵃ ᴶᶜᴮ. ✀
closed August-first week September, first week January, Saturday lunch, Sunday and Mon-
day – **Meals** *Lunch* 37 – a la carte 59/74 ♀ ♀.

at Gasperich *(Gaasperech) South : 4 km* ⓒ *Luxembourg :*

🏨 **Inn Side** Ⓜ, r. Henri Schnadt 1 (Cloche d'Or), ⊠ 2530, ℰ 490 00 61, luxembourg@i
nnside.com, Fax 49 06 80, 佘, « Design », ₤₅, 龠, ♣⅙ – ▥ ✤ 🔟 & ⇔ – ⚓ 25-200.
ÆÕ ⑩ ⑩Ⓞ ᵛⁱˢᵃ
Meals *(closed Saturday) Lunch* 29 – a la carte 41/51 – **158 rm** ⊷ 175/240.

Upland of Kirchberg *(Kiirchbierg) :*

🏨 **Sofitel** Ⓜ ⊱, r. Fort Niedergrünewald 6 (European Centre), ⊠ 2015, ℰ 43 77 61
H1314@accor-hotels.com, Fax 42 50 91 – ▥ ✤ ▤ 🔟 & ⇔ ℙ – ⚓ 25-75. ÆÕ ⑩ ⑩Ⓞ
ᵛⁱˢᵃ. ✀ rest
EY a
Meals Oro e Argento *(closed August and Saturday) Lunch* 37 – à la carte approx. 51 –
⊷ 19 – **100 rm** 273, 4 suites.

🏨 **Novotel** ⊱, r. Fort Niedergrünewald 6 (European Centre), ⊠ 2226, ℰ 429 84 81
H1930@accor-hotels.com, Fax 43 86 58, 佘, 龠, 🏊 – ▥ ✤ ▤ 🔟 & ℙ – ⚓ 25-300
ÆÕ ⑩ ⑩Ⓞ ᵛⁱˢᵃ. ✀ rest
EY a
Meals 22 b.i./42 – ⊷ 14 – **260 rm** 135.

at the skating-rink of Kockelscheuer *(Kockelscheier) South by N 31 :*

XXX **Patin d'Or** (Berring), rte de Bettembourg 40, ⊠ 1899, ℰ 22 64 99, contact@patin
繺 or.lu, Fax 40 40 11, « Floral terrace » – ▤ ℙ. ÆÕ ⑩Ⓞ ᵛⁱˢᵃ. ✀
closed carnival week, last 2 weeks August, Christmas-New Year, Saturday and Sunday
Meals 50, a la carte 63/74 ♀
Spec. Nage de homard et St-Jacques au beurre de Sauternes. Filet de rouget en croustillan
de pommes de terre. Pied de porc farci à l'ancienne. **Wines** Pinot gris, Riesling.

at Neudorf *(Neiduerf) Northeast : 4 km* ⓒ *Luxembourg :*

🏨 **Ponte Vecchio** without rest, r. Neudorf 271, ⊠ 2221, ℰ 424 72 01, pontevecchi
@corcelli.com, Fax 424 72 08 88 – ▥ ▤ 🔟 ℙ. ÆÕ ⑩ ⑩Ⓞ ᵛⁱˢᵃ
46 rm ⊷ 105/112.

at Pulvermühl *(Polfermillen) East : 2 km* ⓒ *Luxembourg :*

XX **L'Espadon and Hotel la Cascade** with rm, r. Pulvermühl 2, ⊠ 2356, ℰ 42 87 36
繺 lrgcv@pt.lu, Fax 42 47 88, 佘, « Late 19C villa, Alzette-side terrace » – ▤ 🔟 ℙ. ÆÕ ⑩
⑩Ⓞ ᵛⁱˢᵃ
closed 24 February-3 March and 22 to 29 December – **Meals** *(closed Tuesday and Saturda*
dinner) – 30/42 ♀ – ⊷ 7 – **7 rm** 81/113.

at Rollingergrund *(Rolléngergronn) Northwest : 3 km* ⓒ *Luxembourg :*

🏨 **Sieweburen**, r. Septfontaines 36, ⊠ 2534, ℰ 44 23 56, Fax 44 23 53, ≪, 佘,
« Woodland setting », ✀ – 🔟 ℙ. ⑩Ⓞ ᵛⁱˢᵃ ᴶᶜᴮ
Meals *(closed Wednesday) (Pub rest) Lunch* 11 – a la carte approx. 26 – **14 rm** ⊷ 80/11

Environs

at Bridel (*Briddel*) *by N 12 : 7 km* Ⓖ *Kopstal pop. 3050 :*

XX **Le Rondeau,** r. Luxembourg 82, ✉ 8140, ℰ 33 94 73, Fax 33 37 46, 🍽 – 🄿 AE ⓞ
🞉 ⓜⓞ VISA
closed 2 weeks March, 3 weeks August, Monday and Tuesday – **Meals** 28/54.

at Hesperange (*Hesper*) *Southeast : 5,5 km. pop. 10111*

XXX **L'Agath** (Steichen), rte de Thionville 274 (Howald), ✉ 5884, ℰ 48 86 87, *agath@email.lu*,
🞉 Fax 48 55 05, 🍽 – 🄿 – 🅐 60. AE ⓞ ⓜⓞ VISA
closed 1 to 20 August, 1 to 15 January, Saturday lunch, Sunday, Monday and Bank Holidays
– **Meals** *Lunch 42* – a la carte 63/78 ⓨ
Spec. Foie gras de canard sauté aux girolles, sauce au cidre. Raviolis de homard et bisque
mousseuse. Suprême de pigeon, pâtes farcies aux épinards. **Wines** Pinot gris, Riesling.

at Strassen (*Strossen*) *West : 4 km. pop. 5847*

🏨 **L'Olivier** with apartments, rte d'Arlon 140, ✉ 8008, ℰ 31 36 66, *ollvier@mail.lu*,
Fax 31 36 66 – ❦ 🛏 TV 🅿 – 🅐 25-50. AE ⓞ ⓜⓞ VISA
Meals see *La Cime* below – **38 rm** ⬜ 133/190, 4 suites.

XX **La Cime** - Hotel L'Olivier, rte d'Arlon 140a, ✉ 8008, ℰ 31 88 13, *lolivier@mail.lu*,
Fax 31 36 27, 🍽 – 🄿 AE ⓞ ⓜⓞ VISA
closed Saturday lunch and Bank Holidays – **Meals** 32/41.

XX **Le Nouveau Riquewihr,** rte d'Arlon 373, ✉ 8011, ℰ 31 99 80, Fax 31 97 05, 🍽
🞉 – 🄿 AE ⓞ ⓜⓞ VISA
closed Sunday – **Meals** *Lunch 31* – a la carte approx. 51.

at Walferdange (*Walfer*) *North : 5 km. pop. 6600*

🏨 **Moris,** pl. des Martyrs, ✉ 7201, ℰ 330 10 51, *contact@morishotel.lu*, Fax 33 30 70, 🍽
– ❦, 🍽 rest, TV 🅿 – 🅐 50. AE ⓞ ⓜⓞ VISA
Meals *(closed 29 July-18 August, 27 December-5 January and Friday)* *Lunch 31* – a la carte
29/43 ⓨ – **24 rm** ⬜ 82/107.

XX **l'Etiquette,** rte de Diekirch 50, ✉ 7220, ℰ 33 51 68, Fax 33 51 69, 🍽 – 🄿 AE ⓞ
🞉 ⓜⓞ VISA
closed 20 August-4 September, 27 December-5 January and Sunday dinner – **Meals** *Lunch*
17 – 20/40.

Echternach (*Iechternach*) 🔲 X 24 and 🔲 M 6. pop. 4000 – 36 km.

at Geyershaff (*Geieschhaff*) *Southwest : 6,5 km by E 27* Ⓖ *Bech pop. 720 :*

XXX **La Bergerie** (Phal), ✉ 6251, ℰ 79 04 64, *phall@gms.lu*, Fax 79 07 71, ❦, 🍽, « Floral
🞉🞉 country setting » – 🄿 AE ⓞ ⓜⓞ VISA
closed 15 January-14 February and Monday except Bank Holidays – **Meals** *(dinner only*
except Sunday and Bank Holidays) 71/105, a la carte 79/113
Spec. Salade de homard aux senteurs méditerranéennes. La symphonie de noix de St-
Jacques. Le soufflé chaud aux fruits de saison. **Wines** Pinot gris, Riesling.

Paliseul *6850 Luxembourg belge* (*Belgium*) 🔲 P 23 and 🔲 I 6. pop. 5006 – 94 km.

XXX **Au Gastronome** (Libotte) with rm, r. Bouillon 2 (Paliseul-Gare) ℰ 0 61 55 30 64,
🞉🞉 Fax 0 61 53 38 91, « Ardennes country inn, floral garden with 🛁 » – 🍽 TV 🄿 AE ⓜⓞ
VISA
closed last week June-first week July, 1 January dinner-7 February, Sunday dinner, Monday
and Tuesday lunch – **Meals** *Lunch 37* – 57/89, a la carte approx. 70 – **8 rm** ⬜ 82/129
Spec. Langoustines poêlées aux piments d'Espelette, tarte Tatin de pied de porc cara-
mélisée. Grenouilles au jus de persil et aux croquettes d'ail. Pigeonneau en crapaudine cuit
à la broche au caramel d'épices.

AMSTERDAM

Noord-Holland **210** O 8 – ㉘ ㉙, **211** O 8 *and* **908** G 4 – ㉗ S – *pop. 731 288.*

Brussels 204 – Düsseldorf 227 – The Hague 60 – Luxembourg 419 – Rotterdam 76.

TOURIST OFFICE

VVV Amsterdam, Stationsplein 10, ✉ *1012 AB,* ℘ *0900-400 40 40, info@amsterdam tourist.nl, Fax (0 20) 625 28 69.*

For more information on tourist attractions consult our Green Guide to Amsterdam and our Map N° 36.

GOLF COURSES

🏌 *West : 6 km at Halfweg, Machineweg 1b,* ✉ *1165 NB,* ℘ *(0 23) 513 29 39, Fax (0 23) 513 29 35 –* 🏌 *South : 5 km at Duivendrecht, Zwarte Laantje 4,* ✉ *1099 CE, ℘ (0 20) 694 36 50, Fax (0 20) 663 46 21 –* 🏌 *Buikslotermeerdijk 141,* ✉ *1027 AC, ℘ (0 20) 632 56 50, Fax (0 20) 634 35 06 –* 🏌 *Southeast at Holendrecht, Abcouderstraatweg 46,* ✉ *1105 AA,* ℘ *(0 294) 28 12 41, Fax (0 294) 28 63 47 –* 🏌 *Bauduinlaan 35,* ✉ *1047 HK,* ℘ *(0 20) 497 78 66, Fax (0 20) 497 59 66.*

CASINO

Holland Casino KY, Max Euweplein 62, ✉ *1017 MB (near Leidseplein),* ℘ *(0 20) 521 11 11, Fax (0 20) 521 11 10.*

PLACES OF INTEREST

VIEUWPOINTS

Keizersgracht★★ KVY – from the sluice bridge on the Oudezijds Kolk and the Oudezijds Voorburgwal★ LX.

HISTORICAL MONUMENTS

Dam : Royal Palace★ KX – Beguine Convent★★ KX – Cromhout Houses★ KY **A⁴** *– Westerkerk★ KX – Nieuwe Kerk★★ KX – Oude Kerk★ LX.*

HISTORICAL MUSEUMS

Amsterdam Historical Museum★★ KX – Jewish Museum★ LY – Allard Pierson Museum★ : archeological finds LXY – the House of Anne Frank★★ KX – Netherlands Maritime History Museum★★ MX – Tropical Museum★ – Van Loon Museum★ LY – Willet-Holthuysen Museum★ LY.

FAMOUS COLLECTIONS

Rijksmuseum★★★ KZ – Van Gogh Museum★★★ (Rijksmuseum) JZ – Museum of Modern Art★★★ JZ – Amstelkring "Our Dear Lord in the Attic"★ (Museum Amstelkring Ons' Lieve Heer op Solder) : clandestine chapel LX – Rembrandt's House★ : works by the master LX – Cobra★ (Modern Art).

MODERN ARCHITECTURE

Housing in the Jordaan district and around the Nieuwmarkt – Contemporary structures at Amsterdam Zuid-Oost (ING bank).

SCENIC AREAS AND PARKS

Old Amsterdam★★★ – Herengracht★★★ KVY – Canals★★★ (Grachten) with hotel-boats (Amstel) – The Jordaan (Prinsengracht★★, Brouwersgracht★, Lijnbaansgracht, Looiersgracht, Egelantiersgracht★, Bloemgracht★) KX – JKY – Regullersgracht★ LY – Realeneiland Dam★ KX – Thin Bridge★ (Magere Brug) LY – The Walletjes★★ (red light district) LX – Sarphatipark – Oosterpark – Vondelpark JZ – Artis★ MY (zoological park) – Singel★★ KY.

AMSTERDAM

0   200 m

HET IJ

de Ruijter Kade

Oost Haven

Centraal
Station
Stationspl.

AIR
TERMINAL

Front

PASSAGIERS-
TERMINAL

S 116

IJ-tunnel

S 100

NIEUWE
ZIJDE

Damrak

dijk

Nieuwendijk

BEURS
VAN
BERLAGE

Dam

MUSEUM
AMSTELKRING

OUDE KERK

OUDE
ZIJDE

Warmoesstraat

Nieuwezijds Voorburgwal

Scheepvaart
huis

Prins Hendrikkade

OOSTERDOK

NEMO

156

Waag

Nieuw
markt

Geldersekade

Waals Eilandsgracht

22

Montelbaanstoren

OUDE

SCHANS

NEDERLANDS
SCHEEPVAART
MUSEUM

Prinsenhof

Zeedijk

Kloveniersburgwal

Zuiderkerk

93

Uilenburgergracht

Entrepot

dok

REMBRANDT
HUIS

88

Valkenburgerstr.

ALLARD
PIERSON M.

Zwanenburgwal

Waterlool.

H

Muziektheater

Mr. Visser Plein

Herengr.

AMSTEL

Waterlooplein

Blauwbrug

JOODS
HISTORISCH
MUSEUM

Hortus
Botanicus

Plantage

ARTIS

Muntplein

REMBRANDTPL.

Amstelstr.

Nieuwe

MUSEUM
WILLET-HOLTHUYSEN

AMSTELHOF

Nieuwe

Keizersgr.

PLANTAGE

Plantage Muidergr.

Middenlaan

Roeters-

str.

MUSEUM
VAN LOON

Utrechtsestr.

Amstel

Nieuwe

Prinsengracht

Achter

gracht

Kerkstr.

Amstel
Kerk

MAGERE
BRUG

Nieuwe

T

De Duif

Amstelsluizen

Weesperplein

Sarphatistr.

S 100

Reguliersgr.

Frederiksplein

Hogesluis
Brug

Sarphatistr.

Mauritskade

Wibautstraat

Wetering-

schans

Westeinde

Oosteinde

Amstel

Ruyschstr.

Singelgracht

Stadhouderskade

LUXEMBOURG

STREET INDEX TO AMSTERDAM TOWN PLAN

Alphabetical listing of hotels and restaurants

H

11 Haesje Claes
14 Herbergh (De)
12 Hilton
14 Hilton Schiphol
11 Hofpark and Résidence
13 Holiday Inn
13 Hollandais (Le)
11 Hosokawa

I – J

10 Indrapura
9 Inntel
11 Jan Luyken
14 Jagershuis ('t)
8 Jolly Carlton
13 Jonge Dikkert (De)

K – L

14 Kaatje bij de Sluis (at Blokzijl)
13 Kas (De)
12 Keyzer
11 Lairesse
10 Lancaster

M – N

10 Manchurian
12 Mangerie de Kersentuin
   (H. Bilderberg Garden)
11 Marriott
11 Memphis
13 Mercure Airport
12 Mercure a/d Amstel
9 Mercure Arthur Frommer
12 Meridien Apollo (Le)
14 Nederlanden (De) (at Vreeland)
13 Novotel

O – P – Q

11 Oesterbar
12 Okura
12 Omega
14 Paardenburg
13 Pakistan
10 Pêcheur (Le)
9 Port van Cleve (Die)
8 Pulitzer

R

12 Radèn Mas
8 Radisson SAS
14 Radisson SAS Airport
10 Rembrandt
8 Renaissance
13 Résidence Fontaine Royale
   (Grand Hotel)
10 Rive (La) (H. Amstel)
14 Ron Blaauw
13 Rosarium
13 Royal San Kong

S

9 Schiller
9 Seven One Seven
14 Sheraton Airport
10 Sichuan Food
13 Sirène (La)
   (H. Le Méridien Apollo)
9 Sofitel
12 Spring
8 Swissôtel

T

11 Takens
11 theeboom (d')
9 Toren
11 Toro
10 Tulip Inn
9 Tulip Inn Art
10 Tuynhuys (Het)

V – W – Y – Z

11 Van Vlaanderen
10 Vermeer
   (H. Barbizon Palace)
8 Victoria
13 visaandeschelde
11 Vondel
12 Vossius
10 Vijff Vlieghen (d')
10 Wiechmann
13 Yamazato (H. Okura)

Establishments according to style of cuisine

Buffets _____

14 Greenhouse (H. Hilton Schiphol)
Env. at Schiphol

Pub rest – Brasseries _____

8 American *Centre*
8 Amstel Bar and Brasserie (The)
(H. Amstel) *Centre*
12 Brasserie Camelia (H. Okura)
South and West Q.
8 Brasserie De Palmboom
(H. Radisson SAS) *Centre*
8 Brasserie Le Relais
(H. de l'Europe) *Centre*
12 Brasserie van Baerle
Rijksmuseum
10 Café Roux
(H. The Grand Sofitel Demeure)
Centre
9 Doelen *Centre*
9 Eden *Centre*
12 Garage (Le) *Rijksmuseum*
12 Keyzer *Rijksmuseum*
13 Novotel *Buitenveldert*
9 Port van Cleve (Die) *Centre*
9 Schiller *Centre*
10 Tulip Inn *Centre*

Seafood – Oyster bar _____

11 Oesterbar *Centre*
10 Pêcheur (Le) *Centre*
12 Sirène (La) (H. Le Meridien Apollo)
South and West Q.
13 visaandeschelde
South and West Q.

American _____

13 Vermont *(H. Holiday Inn)*
Buitenveldert

Asian _____

14 East West *(H. Hilton Schiphol)*
Env. at Schiphol
8 Blakes *Centre*

Chinese _____

13 Royal San Kong
Env. at Amstelveen
10 Sichuan Food *Centre*

Dutch regional _____

8 Dorrius
(H. Crowne Plaza City Centre) *Centre*
9 Roode Leeuw (De)
(H. Amsterdam) *Centre*

Indian _____

13 Pakistan *South and West Q.*

Indonesian _____

10 Indrapura *Centre*
12 Radèn Mas *Rijksmuseum*

Italian _____

10 Bice (H. Golden Tulip Centre)
Rijksmuseum
8 Caruso (H. Jolly Carlton)
Centre
14 Radisson SAS Airport
Env. at Schiphol
12 Roberto's (H. Hilton)
South and West Q.
8 Swissôtel *Centre*
8 Talavera *(H. Radisson SAS) Centre*
9 Tulip Inn *Centre*

Japanese _____

11 Hosokawa *Centre*
12 Sazanka (H. Okura)
South and West Q.
13 Yamazato (H. Okura)
South and West Q.

Oriental _____

10 Dynasty *Centre*
10 Manchurian *Centre*

Centre

Amstel ⌂, Prof. Tulpplein 1, ⊠ 1018 GX, ℰ (0 20) 622 60 60, *maikel_ginsheumer@i nterconti.com*, Fax (0 20) 622 58 08, ≼, 龠, ₤ᵈ, ⊜ₛ, ⊠, ⊥–⫟ 灬 ≡ ⊡ P.– ⩍ 25-180. AE ⓞ ⓜⓞ VISA JCB. ⅜
MZ a
Meals see *La Rive* below – *The Amstel Bar and Brasserie* (Open until 11.30 p.m.) a la carte approx. 54 ♀ – ⊡ 27 – **63 rm** 520, 15 suites.

The Grand Sofitel Demeure ⌂, O.Z. Voorburgwal 197, ⊠ 1012 EX, ℰ (0 20) 555 31 11, *hotel@thegrand.nl*, Fax (0 20) 555 32 22, « Historic building, authentic Art Nouveau lounges, inner garden », ₤ᵈ, ⊜ₛ, ⊠, 灬, 屾, ℺, ⊥–⫟ 灬 ≡ ⊡ P.– ⩍ 25-300. AE ⓞ ⓜⓞ VISA JCB. ⅜
LX b
Meals see *Café Roux* below – ⊡ 20 – **169 rm** 395/440, 13 suites.

Gd H. Krasnapolsky, Dam 9, ⊠ 1012 JS, ℰ (0 20) 554 91 11, *info@krasnapolsky.nl*, Fax (0 20) 622 86 07, « 19C winter garden », ₤ᵈ, ⊥–⫟ 灬 ≡ ⊡ ⅙ ⬷ – ⩍ 25-750. AE ⓞ ⓜⓞ VISA. ⅜
LX k
Meals *Reflet* Lunch 34 – a la carte 42/57 ♀ – *Edo and Kyo* (Japanese cuisine with Teppan-Yaki) Lunch 27 – 59 – *Winter Garden* (Buffets, lunch only) 25 – ⊡ 20 – **461 rm** 265/400, 7 suites.

de l'Europe, Nieuwe Doelenstraat 2, ⊠ 1012 CP, ℰ (0 20) 531 17 77, *hotel@leurop e.nl*, Fax (0 20) 531 17 78, ≼, 龠, « Collection of Dutch landscape paintings in late 19C lounge », ₤ᵈ, ⊜ₛ, ⊠, 屾, ⊥–⫟ 灬 ≡ ⊡ P.– ⩍ 25-80. AE ⓞ ⓜⓞ VISA JCB. ⅜
LY c
Meals see *Excelsior* below – *Brasserie Le Relais* (Open until 11 p.m.) Lunch 22 – 27 – ⊡ 23 – **94 rm** 280/395, 6 suites.

Barbizon Palace, Prins Hendrikkade 59, ⊠ 1012 AD, ℰ (0 20) 556 45 64, *sales@g tbpalace.goldentulip.nl*, Fax (0 20) 624 33 53, ₤ᵈ, ⊜ₛ, ⊥–⫟ 灬 ≡ ⊡ ⬷ – ⩍ 25-300. AE ⓞ ⓜⓞ VISA JCB. ⅜
LV d
Meals see *Vermeer* below – *Hudson's Terrace and Restaurant* (Open until 11 p.m.) Lunch 35 – a la carte 47/55 – ⊡ 19 – **271 rm** 265/380, 3 suites.

Radisson SAS M ⌂, Rusland 17, ⊠ 1012 CK, ℰ (0 20) 623 12 31, *reservations.am sterdam@radissonsas.com*, Fax (0 20) 520 82 00, « Patio with 18C presbytery », ₤ᵈ, ⊜ₛ, ⊥–⫟ 灬 ≡ ⊡ VISA JCB. ⅜ – ⩍ 25-180. AE ⓞ ⓜⓞ VISA JCB. ⅜
LX h
Meals *Talavera* (Partly Italian cuisine) Lunch 29 – a la carte 22/36 ♀ – *Brasserie De Palm-boom* (dinner only) a la carte 25/35 ♀ – ⊡ 19 – **242 rm** 260/330, 1 suite.

Pulitzer ⌂, Prinsengracht 323, ⊠ 1016 GZ, ℰ (0 20) 523 52 35, *sales_amsterdam @sheraton.com*, Fax (0 20) 627 67 53, « 24 terraced canalside houses from 17 and 18C », 灬, ⊥–⫟ 灬 ≡ ⊡ ⬷ – ⩍ 25-150. AE ⓞ ⓜⓞ VISA JCB. ⅜
KX m
Meals *Pulitzers* (Open until 11 p.m.) Lunch 31 – a la carte 42/61 ♀ – ⊡ 23 – **227 rm** 425/500, 3 suites.

Renaissance, Kattengat 1, ⊠ 1012 SZ, ℰ (0 20) 621 22 23, Fax (0 20) 627 52 45, ₤ᵈ, ⊜ₛ, ⊥–⫟ 灬 ≡ ⊡ 屾 ⬷ – ⩍ 25-400. AE ⓞ ⓜⓞ VISA. ⅜ rest
LV e
Meals a la carte 37/48 ♀ – ⊡ 18 – **399 rm** 340/386, 6 suites.

Crowne Plaza City Centre, N.Z. Voorburgwal 5, ⊠ 1012 RC, ℰ (0 20) 620 05 00 and 420 22 24 (rest), *info@crowneplaza.nl*, Fax (0 20) 620 11 73, ₤ᵈ, ⊜ₛ, ⊠, 屾, – ⫟ 灬 ≡ ⊡ VISA ⬷ – ⩍ 25-270. AE ⓞ ⓜⓞ VISA. ⅜
LV q
Meals *Dorrius* (Partly Dutch regional cooking, dinner only until 11 p.m.) Lunch 19 – a la carte 35/43 – ⊡ 21 – **268 rm** 305/415, 2 suites.

Victoria, Damrak 1, ⊠ 1012 LG, ℰ (0 20) 623 42 55, *victres@parkplazahotels.nl*, Fax (0 20) 625 29 97, ₤ᵈ, ⊜ₛ, ⊠, ⊥–⫟ 灬 ≡ ⊡ 屾 – ⩍ 30-150. AE ⓞ ⓜⓞ VISA JCB. ⅜
LV j
Meals Lunch 24 – a la carte approx. 30 ♀ – ⊡ 19 – **295 rm** 310/360, 10 suites.

Blakes M ⌂, Keizersgracht 384, ⊠ 1016 GB, ℰ (0 20) 530 20 10, *hotel@blakes.nl*, Fax (0 20) 530 20 10, 龠, « Period residence, Oriental inspired design », 屾, – ⫟, rm, ⊡ AE ⓞ ⓜⓞ VISA. ⅜
KX a
Meals (closed Sunday dinner) (Partly Asian cuisine) Lunch 27 – a la carte approx. 66 ♀ – ⊡ 16 – **38 rm** 350/450, 3 suites.

American, Leidsekade 97, ⊠ 1017 PN, ℰ (0 20) 556 30 00, *american@basshotels.com*, Fax (0 20) 556 30 01, 龠, ₤ᵈ, ⊜ₛ, ⊥–⫟ 灬, ≡ rm, ⊡ – ⩍ 25-150. AE ⓞ ⓜⓞ VISA. ⅜
JY q
Meals (Art Deco style pub rest) a la carte 31/41 – ⊡ 20 – **186 rm** 305/455, 2 suites.

Jolly Carlton, Vijzelstraat 4, ⊠ 1017 HK, ℰ (0 20) 622 22 66 and 623 83 20 (rest), *banquetting@jollycarlton.nl*, Fax (0 20) 626 61 83 – ⫟ 灬 ≡ ⊡ 屾 ⬷ – ⩍ 25-180. AE ⓞ ⓜⓞ VISA JCB. ⅜
LY n
Meals *Caruso* (closed 23 December) (Italian cuisine, dinner only until 11 p.m.) 31 ♀ – ⊡ 15 – **218 rm** 200/454.

Swissôtel M, Damrak 96, ⊠ 1012 LP, ℰ (0 20) 522 30 00, *emailus.amsterdam@swi ssotel.com*, Fax (0 20) 522 32 23 – ⫟ 灬 ≡ ⊡ 屾 – ⩍ 25-45. AE ⓞ ⓜⓞ VISA JCB. ⅜
LX s
Meals (Partly Italian cuisine) 22 – ⊡ 17 – **106 rm** 270/335.

NETHERLANDS

Sofitel, N.Z. Voorburgwal 67, ✉ 1012 RE, ℰ (0 20) 627 59 00, *h1159@accor-hotels. com*, Fax (0 20) 623 89 32, 🛁 – 🕴 ↩ 📼 ⟨⟩ – ⚑ 25-55. 🖭 ⑩ ⓞⓞ 𝘝𝘐𝘚𝘈 ᴊᴄʙ.
KX q
Meals a la carte approx. 36 – ⊐ 18 – **148 rm** 289/360.

Toren 🌸 without rest, Keizersgracht 164, ✉ 1015 CZ, ℰ (0 20) 622 63 52, *hotel.to ren@tip.nl*, Fax (0 20) 626 97 05, 🌿 – 🕴 📼. 🖭 ⑩ ⓞⓞ 𝘝𝘐𝘚𝘈 ᴊᴄʙ
KV w
⊐ 12 – **39 rm** 120/180, 1 suite.

Doelen, Nieuwe Doelenstraat 24, ✉ 1012 CP, ℰ (0 20) 554 06 00, *sales@gtdoelen.g oldentulip.nl*, Fax (0 20) 622 10 84, ≼, « 19C Amstel-side residence », 🔽 – 🕴 ↩ 📼 –
⚑ 25-100. 🖭 ⑩ ⓞⓞ 𝘝𝘐𝘚𝘈 ᴊᴄʙ. ⅗
LY z
Meals (Pub-rest, dinner only) a la carte approx. 36 ♀ – ⊐ 15 – **85 rm** 220/270.

Seven One Seven 🌸 without rest, Prinsengracht 717, ✉ 1017 JW, ℰ (0 20) 427 07 17, Fax (0 20) 423 07 17, « Small charming hotel along a picturesque canal », 🔽 – 📼 ⟨⟩. 🖭 ⑩ ⓞⓞ 𝘝𝘐𝘚𝘈 ᴊᴄʙ. ⅗
KY c
8 rm ⊐ 337/405.

Ambassade without rest, Herengracht 341, ✉ 1016 AZ, ℰ (0 20) 555 02 22, *info @ambassade-hotel.nl*, Fax (0 20) 555 02 77, ≼, « Typical 17C terraced houses », 🚲
🕴 🔽. 🖭 ⑩ ⓞⓞ 𝘝𝘐𝘚𝘈
KX x
⊐ 14 – **52 rm** 152/180, 7 suites.

Estheréa without rest, Singel 305, ✉ 1012 WJ, ℰ (0 20) 624 51 46, *estherea@xs4all.nl*, Fax (0 20) 623 90 01 – 🕴 ↩ 📼. 🖭 ⑩ ⓞⓞ 𝘝𝘐𝘚𝘈 ᴊᴄʙ. ⅗
KX y
⊐ 14 – **71 rm** 207/243.

Inntel Ⓜ without rest, Nieuwezijdskolk 19, ✉ 1012 PV, ℰ (0 20) 530 18 18, *infoam sterdam@hotelinntel.com*, Fax (0 20) 422 19 19 – 🕴 ↩ 🛏 📼 ⟨⟩. 🖭 ⑩ ⓞⓞ 𝘝𝘐𝘚𝘈 ᴊᴄʙ
⊐ 16 – **236 rm** 190/270.
LVX a

Tulip Inn Art Ⓜ, Spaarndammerdijk 302 (Westerpark), ✉ 1013 ZX, ℰ (0 20) 410 96 70, *info@tulipinnart.nl*, Fax (0 20) 681 08 02, 🍴, « Permanent exhibition of modern paintings by local artists » – 🕴 ↩ 🛏 📼 ⟨⟩ – ⚑ 25. 🖭 ⑩ ⓞⓞ 𝘝𝘐𝘚𝘈. ⅗
Meals Lunch 19 – a la carte 22/37 – ⊐ 13 – **130 rm** 175.

Schiller, Rembrandtsplein 26, ✉ 1017 CV, ℰ (0 20) 554 07 00, *sales@gtschiller.gold entulip.nl*, Fax (0 20) 624 00 98, 🍴 – 🕴 ↩ 📼. 🖭 ⑩ ⓞⓞ 𝘝𝘐𝘚𝘈 ᴊᴄʙ. ⅗ rm
LY x
Meals (Brasserie, open until 11 p.m.) a la carte 34/41 – ⊐ 15 – **91 rm** 180/270, 1 suite.

Caransa without rest, Rembrandtsplein 19, ✉ 1017 CT, ℰ (0 20) 554 08 00, *sales@g tcaransa.goldentulip.nl*, Fax (0 20) 622 27 73 – 🕴 ↩ 📼 – ⚑ 25-140. 🖭 ⑩ ⓞⓞ 𝘝𝘐𝘚𝘈 ᴊᴄʙ. ⅗
LY v
⊐ 15 – **66 rm** 180/270.

Dikker and Thijs Fenice without rest, Prinsengracht 444, ✉ 1017 KE, ℰ (0 20) 620 12 12, *info@dtfh.nl*, Fax (0 20) 625 89 86, 🔽 – 🕴 📼. 🖭 ⑩ ⓞⓞ 𝘝𝘐𝘚𝘈 ᴊᴄʙ KY v
42 rm ⊐ 145/345.

Eden, Amstel 144, ✉ 1017 AE, ℰ (0 20) 530 78 78, *info.eden@edenhotelgroup.com*, Fax (0 20) 623 32 69, 🔽 – 🕴 ↩ 📼 ⟨⟩. 🖭 ⑩ ⓞⓞ 𝘝𝘐𝘚𝘈 ᴊᴄʙ. ⅗
LY r
Meals (Pub rest) 23/34 ♀ – ⊐ 14 – **340 rm** 148/275.

Mercure Arthur Frommer without rest, Noorderstraat 46, ✉ 1017 TV, ℰ (0 20) 622 03 28, *h1032@accor-hotels.com*, Fax (0 20) 620 32 08 – 🕴 ↩ 🛏 📼 ⟨⟩. ℙ. 🖭 ⑩ ⓞⓞ 𝘝𝘐𝘚𝘈 ᴊᴄʙ
LYZ j
⊐ 13 – **90 rm** 130/148.

De Compagnie without rest, Vijzelstraat 49, ✉ 1017 HE, ℰ (0 20) 530 62 00, *info @compagnie-hotel.nl*, Fax (0 20) 530 62 99 – 🕴 📼. 🖭 ⑩ ⓞⓞ 𝘝𝘐𝘚𝘈 ᴊᴄʙ. ⅗
LY g
⊐ 13 – **74 rm** ⊐ 152/191.

City Center without rest, N.Z. Voorburgwal 50, ✉ 1012 SC, ℰ (0 20) 422 00 11, *info @ams.nl*, Fax (0 20) 420 03 57, 🚲 – 🕴 ↩ 📼. 🖭 ⑩ ⓞⓞ 𝘝𝘐𝘚𝘈. ⅗
LV f
106 rm ⊐ 149/160.

Canal House 🌸 without rest, Keizersgracht 148, ✉ 1015 CX, ℰ (0 20) 622 51 82, *info@canalhouse.nl*, Fax (0 20) 624 13 17, « Antique furniture » – 🕴. ⑩ ⓞⓞ 𝘝𝘐𝘚𝘈 ᴊᴄʙ. ⅗
KV k
26 rm ⊐ 150/180.

die Port van Cleve, N.Z. Voorburgwal 178, ✉ 1012 SJ, ℰ (0 20) 624 48 60, *hoteli nfo@dieportvancleve.com*, Fax (0 20) 622 02 40 – 🕴 ↩, 🛏 rest, 📼 – ⚑ 40. 🖭 ⑩ ⓞⓞ 𝘝𝘐𝘚𝘈 ᴊᴄʙ. ⅗ rm
KX w
Meals (Brasserie) Lunch 19 – a la carte 27/58 – ⊐ 15 – **119 rm** 195, 1 suite.

Amsterdam, Damrak 93, ✉ 1012 LP, ℰ (0 20) 555 06 66, *info@hotelamsterdam.nl*, Fax (0 20) 620 47 16 – 🕴 ↩ 🛏 📼. 🖭 ⑩ ⓞⓞ 𝘝𝘐𝘚𝘈 ᴊᴄʙ. ⅗ rest
LX s
Meals **De Roode Leeuw** (Partly Dutch regional cooking) Lunch 16 – 25/35 ♀ – ⊐ 15 – **79 rm** 180/200.

Tulip Inn, Spuistraat 288, ⊠ 1012 VX, 𝒫 (0 20) 420 45 45, *sales@tiamsterdam.gold entulip.nl, Fax (0 20) 420 43 00,* 🛄 – |⚑| ⚑ 📺 ⬩ ⇔. 🅰🅴 🅞 🄼🄾 *VISA* 🄹🄲🄱. ⅍ KX **g**
Meals (Pub rest., partly Italian cuisine) a la carte approx. 34 – ⊒ 14 – **209 rm** 155/195.

Rembrandt without rest, Herengracht 255, ⊠ 1016 BJ, 𝒫 (0 20) 622 17 27, *info@r embrandtresidence.nl, Fax (0 20) 625 06 30,* 🛄 – |⚑| ⚑ 📺 – 🄴 25. 🅰🅴 🅞 🄼🄾 *VISA*. ⅍
111 rm ⊑ 145/175. KX **t**

Lancaster without rest, Plantage Middenlaan 48, ⊠ 1018 DH, 𝒫 (0 20) 535 68 88, *info.lan casterhotel@ edenhotelgroup.com, Fax (0 20) 535 68 89* – |⚑| 📺. 🅰🅴 🅞 🄼🄾 *VISA* 🄹🄲🄱. ⅍
⊑ 14 – **93 rm** 150/164. MY **e**

Wiechmann without rest, Prinsengracht 328, ⊠ 1016 HX, 𝒫 (0 20) 626 33 21,
Fax (0 20) 626 89 62 – 📺. 🄼🄾 *VISA*. ⅍ KX **d**
37 rm ⊑ 70/135.

🍴🍴🍴🍴 **La Rive** - Hotel Amstel, Prof. Tulpplein 1, ⊠ 1018 GX, 𝒫 (0 20) 622 60 60, *maikel_gi*
❀❀ *nsheumer@interconti.com, Fax (0 20) 622 58 08,* ≤, 🍽, « Amstel-side setting », 🛄 – ▤
🄿. 🅰🅴 🅞 🄼🄾 *VISA*. ⅍ MZ **a**
closed 22 July-11 August, 31 December-5 January, Saturday lunch and Sunday – **Meals**
Lunch 35 – 65/95, – a la carte 68/83 ♀.
Spec. Croquettes de morue, pomme de terre et huîtres belons aux poireaux et caviar
(October-April). Turbot et truffe enrobés de pommes de terre, blettes et léger jus de veau.
Gâteau chaud au chocolat pur, glace à l'anis étoilé.

🍴🍴🍴🍴 **Excelsior** - Hotel de l'Europe, Nieuwe Doelenstraat 2, ⊠ 1012 CP, 𝒫 (0 20) 531 17 77,
hotel@leurope.nl, Fax (0 20) 531 17 78, 🍽, Open until 11 p.m., « Amstel-side terrace with
≤ Mint Tower (Munttoren) », 🛄 – ▤ 🄿. 🅰🅴 🅞 🄼🄾 *VISA* 🄹🄲🄱 LY **c**
closed 1 to 7 January and lunch Saturday and Sunday October-Easter – **Meals** Lunch 41 –
a la carte 62/89 ♀.

🍴🍴🍴 **Vermeer** - Hotel Barbizon Palace, Prins Hendrikkade 59, ⊠ 1012 AD, 𝒫 (0 20)
❀ 556 48 85, *vermeer@gtbpalace.goldentulip.nl, Fax (0 20) 556 48 58,* 🛄 – ▤ 🄿. 🅰🅴 🅞 🄼🄾
VISA 🄹🄲🄱. ⅍ LV **d**
closed 14 July-12 August, 26 December-6 January, Saturday lunch and Sunday – **Meals**
Lunch 30 – 60, a la carte 64/77
Spec. St-Jacques à l'avocat et beurre d'oranges. Turbot en croûte d'herbes et ravioli au
céleri. Bombe glacée à l'ananas grillé

🍴🍴🍴 **Christophe** (Royer), Leliegracht 46, ⊠ 1015 DH, 𝒫 (0 20) 625 08 07, *info@christop*
❀ *he.nl, Fax (0 20) 638 91 32* – ▤. 🅰🅴 🅞 🄼🄾 *VISA* KVX **c**
closed 22 December-6 January, Sunday and Monday – **Meals** (dinner only) 43/62, a la carte
approx. 67 ♀
Spec. Brochette de St-Jacques et merguez, légumes marinés au curry. Homard rôti à l'ail
doux. Pigeonneau rôti en bécasse.

🍴🍴🍴 **Dynasty,** Reguliersdwarsstraat 30, ⊠ 1017 BM, 𝒫 (0 20) 626 84 00, 🍽, Oriental cuisine, open until 11 p.m. « Terrace » – ▤. 🅰🅴 🅞 🄼🄾 *VISA*. ⅍ KY **q**
closed 27 December-27 January and Tuesday – **Meals** (dinner only until 11 p.m.) a la carte
32/45.

🍴🍴 **d'Vijff Vlieghen,** Spuistraat 294 (by Vlieghendesteeg), ⊠ 1012 VX, 𝒫 (0 20)
530 40 60, *restaurants@ d-vijfvlieghen.com, Fax (0 20) 623 64 04,* 🍽, « Suite of intimate
dining rooms in a rustic Dutch style in a 17C building », 🛄 – 🅰🅴 🅞 🄼🄾 *VISA* 🄹🄲🄱. ⅍ KX **p**
closed 25 December-1 January – **Meals** (dinner only) a la carte approx. 52. KX **p**

🍴🍴 **Café Roux** - Hotel The Grand Sofitel Demeure, O.Z. Voorburgwal 197, ⊠ 1012 EX,
🖐 𝒫 (0 20) 555 35 60, *caferoux@thegrand.nl, Fax (0 20) 555 32 22,* 🍽 – ▤ 🄿. 🅰🅴 🅞 🄼🄾
VISA 🄹🄲🄱. ⅍ LX **b**
Meals 30/45 ♀.

🍴🍴 **Het Tuynhuys,** Reguliersdwarsstraat 28, ⊠ 1017 BM, 𝒫 (0 20) 627 66 03, *Fax (0 20)*
423 59 99, 🍽, « Terrace » – ▤. 🅰🅴 🅞 🄼🄾 *VISA* 🄹🄲🄱 KY **q**
Meals Lunch 27 – a la carte 38/49.

🍴🍴 **Le Pêcheur,** Reguliersdwarsstraat 32, ⊠ 1017 BM, 𝒫 (0 20) 624 31 21, *Fax (0 20)*
624 31 21, 🍽, Seafood – 🅰🅴 🅞 🄼🄾 *VISA* 🄹🄲🄱. ⅍ KY **w**
closed Sunday – **Meals** Lunch 29 – a la carte 33/41.

🍴🍴 **Indrapura,** Rembrandtplein 42, ⊠ 1017 CV, 𝒫 (0 20) 623 73 29, *info@indrapura.nl,*
Fax (0 20) 624 90 78, Indonesian cuisine – ▤. 🅰🅴 🅞 🄼🄾 *VISA* 🄹🄲🄱. ⅍ LY **h**
closed 31 December – **Meals** (dinner only) 24/37 ♀.

🍴🍴 **Manchurian,** Leidseplein 10a, ⊠ 1017 PT, 𝒫 (0 20) 623 13 30, *Fax (0 20) 626 21 05,*
Oriental cuisine – ▤. 🅰🅴 🅞 🄼🄾 *VISA* 🄹🄲🄱. ⅍ KY **x**
closed 30 April and 31 December – **Meals** a la carte approx. 33.

🍴🍴 **Sichuan Food,** Reguliersdwarsstraat 35, ⊠ 1017 BK, 𝒫 (0 20) 626 93 27, *Fax (0 20)*
❀ 627 72 81, Chinese cuisine – ▤. 🅰🅴 🅞 🄼🄾 *VISA*. ⅍ KY **u**
closed 31 December – **Meals** (dinner only, booking essential) 28/36, a la carte 37/63
Spec. Dim Sum. Canard laqué à la pékinoise. Huîtres sautées maison.

NETHERLANDS

XX **Hosokawa,** Max Euweplein 22, ⊠ 1017 MB, 𝒫 (0 20) 638 80 86, *info@hosokawa.nl*, *Fax (0 20) 638 22 19*, Japanese cuisine with Teppan-Yaki – AE ① ⓞⓞ VISA JCB. ※
KY a
closed last week July-first 2 weeks August – **Meals** (dinner only) a la carte 49/66.

XX **Van Vlaanderen** (Philippart), Weteringschans 175, ⊠ 1017 XD, 𝒫 (0 20) 622 82 92, ✿ 🖀, ⏸ – 🍽. AE ⓞⓞ VISA
KZ k
closed 30 June-22July, 29 December-6 January, Sunday and Monday – **Meals** (dinner only, booking essential) 32/39, a la carte 57/70
Spec. Poularde fermière au foie gras et à la truffe. Turbot au four aux salsifis et béarnaise. Compote de coings, glace vanille et pain perdu.

XX **Takens,** Runstraat 17d, ⊠ 1016 GJ, 𝒫 (0 20) 627 06 18, *Fax (0 20) 624 28 61*, Open until 11 p.m. – AE ① ⓞⓞ VISA
KX s
closed 25 December-5 January – **Meals** (lunch by arrangement) a la carte approx. 43 ⬩.

XX **Breitner,** Amstel 212, ⊠ 1017 AH, 𝒫 (0 20) 627 78 79, *Fax (0 20) 330 29 98* – AE ① ⓞⓞ VISA. ※
.LY p
closed 23 December-2 January and Sunday – **Meals** (dinner only) a la carte 42/56.

XX **d'theeboom,** Singel 210, ⊠ 1016 AB, 𝒫 (0 20) 623 84 20, *theeboom@xs4all.nl*, *Fax (0 20) 421 25 12*, ✿ – AE ① ⓞⓞ VISA JCB
KX b
closed 24 December-5 January, Sunday and lunch Monday and Saturday – **Meals** 30/35.

XX **Oesterbar,** Leidseplein 10, ⊠ 1017 PT, 𝒫 (0 20) 623 29 88, *Fax (0 20) 623 21 99*, Seafood, open until midnight – 🍽. AE ① ⓞⓞ VISA. ※
KY x
closed 25, 26 and 31 December – **Meals** *Lunch 30* – a la carte 48/60.

X **Bordewijk,** Noordermarkt 7, ⊠ 1015 MV, 𝒫 (0 20) 624 38 99, *Fax (0 20) 420 66 03*, « Fashionable Amsterdam atmosphere » – AE ① ⓞⓞ VISA. ※
KV a
closed mid July-early August, 27 December-4 January and Monday – **Meals** (dinner only) 33/45 ⬩.

X **De Gouden Reael,** Zandhoek 14, ⊠ 1013 KT, 𝒫 (0 20) 623 38 83, ✿, « 17C house on old harbour site », ⏸ – AE ① ⓞⓞ VISA
closed Sunday and Bank Holidays – **Meals** (dinner only until 11 p.m.) 30/34 ⬩.

X **Haesje Claes,** Spuistraat 275, ⊠ 1012 VR, 𝒫 (0 20) 624 99 98, *info@haesjeclaes.nl*, *Fax (0 20) 627 48 17*, ✿, « Amsterdam atmosphere » – 🍽. AE ① ⓞⓞ VISA JCB. ※
Meals 18/27.
KX f

X **Entresol,** Geldersekade 29, ⊠ 1011 EJ, 𝒫 (0 20) 623 79 12, *entresol@chello.nl* – 🍽. ⓞⓞ VISA
LX t
closed Monday, Tuesday and Bank Holidays – **Meals** (dinner only) a la carte approx. 39.

Rijksmuseum (Vondelpark)

🏨🏨 **Marriott,** Stadhouderskade 12, ⊠ 1054 ES, 𝒫 (0 20) 607 55 55, *mhrs.amsnt.market ing.assistant@marriott.com*, *Fax (0 20) 607 55 11*, ↥, 🛌, 🚴 – 🔌 ✦ 🍽 📺 ₺ 🚗 – 🔏 25-450. AE ① ⓞⓞ VISA. ※ rest
JY f
Meals (Light meals served until 11 p.m.) – ⬩ 18 – **387 rm** 265/315, 5 suites.

🏨 **Golden Tulip Centre,** Stadhouderskade 7, ⊠ 1054 ES, 𝒫 (0 20) 685 13 51, *info@g tacentre.goldentulip.nl*, *Fax (0 20) 685 16 11*, ↥, 🛌 – 🔌 ✦ 🍽 📺 ₺ – 🔏 25-200. AE ① ⓞⓞ VISA JCB. ※ rest
JY p
Meals (Open until 1 a.m.) a la carte 32/43 – **Bice** (*closed Saturday lunch and Sunday*) (Italian cuisine, open until 11 p.m.) (dinner only July-August) *Lunch 25* – a la carte approx. 40 – ⬩ 19 – **227 rm** 290/320, 2 suites.

🏨 **Memphis** without rest, De Lairessestraat 87, ⊠ 1071 NX, 𝒫 (0 20) 673 31 41, *info @memphishotel.nl*, *Fax (0 20) 673 73 12*, ↥ – 🔌 ✦ 📺 – 🔏 40. AE ① ⓞⓞ VISA JCB
⬩ 18 – **74 rm** 195/285.

🏨 **Jan Luyken** without rest, Jan Luykenstraat 58, ⊠ 1071 CS, 𝒫 (0 20) 573 07 30, *jan-l uyken@bilderberg.nl*, *Fax (0 20) 676 38 41*, 🚴 – 🔌 ✦ 🍽 📺. AE ① ⓞⓞ VISA JCB. ※
⬩ 14 – **62 rm** 225/245.
JZ m

🏨 **Toro** ⚘ without rest, Koningslaan 64, ⊠ 1075 AG, 𝒫 (0 20) 673 72 23, *Fax (0 20) 675 00 31*, « Waterside terrace, overlooking the park » – 🔌 📺. AE ① ⓞⓞ VISA JCB.
⬩ 14 – **22 rm** 173/185.

🏨 **Vondel** (annex) without rest, Vondelstraat 28, ⊠ 1054 GE, 𝒫 (0 20) 612 01 20, *vond el@bhs.nl*, *Fax (0 20) 685 43 21*, « Opulent interior », ✿ – 🔌 📺. AE ① ⓞⓞ VISA JCB
⬩ 15 – **70 rm** 210.
JY m

🏨 **Lairesse** without rest, De Lairessestraat 7, ⊠ 1071 NR, 𝒫 (0 20) 671 95 96, *info@a ms.nl*, *Fax (0 20) 671 17 56* – 🔌 📺. AE ① ⓞⓞ VISA. ※
34 rm ⬩ 172/190.

🏨 **Hofpark and Résidence,** Koninginneweg 34, ⊠ 1075 CZ, 𝒫 (0 20) 664 61 11, *info @ams.nl*, *Fax (0 20) 573 71 30* – 🔌 ✦ 🍽 📺 – 🔏 40. AE ① ⓞⓞ VISA. ※
Meals (dinner only) a la carte approx. 33 – **142 rm** ⬩ 140/155, 1 suite.

Omega without rest, Jacob Obrechtstraat 33, ⊠ 1071 KG, ℘ (0 20) 664 51 82, *info @ams.nl, Fax (0 20) 664 08 09* – |⋮| ⅍ ▤ ☎ ﺔ ◑ ⑳ 𝗩𝗜𝗦𝗔. ⅍
⌐ 16 – **32 rm** 140/205.

Fita without rest, Jan Luykenstraat 37, ⊠ 1071 CL, ℘ (0 20) 679 09 76, *info@fita.nl, Fax (0 20) 664 39 69* – |⋮| ☎ ﺔ ◑ ⑳ 𝗩𝗜𝗦𝗔.   JZ s
closed 16 December-16 January – **16 rm** ⌐ 86/134.

Borgmann Villa ⊗ without rest, Koningslaan 48, ⊠ 1075 AE, ℘ (0 20) 673 52 52, *borgmann@xs4all.nl, Fax (0 20) 676 25 80,* ⚲ – |⋮| ☎ ﺔ ◑ ⑳ 𝗩𝗜𝗦𝗔 𝗝𝗖𝗕. ⅍
15 rm ⌐ 95/145.

De Filosoof ⊗ without rest, Anna van den Vondelstraat 6, ⊠ 1054 GZ, ℘ (0 20) 683 30 13, *reservations@hotelfilosoof.nl, Fax (0 20) 685 37 50,* « Decor inspired by cultural and philosophical themes » – |⋮| ☎ – ☕ 25. ﺔ ◑ ⑳ 𝗩𝗜𝗦𝗔. ⅍
27 rm ⌐ 122/135.

※※※ **Vossius** (Kranenborg), Hobbemastraat 2, ⊠ 1071 7A, ℘ (0 20) 557 41 00, *Fax (0 20) ⅏⅏⅏ 557 41 41* – ☕ 25. ﺔ ◑ ⑳ 𝗩𝗜𝗦𝗔. ⅍   KY z
✿   *closed 29 July-13 August, 31 December-8 January and Sunday* – **Meals** *Lunch* 44 – 75, a la carte approx. 93 ⅀
Spec. Sot-l'y-laisse crème de foie gras à la truffe blanche. St-Pierre clouté à l'anguille fumée, jus d'anchois aux câpres. Moelleux aux chocolat et abricots.

※※※ **Radèn Mas,** Stadhouderskade 6, ⊠ 1054 ES, ℘ (0 20) 685 40 41, *Fax (0 20) 685 39 81,* Indonesian cuisine – ▤. ﺔ ◑ ⑳ 𝗩𝗜𝗦𝗔 𝗝𝗖𝗕. ⅍   JY k
closed 30 April and 31 December – **Meals** (dinner only until 11 p.m.) a la carte 35/44.

※※ **Le Garage,** Ruysdaelstraat 54, ⊠ 1071 XE, ℘ (0 20) 679 71 76, *Fax (0 20) 662 22 49,*
☺ Open until 1 a.m., « Artistic atmosphere in a contemporary and cosmopolitan brasserie »
– ▤. ﺔ ◑ ⑳ 𝗩𝗜𝗦𝗔
closed last 2 weeks July-first week August and Bank Holidays – **Meals** *Lunch* 25 – 27/40 ⅀.

※※ **Keyzer,** Van Baerlestraat 96, ⊠ 1071 BB, ℘ (0 20) 671 14 41, *Fax (0 20) 673 73 53,*
۞, Pub rest, open until 11.30 p.m., « Amsterdam atmosphere » – ﺔ ◑ ⑳ 𝗩𝗜𝗦𝗔. ⅍
Meals 34.

※ **Spring,** Willemsparkweg 177, ⊠ 1071 GZ, ℘ (0 20) 675 44 21, *Fax (0 20) 676 94 14,* ۞
– ▤. ﺔ ◑ ⑳ 𝗩𝗜𝗦𝗔. ⅍ rest
closed Sunday – **Meals** *Lunch* 25 – a la carte 40/60.

※ **Brasserie van Baerle,** Van Baerlestraat 158, ⊠ 1071 BG, ℘ (0 20) 679 15 32,
Fax (0 20) 671 71 96, ۞, Pub rest, open until 11 p.m. – ﺔ ◑ ⑳ 𝗩𝗜𝗦𝗔
closed 25 December-1 January – **Meals** *Lunch* 27 – 31 ⅀.

South and West Quarters

🏨🏨🏨 **Okura** Ⓜ ⊗, Ferdinand Bolstraat 333, ⊠ 1072 LH, ℘ (0 20) 678 71 11, *sales@okura.nl, Fax (0 20) 671 23 44,* ≼, « Restaurant on the 23th floor vith ≼ town », ℉⅊, ⋑s, ▦, ▣
– |⋮| ⅍ ▤ ☎ ⚭ ⇔ P – ☕ 25-1200. ﺔ ◑ ⑳ 𝗩𝗜𝗦𝗔 𝗝𝗖𝗕. ⅍
Meals see *Yamazato* below – *Ciel Bleu* (dinner only) 45/65 ⅀ – *Sazanka* (Japanese cuisine with Teppan-Yaki) 45/73 ⅀ – *Brasserie Le Camelia* (Open until 11 p.m.) a la carte 37/66
⅀ – ⌐ 25 – **358 rm** 320/390, 12 suites.

🏨🏨 **Hilton** Ⓜ. Apollolaan 138, ⊠ 1077 BG, ℘ (0 20) 710 60 00, *cb_amsterdam@hilton.com, Fax (0 20) 710 90 00,* ⚖s, « Canalside garden and terraces », ℉⅊, ⋑s, ▣ – |⋮| ⅍⊨ ▤ ☎
⚭ P – ☕ 25-550. ﺔ ◑ ⑳ 𝗩𝗜𝗦𝗔. ⅍ rest
Meals *Roberto's* (Italian cuisine with buffet) 31 – ⌐ 16 – **267 rm** 420/480, 4 suites.

🏨🏨 **Bilderberg Garden** Ⓜ, Dijsselhofplantsoen 7, ⊠ 1077 BJ, ℘ (0 20) 570 56 00, *gard en@bilderberg.nl, Fax (0 20) 570 56 54* – |⋮| ⅍⊨ ▤ ☎ P – ☕ 25-150. ﺔ ◑ ⑳ 𝗩𝗜𝗦𝗔
𝗝𝗖𝗕
Meals see *Mangerie De Kersentuin* below – ⌐ 19 – **122 rm** 279/309, 2 suites.

🏨🏨 **Le Meridien Apollo,** Apollolaan 2, ⊠ 1077 BA, ℘ (0 20) 673 59 22, *info@meridien.nl, Fax (0 20) 570 57 44,* « Terrace with ≼ canal », ℉⅊, ⚲, ▣ – |⋮| ⅍⊨ ▤ ☎ P – ☕ 25-200.
ﺔ ◑ ⑳ 𝗩𝗜𝗦𝗔 𝗝𝗖𝗕. ⅍
Meals see *La Sirène* below – ⌐ 20 – **217 rm** 305/440, 2 suites.

🏨🏨 **Mercure a/d Amstel,** Joan Muyskenweg 10, ⊠ 1096 CJ, ℘ (0 20) 665 81 81, *h1244@accor-hotels.com, Fax (0 20) 694 87 35,* ℉⅊, ⋑s, ▣ – |⋮| ⅍⊨ ▤ ☎ ⚭ P – ☕ 25-450. ﺔ ◑ ⑳ 𝗩𝗜𝗦𝗔. ⅍
Meals *(closed 1 January and Sunday) Lunch* 23 – 30/43 ⅀ – ⌐ 16 – **178 rm** 240.

※※ **Aujourd'hui,** C. Krusemanstraat 15, ⊠ 1075 NB, ℘ (0 20) 679 08 77, *aujourdhui@w xs.nl, Fax (0 20) 676 76 27,* ۞ – ﺔ ◑ ⑳ 𝗩𝗜𝗦𝗔 𝗝𝗖𝗕
closed 22 December-1 January, Saturday lunch and Sunday – **Meals** *Lunch* 30 – 43.

※※ **Mangerie De Kersentuin** - Hotel Bilderberg Garden, Dijsselhofplantsoen 7, ⊠ 1077 BJ, ℘ (0 20) 570 56 00, *garden@bilderberg.nl, Fax (0 20) 570 56 54,* ۞ – ▤
P. ﺔ ◑ ⑳ 𝗩𝗜𝗦𝗔 𝗝𝗖𝗕. ⅍
closed 31 December-1 January, Saturday lunch and Sunday – **Meals** *Lunch* 28 – 36/41 ⅀.

121

XX **La Sirène** - Hotel Le Méridien Apollo, Apollolaan 2, ⊠ 1077 BA, ℰ (0 20) 673 59 22, *info@meridien.nl, Fax (0 20) 570 57 44*, ≤, Seafood, « Canaside terrace » – ▤ 🅿 🆎 ⓪ 🔞 VISA JCB. 🕸
Meals à la carte 39/53.

XX **visaandeschelde,** Scheldeplein 4, ⊠ 1078 GR, ℰ (0 20) 675 15 83, *info@visaandes chelde.nl, Fax (0 20) 670 46 17,* �, Seafood, open until 11 p.m. – ▤. 🆎 🔞 VISA JCB. 🕸
closed 23 December-5 January, Saturday lunch and Sunday – **Meals** Lunch 27 – à la carte approx. 48 🗜.

XX **Yamazato** - Hotel Okura, Ferdinand Bolstraat 333, ⊠ 1072 LH, ℰ (0 20) 678 83 51, *sales*
🟢 *@okura.nl, Fax (0 20) 678 77 88,* Japanese cuisine, 🔟 – ▤ 🅿 🆎 ⓪ 🔞 VISA JCB. 🕸
Meals Lunch 37 – 53/65, – à la carte approx. 70 🗜
Spec. Tempura moriawase (mixed Tempura). Gyu rosu shabu-shabu (boiled beef). Miso-wan (soup).

X **Blender,** Van der Palmkade 16, ⊠ 1051 RE, ℰ (0 20) 486 98 60, *Fax (0 20) 486 98 54,* �, « Trendy ambience » – 🆎 🔞 VISA   JV k
closed 1 January – **Meals** (dinner only until 11 p.m.) à la carte approx. 39 🗜.

X **Le Hollandais,** Amsteldijk 41, ⊠ 1074 HV, ℰ (0 20) 679 12 48, *lehollandais@planet.nl*
🟢 – ▤. 🔞 VISA JCB
closed Sunday – **Meals** (dinner only) 29.

X **Pakistan,** Scheldestraat 100, ⊠ 1078 GP, ℰ (0 20) 675 39 76, *Fax (0 20) 675 39 76,*
🟢 Indian cuisine – 🆎 ⓪ 🔞 VISA
Meals (dinner only until 11 p.m.) 19/32.

Buitenveldert (RAI)

🏠 **Holiday Inn,** De Boelelaan 2, ⊠ 1083 HJ, ℰ (0 20) 646 23 00, *sales@holidayinn.nl, Fax (0 20) 646 47 90,* 🎣 – 📶 ⇔ ▤ 📺 🕭 🅿 – 🏛 25-350. 🆎 ⓪ 🔞 VISA JCB. 🕸 rest
Meals (American cuisine, open until 11 p.m.) à la carte 38/51 – ⊃ 20 – **256 rm** 255/405, 2 suites.

🏠 **Novotel,** Europaboulevard 10, ⊠ 1083 AD, ℰ (0 20) 541 11 23, *h0515-5a@accor-h otels.com, Fax (0 20) 642 40 85,* 🚲 – 📶 ⇔ ▤ 📺 🕭 🅿 – 🏛 25-225. 🆎 ⓪ 🔞 VISA JCB. 🕸 rest
Meals (Pub rest, open until midnight) Lunch 23 – à la carte 22/37 🗜 – ⊃ 16 – **611 rm** 185/205.

🏠 **Rosarium,** Amstelpark 1, ⊠ 1083 HZ, ℰ (0 20) 644 40 85, *info@rosarium.net, Fax (0 20) 646 60 04,* ≤, �, « Rotunda in park » – 🅿 – 🏛 25-250. *closed Saturday and Sunday* – **Meals** Lunch 34 – 41/53.

Southeast Quarter

X **De Kas,** Kamerlingh Onneslaan 3, ⊠ 1097 DE, ℰ (0 20) 462 45 62, *info@restaurantd ekas.nl, Fax (0 20) 462 45 63,* �, « Former greenhouse used for the city's gardening, vegetable garden » – 🆎 ⓪ 🔞 VISA JCB. 🕸
closed 23 December-9 January, Saturday lunch, Sunday and Bank Holidays – **Meals** (only one menu) 30.

by motorway The Hague (A 4)

🏠 **Mercure Airport,** Oude Haagseweg 20 (exit ① Sloten), ⊠ 1066 BW, ℰ (0 20) 617 90 05, *h1315-gm@accor-hotels.com, Fax (0 20) 615 90 27* – 📶 ⇔ ▤ 📺 🕭 🅿 – 🏛 25-300. 🆎 ⓪ 🔞 VISA. 🕸
Meals Lunch 18 – à la carte approx. 38 – ⊃ 16 – **152 rm** 160/215.

Environs

at Amstelveen South : 11 km. pop. 77 623.
🛈 Thomas Cookstraat 1, ⊠ 1181 ZS, ℰ (0 20) 441 55 45, *Fax (0 20) 647 19 66*

🏠 **Grand Hotel,** Bovenkerkerweg 81 (South : 2,5 km direction Uithoorn), ⊠ 1187 XC, ℰ (0 20) 645 55 58, *info@grand-hotel-amstelveen.nl, Fax (0 20) 641 21 21,* 🍴 – 📶 ⇔ ▤ 📺 🕭 🅿 🆎 ⓪ 🔞 VISA. 🕸
Meals see *Résidence Fontaine Royale* below, shuttle service – ⊃ 13 – **81 rm** 148/168, 10 suites.

XXX **De Jonge Dikkert,** Amsterdamseweg 104a, ⊠ 1182 HG, ℰ (0 20) 643 33 33, *info*
🟢 *@jongedikkert.nl, Fax (0 20) 645 91 62,* 🌣, « 17C windmill » – 🅿 🆎 ⓪ 🔞 VISA
closed 24 and 31 December and 1 January – **Meals** 31/45 🗜.

XX **Résidence Fontaine Royale** - Grand Hotel, Dr Willem Dreesweg 1 (South : 2 km, direction Uithoorn), ⊠ 1185 VA, ℰ (0 20) 640 15 01, *reservering@fontaine.royale.nl, Fax (0 20) 640 16 61,* 🌣 – 🏛 25-225. 🆎 ⓪ 🔞 VISA JCB. 🕸
closed Sunday – **Meals** Lunch 26 – 31/54.

XX **Royal San Kong,** Dorpsstraat 57 (Oude Dorp), ⊠ 1182 JC, ℰ (0 20) 647 79 02, *Fax (0 20) 647 78 63,* Chinese cuisine – ▤. 🆎 🔞 VISA JCB
Meals Lunch 13 – 34/61.

at Badhoevedorp Southwest : 15 km Ⓖ Haarlemmermeer pop. 111 155 :

🏠🏠🏠 **Dorint** Ⓜ, Sloterweg 299, ✉ 1171 VB, ℰ (0 20) 658 81 11, info@dha.dorint.nl,
Fax (0 20) 658 81 00, Ⅰゟ, �, ⬛, 🗡, ぬ – |彙| 🏧, 🗏 rm, 🔳 ⅃ 🄿 – 🟰 25-150. 🕰
Ⓞ 🕅 ⒱⒤⒮⒜ ⒿⒸⒷ
Meals (closed Saturday and Sunday) Lunch 20 – a la carte 28/37 ⅄ – ➯ 17 – **211 rm** 217,
9 suites.

🍴🍴 **De Herbergh** with rm, Sloterweg 259, ✉ 1171 CP, ℰ (0 20) 659 26 00, postbus@h
otelherbergh.demon.nl, Fax (0 20) 659 83 90, 🏡 – 🗏 rest, 🔳 🄿 – 🟰 35. 🕰 Ⓞ 🕅 ⒱⒤⒮⒜.
🦐 rm
Meals Lunch 24 – 36 ⅄ – ➯ 22 – **24 rm** 102/113.

at Ouderkerk aan de Amstel South : 10 km Ⓖ Amstelveen pop. 77 623 :

🍴🍴🍴 **Paardenburg,** Amstelzijde 55, ✉ 1184 TZ, ℰ (0 20) 496 12 10, Fax (0 20) 496 40 17,
🏡, « 19C murals, riverside terrace », 🄻 – 🄿 – 🟰 25-200. 🕰 Ⓞ 🕅 ⒱⒤⒮⒜. 🦐
closed 27 December-8 January and Sunday – **Meals** Lunch 31 – a la carte 50/64 ⅄.

🍴🍴 **'t Jagershuis** with rm Amstelzijde 2, ✉ 1184 VA, ℰ (0 20) 496 20 20, info@jager
shuis.com, Fax (0 20) 496 45 41, ≤, 🏡, « Inn with Amstel-side terrace », ぬ, 🄻 – 🗏 🔳
🄿 – 🟰 30. 🕰 Ⓞ 🕅 ⒱⒤⒮⒜. 🦐 rm
closed 29 December-2 January – **Meals** (closed Saturday lunch) Lunch 33 – 47 – ➯ 10 –
12 rm 152/165.

🍴🍴 **Ron Blaauw,** Kerkstraat 56, ✉ 1191 JE, ℰ (0 20) 496 19 43, ron.blaauw@worldonli
ne.nl, Fax (0 20) 496 57 01, 🏡 🕰 Ⓞ 🕅 ⒱⒤⒮⒜ ⒿⒸⒷ
closed 25 and 26 December, 30 December-2 January and Sunday – **Meals** Lunch 34 – a la
carte 56/68 ⅄.

at Schiphol (international airport) Southwest . 15 km Ⓖ Haarlemmermeer pop. 111 155 – Casino,
Schiphol airport - Terminal Centraal ℰ (0 23) 574 05 74, Fax (0 23) 574 05 77 :

🏨🏨🏨 **Sheraton Airport** Ⓜ, Schiphol bd 101, ✉ 1118 BG, ℰ (0 20) 316 43 00, sales_am
sterdam@sheraton.com, Fax (0 20) 316 43 99, Ⅰゟ, �, ⬛ – |彙| 🏧 🗏 🔳 ⅃ 🖧 –
🟰 25-500. 🕰 Ⓞ 🕅 ⒱⒤⒮⒜ ⒿⒸⒷ. 🦐
Meals **Voyager** (Open until 11 p.m.) Lunch 36 – 41 – ➯ 23 – **400 rm** 380, 8 suites.

🏨🏨🏨 **Hilton Schiphol,** Herbergierstraat 1, ✉ 1118 CA, ℰ (0 20) 710 40 00, schiphil@cis
tron.nl, Fax (0 20) 710 40 90, Ⅰゟ, � – |彙| 🏧 🗏 🔳 ⅃ 🄿 – 🟰 25-60. 🕰 Ⓞ 🕅 ⒱⒤⒮⒜
ⒿⒸⒷ. 🦐 rest
Meals **East West** (Partly Asian cuisine, dinner only until 11 p.m.) a la carte 47/66 ⅄ –
Greenhouse (Buffets, open until 11.30 p.m.) 33/37⅄ – ➯ 22 – **278 rm** 320/390, 2 suites.

🏨🏨🏨 **Radisson SAS Airport** Ⓜ 🦐, Boeing Avenue 2 (Rijk), ✉ 1119 PB, ℰ (0 20) 655 31 31,
reservations.amsterdam.airport@radissonsas.com, Fax (0 20) 655 31 00, 🏡, Ⅰゟ, 🚯 – |彙|
🏧 🗏 🔳 ⅃ 🄿 – 🟰 25-600. 🕰 Ⓞ 🕅 ⒱⒤⒮⒜ ⒿⒸⒷ
Meals (Italian cuisine) Lunch 33 – a la carte approx. 43 ⅄ – ➯ 19 – **277 rm** 235/305, 2 suites.

Blokzijl Overijssel Ⓖ Steenwijk pop. 22 656 **210** U 6 and **908** I 3 – 102 km.

🏠 **Kaatje bij de Sluis** 🦐, Brouwerstraat 20, ✉ 8356 DV, ℰ (0 527) 29 18 33, kaatj
❀❀❀ e@planet.nl, Fax (0 527) 29 18 36, ≤, 🏡, « Terrace and garden along an intersection of
canals », ஜ, 🄻 – 🗏 🔳 🄿 🄻 🕰 Ⓞ 🕅 ⒱⒤⒮⒜
closed February, 1 week after Christmas, Monday, Tuesday and Saturday lunch – **Meals**
Lunch 42 – 57/120, a la carte 64/82 – ➯ 17 – **8 rm** 110/143
Spec. Brochette et salade de homard sauce mousseline. Canapé au foie d'oie et tartare
de coquilles St-Jacques. Sandre grillé aux girolles (June-March).

Haarlem Noord-Holland **210** M 8, **211** M 8 and **908** E 4. pop. 148 484 – 20 km.

at Overveen West : 4 km Ⓖ Bloemendaal pop. 16 716 :

🍴🍴🍴🍴 **De Bokkedoorns,** Zeeweg 53 (West : 2 km), ✉ 2051 EB, ℰ (0 23) 526 36 00, bokk
❀❀❀ edoorns@alliance.nl, Fax (0 23) 527 31 43, ≤ lake, 🏡, « Pavilion with design interior surrounded by wooded dunes » – 🗏 🄿 🕰 Ⓞ 🕅 ⒱⒤⒮⒜. 🦐
closed 30 April, 5 and 24 December, 27 December-6 January, Monday and Saturday lunch
– **Meals** Lunch 43 – 57/84, a la carte 61/87 ⅄
Spec. Risotto à la truffe, poulpe et huîtres de Zélande pochées (October-April). Filet de
barbue vapeur, bouillon de carottes au beurre clarifié. St-Jacques grillées au witlof braisé
et jambon (September-March).

Vreeland Utrecht Ⓖ Loenen pop. 8 415 **211** P 9 and **908** G 5 – 22 km.

🍴🍴🍴 **De Nederlanden** (de Wit) 🦐 with rm, Duinkerken 3, ✉ 3633 EM, ℰ (0 294) 23 23 26,
❀❀❀ denederlanden@hetnet.nl, Fax (0 294) 23 14 07, ≤, 🏡, « Vecht-side setting near a typical drawbridge », ஜ, 🄻 – 🗏 rest, 🔳 ⅃ 🟰 30. 🕰 Ⓞ 🕅 ⒱⒤⒮⒜. 🦐
closed last 3 weeks July-first week August, last week December-first week January, Sunday
and Monday – **Meals** (dinner only) 71/89, a la carte 76/93 – ➯ 16 – **7 rm** 148/175
Spec. Thon rôti aux sésames et couscous fumé. Turbot grillé beurre noisette aux amandes
et fenouil. Biscuit soufflé à la vanille, citron vert et marmelade de framboises.

NETHERLANDS

The HAGUE (Den HAAG or 's GRAVENHAGE) Zuid-Holland 🄫🄫🄫 K 10 - ① ② and 🄫🄫🄫
D 5. pop. 441094.

See : Binnenhof★ : The Knight's Room★ (Ridderzaal) JY – Court pool (Hofvijver) ≤★ HJY
– Lange Voorhout★ HJX – Madurodam★★ – Scheveningen★★.

Museums : Mauritshuis★★★ JY – Prince William V art gallery★ (Schilderijengalerij Prins Willem V) HY M² – Panorama Mesdag★ HX – Mesdag★ – Municipal★★ (Gemeentemuseum) –
Bredius★ JY – The seaside sculpture museum★★ (Museum Beelden aan Zee) at Scheveningen.

🅱 Southeast : 5 km at Rijswijk, Delftweg 58, ✉ 2289 AL, ℘ (0 70) 319 24 24, Fax (0 70)
399 50 40 - 🅱 Northeast : 11 km at Wassenaar, Groot Haesebroekseweg 22, ✉ 2243 EC,
℘ (0 70) 517 96 07, Fax (0 70) 514 01 71 and 🅱 Dr Mansveltkade 15, ✉ 2242 TZ,
℘ (0 70) 517 88 99, Fax (0 70) 551 93 02.

✈ Amsterdam-Schiphol Northeast : 37 km ℘ (0 20) 601 91 11, Fax (0 20) 604 14 75
– Rotterdam-Zestienhoven Southeast : 17 km ℘ (0 10) 446 34 44, Fax (0 20) 446 34 99.

🅱 Kon. Julianaplein 30, ✉ 2595 AA, ℘ 0 900-340 35 05, infovvvdenhaag.nl, Fax (0 70)
347 21 02.

Amsterdam 55 – Brussels 182 – Rotterdam 27 – Delft 13.

Plan opposite

Centre

Des Indes, Lange Voorhout 54, ✉ 2514 EG, ℘ (0 70) 361 23 45, hotel_desindes@d
esindes.com, Fax (0 70) 361 23 50, « Late 19C residence » – 📳 📺 🅿 - 🛗 25-75. 🆎 ⓞ
ⓜⓒ 𝖵𝖨𝖲𝖠 𝖩𝖢𝖡. ⅏   JX s
closed July-August – Meals **Le Restaurant** (closed Sunday dinner) Lunch 25 – 35/55 ⴼ –
ⴼ 20 – **71 rm** 250/375, 5 suites.

Crowne Plaza Promenade, van Stolkweg 1, ✉ 2585 JL, ℘ (0 70) 352 51 61, info
@promenadehotel.nl, Fax (0 70) 354 10 46, ≤, ⴼ, « Collection of modern Dutch
paintings », 🅵ⴼ, ⴼ – 📳 ⴼ 📺 🅿 - 🛗 25-400. 🆎 ⓞ ⓜⓒ 𝖵𝖨𝖲𝖠 𝖩𝖢𝖡
Meals **Brasserie Promenade** Lunch 27 – 30 ⴼ – **Trattoria dell'Arte** (Italian cuisine, open
until midnight and July-August dinner only) Lunch 27 – a la carte approx. 40 – ⴼ 21 – **94 rm**
255/270.

Dorint Ⓜ, Johan de Wittlaan 42, ✉ 2517 JR, ℘ (0 70) 416 91 11, info@dhd.dorint.nl,
Fax (0 70) 416 91 00, 🅵ⴼ, ⴼ, ⴼ – 📳 ⴼ, ⴼ rm, 📺 ⴼ ⴼ – 🛗 25-2000. 🆎 ⓞ ⓜⓒ
𝖵𝖨𝖲𝖠 𝖩𝖢𝖡. ⅏
Meals (closed 26 January-2 February, 6 to 24 April and 12 to 15 July) Lunch 28 – a la carte
39/55 ⴼ – ⴼ 16 – **214 rm** 260/320, 2 suites.

Carlton Ambassador Ⓜ ⴼ, Sophialaan 2, ✉ 2514 JP, ℘ (0 70) 363 03 63, amba
ssador@carlton.nl, Fax (0 70) 360 05 35, ⴼ, « Dutch and English style interior » – 📳 ⴼ
ⴼ 📺 🅿 - 🛗 25-150. 🆎 ⓞ ⓜⓒ 𝖵𝖨𝖲𝖠 𝖩𝖢𝖡. ⅏   HX c
Meals **Henricus** Lunch 25 – 30 – ⴼ 17 – **78 rm** 266/288, 1 suite.

Sofitel, Koningin Julianaplein 35, ✉ 2595 AA, ℘ (0 70) 381 49 01, h0755@accor-ho
tels.com, Fax (0 70) 382 59 27 – 📳 ⴼ ⴼ 📺 ⴼ 🅿 - 🛗 25-150. 🆎 ⓞ ⓜⓒ 𝖵𝖨𝖲𝖠 𝖩𝖢𝖡
Meals Lunch 30 – 34 – ⴼ 18 – **143 rm** 210/255.

Bel Air, Johan de Wittlaan 30, ✉ 2517 JR, ℘ (0 70) 352 53 54, info@belairhotel.nl,
Fax (0 70) 352 53 53, ⴼ – 📳 ⴼ, ⴼ rm, 📺 ⴼ 🅿 - 🛗 25-250. 🆎 ⓞ ⓜⓒ 𝖵𝖨𝖲𝖠 𝖩𝖢𝖡
Lunch 16 – a la carte approx. 46 – ⴼ 13 – **348 rm** 180.

Mercure Central, Spui 180, ✉ 2511 BW, ℘ (0 70) 363 67 00, h1317@accor-hotel
s.com, Fax (0 70) 363 93 98 – 📳 ⴼ ⴼ 📺 ⴼ 🅿 - 🛗 25-130. 🆎 ⓞ ⓜⓒ 𝖵𝖨𝖲𝖠 𝖩𝖢𝖡. ⅏
Meals (dinner only) a la carte approx. 38 – ⴼ 13 – **156 rm** 145/180, 3 suites.   JZ v

Corona without rest, Buitenhof 42, ✉ 2513 AH, ℘ (0 70) 363 79 30, info@corona.nl,
Fax (0 70) 361 57 85 – 📳 📺 ⴼ – 🛗 30-100. 🆎 ⓞ ⓜⓒ 𝖵𝖨𝖲𝖠 𝖩𝖢𝖡   HY v
ⴼ 15 – **36 rm** 140/160.

Parkhotel without rest, Molenstraat 53, ✉ 2513 BJ, ℘ (0 70) 362 43 71, reserverin
gen@parkhoteldenhaag.nl, Fax (0 70) 361 45 25 – 📳 📺 – 🛗 25-100. 🆎 ⓞ ⓜⓒ 𝖵𝖨𝖲𝖠 𝖩𝖢𝖡.
⅏   HY a
114 rm ⴼ 125/218.

Novotel, Hofweg 5, ✉ 2511 AA, ℘ (0 70) 364 88 46, h1180@accor-hotels.com,
Fax (0 70) 356 28 89, ⴼ – 📳 ⴼ, ⴼ rest, 📺 ⴼ - 🛗 25-100. 🆎 ⓞ ⓜⓒ 𝖵𝖨𝖲𝖠 𝖩𝖢𝖡. ⅏
Meals Lunch 16 – a la carte 22/32 – ⴼ 14 – **106 rm** 145/150.   HJY e

Royal Dutch Lion, Laan van Meerdervoort 108, ✉ 2517 AS, ℘ (0 70) 360 53 85,
info@royaldutchlion.nl, Fax (0 70) 360 54 07 – 📳 ⴼ 📺 ⴼ 𝖵𝖨𝖲𝖠 𝖩𝖢𝖡. ⅏
Meals (closed 24 December-1 January) Lunch 14 – 22 – ⴼ 13 – **47 rm** 139.

De Hoogwerf, Zijdelaan 20, ✉ 2594 BV, ℘ (0 70) 347 55 14, info@hoogwerf.nl,
Fax (0 70) 381 95 96, ⴼ, « 17C farmhouse, garden » – 🆎 ⓞ ⓜⓒ 𝖵𝖨𝖲𝖠. ⅏
closed Sunday and Bank Holidays – Meals Lunch 27 – 45.

124

DEN HAAG

XX **Calla's** (van der Kleijn), Laan van Roos en Doorn 51a, ⊠ 2514 BC, ℘ (0 70) 345 58 66,
✿ Fax (0 70) 345 57 10 – ⒶⒺ ① ⑩⑨ 𝖵𝖨𝖲𝖠. ⅗⅗ JX u
closed mid July-early August, 25 December-4 January and Monday – **Meals** Lunch 35 –
45/53, – a la carte approx. 80
Spec. Capuccino de céleri-rave au lard et aux truffes. Turbot en soufflé de pommes de
terre aillées. Crêpes farcies glacées et glace vanille.

XX **Saur,** Lange Voorhout 47, ⊠ 2514 EC, ℘ (0 70) 346 25 65, restaurant.saur@12move.nl,
Fax (0 70) 362 13 13, ⅋̂, Seafood – ⒶⒺ ① ⑩⑨ 𝖵𝖨𝖲𝖠 ᴊᴄʙ JX h
closed Sunday and Bank Holidays – **Meals** Lunch 31 – a la carte 47/56 ⅊.

XX **Rousseau,** Van Boetzelaerlaan 134, ⊠ 2581 AX, ℘ (0 70) 355 47 43, ⅋̂ – ⒶⒺ ① ⑩⑨
𝖵𝖨𝖲𝖠
closed 13 to 21 February, 28 July-29 August, 22 December-2 January, Saturday lunch,
Sunday and Monday – **Meals** Lunch 25 – 30/45 ⅊.

XX **Julien,** Vos in Tuinstraat 2a, ⊠ 2514 BX, ℘ (0 70) 365 86 02, info@julien.nl, Fax (0 70)
365 31 47, « Art Deco interior » – ⒶⒺ ① ⑩⑨ 𝖵𝖨𝖲𝖠 JX s
closed first 2 weeks August and Sunday – **Meals** Lunch 22 – 27/32.

XX **The Raffles,** Javastraat 63, ⊠ 2585 AG, ℘ (0 70) 345 85 87, Indonesian cuisine – ▤.
ⒶⒺ ① ⑩⑨ 𝖵𝖨𝖲𝖠 ᴊᴄʙ
closed 22 July-5 August, 1 to 7 January and Sunday – **Meals** (dinner only) a la carte 29/39 ⅊.

XX **Shirasagi,** Spui 170, ⊠ 2511 BW, ℘ (0 70) 346 47 00, shirasagi@planet.nl, Fax (0 70)
346 26 01, Japanese cuisine with Teppan-Yaki – ▤. ⒶⒺ ① ⑩⑨ 𝖵𝖨𝖲𝖠 ᴊᴄʙ. ⅗⅗ JZ v
closed 30 December-2 January and lunch Saturday, Sunday and Monday – **Meals** Lunch 22
– 30/70.

XX **Marc Smeets,** Buitenhof 42, ⊠ 2513 AH, ℘ (0 70) 363 79 30, rest.marcsmeets@p
lanet.nl, Fax (0 70) 361 57 85, ⅋̂ – ▤. ⅗⅗ HY v
Meals Lunch 27 – 30/43.

at **Scheveningen** ⓒ 's-Gravenhage – Seaside resort★★ – Casino, Kurhausweg 1, ⊠ 2587 RT,
℘ (0 70) 306 77 77, Fax (0 70) 306 88 88.
🄱 Gevers Deijnootweg 1134, ⊠ 2586 BX, ℘ 0-900-340 35 05, info_denhaag.com, Fax
(0 70) 352 04 26

🄷🄰🄷🄰 **Kurhaus,** Gevers Deijnootplein 30, ⊠ 2586 CK, ℘ (0 70) 416 26 36, info@kurhaus.nl,
Fax (0 70) 416 26 46, ⩽, ⅋̂, « Late 19C former concert hall », Ⅼₐ – ⧖ ⅗⩾, ▤ rest, ⓣⓥ
⅄ ℙ – ⅍ 35-480. ⒶⒺ ① ⑩⑨ 𝖵𝖨𝖲𝖠 ᴊᴄʙ. ⅗⅗ rest
Meals *Kandinsky* (closed Sunday) Lunch 23 – 55 ⅊ – **Kurzaal** (Buffets) Lunch 23 – 30 –
⊐ 19 – **247 rm** 245/315, 8 suites.

🄷🄰🄷 **Europa,** Zwolsestraat 2, ⊠ 2587 VJ, ℘ (0 70) 416 95 95, europa@bilderberg.nl,
Fax (0 70) 461 95 55, ⅋̂, Ⅼₐ, ⅀s, ▨, – ⧖ ⅗⩾ ⓣⓥ ⬅➡ – ⅍ 25-460. ⒶⒺ ① ⑩⑨ 𝖵𝖨𝖲𝖠 ᴊᴄʙ.
⅗⅗ rest
Meals *Oxo* (dinner only until 11 p.m.) 27 – ⊐ 16 – **174 rm** 177/248.

🄷🄰🄷 **Carlton Beach,** Gevers Deijnootweg 201, ⊠ 2586 HZ, ℘ (0 70) 354 14 14, beach@c
arlton.nl, Fax (0 70) 355 86 30, ⩽, Ⅼₐ, ⅀s, ▨, ♿ – ⧖ ⅗⩾ ⓣⓥ ℙ – ⅍ 25-250. ⒶⒺ ①
⑩⑨ 𝖵𝖨𝖲𝖠
Meals 34 – ⊐ 18 – **183 rm** 185/205.

🄷🄷 **Badhotel,** Gevers Deijnootweg 15, ⊠ 2586 BB, ℘ (0 70) 351 22 21, info@badhotel
scheveningen.nl, Fax (0 70) 355 58 70, ♿ – ⧖ ⅗⩾, ▤ rm, ⓣⓥ ℙ – ⅍ 25-150. ⒶⒺ ①
⑩⑨ 𝖵𝖨𝖲𝖠 ᴊᴄʙ. ⅗⅗ rest
Meals (dinner only) 25 – ⊐ 13 – **90 rm** 105/150.

XXX **Seinpost,** Zeekant 60, ⊠ 2586 AD, ℘ (0 70) 355 52 50, mail@seinpost.nl, Fax (0 70)
355 50 93, ⩽, Seafood – ▤. ⒶⒺ ① ⑩⑨ 𝖵𝖨𝖲𝖠 ᴊᴄʙ
closed Saturday lunch, Sunday and Bank Holidays – **Meals** Lunch 34 – a la carte 42/61 ⅊.

XXX **Radèn Mas,** Gevers Deijnootplein 125, ⊠ 2586 CR, ℘ (0 70) 354 54 32, Fax (0 70)
350 60 42, Partly Indonesian cuisine – ▤. ⒶⒺ ① ⑩⑨ 𝖵𝖨𝖲𝖠 ᴊᴄʙ. ⅗⅗
Meals (dinner only) a la carte 40/65.

XX **Rederserf,** Schokkerweg 37, ⊠ 2583 BH, ℘ (0 70) 350 50 23, info@rederserf.nl,
Fax (0 70) 350 84 54, ⩽, ⅋̂, « Overlooking harbour and yachts » – ▤. ⒶⒺ ① ⑩⑨ 𝖵𝖨𝖲𝖠
ᴊᴄʙ
Meals 27.

XX **China Delight,** Dr Lelykade 116, ⊠ 2583 CN, ℘ (0 70) 355 54 50, info@chinadelight.nl,
Fax (0 70) 354 66 52, Chinese cuisine, open until 11 p.m. – ① ⑩⑨ 𝖵𝖨𝖲𝖠 ᴊᴄʙ
Meals Lunch 11 – a la carte 31/49.

à **Kijkduin** West : 4 km ⓒ 's-Gravenhage :

🄷🄷 **Atlantic** Ⓜ, Deltaplein 200, ⊠ 2554 EJ, ℘ (0 70) 448 24 82, info@atlantichotel.nl,
Fax (0 70) 368 67 21, ⩽, ⅋̂, ⅀s, ▨, ♿ – ⧖ ⅗⩾ ⓣⓥ ℙ – ⅍ 25-300. ⒶⒺ ① ⑩⑨ 𝖵𝖨𝖲𝖠
ᴊᴄʙ. ⅗⅗
Meals (Buffet) 30/34 – **142 rm** ⊐ 140/210.

Environs

at Leidschendam *East : 6 km. pop. 37 472*

🏨🏨 **Green Park,** Weigelia 22, ✉ 2262 AB, 𝒫 (0 70) 320 92 80, *info@ greenpark.nl,*
Fax (0 70) 327 49 07, ≼, 𝕝⅃ – 🕼 ✦⇄ 📺 🄿 – 🛓 25-250. 🆎 🕦 🐵 𝘝𝘐𝘚𝘈 ᴊᴄʙ
Meals *Chiparus* Lunch 30 – a la carte approx. 47 ♈ – ⊑ 15 – **92 rm** 110/138, 3 suites.

❌❌❌ **Villa Rozenrust,** Veursestraatweg 104, ✉ 2265 CG, 𝒫 (0 70) 327 74 60, *info@ villa
-rozenrust.nl,* Fax (0 70) 327 74 60, 🌤, « Terrace » – 🄿. 🆎 🕦 🐵 𝘝𝘐𝘚𝘈 ᴊᴄʙ
closed 27 December-5 January and Sunday – **Meals** Lunch 33 – a la carte 49/61 ♈.

❌❌❌ **Christian van der Linden,** Veursestraatweg 8, ✉ 2265 CD, 𝒫 (0 70) 327 34 79,
info@ restaurantchristian.nl, Fax (0 70) 327 02 51, 🌤 – ▤ 🄿. 🆎 🕦 🐵 𝘝𝘐𝘚𝘈 ᴊᴄʙ
closed 27 December-8 January, Monday and Saturday lunch – **Meals** Lunch 30 – a la carte
48/68 ♈.

at Rijswijk South : 5 km. pop. 51 922

❌❌❌ **Savarin,** Laan van Hoornwijck 29, ✉ 2289 DG, 𝒫 (0 70) 307 20 50, *savarin@ wxs.nl,*
Fax (0 70) 307 20 55, 🌤 – ▤ 🄿. – 🛓 25 175. 🆎 🕦 🐵 𝘝𝘐𝘚𝘈 ᴊᴄʙ, ❀
closed 27 December-6 January – **Meals** Lunch 25 – 34/48 ♈.

❌❌ ❀ **'t Ganzenest** (Visbeen), Delftweg 58 (near A 4 - E 19, exit ⑨), ✉ 2289 AL, 𝒫 (0 70)
414 06 42, *ganzenest@ wxs.nl,* Fax (0 70) 414 07 05, ≼, 🌤, « Golf course setting » 🄿.
🆎 🕦 🐵 𝘝𝘐𝘚𝘈 ❀
closed late July-early August, Christmas-New Year, Saturday lunch, Sunday and Monday
– **Meals** Lunch 32 – 34/59, – a la carte approx. 52 ♈
Spec. Vichyssoise aux crevettes grises et à la ciboulette (July-February). Paupiette de thon
mariné aux petits légumes. Volvert au chutney de courge et ragoût de lentilles aux girolles
(September-December).

❌ ❀ **Paul van Waarden,** Tollensstraat 10, ✉ 2282 BM, 𝒫 (0 70) 414 08 12, *info@ paul
vanwaarden.nl,* Fax (0 70) 414 09 91, 🌤, « Terrace » – 🆎 🐵 𝘝𝘐𝘚𝘈
closed Sunday and Bank Holidays – **Meals** Lunch 30 – 35, a la carte 41/56 ♈
Spec. Aile de raie pochée à l'anguille fumée. Caille farcie aux champignons sauvages. Tatin
à la rhubarbe.

at Voorburg East : 5 km. pop. 38 496

🏨🏨 **Mövenpick** Ⓜ, Stationsplein 8, ✉ 2275 AZ, 𝒫 (0 70) 337 37 37, *hotel.den-haag@ m
oevenpick.com,* 🌤, 🚲 – 🕼 ✦⇄ 📺 🄿 ⟵ – 🛓 25-160. 🆎 🕦 🐵 𝘝𝘐𝘚𝘈 ᴊᴄʙ
Meals *(closed 31 December dinner)* (Buffets) Lunch 19 – 23 – ⊑ 13 – **125 rm** 120/145.

❌❌❌❌ ❀ **Savelberg** ⓢ with rm, Oosteinde 14, ✉ 2271 EH, 𝒫 (0 70) 387 20 81, *info@ resta
uranthotelsavelberg.nl,* Fax (0 70) 387 77 15, ≼, 🌤, « 17C residence with terrace in public
park » – 🕼 ✦⇄ 📺 🄿 – 🛓 35. 🆎 🕦 🐵 𝘝𝘐𝘚𝘈 ᴊᴄʙ
closed 29 December-7 January – **Meals** *(closed Sunday and Monday)* Lunch 43 – 58/83, a
la carte 67/77 ♈ – ⊑ 16 – **14 rm** 138/195
Spec. Salade de homard maison. Turbot façon saisonnier. Filet de bœuf "Rossini".

❌❌ **Villa la Ruche,** Prinses Mariannelaan 71, ✉ 2275 BB, 𝒫 (0 70) 386 01 10, *rest.villar
uche@ worldonline.nl,* Fax (0 70) 386 50 64, 🌤 – ▤. 🆎 🕦 🐵 𝘝𝘐𝘚𝘈
closed 25 December-5 January and Sunday – **Meals** Lunch 34 – a la carte 45/58 ♈.

❌❌ **De Barbaars,** Kerkstraat 52, ✉ 2271 CT, 𝒫 (0 70) 386 29 00, *marcel@ debarbaars.nl,*
Fax (0 70) 387 70 31, 🌤, Open until 11 p.m., « 19C listed houses » – ▤. 🆎 🕦 🐵 𝘝𝘐𝘚𝘈
closed Sunday and Monday – **Meals** Lunch 28 – a la carte 44/70 ♈.

❌ **Brasserie Savelberg - De Koepel,** Oosteinde 1, ✉ 2271 EA, 𝒫 (0 70) 369 35 72,
🌤, « Rotunda with cupola in public park » – 🆎 🕦 🐵 𝘝𝘐𝘚𝘈 ᴊᴄʙ
closed 31 December-1 January – **Meals** (dinner only until 11 p.m. except Sunday) a la carte
30/41 ♈.

❌ **Papermoon,** Herenstraat 175, ✉ 2271 CE, 𝒫 (0 70) 387 31 61, *info@ papermoon.nl,*
Fax (0 70) 387 75 20, 🌤 – ▤. 🐵 𝘝𝘐𝘚𝘈
closed 31 December-1 January and Monday July-August – **Meals** (dinner only) 24 ♈.

at Wassenaar Northeast : 11 km. pop. 25 999

🏨 **Aub. de Kieviet** ⓢ, Stoeplaan 27, ✉ 2243 CX, 𝒫 (0 70) 511 92 32, *receptie@ dek
ieviet.nl,* Fax (0 70) 511 09 69, 🌤, « Floral terrace », 🚲 – 🕼 ▤ 📺 🄿 – 🛓 25-90.
🆎 🕦 🐵 𝘝𝘐𝘚𝘈
closed 31 December and 1 January – **Meals** Lunch 35 – a la carte approx. 51 ♈ – ⊑ 15 –
24 rm 100/125.

In addition to establishments indicated by ❌❌❌❌❌ ... ❌ ,
many hotels possess good class restaurants.

ROTTERDAM Zuid-Holland 𝟤𝟣𝟣 L 11 - ㊴ ㊵ and 𝟫𝟢𝟪 E 6 - ㉕ N. pop. 592 673 – Casino JY, Plaza-Complex, Weena 624 ⊠ 3012 CN, ℰ (0 10) 206 82 06, Fax (0 10) 206 85 00.

See : Lijnbaan★ JY – St. Laurence Church (Crote- of St-Laurenskerk) : interior★ KY – Euromast★ (Tower) ⁕★★, ≼★ JZ – The harbour★★ ★★ KZ – Willemsbrug★★ – Erasmusbrug★★ KZ – Delftse Poort (building)★ JY C – World Trade Center★ KY Y – The Netherlands architectural institute★ JZ W – Boompjes★ KZ – Willemswerf (building)★ KY.
Museums : History Museum Het Schielandshuis★ KY M⁴ – Boijmans-van Beuningen★★★ JZ – History "De Dubbelde Palmboom"★.

Envir : Southeast : 7 km, Kinderdijk Windmils★★.

🖪 East : 8 km at Capelle aan den IJssel, 's Gravenweg 311, ⊠ 2905 LB, ℰ (0 10) 442 21 09, Fax (0 10) 284 06 06 - 🖪 Southwest : 11 km at Rhoon, Veerweg 2a, ⊠ 3161 EX, ℰ (0 10) 501 80 58, Fax (0 10) 501 56 04 - 🖪 Kralingseweg 200, ⊠ 3062 CG, ℰ (0 10) 452 22 83.
✈ Zestienhoven ℰ (0 10) 446 34 44, Fax (0 10) 446 34 99.
🚢 Europoort to Hull : P and O North Sea Ferries Ltd ℰ (0 181) 25 55 00 (information) and (0 181) 25 55 55 (reservations), Fax (0 181) 25 52 15.

🛈 Coolsingel 67, ⊠ 3012 AC, ℰ 0 900-403 40 65, infovvv.rotterdam.nl, Fax (0 10) 413 01 24 and – Central Station, Stationsplein 1, ⊠ 3013 AJ, ℰ 0-900-403 40 65.
Amsterdam 76 – The Hague 24 – Antwerp 103 – Brussels 148 – Utrecht 57.

Plan opposite

Centre

🏨 **Parkhotel** Ⓜ, Westersingel 70, ⊠ 3015 LB, ℰ (0 10) 436 36 11, parkhotel@bilderberg.nl, Fax (0 10) 436 42 12, 🍴, 🕼, 🕿 – 🛗 ⁕ ≣ 📺 🅿 – 🛎 25-60. 🆎 ⓞ ⓜⓞ 𝘝𝘐𝘚𝘈 🄹🄲🄱. ⁕ rest
JZ a
Meals Lunch 21 – a la carte approx. 50 – � 20 – **187 rm** 150/290, 2 suites.

🏨 **The Westin** Ⓜ, Weena 686, ⊠ 3012 CN, ℰ (0 10) 430 20 00, rotterdam.westin@westin.com, Fax (0 10) 430 20 01, 🕼 – 🛗 ⁕ ≣ 📺 ᴴ – 🛎 25-100. 🆎 ⓞ ⓜⓞ 𝘝𝘐𝘚𝘈 ⁕ JY z
Meals (Open until 11 p.m.) Lunch 22 – a la carte 36/48 – ⊇ 21 – **227 rm** 290/315, 4 suites.

🏨 **Hilton** without rest, Weena 10, ⊠ 3012 CM, ℰ (0 10) 710 80 00, info-rotterdam@hilton.com, Fax (0 10) 710 80 80 – 🛗 ⁕ ≣ 📺 ᴴ 🅿 – 🛎 25-365. 🆎 ⓞ ⓜⓞ 𝘝𝘐𝘚𝘈 🄹🄲🄱
⊇ 20 – **246 rm** 345/370, 8 suites.
JY s

🏨 **Golden Tulip**, Aert van Nesstraat 4, ⊠ 3012 CA, ℰ (0 10) 206 78 00, sales@grotterdam.goldentulip.nl, Fax (0 10) 413 53 20 – 🛗 ⁕ 📺 ᴴ 🚗 – 🛎 25-325. 🆎 ⓞ ⓜⓞ 𝘝𝘐𝘚𝘈 🄹🄲🄱
Meals 27 – ⊇ 15 – **213 rm** 197/251, 2 suites.
JY r

🏨 **Holiday Inn City Centre**, Schouwburgplein 1, ⊠ 3012 CK, ℰ (0 10) 206 25 55, hiccrotterdam@bilderberg.nl, Fax (0 10) 206 25 50 – 🛗 ⁕ 📺 🚗 – 🛎 25-300. 🆎 ⓞ ⓜⓞ 𝘝𝘐𝘚𝘈 🄹🄲🄱. ⁕ rest
JY e
Meals a la carte 31/48 – ⊇ 17 – **100 rm** 180/265.

🏨 **New York**, Koninginnehoofd 1, ⊠ 3072 AD, ℰ (0 10) 439 05 00, Fax (0 10) 484 27 01, ≼, 🍴, « Former head office of the Holland-America Line maritime company » – 🛗 📺 – 🛎 25-120. 🆎 ⓞ ⓜⓞ 𝘝𝘐𝘚𝘈 ⁕
KZ m
Meals (Open until 11 p.m.) a la carte 25 – ⊇ 9 – **72 rm** 139/200.

🏨 **Inntel**, Leuvehaven 80, ⊠ 3011 EA, ℰ (0 10) 413 41 39, inforotterdam@hotelinntel.com, Fax (0 10) 413 32 22, ≼, 🕼, 🕿, 🅺 – 🛗 ⁕ ≣ 📺 🅿 – 🛎 25-250. 🆎 ⓞ ⓜⓞ 𝘝𝘐𝘚𝘈. ⁕ rest
KZ d
Meals 22/30 ♀ – ⊇ 17 – **150 rm** 177/250.

🏨 **Tulip Inn**, Willemsplein 1, ⊠ 3016 DN, ℰ (0 10) 413 47 90, Fax (0 10) 412 78 90, ≼ – 🛗 ⁕ 📺 – 🛎 25-60. 🆎 ⓞ ⓜⓞ 𝘝𝘐𝘚𝘈 🄹🄲🄱. ⁕
KZ s
closed 22 December-2 January – Meals (closed Saturday and Sunday) a la carte approx. 34 – **107 rm** ⊇ 81/128.

🏨 **Savoy** without rest, Hoogstraat 81, ⊠ 3011 PJ, ℰ (0 10) 413 92 80, info.savoy@edenhotelgroup.com, Fax (0 10) 404 57 12, 🕼 – 🛗 ⁕ ≣ 📺 – 🛎 25-60. 🆎 ⓞ ⓜⓞ 𝘝𝘐𝘚𝘈 🄹🄲🄱. ⁕
KY C
⊇ 15 – **94 rm** 202/216.

🏨 **Van Walsum**, Mathenesserlaan 199, ⊠ 3014 HC, ℰ (0 10) 436 32 75, reservations@hotelvanwalsum.nl, Fax (0 10) 436 44 10 – 🛗 📺 🅿 🆎 ⓞ ⓜⓞ 𝘝𝘐𝘚𝘈 🄹🄲🄱. ⁕ rest
Meals (residents only) – **29 rm** ⊇ 80/105.

🏨 **Pax** without rest, Schiekade 658, ⊠ 3032 AK, ℰ (0 10) 466 33 44, pax@bestwestern.nl, Fax (0 10) 467 52 78 – 🛗 ≣ 📺 🅿 🆎 ⓞ ⓜⓞ 𝘝𝘐𝘚𝘈 🄹🄲🄱. ⁕
116 rm ⊇ 86/150.

🍴🍴🍴🍴 **Parkheuvel** (Helder), Heuvellaan 21, ⊠ 3016 GL, ℰ (0 10) 436 07 66, Fax (0 10) 436 71 40, 🍴, « Terrace and ≼ maritime trade » – 🅿. 🆎 ⓞ ⓜⓞ 𝘝𝘐𝘚𝘈 🄹🄲🄱
❀❀❀
JZ n
closed 29 July-10 August, 27 December-3 January, Saturday lunch and Sunday – Meals Lunch 43 – 57/90, – a la carte 54/74 ♀
Spec. Sole poêlée aux morilles et foie d'oie fondu (March-May). Turbot grillé à la crème d'anchois et basilic. Râble de lièvre au thym et petite côte à la royale (20 October-30 December).

ROTTERDAM

NETHERLANDS

NETHERLANDS

XXX **Old Dutch,** Rochussenstraat 20, ⌧ 3015 EK, ℰ (0 10) 436 03 44, Fax (0 10) 436 78 26, 🍴 – 🗏 ℙ. ㏂ ㏘ ㏒ ☑. ⁒
JZ r
closed Saturday July-August, Sunday and Bank Holidays – **Meals** *Lunch 31* – a la carte 51/59.

XXX **Radèn Mas** 1st floor, Kruiskade 72, ⌧ 3012 EH, ℰ (0 10) 411 72 44, Fax (0 10) 411 97 11, Indonesian cuisine – 🗏. ㏂ ㏘ ㏒ ☑
JY a
Meals (dinner only) a la carte 38/75.

XX **La Vilette,** Westblaak 160, ⌧ 3012 KM, ℰ (0 10) 414 86 92, Fax (0 10) 414 33 91 – 🗏. ㏂ ㏘ ㏒ ☑ ㏊. ⁒
JY t
closed 22 July-11 August, 22 December-5 January, Sunday and Bank Holidays – **Meals** *Lunch 27* – 34/39 ℤ.

XX **Melridge Castellane,** Eendrachtsweg 22, ⌧ 3012 LB, ℰ (0 10) 414 11 59, melridg ecaste@cs.com, Fax (0 10) 433 49 21, 🍴, « Terrace » – ㏂ ㏒ ☑ ㏊. ⁒ JZ h
closed 3 weeks August, Sunday and Monday – **Meals** *Lunch 34* – 41/52 ℤ.

XX **Brancatelli,** Boompjes 264, ⌧ 3011 XD, ℰ (0 10) 411 41 51, pino@brancatelli.nl, Fax (0 10) 404 57 34, Italian cuisine, open until 11 p.m. – 🗏. ㏂ ㏘ ㏒ ☑. ⁒ KZ n
closed lunch Saturday and Sunday – **Meals** *Lunch 30* – a la carte approx. 47 ℤ.

XX **7eeZout,** Westorkado 11b, ⌧ 3016 CL, ℰ (0 10) 436 50 49, Fax (0 10) 225 18 47, 🍴, Seafood – ㏂ ㏘ ㏒ JZ e
closed 25, 26 and 31 December, 1 January, Sunday and Monday – **Meals** *Lunch 25* – a la carte 37/49 ℤ.

X **de Engel,** Eendrachtsweg 19, ⌧ 3012 LB, ℰ (0 10) 413 82 56, restaurant@engel.nl, Fax (0 10) 412 51 96 – ℙ. ㏂ ㏘ ㏒ ☑ ㏊ JZ h
closed 24, 25 and 26 December and Sunday – **Meals** (dinner only) a la carte 42/52 ℤ.

X **Foody's,** Nieuwe Binnenweg 151, ⌧ 3014 GK, ℰ (0 10) 436 51 63, Fax (0 10) 436 54 42, 🍴 – 🗏. ㏂ ㏘ ☑ JZ k
closed last week July-first week August, 25 December-4 January and Monday – **Meals** (dinner only until 11 p.m.) 36 ℤ.

X **Engels,** Stationsplein 45, ⌧ 3013 AK, ℰ (0 10) 411 95 50, info@engels.nl, Fax (0 10) 413 94 21, Multinational cuisines – ℙ – ㏌ 25-800. ㏂ ㏘ ㏒ ☑ ㏊ JY v
Meals *Lunch 24* – 29 ℤ.

X **Anak Mas,** Meent 72a, ⌧ 3011 JN, ℰ (0 10) 414 84 87, pturina@hotmail.com, Fax (0 10) 412 44 74, Indonesian cuisine – 🗏. ㏂ ㏘ ㏒ ☑ ㏊ KY s
closed Sunday – **Meals** (dinner only) a la carte approx. 29.

Suburbs

Airport *North : 2,5 km :*

🏨 **Airport,** Vliegveldweg 59, ⌧ 3043 NT, ℰ (0 10) 462 55 66, info@airporthotel.nl, Fax (0 10) 462 22 66, 🍴, 🚲 – 🛗 🍴 📺 ♿ ℙ – ㏌ 25-425. ㏂ ㏘ ㏒ ☑. ⁒
Meals *Lunch 19* – 30 ℤ – ☲ 15 – **98 rm** 130/155.

at Hillegersberg *Northeast : 10 km © Rotterdam :*

X **Mangerie Lommerrijk,** Straatweg 99, ⌧ 3054 AB, ℰ (0 10) 422 00 11, info@lom merrijk.nl, Fax (0 10) 422 64 96, ≤, 🍴, 🍴 – ℙ – ㏌ 25-250. ㏂ ㏘ ㏒ ☑
closed 24 to 31 December, Monday and Tuesday – **Meals** (lunch by arrangement) 26.

at Kralingen *East : 2 km © Rotterdam :*

🏨 **Novotel Brainpark,** K.P. van der Mandelelaan 150 (near A 16), ⌧ 3062 MB, ℰ (0 10) 253 25 32, H1134@accor-hotels.com, Fax (0 10) 253 25 32, 🍴 – 🛗 🍴 📺 ℙ – ㏌ 25-400. ㏂ ㏘ ㏒ ☑
Meals (Open until midnight) *Lunch 16* – a la carte 22/30 ℤ – ☲ 14 – **196 rm** 113/147.

XX **In den Rustwat,** Honingerdijk 96, ⌧ 3062 NX, ℰ (0 10) 413 41 10, info@indenrus twat.nl, Fax (0 10) 404 85 40, 🍴, « 16C residence in floral garden » – 🗏 ℙ. ㏂ ㏘ ㏒ ☑ ㏊
closed 24 December-8 January, Sunday and Monday – **Meals** *Lunch 30* – a la carte 44/53 ℤ.

Europoort zone *West : 25 km :*

🏨 **De Beer Europoort,** Europaweg 210 (N 15), ⌧ 3198 LD, ℰ (0 181) 26 23 77, info @hotelbeer.nl, Fax (0 181) 26 29 23, ≤, 🍴, 🍴, 🍴, 🚲 – 🛗 📺 ℙ – ㏌ 25-180. ㏂ ㏘ ㏒ ☑. ⁒ rm
Meals *Lunch 17* – a la carte 22/30 – **78 rm** ☲ 78/94.

Environs

at Capelle aan den IJssel *East : 8 km. pop. 64 251*

🏨 **Golden Tulip** Ⓜ, Barbizonlaan 2 (near A 20), ⌧ 2908 MA, ℰ (0 10) 456 44 55, sale s@gtcapelle.goldentulip.nl, Fax (0 10) 456 78 58, ≤, 🍴 – 🛗 🍴 📺 ℙ – ㏌ 30-250. ㏂ ㏘ ㏒ ☑ ㏊. ⁒ rest
Meals (closed Sunday dinner) 41 ℤ – ☲ 17 – **100 rm** 100, 1 suite.

at Rhoon *South : 10 km* Ⓖ *Albrandswaard pop. 16 420 :*

XXX **Het Kasteel van Rhoon,** Dorpsdijk 63, ✉ 3161 KD, ℰ (0 10) 501 88 96, *info@he tkasteelvanrhoon.nl*, Fax (0 10) 506 72 59, ≤, 😊, « Situated in the outbuildings of the mansion » – Ⓟ. 🅰🅴 ⑩ ⑩⑨ *VISA*. 🐾
Meals *Lunch 36* – 41/54.

at Schiedam *West : 6 km. pop. 75 589.*

🅱 *Buitenhavenweg 9,* ✉ *3113 BC,* ℰ *(0 10) 473 30 00, vvv.schiedamkabelfoon.nl, Fax (0 10) 473 66 95*

🏨 **Novotel,** Hargalaan 2 (near A 20), ✉ 3118 JA, ℰ (0 10) 471 33 22, *H0517@accor-h otels.com*, Fax (0 10) 470 06 56, 😊, ⬛, 🍽, 🚲 – 📳 ✳ 🟰 📺 Ⓟ – 🛗 25-200. 🅰🅴 ⑩ ⑩⑨ *VISA*. 🐾 rest
Meals *Lunch 15* – a la carte approx. 31 – ⬜ 12 – **134 rm** 125.

XXX **Duchesse,** Maasboulevard 7, ✉ 3114 HB, ℰ (0 10) 426 46 25, *duchesse@planet.nl*, Fax (0 10) 473 25 01, ≤ Nieuwe Maas (Meuse), 😊 – Ⓟ. 🅰🅴 ⑩ ⑩⑨ *VISA* JCB
closed 31 December and Sunday – **Meals** *Lunch 33* – 36 ⚴.

X **Bistrot Hosman Frères,** Korte Dam 10, ✉ 3111 DG, ℰ (0 10) 426 40 96, Fax (0 10) 426 90 41 – 🟰. 🅰🅴 ⑩ ⑩⑨ *VISA* JCB
closed 31 December-1 January and Monday – **Meals** 25/39 ⚴.

X **Orangerie Duchesse,** Maasboulevard 7, ✉ 3114 HB, ℰ (0 10) 426 46 25, *duchess e@planet.nl*, Fax (0 10) 473 25 01, ≤ Nieuwe Maas (Meuse), 😊 – Ⓟ. 🅰🅴 ⑩ ⑩⑨ *VISA* JCB
closed 31 December and Sunday – **Meals** (dinner only) 33 ⚴.

Czech Republic

Česká Republika

PRAGUE

PRACTICAL INFORMATION

LOCAL CURRENCY

Crown : *100 CZK = 3,04 euro (€) (Dec. 2001)*
National Holiday in the Czech Republic : *28 October.*

PRICES

Prices may change if goods and service costs in the Czech Republic are revised and it is therefore always advisable to confirm rates with the hotelier when making a reservation.

FOREIGN EXCHANGE

It is strongly advised against changing money other than in banks, exchange offices or authorised offices such as large hotels, tourist offices, etc... Banks are usually open on weekdays from 9am to 5pm. Some exchange offices in the old city are open 24 hours a day.

HOTEL RESERVATIONS

In case of difficulties in finding a room through our hotel selection, it is always possible to apply to AVE Wilsonova 8, Prague 2, ☎ (02) 24 22 35 21. CEDOK Na příkopě 18, Prague 1 ☎ (02) 24 19 76 15.

POSTAL SERVICES

Post offices are open from 8am to 6pm on weekdays and 12 noon on Saturdays. The **General Post Office** *is open 7am to 8pm : Jindřišska 14, Prague 1, ☎ (02) 21 13 14 45. There is a 24 hr postal service at Hybernská 13 ☎ (02) 24 22 58 45.*

SHOPPING IN PRAGUE

In the index of street names, those printed in red are where the principal shops are found. Typical goods to be bought include embroidery, puppets, Bohemian glass, porcelain, ceramics, wooden toys... Shops are generally open from 9am to 7pm.

TIPPING

Hotel, restaurant and café bills include service in the total charge but it is up to you to tip the staff.

CAR HIRE

The international car hire companies have branches in Prague. Your hotel porter should be able to give details and help you with your arrangements.

BREAKDOWN SERVICE

A 24 hour breakdown service is operated by ABA Autoservice, 5 Kováků str., Prague 5. ☎ (02) 1240.

SPEED LIMITS - SEAT BELTS - MOTORWAYS TAX

The maximum permitted speed on motorways is 130 km/h - 80 mph, 90 km/h - 56 mph on other roads and 50 km/h - 31 mph in built up areas except where a lower speed limit is indicated.
The wearing of seat belts is compulsory for drivers and all passengers.
Driving on motorways is subject to the purchase of a single rate annual road tax obtainable from border posts and tourist offices.
In the Czech Republic, drivers must not drink alcoholic beverages at all.

PRAGUE
(PRAHA)

Česká Republika 976 F 3 – *Pop. 1 203 230*

Berlin 344 – Dresden 152 – Munich 384 – Nürnberg 287 – Wrocław 272 – Vienna 291.

🚹 *Prague Information Service : Na Příkopě 20 (main office), Staroměstsk a radnice, and Main Railway Station ℰ (02) 12444*
CEDOK : Na příkopě 10, Prague 1 ℰ (02) 24 19 71 11, Fax (02) 2422 3479.
🏌 *Golf Club Praha, Motol-Praha 5, ℰ (02) 57 21 65 84.*
✈ *Ruzyně (Prague Airport) NW 20 km, by road n° 7 ℰ (02) 20 11 33 14.*
Bus to airport : Cedaz Bus at airlines Terminal Namesti Republicky ℰ (02) 20 11 42 96.
CZECH AIRLINES (ČESKÉ AEROLINIE) V. Celnici 5, PRAGUE 1 ℰ (02) 20 10 41 11.

See: *Castle District*★★★ *(Hradčany)* **ABX** : *Prague Castle*★★★ *(Pražský Hrad)* **BX**, *St Vitus' Cathedral*★★★ *(Chrám sv. Víta)* **DX**, *Old Royal Palace*★★ *(Královský palác)* **BX**, *St George's Convent*★★ *(National Gallery's Early Bohemian Art*★★*) (Bazilika sv. Jiří/ Jiřský Klášter)* **BX**, *Hradčany Square*★★ *(Hradčanské náměstí)* **BX 37**, *Schwarzenberg Palace*★ *(Schwarzenberský Palác)* **AX** **R¹**, *Loretto Shrine*★★★ *(Loreta)* **AX**, *Strahov Abbey*★★ *(Strahovský Klášter)* **AX** – *Lesser Town*★★★ *(Malá Strana)* **BX** : *Charles Bridge*★★★ *(Karlův Most)* **BCX**, *Lesser Town Square*★ *(Malostranské náměstí)* **BX**, *St Nicholas Church*★★★ *(Sv. Mikuláše)* **BX**, *Neruda Street*★★ *(Nerudova)* **BX**, *Wallenstein Palace*★★ *(Valdštejnský Palác)* **BX** – *Old Town*★★★ *(Staré Město)* **CX** : *Old Town Square*★★★ *(Staroměstské náměstí)* **CX**, *Astronomical Clock*★★★ *(Orloj)* **CX R²**, *Old Town Hall*★ *– Extensive view*★★ *(Staroměstská radnice)* **CX R²**, *St Nicholas*★★ *(Sv. Mikuláše)* **CX**, *Týn Church*★★ *(Týnský chrám)* **CX**, *Jewish Quarter*★★★ *(Josefov)* **CX**, *Old-New Synagogue*★★★ *(Staranová Synagóga)* **CX**, *Old Jewish Cemetery*★★★ *(Starý židovský hřbitov)* **CX R³**, *St Agnes Convent*★★ *(National Gallery's Collection of 19 C Czech Painting and Sculpture) (Anežský klášter)* **CX**, *Celetná Street*★★ *(Celetná)* **CX**, *Powder Tower*★ *(Prašná Brána)* **DX**, *House of the black Madonna*★ *(Dům u černe Matky boží)* **CX E**, *Municipal House*★★★ *(Obecní Dům)* **DX N²** – *New Town*★ *(Nové Město)* **CDY** : *Wenceslas Square*★★★ *(Václavské náměstí)* **CDXY**.

Museums: *National Gallery*★★★ *(Národní Galérie)* **AX**, *National Museum*★ *(Národní muzeum)* **DY**, *National Theatre*★★ *(Národní divadlo)* **CY T²**, *Decorative Arts Museum*★ *(Umělecko průmyslové muzeum)* **CX M⁶**, *City Museum*★ *(Prague model*★★*) (Muzeum hlavního města Prahy)* **DX M³**, *Vila America*★ *(Dvořák Museum)* **DY**.

Outskirts: *Karlštejn Castle SW : 30 km* **ET** – *Konopiště Castle SW : 40 km* **FT**.

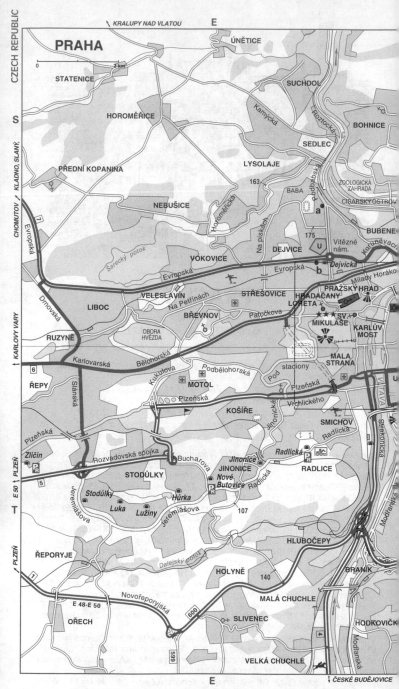

CZECH REPUBLIC

PRAHA

0   2 km

↘ KRALUPY NAD VLTAVOU   E

STATENICE

S

HOROMĚŘICE

CHOMUTOV / KLADNO, SLANÝ

PŘEDNÍ KOPANINA

NEBUŠICE

VOKOVICE

Šárecký potok

VELESLAVÍN

LIBOC

Drnovská

RUZYNĚ

↑ KARLOVY VARY

6

Karlovarská   Bělohorská

ŘEPY

Slánská

Plzeňská

Zličín

E 50 / PLZEŇ

5

Jeremiášova

Stodůlky

Luka   Lužiny

T

PLZEŇ

ŘEPORYJE

7

E 48-E 50

OŘECH

ÚNĚTICE

SUCHDOL

Kamýcká

Roztocká

BOHNICE

SEDLEC

LYSOLAJE

163

BABA

Podbabská

ZOOLOGICKÁ
ZAHRADA

CÍSAŘSKÝ OSTROV

BUBENE

175

U

Vítězné
nám.

Korunovační

Horoměřická

Na pískách

DEJVICE

Dejvická

a

Evropská

b   Dejvická

STŘEŠOVICE

Na Petřinách

HRADČANY
LORETA

Milady Horáko

PRAŽSKÝ HRAD

BŘEVNOV

Patočkova

SV.
MIKULÁŠE

KARLŮV
MOST

OBORA
HVĚZDA

Kukulova

Podbělohorská

Pod

stadiony

MALÁ
STRANA

Plzeňská

MOTOL

Plzeňská

Vrchlického

VLTAVA

U

KOŠÍŘE

Jinonická

SMÍCHOV

Radlická

Strakonická

Rozvadovská spojka

Bucharova

Jinonice

Radlická

JINONICE

Nové
Butovice

Radlická

RADLICE

Hůrka

Jeremiášova

107

Stodůlky

Dalejský potok

HLUBOČEPY

Modřanka

HOLYNĚ   140

BRANÍK

Novořeporyjská

600

MALÁ CHUCHLE

SLIVENEC

HODKOVIČK

599

VELKÁ CHUCHLE

Modřanská

4

E

↓ ČESKÉ BUDĚJOVICE

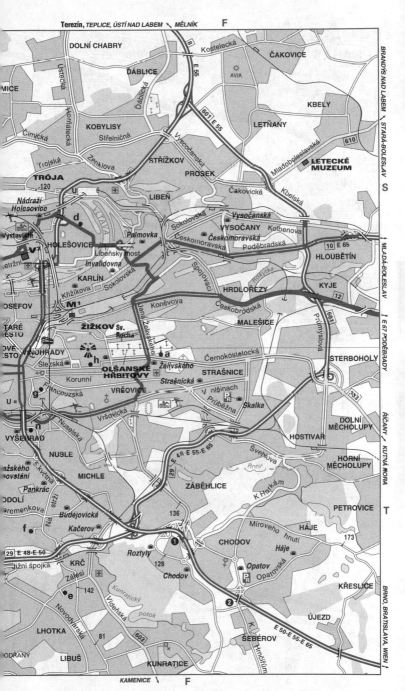

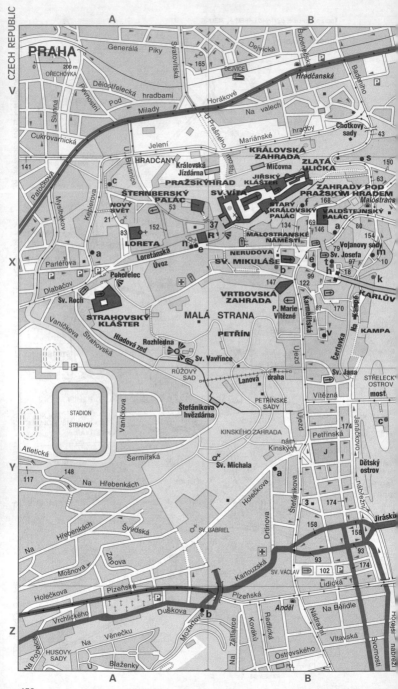

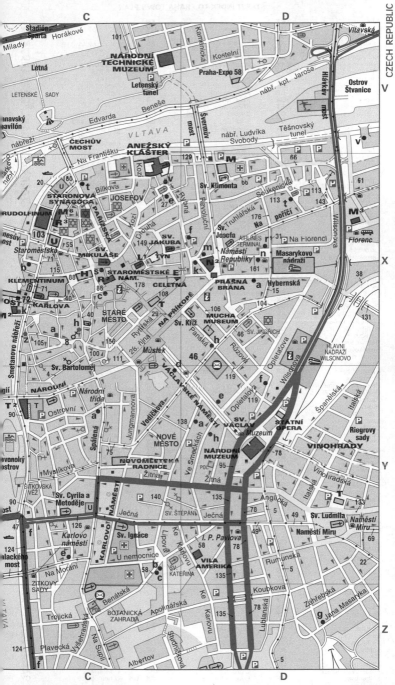

CZECH REPUBLIC

Four Seasons, Veleslavínova 2a, ✉ 110 00, ℘ (02) 2142 7000, prg.reservations@fourseasons.com, Fax (02) 2142 6000, ₤ڏ, ⇆s – ⊫, ⇄ rm, ▤ ⊤⊽ ℃ ₺ – ⅍ 120. ◑◔ ⌶⌶ ⒶⒺ ⑩ ⓥⓘⓢⓐ ⌓⌥⌶ ⅏ rest CX b
Allegro : Meals - Italian - 1150 (lunch) and a la carte 1040/2110 ₤ 550 – ⌷ 670 – **142 rm** 9100/9700, 20 suites.

Inter-Continental, Nám. Curieových 43-45, ✉ 110 00, ℘ (02) 2488 1111, prague@interconti.com, Fax (02) 2481 1216, ≼, ₤ڏ, ⇆s, ◨ – ⊫, ⇄ rm, ▤ ⊤⊽ ℃ ₺ ⇐ – ⅍ 500. ◑◔ ⌶⌶ ⒶⒺ ⑩ ⓥⓘⓢⓐ ⌓⌥⌶ CX t
Meals 600 and a la carte 1250/2450 ₤ 900 (see also **Zlatá Praha** below) – ⌷ 600 – **364 rm** 10900/11300, 25 suites.

Marriott Ⓜ, V Celnici 8, ✉ 110 00, ℘ (02) 2288 8888, prague.marriott@marriott.cz, Fax (02) 2288 8889, ₤ڏ, ⇆s, ◨ – ⊫, ⇄ rm, ▤ ⊤⊽ ℃ ₺ ⇐ – ⅍ 350. ◑◔ ⒶⒺ ⑩ ⓥⓘⓢⓐ ⌓⌥⌶ ⅏ rest DX n
Meals 350 and a la carte 440/740 ₤ 300 – ⌷ 500 – **258 rm** 12150, 35 suites.

Radisson SAS Alcron Ⓜ, Štěpánská 40, ✉ 110 00, ℘ (02) 2282 0000, sales.prague@radissonsas.com, Fax (02) 2282 0100, ⇆, « Art Deco style », ₤ڏ, ⇆s – ⊫ ⇄ ⊤⊽ ℃ ₺ – ⅍ 150. ◑◔ ⒶⒺ ⑩ ⓥⓘⓢⓐ ⌓⌥⌶, ⅏ DY a
La Rotonde : Meals 490 and a la carte 1000/1500 ₤ 690 (see also **Alcron** below) – ⌷ 500 – **205 rm** 7800, 6 suites.

Palace, Panská 12, ✉ 111 21, ℘ (02) 2409 3111, salesmanager@palacehotel.cz, Fax (02) 2422 1240, ⇆s – ⊫, ⇄ rm, ▤ ⊤⊽ ℃ ₺ ⇐ – ⅍ 50. ◑◔ ⒶⒺ ⑩ ⓥⓘⓢⓐ ⌓⌥⌶ Meals a la carte 400/1235 ₤ 550 – **Gourmet Club Restaurant :** Meals (dinner only) 1000 and a la carte 1630/4340 – **121 rm** ⌷ 9300/10000, 3 suites. DX h

Savoy, Keplerova Ul. 6, ✉ 118 00, ℘ (02) 2430 2430, info@hotel-savoy.cz, Fax (02) 2430 2128, ₤ڏ, ⇆s – ⊫, ⇄ rm, ▤ ⊤⊽ ℃ ₺ ⇐ – ⅍ 60. ◑◔ ⒶⒺ ⑩ ⓥⓘⓢⓐ ⌓⌥⌶. ⅏ AX a
Meals (see **Hradčany** below) – **60 rm** ⌷ 10000/11000, 1 suite.

Hilton Prague, Pobřežní 1, ✉ 186 00, ℘ (02) 2484 1111, salesprague@hilton.com, Fax (02) 2484 2378, ≼, ⇆, – ⊫, ⇄ rm, ▤ ⊤⊽ ℃ ₺ ⇐ Ⓟ – ⅍ 1500. ◑◔ ⒶⒺ ⑩ ⓥⓘⓢⓐ ⌓⌥⌶ ⅏ rest DV v
We Like To Cook : Meals (dinner only) a la carte 670/1290 ₤ 760 – **Atrium :** Meals (buffet only) 795 – **Café Bistro :** Meals 450/550 (lunch) and a la carte 690/970 – ⌷ 570 – **765 rm** 6825/10675, 23 suites.

Renaissance Ⓜ, V Celnici 7, ✉ 111 21, ℘ (02) 2182 1111, renaissance.prague@renaissance.com, Fax (02) 2182 2100, ₤ڏ, ⇆s, ◨ – ⊫, ⇄ rm, ▤ ⊤⊽ ℃ ₺ ⇐ – ⅍ 120. ◑◔ ⒶⒺ ⑩ ⓥⓘⓢⓐ ⌓⌥⌶. ⅏ rest DX r
Potomac Steakhouse (℘ (02) 2182 2431) : Meals (dinner only) 340/520 and a la carte 630/890 ₤ 400 – **U Korbele** (℘ (02) 2182 2433) : Meals 400/800 and a la carte – ⌷ 500 – **314 rm** 10800.

Diplomat, Evropská 15, ✉ 160 41, ℘ (02) 9655 9111, hotel@diplomat.praha.cz, Fax (02) 9655 9215, ⇆, ₤ڏ, ⇆s – ⊫, ⇄ rm, ▤ ⊤⊽ ℃ ₺ ⇐ – ⅍ 250. ◑◔ ⒶⒺ ⑩ ⓥⓘⓢⓐ ⌓⌥⌶ ES b
Meals 460 and a la carte 470/1115 ₤ 365 – **383 rm** ⌷ 6000/8000, 13 suites.

Dorint Don Giovanni Ⓜ, Vinohradská 157a, ✉ 130 20, ℘ (02) 6703 1111, info.prgdon@dorint.com, Fax (02) 6703 6717, ≼, ₤ڏ, ⇆s – ⊫, ⇄ rm, ▤ ⊤⊽ ℃ ₺ ⇐ – ⅍ 200. ◑◔ ⒶⒺ ⑩ ⓥⓘⓢⓐ ⌓⌥⌶. ⅏ rest FT a
Meals (buffet lunch) 690/800 and dinner a la carte 640/1090 ₤ 360 – ⌷ 400 – **355 rm** 6300/6800, 42 suites.

Mövenpick Ⓜ, Mozartova 261/1, ✉ 151 33, ℘ (02) 5715 1111, reservation@moevenpick.cz, Fax (02) 5715 3131, ⇆, ₤ڏ, ⇆s, ⇄ – ⊫ ⇄ ▤ ⊤⊽ ₺ ⇐ – ⅍ 250. ◑◔ ⒶⒺ ⑩ ⓥⓘⓢⓐ ⌓⌥⌶. ⅏ rest AZ b
Meals (buffet lunch) 640 and a la carte 400/940 – **427 rm** ⌷ 7200/8700, 7 suites.

Grand Hotel Bohemia, Králodvorská 4, ✉ 110 00, ℘ (02) 2480 4111, grand-hotel-bohemia@austria-hotels.icom.cz, Fax (02) 232 9545, « Ballroom » – ⊫, ⇄ rm, ▤ ⊤⊽ ℃ ₺ – ⅍ 140. ◑◔ ⒶⒺ ⑩ ⓥⓘⓢⓐ ⌓⌥⌶. ⅏ rest DX k
Meals a la carte 470/900 ₤ 360 – **78 rm** ⌷ 7700/11200.

CZECH RE...

Crowne Plaza, Koulova 15, ✉ 160 45, ✆ (02) 2439 3111, *res@crowneplaza.cz*, Fax (02) 2431 0616, 佘, 𝄐, 🛌, 🏊, ⚡ – |≢|, ✲ rm, ▤ TV ✆ & ℙ. – 🅰 250. ⑩⑩ AE ① ⓥⓘⓢⓐ ⒿⒸⒷ
ES a
Meals (buffet lunch) 400/1200 and a la carte approx. 800 – ⌐ 400 – **237 rm** 8800, 4 suites.

Corinthia Towers, Kongresová 1, ✉ 140 69, ✆ (02) 6119 1111, *towers@corinthia.cz*, Fax (02) 6121 1673, ≤, 🛌, 𝄐, 🏊, squash – |≢|, ✲ rm, ▤ TV ✆ & ⇔ – 🅰 390. ⑩⑩ ① ⓥⓘⓢⓐ ⒿⒸⒷ ✺
FT n
Let's Eat : Meals (dinner only and Sunday lunch) 700 and a la carte 1400/1900 🍷 600 – *Rickshaw :* Meals (closed Sunday) (dinner only) 1200 and a la carte 1100/1500 – *Toscana :* Meals (closed Monday and Sunday lunch) 700 and a la carte 800/1000 – **522 rm** ⌐ 7700/9000, 22 suites.

Hoffmeister, Pod Bruskou 7, ✉ 118 00, ✆ (02) 5101 7111, *hotel@hoffmeister.cz*, Fax (02) 5101 7120, 佘, « Collection of Adolf Hoffmeister's artwork » – |≢| ▤ TV ⇔.
⑩⑩ AE ① ⓥⓘⓢⓐ ⒿⒸⒷ
BX s
Meals a la carte 660/3160 🍷 360 – **33 rm** ⌐ 7480/10540, 4 suites.

Paříž, U obecního domu 1, ✉ 110 00, ✆ (02) 2219 5195, *booking@hotel-pariz.cz*, Fax (02) 2422 5475, « Neo-Gothic and Art Nouveau architecture » – |≢|, ✲ rm, ▤ TV ✆ ⇔ – 🅰 55. ⑩⑩ AE ① ⓥⓘⓢⓐ ⒿⒸⒷ
DX m
Meals - French - 400/1500 and a la carte 730/1350 🍷 380 – *Sarah Bernhardt :* Meals 400/1500 and a la carte 730/1350 🍷 380 – ⌐ 300 – **93 rm** 7500/11300, 1 suite.

Esplanade, Washingtonova 19, ✉ 110 00, ✆ (02) 2450 1111, *esplanade@esplanade.cz*, Fax (02) 2422 9306, « Art Nouveau building » – |≢| TV – 🅰 60. ⑩⑩ AE ① ⓥⓘⓢⓐ ⒿⒸⒷ
DY f
Meals a la carte 450/1160 🍷 375 – **74 rm** ⌐ 6600/8950.

Residence Nosticova ⚘ without rest., Nosticova 1, ✉ 118 00, ✆ (02) 5731 2513, *nostic@bohem-net.cz*, Fax (02) 5731 2517, « Tastefully refurbished 17C burgher's house » – |≢| TV ✆ ℙ. ⑩⑩ AE ① ⓥⓘⓢⓐ ⒿⒸⒷ
BX v
⌐ 300 **5 rm** 7100, **5 suites** 10000/17650.

U Prince, Staroměstské Nám. 29, ✉ 110 00, ✆ (02) 2421 3807, *reserve@hoteluprince.cz*, Fax (02) 2421 3807, 佘, « Refurbished 17C house with antique furnishings, roof terrace with ≤ Prague » – |≢| ▤ TV ⑩⑩ AE ① ⓥⓘⓢⓐ
CX c
Meals a la carte 320/1380 – **24 rm** ⌐ 6990/10990.

Villa Voyta (and Voyta Garni) ⚘, K Novému Dvoru 124-54, ✉ 142 00, ✆ (02) 6171 1307, *info@villavoyta.cz*, Fax (02) 4447 1248, 佘, ✲ – |≢| ▤ TV ✆ ℙ. – 🅰 25. ⑩⑩ AE ① ⓥⓘⓢⓐ ⒿⒸⒷ
FT e
Meals 395/1200 and a la carte 640/1360 🍷 395 – **19 rm** ⌐ 4700/5300, 1 suite.

Kinsky Garden, Holečkova 7, ✉ 150 00, ✆ (02) 5731 1173, *kinskygarden@vol.cz*, Fax (02) 5731 1184 – |≢|, ✲ rm, ▤ TV & – 🅰 30. ⑩⑩ AE ① ⓥⓘⓢⓐ ⒿⒸⒷ ✺ BY a
Meals 525 and a la carte 630/830 – **60 rm** ⌐ 5200/6300.

K + K Fenix Ⓜ, Ve Smečkách 30, ✉ 110 00, ✆ (02) 3309 2222, *hotel.fenix@kkhotels.cz*, Fax (02) 2221 2141, 🛌, 𝄐 – |≢|, ✲ rm, ▤ TV & ⇔ – 🅰 40. ⑩⑩ AE ① ⓥⓘⓢⓐ ⒿⒸⒷ
DY h
Meals (in bar) a la carte 420/740 🍷 420 – **128 rm** ⌐ 7300/8300.

Jalta, Václavské Nám. 45, ✉ 110 00, ✆ (02) 2282 2111, *jalta@jalta.cz*, Fax (02) 2421 3866 – |≢| ▤ TV ✆ – 🅰 100. ⑩⑩ AE ① ⓥⓘⓢⓐ ⒿⒸⒷ ✺ rest DY e
Meals 335 (lunch) and a la carte 430/1110 🍷 375 - also Japanese (Teppan-Yaki) - 600/2200 and a la carte 510/990 🍷 375 – **89 rm** ⌐ 8150/9500, 5 suites.

U Zlaté Studně ⚘, U Zlaté Studně, ✉ 118 00, ✆ (02) 5701 1213, *hotel@zlatastudna.cz*, Fax (02) 5753 3320, « 16C Renaissance building with stylish furnishing » – |≢| ▤ TV ✆. ⑩⑩ AE ① ⓥⓘⓢⓐ
BX f
Meals (see *U Zlaté Studně* below) – **17 rm** ⌐ 8500/9200, 3 suites.

Maximilian ⚘ without rest., Haštalská 14, ✉ 110 00, ✆ (02) 2180 6111, *maximilianhotel@hotmail.com*, Fax (02) 2180 6110 – |≢| ✲ ▤ TV & ⇔ – 🅰 50. ⑩⑩ AE ① ⓥⓘⓢⓐ ⒿⒸⒷ
CX e
72 rm ⌐ 4200/7000.

Elite ⚘, Ostrovní 32, ✉ 110 00, ✆ (021) 2493 2250, *sales@hotelelite.cz*, Fax (021) 2493 0787 – |≢|, ✲ rm, ▤ TV ✆ & ⇔. ⑩⑩ AE ① ⓥⓘⓢⓐ ⒿⒸⒷ ✺ rest
CY a
Meals a la carte 345/575 – **79 rm** ⌐ 5200/5950.

Zlatá Hvězda, Nerudova 48, ✉ 118 00, ✆ (02) 5753 2867, *hvezda@ok.cz*, Fax (02) 5753 3624, 佘 – |≢|, ✲ rm, TV ✆. ⑩⑩ AE ⓥⓘⓢⓐ
AX x
Meals a la carte 240/430 🍷 250 – **24 rm** ⌐ 6300/6900, 2 suites.

U Modrého Klíče without rest., Letenská 14, ✉ 118 00, ✆ (02) 5753 4361, *bluekey@mbox.vol.cz*, Fax (02) 5753 4372, « 14C restored monastery with modern interior », 𝄐 – |≢| ✲ ▤ TV ⑩⑩ AE ① ⓥⓘⓢⓐ ⒿⒸⒷ
BX a
22 rm ⌐ 4300/7800, 6 suites.

Meteor Plaza, Hybernská 6, ✉ 110 00, ✆ (02) 2419 2111, *alltours@hotel-meteor.cz*, Fax (02) 2419 2130, 佘, 🛌, 𝄐 – |≢| ▤ TV ✆. ⑩⑩ AE ① ⓥⓘⓢⓐ ⒿⒸⒷ ✺
DX a
Meals a la carte 150/810 🍷 450 – **82 rm** ⌐ 4900/6000, 6 suites.

🏨 **Novotel** Ⓜ, Kateřinská 38, ✉ 120 00, ℰ (02) 2110 4999, *h3194@accor-hotels.c* *Fax (02) 2110 4888*, 🍴, 🛏, 🏊, 🈺 – 📶, 🔄 rm, 🗐 📺 ✦ & 🚗 – 🚗 80. 🐕🕒 🗚 CY b
Meals 350/380 (lunch) and a la carte 495/920 – 🍷 325 – **145 rm** 5100/5350.

🏨 **U Krále Karla**, ¿voz 4, ✉ 118 00, ℰ (02) 5753 1211, *ukrale@tnet.cz*, *Fax (02) 5753 3591*, « 17C baroque house, antique furnishings » – 📶, 🈺 rm, 📺. 🐕🕒 🗚 ① 🗚 AX n
Meals 220 and a la carte 580/900 🍴 450 – **19 rm** 🍷 6100/7900.

🏨 **Adria,** Václavské Nám. 26, ✉ 110 00, ℰ (02) 2108 1111, *mailbox@hoteladria.cz*, *Fax (02) 2108 1300* – 📶, 🈺 rm, 🗐 📺 ✦ & 🚗 – 🚗 50. 🐕🕒 🗚 ① 🗚 🗚 🔄
Triton : **Meals** (dinner booking essential) a la carte 600/870 🍴 640 – **83 rm** 🍷 5400/6400, 5 suites. CY d

🏨 **Casa Marcello** 🦢, Řásnovka 783, ✉ 110 00, ℰ (02) 2231 1230, *casa@casa-marce* *llo.cz, Fax (02) 2231 3323*, 🍴 – 🈺 rm, 📺 ✦. 🐕🕒 🗚 ① 🗚 🔄 CX v
Meals (dinner only October-March) a la carte 380/510 🍴 250 – **26 rm** 🍷 8700, 6 suites.

🏨 **U Páva,** U Lužického Semináře 30, ✉ 118 00, ℰ (02) 5753 5360, *hotelupava@iol.cz*, *Fax (02) 5753 0919*, « Tastefully decorated », 🛏 – 📶 📺 ✦. 🐕🕒 🗚 ① 🗚. 🔄 rest BX m
Meals a la carte 520/890 🍴 560 – **18 rm** 🍷 5400/7900, 9 suites.

🏨 **City H. Moran,** Na Moráni 15, ✉ 120 00, ℰ (02) 2491 5208, *bw-moran@login.cz*, *Fax (02) 2492 0625* – 📶 🗐 📺. 🐕🕒 🗚 ① 🗚 CY e
Meals a la carte 340/680 🍴 280 – **57 rm** 🍷 3800/6300.

🏨 **U Raka** without rest., Černínská 10, ✉ 110 00, ℰ (02) 2051 1100, *uraka@login.cz*, *Fax (02) 2051 5361*, 🚗 🗐 📺 🅿. 🐕🕒 🗚 🗚. 🔄 AX c
6 rm 🍷 6200/7900.

🏨 **Astoria** Ⓜ, Rybná 10, ✉ 110 00, ℰ (02) 2177 5711, *info@hotelastoria.cz*, *Fax (02) 2177 5712* – 📶, 🈺 rm, 🗐 📺 ✦ &. 🐕🕒 🗚 ① 🗚 🔄 DX f
Meals a la carte 330/650 – **74 rm** 🍷 6000.

🏨 **Ametyst,** Jana Masaryka 11, ✉ 120 00, ℰ (02) 2425 4185, *mailbox@hotelametyst.cz*, *Fax (02) 2425 1315*, 🔄 – 📶, 🈺 rm, 🗐 rest, 📺 &. 🐕🕒 🗚 ① 🗚 🔄 DZ g
Meals a la carte 665/1290 🍴 385 – **84 rm** 🍷 3500/6800.

🏨 **Alta,** Ortenovo Nám. 22, ✉ 170 00, ℰ (02) 800 252, *alta@login.cz, Fax (02) 6671 2011* – 📶, 🈺 rm, 🗐 rest, ✦ 🚗. 🐕🕒 🗚 ① 🗚 🔄 🔄 rest FS d
Meals a la carte 290/705 🍴 180 – **82 rm** 🍷 2850/3850, 5 suites.

🏨 **Biskupský Dům,** Dražického Nám. 6, ✉ 110 00, ℰ (02) 5753 2320, *biskup@ok.cz*, *Fax (02) 5753 1840*, 🍴 – 📶 📺 &. 🐕🕒 🗚 🗚 BX t
Meals 200/550 and a la carte 330/795 🍴 225 – **29 rm** 🍷 6300/6900.

🏨 **The Charles** without rest., Josefská 1, ✉ 118 00, ℰ (02) 5753 2913, *thecharles@b* *on.cz, Fax (02) 5753 2910* – 📶 🈺 📺. 🐕🕒 🗚 🗚. 🔄 BX e
27 rm 🍷 5000/8000, 3 suites.

🏨 **Sieber,** Slezská 55, ✉ 130 00, ℰ (02) 2425 0025, *reservations@sieber.cz*, *Fax (02) 2425 0027* – 📶 🗐 📺. 🐕🕒 🗚 ① 🗚 🔄 FT h
Meals (closed 24 and 31 December) (dinner only) a la carte 505/1150 🍴 250 – **11 rm** 🍷 4480/5480.

🏨 **Vladař** 🦢, Na Dvorcích 144-9, ✉ 140 00, ℰ (02) 4144 3609, *mvladar@login.cz*, *Fax (02) 4144 2423* – 📺. 🐕🕒 🗚 ① 🗚 🔄 FT f
Meals 95 (lunch) and a la carte 225/305 – 🍷 220 – **16 rm** 2400/4800.

🏨 **Černá Liška,** Mikulášská 2, Staroměstské Nám., ✉ 110 00, ℰ (02) 2423 2250, *Fax (02) 2423 2249*, 🍴 – 📶 🐕🕒 🗚 🔄 CX s
Meals a la carte approx. 300 – **11 rm** 🍷 4300/5500, 1 suite.

🏨 **Bílá Labuť,** Biskupská 9, ✉ 110 00, ℰ (02) 232 4524, *cchotels@login.cz*, *Fax (02) 232 2905*, 🔄 – 📶, 🈺 rm, 📺. 🐕🕒 🗚 ① 🗚 DX t
Meals a la carte 400/420 – **54 rm** 🍷 4700/6000.

🏨 **Ibis Praha City** Ⓜ, Kateřinská 36, ✉ 110 00, ℰ (02) 2286 5777, *h3195-rc@accor* *-hotels.com, Fax (02) 2286 5666*, 🍴 – 📶, 🈺 rm, 🗐 📺 ✦ & 🚗. 🐕🕒 ① 🗚 🔄
Meals 350 and a la carte 280/370 – 🍷 200 – **180 rm** 2590/3190. CY c

🍴🍴🍴🍴 **Zlatá Praha** (at Inter-Continental H.), Nám. Curieových 43-45, ✉ 110 00, ℰ (02) 2488 9914, *prague@interconti.com, Fax (02) 2481 1216*, ≤ Prague, 🍴 – 🐕🕒 🗚 ① 🗚 🔄 CX t
Meals 600/2400 and a la carte 800/1800 🍴 890.

🍴🍴🍴🍴 **Hradčany** (at Savoy H.), Keplerova Ul. 6, ✉ 118 00, ℰ (02) 2430 2150, *savhoprg@m* *box.vol.cz, Fax (02) 2430 2128* – 🗐. 🐕🕒 🗚 ① 🗚 🔄. 🔄 AX a
Meals 590/1300 and a la carte 1020/1490 🍴 650.

Flambée, Husova 5, ⊠ 110 00, ℰ (02) 2424 8512, *flambee@flambee.cz,*
Fax (02) 2424 8513, « Vaulted cellar with elegant interior » – ▤. **MC** **AE** **①** **VISA** **JCB.** ⚘
Meals 1000/2000 and a la carte 1070/2640 ⏷ 600 – **Cafe Flambée :** Meals a la carte
305/585 ⏷ 600.   CX h

Alcron (at Radisson SAS Alcron H.), Štěpánská 40, ⊠ 110 00, ℰ (02) 2228 0000,
Fax (02) 2282 0100 – ▤ ☜. **MC** **AE** **①** **VISA** ⚘   DY a
Meals (booking essential) (dinner only) 1300/2000 and a la carte 1350/1700.

La Perle de Prague, Dancing House (7th floor), Rašínovo Nábřeží 80, ⊠ 120 00, ℰ (02)
2198 4160, *laperle@volny.cz, Fax (02) 2198 4179,* ≼, 🍽 – 🏮 ▤. **MC** **AE** **VISA** CY f
closed Sunday and Monday lunch – **Meals** - French - 490/2500 and a la carte 810/1320
⏷ 450.

Bellevue, Smetanovo Nábřeží 18, ⊠ 110 00, ℰ (02) 2222 1443, *bellevue@zatisgrou*
p.cz, Fax (02) 2222 0453, ≼, 🍽 – **MC** **AE** **VISA** ⚘   CX z
closed 24 December – **Meals** 1250 and a la carte 1040/1870 ⏷ 490.

Circle Line, Malostranske Nám. 12, ⊠ 118 00, ℰ (02) 5753 0021, *circleline@prague*
finedining.cz, Fax (02) 5753 0023 – **MC** **AE** **VISA**   BX b
closed 24 December – **Meals** 675/1475 and a la carte 785/1585 ⏷ 790.

U Zlate Studně (at U Zlaté Studně H.), U Zlaté Studně 4, ⊠ 118 00, ℰ (02) 5753 3322,
zlata.studne@email.cz, Fax (02) 5753 5044, ≼ Prague, 🍽, « Panoramic roof terrace »
– ▤. **MC** **AE** **VISA**   BX f
Meals a la carte 800/1330 ⏷ 600.

Mlynec, Novotncho Lavka 9, ⊠ 110 00, ℰ (02) 2108 2208, *mylnec@pfd.cz,*
Fax (02) 92108 2391, 🍽, « Terrace ≼ Charles Bridge » – **MC** **AE** **VISA.** ⚘   CX k
closed 24 December – **Meals** a la carte 635/1535 ⏷ 490.

River Club, U Plovárny 8, ⊠ 110 00, ℰ (02) 5731 2578, *reservace@riverclub.cz,*
Fax (02) 5731 2574, 🍽, « Riverside terrace » – ▤ **P.** **MC** **AE** **①** **VISA** **JCB.** ⚘ CX x
Meals a la carte 955/1485.

Ostroff, Střelecký Ostrov 336, ⊠ 110 00, ℰ (02) 2491 9235, *ostroff@seznam.cz,*
Fax (02) 2492 0227, ≼, « Island setting, summer roof terrace » – ▤. **MC** **AE** **VISA**
Meals - Italian - *(closed Saturday lunch and Sunday November-March)* 420 (lunch) and a
la carte 990/1250 ⏷ 600.   BY c

Vinárna V Zátiši, Liliová 1, Betlémské Nám., ⊠ 110 00, ℰ (02) 2222 1155, *vzatisi*
@pfd.cz, Fax (02) 2222 0629 – ⚘ rest, ▤. **MC** **AE** **VISA**   CX a
closed 24 December – **Meals** (dinner booking essential) 595/795 (lunch) and a la carte
665/1965.

U Patrona, Dražického Nám. 4, ⊠ 118 00, ℰ (02) 5753 0725, *upatrona@uhi.cz,*
Fax (02) 5753 0723 – ⚘. **MC** **AE** **VISA**   BX h
closed Sunday – **Meals** (dinner only) a la carte 630/1060 ⏷ 450.

Kampa Park, Na Kampě 8b, ⊠ 110 00, ℰ (02) 5753 2685, *kampapark@anet.cz,*
Fax (02) 5753 3223, 🍽, « Vltava riverside setting, ≼ Charles Bridge » – **MC** **AE** **①** **VISA**
closed 24-26 December – **Meals** (dinner booking essential) 1000/1300 and a la carte
1050/1505 ⏷ 850.   BX k

Bistrot de Marlène, Plavecká 4, ⊠ 120 00, ℰ (02) 2491 1853, *Fax (02) 2492 0743*
– **MC** **AE** **VISA**   CZ f
closed 23 December-4 January, Sunday and Saturday lunch – **Meals** (booking essential at
dinner) a la carte 920/1225 ⏷ 640.

Denmark

Danmark

COPENHAGEN

PRACTICAL INFORMATION

LOCAL CURRENCY
Danish Kroner: *100 DKK = 13,44 euro (€) (Dec. 2001)*

TOURIST INFORMATION
The telephone number and address of the Tourist Information office is given in the text under 🛈.
National Holiday in Denmark: *5 June.*

FOREIGN EXCHANGE
Banks are open between 9.30am and 4.00pm (6.00pm on Thursdays) on weekdays except Saturdays. The main banks in the centre of Copenhagen, the Central Station and the Airport have exchange facilities outside these hours.

AIRLINES
SAS/LUFTHANSA: *Hamerichsgade 1, ☎ 70 10 20 00*
AIR FRANCE: *Ved Versterpot 6, ☎ 33 12 76 76*
BRITISH AIRWAYS: *Rådhuspladsen 16, ☎ 33 14 60 00*

MEALS
At lunchtime, follow the custom of the country and try the typical buffets of Danish specialities (smørrebrød).
At dinner, the a la carte and set menus will offer you more conventional cooking.

SHOPPING IN COPENHAGEN
Strøget (Department stores, exclusive shops, boutiques).
Kompagnistræde (Antiques). Shops are generally open from 10am to 7pm (Saturday 9am to 4pm).
See also in the index of street names, those printed in red are where the principal shops are found.

THEATRE BOOKINGS
Your hotel porter will be able to make your arrangements or direct you to Theatre Booking Agents.

CAR HIRE
The international car hire companies have branches in Copenhagen. Your hotel porter should be able to give details and help you with your arrangements.

TIPPING
In Denmark, all hotels and restaurants include a service charge. As for the taxis, there is no extra charge to the amount shown on the meter.

SPEED LIMITS
The maximum permitted speed in cities is 50 km/h - 31 mph, outside cities 80 km/h - 50 mph and 110 km/h - 68 mph on motorways. Cars towing caravans 70 km/h – 44 mph and buses 80 km/h – 50 mph also on motorways.
Local signs may indicate lower or permit higher limits. On the whole, speed should always be adjusted to prevailing circumstances. In case of even minor speed limit offences, drivers will be liable to heavy fines to be paid on the spot. If payment cannot be made, the car may be impounded.

SEAT BELTS
The wearing of seat belts is compulsory for drivers and all passengers except children under the age of 3 and taxi passengers.

COPENHAGEN
(KØBENHAVN)

Danmark 985 *Q 9 – pop. 622 000, Greater Copenhagen 1 354 000.*

Berlin 385 – Hamburg 305 – Oslo 583 – Stockholm 630.

🛈 *Copenhagen Tourist Information, Bernstorffsgade 1,* ✉ *1577 V* 𝄐 *70 22 24 42, Fax 70 22 24 52.*

🛈 *Dansk Golf Union 56* 𝄐 *43 45 55 55.*

✈ *Copenhagen/Kastrup SE : 10 km* 𝄐 *32 31 32 31 – Air Terminal : main railway station* 𝄐 *33 14 17 01.*

🚗 *Motorail for Southern Europe :* 𝄐 *33 14 17 01.*

🚢 *Further information from the D S B, main railway station or tourist information centre (see above).*
Øresund Bridge-high speed road and rail link between Denmark and Sweden.

See : *Rosenborg Castle*★★★ *(Rosenborg Slot) CX – Amalienborg Palace*★★ *(Amalienborg) DY – Nyhavn*★★★ *(canal) DY – Tivoli*★★ *: May to mid September BZ – Christiansborg Palace*★ *(Christiansborg) CZ – Citadel*★ *(Kastellet) DX – Gråbrødretorv*★ *CY 28 – Little Mermaid*★★ *(Den Lille Havfrue) DX – Marble Bridge*★ *(Marmorbroen) CZ 50 – Marble Church*★ *(Marmorkirke) DY – Kongens Nytorv*★ *DX – Round Tower*★ *(Rundetårn) CY E – Stock Exchange*★ *(Børsen) CDZ – Strøget*★ *BCYZ – Town Hall (Rådhuset) BZ H : Jens Olsen's astronomical clock*★ *BZ H – Bibliothek*★ *CZ.*

Museums : *National Museum*★★★ *(Nationalmuseet) CZ – Ny Carlsberg Glyptotek*★★★ *: art collection BZ – National Fine Arts Museum*★★ *(Statens Museum for Kunst) CX – Thorvaldsen Museum*★★ *(Thorvaldsens Museum) CZ M*[1] *– Den Hirschsprungske Samling*★ *CX – Davids Samling*★ *CY.*

Outskirts : *Ordrupgård*★★ *: art collection (Ordrupgårdsamlingen) N : 10 km CX – Louisiana Museum of Modern Art*★★★ *(Museum for Moderne Kunst) N : 35 km CX – Arken Museum of Modern Art*★★ *SW : 17 km by 02 (BN) and 151 – Dragør*★ *SW : 13 km CZ – Rungstedlund*★ *: Karen Blixen Museum N : 25 km CX – Open-Air Museum*★ *(Frilandsmuseet) NW : 12 km AX.*

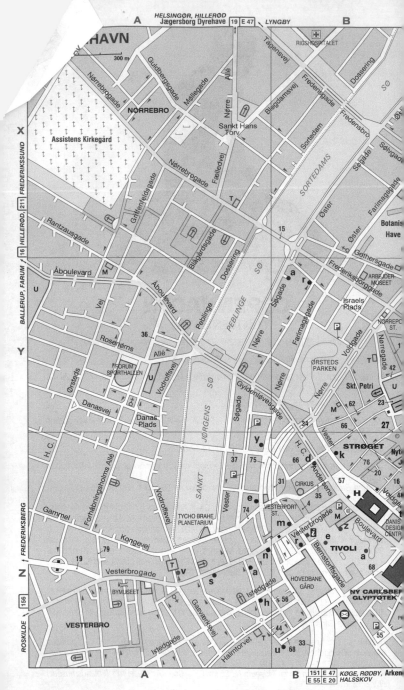

KØBENHAVN

300 m

RIGSHOSPITALET

Guldbergsgade

Nørrebrogade

NØRREBRO

Møllegade

Nørre Allé

Tagensvej

Blegdamsvej

Fredensgade

Dossering

SØ

Sankt Hans Torv

X

Assistens Kirkegård

Nørrebrogade

Fælledvej

Sortedam

Fredensbro

Fredensgade

Sølvgade

FREDERIKSSUND 211 HILLERØD 16

Griffenfeldsgade

Blågårdsgade

Dossering

SORTEDAMS

SØ

Øster Farimagsgade

Botanisk

Have

Rantzausgade

Åboulevard

M

Åboulevard

Peblinge

Dossering

SØ

PEBLINGE

SØ

Gothersgade

Frederiksborggade

ARBEJDER-
MUSEET

a r

Israels Plads

NØRREPO
ST.

BALLERUP, FARUM

U

Vej

Rosenørns

36

Allé

Peblinge

Nørre Søgade

Nørre

Farimagsgade

P

Nørregade

42

Y

FORUM
SPORTHALLEN

Ørsteds

U

Vodroffsvej

Danasvej

Danas Plads

Gyldenløvesgade

SØ

Søgade

ØRSTEDS
PARKEN

Nørre

Skt. Petri

62

M

23

T

U

H. C.

FREDERIKSBERG

Forhåbningsholms Allé

Vodroffsvej

SANKT

JØRGENS

SØ

Søgade

P

34

66

Vester

27

STRØGET

k

Nyt

y

d

66

H. C. Andersens

57

76

20

16

Voldga

37

75

31

CIRKUS

35

e

VESTERPORT
ST.

74

Vester

m

Vesterbrogade

P

M

z

r

Z

e

DANISH
DESIGN
CENTR

TIVOLI

a

Gammel

Kongevej

19

79

Vesterbrogade

T

V

BYMUSEET

Z

n

a

s

Gasværksvej

Isteedgade

h

HOVEDBANE
GÅRD

Bernstorffsgade

68

NY CARLSBER
GLYPTOTEK

ROSKILDE 156

VESTERBRO

Istedgade

Halmtorvet

T

44

56

33

u 68

P

55

A B

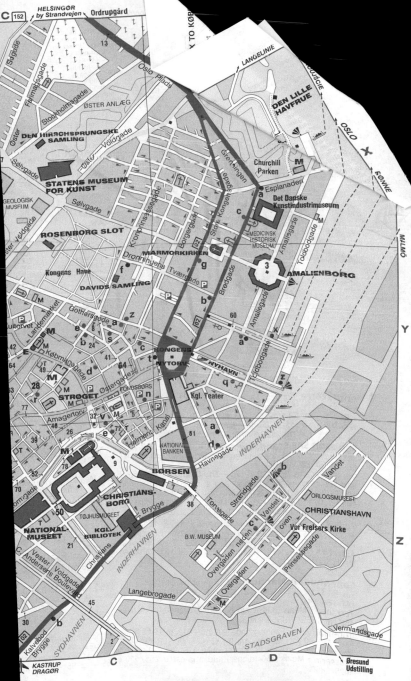

C 152 HELSINGØR by Strandvejen Ordrupgård

13

ÅX TO KØB

LANGELINIE

OSLO PLADS

KOUSCHE

DEN LILLE HAVFRUE

Søgade
Farimalsgade
Stockholmsgade

ØSTER ANLÆG

DEN HIRSCHSPRUNGSKE SAMLING

Øster
Sølvgade

Øster Voldgade

Øster Voldgade

Sølvgade

STATENS MUSEUM FOR KUNST

GEOLOGISK MUSEUM

ROSENBORG SLOT

Kronprinsessegade

Sølvgade

Borgergade

Store Kongensgade

Grønningen

OSLO

KØNNE

MILMØ

Churchill Parken

Esplanaden

a

Det Danske Kunstindustrimuseum

c

MEDICINSK HISTORISK MUSEUM

Toldbodgade

M

MARMORKIRKEN

Dronningens Tværgade

Kongens Have

f

DAVIDS SAMLING

g

Bredgade

Amaliegade

3

AMALIENBORG

X

Y

Gothersgade

a

z

e

b

8

s

P

b

60

O

a

Købmagergade

24

c

t

KONGENS NYTORV

NYHAVN

q

64

d

Østergade

STRØGET

M

FONDSBØRS

P

n

Kgl. Teater

Amagertorv

32

V

M

5

P

e

77

a

r

Holmens Kanal

NATIONAL BANKEN

26

39

51

M

78

9

Havnegade

INDERHAVNEN

b

BØRSEN

Vandet

Strandgade

Vandet

ORLOGSMUSEET

CHRISTIANS-BORG

Børsgade

38

Torvegade

CHRISTIANSHAVN

c

Vandet

oven

Vor Frelsers Kirke

TØJHUSMUSEET

Brygge

KGL. BIBLIOTEK

B.W. MUSEUM

Overgaden neden

Prinsessegade

NATIONAL MUSEET

21

Christians

INDERHAVNEN

Overgaden

Overgaden

Vester Voldgade

H. C. Andersens Boulevard

Langebrogade

M

45

30

b

Kalvebod Brygge

2

SYDHAVNEN

STADSGRAVEN

Vermlandsgade

KASTRUP DRAGØR

C

D

Øresund Udstilling

🏨🏨🏨🏨 **Angleterre,** Kongens Nytorv 34, ⌂ 1021 K, ℰ 33 12 00 95, remmen@remmen.dk, Fax 33 12 11 18, « Elegant 18C hotel overlooking the New Royal Square », ⌕, ⊜, ▨ – ▤, ⥊ rm, 📺 ⫝̸ ⛬ ⓪ VISA ⥥ 400. ⓂⓄ ⒶⒺ ⓪ VISA ⥥
CDY t
Wiinblad (ℰ 33 37 06 45) : **Meals** 295/355 (dinner) and a la carte 365/570 ⋔ 245 – ⌸ 130 – **104 rm** 2170/3470, 20 suites.

🏨🏨🏨🏨 **Radisson SAS Scandinavia** Ⓜ, Amager Boulevard 70, ⌂ 2300 S, ℰ 33 96 50 00, Fax 33 96 55 00, ≤ Copenhagen, ⌕, ⊜, ▨, squash – ▤, ⥊ rm, 📺 ⫝̸ ⛬ ⓔ – ⬛ 1200. ⓂⓄ ⒶⒺ ⓪ VISA JCB ⥥ rest
CZ
Meals a la carte 250/420 ⋔ 170 – **The Dining Room** (26th floor) : **Meals** (closed Sunday and Saturday lunch) 500/550 and a la carte approx. 400 ⋔ 170 – **Blue Elephant** (ℰ 33 96 59 70) : **Meals** - Thai - (closed lunch Saturday and Sunday) 205/495 and a la carte 330/535 ⋔ 170 – **Kyoto** : **Meals** - Japanese - (dinner only) 250/390 and a la carte ⋔ 170 – ⌸ 140 – **540 rm** 1830/2030, 2 suites.

🏨🏨🏨🏨 **Radisson SAS Royal,** Hammerichsgade 1, ⌂ 1611 V, ℰ 33 42 60 00, sales-cphzh @cphzh.com, Fax 33 42 61 00, ≤, « Panoramic restaurant on 20th floor », ⌕, ⊜ – ▤, ⥊ rm, ▤ 📺 ⛬ ⓔ – ⬛ 220. ⓂⓄ ⒶⒺ ⓪ VISA JCB ⥥ rest
BZ m
Alberto K : **Meals** (closed Sunday) 245/645 and a la carte 460/530 ⋔ 215 – **Café Royal** : **Meals** (buffet lunch) 220 and a la carte 260/335 ⋔ 200 – ⌸ 135 – **258 rm** 2590/3490, 2 suites.

🏨🏨🏨 **Copenhagen Marriott** Ⓜ, Kalvebod Brygge 5, ⌂ 1560, ℰ 88 33 99 00, Fax 88 33 99 99, ≤, ⌖, ⌕, ⊜ – ▤, ⥊ rm, ▤ 📺 ⫝̸ ⛬ ⓔ – ⬛ 570. ⓂⓄ ⒶⒺ ⓪ VISA JCB ⥥
CZ b
Terraneo : **Meals** (buffet lunch) 200/320 and a la carte 245/340 ⋔ 165 – ⌸ 140 – **386 rm** 1695/2195, 9 suites.

🏨🏨🏨 **Imperial,** Vester Farimagsgade 9, ⌂ 1606 V, ℰ 33 12 80 00, imperial@imperialhotel.dk, Fax 33 93 80 31 – ▤, ⥊ rm, 📺 ⛬ ⓔ – ⬛ 150. ⓂⓄ ⒶⒺ ⓪ VISA JCB ⥥ rest
Imperial Garden : **Meals** (dinner only) 410 and a la carte 365/555 ⋔ 185 – **Imperial Brasserie** : **Meals** 230 (dinner) and a la carte 255/310 ⋔ 185 – ⌸ 95 – **163 rm** 1425/2850.
AZ e

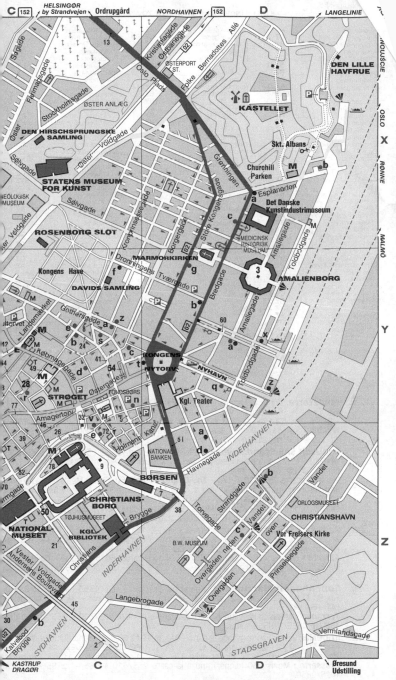

STREET INDEX TO KØBENHAVN TOWN PLAN

🏨🏨🏨🏨🏨 **Angleterre,** Kongens Nytorv 34, ✉ 1021 K, 𝒫 33 12 00 95, *remmen@remmen.dk,* Fax 33 12 11 18, « Elegant 18C hotel overlooking the New Royal Square », 𝐿𝑏, ≘s, 🔲 – 🛗, ✳ rm, 📺 🗘 – 🍴 400. 🟣🟢 🄰🄴 ① 𝗩𝗜𝗦𝗔 🐾
CDY t
Wiinblad (𝒫 33 37 06 45) : **Meals** 295/355 (dinner) and a la carte 365/570 ⓐ 245 – ⌷ 130 – **104 rm** 2170/3470, 20 suites.

🏨🏨🏨🏨 **Radisson SAS Scandinavia** 🅼, Amager Boulevard 70, ✉ 2300 S, 𝒫 33 96 50 00, Fax 33 96 55 00, ≤ Copenhagen, 𝐿𝑏, ≘s, 🔲, squash – 🛗, ✳ rm, 📺 🗘 🖵 – 🍴 1200. 🟣🟢 🄰🄴 ① 𝗩𝗜𝗦𝗔 🐾 rest
CZ
Meals a la carte 250/420 ⓐ 170 – **The Dining Room** *(26th floor)* : **Meals** *(closed Sunday and Saturday lunch)* 500/550 and a la carte approx. 400 ⓐ 170 – **Blue Elephant** (𝒫 33 96 59 70) : **Meals** - Thai - *(closed lunch Saturday and Sunday)* 205/495 and a la carte 330/535 ⓐ 170 – **Kyoto** : **Meals** - Japanese - *(dinner only)* 250/390 and a la carte ⓐ 170 – ⌷ 140 – **540 rm** 1830/2030, 2 suites.

🏨🏨🏨🏨 **Radisson SAS Royal,** Hammerichsgade 1, ✉ 1611 V, 𝒫 33 42 60 00, *sales-cphzh @cphzh.com, Fax 33 42 61 00,* ≤, « Panoramic restaurant on 20th floor », 𝐿𝑏, ≘s – 🛗, ✳ rm, 🔲 📺 🗘 🖵 🚗 🖵 – 🍴 220. 🟣🟢 🄰🄴 ① 𝗩𝗜𝗦𝗔 🄹🄲🄱 🐾 rest
BZ m
Alberto K : **Meals** *(closed Sunday)* 245/645 and a la carte 460/530 ⓐ 215 – **Café Royal :** **Meals** *(buffet lunch)* 220 and a la carte 260/335 ⓐ 200 – ⌷ 135 – **258 rm** 2590/3490, 2 suites.

🏨🏨🏨🏨 **Copenhagen Marriott** 🅼, Kalvebod Brygge 5, ✉ 1560, 𝒫 88 33 99 00, Fax 88 33 99 99, ≤, 🍽, 𝐿𝑏, ≘s – 🛗, ✳ rm, 🔲 📺 🗘 🖵 🚗 – 🍴 570. 🟣🟢 🄰🄴 ① 𝗩𝗜𝗦𝗔 🄹🄲🄱 🐾
CZ b
Terraneo : **Meals** *(buffet lunch)* 200/320 and a la carte 245/340 ⓐ 165 – ⌷ 140 – **386 rm** 1695/2195, 9 suites.

🏨🏨🏨 **Imperial,** Vester Farimagsgade 9, ✉ 1606 V, 𝒫 33 12 80 00, *imperial@imperialhotel.dk,* Fax 33 93 80 31 – 🛗, ✳ rm, 📺 🗘 🖵 – 🍴 150. 🟣🟢 🄰🄴 ① 𝗩𝗜𝗦𝗔 🄹🄲🄱 🐾 rest
Imperial Garden : **Meals** *(dinner only)* 410 and a la carte 365/555 ⓐ 185 – **Imperial Brasserie :** **Meals** 230 (dinner) and a la carte 255/310 ⓐ 185 – ⌷ 95 – **163 rm** 1425/2850.
AZ e

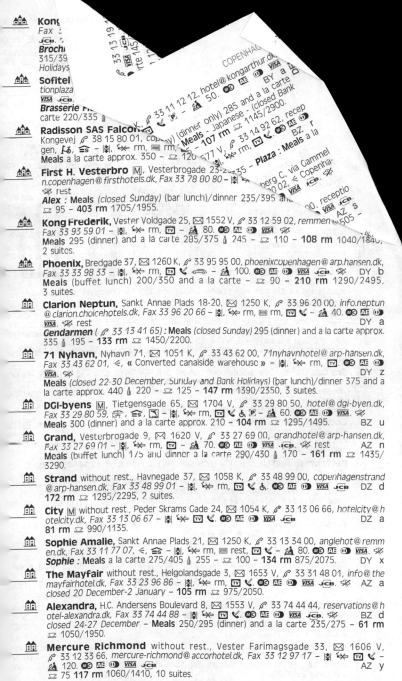

🏨 **Kong** ...
Fax ...
Broch...
315/39...
Holidays...

🏨 **Sofitel** ...
tionplaza...
VISA **JCB**...
Brasserie F...
carte 220/335 ...

COPENHA...

..., hotel@kongarthur.dk ...
... 50. **MB** **AE** **①** ... BY a
Meals (dinner only) 285 and a la carte
– **107 rm** ⊆ 1145/2900.

🏨 **Radisson SAS Falcon...**
Kongevej ℰ 38 15 80 01, cop...
gen., **⅃ઠ**, **⬱** – |‡|, **⥅** rm, **rm**, ... 33 14 92 62, recep
Meals a la carte approx. 350 – ⊆ 120 ... V, ... Plaza : *Meals* a la

🏨 **First H. Vesterbro** M, Vesterbrogade 23-... 235 ...
n.copenhagen@firsthotels.dk, Fax 33 78 80 80 – |‡| ...berg C, via Copenha-
⅏ rest ... 02, ... reception
Alex : *Meals* (closed Sunday) (bar lunch)/dinner 235/395 ... **VISA** **JCB** s
⊆ 95 – **403 rm** 1705/1955.

🏨 **Kong Frederik,** Vester Voldgade 25, ⊠ 1552 V, ℰ 33 12 59 02, remmen... AZ s
Fax 33 93 59 01 – |‡|, **⥅** rm, **TV** – **△** 80. **MB** **AE** **①** **VISA** **⅏**
Meals 295 (dinner) and a la carte 285/375 ‡ 245 – ⊆ 110 – **108 rm** 1040/1840,
2 suites.

🏨 **Phoenix,** Bredgade 37, ⊠ 1260 K, ℰ 33 95 95 00, phoenixcopenhagen@arp.hansen.dk,
Fax 33 33 98 33 – |‡|, **⥅** rm, **TV** **☎** **⇐⇒** – **△** 100. **MB** **AE** **①** **VISA** **JCB**. **⅏** DY b
Meals (buffet lunch) 200/350 and a la carte – ⊆ 90 – **210 rm** 1290/2495,
3 suites.

🏨 **Clarion Neptun,** Sankt Annae Plads 18-20, ⊠ 1250 K, ℰ 33 96 20 00, info.neptun
@clarion.choicehotels.dk, Fax 33 96 20 66 – |‡|, **⥅** rm, **⊟** rm, **TV** **☎** – **△** 40. **MB** **AE** **①**
VISA. **⅏** rest DY a
Gendarmen (ℰ 33 13 41 65) : *Meals* (closed Sunday) 295 (dinner) and a la carte approx.
335 ‡ 195 – **133 rm** ⊆ 1450/2200.

🏨 **71 Nyhavn,** Nyhavn 71, ⊠ 1051 K, ℰ 33 43 62 00, 71nyhavnhotel@arp-hansen.dk,
Fax 33 43 62 01, ≤, « Converted canalside warehouse » – |‡|, **⥅** rm, **TV**. **MB** **AE** **①**
VISA. DY z
Meals (closed 22-30 December, Sunday and Bank Holidays) (bar lunch)/dinner 375 and a
la carte approx. 440 ‡ 220 – ⊆ 125 – **147 rm** 1390/2350, 3 suites.

🏨 **DGI-byens** M, Tietgensgade 65, ⊠ 1704 V, ℰ 33 29 80 50, hotel@dgi-byen.dk,
Fax 33 29 80 59, **⇱**, **⥄**, **⌷** – |‡|, **⥅** rm, **TV** **☎** **ઠ** **⌷** – **△** 60. **MB** **AE** **①** **VISA**. **⅏**
Meals 300 (dinner) and a la carte approx. 210 – **104 rm** ⊆ 1295/1495. BZ u

🏨 **Grand,** Vesterbrogade 9, ⊠ 1620 V, ℰ 33 27 69 00, grandhotel@arp-hansen.dk,
Fax 33 27 69 01 – |‡|, **⥅** rm, **TV** – **△** 70. **MB** **AE** **①** **VISA** **JCB**. **⅏** rest AZ n
Meals (buffet lunch) 175 and dinner a la carte 290/430 ‡ 170 – **161 rm** ⊆ 1435/
3290.

🏨 **Strand** without rest., Havnegade 37, ⊠ 1058 K, ℰ 33 48 99 00, copenhagenstrand
@arp-hansen.dk, Fax 33 48 99 01 – |‡|, **⥅** rm, **TV** **☎** **ઠ**. **MB** **AE** **①** **VISA** **JCB** DZ d
172 rm ⊆ 1295/2295, 2 suites.

🏨 **City** M without rest., Peder Skrams Gade 24, ⊠ 1054 K, ℰ 33 13 06 66, hotelcity@h
otelcity.dk, Fax 33 13 06 67 – |‡| **⥅** **TV** **☎**. **MB** **AE** **①** **VISA** **JCB** DZ a
81 rm ⊆ 990/1135.

🏨 **Sophie Amalie,** Sankt Annae Plads 21, ⊠ 1250 K, ℰ 33 13 34 00, anglehot@remm
en.dk, Fax 33 11 77 07, ≤, **⥄** – |‡|, **⥅** rm, **⊟** rest, **TV** **☎** – **△** 80. **MB** **AE** **①** **VISA**. **⅏**
Sophie : *Meals* a la carte 275/405 ‡ 255 – ⊆ 100 – **134 rm** 875/2075. DY x

🏨 **The Mayfair** without rest., Helgolandsgade 3, ⊠ 1653 V, ℰ 33 31 48 01, info@the
mayfairhotel.dk, Fax 33 23 96 86 – |‡|, **⥅** rm, **TV** **☎**. **MB** **AE** **①** **VISA** **JCB**. **⅏** AZ a
closed 20 December-2 January – **105 rm** ⊆ 975/2050.

🏨 **Alexandra,** H.C. Andersens Boulevard 8, ⊠ 1553 V, ℰ 33 74 44 44, reservations@h
otel-alexandra.dk, Fax 33 74 44 88 – |‡| **⥅** **TV** **☎**. **MB** **AE** **①** **VISA** **JCB**. **⅏** BZ d
closed 24-27 December – *Meals* 250/295 (dinner) and a la carte 235/275 – **61 rm**
⊆ 1050/1950.

🏨 **Mercure Richmond** without rest., Vester Farimagsgade 33, ⊠ 1606 V,
ℰ 33 12 33 66, mercure-richmond@accorhotel.dk, Fax 33 12 97 17 – |‡| **⥅** **TV** **☎** –
△ 120. **MB** **AE** **①** **VISA** **JCB** AZ y
⊆ 75 **117 rm** 1060/1410, 10 suites.

..., hotel@ibsenshotel.dk

BY

Ibsens, ...20 ᴙ 85 – **118 rm** ☲ 925/2100

Fax 33 13...

La Rocca, ...de 15, ⊠ 1653 V, ℘ 33 24 22 11, info@absalon...

..60 K, ℘ 33 48 10 00, info-esplanade...

..0 60 – |‖| ✦ 📺 • 🐾 AE ① VISA

DX a

AZ h

Esplan ...n@ c... – **179 rm** ☲ 850/1700.

...116 ..ester Voldgade 89, ⊠ 1552 V, ℘ 33 11 48 06, hotel@hot...

...36 30 – |‖| ✦ 📺 🐾 ⟿ ⬛ 🐾 AE ① VISA JCB

BZ t

Ab ..2 suites.

...ixnout rest., Dronningens Tvaergade 45, ⊠ 1302 K, ℘ 33 32 10 44

...iv@arp-hansen.dk, Fax 33 32 07 06 – |‖| ✦ 📺 ⬛ 🐾 AE ①

CY 1

...ristmas – **42 rm** ☲ 1090/1390.

g Hans Kaelder, Vingårdsstraede 6, ⊠ 1070 K, ℘ 33 11 68 68, konghans@m...

...il.tele.dk, Fax 33 32 67 68, « Vaulted Gothic cellar » – 🐾 AE ① VISA JCB. ✦ CY n

closed Easter, 21 July-4 August, Christmas and Bank Holidays – **Meals** (booking essential)

(dinner only) a la carte 640/840 ᴙ 195

Spec. Foie gras with dried fruit compote, Banyuls sauce. Variations of Valhrona chocolate

XX **Kommandanten**, Ny Adelgade 7, ⊠ 1104 K, ℘ 33 12 09 90, kommandanten@kc...

✿✿ mmandanten.dk, Fax 33 93 12 23, « 17C town house, contemporary furnishings » – 🐾

AE ① VISA JCB. ✦ CY c

closed 14-28 July, 23 December-4 January, Sunday, Saturday lunch and Bank Holidays –

Meals (booking essential) 380/730 and a la carte 420/760

Spec. Fried lobster tails with sesame biscuit and aniseed. Chocolate desserts.

XX **Pierre André** (Houdet), Ny Østergade 21, ⊠ 1101 K, ℘ 33 16 17 19, Fax 33 16 17 72

✿ – 🐾 AE ① VISA CY s

closed Easter, last 2 weeks July-first week August, 23-26 and 31 December, 1 January,

Sunday, Saturday lunch, lunch June-mid August and Bank Holidays – **Meals** (booking essential)

320/980 and a la carte 405/640 ᴙ 195

Spec. Foie gras "Emilia Romagna". Chevreuil aux épices. Gâteau chaud au chocolat, glace

Gianduja.

XX **Era Ora** (Milleri), Overgaden neden Vandet 33B, ⊠ 1414 K, ℘ 32 54 06 93, era-ora

✿ @era-ora.dk, Fax 32 96 02 09 – ⬛. 🐾 AE ① VISA. ✦ DZ x

closed Easter, 24-25 December, 1 January and Sunday – **Meals** - Italian - (booking essential)

(dinner only) 350/725 ᴙ 425

Spec. Assorted antipasto. Homemade pasta. Rare Italian cheeses.

XX **Coquus**, Gothersgade 35, ⊠ 1123 K, ℘ 33 13 62 82, Fax 33 13 72 82 – ✦ ⬛. 🐾 AE

① VISA JCB. ✦ CY a

closed Easter, July, Christmas, Sunday and Bank Holidays – **Meals** (dinner only) (set menu

only) 425/545 ᴙ 250.

XX **Restaurationen** (Jacobsen), M! ntergade 19, ⊠ 1116 K, ℘ 33 14 94 95 – 🐾 AE ①

✿ VISA. ✦ CY e

closed 7 July-5 August, 21 December-6 January, Sunday, Monday and Bank Holidays –

Meals (booking essential) (dinner only except December) (set menu only) 575 ᴙ 325

Spec. Smoked eel and leek brawn. Roast tail of veal with foie gras and truffle sauce. Caramel

ice cream with elderberry jelly.

XX **Krogs**, Gammel Strand 38, ⊠ 1202 K, ℘ 33 15 89 15, krogs@krogs.dk, Fax 33 15 83 19

🍴, 18C house – 🐾 AE ① VISA JCB. ✦ CZ a

closed Easter, 22-26 December, 1 January and Sunday dinner – **Meals** - Seafood - (booking

essential) 300/445 and a la carte 535/925 ᴙ 250.

XX **Gammel Mont**, Gammel Mont 41, ⊠ 1117 K, ℘ 33 15 10 60, Fax 33 15 10 60, « Half

timbered house from 1732 %2" – 🐾 AE ① VISA. ✦ CY b

closed July, 23 December-3 January and Sunday – **Meals** 175/525 and a la carte 275/550

ᴙ 195.

XX **Ketchup Café**, Pilestraede 19, ⊠ 1112 K, ℘ 33 32 30 30, cafeketchup@sovino.dk,

Fax 33 32 30 95, Modern bistro with cigar bar – ⬛. 🐾 AE ① VISA JCB. ✦ CY o

closed 25-26 December, Easter Monday and Sunday – **Meals** (booking essential) a la carte

280/510 ᴙ 250.

XX **Le Sommelier**, Bredgade 63-65, ⊠ 1260 K, ℘ 33 11 45 15, mail@lesommelier.dk

Fax 33 11 59 79 – 🐾 ① VISA JCB. ✦ DX c

closed July, 23 December-3 January, Saturday and Sunday lunch – **Meals** 245/315 and

a la carte 255/435.

X **Godt** (Rice), Gothersgade 38, ✉ 1123 K, 𝒫 33 15 21 22, *godt@get2net.dk* – ☜
🕸 ᴊᴄʙ.
closed Easter, July, Christmas-New Year, Sunday, Monday and Bank Holidays – .
(booking essential) (dinner only) (set menu only) 420/540 🍷 305
Spec. Wild duck consommé with foie gras. Turbot with beurre blanc of orange and ba.
Stuffed pheasant with glazed chestnuts.

X **Lumskebugten,** Esplanaden 21, ✉ 1263 K, 𝒫 33 15 60 29, Fax 33 32 07 18, 🌣,
📠 « Mid 19C café-pavilion » – ⓂⓈ ᴀᴇ ① 𝐕𝐈𝐒𝐀 ᴊᴄʙ. 🛇   DX b
closed 23 December-2 January, Saturday lunch, Sunday and Bank Holidays – **Meals**
275/850 and a la carte 330/825.

X **Kanalen,** Christianshavn-Wilders Plads 2, ✉ 1403 K, 𝒫 32 95 13 30, *info@restaurant-*
🍴 *kanalen.dk*, Fax 32 95 13 38, ≤, « Canalside house and terrace » – 🅿. ⓂⓈ ᴀᴇ ① 𝐕𝐈𝐒𝐀 ᴊᴄʙ.
🛇   DZ b
closed 25 March-2 April, 23-30 December, Sunday and Bank Holidays – **Meals** (booking
essential) 180/325 and a la carte 320/425 🍷 190.

X **M/S Amerika**, Dampfaergevej 8 (Pakhus 12, Amerikakaj), ✉ 2100 K, via Folke Ber-
🍴 nadettes Allée 𝒫 35 26 90 30, *info@msamerika.dk*, Fax 35 26 91 30, 🌣, « 19C former
warehouse » – ⓂⓈ ᴀᴇ ① 𝐕𝐈𝐒𝐀 ᴊᴄʙ. 🛇
closed 24 December-2 January, Sunday and Bank Holidays – **Meals** (set menu only at dinner)
180/295 and lunch a la carte 295 🍷 170.

X **Restaurant Gastronomique,** Frederiksberg Runddel 1, ✉ 2000 F, via Frederiksberg
Allé 𝒫 38 34 84 36, Fax 38 34 84 36, « 18C pavilion with terrace in Royal Park » – ⓂⓈ
ᴀᴇ ① 𝐕𝐈𝐒𝐀 ᴊᴄʙ. 🛇 *– April-22 December –* **Meals** *(closed Sunday, Saturday lunch and lunch
October-22 December)* 330/530 🍷 360.

X **Den Gyldne Fortun,** Ved Stranden 18, ✉ 1061 K, 𝒫 33 12 20 11, *den-gyldne for*
tun@den-gyldne-fortun.dk, Fax 33 93 35 11, 🌣, « Late 16C former inn » – ⓂⓈ ᴀᴇ ①
𝐕𝐈𝐒𝐀 ᴊᴄʙ. 🛇   CZ e
closed 22-26 December and Sunday lunch in winter **Meals** - Seafood - 370 (dinner) and a
la carte 355/515 🍷 230.

X **Den Sorte Ravn,** Nyhavn 14, ✉ 1051 K, 𝒫 33 13 12 33, *rest@sorteravn.dk*,
Fax 33 13 24 72 – ▤. ⓂⓈ ᴀᴇ ① 𝐕𝐈𝐒𝐀 ᴊᴄʙ. 🛇   DY q
*closed 28 March-1 April, 19-20 May, 2 weeks July, 24-26 December, first week January
and Sunday –* **Meals** 200/400 and a la carte 280/500 🍷 175.

X **Grabrodre Torv 21,** Grabrodre Torv 21, ✉ 1154 K, 𝒫 33 11 47 07, *grabrodre21@m*
ail.tele.dk, Fax 33 12 60 19, 🌣 – ⓂⓈ ᴀᴇ ① 𝐕𝐈𝐒𝐀 ᴊᴄʙ. 🛇   CY r
closed 23-26 and 31 December and first week January – **Meals** 200/400 and a la carte
220/465 🍷 160.

X **Passagens Spisehus,** Vesterbrogade 42, ✉ 1620 V, 𝒫 33 22 47 57, *info@passag*
ens.dk, Fax 33 22 47 87, 🌣 – ⓂⓈ ᴀᴇ ① 𝐕𝐈𝐒𝐀. 🛇   AZ v
closed 1 week Easter, 8 days Christmas and Sunday – **Meals** (dinner only) 265/325 and
a la carte.

in Tivoli : *Vesterbrogade 3* ✉ *1620 V (Entrance fee payable)*

XXX **Divan 2,** 𝒫 33 12 51 51, *restaurant@divan2.dk*, Fax 33 91 08 82, ≤, 🌣, « Floral decoration and terrace » – ⓂⓈ ᴀᴇ ① 𝐕𝐈𝐒𝐀 ᴊᴄʙ. 🛇   BZ a
20 April-21 September and 23 November-21 December – **Meals** 345/495 and a la carte
475/795 🍷 280.

XX **La Crevette,** Bernstorffsgade 5, ✉ 1577 V, 𝒫 33 14 68 47, *restaurant@nimb.dk*,
Fax 33 14 60 06, ≤, 🌣, « Terrace overlooking flowered garden » – ⓂⓈ ᴀᴇ ① 𝐕𝐈𝐒𝐀 ᴊᴄʙ.
🛇   BZ e
19 April-23 September – **Meals** - Seafood - 335/455 and a la carte 555/780 🍷 250.

X **Bagatellen,** ✉ 1630 V, 𝒫 33 75 07 51, *mail@bagatellen.dk*, Fax 33 75 07 52, 🌣,
« Modern-style brasserie in mid 19C pavilion » – ⓂⓈ ᴀᴇ ① 𝐕𝐈𝐒𝐀. 🛇   BZ z
closed 23 September-15 November and 23 November-15 April – **Meals** 195/495 (dinner)
and a la carte 335/500 🍷 285.

SMØRREBRØD

**The following list of simpler restaurants and cafés/bars specialize in Danish
open sandwiches and are generally open from 10.00am to 4.00pm.**

X **Ida Davidsen,** St Kongensgade 70, ✉ 1264 K, 𝒫 33 93 64 54, Fax 33 11 36 55 – ⓂⓈ
🍴 ᴀᴇ ① 𝐕𝐈𝐒𝐀 ᴊᴄʙ. 🛇   DY g
closed July, Christmas-New Year, Saturday and Sunday – **Meals** (buffet lunch only) a la carte
45/200 🍷 120.

X **Slotskaelderen-Hos Gitte Kik,** Fortunstraede 4, ✉ 1065 K, 𝒫 33 11 15 37,
Fax 33 11 15 37 – ⓂⓈ ᴀᴇ ① 𝐕𝐈𝐒𝐀 ᴊᴄʙ. 🛇   CYZ v
closed Sunday and Monday – **Meals** (buffet lunch only) a la carte 75/155.

X **Sankt Annae,** Sankt Annae Plads 12, ✉ 1250 K, 𝒫 33 12 54 97, Fax 33 15 16 61 –
ⓂⓈ ᴀᴇ ① 𝐕𝐈𝐒𝐀. 🛇   DY a
closed Sunday and Bank Holidays – **Meals** (lunch only) a la carte 40/85.

7 ½ km by Østbanegade DX and Road 2 – ⊠ 2900 Hellerup :

...arkhotel, Strandvejen 203, ℰ 39 62 40 44, info@hellerupparkhotel.dk, ...56 57, ⅃ᵟ, ⇌ – ❘𝖘❘, ⅄⇆ rm, 🆅 ℂ 🅟 – 🅐 150. 🆎 🅰🅴 🅾 🆅🅸🆂🅰 🅹🅲🅱, ❀ rest
...23-26 December – **Saison :** Meals (closed Sunday and Bank Holiday lunch) 225/395 ...a la carte 350/510 ⬥ 160 – **Via Appia :** Meals - Italian - (dinner only) 220/325 and a la carte 170/320 ⬥ 160 – **71 rm** ⊑ 1165/1950.

...øllerød North : 20 km by Tagensvej BX and Road 19 – ⊠ 2840 Holte :

🏯🏯🏯 **Søllerød Kro,** Søllerødvej 35, ⊠ 2840 K, ℰ 45 80 25 05, mail@soelleroed-kro.dk, Fax 45 80 22 70, ⇞, « 17C thatched inn, terrace » – 🅿. 🆎 🅰🅴 🅾 🆅🅸🆂🅰 🅹🅲🅱. ❀ closed 8-28 July, 24 December and 1 January – **Meals** 250/520 and a la carte 435/575 ⬥ 245.

at Kastrup Airport Southeast : 10 km by Amager Boulevard CZ – ⊠ 2300 S :

🏨🏨🏨 **Hilton Copenhagen Airport** 🅼, Ellehammersvej 20, Kastrup, ⊠ 2770, ℰ 32 50 15 01, rescopenhagen-airport@hilton.com, Fax 32 52 85 28, ⩽, ⅃ᵟ, ⇌, 🝔 – ❘𝖘❘, ⅄⇆ rm, 🗐 🆅 ℂ ⅄ ⅋ – 🅐 450. 🆎 🅰🅴 🅾 🆅🅸🆂🅰 ❀
Hamlet : Meals (closed 23 December-1 January) 350/425 (dinner) and a la carte 340/495 ⬥ 185 – **Horizon :** Meals (closed 23 December-1 January) (buffet lunch) 210/220 and a la carte 190/385 ⬥ 185 – ⊑ 140 – **376 rm** 2250/3250, 6 suites.

🏨🏨 **Quality Airport H. Dan** 🅼, Kastruplundgade 15, Kastrup, ⊠ 2770, North : 2 ½ km by coastal rd ℰ 32 51 14 00, info.airport.dan@quality.choicehotels.dk, Fax 32 51 37 01, ⇞, ⅃ᵟ, ⇌ – ❘𝖘❘, ⅄⇆ rm, 🗐 rest, 🆅 ⅍ 🅿 – 🅐 120. 🆎 🅰🅴 🅾 🆅🅸🆂🅰 ❀ rest closed 21 December-2 January – **Amadeus :** Meals 170/335 and a la carte ⬥ 175 – **Valentino :** Meals (buffet lunch) 150/335 ⬥ 175 – **228 rm** ⊑ 1095/2695.

🏨🏨 **Radisson SAS Globetrotter,** Engvej 171, ⊠ 2770, Northwest : 3 km by coastal rd ℰ 32 87 02 02, sales.globetrotter.copenhagen@radissonsas.com, Fax 32 87 02 20, ⅃ᵟ, ⇌, 🝔 – ❘𝖘❘, ⅄⇆ rm, 🆅 ℂ 🅟 – 🅐 360. 🆎 🅰🅴 🅾 🆅🅸🆂🅰 🅹🅲🅱 ❀ rest
Meals (buffet lunch) 180 and a la carte approx. 200 – ⊑ 120 – **197 rm** 1460/2460.

Finland

Suomi

HELSINKI

PRACTICAL INFORMATION

CURRENCY

uro (€) = 0,89 USD ($) (Dec. 2001)

TOURIST INFORMATION

The Tourist Office is situated near the Market Square, Pohjoisesplanadi 19 ℘ (09) 169 3757. Open from 2 May to 30 September, Monday to Friday 9am - 8pm, Saturday and Sunday 9am - 6pm, and from 1 October to 30 April, Monday to Friday 9am - 6pm Saturday and Sunday from 10am to 4pm. Hotel bookings are possible from a reservation board situated in the airport arrival lounge and in the main railway station; information is also available free.

National Holiday in Finland: *6 December.*

FOREIGN EXCHANGE

Banks are open between 9.15am and 4.15pm on weekdays only. Exchange offices at Helsinki-Vantaa airport and Helsinki harbour open daily between 6.30am and 11pm and at the railway station between 7am and 10pm.

MEALS

At lunchtime, follow the custom of the country and try the typical buffets of Scandinavian specialities.
At dinner, the a la carte and set menus will offer you more conventional cooking. Booking is essential.
Many city centre restaurants are closed for a few days over the Midsummer Day period.

SHOPPING IN HELSINKI

Furs, jewellery, china, glass and ceramics, Finnish handicraft and wood.
In the index of street names, those printed in red are where the principal shops are found. Your hotel porter will be able to help you with information.

THEATRE BOOKINGS

The following agents sell tickets for opera, theatre, concerts, cinema and sports events: Lippupalvelu ℘ 0600 108 00, Lippupiste ℘ 0600 900 900, Tiketti ℘ 0600 116 16.

CAR HIRE

The international car hire companies have branches in Helsinki and at Vantaa airport. Your hotel porter should be able to help you with your arrangements.

TIPPING

Service is normally included in hotel and restaurant bills. Doormen, baggage porters etc. are generally given a gratuity; taxi drivers are not usually tipped.

SPEED LIMITS

The maximum permitted speed on motorways is 120 km/h - 74 mph (in winter 100 km/h - 62 mph), 80 km/h - 50 mph on other roads and 50 km/h - 31 mph in built-up areas.

SEAT BELTS

The wearing of seat belts in Finland is compulsory for drivers and all passengers.

HELSINKI
(HELSINGFORS)

Finland 985 L 21 – Pop. 546 317.

Lahti 103 – Tampere 176 – Turku 165.

🛈 City Tourist Office Pohjoisesplanadi 19 ☎ (09) 169 37 57, Fax (09) 169 38 39.

🖾 Helsingin golfklubi ☎ (09) 550 235.

✈ Helsinki-Vantaa N. 19 km ☎ 0200 4636 (information) – Finnair Head Office, Tietotie 11 A – 01053 ☎ 818 8383 – Air Terminal : Scandic H. Continental, Mannerheimintie 46 – Finnair City Terminal : Asema – Aukio 3, ☎ 0203 140 160 (reservations).

⛴ To Sweden, Estonia and boat excursions : contact the City Tourist Office (see above) – Car Ferry: Silja Line ☎ 0203 74 552 – Viking Line ☎ 123577 – Eckerö Line ☎ 228 8544 – Nordic Jetline ☎ 681 770 – Tallink ☎ 2282 1277.

See: Senate Square★★★ (Senaatintori) DY **53** – Market Square★★ (Kauppatori) DY **26** – Esplanadi★★ CDY **8/43** – Railway Station★★ (Rautatiesema) CX – Finlandia Hall★★ (Finlandia-talo) BX – National Opera House★★ (Kansallisoopera) BX – Church in the Rock★★ (Temppeliaukion kirkko) BX – Ateneum Art Museum★★ (Ateneum, Suomen Taiteen Museo) CY **M¹** – National Museum★★ (Kansallismuseo) BX **M²** – Lutheran Cathedral★★ (Tuomiokirkko) DY – Parliament House★ (Eduskuntatalo) BX – Amos Anderson Collection★ (Amos Andersinin taidemuseo) BY **M⁴** – Uspensky Cathedral★ (Uspenskin katedraali) DY – Cygnaeus home and collection★ (Cynaeuksen galleria) DZ **B** – Mannerheim home and collection★ (Mannerheim-museo) DZ **M⁵** – Olympic Stadium★ (Olympiastadion) ☀★★ BX **21** – Museum of Applied Arts★★ (Taideteollisuusmuseo) CZ **M⁶** – Sibelius Monument★ (Sibelius-monumentti) AX **S** – Ice-breaker fleet★ DX.

Outskirts: Fortress of Suomenlinna★★ by boat DZ – Seurasaari Open-Air Museum★★ BX – Urho Kekkonen Museum★ (Urho Kekkosen museo) BX.

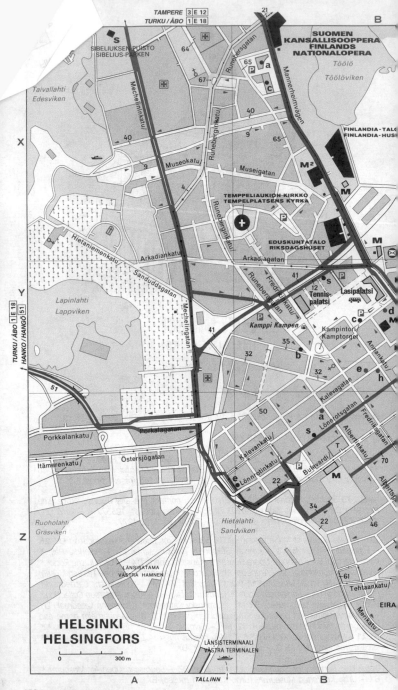

TAMPERE 3 E 12
TURKU / ÅBO 1 E 18

B

SUOMEN
KANSALLISOOPPERA
FINLANDS
NATIONALOPERA

S
SIBELIUKSEN PUISTO
SIBELIUS-PARKEN

64

Töölö
Töölöviken

65 P a
c
67

40

X

Taivallahti
Edesviken

Mechelininkatu/

Runebergingatan

Mannerheimvägen

FINLANDIA - TALO
FINLANDIA - HUS

40

9

65

9

Museokatu/

Museigatan

Runeberginkatu/

M²

M

TEMPPELIAUKION KIRKKO
TEMPELPLATSENS KYRKA

4

P

M

Hietaniemenkatu/

Arkadiankatu/

Sanduddsgatan

EDUSKUNTATALO
RIKSDAGSHUSET

Arkadiagatan

M

Y

Lapinlahti
Lappviken

Mechelingatan

Runebergsgatan

41

Fredriksgatan

12 s P
Tennis-
palatsi

Lasipalatsi

Runebergingatan

TURKU / ÅBO 1 E 18
HANKO / HANGÖ 51

41

Kamppi Kampen

35

32

b

P c d
M

Kampintori/
Kamptorget

Annankatu/

51

32

e

h

Kalevagatan

50

a

Lönnrotsgatan

s

Fredriksgatan

Albertsgatan

Porkkalankatu/

Porkalagatan

Kalevankatu/

Lönnrotinkatu/

Bulevardi/

P

70

Albertsin

Itämerenkatu/

Östersjögatan

e
Lönnrotinkatu/

22

M

T

34

22

46

Z

Ruoholahti
Gräsviken

Hietalahti
Sandviken

61

Tehtaankatu/

LÄNSISATAMA
VÄSTRA HAMNEN

EIRA

Merikatu/

HELSINKI
HELSINGFORS

0   300 m

LÄNSITERMINAALI
VÄSTRA TERMINALEN

A

TALLINN

B

158

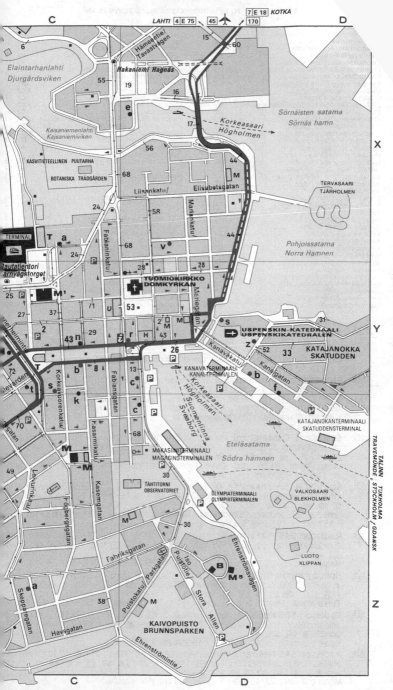

Kämp M, Pohjoisesplanadi 29, ⊠ 00100, ℰ (09) 576 111, hotelkamp@luxurycollecti on.com, Fax (09) 576 1122, 𝓕ᵬ, ⬧ – 📶 ⤬ 🖃 📺 ✶ 🗲 ⟷ – 🔏 120. 🆔 🆎 ⓪ 𝓥𝓘𝓢𝓐 ⋟ CY n
CK's Brasserie : Meals 24/46 and dinner a la carte 30/46 🍴 36 (see also **Kämp** below)
– ⌧ 29 – **172 rm** 330, 7 suites.

Strand Inter-Continental M, John Stenbergin Ranta 4, ⊠ 00530, ℰ (09) 39 351, stran d@interconti.com, Fax (09) 3935 255, ⟨, « Contemporary Finnish architecture and decor », ⬧, ⬛ – 📶, ⤬ rm, 🖃 📺 ⟷ – 🔏 120. 🆔 🆎 ⓪ 𝓥𝓘𝓢𝓐 𝓙𝓬𝓑. ⋟ rest closed Easter and Christmas – **Pamir** : Meals (dinner only) 70 and a la carte 49/83 🍴 33 – **Atrium Plaza** : Meals (buffet lunch) 30/36 and a la carte 23/51 🍴 33 – ⌧ 20 – **192 rm** 280/362, 8 suites. DX e

Scandic H. Continental, Mannerheimintie 46, ⊠ 00260, ℰ (09) 40 551, continen talhelsinki@scandic-hotels.com, Fax (09) 4055 3255, ⟨, 🍽, 𝓕ᬆ, ⬧, ⬛ – 📶, ⤬ rm, 🖃 📺 ⟷ 𝓟 – 🔏 800. 🆔 🆎 ⓪ 𝓥𝓘𝓢𝓐 ⋟ rest BX c closed Easter and Christmas – **Olivo** : Meals (closed Sunday) 40/45 (dinner) and a la carte 24/41 🍴 28 – **500 rm** ⌧ 216/251, 12 suites.

Scandic H. Simonkenttä M, Simonkatu 9, ⊠ 00100, ℰ (09) 68 380, simonkentt a@scandic-hotels.com, Fax (09) 683 811, 𝓕ᬆ, ⬧ – 📶, ⤬ rm, 🖃 📺 ✶ 🗲 – 🔏 80. 🆔 🆎 ⓪ 𝓥𝓘𝓢𝓐 𝓙𝓬𝓑. ⋟ rest BY c closed 20-27 December – **Simonkatu** : Meals (closed Sunday) 21/31 and a la carte 22/38 – **357 rm** ⌧ 183/258, 3 suites.

Radisson SAS Plaza M, Mikonkatu 23, ⊠ 00100, ℰ (09) 77 590, info.plazahelsink @radissonsas.com, Fax (09) 7759 7100, ⬧ – 📶 ⤬ 🖃 📺 ✶ 🗲 – 🔏 100. 🆔 🆎 ⓪ 𝓥𝓘𝓢𝓐 ⋟ CX a
Meals a la carte 24/38 🍴 25 – ⌧ 16 **295 rm** 250, 6 suites.

Holiday Inn Helsinki M, Messuaukio 1, ⊠ 00520, North : 4 km by Mannerheimintie ℰ (09) 150 900, holidayinn@iaf.fi, Fax (09) 150 901, ⬧ – 📶, ⤬ rm, 🖃 📺 🗲 🗲 ⟷ – 🔏 1200. 🆔 🆎 ⓪ 𝓥𝓘𝓢𝓐 ⋟
Terra Nova : Meals a la carte approx. 34 🍴 25 – **239 rm** ⌧ 190/202, 5 suites.

Radisson SAS Royal M, Runeberginkatu 2, ⊠ 00100, ℰ (09) 69 580, info.royalhe sinki@radissonsas.com, Fax (09) 6958 7100, 𝓕ᬆ, ⬧ – 📶, ⤬ rm, 🖃 📺 🗲 ⟷ – 🔏 300. 🆔 🆎 ⓪ 𝓥𝓘𝓢𝓐 𝓙𝓬𝓑. ⋟ BY b
Meals a la carte 24/40 🍴 29 – ⌧ 16 **254 rm** 230, 8 suites.

Radisson SAS Hesperia, Mannerheimintie 50, ⊠ 00260, ℰ (09) 43 101, info.hesp eriahelsinki@radissonsas.com, Fax (09) 431 0995, 🍽, 𝓕ᬆ, ⬧, ⬛ – 📶, ⤬ rm, 🖃 📺 ⟷ 𝓟 – 🔏 450. 🆔 🆎 ⓪ 𝓥𝓘𝓢𝓐 𝓙𝓬𝓑. ⋟ BX a
Meals a la carte 27/46 🍴 29 – ⌧ 16 **380 rm** 185, 3 suites.

Palace Ⓜ, Eteläranta 10, ✉ 00130, ✆ (09) 134 561, *sales@palacehotel.fi*, *Fax (09) 654 786*, ⟨, 🍴 – |▲|, ✎ rm, 🖵 📺 ✆ ⟶ – 🚗 120. 💳 🏧 ⓪ 𝗩𝗜𝗦𝗔 🇯🇨🇧. ✂️ DZ c
PalacenRanta : Meals *(closed Saturday lunch, Sunday and Bank Holidays)* 28/50 and dinner a la carte 31/49 ⓘ 39 (see also *Palace Gourmet* below) – **37 rm** ⚏ 220/305, 2 suites.

Scandic H. Marski, Mannerheimintie 10, ✉ 00100, ✆ (09) 68 061, *marski@scandic-hotels.com*, *Fax (09) 642 377*, 🍴 – |▲|, ✎ rm, 🖵 📺 ✆ & ⟶ – 🚗 30. 💳 🏧 ⓪ 𝗩𝗜𝗦𝗔 🇯🇨🇧. ✂️ rest CY d
closed 21-29 December – *Marski :* Meals *(closed Sunday)* (light lunch)/dinner 32/35 and a la carte 22/41 ⓘ 23 – **283 rm** ⚏ 199/234, 6 suites.

Seaside, Ruoholahdenranta 3, ✉ 00180, ✆ (09) 69 360, *seaside@seasidehotel.fi*, *Fax (09) 693 2123*, 🍴 – |▲|, ✎ rm, 🖵 & ⟶ – 🚗 50. 💳 🏧 ⓪ 𝗩𝗜𝗦𝗔. ✂️ rest
Swing Boat : Meals a la carte approx. 34 – **359 rm** ⚏ 106/204, 5 suites. ABZ e

Vaakuna, Asema-aukio 2, ✉ 00100, ✆ (09) 433 70, *sokos.hotels@sok.fi*, *Fax (09) 4337 7100*, ☞, 🍴 – |▲|, ✎ rm, 📺 &. 🏧 ⓪ 𝗩𝗜𝗦𝗔 🇯🇨🇧. ✂️ rest
closed Easter and Christmas – Meals 21 (lunch) and a la carte 22/26 ⓘ 20 – **266 rm** ⚏ 212/241, 11 suites. BY n

Ramada H. Presidentti, Eteläinen Rautatiekatu 4, ✉ 00100, ✆ (09) 6911, *presidentti.ramada@restel.fi*, *Fax (09) 694 7886*, 🍴, 🖳 – |▲|, ✎ rm, 📺 & ⟶ – 🚗 30. 💳 🏧 ⓪ 𝗩𝗜𝗦𝗔 🇯🇨🇧. ✂️ rest BY s
Meals a la carte 20/47 ⓘ 31 – **491 rm** ⚏ 183, 4 suites.

Scandic H. Grand Marina, Katajanokanlaituri 7, ✉ 00160, ✆ (09) 16 661, *grandmarina@scandic-hotels.com*, *Fax (09) 664 764*, 🍴 – |▲|, ✎ rm, 🖵 📺 ✆ & ⟶ 📠 – 🚗 40. 💳 🏧 ⓪ 𝗩𝗜𝗦𝗔 🇯🇨🇧. ✂️ rest DY f
Makasiim : Meals *(closed lunch Saturday and Sunday and Bank Holidays)* a la carte 23/43 ⓘ 23 – **442 rm** ⚏ 154/189, 20 suites.

Pasila Ⓜ, Maistraatinportti 3, ✉ 00240, North : 4 km by Mannerheimintie ✆ (09) 148 841, *sokos.hotels@sok.fi, Fax (09) 143 771*, 🍴, squash – |▲| ✎ rm 🖵 📺 ✆ 📠 – 🚗 90. 💳 🏧 ⓪ 𝗩𝗜𝗦𝗔 🇯🇨🇧. ✂️ rest – *closed Easter and Christmas* – *Sevilla :* Meals a la carte 15/28 ⓘ 23 – **177 rm** ⚏ 155/186, 1 suite.

Sokos H. Klaus Kurki, Bulevardi 2, ✉ 00120, ✆ (09) 618 911, *sokos.hotels@sok.fi, Fax (09) 6189 1234*, 🍴 – |▲|, ✎ rm, 📺. 💳 🏧 ⓪ 𝗩𝗜𝗦𝗔 🇯🇨🇧. ✂️ rest CY t
Bulevardi Kaksi : Meals 25/50 and a la carte 31/47 ⓘ 25 – **132 rm** ⚏ 180/218, 2 suites.

Lord ⌂, Lönnrotinkatu 29, ✉ 00180, ✆ (09) 615 815, *lord.hotel@c.o.inet.fi*, *Fax (09) 680 1315*, « Restaurant in part Jugendstil (Art Nouveau) building, fireplaces », 🍴 – |▲|, ✎ rm, 📺 & ⟶ – 🚗 200. 💳 🏧 ⓪ 𝗩𝗜𝗦𝗔. ✂️ rest BZ x
closed 23-26 December – Meals *(closed Sunday and Bank Holidays)* 20/42 and a la carte 34/46 ⓘ 25 – **47 rm** ⚏ 131/160, 1 suite.

Rivoli Jardin ⌂ without rest., Kasarmikatu 40, ✉ 00130, ✆ (09) 681 500, *rivoli.jardin@rivoli.fi*, *Fax (09) 656 988*, 🍴 – |▲| ✎ 📺 ✆ &. 💳 🏧 ⓪ 𝗩𝗜𝗦𝗔 CYZ k
55 rm ⚏ 195/325.

Sokos H. Torni, Yrjönkatu 26, ✉ 00100, ✆ (09) 131 131, *torni.reception@sok.fi*, *Fax (09) 131 1361*, 🍴 – |▲|, ✎ rm, 📺 – 🚗 35. 💳 🏧 ⓪ 𝗩𝗜𝗦𝗔. ✂️ rest BY r
closed 21-29 December – *Torni :* Meals *(closed Sunday and Bank Holidays)* 27/62 and a la carte 31/55 ⓘ 34 – **154 rm** ⚏ 185/340.

Seurahuone, Kaivokatu 12, ✉ 00100, ✆ (09) 69 141, *cumulus.seurahuone@restel.fi*, *Fax (09) 691 4010*, 🍴 – |▲|, ✎ rm, 📺 – 🚗 60. 💳 🏧 ⓪ 𝗩𝗜𝗦𝗔. ✂️ rest CY e
Meals a la carte 19/30 – **118 rm** ⚏ 160/225.

🗙🗙🗙 **Kämp** (at Kämp H.), Pohjoisesplanadi 29, ✉ 00100, ✆ (09) 5761 1910, *hotelkamp@luxurycollection.com*, *Fax (09) 576 1122* – 🖳. 💳 🏧 ⓪ 𝗩𝗜𝗦𝗔 🇯🇨🇧. ✂️ CY n
closed Sunday and Monday – Meals (dinner only) a la carte 60/76 ⓘ 36.

🗙🗙🗙 **Russkij,** Katajanokanlaituri 5, ✉ 00160, ✆ (09) 6813 1770, *Fax (09) 6813 1771*, ☞, « Elegant wood panelled interior, 1903 former harbour warehouse » – 🖳. 💳 🏧 ⓪ 𝗩𝗜𝗦𝗔,
closed Easter, 22 December-1 January, Sunday and Saturday lunch – Meals - Russian - a la carte 28/46 ⓘ 25. DY b

🗙🗙🗙 **G.W.Sundmans,** Eteläranta 16 (1st floor), ✉ 00130, ✆ (09) 622 6410, *ursula.zitting@royalravintolat.com, Fax (09) 661 331*, ⟨, « 19C Empire style house, vaulted wine
❀ cellar » – 🖳 – 🚗 60. 💳 🏧 ⓪ 𝗩𝗜𝗦𝗔 🇯🇨🇧. ✂️ DY c
closed Easter, 23 December-7 January, Sunday and lunch July and Saturday – Meals 28/76 and a la carte 54/92 ⓘ 34 – *Krog (ground floor) :* Meals 31/39 (dinner) and a la carte 25/44 ⓘ 29
Spec. Terrine of perch and lobster. Smoked char with dill sauce. Mango soufflé, raspberry sorbet.

🗙🗙🗙 **Savoy,** Eteläesplanadi 14 (8th floor), ✉ 00130, ✆ (09) 684 4020, *terhi.oksanen@royalravintolat.com, Fax (09) 628 715*, ⟨, ☞, « Typical Finnish design dating from 1937 » – |▲|, 💳 🏧 ⓪ 𝗩𝗜𝗦𝗔. ✂️ CY b
closed Easter, 22 December-6 January, Saturday and Sunday – Meals 47/80 and dinner a la carte 51/79 ⓘ 49.

XXX **Palace Gourmet** (at Palace H.), Eteläranta 10 (10th floor), ✉ 00130, ℰ (09) 134 561,
Fax (09) 654 786, ≤ Helsinki and harbour – |✦| ▤. ✪❸ ℄ ⓞ VISA. ✧⁄⁄ DZ c
closed 3 weeks July, Saturday, Sunday and Bank Holidays – **Meals** 40/69 and dinner a la
carte 56/69 ⑂ 39.

XXX **Alexander Nevski,** Pohjoisesplanadi 17, ✉ 00170, ℰ (09) 6869 6510, sirkka.jarven
paa@royalravintolat.com, Fax (09) 6869 6535 – ▤. ✪❸ ℄ ⓞ VISA. ✧⁄⁄ DY r
closed 25-26 December and lunch July and Sunday – **Meals** - Russian - 22/71 and dinner
a la carte 42/71 ⑂ 38.

XX **Sipuli,** Kanavaranta 3 (2nd floor), ✉ 00160, ℰ (09) 179 900, juha.hyytia@royalravint
olat.com, Fax (09) 622 3559, « Picture window ≤ Uspensky Cathedral (orthodox) » – ✪❸
℄ ⓞ VISA. ✧⁄⁄ DY s
closed Easter, 21 June-3 August, 23 December-5 January, Saturday and Sunday – **Meals**
(booking essential) 42/54 and a la carte 43/61 ⑂ 40.

XX **Havis Amanda,** Pohjoisesplanadi 17, ✉ 00170, ℰ (09) 6869 5660, jan.ingstrom@r
oyalravintolat.com, Fax (09) 631 435 – ▤. ✪❸ ℄ ⓞ VISA. ✧⁄⁄ DY r
closed Easter, Christmas and Sunday in winter – **Meals** - Seafood - (booking essential)
34/56 and a la carte approx. 50 ⑂ 36.

XX **George,** Kalevankatu 17, ✉ 00100, ℰ (09) 647 662, george@george.fi,
Fax (09) 647 110 – ▤. ✪❸ ℄ ⓞ VISA. ✧⁄⁄ BY e
closed midsummer, 25 December, Sunday, Saturday lunch and Monday dinner – **Meals**
17/66 and dinner a la carte 41/58 ⑂ 37.

XX **Kartano,** Simonkatu 6, ✉ 00100, ℰ (09) 5860 7121, ravintola.kartano.helsinki@sok.fi,
Fax (09) 5860 7110, « Modern Finnish interior » – ▤. ✪❸ ℄ ⓞ VISA JCB. ✧⁄⁄ BY d
closed 29 March-1 April, 21-23 June, 23-26 December and Sunday lunch – **Meals** - Finnish
- 29/38 and a la carte 21/42 ⑂ 29.

XX **Bellevue,** Rahapajankatu 3, ✉ 00160, ℰ (09) 179 560, info@restaurantbellevue.com,
Fax (09) 636 985 – ▤. ✪❸ ℄ ⓞ VISA DY z
closed 21-28 December and lunch July, Saturday and Sunday – **Meals** - Russian - 22/76
and a la carte 35/58 ⑂ 35.

XX **Rivoli,** Albertinkatu 38, ✉ 00180, ℰ (09) 643 455, kala.cheri@rivoli.inet.fi,
Fax (09) 647 780 – ▤. ✪❸ ℄ ⓞ VISA JCB. ✧⁄⁄ BZ a
closed 1 week spring, midsummer, Christmas, Sunday and Bank Holidays – **Meals** 36 (dinner)
and a la carte approx. 68 ⑂ 32.

X **Chez Dominique,** Ludviginkatu 3-5, ✉ 00130, ℰ (09) 612 7393, info@chezdomini
☸ que.fi, Fax (09) 6124 4220 – ✪❸ ℄ ⓞ VISA. ✧⁄⁄ CY s
closed July, 22 December-2 January, Sunday, Monday, Saturday lunch and Bank Holidays
– **Meals** (booking essential) 55/70 and a la carte 56/76 ⑂ 60
Spec. Cream of chestnuts and truffles, artichoke ravioli. Roast pigeon with foie gras, Albu-
féra sauce. Chocolate fondant, coconut sorbet.

X **La Petite Maison,** Huvilakatu 28A, ✉ 00150, ℰ (09) 260 9680, lapetite.maison@k
olumbus.fi, Fax (09) 684 25 666 – ✪❸ ℄ ⓞ VISA. ✧⁄⁄ CZ a
closed Easter, Christmas and Sunday – **Meals** (booking essential) (dinner only) 40/45 and
a la carte 39/50 ⑂ 29.

X **Safka,** Vironkatu 8, ✉ 00170, ℰ (09) 135 7287, safka@safka.fi, Fax (09) 135 7287 –
☸ ✪❸ ℄ ⓞ VISA. ✧⁄⁄ DX v
closed 24 June-15 July, 24-26 December, Monday and Saturday lunch – **Meals** (booking
essential) 25/37 and a la carte 27/48.

X **Lappi,** Annankatu 22, ✉ 00100, ℰ (09) 645 550, Fax (09) 645 551, « Typical Lapland
atmosphere » – ✪❸ ℄ ⓞ VISA JCB. ✧⁄⁄ BY h
closed Easter, Christmas and lunch 26 June-9 August – **Meals** - Finnish - (booking essential)
a la carte 24/52 ⑂ 26.

at Vantaa North : 19 km by A 137 DX :

🏨 **Holiday Inn Garden Court Helsinki Airport,** Rälssitie 2, ✉ 01510, ℰ (09)
870 900, inn.holiday@tradeka.fi, Fax (09) 8709 0101, ⎌, ≋ – |✦|, ✷ rm, TV ৬ 🅿 –
🔏 25. ✪❸ ℄ ⓞ VISA. ✧⁄⁄ rest
Meals - Bistro - (closed Saturday and Sunday lunch) a la carte approx. 34 – **283 rm** ⚌ 162.

🏨 **Vantaa,** Hertaksentie 2 (near Tikkurila Railway Station), ✉ 01300, ℰ (09) 857 851,
Fax (09) 8578 5555, ☗, ≋ – |✦|, ✷ rm, TV ৬ ⇔ 🅿 – 🔏 280. ✪❸ ℄ ⓞ VISA.
✧⁄⁄ rest
Sevilla : Meals 14/34 and a la carte – **Tulisuudelma :** Meals (closed Sunday) 18.50/20.50
and a la carte – **154 rm** ⚌ 130/154, 8 suites.

🏨 **Cumulus Airport,** Robert Huberin Tie 4, ✉ 01510, ℰ (09) 415 77100, airport.cum
ulus@restel.fi, Fax (09) 415 77101, ≋, ⬛ – |✦|, ✷ rm, TV ৬ 🅿 – 🔏 250. ✪❸ ℄ ⓞ
VISA. ✧⁄⁄ rest
Meals (closed lunch Saturday and Sunday) (buffet lunch) 21 and a la carte approx. 34 –
260 rm ⚌ 135/163, 4 suites.

France

PARIS AND ENVIRONS – BORDEAUX
CANNES – LILLE – LYONS
MARSEILLES – PRINCIPALITY OF MONACO
NICE – STRASBOURG
TOULOUSE

PRACTICAL INFORMATION

LOCAL CURRENCY

Euro: *1 euro (€) = 0,89 USD ($) (Dec 2001)*

TOURIST INFORMATION IN PARIS

Paris "Welcome" Office *(Office du Tourisme de Paris): 127 Champs-Élysées, 8th,* ℰ *08 36 68 31 12, Fax 01 49 52 53 20*

American Express *9, rue Auber, 9th,* ℰ *01 47 14 50 00, Fax 01 42 68 17 17*

National Holiday in France: *14 July*

AIRLINES

AMERICAN AIRLINES: *Roissy Airport, Terminal 2A,* ℰ *08 01 87 28 72, Fax 01 42 99 99 95*

UNITED AIRLINES: *106 bd. Haussmann, 8th,* ℰ *08 10 72 72 72*

DELTA AIRLINES: *119 Av. des Champs-Élysées, 8th,* ℰ *0800 35 40 80, Fax 01 55 69 55 36*

BRITISH AIRWAYS: *13 boulevard de la Madeleine, 1st,* ℰ *08 25 82 54 00, Fax 04 78 53 34 43*

AIR FRANCE: *119 Champs-Élysées, 8th,* ℰ *08 20 82 08 20, Fax 01 42 99 21 99*

FOREIGN EXCHANGE OFFICES

Banks: *close at 4.30pm and at weekends*

Orly Sud Airport: *daily 6.30am to 11pm*

Roissy-Charles-de-Gaulle Airport: *daily 6am to 11.30pm*

TRANSPORT IN PARIS

Taxis: *may be hailed in the street when showing the illuminated sign-available day and night at taxi ranks or called by telephone*

Bus-Métro (subway): *for full details see the Michelin Plan de Paris n° 11. The metro is quicker but the bus is good for sightseeing and practical for short distances.*

POSTAL SERVICES

Local post offices: *open Mondays to Fridays 8am to 7pm; Saturdays 8am to noon*

General Post Office: *52 rue du Louvre, 1st: open 24 hours,* ℰ *01 40 28 76 00*

SHOPPING IN PARIS

Department stores: *Boulevard Haussmann, Rue de Rivoli and Rue de Sèvres*

Exclusive shops and boutiques: *Faubourg St-Honoré, Rue de la Paix and Rue Royale, Avenue Montaigne.*

Antiques and second-hand goods: *Swiss Village (Avenue de la Motte Picquet), Louvre des Antiquaires (Place du Palais Royal), Flea Market (Porte Clignancourt).*

TIPPING

Service is generally included in hotel and restaurants bills but you may choose to leave more than the expected tip to the staff. Taxi-drivers, porters, barbers and theatre or cinema attendants also expect a small gratuity.

BREAKDOWN SERVICE

Some garages in central and outer Paris operate a 24 hour breakdown service. If you breakdown the police are usually able to help by indicating the nearest one.

SPEED LIMITS

The maximum permitted speed in built up areas is 50 km/h - 31 mph; on motorways the speed limit is 130 km/h - 80 mph and 110 km/h - 68 mph on dual carriageways. On all other roads 90 km/h - 56 mph.

SEAT BELTS

The wearing of seat belts is compulsory for drivers and all passengers.

PARIS AND ENVIRONS

Maps:  10, 11, 12 G. Paris.

Population: *Paris 2 125 246 ; Ile-de-France region : 10 952 011.*

Altitude: *Observatory : 60 m ; Place Concorde : 34 m*

Air Terminals:

To ORLY

Orly Bus *(RATP)* ℰ *08 36 68 77 14 from: Place Denfert-Rochereau – 14th (exit RER)*

to ROISSY

Roissy Bus *(RATP)* ℰ *08 36 68 77 14 from: Opéra, rue Scribe (angle r. Auber) 9th*

ORLY *(Air France Bus)* ℰ *01 41 56 89 00 from: Montparnasse, rue du Cdt-Mouchotte, Near SNCF station, 14th; from: Invalides Aérogare, 2 rue Pelterie, 7th*

Roissy – CDG1 – CDG2 *(Air France Bus) from: Etoile, place Ch.-De-Gaulle, angle 1 av. Carnot 17th, from: Porte Maillot, Palais des Congrès, near Méridien Hôtel, 17th*

Paris'Airports: *see Orly and Charles de Gaulle (Roissy)*

Railways, motorail: *information* ℰ *01 53 90 20 20.*

ARRONDISSEMENTS

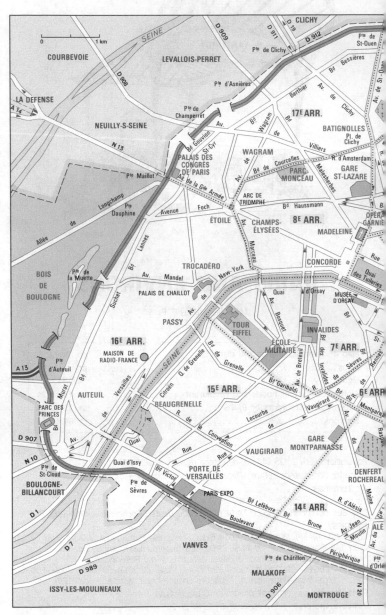

AND DISTRICTS

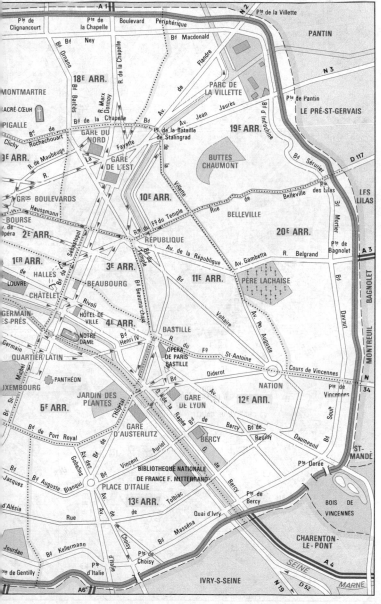

0   200 m

FRAN

PORTE DE CHAMPERRET

Pl. de la Porte de Champerret
Sqre de l'Amerique Latine
Pl. Stuart Merrill
Square J.-Bellan

BERTHIER

AVENUE

LYCÉE STE URSULE LOUISE DE BETTIGNIES

Pl. du Mal JUIN

PÉREIRE-LEVALLOIS (R.E.R.)

PÉREIRE

DE VILLIERS

PL. WAGRAM
du Brésil AV.

D 7

D 8

PÉREIRE

NIEL

AVENUE

Rue

PRONY

WAGRAM

AVENUE

DE

Rue

MARCHÉ DES TERNES

BOULEVARD

Pl. Tristan Bernard

DES

TERNES

Pl. des Ternes

TERNES

BOULEVARD

COURCEL

M COURCEL

E 8

E 7

HÔPITAL MARMOTTAN

ST FERDINAND
STE THÉRÈSE DE L'ENFANT JÉSUS

ESPACE WAGRAM

Acacias

AVENUE

MAC MAHON

AVENUE

CARNOT

SALLE PLEYEL

CATHÉDRALE ST ALEXANDRE NEVSKY

N.D. DE L'ANNONCIATION

ST JOSEPH

ARGENTINE

AV. DE LA GRANDE ARMÉE

CH. DE GAULLE ÉTOILE (R.E.R.)
PLACE

AVENUE

St-Honoré

Beaujon

FRIEDLAND

CORPUS CHRISTI

ARC DE TRIOMPHE (R.E.R.)

CHARLES DE GAULLE

F 8

CHAMBRE DE COMMERCE ET D'INDUSTRIE DE PARIS

AVENUE

OFFICE DU TOURISME

AIR FRANCE

GEORGE V

DES

AV. FOCH

F 7

AV. VICTOR HUGO

KLÉBER

CLIN V. HUGO

CENTRE DE CONFÉRENCES INTERNATIONALES

R. Newton

ST GEORGES

AVENUE

AVENUE

Euler

Vernet

RÉSERVOIRS DE PASSY

Copernic

KLÉBER

D'IÉNA

Pl. de l'Uruguay

Pl. de Beyrouth

SERBIE

Place des

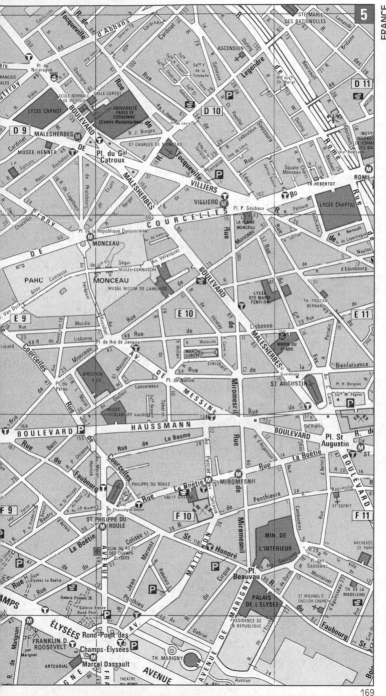

5

D 11

D 10

D 9

E 9

E 10

E 11

F 9

F 10

F 11

STE-MARIE
DES BATIGNOLLES

R. de Tocqueville

R. d'Abbans

Cardinet

ASCENSION

Legendre

Rue

LYCEE CARNOT

BOULEVARD

ECOLE NORMALE
DE MUSIQUE

SALLE CORTOT

UNIVERSITÉ
PARIS IV
SORBONNE
(Centre Malesherbes)

MALESHERBES

MUSÉE HENNER

ST CHARLES DE MONCEAU

Pl. du Gal
Catroux

R. de Tocqueville

DE

MALESHERBES

de

VILLIERS

VILLIERS

Pl. P. Goubaux

LYCÉE CHAPTAL

COURCELLES

Rue

ROME

TH. HEBERTOT

Square
Monceau

LA PLAINE
MONCEAU

MONCEAU

Pl. de la République Dominicaine

MONCEAU

Av. Velasquez

BOULEVARD

LYCÉE
STE MARIE
FÉNELON

PARC

MONCEAU

MUSÉE-CERNUSCHI

MUSÉE NISSIM DE CAMONDO

de

Lisbonne

MALESHERBES

TH TRISTAN
BERNARD

Van Dyck

Rue

Lisbonne

Rue

de

Murillo

Pl. de Rio de Janeiro

MARCHÉ
EUROPE

MAIRIE DU
8e ARR.

DIRECTION
E.D.F.

A.V.

DE

MESSINE

Pl. de Narvik

Miromesnil

ST AUGUSTIN

Bienfaisance

Pl. du
Pérou

MUSÉE
JACQUEMART ANDRÉ

BOULEVARD

HAUSSMANN

BOULEVARD

Pl. St
Augustin

Rue

de

La Baume

Rue

Courcelles

du

Faubourg

ST PHILIPPE DU ROULE

La Boétie

SALLE GAVEAU

MIROMESNIL

ST ESPRIT

BOULEVARD

ST

ST PHILIPPE DU
ROULE

La Boétie

Rue

de

Penthièvre

de

Coliseo

St.

Honoré

MIN. DE
L'INTÉRIEUR

ARCHEVÉCHÉ
DE PARIS

CLIN DU RD PT
DES CHAMPS
ÉLYSÉES

Galerie Élysées

Galerie Élysée
Rond Point

Pl.
Beauvau

ST MICHAEL'S
ENGLISH CHURCH

TH. DE LA
MADELEINE

ÉLYSÉES

FRANKLIN D.
ROOSEVELT

Rond Point des

Champs-Élysées

Marcel Dassault

ARTCURIAL

PALAIS
DE L'ÉLYSÉE

PRÉSIDENCE DE
LA RÉPUBLIQUE

AVENUE

DE

MARIGNY

TH. MARIGNY

AVENUE

Faubourg

St.

169

D 11
D 12
D 13

Rue Caulaincourt

THÉÂTRE DES 2 ÂNES
BAL DU MOULIN ROUGE
LYCÉE J. FERRY
STE RITA
Pl. Blanche
BLANCHE
COMÉDIE DE PARIS

ESPACE EUROPÉEN
de Clichy
CLINIQUE VINTIMILLE
PL. DE CLICHY
Pl. A. Max
BATIGNOLLES

INSTITUT UNIVERSITAIRE DE FORMATION DES MAÎTRES
DESCENTE DU ST-ESPRIT ET ÉGLISE RÉFORMÉE DES BATIGNOLLES
ROME
Pl. Lili Boulanger
R. de Calais
MUSÉE DE LA VIE ROMANTIQUE
TH. FONTAINE

ST ANDRÉ DE L'EUROPE
Pl. de Dublin
TH. DE L'ŒUVRE
LYCÉE ST LOUIS
FÉDÉRATION PROTESTANTE DE FRANCE
DEUTSCHE EVANGELISCHE CHRISTUSKIRCHE
TH. LA BRUYÈRE
MUSÉE GUSTAVE MOREAU

Constantinople
CLIN TURIN
LIÈGE
Liège
TH. DE PARIS

Pl. de l'Europe
EUROPE
E 11
CLIN MILAN
E 12
d'Athènes
CASINO DE PARIS
E 13

Pl. de Budapest
R. de la Tour des Dames

GARE ST LAZARE
STE TRINITÉ

CEYCEE RACINE
Stockholm
TRINITÉ
Pl. d'Estienne d'Orves

Laborde
ST LAZARE
Cour de Rome
Cour du Havre
TH. MOGADOR

R. de la Pépinière
Pl. G. Péri
Rue de l'Isly
du Havre
LYCÉE CONDORCET
ST LOUIS D'ANTIN
de Joubert

ST AUGUSTIN
Lavoisier
de Provence
Cité d'Antin

HAUSSMANN
MAGASINS DU PRINTEMPS
GALERIES LAFAYETTE
HAUSSMANN-ST LAZARE

ARCHEVÊCHÉ DE PARIS
F 11
TH. DES MATHURINS
TH. MICHEL
HAVRE-CAUMARTIN
Mathurins
Pl. Diaghilev
CHAUSSÉE D'ANTIN
F 1

MALESHERBES
CHAPELLE EXPIATOIRE
Marché de la Madeleine
F 12
PARISTORIO
AUBER
OPÉRA
GARNIER
MUSÉE DE LA PARFUMERIE

TH. ATHÉNÉE L. JOUVET
COMÉDIE CAUMARTIN
Pl. Ch. Garnier
Pl. de

ARCHEVÊCHÉ DE PARIS
KIOSQUE THÉÂTRE
Pl. de la Madeleine
TH. ÉDOUARD VII SACHA GUITRY
OLYMPIA
CAPUCINES
l'Opéra

STE MARIE MADELEINE
BD DE LA MADELEINE
MADELEINE
DES
OPÉRA
QUATRE-
SEPTEMBRE

GALERIE DES TROIS QUARTIERS
CRÉDIT FONCIER DE FRANCE
MICHELIN
TH. DES BOUFFES PARISIENS

MINISTÈRE DE LA JUSTICE

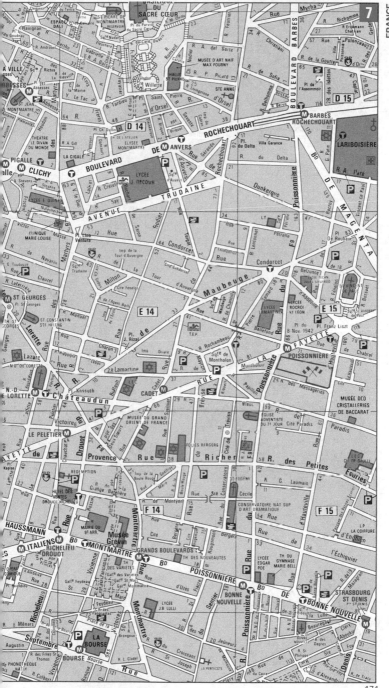

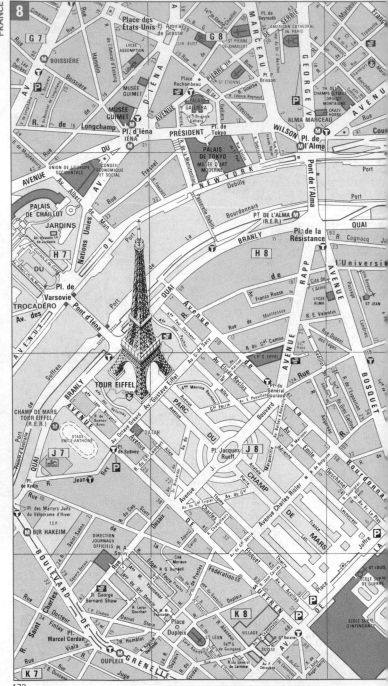

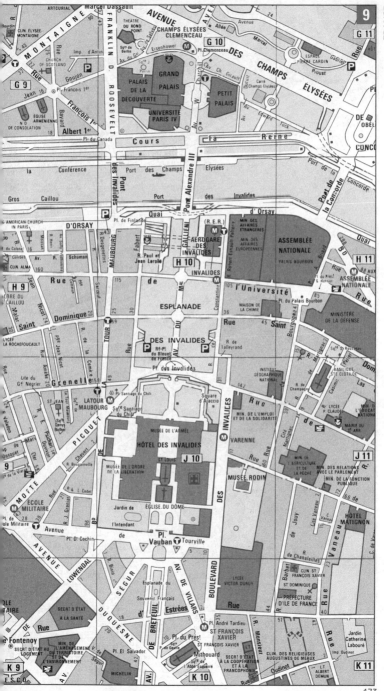

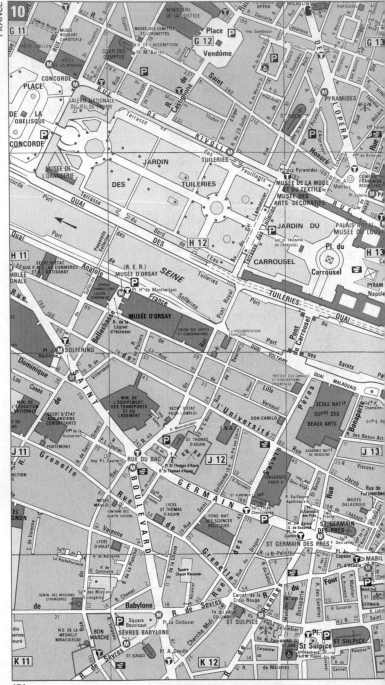

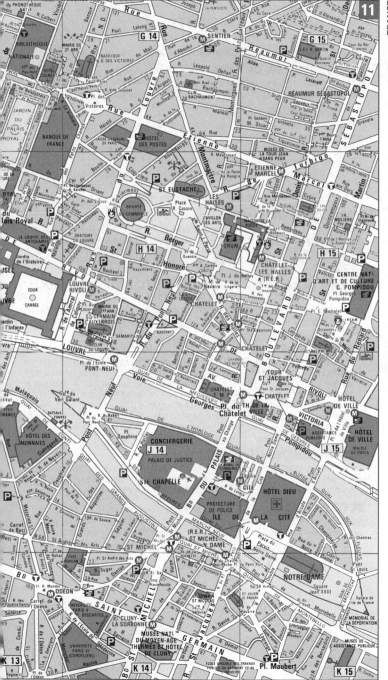

SIGHTS

How to make the most of a trip to Paris – some ideas :

A BIRD'S-EYE VIEW OF PARIS

★★★ *Eiffel Tower* J 7 – ★★★ *Montparnasse Tower* LM 11 – ★★★ *Notre-Dame Towers* K 15 –
★★★ *Sacré Cœur Dome* D 14 – ★★★ *Arc de Triomphe platform* F 8.

FAMOUS PARISIAN VISTAS

★★★ *Arc de Triomphe – Champs-Élysées – Place de la Concorde :* ≼ *from the Rond Point
on the Champs-Élysées* G 10.

★★ *The Madeleine – Place de la Concorde – Palais Bourbon (National Assembly) :* ≼ *from
the Obelisk in the middle of Place de la Concorde* G 11.

★★★ *The Trocadéro – Eiffel Tower – Ecole Militaire :* ≼ *from the terrace of the Palais
de Chaillot* H 7.

★★ *The Invalides – Grand and Petit Palais :* ≼ *from Pont Alexandre III* H 10.

MAIN MONUMENTS

The Louvre★★★ *(Cour Carrée, Perrault's Colonnade, Pyramid)* H 13 – *Eiffel Tower*★★★
J 7 – *Notre-Dame Cathedral*★★★ K 15 – *Sainte-Chapelle*★★★ J 14 – *Arc de Triomphe*★★★
F 8 – *The Invalides*★★★ *(Napoleon's Tomb)* J 10 – *Palais-Royal*★★ H 13 – *The Opéra*★★
F 12 – *The Conciergerie*★★ J 14 – *The Panthéon*★★ L 14 – *Luxembourg*★★ *(Palace and
Gardens)* KL 13.

Churches : *The Madeleine*★★ G 11 – *Sacré Cœur*★★ D 14 – *St-Germain-des-Prés*★★ J 13
– *St-Etienne-du-Mont*★★ – *St-Germain-l'Auxerrois*★★ H 14.

In the Marais : *Place des Vosges*★★ – *Hôtel Lamoignon*★★ – *Hôtel Guénégaud*★★ *(Museum
of the Chase and of Nature)* – *Hôtel de Soubise*★★ *(Historical Museum of France)* by
HJ 15.

MAIN MUSEUMS

The Louvre★★★ H 13 – *Musée d'Orsay*★★★ *(mid-19C to early 20C)* H 12 – *National
Museum of Modern Art*★★★ *(Centre Georges-Pompidou)* H 15 – *Army Museum*★★★
(Invalides) J 10 – *Guimet*★★★ *(musée national des arts asiatiques)* G 7 – *Museum of
Decorative Arts*★★ *(107 rue de Rivoli)* H 13 – *Hôtel de Cluny*★★ *(Museum of the Middle
Ages and Roman Baths)* K 14 – *Rodin*★★ *(Hôtel de Biron)* J 10 – *Carnavalet*★★ *(History
of Paris)* J 17 – *Picasso*★★ H 17 – *Cité de la Science et de l'Industrie*★★★ *(La Villette)*
– *Marmottan*★★ *(Impressionist artists)* – *Orangerie*★★ *(from the Impressionists until 1930)*
H 11.

MODERN MONUMENTS

La Défense★★ *(CNIT, Grande Arche)* – *Centre Georges-Pompidou*★★ H 15 – *Forum
des Halles* H 14 – *Institut du Monde Arabe*★ – *Opéra Paris-Bastille*★ – *Bercy (Palais
Omnisports, Ministry of Finance)* – *Bibliothèque Nationale de France.*

PRETTY AREAS

Montmartre★★★ D 14 – *Ile St-Louis*★★ J 14 J 15 – *the Quays*★★ *(between Pont des
Arts and Pont de Sully)* J 14 J 15 – *St Séverin district*★★ K 14 – *the Marais*★★★.

K 14, G 10 *: Reference letters and numbers on the town plans.*

Use MICHELIN *Green Guide* Paris *for a well-informed visit.*

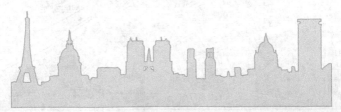

Alphabetical list (Hotels and restaurants)

HOTELS, RESTAURANTS

Listed by districts and arrondissements

(List of Hotels and Restaurants in alphabetical order, see pp 13 to 21)

G 12: These reference letters and numbers correspond to the squares on the Michelin Map of Paris no ⬜⬜. Paris Atlas no ⬜⬜. Map with street index no ⬜⬜ and Map of Paris no ⬜⬜.

Consult any of the above publications when looking for a car park nearest to a listed establishment.

Opéra,
Palais-Royal,
Halles, Bourse.

1st and 2nd arrondissements.

1st: ✉ 75001
2nd: ✉ 75002

Ritz, 15 pl. Vendôme (1st) ✆ 01 43 16 30 30, *resa@ritzparis.com*, Fax 01 43 16 36 68
⬜, « Attractive pool and luxurious fitness centre », ⬜, ⬜ – ⬜ ⬜ ⬜ ⬜ – ⬜ 30 - 80
⬜ ⬜ ⬜ ⬜. ⬜   G 12
see **L'Espadon** below - **Ritz Club** (dinner only) *(closed August, Sunday and Bank Holidays)*
Meals a la carte 65/80 – **Bar Vendôme** (lunch only) Meals a la carte 65/75 ⬜ – ⬜ 32,50
– **133 rm** 630/730, 42 suites.

Meurice, 228 r. Rivoli (1st) ✆ 01 44 58 10 10, *reservations@meuricehotel.com*
Fax 01 44 58 10 15, ⬜ – ⬜, ⬜ rm, ⬜ ⬜ ⬜ ⬜ – ⬜ 40 - 70. ⬜ ⬜ ⬜
⬜. ⬜   G 12
see **Le Meurice** below - **Jardin d'Hiver** ✆ 01 44 58 10 44 Meals 42bi (lunch) and a la
carte 44/84 ⬜ – ⬜ 30 – **135 rm** 550/740, 25 suites.

Inter-Continental, 3 r. Castiglione (1st) ✆ 01 44 77 11 11, *paris@interconti.com*
Fax 01 44 77 14 60, ⬜, ⬜ – ⬜, ⬜ rm, ⬜ ⬜ ⬜ ⬜ – ⬜ 15 - 350. ⬜ ⬜ ⬜ ⬜
⬜ rest   G 12
234 Rivoli ✆ 01 44 77 10 40 Meals a la carte 48/72 – **Terrasse Fleurie** *(2 May to
15 September)* Meals a la carte 45/62 – ⬜ 30 – **410 rm** 600/970, 33 suites.

Costes ⬜, 239 r. St-Honoré (1st) ✆ 01 42 44 50 00, *Fax 01 42 44 50 01*, ⬜, « Elegant
mansion tastefully decorated », ⬜, ⬜ – ⬜ ⬜ ⬜ ⬜ ⬜. ⬜ ⬜ ⬜ ⬜   G 12
Meals 70/90 ⬜ – ⬜ 25 – **80 rm** 300/540, 3 duplex.

Vendôme ⬜, 1 pl. Vendôme (1st) ✆ 01 55 04 55 00, *reservations@hoteldevendom
e.com*, Fax 01 49 27 97 89, « 18C mansion » – ⬜ ⬜ ⬜ ⬜ ⬜ ⬜. ⬜ ⬜ ⬜
⬜. ⬜   G 12
Café de Vendôme ✆ 01 55 04 55 55 Meals 38(lunch), 46/50 ⬜ – **Les Perles de Ven-
dôme** ✆ 01 55 04 55 62 *(closed Saturday and Sunday)* Meals 35 – ⬜ 28 – **24 rm**
488/840, 5 suites.

Sofitel Castille ⬜, 37 r. Cambon (1st) ✆ 01 44 58 44 58, *reservations@castille.com*
Fax 01 44 58 44 00 – ⬜, ⬜ rm, ⬜ ⬜ ⬜ – ⬜ 30. ⬜ ⬜ ⬜ ⬜   G 12
see **Il Cortile** below – ⬜ 25 – **86 rm** 455/940, 7 suites, 14 duplex.

Louvre, pl. A. Malraux (1st) ✆ 01 44 58 38 38, *hoteldulouvre@hoteldulouvre.com*
Fax 01 44 58 38 01, ⬜ – ⬜, ⬜ rm, ⬜ ⬜ ⬜ ⬜ – ⬜ 20 - 80. ⬜ ⬜
⬜ ⬜   H 13
Brasserie Le Louvre ✆ 01 42 96 27 98 Meals 190 ⬜ – ⬜ 21 – **195 rm** 420/515.

🏨🏨🏨 **Westminster,** 13 r. Paix (2nd) ℰ 01 42 61 57 46, *resa-westminster@warwickhotels.com*, *Fax 01 42 60 30 66*, 🕭 – |‡|, ⟷ rm, ▤ 🖵 ✆ ⟵ – 🛦 15 - 40. 🕮 ⓞ GB JCB
G 12
see *Céladon* below **- Petit Céladon** (weekend only) *(closed August)* Meals 41,16bi – ⌷ 20 – **82 rm** 390/650, 20 suites.

🏨🏨🏨 **Lotti,** 7 r. Castiglione (1st) ℰ 01 42 60 37 34, *hotel.lotti@wanadoo.fr*, *Fax 01 40 15 93 56* – |‡|, ⟷ rm, ▤ rm, 🖵 ✆. 🕮 ⓞ GB JCB
G 12
see *Gualtiero Marchesi pour le Lotti* below – ⌷ 23 – **129 rm** 315/530.

🏨🏨 **Royal St-Honoré** Ⓜ without rest, 221 r. St-Honoré (1st) ℰ 01 42 60 32 79, *rsh@hotel-royal-st-honore.com*, *Fax 01 42 60 47 44* – |‡| ▤ 🖵 ✆ 🕭 – 🛦 15. 🕮 ⓞ GB JCB ⌕
G 12
⌷ 18 – **67 rm** 280/350, 5 suites.

🏨🏨 **Edouard VII** without rest, 39 av. Opéra (2nd) ℰ 01 42 61 56 90, *info@edouard7hotel.com*, *Fax 01 42 61 47 73* – |‡| ▤ 🖵 ✆ – 🛦 15 - 25. 🕮 ⓞ GB JCB
G 13
⌷ 18 – **65 rm** 315/380, 4 suites.

🏨🏨 **Normandy,** 7 r. Échelle (1st) ℰ 01 42 60 30 21, *normandy@hotelsparis.fr*, *Fax 01 42 60 45 81* – |‡|, ⟷ rm, 🖵 ✆ – 🛦 15 - 30. 🕮 ⓞ GB JCB. ⌕
H 13
Il Palazzo ℰ 01 42 60 91 20 - Italian rest. - Meals a la carte 53/77 – ⌷ 22,87 – **117 rm** 335/442, 4 suites.

🏨🏨 **Regina,** 2 pl. Pyramides (1st) ℰ 01 42 60 31 10, *reservation@regina-hotel.com*, *Fax 01 40 15 95 16*, ⌖, « "Art Nouveau" lobby » – |‡| ▤ 🖵 ✆ – 🛦 20 - 60. 🕮 ⓞ GB JCB
H 13
Meals *(closed August, Saturday, Sunday and Bank Holidays)* 29/49 ♀ – ⌷ 16 – **116 rm** 305/415, 15 suites.

🏨🏨 **Washington Opéra** Ⓜ without rest, 50 r. Richelieu (1st) ℰ 01 42 96 68 06, *hotel @washingtonopera.com*, *Fax 01 40 15 01 12*, « Marquise de Pompadour's mansion house, terrace ⩽ Palais Royal » – |‡| ▤ 🖵 ✆ 🕭. 🕮 ⓞ GB JCB. ⌕
G 13
⌷ 14 – **36 rm** 214/275.

🏨🏨 **Opéra Richepanse** without rest, 14 r. Richepanse (1st) ℰ 01 42 60 36 00, *richepanseotel@wanadoo.fr*, *Fax 01 42 60 13 03* – |‡| ▤ 🖵 ✆. 🕮 ⓞ GB JCB
G 12
⌷ 13 – **35 rm** 257/298, 3 suites.

🏨🏨 **Cambon** Ⓜ without rest, 3 r. Cambon (1st) ℰ 01 44 58 93 93, *cambon@cybercable.fr*, *Fax 01 42 60 30 59* – |‡| ▤ 🖵 ✆. 🕮 ⓞ GB JCB. ⌕
G 12
⌷ 13 – **40 rm** 241/287.

🏨🏨 **Stendhal** without rest, 22 r. D. Casanova (2nd) ℰ 01 44 58 52 52, *h1610@accor-hotels.com*, *Fax 01 44 58 52 00* – |‡| ▤ 🖵 ✆. 🕮 ⓞ GB JCB
G 12
⌷ 16 – **20 rm** 260/328.

🏨🏨 **Mansart** without rest, 5 r. Capucines (1st) ℰ 01 42 61 50 28, *hotel.mansart@wanadoo.fr*, *Fax 01 49 27 97 44* – |‡| 🖵 ✆. 🕮 ⓞ GB JCB. ⌕
G 12
⌷ 9,15 – **57 rm** 119/275.

🏨🏨 **L'Horset Opéra** Ⓜ without rest, 18 r. d'Antin (2nd) ℰ 01 44 71 87 00, *lopera@paris-hotels-charm.com*, *Fax 01 42 66 55 54* – |‡|, ⟷ rm, ▤ 🖵. 🕮 ⓞ GB JCB
G 13
55 rm ⌷ 222/252.

🏨🏨 **Novotel Les Halles** Ⓜ, 8 pl. M.-de-Navarre (1st) ℰ 01 42 21 31 31, *H0785@accor-hotels.com*, *Fax 01 40 26 05 79* – |‡|, ⟷ rm, ▤ 🖵 ✆ 🕭 – 🛦 15 - 20. 🕮 ⓞ GB JCB
H 14
Meals 23 ♀ – ⌷ 14 – **285 rm** 292/437.

🏨 **États-Unis Opéra** without rest, 16 r. d'Antin (2nd) ℰ 01 42 65 05 05, *us-opera@wanadoo.fr*, *Fax 01 42 65 93 70* – |‡| ▤ 🖵 ✆ – 🛦 25. 🕮 ⓞ GB JCB. ⌕
G 13
⌷ 10 – **45 rm** 116/182.

🏨 **Noailles** Ⓜ without rest, 9 r. Michodière (2nd) ℰ 01 47 42 92 90, *goldentulip.denoailles@wanadoo.fr*, *Fax 01 49 24 92 71*, contemporary decor, 🕭 – |‡|, ⟷ rm, 🖵 ✆ 🕭 – 🛦 20. 🕮 ⓞ GB JCB
G 13
⌷ 14 – **55 rm** 210/240, 6 suites.

🏨 **Place du Louvre** without rest, 21 r. Prêtres-St-Germain-L'Auxerrois (1st) ℰ 01 42 33 78 68, *hotel.place.louvre@wanadoo.fr*, *Fax 01 42 33 09 95* – |‡| 🖵. 🕮 ⓞ GB JCB
H 14
⌷ 9,15 – **20 rm** 87/141.

🏨 **Victoires Opéra** Ⓜ without rest, 56 r. Montorgueil (2nd) ℰ 01 42 36 41 08, *hotel @victoiresopera.com*, *Fax 01 45 08 08 79* – |‡| ▤ 🖵 ✆ 🕭. 🕮 ⓞ GB JCB. ⌕
G 14
⌷ 15 – **24 rm** 220/275.

🏨 **Favart** without rest, 5 r. Marivaux (2nd) ℰ 01 42 97 59 83, *favart.hotel@wanadoo.fr*, *Fax 01 40 15 95 58* – |‡| 🖵 ✆. 🕮 ⓞ GB JCB
F 13
⌷ 3,05 – **37 rm** 83,85/105,95.

🏨 **Louvre Rivoli** without rest, 20 r. Molière (1st) ℘ 01 42 60 31 20, *louvre@hotelsparis.fr*, Fax 01 42 60 32 06 – 🛗 🖩 📺 ✦ 🕭. 🖭 ⓪ ⮽ 🎅. ✀ G 13
⛉ 15 – **29 rm** 181/212.

🏨 **Baudelaire Opéra** without rest, 61 r. Ste Anne (2nd) ℘ 01 42 97 50 62, *hotel@cy bercable.fr*, Fax 01 42 86 85 85 – 🛗 📺 ✦. 🖭 ⓪ ⮽ 🎅. ✀ G 13
⛉ 7,50 – **24 rm** 99/130, 5 duplex.

🏨 **Louvre Ste-Anne** without rest, 32 r. Ste-Anne (1st) ℘ 01 40 20 02 35, *ste-anne@w orldonline.fr*, Fax 01 40 15 91 13 – 🛗 🖩 📺 ✦ 🕭. 🖭 ⓪ ⮽ 🎅. ✀ G 13
⛉ 9,15 – **20 rm** 121,35/181,40.

🏨 **Vivienne** without rest, 40 r. Vivienne (2nd) ℘ 01 42 33 13 26, *paris@hotel-vivienne.c om*, Fax 01 40 41 98 19 – 🛗 📺. ⮽ F 14
⛉ 6 – **44 rm** 63/84.

XXXXX **L'Espadon** - Hôtel Ritz, 15 pl. Vendôme (1st) ℘ 01 43 16 30 80, *food-bev@ritzparis.com*, 🕸 Fax 01 43 16 33 75, 🍽 – 🗏. 🖭 ⓪ ⮽ 🎅. ✀ G 12
Meals 56,50 (lunch)/141,80 and a la carte 115/160
Spec. Homard bleu aux jeunes salades. Tronçon de turbot rôti au jus acidulé et poivre concassé. Rosettes d'agneau en éulln de champignons..

XXXXX **Le Meurice** - Hôtel Meurice, 228 r. Rivoli (1st) ℘ 01 44 58 10 55, *restauration@meu 🕸 ricehotel.com*, Fax 01 44 58 10 15 – 🗏. 🖭 ⓪ ⮽ 🎅. ✀ G 12
closed 29 July-25 August – **Meals** 55 (lunch)/95 and a la carte 80/110
Spec. Langoustines de Bretagne au caramel d'ail doux. Noisette de bar au sévruga, charlotte aux oursins (Autumn-Winter). Fine tarte moelleuse chocolat-café, glace vanille.

XXXX **Grand Vefour**, 17 r. Beaujolais (1st) ℘ 01 42 96 56 27, *grand.vefour@wanadoo.fr*, 🕸🕸🕸 Fax 01 42 86 80 71, « Pre-Revolutionary (late 18C) café style » – 🗏. 🖭 ⓪ ⮽ 🎅. ✀ *closed 1 to 7 April, 2 August-2 September, 31 to 31 December, Friday Dinner, Saturday and Sunday* – **Meals** 73,17 (lunch)/221,05 and a la carte 145/190
Spec. Cuisses de grenouilles blondes dorées, panais et moelle en pluches de persil. Filet de sole meunière, fenouil à l'essence d'agrumes et jus au tarama. Canard colvert cuit sur son coffre, jus aux figues et feuille de laurier..

XXXX **Carré des Feuillants** (Dutournier), 14 r. Castiglione (1st) ℘ 01 42 86 82 82, 🕸🕸 Fax 01 42 86 07 71 – 🗏. 🖭 ⓪ ⮽ 🎅. ✀ G 12
closed August, Saturday lunch, Sunday and Monday – **Meals** 58 (lunch)/138 and a la carte 90/115
Spec. Cèpes marinés à l'huile de noisette, chapeau poêlé et pied en pâté chaud (Summer-Autumn). Canette fermière de Challans "sauvageonne" (April-September). Pêche "dans tous ses états" (June-September)..

XXXX **Drouant** see also *Café Drouant*, pl. Gaillon (2nd) ℘ 01 42 65 15 16, *drouantrv@elio 🕸 r.com*, Fax 01 49 24 02 15, « Home of the Academie Goncourt since 1914 » – 🗏. 🖭 ⓪ ⮽ 🎅 G 13
closed August, Saturday and Sunday – **Meals** 53 (lunch)/104 (dinner) and a la carte 90/125 ♀
Spec. Raviole d'œuf au coulis de truffe. Fricassée de homard au poivre et gingembre. Filet de veau à la ficelle et chartreuse de légumes..

XXXX **Gérard Besson**, 5 r. Coq Héron (1st) ℘ 01 42 33 14 74, *gerard.besson4@libertysurf.fr*, 🕸🕸 Fax 01 42 33 85 71 – 🗏. 🖭 ⓪ ⮽ 🎅 H 14
closed Monday lunch except July-August, Saturday except dinner from September-June and Sunday – **Meals** 49 (lunch)/95 (dinner) and a la carte 90/120 ♀
Spec. Homard de Bretagne. Gibier (1 October-15 December). Truffes (15 December-15 March).

XXXX **Goumard**, 9 r. Duphot (1st) ℘ 01 42 60 36 07, *goumard.philippe@wanadoo.fr*, 🕸 Fax 01 42 60 04 54 – 🛗 🗏. 🖭 ⓪ ⮽ 🎅 G 12
closed 3 to 20 August – **Meals** - Seafood - 40 (lunch) and a la carte 60/95 ♀
Spec. Saint-Jacques à la plancha (October-April). Turbot de ligne en cocotte au jus de volaille. Biscuit au chocolat, glace pistache.

XXX **Céladon** - Hôtel Westminster, 15 r. Daunou (2nd) ℘ 01 47 03 40 42, *resa@westmins 🕸 ter.hepta.fr*, Fax 01 42 61 33 78 – 🗏. 🖭 ⮽ 🎅 G 12
closed August, Saturday, Sunday and Bank Holidays – **Meals** 44,21 (lunch)/57,93 (dinner) and a la carte 70/100
Spec. Bouquet poêlé au beurre salé, bouillon mousseux au curry (September-December). Rouget farci et rôti aux épices chermoula. Petites poires pochées et caramélisées, crème à la chicorée..

XXX **Gualtiero Marchesi pour le Lotti** - Hôtel Lotti, 9 r. Castiglione (1st) 🕸 ℘ 01 42 60 40 62, Fax 01 42 60 55 03 – 🗏. 🖭 ⓪ ⮽ 🎅. ✀ G 11
Meals - Italian rest. - 35,06 (lunch), 85,37/112,81 and a la carte 57/100
Spec. Risotto à l'encre de seiche et sardines. Strates de pâtes au ragoût de veau. Tiramisu..

XXX **Macéo**, 15 r. Petits-Champs (1st) ℘ 01 42 97 53 85, *info@maceorestaurant.com*, Fax 01 47 03 36 93 – 🗏. ⮽. ✀ G 13
closed Saturday lunch and Sunday – **Meals** 28,97 (lunch), 35,06/38,11 and a la carte 45/64 ♀

XXX ⌘ **Il Cortile** - Hôtel Sofitel Castille, 37 r. Cambon (1st) ✆ 01 44 58 45 67, *ilcortile@casti llc.com*, Fax 01 44 58 45 69, 🏠 – 🗏. 🆎 ⓞ ᴳᴮ ᴶᶜᴮ
closed Saturday, Sunday and Bank Holidays – **Meals** - Italian rest. - 42 (lunch) and a la carte 55/70
Spec. Cannelloni à l'encre, chair de tourteau et homard. Piccata de veau au citron vert. Palet or moelleux au chocolat, noisettes et amandes..

XXX **Pierre " A la Fontaine Gaillon "**, pl. Gaillon (2nd) ✆ 01 47 42 63 22,
Fax 01 47 42 82 84, 🏠 – 🗏. 🆎 ⓞ ᴳᴮ ᴶᶜᴮ   G 13
closed August, Saturday lunch and Sunday – **Meals** 32 and a la carte 40/68 ℥.

XX **Pierre - Jean-Paul Arabian**, 10 r. Richelieu (1st) ✆ 01 42 96 09 17,
Fax 01 42 96 09 62 – 🗏. 🆎 ⓞ ᴳᴮ   H 13
closed 24 December-2 January – **Meals** a la carte 51/90 ℥.

XX **Palais Royal**, 110 Galerie de Valois - Jardin du Palais Royal (1st) ✆ 01 40 20 00 27,
palaisrest@aol.com, Fax 01 40 20 00 82, 🏠, « Terrace in Palais Royal garden » – 🆎 ⓞ
ᴳᴮ   G 13
closed 15 December-30 January, Saturday from October-May and Sunday – **Meals** a la carte 43/80 ℥.

XX **Chez Pauline**, 5 r. Villédo (1st) ✆ 01 42 96 20 70, *chezpauline@wanadoo.fr*,
Fax 01 49 27 99 89 – 🗏. 🆎 ⓞ ᴳᴮ ᴶᶜᴮ   G 13
closed Saturday except dinner in Winter and Sunday – **Meals** 35 (lunch)/40 and a la carte 35/50 🍷.

XX **Café Drouant**, pl. Galion (2nd) ✆ 01 42 65 15 16, Fax 01 49 24 02 15, 🏠 – 🗏. 🆎 ⓞ
ᴳᴮ ᴶᶜᴮ   G 13
closed August, Saturday and Sunday – **Meals** 38 and a la carte 39/81 ℥.

XX **Cabaret**, 2 pl. Palais Royal (1st) ✆ 01 58 62 56 25, Fax 01 58 62 56 40 – 🗏. 🆎 ᴳᴮ
Closed saturday lunch and Sunday – **Meals** a la carte 44/70 ℥.

XX **Au Pied de Cochon** (24 hr service), 6 r. Coquillière (1st) ✆ 01 40 13 77 00,
Fax 01 40 13 77 09, 🏠, brasserie – 🛗 🗏. 🆎 ⓞ ᴳᴮ   H 14
Meals a la carte 35/58 ℥.

XX **Aristippe**, 8 r. J. J. Rousseau (1st) ✆ 01 42 60 08 80, *aristippe@wanadoo.fr*,
Fax 01 42 60 11 13 – 🗏. 🆎 ᴳᴮ ᴶᶜᴮ
closed 1 to 21 August, Saturday lunch and Sunday – **Meals** - Seafood - 30 (lunch)/39 and a la carte 41/57 ℥.

XX **Pays de Cocagne**, -Espace Tarn- 111 r. Réaumur (2nd) ✆ 01 40 13 81 81,
Fax 01 40 13 87 70 – 🗏. 🆎 ⓞ ᴳᴮ ᴶᶜᴮ   G 14
closed 12 to 25 August, Saturday lunch, Sunday and Bank Holidays – **Meals** -South West of France rest.- 27,10/49 b.i. and a la carte 35/55 ℥.

XX 🍷 **Gallopin**, 40 r. N.-D.-des Victoires (2nd) ✆ 01 42 36 45 38, Fax 01 42 36 10 32, « Late
19C brasserie » – 🗏. 🆎 ⓞ ᴳᴮ   G 14
closed Sunday – **Meals** 25,50/30,50 b.i. and a la carte 28/58 ℥.

XX **Delizie d'Uggiano**, 18 r. Duphot (1st) ✆ 01 40 15 06 69, *losapiog@wanadoo.fr*,
Fax 01 40 15 03 90 – 🆎 ⓞ ᴳᴮ ᴶᶜᴮ   G 12
closed Saturday lunch and Sunday – **Meals** - Italian rest. - 36/49 and a la carte 34/46 ℥.

XX **Grand Colbert**, 2 r. Vivienne (2nd) ✆ 01 42 86 87 88, *le.grand.colbert@wanadoo.fr*,
Fax 01 42 86 82 65, brasserie – 🗏. 🆎 ⓞ ᴳᴮ ᴶᶜᴮ   G 13
Meals 24,40 and a la carte 31/53 ℥.

XX **Soufflé**, 36 r. Mont-Thabor (1st) ✆ 01 42 60 27 19, *c_rigaud@club-internet.fr*,
Fax 01 42 60 54 98 – 🗏. 🆎 ⓞ ᴳᴮ ᴶᶜᴮ   G 12
closed Sunday and Bank Holidays – **Meals** 28,20/35,83 and a la carte 40/50 ℥.

XX 🍷 **Vaudeville**, 29 r. Vivienne (2nd) ✆ 01 40 20 04 62, Fax 01 49 27 08 78, brasserie – 🆎
ⓞ ᴳᴮ ᴶᶜᴮ   G 14
Meals 21,04 b.i. (lunch)/30,18 b.i. and a la carte 42/55 ℥.

X **Chez Georges**, 1 r. Mail (2nd) ✆ 01 42 60 07 11, bistro – 🆎 ᴳᴮ   G 14
closed 29 July-19 August, Sunday and Bank Holidays – **Meals** a la carte 45/65.

X **L'Atelier Berger**, 49 r. Berger (1st) ✆ 01 40 28 00 00, *contact@atelierberger.com*,
Fax 01 40 28 10 65 – 🆎 ᴳᴮ   H 14
closed 11 to 18 August and Sunday – **Meals** 32.

X **Bistrot St-Honoré**, 10 r. Gomboust (1st) ✆ 01 42 61 77 78, Fax 01 42 61 77 78 – 🆎
ᴳᴮ ᴶᶜᴮ   G 13
closed August, 24 December-2 January, Saturday dinner and Sunday – **Meals** 23 and a la carte 35/52 ℥.

X **Café Marly**, 93 r. Rivoli - Cour Napoléon (1st) ✆ 01 49 26 06 60, Fax 01 49 26 07 06,
🏠, « Original decor at the Louvre museum » – 🗏. 🆎 ⓞ ᴳᴮ   H 13
Meals a la carte 31/57.

✗ **Aki,** 2 bis r. Daunou (2nd) ✆ 01 42 61 48 38, *Fax 01 47 03 37 52* – ◬ ⒼⒷ ⒿⒸⒷ. ✻
closed Easter Holidays, August, Saturday lunch and Sunday – **Meals** - Japanese rest. - 24,50
(lunch), 30,50/58,50 and a la carte 40/55.

✗ **Café Runtz,** 16 r. Favart (2nd) ✆ 01 42 96 69 86, *Fax 01 40 20 92 95*, bistro – ◬ ⑩
ⒼⒷ   F 13
*closed 5 to 12 May, 27 July-25 August, Saturday (except dinner from October-June), Sunday
and Bank Holidays* – **Meals** - Alsatian rest. - 17,54 (lunch), 21,96/33,54 and a la carte 30/40.

✗ **Pierrot,** 18 r. Étienne Marcel (2nd) ✆ 01 45 08 00 10 – ▤.
🦞 ◬ ⒼⒷ   H 15
closed August, 1 to 7 January and Sunday – **Meals** a la carte 28/34 ♖.

✗ **Mellifère,** 8 r. Monsigny (2nd) ✆ 01 42 61 21 71, *Fax 01 42 61 31 71* – ◬ ⒼⒷ
Meals 22,71 and a la carte 29/37.   G 13

✗ **L'Ardoise,** 28 r. Mont-Thabor (1st) ✆ 01 42 96 28 18 – ⒼⒷ   AX 7
closed August, 23 December-3 January, Monday and Tuesday – **Meals** 29 ♖.

✗ **Relais Chablisien,** 4 r. B. Poirée (1st) ✆ 01 45 08 53 73, *Fax 01 45 08 53 73*, « 17C
house » – ▤. ⒼⒷ. ✻   J 14
closed 1 to 21 August, Saturday and Sunday – **Meals** a la carte 28/39 ♖.

✗ **Tour de Montlhéry, Chez Denise** (open 24 h.), 5 r. Prouvaires (1st)
✆ 01 42 36 21 82, *Fax 01 45 08 81 99* – ▤. ⒼⒷ   H 14
closed 14 July-19 August, Saturday and Sunday – **Meals** a la carte 35/53.

✗ **Chez La Vieille "Adrienne",** 1 r. Bailleul (1st) ✆ 01 42 60 15 78, *Fax 01 42 33 85 71*
– ◬ ⒼⒷ ⒿⒸⒷ   H 14
closed 10 to 18 August, Saturday, Sunday and dinner except Thursday – **Meals** (booking
essential) 26 and a la carte 40/45.

✗ **Souletin,** 6 r. Vrillière (1st) ✆ 01 42 61 43 78, *Fax 01 42 61 43 78*, bistro – ⒼⒷ
closed Saturday lunch, Sunday and Bank Holidays – **Meals** 30,49 ♖.   G 14

✗ **Lescure,** 7 r. Mondovi (1st) ✆ 01 42 60 18 91, bistro – ▤. ⒼⒷ   G 11
closed 1 to 23 August, 24 December to 1 January, Saturday and Sunday – **Meals** 19,82
and a la carte 25/35 ♖.

✗ **Dauphin,** 167 r. St-Honoré (1st) ✆ 01 42 60 40 11, *Fax 01 42 60 01 18* – ◬ ⑩ ⒼⒷ
ⒿⒸⒷ   H 13
Meals 22,10 (lunch)/30,94 and a la carte 31/44.

✗ **Issé,** 56 r. Ste-Anne (2nd) ✆ 01 42 96 67 76, *Fax 01 42 96 82 63* – ▤. ⒼⒷ   G 13
closed 5 to 19 August, 23 December-6 January, Monday lunch, Saturday lunch and Sunday
– **Meals** 23/30,49 and a la carte 48/80.

Bastille,
République,
Hôtel de Ville.

3rd, 4th and 11th arrondissements.
3rd: ✉ *75003*
4th: ✉ *75004*
11th: ✉ *75011*

🏨🏨 **Pavillon de la Reine** ⑤ without rest, 28 pl. Vosges (3rd) ✆ 01 40 29 19 19, *pavillon@club-internet.fr, Fax 01 40 29 19 20* – ▤ ▤ ☰ ⒯⒱ ✆ ⇦. ◬ ⑩ ⒼⒷ ⒿⒸⒷ   J 17
⊆ 20 – **31 rm** 330/385, 14 suites, 10 duplex.

🏨🏨 **Holiday Inn** Ⓜ, 10 pl. République (11th) ✆ 01 43 14 43 50, *holiday.inn.paris.republique@wanadoo.fr, Fax 01 47 00 32 34*, ▰ – ▤ ☰ ⒯⒱ ✆ ⅗ – ▱ 25 - 150. ◬ ⑩
ⒼⒷ ⒿⒸⒷ   G 17
Au 10 de la République : **Meals** 14,48/45 – ⊆ 25,15 – **318 rm** 305/478.

🏨🏨 **Villa Beaumarchais** Ⓜ ⑤, 5 r. Arquebusiers (3rd) ✆ 01 40 29 14 00, *beaumarchais@hotelsparis.fr, Fax 01 40 29 14 01* – ▤ ⅗ rm, ☰ ⒯⒱ ✆ ⅙ – ▱ 15. ◬ ⑩ ⒼⒷ ⒿⒸⒷ
Meals (*closed August, Saturday lunch, Sunday and Monday*) 25 (lunch), 30/53 ♖ – ⊆ 24
– **50 rm** 305/488.

🏨🏨 **Jeu de Paume** ⑤ without rest, 54 r. St-Louis-en-l'Ile (4th) ✆ 01 43 26 14 18, *info@jeudepaumehotel.com, Fax 01 40 46 02 76*, « 17C tennis court », ▰ – ▤ ⒯⒱ ✆ –
▱ 25. ◬ ⑩ ⒼⒷ ⒿⒸⒷ   K 16
⊆ 14 – **30 rm** 151/263.

Bourg Tibourg without rest, 19 r. Bourg Tibourg (4th) ℘ 01 42 78 47 39, *hotel.du. bourg.tibourg@ wanadoo fr*, Fax 01 40 29 07 00 – 🔊 🖃 🖂 📺 📞 👤. 🖭 💿 ☰☷
JCB. 🕸   J 16
🖴 12 – **30 rm** 170/270.

Bretonnerie without rest, 22 r. Ste-Croix-de-la-Bretonnerie (4th) ℘ 01 48 87 77 63, *hotel@bretonnerie.com*, Fax 01 42 77 26 78 – 🔊 📺 📞 ☰☷. 🕸   J 16
closed 29 July-27 August – 🖴 9,50 – **22 rm** 108/140, 4 suites, 3 duplex.

Caron de Beaumarchais without rest, 12 r. Vieille-du-Temple (4th)
℘ 01 42 72 34 12, Fax 01 42 72 34 63 – 🔊 🖃 📺 📞. 🖭 💿 ☰☷. 🕸   J 16
🖴 9 – **19 rm** 128/142.

Méridional without rest, 36 bd Richard Lenoir (11th) ℘ 01 48 05 75 00, *hotel.meridi onal@wanadoo.fr*, Fax 01 43 57 42 85 – 🔊 📺 📞. 🖭 💿 ☰☷   J18
🖴 6,87 – **36 rm** 121,96/137,21.

Beaubourg without rest, 11 r. S. Le Franc (4th) ℘ 01 42 74 34 24, *hltbeaubourg@ h otellerie.net*, Fax 01 42 78 68 11 – 🔊 📺 📞. 🖭 💿 ☰☷ JCB   H 15
🖴 6 – **28 rm** 101/113.

Verlain without rest, 97 r. St-Maur (11th) ℘ 01 43 57 44 88, *verlain@ 3and1hotels.com*, Fax 01 43 57 32 06 – 🔊 🖃 📺 📞. 🖭 💿 ☰☷ JCB   G 19
🖴 7,62 – **38 rm** 92,38/112,35.

Lutèce without rest, 65 r. St-Louis-en-l'Ile (4th) ℘ 01 43 26 23 52, *hotel.lutece@ free.fr*, Fax 01 43 29 60 25 – 🔊 🖃 📺 📞. 🖭 ☰☷. 🕸   K 16
🖴 10 – **23 rm** 122/148.

Croix de Malte without rest, 5 r. Malte (11th) ℘ 01 48 05 09 36, *H2752-gm@ acco r-hotels.com*, Fax 01 43 57 02 54 – 🔊, ✜ rm, 📺. 🖭 💿 ☰☷ .JCB   H 17
🖴 8 – **29 rm** 95/105.

Grand Hôtel Français without rest, 223 bd Voltaire (11th) ℘ 01 43 71 27 57, Fax 01 43 48 40 05 – 🔊 📺 📞. 🖭 💿 ☰☷ JCB   K 20
🖴 6,10 – **40 rm** 83,85/114,34.

Beaumarchais without rest, 3 r. Oberkampf (11th) ℘ 01 53 36 86 86, *hotel.beauma rchais@ libertysurf.fr*, Fax 01 43 38 32 86 – 🔊 📺. 🖭 ☰☷ JCB   H 17
🖴 9 – **31 rm** 69/99.

Grand Prieuré without rest, 20 r. Grand Prieuré (11th) ℘ 01 47 00 74 14, Fax 01 49 23 06 64 – 🔊 📺. 🖭 💿 ☰☷ JCB. 🕸   G 17
🖴 5 – **32 rm** 54,90/62,60.

Lyon-Mulhouse without rest, 8 bd Beaumarchais (11th) ℘ 01 47 00 91 50, *hotelyo nmulhouse@ wanadoo.fr*, Fax 01 47 00 06 31 – 🔊 📺 📞. 🖭 💿 ☰☷ JCB   J17
🖴 5 – **40 rm** 55/83.

Nice without rest, 42 bis r. Rivoli (4th) ℘ 01 42 78 55 29, Fax 01 42 78 36 07 – 🔊 📺
📞. ☰☷   J 16
🖴 6 – **23 rm** 60/95.

L'Ambroisie (Pacaud), 9 pl. des Vosges (4th) ℘ 01 42 78 51 45 – 🖃. 🖭 ☰☷.
🕸   J 17
closed August, February Holidays, Sunday and Monday – **Meals** a la carte 155/ 200
Spec. Feuillantine de langoustines aux graines de sésame, sauce au curry. Suprêmes de pigeon de Bresse au jus tranché, cuisses en pastilla. Tarte fine sablée au chocolat, glace à la vanille..

Hiramatsu, 7 quai Bourbon (4th) ℘ 01 56 81 08 80, *paris@ hiramatsu.co.jp*, Fax 01 56 81 08 81 – 🖃. 🖭 💿 ☰☷   K 16
closed 4 to 26 August, 22 December-6 January, Sunday and Monday – **Meals** (booking essential) 45,70 (lunch)/92 and a la carte 85/105
Spec. Aiguillettes de pigeonneau au foie gras. Noix de veau au sésame, sauce vin jaune au curry. Cassonade brûlée de café corsé..

Ambassade d'Auvergne, 22 r. Grenier St-Lazare (3rd) ℘ 01 42 72 31 22, *info@ a mbassade-auvergne.com*, Fax 01 42 78 85 47 – 🖃. 🖭 ☰☷ JCB   H 15
Meals 25,92 and a la carte 35/40.

Bofinger, 5 r. Bastille (4th) ℘ 01 42 72 87 82, Fax 01 42 72 97 68, brasserie, « Belle Epoque decor » – 🖃. 🖭 💿 ☰☷   J 17
Meals 30,50 b.i. and a la carte 35/57.

L'Aiguière, 37bis r. Montreuil (11th) ℘ 01 43 72 42 32, *patrick-masbatin1@ libertysu rf.com*, Fax 01 43 72 96 36 – 🖃. 🖭 💿 ☰☷ JCB   K 20
closed Saturday lunch and Sunday – **Meals** 22,50 b.i./45 b.i. and a la carte 41/ 58.

XX 🕸 **Benoît,** 20 r. St-Martin (4th) ℘ 01 42 72 25 76, Fax 01 42 72 45 68, bistro – ▤. ᴀᴇ
closed August – **Meals** 38 (lunch)and a la carte 60/90 ⅋
Spec. Tête de veau sauce ravigote. Cassoulet. Gibier (season).

XX **A Sousceyrac,** 35 r. Faidherbe (11th) ℘ 01 43 71 65 30, Fax 01 40 09 79 75 – ▤. ᴀᴇ
ⓞ ᴳᴮ   J 19
closed August – **Meals** 30 and a la carte 40/50 ⅋.

XX 🐸 **Dôme du Marais,** 53 bis r. Francs-Bourgeois (4th) ℘ 01 42 74 54 17,
Fax 01 42 77 78 17 – ᴀᴇ ᴳᴮ   H16 J16
closed 15 to 31 August, 1 to 8 January, Sunday and Monday – **Meals** 23 (lunch), 28/38
and a la carte 39/44 ⅋.

XX **Vin et Marée,** 276 bd Voltaire (11th) ℘ 01 43 72 31 23, vin.maree@wanadoo.fr,
Fax 01 40 24 00 23 – ▤. ᴀᴇ ᴳᴮ   K 21
Meals - Seafood - a la carte 30/37 ⅋.

XX **Mansouria,** 11 r. Faidherbe (11th) ℘ 01 43 71 00 16, Fax 01 40 24 21 97 – ▤. ᴳᴮ
✸   K 19
closed 12 to 19 August, Sunday, lunch Tuesday and Monday – **Meals** - Moroccan rest. -
29/43,50 b.i. and a la carte 35/45.

XX **Les Amognes,** 243 r. Fg St-Antoine (11th) ℘ 01 43 72 73 05, Fax 01 43 28 77 23 –
ᴳᴮ   K 20
closed 1 to 19 August, 24 December-2 January, Sunday, lunch Monday and Saturday –
Meals 30 ⅋.

X 🐸 **Pamphlet,** 38 r. Debelleyme (3rd) ℘ 01 42 72 39 24, Fax 01 42 72 12 53 –
▤. ᴳᴮ   H 17
closed 8 to 27 August, 1 to 15 January, Saturday lunch and Sunday – **Meals** 27.

X **Repaire de Cartouche,** 99 r. Amelot (11th) ℘ 01 47 00 25 86, Fax 01 43 38 85 91
– ᴳᴮ   H 17
closed 25 July-25 August, Sunday and Monday – **Meals** 21 and a la carte 28/32.

X **Péché Mignon,** 5 r. Guillaume Bertrand (11th) ℘ 01 43 57 68 68, Fax 01 49 83 91 62
– ᴀᴇ ᴳᴮ   H 19
closed August, Sunday dinner and Monday – **Meals** 26 and a la carte 30/38.

X **Auberge Pyrénées Cévennes,** 106 r. Folie-Méricourt (11th) ℘ 01 43 57 33 78 – ▤.
ᴀᴇ ᴳᴮ   G 17
closed 29 July-22 August, 1 to 7 January, Saturday lunch and Sunday – **Meals** 25 and a
la carte 33/40.

X 🐸 **Astier,** 44 r. J.-P. Timbaud (11th) ℘ 01 43 57 16 35, bistro – ᴳᴮ   G 18
closed Easter Holidays, August, Christmas-New Year, Saturday and Sunday – **Meals**
(booking essential) 19,50 (lunch)/23,50.

X **Au Bascou,** 38 r. Réaumur (3rd) ℘ 01 42 72 69 25, Fax 01 42 72 69 25, bistro – ᴀᴇ ᴳᴮ
closed 28 July-27 August, 23 December-1 January, Sunday, lunch Saturday and Monday
– **Meals** a la carte 29/34 ⅋.

X **C'Amelot,** 50 r. Amelot (11th) ℘ 01 43 55 54 04, Fax 01 43 14 77 05 – ᴳᴮ   H 17
closed August, Saturday lunch, Sunday and Monday – **Meals** 30 ⅋.

X **Monde des Chimères,** 69 r. St-Louis-en-l'Ile (4th) ℘ 01 43 54 45 27,
Fax 01 43 29 84 88 – ᴳᴮ   K 16
closed Sunday and Monday – **Meals** 13,60 (lunch)/25,15 and a la carte 39/63.

X **Grizzli Café,** 7 r. St-Martin (4th) ℘ 01 48 87 77 56, �, bistro – ᴀᴇ ᴳᴮ   J 15
Meals a la carte 29/41 ⅋.

X **Les Fernandises Chez Fernand,** 19 r. Fontaine au Roi (11th) ℘ 01 48 06 16 96,
bistro – ᴳᴮ   G 18
closed August, Sunday and Monday – **Meals** 16,77 (lunch)/20,58 and a la carte
30/40.

X **Clos du Vert Bois,** 13 r. Vert Bois (3rd) ℘ 01 42 77 14 85 – ᴀᴇ ᴳᴮ ᴊᴄʙ   G 16
closed 1 to 25 August, Saturday lunch and Monday – **Meals** 20,59/44,98 and a la carte
43/56.

X **Anjou-Normandie,** 13 r. Folie-Méricourt (11th) ℘ 01 47 00 30 59, Fax 01 47 00 30 59
– ᴳᴮ. ✸   H 18
closed August, Saturday and Sunday – **Meals** (lunch only) 17,50/20 and a la carte 27/
38 ⅋.

X **Piton des Iles,** 174 r. Roquette (11th) ℘ 01 43 48 61 89 – ᴀᴇ ᴳᴮ   H 20
closed Monday lunch and Sunday – **Meals** - Specialities of Reunion Island - 11 (lunch) and
a la carte 16/20 ⅋.

X **Balibar,** 9 r. St-Sabin (11e) ℘ 01 47 00 25 47, Fax 01 43 14 98 32 – ᴀᴇ ⓞ ᴳᴮ ᴊᴄʙ
closed August and Sunday – **Meals** (dinner only) a la carte 33/42.

Quartier Latin, Luxembourg, Jardin des Plantes.

5th and 6th arrondissements.
5th: ✉ 75005
6th: ✉ 75006

Lutétia, 45 bd Raspail (6th) ✆ 01 49 54 46 46, *lutetia-paris@lutetia-paris.com*, Fax 01 49 54 46 00, ₤ – ▯, ← rm, ▭ TV ✆ – ▲ 300. AE ⓞ GB JCB ━━━━━━ K 12 see *Paris* below - *Brasserie Lutétia* ✆ 01 49 54 46 76 **Meals** 29/35 ♀ – ⌷ 21 – **240 rm** 380/600, 10 suites.

Victoria Palace without rest, 6 r. Blaise-Desgoffe (6th) ✆ 01 45 49 70 00, *victoria @club-internet.fr*, Fax 01 45 49 23 75 – ▯, ← rm, ▭ TV ✆ ₺ ⇌ – ▲ 20. AE ⓞ GB JCB ━━━ L 11 ⌷ 16 – **62 rm** 280/345.

Aubusson without rest, 33 r. Dauphine (6th) ✆ 01 43 29 43 43, *reservationherve@h oteldaubusson.com*, Fax 01 43 29 12 62, « Elegantly decorated mansion » – ▯, ← rm, ▭ TV ✆ ₺ ⇌. ⓞ GB JCB ━━━━━━━━━━━━━━━━━━━━━━━━━━━━━━━━ BX 9 ⌷ 20 – **47 rm** 250/390, 3 studios.

Relais Christine M ⚭ without rest, 3 r. Christine (6th) ✆ 01 40 51 60 80, *contac t@relais-christine.com*, Fax 01 40 51 60 81, « Elegant decor » – ▯, ← rm, ▭ TV ✆ ⇌ – ▲ 20. AE ⓞ GB JCB ━━━━━━━━━━━━━━━━━━━━━━━━━━━━━━━━ J 14 ⌷ 20 – **35 rm** 315/410, 16 duplex.

Littré without rest, 9 r. Littré (6th) ✆ 01 53 63 07 07, *hotellittre@hotellittreparis.com*, Fax 01 45 44 88 13 – ▯, ← rm, ▭ TV ✆ – ▲ 25. AE ⓞ GB JCB. ❄ ━━━━━━━ L 11 ⌷ 13 – **79 rm** 222/321, 11 suites.

Bel Ami St-Germain-des-Prés M without rest, 7-11 r. St-Benoit (6th) ✆ 01 42 61 53 53, *contact@hotel-bel-ami.com*, Fax 01 49 27 09 33, « Fine contemporary decor » – ▯ ▭ TV ✆ ₺ ₺. AE ⓞ GB JCB ━━━━━━━━━━━━━━━━━━━━━━ J 13 ⌷ 16 – **115 rm** 270/420.

Buci M without rest, 22 r. Buci (6th) ✆ 01 55 42 74 74, *hotelbuci@wanadoo.fr*, Fax 01 55 42 74 44 – ▯ ▭ TV ✆ ₺. AE ⓞ GB JCB. ❄ ━━━━━━━━━━━━━━━━━━ J 13 ⌷ 14 – **24 rm** 240/315.

L'Abbaye ⚭ without rest, 10 r. Cassette (6th) ✆ 01 45 44 38 11, *hotel.abbaye@wa nadoo.fr*, Fax 01 45 48 07 86 – ▯ ▭ TV ✆. AE GB. ❄ ━━━━━━━━━━━━━━━ K 12 **42 rm** ⌷ 253,07, 4 duplex.

L'Hôtel, 13 r. Beaux Arts (6th) ✆ 01 44 41 99 00, *reservation@l-hotel.com*, Fax 01 43 25 64 31, ▯ – ▯ ▭ TV ✆. AE ⓞ GB JCB. ❄ ━━━━━━━━━━━━━━━━━━━ J 13 **Meals** a la carte 30/54 ♀ – ⌷ 16,77 – **16 rm** 259,16/594,60, 4 suites.

Relais St-Germain M without rest, 9 carrefour de l'Odéon (6th) ✆ 01 44 27 07 97, Fax 01 46 33 45 30, « Attractive interior » – ▯ kitchenette ▭ TV ✆. AE ⓞ GB JCB **18 rm** ⌷ 196,66/266,79, 4 studios.

Madison M without rest, 143 bd St-Germain (6th) ✆ 01 40 51 60 00, *resa@hotel-m adison.com*, Fax 01 40 51 60 01, « Fine furniture » – ▯ ▭ TV. AE ⓞ GB JCB J 13 **54 rm** ⌷ 150/305.

Relais Médicis M without rest, 23 r. Racine (6th) ✆ 01 43 26 00 60, *relais edicis@w anadoo.fr*, Fax 01 40 46 83 39 – ▯ ▭ TV ✆. AE ⓞ GB JCB. ❄ ━━━━━━━━━ K 13 **16 rm** ⌷ 188/258.

Villa Panthéon M without rest, 41 r. Écoles (5th) ✆ 01 53 10 95 95, *pantheon@h otelsparis.fr*, Fax 01 53 10 95 96 – ← rm, ▭ TV ✆ ₺. AE ⓞ GB JCB ━━━━━━━ K 14 ⌷ 26 – **59 rm** 252/426.

Left Bank St-Germain without rest, 9 r. Ancienne Comédie (6th) ✆ 01 43 54 01 70, *lb@paris-hotels-charm.com*, Fax 01 43 26 17 14 – ▯ ▭ TV. AE ⓞ GB JCB. ❄ ━━━━━━ K 13 **31 rm** ⌷ 206/251.

Holiday Inn St-Germain-des-Prés M without rest, 92 r. Vaugirard (6th) ✆ 01 49 54 87 00, *holiday-inn.psg@wanadoo.fr*, Fax 01 49 54 87 01 – ▯, ← rm, ▭ TV ₺ ⇌ – ▲ 60. AE ⓞ GB JCB ━━━━━━━━━━━━━━━━━━━━━━━━━━━━━━━━━ L 12 ⌷ 14 – **134 rm** 215/260.

🏨 **Angleterre** without rest, 44 r. Jacob (6th) ℰ 01 42 60 34 72, anglotel@wanadoo.fr, Fax 01 42 60 16 93 – 🛗 📺 📶 ஊ ⓪ GB ᴊᴄʙ. ❀   J 13
🖿 9,15 – **23 rm** 125/210, 4 suites.

🏨 **Villa** Ⓜ without rest, 29 r. Jacob (6th) ℰ 01 43 26 60 00, hotel@villa-saintgermain.com, Fax 01 46 34 63 63, « Contemporary decor » – 🛗, ❄ rm, 📺 📶 ஊ ⓪ GB ᴊᴄʙ   L 12
🖿 **13 – 31 rm** 225/400.

🏨 **St-Grégoire** Ⓜ without rest, 43 r. Abbé Grégoire (6th) ℰ 01 45 48 23 23, hotel@saintgregoire.com, Fax 01 45 48 33 95 – 🛗 📺 📶 ஊ ⓪ GB ᴊᴄʙ. ❀   L 12
🖿 12 – **20 rm** 145/236.

🏨 **Millésime Hôtel** ⑤ without rest, 15 r. Jacob (6th) ℰ 01 44 07 97 97, reservation@millesimehotel.com, Fax 01 46 34 55 97 – 🛗 📺 📶 ஊ ⓪ GB ᴊᴄʙ   J 13
🖿 12 – **22 rm** 150/210.

🏨 **Résidence Henri IV** Ⓜ without rest, 50 r. Bernardins (5th) ℰ 01 44 41 31 81, hotel.residence.henri4@wanadoo.fr, Fax 01 46 33 93 22 – 🛗 kitchenette 📺 📶 ஊ ⓪ GB ᴊᴄʙ. ❀   K 15
🖿 8 – **8 rm** 145, 5 suites.

🏨 **Rives de Notre-Dame** Ⓜ without rest, 15 quai St-Michel (5th) ℰ 01 43 54 81 16, hotel@rivesdenotredame.com, Fax 01 43 26 27 09, ≤, « 16C house, Provencal decor » – 🛗 📺 📶 – 🕍 15. ஊ ⓪ GB ᴊᴄʙ   J 14
🖿 10,70 – **10 rm** 213/381.

🏨 **Au Manoir St-Germain-des-Prés** without rest, 153 bd St-Germain (6th) ℰ 01 42 22 21 65, msg@paris-hotels-charm.com, Fax 01 45 48 22 25 – 🛗 📺 📶 ஊ ⓪ GB ᴊᴄʙ. ❀   J 12
33 rm 🖿 168/222.

🏨 **Ste-Beuve** Ⓜ without rest, 9 r. Ste-Beuve (6th) ℰ 01 45 48 20 07, saintebeuve@wanadoo.fr, Fax 01 45 48 67 52 – 🛗 📺 📶 ஊ ⓪ GB ᴊᴄʙ. ❀   L 12
🖿 12,96 – **22 rm** 122/222.

🏨 **Panthéon** without rest, 19 pl. Panthéon (5th) ℰ 01 43 54 32 95, hotel.pantheon@wanadoo.fr, Fax 01 43 26 64 65, ≤ – 🛗 📺 ஊ ⓪ GB ᴊᴄʙ. ❀   L 14
🖿 12 – **36 rm** 183.

🏨 **Jardins du Luxembourg** Ⓜ ⑤ without rest, 5 imp. Royer-Collard (5th) ℰ 01 40 46 08 88, jardinslux@wanadoo.fr, Fax 01 40 46 02 28 – 🛗 📺 ஊ ⓪ GB ᴊᴄʙ. ❀   L 14
🖿 9 – **26 rm** 130/140.

🏨 **Tour Notre-Dame** without rest, 20 r. Sommerard (5th) ℰ 01 43 54 47 60, tour-notre-dame@magic.fr, Fax 01 43 26 42 34 – 🛗 📺 📶 ஊ ⓪ GB ᴊᴄʙ   K 14
🖿 10 – **48 rm** 152/243.

🏨 **Villa des Artistes** Ⓜ ⑤ without rest, 9 r. Grande Chaumière (6th) ℰ 01 43 26 60 86, hotel@villa-artistes.com, Fax 01 43 54 73 70 – 🛗 📺 📶 ஊ ⓪ GB ᴊᴄʙ. ❀   L 12
🖿 8,50 – **59 rm** 120/205.

🏨 **Relais St-Sulpice** Ⓜ ⑤ without rest, 3 r. Garancière (6th) ℰ 01 46 33 99 00, relaissstsulpice@wanadoo.fr, Fax 01 46 33 00 10 – 🛗, ❄ rm, 📺 & ஊ ⓪ GB ᴊᴄʙ. ❀
🖿 10 – **26 rm** 155/190.

🏨 **Grand Hôtel St-Michel** without rest, 19 r. Cujas (5th) ℰ 01 46 33 33 02, grand.hotel@st.michel.com, Fax 01 40 46 96 33 – 🛗 📺 & ஊ ⓪ GB ᴊᴄʙ   K 14
🖿 10 – **45 rm** 160, 7 suites.

🏨 **Fleurie** without rest, 32 r. Grégoire de Tours (6th) ℰ 01 53 73 70 00, bonjour@hotel-de-fleurie.tm.fr, Fax 01 53 73 70 20 – 🛗 📺 📶 ஊ ⓪ GB. ❀   K 13
🖿 9 – **29 rm** 145/274.

🏨 **St-Germain-des-Prés** without rest, 36 r. Bonaparte (6th) ℰ 01 43 26 00 19, hotel-saint-germain-des-pres@wanadoo.fr, Fax 01 40 46 83 63 – 🛗, ❄ rm, 📺 📶 ஊ ⓪ GB. ❀
🖿 8 – **30 rm** 150/245.

🏨 **Saints-Pères** without rest, 65 r. Sts-Pères (6th) ℰ 01 45 44 50 00, hotelsts.peres@wanadoo.fr, Fax 01 45 44 90 83 – 🛗 📺. ஊ GB. ❀   J 12
🖿 11 – **36 rm** 120/195, 3 suites.

🏨 **Royal St-Michel** Ⓜ without rest, 3 bd St-Michel (5th) ℰ 01 44 07 06 06, hotel.royalst.michel@wanadoo.fr, Fax 01 44 07 36 25 – 🛗, ❄ rm, 📺 📶 ஊ ⓪ GB ᴊᴄʙ
🖿 10 – **39 rm** 175/200.

🏨 **Notre Dame** without rest, 1 quai St-Michel (5th) ℰ 01 43 54 20 43, hotel.lenotredame@libertysurf.fr, Fax 01 43 26 61 75, ≤ – 🛗, ❄ rm, 📺 ஊ ⓪ GB. ❀   K 14
🖿 6 – **23 rm** 150/199, 2 duplex.

🏨 **Relais St-Jacques** without rest, 3 r. Abbé de l'Épée (5th) ℰ 01 53 73 26 00, sanevers@wanadoo.fr, Fax 01 43 26 17 81 – 🛗 📺 & – 🕍 20. ஊ ⓪ GB ᴊᴄʙ. ❀   L 14
🖿 11 – **23 rm** 186/224.

🏠 **St-Christophe** without rest, 17 r. Lacépède (5th) ℰ 01 43 31 81 54, *saintchristophe
@wanadoo.fr*, Fax 01 43 31 12 54 – |📶| 📺. 🗚 ⓪ 🆖   L 15
🛏 8 – **31 rm** 102/114.

🏠 **Sully St-Germain** Ⓜ without rest, 31 r. Écoles (5th) ℰ 01 43 26 56 02, *sully@sequ
anahotels.com*, Fax 01 43 29 74 42, 🛋 – |📶| 📺. 🗚 ⓪ 🆖 🆓. 🛇   K 15
🛏 12 – **58 rm** 145/200.

🏠 **Parc St-Séverin** without rest, 22 r. Parcheminerie (5th) ℰ 01 43 54 32 17, *hotel.pa
rc.severin@wanadoo.fr*, Fax 01 43 54 70 71 – |📶| 📺. 🗚 ⓪ 🆖 🆓. 🛇   K 14
🛏 9,15 – **27 rm** 91,50/175,30.

🏠 **Jardin de Cluny** without rest, 9 r. Sommerard (5th) ℰ 01 43 54 22 66, *hotel.declun
y@wanadoo.fr*, Fax 01 40 51 03 36 – |📶| 🗖 📺 🗚 ⓪ 🆖 🆓. 🛇   K 14
🛏 10 – **40 rm** 125/185.

🏠 **Libertel Quartier Latin** Ⓜ without rest, 9 r. Écoles (5th) ℰ 01 44 27 06 45, *H2782@a
ccor-hotels.com*, Fax 01 43 25 36 70 – |📶| 🗖 📺 ♿. 🗚 ⓪ 🆖 🆓   L 15
🛏 13 – **29 rm** 210/242.

🏠 **Jardin de l'Odéon** Ⓜ without rest, 7 r. Casimir Delavigne (6th) ℰ 01 53 10 28 50,
hotel@jardindelodeon.com, Fax 01 43 25 28 12 – |📶| 📺 ♿. 🗚 🆖   K 13
🛏 9 – **41 rm** 113/181.

🏠 **Prince de Conti** without rest, 8 r. Guénégaud (6th) ℰ 01 44 07 30 40,
Fax 01 44 07 36 34 – |📶|, 🛏 rm, 🗖 📺 ♿. 🗚 ⓪ 🆖 🆓   J 13
🛏 12,96 – **26 rm** 210/310.

🏠 **Clos Médicis** Ⓜ without rest, 56 r. Monsieur Le Prince (6th) ℰ 01 43 29 10 80, *mess
age@closmedicis.com*, Fax 01 43 54 26 90 – |📶| 🗖 📺 🗘 ♿. 🗚 ⓪ 🆖 🆓   K 14
🛏 10 – **38 rm** 125/220.

🏠 **Odéon Hôtel** Ⓜ without rest, 3 r. Odéon (6th) ℰ 01 43 25 90 67, *odeon@odeonho
tel.fr*, Fax 01 43 25 55 98, « 17C house » – |📶|, 🛏 rm, 🗖 📺 🗘. 🗚 ⓪ 🆖 🆓. 🛇 K 13
🛏 10 – **33 rm** 120/240.

🏠 **Grands Hommes** without rest, 17 pl. Panthéon (5th) ℰ 01 46 34 19 60, *hotel-gran
ds-hommes@wanadoo.fr*, Fax 01 43 26 67 32, ≼ – |📶| 🗖 📺 – 🛆 20. 🗚 ⓪ 🆖 🆓.
🛇   L 14
🛏 9 – **32 rm** 198/381.

🏠 **de l'Odéon** without rest, 13 r. St-Sulpice (6th) ℰ 01 43 25 70 11, *hotelodeon@wana
doo.fr*, Fax 01 43 29 97 34, « 16C house » – |📶| 🗖 📺 🗘. 🗚 ⓪ 🆖 🆓   K 13
🛏 11 – **29 rm** 145/237.

🏠 **Prince de Condé** without rest, 39 r. Seine (6th) ℰ 01 43 26 71 56, Fax 01 46 34 27 95
– |📶|, 🛏 rm, 🗖 📺. 🗚 ⓪ 🆖 🆓   K 12
🛏 12,96 – **12 rm** 210/310.

🏠 **Régent** without rest, 61 r. Dauphine (6th) ℰ 01 46 34 59 80, *hotel.leregent@wanad
oo.fr*, Fax 01 40 51 05 07 – |📶| 🗖 📺. 🗚 ⓪ 🆖 🆓. 🛇   J 13
🛏 10,67 – **25 rm** 121,96/182,94.

🏠 **Select** Ⓜ without rest, 1 pl. Sorbonne (5th) ℰ 01 46 34 14 80, *select.hotel@wanadoo.fr*,
Fax 01 46 34 51 79 – |📶| 🗖 📺 🗘. 🗚 ⓪ 🆖 🆓   K 14
🛏 6 – **68 rm** 137.

🏠 **Albe** without rest, 1 r. Harpe (5th) ℰ 01 46 34 09 70, *albehotel@wanadoo.fr*,
Fax 01 40 46 85 70 – |📶| 🗖 📺 🗘. 🗚 ⓪ 🆖 🆓. 🛇   K 14
🛏 10 – **45 rm** 103/148.

🏠 **Ferrandi** without rest, 92 r. Cherche-Midi (6th) ℰ 01 42 22 97 40, *hotel.ferrandi@w
anadoo.fr*, Fax 01 45 44 89 97 – |📶| 🗖 📺 🗘. 🗚 ⓪ 🆖 🆓   L 11
🛏 10 – **42 rm** 105/220.

🏠 **Dacia-Luxembourg** without rest, 41 bd St-Michel (5th) ℰ 01 53 10 27 77, *info@h
oteldacia.com*, Fax 01 44 07 10 33 – |📶| 🗖 📺 🗘. 🗚 ⓪ 🆖 🆓. 🛇   K 14
🛏 8 – **38 rm** 100/130.

🏠 **Marronniers** � without rest, 21 r. Jacob (6th) ℰ 01 43 25 30 60, Fax 01 40 46 83 56
– |📶| 🗖 📺 🗘. 🆖. 🛇   J 13
🛏 12 – **37 rm** 180/200.

🏠 **Pierre Nicole** 🌿 without rest, 39 r. Pierre Nicole (5th) ℰ 01 43 54 76 86,
Fax 01 43 54 22 45 – |📶| 📺 🗘. 🗚 ⓪ 🆖. 🛇   M 13
🛏 6 – **33 rm** 60/70.

🏠 **St-Jacques** without rest, 35 r. Écoles (5th) ℰ 01 44 07 45 45, *hotelsaintjacques@wa
nadoo.fr*, Fax 01 43 25 65 50 – |📶| 📺 🗘. 🗚 ⓪ 🆖 🆓. 🛇   K 15
🛏 6,10 – **35 rm** 67,84/102,14.

🏠 **Maxim** without rest, 28 r. Censier (5th) ℰ 01 43 31 16 15, Fax 01 43 91 93 87 – |📶|,
🛏 rm, 📺. 🗚 ⓪ 🆖 🆓   M 15
🛏 8 – **36 rm** 105/115.

Familia without rest, 11 r. Écoles (5th) ℰ 01 43 54 55 27, *familia.hotel@libertysurf.fr*, Fax 01 43 29 61 77 – 📶 📺 🖭 ⑩ 🅶🅱 🅹🅲🅱. ⚒ **K-L 15**
⌧ 6,10 – **30 rm** 68,60/106.

Dauphine St-Germain without rest, 36 r. Dauphine (6th) ℰ 01 43 26 74 34, Fax 01 43 26 49 09 – 📶, ≪ rm, 🖃 📺 🖳 🆔 ⑩ 🅶🅱 🅹🅲🅱 **J 13**
⌧ 14 – **30 rm** 170/210.

Sèvres Azur without rest, 22 r. Abbé-Grégoire (6th) ℰ 01 45 48 84 07, *sevres.azur@wanadoo.fr*, Fax 01 42 84 01 55 – 📶 📺. 🆔 ⑩ 🅶🅱 🅹🅲🅱 **K 11-12**
⌧ 7 – **31 rm** 74/89.

California without rest, 32 r. Écoles (5th) ℰ 01 46 34 12 90, *california@sequanahotels.com*, Fax 01 46 34 75 52 – 📶, ≪ rm, 🖃 📺. 🆔 ⑩ 🅶🅱. ⚒ **K 14-15**
⌧ 10 – **44 rm** 120/200.

XXXXX ❀❀ **Tour d'Argent** (Terrail), 15 quai Tournelle (5th) ℰ 01 43 54 23 31, Fax 01 44 07 12 04, ≪ Notre-Dame, « Small museum showing the development of eating utensils. In the cellar : an illustrated history of wine » – 🖃. 🆔 ⑩ 🅶🅱 🅹🅲🅱 **K 16**
closed Monday – **Meals** 59,46 (lunch)/182,94 and à la carte 130/190
Spec. Quenelles de brochet "André Terrail". Caneton "Tour d'Argent". Flambée de pêche..

XXX ❀ **Jacques Cagna**, 14 r. Grands Augustins (6th) ℰ 01 43 26 49 39, Fax 01 43 54 54 48, « Old Parisian house » – 🖃. 🆔 ⑩ 🅶🅱 🅹🅲🅱 **J 14**
closed 3 to 27 August, Sunday, lunch Saturday and Monday – **Meals** 41 (lunch)/80 and à la carte 85/125
Spec. Foie gras de canard poêlé aux fruits confits caramélisés. Pigeon de Vendée à la chartreuse verte. Gibier (Season)..

XXX ❀ **Paris** - Hôtel Lutétia, 45 bd Raspail (6th) ℰ 01 49 54 46 90, *lutetia-paris@lutetia-paris.com*, Fax 01 49 54 46 00, « "Art Deco" décor » – 🖃. 🆔 ⑩ 🅶🅱 🅹🅲🅱 **K 12**
closed August, Saturday, Sunday and Bank Holidays – **Meals** 45 (lunch), 60/121 and à la carte 70/100
Spec. Cannelloni de foie gras de canard à la truffe noire. Turbot cuit sur le sel de Guérande et aux algues bretonnes. Jarret de veau en cocotte aux pommes fondantes et champignons des bois..

XXX ❀❀ **Relais Louis XIII** (Martinez), 8 r. Grands Augustins (6th) ℰ 01 43 26 75 96, *rl13@free.fr*, Fax 01 44 07 07 80, « Historical house, 16C cellar » – 🖃. 🆔 🅶🅱 🅹🅲🅱. ⚒ **J 14**
closed 5 to 27 August, Sunday and Monday – **Meals** 41 (lunch)/89 and à la carte 100/120
Spec. Ravioli de homard, foie gras, estragon et crème de cèpes. Pavé de gros turbot sauvage en cocotte, petits oignons, champignons et œuf meurette. Assiette "tout chocolat".

XXX **Closerie des Lilas,** 171 bd Montparnasse (6th) ℰ 01 40 51 34 50, *closerie@club-internet.fr*, Fax 01 43 29 99 94, 🍽, « Former literary café » – 🆔 ⑩ 🅶🅱 🅹🅲🅱 **M 13**
Meals 42,70 b.i. (lunch)and à la carte 50/67 - ***Brasserie* :** **Meals** à la carte 30/50 ⓨ.

XXX ❀ **Hélène Darroze,** 4 r. d'Assas (6th) ℰ 01 42 22 00 11, *helene.darroze@wanadoo.fr*, Fax 01 42 22 25 40 – 🖃. 🆔 🅶🅱 **K 12**
closed Sunday and Monday – **Meals** 59,50/109,75 and à la carte 65/100 ***Salon* :** **Meals** 28,20b.i. and à la carte 30/45 ⓨ
Spec. Soupe de lièvre, quenelles, râble rôti et crème glacée au foie gras (Season). Foie gras de canard des Landes grillé au feu de bois. Baba au vieil armagnac.

XXX **Procope,** 13 r. Ancienne Comédie (6th) ℰ 01 40 46 79 00, *de.procope@blanc.net*, Fax 01 40 46 79 09, « Former 18C literary café » – 🖃. 🆔 ⑩ 🅶🅱. ⚒ **K 13**
Meals 22 (lunch)/27,90 and à la carte 36/55.

XXX **Lapérouse,** 51 quai Grands Augustins (6th) ℰ 01 43 26 68 04, Fax 01 43 26 99 39 – 🖃. 🆔 ⑩ 🅶🅱 **J 14**
closed 25 July-20 August, Saturday lunch and Sunday – **Meals** 29,72 (lunch)/83,85 and à la carte 65/98.

XX **Mavrommatis,** 42 r. Daubenton (5th) ℰ 01 43 31 17 17, Fax 01 43 36 13 08 – 🖃. 🅶🅱 🅹🅲🅱. ⚒ **M 15**
closed Monday – **Meals** - Greek rest. - 27,45 and à la carte 34/49 ⓨ.

XX **Marty,** 20 av. Gobelins (5th) ℰ 01 43 31 39 51, *restaurant.marty@wanadoo.fr*, Fax 01 43 37 63 70, brasserie, « 1930 décor » – 🖃. 🆔 ⑩ 🅶🅱 🅹🅲🅱 **M 15**
Meals 33 and à la carte 37/58 ⓨ.

XX ❀ **Maxence** (Van Laer), 9 bis bd Montparnasse (6th) ℰ 01 45 67 24 88, Fax 01 45 67 10 22 – 🖃. 🆔 ⑩ 🅹🅲🅱 **L 11**
closed 1 to 15 August – **Meals** 28,96 (lunch)/57,93 and à la carte 60/80 ⓨ
Spec. Tempura de langoustines. Pigeon rôti, sauce bécasse, cromesquis de foie gras Grande assiette de chocolat corsé..

XX **Atelier Maître Albert,** 1 r. Maître Albert (5th) ℰ 01 46 33 13 78, Fax 01 44 07 01 86 – 🖃. 🆔 🅶🅱 **K 15**
closed 5 to 20 August, Sunday and Bank Holidays – **Meals** 34.

XX **Ziryab,** 1 r. Fossés St-Bernard (5th) at Institut du Monde Arabe ℰ 01 53 10 10 20, Fax 01 44 07 30 98, ⇐ Paris, ☆, « Panoramic terrace » – ▤. ᴬᴱ ⓞ ᴳᴮ ᴶᶜᴮ. closed Sunday dinner and Monday – **Meals** Oriental rest. a la carte 44/49.　　K 16

XX **Méditerranée,** 2 pl. Odéon (6th) ℰ 01 43 26 02 30, Fax 01 43 26 18 44 – ▤. ᴬᴱ ᴳᴮ **Meals** 29 and a la carte 38/67 ☿.

XX **Bastide Odéon,** 7 r. Corneille (6th) ℰ 01 43 26 03 65, bastide.odeon@wanadoo.fr, Fax 01 44 07 28 93 – ▤. ᴬᴱ ᴳᴮ　　　　　　　　　　　　　　　　　　　K 13 closed 5 to 30 August, 30 December-7 January, Sunday and Monday – **Meals** 32.

XX **Yugaraj,** 14 r. Dauphine (6th) ℰ 01 43 26 44 91, Fax 01 46 33 50 77 – ▤. ᴬᴱ ⓞ ᴳᴮ ᴶᶜᴮ　　　　　　　　　　　　　　　　　　　　　　　　　　　　　　　J 13 closed August, Thursday lunch and Monday – **Meals** - Indian rest. - 15,09 (lunch), 27,44/44,21 and a la carte 32/54.

XX **Alcazar,** 62 r. Mazarine (6th) ℰ 01 53 10 19 99, atlanticblue@wanadoo.fr, Fax 01 53 10 23 23, « Original contemporary decor » – ▤. ᴬᴱ ⓞ ᴳᴮ ᴶᶜᴮ. ❀　　J 13 **Meals** 25 b.i. (lunch)and a la carte 39/60.

XX
🍷 **Chez Maître Paul,** 12 r. Monsieur-le-Prince (6th) ℰ 01 43 54 74 59, chezmaitrepaul @aol.com, Fax 01 43 54 43 74 – ▤. ᴬᴱ ⓞ ᴳᴮ. ❀　　　　　　　　　　　　K 13 closed 20 to 27 December, Sunday and Monday in July-August – **Meals** 26/31 b.i. and a la carte 32/51.

XX **Chez Toutoune,** 5 r. Pontoise (5th) ℰ 01 43 26 56 81, cheztoutoune@wanadoo.fr, Fax 01 40 46 80 34 – ᴬᴱ ᴳᴮ ᴶᶜᴮ　　　　　　　　　　　　　　　　　　K 15 closed Monday – **Meals** 22,56 (lunch)/33,23 ☿.

XX **Inagiku,** 14 r. Pontoise (5th) ℰ 01 43 54 70 07, Fax 01 40 51 74 44 – ▤. ᴬᴱ ᴳᴮ closed 6 to 19 August and Sunday – **Meals** - Japanese rest. - 14,99 (lunch), 27,22/65,33 and a la carte 35/47.　　　　　　　　　　　　　　　　　　　　　　　K 15

XX **Yen,** 22 r. St-Benoît (6th) ℰ 01 45 44 11 18, OKFIH@wanadoo.fr, Fax 01 45 44 19 48 – ▤. ᴬᴱ ᴳᴮ ᴶᶜᴮ　　　　　　　　　　　　　　　　　　　　　　　　　J 13 closed Monday lunch and Sunday – **Meals** - Japanese rest. - a la carte 15/40.

X **Rotonde,** 105 bd Montparnasse (6th) ℰ 01 43 26 68 84, Fax 01 46 34 52 40, brasserie – ▤. ᴬᴱ ᴳᴮ ᴶᶜᴮ　　　　　　　　　　　　　　　　　　　　　　　　　L 12 **Meals** 22/30 and a la carte 35/45.

X **Café des Délices,** 87 r. Assas (6th) ℰ 01 43 54 70 00, Fax 01 43 26 42 05 – ▤. ᴬᴱ ᴳᴮ　　　　　　　　　　　　　　　　　　　　　　　　　　　　　LM 13 closed 29 july-20 August, Saturday lunch and Sunday – **Meals** a la carte approx. 33

X **Quai V,** 25 quai Tournelle (5th) ℰ 01 43 54 05 17, Fax 01 43 29 74 93 – ▤. ᴬᴱ ᴳᴮ closed 5 to 26 August, Sunday, lunch Saturday and Monday – **Meals** 22 b.i. (lunch)/37,50 and a la carte 50/55.　　　　　　　　　　　　　　　　　　　　　　　K 15

X
🍷 **L'Épi Dupin,** 11 r. Dupin (6th) ℰ 01 42 22 64 56, lepidupin@wanadoo.fr, Fax 01 42 22 30 42, ☆ – ᴬᴱ ᴳᴮ. ❀　　　　　　　　　　　　　　　　K 12 closed 27 July-20 August, Monday lunch, Saturday and Sunday – **Meals** (booking essential) 28,20.

X **Dominique,** 19 r. Bréa (6th) ℰ 01 43 27 08 80, restaurant.dominique@mageos.com, Fax 01 43 27 03 76 – ▤. ᴬᴱ ᴳᴮ ᴶᶜᴮ　　　　　　　　　　　　　　　　L 12 closed 22 July-20 August, Sunday and Monday – **Meals** - Russian rest. - (dinner only) 40/55 and a la carte 30/49.

X **Brasserie Lipp,** 151 bd St-Germain (6th) ℰ 01 45 48 53 91, lipp@magic.fr, Fax 01 45 44 33 20 – ▤. ᴬᴱ ⓞ ᴳᴮ　　　　　　　　　　　　　　　　J 13 **Meals** a la carte 32/52.

X **Les Bookinistes,** 53 quai Grands Augustins (6th) ℰ 01 43 25 45 94, bookinistes@g uysavoy.com, Fax 01 43 25 23 07 – ▤. ᴬᴱ ⓞ ᴳᴮ ᴶᶜᴮ　　　　　　　　J 14 closed Saturday lunch and Sunday – **Meals** 24,39 (lunch).

X **Bouillon Racine,** 3 r. Racine (6th) ℰ 01 44 32 15 60, bouillon.racine@wanadoo.fr, Fax 01 44 32 15 61, « ''Art Nouveau'' decor » – ᴬᴱ ᴳᴮ　　　　　　　　　K 14 **Meals** -Flemish rest.- 20 (lunch)/27,29 and a la carte 27/43 ☿ - **L'Arrière Cuisine** (closed Monday) **Meals** a la carte 16/28 ☿.

X **L'Espadon Bleu,** 25 r. Grands Augustins (6th) ℰ 01 46 33 00 85 – ▤. ᴬᴱ ⓞ ᴳᴮ ᴶᶜᴮ closed 2 to 27 August, Sunday and Monday – **Meals** - Seafood - 26 (lunch)/36.

X **Emporio Armani Caffé,** 149 bd St-Germain (6th) ℰ 01 45 48 62 15, maximori@a ol.com, Fax 01 45 48 53 17 – ▤. ᴬᴱ ⓞ ᴳᴮ　　　　　　　　　　　　J 13 closed Sunday – **Meals** - Italian rest. - a la carte 35/50.

X **Les Délices d'Aphrodite,** 4 r. Candolle (5th) ℰ 01 43 31 40 39, Fax 01 43 36 13 08, bistro – ▤. ᴬᴱ ᴳᴮ ᴶᶜᴮ. ❀　　　　　　　　　　　　　　　　　M 15 closed Sunday – **Meals** - Greek rest. - 14,65 (lunch) and a la carte 26/39 ☿.

X **Joséphine "Chez Dumonet"**, 117 r. Cherche Midi (6th) ℘ 01 45 48 52 40,
Fax 01 42 84 06 83, bistro – ▥ ⒼⒷ   L 11
closed August, Saturday and Sunday – **Meals** a la carte 39/46.

X **Allard,** 41 r. St-André-des-Arts (6th) ℘ 01 43 26 48 23, Fax *01 46 33 04 02, bistro* – ▤.
ⒶⒺ ⓪ ⒼⒷ ⒿⒸⒷ ⅍   K 14
closed 5 to 26 August and Sunday – **Meals** 30,49 and a la carte 46/73.

X **Moissonnier,** 28 r. Fossés-St-Bernard (5th) ℘ 01 43 29 87 65, Fax *01 43 29 87 65*, bis-
Ⓐ tro – ⒼⒷ   K 15
closed 1 August-1 September, Sunday and Monday –**Meals** 22,90 (lunch) and a la carte 31/47.

X **Bistrot de la Catalogne,** 4 cour du Commerce St-André (6th) ℘ 01 55 42 16 19,
office.tourisme.catalogne.infotourisme.com, Fax 01 55 42 16 33   K 13
closed Sunday and Monday – **Meals** - Catalan rest. - a la carte approx. 27,44.

X **Bauta,** 129 bd Montparnasse (6th) ℘ 01 43 22 52 35, *Fax 01 43 22 10 99* – ⒶⒺ ⓪ ⒼⒷ
ⒿⒸⒷ   M 12
closed Saturday lunch and Sunday – **Meals** - Italian rest. - 38 b.i. and a la carte 47/61.

X **Coco de Mer,** 34 bd St-Marcel (5th) ℘ 01 47 07 06 64, *frichot@seychelles-saveurs.
com, Fax 01 47 07 41 88* – ⒶⒺ ⒼⒷ   M 16
closed August, Monday lunch and Sunday – **Meals** - Seychellian rest. - 20/26 ♀.

X **Casa Corsa,** 25 r. Mazarine (6th) ℘ 01 44 07 38 98, *Fax 01 43 54 14 79* – ▤. ⒶⒺ ⓪
ⒼⒷ. ⅍   J 13
closed August, Monday lunch and Sunday – **Meals** - Corsican rest. - a la carte 30/50.

X **Au Moulin à Vent,** 20 r. Fossés-St-Bernard (5th) ℘ 01 43 54 99 37,
Fax 01 40 46 92 23, bistro – ⒼⒷ. ⅍   K 15
closed 2 to 31 August, 23 December-2 January, Saturday lunch, Sunday and Monday –
Meals a la carte 38/52.

X **Rôtisserie d'en Face,** 2 r. Christine (6th) ℘ 01 43 26 40 98, *rotisface@aol.fr,
Fax 01 43 54 22 71* – ▤. ⒶⒺ ⓪ ⒼⒷ ⒿⒸⒷ   J 14
closed Saturday lunch and Sunday – **Meals** 25,70 (lunch)/39.

X **Les Bouchons de François Clerc,** 12 r. Hôtel Colbert (5th) ℘ 01 43 54 15 34,
Fax 01 46 34 68 07, « Old Parisian house » – ⒶⒺ ⒼⒷ ⒿⒸⒷ   K 15
closed Saturday lunch and Sunday – **Meals** 40,86.

X **Rôtisserie du Beaujolais,** 19 quai Tournelle (5th) ℘ 01 43 54 17 47,
Fax 01 56 24 43 71 – ▤. ⒼⒷ   K 15
closed Monday – **Meals** a la carte 31/48.

X **Buisson Ardent,** 25 r. Jussieu (5th) ℘ 01 43 54 93 02, Fax *01 46 33 34 77,* ☞ – ⒶⒺ
ⒼⒷ   L 15
closed 1 August-2 September, Saturday and Sunday – **Meals** 14,50 (lunch)/27 and a la
carte 26/35 ♀.

X **Balzar,** 49 r. Écoles (5th) ℘ 01 43 54 13 67, *Fax 01 44 07 14 91*, brasserie – ▤. ⒶⒺ ⒼⒷ
Meals a la carte 24/46.

X **Cafetière,** 21 r. Mazarine (6th) ℘ 01 46 33 76 90, *Fax 01 43 25 76 90* – ▤. ⒼⒷ J 13
closed August, 25 December-2 January, Sunday and Monday – **Meals** - Italian rest. - 24
(lunch) and a la carte 31/48.

X **Ma Cuisine,** 26 bd St-Germain (5th) ℘ 01 40 51 08 27, *Fax 01 40 51 08 52* – ⒼⒷ
closed Sunday – **Meals** 24,39 and a la carte 31/39 ♀.

X **Marmite et Cassolette,** 157 bd Montparnasse (6th) ℘ 01 43 26 26 53,
Fax 01 43 26 43 40 – ⒼⒷ   M 13
closed Saturday lunch and Sunday – **Meals** 19 and a la carte 25/30 ♀.

X **Reminet,** 3 r. Grands Degrés (5th) ℘ 01 44 07 04 24 – ⒼⒷ   K 15
closed 12 August-1 September, 18 February-3 March, Tuesday and Wednesday – **Meals**
13 (lunch) (weekends a la carte) and a la carte 32/48.

X **Chez Marcel,** 7 r. Stanislas (6th) ℘ 01 45 48 29 94 – ⒼⒷ   L 12
closed August, Saturday and Sunday – **Meals** a la carte 27/43 ♀.

X **Ze Kitchen,** 4 r. Grands Augustins (6th) ℘ 01 44 32 00 32, *Fax 01 44 32 00 33* – ▤.
ⒶⒺ ⓪ ⒼⒷ ⒿⒸⒷ   J 14
closed Saturday lunch and Sunday – **Meals** a la carte 31/36.

X **Palanquin,** 12 r. Princesse (6th) ℘ 01 43 29 77 66, *info@lepalanquin.com* – ▤. ⒼⒷ
closed 5 to 18 August, Monday lunch and Sunday – **Meals** - Vietnamese rest. - 11,89 (lunch),
19,66/25,61 and a la carte 32/39.

X **Table de Fès,** 5 r. Ste-Beuve (6th) ℘ 01 45 48 07 22 – ⒼⒷ   F 12
closed 27 July-31 August and Sunday – **Meals** - Moroccan rest. - (dinner only) a la carte 37/50.

X **Petit Pontoise,** 9 r. Pontoise (5th) ℘ 01 43 29 25 20, *Fax 01 43 25 35 93* – ▤. ⒶⒺ ⒼⒷ
closed Sunday dinner and Monday – **Meals** a la carte 25/36 ♀.

X **Lhassa,** 13 r. Montagne Ste-Geneviève (5th) ℘ 01 43 26 22 19, *Fax 01 42 17 00 08* –
ⒼⒷ   K 15
closed Monday – **Meals** - Tibetan rest. - 10,67 (lunch), 12,95/20,73 and a la carte 25/38 ♣.

Faubourg-St-Germain, Invalides, École Militaire.

7th arrondissement.
7th: ✉ 75007

Pont Royal M, 7 r. Montalembert ☎ 01 42 84 70 00, *hpr@hotel-pont-royal.com, Fax 01 42 84 71 00,* – 🛗 ▤ TV ☎ ♿ – 25 40. AE ⓓ GB JCB. ✗ rest
Meals *(closed August, Saturday and Sunday)* a la carte 30/67 ♀ – ☕ 26 – **75 rm** 350/400.

Montalembert M, 3 r. Montalembert ☎ 01 45 49 68 68, *welcome@hotel-montalembert.fr, Fax 01 45 49 69 49,* , « Original decor » – 🛗 ▤ TV ☎ – 25. AE ⓓ GB JCB — J 12
Meals a la carte 45/75 – ☕ 20 – **48 rm** 350/440, 8 suites.

Duc de Saint-Simon without rest, 14 r. St-Simon ☎ 01 44 39 20 20, *duc.de.saint.simon@wanadoo.fr, Fax 01 45 48 68 25* – 🛗 TV ☎. AE GB. ✗ — J 11
☕ 14 – **29 rm** 220/255, 5 suites.

Cayré M without rest, 4 bd Raspail ☎ 01 45 44 38 88, *reservations@kkhotels.fr, Fax 01 45 44 98 13* – 🛗, ✗ rm, ▤ TV ☎. AE ⓓ GB JCB — J 12
☕ 17 – **120 rm** 314/337.

Bourgogne et Montana without rest, 3 r. Bourgogne ☎ 01 45 51 20 22, *bmontana@bourgogne-montana.com, Fax 01 45 56 11 98* – 🛗 ▤ TV ☎. AE ⓓ GB JCB
28 rm ☕ 155/350, 4 suites. — H 11

Tourville M without rest, 16 av. Tourville ☎ 01 47 05 62 62, *hotel@tourville.com, Fax 01 47 05 43 90* – 🛗 ▤ TV ☎. AE ⓓ GB JCB — J 9
☕ 12 – **30 rm** 175/310.

Verneuil without rest, 8 r. Verneuil ☎ 01 42 60 82 14, *verneuil@noos.fr, Fax 01 42 61 40 38,* « Fine decor » – 🛗 TV. AE ⓓ GB. ✗ — J 12
☕ 10 – **26 rm** 115/175.

Lenox Saint-Germain without rest, 9 r. Université ☎ 01 42 96 10 95, *hotel@lenoxsaintgermain.com, Fax 01 42 61 52 83* – 🛗 ▤ TV ☎. AE ⓓ GB JCB. ✗ — J 12
☕ 9 – **34 rm** 117/196.

Bellechasse M without rest, 8 r. Bellechasse ☎ 01 45 50 22 31, *Fax 01 45 51 52 36* – 🛗, ✗ rm, TV ☎ ♿. AE ⓓ GB JCB — H 11
☕ 13 – **41 rm** 189/252.

Eiffel Park Hôtel M without rest, 17 bis r. Amélie ☎ 01 45 55 10 01, *reservation@eiffelpark.com, Fax 01 47 05 28 68* – 🛗 ▤ TV. AE ⓓ GB JCB. ✗ — J 9
☕ 9 – **36 rm** 153/183.

Cadran M without rest, 10 r. Champ-de-Mars ☎ 01 40 62 67 00, *lecadran@worldnet.fr, Fax 01 40 62 67 13* – 🛗, ✗ rm, ▤ TV ☎. AE ⓓ GB. ✗ — J 9
☕ 9 – **42 rm** 145/159.

Muguet M without rest, 11 r. Chevert ☎ 01 47 05 05 93, *muguet@wanadoo.fr, Fax 01 45 50 25 37* – 🛗, ✗ rm, ▤ TV ☎. AE GB — J 9
☕ 7,50 – **48 rm** 83/100.

Les Jardins d'Eiffel M without rest, 8 r. Amélie ☎ 01 47 05 46 21, *paris@hoteljardinseiffel.com, Fax 01 45 55 28 08* – 🛗, ✗ rm, ▤ TV ☎ 🚗. AE ⓓ GB JCB — H 9
☕ 11 – **80 rm** 110/150.

Relais Bosquet M without rest, 19 r. Champ-de-Mars ☎ 01 47 05 25 45, *hotel@relaisbosquet.com, Fax 01 45 55 08 24* – 🛗 ▤ TV ☎. AE ⓓ GB JCB — J 9
☕ 9,50 – **40 rm** 144,80/160.

Timhôtel Invalides M without rest, 35 bd La Tour Maubourg ☎ 01 45 56 10 78, *invalides@timhotel.fr, Fax 01 47 05 65 08* – 🛗, ✗ rm, ▤ TV ☎. AE ⓓ GB JCB
☕ 10 – **30 rm** 180/260. — H 10

Londres Eiffel without rest, 1 r. Augereau ☎ 01 45 51 63 02, *info@londres-eiffel.com, Fax 01 47 05 28 96* – 🛗 TV ☎. AE ⓓ GB JCB. ✗ — J 8
☕ 6,86 – **30 rm** 93/115.

St-Germain without rest, 88 r. Bac ☎ 01 49 54 70 00, *info@hotel-saint-germain.fr, Fax 01 45 48 26 89* – 🛗 TV ☎. AE GB. ✗ — J 11
☕ 11 – **29 rm** 150/170.

Splendid M without rest, 29 av. Tourville ☎ 01 45 51 29 29, *splendid@club-internet.fr, Fax 01 44 18 94 60* – 🛗 TV ☎ ♿. AE ⓓ GB — J 9
☕ 8,50 – **48 rm** 106/197.

🏨 **Sèvres Vaneau** without rest, 86 r. Vaneau ℘ 01 45 48 73 11, Fax 01 45 49 27 74
|🛗|, 🛌 rm, 📺. 🆎 ⓪ ⅅ 🈺   K 11
≥ 13 – **39 rm** 169/184.

🏨 **La Bourdonnais** without rest, 111 av. La Bourdonnais ℘ 01 47 05 45 42, otlbourc
@ club-internet.fr, Fax 01 45 55 75 54 – |🛗| ▤ 📺 🍷. 🆎 ⓪ ⅅ 🈺   J 9
≥ 8 – **57 rm** 110/140, 3 suites.

🏨 **Varenne** 🐾 without rest, 44 r. Bourgogne ℘ 01 45 51 45 55, info@ hotelvarenne.com,
Fax 01 45 51 86 63 – |🛗| ▤ 📺. 🆎 ⅅ   J 10
≥ 9 – **24 rm** 105/124.

🏨 **Beaugency** without rest, 21 r. Duvivier ℘ 01 47 05 01 63, infos@ hotel-beaugency.c
om, Fax 01 45 51 04 96 – |🛗| ▤ 📺 🍷. 🆎 ⓪ ⅅ. 🈺   J 9
≥ 7,50 – **30 rm** 84/112.

🏨 **Champ-de-Mars** without rest, 7 r. Champ-de-Mars ℘ 01 45 51 52 30, stg@ club-inte
rnet.fr, Fax 01 45 51 64 36 – |🛗| 📺 🍷. 🆎. 🈺   J 9
≥ 6,50 – **25 rm** 66/76.

🏨 **Bersoly's** without rest, 28 r. Lille ℘ 01 42 60 73 79, bersolys@ wanadoo.fr
Fax 01 49 27 05 55 – |🛗| 📺 🍷. 🆎 ⓪ ⅅ   J 13
closed August – ≥ 10 – **16 rm** 97/122.

🏨 **France** without rest, 102 bd La Tour Maubourg ℘ 01 47 05 40 49, hoteldefrance@ w
anadoo.fr, Fax 01 45 56 96 78 – |🛗| 📺 🍷. 🆎 ⓪ ⅅ 🈺   J 9
≥ 7 – **60 rm** 64/81.

🏨 **L'Empereur** without rest, 2 r. Chevert ℘ 01 45 55 88 02, contact@ hotelempereur.c
om, Fax 01 45 51 88 54, ≤ – |🛗| 📺. 🆎 ⓪ ⅅ 🈺. 🈺   J 9
≥ 7 – **38 rm** 75/85.

🏨 **Lévêque** without rest, 29 r. Clerc ℘ 01 47 05 49 15, info@ hotel-leveque.com
Fax 01 45 50 49 36 – |🛗| 📺 🍷. 🆎 ⅅ. 🈺   J 9
≥ 7 – **50 rm** 53/91.

XXXX
❀❀❀ **Arpège** (Passard), 84 r. Varenne ℘ 01 45 51 47 33, arpege.passard@ wanadoo.fr
Fax 01 44 18 98 39 – ▤. 🆎 ⓪ ⅅ 🈺   J 10
closed Saturday and Sunday – **Meals** 214 and a la carte 140/225
Spec. Homard de l'archipel de Chausey. Légumes de pleine terre du Val d'Anjou. Cuisine
des fruits.

XXXX
❀❀ **Le Divellec,** 107 r. Université ℘ 01 45 51 91 96, ledivellec@ noos.fr, Fax 01 45 51 31 7:
– ▤. 🆎 ⓪ ⅅ 🈺. 🈺   H 11
closed 20 July-20 August, Saturday and Sunday – **Meals** - Seafood - 53/69 (lunch)and a
la carte 80/140
Spec. Homard a la presse avec son corail. Brouillade de pibales aux piments d'Espelette
et brunoise de chorizo (January-March). Turbot braisé aux truffes..

XXX
❀ **Jules Verne,** Eiffel Tower : 2nd platform, lift in south leg ℘ 01 45 55 61 44
Fax 01 47 05 29 41, ≤ Paris – ▤. 🆎 ⓪ ⅅ 🈺. 🈺   J
Meals 49 (lunch)/110 and a la carte 95/120
Spec. Ravioli de Saint-Jacques a la vapeur. Rouget barbet farci de légumes au jus de truffes
Tarte soufflée au citron vert..

XXX
❀ **Violon d'Ingres** (Constant), 135 r. St-Dominique ℘ 01 45 55 15 05, violondingres@
anadoo.fr, Fax 01 45 55 48 42 – ▤. 🆎 ⅅ   J
closed Saturday and Sunday – **Meals** 60,97 (lunch)/89,94 and a la carte 75/90
Spec. Oeufs mollets roulés a la mie de pain, toasts de beurre truffés. Suprême de ba
croustillant aux amandes. Pommes soufflées, mousseline légère a la réglisse..

XXX
❀ **Cantine des Gourmets,** 113 av. La Bourdonnais ℘ 01 47 05 47 96, la.cantine@
-bourdonnais.com, Fax 01 45 51 09 29 – ▤. 🆎 ⅅ   J
Meals 42 (lunch)/80 and a la carte 75/100 ♀
Spec. Foie gras de canard chaud. Saint-Pierre et coquillages au jus de cidre (October
March). Carré et épaule d'agneau des Alpilles, cébettes aux épices et citron confit.

XXX
❀ **Pétrossian,** 144 r. Université ℘ 01 44 11 32 32, Fax 01 44 11 32 35 – 🆎 ⓪ ⅅ 🈺
closed 12 August-3 September, Sunday and Monday – **Meals** 44 (lunch)/136 and a la cart
70/110
Spec. Les "Coupes du Tsar". Rouget poivré et blin soufflé. "Teaser" de goûts et saveur
(dessert)..

XXX **Maison des Polytechniciens,** 12 r. Poitiers ℘ 01 49 54 74 54, info@ maison-de
-x.com, Fax 01 49 54 74 84, « 18C mansion » – 🆎 ⓪ ⅅ   H 1
closed 29 July-28 August, 23 December-7 January, Saturday, Sunday and Bank Holiday
– **Meals** 33,54/59,46 and a la carte 63/92.

XXX **Petit Laurent,** 38 r. Varenne ℘ 01 45 48 79 64, Fax 01 45 44 15 95 – 🆎 ⓪ ⅅ
closed August, Sunday, lunch Monday and Saturday – **Meals** 29/43 and a la carte 45,
70 ♀.

FRANCE

XX ⊛ **Bellecour** (Goutagny), 22 r. Surcouf ℰ 01 45 51 46 93, *Fax 01 45 50 30 11* – 🖿. 🖎 ⓪ ⬛ **GB**   H 9
closed August, Saturday and Sunday – **Meals** 40
Spec. Quenelle de brochet. Lasagne champêtre de gibier (15 October-15 January). Lièvre à la royale (15 October-15 January)..

XX ⊛ **Récamier,** 4 r. Récamier ℰ 01 45 48 86 58, *Fax 01 42 22 84 76,* 🌣 – 🖿. 🖎 ⓪ **GB** **JCB**   K 12
closed Sunday – **Meals** a la carte 55/80
Spec. Œufs en meurette. Mousse de brochet sauce Nantua. Gigue de chevreuil sauce Grand Veneur (season).

XX **Maison de l'Amérique Latine**, 217 bd St-Germain ℰ 01 49 54 75 10, *commercia l@mal217.org, Fax 01 40 49 03 94,* 🌣, « 18C mansion, terrace opening onto the garden », 🌿 – 🖎 **GB**. ✼   J 9
closed August, 20 December-1 January, Saturday, Sunday and dinner from October-April – **Meals** 37 and a la carte 39/49.

XX **Beato,** 8 r. Malar ℰ 01 47 05 94 27, *beato.rest@wanadoo.fr, Fax 01 45 55 64 41* – 🖿. 🖎 **GB** **JCB**   H 9
closed 28 July-18 August, 22 December-1 January and Sunday – **Meals** - Italian rest. - 23 (lunch) and a la carte 35/54 ⥣.

XX **Tante Marguerite,** 5 r. Bourgogne ℰ 01 45 51 79 42, *tante.marguerite@wanadoo.fr, Fax 01 47 53 79 56* – 🖿. 🖎 ⓪ **GB**. ✼   H 11
closed August, Saturday and Sunday – **Meals** 32 (lunch)/36,60 and a la carte 46/76 ⥣.

XX **Ferme St-Simon**, 6 r. St-Simon ℰ 01 45 48 35 74, *fermestsimon@wanadoo.fr, Fax 01 40 49 07 31* – 🖿. 🖎 ⓪ **GB**   J 11
closed 3 to 18 August, Saturday lunch and Sunday – **Meals** 27,75 (lunch)/30,18 and a la carte 42/61.

XX **Vin sur Vin,** 20 r. Monttessuy ℰ 01 47 05 14 20 – 🖿. **GB**   H 8
closed 1 to 21 August, 23 December-3 January, Sunday and lunch Saturday and Sunday – **Meals** a la carte 46/64.

XX **Bamboche,** 15 r. Babylone ℰ 01 45 49 14 40, *ccolliot@club-internet.fr, Fax 01 45 49 14 44* – 🖿. **GB**   K 11
closed Saturday lunch and Sunday – **Meals** 29 (lunch)/50 and a la carte 54/71 ⥣.

XX **Tan Dinh,** 60 r. Verneuil ℰ 01 45 44 04 84, *Fax 01 45 44 36 93*   J 12
closed 1 August-1 September and Sunday – **Meals** - Vietnamese rest. - a la carte 40/45.

XX **Chez Françoise,** Invalides airport station ℰ 01 47 05 49 03, *pm@chezfrançoise.com, Fax 01 45 51 96 20,* 🌣 – 🖎 ⓪ **GB** **JCB**   H 10
Meals 28,97 and a la carte 36/62 ⥣.

XX ⊛ **Champ de Mars,** 17 av. La Motte-Picquet ℰ 01 47 05 57 99, *Fax 01 44 18 94 69* – 🖎 ⓪ **GB** **JCB**   J 9
closed 15 July-22 August, Tuesday lunch and Monday – **Meals** 25,16 b.i./30,19 b.i. and a la carte 28/46.

X **Cigale,** 11 bis r. Chomel ℰ 01 45 48 87 87, *Fax 01 45 48 87 87* – **GB**. ✼   K 12
closed Saturday lunch and Sunday – **Meals** a la carte approx. 47 ⥣.

X ⊛ **Les Olivades,** 41 av. Ségur ℰ 01 47 83 70 09, *Fax 01 42 73 04 75* – 🖎 **GB**   K 9
closed 13 to 16 August, Sunday, lunch Saturday and Monday – **Meals** 28 and a la carte 40/50.

X **Bistrot de Paris,** 33 r. Lille ℰ 01 42 61 15 84, *ecorail@noos.fr, Fax 01 49 27 06 09,* 1900 bistro – 🖎 **GB**   J 12
Meals 29,70 and a la carte 40/50 ⥣.

X **Nabuchodonosor,** 6 av. Bosquet ℰ 01 45 56 97 26, *Fax 01 45 56 98 44* – 🖿. 🖎 **GB**
closed 3 to 25 August, Saturday lunch, Sunday and Bank Holidays – **Meals** a la carte 32/56 ⥣.

X ⊛ **P'tit Troquet,** 28 r. Exposition ℰ 01 47 05 80 39, *Fax 01 47 05 80 39*, bistro – **GB**. ✼   J 9
closed 1 to 23 August, 23 December-2 February, Sunday, lunch Saturday and Monday – **Meals** (booking essential) 26,50 ⥣.

X ⊛ **Maupertu,** 94 bd La Tour Maubourg ℰ 01 45 51 37 96, *Fax 01 53 59 94 83* – **GB**. ✼   J 10
closed 10 to 25 August, February Holidays, Saturday and Sunday – **Meals** 27,50.

X **Fontaine de Mars,** 129 r. St-Dominique ℰ 01 47 05 46 44, *Fax 01 47 05 11 13,* 🌣, bistro – 🖎 **GB**   J 9
Meals a la carte 30/36 ⥣.

X **Chez Collinot,** 1 r. P. Leroux ℰ 01 45 67 66 42 – **GB**   K 11
closed August, Saturday and Sunday – **Meals** 22,87.

※ **Au Bon Accueil,** 14 r. Monttessuy 𝒫 01 47 05 46 11 – 🍽. ⌷ᴮ   H 8
closed 10 to 25 August, Saturday and Sunday – **Meals** 25,20 (lunch)/28,20 (dinner) and a la carte 40/50.

※ **Florimond,** 19 av. La Motte-Picquet 𝒫 01 45 55 40 38, Fax 01 45 55 40 38 – ⌷ᴮ   H 9
closed 2 to 27 August, 23 December-2 January, Saturday lunch and Sunday. – **Meals** 17,10 (lunch)/27,40 and a la carte 30/45.

※ Léo Le Lion, 23 r. Duvivier 𝒫 01 45 51 41 77   J 9

※ **Bistrot du 7ᵉ,** 56 bd La Tour-Maubourg 𝒫 01 45 51 93 08, Fax 01 45 50 33 24 – ᴬᴱ
⌷ᴮ   J 10
closed Saturday lunch and Sunday lunch – **Meals** 12 (lunch)/16 ♀.

Champs-Élysées,
St-Lazare,
Madeleine.

8th arrondissement.
8th: ✉ *75008*

Plaza Athénée, 25 av. Montaigne 𝒫 01 53 67 66 65, reservation@plaza-athenee-pa ris.com, Fax 01 53 67 66 66, 🍴, ₺₆ – ▮ ⫘ rm, ▤ ᴛᴠ ✆ – ▲ 20 - 60. ᴬᴱ ① ⌷ᴮ
ᴶᴄᴮ   G 9
see *Plaza Athénée* below - **Relais-Plaza** 𝒫 01 53 67 64 00 (closed August) Meals 40 ♀ – **La Cour Jardin** (terrace) 𝒫 01 53 67 66 02 (May-September) Meals a la carte 62/88 – ⫧ 32 – **121 rm** 508/808, 66 suites.

Bristol, 112 r. Fg St-Honoré 𝒫 01 53 43 43 00, resa@hotel-bristol.com, Fax 01 53 43 43 01, « Attractive courtyard with French-style garden », ₺₆, ⬚, 🌳 – ▮
▤ rm, ᴛᴠ ✆ 🐾 – ▲ 30 - 60. ᴬᴱ ① ⌷ᴮ   F 10
Meals see *Bristol* below – ⫧ 30 – **152 rm** 540/710, 26 suites.

Four Seasons George V, 31 av. George V 𝒫 01 49 52 70 00, par.reservations@fc urseasons.com, Fax 01 49 52 70 20, ₺₆, ⬚ – ▮ ⫘ rm, ▤ ᴛᴠ ✆ & – ▲ 30 - 400. ᴬᴱ
① ⌷ᴮ ᴶᴄᴮ   F 8
see *Le Cinq* below – ⫧ 38 – **184 rm** 570/870, 61 suites.

Crillon, 10 pl. Concorde 𝒫 01 44 71 15 00, crillon@crillon.com, Fax 01 44 71 15 02, ₺₆
– ▮ ⫘ rm, ▤ ᴛᴠ ✆ – ▲ 30 - 60. ᴬᴱ ① ⌷ᴮ ᴶᴄᴮ   G 11
see *Les Ambassadeurs* and *L'Obélisque* below – ⫧ 30 – **114 rm** 550/725, 43 suites

Prince de Galles, 33 av. George-V 𝒫 01 53 23 77 77, hotel_prince_de_galles@she aton.com, Fax 01 53 23 78 78, 🍴 – ▮ ⫘ rm, ▤ ᴛᴠ ✆ – ▲ 25 - 100. ᴬᴱ ① ⌷ᴮ ᴶᴄᴮ
🍽 rest   G 8
Jardin des Cygnes 𝒫 01 53 23 78 50 Meals 44 (lunch), 47/49,50 ♀ – ⫧ 24,50 – **138 rm** 570/700, 30 suites.

Royal Monceau, 37 av. Hoche 𝒫 01 42 99 88 00, royalmonceau@jetmultimedia.fr Fax 01 42 99 89 90, 🍴, « Pool and fitness centre », ₺₆, ⬚ – ▮ ⫘ rm, ▤ ᴛᴠ ✆ –
▲ 25 - 100. ᴬᴱ ① ⌷ᴮ ᴶᴄᴮ 🍽   E 8
see *Le Jardin* and *Carpaccio* below – ⫧ 26 – **156 rm** 442/488, 47 suites.

Lancaster, 7 r. Berri 𝒫 01 40 76 40 76, reservations@hotel-lancaster.fr Fax 01 40 76 40 00, 🍴, « Tasteful decor », ₺₆ – ▮ ⫘ rm, ▤ ᴛᴠ ✆. ᴬᴱ ① ⌷ᴮ. 🍽
Meals (residents only) a la carte 50/75 – ⫧ – **49 rm** 400/545, 11 suites.

Vernet, 25 r. Vernet 𝒫 01 44 31 98 00, hotelvernet@jetmultimedia.fr Fax 01 44 31 85 69 – ▮▮ ▤ ᴛᴠ ✆. ᴬᴱ ① ⌷ᴮ ᴶᴄᴮ   F 8
see *Les Élysées* below – ⫧ 32 – **42 rm** 340/535, 9 suites.

Sofitel Astor Ⓜ, 11 r. d'Astorg 𝒫 01 53 05 05 05, hotelastor@aol.com Fax 01 53 05 05 30, ₺₆ – ▮ ⫘ rm, ▤ rm, ᴛᴠ ✆ &. ᴬᴱ ① ⌷ᴮ ᴶᴄᴮ. 🍽 rest
Meals see *L'Astor* below – ⫧ 25 – **129 rm** 298/590, 5 suites.   F 11

San Régis, 12 r. J. Goujon 𝒫 01 44 95 16 16, message@hotel-sanregis.fr Fax 01 45 61 05 48, « Tasteful decor » – ▮ ▤ ᴛᴠ ✆. ᴬᴱ ① ⌷ᴮ ᴶᴄᴮ. 🍽   G 9
Meals (closed August) a la carte 48/69 ♀ – ⫧ 20 – **33 rm** 290/518, 11 suites.

Sofitel Le Faubourg Ⓜ, 15 r. Boissy d'Anglas 𝒫 01 44 94 14 14, h1295@accor-h otels.com, Fax 01 44 94 14 28, ₺₆, ⫘ rm, ▤ ᴛᴠ ✆ & 🚗. ᴬᴱ ① ⌷ᴮ ᴶᴄᴮ. 🍽
Café Faubourg 𝒫 01 44 94 14 24 Meals a la carte 40/64 ♀ – ⫧ 23 – **154 rm** 425/670 7 suites, 3 duplex.

🏨 **Sofitel Arc de Triomphe,** 14 r. Beaujon ℘ 01 53 89 50 50, h1296@accor-hotels. com, Fax 01 53 89 50 51 – |⚐|, ⟨⟨❀⟩⟩ rm, 🗐 📺 📞 ⓖ – 🏛 40. 🗚 ⓞ 🈺   F 8
see **Clovis** below – ⌷ 25,91 – **135 rm** 445/750.

🏨 **Hyatt Regency** Ⓜ, 24 bd Malesherbes ℘ 01 55 27 12 34, madeleine.concierge@p aris.hyatt.com, Fax 01 55 27 12 35, ℥ – |⚐|, ⟨⟨❀⟩⟩ rm, 🗐 📺 📞 ⓖ – 🏛 20. 🗚 ⓞ 🈺
🈔. 🗷 rest   F 11
Café M : Meals a la carte 41/46 ⌷ – ⌷ 25 – **81 rm** 530/620, 5 suites.

🏨 **de Vigny,** 9 r. Balzac ℘ 01 42 99 80 80, de-vigny@wanadoo.fr, Fax 01 42 99 80 40, « Tasteful decor » – |⚐|, ⟨⟨❀⟩⟩ rm, 🗐 rm, 📺 📞 ⟨❀⟩. 🗚 ⓞ 🈺 🈔   F 8
Meals a la carte 50/80 ⌷ – ⌷ 21 – **26 rm** 395/610, 8 suites.

🏨 **Concorde St-Lazare,** 108 r. St-Lazare ℘ 01 40 08 44 44, stlazare@concordestlazar e-paris.com, Fax 01 42 93 01 20, « Late 19C lobby » – |⚐|, ⟨⟨❀⟩⟩ rm, 🗐 📺 📞 – 🏛 25 - 150. 🗚 ⓞ 🈺 🈔   E 12
Café Terminus : Meals 30/42bi. ⌷ – ⌷ 22 – **251 rm** 300/430, 11 suites.

🏨 **Marriott** Ⓜ, 70 av. Champs-Élysées ℘ 01 53 93 55 00, Fax 01 53 93 55 01, 🗮, ℥ – |⚐|, ⟨⟨❀⟩⟩ rm, 🗐 📺 📞 ⓖ ⟨❀⟩ – 🏛 15 - 165. 🗚 ⓞ 🈺 🈔. 🗷 rest   F 9
Pavillon ℘ 01 53 93 55 44 (closed Sunday dinner and Saturday) **Meals** 52bi. (lunch) and a la carte 60/70 ⌷ – ⌷ 22 – **174 rm** 670/760, 18 suites.

🏨 **Balzac** Ⓜ, 6 r. Balzac ℘ 01 44 35 18 00, hbalzac@cybercable.fr, Fax 01 44 35 18 05 – |⚐|, 🗐 rm, 📺 📞. 🗚 ⓞ 🈺 🈔   F 8
see **Pierre Gagnaire** below – ⌷ 21 – **56 rm** 395/545, 14 suites.

🏨 **Warwick** Ⓜ, 5 r. Berri ℘ 01 45 63 14 11, cesa.whparis@warwickhotels.com, Fax 01 45 63 75 81 – |⚐|, ⟨⟨❀⟩⟩ rm, 🗐 📺 📞 – 🏛 30 - 110. 🗚 ⓞ 🈺 🈔. 🗷 rest
see **Le W** below – ⌷ 28 – **147 rm** 420/570.   Г 9

🏨 **Napoléon,** 40 av. Friedland ℘ 01 56 68 43 21, napoleon@hotelnapoleonparis.com, Fax 01 47 66 82 33 – |⚐|, 🗐 rm, 📺 📞 – 🏛 15 - 80. 🗚 ⓞ 🈺 🈔   F 8
Meals a la carte 30/48 ⌷ – ⌷ 18,30 – **102 rm** 320/550.

🏨 **California,** 16 r. Berri ℘ 01 43 59 93 00, eg@hroy.com, Fax 01 45 61 03 62, 🗮, « Important collection of paintings » – |⚐|, ⟨⟨❀⟩⟩ rm, 🗐 📺 📞 – 🏛 20 - 100. 🗚 ⓞ 🈺
🈔. 🗷 rm   F 9
Meals (closed August, Saturday and Sunday) (lunch only) 31/43 ⌷ – ⌷ 21 – **161 rm** 450/470, 13 duplex.

🏨 **Château Frontenac** without rest, 54 r. P. Charron ℘ 01 53 23 13 13, hotel@hfro ntenac.com, Fax 01 53 23 13 01 – |⚐| 🗐 📺 📞 – 🏛 25. 🗚 ⓞ 🈺   G 9
⌷ 15 – **104 rm** 205/295, 6 suites.

🏨 **Bedford,** 17 r. de l'Arcade ℘ 01 44 94 77 77, contact@hotel-bedford.com, Fax 01 44 94 77 97 – |⚐| 🗐 📺 📞 – 🏛 15 - 50. 🗚 🈺 🈔. 🗷 rest   F 11
Meals (closed Saturday and Sunday) (lunch only) 32 – ⌷ – **134 rm** 162/180, 11 suites.

🏨 **Queen Elizabeth,** 41 av. Pierre-1er-de-Serbie ℘ 01 53 57 25 25, reservation@hotel -queen.com, Fax 01 53 57 25 26 – |⚐| 🗐 📺 📞 – 🏛 30. 🗚 ⓞ 🈺 🈔   G 8
Meals (closed August, Saturday and Sunday) (lunch only) 27 – ⌷ 19 – **48 rm** 290/455, 12 suites.

🏨 **Montaigne** Ⓜ without rest, 6 av. Montaigne ℘ 01 47 20 30 50, contact@hotel-mo ntaigne.com, Fax 01 47 20 94 12 – |⚐| 🗐 📺 📞 ⓖ. 🗚 ⓞ 🈺 🈔   G 9
⌷ 17 – **29 rm** 245/385.

🏨 **Élysées Star** Ⓜ without rest, 19 r. Vernet ℘ 01 47 20 41 73, star@easynet.fr, Fax 01 47 23 32 15 – |⚐|, 🗐 rm, 📞 – 🏛 30. 🗚 ⓞ 🈺 🈔   F 8
⌷ 20 – **38 rm** 280/650, 4 suites.

🏨 **François 1er** Ⓜ without rest, 7 r. Magellan ℘ 01 47 23 44 04, hotel@francois1er.fr, Fax 01 47 23 93 43 – |⚐|, ⟨⟨❀⟩⟩ rm, 🗐 📺 📞 – 🏛 15. 🗚 ⓞ 🈺 🈔   F 8
⌷ 24 – **40 rm** 300/457.

🏨 **Royal** Ⓜ without rest, 33 av. Friedland ℘ 01 43 59 08 14, rh@royal-hotel.com, Fax 01 45 63 69 92 – |⚐| 🗐 📺 📞. 🗚 ⓞ 🈺 🈔   F 8
⌷ 20 – **58 rm** 260/400.

🏨 **Sofitel Champs-Élysées** Ⓜ, 8 r. J. Goujon ℘ 01 40 74 64 64, H1184-RE@accor-h otels.com, Fax 01 40 74 79 66, 🗮 – |⚐|, ⟨⟨❀⟩⟩ rm, 🗐 📺 📞 ⟨❀⟩ – 🏛 15 - 150. 🗚 ⓞ 🈺
🈔   G 9
Les Signatures ℘ 01 40 74 64 94 (lunch only)(closed 1 to 18 August, 25 December-1 January, Saturday, Sunday) **Meals** a la carte 40/51 ⌷ – ⌷ 23 – **40 rm** 435/560.

🏨 **Élysées-Ponthieu and Résidence** without rest, 24 r. Ponthieu ℘ 01 53 89 58 58, Fax 01 53 89 59 59 – |⚐| kitchenette, ⟨⟨❀⟩⟩ rm, 📺 ⓖ. 🗚 ⓞ 🈺 🈔   F 9
⌷ 13 – **91 rm** 185/305, 6 suites.

🏨 **Powers** without rest, 52 r. François 1er ℘ 01 47 23 91 05, contact@hotel-powers.com, Fax 01 49 52 04 63 – |⚐| 🗐 📺 📞. 🗚 ⓞ 🈺 🈔   G 9
⌷ 13 – **55 rm** 100/300.

Résidence du Roy Ⓜ without rest, 8 r. François 1er ℰ 01 42 89 59 59, rdr@resid
ence-du-roy.com, Fax 01 40 74 07 92 – |‡| kitchenette 🔲 📺 ⚡ �& 🚗 – 🔬 25. 🎴 ⓪
GB JCB G 9
⌂ 18, 28 suites, 4 studios, 3 duplex.

Chateaubriand without rest, 6 r. Chateaubriand ℰ 01 40 76 00 50, chateaubrianc
@copatel.com, Fax 01 40 76 09 22 – |‡| 🔲 📺 ⚡. 🎴 ⓪ GB JCB F 9
⌂ 16 – **28 rm** 306/336.

Résidence Monceau without rest, 85 r. Rocher ℰ 01 45 22 75 11, residencemonc
eau@wanadoo.fr, Fax 01 45 22 30 88 – |‡| 📺 �&. 🎴 ⓪ GB JCB. ⠩ E 11
⌂ 9 – **51 rm** 122.

Pershing Hall Ⓜ, 49 r. P. Charon ℰ 01 58 36 58 00, info@pershinghall.com,
Fax 01 58 36 58 01 – |‡| 🔲 📺 ⚡ �& – 🔬 60. 🎴 ⓪ GB JCB G 9
Meals (closed Sunday) 39 and a la carte 40/60 – ⌂ 26 – **26 rm** 380/720, 6 suites.

L'Arcade Ⓜ without rest, 7 r. de l'Arcade ℰ 01 53 30 60 00, contact@hotel-arcade.fr
Fax 01 40 07 03 07 – |‡| 🔲 📺 ⚡ – 🔬 25. 🎴 GB JCB F 11
⌂ 9 – **37 rm** 132/169, 4 duplex.

Monna Lisa Ⓜ, 97 r la Boétic ℰ 01 56 43 38 38, contact@hotelmonnalisa.com,
Fax 01 45 62 39 90 – |‡| 🔲 📺 ⚡. 🎴 ⓪ GB JCB. ⠩ F 9
Caffe Ristretto - Italian rest. (closed 3 to 25 August, Saturday and Sunday) **Meals** 30,49
♀ – ⌂ 16,77 – **22 rm** 221,05/237,82.

Lavoisier Ⓜ without rest, 21 r. Lavoisier ℰ 01 53 30 06 06, info@hotellavoisier.com
Fax 01 53 30 23 00 – |‡| 🔲 📺 ⚡ �&. 🎴 ⓪ GB JCB. ⠩ F 11
⌂ 12 – **30 rm** 199/305.

Sofitel Marignan Élysées without rest, 12 r. Marignan ℰ 01 40 76 34 56, H2801@a
ccor-hotels.com, Fax 01 40 76 34 34 – |‡|, ⠶ rm, 🔲 📺 ⚡ – 🔬 15 - 50. 🎴 ⓪ GB JCB
⌂ 25 – **57 rm** 450/600, 16 duplex.

Élysées Mermoz Ⓜ without rest, 30 r. J. Mermoz ℰ 01 42 25 75 30, elymermoz@w
orldnet.fr, Fax 01 45 62 87 10 – |‡| 🔲 📺 ⚡ �& – 🔬 15. 🎴 ⓪ GB JCB F 10
⌂ 7,70 – **22 rm** 126/156, 5 suites.

Franklin Roosevelt without rest, 18 r. Clément-Marot ℰ 01 53 57 49 50, franklir
@iway.fr, Fax 01 47 20 44 30 – |‡| 📺 �&. 🎴 GB. ⠩ G 9
⌂ 15 – **48 rm** 180/285.

Queen Mary Ⓜ without rest, 9 r. Greffulhe ℰ 01 42 66 40 50, hotelqueenmary@w
anadoo.fr, Fax 01 42 66 94 92 – |‡| 🔲 📺. 🎴 ⓪ GB JCB. ⠩ F 12
⌂ 14 – **36 rm** 125/165.

Vignon Ⓜ without rest, 23 r. Vignon ℰ 01 47 42 93 00, h-vignon@club-internet.fr
Fax 01 47 42 04 60 – |‡| 🔲 📺 ⚡ �&. 🎴 ⓪ GB F 12
⌂ 12 – **30 rm** 185/305.

Relais Mercure Opéra Garnier Ⓜ without rest, 4 r. de l'Isly ℰ 01 43 87 35 50
H1913@accor-hotels.com, Fax 01 43 87 03 29 – |‡|, ⠶ rm, 🔲 📺 ⚡. 🎴 ⓪ GB JCB
⌂ 13 – **140 rm** 190/230.

Étoile Friedland without rest, 177 r. Fg St-Honoré ℰ 01 45 63 64 65, friedlan@pa
ris-honotel.com, Fax 01 45 63 88 96 – |‡| 🔲 📺 ⚡ �&. 🎴 ⓪ GB JCB. ⠩ F 9
⌂ 16,72 – **40 rm** 244/275.

Élysées Céramic without rest, 34 av. Wagram ℰ 01 42 27 20 30, cerotel@aol.com
Fax 01 46 22 95 83, « "Art Nouveau" facade » – |‡| 🔲 📺 ⚡. 🎴 ⓪ GB JCB
⌂ 10 – **57 rm** 160/207.

Atlantic without rest, 44 r. Londres ℰ 01 43 87 45 40, reserv@atlantic-hotel.fr
Fax 01 42 93 06 26 – |‡| 🔲 📺 ⚡. 🎴 ⓪ GB JCB. ⠩ E 12
⌂ 9 – **86 rm** 95/150.

L'Élysée without rest, 12 r. Saussaies ℰ 01 42 65 29 25, hotel-de-l-elysee@wanadoo.fr
Fax 01 42 65 64 28 – |‡| 🔲 📺 ⚡. 🎴 ⓪ GB JCB F 11
⌂ 10 – **32 rm** 105/220.

Pavillon Montaigne Ⓜ without rest, 34 r. J. Mermoz ℰ 01 53 89 95 00
Fax 01 42 89 33 00 – |‡| 🔲 📺 ⚡. 🎴 ⓪ GB JCB. ⠩
⌂ 8 – **18 rm** 130/165.

Alison without rest, 21 r. de Surène ℰ 01 42 65 54 00, hotel.alison@wanadoo.fr
Fax 01 42 65 08 17 – |‡| 📺. 🎴 ⓪ GB JCB. ⠩
⌂ 7 – **35 rm** 75/135.

Newton Opéra without rest, 11 bis r. de l'Arcade ℰ 01 42 65 32 13, newtonopera
@easynet.fr, Fax 01 42 65 30 90 – |‡| 🔲 📺 ⚡. 🎴 ⓪ GB. ⠩ F 11
⌂ 12 – **31 rm** 150/183.

Comfort Malesherbes without rest, 11 pl. St-Augustin ℰ 01 42 93 27 66, hotelm
alesherbes@gofornet.com, Fax 01 42 93 27 51 – |‡| 🔲 📺 ⚡. 🎴 ⓪ GB JCB. ⠩ F 11
⌂ 11 – **24 rm** 117/168.

XXXXX ✿✿✿ **Le "Cinq"** - Hôtel Four Seasons George V, 31 av. George V ✆ 01 49 52 71 54, *Fax 01 49 52 71 81*, 🍴 – 🗏. 🖭 ⑪ ☷ 🃏. ✆
Meals 60 (lunch)/200 and a la carte 100/150
Spec. Blanc-manger au caviar d'Aquitaine (Spring). Fricassée de langoustines à la coriandre, lasagne au vieux parmesan. Lièvre à la royale (Season)..

XXXXX ✿✿✿ **Les Ambassadeurs** - Hôtel Crillon, 10 pl. Concorde ✆ 01 44 71 16 16, *restaurants @ crillon.com, Fax 01 44 71 15 02*, « 18C decor » – 🗏. 🖭 ⑪ ☷ 🃏. ✆   G 11
Meals 62 (lunch)/135 and a la carte 120/175
Spec. Turbot rôti aux agrumes, jus de poulet et vinaigre balsamique. Aiguillette de canette au pain d'épice. Vacherin "comme en Alsace"..

XXXXX ✿✿✿ **Ledoyen,** carré Champs-Élysées (1st floor) ✆ 01 53 05 10 01, *Fax 01 47 42 55 01* – 🗏 🖪. 🖭 ☷. ✆   G 10
closed 29 July-26 August, Saturday, Sunday and Bank Holidays – **Meals** 58 (lunch), 119/192 b.i. and a la carte 120/160 ♀
Spec. Grosses langoustines bretonnes croustillantes. Blanc de turbot braisé, pommes rattes au beurre de truffe. Millefeuille de fines "krampouz" craquantes au citron..

XXXXX ✿✿✿ **Plaza Athénée** - Hôtel Plaza Athénée, 25 av. Montaigne ✆ 01 53 67 65 00, *adpa@a lain-ducasse.com, Fax 01 53 67 65 12* – 🗏. 🖭 ⑪ ☷ 🃏. ✆   G 9
closed 12 July-19 August, 20 to 30 December, Saturday, Sunday, Bank Holidays, lunch Monday, Tuesday and Wednesday – **Meals** 190/250 and a la carte 165/225
Spec. Langoustines rafraîchies, nage réduite, caviar osciètre. Volaille de Bresse, chapelure d'herbes et jus perlé. Coupe glacée de saison..

XXXXX ✿✿ **Bristol** - Hôtel Bristol, 112 r. Fg St-Honoré ✆ 01 53 43 43 40, *resa@hotel-bristol.com, Fax 01 53 43 43 01*, 🍴 – 🗏. 🖭 ⑪ ☷ 🃏. ✆   F 10
Meals 60/120 and a la carte 100/145
Spec. Macaroni farcis d'artichaut, truffe et foie gras de canard, gratinés au vieux parmesan. Poularde de Bresse en vessie parfumée au Vin Jaune. Biscuit mi-cuit au chocolat..

XXXXX ✿✿ **Taillevent** (Vrinat), 15 r. Lamennais ✆ 01 44 95 15 01, *mail@taillevent.com, Fax 01 42 25 95 18* – 🗏. 🖭 ⑪ ☷ 🃏. ✆   F 9
closed 27 July-26 August, Saturday, Sunday and Bank Holidays – **Meals** (booking essential) 130 and a la carte 105/130 ♀
Spec. Quenelles de volaille aux écrevisses. Foie de canard poêlé au banyuls. Beignet au chocolat..

XXXXX ✿✿ **Lucas Carton** (Senderens), 9 pl. Madeleine ✆ 01 42 65 22 90, *lucas.carton@lucascar ton.com, Fax 01 42 65 06 23*, « Authentic 1900 decor » – 🗏. 🖭 ⑪ ☷ 🃏. ✆   G 11
closed August, Christmas-New Year, Sunday, lunch Monday and Saturday – **Meals** 64 (lunch)/131 and a la carte 140/250
Spec. Homard à la vanille "Bourbon de Madagascar". Foie gras de canard des Landes au chou, à la vapeur. Canard Apicius rôti au miel et aux épices..

XXXXX ✿✿ **Lasserre,** 17 av. F.-D.-Roosevelt ✆ 01 43 59 53 43, *Fax 01 45 63 72 23*, « Retractable roof » – 🗏. 🖭 ⑪ ☷ 🃏. ✆   G 10
closed 4 August-2 September, Sunday and Monday – **Meals** 55 (lunch)/150 and a la carte 110/160 ♀
Spec. Galette de truffe noire au céleri (mid-December-mid-March). Bar de ligne en croûte blonde aux citrons confits. Tarte soufflée pralinée au gingembre et cacao amer.

XXXXX ✿✿ **Laurent,** 41 av. Gabriel ✆ 01 42 25 00 39, *info@le-laurent.com, Fax 01 45 62 45 21*, 🍴, « Pleasant summer terrace » – 🖭 ⑪ ☷. ✆   G 10
closed Saturday lunch, Sunday and Bank Holidays – **Meals** 65/130 and a la carte 100/180
Spec. Araignée de mer dans ses sucs en gelée, crème de fenouil. Foie gras de canard aux haricots noirs pimentés. Variation sur le chocolat..

XXXX ✿✿ **Les Élysées** - Hôtel Vernet, 25 r. Vernet ✆ 01 44 31 98 98, *hotelvernet@jetmultim edia.fr, Fax 01 44 31 85 69*, « Fine glass roof » – 🗏. 🖭 ⑪ ☷ 🃏. ✆   F 8
closed 22 July-25 August, Monday lunch, Saturday, Sunday and Bank Holidays – **Meals** 52 (lunch)/150 and a la carte 115/160
Spec. Epeautre "comme un risotto" et râpée de truffe noire (December-February). Bar de ligne à l'étouffé, cèpes, cébettes et artichauts violets. Gnocchi d'herbes fraîches, pain grillé aux noix, et sorbet à l'huile d'olive..

XXXX ✿✿✿ **Pierre Gagnaire** - Hôtel Balzac, 6 r. Balzac ✆ 01 58 36 12 50, *p.gagnaire@wanadoo.fr, Fax 01 58 36 12 51* – 🗏. 🖭 ⑪ ☷   F 8
closed 15 to 31 July, All Saints Holidays, February Holidays, Sunday lunch, Saturday and Bank Holidays – **Meals** 83,85 (lunch)/182,94 and a la carte 155/215
Spec. Langoustines bretonnes : grillées, en tartare et mousseline, sabayon au macvin. Coffre de canard rôti entier, crumble de mangue, peau laquée et cuisse en terrine. Biscuit soufflé au chocolat pur Caraïbes.

XXXX **L'Astor** - Hôtel Sofitel Astor, 11 rue d'Astorg ℂ 01 53 05 05 20, *hotelastor@aol.com*,
★★ Fax *01 53 05 05 30* – ▤. 🅰🄴 ① 🄶🄱 🄹🄲🄱   F 11
closed 5 August-2 September, Saturday and Sunday – **Meals** 49,55 b.i. (lunch)/99,09 b.i.
and a la carte 85/125 ♀
Spec. Araignée de mer à la crème de chou fleur et caviar. Lièvre à la royale (October-
December). Pomme verte en cristalline, crème croustillante au thé.

XXXX **La Marée,** 1 r. Daru ℂ 01 43 80 20 00, Fax *01 48 88 04 04* – ▤. 🅰🄴 ① 🄶🄱   E 8
★ *closed 26 July-28 August, Saturday lunch and Sunday* – **Meals** - Seafood - a la carte 80/100♀
Spec. Croustillant de langoustines à la sauce aigre douce. Petite marmite tropézienne.
Millefeuille chaud caramélisé aux amandes..

XXXX **Chiberta,** 3 r. Arsène-Houssaye ℂ 01 53 53 42 00, *info@lechiberta.com*,
★ Fax *01 45 62 85 08* – ▤. 🅰🄴 ① 🄶🄱   a la carte
closed August, Saturday lunch and Sunday – **Meals** 44,21 (lunch)/89,94 and a la carte
70/110 ♀
Spec. Cuisses de grenouilles poêlées à l'ail doux. Saint-Pierre serti à la feuille de laurier.
Truffe noire de Provence cuite au champagne, à la croque au sel (mid-November-Late
February).

XXXX **Clovis** - Hôtel Sofitel Arc de Triomphe, 14 r. Beaujon ℂ 01 53 89 50 53, *h1296@acc*
★ *or-hotels.com*, Fax *01 53 89 50 51* – ▤. 🅰🄴 ① 🄶🄱   F 8
closed 24 July-24 August, 24 December-2 January, Saturday, Sunday and Bank Holidays
– **Meals** 45,42/88,42 and a la carte 62/76 ♀
Spec. Duo de foie gras de canard, figues vigneronnes. Tournedos de lotte grillé, tranches
de lomo, blettes braisées. Coeur de filet de boeuf normand aux câpres..

XXX **Maison Blanche,** 15 av. Montaigne (6th floor) ℂ 01 47 23 55 99, Fax *01 47 20 09 56*,
<, 🏠 – 🛗 ▤. 🅰🄴 ① 🄶🄱   G 9
closed lunch Saturday and Sunday – **Meals** a la carte 78/83.

XXX **Jardin** - Hôtel Royal Monceau, 37 av. Hoche ℂ 01 42 99 98 70, Fax *01 42 99 89 94*, 🏠
★ – ▤. 🅰🄴 ① 🄶🄱 🄹🄲🄱. ✀   E 8
closed Saturday and Sunday – **Meals** 61 (lunch)/99,13 and a la carte 90/110
Spec. "Fougassette" de jeunes légumes à la purée d'écrevisses (Summer). Bar de ligne
braisé en feuille de figue (Autumn). Filet de veau de lait rôti, chicons au jus de truffe et
vieux jambon (Spring and Winter)..

XXX **Fouquet's,** 99 av. Champs Élysées ℂ 01 47 23 50 00, *fouquets@lucienbarriere.com*,
Fax *01 47 23 50 55*, 🏠 – 🅰🄴 ① 🄶🄱 🄹🄲🄱 – **Meals** 50 and a la carte 65/78.

XXX **Le W** - Hôtel Warwick, 5 r. Berri ℂ 01 45 61 82 08, *lerestaurantw@warwickhotels.com*,
★ Fax *01 45 63 75 81* – ▤. 🅰🄴 ① 🄶🄱   F 9
closed 28 July-2 September, 20 December-6 January, Saturday and Sunday – **Meals** 40
(lunch)/55 and a la carte 60/85
Spec. Champignons sauvages et foie gras de canard poêlé. Saint-Jacques aux topinam-
bours et patate douce. Côte épaisse de cochon en croûte de sel..

XXX **L'Obélisque** - Hôtel Crillon, 6 r. Boissy d'Anglas ℂ 01 44 71 15 15, *restaurants@crillo*
n.com, Fax *01 44 71 15 02* – ▤. 🅰🄴 ① 🄶🄱 🄹🄲🄱   G 11
closed 27 July-26 August – **Meals** 48.

XXX **Marcande,** 52 r. Miromesnil ℂ 01 42 65 19 14, *info@marcande.com*,
Fax *01 42 65 76 85*, 🏠 – 🄶🄱   F 10
closed 5 to 19 August, 25 December-2 January, Saturday and Sunday – **Meals** 38,11 and
a la carte 49/78 ♀.

XXX **Copenhague,** 142 av. Champs-Élysées (1st floor) ℂ 01 44 13 86 26, *floricadanica@w*
★ *anadoo.fr*, Fax *01 44 13 89 44*, 🏠 – ▤. 🅰🄴 🄶🄱
closed 29 July-25 August, Saturday lunch, Sunday and Bank Holidays – **Meals** - Danish rest. -
49/73 and a la carte 60/95 - *Flora Danica*: **Meals** 30 and a la carte 44/68♀   F 8
Spec. Assiette gourmande "Copenhague". Noisettes de renne frottées de poivre noir,
rôties au sautoir. Rhubarbe confite et sorbet, gâteau aux amandes (April-September)..

XXX **El Mansour,** 7 r. Trémoille ℂ 01 47 23 88 18, Fax *01 40 70 13 53* – ▤. 🅰🄴 ① 🄶🄱
closed 11 to 19 August, Monday lunch and Sunday – **Meals** - Moroccan rest. - 42,69 b.i.
(lunch), 53,36 b.i./68,60 b.i..

XXX **Yvan,** 1bis r. J. Mermoz ℂ 01 43 59 18 40, Fax *01 42 89 30 95* – ▤. 🅰🄴 ① 🄶🄱 🄹🄲🄱 F-G 10
closed Saturday lunch and Sunday – **Meals** 29,73 (lunch)/43,45 and a la carte 50/80.

XXX **Bath's,** 9 r. La Trémoille ℂ 01 40 70 01 09, *restaurantbath@wanadoo.fr*,
★ Fax *01 40 70 01 22* – ▤. 🅰🄴 🄶🄱   G 9
closed 2 August to 2 September, 23 to 26 December, Saturday, Sunday and Bank Holidays
– **Meals** 30 (lunch)/70 and a la carte 65/90 ♀
Spec. Crème de lentilles, bonbons de foie gras et truffes. Cassoulet de homard. Côte de
veau du Limousin, macaroni rôtis aux morilles hachées..

XXX **Indra,** 10 r. Cdt-Rivière ℂ 01 43 59 46 40, Fax *01 42 25 00 32* – ▤. 🅰🄴 ① 🄶🄱   F 9
closed Saturday lunch and Sunday – **Meals** - Indian rest. - 34 (lunch), 38/58 and a la carte
41/51.

XX **Spoon,** 14 r. Marignan ℰ 01 40 76 34 44, *spoonfood@aol.com, Fax 01 40 76 34 37,*
« Contemporary decor » – 🗐. AE ➊ GB JCB. ❄️   G 9
closed 22 July-19 August, 23 December-1 January, Saturday and Sunday – **Meals** - cosmopolitan cuisine and international wines - a la carte 54/89.

XX **Rue Balzac,** 3 r. Balzac ℰ 01 53 89 90 91, *rostang@relaischateaux.fr,*
Fax 01 53 89 90 94 – 🗐. AE   F 8
closed 13 to 19 August and lunch Saturday and Sunday – **Meals** a la carte 43/51 ♀.

XX **Carpaccio** - Hôtel Royal Monceau, 37 av. Hoche ℰ 01 42 99 98 90 – 🗐 AE ➊ GB JCB
💮 *closed 20 July-26 August –* **Meals** a la carte 55/91
Spec. Gnocchi verts au parmesan. Tagliatelle au ragoût de veau. Pigeon rôti sur polenta et truffes noires..

XX **Luna,** 69 r. Rocher ℰ 01 42 93 77 61, Fax 01 40 08 02 44 – 🗐. AE GB   E 11
💮 *closed 6 to 27 August and Sunday –* **Meals** - Seafood - a la carte 53/73 ♀
Spec. Grosses gambas rôties à l'huile de vanille. Cassolette de homard au lard fumé. "Vrai baba" de Zanzibar..

XX **Tante Louise,** 41 r. Boissy-d'Anglas ℰ 01 42 65 06 85, *tante.louise@wanadoo.fr,*
Fax 01 42 65 28 19 – 🗐. AE ➊ GB JCB   F 11
closed August, Saturday and Sunday – **Meals** a la carte 44/68 ♀.

XX **Shozan,** 11 r. de la Trémoille ℰ 01 47 23 37 32, Fax 01 47 23 67 30 – 🗐. AE ➊ GB
JCB   G 9
closed 1 to 29 August, Saturday and Sunday – **Meals** - French and Japanese rest. - 30 (lunch), 60,50/75,50 and a la carte 59/65 ♀

XX **Korova,** 33 r. Marbeuf ℰ 01 53 89 93 93, *info@korova.fr, Fax 01 53 89 93 94,* « Design
decor » – 🗐. AE ➊ GB JCB   G 9
closed 1 to 15 August, lunch Saturday and Sunday – **Meals** a la carte 41/69 ♀.

XX **Grenadin,** 46 r. Naples ℰ 01 45 63 28 92, Fax 01 45 61 24 76 – 🗐. AE GB   E 11
closed Saturday lunch, Monday dinner and Sunday – **Meals** 33,54/40,86 and a la carte approx. 60.

XX **Hédiari,** 21 pl. Madeleine ℰ 01 43 12 88 99, *restaurant@hediard.fr,*
Fax 01 43 12 88 98 – 🗐. AE ➊ GB. ❄️   F 11
closed 25 December-1 January and Sunday – **Meals** a la carte 41/58 ♀.

XX **Sarladais,** 2 r. Vienne ℰ 01 45 22 23 62, Fax 01 45 22 23 62 – 🗐. AE GB JCB
closed 4 to 13 May, 3 August-3 September, Saturday except dinner from October-April,
Sunday and Bank Holidays – **Meals** 33 ♀.   E 11

XX **Fermette Marbeuf 1900,** 5 r. Marbeuf ℰ 01 53 23 08 00, Fax 01 53 23 08 09,
« 1900 decor with original ceramics and stained glass windows » – 🗐. AE ➊ GB
Meals 27,90 and a la carte 36/54 ♀.   G 9

XX **Marius et Janette,** 4 av. George-V ℰ 01 47 23 41 88, Fax 01 47 23 07 19, 🛋 – 🗐.
💮 AE ➊ GB JCB   G 8
Meals - Seafood - 51,84 b.i. and a la carte 60/90
Spec. Poissons crus. Merlan frit sauce tartare (May-October). Saint-Jacques poêlées aux cèpes (October-February).

XX **Stella Maris,** 4 r. Arsène Houssaye ℰ 01 42 89 16 22, *stella.maris.paris@wanadoo.fr,*
Fax 01 42 89 16 01 – 🗐. AE ➊ GB JCB. ❄️   F 8
closed 10 to 22 August, Sunday, lunch Saturday and Monday – **Meals** 42,70 (lunch)/103,68 and a la carte 75/85.

XX **Il Sardo,** 11 r Treilhard ℰ 01 45 61 09 46 – 🗐. AE GB   E 10
closed August, Saturday lunch, Sunday and Bank Holidays – **Meals** - Italian rest. - a la carte 25/49 ♀.

XX **Les Bouchons de François Clerc "Étoile",** 6 r. Arsène Houssaye ℰ 01 42 89 15 51,
siegebouchons@wanadoo.fr, Fax 01 42 89 28 67 – 🗐. AE GB JCB. ❄️   F 8
closed Saturday lunch and Sunday – **Meals** - Seafood - 40,86 ♀.

XX **Stresa,** 7 r. Chambiges ℰ 01 47 23 51 62 – 🗐. AE ➊ GB. ❄️   G 9
closed August, 20 December-3 January, Saturday and Sunday – **Meals** - Italian rest. - (booking essential) a la carte 42/79.

XX **Berkeley,** 7 av. Matignon ℰ 01 42 25 72 25, Fax 01 45 63 30 06, 🛋 – 🗐. AE ➊ GB
JCB   G 10
Meals a la carte 38/45 ♀.

XX **Bistrot du Sommelier,** 97 bd Haussmann ℰ 01 42 65 24 85, *bistrot-du-sommelier*
@noos.fr, Fax 01 53 75 23 23 – 🗐. AE GB   F 11
closed 27 July-25 August, 21 December-1 January, Saturday and Sunday – **Meals** 38,11 (lunch), 59,46 b.i./99,09 b.i..

XX **Nobu,** 15 r. Marbeuf ℰ 01 56 89 53 53, Fax 01 56 89 53 54 – 🗐. AE ➊ GB JCB G 9
closed Sunday lunch and Saturday – **Meals** - Japanese rest. - a la carte approx. 90 ♀.

XX **Kinugawa,** 4 r. St-Philippe du Roule ☎ 01 45 63 08 07, *Fax 01 42 60 45 21* – ▤. AE ⓓ GB JCB. ✗ F 9
closed 24 December-7 January and Sunday – **Meals** - Japanese rest. - 26 (lunch), 86/107 and a la carte 80/110 ♀.

XX ✿ **L'Angle du Faubourg,** 195 r. Fg St-Honoré ☎ 01 40 74 20 20, *Fax 01 40 74 20 21* – ▤. AE ⓓ GB JCB E 9
closed 27 July-20 August, Saturday and Sunday – **Meals** 35/73 and a la carte 50/60 ♀
Spec. Lomo de thon rôti aux épices. Joues de veau braisées, gratin de macaroni aux artichauts. Entremets au chocolat, glace à l'amande amer..

XX **Les Bouchons de François Clerc,** 7 r. Boccador ☎ 01 47 23 57 80, *Fax 01 47 23 74 54* – AE GB JCB G 9
closed Saturday lunch and Sunday – **Meals** 40,86 ♀.

XX **Al Ajami,** 58 r. François 1er ☎ 01 42 25 38 44, *Fax 01 42 25 38 39* – ▤. AE ⓓ GB. ✗ G 9
Meals - Lebanese rest - 19,67/28,81 and a la carte 30/52 ♀.

XX **Village d'Ung et Li Lam,** 10 r. J. Mermoz ☎ 01 42 25 99 79, *Fax 01 42 25 12 06* – ▤. AE ⓓ GB JCB F 10
closed lunch Saturday and Sunday – **Meals** - Chinese and Thai rest. - 18 (lunch), 22/29 and a la carte approx. 35 ♀.

XX **Pichet de Paris,** 68 r. P. Charron ☎ 01 43 59 50 34, *Fax 01 42 89 68 91* – ▤. AE ⓓ GB GF 9
closed Saturday except dinner from September-April and Sunday – **Meals** a la carte 50/90.

XX **Bistro de l'Olivier,** 13 r. Quentin Bauchart ☎ 01 47 20 78 63, *Fax 01 47 20 74 58* – ▤. AE GB G 8
Meals (booking essential) 32,01 and a la carte 61/66 ♀.

XX **Market,** 15 r. Matignon ☎ 01 56 43 40 90, *Fax 01 43 59 10 87* – ▤. AE GB F 10
Meals 39 (lunch) and a la carte 45/65 ♀.

X **Cap Vernet,** 82 av. Marceau ☎ 01 47 20 20 40, *capvernet@guysavoy.com, Fax 01 47 20 95 36,* 帝 – ▤. AE ⓓ GB JCB F 8
Meals - Seafood - a la carte 42/58.

X **L'Appart',** 9 r. Colisée ☎ 01 53 75 16 34, *restapart@aol.com, Fax 01 53 76 15 39* – ▤. AE GB JCB F 9
Meals 29/39,60 ♀.

X **Saveurs et Salon,** 3 r. Castellane ☎ 01 40 06 97 97, *Fax 01 40 06 98 06* – ▤. AE GB
closed Saturday lunch and Sunday – **Meals** 30 ♁.

X **L'Atelier Renault,** 53 av. Champs Élysées ☎ 01 49 53 70 70, *Fax 01 49 53 70 71* – ▤
Meals 28 and a la carte 35/42.

X **Cô Ba Saigon,** 181 r. Fg St-Honoré ☎ 01 45 63 70 37, *Fax 01 42 25 18 31* – ▤. AE GB F 9
closed 27 July-18 August, Saturday lunch in July-August and Sunday – **Meals** - Vietnamese rest. - 14,94 (lunch)/22,87 and a la carte 23/30.

X **Zo,** 13 r. Montalivet ☎ 01 42 65 18 18, *restzo@club-internet.fr, Fax 01 42 65 10 91* – ▤. AE GB JCB F 11
closed 9 to 19 August., lunch Saturday and Sunday – **Meals** a la carte 35/40.

X **Xu,** 19 r. Bayard ☎ 01 47 20 82 24, *Fax 01 47 20 20 21* – ▤. AE ⓓ GB G 9
closed 13 to 20 August and Sunday dinner – **Meals** a la carte 34/56.

X **Bistrot de Marius,** 6 av. George V ☎ 01 40 70 11 76, 帝 – AE ⓓ GB. ✗ G 8
Meals a la carte 33/54.

X **Rocher Gourmand,** 89 r. Rocher ☎ 01 40 08 00 36, *Fax 01 40 08 05 29* – GB
closed 27 July-27 August, Saturday lunch and Sunday – **Meals** 30/45. E 10

X **Daru,** 19 r. Daru ☎ 01 42 27 23 60, *Fax 01 47 54 08 14* – ▤. AE GB E 9
closed August, Sunday and Bank Holidays – **Meals** - Russian rest. - a la carte 45/80.

X ☺ **Ferme des Mathurins,** 17 r. Vignon ☎ 01 42 66 46 39, *Fax 01 42 66 00 27* – ⓓ GB JCB F 12
closed August, Sunday and Bank Holidays – **Meals** 27,45/36,60 and a la carte 45/50.

X **Maline,** 40 r. Ponthieu ☎ 01 45 63 14 14, *Fax 01 48 78 35 30* – GB F 9
closed 1 to 8 May, Saturday and Sunday – **Meals** 28,20 and a la carte 21/37 ♀.

X **Version Sud,** 3 r. Berryer ☎ 01 40 76 01 40, *Fax 01 40 76 03 96* – ▤. AE ⓓ GB JCB. ✗ F 9
closed 5 to 19 August, Saturday lunch and Sunday – **Meals** (booking essential) a la carte 36/47 ♀.

X **Café Indigo,** 12 av. George V ☎ 01 47 20 89 56, *Fax 01 47 20 76 16* – ▤. AE ⓓ GB JCB G 8
Meals a la carte 34/56.

✗ **Boucoléon,** 10 r. Constantinople ℘ 01 42 93 73 33, *claval.jeremy@fnac.net,*
🍴 Fax 01 42 93 17 44 – **GB**. ✗   E 11
closed 1 to 18 August, Saturday and Sunday – **Meals** (booking essential) a la carte 24/35.

✗ **Shin Jung,** 7 r. Clapeyron ℘ 01 45 22 21 06   D 11
closed Bank Holidays and lunch Saturday and Sunday – **Meals** Corean rest. 13,50/29 and
a la carte 28/45 ♨.

Opéra, Gare du Nord, Gare de l'Est, Grands Boulevards.

9th and 10th arrondissements.
9th: ✉ 75009
10th: ✉ 75010

🏨 **Scribe** M, 1 r. Scribe (9th) ℘ 01 44 71 24 24, *scribe.reservation@wanadoo.fr,*
Fax 01 42 65 39 97 – |☰|, ✲ rm, ▤ ▥ ✆ &. – ⚒ 50. ⅀ ⓪ **GB** ⫶⫶   F 12
see **Les Muses** below - *Jardin des Muses :* **Meals** 29 (lunch) and a la carte 29/50 ♀ –
⌷ 24 – **206 rm** 419//05, 11 suites.

🏨 **Millennium Opéra** M, 12 bd Haussmann (9th) ℘ 01 49 49 16 00, *opera@mill cop.c
om,* Fax 01 49 49 17 00, 🍴 – |☰|, ✲ rm, ▤ rm, ▥ ✆ &. – ⚒ 80. ⅀ ⓪ **GB**
⫶⫶   F 13
Brasserie Haussmann ℘ 01 49 49 16 64 **Meals** 36 ♀ – ⌷ 25 – **150 rm** 400/500,
13 suites.

🏨 **Ambassador,** 16 bd Haussmann (9th) ℘ 01 44 83 40 40, *ambass@concorde-hotels.
com,* Fax 01 42 46 19 84 – |☰|, ✲ rm, ▤ ▥ ✆ – ⚒ 110. ⅀ ⓪ **GB** ⫶⫶   F 13
see **16 Haussmann** below – ⌷ 23 – **292 rm** 360/450, 4 suites.

🏩 **Villa Opéra Drouot** M without rest, 2 r. Geoffroy Marie (9th) ℘ 01 48 00 08 08, *drou
ot@hotelsparis.fr,* Fax 01 48 00 80 60, « Baroque decor » – |☰| ▤ ▥ ✆ &. ⅀ ⓪ **GB**
⫶⫶   F 14
⌷ 18 – **27 rm** 390/442, 3 duplex.

🏩 **Terminus Nord** M without rest, 12 bd Denain (10th) ℘ 01 42 80 20 00,
Fax 01 42 80 63 89 – |☰|, ✲ rm, ▥ ✆ &. – ⚒ 70. ⅀ ⓪ **GB** ⫶⫶   E 16
⌷ 13 – **236 rm** 216/229.

🏩 **Holiday Inn Paris Opéra,** 38 r. Échiquier (10th) ℘ 01 42 46 92 75, *information@h
i-parisopera.com,* Fax 01 42 47 03 97 – |☰|, ✲ rm, ▤ ▥ ✆ &. – ⚒ 60. ⅀ ⓪
GB ⫶⫶   F 15
Meals 32 b.i./35 b.i. – ⌷ 20 – **92 rm** 228/273.

🏩 **Pavillon de Paris** M without rest, 7 r. Parme (9th) ℘ 01 55 31 60 00, *mail@pavillo
ndeparis.com,* Fax 01 55 31 60 01 – |☰| ▤ ▥ ✆ &. ⅀ ⓪ **GB**   D 12
⌷ 13,75 – **30 rm** 229/275.

🏩 **Lafayette** M without rest, 49 r. Lafayette (9th) ℘ 01 42 85 05 44, *h2802-gm@acc
or-hotels.com,* Fax 01 49 95 06 60 – |☰| kitchenette, ✲ rm, ▥ ✆ &. ⅀ ⓪
GB ⫶⫶   F 14
⌷ 13 – **96 rm** 174/305, 7 suites.

🏩 **St-Pétersbourg,** 33 r. Caumartin (9th) ℘ 01 42 66 60 38, *hotel.st-petersbourg@wa
nadoo.fr,* Fax 01 42 66 53 54 – |☰| ▤ ▥ ✆ – ⚒ 25. ⅀ ⓪ **GB** ⫶⫶. ✗ rest   F 12
Relais ℘ 01 42 66 85 90 *(closed August, Saturday and Sunday)* **Meals** 23 ♀ – **100 rm**
⌷ 158/199.

🏩 **Astra** without rest, 29 r. Caumartin (9th) ℘ 01 42 66 15 15, *hotel.astra@astotel.com,*
Fax 01 42 66 98 05 – |☰|, ✲ rm, ▤ ▥ ✆. ⅀ ⓪ **GB** ⫶⫶. ✗   F 12
⌷ 21 – **82 rm** 258/304.

🏨 **Richmond Opéra** without rest, 11 r. Helder (9th) ℘ 01 47 70 53 20, *paris@richmo
nd-hotel.com,* Fax 01 48 00 02 10 – |☰| ▤ ▥ ✆. ⅀ ⓪ **GB** ⫶⫶. ✗   F 13
⌷ 10 – **59 rm** 122/143.

🏨 **Carlton's Hôtel** without rest, 55 bd Rochechouart (9th) ℘ 01 42 81 91 00, *carltons
@club-internet.fr,* Fax 01 42 81 97 04, « Rooftop panoramic terrace » – |☰| ▥ ✆. ⅀ ⓪
GB ⫶⫶   D 14
⌷ 8,40 – **108 rm** 122/167,70.

🏨 **Albert 1er** Ⓜ without rest, 162 r. Lafayette (10th) ℰ 01 40 36 82 40, *resa@hotel-albert1er-paris.com*, Fax 01 40 35 72 52 – 🛗 ▤ 🖵 ✆. AE ◑ GB JCB   E 16
🖵 9 – **55 rm** 85/101.

🏨 **Opéra Cadet** Ⓜ without rest, 24 r. Cadet (9th) ℰ 01 53 34 50 50, *infos@hotel-opera-cadet.fr*, Fax 01 53 34 50 60 – 🛗 ▤ 🖵 ✆ 🛋. – 🔏 50. AE ◑ GB JCB   F 14
🖵 12 – **85 rm** 150/170, 3 suites.

🏨 **Bergère Opéra** without rest, 34 r. Bergère (9th) ℰ 01 47 70 34 34, *hotel.bergere @astotel.com*, Fax 01 47 70 36 36 – 🛗 ▤ 🖵 – 🔏 40. AE ◑ GB JCB   F 14
🖵 14 – **134 rm** 167/182.

🏨 **Franklin** without rest, 19 r. Buffault (9th) ℰ 01 42 80 27 27, *H2779@ accor-hotels.com*, Fax 01 48 78 13 04 – 🛗, ↳⟵ rm, 🖵 ✆. AE ◑ GB JCB   E 14
🖵 13 – **68 rm** 157/207.

🏨 **Caumartin** without rest, 27 r. Caumartin (9e) ℰ 01 47 42 95 95, *h2811@ accor-hotels.com*, Fax 01 47 42 88 19 – 🛗, ↳⟵ rm, ▤ ✆. AE ◑ GB JCB   F 12
🖵 12 – **40 rm** 177.

🏨 **Blanche Fontaine** ⌂ without rest, 34 r. Fontaine (9th) ℰ 01 44 63 54 95, Fax 01 42 81 05 52 – 🛗, ↳⟵ rm, 🖵 ✆ 🛋.   D 13
🖵 14,48 – **62 rm** 168/206, 4 suites.

🏨 **Anjou-Lafayette** without rest, 4 r. Riboutté (9th) ℰ 01 42 46 83 44, *hotel.anjou.lafayette@ wanadoo.fr*, Fax 01 48 00 08 97 – 🛗 🖵 ✆. AE ◑ GB JCB   E 14
🖵 10 – **39 rm** 130/145.

🏨 **Touraine Opéra** without rest, 73 r. Taitbout (9th) ℰ 01 48 74 50 49, *H2803@ accor-hotels.com*, Fax 01 42 81 26 09 – 🛗, ↳⟵ rm, 🖵 ✆. AE ◑ GB JCB   E 13
🖵 13 – **39 rm** 151/207.

🏨 **Paris-Est** without rest, 4 r. 8 Mai 1945 (main courtyard East Railwaystation)(10th) ℰ 01 44 89 27 00, *hotelparisest-bestwestern@ autogrill.fr*, Fax 01 44 89 27 49 – 🛗 ▤ 🖵. AE ◑ GB   E 16
🖵 9 – **45 rm** 95/182.

🏨 **Trois Poussins** Ⓜ without rest, 15 r. Clauzel (9th) ℰ 01 53 32 81 81, *h3p@les3poussins.com*, Fax 01 53 32 81 82 – 🛗 kitchenette, ↳⟵ rm, 🖵 ✆ &. AE ◑ GB JCB. ⚓   E 13
🖵 10 – **40 rm** 130/185.

🏨 **Pavillon République Les Halles** without rest, 9 r. Pierre Chausson (10th) ℰ 01 40 18 11 00, *republique@ hotelsparis.fr*, Fax 01 40 18 11 06 – ↳⟵ rm, 🖵 ✆ &. AE ◑ GB JCB   F 16
🖵 11 – **58 rm** 153/200.

🏨 **Mercure Monty** without rest, 5 r. Montyon (9th) ℰ 01 47 70 26 10, Fax 01 42 46 55 10 – 🛗, ↳⟵ rm, ▤ 🖵 ✆ – 🔏 50. AE ◑ GB JCB   F 14
🖵 11 – **70 rm** 152/160.

🏨 **Paix République** without rest, 2 bis bd St-Martin (10th) ℰ 01 42 08 96 95, *hotelpaix@ wanadoo.fr*, Fax 01 42 06 36 30 – 🛗 🖵. AE ◑ GB JCB. ⚓   G 16
🖵 7 – **45 rm** 106/197.

🏨 **Corona** ⌂ without rest, 8 cité Bergère (9th) ℰ 01 47 70 52 96, *hotelcoronaopera@r egetel.com*, Fax 01 42 46 83 49 – 🛗 🖵 ✆ &. AE ◑ GB JCB   F 14
🖵 12 – **56 rm** 151/191, 4 suites.

🏨 **Alba** ⌂ without rest, 34 ter r. La Tour d'Auvergne (9th) ℰ 01 48 78 80 22, Fax 01 42 85 23 13 – 🛗 kitchenette 🖵 ✆. AE ◑ GB JCB. ⚓   E 14
🖵 7 – **24 rm** 90/121.

🏨 **Amiral Duperré** Ⓜ without rest, 32 r. Duperré (9th) ℰ 01 42 81 55 33, *h2756@ accor-hotels.com*, Fax 01 44 63 04 73 – 🛗, ↳⟵ rm, 🖵 ✆. AE ◑ GB JCB   D 13
🖵 8 – **52 rm** 101,62/131,11.

🏨 **Relais du Pré** without rest, 16 r. P. Sémard (9th) ℰ 01 42 85 19 59, Fax 01 42 85 70 59 – 🛗 🖵 ✆. AE ◑ GB   E 15
🖵 9 – **34 rm** 78/95.

🏨 **Ibis Gare de l'Est** Ⓜ, 197 r. Lafayette (10th) ℰ 01 44 65 70 00, Fax 01 44 65 70 07 – 🛗, ↳⟵ rm, ▤ rm, 🖵 ✆ & 🛋. AE ◑ GB. ⚓ rest   E 17
Meals 14,78 ♈ – 🖵 6 – **165 rm** 69.

🏨 **Aulivia Opéra** without rest, 4 r. Petites Écuries (10th) ℰ 01 45 23 88 88, *hotel.aulivia@ astotel.com*, Fax 01 45 23 88 89 – 🛗 ▤ 🖵 ✆. AE ◑ GB JCB. ⚓   F 15
🖵 10 – **31 rm** 106/151.

✗✗✗✗ **Les Muses** - Hôtel Scribe, 1 r. Scribe (9th) ℰ 01 44 71 24 26, Fax 01 44 71 24 64 – ▤
❀❀ AE ◑ GB JCB   F 12
closed August, Saturday and Sunday – **Meals** 44 (lunch), 60/95 and a la carte 55/65 ♈
Spec. Pinces de tourteau décortiquées, bavaroise d'avocat au caviar d'Aquitaine. Gibier (October-December). Feuilleté aux amandes à la crème praliné.

XXX **Table d'Anvers,** 2 pl. Anvers (9th) *℘* 01 48 78 35 21, *conticini@ latabledanvers.fr,*
Fax 01 45 26 66 67 – ▤. 𝔸𝔼 ᴳᴮ ᴶᶜᴮ   D 14
closed Saturday lunch and Sunday – **Meals** 41 (lunch)/53 (din. except Friday-Saturday)and
a la carte 90/110 ♀.

XXX **Charlot "Roi des Coquillages",** 12 pl. Clichy (9th) *℘* 01 53 20 48 00, *de.charlot
@blanc.net, Fax 01 53 20 48 09* – ▤. 𝔸𝔼 ⓞ ᴳᴮ   D 12
Meals - Seafood - 27,90 (lunch)and a la carte 37/63 ♀.

XX **Au Chateaubriant,** 23 r. Chabrol (10th) *℘* 01 48 24 58 94, *Fax 01 42 47 09 75*, Collection of paintings – ▤. 𝔸𝔼 ᴳᴮ ᴶᶜᴮ   E 15
closed August, Sunday and Monday – **Meals** - Italian rest. - 26,03 ♀.

XX **16 Haussmann** - Hôtel Ambassador, 16 bd Haussmann (9th) *℘* 01 44 83 40 40,
Fax 01 42 46 19 84 – ▤. 𝔸𝔼 ⓞ ᴳᴮ
closed Saturday lunch and Sunday – **Meals** 36,59 ♀.

XX **Au Petit Riche,** 25 r. Le Peletier (9th) *℘* 01 47 70 68 68, *Fax 01 48 24 10 79*, bistro,
« Late 19C decor » – ▤. 𝔸𝔼 ⓞ ᴳᴮ ᴶᶜᴮ   F 13
closed Sunday – **Meals** 25,15 (lunch)/27,45 and a la carte 30/48 ♀.

XX **Bistrot Papillon,** 6 r. Papillon (9th) *℘* 01 47 70 90 03, *Fax 01 48 24 05 59* – ▤. 𝔸𝔼 ⓞ
ᴳᴮ ᴶᶜᴮ   E 15
*closed 3 to 25 August, 4 to 13 May, Saturday except dinner from October to April and
Sunday from May to September* – **Meals** 27 and a la carte 35/47 ♀.

XX **Julien,** 16 r. Fg St-Denis (10th) *℘* 01 47 70 12 06, *Fax 01 42 47 00 65,* « Belle Epoque
brasserie » – ▤. 𝔸𝔼 ⓞ ᴳᴮ   F 15
Meals 21,50 b.i. (lunch)/30,50 b.i. and a la carte 28/43 ♀.

XX **Grand Café** (24 hr service), 4 bd Capucines (9th) *℘* 01 43 12 19 00, *Fax 01 43 12 19 09,*
brasserie, « Belle Epoque decor » – ▤. 𝔸𝔼 ⓞ ᴳᴮ   F 13
Meals 27,90 and a la carte 40/55 ♀.

XX **Quercy,** 36 r. Condorcet (9th) *℘* 01 48 78 30 61, *Fax 01 48 78 16 29* – 𝔸𝔼 ⓞ ᴳᴮ ᴶᶜᴮ
closed August, Sunday and Bank Holidays – **Meals** 23,20 and a la carte 30/44.

XX **Grange Batelière,** 16 r. Grange Batelière (9th) *℘* 01 47 70 85 15, *Fax 01 47 70 85 15*
– ▤. 𝔸𝔼 ᴳᴮ   G 10
closed 5 to 19 August, Saturday lunch and Sunday – **Meals** 26,53/30,34 ♀.

XX **Bubbles,** 6 r. Édouard VII (9th) *℘* 01 47 42 77 95, *Fax 01 47 42 31 32,* 斎 – ▤. 𝔸𝔼 ⓞ
ᴳᴮ. ✻   F 12
closed Saturday lunch, Monday dinner and Sunday – **Meals** 25,14 (lunch)/38,11 and a la
carte 43/50 ♀.

XX **Brasserie Flo,** 7 cour Petites-Écuries (10th) *℘* 01 47 70 13 59, *Fax 01 42 47 00 80,*
« 1900 decor » – ▤. 𝔸𝔼 ⓞ ᴳᴮ ᴶᶜᴮ   H 15
Meals 29 b.i. (lunch)/30,50 b.i. ♀.

XX **Terminus Nord,** 23 r. Dunkerque (10th) *℘* 01 42 85 05 15, *Fax 01 40 16 13 98*, brasserie – ▤. 𝔸𝔼 ⓞ ᴳᴮ   E 16
Meals 30,50 b.i. and a la carte 28/50.

XX **Brasserie Flo,** Printemps department store (6th floor), 64 bd Haussmann (9th)
℘ 01 42 82 58 81, *Fax 01 42 82 51 88* – ▤. 𝔸𝔼 ⓞ ᴳᴮ   F 12
closed Sunday and Bank Holidays – **Meals** (lunch only) 21,65 b.i./36,13 b.i. and a la carte
28/43.

XX **Paprika,** 28 av. Trudaine (9th) *℘* 01 44 63 02 91, *Fax 01 44 63 09 62* – 𝔸𝔼 ᴳᴮ ᴶᶜᴮ
closed 1 to 20 August – **Meals** - Hungarian rest. - 13 (lunch), 19,80/38 ♀.

XX **Wally Le Saharien,** 36 r. Rodier (9th) *℘* 01 42 85 51 90, *Fax 01 45 86 08 35* – ▤. ᴳᴮ.
✻   E 14
closed Monday lunch and Sunday – **Meals** - North African rest. - 40,39 and a la carte 35/51.

X **Cotriade,** 62 r. Fg Montmartre (9th) *℘* 01 42 80 39 92, *Fax 01 42 80 53 38* – 𝔸𝔼 ⓞ
ᴳᴮ   E 14
closed 1 to 18 August, Saturday lunch and Sunday – **Meals** 20 (lunch)/26 ♀.

X **Petite Sirène de Copenhague,** 47 r. N.-D. de Lorette (9th) *℘* 01 45 26 66 66 – ᴳᴮ.
✻   E 13
closed 29 July-20 August, 3 to 10 February, Sunday and Monday – **Meals** - Danish rest.
- (booking essential) 22 (lunch)/27 and a la carte 37/57.

X **L'Oenothèque,** 20 r. St-Lazare (9th) *℘* 01 48 78 08 76, *loenotheque@ free.fr,*
Fax 01 40 16 10 27 – ▤. 𝔸𝔼 ⓞ ᴳᴮ ᴶᶜᴮ   E 13
closed 10 August-1 September, Saturday and Sunday – **Meals** 27,50 and a la carte 32/57.

X **I Golosi,** 6 r. Grange Batelière (9th) *℘* 01 48 24 18 63, *i.golosi@ wanadoo.fr,*
Fax 01 45 23 18 96, « Venetian decor » – ▤. ᴳᴮ   F 14
closed August, Saturday dinner and Sunday – **Meals** - Italian rest - a la carte 28/42 ♀.

X **Pré Cadet,** 10 r. Saulnier (9th) ℰ 01 48 24 99 64, Fax 01 47 70 55 96 – 🖹. ⒶⒺ ⓪ ⒼⒷ
🏵️   F 14
closed 1 to 8 May, 4 to 24 August, Christmas-New Year, Saturday lunch and Sunday – **Meals**
(booking essential) 25.

X **Bistro de Gala,** 45 r. Fg Montmartre (9th) ℰ 01 40 22 90 50, Fax 01 40 22 98 30 – 🖹
ⒶⒺ ⓪ ⒼⒷ   F 14
closed Saturday lunch and Sunday lunch – **Meals** 29/34.

X **Bistro des Deux Théâtres,** 18 r. Blanche (9th) ℰ 01 45 26 41 43, Fax 01 48 74 08 92
– 🖹. ⒶⒺ ⒼⒷ   E 12
Meals 28,81.

X **Aux Deux Canards,** 8 r. Fg Poissonnière (10th) ℰ 01 47 70 03 23, Fax 01 47 70 18 85
– 🖹. ⒶⒺ ⓪ ⒼⒷ   F 15
closed 29 July-25 August, 1 to 6 January, Sunday, lunch Saturday and Monday – **Meals**
a la carte 28/30.

X **Chez Catherine,** 65 r. Provence (9th) ℰ 01 45 26 72 88, Fax 01 45 80 96 88, bistro
– ⓪ ⒼⒷ   F 13
closed August, 1 to 5 January, Monday dinner, Saturday and Sunday – **Meals** a la carte
44/61.

X **Petit Batailley,** 26 r. Bergère (9th) ℰ 01 47 70 85 81, fantaisie@net.up.com – ⒶⒺ ⒼⒷ
closed 15 August-1 September, 20 to 27 December, Saturday lunch and Sunday – **Meals**
24,39 and a la carte 39/47.   F 14

X **Relais Beaujolais,** 3 r. Milton (9th) ℰ 01 48 78 77 91, bistro – ⒼⒷ   E 14
closed August, Saturday, Sunday and Bank Holidays – **Meals** a la carte 25/35 ॐ.

X **Chez Michel,** 10 r. Belzunce (10th) ℰ 01 44 53 06 20, Fax 01 44 53 61 31 – ⒼⒷ
closed August, Sunday and Monday – **Meals** 18,29 (lunch)/29,73 Ⓨ.   F 15

X **L'Alsaco Winstub,** 10 r. Condorcet (9th) ℰ 01 45 26 44 31, Fax 01 42 85 11 05 – ⒶⒺ
ⒼⒷ   E 15
closed 14 July-early September, Saturday lunch, Monday lunch and Sunday – **Meals** 20/30
b.i. and a la carte 28/45 Ⓨ.

Bastille, Gare de Lyon, Place d'Italie, Bois de Vincennes.

12th and 13th arrondissements.
12th: ✉ 75012
13th: ✉ 75013

🏨🏨🏨 **Sofitel Paris Bercy** Ⓜ, 1 r. Libourne (12th) ℰ 01 44 67 34 00, h2192@accor-hote
ls.com, Fax 01 44 67 34 01, 🍴, Ⓕ🔸 – 🛗, 🌬️ rm, 🖹 📺 📶 ♿ – 🔏 250. ⒶⒺ ⓪
ⒼⒷ ⒿⒸⒷ   NP 20
Café Ké ℰ 01 44 67 34 71 Meals 28Ⓨ – 🖵 21 – **376 rm** 345/500, 10 suites, 10 studios.

🏨🏨 **Novotel Gare de Lyon** Ⓜ, 2 r. Hector Malot (12th) ℰ 01 44 67 60 00, h1735@a
cor-hotels.com, Fax 01 44 67 60 60, 🍴, 🔲 – 🛗, 🌬️ rm, 🖹 📺 📶 ♿ ⟷ – 🔏 75. Ⓐ
⓪ ⒼⒷ ⒿⒸⒷ   L 18
Meals 15,50 Ⓨ – 🖵 12,96 – **253 rm** 175/230.

🏨🏨 **Holiday Inn Bastille** Ⓜ without rest, 11 r. Lyon (12th) ℰ 01 53 02 20 00, resa.hi
n@guichard.fr, Fax 01 53 02 20 01 – 🛗, 🌬️ rm, 🖹 📺 📶 ♿ – 🔏 75. ⒶⒺ ⓪ ⒼⒷ ⒿⒸ
🖵 14 – **125 rm** 152.

🏨🏨 **Novotel Bercy** Ⓜ, 86 r. Bercy (12th) ℰ 01 43 42 30 00, h0935@accor-hotels.com
Fax 01 43 45 30 60, 🍴 – 🛗, 🌬️ rm, 🖹 📺 📶 ♿ – 🔏 80. ⒶⒺ ⓪ ⒼⒷ   M 19
Meals a la carte approx. 27 Ⓨ – 🖵 12,96 – **129 rm** 146/222.

🏨🏨 **Holiday Inn Bibliothèque de France** Ⓜ, 21 r. Tolbiac (13th) ℰ 01 45 84 61 61,
tolbiac@club-internet.com, Fax 01 45 84 43 38 – 🛗, 🌬️ rm, 🖹 rm, 📺 📶 ♿ – 🔏 25
ⒶⒺ ⓪ ⒼⒷ ⒿⒸⒷ. 🍴 rest   P 19
Meals (dinner only) a la carte 32/44 – 🖵 12 – **69 rm** 185/212.

🏨🏨 **Mercure Pont de Bercy** Ⓜ without rest, 6 bd Vincent Auriol (13th)
ℰ 01 45 82 48 00, h0934@accor-hotels.com, Fax 01 45 82 19 16 – 🛗 🖹 📺 📶 – 🔏 35
ⒶⒺ ⓪ ⒼⒷ ⒿⒸⒷ   M 18
🖵 13 – **89 rm** 136/144.

🏨🏨 **Mercure Place d'Italie** M without rest, 25 bd Blanqui (13th) ✆ 01 45 80 82 23, H1191@accor-hotels.com, Fax 01 45 81 45 84 – |$|, ✻ rm, 🔲 📺 ✆ 🔥 – 🔏 20. 🆎 ⑩
🔤 🔤
 ☎ 11 – **50 rm** 183/201. P 15

🏨🏨 **Mercure Gare de Lyon** M without rest, 2 pl. Louis Armand (12th) ✆ 01 43 44 84 84, H2217@accor-hotels.com, Fax 01 43 47 41 94 – |$|, ✻ rm, 🔲 📺 ✆ 🔥 – 🔏 15 - 90.
🆎 ⑩ 🔤 🔤
 ☎ 13 – **315 rm** 146/154. L 18

🏨 **Pavillon Bastille** without rest, 65 r. Lyon (12th) ✆ 01 43 43 65 65, hotel-pavillon@a kamail.com, Fax 01 43 43 96 52, « Elegant contemporary decor » – |$|, ✻ rm, 📺 ✆. 🆎
⑩ 🔤 🔤
 ☎ 12 – **25 rm** 130. K 18

🏨 **Paris Bastille** M without rest, 67 r. Lyon (12th) ✆ 01 40 01 07 17, infos@hotelpar isbastille.com, Fax 01 40 01 07 27 – |$| 🔲 📺 ✆ – 🔏 25. 🆎 ⑩ 🔤
 ☎ 12 – **37 rm** 134/199. K 18

🏨 **Manufacture** M without rest, 8 r. Philippe de Champagne (13th) ✆ 01 45 35 45 25, lamanufacturehot@aol.com, Fax 01 45 35 45 40 – |$| 🔲 📺 ✆. 🆎 ⑩ 🔤 🔤 N 16
 ☎ 7 – **57 rm** 119/128.

🏨 **Ibis Gare de Lyon Diderot** M without rest, 31 bis bd Diderot (12th)
✆ 01 43 46 12 72, h32110@accor-hotels.com, Fax 01 43 41 68 01 – |$|, ✻ rm, 🔲 📺
✆ 🔥 – 🔏 25 🆎 ⑩ 🔤
 ☎ 6 – **89 rm** 87. L 18

🏨 **Bercy Gare de Lyon** M without rest, 209 r. Charenton (12th) ✆ 01 43 40 80 30, bercy@hotelsparis.fr, Fax 01 43 40 81 30 – |$| 📺 ✆ 🔥 – 🔏 20. 🆎 ⑩ 🔤 🔤 ✻
 ☎ 10 – **48 rm** 137/168.

🏨 **Lux Hôtel Picpus** without rest, 74 bd Picpus (12th) ✆ 01 43 43 08 46, lux-hotel@w anadoo.fr, Fax 01 43 43 05 22 – |$| 📺. 🔤 L 22
 ☎ 5,50 – **38 rm** 43/60.

🏨 **Ibis Gare de Lyon** M without rest, 43 av. Ledru-Rollin (12th) ✆ 01 53 02 30 30, H1937@accor-hotels.com, Fax 01 53 02 30 31 – |$|, ✻ rm, 🔲 📺 ✆ 🔥 ⟵ – 🔏 25
 ☎ 6 – **119 rm** 84.

🏨 **Ibis Place d'Italie** M without rest, 25 av. Stephen Pichon (13th) ✆ 01 44 24 94 85, Fax 01 44 24 20 70 – |$|, ✻ rm, 📺 ✆ 🔥 ⟵. 🆎 ⑩ 🔤 N 16
 ☎ 6 – **58 rm** 75.

🏨 **Agate** without rest, 8 cours Vincennes (12th) ✆ 01 43 45 13 53, agate-hotel@wanad oo.fr, Fax 01 43 42 09 39 – |$| 📺. 🆎 🔤. ✻ L 22
 ☎ 5,35 – **49 rm** 52/69.

🏨 **Ibis Italie Tolbiac** M without rest, 177 r. Tolbiac (13th) ✆ 01 45 80 16 60, h0923@a ccor-hotels.com, Fax 01 45 80 95 80 – |$|, ✻ rm, 📺 ✆ 🔥. 🆎 ⑩ 🔤 P 15
 ☎ 6 – **60 rm** 75.

🏨 **Touring Hôtel Magendie** M without rest, 6 r. Corvisart (13th) ✆ 01 43 36 13 61, magendie@vvf-vacances.fr, Fax 01 43 36 47 48 – |$| 📺 🔥 – 🔏 30. 🔤 N 14
 ☎ 5,34 – **112 rm** 56/65.

🏨 **Nouvel H.** without rest, 24 av. Bel Air (12th) ✆ 01 43 43 01 81, nouvelhotel@wanad oo.fr, Fax 01 43 44 64 13 – 📺 ✆. 🆎 ⑩ 🔤 L 21
 ☎ 7 – **28 rm** 58/91.

XXX ☼ **Au Pressoir** (Seguin), 257 av. Daumesnil (12th) ✆ 01 43 44 38 21, Fax 01 43 43 81 77
 – 🔲. 🆎 🔤 🔤 M 22
 closed August, Saturday and Sunday – **Meals** 65,55 and a la carte 66/96 ♀
 Spec. Millefeuille de champignons aux truffes (winter). Fricassée de homard aux girolles.
 Lièvre à la royale (October-November).

XXX **Train Bleu**, Gare de Lyon (12th) ✆ 01 43 43 09 06, isabell.car@compass-group.fr, Fax 01 43 43 97 96, brasserie, « Murals depicting the journey from Paris to the Mediterranean » – 🆎 ⑩ 🔤 🔤 L 18
 Meals (1st floor) 40 and a la carte 45/60 ♀.

XXX **L'Oulette**, 15 pl. Lachambeaudie (12th) ✆ 01 40 02 02 12, info@l-oulette.com, Fax 01 40 02 04 77, � – 🆎 ⑩ 🔤 🔤 N 20
 closed Saturday and Sunday – **Meals** - South-West of France cuisine - 27 (lunch)/44 b.i. and a la carte 45/54 ♀.

XX **Au Trou Gascon**, 40 r. Taine (12th) ✆ 01 43 44 34 26, Fax 01 43 07 80 55 – 🔲. 🆎
⑩ 🔤 🔤 M 21
 closed August, 29 December-6 January, Saturday lunch and Sunday – **Meals** 36 (lunch)and a la carte 50/65.

XX **Gourmandise**, 271 av. Daumesnil (12th) ✆ 01 43 43 94 41, Fax 01 43 45 59 78 – 🔲.
🆎 🔤 🔤 M 22
 closed August, Sunday dinner and Monday – **Meals** 28 and a la carte 39/61.

XX **Petit Marguery**, 9 bd Port-Royal (13th) ✆ 01 43 31 58 59, bistro – AE ① GB JCB
✗
M 15
closed August, 23 December-3 January, Sunday and Monday – **Meals** 25,15 (lunch)/
33,54.

XX **Traversière**, 40 r. Traversière (12th) ✆ 01 43 44 02 10, *Fax 01 43 44 64 20* – AE ①
GB JCB
K 18
closed 29 July-25 August, 25 December-1 January, Sunday dinner and Monday – **Meals**
20 (lunch), 27/37,50 and a la carte 40/45.

XX **Les Marronniers**, 53 bis bd Arago (13th) ✆ 01 47 07 58 57, *Fax 01 47 07 46 09* – ▤.
AE GB
N 14
closed August, Saturday lunch and Sunday dinner – **Meals** 22,87/28,20 and a la carte 30/
38 ♀.

XX **Sologne**, 164 av. Daumesnil (12th) ✆ 01 43 07 68 97, *Fax 01 43 44 66 23* – ▤. AE GB
closed Saturday lunch and Sunday – **Meals** 28,75 ♀.

XX **Janissaire**, 22 allée Vivaldi (12th) ✆ 01 43 40 37 37, *Fax 01 43 40 38 39*, 斎 – AE ①
GB. ✗
M 20
closed Saturday lunch and Sunday – **Meals** Turkish rest. 10,52 (lunch)/22,10 and a la carte
25/34 ♣.

XX **Frégate**, 30 av. Ledru-Rollin (12th) ✆ 01 43 43 90 32 – ▤. AE GB
L 18
closed 3 to 26 August, Saturday and Sunday – **Meals** - Seafood - 25/30 ♀.

X **L'Avant Goût**, 26 r. Bobillot (13th) ✆ 01 53 80 24 00, *Fax 01 53 80 00 77*, bistro – ▤.
GB. ✗
P 15
closed 1 to 7 May, 7 to 27 August, 1 to 7 January, Sunday and Monday – **Meals** (booking
essential) 26/40,40 ♀.

X **Jean-Pierre Frelet**, 25 r. Montgallet (12th) ✆ 01 43 43 76 65, *frelet@infonie.fr* – ▤
GB
L 20
closed August, February Holidays, Saturday lunch and Sunday – **Meals** 24 (dinner)and a
la carte 26/40 ♀.

X **Pataquès**, 40 bd Bercy (12th) ✆ 01 43 07 37 75, *Fax 01 43 07 36 64* – AE ①
GB
M 19
closed Sunday – **Meals** 26 ♀.

X **Bistrot de la Porte Dorée**, 5 bd Soult (12th) ✆ 01 43 43 80 07, *Fax 01 43 43 80 07*
– ▤. GB
N 22
Meals 31 b.i..

X **Quincy**, 28 av. Ledru-Rollin (12th) ✆ 01 46 28 46 76, *Fax 01 46 28 46 76*, bistro
– ▤
L 17
closed 10 August-10 September, Saturday, Sunday and Monday – **Meals** a la carte 40/69.

X **Anacréon**, 53 bd St-Marcel (13th) ✆ 01 43 31 71 18, *Fax 01 43 31 94 94* – ▤. AE ①
GB JCB
M 16
closed 4 to 13 May, August, Wednesday lunch, Sunday and Monday – **Meals** 19 (lunch),
30.

X **Chez Jacky**, 109 r. du Dessous-des-Berges (13th) ✆ 01 45 83 71 55,
Fax 01 45 86 57 73 – ▤. GB
P 19
closed 27 July-26 August, 21 to 28 December, Saturday and Sunday – **Meals** 30 and
la carte 43/69.

X **Potinière du Lac**, 4 pl. E. Renard (12th) ✆ 01 43 43 39 98, *Fax 01 43 43 32 43* -
GB
N 23
closed Monday, dinner Sunday and Tuesday – **Meals** - Seafood - 22/33 ♀.

X **Biche au Bois**, 45 av. Ledru-Rollin (12th) ✆ 01 43 43 34 38 – AE ① GB
K 18
closed 20 July-20 August, Saturday and Sunday – **Meals** 20,20 and a la carte
25/30 ♀.

X **Sukhothaï**, 12 r. Père Guérin (13th) ✆ 01 45 81 55 88 – GB
P 19
closed 1 to 15 August and Sunday – **Meals** Chinese and Thaï rest. 8,84 (lunch), 14,48/17,5
and a la carte 18/27 ♣.

X **Temps des Cerises**, 216 r. Fg St-Antoine (12th) ✆ 01 43 67 52 08, *resto.tdc@free.fr*
Fax 01 43 67 60 91 – ▤. AE ① GB JCB
K 20
closed 5 to 25 August, 22 to 31 December and Monday – **Meals** 16,77/38,11 ♀.

X **L'Auberge Aveyronnaise**, 40 r. Lamé (12th) ✆ 01 43 40 12 24, *Fax 01 43 40 12 15*
– ▤. AE GB
N 20
closed 14 July-15 August, Sunday dinner and Monday – **Meals** 19,82/21,34 ♀.

X **Auberge Etchegorry**, 41 r. Croulebarbe (13th) ✆ 01 44 08 83 51 – AE ①
GB JCB
N 16
closed 8 to 24 August, Sunday and Monday – **Meals** - basque cooking - 24/35 and a la
carte 31/46 ♀.

Vaugirard,
Gare Montparnasse, Grenelle,
Denfert-Rochereau.

14th and 15th arrondissements.
14th: ✉ 75014
15th: ✉ 75015

🏨🏨🏨 **Méridien Montparnasse** Ⓜ, 19 r. Cdt Mouchotte (14th) ✆ 01 44 36 44 36, *merid ien.montparnasse@lemeridien-hotels.com*, Fax 01 44 36 49 00, ≼, � – |🛄|, ✙ rm, 🗏 📺 ✅ 🔥 – 🔬 25 - 500. 🆎 ⓞ 🕮 🇯🇨🇧 ❄ rest .... M 11
see *Montparnasse 25* below - *Justine* ✆ 01 44 36 44 00 Meals 32,50 ₤ – ⨅ 24,50 –
916 rm 335/380, 37 suites.

🏨🏨🏨 **Sofitel Porte de Sèvres** Ⓜ, 8 r. L. Armand (15th) ✆ 01 40 60 30 30, *h0572@ac cor-hotels.com*, Fax 01 45 57 04 22, ≼, 𝕝𝕤, 🔲 – |🛄|, ✙ rm, 🗏 📺 ✅ 🔥 ⇦ – 🔬 450.
🆎 ⓞ 🕮 🇯🇨🇧 .... N 5
see *Relais de Sèvres* below - *Brasserie* ✆ 01 40 60 33 77 Meals 22,50, ₤ – ⨅ 20 –
579 rm 230/380, 15 suites.

🏨🏨 **Novotel Porte d'Orléans** Ⓜ, 15-19 bd R. Rolland (14th) ✆ 01 41 17 26 00, *H1834@a ccor-hotels.com*, Fax 01 41 17 26 26 – |🛄|, ✙ rm, 🗏 📺 ✅ 🔥 ⇦ – 🔬 100. 🆎 ⓞ 🕮
🇯🇨🇧 .... S 12
Meals 21,50 ₤ – ⨅ 13 – **150 rm** 190/320.

🏨🏨 **Novotel Vaugirard** Ⓜ, 253 r. Vaugirard (15th) ✆ 01 40 45 10 00, *h1978@accor-h otels.com*, Fax 01 40 45 10 10, 🌫, 𝕝𝕤 – |🛄|, ✙ rm, 🗏 📺 ✅ 🔥 ⇦ – 🔬 25 - 300.
🆎 ⓞ 🕮 .... M 9
Transatlantique : Meals à la carte approx 26 – ⨅ 12,96 – **189 rm** 180/228.

🏨🏨 **Mercure Montparnasse** Ⓜ, 20 r. Gaîté (14th) ✆ 01 43 35 28 28, *h0905@accor-h otels.com*, Fax 01 43 35 78 00 – |🛄|, ✙ rm, 🗏 📺 ✅ 🔥 ⇦. 🆎 ⓞ 🕮 🇯🇨🇧 M 11
Bistrot de la Gaîté ✆ 01 43 22 86 46 *(closed Sunday lunch)* Meals 23 ₤ – ⨅ 13,42 –
180 rm 225, 5 suites.

🏨🏨 **L'Aiglon** without rest, 232 bd Raspail (14th) ✆ 01 43 20 82 42, *hotelaiglon@wanadoo.fr*,
Fax 01 43 20 98 72 – |🛄| 🗏 📺 ✅. 🆎 ⓞ 🕮 🇯🇨🇧 .... M 12
⨅ 6,50 – **34 rm** 104/138, 4 suites.

🏨🏨 **Mercure Porte de Versailles** Ⓜ without rest, 69 bd Victor (15th) ✆ 01 44 19 03 03,
h1131@accor-hotels.com, Fax 01 48 28 22 11 – |🛄|, ✙ rm, 🗏 📺 ✅ ⇦ – 🔬 50 - 250.
🆎 ⓞ 🕮 🇯🇨🇧 .... N 7
⨅ 14 – **91 rm** 145/259.

🏨🏨 **Mercure Tour Eiffel** Ⓜ without rest, 64 bd Grenelle (15th) ✆ 01 45 78 90 90, *hote l@mercuretoureiffel.com*, Fax 01 45 78 95 55, 𝕝𝕤 – |🛄|, ✙ rm, 🗏 📺 ✅ 🔥 ⇦ – 🔬 25
- 40. 🆎 ⓞ 🕮 🇯🇨🇧 .... K 7
⨅ 15 – **76 rm** 230/250.

🏨🏨 **Holiday Inn Paris Montparnasse** without rest, 10 r. Gager Gabillot (15th)
✆ 01 44 19 29 29, *reservations@holidayinn-paris.com*, Fax 01 44 19 29 39 – |🛄| 🗏 📺 ✅
🔥 ⇦ – 🔬 30. 🆎 ⓞ 🕮 🇯🇨🇧 .... M 9
⨅ 13 – **60 rm** 215/245.

🏨🏨 **Raspail Montparnasse** without rest, 203 bd Raspail (14th) ✆ 01 43 20 62 86, *rasp ailm@aol.com*, Fax 01 43 20 50 79 – |🛄| 🗏 📺 ✅. 🆎 ⓞ 🕮 🇯🇨🇧 ❄
⨅ 9 – **38 rm** 96/199. .... M 12

🏨🏨 **Lenox Montparnasse** without rest, 15 r. Delambre (14th) ✆ 01 43 35 34 50,
Fax 01 43 20 46 64 – |🛄| 📺 ✅. 🆎 🕮 🇯🇨🇧 ❄ .... M 12
⨅ 9 – **52 rm** 102/122.

🏨🏨 **Delambre** Ⓜ without rest, 35 r. Delambre (14th) ✆ 01 43 20 66 31, Fax 01 45 38 91 76
– |🛄| 📺 ✅ 🔥. 🕮 ❄ .... M 12
⨅ 8 – **30 rm** 80/90.

🏨🏨 **Mercure Paris XV** Ⓜ without rest, 6 r. St-Lambert (15th) ✆ 01 45 58 61 00, *h0903@a ccor-hotels.com*, Fax 01 45 54 10 43 – |🛄|, ✙ rm, 🗏 📺 ✅ 🔥 ⇦ – 🔬 30. 🆎 ⓞ 🕮
⨅ 11 – **56 rm** 131/137.

Apollinaire without rest, 39 r. Delambre (14th) ℰ 01 43 35 18 40, *infos@hotel.apoll inaire.com*, Fax 01 43 35 30 71 – 🛗 📺 📺 🖫. ᴁ Ⓞ ᴳᴮ M 12
⛟ 7 – **36 rm** 100/122.

Relais Mercure Raspail Montparnasse without rest, 207 bd Raspail (14th) ℰ 01 43 20 62 94, *h0351@accor-hotels.com*, Fax 01 43 27 39 69 – 🛗, ✦ rm, 🖃 📺 🖫 ♿. ᴁ Ⓞ ᴳᴮ M 12
⛟ 12 – **63 rm** 126/153.

Nouvel Orléans M̄ without rest, 25 av. Gén. Leclerc (14th) ℰ 01 43 27 80 20, *nouv elorleans@aol.com*, Fax 01 43 35 36 57 – 🛗 🖃. ᴁ Ⓞ ᴳᴮ ᴶᶜᴮ. ✼ P 12
⛟ 7 – **46 rm** 107/144.

Daguerre M̄ without rest, 94 r. Daguerre (14th) ℰ 01 43 22 43 54, *hotel.daguerre.p aris14@gofornet.com*, Fax 01 43 20 66 84 – 🛗 📺 🖫 ♿. ᴁ Ⓞ ᴳᴮ ᴶᶜᴮ. ✼ N 11
⛟ 8 – **30 rm** 69/104.

Lilas Blanc without rest, 5 r. Avre (15th) ℰ 01 45 75 30 07, *hotellilasblanc@minitel.net*, Fax 01 45 78 66 65 – 🛗 📺. ᴁ Ⓞ ᴳᴮ K 8
⛟ 6 – **32 rm** 61/73.

Istria without rest, 29 r. Campagne Première (14th) ℰ 01 43 20 91 82, *hotelistria@w anadoo.fr*, Fax 01 43 22 48 45 – 🛗 📺 🖫. ᴁ Ⓞ ᴳᴮ ᴶᶜᴮ. ✼ M 12
⛟ 8 – **26 rm** 90/100.

Apollon Montparnasse without rest, 91 r. Ouest (14th) ℰ 01 43 95 62 00, *apollo nm@club-internet.fr*, Fax 01 43 95 62 10 – 🛗 📺 🖫. ᴁ Ⓞ ᴳᴮ ᴶᶜᴮ. N 10-11
⛟ 6 – **33 rm** 65/78.

Ibis Brancion M̄ without rest, 105 r. Brancion (15th) ℰ 01 56 56 62 30 Fax 01 56 56 62 31 – 🛗, ✦ rm, 🖃 📺 🖫 ♿. ᴁ Ⓞ ᴳᴮ. ✼ P 8-9
⛟ 6 – **71 rm** 79.

Carladez Cambronne without rest, 3 pl. Gén. Beuret (15th) ℰ 01 47 34 07 12, *car adez@club-internet.fr*, Fax 01 40 65 95 68 – 🛗 📺 🖫. ᴁ Ⓞ ᴳᴮ ᴶᶜᴮ M 9
⛟ 7 – **28 rm** 71/76.

Val Girard without rest, 14 r. Pétel (15th) ℰ 01 48 28 53 96, *valgirar@club-internet.fr* Fax 01 48 28 69 94 – 🛗 📺. ᴁ ᴳᴮ ᴶᶜᴮ M 8
⛟ 8 – **39 rm** 83/120.

Montparnasse 25 - Hôtel Méridien Montparnasse, 19 r. Cdt Mouchotte (14th) ℰ 01 44 36 44 25, *meridien.montparnasse@lemeridien.com*, Fax 01 44 36 49 03 – 🖃 📺 ᴁ Ⓞ ᴳᴮ ᴶᶜᴮ. ✼ M 11
closed August, Saturday, Sunday and Bank Holidays – **Meals** 42 (lunch), 60,50/85 and a la carte 60/75 ♀
Spec. Saint-Jacques poêlées aux lanières d'endives et pommes granny (October-May). Tur bot cuit sur l'arête, caramélisé au citron. Poitrine de canard sauvage au pilé de noix e noisettes (October-January)..

Relais de Sèvres - Hôtel Sofitel Porte de Sèvres, 8 r. L. Armand (15th) ℰ 01 40 60 33 66, *h0572@accor-hotels.com*, Fax 01 45 57 04 22 – 🖃 📺 ᴁ Ⓞ ᴳᴮ ᴶᶜ *closed 30 July-26 August, Saturday, Sunday and Bank Holidays* – **Meals** 61 b.i./68 and a la carte 55/75 ♀
Spec. Emietté de tourteau et crème de petits oignons nouveaux. Carré d'agneau du Querc et millefeuille de légumes confits. Petit sablé et marmelade de poire à la fève tonka..

Ciel de Paris, Maine Montparnasse Tower, at 56th floor (15th) ℰ 01 40 64 77 64, *cie -de-paris.rv@elior.com*, Fax 01 40 64 59 71, ≤ Paris – 🛗 🖃. ᴁ Ⓞ ᴳᴮ ᴶᶜᴮ. ✼ M 11
Meals 30,18 (lunch)/48,78 and a la carte 58/75.

Le Duc, 243 bd Raspail (14th) ℰ 01 43 20 96 30, Fax 01 43 20 46 73 – 🖃. ᴁ Ⓞ ᴳᴮ ᴶᶜᴮ M 12
closed 27 July-19 August, 21 December-2 January, Saturday lunch, Sunday and Monda – **Meals** - Seafood - 44 (lunch)and a la carte 55/85
Spec. Poissons crus. Escalopes de Saint-Pierre, beurre vodka. Sole meunière..

Le Dôme, 108 bd Montparnasse (14th) ℰ 01 43 35 25 81, Fax 01 42 79 01 19, brasseri – 🖃. ᴁ Ⓞ ᴳᴮ ᴶᶜᴮ LM 11
Meals - Seafood - a la carte 52/82 ♀.

Chen-Soleil d'Est, 15 r. Théâtre (15th) ℰ 01 45 79 34 34, Fax 01 45 79 07 53 – 🖃 ᴁ ᴳᴮ ᴶᶜᴮ K
closed August and Sunday – **Meals** - Chinese rest. - 40/75 and a la carte 55/75
Spec. "Promenade de caviar à Shanghai". Mijoté de chevreau au ginseng. Fondant de poir au vin de litchis..

Maison Courtine (Charles), 157 av. Maine (14th) ℰ 01 45 43 08 04, Fax 01 45 45 91 3 – 🖃. ᴁ. ᴳᴮ. ✼ N 11
closed 4 to 25 August, Saturday lunch, Monday lunch and Sunday – **Meals** 29 ♀
Spec. Andouille de Guéméné à la crème. Canette des Dombes en deux services. Tourtièr aux pommes..

XX **La Coupole**, 102 bd Montparnasse (14th) ℰ 01 43 20 14 20, Fax 01 43 35 46 14, « 1920's Parisian brasserie » – 🗏. ᴁ ⓪ ⓰ ᴊᴄʙ L 12
Meals 29 (lunch)/51 and a la carte 35/40 ♈.

XX **La Dînée**, 85 r. Leblanc (15th) ℰ 01 45 54 20 49, Fax 01 40 60 73 76 – ᴁ ⓰ ᴊᴄʙ
closed Saturday and Sunday – Meals 30 ♈.

XX **Gauloise**, 59 av. La Motte-Picquet (15 th) ℰ 01 47 34 11 64, Fax 01 40 61 09 70, 🍽
– ᴁ ⓰ ᴊᴄʙ K 8
Meals 26 and a la carte 37/54 ♨.

XX **Philippe Detourbe**, 8 r. Nicolas Charlet (15th) ℰ 01 42 19 08 59, Fax 01 45 67 09 13
– 🗏. ᴁ ⓰ ᴊᴄʙ L 10
closed Sunday, lunch Monday and Saturday – Meals 30 (lunch)/37.

XX **Caroubier**, 82 bd Lefèbvre (15th) ℰ 01 40 43 16 12 – 🗏. ⓰ N 11
⊕ closed 15 July-15 August and Monday – Meals - Morrocan rest. - 22,87 and a la carte 30/
37 ♈.

XX **Les Vendanges**, 40 r. Friant (14th) ℰ 01 45 39 59 98, Fax 01 45 39 74 13 – ᴁ ⓪
⓰ ᴊᴄʙ R 11
closed August, 21 to 29 December, Saturday and Sunday – Meals 35 ♈.

XXX **Fontanarosa**, 28 bd Garibaldi (15th) ℰ 01 45 66 97 84, Fax 01 47 83 96 30, 🍽 – 🗏.
ᴁ ⓰ ᴊᴄʙ L 9
Meals - Italian rest. - 18,29 (lunch)and a la carte 33/53 ♈.

XX **Erawan**, 76 r. Fédération (15th) ℰ 01 47 83 55 67, Fax 01 47 34 85 98 – 🗏. ᴁ ⓰.
🍱 K 8
closed August and Sunday – Meals - Thai rest. - 22,87/38,11 and a la carte 26/36.

XX **L'Épopée**, 89 av. É. Zola (15th) ℰ 01 45 77 71 37, Fax 01 45 77 71 37 – ᴁ ⓰ ᴊᴄʙ L 7
closed 28 July-28 August, 24 December-2 January, Saturday lunch and Sunday – Meals
30 ♈.

XX **L'Étape**, 89 r. Convention (15th) ℰ 01 45 54 73 49, Fax 01 45 58 20 91 – 🗏. ᴁ ⓰
closed 3 to 26 August, Saturday lunch and Sunday – Meals 20/26.

X **Troquet**, 21 r. F. Bonvin (15th) ℰ 01 45 66 89 00, Fax 01 45 66 89 83 – ⓰.
⊛ 🍱 L 9
closed August, 24 December-2 January, Sunday and Monday – Meals 22 (lunch), 28/30♈.

X **L'O à la Bouche**, 124 bd Montparnasse (14th) ℰ 01 56 54 01 55, Fax 01 43 21 07 87
– 🗏. ᴁ ⓰ M 12
closed 15 to 23 April, 5 to 26 August, 1 to 7 January, Sunday and Monday – Meals 19
(lunch)/29,90 and a la carte 40/45 ♈.

X **Bistro d'Hubert**, 41 bd Pasteur (15th) ℰ 01 47 34 15 50, message@bistrodhubert.
com, Fax 01 45 67 03 09 – ᴁ ⓰ ᴊᴄʙ L 10
closed Saturday lunch – Meals 37.

X **Stéphane Martin**, 67 r. Entrepreneurs (15th) ℰ 01 45 79 03 31, resto.stephanema
rtin@free.fr, Fax 01 45 79 44 69 – 🗏. ᴁ ⓰. 🍱 L 7
closed 4 to 26 August, Sunday and Monday – Meals 22,87 b.i. (lunch), 28,20/35,82.

X **Contre-Allée**, 83 av. Donfert-Rochereau (14th) ℰ 01 43 54 99 86, Fax 01 43 25 08 11
– ᴁ ⓰. 🍱 N 13
closed Saturday lunch – Meals 28,96/34,30.

X **Gastroquet**, 10 r. Desnouettes (15th) ℰ 01 48 28 60 91, Fax 01 45 33 23 70 –
⊛ ᴁ ⓰ N 7
closed August, Monday lunch, Saturday and Sunday – Meals 27 50and a la carte 41/50.

X **Pascal Champ**, 5 r. Mouton-Duvernet (14th) ℰ 01 45 39 39 61, Fax 01 45 39 39 61 –
🗏. ᴁ ⓰ N 12
closed August, Sunday and Monday – Meals 19 (lunch), 22/28 and a la carte 30/45 ♈.

X **St-Vincent**, 26 r. Croix-Nivert (15th) ℰ 01 47 34 14 94, Fax 01 45 66 46 58, bistro –
🗏. ᴁ ⓰ L 8
closed in August, Saturday lunch and Sunday – Meals a la carte 30/42.

X **Les P'tits Bouchons de François Clerc**, 32 bd Montparnasse (15th)
ℰ 01 45 48 52 03, Fax 01 45 48 52 17 – ᴁ ⓰ ᴊᴄʙ L 11
closed Saturday lunch and Sunday – Meals 31,25 ♈.

X **Régalade**, 49 av. J. Moulin (14th) ℰ 01 45 45 68 58, Fax 01 45 40 96 74, bistro – 🗏.
⓰ R 11
closed August, Saturday lunch, Sunday and Monday – Meals (booking essential) 30.

X **L'Os à Moelle**, 3 r. Vasco de Gama (15th) ℰ 01 45 57 27 27, Fax 01 45 57 27 27, bistro
– M 6
closed August, Sunday and Monday – Meals 27 (lunch), 32/38 ♈.

X **Bistrot du Dôme**, 1 r. Delambre (14th) ℰ 01 43 35 32 00 – 🗏. ᴁ ⓰. 🍱 M 12
closed Sunday and Monday in August – Meals - Seafood - a la carte 30/44.

X **Les Gourmands,** 101 r. Ouest (14th) ℰ 01 45 41 40 70, *Fax 01 45 41 17 66* – 🆎 🄖
closed mid July-mid August, Sunday and Monday – **Meals** 24/30.

X **A La Bonne Table,** 42 r. Friant (14th) ℰ 01 45 39 74 91, *Fax 01 45 43 66 92* – 🆎 🄖
🄐 🄶🄱
closed 14 to 28 July, 23 February-2 March, Saturday lunch and Sunday – **Meals** 22,70 an
a la carte 35/45.

X **Petit Bofinger,** 46 bd Montparnasse (15th) ℰ 01 45 48 49 16, *Fax 01 45 44 92 05*
🄪. 🆎 🄶🄱   L 1
Meals 27 b.i. (dinner) 30.

X **Sept/Quinze,** 29 av. Lowendal (15th) ℰ 01 43 06 23 06, *Fax 01 45 67 14 11* – 🄖🄱
closed 3 to 26 August and Sunday – **Meals** 21 (lunch), 23,30/29,40 and a la carte 25
35 ♈.

X **Beurre Noisette,** 68 r. Vasco de Gama (15e) ℰ 01 48 56 82 49, *Fax 01 48 56 82 4*
🄐 – 🆎 🄶🄱. ✿   N
closed 1 to 25 August, Sunday and Monday – **Meals** 27 ♈.

X **Château Poivre,** 145 r. Château (14th) ℰ 01 43 22 03 68, *chateaupoivre@noos.fr*
🆎 🄾 🄶🄱 🄹🄲🄱   N 1
closed 10 to 25 August, 22 December-3 January, Sunday and Bank Holidays – **Meals** 1
and a la carte 26/37 ♈.

X **Les Petites Sorcières,** 12 r. Liancourt (14th) ℰ 01 43 21 95 68, *Fax 01 43 21 95 6*
🄐 – 🄶🄱   N 1
closed Sunday, lunch Monday and Saturday – **Meals** a la carte 29/38.

X **du Marché,** 59 r. Dantzig (15th) ℰ 01 48 28 31 55, *restaurant.du.marche@wanadoo.f*
🄐 *Fax 01 48 28 18 31* – 🆎 🄶🄱 🄹🄲🄱   N
closed 1 to 15 August, Sunday, lunch Monday and Saturday – **Meals** 26 and a la cart
43/82.

X. **Au Soleil de Minuit,** 15 r. Desnouettes (15th) ℰ 01 48 28 15 15, *Fax 01 48 28 17 1*
🄐 – 🆎 🄶🄱
closed 28 July to 19 August, 23 to 26 December, Sunday dinner and Monday – **Meal**
Finnish rest. 20/42 and a la carte 31/46 ♈.

X **Mûrier,** 42 r. Olivier de Serres (15th) ℰ 01 45 32 81 88 – 🄶🄱. ✿   N
closed 5 to 25 August, Sunday, lunch Monday and Saturday – **Meals** 16,61 (lunch
19,05/22,71 ♈.

X **Folletterie,** 35 r. Letellier (15th) ℰ 01 45 75 55 95 – 🄶🄱 🄹🄲🄱   L
closed 28 July-19 August, Sunday and Monday – **Meals** 20 (lunch)/23 and a la carte 26/30♈.

X **Autour du Mont,** 58 r. Vasco de Gama (15th) ℰ 01 42 50 55 63, *Fax 01 42 50 55 6*
🄐 – 🆎 🄶🄱 🄹🄲🄱   N
closed August, Sunday and Monday – **Meals** a la carte 25/40 ♈.

X **Flamboyant,** 11 r. Boyer-Barret (14th) ℰ 01 45 41 00 22 – 🆎 🄶🄱   N 1
closed August, Sunday dinner, Tuesday lunch and Monday – **Meals** specialities of th
French Antilles 12 (lunch), 28 b.i./42 b.i. and a la carte 25/34 🍴.

X **Les Coteaux,** 26 bd Garibaldi (15th) ℰ 01 47 34 83 48, bistro – 🄶🄱   L
closed August, Saturday, Sunday and Monday – **Meals** 23.

X **Severo,** 8 r. Plantes (14th) ℰ 01 45 40 40 91 – 🄶🄱   N 1
🄐 *closed 10 to 31 July, Christmas Holidays, Saturday dinner, Sunday and Bank Holidays*
Meals a la carte 25/35.

Passy, Auteuil,
Bois de Boulogne,
Chaillot, Porte Maillot.

16th arrondissement.
16th: ✉ 75016 or 75116

🏨 **Raphaël,** 17 av. Kléber ✉ 75116 ℰ 01 53 64 32 00, *management@raphael-hotel.com*
Fax 01 53 64 32 01, 🌫, « Elegant period decor and panoramic terrace with < Paris
– 📳, ✲ rm, 🄪 📺 ✆ – 🄐 50. 🆎 🄾 🄶🄱 🄹🄲🄱   F
Jardins Plein Ciel ℰ 01 53 64 32 30 (7th floor)-buffet *(May-October)* **Meals** 60 (lunch)/7
♈ – **Salle à Manger** ℰ 01 53 64 32 11 *(closed August, Saturday and Sunday)* **Meal**
48 b.i.(lunch)/58 ♈ – ☒ 25 – **62 rm** 420/505, 25 suites.

Sofitel Le Parc ⚘, 55 av. R. Poincaré ✉ 75116 ✆ 01 44 05 66 66, *le-parc@comp userve.com*, Fax 01 44 05 66 00, 佘, « Fine English furniture » – 🛗, ✻ rm, 🔲 📺 🕯
🕭 – � 30 - 250. 🖭 ⑩ 🆖 🄵

                                                G 6

see **59 Poincaré** below - **Les Jardins du 59** *(May-September)* **Meals** 44,21 ♀ – ☷ 26 – **113 rm** 340/754, 3 duplex.

St-James Paris ⚘, 43 av. Bugeaud ✉ 75116 ✆ 01 44 05 81 81, *contact@saint-ja mes-paris.com*, Fax 01 44 05 81 82, 佘, « Attractive 19C mansion », 🛏, ✿ – 🛗 🔲 📺
🕯 🄿 – 🚫 25. 🖭 ⑩ 🆖 🄵

                                                F 5

Meals *(closed week-ends and Bank Holidays)* (residents only) 46 – ☷ 20 – **12 rm** 420/465, 28 suites580/730, 8 duplex.

Costes K. Ⓜ without rest, 81 av. Kléber ✉ 75116 ✆ 01 44 05 75 75, *costes.k@wa nadoo.fr*, Fax 01 44 05 74 74, « Contemporary decor », 🛏 – 🛗, ✻ rm, 🔲 📺 🕯 🕭 ☞.
🖭 ⑩ 🆖. �

                                                G 7

☷ 19 – **83 rm** 300/540.

Sofitel Baltimore, 88bis av. Kléber ✉ 75116 ✆ 01 44 34 54 54, *welcome@hotelb latimore.com*, Fax 01 44 34 54 44, 🛏 – 🛗, ✻ rm, 🔲 📺 🕯 – 🚫 50. 🖭 ⑩
🆖 🄵

                                                G 7

Table du Baltimore *(closed 27 July-26 August, Saturday, Sunday and Bank Holidays)*
Meals a la carte 36/57 – ☷ 23 – **105 rm** 425/690.

Square Ⓜ, 3 r. Boulainvilliers ✉ 75016 ✆ 01 44 14 91 90, *hotel.square@wanadoo.fr*, Fax 01 44 14 91 99, « Contemporary decor » – 🛗 🔲 📺 🕯 🕭 ☞. 🖭 ⑩ 🆖
🄵. �

                                                K 5

Meals see **Zébra Square** below – ☷ 17 – **22 rm** 250/370.

Trocadero Dokhan's without rest, 117 r. Lauriston ✉ 75116 ✆ 01 53 65 66 99, *hotel.trocadero.dokhans@wanadoo.fr*, Fax 01 53 65 66 88, « Elegant decor and fine furniture » – 🛗, ✻ rm, 🔲 📺 🕯 🖭 🖭 ⑩ 🆖 🄵. �

                                                G 6

☷ 23 – **41 rm** 480/991, 4 suites.

Villa Maillot Ⓜ without rest, 143 av. Malakoff ✉ 75116 ✆ 01 53 64 52 52, *resa@l avillamaillot.fr*, Fax 01 45 00 60 61, « Elegant contemporary decor » – 🛗, ✻ rm, 🔲 📺
🕯 🕭 – 🚫 25. 🖭 ⑩ 🆖 🄵. �

                                                F 6

☷ 21 – **39 rm** 300/335, 3 suites.

Élysées Régencia Ⓜ without rest, 41 av. Marceau ✉ 75116 ✆ 01 47 20 42 65, *info @regencia.com*, Fax 01 49 52 03 42, « Attractive decor » – 🛗, ✻ rm, 🔲 📺 🕯 – 🚫 20.
🖭 ⑩ 🆖 🄵. �

                                                G 8

☷ 18 – **43 rm** 275/335.

Libertel Auteuil Ⓜ without rest, 8 r. F. David ✉ 75016 ✆ 01 40 50 57 57, *H2777@a ccor-hotels.com*, Fax 01 40 50 57 50 – 🛗, ✻ rm, 🔲 📺 🕯 🕭 ☞ – 🚫 35. 🖭 ⑩ 🆖

                                                G 7

☷ 13 – **94 rm** 200/240.

Pergolèse Ⓜ without rest, 3 r. Pergolèse ✉ 75116 ✆ 01 53 64 04 04, *hotel@perg olese.com*, Fax 01 53 64 04 40, « Contemporary decor » – 🛗, ✻ rm, 🔲 📺 🕯. 🖭 ⑩
🆖 🄵

                                                E 6

☷ 12 – **40 rm** 195/320.

Argentine Ⓜ without rest, 1 r. Argentine ✉ 75116 ✆ 01 45 02 76 76, *H2757@ac cor-hotels.com*, Fax 01 45 02 76 00 – 🛗, ✻ rm, 📺 🕯 🕭. 🖭 ⑩ 🆖 🄵

                                                E 7

☷ 13 – **40 rm** 228/250.

Majestic without rest, 29 r. Dumont d'Urville ✉ 75116 ✆ 01 45 00 83 70, *managem ent@majestic-hotel.com*, Fax 01 45 00 29 48 – 🛗, ✻ rm, 🔲 📺 🕯. 🖭 ⑩
🆖 🄵

                                                F 7

☷ 13,75 – **27 rm** 192/409, 3 suites.

Garden Élysée Ⓜ ⚘ without rest, 12 r. St-Didier ✉ 75116 ✆ 01 47 55 01 11, *gard en.elysee@wanadoo.fr*, Fax 01 47 27 79 24 – 🛗, ✻ rm, 🔲 📺 🕯 🕭. 🖭 ⑩ 🆖 🄵.
�

                                                G 7

☷ 18,50 – **48 rm** 214/335.

Élysées Union without rest, 44 r. Hamelin ✉ 75116 ✆ 01 45 53 14 95, *unionetoil @aol.com*, Fax 01 47 55 94 79 – 🛗 kitchenette 📺 🕯 🕭. 🖭 ⑩ 🆖. �

                                                G 7

☷ 10 – **47 rm** 154/202, 12 suites.

Élysées Bassano without rest, 24 r. Bassano ✉ 75116 ✆ 01 47 20 49 03, *h2815-g m@accor-hotels.com*, Fax 01 47 23 06 72 – 🛗, ✻ rm, 🔲 📺 🕯. 🖭 ⑩ 🆖 🄵

                                                G 8

☷ 13 – **40 rm** 180/240.

Alexander without rest, 102 av. V. Hugo ✉ 75116 ✆ 01 56 90 61 00, *melia.alexand er@solmelia.com*, Fax 01 56 90 61 01 – 🛗 🔲 📺. 🖭 ⑩ 🆖 🄵. �

                                                G 6

☷ 21,50 – **61 rm** 320/442.

Frémiet without rest, 6 av. Frémiet ✉ 75016 ✆ 01 45 24 52 06, *hotel.fremiet@wa nadoo.fr*, Fax 01 53 92 06 46 – 📺 🕯. 🖭 ⑩ 🆖 🄵

                                                J 6

☷ 11,50 – **36 rm** 160/206.

Résidence Bassano Ⓜ without rest, 15 r. Bassano ⊠ 75116 ℘ 01 47 23 78 23, info@hotel-bassano.com, Fax 01 47 20 41 22 – 🛗, ⇔ rm, ▤ 📺 📞. 🕮 ⓪ GB. ⛆
G

⌑ 18 – **28 rm** 275/335, 3 suites.

Résidence Impériale without rest, 155 av. Malakoff ⊠ 75116 ℘ 01 45 00 23 45, res.imperiale@wanadoo.fr, Fax 01 45 01 88 82 – 🛗, ⇔ rm, ▤ 📺 📞 &. 🕮 ⓪ GB
E

⌑ 11 – **37 rm** 130/195.

Passy Eiffel without rest, 10 r. Passy ⊠ 75016 ℘ 01 45 25 55 66, Fax 01 42 88 89 85 – 🛗 📺 📞. 🕮 ⓪ GB JCB
J

⌑ 10 – **48 rm** 122/128.

Élysées Sablons Ⓜ without rest, 32 r. Greuze ⊠ 75116 ℘ 01 47 27 10 00, h2778-m@accor-hotels.com, Fax 01 47 27 47 10 – 🛗, ⇔ rm, 📺 📞 &. 🕮 ⓪ GB JCB
G

⌑ 13 – **41 rm** 170/180.

Chambellan Morgane without rest, 6 r. Keppler ⊠ 75116 ℘ 01 47 20 35 72, Fax 01 47 20 95 69 – 🛗 ▤ 📺 📞 – ⚉ 20. 🕮 ⓪ GB JCB. ⛆
GF

⌑ 10 – **20 rm** 156/157.

Floride Étoile without rest, 14 r. St-Didier ⊠ 75116 ℘ 01 47 27 23 36, floridetc@aol.com, Fax 01 47 27 82 87 – 🛗 ▤ 📺 📞 – ⚉ 30. 🕮 ⓪ GB JCB. ⛆
G

⌑ 11 – **63 rm** 122/192.

Hameau de Passy Ⓜ ⛱ without rest, 48 r. Passy ⊠ 75016 ℘ 01 42 88 47 55, hameau.passy@wanadoo.fr, Fax 01 42 30 83 72 – 🛗 📺. 🕮 ⓪ GB JCB
J 5-6

⌑ 4,57 – **32 rm** 89,20/101,40.

Boileau without rest, 81 r. Boileau ⊠ 75016 ℘ 01 42 88 83 74, boileau@cybercable.fr, Fax 01 45 27 62 98 – 📺 📞 – ⚉ 15. 🕮 ⓪ GB
M

⌑ 6,10 – **30 rm** 67,84/85,37.

Bois without rest, 11 r. Dôme ⊠ 75116 ℘ 01 45 00 31 96, hoteldubois@wanadoo.fr, Fax 01 45 00 90 05 – 📺. 🕮 ⓪ GB JCB
F

⌑ 10 – **41 rm** 95/125.

Queen's Hôtel without rest, 4 r. Bastien Lepage ⊠ 75016 ℘ 01 42 88 89 85, contact@queens-hotel.fr, Fax 01 40 50 67 52 – 🛗, ⇔ rm, 📺 📞. 🕮 ⓪ GB JCB
K

⌑ 6,10 – **22 rm** 68/120.

Nicolo ⛱ without rest, 3 r. Nicolo ⊠ 75116 ℘ 01 42 88 83 40, hotel.nicolo@wanadoo.fr, Fax 01 42 24 45 41 – 🛗 📺. 🕮 ⓪ GB JCB
J

⌑ 6 – **28 rm** 71/112.

Palais de Chaillot without rest, 35 av. R. Poincaré ⊠ 75116 ℘ 01 53 70 09 09, hapc@wanadoo.fr, Fax 01 53 70 09 08 – 🛗 📺 📞. 🕮 ⓪ GB JCB. ⛆
G

⌑ 8 – **28 rm** 95/130.

Gavarni without rest, 5 r. Gavarni ⊠ 75116 ℘ 01 45 24 52 82, reservation@gavarni.com, Fax 01 40 50 16 95 – 🛗 📺 📞. 🕮 ⓪ GB JCB. ⛆
J

⌑ 8,50 – **25 rm** 92/145.

Longchamp without rest, 68 r. Longchamp ⊠ 75116 ℘ 01 44 34 24 14, info@hotel-paris-hotels.com, Fax 01 44 34 24 24 – 🛗 📺 📞. 🕮 ⓪ GB
G

⌑ 10 – **23 rm** 100/159.

Faugeron, 52 r. Longchamp ⊠ 75116 ℘ 01 47 04 24 53, faugeron@wanadoo.fr, Fax 01 47 55 62 90, « Attractive decor » – ▤. 🕮 GB JCB. ⛆
G
closed August, 23 December-3 January, Saturday and Sunday – **Meals** 54 (lunch)/114 b. and a la carte 90/130

Spec. Oeufs coque à la purée de truffes. Truffes (January-March). Gibier (15 October-10 January)..

Ghislaine Arabian, 16 av. Bugeaud ⊠ 75116 ℘ 01 56 28 16 16, Fax 01 56 28 16 78 – ▤. 🕮 ⓪ GB JCB
F
closed Saturday and Sunday – **Meals** 45 and a la carte 56/91

Spec. Croquettes de crevettes grises. Filet de bœuf à la Gueuze. Parfait glacé à la chicorée.

59 Poincaré, 59 av. R. Poincaré ⊠ 75116 ℘ 01 47 27 59 59, 59poincare@leparc-paris.com, Fax 01 47 27 59 00 – ▤. 🕮 ⓪ GB JCB. ⛆
G
closed Sunday and Monday – **Meals** a la carte 54/69.

Jamin (Guichard), 32 r. Longchamp ⊠ 75116 ℘ 01 45 53 00 07, Fax 01 45 53 00 15 – ▤. 🕮 ⓪ GB
G
closed 26 July-26 August, February Holidays, Saturday and Sunday – **Meals** 48 (lunch)/80 and a la carte 90/130

Spec. Poêlée de langoustines de petite pêche (Summer). Blanc de bar en peau croustillante. Carré d'agneau rôti au thym.

XXX **Relais d'Auteuil** (Pignol), 31 bd Murat ⊠ 75016 ✆ 01 46 51 09 54, *Fax 01 40 71 05 03*
🕸🕸 – ▤, ᴁ ⓪ ᴊᴄ🅱 L 3
closed August, Monday lunch, Saturday lunch and Sunday – **Meals** 44,25 (lunch),
89,95/120,45 and a la carte 85/110
Spec. Amandine de foie gras de canard et lobe poêlé. Dos de bar à la croûte poivrée.
Madeleines au miel de bruyère, glace miel et noix..

XXX **Pergolèse** (Corre), 40 r. Pergolèse ⊠ 75116 ✆ 01 45 00 21 40, *le-pergolese@wana*
🕸 *doo.fr, Fax 01 45 00 81 31* – ▤, ᴁ ᴳᴮ ᴊᴄ🅱 F 6
closed 2 August-2 September, Saturday and Sunday – **Meals** 35,83/64,03 and a la carte
55/75
Spec. Ravioli de langoustines au beurre de foie gras. Saint-Jacques rôties en robe des
champs (November-March). Moelleux au chocolat, glace vanille.

XXX **Tsé-Yang**, 25 av. Pierre 1er de Serbie ⊠ 75116 ✆ 01 47 20 70 22, *Fax 01 49 52 03 68*,
« Tasteful decor » – ▤, ᴁ ⓪ ᴳᴮ ⬚ G 8
Meals - Chinese rest. - 40,40/43,45 and a la carte 42/59.

XXX **Pavillon Noura**, 21 av. Marceau ⊠ 75116 ✆ 01 47 20 33 33, *Fax 01 47 20 60 31* –
▤, ᴁ ⓪ ᴳᴮ. ⬚ G 8
Meals - Lebanese rest. - 27,14 (lunch), 43,91/51,33 and a la carte 35/60 ⬚.

XXX **Les Arts**, 9 bis av. Iéna ⊠ 75116 ✆ 01 40 69 27 53, *maison.des.am@sodexho.presti*
ge.fr, Fax 01 40 69 27 08, ⬚ – ▤, ᴁ ⓪ ᴳᴮ G 7
closed August, Saturday and Sunday – **Meals** 36 and a la carte 50/62.

XXX **Passiflore** (Durand), 33 r. Longchamp ⊠ 75016 ✆ 01 47 04 96 81, *Fax 01 47 04 32 27*
🕸 – ▤, ᴁ ⓪ ᴳᴮ. ⬚ G 7
closed 4 to 26 August, Saturday lunch and Sunday – **Meals** 30/38 and a la carte 45/67⬚
Spec. Foie gras de canard. Côte de bœuf de Bavière en sautoir. Tarte fine au chocolat..

XXX **L'Étoile**, 12 r. Presbourg ⊠ 75116 ✆ 01 45 00 78 70, *Fax 01 45 00 78 71* – ▤, ᴁ ᴳᴮ F 7
closed August, 23 December-2 January, lunch Saturday and Sunday – **Meals** 44,21 b.i.
(lunch) and a la carte 52/68.

XXX **Port Alma** (Canal), 10 av. New-York ⊠ 75116 ✆ 01 47 23 75 11, *Fax 01 47 20 42 92*
🕸 – ▤, ᴁ ⓪ ᴊᴄ🅱 H 8
closed August, 24 December-2 January, Sunday and Monday – **Meals** - Seafood - a la carte
46/70
Spec. Salade de homard. Pétales de Saint-Jacques marinées à l'huile d'argan (October-May).
Fricassée de sole poêlée au foie gras.

XX **Astrance** (Barbot), 4 r. Beethoven ⊠ 75016 ✆ 01 40 50 84 40, *Fax 01 40 50 11 45* –
🕸 ᴁ ⓪ ᴳᴮ J 7
closed 1 to 21 August, February Holidays, Tuesday lunch and Monday – **Meals** (booking
essential) 30 (lunch), 58/76 b.i. and a la carte 55/75 ⬚
Spec. Crabe en fines ravioles d'avocat, huile d'amande douce. Noix de Saint-Jacques,
velouté au curry et coco (saison). Le lait "dans tous ses états".

XX **Giulio Rebellato**, 136 r. Pompe ⊠ 75116 ✆ 01 47 27 50 26 – ▤, ᴁ ᴳᴮ. ⬚ G 6
closed August – **Meals** - Italian rest. - a la carte 50/70.

XX **Fakhr el Dine**, 30 r. Longchamp ⊠ 75116 ✆ 01 47 27 90 00, *resa@fakhreldine.com*,
Fax 01 53 70 01 81 – ▤, ᴁ ⓪ ᴳᴮ G 7
Meals - Lebanese rest. - 23/26 and a la carte 25/40.

XX **San Francisco**, 1 r. Mirabeau ⊠ 75016 ✆ 01 46 47 84 89, *Fax 01 46 47 75 45*, ⬚
– ᴁ ⓪ ᴳᴮ ᴊᴄ🅱
closed Sunday – **Meals** - Italian rest. - a la carte 40/55 ⬚.

XX **Bellini**, 28 r. Lesueur ⊠ 75116 ✆ 01 45 00 54 20, *Fax 01 45 00 11 74* – ▤, ᴁ ᴳᴮ
closed August, Saturday and Sunday – **Meals** - Italian rest. - 27,44 (lunch) and a la carte
45/50.

XX **Paul Chêne**, 123 r. Lauriston ⊠ 75116 ✆ 01 47 27 63 17, *Fax 01 47 27 53 18* – ▤,
ᴁ ⓪ ᴳᴮ. ⬚ G 6
closed August, 23 December-1er January, Saturday lunch and Sunday – **Meals** 33,54/41,16
and a la carte 40/56.

XX **Tang,** 125 r. de la Tour ⊠ 75116 ✆ 01 45 04 35 35, *Fax 01 45 04 58 19* – ▤, ᴁ ᴳᴮ.
🕸 ⬚ H 5
closed 1 to 26 August, 23 December-1 January, Sunday and Monday – **Meals** - Chinese
and Thai rest. - 39 (lunch)/65 and a la carte 50/100
Spec. Ravioli thaï au gingembre et coriandre. Croustillants de langoustines en sauce cara-
mélisée. Pigeonneau laqué aux cinq parfums.

XX **Zébra Square**, 3 pl. Clément Ader ⊠ 75016 ✆ 01 44 14 91 91, *Fax 01 45 20 46 41*,
« Original contemporary decor » – ▤, ᴁ ⓪ ᴳᴮ ᴊᴄ🅱 K 5
Meals a la carte 38/45 ⬚.

XX **Conti**, 72 r. Lauriston ⊠ 75116 ✆ 01 47 27 74 67, *Fax 01 47 27 37 66* – ▤, ᴁ ⓪ ᴳᴮ
closed 3 to 25 August, 25 December-1 January, Saturday, Sunday and Bank Holidays –
Meals - Italian rest. - a la carte 50/65 ⬚.

XX **Vinci,** 23 r. P. Valéry ⊠ 75116 ℰ 01 45 01 68 18, *Fax 01 45 01 60 37* – ▤. ☒☒
closed 1 to 19 August, Saturday and Sunday – **Meals** - Italian rest. - 29 and a la carte
40/52 ⌇.　　　　　　　　　　　　　　　　　　　　　　　　　　　　　　　F 7

XX **Marius,** 82 bd Murat ⊠ 75016 ℰ 01 46 51 67 80, *Fax 01 47 43 10 24,* ☞ – ☒☒ ☒☒
closed 1 to 19 August, Saturday lunch and Sunday – **Meals** a la carte 32/45 ⌇.

XX **Essaouira,** 135 r. Ranelagh ℰ 01 45 27 99 93, *Fax 01 45 27 56 36* – ☒☒
Closed 23 July-31 August, Tuesday and Monday – **Meals** North-African rest.- a la carte
33/44.

XX **Chez Géraud,** 31 r. Vital ⊠ 75016 ℰ 01 45 20 33 00, *Fax 01 45 20 46 60,* « Longwy
porcelain mural » – ☒☒　　　　　　　　　　　　　　　　　　　　　　　　　H 5
closed 26 July-26 August, Saturday and Sunday – **Meals** 28 and a la carte 50/82.

XX **Fontaine d'Auteuil,** 35bis r. La Fontaine ⊠ 75016 ℰ 01 42 88 04 47,
Fax 01 42 88 95 12 – ▤. ☒☒ ☒ ☒☒　　　　　　　　　　　　　　　　　　K 5
closed 4 to 28 August, Saturday lunch and Sunday – **Meals** 28,20 ⌇.

XX **Petite Tour,** 11 r. de la Tour ⊠ 75116 ℰ 01 45 20 09 31, *Fax 01 45 20 09 31* – ☒☒
☒ ☒☒ ☒☒☒　　　　　　　　　　　　　　　　　　　　　　　　　　　　　H 6
closed August and Sunday – **Meals** a la carte 48/78 ⌇.

XX **Butte Chaillot,** 110 bis av. Kléber ⊠ 75116 ℰ 01 47 27 88 88, *Fax 01 47 04 85 70*
– ▤. ☒☒ ☒ ☒☒ ☒☒☒　　　　　　　　　　　　　　　　　　　　　　　　G 7
closed 12 to 27 August and Saturday lunch – **Meals** 29,73 and a la carte 40/55 ⌇.

XX **Murat,** 1 bd Murat ⊠ 75016 ℰ 01 46 51 33 17, *Fax 01 46 51 88 54* – ▤. ☒☒ ☒☒
Meals a la carte 38/55 ⌇.　　　　　　　　　　　　　　　　　　　　　　K 3

X **Natachef,** 9 r. Duban ⊠ 75016 ℰ 01 42 88 10 15, *natachef@noos.fr,*
Fax 01 45 25 74 71 – ☒☒ ☒☒　　　　　　　　　　　　　　　　　　　　　J 5
Closed August, Saturday and Sunday – **Meals** a la carte approx. 35.

X **A et M Le Bistrot,** 136 bd Murat ⊠ 75016 ℰ 01 45 27 39 60, *am-bistrot-16@wa*
nadoo.fr, ☞ – ☒☒ ☒ ☒☒ ☒☒☒. ⌇⌇　　　　　　　　　　　　　　　　　M 3
closed 1 to 20 August, Saturday lunch and Sunday – **Meals** 27,44.

X **Les Ormes** (Molé), 8 r. Chapu ⊠ 75016 ℰ 01 46 47 83 98, *Fax 01 46 47 83 98* – ▤
ⒶⒼ ☒☒ ☒☒　　　　　　　　　　　　　　　　　　　　　　　　　　　　　M 4
closed 4 August-3 September, 5 to 14 January, Sunday and Monday – **Meals** (booking
essential) 25,92 (lunch)/32 and a la carte 32/44
Spec. Quenelle de volaille gratinée. Jarret de veau braisé et gnocchi de pommes de terre.
Tarte aux figues et amandes..

X **Vin et Marée,** 183 bd Murat ⊠ 75016 ℰ 01 46 47 91 39, *vin.maree@wanadoo.fr,*
Fax 01 46 47 69 07 – ☒☒ ☒☒ – **Meals** - Seafood - a la carte 29/43.

X **Les Bouchons de François Clerc,** 79 av. Kléber ⊠ 75116 ℰ 01 47 27 87 58,
Fax 01 47 04 60 97 – ☒☒ ☒☒ ☒☒☒　　　　　　　　　　　　　　　　　　G 7
closed Saturday lunch and Saturday – **Meals** 29,73 (lunch)/40,86 ⌇.

X **Bistrot de l'Étoile Lauriston,** 19 r. Lauriston ⊠ 75116 ℰ 01 40 67 11 16,
Fax 01 45 00 99 87 – ▤. ☒☒ ☒ ☒☒ ☒☒☒. ⌇⌇　　　　　　　　　　　　　F 7
Meals 25,15 (lunch)and a la carte 34/48 ⌇.

X **Rosimar,** 26 r. Poussin ⊠ 75016 ℰ 01 45 27 74 91, *Fax 01 45 20 75 05* – ▤. ☒☒ ☒☒
☒☒☒　　　　　　　　　　　　　　　　　　　　　　　　　　　　　　　　K 3
*closed 3 August-2 September, 24 December-1 January, Saturday, Sunday and Bank Holi-
days* – **Meals** - Spanish rest- 28,20/29,73 b.i. and a la carte 34/47.

X **Victor,** 101 bis r. Lauriston ⊠ 75116 ℰ 01 47 27 72 21, *Fax 01 47 27 72 22,* bistro –
▤. ☒☒ ☒☒. ⌇⌇　　　　　　　　　　　　　　　　　　　　　　　　　　　G 7
closed 5 to 25 August, Saturday lunch and Sunday – **Meals** a la carte 34/45 ⌇.

X **Gare,** 19 chaussée de la Muette ⊠ 75016 ℰ 01 42 15 15 31, *Fax 01 42 15 15 23,* ☞
« Original decor in converted 1854 railway station » – ☒☒ ☒☒. ⌇⌇　　　J 5
Meals a la carte 29/47 ⌇.

in the Bois de Boulogne :

XXXX **Pré Catelan,** rte Suresnes ⊠ 75016 ℰ 01 44 14 41 14, *Fax 01 45 24 43 25,* ☞
ⒼⒼ « Napoleon III pavilion », ☞ – ▤ Ⓟ. ☒☒ ☒ ☒☒ ☒☒☒　　　　　　　H 2
*closed 27 October-5 November, 1 to 24 February, Sunday except lunch from 6 May-
28 October and Monday* – **Meals** 55 (lunch), 87/115 and a la carte 75/120
Spec. Étrille en coque, gelée au caviar et crème fondante d'asperges vertes. Truffe en
fins copeaux à la croque au sel (October-March). Pigeonneau poché dans un bouillon aux
épices.

XXXX **Grande Cascade,** allée de Longchamp (opposite the hippodrome) ⊠ 75016
Ⓖ ℰ 01 45 27 33 51, *grandecascade@wanadoo.fr,* *Fax 01 42 88 99 06,* ☞, « Second
Empire pavilion » – Ⓟ. ☒☒ ☒ ☒☒ ☒☒☒
closed 18 February-16 March – **Meals** 55/130 and a la carte 100/135
Spec. Macaroni aux truffes noires, foie gras et céleri. Porcelet et lard paysan à la broche,
jus corsé aux châtaignes et sarriette. Grande assiette aux quatre chocolats.

Clichy, Ternes, Wagram.

17th arrondissement.
17th: ⊠ 75017

Meridien Étoile Ⓜ, 81 bd Gouvion St-Cyr ℰ 01 40 68 34 34, *guest.etoile@lemeridi en-hotels.com*, Fax 01 40 68 31 31 – 🛗, ⇥ rm, ⊟ rest, 📺 ⚓ ₲ – 🏛 50 - 1 200. 🄰🄴 Ⓞ ⊕ ⒿⒸⒷ
E 6
Meals a la carte 50/60 ♀ *L'Orenoc* : Meals a la carte 38/60 ♀ – *Terrasse* : Meals a la carte 30/45 ♀ – ⚏ 22,20 – **1 008 rm** 365/450, 17 suites.

Concorde La Fayette Ⓜ, 3 pl. Gén. Koenig ℰ 01 40 68 50 68, *info@concorde-laf ayette.com*, Fax 01 40 68 50 43, ⇐ – 🛗, ⇥ rm, ⊟ 📺 ⚓ – 🏛 40 - 2 000. 🄰🄴 ⓄⒸⒷ ⒿⒸⒷ
E 6
La Fayette ℰ 01 40 68 51 19 Meals 27 ♀ – ⚏ 20,50 – **917 rm** 285/440, 33 suites.

Splendid Étoile without rest, 1bis av. Carnot ℰ 01 45 72 72 00, *hotel@splendid.com*, Fax 01 45 72 72 01 – 🛗 📺 ⚓. 🄰🄴 ⓄⒸⒷ
F 7
⚏ 15 – **52 rm** 205/295, 5 suites.

Regent's Garden without rest, 6 r. P. Demours ℰ 01 45 74 07 30, *hotel.regents.ga rden@wanadoo.fr*, Fax 01 45 55 01 42, ⟿ – 🛗 ⊟ 📺. 🄰🄴 ⓄⒸⒷ ⒿⒸⒷ. ⚘
E 7
⚏ 10 – **39 rm** 124,40/230,50.

Balmoral without rest, 6 r. Gén. Lanrezac ℰ 01 43 80 30 50, Fax 01 43 80 51 56 – 🛗 ⊟ 📺 ⚓. 🄰🄴 ⓄⒸⒷ
E 7
⚏ 9,15 – **57 rm** 110/150.

Banville without rest, 166 bd Berthier ℰ 01 42 67 70 16, *hotelbanville@wanadoo.fr*, Fax 01 44 40 42 77, « Elegant atmosphere » – 🛗 ⊟ 📺 ⚓. 🄰🄴 ⓄⒸⒷ ⒿⒸⒷ
D 8
⚏ 11 – **38 rm** 127/183.

Quality Inn Pierre Ⓜ without rest, 25 r. Th.-de-Banville ℰ 01 47 63 76 69, *hotel @qualitypierre.com*, Fax 01 43 80 63 96 – 🛗, ⇥ rm, ⊟ 📺 ⚓ ₲ – 🏛 30. 🄰🄴 ⓄⒸⒷ ⒿⒸⒷ
D 8
⚏ 15 – **50 rm** 260/290.

Ampère Ⓜ, 102 av. Villiers ℰ 01 44 29 17 17, *resa@hotelampere.com*, Fax 01 44 29 16 50, ⟿ – 🛗 ⊟ 📺 ⚓ ₲ ⟿ – 🏛 40 - 100. 🄰🄴 ⓄⒸⒷ
D 8
Jardin d'Ampère ℰ 01 44 29 16 54 *(closed 5 to 26 August and Sunday dinner)* Meals 28 ♀ – ⚏ 12 – **100 rm** 165/320.

Villa Alessandra Ⓜ ⚘ without rest, 9 pl. Boulnois ℰ 01 56 33 24 24, *alessandra @hotelsparis.fr*, Fax 01 56 33 24 30 – 🛗 ⊟ 📺 ⚓ ⟿. 🄰🄴 ⓄⒸⒷ ⒿⒸⒷ
E 8
⚏ 18,29 – **49 rm** 223/380.

Villa Eugénie without rest, 167 r. Rome ℰ 04 44 29 06 06, *eugenie@hotelsparis.fr*, Fax 01 44 29 06 07 – 🛗 ⊟ 📺 ⚓. 🄰🄴 ⓄⒸⒷ ⒿⒸⒷ
C 10
⚏ 18 – **36 rm** 196/272.

Champerret Élysées without rest, 129 av. Villiers ℰ 01 47 64 44 00, *champerret-e lysees@cybercable.fr*, Fax 01 47 63 10 58 – 🛗, ⇥ rm, ⊟ 📺 ⚓. 🄰🄴 ⓄⒸⒷ ⒿⒸⒷ. ⚘
⚏ 11 – **45 rm** 107/123.

Mercure Wagram Arc de Triomphe Ⓜ without rest, 3 r. Brey ℰ 01 56 68 00 01, *h2053@accor-hotels.com*, Fax 01 56 68 00 02 – 🛗, ⇥ rm, ⊟ 📺 ⚓ ₲. 🄰🄴 ⓄⒸⒷ ⒿⒸⒷ. ⚘
E 8
⚏ 13 – **43 rm** 183/200.

Ternes Arc de Triomphe Ⓜ without rest, 97 av. Ternes ℰ 01 53 81 94 94, *hote l@hotelternes.com*, Fax 01 53 81 94 95 – 🛗, ⇥ rm, ⊟ 📺 ⚓ ₲. 🄰🄴 ⓄⒸⒷ ⒿⒸⒷ
E 6
⚏ 12 – **39 rm** 150/240.

Magellan ⚘ without rest, 17 r. J.B.-Dumas ℰ 01 45 72 44 51, *hotel.magellan@wan adoo.fr*, Fax 01 40 68 90 36, ⟿ – 🛗 📺 ⚓. 🄰🄴 ⓄⒸⒷ. ⚘
D 7
⚏ 7,50 – **75 rm** 103/110.

Mercure Étoile Ⓜ without rest, 27 av. Ternes ℰ 01 47 66 49 18, *h0372@accor-h otels.com*, Fax 01 47 63 77 91 – 🛗, ⇥ rm, ⊟ 📺 ⚓. 🄰🄴 ⓄⒸⒷ ⒿⒸⒷ
E 8
⚏ 12,96 – **56 rm** 183/200.

Étoile St-Ferdinand without rest, 36 r. St-Ferdinand ℰ 01 45 72 66 66, *ferdinand @paris-honotel.com*, Fax 01 45 74 12 92 – 🛗 ⊟ 📺 ⚓. 🄰🄴 ⓄⒸⒷ ⒿⒸⒷ
E 6-7
⚏ 12 – **42 rm** 136/206.

🏠🏠 **Jardin de Villiers** without rest, 18 r. C. Pouillet ℰ 01 42 67 15 60, jardindevillier@ anadoo.fr, Fax 01 42 67 32 11 – 🛗 📺. ፴ ⓸ ⒼⒷ ⒿⒸⒷ. ⅍   D 1
⌷ 6,10 – **26 rm** 83,85/144,83.

🏠🏠 **Étoile Park Hôtel** without rest, 10 av. Mac Mahon ℰ 01 42 67 69 63, ephot@eas net.fr, Fax 01 43 80 18 99 – 🛗 🗐 📺 ⓒ. ፴ ⓸ ⒼⒷ ⒿⒸⒷ   E
⌷ 9 – **28 rm** 84/136.

🏠 **Star Hôtel Étoile** without rest, 18 r. Arc de Triomphe ℰ 01 43 80 27 69, star.etc e.hotel@ wanadoo.fr, Fax 01 40 54 94 84 – 🛗 🗐 📺 ⓒ. ፴ ⓸ ⒼⒷ. ⅍   E
⌷ 10 – **62 rm** 130/165.

🏠 **Astrid** without rest, 27 av. Carnot ℰ 01 44 09 26 00, paris@hotel-astrid.con Fax 01 44 09 26 01 – 🛗 📺 ⓒ. ፴ ⓸ ⒼⒷ ⒿⒸⒷ   E
⌷ 8 – **41 rm** 92,50/129.

🏠 **Flaubert** without rest, 19 r. Rennequin ℰ 01 46 22 44 35, Fax 01 43 80 32 34 – 🛗 📺 ⓒ ♿. ፴ ⓸ ⒼⒷ   D
⌷ 7,50 – **40 rm** 86/99.

🏠 **Campanile,** 4 bd Berthier ℰ 01 46 27 10 00, resa@campanile-berthier.con Fax 01 46 27 00 57, 🌤 – 🛗, 🗏 📺 ⓒ ♿ ⇔ – 🔬 15 - 40. ፴ ⓸ ⒼⒷ
Meals 14/18,50 ⵎ – ⌷ 6,50 – **246 rm** 79.   B 1

XXXX ✿✿✿ **Guy Savoy,** 18 r. Troyon ℰ 01 43 80 40 61, reserv@guysavoy.com, Fax 01 46 22 43 0 – 🗐. ፴ ⓸ ⒼⒷ ⒿⒸⒷ   E
closed August, Saturday lunch, Sunday and Monday – **Meals** 170/200 and a la cart 135/175
Spec. Petits médaillons de foie gras de canard au sel gris. Soupe d'artichaut à la truff noire et brioche feuilletée aux champignons. Côte de veau rôtie et purée de pommes d terre à la truffe..

XXXX ✿✿ **Michel Rostang,** 20 r. Rennequin ℰ 01 47 63 40 77, rostang@relaischateaux.f Fax 01 47 63 82 75, « Elegant decor » – 🗐. ፴ ⓸ ⒼⒷ ⒿⒸⒷ   D
closed 1 to 15 August, Sunday, lunch Monday and Saturday – **Meals** 59 (lunch)/150 an a la carte 110/160
Spec. Carte des truffes noires (December-March). Grosse sole de ligne "cuisson meunière Soufflé au fenouil et safran.

XXX ✿✿ **Apicius** (Vigato), 122 av. Villiers ℰ 01 43 80 19 66, Fax 01 44 00 09 57 – 🗐. ፴ ⓸ Ⓖ ⒿⒸⒷ   D
closed August, Saturday and Sunday – **Meals** 103,67 and a la carte 75/105
Spec. Foie gras de canard poêlé en aigre-doux. Rouget en "sandwich" de cresson, huître et échalotes au curry. Soufflé au chocolat..

XXX ✿ **Faucher,** 123 av. Wagram ℰ 01 42 27 61 50, Fax 01 46 22 25 72, 🌤 – 🗐 ፴ ⒼⒷ   D
closed Saturday and Sunday – **Meals** 46 (lunch)/92 and a la carte 65/90
Spec. Œuf au plat, foie gras chaud et coppa grillée. Montgolfière de Saint-Jacques (Octo ber-March). Canette rôtie et ses filets laqués..

XXX ✿ **Sormani** (Fayet), 4 r. Gén. Lanrezac ℰ 01 43 80 13 91, Fax 01 40 55 07 37 – 🗐. ⒼⒷ
closed 1 to 26 August, 20 December-3 January, Saturday, Sunday and Bank Holidays **Meals** - Italian rest. - 44 (lunch)and a la carte 55/80 ⵎ
Spec. Tagliatelle à la truffe blanche (October-December). Veau farci à la truffe noir (December-March). Risotto paysan à la saucisse de Naples.

XXX **Pétrus,** 12 pl. Mar. Juin ℰ 01 43 80 15 95, Fax 01 47 66 49 86 – 🗐. ፴ ⓸ ⒼⒷ ⒿⒸⒷ   D
closed 10 to 25 August – **Meals** - Seafood - 38,11 (lunch)/85,37 and a la carte 49 93 ⵎ.

XXX **Amphyclès,** 78 av. Ternes ℰ 01 40 68 01 01, amphycles@aol.com, Fax 01 40 68 91 8 – 🗐. ፴ ⓸ ⒼⒷ ⒿⒸⒷ   E
closed 8 to 31 July, 24 to 28 February, Saturday lunch and Sunday – **Meals** 44,9 (lunch)/103,67.

XXX ✿ **Timgad,** 21 r. Brunel ℰ 01 45 74 23 70, Fax 01 40 68 76 46, « Moorish decor » – 🗐 ፴ ⓸ ⒼⒷ. ⅍   E
Meals - Moorish rest. - a la carte 40/60
Spec. Couscous méchoui. Pastilla. Tagine d'agneau..

XX **Petit Colombier,** 42 r. Acacias ℰ 01 43 80 28 54, Fax 01 44 40 04 29 – 🗐. Ⓐ ⒼⒷ   E
closed 1 to 27 August, Saturday (except dinner from September-March) and Sunday **Meals** 34/60 and a la carte 55/75 ⵎ.

XX **Dessirier,** 9 pl. Mar. Juin ℰ 01 42 27 82 14, restaurantdessirier@ wanadoo.fr Fax 01 47 66 82 07 – 🗐. ፴ ⓸ ⒼⒷ ⒿⒸⒷ   D
closed 12 to 18 August – **Meals** - Seafood - 35/80 b.i. and a la carte 49/82.

XX **Les Béatilles** (Bochaton), 11 bis r. Villebois-Mareuil ℘ 01 45 74 43 80,
⊗ Fax 01 45 74 43 81 – ▤. 쟈 ⬛ 예 E 7
closed 30 July-26 August, 24 to 30 December, Saturday and Sunday – **Meals** 38,20 (lunch),
44,20/65,60 and a la carte 65/90
Spec. Nems d'escargots et champignons des bois. Pastilla de pigeon et foie gras aux épices.
La "Saint-Cochon" (November-March)..

XX **Graindorge,** 15 r. Arc de Triomphe ℘ 01 47 54 00 28, Fax 01 47 54 00 28 –
🅰 ⬛ E 7
closed Saturday lunch and Sunday – **Meals** flemish rest. 27 (lunch)/32 and a la carte 38/53.

XX **L'Atelier Gourmand,** 20 r. Tocqueville ℘ 01 42 27 03 71, Fax 01 42 27 03 71 – 🅰
⬛ D 10
closed 5 to 26 August, Saturday except dinner from 15 September 15 June and Sunday
– **Meals** 25,50 (lunch)/30 and a la carte 36/40 ♈.

XX **Beudant,** 97 r. des Dames ℘ 01 43 87 11 20, Fax 01 43 87 27 35 – ▤. 🅰 ⬛ 예 ⬛ 🇯🇨🇧
closed 6 to 26 August, Saturday lunch and Sunday – **Meals** 26,75/48,85 and a la carte
37/46 ♈. D 11

XX **Coco et sa Maison,** 18 r. Bayen ℘ 01 45 74 73 73, Fax 01 45 74 73 52 – 🅰 예 ⬛
🇯🇨🇧 E 7
closed 1 to 20 August, 24 December-2 January, Sunday, lunch Saturday and Monday –
Meals a la carte 32/48.

XX **Truite Vagabonde,** 17 r. Batignolles ℘ 01 43 87 77 80, Fax 01 43 87 31 50, 🍴 – 🅰
⬛ D 11
Meals 32 and a la carte 48/52 ♈.

XX **Ballon des Ternes,** 103 av. Ternes ℘ 01 45 74 17 98, leballondesternes@wanadoo.fr,
Fax 01 45 72 18 84, brasserie – 🅰 ⬛ 🇯🇨🇧 E 6
closed 28 July-27 August – **Meals** a la carte 34/47 ♈.

XX **Paolo Petrini,** 6 r. Débarcadère ℘ 01 45 74 25 95, paolo.petrini@wanadoo.fr,
Fax 01 45 74 12 95 – ▤. 🅰 예 ⬛ 🇯🇨🇧 E 6
closed 1 to 21 August, Saturday lunch and Sunday – **Meals** Italian rest. - 20 (lunch)/29
and a la carte 41/44.

XX **Tante Jeanne,** 116 bd Péreire ℘ 01 43 80 88 68, tantejeanne@bernard.loiseau.com,
Fax 01 47 66 53 02 – ▤. 🅰 예 ⬛ D 8
(closed August, Saturday and Sunday) – **Meals** 30 (lunch)/37 and a la carte 40/63 ♈.

XX **Taûra,** 10 r. Acacias ℘ 01 47 66 74 14, tairacuisinedelamer@hotmail.com,
Fax 01 47 66 74 14 – ▤. 🅰 예 ⬛. 🍴 E 7
closed 15 to 31 August, Saturday lunch and Sunday – **Meals** - Seafood - 32/61 and a la
carte 43/67 ♈.

XX **Chez Georges,** 273 bd Péreire ℘ 01 45 74 31 00, Fax 01 45 74 02 56, bistro – ⬛
🇯🇨🇧. 🍴 – **Meals** a la carte 37/54 ♈. E 6

XX **Chez Léon,** 32 r. Legendre ℘ 01 42 27 06 82, Fax 01 46 22 63 67, bistro – 🅰 예 ⬛.
🍴 D 10
closed 30 July-19 August, Christmas Holidays, Saturday and Sunday – **Meals** (booking
essential) 50 b.i. and a la carte 38/60.

X **Rôtisserie d'Armaillé,** 6 r. Armaillé ℘ 01 42 27 19 20, Fax 01 40 55 00 93 – ▤. 🅰
예 ⬛ 🇯🇨🇧 E 7
closed 6 to 19 August, Saturday lunch and Sunday – **Meals** 38.

X **Soupière,** 154 av. Wagram ℘ 01 42 27 00 73, Fax 01 46 22 27 09 – ▤. 🅰 ⬛
⊗ closed 5 to 25 August, Saturday lunch and Sunday – **Meals** 24 (lunch), 27/48 and a la carte
33/60. D 9

X **Table des Oliviers,** 38 r. Laugier ℘ 01 47 63 85 51, Fax 01 47 63 85 81 – ▤. 🅰
⬛ D 7-8
closed 12 to 26 August, Saturday lunch and Sunday – **Meals** (booking essential) 25,15.

X **A et M le Bistrot,** 105 r. Prony ℘ 01 44 40 05 88, AM.Bistrot.17eme@wanadoo.fr,
⊗ Fax 01 44 40 05 89, 🍴 – ▤. 🅰 예 ⬛. 🍴 D 8
closed August, Saturday lunch and Sunday – **Meals** 27,44.

X **Troyon,** 4 r. Troyon ℘ 01 40 68 99 40, Fax 01 40 68 99 57 – 🅰 ⬛. 🍴 E 8
closed 1 to 20 August, 23 December-4 January, Saturday and Sunday – **Meals** (booking
essential) 30,18.

X **Les Dolomites,** 38 r. Poncelet ℘ 01 47 66 38 54, Fax 01 42 27 39 57 – 🅰
⬛ 🇯🇨🇧 E 8
closed 12 to 18 August and Sunday – **Meals** 21/30 ♈.

X **Café d'Angel,** 16 r. Brey ℘ 01 47 54 03 33, Fax 01 47 54 03 33 – ⬛ E 8
⊗ closed August, Christmas-New Year, Saturday and Sunday – **Meals** 19,06/30,49 and a la
carte 25/35 ♈.

X **L'Impatient,** 14 passage Geffroy Didelot ℰ 01 43 87 28 10, Fax 01 43 87 28 1●
– GB   D 10-1
closed Saturday lunch, Sunday and Monday – **Meals** 17 (lunch), 21,50/51 and a la cart●
36/50.

X **Caves Petrissans,** 30 bis av. Niel ℰ 01 42 27 52 03, cavespetrissans@noos.fr
Fax 01 40 54 87 56, 畲, bistro – GB   D ●
closed 27 July-25 August, 28 December-5January, Saturday and Sunday – **Meals** 29 an●
a la carte 35/59.

X **Petit Gervex,** 2 r. Gervex ℰ 01 43 80 53 63, 畲 – GB ① GB   C ●
closed 26 July-22 August, Sunday dinner and Saturday – **Meals** 23 and a la carte 29,
46 ♀.

X **Le Clou,** 132 r. Cardinet ℰ 01 42 27 36 78, le.clou@wanadoo.fr, Fax 01 42 27 89 9●
bistro – GB GB JCB   C 1●
closed 6 to 19 August, Saturday and Sunday – **Meals** 18 and a la carte 29/41.

X **Huîtrier et Presqu'île,** 16 r. Saussier-Leroy ℰ 01 40 54 83 44, Fax 01 40 54 83 86 –
▣. GB GB   E ●
closed August, Sunday from May-August and Monday – **Meals** - Seafood - a la cart●
41/63.

Montmartre, La Villette, Belleville.

18th, 19th and 20th arrondissements.
18th: ✉ *75018*
19th: ✉ *75019*
20th: ✉ *75020*

🏛️ **Terrass'Hôtel** M, 12 r. J. de Maistre (18th) ℰ 01 46 06 72 85, reservation@terras
-hotel.com, Fax 01 42 52 29 11, 畲, « Panoramic rooftop terrace » – ₪, ⇔ rm, ▤ ▣
◦ – ▵ 25 - 100. GB ① GB JCB   C 1.
Terrasse : **Meals** 28 ₰ – ⊡ 12 – **78 rm** 188/302, 13 suites.

🏛️ **Holiday Inn** M, 216 av. J. Jaurès (19th) ℰ 01 44 84 18 18, hilavillette@alliance-hos
itality.com, Fax 01 44 84 18 20, 畲, ₤₆ – ₪, ⇔ rm, ▤ ▣ ◦ & ▣ – ▵ 15 - 140. ▣
① GB JCB. ٪ rest   C 2
Meals 30 ♀ – ⊡ 15 – **174 rm** 220/240, 8 suites.

🏨 **Mercure Montmartre** without rest, 1 r. Caulaincourt (18th) ℰ 01 44 69 70 7C
h0373@accor-hotels.com, Fax 01 44 69 70 71 – ₪, ⇔ rm, ▤ ▣ ◦ & – ▵ 20 - 7C
GB ① GB JCB   D 1:
⊡ 12,96 – **305 rm** 161/171.

🏨 **Holiday Inn Garden Court** M without rest, 23 r. Damrémont (18th
ℰ 01 44 92 33 40, hiparmm@aol.com, Fax 01 44 92 09 30 – ₪, ⇔ rm, ▤ ▣ ◦ &
▵ 20. GB ① GB JCB   C 1:
⊡ 13 – **54 rm** 145/221.

🏨 **Parc des Buttes Chaumont** without rest, 1 pl. Armand Carrel (19th
ℰ 01 42 08 08 37, HPBC@wanadoo.fr, Fax 01 42 45 66 91 – ₪ ▤ ▣ ◦. GB ① GB
⊡ 8 – **45 rm** 84/124.

🏨 **Kyriad** M, 147 av. Flandres (19th) ℰ 01 44 72 46 46, kyriad-paris-villette@wanadoo.f●
Fax 01 44 72 46 47 – ₪, ⇔ rm, ▤ rest, ▣ ◦ & ⟷ – ▵ 70. GB ① GB JCB
Meals 11,50 ♀ – ⊡ 6 – **207 rm** 65/90.   B 1●

🏨 **Roma Sacré Cœur** without rest, 101 r. Caulaincourt (18th) ℰ 01 42 62 02 0●
Fax 01 42 54 34 92 – ₪ ▣. GB ① GB JCB   C 1●
⊡ 6 – **57 rm** 75/86.

🏨 **Palma** without rest, 77 av. Gambetta (20th) ℰ 01 46 36 13 65, hotel.palma@wanad●
o.fr, Fax 01 46 36 03 27 – ₪ ▣. GB ① GB JCB   G 2
⊡ 5,65 – **32 rm** 58/73.

🏨 **Crimée** without rest, 188 r. Crimée (19th) ℰ 01 40 36 75 29, hotel.crimee@free.f●
Fax 01 40 36 29 57 – ₪ ▤ ▣ ◦. GB GB JCB   C 1
⊡ 5,50 – **31 rm** 50/56,50.

🏠 **Laumière** without rest, 4 r. Petit (19th) 𝒫 01 42 06 10 77, *le-laumiere@wanadoo.fr,*
Fax 01 42 06 72 50 – 🛗 📺 ☻ D 19
🛏 6,40 – **54 rm** 46/63.

🏠 **Abricôtel** without rest, 15 r. Lally Tollendal (19th) 𝒫 01 42 08 34 49, *abricotel@wan
adoo.fr, Fax 01 42 40 83 95* – 🛗 📺 📞 ♿ ⚼ ⑩ ☻ ⚗ D 18
🛏 5,50 – **39 rm** 59/65.

🏠 **Damrémont** without rest, 110 r. Damrémont (18th) 𝒫 01 42 64 25 75, *hotel-damre
mont@easynet.fr, Fax 01 46 06 74 64* – 🛗 🔁 rm, 📺 📞 ⚼ ⑩ ☻ ⱼᴄʙ ⚗ B 13
🛏 6,10 – **35 rm** 82,32.

XXX **Beauvilliers,** 52 r. Lamarck (18th) 𝒫 01 42 54 54 42, *beauvilliers@club-internet.fr,*
Fax 01 42 62 70 30, ☀, « 1900 decor, terrace » – ▦ ⚼ ☻ ⱼᴄʙ C 14
closed Monday lunch and Sunday (except Summer) – Meals 30 (lunch)/61 b.i. and a la carte
70/75.

XXX **Pavillon Puebla,** Parc Buttes-Chaumont, entrance : av. Bolivar, r. Botzaris (19th)
𝒫 01 42 08 92 62, *Fax 01 42 39 83 16,* ☀, « Pleasant setting in the park » – 🅿 ⚼ ☻
closed Sunday and Monday – Meals 29/40 and a la carte 56/85. E 19

XX **Cottage Marcadet,** 151 bis r. Marcadet (18th) 𝒫 01 42 57 71 22 ▦ ☻ ⚗ C 13
closed April, 27 July-27 August and Sunday – Meals 26,50 (lunch)/36,50 b.i. and a la carte
40/66.

XX **Les Allobroges,** 71 r. Grands-Champs (20th) 𝒫 01 43 73 40 00 ⚼ ☻ K 22
closed 28 July-28 August, Sunday and Monday – Meals 15,24/28,97.

XX **Relais des Buttes,** 86 r. Compans (19th) 𝒫 01 42 08 24 70, *Fax 01 42 03 20 44,* ☀
– ☻ E 20
closed August, Saturday lunch and Sunday – Meals 29 and a la carte 38/57 ℤ.

XX **Wepler,** 14 pl. Clichy (18th) 𝒫 01 45 22 53 24, *wepler@club-internet.fr,*
Fax 01 44 70 07 50 – ⚼ ⑩ ☻ ⱼᴄʙ D 12
Meals 24,10 and a la carte 30/49 ℤ.

XX **Chaumière,** 46 av. Secrétan (19th) 𝒫 01 42 06 54 69, *Fax 01 42 06 28 12* – ▦ ⚼ ⑩
☻ E 18
closed 5 to 21 August, Saturday lunch, Sunday dinner and Monday – Meals 21,80/28,97
and a la carte 43/59.

XX **Au Clair de la Lune,** 9 r. Poulbot (18th) 𝒫 01 42 58 97 03, *Fax 01 42 55 64 74* – ⚼
☻ ⱼᴄʙ D 14
closed 20 August-15 September, Monday lunch and Sunday – Meals 26 and a la carte
30/47.

X **Poulbot Gourmet,** 39 r. Lamarck (18th) 𝒫 01 46 06 86 00, *Fax 01 46 06 86 00* – ☻.
⚗ C 14
closed 12 to 19 August and Sunday except lunch from October-May – Meals 51,25 and
a la carte 34/53.

X **L'Oriental,** 76 r. Martyrs (18th) 𝒫 01 42 64 39 80, *Fax 01 42 64 39 80.* ⚗
closed 22 July-28 August, Sunday and Monday – Meals - North-African rest. - 35,58 b.i.
and a la carte 27/35.

X **Basilic,** 33 r. Lepic (18th) 𝒫 01 46 06 78 43, *Fax 01 46 06 39 26* – ⚼ ☻ D 13
closed August, Tuesday lunch and Monday – Meals 19,82 (lunch)/22,87 and a la carte
31/43 ℤ.

X **Cave Gourmande,** 10 r. Gén. Brunet (19th) 𝒫 01 40 40 03 30, *Fax 01 40 40 03 30* –
▦. ⚼ ☻ E 20
Meals 28,97 and a la carte 29/35.

X **Bouclard,** 1 r. Cavallotti (18th) 𝒫 01 45 22 60 01, *michel.bonnemort@wanadoo.fr,*
Fax 01 53 42 33 01, bistro – ▦ ⚼ ☻ D 12
closed Saturday lunch and Sunday – Meals 21 b.i. and a la carte 39/55.

X **Village Kabyle,** 4 r. Aimé Lavy (18th) 𝒫 01 42 55 03 34, *Fax 01 45 86 08 35* – ☻.
⚗ B 14
closed Monday lunch and Sunday – Meals - North-African rest. - 25,92 and a la carte 27/35.

X **Histoire de...,** 14 r. Ferdinand Flocon (18th) 𝒫 01 42 52 24 60 – ☻ C 14
closed 23 to 27 April, 30 July-21 August, Sunday and Monday – Meals 30.

X **Perroquet Vert,** 7 r. Cavalotti (18th) 𝒫 01 45 22 49 16, *perroquetvert@moos.fr,*
Fax 01 42 93 70 29 – ⚼ ☻ ⱼᴄʙ D 12
closed 1 to 19 August, Sunday, lunch Saturday and Monday – Meals 27/38,73.

X **Bistrot des Soupirs "Chez Raymonde",** 49 r. Chine (20th) 𝒫 01 44 62 93 31,
Fax 01 44 62 77 83 – ☻ G 21
closed 15 to 30 August, Sunday and Monday – Meals 13,57 and a la carte 31/47.

X **Chez Vincent,** 5 r. Tunnel (19th) 𝒫 01 42 02 22 45 – ▦. ⚼ ⑩ ☻ E 20
closed Saturday lunch and Sunday – Meals - Italian rest ; - (booking essential) 34,30 and
a la carte 40/53 ♨.

ENVIRONS

The outskirts of Paris up to 25Km

K 11: These reference letters and numbers correspond to the squares on the **Michelin plans of Parisian suburbs** nos 🔟, 🔟, 🔟, 🔟.

Cergy-Pontoise-Ville-Nouvelle 95 Val-d'Oise 🔟 ⑳, 🔟 ②.
Paris 36.

à Cormeilles-en-Vexin – pop. 802 alt. 111 – ⊠ 95830 :

XXX **Relais Ste-Jeanne** (Cagna), on D 915 ℰ 01 34 66 61 56, saintejeanne@hotmail.com
❀❀ Fax 01 34 66 40 31, 🚗 – 🄿. 🅰🅴 ⲟ 🅶🅱
closed 28 July-28 August, 22 to 27 December, Sunday dinner, Monday and Tuesday –
Meals 45/85 and a la carte 85/105
Spec. Dégustation de homard bleu en deux services. Pavé de bœuf "Waguy" au poivre
noir. Fondant au praliné, sorbet chocolat..

La Défense 92 Hauts-de-Seine 🔟 ⑭, 🔟 – ⊠ 92400 Courbevoie.
See : Quarter★★ : perspective★ from the parvis.
Paris 8,5.

🏨 **Sofitel Grande Arche** M, 11 av. Arche, exit Défense 6 ℰ 01 71 00 50 00, h3013@a
ccor-hotels.com, Fax 01 71 00 56 78, 🎜 – 🛗, 🖐 rm, 🔲 📺 🛎 ㅎ 🚗 – 🖾 100. 🅰🅴 ⲟ
🅶🅱 🅹🅲🅱   AW 4(
Avant Seine ℰ 01 71 00 59 99 (closed Saturday and Sunday) **Meals** a la carte 40/48 ⵛ
– ☲ 21 – **368 rm** 490/685, 16 suites.

🏨 **Renaissance** M, 60 Jardin de Valmy, by ring road, exit La Défense 7 ⊠ 92918 Puteau»
ℰ 01 41 97 50 50, rhi.parld.sales.mgr@renaissancehotels.com, Fax 01 41 97 51 51, 🎜 –
🛗, 🖐 rm, 🔲 📺 🛎 ㅎ 🚗 – 🖾 160. 🅰🅴 ⲟ 🅶🅱 🅹🅲🅱   AW 4(
Meals 30 ⵛ – ☲ 20,50 – **331 rm** 350/395, 20 suites.

🏨 **Sofitel CNIT** M 🕭, 2 pl. Défense 🖂 92053 ℰ 01 46 92 10 10, h1089@accor-hote
ls.com, Fax 01 46 92 10 50 – 🛗, 🖐 rm, 🔲 📺 🛎 ㅎ – 🖾 20 - 60. 🅰🅴 ⲟ
🅶🅱 🅹🅲🅱   AV-AW4(
Les Communautés (closed Friday dinner, Saturday, Sunday and Bank Holidays) **Meals**
54,88 and a la carte 61/71 ⵛ – ☲ 22,86 – **141 rm** 285/430, 6 suites.

🏨 **Sofitel Centre** M 🕭, 34 cours Michelet by ring road, exit La Défense 4 🖂 9206(
Puteaux ℰ 01 47 76 44 43, h0912@accor-hotels.com, Fax 01 47 76 72 10, 🍴 – 🛗
🖐 rm, 🔲 📺 🛎 ㅎ 🚗 – 🖾 100. 🅰🅴 ⲟ 🅶🅱. 🎜   AW 4
Les 2 Arcs ℰ 01 47 76 72 30 (closed Friday dinner, Saturday and Sunday) **Meals** 54 ⵛ
– **Botanic** ℰ 01 47 76 72 40 **Meals** a la carte approx. 39 ⵛ – ☲ 21 – **151 rm** 430/485

🏨 **Novotel La Défense** M, 2 bd Neuilly ℰ 01 41 45 23 23, H0747@accor-hotels.com
Fax 01 41 45 23 24, ⩽ – 🛗, 🖐 rm, 🔲 📺 🛎 ㅎ – 🖾 130. 🅰🅴 ⲟ 🅶🅱 🅹🅲🅱   AW 42
Meals a la carte approx. 27 ⵛ – ☲ 12,96 – **280 rm** 230/275.

🏨 **Ibis La Défense** M, 4 bd Neuilly ℰ 01 41 97 40 40, h0771@accor-hotels.com
Fax 01 41 97 40 50, 🖐 – 🛗, 🖐 rm, 🔲 📺 🛎 ㅎ – 🖾 40. 🅰🅴 ⲟ 🅶🅱   AW 42
Meals a la carte approx. 22 – ☲ 6 – **286 rm** 103.

Marne-la-Vallée 77206 S.-et-M. 🔟 ⑲.
🏌 of Bussy-St-Georges (private) ℰ 01 64 66 00 00 ; 🏌 🏌 of Disneyland Paris
ℰ 01 60 45 68 90.
🛈 Tourist Office pl. des passagers du vent - Disneyland Paris ℰ 01 60 30 60 30.
Paris 28.

at Disneyland Paris access by Highway A 4 and Disneyland exit.
See : Disneyland Paris★★★

🏨 **Disneyland Hôtel** M, ℰ 01 60 45 65 00, Fax 01 60 45 65 33, ⩽, « Victorian style
architecture, at the entrance to the Disneyland Resort », 🎜, 🔲, 🚗 – 🛗, 🖐 rm, 🔲
📺 ㅎ 🄿 – 🖾 25 - 50. 🅰🅴 ⲟ 🅶🅱 🅹🅲🅱. 🎜
California Grill (dinner only) **Meals** 44/65 – **Inventions** (buffet) **Meals** 28 (lunch)/39 –
478 rm ☲ 492, 18 suites.

🏨 **New-York** M, ℰ 01 60 45 73 00, Fax 01 60 45 73 33, ⩽, 🍴, « Evokes the architecture
of Manhattan », 🎜, 🔲, 🔲, 🎜 – 🛗, 🖐 rm, 🔲 📺 🛎 ㅎ 🄿 – 🖾 2 200. 🅰🅴 ⲟ 🅶🅱
🅹🅲🅱.
Manhattan Restaurant (dinner only) **Meals** 32 ⵛ – **Parkside Diner** : **Meals** 20 ⵛ – **536 rm**
☲ 300, 27 suites.

🏨 **Newport Bay Club** Ⓜ, ℰ 01 60 45 55 00; *Fax 01 60 45 55 33*, ≤, 🍴, Convention centre, « In the style of a New England seaside resort », 🛋, 🏊, 🏊 – 🕴, ≶ rm, 🗏 rest, 📺 & 🅿 – 🛠 1 500. 🆎 ① 🆖 🗝 ❄
Cape Cod : Meals 25(lunch)/20(dinner) – *Yacht Club* (dinner only) Meals 30/38 –
1 082 rm ☲ 260, 13 suites.

🏨 **Séquoia Lodge** Ⓜ, ℰ 01 60 45 51 00, *Fax 01 60 45 51 33*, ≤, 🍴, « The atmosphere of an American mountain lodge », 🛋, 🏊, 🏊, 🌳 – 🕴, ≶ rm, 🗏 rest, 📺 & 🅿 –
🛠 75. 🆎 ① 🆖 🗝 ❄
Hunter's Grill (dinner only) Meals 26 – *Beaver Creek Tavern* (dinner only) Meals 20 –
1 001 rm ☲ 243, 10 suites.

🏨 **Cheyenne,** ℰ 01 60 45 62 00, *Fax 01 60 45 62 33*, 🍴, « Resembles a frontier town of the American Wild West », 🌳 – ≶ rm, 🗏 rest, 📺 & 🅿 🆎 ① 🆖 🗝 ❄
Chuck Wagon Café (coffee shop) Meals a la carte approx 20 – **1 000 rm** ☲ 198.

🏨 **Santa Fé,** ℰ 01 60 45 78 00, *Fax 01 60 45 78 55*, « Evokes a New Mexican pueblo » –
≶ rm, 📺 & 🅿 🆎 ① 🆖 🗝. ❄
La Cantina (coffee shop) Meals a la carte approx. 20 – **1 000 rm** ☲ 174.

Orly (Paris Airports) *94396 Val-de-Marne* 🔟🔟🔟 ㉖, ㉔ – *pop. 21 646*
🛬 ℰ 01 49 75 15 15.
Paris 15.

🏨 **Hilton Orly** Ⓜ, near airport station ⊠ 94544 ℰ 01 45 12 45 12, *fb-orly@hilton.com,
Fax 01 45 12 45 00*, 🛋 – 🕴, ≶ rm, 🗏 📺 🅿 – 🛠 280. 🆎 ① 🆖 🗝 BR 51
Meals (lunch buffet) 25,15 (lunch)/31,71 (dinner) and a la carte 30/52 ☲ – ☲ 15,24 – **352 rm** 105/190.

🏨 **Mercure** Ⓜ, N 7, Z.I. Nord, Orlytech ⊠ 94547 ℰ 01 46 87 23 37, *h1246@accor-hot els.com, Fax 01 46 87 71 92* – 🕴, ≶ rm, 🗏 📺 & 🅿 – 🛠 40. 🆎 ① 🆖 🗝
Meals (closed Sunday lunch and Saturday) 22,10 ☲ – ☲ 11 – **190 rm** 126/149.

See also *Rungis*

Roissy-en-France (Paris Airports) *95700 Val-d'Oise* 🔟🔟🔟 ⑧ – *pop. 2 054 alt. 85.*
🛬 ℰ 01 48 62 22 80.
Paris 26.

at Roissy-Town :

🏨 **Copthorne** Ⓜ, allée Verger ℰ 01 34 29 33 33, *resa.cdg@mill-cop.com,
Fax 01 34 29 03 05*, 🍴, 🛋, 🏊 – 🕴, ≶ rm, 🗏 📺 & 🅿 🖘 – 🛠 150. 🆎 ① 🆖
🗝
Meals 25,92 b.i./28 b.i. – ☲ 17,55 – **239 rm** 250/300.

🏨 **Mercure** Ⓜ, allée Verger ℰ 01 34 29 40 00, *h1245@accor-hotels.com,
Fax 01 34 29 00 18*, 🍴 – 🕴, ≶ rm, 🗏 📺 & 🅿 – 🛠 90. 🆎 ① 🆖
Meals 34/37 🍷 – ☲ 12 – **203 rm** 180/187.

🏨 **Bleu Marine** Ⓜ, Z.A. parc de Roissy ℰ 01 34 29 00 00, *bleu.roissy@wanadoo.fr,
Fax 01 34 29 00 11*, 🍴, 🛋 – 🕴, ≶ rm, 🗏 📺 & 🖘 🅿 – 🛠 80. 🆎 ① 🆖 🗝
Meals 25,50 and a la carte Sunday ☲ – ☲ 9,90 – **153 rm** 135.

🏨 **Ibis** Ⓜ, av. Raperie ℰ 01 34 29 34 34, *Fax 01 34 29 34 19* – 🕴, ≶ rm, 🗏 📺 & 🖘
🅿 – 🛠 70. 🆎 ① 🆖 🗝
Meals 16 🍷 – ☲ 7 – **300 rm** 75.

at Airport terminal n° 2 :

🏨 **Sheraton** Ⓜ 🌊, ℰ 01 49 19 70 70, *Fax 01 49 19 70 71*, ≤, « Original contemporary architecture », 🛋 – 🕴, ≶ rm, 🗏 📺 & 🅿 – 🛠 110. 🆎 ① 🆖
Les Étoiles (closed 29/07-28/08, 23/12-5/01, Saturday, Sunday and Bank Holidays) Meals
47,50(lunch)/53,50 ☲ – *Les Saisons :* Meals 39 ☲ – ☲ 22 – **244 rm** 535/670, 12 suites.

at Roissypole :

🏨 **Hilton** Ⓜ 🌊, ℰ 01 49 19 77 77, *CDGHITWSAL@hilton.com, Fax 01 49 19 77 78*, 🛋, 🏊
– 🕴, ≶ rm, 🗏 📺 & 🖘 – 🛠 500. 🆎 ① 🆖 🗝. ❄ rest
Gourmet (closed 1 July-31 August, Saturday and Sunday) Meals 38,11 ☲ – *Aviateurs* -
brasserie Meals 33,54 ☲ – *Oyster bar* - Seafood (closed July, August, Saturday and Sunday)
Meals a la carte 38/45 ☲ – ☲ 22,11 – **383 rm** 500/560, 4 suites.

🏨 **Sofitel** Ⓜ, Zone centrale Ouest ℰ 01 49 19 29 29, *Fax 01 49 19 29 00*, ❄ – 🕴, ≶ rm, 🗏 📺 & 🅿 – 🛠 60. 🆎 ① 🆖 🗝.
Meals brasserie (lunch only) 24,39 ☲ *L'Escale* -Seafood Meals 24,39(lunch) and a la carte approx. 36 ☲ – ☲ 12,20 – **336 rm** 335,39/411,61, 6 suites.

🏨 **Novotel** Ⓜ, ℰ 01 49 19 27 27, *h1014@accor-hotels.com, Fax 01 49 19 27 99* – 🕴, ≶ rm, 🗏 📺 & 🅿 – 🛠 60. 🆎 ① 🆖 🗝
Meals a la carte approx. 28 ☲ – ☲ 11 – **201 rm** 135.

Z.I. Paris Nord II – ⊠ *95912* :

🏨 **Hyatt Regency** Ⓜ ⑤, 351 av. Bois de la Pie ✆ 01 48 17 12 34, sales@paris.hyatt.com
Fax 01 48 17 17 17, « Original contemporary decor », ⅙, ⬛, ❊ – ➌, ❊ rm, ■ 📺
✔ & 🄿 – 🚗 300. 🖭 ⓞ 🄶🄱 🄹🄲🄱
Meals 35/45 ♀ – ☲ 21 – **383 rm** 295/475, 5 suites.

Rungis *94150* Val-de-Marne ⑩⑪ ㉖, ㉔ – pop. *2 939* alt. *80*.
Paris 14.

at Pondorly : Access : from Paris, Highway A 6 and take Orly Airport exit ; from outside of Paris
A 6 and Rungis exit :

🏨 **Holiday Inn** Ⓜ, 4 av. Ch. Lindbergh ✆ 01 49 78 42 00, hiorly.manager@alliance-hos
itality.com, Fax 01 45 60 91 25 – ➌, ❊ rm, ■ 📺 & 🄿 – 🚗 15 - 150. 🖭 ⓞ 🄶🄱 🄹🄲🄱
❊ rest   BM 5⓿
Meals 24,50 ♀ – ☲ 15 – **171 rm** 130/191.

🏨 **Grand Hôtel Mercure Orly** Ⓜ, 20 av. Ch. Lindbergh ✆ 01 56 70 56 70, h1298@
ccor-hotels.com, Fax 01 56 70 56 56, ⬛ – ➌, ❊ rm, ■ 📺 & 🚗 🄿 – 🚗 15 - 14⓿
🖭 ⓞ 🄶🄱. ❊ rest   BM 5⓿
Meals (closed lunch Saturday and Sunday) 32,77 ♀ – ☲ 11,43 – **190 rm** 152/190.

🏨 **Novotel** Ⓜ, Zone du Delta, 1 r. Pont des Halles ✆ 01 45 12 44 12, h1628@accor-h
tels.com, Fax 01 45 12 44 13, ⬛ – ➌, ❊ rm, ■ 📺 ✔ & 🄿 – 🚗 15 - 150. 🖭
ⓞ 🄶🄱   BM 5⓿
Meals a la carte 22/28 ♀ – ☲ 11,28 – **187 rm** 136/142.

Versailles *78000* Yvelines ⑩⑪ ㉒, ㉒㉒ – pop. *87 789* alt. *130*.
See : Palace★★★ Y – Gardens★★★ (fountain display★★★ (grandes eaux) and illuminate
night performances★★★ (fêtes de nuit) in summer) – Ecuries Royales★ Y – The Trianons★★
– Lambinet Museum★ Y M.
⛳ ⛳ of la Boulie (private) ✆ 01 39 50 59 41 by ③ : 2,5 km.
🄱 Tourist Office 2 bis av. Paris ✆ 01 39 24 88 88, Fax 01 39 24 88 89.
Paris 20 ①

Plan opposite

🏨 **Trianon Palace** Ⓜ ⑤, 1 bd Reine ✆ 01 30 84 50 00, trian@westin.com
Fax 01 30 84 50 01, ≤, « Tasteful early 20C decor », ⅙, ⬛, ❊, ⚤ – ➌, ■ rm, 📺 ✔
🚗 🄿 – 🚗 15 - 200. 🖭 ⓞ 🄶🄱 🄹🄲🄱. ❊   X
see **Les Trois Marches** below - **Café Trianon** : Meals a la carte 44/70 ♀ – ☲ 25 – **166 rm**
280/540, 26 suites.

🏨 **Sofitel Château de Versailles** Ⓜ, 2 bis av. Paris ✆ 01 39 07 46 46, h1300@ac
or-hotels.com, Fax 01 39 07 46 47, ⅙ – ➌, ❊ rm, ■ 📺 ✔ & 🚗 – 🚗 90. 🖭 ⓞ
🄶🄱 🄹🄲🄱. ❊ rest   Y
Meals (closed 27 July-25 August, 21 to 26 December and Saturday) 27 – ☲ 19,50
146 rm 228, 6 suites.

🏨 **Versailles** Ⓜ ⑤ without rest, 7 r. Ste-Anne ✆ 01 39 50 64 65, info@hotel-le-vers
illes.fr, Fax 01 39 02 37 85 – ➌, ❊ rm, 📺 ✔ & 🄿 – 🚗 25. 🖭 ⓞ 🄶🄱 🄹🄲🄱   Y
☲ 10 – **46 rm** 84/105.

🏨 **Résidence du Berry** Ⓜ without rest, 14 r. Anjou ✆ 01 39 49 07 07, resa@hotel-
erry.com, Fax 01 39 50 59 40 – ➌, ❊ rm, 📺 ✔. 🖭 ⓞ 🄶🄱 🄹🄲🄱   Z
☲ 10 – **38 rm** 100/120.

🏨 **Relais Mercure** Ⓜ without rest, 19 r. Ph. de Dangeau ✆ 01 39 50 44 10, hotel@
ercure-versaille.com, Fax 01 39 50 65 11 – ➌ 📺 ✔ & 🚗 – 🚗 35. 🖭 ⓞ 🄶🄱 🄹🄲🄱
☲ 7,50 – **60 rm** 79/86.   Y

🏨 **Ibis** without rest, 4 av. Gén. de Gaulle ✆ 01 39 53 03 30, Fax 01 39 50 06 31 – ➌, ❊ rm
📺 & 🚗. 🖭 ⓞ 🄶🄱
☲ 5,95 – **85 rm** 69,36.   Y

🍴 **Les Trois Marches** - Hôtel Trianon Palace, 1 bd Reine ✆ 01 39 50 13 21, gerard.v
❀ @westin.com, Fax 01 30 21 01 25, ≤, ❊ – ■ 🄿. 🖭 ⓞ 🄶🄱 🄹🄲🄱   X
closed August, Sunday and Monday – Meals 58 (lunch)/130 ♀
Spec. Penne "al dente" au balsamic et à la mirepoix de homard. Parmentier de lar
goustines et huîtres en tartare. Semoule de rave aux truffes (mid-January-lat
March)..

🍴 **Marée de Versailles,** 22 r. au Pain ✆ 01 30 21 73 73, Fax 01 39 49 98 29, ❊ – ■
🖭 🄶🄱   Y
closed 3 to 18 August, February Holidays, Sunday and Monday – Meals - Seafood - a
carte 38/51 ♀.

VERSAILLES

FRANCE

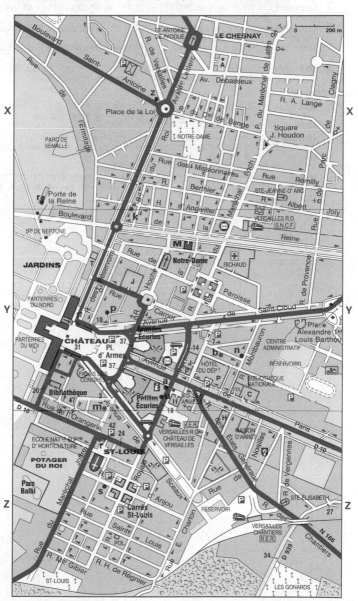

XX **Potager du Roy,** 1 r. Mar.-Joffre ℰ 01 39 50 35 34, Fax 01 30 21 69 30 – ▤
⬛ GB   Z ▮
closed Saturday lunch, Sunday dinner and Monday – **Meals** 30/45 ♀.

XX **Étape Gourmande,** 125 r. Yves Le Coz ℰ 01 30 21 01 63, ☎ – GB   V r
closed 28 July-22 August, Wednesday and dinner Sunday and Tuesday – **Meals** 37 ♀.

X **Chevalet,** 6 r. Ph. de Dangeau ℰ 01 39 02 03 13, Fax 01 39 50 81 41 – ⬛ GB   Y b
closed 6 to 21 August, Sunday and Monday – **Meals** 26 ♀.

X **Cuisine Bourgeoise,** 10 bd Roi ℰ 01 39 53 11 38, *la.cuisine.bougeoise@wanadoo.fr*
Fax 01 39 53 25 26 – ⬛ GB   XY k
closed 3 to 26 August, Saturday lunch, Sunday and Monday – **Meals** 29,50 (lunch), 39/57
b.i..

X **Le Falher,** 22 r. Satory ℰ 01 39 50 57 43, Fax 01 39 49 04 66 – ⬛ GB. ⚄   Y m
closed Saturday lunch, Sunday and Monday – **Meals** 23 (lunch), 26/32.

at Le Chesnay – *pop. 29542 alt. 120* – ✉ 78150 :

🏨 **Novotel** M, 4 bd St-Antoine ℰ 01 39 54 96 96, *h1022@accor-hotels.com*
Fax 01 39 54 94 40 – 🛗, ⇔ rm, ▤ 📺 ❦ & ⬅ – 🛎 90. ⬛ ⓞ GB   X z
Meals 21 ♀ – ☷ 11 – **105 rm** 107/115.

🏨 **Mercure** M without rest, r. Marly-le-Roi, in front of Commercial Centre Parly
ℰ 01 39 55 11 41, *h0379@accor-hotels.com*, Fax 01 39 55 06 22 – 🛗, ⇔ rm, 📺 ❦ &
🅿 – 🛎 15. ⬛ ⓞ GB ᴊᴄᴮ
☷ 11 – **89 rm** 107/145.

🏨 **Ibis** without rest, av. Dutartre, Commercial Centre Parly II ℰ 01 39 63 37 93
H0939-ACT2003@accor-hotels.com, Fax 01 39 55 18 66 – 🛗, ⇔ rm, ▤ 📺 &. ⬛ ⓞ
GB
☷ 6,02 – **72 rm** 69.

AND BEYOND...

Joigny *89300 Yonne* 🔢 ④ *- pop. 9697 alt. 79.*
See : *Vierge au Sourire★ in St-Thibault's Church – Côte St-Jacques ≤★ 1,5 km by D 20.*
🏌 *of Roncemay ℘ 03 86 73 50 50.*
🛈 *Tourist Office 4 quai H.-Ragobert ℘ 03 86 62 11 05, Fax 03 86 91 76 38.*
Paris 147 – Auxerre 27 – Gien 75 – Montargis 59 – Sens 30 – Troyes 76.

🏨 **Côte St-Jacques** (Lorain) Ⓜ ⚓, 14 fg Paris ℘ 03 86 62 09 70, lorain@relaischatea
🌼🌼 ux.fr, Fax 03 86 91 49 70, ≤, 🍴, 🔲, 🌿 – 🛗, 🛏 rest, 📺 ✆ 🅿 – 🛎 30. 🆎 ⓪
🆖 🄾🄲🄱
closed 6 January-5 February – **Meals** (Sunday booking essential) 64 (lunch), 95/128 and
a la carte 95/150 ♀ – ☕ 22 – **32 rm** 125/305
Spec. Huîtres creuses en petite terrine océane. Tronçon de turbot cuit en croûte de sel,
émulsion au lait d'amande. Canard croisé aux lentilles vertes, sauce cresson au thé vert..
Wines Chardonnay de Bourgogne, Irancy..

Rheims (Reims) *51100 Marne* 🔢 ⑥ ⑯ *– pop. 180 620 alt. 85.*
See : *Cathedral★★★ – St-Remi Basilica★★ : interior★★★ – Palais du Tau★★ – Champagne
cellars★ – Place Royale★ – Porte Mars★ – Hôtel de la Salle★ – Foujita Chapel★ – Library★
of Ancien Collège des Jésuites – St-Remi Museum★★ – Hôtel le Vergeur Museum★ – Fine
Arts Museum★ – French Automobile Heritage Centre★.*
Envir. : *Fort de la Pompelle : German helmets★ 9 km to the SE by N 44.*
🏌 *Rheims-Champagne ℘ 03 26 05 46 10 at Gueux ; to the NW by N 31-E 46 : 9,5 km.*
🏌 *Rheims-Champagne ℘ 03 26 07 15 15 : 6 km.*
🚗 *℘ 08 36 35 35 35.*
🛈 *Tourist Office 12 bd Gén.-Leclerc ℘ 03 26 77 45 00, Fax 03 26 77 45 19,
TourismReimsnet – Automobile Club de Champagne 7 bd Lundy ℘ 03 26 47 34 76, Fax
03 26 88 52 24.*
Paris 144 – Brussels 214 – Châlons-sur-Marne 48 – Lille 199 – Luxembourg 232.

🏨 **Boyer "Les Crayères"** (Boyer) Ⓜ ⚓, 64 bd Vasnier ℘ 03 26 82 80 80, crayeres@r
🌼🌼🌼 elaischateaux.com, Fax 03 26 82 65 52, ≤, 🍴, « Elegant mansion in park », 🎾, 🛗 – 🛗
🛏 📺 ✆ 🅿 🆎 ⓪ 🆖 🄾🄲🄱
closed 23 December-13 January – **Meals** (closed Tuesday lunch and Monday) (booking
essential) 165 b.i./189 b.i. and a la carte 85/115 – ☕ 22,90 – **16 rm** 242,50/350,70,
3 suites
Spec. Langoustines poêlées sur un tiramisu de volaille. Filet de bar rôti sous un manteau
croustillant au gingembre et citron. Petits grenadins de veau de lait enrobés de girolles
façon crépinette. **Wines** Champagne..

Saulieu *21210 Côte-d'Or* 🔢 ⑰ *– pop. 2917 alt. 535.*
See : *St-Andoche Basilica★ : capitals★★.*
🛈 *Tourist Office 24 r. d'Argentine ℘ 03 80 64 00 21, Fax 03 80 64 21 96,
Saulieu-tourismowanadoo.fr.*
Paris 249 – Autun 41 – Avallon 38 – Beaune 64 – Clamecy 76 – Dijon 73.

🏨 **Côte d'Or** (Loiseau) Ⓜ ⚓, 2 r. Argentine ℘ 03 80 90 53 53, loiseau@relaischateaux
🌼🌼🌼 .com, Fax 03 80 64 08 92, « Tasteful inn with flowered garden », 🛁, 🏊, 🌿 – 🛗 📺 ✆
🚗 – 🛎 30. 🆎 ⓪ 🆖 🄾🄲🄱
Meals 122/185 and a la carte 130/200 – ☕ 25 – **23 rm** 195/380, 7 suites, 3 duplex
Spec. Jambonnettes de grenouilles à la purée d'ail et au jus de persil. Sandre à la fondue
d'échalotes au vin rouge. Blanc de volaille fermière lardé de truffes.. **Wines** Vin des Coteaux
de l'Auxois, Mercurey.

Pleasant hotels and restaurants
are shown in the Guide by a **red sign**.

Please send us the names
of any where you have enjoyed your stay.

Your **Michelin Guide** will be even better.

C D

37

P

64
P

Turenne

R. Fondaudège 139

Barraud

Rue Turenne

A.

R. R. Allo

R. du

Espl. d[u]
Quincon[ces]

L

Pl.
de Tourny

R. Huguerie

Clemenceau

A. de Tourny

Z

P

MAISON DU
[VIN] DE BORDE[AUX]

S n

43

X

30

St-Seurin

R. Thiac

POL.

Abbé

Palais

de

l'Épée

de

Gallien

Pl. des Martyrs
de la Résistance

75

P p

P

G

Pl. du
Chapelet

100

P

N.-DAME

133

l'Intendance

de Grassi

Crs.

R. de
Grassi

21

GRAN[D]
THÉÂT[RE]

e

Judaïque

Pl.
Gambetta

V

k

m

Rue

Rue

r

Bonnac

40

R. des Remparts

48

R. V. Dijeaux

Pte Dijeaux

VIEUX

Pl.
Dijeaux

G.

BORDEAUX

PEY
BERLAND

M 3

Carles

Centre
Jean Moulin

3 Conils

130

P

n

Rue

Bonnier

40

N

M 4

H

CATH. ST-ANDRÉ

P

R.

Crs.

d' Alsace

St[e]

C.

HÔTEL
DU DEPT

MÉRIADECK

4m

C rs.

ST-PAUL

ST-BRUNO

Esplanade
Ch. de Gaulle

R. Mal

d' Alsace

57

PALAIS
DES
SPORTS

Hôtel
de Région

P

P

m

d'Albret

CITÉ
JUDICIAIRE

Joffre

U

Crs.

M 1

63

Y

P

Rue

Juin

M al

Rue

de

Pl. de la
République

J

R. de Cursol

STE-EULALIE

C rs

Crs.

Lande

L

Pasteur

Crs.

François

Molneyra

Belleville

R.

de la

Libération

R. J. Burguet

Pl. de
Pressensé

Po[nt]
d'Aqu[i]

de

Belfort

A.

P

Rue

ST-VICTOR

Sourdis

du

Tondu

R. L.

Mle

Pessac

R. de Lamourous

St-Genès

R. Ed.
Costedoat

Briand

R. Villedieu

Lebrethon

Pl. de
Victoi[re]

Z

Rue

R. F.
Audeguil

de

R. P.

Duhen

de

Rue

Mazarin

Rue

d' Argonne

Cadroin

R. St-Nicolas

Barrière
de Pessac

N.-D.
DES ANGES

des

Treuils

Rue

R. A. Baysselance

R. G.
Rioux

Cre.

ST-NICOLAS

C D

234

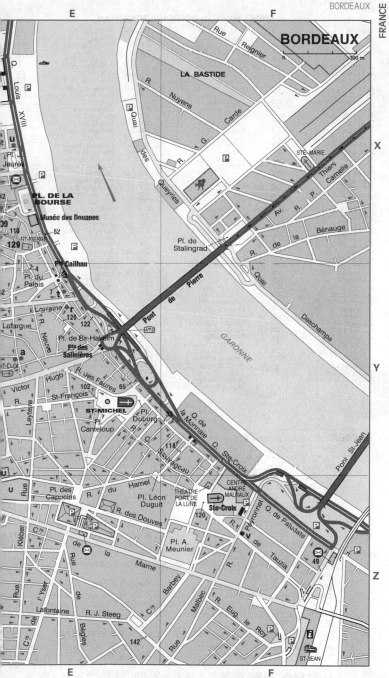

BORDEAUX

300 m

LA BASTIDE

Rue Reignier

Rue Nuvens

Carde

G.

R.

Quai

Q. Louis XVIII

P

P

PL. Jaures

P

PL. DE LA BOURSE

Musée des Douanes

ST-PIERRE

52

129

110

P

Pte Cailhau

4

Pl. du Palais

7

Lorraine

R.

126

122

Lafargue

R. Neuve

a

ST-CLO.

Pl. de Bir-Hakeim

Pte des Salinières

Victor

Hugo

Leyteire

R.

R. des Faures

65

102

St-François

ST-MICHEL

Pl. Duburg

33

Canteloup

R.

C.

118

Sauvageau

U

U

Rue

Pl. des Capucins

R.

du

Hamel

Pl. Léon Duguit

THEATRE

PORT DE LA LUNE

120

R. des Douves

Kléber

Crs

P

P

de

la

Marne

Pl. A. Meunier

Rue

de

l'Yser

Rue

Lafontaine

R. J. Steeg

Crs

Bègles

Bardey

Malbec

R.

R. Eug. le Roy

142

ST-JEAN

STE-MARIE

Thiers

Camélia

Av.

R.

P.

de

la

Bénauge

Pl. de Stalingrad

R.

de

Quai

Pont

de

Pierre

4m2

GARONNE

Deschamps

Q. de la Monnaie

Q. Ste-Croix

Pont St-Jean

CENTRE ANDRÉ MALRAUX

Ste-Croix

Peyronnet

Q. de Palujate

R.

de

Tauzia

49

P

P

Queyries

P

Quai des

X

Y

Z

STREET INDEX TO BORDEAUX TOWN PLAN

BORDEAUX 33000 Gironde 🔟 ⑨ – pop. 210 336 alt. 4 Greater Bordeaux 696 364 h.

See : 18C Bordeaux : façades along the quayside★★ EX, Esplanade des Quinconces DX★ Grand Théâtre★★ DX, Notre-Dame Church★ DX, Allées de Tourny DX, – Cours Clemenceau DX, Place Gambetta DX, Cours de l'Intendance DX – Old Bordeaux★★ : Place de la Bourse★★ EX, Place du Parlement★ EX **109**, St-Michel Basilica★ EY, Great Bell★ (Grosse Cloche) EY D – Pey-Berland district : St-André Cathedral★ DY (Pey-Berland Tower★ : ≼★★ E) – Méradeck district CY – Battle-Cruiser Colbert★★ – Museums : Fine Arts★ (Beaux-Arts) CDY M³, Decorative Arts★ DY M², Aquitaine★★ DY M⁴ – Entrepôt Laîné★★ : Museum of Contemporary Art★.

🛈ᵦ Golf Bordelais ℘ 05 56 28 56 04 by av. d'Eysines : 4 km ; 🛈ᵦ 🛈ᵦ of Bordeaux Lac ℘ 05 56 50 92 72, to the N by D 209 : 10 km ; 🛈ᵦ 🛈ᵦ of Medoc at Louens ℘ 05 56 70 11 90 to the NW by D 6 : 6 km ; 🛈 🛈ᵦ Internat. of Bordeaux-Pessac ℘ 05 57 26 03 33 by N 250 🛈ᵦ Bordeaux-Cameyrac ℘ 05 56 72 96 79 by N 89 : 18 km.

🛪 of Bordeaux-Mérignac : ℘ 05 56 34 50 50 to the W : 11 km.

🚄 ℘ 08 36 35 35 35.

🛈 Tourist Office 12 cours 30 Juillet ℘ 05 56 00 66 00, Fax 05 56 00 66 01 otbbordeaux-tourisme.com – Automobile Club du Sud-Ouest 8 pl. des Quinconces ℘ 05 56 44 22 92, Fax 05 56 48 57 47 – Bordeaux wine Exhibition (Maison du vin de Bordeaux) 1 cours 30 juil. (closed weekend from mid Oct.-mid May) ℘ 05 56 00 22 66, Fax 05 56 00 22 77 DX.

Paris 579 – Lyons 531 – Nantes 324 – Strasbourg 919 – Toulouse 245.

Burdigala Ⓜ, 115 r. G. Bonnac ℘ 05 56 90 16 16, burdigala@burdigala.com Fax 05 56 93 15 06, « Tasteful decor » – 🛗 🖿 📺 📞 🕭 ⊜ – 🕭 25 - 100. 🜂 ⓪ ⒼⒷ CX

Jardin de Burdigala : Meals 31 – 🖵 16 – **68 rm** 159/240, 8 suites, 7 duplex.

🏨 **Mercure Château Chartrons** Ⓜ, 81 cours St-Louis ⊠ 33300 ℰ 05 56 43 15 00, h1810@accor-hotels.com, Fax 05 56 69 15 21, 🍴, 🐕 – 🛗, ✳ rm, 🖥 📺 ✆ 🕭 – 🛗 150 🖭 ⓪ ⬛
Meals 23,65 ♀ – ☲ 10 – **144 rm** 97/112.

🏨 **Claret** Ⓜ ⚓, Cité Mondiale du Vin, 18 parvis des Chartrons ℰ 05 56 01 79 79, h2877@a ccor.hotels.com, Fax 05 56 01 79 00, 🍴 – 🛗, ✳ rm, 🖥 📺 ✆ 🕭 – 🛗 25 - 800. 🖭 ⓪ ⬛ 🗾 ✂ rest
Le 20 wine bar-rest. *(closed 22 December-2 January, Friday dinner, Saturday and Sunday)*
Meals 18 ♀ – ☲ 10,50 – **96 rm** 98/196.

🏨 **Mercure Mériadeck** Ⓜ, 5 r.-Lateulade ℰ 05 56 56 43 43, h1281@accor-hotels.com, Fax 05 56 96 50 59 – 🛗, ✳ rm, 🖥 📺 ✆ – 🛗 15 - 150. 🖭 ⓪ ⬛ 🗾   CY v
Festival (closed Saturday, Sunday and Bank Holidays) **Meals** 17 ♀ – ☲ 10 – **194 rm** 95/116.

🏨 **Holiday Inn** Ⓜ, 30 r. de l'auzia ⊠ 33800 ℰ 05 56 92 21 21, hiBordeauxCentre@all iance hotellerie.fr, Fax 05 56 91 08 06, 🍴 – 🛗, ✳ rm, 🖥 📺 ✆ 🕭, 🚗 – 🛗 65. 🖭 ⓪ ⬛ 🗾   FZ v
Meals *(closed lunch Saturday and Sunday)* 14/23 🍷 – ☲ 12,50 – **89 rm** 105/120.

🏨 **Novotel Bordeaux-Centre** Ⓜ, 45 cours Mar. Juin ℰ 05 56 51 46 46, h1023@acc or-hotels.com, Fax 05 56 98 25 56, 🍴 – 🛗, ✳ rm, 🖥 📺 ✆ 🕭 – 🛗 80. 🖭 ⓪ ⬛ 🗾   CY m
Meals a la carte 23/30 🍷 – ☲ 10 – **138 rm** 93/99.

🏨 **Ste-Catherine** Ⓜ without rest, 27 r. Parlement Ste-Catherine ℰ 05 56 81 95 12, Fax 05 56 44 50 51 – 🛗, ✳ rm, 🖥 📺 ✆ 🕭 – 🛗 40. 🖭 ⓪ ⬛ 🗾   DX m
☲ 11 – **84 rm** 107/155.

🏨 **Normandie** without rest, 7 cours 30-Juillet ℰ 05 56 52 16 80, Fax 05 56 51 68 91 – 🛗 📺 ✆ – 🛗 30. 🖭 ⓪ ⬛ 🗾   DX z
☲ 12 – **100 rm** 52/137.

🏨 **Bayonne Etche-Ona** without rest, 4 r. Martignac ℰ 05 56 48 00 88, bayetche@bo rdeaux-hotel.com, Fax 05 56 48 41 60 – 🛗 🖥 📺 ✆ – 🛗 35. 🖭 ⓪ ⬛ 🗾 ✂   DX f
☲ 10 – **63 rm** 90/200.

🏨 **Majestic** without rest, 2 r. Condé ℰ 05 56 52 60 44, mail-majestic@hotel-majestic.com, Fax 05 56 79 26 70 – 🛗 🖥 📺 ✆ 🖭 ⓪ ⬛ 🗾   DX a
☲ 9 – **50 rm** 70/95.

🏨 **Grand Hôtel Français** without rest, 12 rue Temple ⊠ 33000 ℰ 05 56 48 10 35, info@grand-hotel-francais.com, Fax 05 56 81 76 18 – ✆ 🕭. 🖭 ⓪ ⬛ 🗾   DX v
☲ 10 – **35 rm** 74/112.

🏨 **Presse** without rest, 6 r. Porte Dijeaux ℰ 05 56 48 53 88, cjourdian@free.fr, Fax 05 56 01 05 82 – 🛗 🖥 📺 ✆. 🖭 ⓪ ⬛ 🗾   DX k
closed 25 December-2 January – ☲ 7 – **27 rm** 46/80.

🏨 **Continental** without rest, 10 r. Montesquieu ℰ 05 56 52 66 00, continental@hotel-l e continental.com, Fax 05 56 52 77 97 – 🛗 📺 ✆. 🖭 ⓪ ⬛ 🗾   DX b
☲ 6,10 – **50 rm** 51/90.

🏨 **Quatre Sœurs** without rest, 6 cours 30-Juillet ℰ 05 57 81 19 20, 4sœurs@marluty .com, Fax 05 56 01 04 28 – 🛗 🖥 📺 ✆. 🖭 ⬛   DX s
☲ 8 – **34 rm** 60/70.

🏨 **Opéra** without rest, 35 r. Esprit des Lois ℰ 05 56 81 41 27, hotel.opera.bx@wanadoo.fr, Fax 05 56 51 78 80 – 🛗 🖥 📺 ✆. ⬛ ✂   DX n
closed 23 December-3 January – ☲ 6,10 – **27 rm** 32,10/48,80.

❈❈❈ **Chapon Fin** (Garcia), 5 r. Montesquieu ℰ 05 56 79 10 10, Fax 05 56 79 09 10, ✿ « Authentic 1900 rocaille decor » – 🖥. 🖭 ⓪ ⬛ 🗾. ✂   DX p
closed 15 August-3 September, Sunday and Monday – **Meals** 30 (lunch), 43/73 and a la carte 63/88 ♀
Spec. Soupe de potimaron, crème aux herbes potagères (September-March). Cabillaud poché au cerfeuil. Minute de macaron tiède au café torréfié.. **Wines** Pessac-Léognan blanc, Moulis..

❈❈❈ **Pavillon des Boulevards** (Franc), 120 r. Croix de Seguey ℰ 05 56 81 51 02, ✿ pavillon.des.boulevards@wanadoo.fr, Fax 05 56 51 14 58, 🍴 – 🖥. 🖭 ⓪ ⬛ 🗾
closed 11 to 26 August, 1 to 8 January, Sunday and lunch Monday and Saturday – **Meals** 40 (lunch), 50/74 and a la carte 65/80
Spec. Macaroni au pressé de ratatouille et langoustines rôties. Morceau de cochon "cul noir", jus de boudin et frites de pommes vertes. Cigarette noisette, mousse de chocolat et sorbet mandarine.. **Wines** Premières Côtes de Bordeaux blanc et rouge..

XXX **Les Plaisirs d'Ausone** (Gauffre), 10 r. Ausone ℰ 05 56 79 30 30, Fax 05 56 51 38 16
✿ « Vaulted restaurant elegantly decorated » – 🆔 ⓐ 🅶🅱 ⌚ᴄ🅱   EY ↑
closed 26 August-9 September, 2 to 8 January, Sunday, lunch Saturday and Monday –
Meals 27,44/68,60 and a la carte 55/70 ♀
Spec. Gourmandise de foies de canard. Fricassée de sole aux cèpes (early September-mid
October). Lamproie à la bordelaise (January- March).. **Wines** Bordeaux Supérieur, Canon-
Fronsac..

XXX **Jean Ramet**, 7 pl. J. Jaurès ℰ 05 56 44 12 51, ramet@ramet-jean.com,
✿ Fax 05 56 52 19 80 – 🔲. 🆔 🅶🅱   EX u
closed 3 to 25 August, 2 to 7 January, Sunday and Monday – **Meals** 28 (lunch), 45/56
and a la carte 62/76
Spec. Les trois salades. Dos et ventre de bar à la crème d'aulx. Croquant aux fruits de
saison.. **Wines** Graves blanc et rouge..

XXX **Vieux Bordeaux**, 27 r. Buhan ℰ 05 56 52 94 36, Fax 05 56 44 25 11, 🍽 – 🔲. 🆔 ⓐ
🅶🅱   EY a
closed 5 to 26 August, 10 to 24 February, Sunday, lunch Monday and Saturday – **Meals**
25,92/45,73 and a la carte 42/50.

XXX **L'Alhambra,** 111 bis r. Judaûque ℰ 05 56 96 06 91, Fax 05 56 98 00 52 – 🔲. 🅶🅱
closed 25 July-20 August, Sunday, Bank Holidays, lunch Monday and Saturday – **Meals** 17
(lunch), 26/36 and a la carte 40/55 ♀   CX e

XX **Didier Gélineau**, 26 r. Pas St-Georges ℰ 05 56 52 84 25, Fax 05 56 51 93 25 – 🔲. 🆔
ⓐ 🅶🅱 ⌚ᴄ🅱   EX n
closed 12 to 25 August, Sunday, lunch Monday and Saturday – **Meals** (booking essential)
20 (lunch), 34/50 ♀.

XX **Chamade,** 20 r. Piliers de Tutelle ℰ 05 56 48 13 74, la-chamade@la-chamade.com
Fax 05 56 79 29 67 – 🔲. 🆔 ⓐ 🅶🅱 ⌚ᴄ🅱   DX c
closed 20 July-5 August, 2 to 8 January, Saturday lunch and Wednesday – **Meals** 21/45
♀.

XX **L'Oiseau Bleu,** 65 cours Verdun ℰ 05 56 81 09 39, Fax 05 56 81 09 39 – 🔲. 🆔 ⓐ
🅶🅱
closed 28 July-18 August, 1 to 8 January, Saturday lunch and Sunday – **Meals** 17 (lunch)
32,50/54 ♀.

XX **Buhan,** 28 r. Buhan ℰ 05 56 52 80 86, lebuhan@wanadoo.fr, Fax 05 56 52 80 86 – 🆔
🅶🅱   EY a
closed 29 July-20 August, February Holidays, Sunday and Monday – **Meals** 24,50/43 ♀

X **Croc-Loup,** 35 r. Loup ℰ 05 56 44 21 19 – 🅶🅱   DY r
closed 28 July-28 August, Sunday and Monday – **Meals** 12,04 (lunch), 22,87/27,44.

at Bordeaux-Lac (Parc des Expositions) North of the town – ✉ 33300 Bordeaux :

🏨 **Sofitel Aquitania** Ⓜ, ℰ 05 56 69 66 66, h0669@accor-hotels.com,
Fax 05 56 69 66 00, 🍽, 🏊 – 🛗, ✱ rm, 🔲 📺 ⌚ 🅿 – 🛗 15 - 400. 🆔 ⓐ 🅶🅱 ⌚ᴄ🅱
Flore : Meals a la carte 38/48 ⅃ – ⌚ 14 – **183 rm** 130/140.

🏨 **Novotel-Bordeaux Lac** Ⓜ, ℰ 05 56 43 65 00, h0403@accor-hotels.com,
Fax 05 56 43 65 01, 🍽, 🏊, 🌳 – 🛗, ✱ rm, 🔲 📺 ⌚ 🅳 🅿 – 🛗 120. 🆔 ⓐ 🅶🅱 ⌚ᴄ🅱
Meals a la carte 25/35 ♀ – ⌚ 10 – **176 rm** 88/99.

at Bouliac SE : 8 km – alt. 74 – ✉ 33270 :

🏨 **St-James** (Amat) Ⓜ 🌿, pl. C. Hostein, near church ℰ 05 57 97 06 00, stjames@jn
✿ -amat.com., Fax 05 56 20 92 58, ≤ Bordeaux, 🍽, « Original contemporary decor », 🏊
🌳 – 🛗, 🔲 rm, 📺 ⌚ 🅳 🅿 – 🛗 25 - 40. 🆔 ⓐ 🅶🅱 ⌚ᴄ🅱 🍽
closed January – **Meals** (closed Monday and Tuesday except June-July) 70,13 and a la carte
70/95 ♀ - **Le Bistroy** ℰ 05 56 20 92 58 (closed March) **Meals** a la carte 30/35 ♀ –
⌚ 15,25 – **18 rm** 152,45/182,94
Spec. Salade d'huîtres au caviar de Gironde, crépinette grillée. Ravioli de cèpes frais. Agneau
de Pauillac rôti rosé aux tomates confites.. **Wines** Bordeaux Supérieur, Pomerol..

to the W :

at the airport of Mérignac 11 km by A 630 : from the North, exit n° 11=b, from the South,
exit n°11 – ✉ 33700 Mérignac :

🏨 **Mercure Aéroport** Ⓜ, 1 av. Ch. Lindbergh ℰ 05 56 34 74 74, h1508@accor-hote
s.com, Fax 05 56 34 30 84, 🍽, 🏊 – 🛗, ✱ rm, 🔲 📺 ⌚ 🅳 🅿 – 🛗 110. 🆔 ⓐ 🅶🅱
Meals 20 ♀ – ⌚ 10,50 – **148 rm** 122/130.

🏨 **Novotel Aéroport** Ⓜ, av. J. F. Kennedy ℰ 05 56 34 10 25, h0402@accor-hotels.com,
Fax 05 56 55 99 64, 🍽, 🏊, 🌳 – 🛗, ✱ rm, 🔲 📺 ⌚ 🅳 🅿 – 🛗 70. 🆔 ⓐ 🅶🅱 ⌚ᴄ🅱
Meals 15,55 ♀ – ⌚ 10 – **137 rm** 92/98.

Eugénie-les-Bains 40320 Landes 🅱🅾 ① – pop. 467 alt. 65 – Spa (Feb.-Nov.).

🏌 Golf du Tursan ℘ 05 58 51 11 63 by D 11 and D 62 : 2 km.

🅱 Tourist Office 147 r. René Vielle (Feb.-Nov.) ℘ 05 58 51 13 16, Fax 05 58 51 12 02.
Bordeaux 151.

🏨 **Les Prés d'Eugénie** (Guérard) Ⓜ ⚜, ℘ 05 58 05 06 07, guerard@relaischateaux.fr,
🏵🏵🏵 Fax 05 58 51 10 10, ≤, 🏖, « Elegantly decorated 19C mansion, park », 🛌, ⌁, %, 🏊
– 🛗 📺 🕻 🕹 🅿 – 🛄 40. 🆎 ⓞ 🇬🇧. %
closed 2 to 20 December and 3 January-21 March – (low-calorie menu for residents only)
- rest. Michel Guérard (booking essential)(set menu only at lunch) (closed Monday and
Tuesday except August and Bank Holidays) Meals 70(lunch), dinner and Sunday : 110/150
and a la carte 110/140 – ⇌ 28 – **29 rm** 285/300, 6 suites
Spec. Huîtres "d'une bouchée" et papillote de farce fine truffée à l'ancienne. Poitrine de
volaille des Landes cuisinée au lard sur la braise. Pêche blanche brûlée au sucre en Melba
de fruits rouges.. **Wines** Tursan blanc et rosé..
Couvent des Herbes Ⓜ ⚜, ≤, « 18C convent », 🏊 – 📺 🕻 🅿. % rest
closed 2 to 20 December and 3 January-7 February - **Meals** see **Les Prés d'Eugénie** and
Michel Guérard – ⇌ 28 – **5 rm** 360, 3 suites.

🏨 **Maison Rose** Ⓜ ⚜ (see also **rest. Michel Guérard**), ℘ 05 58 05 06 07, guerard@r
elaischateaux.fr, Fax 05 58 51 10 10, « Guesthouse ambience », ⌁, %, 🏊 – kitchenette
📺 🕻 🅿
(closed December and 5 January-9 February) – **Meals** (residents only) – ⇌ 17 – **31 rm**
90/160.

❌ **Ferme aux Grives** Ⓜ ⚜ with rm, ℘ 05 58 05 05 06, guerard@relaischateaux.fr,
Fax 05 58 51 10 10, ≤, « Old country inn », ⌁, %, 🏊 – 📺 🕻 🅿. 🇬🇧
closed 5 January-7 February – **Meals** (closed Monday and Tuesday except from 11 July-
1 September and Bank Holidays) 37 – ⇌ 20 – **4 rm** 360/470.

Pauillac 33250 Gironde 🔟 ⑦ – pop. 5 670 alt. 20.
Bordeaux 53.

🏨 **Château Cordeillan Bages** Ⓜ ⚜, to the S : 1 km by D 2 ℘ 05 56 59 24 24, cord
🏵🏵 eillan@relaischateaux.fr, Fax 05 56 59 01 89, 🏖 – 🛗 📺 🕻 🕹 🅿 🆎 ⓞ 🇬🇧 🇯🇨🇧. % rest
closed 13 December-31 January – **Meals** (closed Monday and lunch Saturday and Tuesday)
45 (lunch)/75 and a la carte 63/83 – ⇌ 15,24 – **25 rm** 157,07/223,34
Spec. Pressé d'anguilles fumées "terre et estuaire". Pigeon en coque de pois chiches.
Aubergine cristallisée au sucre.. **Wines** Entre-deux-Mers, Pauillac.

If you write to a hotel abroad,
enclose an International Reply Coupon (available from Post Offices).

CANNES 06400 Alpes-Mar. 🅱🅾 ⑨, 🔢🔢🔢 ㉟ ㊳ – pop. 68 676 alt. 2 – Casinos Carlton Casino Club
BYZ, Croisette BZ.

See : Site★★ – Seafront★★ : Boulevard★★ BCDZ and Pointe de la Croisette★ X – ≤★ from the
Mont Chevalier Tower AZ V – The Castre Museum★ (Musée de la Castre) AZ – Tour Into the
Hills▲ (Chemin des Collines) NE : 4 km V – The Croix des Gardes X E ≤★ W : 5 km then 15 mn.

🏌 of Cannes-Mougins ℘ 04 93 75 79 13 by ⑤ : 9 km ; 🏌 of Cannes-Mandelieu
℘ 04 92 97 32 00 by ② ; 🏌 Royal Mougins Golf Club at Mougins ℘ 04 92 92 49 69 by ④ :
10 km ; 🏌 Riviera Golf Club at Mandelieu ℘ 04 92 97 49 49 by ② : 8 km.

🅱 Tourist Office "SEMEC", Palais des Festivals ℘ 04 93 39 24 53, Fax 04 92 99 84 23
and railway station, first floor ℘ 04 93 99 19 77, Fax 04 92 99 84 23,
semoftouPalais-Festivals-Cannes.fr – Automobile Club 12 bis r. L.-Blanc ℘ 04 93 39 38 94,
Fax 04 93 38 30 65.

Paris 903 ⑤ – Aix-en-Provence 146 ⑤ – Grenoble 312 ⑤ – Marseilles 159 ⑤ – Nice 32
⑤ – Toulon 121 ⑤.

Plans on following pages

🏨 **Carlton Inter-Continental,** 58 bd Croisette ℘ 04 93 06 40 06, cannes@intercont
i.com, Fax 04 93 06 40 25, ≤, 🏖, 🛌, 🛞 – 🛗, ⤢ rm, 🗄 📺 🕻 🕹 🚗 – 🛄 25 - 250.
🆎 ⓞ 🇬🇧 🇯🇨🇧. % rest   CZ e
La Côte ℘ 04 93 06 40 23 (dinner only) (July-September and closed Sunday and Monday)
Meals 103,67 ⚑ – **Brasserie Carlton** ℘ 04 93 06 40 21 Meals 33,54/39,64 ⚑ – **Plage**
℘ 04 93 06 44 94 - (lunch only) (April-mid-October) Meals 45 – ⇌ 25,92 – **310 rm**
370/750, 28 suites.

🏨 **Majestic Barrière,** 14 bd Croisette ℘ 04 92 98 77 00, majestic@lucienbarriere.com,
Fax 04 93 38 97 90, ≤, 🛌, ⌁, 🛞 – 🛗 🗄 📺 🕻 🕹 🚗 – 🛄 400. 🆎 ⓞ 🇬🇧 🇯🇨🇧
closed mid- November-late December - - see **Villa des Lys** below- **Fouquet's :** Meals a
la carte 38/65 ⚑ – **Plage** (lunch only) (April-October) Meals a la carte 40/60 ⚑ – ⇌ 23
– **282 rm** 405/760, 23 suites.   BZ n

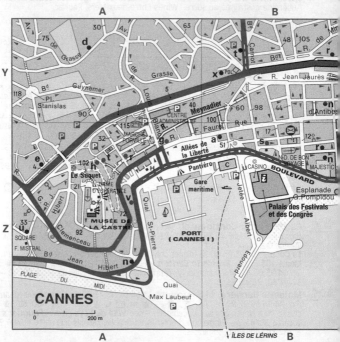

CANNES

0   200 m

A

↓ ÎLES DE LÉRINS   B

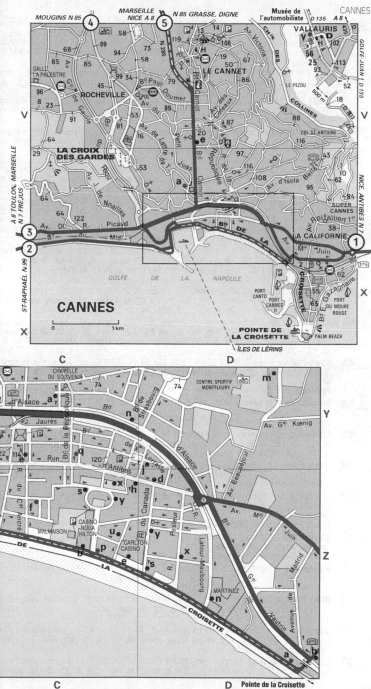

CANNES
FRANCE

MOUGINS N 85   MARSEILLE   N 85 GRASSE, DIGNE   Musée de   CANNES
                NICE A 8   l'automobiliste

VALLAURIS

CANNES

GOLFE DE LA NAPOULE

POINTE DE
LA CROISETTE

ÎLES DE LÉRINS

CROISETTE

Pointe de la Croisette

241

Martinez, 73 bd Croisette ℘ 04 92 98 73 00, martinez@concorde-hotels.com, Fax 04 93 39 67 82, ≤, 佘, 丛, 為。– 園 圓 ⊡ ✔ も – 益 600. ஊ ⓪ ⒼⒷ 亞 DZ n see *Palme d'Or* below - *Relais Martinez* ℘ 04 92 98 74 12 *(closed 1 to 7 January)* Meals 34/49 ♀ – *Plage* (lunch only) *(April-October)* Meals a la carte 40/80 ♀ – ⊡ 22 – **397 rm** 430/740, 33 suites.

Noga Hilton Ⓜ, 50 bd Croisette ℘ 04 92 99 70 00, sales_cannes@hilton.com, Fax 04 92 99 70 11, 佘, « Panoramic rooftop swimming pool and terrace », 丛, 丛, 為。 – 園, ⊱ rm, 圓 ⊡ ✔ も ⇔. 園 ⓪ ⒼⒷ 亞. ⅍ rm   CZ b *Scala :* ℘ 04 92 99 70 23 *(closed lunch July-August)* Meals 36/52,75 ♀ – *Plage* ℘ 04 92 99 70 27 *(April-September)* Meals a la carte 40/69 ♀ – ⊡ 23,75 – **186 rm** 329/719, 48 suites.

Sofitel Méditerranée Ⓜ, 2 bd J. Hibert ℘ 04 92 99 73 00, sofimedcannes@gofcrnet.com, Fax 04 92 99 73 29, ≤, 佘, « Panoramic rooftop swimming pool and restaurant », 丛 – 園, ⊱ rm, 圓 ⊡ ✔ も ⇔ – 益 70. 園 ⓪ ⒼⒷ 亞   AZ n *Méditerranée* (7th floor) ℘ 04 92 99 73 02 *(dinner only in July-August) (closed 23 November-24 December, Sunday and Monday from September-June)* Meals 35,06(lunch), 44,97/64,03 ♀ – *Chez Panisse* - Provencal decor - Meals 25,10 ♀ – ⊡ 22,11 – **149 rm** 221/358.

Radisson SAS Montfleury Ⓜ ⅀, 25 av. Beauséjour ℘ 04 93 68 86 86, info.mortfleury@radissonsas.com, Fax 04 93 68 87 87, ≤, 佘, 丛, 爲, ℀ – 園, ⊱ rm, 圓 ⊡ ✔ も ⇔ – 益 260. 園 ⓪ ⒼⒷ 亞. ⅍   DY m (swimming pool grill in July-August) *L'Olivier* (closed July, August and Sunday from September-June) Meals 22/34 ♀ – ⊡ 17 – **182 rm** 199/350.

Gray d'Albion Ⓜ, 38 r. Serbes ℘ 04 92 99 79 79, graydalbion@lucienbarriere.com Fax 04 93 99 26 10, 佘, 為。– 園, ⊱ rm, 圓 ⊡ ✔ も – 益 150. 園 ⓪ ⒼⒷ BZ c *Royal Gray* ℘ 04 92 99 79 60 *(closed Sunday dinner and Monday)* Meals 38 ♀ – 19 – **191 rm** 250/395, 8 suites.

Croisette Beach Ⓜ without rest, 13 r. Canada ℘ 04 92 18 88 00, croisettebea@aws.fr, Fax 04 93 68 35 38, 丛 – 園, ⊱ rm, 圓 ⊡ ✔ も ⇔. 園 ⓪ ⒼⒷ 亞 DZ y closed 20 November-27 December – ⊡ 16 – **94 rm** 190/290.

Amarante Ⓜ, 78 bd Carnot ℘ 04 93 39 22 23, cannes@amarantehotels.com Fax 04 93 39 40 22, 佘, 丛 – 園, ⊱ rm, 圓 ⊡ ✔ も ⇔ – 益 25. 園 ⓪ ⒼⒷ 亞 closed December, Saturday and Sunday from January-March – Meals 25/31 b.i. ♀ – ⊡ 13 – **71 rm** 230/520.   V e

Savoy Ⓜ, 5 r. F. Einesy ℘ 04 92 99 72 00, Fax 04 93 68 25 59, 佘, « Rooftop swimming pool and terrace », 丛, 為。– 園, ⊱ rm, 圓 ⊡ ✔ ⇔ – 益 15 - 80. 園 ⓪ ⒼⒷ 亞. ⅍   CZ u *Roseraie* ℘ 04 92 99 72 09 Meals 25/28 ♀ – ⊡ 16 – **101 rm** 182/261, 5 suites.

Sun Riviera Ⓜ without rest, 138 r. d'Antibes ℘ 04 93 06 77 77, sun-riviera-hotel.cannes@wanadoo.fr, Fax 04 93 38 31 10, 丛, 爲 – 園, ⊱ rm, 圓 ⊡ ✔ も ⇔. 園 ⓪ ⒼⒷ 亞 – closed 17 November-28 December – ⊡ 14 – **42 rm** 142/210.   CZ h

Splendid without rest, 4 r. F. Faure ℘ 04 97 06 22 22, hotel.splendid.cannes@wanadoo.fr, Fax 04 93 99 55 02, ≤ harbour – 園 kitchenette 圓 ⊡ ✔. 園 ⓪ ⒼⒷ BZ a ⊡ 10 – **64 rm** 99/198.

Belle Plage Ⓜ without rest, 6 r. J. Dollfus ℘ 04 93 06 25 50, belleplage@wanadoo.fr Fax 04 93 99 61 06, « Panoramic rooftop terrace » – 園 圓 ⊡ ✔ も ⇔. 園 ⓪ ⒼⒷ 亞 1 February-1 November – ⊡ 14 – **48 rm** 200/300.   AZ u

Cristal Ⓜ, 15 rd-pt Duboys d'Angers ℘ 04 93 39 45 45, reservation@hotel-cristal.com Fax 04 93 38 64 66, 佘 – 園, ⊱ rm, 圓 ⊡ ✔ も ⇔. 園 ⓪ ⒼⒷ 亞. ⅍ rm   CZ s closed 25 November-28 December – Meals 27,50/53,40 ♀ – ⊡ 15 – **50 rm** 165/370

Cavendish Ⓜ without rest, 11 bd Carnot ℘ 04 97 06 26 00, Fax 04 97 06 26 01 – 園 ⊱ rm, 圓 ⊡ ✔. 園 ⓪ ⒼⒷ   BY v closed 6 December-15 January – ⊡ 18 – **34 rm** 210/260.

Fouquet's without rest, 2 rd-pt Duboys d'Angers ℘ 04 92 59 25 00, info@le-fouquets.com, Fax 04 92 98 03 39 – 圓 ⊡ ✔ ⇔. 園 ⓪ ⒼⒷ   CZ y 1 April-15 November – ⊡ 12 – **10 rm** 140/185.

Bleu Rivage without rest, 61 bd Croisette ℘ 04 93 94 24 25, hotel.bleu-rivage@libertysurf.fr, Fax 04 93 43 74 92 – 圓 ⊡ も. 園 ⓪ ⒼⒷ. ⅍   DZ s ⊡ 10 – **19 rm** 122/260.

Cézanne Ⓜ without rest, 40 bd Alsace ℘ 04 93 38 50 70, cezanne@worldnet.fr Fax 04 92 99 20 99, 爲 – 園 圓 ⊡ ✔ も ⇔ – 益 40. 園 ⓪ ⒼⒷ 亞   CY r ⊡ 9 – **29 rm** 108/138.

Cannes Riviera Ⓜ without rest, 16 bd Alsace ℘ 04 97 06 20 40, reservation@cannesriviera.com, Fax 04 93 39 20 75, 丛 – 園 圓 ⊡ ✔ も ⇔ – 益 20. 園 ⓪ ⒼⒷ 亞. BY ⊡ 10 – **59 rm** 100/160.

🏨 **Paris** without rest, 34, bd Alsace 📞 04 93 38 30 89, *reservation@hotel-de-paris.com*, Fax 04 93 39 04 61, ≥, 🐟, – 🛠 25. 🆎 ⓪ 🆖 🆑 ⚙ CY a
closed 16 November-26 December – ⊑ 13 – **47 rm** 105/120, 3 suites.

🏨 **America** Ⓜ without rest, 13 r. St-Honoré 📞 04 93 06 75 75, *info@hotel-america.com*, Fax 04 93 68 04 58 – 🛗 🗏 📺 🔦 🆎 ⓪ 🆖 🆑 BZ r
closed 26 November-26 December – ⊑ 11 – **28 rm** 105/152.

🏨 **Eden Hôtel** Ⓜ without rest, 133 r. Antibes 📞 04 93 68 78 00, *reception@eden-hotel-cannes.com*, Fax 04 93 68 78 01 – 🛗, ⇥ rm, 🗏 📺 🔦 🐟 – 🛠 60. 🆎 ⓪ 🆖
⊑ 14 – **40 rm** 167,69/228,67. DZ d

🏨 **Renoir** without rest, 7 r. Edith Cavell 📞 04 92 99 62 62, *renoir@worldnet.fr*, Fax 04 92 99 62 82 – 🛗 kitchenette 🗏 📺 🔦 🆎 ⓪ 🆖 🆑 BY x
⊑ 12 – **27 rm** 137/243.

🏨 **Victoria** without rest, rd-pt Duboys d'Angers 📞 04 92 59 40 00, *hotelvicto@aol.com*, Fax 04 93 38 03 91 – 🛗 🗏 📺 🔦 🐟 🆎 ⓪ 🆖 CZ x
closed 22 November-27 December – ⊑ 13,72 – **25 rm** 182,93/243,91.

🏨 **Mondial** without rest, 1 r. Teisseire 📞 04 93 68 70 00, *mondial@dial.oleane.com*, Fax 04 93 99 39 11 – 🛗, ⇥ rm, 🗏 📺 🔦 ♿ 🆎 ⓪ 🆖 🆑 CY e
⊑ 12 – **58 rm** 110/134.

🏨 **Villa de l'Olivier** without rest, 5 r. Tambourinaires 📞 04 93 39 53 28, *reception@hotelolivier.com*, Fax 04 93 39 55 85, ≥ – 🗏 📺 🅿 🆎 ⓪ 🆖. ⚙ AZ e
closed 1 to 22 December – ⊑ 9 – **24 rm** 91/120.

🏨 **Régina** Ⓜ without rest, 31 r. Pasteur 📞 04 93 94 05 43, *reception@hotel-regina-cannes.com*, Fax 04 93 43 20 54 – 🛗 🗏 📺 🔦 🅿 🆖 🆑. ⚙ DZ x
closed 9 November-27 December – ⊑ 10 – **19 rm** 145.

🏨 **Embassy**, 6 r. Bône 📞 04 97 06 99 00, *embassy@wanadoo.fr*, Fax 04 93 99 07 98 – 🛗 🗏 📺 🔦 🆎 ⓪ 🆖 🆑 DY j
Meals 25/34 ⊑ – ⊑ 10 – **60 rm** 117/182.

🏨 **California's** Ⓜ without rest, 8 traverse Alexandre III 📞 04 93 94 12 21, *nadia@californias-hotel.com*, Fax 04 93 43 55 17, ≥, 🐟 – 🛗 🗏 📺 🔦 ♿ – 🛠 15. 🆎 ⓪ 🆖
⊑ 11 – **33 rm** 132/214. DZ h

🏨 **Albert 1er** without rest, 68 av. Grasse 📞 04 93 39 24 04, Fax 04 93 38 83 75 – 📺 🅿. 🆖 AY d
closed 17 November-16 December – ⊑ 5,50 – **11 rm** 50/58.

🏨 **Beverly** without rest, 14 r. Hoche 📞 04 93 39 10 66, *contact@hotel-beverly.com*, Fax 04 93 98 65 63 – 🛗 📺 🔦 🆎 ⓪ 🆖 🆑. ⚙ BY n
⊑ 6 – **19 rm** 46/70.

🍴🍴🍴🍴 **Palme d'Or** - Hôtel Martinez, 73 bd Croisette 📞 04 92 98 74 14, *martinez@concorde-hotels.com*, Fax 04 93 39 03 38, ≤, 🍴 – 🛗 🗏 🅿 🆎 ⓪ 🆖 DZ u
🌹🌹 closed mid-November-mid-December, Monday and Tuesday – **Meals** 43 (lunch), 65/130 and a la carte 95/130
Spec. Cassolette de haricots cocos, persillé de poulpes et supions (Spring-Summer). Bouillabaisse de légumes, crevettes, bulots et champignons (Spring-Summer). Chocolat "Palme d'Or" aux éclats de noisettes. **Wines** Coteaux Varois, Côtes de Provence.

🍴🍴🍴🍴 **Villa des Lys** - Hôtel Majestic, 14 bd Croisette 📞 04 92 98 77 00, *majestic@lucienbarriere.com*, Fax 04 93 38 97 90, 🍴 – 🗏. 🆎 ⓪ 🆖 🆑 BZ n
🌹 closed mid November-late December, lunch July-August, Sunday and Monday – **Meals** 42,69 (lunch)/118,91 and a la carte 90/130 ⊑
Spec. Sauté de crustacés à l'aïoli. Côte de veau cuite en cocotte et légumes braisés au jus. Diplomate arabica, fondant au chocolat et sorbet cacao **Wines** Bandol, Côtes de Provence.

🍴🍴🍴 **Neat**, 11 square Mérimée 📞 04 93 99 29 19, *neat.resto@wanadoo.fr*, Fax 04 93 68 84 48, 🍴 – 🗏. 🆎 ⓪ 🆖 🆑 BZ s
🌹 closed 28 July-11 August, 17 November-12 January, lunch in July-August, Sunday and Monday – **Meals** 42,70/105 and a la carte 85/120 ⊑
Spec. Escargots aux morilles et purée d'ail doux. Foie gras fumé minute, purée d'oignons caramélisés. Magret de canard au beurre de lentilles (October-April). **Wines** Côtes de Provence, Coteaux d'Aix en Provence.

🍴🍴🍴 **Mesclun**, 16 r. St-Antoine 📞 04 93 99 45 19, *lemesclun@wanadoo.fr*, Fax 04 93 47 68 29 – 🗏. 🆎 🆖 🆑 AZ t
closed 20 November-20 December, 20 to 28 February and Wednesday – **Meals** (dinner only) 31 ⊑.

🍴🍴 **Festival**, 52 bd Croisette 📞 04 93 38 04 81, *contact@lefestival.fr*, Fax 04 93 38 13 82, 🍴 – 🗏. 🆎 ⓪ 🆖 🆑 CZ p
closed 17 November-27 December – **Meals** 36,20 ⊑ - **Grill :** **Meals** a la carte 27/51 ⊑.

🍴🍴 **Gaston et Gastounette**, 7 quai St-Pierre 📞 04 93 39 47 92, Fax 04 93 99 45 34, 🍴 – 🗏. 🆎 ⓪ 🆖 AZ v
closed 1 to 20 December – **Meals** 22,50 (lunch)/33,50 ⊑.

XX **Rest. Arménien,** 82 bd Croisette ✆ 04 93 94 00 58, *lucieetchristian@lerestauranta rmenien.com, Fax 04 93 94 56 12* – ▤. ◑ GB DZ a
closed 18 November-10 December, lunch in July-August and Monday – **Meals** - Armenian rest. - set menu only 40.

XX **Côté Jardin,** 12 av. St-Louis ✆ 04 93 38 60 28, *contact@chef-cotejardin.com, Fax 04 93 38 60 28,* 佘 – ▤. AE GB X a
closed February, Sunday and Monday – **Meals** 35.

XX **3 Portes,** 16 r. Frères Pradignac ✆ 04 93 38 91 70, *Fax 04 93 38 95 52,* 佘 – ▤. AE GB CZ
closed 1 to 15 December, Monday lunch and Saturday in winter and Sunday – **Meals** 19,80 (lunch)/25,90 b.i. ♀.

X **Mi-Figue, Mi-Raisin,** 27 r. Suquet ✆ 04 93 39 51 25, *Fax 04 93 39 51 25,* 佘 – AE GB AY h
closed 20 November-7 December and Wednesday – **Meals** (dinner only) a la carte 40/50

X **Rendez-Vous,** 35 r. F. Faure ✆ 04 93 68 55 10, *Fax 04 93 38 96 21,* 佘 – ▤. AE GB AZ g
closed 1 to 20 December – **Meals** 17/24 ♀.

X **La Cave,** 9 bd République ✆ 04 93 99 79 87 – ▤. AE GB JCB CY c
closed Saturday lunch and Sunday – **Meals** 27,14.

X **Aux Bons Enfants,** 80 r. Meynadier, 佘 – ⚘ AZ
closed 4 August-1 September, 24 December-2 January, Saturday dinner from October-April and Sunday – **Meals** 15.

Grasse *06130 Alpes-Mar.* 84 ⑧, 114 ⑬, 115 ㉔ – *pop. 41388 alt. 250.*
Victoria Golf Club ✆ 04 93 12 23 26 by D 4, D 3 and D 103 : 13 km ; Grande Bastide at Opio ✆ 04 93 77 70 08, E : 6 km by D 7 ; of St-Donat ✆ 04 93 09 76 60 : 5,5 km Opio-Valbonne ✆ 04 93 12 00 08 by D 4 : 11 km.
Tourist Office 22 Crs H. Cresp ✆ 04 93 36 66 66, Fax 04 93 36 86 36, tourismeville-grasse.fr.
Cannes 17.

XXXX ✿✿ **Bastide St-Antoine** (Chibois) with rm, 48 av. H. Dunant (quartier St-Antoine) by road of Cannes : 1,5 km ✆ 04 93 70 94 94, *info@jacques-chibois.com, Fax 04 93 70 94 95,* ←, 佘, « 18C country farm in an olive-grove », – ▤ TV P – 20 - 80. AE ◑ GB JCB
Meals 44 (lunch), 99/130 and a la carte 80/120 ♀ – 21 – **11 rm** 235/285
Spec. Fleur de Saint-Jacques à la citronnelle (15 October-15 March). Denti à l'infusion de verveine sur mitonnée de légumes au basilic. Fraises cuites au vin d'épices et glace à l'huile d'olive (April-October). **Wines** Bellet, Coteaux d'Aix-en-Provence.

Juan-les-Pins *06160 Alpes-Mar.* 84 ⑨, 115 ㉟ ㊴
Tourist Office 51 bd Ch.-Guillaumont ✆ 04 92 90 53 05, Fax 04 93 61 55 13, acceuilantibes6juanlespins.com.
Cannes 8,5.

✿✿ **Juana**, la Pinède, av. G. Gallice ✆ 04 93 61 08 70, *info@hotel-juana.com Fax 04 93 61 76 60,* 佘, – ▤ rm, TV P – 25. AE GB JCB
10 April-31 October – ***Terrasse-Christian Morisset*** ✆ 04 93 61 20 37-(dinner only in July-August) *(closed Monday lunch, Thursday lunch and Wednesday except July-August)* **Meals** 52(lunch), 92/120 and a la carte 90/140 ♀ – 19 – **45 rm** 185/457, 5 suites
Spec. Cannelloni de supions et palourdes à l'encre de seiche. Selle d'agneau de Pauillac cuite en terre d'argile de Vallauris. Millefeuille de fraises des bois à la crème de mascarpone. **Wines** Bellet, Côtes de Provence.

La Napoule *06210 Alpes-Mar.* 84 ⑧, 115 ㉞.
of Mandelieu ✆ 04 92 97 32 00 ; Riviera Golf Club ✆ 04 92 97 49 49.
Tourist Office av. Cannes at Mandelieu ✆ 04 92 97 86 46, Fax 04 92 97 67 79.
Cannes 9,5.

XXXX ✿✿ **L'Oasis** (Raimbault), r. J. H. Carle ✆ 04 93 49 95 52, *message@oasis-raimbault.com Fax 04 93 49 64 13,* 佘, « Shaded and flowered patio » – ▤. AE ◑ GB JCB
closed Sunday dinner and Monday from October-28 February – **Meals** 43 (lunch), 58/115 and a la carte 90/115
Spec. "Soleil levant" de rouget de roche en salade aux saveurs d'Orient. Chapon de pêche locale au four rôti en tian aux senteurs de Provence. Filet mignon de veau et foie gras au gingembre, mangue rôtie.. **Wines** Côteaux d'Aix-en-Provence.

Don't get lost, use **Michelin Maps** which are updated annually.

LILLE 59000 Nord 💵 ⑯, 💵 ⑫ – pop. 172 142 alt. 10.

See : Old Lille★★ : Old Stock Exchange★★ (Vieille Bourse) EY, Place du Général-de-Gaulle★ EY 66, Hospice Comtesse★ (panelled timber vault★★) EY, – Ruc de la Monnaie★ EY 120 – Vauban's Citadel★ EY – St-Sauveur district : Paris Gate★ EFZ, ≼★ from the top of the belfry of the Hôtel de Ville FZ – Fine Arts Museum★★★ (Musée des Beaux-Arts) EZ – Général de Gaulle's Birthplace (Maison natale) EY.

🅱 of Flandres (private) 𝜙 03 20 72 20 74 : 4,5 km ; 🅱 of Sart (private) 𝜙 03 20 72 02 51 : 7 km ; 🅱 of Brigode at Villeneuve d'Ascq 𝜙 03 20 91 17 86 : 9 km ; 🅱 🅱 of Bondues 𝜙 03 20 23 20 62 : 9,5 km.

✈ of Lille-Lesquin : 𝜙 03 20 49 68 68 : 8 km.

🚗🚃 𝜙 08 36 35 35 35.

🛈 Tourist Office Palais Rihour 𝜙 03 20 21 94 21, Fax 03 20 21 94 20, infolilletourism.com.
Paris 221 ④ – Brussels 116 ② – Ghent 71 ② – Luxembourg 312 ④ – Strasbourg 525 ④

Plans on following pages

🏨🏨🏨 **Alliance** 🅼 ♨, 17 quai du Wault ⊠ 59800 𝜙 03 20 30 62 62, alliancelille@alliance-hospitality.com, Fax 03 20 42 94 25, « 17C former convent » – 📳, ⇻ rm, 📺 ✆ & 🅿 – 🔄 35 - 100. 🆎 ⓪ 🆖 🃏   BV d
Meals (closed 15 July-31 August) 26,68/31,25 b.i. ♈ – � 14 – **80 rm** 185/255, 3 suites.

🏨🏨🏨 **Carlton** without rest, 3 r. Paris ⊠ 59800 𝜙 03 20 13 33 13, carlton@carltonlille.com, Fax 03 20 51 48 17, 🎬 – 📳, ⇻ rm, 🗐 📺 ✆ & 🚗 – 🔄 15 - 170. 🆎 ⓪ 🆖 🃏
⊇ – **59 rm** 150/224.   FY u

🏨🏨 **Novotel Flandres** 🅼, 49 r. Tournai ⊠ 59800 𝜙 03 28 38 67 00, H3165@accor-hotels.com, Fax 03 28 38 67 10, 🎬 – 📳, ⇻ rm, 🗐 📺 ✆ & – 🔄 80   FZ w
Meals 21,90 ♈ – ⊇ 10,50 – **88 rm** 114/125, 5 suites.

🏨🏨 **Grand Hôtel Bellevue** without rest, 5 r. J. Roisin 𝜙 03 20 57 45 64, grand.hotel.bellevue@wanadoo.fr, Fax 03 20 40 07 93 – 📳, ⇻ rm, 📺 ✆ – 🔄 50.
⊇ 9,90 – **60 rm** 135,67/182,94.   EY a

🏨🏨 **Novotel Centre** 🅼, 116 r. Hôpital Militaire ⊠ 59800 𝜙 03 28 38 53 53, h0918-gm@accor-hotels.com, Fax 03 28 38 53 54 – 📳, ⇻ rm, 🗐 📺 ✆ & – 🔄 50. 🆎 ⓪ 🆖 🃏   FY s
Meals 20,58 ♈ – ⊇ 10,06 – **102 rm** 109/144.

🏨🏨 **Mercure Royal** 🅼 without rest, 2 bd Carnot ⊠ 59800 𝜙 03 20 14 71 47, h0802@accor-hotels.com, Fax 03 20 14 71 48 – 📳, ⇻ rm, 🗐 📺 ✆ & – 🔄 25. 🆎 ⓪ 🆖 🃏
⊇ 10 – **101 rm** 145/155.   EY h

🏨🏨 **Express by Holiday Inn** 🅼, 75 bis r. Gambetta 𝜙 03 20 42 90 90, expresslille@alliance-hotellerie.fr, Fax 03 20 57 14 24 – 📳, ⇻ rm, 📺 ✆ & 🚗 – 🔄 15 - 100. 🆎 ⓪ 🆖 🃏   EZ e
Meals (closed August, Saturday and Sunday) a la carte approx. 26 ⅋ – **97 rm** ⊇ 150.

🏨🏨 **Paix** without rest, 46 bis r. Paris ⊠ 59800 𝜙 03 20 54 63 93, hotelpaixlille@aol.com, Fax 03 20 63 98 97 – 📳 📺 ✆. 🆎 ⓪ 🆖 🃏   EY r
⊇ 7,62 – **35 rm** 61/84.

🏨 **Ibis Gare** 🅼, 29 av. Ch. St-Venant ⊠ 59800 𝜙 03 28 36 30 40, h0901@accor hotels.com, Fax 03 28 36 30 99, 🎬 – 📳, ⇻ rm, 📺 ✆ & 🚗 – 🔄 20 60. 🆎 ⓪ 🆖
Meals a la carte approx. 22 ⅋ – ⊇ 5,50 – **151 rm** 68.   FYZ a

🏨 **Brueghel** without rest, parvis St-Maurice 𝜙 03 20 06 86 69, Fax 03 20 63 25 27 – 📳 📺 ✆. 🆎 ⓪ 🆖   EY x
⊇ 7 – **66 rm** 62/96.

🏨 **Lille Europe** 🅼 without rest, av. Le Corbusier 𝜙 03 28 36 76 76, lilleeurope@citadines.com, Fax 03 28 36 77 77 – 📳 📺 & 🚗. 🆎 ⓪ 🆖 🃏   FY m
⊇ 8 – **97 rm** 75.

🍴🍴🍴 **A L'Huîtrière**, 3 r. Chats Bossus ⊠ 59800 𝜙 03 20 55 43 41, poisson.huitriere@libertysurf.fr, Fax 03 20 55 23 10, « Original decoration with ceramics in the fish shop » – 🗐. 🆎 ⓪ 🆖 🃏   EY g
closed 22 July-24 August, dinner Sunday and Bank Holidays – **Meals** 43 (lunch), 75/100 and a la carte 65/100 ♈
Spec. Pressé d'anguille fraîche et d'anguille fumée de la Somme. Filet de turbot en croûte de pomme de terre. Produits de la mer.

🍴🍴 **Sébastopol** (Germond), 1 pl. Sébastopol 𝜙 03 20 57 05 05, Fax 03 20 40 11 31 – 🆎 🆖 🃏   EZ a
closed 4 to 26 August, Sunday except lunch from September-June and Saturday lunch – **Meals** 26 (lunch)/41 and a la carte 36/63 ♈
Spec. Mousseline de brocheton au foie gras. Filet de bœuf, ravioli au Maroilles et jus à la bière. Opéra glacé au café, coulis à la chicorée.

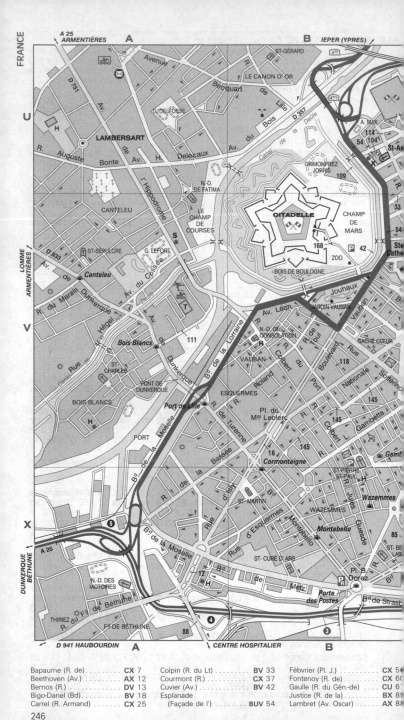

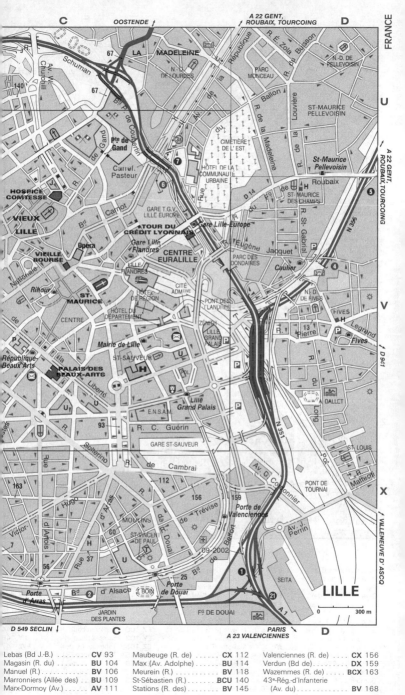

FRANCE

C OOSTENDE

A 22 GENT,
ROUBAIX, TOURCOING D

U

A 22 GENT,
ROUBAIX,TOURCOING

V

/ D 941

X

/ VILLENEUVE D'ASCQ

LA MADELEINE

N.-D. DE
PELLEVOISIN

PARC
MONCEAU

N.-D.
DE LOURDES

ST-MAURICE
PELLEVOISIN

Pte de
Gand

Carref.
Pasteur

CIMETIÈRE
DE L'EST

HÔTEL DE LA
COMMUNAUTÉ
URBAINE

St-Maurice
Pellevoisin

Roubaix

HOSPICE
COMTESSE

VIEUX
LILLE

ST-MAURICE
DES CHAMPS

GARE T.G.V.
LILLE EUROPE

TOUR DU
CRÉDIT LYONNAIS

Gare Lille-Europe

VIEILLE
BOURSE

Opéra

Gare Lille
Flandres

CENTRE
EURALILLE

Eugène Jacquet

PARC DES
DONDAINES

Caulier

LILLE-
FLANDRES

ST-
MAURICE

Rihour

CITÉ
ADMIVE

HÔTEL
DE RÉGION

CENTRE

HÔTEL DU
DÉPARTEMENT

PONT DES
FLANDRES

N.-D.
DE RIVES

FIVES

République-
Beaux-Arts

Mairie de Lille

ST-SAUVEUR

ZÉNITH
LILLE
GRAND PALAIS

Pierre

13

Fives

PALAIS DES
BEAUX-ARTS

Liberté

Lille
Grand Palais

DALLET

ST-LOUIS

E.N.S.A.M.

93

R. C. Guérin

GARE ST-SAUVEUR

Matteoli

de Cambrai

112

156

159

Porte de
Valenciennes

PONT DE
TOURNAI

163

MOULINS

ST-VINCENT
DE PAUL

60

Av. J.
Perrin

Av. G. Cordonnier

7

56

37

Porte
d'Arras

2

d'Alsace

BOIN

25

Porte
de Douai

09-2002

1

21

SEITA

LILLE

0   300 m

D 549 SECLIN

C

JARDIN
DES PLANTES

Fg DE DOUAI

PARIS
A 23 VALENCIENNES

D

LILLE

0   300 m

XXX **Laiterie,** 138 av. Hippodrome at Lambersart ✉ 59130 *Lambersart* ☎ 03 20 92 79 73, *Fax 03 20 22 16 19,* 🏠, ☂ - **P**. AE GB JCB AV s
closed 14 to 18 August, Monday, dinner Sunday and Wednesday – **Meals** 20/45 ♀.

XXX **Cour des Grands,** 61 r. Monnaie ✉ 59800 ☎ 03 20 06 83 61, *Fax 03 20 14 03 75* – AE ◑ GB EY v
closed 1 to 19 August, 15 February-2 March, Sunday, lunch Saturday and Monday – **Meals** (booking essential) 28,20/48,02 and a la carte 45/65 ♀.

XX **Varbet,** 2 r. Pas ✉ 59800 ☎ 03 20 54 81 40, *levarbet@aol.com, Fax 03 20 57 55 18* – AE GB EY t
closed 16 July-17 August, 24 December-4 January, Sunday, Monday and Bank Holidays – **Meals** 28/74.

XX **Cardinal,** 84 façade Esplanade ✉ 59800 ☎ 03 20 06 58 58, *Fax 03 20 51 42 59* – AE GB JCB BV x
closed 13 to 19 August and Sunday – **Meals** 22,10 (lunch), 25,15/29,73 ♀.

XX **Baan Thaû,** 22 bd J.-B. Lebas ☎ 03 20 86 06 01, *Fax 03 20 86 03 23* – ▤. AE GB EZ s
closed 27 July-25 August, Saturday lunch and Sunday dinner – **Meals** - Thai rest. - 23 and a la carte 33/40.

XX **Clément Marot,** 16 r. Pas ✉ 59800 ☎ 03 20 57 01 10, *cmarot@nordnet.fr, Fax 03 20 57 39 69* – ▤. AE ◑ GB EY n
closed Sunday dinner – **Meals** 21,95 (lunch), 30,95/44,97 ♀.

XX **Lanathaû,** 189 r. Solférino ☎ 03 20 57 20 20, 🏠 – AE GB. ✂ EZ t
closed Sunday – **Meals** - Thai rest. - 23 (lunch), 32/40.

XX **L'Écume des Mers,** 10 r. Pas ✉ 59800 ☎ 03 20 54 95 40, *aproye@nordnet.com, Fax 03 20 54 96 66* – ▤. AE ◑ GB JCB EY n
closed 28 July- 27 August and Sunday dinner – **Meals** - Seafood - 20,50 (weekdays dinner)and a la carte 27/39.

XX **Brasserie de la Paix,** 25 pl. Rihour ☎ 03 20 54 70 41, *Fax 03 20 40 15 52* – ▤. AE GB
closed Sunday – **Meals** 15 (lunch)/23 ♀.

XX **Bistrot Tourangeau,** 61 bd Louis XIV ✉ 59800 ☎ 03 20 52 74 64, *hehochart@nordnet.fr, Fax 03 20 85 06 39* – ▤. AE GB FZ t
closed Saturday lunch and Sunday – **Meals** 24,50 ♀.

XX **Champlain,** 13 r. N. Leblanc ☎ 03 20 54 01 38, *le.champlain@wanadoo.fr, Fax 03 20 40 07 28,* 🏠 – AE GB. ✂ EZ u
closed 28 July-25 August, Saturday lunch and Sunday dinner – **Meals** 23,64 b.i. (lunch), 25,92/38,12 ♀.

X **Coquille,** 60 r. St-Étienne ✉ 59800 ☎ 03 20 54 29 82, *Fax 03 20 54 29 82* – GB EY e
closed 5 to 25 August, Saturday lunch and Sunday – **Meals** 27 ♀.

XX **Alcide,** 5 r. Débris St-Étienne ✉ 59800 ☎ 03 20 12 06 95, *bigarade@easynet.fr, Fax 03 20 55 93 83* – ▤. AE ◑ GB EY l
Meals 20/32 🍷.

at Marcq-en-Barœul – *pop. 36 601 alt. 15* – ✉ *59700* :

🏨 **Sofitel** M, av. Marne, by N 350 : 5 km ☎ 03 28 33 12 12, *h1099@accor-hotels.com, Fax 03 28 33 12 24* |◆|, ⇢ rm, ▤ TV ☎ ♿ **P** – 🏛 15 - 150. AE ◑ GB
Europe *(closed Saturday lunch and Sunday dinner)* **Meals** 21,34/38,11 ♀ – ☕ – **125 rm** 190/228.

XXX **L'Auberge de Didier Beckaert,** 287 bd Clemenceau ☎ 03 20 45 90 00, *Fax 03 20 45 90 45,* 🏠 – ▤ **P**. AE ◑ GB JCB
closed 1 to 31 August, Saturday, Sunday and dinner weekdays except Friday – **Meals** 24,24/53,36 b.i..

XXX **Septentrion,** parc du Château Vert Bois, by N 17 : 9 km ☎ 03 20 46 26 98, *Fax 03 20 46 38 33,* 🏠, « In a park with a lake », 🌳 – **P**. AE GB
closed 24 July-14 August, Monday, dinner Tuesday and Wednesday – **Meals** 28,13 b.i./56,48 b.i..

XX **Auberge de la Garenne,** 17 chemin de Ghesles ☎ 03 20 46 20 20, *contact@aubergegarenne.fr, Fax 03 20 46 32 33,* 🏠, ☂ – **P**. AE GB JCB
closed 30 July-23 August, Tuesday from October-April, Sunday dinner and Monday – **Meals** 29 b.i./68 b.i..

at Lille-Lesquin airport *by A 1 : 8 km –* ✉ *59810 Lesquin :*

🏨 **Mercure Aéroport,** 🕿 03 20 87 46 46, *h1098@ hotels-accor.com*, Fax 03 20 87 46 47, 🍴 – 📶, ⇔ rm, 🔲 📺 📶 ⚫ 🅿 – 🚗 900. 🆎 ⓞ ⅁⅊ ⌿⌿⌿
Flamme : Meals 22/36b.i. ⅄ – **Poêlon** (lunch only) (closed Saturday and Sunday) Meals a la carte approx. 20 ⅄ – ⌷ 10 – **212 rm** 86/97.

🏨 **Suite Hôtel** Ⓜ without rest, 🕿 03 28 54 24 24, *H2855@ accor-hotels.com*, Fax 03 28 54 24 99 – 📶 kitchenette, ⇔ rm, 🔲 📺 📶 ⚫ 🅿 🆎 ⓞ ⅁⅊   HT u ⌷ 10 – **73 rm** 72.

🏨 **Novotel Aéroport,** 🕿 03 20 62 53 53, *H0427@ accor-hotels.com*, Fax 03 20 97 36 12, 🌳, ⇔ rm, 🔲 📺 📶 ⚫ 🅿 – 🚗 25 - 140. 🆎 ⓞ ⅁⅊ ⌿⌿⌿
Meals 22 ⅄ – ⌷ 10,50 – **92 rm** 82/89.

🏨 **Agena** without rest, ✉ 59155 Faches-Thumesnil 🕿 03 20 60 13 14, Fax 03 20 97 31 79 – 📺 📶 ⚫ 🅿 🆎 ⓞ ⅁⅊ ⌿⌿⌿
⌷ 8 – **40 rm** 55/60.

🍴🍴 **Septième Ciel,** highest level of the airport station 🕿 03 20 49 67 77, Fax 03 20 49 67 75, ⇐ – 🔲. 🆎 ⅁⅊
Meals 19,06/25,13 - **Zingue** : brasserie Meals 14,48 ⅄.

at Englos *by A 25 : 10 km (exit Lomme) – alt. 46 –* ✉ *59320 :*

🏨 **Novotel Englos** Ⓜ, 🕿 03 20 10 58 58, *h0429@ accor-hotels.com*, Fax 03 20 10 58 59, 🌳, 🏊, 🌳 – ⇔ rm, 🔲 📺 📶 ⚫ 🅿 – 🚗 130. 🆎 ⓞ ⅁⅊
Meals 22 ⅄ – ⌷ 10 – **124 rm** 80/84.

Béthune *62400 P.-de-C.* 🗺 ⑭ *– pop. 24 556 alt. 34.*
🛈 *Tourist Office Le Beffroi Gd Place* 🕿 *03 21 57 25 47, Fax 03 21 57 01 60.*
Lille 39.

🍴🍴🍴 **Meurin and Résidence Kitchener** Ⓜ with rm, 15 pl. République 🕿 03 21 68 88 88, ✿✿ *marc.meurin@ le-meurin.fr, Fax 03 21 68 88 89,* 🌳 – kitchenette, 🔲 rest, 📺 📶 🆎 ⓞ ⅁⅊ ⌿⌿⌿
closed 1 to 25 August, 2 to 10 January, Tuesday lunch, Sunday dinner and Monday – **Meals** 33,54 (lunch), 45,73/91,47 and a la carte 72/92 ⅄ – ⌷ 11,43 – **7 rm** 83,85/129,58
Spec. Anguille de la Somme au pain perdu d'herbes du jardin. Turbot côtier et salade de pieds de porc à l'encre de seiche. Flan de réglisse chocolaté au sirop de thé vert.

In this Guide,
a symbol or a character, printed in **red** or **black**,
does not have the same meaning.
Please read the explanatory pages carefully.

LYONS (LYON) *69000 RhCone* 🗺 ⑪ ⑫ *– pop. 415 487 alt. 175.*
See : *Site★★★ (panorama★★ from Fourvière) – Fourvière hill : Notre-Dame Basilica* EX*, Museum of Gallo-Roman Civilization★★ (Claudian tablet★★★)* EY M³*, Roman ruins* EY – Old Lyons★★★ : Rue St-Jean★* FX*, St-Jean Cathedral★* FY*, Hôtel de Gadagne★ (Lyons Historical Museum★ and International Marionette Museum★)* EX M¹ *– Guignol de Lyon* FX N *– Central Lyons (Peninsula) : to the North, Place Bellecour* FY*, Hospital Museum (pharmacy★)* FY M⁸*, Museum of Printing and Banking★★* FX M⁶*, – Place des Terreaux* FX*, Hôtel de Ville* FX*, Palais St-Pierre, Fine Arts Museum (Beaux-Arts)★★* FX M⁴ *– to the South, St-Martin-d'Ainay Basilica (capitals★)* FY*, Weaving and Textile Museum★★★* FY M²*, Decorative Arts Museum★★* FY M⁵ *– La Croix-Rousse : Silkweavers' House* FV M¹¹*, Trois Gaules Amphitheatre* FV E *– Tête d'Or Park★* GHV *– Guimet Museum of Natural History★★* GV M⁷ *– Historical Information Centre on the Resistance and the Deportation★* FZ M⁹*.*
Envir. : *Rochetaillée : Henri Malartre Car Museum★★, 12 km to the North.*
🏌 *Verger-Lyon at St-Symphorien-d'Ozon* 🕿 *04 78 02 84 20, S : 14 km ;* 🏌 *Lyon-Chassieu at Chassieu* 🕿 *04 78 90 84 77, E : 12 km by D 29 ;* 🏌 *Salvagny (private) at the Tour de Salvagny* 🕿 *04 78 48 88 48 ; junctio* n *Lyon-Ouest : 8 km ;* 🏌 🏌 *Golf Club of Lyon at Villette-d'Anthon* 🕿 *04 78 31 11 33.*
✈ *of Lyon-Saint-Exupery* 🕿 *04 72 22 72 21 to the E : 27 km.*
🚕🚕 🕿 *08 36 35 35 35.*
🛈 *Tourist Office pl. Bellecour* 🕿 *04 72 77 69 69, Fax 04 78 42 04 32, lyoncvblyon-france.com – Automobile Club du Rhône 7 r. Grolée* 🕿 *04 78 42 51 01, Fax 04 78 37 73 74.*
Paris 462 – Geneva 151 – Grenoble 105 – Marseilles 313 – St-Étienne 60 – Turin 300.

Town Centre (Bellecour-Terreaux) :

Sofitel M, 20 quai Gailleton ✉ 69002 ☎ 04 72 41 20 20, *h0553@accor-hotels.com, Fax 04 72 40 05 50,* ← – |‡|, ⇹ rm, ▤ TV ☎ ♿ 🚗 – 🏛 15 - 200. AE ⊕ GB JCB
Les Trois Dômes (8th floor) ☎ 04 72 41 20 97 *(closed August)* **Meals** 47(lunch), 63/114bc ♀ – ***Sofishop*** (ground floor) ☎ *04 72 41 20 80* **Meals** 22bc/24 ♀ – ☕ 21 – **138 rm** 239/330, 29 suites. FY p

Grand Hôtel Concorde without rest, 11 r. Grolée ✉ 69002 ☎ 04 72 40 45 45, *reservation@lyon.boscolo.com, Fax 04 78 37 52 55* – |‡|, ⇹ rm, ▤ TV ☎ – 🏛 15 - 60. AE ⊕ GB JCB FX y
☕ 12,96 – **137 rm** 131,11/195,13, 3 suites.

Royal, 20 pl. Bellecour ✉ 69002 ☎ 04 78 37 57 31, *h2952@accor-hotels.com, Fax 04 78 37 01 36* – |‡|, ⇹ rm, ▤ TV ☎. AE ⊕ GB JCB FY g
Meals *(closed August and Saturday)* 23/26 ♀ – ☕ 15 – **80 rm** 158/218.

Carlton without rest, 4 r. Jussieu ✉ 69002 ☎ 04 78 42 56 51, *h2950@accor-hotels.com, Fax 04 78 42 10 71* – |‡|, ⇹ rm, ▤ TV ☎. AE ⊕ GB JCB FX b
☕ 10,50 – **83 rm** 144.

Mercure Plaza République M without rest, 5 r. Stella ✉ 69002 ☎ 04 78 37 50 50, *h2951-gm@accor-hotels.com, Fax 04 78 42 33 34* – |‡|, ⇹ rm, ▤ TV ☎ ♿ – 🏛 20 - 35. AE ⊕ GB JCB FY k
☕ 11 – **78 rm** 96/137.

Globe et Cécil without rest, 21 r. Gasparin ✉ 69002 ☎ 04 78 42 58 95, *globe.et.cecil@wanadoo.fr, Fax 04 72 41 99 06* – |‡| ▤ TV ☎ – 🏛 25. AE ⊕ GB JCB FY b
60 rm ☕ 107/125.

Beaux-Arts without rest, 75 r. Prés. E. Herriot ✉ 69002 ☎ 04 78 38 09 50, *h2949@accor-hotels.com, Fax 04 78 42 19 19* – |‡|, ⇹ rm, ▤ TV ☎ – 🏛 15. AE ⊕ GB JCB FX t
☕ 10 – **75 rm** 76/136.

Grand Hôtel des Terreaux without rest, 16 r. Lanterne ✉ 69001 ☎ 04 78 27 04 10, *ght@hotel-lyon.fr, Fax 04 78 27 97 75,* 🏊 – |‡| TV ☎. AE ⊕ GB FX l
☕ 8,50 – **50 rm** 72,50/125.

Résidence without rest, 18 r. V. Hugo ✉ 69002 ☎ 04 78 42 63 28, *hotel-la-residence@wanadoo.fr, Fax 04 78 42 85 76* – |‡| ▤ TV ☎. AE ⊕ GB JCB FY s
☕ 6 – **67 rm** 57/62.

Perrache :

Grand Hôtel Mercure Château Perrache, 12 cours Verdun ✉ 69002 ☎ 04 72 77 15 00, *h1292@accor-hotels.com, Fax 04 78 37 06 56,* « Art Nouveau decor » – |‡|, ⇹ rm, ▤ TV ☎ 🚗 – 🏛 20 - 200. AE ⊕ GB JCB EY a
Les Belles Saisons : **Meals** 24/31,50 ♀ – ☕ 12,50 – **111 rm** 92/164.

Charlemagne M, 23 cours Charlemagne ✉ 69002 ☎ 04 72 77 70 00, *charlemagne@hotel-lyon.fr, Fax 04 78 42 94 84,* 🍽 – |‡| ▤ TV ☎ 🚗 – 🏛 120. AE ⊕ GB EZ t
Meals *(closed Saturday dinner and Sunday)* 17,10/21,65 – ☕ 9 – **116 rm** 82/106.

at Vaise :

Saphir M, 18 r. L. Loucheur ✉ 69009 ☎ 04 78 83 48 75, *com-hotel-saphir@wanadoo.fr, Fax 04 78 83 30 81* – |‡|, ⇹ rm, ▤ TV ☎ ♿ 🚗 – 🏛 50. AE ⊕ GB
Meals 15,25/29,30 ♀ – ☕ 10 – **111 rm** 108/146.

Vieux-Lyon :

Villa Florentine M 🐌, 25 montée St-Barthélémy ✉ 69005 ☎ 04 72 56 56 56, *florentine@relaischateaux.com, Fax 04 72 40 90 56,* ← Lyon, 🍽, 🏊, 🌳 – |‡| ▤ TV ☎ 🚗 P – 🏛 15. AE ⊕ GB JCB EFX s
✿ ***Les Terrasses de Lyon*** (dinner only except Sunday) **Meals** 55/120 and a la carte 75/90 – **16 rm** 335/460, 3 suites
Spec. Moelleux d'anchois frais marinés aux épices (15 April-30 September). Courgette-fleur farcie aux saveurs du Midi (May-September). Caneton de Challans aux herbes du jardin..
Wines Saint-Joseph blanc, Cornas..

Cour des Loges M 🐌, 6 r. Boeuf ✉ 69005 ☎ 04 72 77 44 44, *contact@courdesloges.com, Fax 04 72 40 93 61,* 🍽, « Original decor in houses of Old Lyons », 🏋 – |‡| ▤ TV ☎ 🚗 – 🏛 15 - 50. AE ⊕ GB JCB FX n
Les Loges ☎ 04 72 77 44 40 *(closed 5 to 25 August, 10 to 23 February, Sunday and Monday)* **Meals** 42 (lunch) 65/90 ♀ – ☕ 20 – **58 rm** 200/420, 4 suites.

Tour Rose M 🐌, 22 r. Boeuf ✉ 69005 ☎ 04 78 92 69 10, *chavent@asi.fr, Fax 04 78 42 26 02,* « 17C house, tasteful silk themed decor » – |‡| ▤ TV ☎ 🚗 – 🏛 25. AE ⊕ GB JCB EFX e
Meals *(closed lunch in August and Sunday)* 49/107 – ☕ 18 – **8 rm** 239/315, 4 duplex.

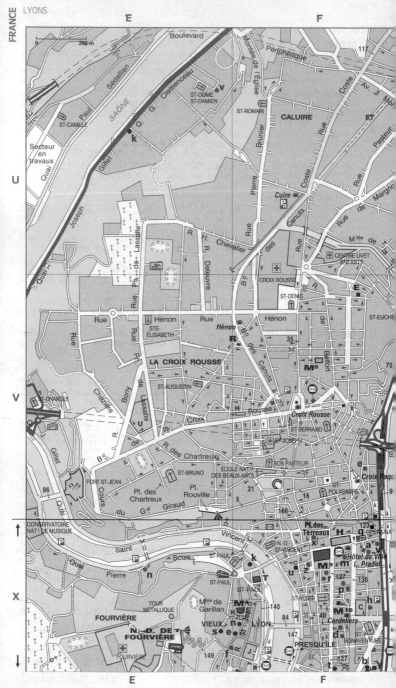

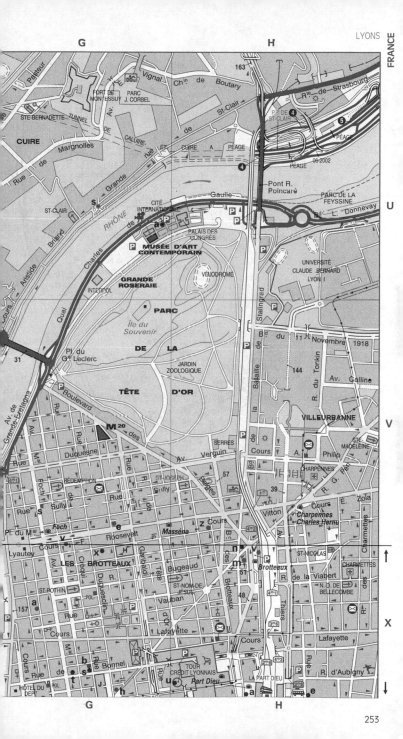

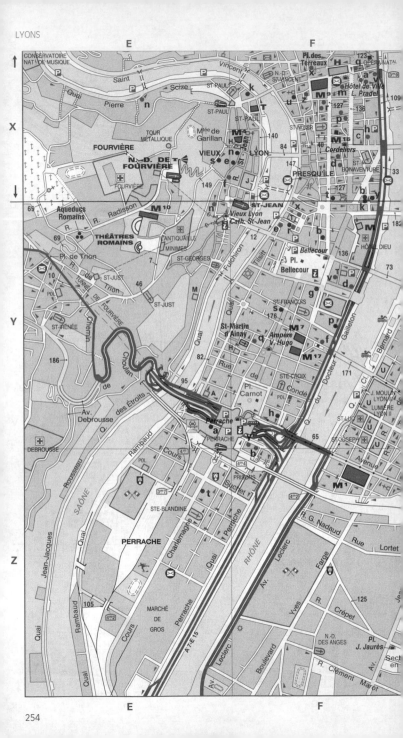

STREET INDEX TO LYON TOWN PLAN

🏨 **Phénix Hôtel** without rest, 7 quai Bondy ⊠ 69005 ℘ 04 78 28 24 24, *phenix-hotel@ wanadoo.fr*, Fax 04 78 28 62 86 – 📶 ≣ 📺 ✆ 🕭 ⟷ – 🔏 30. 🖭 ⓵ ⅏ 🔃
36 rm ☲ 125/168.
FX k

La Croix-Rousse (bank of the River Saône) :

🏨 **Lyon Métropole** Ⓜ, 85 quai J. Gillet ⊠ 69004 ℘ 04 72 10 44 44, *metropole@wan adoo.fr*, Fax 04 72 10 44 42, 😄, ⅃, ⅌ – 📶 ≣ 📺 ✆ 🕭 ⟷ 🅿 – 🔏 15 - 300. 🖭 ⓵ ⅏ 🔃
closed 23 December-2 January – **Brasserie Lyon Plage :** Meals 26(lunch)/41 – ☲ 15
– **118 rm** 153/211.
EU u

Les Brotteaux :

🏨 **Hilton** Ⓜ ॐ, 70 quai Ch. de Gaulle ⊠ 69006 ℘ 04 78 17 50 50, *rm-lyon@hilton.com*, Fax 04 78 17 52 52, 😄 – ⅃, ⅌ rm, ≣ 📺 ✆ 🕭 ⟷ – 🔏 15 - 400. 🖭 ⓵ ⅏ 🔃
Blue Elephant *(closed 15 July-15 August, Saturday lunch and Sunday)* **Meals** 25,92(lunch),
38,11/47,26 – **Brasserie Belge** ℘ 04 78 17 51 00 **Meals** 22b.i.(lunch) and a la carte 25/30
ⵀ – ☲ 23 – **196 rm** 300/455, 5 suites.
GU a

🏠 **Roosevelt** Ⓜ without rest, 48 r. Sèze ⊠ 69006 ℰ 04 78 52 35 67, *hotel.roosevelt @ wanadoo.fr*, Fax 04 78 52 39 82 – |≐|, ↳× rm, 🗐 📺 ✔ & ⟵ 🅿 – 🕍 15 - 40. 🖭 ⑩
GB   GX x
  ☲ 9,50 – **48 rm** 92/122.

🏠 **Holiday Inn Garden Court** Ⓜ without rest, 114 bd Belges ⊠ 69006
ℰ 04 78 24 44 68, *hollilyon@ imaginet.fr*, Fax 04 78 24 82 36 – |≐|, ↳× rm, 🗐 📺 ✔ 🖭
⑩ GB   HX n
  ☲ 9,50 – **55 rm** 92/102.

La Part-Dieu :

🏨 **Méridien Part-Dieu** Ⓜ ॐ, 129 r. Servient (32nd floor) ⊠ 69003 ℰ 04 78 63 55 00,
info@ lemeridien-lyon.com, Fax 04 78 63 55 20, ≤ Lyons and Rhône Valley – |≐|, ↳× rm,
🗐 📺 ✔ ⟵ – 🕍 110. 🖭 ⑩ GB 🇯🇨🇧   GX u
L'Arc-en-Ciel (closed 15 July-25 August, Saturday lunch and Sunday) **Meals** 32/50 ♀ –
Bistrot de la Tour (ground floor) (closed Friday dinner, Sunday lunch and SaturdayÑ **Meals**
18 ♀ – ☲ 16 – **245 rm** 180/260.

🏨 **Grand Hôtel Mercure Saxe-Lafayette**, 29 r. Bonnel ⊠ 69003 ℰ 04 72 61 90 90,
h2057@ accor-hotels.com, Fax 04 72 61 17 54, 🕩 – |≐|, ↳× rm, 🗐 📺 ✔ & ⟵ – 🕍 20
- 120. 🖭 ⑩ GB 🇯🇨🇧   GX t
Meals 20,50/25,15 ♀ – ☲ 12,20 – **156 rm** 136/166.

🏨 **Novotel La Part-Dieu** Ⓜ, 47 bd Vivier-Merle ⊠ 69003 ℰ 04 72 13 51 51, *h0735@ a ccor-hotels.com*, Fax 04 72 13 51 99 – |≐|, ↳× rm, 🗐 📺 ✔ & ⟵ – 🕍 15 - 70. 🖭 ⑩
GB 🇯🇨🇧   HX a
Meals a la carte 19/31 ♀ – ☲ 10,50 – **124 rm** 120/141.

🏨 **de Créqui** without rest, 158 r. Créqui ⊠ 69003 ℰ 04 78 60 20 47, Fax 04 78 62 21 12
– |≐|, ↳× rm, 🗐 📺 🖭 GB   GX s
  ☲ 7 – **28 rm** 79/199.

🏨 **Ibis La Part-Dieu Gare**, pl. Renaudel ⊠ 69003 ℰ 04 78 95 42 11, Fax 04 78 60 42 85,
🏡 – |≐|, ↳× rm, 🗐 📺 ✔ & ⟵ – 🕍 20. 🖭 ⑩ GB   HY k
Meals 12,96/16,01 ♀ – ☲ 5,50 – **144 rm** 75.

La Guillotière :

🏠 **Libertel Wilson** Ⓜ without rest, 6 r. Mazenod ⊠ 69003 ℰ 04 78 60 94 94, *h2780-g m@ accor-hotels.com*, Fax 04 78 62 72 01 – |≐|, ↳× rm, 🗐 📺 ✔ ⟵. 🖭 ⑩ GB 🇯🇨🇧
  ☲ 11 – **54 rm** 109/145.

🏠 **Noailles** without rest, 30 cours Gambetta ⊠ 69007 ℰ 04 78 72 40 72, *accueil@ hot el-de-noailles-lyon.com*, Fax 04 72 71 09 10 – 🗐 📺 ✔ ⟵. GB   GY s
closed 4 to 27 August – ☲ 9 – **24 rm** 65/80.

Gerland :

🏨 **Mercure Gerland** Ⓜ, 70 av. Leclerc ⊠ 69007 ℰ 04 72 71 11 11, *h0736@ accor-h otels.com*, Fax 04 72 71 11 00, 🏡, ⍽ – |≐|, ↳× rm, 🗐 📺 ✔ & ⟵ – 🕍 90 150. 🖭
⑩ GB 🇯🇨🇧
Meals 20,58 ♀ ☲ 10,50 – **187 rm** 104/149.

Montchat-Monplaisir :

🏨 **Mercure Lumière** Ⓜ, 69 cours A. Thomas ℰ 04 78 53 76 76, Fax 04 72 36 97 65 –
|≐|, ↳× rm, 🗐 📺 ✔ & ⟵ – 🕍 25 - 50. 🖭 ⑩ GB 🇯🇨🇧
Meals (closed Sunday lunch and Saturday) 18 ♀ – ☲ 11 – **78 rm** 113/116.

at Bron – pop. 39 683 alt. 204 – ⊠ 69500 :

🏨 **Novotel Bron** Ⓜ, av. J. Monnet ℰ 04 72 15 65 65, *h0436@ accor-hotels.com*,
Fax 04 72 15 09 09, 🏡, ⍽, 🌲 – |≐|, ↳× rm, 🗐 📺 ✔ & 🅿 – 🕍 15 - 500. 🖭 ⑩ GB
Meals 21,34 ♀ – ☲ 10,50 – **190 rm** 104/109.

Restaurants

XXXXX **Paul Bocuse**, bridge of Collonges N : 12 km by the banks of River Saône (D 433, D 51
❀❀❀ ⊠ 69660 *Collonges-au-Mont-d'Or* ℰ 04 72 42 90 90, *paul.bocuse@ bocuse.fr*,
Fax 04 72 27 85 87, « Fresco depicting great chefs » – 🗐 🄿. 🖭 ⑩ GB 🇯🇨🇧
Meals 100,62/135,68 and a la carte 90/140
Spec. Soupe aux truffes. Rouget en écailles de pommes de terre. Volaille de Bresse.. **Wines**
Saint-Véran, Brouilly..

XXXX **Léon de Lyon** (Lacombe), 1 r. Pleney ⊠ 69001 ℰ 04 72 10 11 12, *leon@ relaischat
❀❀ eaux.fr*, Fax 04 72 10 11 13 – 🗐. 🖭 GB 🇯🇨🇧   FX r
closed 4 to 26 August, Sunday and Monday – **Meals** 52 (lunch), 95/130 and a la carte
85/105 ♀
Spec. Cochon fermier du Cantal, foie gras et oignon confit. Quenelles de brochet à notre
façon. Six petits desserts à la praline de Saint-Genix.. **Wines** Saint-Véran, Chiroubles..

XXXX **Pierre Orsi,** 3 pl. Kléber ⊠ 69006 ℘ 04 78 89 57 68, *orsi@ relaischateaux.fr,*
❀ Fax 04 72 44 93 34, 綵, « Elegant decor » – ▤. Ⅿ 綵 📠 GV e
closed Sunday and Monday except Bank Holidays – **Meals** 43 (lunch), 77/107 and a la carte
70/100 ℤ
Spec. Ravioles de foie gras au jus de porto et truffes. Homard en carapace. Pigeonneau
en cocotte aux gousses d'ail confites.. **Wines** Mâcon-Clessé, Saint-Joseph..

XXX **Christian Têtedoie,** 54 quai Pierre Scize ⊠ 69005 ℘ 04 78 29 40 10,
❀ Fax 04 72 07 05 65 – ▤. ➾. Ⅿ 📠 EX n
closed 6 to 12 May, 29 July-25 August, Saturday lunch and Sunday – **Meals** 26/67/60,97
and a la carte 48/68 ℤ
Spec. Salade de homard rôti au beurre d'orange. Quenelle de brochet au coulis d'écrevisse.
Râble de lièvre aux myrtilles (October-December).. **Wines** Saint-Joseph blanc, Beaujolais-
Villages..

XXX **L'Auberge de Fond Rose** (Vignat), 23 quai G. Clemenceau ⊠ 69300 *Caluire-et-Cuire*
❀ ℘ 04 78 29 34 61, *contact@ aubergedefondrose.com,* Fax 04 72 00 28 67, 綵,
« Shaded and flowered garden, terrace », 綵 – ▤ 📺. Ⅿ 📠 📠 EU v
*closed 6/10-16/11, 3-28/02, Monday dinner and Tuesday lunch from 01/06-31/08, Sun-
day dinner and Monday lunch* – **Meals** 33,54/59,45 and a la carte 55/75 ℤ
Spec. Ravioles de queue de bœuf aux dés de foie gras. Pigeon cuit à la rôtissoire, pommes
de terre paillasson à la lyonnaise. Entremets tiède au chocolat..

XXX **Mère Brazier,** 12 r. Royale ⊠ 69001 ℘ 04 78 28 15 49, Fax 04 78 28 63 63,
« Lyonnaise atmosphere » – ▤. Ⅿ 📠 📠 FV e
closed 14 to 21 April, 26 July-28 August, Saturday lunch, Sunday and Tuesday – **Meals**
46/55 and a la carte 45/65 ℤ.

XXX **St-Alban,** 2 quai J. Moulin ⊠ 69001 ℘ 04 78 30 14 89, Fax 04 72 00 88 82 – ▤. Ⅿ
📠 📠 FX v
closed 20 July-20 August, Saturday lunch, Sunday and Bank Holidays – **Meals** 26,68/56,50
and a la carte 41/61 ℤ.

XX **Auberge de l'Ile** (Ansanay-Alex). sur l'Ile Barbe ⊠ 69009 ℘ 04 78 83 99 49, *info@a*
❀❀ *ubergedelile.com,* Fax 04 78 47 80 46, « 17C house on island of the river Saône » – 📺. Ⅿ
📠 📠
*closed 3 to 10 March, 5 to 26 August, lunch from Tuesday-Friday, Sunday dinner and
Monday* – **Meals** 55/70
Spec. Velouté de champignons comme un capuccino (Autumn). Mousseline de brochet,
nougatine de grenouilles à l'ail doux (Spring). Crème glacée à la réglisse.. **Wines** Saint-Véran,
Morgon..

XX **L'Alexandrin** (Alexanian), 83 r. Moncey ⊠ 69003 ℘ 04 72 61 15 69,
❀ Fax 04 78 62 75 57, 綵 – ▤. Ⅿ 📠 GX h
*closed 28 April-1 May, 24 to 28 May, 29 July-20 August, 23 December-3 January, Snday
and Monday* – **Meals** 25 (lunch), 37/66 and a la carte 60/70
Spec. Mousseline de brochet en quenelle et son crémeux d'écrevisses. Volaille de Bresse
au vinaigre. Le "Tout chocolat".. **Wines** Crozes-Hermitage, Saint-Joseph..

XX **Passage,** 8 r. Plâtre ⊠ 69001 ℘ 04 78 28 11 16, Fax 04 72 00 84 34 – ▤. Ⅿ 📠 📠
📠 FX r
closed 11 to 26 August, Sunday and Monday – **Meals** 29/36 ℤ.

XX **Fleur de Sel,** 3 r. Remparts d'Ainay ⊠ 69002 ℘ 04 78 37 40 37, Fax 04 78 37 26 37
– 📠 FY q
closed 29 July-22 August and Sunday – **Meals** 23 (lunch), 38/61 ℤ.

XX **Mathieu Viannay,** 47 av. Foch ⊠ 69006 ℘ 04 78 89 55 19, Fax 04 78 89 08 39 – ▤
Ⅿ 📠 GV s
closed 5 to 25 August, 30 December-5 January, Saturday and Sunday – **Meals** 23/39 ℤ

XX **Le Nord,** 18 r. Neuve ⊠ 69002 ℘ 04 72 10 69 69, Fax 04 72 10 69 68, 綵 – ▤. Ⅿ
📠 📠 📠 FX p
Meals brasserie 19,60/24,80 ℤ.

XX **Gourmet de Sèze** (Mariller), 129 r. Sèze ⊠ 69006 ℘ 04 78 24 23 42,
❀ Fax 04 78 24 66 81 – ▤. Ⅿ 📠 HV z
closed 5 to 13 May, 27 July-21 August, Sunday and Monday – **Meals** (booking essential)
29,50/48 ℤ
Spec. Croustillants de pieds de cochon. Tendron de veau de lait rôti, jus crémé aux herbes
fraîches. Le "Grand dessert"..

XX **Chez Jean-François,** 2 pl. Célestins ⊠ 69002 ℘ 04 78 42 08 26, Fax 04 72 40 04 51
– ▤. Ⅿ 📠 📠 📠 FY x
closed 27 July-27 August, Sunday and Bank Holidays – **Meals** 16,75/30 ℤ.

XX **Tassée,** 20 r. Charité ⊠ 69002 ℘ 04 72 77 79 00, *jpborgaot@ latassee.fr*
Fax 04 72 40 05 91 – ▤. Ⅿ 📠 FY u
closed Sunday – **Meals** 21,34/44,21 ℤ.

XX **Vivarais,** 1 pl. Gailleton ✉ 69002 ℰ 04 78 37 85 15, Fax 04 78 37 59 49 – 🗏 . 🆎 ⑩
🆑 🏧   FY f
closed 27 July-19 August, 25 December-1 January, Saturday lunch and Sunday – **Meals**
18,29 (lunch), 23,17/30,18 ⌾.

XX **Mère Vittet,** 26 cours de Verdun ✉ 69002 ℰ 04 78 37 20 17, merevittet.lyon@fr
ee.fr, Fax 04 78 42 40 70 – 🗏 . 🆎 🆑   FY y
Meals 18,75/36,59 ⌾.

XX **Grenier des Lyres,** 21 r. Creuzet ✉ 69007 ℰ 04 78 72 81 77, Fax 04 78 72 01 75
– 🗏 . 🆎 🆑   GY e
closed 11 to 27 August, Monday dinner, Saturday lunch and Sunday – **Meals** 13,72 (lunch),
25,15/37,81.

XX **Brasserie Georges,** 30 cours Verdun ✉ 69002 ℰ 04 72 56 54 54, brasserie.georg
es@wanadoo.fr, Fax 04 78 42 51 65, « 1925 brasserie » – 🆎 ⑩ 🆑 🏧   FZ b
Meals 17/24 ⌾.

XX **Machonnerie,** 36 r. Tramassac ✉ 69005 ℰ 04 78 42 24 62, felix@lamachonnerie.c
om, Fax 04 72 40 23 32 – 🗏 . 🆎 ⑩ 🆑   EY n
closed lunch except Saturday and Sunday except lunch from September-December –
Meals 18,50/42 ⌾.

XX **La Voûte - Chez Léa,** 11 pl. A. Gourju ✉ 69002 ℰ 04 78 42 01 33, Fax 04 78 37 36 41
– 🗏 . 🆎 🆑   FY e
closed Sunday – **Meals** 15,10 (lunch), 23/31 ⌾.

XX **Bœuf d'Argent,** 29 r. Boeuf ✉ 69005 ℰ 04 78 42 21 12, Fax 04 72 40 24 65 – 🆎
⑩ 🆑   EFX f
Meals 18/74 ⌾.

X **L'Est,** Gare des Brotteaux, 14 pl. J. Ferry ✉ 69006 ℰ 04 37 24 25 26,
Fax 04 37 24 25 25, 🍴, « Brasserie in an old railway station, travel themed decor » –
🗏 . 🆎 ⑩ 🆑 🏧   HX v
Meals brasserie 19,60/24,80 ⌾.

X **Le Sud,** 11 pl. Antonin Poncet ✉ 69002 ℰ 04 72 77 80 00, Fax 04 72 77 80 01, 🍴
– 🗏 . 🆎 ⑩ 🆑 🏧   FY d
Meals (booking essential) 19,60/24,80 ⌾.

X **Francotte,** 8 pl. Célestins ✉ 69002 ℰ 04 78 37 38 64, Fax 04 78 38 20 35 – 🗏 . 🆎
🆑   FY r
closed Sunday and Monday – **Meals** 14,94 (lunch)and a la carte 24/38 ⌾.

X **Terrasse St-Clair,** 2 Grande r. St-Clair ✉ 69300 Caluire-et-Cuire ℰ 04 72 27 37 37,
Fax 04 72 27 37 30, 🍴 – 🆎 🆑   GU s
closed 2 to 15 January, dinner Monday and Tuesday from 1 October-30 March and Sunday
– **Meals** 20 ⌾.

X **Théodore,** 34 cours Franklin Roosevelt ✉ 69006 ℰ 04 78 24 08 52,
Fax 04 72 74 41 21, 🍴 – 🗏 . 🆎 ⑩ 🆑 🏧   GVX v
closed 11 to 18 August, 22 to 25 December, 29 December-1 January, Sunday and Bank
Holidays – **Meals** 16 (lunch), 18/37,50.

X **Assiette et Marée,** 49 r. Bourse ✉ 69002 ℰ 04 78 37 36 58, Fax 04 78 37 98 52,
🍴 – 🗏 . 🆎 🆑   FX h
closed Sunday – **Meals** - Seafood - a la carte 25/32 ⌾.

X **Les Muses de l'Opéra,** pl. Comédie, 7th floor of the Opera ✉ 69001
ℰ 04 72 00 45 58, Fax 04 78 29 34 01, ≤ Fourvière, 🍴, « Contemporary decor » – 🗏 .
🆎 🆑   FX q
closed Sunday – **Meals** 21,19 (lunch)/25,76 ⌾.

X **L'Étage,** 4 pl. Terreaux (2nd floor) ✉ 69001 ℰ 04 78 28 19 59 – 🗏 . 🆑
🕸   FX x
closed 22 July-21 August, 10 to 17 February, Sunday and Monday – **Meals** (booking essential) 17/49 ⌾.

X **Assiette et Marée,** 26 r. Servient ✉ 69003 ℰ 04 78 62 89 94, Fax 04 78 60 39 27
– 🗏 . 🆎 🆑   GY n
closed Monday dinner, Saturday lunch and Sunday – **Meals** - Seafood - a la carte 25/32
⌾.

X **Daniel et Denise,** 156 r. Créqui ✉ 69003 ℰ 04 78 60 66 53, Fax 04 78 60 66 53,
bistro – 🗏 . 🆑   GX s
closed August, Saturday, Sunday and Bank Holidays – **Meals** a la carte 28/40.

X **Tablier de Sapeur,** 16 r. Madeleine ✉ 69007 ℰ 04 78 72 22 40, Fax 04 78 72 22 40
– 🗏 .   GY k
closed Saturday from June-September, Monday from October-May and Sunday – **Meals**
17,50/33,56.

BOUCHONS : *Regional specialities and wine tasting in a Lyonnaise atmosphere*

X
@
Garet, 7 r. Garet ⊠ 69001 ✆ 04 78 28 16 94, *Fax 04 72 00 06 84* – ▤. 🄰🄴 🄶🄱   FX **a**
closed 20 July-20 August, Saturday and Sunday – **Meals** (booking essential) 15,24
(lunch)/19,82 ♈.

X
Chez Hugon, 12 rue Pizay ⊠ 69001 ✆ 04 78 28 10 94, *Fax 04 78 28 10 94* –
🄶🄱   FX **m**
closed August, Saturday and Sunday – **Meals** (booking essential) a la carte 21/34.

X
Café des Fédérations, 8 r. Major Martin ⊠ 69001 ✆ 04 78 28 26 00, *yr@lesfed*
eslyon.com, Fax 04 72 07 74 52 – ▤. 🄶🄱 🄹🄲🄱   FX **z**
closed 5 to 31 August, Saturday and Sunday – **Meals** (booking essential) 18,20
(lunch)/23.

X
@
Au Petit Bouchon "Chez Georges", 8 r. Garet ⊠ 69001 ✆ 04 78 28 30 46
– 🄶🄱   FX **a**
closed August, Saturday and Sunday – **Meals** 14,33/19,51 (lunch) and dinner a la carte.

X
Jura, 25 r. Tupin ⊠ 69002 ✆ 04 78 42 20 57 – 🄶🄱   FX **d**
*closed 28 July-28 August, Monday from September-April, Saturday from May-September
and Sunday* – **Meals** (booking essential) 16,50 ♈.

X
Meunière, 11 r. Neuve ⊠ 69001 ✆ 04 78 28 62 91 – 🄰🄴 🄶🄱   FX **p**
closed 13 July-17 August, Sunday and Monday – **Meals** (booking essential) 15 (lunch),
18,50/25.

Environs

to the NE :

at Rillieux-la-Pape : *7 km by N 83 and N 84 – pop. 30 791 alt. 269 –* ⊠ 69140 *:*

XXX
❀
Larivoire (Constantin), chemin des Iles ✆ 04 78 88 50 92, *bernard.constantin@larivoi*
re.com, Fax 04 78 88 35 22, � – 🄿. 🄰🄴 🄶🄱 🄹🄲🄱
closed 16 to 28 August, Tuesday, dinner Sunday and Monday – **Meals** 30/71 and a la carte
54/70
Spec. Huîtres gratinées au champagne (October-April). Millefeuille de "pommes cristallines"
et de crabe dormeur. Carré d'agneau de Sisteron rôti en croûte de pain d'épice.. **Wines**
Saint-Véran, Côteaux du Lyonnais..

to the E :

at the Lyon St-Exupéry Airport *: 27 km by A 43 –* ⊠ 69125 Lyon St-Exupéry Airport *:*

🏨
Sofitel Lyon Aéroport Ⓜ without rest, 3rd floor ✆ 04 72 23 38 00, *h913@acco*
r-hotels.com, Fax 04 72 23 98 00 – 🕮, ✸ rm, ▤ 📺 📞. 🄰🄴 🄾 🄶🄱 🄹🄲🄱
☲ 16,20 – **120 rm** 171/218.

XXX
Les Canuts, 1st floor in airport station ✆ 04 72 22 71 76, *Fax 04 72 22 71 72* – ▤. 🄰🄴
🄾 🄶🄱
closed 3 to 25 August, Saturday and Sunday – **Meals** 30 and a la carte approx. 35 ♈.

X
Bouchon, 1st floor in airport station ✆ 04 72 22 72 31, *Fax 04 72 22 71 72* – ▤. 🄰🄴
🄾 🄶🄱
Meals brasserie 23 b.i..

to the W :

at Tour-de-Salvagny *11 km by N 7 – pop. 3 226 alt. 356 –* ⊠ 69890 *:*

XXXX
❀❀
Rotonde, at Casino Le Lyon Vert ✆ 04 78 87 00 97, *rotonde@ifrance.com,*
Fax 04 78 87 81 39, « Art deco decor » – ▤. 🄰🄴 🄾 🄶🄱 🄹🄲🄱
closed 21 July-22 August, Sunday dinner, Tuesday lunch and Monday – **Meals** 38 (lunch),
75/108 and a la carte 77/100
Spec. Quatre foies pressés et salade de fonds d'artichauts. Tajine de homard entier aux
petits farcis. Cannelloni de chocolat amer à la glace de crème brûlée.. **Wines** Condrieu,
Côte-Rôtie..

to the NW :

Porte de Lyon *- motorway junction A6-N6 : 10 km –* ⊠ 69570 Dardilly *:*

🏨
Novotel Lyon Nord Ⓜ, ✆ 04 72 17 29 29, *h0437@accor-hotels.com,*
Fax 04 78 35 08 45, �, 🏊, 🎾 – 🕮, ✸ rm, ▤ 📺 📞 🄿 – 🔬 100. 🄰🄴 🄾
🄶🄱 🄹🄲🄱
Meals 19,67 ♈ – ☲ 10,50 – **107 rm** 102/109.

🏠
Ibis Lyon Nord, ✆ 04 78 66 02 20, *ibis.lyon.nord@wanadoo.fr, Fax 04 78 47 47 93,*
�, 🏊, 🎾 – 🕮, ✸ rm, ▤ 📺 📞 ♿ 🄿 – 🔬 20. 🄰🄴 🄾 🄶🄱
Meals 19/22 ♈ – ☲ 6 – **84 rm** 55/64.

Annecy 74000 H.-Savoie **74** ⑥ – pop. 49 644 alt. 448.

See : Old Annecy★★ : Descent from the Cross★ in church of St-Maurice, Palais de l'Isle★, rue Ste-Claire★, bridge over the Thiou ≤★ – Château★ – Jardins de l'Europe★.

Envir. : Tour of the lake★★★ 39 km (or 1 hour 30 min by boat).

⌐₈ of the lac d'Annecy ℘ 04 50 60 12 89 : 10 km ; ⌐₅ ⌐₁₈ of Giez ℘ 04 50 44 48 41 ; ⌐₉ of Belvédère at St-Martin-Bellevue ℘ 04 50 60 31 78.

✈ of Annecy-Meythet ℘ 04 50 27 30 30 by N 508 and D 14 : 4 km.

🖪 Tourist Office Clos Bonlieu 1 r. J. Jaurès ℘ 04 50 45 00 33, Fax 04 50 51 87 20 – Autombile Club 15 r. Préfecture ℘ 04 50 45 09 12, Fax 04 50 52 96 08.

Lyons 140.

at Veyrier-du-Lac E : 5,5 km – pop. 1 967 alt. 504 – ⌧ 74290

XXXXX ❀❀❀ **Auberge de l'Éridan** (Veyrat) Ⓜ ⌇ with rm, 13 Vieille rte des Pensières ℘ 04 50 60 24 00, contact@marcveyrat.fr, Fax 04 50 60 23 63, ≤ lake, 佘, 舝 – 閶 ▤ ▥ ✆ & ⇔ 🅿 🄰🄴 ⑩ 🄶🄱

mid-May-late October and closed Thursday except dinner in July-August, Monday, lunch Wednesday and Thursday – **Meals** 145/228 and a la carte 190/240 – ⌷ 42 – **12 rm** 404/603

Spec. "Tapas" en folie, ravioles de chénopodes, cacao, berce. Perche du lac, infusion de sapin, écume de sève, arôme de cannelle. Soufflé de cresson, galette de yaourt épicée, sorbet de bourbon.. **Wines** Chignin-Bergeron, Mondeuse d'Arbin..

Le Bourget-du-Lac 73370 Savoie **74** ⑮ – pop. 2 886 alt. 240.

Lyons 103.

XXXX ❀❀ **Bateau Ivre** - Hôtel Ombremont (Jacob), Nord : 2 km par N 504 ℘ 04 79 25 00 23, ombremontbateauivre@wanadoo.fr, Fax 04 79 25 25 77, ≤ lake and mountains, 佘, « Terrace overlooking the lake » – 🅿 🄰🄴 ⑩ 🄶🄱 🄹🄲🄱

early May-early November and closed lunch Monday and Tuesday – **Meals** 45 (lunch), 62/120 and a la carte 90/115

Spec. Foie gras de canard rôti, tranche de melon et jus à la réglisse (June-August). Lavaret cuit en filet, arrosé à l'huile de poivrons rouges aux aromates. Veau de lait rôti en papillote de lard, chutney de fruits d'été.. **Wines** Chignin-Bergeron, Mondeuse d'Arbin..

Chagny 71150 S.-et-L. **69** ⑨ – pop. 5 346 alt. 215.

🖪 Tourist Office 2 r. des Halles ℘ 03 85 87 25 95, Fax 03 85 87 14 44.

Lyons 145.

🏛 ❀❀❀ **Lameloise** Ⓜ, pl. d'Armes ℘ 03 85 87 65 65, reception@lameloise.fr, Fax 03 85 87 03 57, « Old Burgundian house, tasteful decor » – 閶 ▤ ▥ ⇔ 🄰🄴 ⑩ 🄶🄱 🄹🄲🄱

closed 18 December-23 January, Wednesday, lunch Thursday and Tuesday – **Meals** (booking essential) 75/105 and a la carte 72/100 – ⌷ 19 – **16 rm** 170/260

Spec. Ravioli d'escargots de Bourgogne dans leur bouillon d'ail doux. Pigeonneau rôti à l'émietté de truffes. Griottines au chocolat noir sur une marmelade d'oranges amères.. **Wines** Rully blanc, Chassagne-Montrachet rouge..

Megève 74120 H.-Savoie **74** ⑦ ⑧ – pop. 4 509 alt. 1 113.

🖪 Tourist Office Maison des Frères ℘ 04 50 21 27 28, Fax 04 50 93 03 09, megevemegeve.com.

Lyons 182.

XXXX ❀❀❀ **Ferme de mon Père** (Veyrat) (rooms expected), 367 rte Crêt ℘ 04 50 21 01 01, contact@marcveyrat.fr, Fax 04 50 21 43 43 – 🅿 🄰🄴 ⑩ 🄶🄱

mid-December-mid-April and closed Tuesday lunch, Wednesday lunch, Thursday lunch and Monday – **Meals** 145/228 and a la carte 190/240

Spec. Potimaron en soupe, écume de lard fumé. Anchois rôtis, frites de polenta, gelée de parmesan. Morceaux de canette, sève de sapin, calament épicé.. **Wines** Chignin-Bergeron, Mondeuse d'Arbin..

Mionnay 01390 Ain **74** ② – pop. 1 103 alt. 276.

Lyons 23.

XXXX ❀❀ **Alain Chapel** with rm, ℘ 04 78 91 82 02, chapel@relaischateaux.fr, Fax 04 78 91 82 37, 佘, « Flowered garden », 舝 – ▥ ⇔ 🅿 🄰🄴 ⑩ 🄶🄱 🄹🄲🄱

closed January, Monday, lunch Tuesday and Thursday – **Meals** 60 (lunch), 96/130 and a la carte 85/110 ♀ – ⌷ 15 – **12 rm** 103/130

Spec. Petit ragoût d'encornets à l'encre en paupiette d'aile de raie (Spring-Summer). Poulette de Bresse en vessie. Crème de Saint-Jacques aux châtaignes confites et œufs à la neige (Autumn).. **Wines** Mâcon-Clessé, Saint-Joseph.

Montrond-les-Bains 42210 Loire 🔞 ⑱ – pop. 3 627 alt. 356 – Spa (April-November) – Casino.
🏌 Forez 🐌 04 77 30 86 85 at Craintilleux, S : 12 km by N 82 and D 16.
🚹 Syndicat d'Initiative av. Philibert-Gary 🐌 04 77 94 64 74.
Lyons 62.

Hostellerie La Poularde (Etéocle), 🐌 04 77 54 40 06, lapoularde@aol.com,
Fax 04 77 54 53 14, 🗩 – 🖭 📺 🕭 🖙 – 🗛 30. 🆎 ⓞ 🆑 🃏
closed 4 to 20 August, 1 to 22 January, Sunday dinner from November-April, Tuesday lunch
and Monday – **Meals** (Sunday : booking essential) 42,69/103,67 and a la carte 85/115 –
⟐ 15,24 – **8 rm** 60,98/106,41, 6 suites, 3 duplex
Spec. Lobe de foie gras de canard froid poché à la lie de sauvignon. Agneau de lait rôti
et galette de maûs (January-September). Pigeonneau du Forez en pastilla, sauce vigne-
ronne.. **Wines** Condrieu, Saint-Joseph rouge.

Roanne 42300 Loire 🔞 ⑦ – pop. 41 756 alt. 265.
🏌 of Champlong at Villerest 🐌 04 77 69 70 60.
✈ Roanne-Renaison 🐌 04 77 66 85 77 by D 9.
🚹 Tourist Office 1 Crs République 🐌 04 77 71 51 77, Fax 04 77 70 96 62 – Automobile Club
24/26 r. Rabelais 🐌 04 77 71 31 67, Fax 04 77 71 27 00.
Lyons 87.

Troisgros 🅼, pl. Gare 🐌 04 77 71 66 97, troisgros@avo.fr, Fax 04 77 70 39 77,
« Tasteful contemporary decor », 🖼 – 🖭 📺 🕭 🖙 – 🆎 ⓞ 🆑 🃏
closed 30 July-16 August, February Holidays, Tuesday and Wednesday – **Meals** (booking
essential) 117/143 and a la carte 90/140 ⵕ – ⟐ 20 – **13 rm** 148/270, 5 suites
Spec. "Melba" de Saint Jacques, oursins à la moutarde (Autumn-Winter). Acidulé
d'écrevisses à la trévise. Jalousie de pamplemousse au miel de bourdaine (December-May)..
Wines Côte roannaise, Côte Rôtie..

St-Bonnet-le-Froid 43290 H.-Loire 🔞 ⑨ – pop. 180 alt. 1 126.
Lyons 101.

Auberge et Clos des Cimes (Marcon) 🅼 🍴 with rm, 🐌 04 71 59 93 72, contac
t@regismarcon.fr, Fax 04 71 59 93 40, ≤, 🖼 – 🗲 rm, 🖭 rest, 📺 🕭 🗜 🖭 🆎 🆑
closed 1 January-15 March, Monday dinner (except June-September), Tuesday and Wednesday – **Meals** 51 (lunch), 74/100 and a la carte 70/95 – ⟐ 16 – **12 rm** 145/206
Spec. Menu "champignons" (Spring and Autumn). Omble chevalier à l'huile de champignons
grillés. Agneau cuit en croûte de foin.. **Wines** Saint-Joseph, Madargues..

Valence 26000 Drôme 🔞 ⑫ – pop. 63 437 alt. 126.
See : House of the Heads (Maison des Têtes)⋆ – Interior⋆ of the cathedral – Champ de
Mars ⩽⋆ – Red chalk sketches by Hubert Robert⋆⋆ in the museum.
🏌 of Chanalets 🐌 04 75 83 16 23 ; 🏌 New Golf 🐌 04 75 59 48 18 at Montmeyran : 16 km
by ③ ; 🏌 of St-Didier 🐌 04 75 59 67 01, E : 14Km by D 119.
✈ of Valence-Chabeuil 🐌 04 75 85 26 26.
🚹 Tourist Office Parvis de la Gare 🐌 04 75 44 90 40, Fax 04 75 44 90 41,
infotourisme-valence.com – Automobile Club 15 r. Pont du Gat 🐌 04 75 43 61 07, Fax
04 75 42 27 03.
Lyons 101.

Pic 🅼, 285 av. V. Hugo, Motorway exit signposted Valence-Sud 🐌 04 75 44 15 32, pic@r
elaischateaux.com, Fax 04 75 40 96 03, 🖼, 🗩, 🖼 – 🖭 📺 🕭 🗜 🖙 🖭 – 🗛 50.
🆎 ⓞ 🆑 🃏
Meals (closed 1 to 21 January, Tuesday from November-March, Sunday dinner and Monday) (Sunday : booking essential) 42 (lunch)/120 and a la carte 100/130 ⵕ – ⟐ 16 – **12 rm**
145/280, 3 suites
Spec. Salade des pêcheurs. Filet de loup au caviar "Jacques Pic". Cochon de lait fermier
cuit au four et tian de fruits.. **Wines** Saint-Péray, Crozes-Hermitage..

Vienne 38200 Isère 🔞 ⑪ ⑫ – pop. 29 449 alt. 160.
See : Site⋆ – St-Maurice cathedral⋆⋆ – Temple of Augustus and Livia⋆⋆ – Roman
Theatre⋆ – Church⋆ and cloisters⋆ of St-André-le-Bas – Mont Pipet Esplanade ⩽⋆ – Old
church of St-Pierre⋆ : lapidary museum⋆ – Gallo-roman city⋆ of St-Romain-en-Gal – Sculp-
ture group⋆ in the church of Ste-Colombe.
🚹 Tourist Office 3 Crs Brillier 🐌 04 74 53 80 30, Fax 04 74 53 80 31, o-t-viennewanadoo.fr.
Lyons 31.

Pyramide (Henriroux) 🅼, 14 bd F. Point 🐌 04 74 53 01 96, pyramide.f.point@wanadoo.fr,
Fax 04 74 85 69 73, 🖼, 🖼 – 🗲, 🗲 rm, 🖭 📺 🕭 🖙 🖭 – 🗛 25. 🆎 ⓞ 🆑 🃏
closed mid-February-mid-March – **Meals** (closed Tuesday and Wednesday) 48 b.i. (lunch),
76/110 and a la carte 95/125 ⵕ – ⟐ 15,24 – **21 rm** 121/187, 4 suites
Spec. Moelleux de dormeurs à l'artichaut cru. Cul de veau de lait aux légumes de la vallée.
Piano au chocolat en "ut" praliné.. **Wines** Condrieu, Côte-Rôtie..

Vonnas 01540 Ain **74** ② – pop. 2 381 alt. 200.
Lyons 63.

Georges Blanc Ⓜ ⟨⟩, ℘ 04 74 50 90 90, blanc@relaischateaux.fr,
✿✿✿ Fax 04 74 50 08 80, « Elegant inn on the banks of the Veyle, flowered garden », ⟨⟩, ⟨⟩,
⟨⟩ – ⟨⟩ 📺 ℃ ⟨⟩ – ⚛ 80. ⟪ ⑨ ⟨⟩ ⟨⟩
closed January – **Meals** (closed Wednesday lunch, Monday and Tuesday except Bank Holidays) (booking essential) 95/215 and a la carte 90/125 – ⟨⟩ 23 – **32 rm** 165/335, 6 suites
Spec. Sauté de homard éclaté, raviole de truffe et céleri (Winter). Poulet de Bresse aux
gousses d'ail et foie gras. Panouille bressanne glacée à la confiture de lait.. **Wines** Mâcon-
Azé, Chiroubles.

MARSEILLES (MARSEILLE) 13000 B.-du-R. **84** ⑬ – pop. 800 550.
See : Site★★★ – N.-D.-de-la-Garde Basilica ⚜★★★ – Old Port★★ : Fish market (quai des
Belges) ET **5** – Palais Longchamp★ GS : Fine Arts Museum★, Natural History Museum★
– St-Victor Basilica★ : crypt★★ DU – Old Major Cathedral★ DS **N** – Pharo Park ⇐★ DU
– Hôtel du département et Dôme-Nouvel Alcazar★ – Vieille Charité★★ (Mediterranean
archeology) DS **R** – Museums : Grobet-Labadié★★ GS **M**[7], Cantini★ FU **M**[5], Vieux Marseille★
DT **M**[2], History of Marseilles★ ET **M**[1].
Envir. : Corniche road★★ of Callelongue S : 13 km along the sea front.
Exc. : – Château d'If★★ (⚜★★★) 1 h 30.
[18] of Marseilles-Aix ℘ 04 42 24 20 41 to the N : 22 km ; [9] of Allauch-Fonvieille (private)
℘ 04 91 05 09 69 ; junction Marseilles-East : 15 km, by D 2 and D 4=A ; [18] Country Club
of la Salette ℘ 04 91 27 12 16 by A 50.
⊁ Marseilles-Provence : ℘ 04 42 14 14 14 to the N : 28 km.
⟨⟩ ℘ 08 36 35 35 35.
🛈 Tourist Office 4 Canebière, 13001 ℘ 04 91 13 89 00, Fax 04 91 13 89 20 and St-Charles
railway station ℘ 04 91 50 59 18, destination-marseille@wanadoo.fr – Automobile Club of
Provence 149 bd Rabatau, 13010 ℘ 04 91 78 83 00, Fax 04 91 25 74 38.
Paris 772 – Lyons 312 – Nice 188 – Turin 407 – Toulon 64 – Toulouse 401.

Plans on following pages

Sofitel Vieux Port Ⓜ, 36 bd Ch. Livon ⊠ 13007 ℘ 04 91 15 59 00, h0542@acco
r-hotels.com, ⟨⟩ old Port, « Panoramic restaurant », ⟨⟩ – ⟨⟩,
⟨⟩ 📺 ℃ & ⟨⟩ – ⚛ 130. ⟪ ⑨ ⟨⟩ ⟨⟩, ⚜ rest   DU **n**
Les Trois Forts ℘ 04 91 15 59 56 **Meals** 45/58 ⟨⟩ – ⟨⟩ 19 – **127 rm** 220/330, 3 suites.

Petit Nice (Passédat) Ⓜ ⟨⟩, anse de Maldormé (turn off when level with no 160 Corniche
✿✿✿ Kennedy) ⊠ 13007 ℘ 04 91 59 25 92, hotel@petitnice-passedat.com,
Fax 04 91 59 28 08, ⇐ the sea, ⟨⟩, « Villas standing on the rocks, elegant decor », ⟨⟩
– ⟨⟩ ⟨⟩ 📺 🅿 ⟪ ⑨ ⟨⟩ ⟨⟩
closed 27 October-20 November – **Meals** (closed Sunday and Monday except dinner from
mid-April-September) 59 b.i. (lunch), 121/151 and a la carte 120/185 – ⟨⟩ 20 – **16 rm**
244/465 – **Spec.** Onctueux à la cryste marine et médaillons de langouste (June-
September). Tronçon de loup "Lucie Passédat". Déclinaison de chocolats en chaud et froid..
Wines Coteaux d'Aix, Bandol..

Holiday Inn Ⓜ, 103 av. Prado ⊠ 13008 ℘ 04 91 83 10 10, himarseille@alliance-ho
spitality.com, Fax 04 91 79 84 12, [6] – ⟨⟩, ⚐ rm, ⟨⟩ 📺 ⟪ & ⟨⟩ – ⚛ 150. ⟪ ⑨
⟨⟩ ⟨⟩
Meals (closed weekends and Bank Holidays) 14/24 ⟨⟩ – ⟨⟩ 11 – **115 rm** 119/134, 4 suites.

Mercure Beauvau Vieux Port without rest, 4 r. Beauvau ⊠ 13001
℘ 04 91 54 91 00, H1293@accor-hotels.com, Fax 04 91 54 15 76, « Antique furniture »
– ⟨⟩, ⚐ rm, ⟨⟩ 📺 ⟪ ⟪ ⑨ ⟨⟩ ⟨⟩
⟨⟩ 10,50 – **71 rm** 90/120.

Mercure Prado Ⓜ without rest, 11 av. Mazargues ⊠ 13008 ℘ 04 96 20 37 37,
H3004@accor-hotels.com, Fax 04 96 20 37 99, [6] – ⟨⟩, ⚐ rm, ⟨⟩ 📺 ⟪ ⟨⟩ – ⚛ 20.
⟪ ⑨ ⟨⟩   BZ **n**
⟨⟩ 10 – **100 rm** 100/140.

Mercure Euro-Centre Ⓜ, r. Neuve St-Martin ⊠ 13001 ℘ 04 91 17 22 22, h1148@a
ccor-hotels.com, Fax 04 91 17 22 33 – ⟨⟩, ⚐ rm, ⟨⟩ 📺 ⟪ & ⟨⟩ – ⚛ 200. ⟪ ⑨ ⟨⟩
Meals (closed Sunday lunch) 14 ⟨⟩ – ⟨⟩ 11 – **199 rm** 96/114.   EST **g**

Novotel Vieux Port Ⓜ, 36 bd ch. Livon ⊠ 13007 ℘ 04 96 11 42 11, h0911@acc
or-hotels.com, Fax 04 96 11 42 20, ⟨⟩, ⟨⟩ – ⟨⟩, ⚐ rm, ⟨⟩ 📺 ⟪ & ⟨⟩ – ⚛ 250. ⟪
⑨ ⟨⟩ ⟨⟩   DU **n**
Meals a la carte approx. 28 ⟨⟩ – ⟨⟩ 9,90 – **90 rm** 120/150.

New Hôtel Bompard ⟨⟩ without rest, 2 r. Flots Bleus ⊠ 13007 ℘ 04 91 99 22 22,
marseillebompard@new-hotel.com, Fax 04 91 31 02 14, ⟨⟩, ⟨⟩ – ⟨⟩ kitchenette ⟨⟩ 📺
& 🅿 – ⚛ 25. ⟪ ⑨ ⟨⟩ ⟨⟩
⟨⟩ 10 – **50 rm** 87/183.

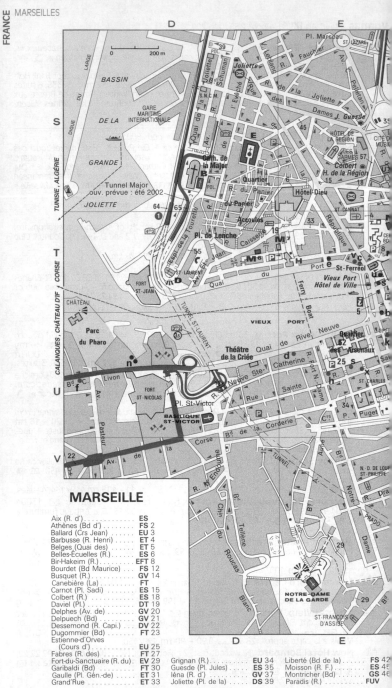

MARSEILLE

🏠🏠 **Résidence du Vieux Port** without rest, 18 quai du Port ⊠ 13002 ℰ 04 91 91 91 22, *hotelresidence@wanadoo.fr*, Fax 04 91 56 60 88, ≤ old port – |‡|, ⇌ rm, 🗏 🗺 📞 👌
– 🖄 30. 🕮 ◑ 🖼 🗾
� 10,50 – **42 rm** 85/190.

🏠🏠 **St-Ferréol's** without rest, 19 r. Pisançon ⊠ 13001 ℰ 04 91 33 12 21, *hotelstferreol@hotmail.com*, Fax 04 91 54 29 97 – |‡| 🗏 🗺. 🕮 ◑ 🖼 🗾   FU h
⊟ 6,55 – **19 rm** 61/94,50.

🏠🏠 **Mascotte** without rest, 5 La Canebière ⊠ 13001 ℰ 04 91 90 61 61, *mascotte-marseille@hotel-sofibra.com*, Fax 04 91 90 95 61 – |‡|, ⇌ rm, 🗏 🗺 – 🖄 30. 🕮 ◑ 🖼   ET s
⊟ 8 – **45 rm** 71/92.

🏠🏠 **Tonic Hôtel** without rest, 43 quai des Belges ⊠ 13001 ℰ 04 91 55 67 46, *tonic.marseille@wanadoo.fr*, Fax 04 91 55 67 56, ≤ – |‡| 🗏 🗺 📞 👌. 🕮 ◑ 🖼 🗾
⊟ 10 – **59 rm** 92/110.

🏠🏠 **New Hôtel Vieux Port** without rest, 3 bis r. Reine Élisabeth ⊠ 13001
ℰ 04 91 99 23 23, *marseillevieux-port@new-hotel.com*, Fax 04 91 90 76 24 – |‡| 🗏 🗺
– 🖄 25. 🕮 ◑ 🖼 🗾   ET u
⊟ 10 – **47 rm** 75/81.

🏠 **Alizé** without rest, 35 quai Belges ⊠ 13001 ℰ 04 91 33 66 97, *alize-hotel@wanadoo.fr*, Fax 04 91 54 80 06, ≤ – |‡| 🗏 🗺 📞. 🕮 ◑ 🖼 🗾   ETU b
⊟ 6,50 – **39 rm** 53/71.

🏠 **Ibis Gare St-Charles** 🅼, esplanade Gare St-Charles ⊠ 13001 ℰ 04 91 95 62 09, *h1390@accor-hotels.com*, Fax 04 91 50 68 42, 😚 – |‡|, ⇌ rm, 🗏 rm, 🗺 📞 👌 – 🖄 40.
🕮 ◑ 🖼   FS k
Meals 14,79 ⅘ – ⊟ 5,34 – **172 rm** 72.

🏠 **Kyriad** without rest, 31 r. Rouet ⊠ 13006 ℰ 04 91 79 56 66, *kyriad.marseille@wanadoo.fr*, Fax 04 91 78 33 85 – |‡|, ⇌ rm, 🗏 🗺 📞. 🕮 ◑ 🖼
⊟ 6 – **53 rm** 50/58.

🏠 **Hermès** 🅼 without rest, 2 r. Bonneterie ⊠ 13002 ℰ 04 96 11 63 63, *hotel.hermes@wanadoo.fr*, Fax 04 96 11 63 64 – |‡|, ⇌ rm, 🗏 🗺 📞. 🕮 ◑ 🖼 🗾   ET e
⊟ 7 – **28 rm** 43/66.

XXX **Miramar** (Minguella), 12 quai Port ⊠ 13002 ℰ 04 91 91 10 40, *contact@bouillabaisse.com*, Fax 04 91 56 64 31, 😚 – 🗏. 🕮 ◑ 🖼 🗾   ET v
❀ closed 5 to 26 August, 5 to 20 January, Sunday and Monday – **Meals** - Seafood - a la carte 54/80 ♀
Spec. Bouillabaisse. Poissons du golfe au beurre de pisala. Sar "à la Raimu".. **Wines** Coteaux Varois, Côtes du Luberon..

XXX **Ferme,** 23 r. Sainte ⊠ 13001 ℰ 04 91 33 21 12, Fax 04 91 33 81 21 – 🗏. 🕮 ◑ 🖼
🗾   EU m
closed August, Saturday lunch and Sunday – **Meals** 36,59 and a la carte approx. 45.

XX **Péron,** 56 corniche Kennedy ⊠ 13007 ℰ 04 91 52 15 22, Fax 04 91 52 17 29, ≤ Frioul islands and Château d'If, 😚 – 🕮 ◑ 🖼   AY a
Meals 33,54/48,78.

XX **Une Table au Sud,** 2 quai Port (1st floor) ⊠ 13002 ℰ 04 91 90 63 53, Fax 04 91 90 63 86, ≤ – 🗏. 🕮 ◑ 🖼   ET c
closed 28 July-21 August, 1 to 7 January, Sunday and Monday – **Meals** 29,73/44,97.

XX **Michel-Brasserie des Catalans,** 6 r. Catalans ⊠ 13007 ℰ 04 91 52 30 63, ❀ Fax 04 91 59 23 05 – 🗏. 🕮 🖼
Meals - Seafood - a la carte 45/75
Spec. Bouillabaisse. Bourride. Poissons grillés et flambés au fenouil.. **Wines** Cassis, Bandol.

XX **Les Échevins,** 44 r. Sainte ⊠ 13001 ℰ 04 96 11 03 11, *echevins@wanadoo.fr*, Fax 04 96 11 03 14 – 🗏. 🕮 ◑ 🖼 🗾   EU x
closed 14 July-16 August, Saturday lunch and Sunday – **Meals** 20,60/41,16 ♀.

XX **L'Ambassade des Vignobles,** 42 pl. aux Huiles ⊠ 13001 ℰ 04 91 33 00 25, Fax 04 91 54 25 60 – 🗏. 🕮 🖼 🗾   EU h
closed August, Saturday lunch and Sunday – **Meals** 35,06/47,26 b.i. ♀.

XX **Les Arcenaulx,** 25 cours d'Estienne d'Orves ⊠ 13001 ℰ 04 91 59 80 30, *restaurant@les-arcenaulx.com*, Fax 04 91 54 76 33, 😚, « Bookshop and restaurant in original decor » – 🗏. 🕮 ◑ 🖼 🗾   EU s
closed 11 to 26 August, 1 to 7 January and Sunday – **Meals** 23,63/45 ♀.

XX **Les Mets de Provence "Chez Maurice Brun",** 18 quai de Rive Neuve (2nd floor) ⊠ 13007 ℰ 04 91 33 35 38, Fax 04 91 33 05 69, « Rustic Provençal ambience » – 🗏
🖼   EU c
closed 1 to 20 August, Monday lunch and Sunday – **Meals** 33,54 (lunch)/48,78.

XX **René Alloin,** 9 pl. Amiral Muselier (by prom. G. Pompidou) ⊠ 13008 ℰ 04 91 77 88 25, *allloinfilipe@aol.com*, Fax 04 91 71 82 46, 😚 – 🗏. 🖼
closed Saturday lunch and Sunday dinner – **Meals** 21 (lunch), 31,25/44,21.

Aix-en-Provence 13100 B.-du-R. 84 ③ – pop. 123 842 alt. 206.

🛈 Tourist Office 2 pl. Gén.-de-Gaulle ℘ 04 42 16 11 61, Fax 04 42 16 11 62 – Automobile Club 7 bd J.-Jaurès ℘ 04 42 23 33 73, Fax 04 42 23 13 77.

Marseilles 31.

XXX
ध्ये ध्ये **Clos de la Violette** (Banzo), 10 av. Violette ℘ 04 42 23 30 71, restaurant@closdel aviolette.fr, Fax 04 42 21 93 03, 😤 – ■. ﷼ GB. ⋇

closed 4 to 18 August, 24 December-6 January, Sunday, lunch Monday and Wednesday – **Meals** (booking essential) 53,36 (lunch)/106,71 and a la carte 78/105

Spec. La truffe sous toutes ses formes (January-April). Sanguette de pigeon à l'ancienne. Trois réflexions chocolatées. **Wines** Côtes de Provence..

Les Baux-de-Provence 13520 B.-du-R. 84 ① – pop. 457 alt. 185.

See : Site★★★ – Château ※★★ – Charloun Rieu monument ≤★ – Place St-Vincent★ – Rue du Trencat★ – Paravelle Tower ≤★ – Yves-Brayer museum★ (in Hôtel des Porcelets) – Shepherds' Festival★★ (Christmas midnight mass) – Cathédrale d'Images★ N : 1 km on the D 27 – ※★★★ of the village N : 2,5 km on the D 27.

🟦 of les Baux-de-Provence ℘ 04 90 54 40 20, S : 2 km.

🛈 Tourist Office Ilôt "Post Tenebras Lux" ℘ 04 90 54 34 39, Fax 04 90 54 51 15.

Marseilles 83.

in the Vallon :

XXXXX
ध्ये ध्ये **Oustaù de Baumanière** (Charial) ☙ with rm, ℘ 04 90 54 33 07, Fax 04 90 54 40 46, ≤, 😤, « 16C period house tastefully decorated », ⊥, 🎋 – ■ 📺 🅿. ﷼ ① GB JCB

closed early January-early March, Tuesday lunch and Wednesday from November-March – **Meals** 85/135 and a la carte 95/130 ♀ – � 18,29 – **9 rm** 235/250, 5 suites

Spec. Ravioli de truffes aux poireaux. Filets de rouget au basilic. Canon d'agneau en croûte, gratin dauphinois.. **Wines** Châteauneuf-du-Pape-blanc, Coteaux d'Aix-en-Provence-les Baux.

Manoir ⌂⌂, ≤, ⊥, 🎋 – ■ rm, 📺 🅿. ﷼ ① GB JCB

Meals see **Oustaù de Baumanière** – ⊶ 18,29 – **7 rm** 250, 7 suites.

road of Arles to the SW by D 78=F road :

⌂⌂ **Cabro d'Or** ☙, à 1 km ℘ 04 90 54 33 21, contact@lacabrodor.com, ध्ये Fax 04 90 54 45 98, ≤, 😤, « Flowered gardens », ⊥, 🎋, ⋇ – ■ rm, 📺 ⋐ 🅿. ﷼ ①
GB

closed 11 November-20 December, Monday from November-March and Tuesday lunch – **Meals** 55 b.i. (lunch), 48/72 and a la carte 60/85 ♀ – ⊶ 13 – **23 rm** 147/205, 8 suites

Spec. Crème onctueuse d'artichauts au parfum de truffes. Suprême de volaille fermière farcie au chèvre frais et rôtie à la broche. Fraîcheur de pêches sur ganache cacao-thé. **Wines** Coteaux d'Aix-en-Provence-les Baux..

Lourmarin 84160 Vaucluse 84 ③ – pop. 1 108 alt. 224.

🛈 Tourist Office 8 av. Ph.-de-Girard ℘ 04 90 68 10 77, Fax 04 90 68 10 77.

Marseilles 63.

⌂⌂ **Moulin de Lourmarin** (Loubet) Ⓜ ☙, r Temple ℘ 04 90 68 06 69, lourmarin@fr ध्ये ध्ये ancemarket.com, Fax 04 90 68 31 76, 😤 – 🕻 ■ 📺 ⋘, ﷼ ① GB. ⋇ rest

closed 27 November-12 December and 13 January-1 March – **Meals** (closed Wednesday lunch and Tuesday) 95/138 and a la carte 105/140 – ⊶ 16 – **22 rm** 280/380

Spec. Cœur de tournesol vinaigrette. Cromesqui de joue de porc en farinette de noisette. Millefeuille de framboises tiédies et fraises des bois en chiboust.. **Wines** Côtes du Lubéron blanc et rouge.

Montpellier 34000 Hérault 83 ⑦ – pop. 207 996 alt. 27.

🟦 of Coulondres ℘ 04 67 84 13 75, N : 12 km ; 🟦 of Fontcaude at Juvignac ℘ 04 67 45 90 10, O : 9 km ; 🟦 of Massane at Baillargues ℘ 04 67 87 87 89, E : 13 km.

✈ of Montpellier-Méditerranée ℘ 04 67 20 85 85 te the SE :.

🛈 Tourist Office Triangle Comédie allée du Tourisme ℘ 04 67 60 60 60, Fax 04 67 60 60 61 and 78 av. du Pirée ℘ 04 67 22 06 16, contactot-montpellier.fr.

Marseilles 171.

XXXX
ध्ये ध्ये ध्ये **Jardin des Sens** (Jacques and Laurent Pourcel) Ⓜ with rm, 11 av. St-Lazare ℘ 04 99 58 38 38, jds@mnet.fr, Fax 04 99 58 38 39, « Elegant contemporary decor », ⊥, 🎋 – 🕻 ■ 📺 ⋎ ⋖ ⊶ 🅿 – 🔏 25. ﷼ ① GB JCB

Meals (closed 2 to 20 January, Sunday and lunch Monday and Wednesday) (booking essential) 42,70 (lunch), 77,70/109,80 and a la carte 100/130 – ⊶ 15,24 – **14 rm** 150/215

Spec. Encornets farcis aux langoustines. Filet de loup aux citrons confits. Pigeon en pastilla, jus au cacao.. **Wines** Coteaux du Languedoc, Faugères..

FRANCE

MONACO (Principality of) (Principauté de) 🆘 ⑩, 🆘 ㉗ ㉘ – *pop. 29 972 alt. 65 – Casino.*

Monaco *Capital of the Principality –* ✉ *98000.*

See : Tropical Garden★★ (Jardin exotique) : ≼★ – Observatory Caves★ (Grotte de l'Observatoire) – St-Martin Gardens★ – Early paintings of the Nice School★★ in Cathedral – Recumbent Christ★ in the Misericord Chapel – Place du Palais★ – Prince's Palace★ – Museums : oceanographic★★★ (aquarium★★, ≼★★ from the terrace), Prehistoric Anthropology★, Napoleon and Monaco History★, Royal collection of vintage cars★.

Urban racing circuit – A.C.M. 23 bd Albert-1er ℘ (00-377) 93 15 26 00, Fax (00-377) 93.

Paris 956 – Nice 21 – San Remo 44.

Monte-Carlo *Fashionable resort of the Principality – Casinos Grand Casino, Monte-Carlo Sporting Club, Sun Casino.*

See : Terrace★★ of the Grand Casino – Museum of Dolls and Automata★.

🛫 Monte-Carlo ℘ 04 92 41 50 70 to the S by N 7 : 11 km.

🅱 Tourist Office 2A bd Moulins ℘ (00-377) 92 16 61 16, Fax (00-377) 92 16 60 00, dtcmonaco-congres.com.

Paris, pl. Casino ℘ (00-377) 92 16 30 00, hp@sbm.mc, Fax (00-377) 92 16 38 50, ≼, 🍴, health centre, 𝄡, 🏊 – 📶, 🔁 rm, 🖵 📺 📞 🚗 – 🏛 70. 🆎 ⓪ 🆖 🆑 JCB. 🎴
see **Louis XV** and **Grill** below - **Côté Jardin** ℘ (00-377) 92 16 68 44 (closed dinner except 13 July-18 August and 6 to 21 January) Meals 50(lunch) and dinner a la carte 61/116 🍷 – **Salle Empire** ℘ (00-377) 92 16 29 52 (dinner only) (open July-August) Meals a la carte 71/148 🍷 – 🍽 30 – **117 rm** 570/685, 73 suites.

Hermitage, square Beaumarchais ℘ (00-377) 92 16 40 00, hh@sbm.mc, Fax (00-377) 92 16 38 52, ≼, 🍴, health centre, 𝄡, 🏊 – 📶 🖵 📺 📞 🚗 – 🏛 80. 🆎 ⓪ 🆖 JCB. 🎴 rest
Meals see **Vistamar** below – 🍽 25 – **211 rm** 460/590, 18 suites.

Métropole Palace Ⓜ, 4 av. Madone ℘ (00-377) 93 15 15 15, metropole@metropole.mc, Fax (00-377) 93 25 24 44, 🍴, 🏊, 🌳 – 📶 🖵 📺 📞 🚗 – 🏛 220. 🆎 🆖 JCB. 🎴 rest
Jardin ℘ (00-377)93 15 15 10 Meals 38(lunch), 53/84 🍷 – 🍽 28 – **150 rm** 290/545, 10 suites.

Méridien Beach Plaza Ⓜ, av. Princesse Grace, à la Plage du Larvotto ℘ (00-377) 93 30 98 80, resa@le-meridien-montecarlo.com, Fax (00-377) 93 50 23 14, ≼, 🍴, « Extensive swimming complex and luxurious conference centre », 𝄡, 🏊, 🏊, 🚲 – 📶 🖵 📺 📞 🚗 – 🏛 300. 🆎 ⓪ 🆖 JCB. 🎴 rm
Les Pergolas : Meals a la carte 50/69 🍷 – **Sea Club** - coffee shop (lunch only) (May-September) Meals a la carte approx. 47 🍷 – 🍽 31 – **330 rm** 335/1100, 8 suites.

Monte-Carlo Grand Hôtel Ⓜ, 12 av. Spélugues ℘ (00-377) 93 50 65 00, grandhotel@monaco.mc, Fax (00-377) 93 30 01 57, ≼, 🍴, Casino and cabaret, 𝄡, 🏊 – 📶 🖵 📺 📞 🚗 – 🏛 1 500. 🆎 ⓪ 🆖 JCB. 🎴 rest
L'Argentin (dinner only) (closed November) Meals a la carte 30/79 – **Pistou** (closed dinner from December-March and Tuesday dinner from April-23 July and 16 September-October) Meals a la carte 30/79 – 🍽 19,50 – **599 rm** 290/450, 20 suites.

Mirabeau Ⓜ, 1 av. Princesse Grace ℘ (00-377) 92 16 65 65, mi@sbm.mc, Fax (00-377) 93 50 84 85, ≼, 🍴, 🏊, 🔁 rm, 🖵 rm, 📺 📞 🚗 – 🏛 40. 🆎 ⓪ 🆖 JCB. 🎴 rest
see **La Coupole** below - **Café Mirabeau** (lunch only) (June-September) Meals a la carte 37/63 – 🍽 25 – **83 rm** 360/530, 10 suites.

Balmoral, 12 av. Costa ℘ (00-377) 93 50 62 37, resa@hotel-balmoral.mc, Fax (00-377) 93 15 08 69, ≼ – 📶, 🖵 rm, 📺 📞 – 🏛 20. 🆎 ⓪ 🆖 JCB. 🎴
Meals coffee shop (closed November, Sunday dinner and Monday) 21,34 – 🍽 14 – **53 rm** 152,45/167,69, 7 suites.

Alexandra without rest, 35 bd Princesse Charlotte ℘ (00-377) 93 50 63 13, hotelalexandra@imcn.com, Fax (00-377) 92 16 06 48 – 📶 🖵 📺. 🆎 ⓪ 🆖 JCB. 🎴
🍽 13 – **56 rm** 89/140.

Louis XV - Hôtel de Paris, pl. Casino ℘ (00-377) 92 16 29 76, lelouisxv@alain-ducasse.com, Fax (00-377) 92 16 69 21, 🍴 – 🖵 🅿. 🆎 ⓪ 🆖 JCB. 🎴
closed 28 November-27 December, 18 February-5 March, Wednesday except dinner from 19 June-21 August and Tuesday – Meals 90 b.i. (lunch), 150/180 and a la carte 130/200 🍷
Spec. Légumes des jardins de Provence mijotés à la truffe noire écrasée. Poitrine de pigeonneau, foie gras de canard et pommes de terre au jus d'abats. Le "Louis XV" au croustillant de pralin.. Wines Côtes-de-Provence, Bandol..

XXXX **Grill de l'Hôtel de Paris,** pl. Casino 🎧 (00-377) 92 16 29 66, hp@sbm.mc, Fax (00-377)
ξξ 92 16 38 40, ≤ the Principality, « Rooftop restaurant with sliding roof » – 🖹 🖹 🖭 🕮
🛈 🖼 🎸 ⊛
closed 6 to 21 January and lunch from 8 July to 28 August – **Meals** a la carte 100/140
♀
Spec. Poissons de Méditerranée grillés au feu de bois. Ravioli de langouste rose aux cour-
gettes et asperges vertes. Soufflé "tradition du grill".. **Wines** Côtes de Provence..

XXXX **La Coupole** - Hôtel Mirabeau, 1 av. Princesse Grace 🎧 (00-377) 92 16 65 65, mi@sbm.mc,
ξξ Fax (00-377) 93 50 84 85 – 🖹 ⇔, 🖭 🛈 🖼 🎸 ⊛
Meals (dinner only in July-August) 55/76 and a la carte 70/110
Spec. Encornet, fines feuilles de lasagne et gousses d'ail confites. Rouget de pays cuit sur
le grill. Veau taillé épais dans la côte, jus à la citronnelle.. **Wines** Côtes de Provence blanc
et rouge..

XXXX **Vistamar** - Hôtel Hermitage, pl. Beaumarchais 🎧 (00-377) 92 16 27 72, hh@sbm.mc,
ξξ Fax (00-377) 92 16 38 52, ≤ Harbour and Principality, 🛱 – 🖹. 🖭 🛈 🖼 🎸 ⊛
closed 23 to 26 May and 29 December-2 January – **Meals** 55 and a la carte 75/100
Spec. Saint-Pierre en cocotte aux morilles et lardons de canard (Spring). Cassolette de thon
à la tomate (Summer). Daurade royale en aiguillettes, sauce vin rouge (Winter).. **Wines**
Bellet, Côtes de Provence..

XXX **Bar et Bœuf,** av. Princesse Grace, au Sporting-Monte-Carlo 🎧 (00-377) 92 16 60 60,
ξξ b.b@sbm.mc, Fax (00-377) 92 16 60 61, ≤, 🛱, « Original decor » – 🖹 🖭 🖭 🛈 🖼
🎸
23 May-29 September – **Meals** (dinner only) a la carte 65/95
Spec. "Tomato et tomates", sorbet tomate et bloody Mary. Pavé de bar en feuille de
figuier, fruits rôtis, tomates et artichauts. Glace au bubble-gum.. **Wines** Côtes de Provence
blanc et rosé.

XXX **Maxim's,** 20 av. Costa 🎧 (00-377) 97 97 84 60, Fax (00-377) 97 97 84 61, 🛱 – 🖹.
🖭 🛈 🖼
Meals 38,11 (lunch), 88,42/137,20 and a la carte 83/128.

XXX **L'Hirondelle,** 2 av. Monte-Carlo (aux Thermes Marins) 🎧 (00-377) 92 16 49 30, Fax (00-
377)92 16 49 02, ≤ Harbour and rock, 🛱 – 🖹. 🖭 🛈 🖼 🎸 ⊛
closed 9 to 16 December – **Meals** (lunch only) 46 and a la carte 55/85 ♀.

XXX **Saint Benoit,** 10 ter av. Costa 🎧 (00-377) 93 25 02 34, lesaintbenoit@montecarlo.mc,
Fax (00-377) 93 30 52 64, ≤ Harbour and Monaco, 🛱 – 🖹. 🖭 🛈 🖼 🎸
closed 23 December-6 January, Sunday dinner and Monday from November-March, lunch
Monday and Saturday July-August – **Meals** 27/38 and a la carte 35/86 ♀.

XX **Café de Paris,** pl. Casino 🎧 (00-377) 92 16 20 20, cp@sbm.mc, Fax (00-377) 92 16
58 58, 🛱, « 1900 brasserie decor » – 🖹 🖭 🛈 🖼 🎸 ⊛
Meals a la carte 34/80,50 ♀.

XX **Bruno Restaurant,** 31 av. Princesse Grace 🎧 (00-377) 93 50 20 03, Fax (00-377) 97
70 87 75, 🛱 – 🖹. 🖭 🛈 🖼 🎸
Meals a la carte 46,50/71,65.

XX **Maison du Caviar,** 1 av. St-Charles 🎧 (00-377) 93 30 80 06, Fax (00-377) 93 30 23
90, 🛱 – 🖼
closed August, Saturday lunch and Sunday – **Meals** 24 (lunch), 30/45 ♀.

XX **Zébra Square,** 10 av. Princesse Grâce (Grimaldi Forum : 2nd floor by lift) 🎧 (00-377)
99 99 25 50, Fax (00-377) 99 99 25 60, ≤, 🛱 – 🖹. 🖭 🛈 🖼 🎸 ⊛
Meals a la carte 32/64 ♀.

X **Polpetta,** 2 r. Paradis 🎧 (00-377) 93 50 67 84 – 🖹. 🖭 🖼
closed 5 to 25 June, Saturday lunch and Tuesday – **Meals** - Italian rest. - 22,87.

at Monte-Carlo-Beach (06 Alpes-Mar.) at 2,5 km – ✉ 06190 Roquebrune-Cap-Martin :

🏨🏨 **Monte-Carlo Beach Hôtel** 🅼 ♨, av. Princesse Grace 🎧 04 93 28 66 66, bh@sb
m.mc, Fax 04 93 78 14 18, ≤ sea and Monaco, 🛱, « Extensive swimming complex », 🏊,
🐾, ⊛ – 🖹, 🖹 rm, 📺 ✆ & 🅿 – 🔏 30. 🖭 🛈 🖼 🎸 ⊛
1 March-24 November – **Salle à Manger** (closed July-August) **Meals** a la carte 50/93 ♀
– **Potinière** 🎧 04 93 28 66 43 (lunch only) (1 June-15 September) **Meals** a la carte 44/112
♀ – **Rivage** 🎧 04 93 28 66 42 (lunch only) (13 April-13 October) **Meals** a la carte 28/76
– **Vigie** 🎧 04 93 28 66 44 (28 June-3 Sept.) **Meals** 46(lunch)/55 (dinner) – ☷ 25 – **46 rm**
460/540.

Send us your comments on the restaurants we recommend
and your opinion on the specialities
and local wines they offer.

NICE *06000 Alpes-Mar.* 🎱🎱 ⑨ ⑩, 🎱🎱🎱 ㉖ ㉗ – *pop. 342 439 alt. 6 – Casino Ruhl FZ.*

See : *Site*★★ – *Promenade des Anglais*★★ *EFZ – Old Nice*★ : *Château* ≤★★ *JZ, Interior*★ *of church of St-Martin-St-Augustin HY* **D** – *Balustraded staircase*★ *of the Palais Lascaris HZ* **K**, *Interior*★ *of Ste-Réparate Cathedral – HZ* **L**, *St-Jacques Church*★ *HZ* **N**, *Decoration*★ *of St-Giaume's Chapel HZ* **R** – *Mosaic*★ *by Chagall in Law Faculty DZ* **U** – *Palais des Arts*★ *HJY – Miséricorde Chapel*★ *HZ* **S** – *Cimiez : Monastery*★ *(Masterpieces*★★ *of the early Nice School in the church) HV* **Q**, *Roman Ruins*★ *HV – Museums : Marc Chagall*★★ *GX, Matisse*★ *HV* **M2**, *Fine Arts Museum*★★ *DZ* **M**, *Masséna*★ *FZ* **M1** – *Modern and Contemporary Art*★★ *HY – Parc Phoenix*★ ★★ *(before Shrove Tuesday).*

Envir. : *St-Michel Plateau* ≤★★ *9,5 km.*

✈ *of Nice-Côte d'Azur* ℘ *04 93 21 30 30 : 7 km.*

🚗 ℘ *08 36 35 35 35.*

🛈 *Tourist Office 5 prom. des Anglais* ℘ *04 92 14 48 00, SNCF Station* ℘ *04 93 87 07 07, Fax 04 93 92 82 98, Nice-Ferber (Near the Airport)* ℘ *04 93 83 32 64, and Airport, Terminal 1* ℘ *04 93 21 44 11, Fax 04 93 21 44 50 – Automobile Club 9 r. Massenet* ℘ *04 93 87 18 17, Fax 04 93 88 90 00.*

Paris 932 – Cannes 32 – Genova 194 – Lyons 472 – Marseilles 188 – Turin 220.

Plans on following pages

🏨🏨🏨🏨 **Négresco,** 37 promenade des Anglais ℘ 04 93 16 64 00, *direction@hotel-negresco.c om, Fax 04 93 88 35 68,* ≤, 🍴, « *17C, 18C, Empire and Napoléon III furnishings* », 🛁 – 📵 🔲 📺 ✆ ⟨⟩ – 🔬 200. 🆎 ⓪ 🆑 FZ k
see **Chantecler** below - **Rotonde : Meals** 29, Sunday a la carte 35/98 ♀ – ♋ 25 – **119 rm** 267/585, 22 suites.

🏨🏨🏨 **Palais Maeterlinck** Ⓜ ⌂, 30 bd Maeterlinck, 6 km by Inferior Corniche ✉ 06300 ℘ 04 92 00 72 00, *info@palais-maeterlinck.com, Fax 04 92 04 18 10,* ≤ the coast, 🍴, « *Swimming pool, garden and terraces overlooking sea* », 🛁, ⌘, ☂, ♨ – 📵 kitche- nette 📶 📺 ✆ ⟨⟩ 🅿 – 🔬 80. 🆎 ⓪ 🆑 🆑 ⛴.
Mélisande : Meals 36/73 ♀ – ♋ 25 – **16 rm** 280/520, 13 suites, 11 duplex.

🏨🏨🏨 **Méridien** Ⓜ, 1 promenade des Anglais ℘ 04 97 03 44 44, *mail@lemeridien-nice.com, Fax 04 97 03 44 45,* « *Panoramic rooftop swimming pool* », 🛁, ⌘ – 📵, ✛ rm, 📶 📺 ✆ – 🔬 300. 🆎 ⓪ 🆑 FZ d
Colonial Café : Meals a la carte 38,11/54,12 ♀ – **Terrasse du Colonial** *(March-November)* **Meals** a la carte 39,63/53,36 ♀ – ♋ 20 – **305 rm** 260/1220, 9 suites.

🏨🏨🏨 **Élysée Palace** Ⓜ, 2, r. Sauvan ℘ 04 93 97 90 90, *reservations@elysee-palace.fr, Fax 04 93 44 50 40,* « *Panoramic rooftop swimming pool* », ⌘ – 📵, ✛ rm, 📶 📺 ✆ ⟨⟩ ⟨⟩ – 🔬 70. 🆎 ⓪ 🆑 ⛴ rest EZ d
Meals *(closed Saturday and Sunday)* 26 (lunch), 29/43 – ♋ 19 – **143 rm** 185/ 595.

🏨🏨🏨 **Radisson SAS** Ⓜ, 223 promenade des Anglais ✉ 06200 ℘ 04 93 37 17 17, *res@n cezh.rdsas.com, Fax 04 93 71 21 71,* ≤, 🍴, « *Panoramic rooftop swimming pool* », 🛁, ⌘ – 📵, ✛ rm, 📶 📺 ✆ ⟨⟩ – 🔬 260. 🆎 ⓪ 🆑 ⛴
Bleu Citron : Meals 27(lunch)/30 ⚐ – ♋ 20 – **318 rm** 265/525, 11 suites.

🏨🏨🏨 **Sofitel** Ⓜ, 2-4 parvis de l'Europe ✉ 06300 ℘ 04 92 00 80 00, *h1119@accor-hotels .com, Fax 04 93 26 27 00,* 🍴, « *Panoramic rooftop swimming pool* », 🛁, ⌘ – 📵, ✛ rm, 📶 📺 ✆ ⟨⟩ – 🔬 35. 🆎 ⓪ 🆑 ⛴ rest JX t
L'Oliveraie *(1 October-1 July)* **Meals** 21,34/38,11 ♀ – **Sundeck** *(July-September)* **Meals** 21,34/38,11 ♀ – ♋ 16,77 – **152 rm** 190,56/259,16.

🏨🏨🏨 **Boscolo Hôtel Plaza,** 12 av. Verdun ℘ 04 93 16 75 75, *info@plaza-hotel-nice.com, Fax 04 93 88 61 11* – 📵 📶 📺 ✆ – 🔬 250. 🆎 ⓪ 🆑 ⛴ GZ u
Meals a la carte 32/43 – ♋ 15 – **172 rm** 183/290, 10 suites.

🏨🏨 **La Pérouse** Ⓜ, 11 quai Rauba-Capéu ✉ 06300 ℘ 04 93 62 34 63, *lp@hroy.com, Fax 04 93 62 59 41,* ≤ Nice and Baie des Anges, 🍴, « *Flowered terraces* », 🛁, ⌘, – 📵, 📶 rm, 📺 ✆ – 🔬 30. 🆎 ⓪ 🆑 ⛴ ⛴ HZ k
Meals grill rest. *(mid-May-mid-September)* a la carte 27/41 ♀ – ♋ 16 – **63 rm** 215/ 373.

🏨🏨 **Masséna** Ⓜ without rest, 58 r. Gioffredo ℘ 04 92 47 88 88, *info@hotel-massena-ni ce.com, Fax 04 92 47 88 89* – 📵, ✛ rm, 📶 📺 ✆ ⟨⟩ ⟨⟩ – 🔬 20. 🆎 ⓪ 🆑 ⛴ GZ x
♋ 14 – **106 rm** 100/180.

🏨🏨 **Boscolo Park Hôtel,** 6 av. Suède ℘ 04 97 03 19 00, *reservation@park.boscolo.com, Fax 04 93 82 29 27,* ≤ – 📵 📶 📺 ✆ ⟨⟩ – 🔬 150. 🆎 ⓪ 🆑 ⛴ FZ a
Meals a la carte 37/61 – ♋ 15,25 – **104 rm** 213,43/282,04.

🏨🏨 **West End,** 31 promenade des Anglais ℘ 04 92 14 44 00, *hotel-westend@hotel-west end.com, Fax 04 93 88 85 07,* ≤, 🍴 – 📵 📶 📺 ✆ – 🔬 60. 🆎 ⓪ 🆑 ⛴ FZ p
Le Siècle : Meals 27 ♀ – ♋ 15 – **114 rm** 200/457, 10 suites.

🏨 **Beau Rivage,** 24 r. St-François-de-Paule ⊠ 06300 ℰ 04 92 47 82 82, *nicebeaurivag e@new-hotel.com*, Fax 04 92 47 82 83, 🏊 – 🛗, ⇥ rm, 🗏 📺 📞 ♿ – 🔥 50. 🖭
GB **JCB** GZ y
Bistrot du Rivage : Meals a la carte 25/35 ♀ – *Plage* 1 April-15 October Meals a la carte 27//45 ♀ – ☲ 15 – **118 rm** 190/220.

🏨 **Mercure Centre Notre Dame** Ⓜ without rest, 28 av. Notre-Dame ℰ 04 93 13 36 36, *h1291@accor-hotels.com*, Fax 04 93 62 61 69, « Hanging garden on 2nd floor », ⌧, 🌳 – 🛗, ⇥ rm, 🗏 📺 📞 – 🔥 90. 🖭 ① **GB** **JCB** FXY q
☲ 14 – **201 rm** 130/245.

🏨 **Holiday Inn** Ⓜ, 20 bd V. Hugo ℰ 04 97 03 22 22, *reservations@holinice.com*, Fax 04 97 03 22 23, 🏋 – 🛗, ⇥ rm, 🗏 📺 📞 ♿ – 🔥 90. 🖭 ① **GB** **JCB** FY a
Meals 24 (lunch), 28/35 ♀ – ☲ 18 – **131 rm** 205/260.

🏨 **Novotel** Ⓜ, 8-10 Parvis de l'Europe ⊠ 06300 ℰ 04 93 13 30 93, H1103@accor-ho tels.com, Fax 04 93 13 09 04, 🌤, « Panoramic rooftop swimming pool », ⌧ – 🛗, ⇥ rm, 🗏 📺 📞 ♿ 🚗 – 🔥 100. 🖭 ① **GB**. 🍴 rest JX v
Meals 19,06 ♀ – ☲ 11 – **175 rm** 117/183.

🏨 **Atlantic,** 12 bd V. Hugo ℰ 04 97 03 89 89, *info@atlantic-hotel.com*, Fax 04 93 88 68 60 – 🛗, ⇥ rm, 🗏 📺 📞 – 🔥 200. 🖭 ① **GB** **JCB** FY d
Meals 21,34 ♀ – ☲ 15,24 – **123 rm** 144,83/266,78.

🏨 **Splendid,** 50 bd V. Hugo ℰ 04 93 16 41 00, *info@splendid-nice.com*, Fax 04 93 16 42 70, 🌤, « Panoramic rooftop swimming pool », 🏋, ⌧ – 🛗, ⇥ rm, 🗏 📺 📞 🚗 – 🔥 15 - 60. 🖭 ① **GB** **JCB**. 🍴 rest FYZ g
Meals 29,73 ♀ – ☲ 15,24 – **112 rm** 175/220, 15 suites.

🏨 **Windsor,** 11 r. Dalpozzo ℰ 04 93 88 59 35, *windsor@webstore.fr*, Fax 04 93 88 94 57, 🌤, « Rooms decorated by modern artist, exotic garden with swimming pool », 🏋, ⌧, 🌳 – 🛗 🗏 📺 🖭 ① **GB**. 🍴 rest FZ f
Meals (coffee shop) *(closed lunch and Sunday)* a la carte approx. 31 – ☲ 8 – **57 rm** 120/135.

🏨 **Grimaldi** without rest, 15 r. Grimaldi ℰ 04 93 16 00 24, *zedde@le-grimaldi.com*, Fax 04 93 87 00 24 – 🛗 🗏 📺 📞. 🖭 ① **GB** FY s
☲ 13 – **46 rm** 105/145.

🏨 **Bleu Marine Victoria** without rest, 33 bd V. Hugo ℰ 04 93 88 39 60, *contact@ho telbleumarine.com*, Fax 04 93 88 07 98, 🌳 – 🛗, ⇥ rm, 🗏 📺 📞. 🖭 ① **GB** **JCB** FZ s
closed 21 to 28 December – ☲ 9,50 – **38 rm** 130/160.

🏨 **Petit Palais** 🐾 without rest, 17 av. E. Bieckert ℰ 04 93 62 19 11, *petitpalais@prov ence-riviera.com*, Fax 04 93 62 53 60, ≼ Nice and sea – 🛗, ⇥ rm, 🗏 📺 📞. 🖭 ① **GB** **JCB** HX p
☲ 9,91 – **25 rm** 94,52/123,48.

🏨 **Kyriad Nice Centre Les Musiciens** without rest, 36 r. Rossini ℰ 04 93 88 85 94, *info@nice-hotel-kyriad.com*, Fax 04 93 88 15 88 – 🛗 🗏 📺. 🖭 ① **GB** FY n
closed 19 to 26 December – ☲ 6,50 – **35 rm** 61/99.

🍴🍴🍴🍴🍴 **Chantecler** - Hôtel Négresco, 37 promenade des Anglais ℰ 04 93 16 64 00, *directio
✿✿ n@hotel-negresco.com*, Fax 04 93 88 35 68 – 🗏. 🖭 ① **GB** **JCB** FZ k
closed mid-November-mid-December – **Meals** 75/90 and a la carte 90/125
Spec. Salade Riviera (summer). Crépinette de rouget à la tapenade. Filet de bœuf, bolognaise aux condiments et pommes de terre soufflées. **Wines** Côtes-de-Provence..

🍴🍴🍴 **L'Ane Rouge** (Devillers), 7 quai Deux-Emmanuel ⊠ 06300 ℰ 04 93 89 49 63, *anero
✿ uge@free.fr*, Fax 04 93 89 49 63, 🏋 – 🗏. 🖭 ① **GB** JZ m
closed 8 to 21 July, February Holidays and Wednesday – **Meals** 24,10 (lunch), 31,70/55 and a la carte 45/65 ♀
Spec. Soupe de tomate en chaud-froid. Poisson du pêcheur aux gnocchi et poivrons confits. Petit baba comme autrefois.. **Wines** Bellet, Gassin..

🍴🍴🍴 **Don Camillo,** 5 r. Ponchettes ⊠ 06300 ℰ 04 93 85 67 95, *vianostephane@wanado o.fr*, Fax 04 93 13 97 43 – 🗏. 🖭 **GB** HZ h
closed 23 to 27 December, Monday lunch and Sunday – **Meals** - Niçoise and Italian specialities - 29 and a la carte 36/70 ♀.

🍴🍴🍴 **Les Viviers,** 22 r. A. Karr ℰ 04 93 16 00 48, Fax 04 93 16 04 06 – 🗏. 🖭 **GB** FY k
closed 28 July-28 August and Sunday – **Meals** 29/68 and a la carte 30/50 ♀.

🍴🍴 **L'Univers-Christian Plumail,** 54 bd J. Jaurès ⊠ 06300 ℰ 04 93 62 32 22, *plumai
✿ lunivers@aol.com*, Fax 04 93 62 55 69 – 🗏. 🖭 ① **GB** HZ u
closed Sunday, lunch Saturday and Monday – **Meals** (booking essential) 33,53/57,16 and a la carte 45/70 ♀
Spec. "Pan bagna" de légumes nouveaux et raie farcie. Rougets de roches et brandade aux olives. Tarte sans fond aux fraises des bois, glace vanille. **Wines** Bellet, Côtes de Provence..

271

NICE

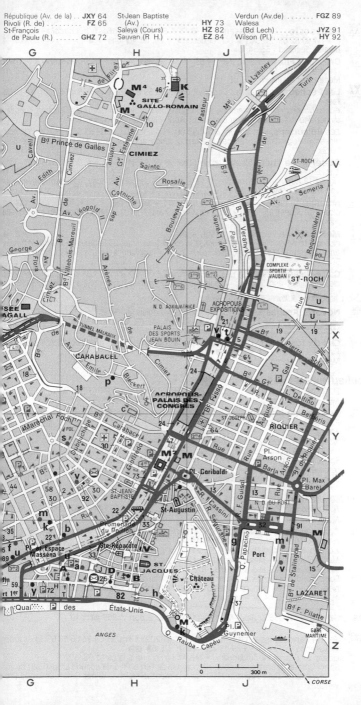

XX **Boccaccio,** 7 r. Masséna ✆ 04 93 87 71 76, *infos@boccaccio-nice.com, Fax 04 93 82 09 06,* ☂, « Carvel decor » – ▤. AE ⓓ GB JCB GZ f
Meals - Seafood - 33,54 ♀.

XX **Brasserie Flo,** 4 r. S. Guitry ✆ 04 93 13 38 38, *Fax 04 93 13 38 39,* brasserie, « Former theatre » – ▤. AE ⓓ GB GYZ m
Meals 19,50 b.i. (lunch)/28 b.i. ♨.

XX **Les Pêcheurs,** 18 quai des Docks ✆ 04 93 89 59 61, *Fax 04 93 55 47 50,* ☂ – ▤. AE GB JZ v
closed November-mid December, Wednesday, Thursday lunch from May-October, Tuesday dinner and Wednesday from December-April – **Meals** - Seafood - 26.

XX **Les Épicuriens,** 6 pl. Wilson ✆ 04 93 80 85 00, *Fax 04 93 85 65 00,* ☂ – ▤. AE GB
closed 6 August-2 September, Saturday lunch and Sunday – **Meals** a la carte 32/50 ♀. HY v

XX **Auberge de Théo,** 52 av. Cap de Croix ✆ 04 93 81 26 19, *Fax 04 93 81 51 73* – ▤. GB BS u
closed 19 August-11 September, 23 December-6 January, Sunday from September-April and Monday – **Meals** 18,29 (lunch), 25,92/32,01.

X **Mireille,** 19 bd Raimbaldi ✆ 04 93 85 27 23 – ▤. AE GB GX d
closed 10 June-4 July, 1 to 9 October, Monday and Tuesday – **Meals** - One dish only : paella - 25,92 ♀.

X **Merenda,** 4 r. Terrasse ✉ 06300 – ▤ HZ a
closed 8 to 14 April, 27 July-18 August, 1 to 10 December, 23 February-2 March, Saturday and Sunday – **Meals** - Niçoise specialities - (booking essential) a la carte 25,50/30,50 ♀.

X **Gaité-Nallino,** 72 av. Cap de Croix à Cimiez ✉ 06100 ✆ 04 93 81 91 86, ☂ – ▤. GB
closed August and Sunday – **Meals** Niçoise specialities (lunch only) a la carte 23/38 ♀.

at the airport : *7 km – ✉ 06200 Nice :*

Novotel Arenas Ⓜ, 455 promenade des Anglais ✆ 04 93 21 22 50, *h0478@accor-hotels.com, Fax 04 93 21 63 50* – 🛗, ⇔ rm, ▤ TV ✆ ♿ 🚗 – 🏛 150. AE ⓓ GB
Meals 15 – ☕ 11 – **131 rm** 110.

XXX **Ciel d'Azur,** airport station 1, 2nd floor ✆ 04 93 21 36 36, *pascal.bourdois@elior.com, Fax 04 93 21 35 31* – ▤. AE ⓓ GB
Meals (lunch only) 38,87 ♀.

Beaulieu-sur-Mer *06310 Alpes-Mar.* 84 ⑩ – *pop. 4 013.*

ℹ *Tourist Office pl. G.-Clemenceau ✆ 04 93 01 02 21, Fax 04 93 01 44 04.*
Nice 10.

✿✿ **Réserve de Beaulieu** 🐦, bd Mar. Leclerc ✆ 04 93 01 00 01, *reserve@wanadoo.fr, Fax 04 93 01 28 99,* ≤ sea, ☂, « Seaside », 🏋, 🏊 – 🛗, ▤ rm, TV 🚗. AE ⓓ GB
closed 1 November-20 December – **Meals** (dinner only from June-September) 46 (lunch), 65/130 and a la carte 120/190 – ☕ 28 – **34 rm** 665/1250, 4 suites
Spec. Thon et poivrons marinés à la julienne de jabugo (Summer-Autumn). Loup de Méditerranée au bellet rouge et poire épicée. Blancs de pigeon rôti au cœur de laitue, truffes et crémeux de parmesan. **Wines** Bellet, Bandol.

Èze *06360 Alpes-Mar.* 84 ⑩ – *pop. 2 446 alt. 390.*

ℹ *Tourisme Office pl. de Gaulle ✆ 04 93 41 26 00, Fax 04 93 41 04 80, ezewebstore.fr.*
Nice 12.

✿✿ **Château de la Chèvre d'Or** 🐦, r. Barri (pedestrian access) ✆ 04 92 10 66 66, *reservation@chevredor.com, Fax 04 93 41 06 72,* ≤ coast and peninsula, ☂, « Picturesque location overlooking the sea », 🏊, 🌳 – ▤ TV ✆ – 🏛 20. AE ⓓ GB JCB
March-November – **Meals** *(closed Wednesday in March and November)* (booking essential) 54 (lunch), 68/122 and a la carte 105/150 – ☕ 23 – **33 rm** 400/720
Spec. Fondant de pigeon et de foie gras de canard aux aubergines. Rouget barbet meunière et risotto de calmars. Longe d'agneau des Alpes de Haute-Provence farci de tomates et ail.. **Wines** Côtes de Provence..

St-Martin-du-Var *06670 Alpes-Mar.* 84 ⑨, 115 ⑯ – *pop. 1 869 alt. 110.*

Nice 26.

XXXX ✿✿ **Jean-François Issautier,** on Nice road (N 202) 3 km ✆ 04 93 08 10 65, *jf.issautier@wanadoo.fr, Fax 04 93 29 19 73* – ▤ P. AE ⓓ GB
closed 23 December-30 January, – **Meals** 44/86 and a la carte 68/107
Spec. Grosses crevettes en robe de pomme de terre. Pied de cochon croustillant au jus de marjolaine. "Cul" d'agneau rôti rosé à la menthe fraîche.. **Wines** Bellet, Côtes de Provence..

Vence 06140 Alpes-Mar. 🔢 ⑨, 🔢 ㉕ – pop. 15 330 alt. 325.
🛈 Tourist Office, pl. Grand-Jardin ℘ 04 93 58 06 38, Fax 04 93 58 91 81.
Nice 23.

XXX   **Jacques Maximin,** 689 chemin de La Gaude, by road of Cagnes : 3 km
🌼🌼   ℘ 04 93 58 90 75, restaurant.maximin@vence-prestige.com, Fax 04 93 58 22 86, 佘,
🍴 – **P**. AE GB
closed mid Nov.-mid Dec., lunch in 07/08 except Sunday, Sunday dinner and Monday from
09/06 except Bank Holidays – **Meals** (booking essential) 40 (lunch), 58/110 and a la carte
90/120
Spec. Soupe de tomates crues aux écrevisses (May-September). Filet de loup sauvage rôti
à la niçoise. Canard rôti à l'ail, sauce poivrade. **Wines** Bellet, Côtes de Provence..

STRASBOURG 67000 B.-Rhin 🔢 ⑩ – pop. 252 338 alt. 143 – Historical Museum★ KZ **M²** –
Museum of Modern Art★ KZ – Guided tours of the Port★ by boat.
See : Cathedral★★★ : Astronomical clock★ – La Petite France★★ : rue du Bains-aux-Plantes★★
HJZ – Barrage Vauban ⁂★ – Ponts couverts★ – Place de la Cathédrale★ KZ **26** : Maison
Kammerzell★ KZ **e** – Mausoleum★★ in St-Thomas Church JZ – Place Kléber★ – Hôtel de Ville★
KY **H** – Orangery★ – Palais de l'Europe★ – Museum of Oeuvre N.-Dame★★ KZ **M¹** – Boat trips
on the Ill river and the canals★ KZ – Museums★★ (decorative Arts, Fine Arts, Archeology) in
the Palais Rohan★ KZ – Alsatian Museum★★ KZ **M²**.

🏌 🏌 at Illkirch-Graffenstaden (private) ℘ 03 88 66 17 22 ; 🏌 of the Wantzenau at Wantzenau (private) ℘ 03 88 96 37 73 ; N by D 468 : 12 km ; 🏌 of Kempferhof at Plobsheim
℘ 03 88 98 72 72, S by D 468 : 15 km.

✈ of Strasbourg International : ℘ 03 88 64 67 67 by D 392 . 12 km FR.

🚂 ℘ 08 36 35 35 35.

🛈 Tourist Office 17 pl. de la Cathédrale ℘ 03 88 52 28 28, Fax 03 88 52 28 29, pl. gare
℘ 03 88 32 51 49, Pont de l'Europe ℘ 03 88 61 39 23 – Automobile Club 5 av. Paix
℘ 03 88 36 04 34, Fax 03 88 36 00 63.

Paris 490 – Basle 145 – Bonn 360 – Bordeaux 915 – Frankfurt 218 – Karlsruhe 81 – Lille
545 – Luxembourg 223 – Lyons 485 – Stuttgart 157

Plans on following pages

🏨 **Hilton,** av. Herrenschmidt ℘ 03 88 37 10 10, Fax 03 88 36 83 27, 佘 – 🛗, 🛏 rm, 🖥
🔲 📺 ☎ ⌾ ⯂ **P** – 🏛 25 - 300. AE ⓞ GB 🔳 ⅏
Jardin ℘ 03 88 35 72 61 **Meals** 26,52/49,23 ⬍ – ☲ 11 – **238 rm** 190/266, 5 suites.

🏨 **Sofitel** Ⓜ, pl. St-Pierre-le-Jeune ℘ 03 88 15 49 00, h0568@accor-hotels.com,
Fax 03 88 15 49 99, 佘, patio – 🛗, 🛏 rm, 🖥 📺 ☎ – 🏛 120. AE ⓞ GB 🔳   JY **s**
L'Alsace Gourmande ℘ 03 88 15 49 10 **Meals** 27 ⬍ – ☲ 17 – **155 rm** 220/275.

🏨 **Régent Petite France** Ⓜ ⳾, 5 r. Moulins ℘ 03 88 76 43 43, rpf@regent-hotels.
com, Fax 03 88 76 43 76, ≤, « Former ice factory on the banks of River Ill, contemporary
decor », 🛀 – 🛗, 🛏 rm, 🖥 📺 ☎ ⌾ – 🏛 30. AE ⓞ GB 🔳   JZ **z**
Meals (closed Monday from June-September and weekends from October-May) 32/59 –
☲ 17 – **64 rm** 200/272, 5 suites, 4 duplex.

🏨 **Holiday Inn,** 20 pl. Bordeaux ℘ 03 88 37 80 00, Fax 03 88 37 07 04, 🔲 – 🛗, 🛏 rm,
🖥 📺 ☎ ⌾ **P** – 🏛 300. AE ⓞ GB 🔳 ⅏ rest
Meals (closed lunch Saturday and Sunday) 25 ⬍ – ☲ 15 – **170 rm** 170/450.

🏨 **Régent Contades** Ⓜ without rest, 8 av. Liberté ℘ 03 88 15 05 05, rc@regent-ho
tels.com, Fax 03 88 15 05 15, « 19C mansion » – 🛗, 🛏 rm, 🖥 📺 ☎. AE ⓞ GB 🔳
☲ 15 – **45 rm** 145/235.   LY **f**

🏨 **Beaucour** Ⓜ without rest, 5 r. Bouchers ℘ 03 88 76 72 00, beaucour@hotel-beauc
our.com, Fax 03 88 76 72 60, « Old Alsatian houses elegantly decorated » – 🛗 🖥 📺 ☎
☎ – 🏛 30. AE ⓞ GB 🔳   KZ **k**
☲ 10 – **49 rm** 86/162.

🏨 **Maison Rouge** Ⓜ without rest, 4 r. Francs-Bourgeois ℘ 03 88 32 08 60, info@maison
-rouge.com, Fax 03 88 22 43 73, « Tasteful decor » – 🛗 📺 ☎ ☎ – 🏛 30. AE ⓞ GB
☲ 12 – **142 rm** 82/109.   JZ **g**

🏨 **Monopole-Métropole** without rest, 16 r. Kuhn ℘ 03 88 14 39 14, infos@bw-mono
pole.com, Fax 03 88 32 82 55, « Alsatian and contemporary decor » – 🛗, 🛏 rm, 📺
☎. AE ⓞ GB 🔳   HY **p**
☲ 10 – **90 rm** 73/125.

🏨 **Europe** without rest, 38 r. Fossé des Tanneurs ℘ 03 88 32 17 88, info@hotel-europ
e.com, Fax 03 88 75 65 45, « Half timbered Alsatian house, beautiful 1/50th model of the
Cathedral » – 🛗, 🛏 rm, 🖥 📺 ☎ – 🏛 30. AE ⓞ GB 🔳   JZ **v**
closed 22 to 29 December – ☲ 9,50 – **60 rm** 69/154.

🏨 **Mercure Centre** Ⓜ without rest, 25 r. Thomann ℘ 03 90 22 70 70, h1106@accor
-hotels.com, Fax 03 90 22 70 71 – 🛗, 🛏 rm, 🖥 📺 ☎ ☎ ⌾. AE ⓞ GB 🔳   JY **q**
☲ 11 – **98 rm** 125/134.

STRASBOURG

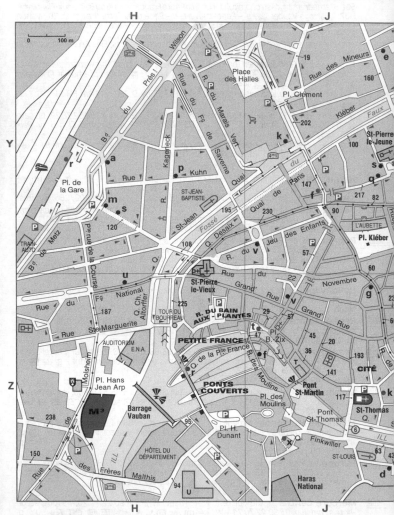

France without rest, 20 r. Jeu des Enfants 📞 03 88 32 37 12, *hotel.de.france.sa@wa nadoo.fr*, Fax 03 88 22 48 08 – 🛗, ✺ rm, 📺 🚗 – 🔬 30. 🖭 ⓞ 🖼 JY v
🚪 12 – **66 rm** 83/119.

Novotel Centre Halles 🅼, 4 quai Kléber 📞 03 88 21 50 50, *h0439@accor-hotels. com*, Fax 03 88 21 50 51 – 🛗, ✺ rm, 📺 ✆ 🔥 – 🔬 80. 🖭 ⓞ 🖼 🗷 JY k
Meals a la carte 23/26 ♀ – 🚪 11 – **98 rm** 129/136.

Grand Hôtel without rest, 12 pl. Gare 📞 03 88 52 84 84, *le.grand.hotel.@wanadoo.fr*, Fax 03 88 52 84 00 – 🛗 📺 ✆. 🖭 ⓞ 🖼 🗷 HY m
🚪 10 – **85 rm** 66/106.

Cathédrale 🅼 without rest, 12 pl. Cathédrale 📞 03 88 22 12 12, *reserv@hotel-cat hedrale.fr*, Fax 03 88 23 28 00, « Facing the Cathedral » – 🛗 🖻 📺 ✆ – 🔬 25. 🖭 ⓞ 🖼 🗷 KZ n
🚪 9,50 – **44 rm** 75/130, 5 duplex.

des Rohan without rest, 17 r. Maroquin 📞 03 88 32 85 11, *info@hotel-rohan.com*, Fax 03 88 75 65 37 – 🛗, ✺ rm, 📺. 🖭 ⓞ 🖼 🗷 KZ u
🚪 10 – **36 rm** 63/122.

Dragon 🅼 without rest, 2 r. Ecarlate 📞 03 88 35 79 80, *hotel@dragon.fr*, Fax 03 88 25 78 95 – 🛗, ✺ rm, 📺. 🖭 ⓞ 🖼. ✺ JZ d
🚪 9,15 – **32 rm** 65,55/107,47.

Diana-Dauphine without rest, 30 r. 1e Armée 📞 03 88 36 26 61, *hotel.dianadauphin e@wanadoo.fr*, Fax 03 88 35 50 07 – 🛗 🖻 📺 ✆ 🚗. 🖭 ⓞ 🖼 🗷
closed 22 December-1 January – 🚪 9 – **45 rm** 76/84.

Gutenberg without rest, 31 r. Serruriers 📞 03 88 32 17 15, Fax 03 88 75 76 67 – 🛗 📺. 🖼. ✺ KZ m
closed 1 to 12 January – 🚪 6,90 – **42 rm** 53/84.

Couvent du Franciscain without rest, 18 r. Fg de Pierre 📞 03 88 32 93 93, *info @hotel-franciscain.com*, Fax 03 88 75 68 46 – 🛗 📺 ✆ 🔥 🅿 – 🔬 15. 🖭 ⓞ 🖼 🗷 JY e
closed 24 December-5 January – 🚪 8 – **43 rm** 52/58.

Pax, 24 r. Fg National 📞 03 88 32 14 54, *info@paxhotel.com*, Fax 03 88 32 01 16, 🏡 – 🛗, ✺ rm, 📺 🔥 🚗 – 🔬 25. 🖭 ⓞ 🖼 🗷 HYZ u
closed 23 December-2 January – **Meals** *(closed Sunday from November-February)* 12/22 ♀ – 🚪 6,90 – **106 rm** 54,88/67,08.

Continental without rest, 14 r. Maire Kuss 📞 03 88 22 28 07, Fax 03 88 32 22 25 – 🛗 📺. 🖭 ⓞ 🖼. ✺ HY s
🚪 6,50 – **48 rm** 58/61.

Au Crocodile (Jung), 10 r. Outre 📞 03 88 32 13 02, *info@au-crocodile.com*, Fax 03 88 75 72 01, « Elegant decor » – 🖻. 🖭 ⓞ 🖼 🗷. ✺ KY x
closed 7 to 29 July, 22 December-6 January, Sunday and Monday – **Meals** 54 (lunch), 74/113 and a la carte 80/110 ♀
Spec. Sandre et laitance de carpe, paysanne de poireau. Pigeon des Vosges rôti, artichauts en barigoule. Symphonie aux trois chocolats.. **Wines** Riesling, Tokay-Pinot gris.

Buerehiesel (Westermann), set in the Orangery Park 📞 03 88 45 56 65, *westermar n@buerehiesel.fr*, Fax 03 88 61 32 00, ≤, « Reconstructed authentic Alsatian farmhouse with conservatory » – 🖻. 🅿. 🖭 ⓞ 🖼
closed 31 July-22 August, 31 December-15 January, Tuesday and Wednesday – **Meals** 51,83 (lunch), 97,57/129,58 and a la carte 105/125
Spec. Schniederspaetle et cuisses de grenouilles poêlées au cerfeuil. Poissons d'eau douce rôtis, jus de volaille à la coriandre fraîche, nouilles à l'alsacienne. Poularde de Bresse cuite entière comme un baeckeoffa.. **Wines** Tokay-Pinot gris, Pinot noir..

Vieille Enseigne (Langs), 9 r. Tonneliers 📞 03 88 32 58 50, Fax 03 88 75 63 80 – 🖻 🖭 ⓞ 🖼 🗷 KZ f
closed Saturday lunch and Sunday – **Meals** 32 (lunch), 56,41/73,18 and a la carte 60/82 ♀
Spec. Foie gras d'oie en terrine. Bar rôti au basilic et citronnelle. Paletot de canette laqué aux épices.. **Wines** Sylvaner, Pinot blanc..

Zimmer, 8 r. Temple Neuf 📞 03 88 32 35 01, Fax 03 88 32 42 28, 🍽 – 🖻. 🖭 ⓞ 🖼. ✺ KY y
closed 30 July-20 August, 23 December-7 January, Sunday and Monday – **Meals** 29,73/54,88 ♀.

Estaminet Schloegel, 19 r. Krütenau 📞 03 88 36 21 98, Fax 03 88 36 21 98 – 🖼 LZ c
closed August, Saturday lunch and Sunday – **Meals** 24,39 (lunch), 36,60/45,70 and a la carte 38/52 ♀.

XXX **Maison des Tanneurs dite "Gerwerstub",** 42 r. Bain aux Plantes ✆ 03 88 32 79 70, *maison.des.tanneurs@wanadoo.fr, Fax 03 88 22 17 26,* « Old Alsatian house on the banks of the River Ill » – AE ⓓ GB JZ t
closed 30 December-20 January, Sunday and Monday – **Meals** a la carte 28/63.

XXX **Maison Kammerzell and Hôtel Baumann** Ⓜ with rm, 16 pl. Cathédrale ✆ 03 88 32 42 14, *infomaison@kammerzell.com, Fax 03 88 23 03 92,* « Attractive 16C Alsatian house » – |♦|, ▤ rm, TV ✆ – 🏃 80. AE ⓓ GB JCB KZ e
hotel : closed February – **Meals** 29/45 and a la carte 35/45 ♀ – ☕ 11 – **9 rm** 69/110.

XX ✿ **Julien,** 22 quai Bateliers ✆ 03 88 36 01 54, *Fax 03 88 35 40 14* – ▤. AE ⓓ GB JCB KZ x
closed 1 to 21 April, 1 to 15 January, Sunday and Monday – **Meals** 32 (lunch), 46/69 and a la carte 55/66
Spec. Foie gras gras de canard poêlé à la rhubarbe. Langoustines rôties à l'infusion de gingembre confit. Moelleux de chocolat "guanaja"et sorbet à l'orange.. **Wines** Riesling, Pinot noir..

XX **S'Staefele,** 2 pl. St-Thomas ✆ 03 88 32 39 03, *Fax 03 88 21 90 80,* ☂ – AE GB
closed 1 to 15 January, 6 to 15 August, Sunday and Monday – **Meals** 17,53 and a la carte 28/39 ♀. JZ k

XX **Pont des Vosges,** 15 quai Koch ✆ 03 88 36 47 75, *Fax 03 88 25 16 85,* ☂ – AE GB
closed Sunday – **Meals** a la carte 30/40 ♀. LY h

XX **Buffet de la Gare-Argentoratum,** pl. Gare ✆ 03 88 32 68 28, *Fax 03 88 32 88 34* – ▤. AE ⓓ GB HY r
Meals 10,40/23 ♀.

X **Au Rocher du Sapin,** 6 r. Noyer ✆ 03 88 32 39 65, *Fax 03 88 75 60 99,* ☂, brasserie – AE GB JY f
closed Sunday – **Meals** 14,48/22,11 ♀.

WINSTUBS : *Regional specialities and wine tasting in a typical Alsatian atmosphere :*

X **Le Clou,** 3 r. Chaudron ✆ 03 88 32 11 67, *Fax 03 88 75 72 83* – ▤. AE GB KY n
closed Wednesday lunch, Sunday and Bank Holidays – **Meals** a la carte 30/38 ♀.

X **Ami Schutz,** 1 r. Ponts Couverts ✆ 03 88 32 76 98, *ami-schutz@strasbourg.com, Fax 03 88 32 38 40,* ☂ – AE ⓓ GB HZ r
closed Christmas Holidays – **Meals** 14,03 b.i. (lunch), 33,54 b.i./38,87 b.i..

X **S'Burjerstuewel (Chez Yvonne),** 10 r. Sanglier ✆ 03 88 32 84 15, *Fax 03 88 23 00 18* – AE GB KYZ r
closed 1 to 15 August, 23 December-2 January, Monday lunch and Sunday – **Meals** (booking essential) 27,44/38,11 ♀.

X **S'Muensterstuewel,** 8 pl. Marché aux Cochons de Lait ✆ 03 88 32 17 63, *munster stuewel@wanadoo.fr, Fax 03 88 21 96 02,* ☂ – ▤. AE ⓓ GB KZ y
closed 20 August-9 September, 18 to 28 February, 5 to 11 March, 30 April-6 May, Sunday and Monday – **Meals** 28,66 (lunch)/39,64.

X **Au Pont du Corbeau,** 21 quai St-Nicolas ✆ 03 88 35 60 68, *corbeau@reperes.com, Fax 03 88 25 72 45* – ▤. GB KZ b
closed 22 April-2 May, August, Sunday lunch and Saturday except December – **Meals** a la carte 25/30 ♀.

X **Fink'Stuebel,** 26 r. Finkwiller ✆ 03 88 25 07 57, *Fax 03 88 36 48 82* – GB JZ x
closed 5 to 20 August, 1 to 10 January, Sunday and Monday – **Meals** a la carte 22/32 ♀.

X **Hailich Graab "Au St-Sépulcre",** 15 r. Orfèvres ✆ 03 88 32 39 97, *Fax 03 88 32 39 97* – ▤. GB KZ d
closed 14 to 31 July, Sunday and Monday – **Meals** 23/29.

X **Zum Strissel,** 5 pl. Gde Boucherie ✆ 03 88 32 14 73, *Fax 03 88 32 70 24* – ▤. AE ⓓ GB KZ a
closed 3 to 31 July, 30 January-10 February, Sunday except Bank Holidays and Monday – **Meals** 10,20/21 ♀.

Environs

at La Wantzenau *NE by D 468 : 12 km – pop. 4 394 alt. 130 – ✉ 67610 :*

🏨 **Hôtel Au Moulin** 🐌, S : 1,5 km by D 468 ✆ 03 88 59 22 22, *moulin-wantzenau@wanadoo.fr, Fax 03 88 59 22 00,* ≤, « Old watermill on a branch of the River Ill », 🌳 – |♦| TV ✆ P. AE GB
closed 24 December-2 January – **Meals** see ***Rest. Au Moulin*** below – ☕ 8,85 – **20 rm** 59/90.

🏠 **Roseraie** without rest, 32 r. Gare ✆ 03 88 96 63 44, *laroseraie67@wanadoo.fr, Fax 03 88 96 64 95* – TV ✆ P. GB
closed 26 July-19 August – ☕ 6,40 – **15 rm** 42,70/50,30.

XXX **Relais de la Poste** with rm, 21 r. Gén. de Gaulle ℘ 03 88 59 24 80, *info@relais-po ste.com*, Fax 03 88 59 24 89, 斎, « Attractive Alsatian decor » – 🛊, 🗏 rest, 🗺 ಈ 🅿.
🆎 ⓪ ☎
closed 2 to 22 January – **Meals** *(closed 22 July-2 August, 2 to 22 January, Saturday lunch, Sunday dinner and Monday)* 28 (lunch), 39/73 and a la carte 62/80 – ☲ 10 – **19 rm** 60/115.

XXX **Zimmer**, 23 r. Héros ℘ 03 88 96 62 08, Fax 03 88 96 37 40 – 🆎 ☎
closed 21 to 30 November, 24 February-11 March, Sunday dinner and Monday except Bank Holidays – **Meals** 26/61 and a la carte 32/38 ♨.

XX **Rest. Au Moulin** - Hôtel Au Moulin, S : 1,5 km by D 468 ℘ 03 88 96 20 01, *philippe .clauss@wanadoo.fr*, Fax 03 88 68 07 97, 斎, « Floral garden », 🐎 – 🗏 🅿 🆎 ⓪ ☎
closed 8 to 29 July, 27 December-5 January, 17 to 23 February, dinner Sunday and Bank Holidays – **Meals** 22/60.

XX **Les Semailles**, 10 r. Petit-Magmod ℘ 03 88 96 38 38, *semailles@reperes.com*, Fax 03 88 68 09 06, 斎 – ☎
closed 4 August-4 September, 19 February-5 March, Sunday dinner, Wednesday and Thursday – **Meals** 35/45 ♀.

Baerenthal 57 Moselle 🟧🟥 ⑱ – pop. 723 alt. 220 – ⊠ 57230 Bitche.
Strasbourg 64.

at Untermuhthal SE : 4 km by D 87 – ⊠ 57230 Baerenthal :
XXXX **L'Arnsbourg** (Klein), ℘ 03 87 06 50 85, *l.arnsbourg@wanadoo.fr*, Fax 03 87 06 57 67,
🌼🌼🌼 斎 – 🗏 🅿. 🆎 ⓪ ☎ 🄹🄲🄱
closed 26 August-11 September, January, Tuesday and Wednesday – **Meals** *(weekends booking essential)* 39 (lunch), 68/83 and a la carte 75/95
Spec. Langoustines et foie gras marinés, petite salade d'artichauts et truffes. Grillade de foie gras de canard au citron confit. Saint-Pierre, compoté de pomelos, fenouil branches confit.. **Wines** Gewürztraminer, Muscat..

Illhaeusern 68970 H.-Rhin 🟦🟥 ⑲ – pop. 578 alt. 173.
Strasbourg 60.

🏠 **Clairière** ⌂ without rest, rte Guémar ℘ 03 89 71 80 80, *hotel.la.clairiere@wanadoo.fr*, Fax 03 89 71 86 22, ⌇, 🐎, 🍴 – 🛊, ᯤ rm, 🗺 🅿. ☎
closed 1 January-14 March – ☲ 12,95 – **25 rm** 74,70/236,29.

XXXXX **Auberge de l'Ill** (Haeberlin), ℘ 03 89 71 89 00, *auberge-de-l-ill@auberge-de-l-ill.com*,
🌼🌼🌼 Fax 03 89 71 82 83, ⩽ flowered gardens, « Elegant installation, on the banks of the River Ill », 🐎 – 🗏 🅿 🆎 ⓪ ☎
closed 28 January-7 March, Monday and Tuesday – **Meals** *(booking essential)* 89,94 (lunch), 105,19/126,53 and a la carte 80/130 ♀
Spec. Assiette de homard aux différentes saveurs. Filet d'omble chevalier à la choucroute et crème de caviar. Canard colvert légèrement laqué (September-December).. **Wines** Riesling, Pinot noir..
Hôtel des Berges 🏯 Ⓜ ⌂, ℘ 03 89 71 87 87, Fax 03 89 71 87 88, ⩽, « Resembling a tobacco shed in the Ried country », 🐎 – 🛊, ᯤ rm, 🗺 🗴 ಈ 🚗. 🆎 ⓪ ☎
closed 28 January-28 February and Tuesday – **Meals** *see* **Aub. de l'Ill** – ☲ 25 – **11 rm** 255/305.

Lembach 67510 B.-Rhin 🟧🟥 ⑲ – pop. 1710 alt. 190.
🅱 Tourist Office 23 rte Bitche ℘ 03 88 94 43 16, Fax 03 88 94 20 04.
Strasbourg 55.

XXXX **Auberge du Cheval Blanc** (Mischler) with rm, 4 rte Wissembourg ℘ 03 88 94 41 86,
🌼🌼 *info@au-cheval-blanc.fr*, Fax 03 88 94 20 74, « Old coaching inn », 🐎 – 🗏 🗺 🗴 ಈ 🅿.
🆎 ⓪ ☎
closed 1 to 19 July and 3 to 28 February – **Meals** *(closed Friday lunch, Monday and Tuesday)* 32,01/81,56 and a la carte 60/75 ♀ – **4 rm** 137,20/198,18, 3 suites
Spec. Filet de bar, fondant de jeunes poireaux au jus d'huître acidulé. Poitrines de pigeon en croûte de noix, ravioles à l'alsacienne. Médaillons de chevreuil à la moutarde de fruits rouges. **Wines** Tokay-Pinot gris, Pinot noir..

Marlenheim 67520 B.-Rhin 🟦🟥 ⑨ – pop. 2956 alt. 195.
Strasbourg 20.

🏨 **Cerf** (Husser), ℘ 03 88 87 73 73, *info@lecerf.com*, Fax 03 88 87 68 08, 斎, « Flowered
🌼🌼 inn » – 🗏 🗺 🅿. 🆎 ⓪ ☎
closed Tuesday and Wednesday – **Meals** 50 b.i. (lunch), 60/110 and a la carte 72/95 ♀ –
☲ 15 – **14 rm** 90/200
Spec. Grands ravioli de foie de canard fumé en pot-au-feu. Goujonnettes d'anguille poêlées aux escargots du Kochersberg. Chausson à la truffe noire du Périgord (January-March)..
Wines Sylvaner, Pinot noir..

TOULOUSE 31000 H.-Gar. 82 ⑧ - pop. 390 350 alt. 146.

🔟 🔟 of Vieille-Toulouse ℘ 05 61 73 45 48 by D 4 : 8 km ; ; 🔟 🔟 of Tournefeuille ℘ 05 61 07 09 09 by D 632 : 8 km ; 🔟 of St-Gabriel at Montrabé ℘ 05 61 84 16 65 by 3 : 9 km.

✈ of Toulouse Blagnac ℘ 05 61 42 44 00.

🚗 ℘ 08 36 35 35 35.

🛈 Tourist Office Donjon du Capitole ℘ 05 61 11 02 22, Fax 05 61 22 03 63, infostoulouse-tourisme-office.com.

Paris 699 – Bordeaux 248 – Lyons 536 – Marseilles 407 – Nantes 569.

Plans on following pages

🏨🏨🏨 **Sofitel Centre** M, 84 allées J. Jaurès ℘ 05 61 10 23 10, h1091@accor-hotels.com, Fax 05 61 10 23 20 – 📶, ❨❩ rm, 🔲 📺 📞 ⌖ ⇔ – 🔼 150. 🆔 ⓪ 🆖 🅹🅲🅱 ⚡ FX v
L'Armagnac (closed Sunday lunch and Saturday) **Meals** 26 ☿ – ☲ 16 – **112 rm** 200/297, 7 suites.

🏨🏨🏨 **Crowne Plaza** M, 7 pl. Capitole ℘ 05 61 61 19 19, dvtlsfr@imaginet.fr, Fax 05 61 23 79 96, 🍴, 🎰 – 📶, ❨❩ rm, 🔲 📺 📞 ⌖ – 🔼 60. 🆔 ⓪ 🆖 🅹🅲🅱 EY t
Meals 23/54 ☿ – ☲ 18,30 – **159 rm** 160/350, 3 suites.

🏨🏨🏨 **Grand Hôtel de l'Opéra** M without rest, 1 pl. Capitole ℘ 05 61 21 82 66, contact@grand-hotel-opera.com, Fax 05 61 23 41 04, 🎰 – 📶 🔲 📺 📞 ⌖ – 🔼 15 - 40. 🆔 ⓪ 🆖 🅹🅲🅱
☲ 18 – **47 rm** 122/245, 3 suites. EY a

🏨🏨🏨 **Grand Hôtel Capoul** M, 13 pl. Wilson ℘ 05 61 10 70 70, Fax 05 61 21 96 70, 🍴 – 📶, ❨❩ rm, 🔲 📺 📞 ⌖ – 🔼 100. 🆔 ⓪ 🆖 🅹🅲🅱 FY n
Brasserie le Capoul ℘ 05 61 21 08 27 **Meals** a la carte 29/40 – ☲ 11 – **130 rm** 106/134, 20 suites.

🏨🏨🏨 **Brienne** M without rest, 20 bd Mar. Leclerc ℘ 05 61 23 60 60, hoteldebrienne@wanadoo.fr, Fax 05 61 23 18 94 – 📶 🔲 📺 📞 ⌖ 🅿 – 🔼 25. 🆔 ⓪ 🆖 🅹🅲🅱 DV n
☲ 8,40 – **71 rm** 67,10/106,80.

🏨🏨🏨 **Mercure Atria** M, 8 espl. Compans Caffarelli ℘ 05 61 11 09 09, h1585@accor-hotels.com, Fax 05 61 23 14 12, 🍴 – 📶, ❨❩ rm, 🔲 📺 📞 ⌖ ⇔ – 🔼 200. 🆔 ⓪ 🆖 🅹🅲🅱 DV k
Meals 19 ☿ – ☲ 11 **136 rm** 99/144.

🏨🏨🏨 **Novotel Centre** M 🐾, pl. A. Jourdain ℘ 05 61 21 74 74, h0906@accor-hotels.com, Fax 05 61 22 81 22, 🍴, 🏊 – 📶, ❨❩ rm, 🔲 📺 📞 ⌖ ⇔ 🔼 100. 🆔 ⓪ 🆖 🅹🅲🅱
Meals a la carte approx. 28 ₰ – ☲ 10,50 – **125 rm** 100/110, 6 suites. DV u

🏨🏨 **Beaux Arts** M without rest, 1 pl. Pont-Neuf ℘ 05 34 45 42 42, contact@hotelsdesbeauxarts.com, Fax 05 34 45 42 43, ≤, « Fine decor » – 📶 🔲 📺 📞. 🆔 🆖 🅹🅲🅱 ⚡
☲ 15 – **19 rm** 99/153. EY v

🏨🏨 **Mermoz** M 🐾 without rest, 50 r. Matabiau ℘ 05 61 63 04 04, reservation@hotel.mermoz.com, Fax 05 61 63 15 64 – 📶 kitchenette 🔲 📺 📞 ⌖ ⇔ – 🔼 30. 🆔 ⓪ 🆖 🅹🅲🅱 DV f
☲ 9,15 – **52 rm** 83,85/105,20.

🏨🏨 **Grand Hôtel Jean Jaurès "Les Capitouls"** M without rest, 29 allées J. Jaurès ℘ 05 34 41 31 21, info@hotel-capitouls.com, Fax 05 61 63 15 17 – 📶, ❨❩ rm, 🔲 📺 📞 ⌖ – 🔼 20. 🆔 ⓪ 🆖 🅹🅲🅱 FX g
☲ 10,50 – **52 rm** 103/145.

🏨🏨 **Mercure Wilson** M without rest, 7 r. Labéda ℘ 05 34 45 40 60, h1260@accor-hotels.com, Fax 05 34 45 40 61 – 📶, ❨❩ rm, 🔲 📺 📞 ⌖ ⇔. 🆔 ⓪ 🆖 🅹🅲🅱 FY m
☲ 11 – **91 rm** 111/155, 4 suites.

🏨🏨 **Mercure St-Georges,** r. St-Jérôme (pl. Occitane) ℘ 05 62 27 79 79, H0370@accor-hotels.com, Fax 05 62 27 79 00, 🍴 – 📶 kitchenette, ❨❩ rm, 🔲 rest, 📺 📞 ⌖ – 🔼 60. 🆔 ⓪ 🆖 🅹🅲🅱 FY s
closed 13 July-26 August – **Meals** (closed Friday dinner, Saturday, Sunday and Bank Holidays) a la carte approx. 23 ☿ – ☲ 11 – **122 rm** 110/130, 26 suites.

🏨🏨 **Président** 🐾 without rest, 43 r. Raymond IV ℘ 05 61 63 46 46, contact@hotel-president.com, Fax 05 61 62 83 60 – 📺 📞 ⇔. 🆔 ⓪ 🆖 🅹🅲🅱 FX k
☲ 7,20 – **31 rm** 45/60.

🏨🏨 **Athénée** without rest, 13 r. Matabiau ℘ 05 61 63 10 63, Fax 05 61 63 87 80 – 📶 🔲 📺 📞 ⌖ 🅿 – 🔼 15 - 25. 🆔 ⓪ 🆖 🅹🅲🅱 FX a
☲ 8,38 – **35 rm** 60,98/83,84.

🏨 **Albert 1er** without rest, 8 r. Rivals ℘ 05 61 21 17 91, hotel.albert.1er@wanadoo.fr, Fax 05 61 21 09 64 – 📶 🔲 📺 📞 – 🔼 15. 🆔 ⓪ 🆖 EX r
☲ 8 – **50 rm** 54/74.

🏨 **Park Hôtel** without rest, 2 r. Porte Sardane ℘ 05 61 21 25 97, contact@au-park-hotel.com, Fax 05 61 23 96 27, 🎰 – 📺 📞. 🆔 ⓪ 🆖 FX s
☲ 6 – **44 rm** 45/57.

TOULOUSE

Alsace-Lorraine (R. d')	**EXY**
Arnaud-Bernard (R.)	**EX** 4
Astorg (R. d')	**FY** 5
Baronie (R.)	**EY** 9
Bilières (Av. E.)	**DV** 13
Bonrepos (Bd)	**DV** 16
Boulbonne (R.)	**FY** 18
Bouquières (R.)	**FZ** 19
Bourse (Pl. de la)	**EY** 20
Cantegril (R.)	**FY** 23
Capitole (Pl. du)	**EY**
Cartailhac (R. E.)	**EX** 26
Chaîne (R. de la)	**EX** 31
Cugnaux (R. de)	**DV** 35
Cujas (R.)	**EY** 36
Daurade (Quai de la)	**EY** 38
Demoiselles (Allées des)	**DV** 40

Esquirol (Pl.)	**EY** 54
Fonderie (R. de la)	**EZ** 60
Frères-Lion (R. des)	**FY** 62
Griffoul-Dorval (Bd)	**DV** 72
Henry-de-Gorsse (R.)	**EZ** 76
Jules-Chalande (R.)	**EY** 79
La Fayette (R.)	**EY**
Lapeyrouse (R.)	**FY** 85
Leclerc (Bd Mar.)	**DV** 87
Magre (R. Genty)	**EY** 91
Malcousinat (R.)	**EY** 92
Marchands (R. des)	**EY** 95
Mercié (R. A.)	**EY** 103
Metz (R. de)	**EFY**
Peyras (R.)	**EY** 113
Pleau (R. de la)	**FZ** 114
Poids-de-l'Huile (R.)	**EY** 115
Polinaires (R. des)	**EZ** 116
Pomme (R. de la)	**EFY** 117
Pompidou (Allée)	**DV** 118

Rémusat (R. de)	**EX**
République (R. de la)	**DV** 124
Riguepels (R.)	**FY** 12?
Romiguières (R.)	**EY** 12?
Roosevelt (Allées)	**FXY** 13?
St-Antoine du T. (R.)	**FY**
St-Étienne (Port)	**DV** 13?
St-Michel (Gde-Rue)	**DV** 13?
Ste-Ursule (R.)	**EY** 13?
St-Rome (R.)	**EY**
Sébastopol (R. de)	**DV** 139
Semard (Bd P.)	**DV** 14?
Suau (R. J.)	**EY** 14?
Temponières (R.)	**EY** 14?
Trinité (R. de la)	**EY** 14?
Vélane (R.)	**FZ** 15?
Wilson (Pl. Près)	**FY**
3-journées (R. des)	**EY** 16?
3-Piliers (R. des)	**EX** 16?

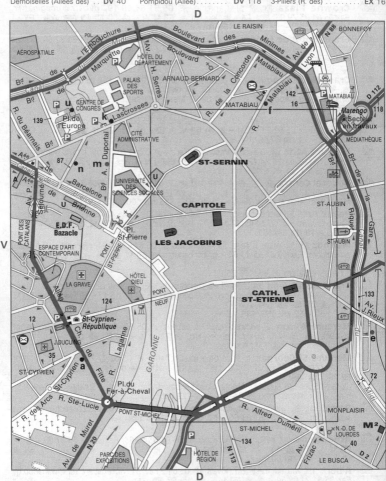

E   F

Pl. Arnaud
Bornard

Bd d'Arcole

R. de la Concorde

R. G. Paulhac

Matabiau

Raymond IV

MATABIAU

4 164

R. Gaten-Arnoult

R. Merly

a

k

Bayard

de

R. B. de Born

e

BASILIQUE
ST-SERNIN

31

MUSÉE
ST-RAYMOND

V

Pl.
St-Sernin

Pl.
Jeanne d'Arc

Rue

de

Pl. de
Belfort

Belfort

X

26

R. du Périgord

R. Denfert-Rochereau

Strasbourg

Jaurès

v

U

R. Lautmann

R. des Lois

R. de Rémusat

R. du Taur

N.-Dame-
du-Taur

Lorraine

Austerlitz

g

Jean Jaurès

A. France

R. Deville

r

Pl.
V. Hugo

s

p

f

R. Gabriel

Péri

argaminières

R. Lakanal

R. Gambetta

129 Pl. du Capitole

CAPITOLE

H
T

Capitole

Donjon

La Fayette

n

Place
Wilson

162

m

Bd

f

R. de la Colombette

LES JACOBINS

t

q a

R. St Rome

115

117

85

z

R. M. Fonvielle

T

P

Rue

d'Aubuisson

Hôtel
de Bernuy

M

79

d'Alsace

R. St-Antoine

117

s

Place
Occitane

ST-GEORGES

Lazare

Y

146

137

R. du May

147

9

91

103

r

Pl.
St.Georges

POL

36

20

R. Peyrolières

113

92

R. des Changes

54

23

18

MUSÉE DES
AUGUSTINS

5

Carnot

HÔTEL
D'ASSÉZAT

38

R. de la Bourse

R. de Metz

Pont Neuf

V

95

P Esquirol

149

c

Arts

18

127

62

R. de Metz

R. des Couteliers

Pl.
Rouaix

R. Croix Baragnon

R. Fermat

CATH.
ST-ÉTIENNE

Allées

François

N.-D. la
Dalbade

116

76

Pl. des
Carmes

19

R. Maye

R. Perchepinte

R. St-Jacques

Ninau

Allées

Poitiers

Verdier

GARONNE

Quai

R. de la Garonnette

R. de Tounis

R. de la Dalbade

Pharaon

R. du

R. Nazareth

Ozenne

114

v

MUSÉE PAUL
DUPUY

158

R. Espinasse

Pl.
Montoulieu

des

Jardin
Royal

Grand
Rond

Z

60

Pl. du Salin

J

Allées Jules Guesde

Av. M. Haurieu

Pl. du
Parlement

P

U

Allées Feuga

ST-EXUPÈRE

MUSÉUM
D'HISTOIRE NATURELLE

Allées Frédéric Mistral

Pont St-Michel

Pl. A.
Lafourcade

R. Alfred Duméril

Jardin
des Plantes

Mt de la
Résistance

0   200 m

E   F

🏠 **Ours Blanc-Wilson** without rest, 2 r. V. Hugo ℰ 05 61 21 62 40, *wilson@hotel-ours* *blanc.com, Fax 05 61 23 62 34* – 🛗 🖭 📺 🕻. 🖪   FX p
⊇ 7 – **37 rm** 49/70.

🏠 **Gascogne** without rest, 25 allées Ch. de Fitte ⊠ 31300 ℰ 05 61 59 27 44
Fax 05 61 42 25 52 – 🛗 📺 ♿ 🅿 – 🔏 15. 🖭 ① 🖪   DV a
⊇ 6,50 – **51 rm** 41,50/49.

🏠 **Bordeaux** without rest, 4 bd Bonrepos ℰ 05 61 62 41 09, *Fax 05 61 63 06 65* – 🛗 📺
🚗. 🖭 ① 🖪   FX e
closed 25 December-1 January – ⊇ 6,10 – **31 rm** 38/49.

🏛🏛🏛🏛 **Toulousy-Les Jardins de l'Opéra,** 1 pl. Capitole ℰ 05 61 23 07 76, *toulousy@wa*
🕸 *nadoo.fr, Fax 05 61 23 63 00* – 🖳. 🖭 ① 🖪 🔤   EY c
closed 28 July-27 August, 1 to 6 January, Sunday and Monday – **Meals** 36 (lunch), 46/84
and a la carte 85/110 ♀
Spec. Ravioli de foie gras de canard au jus de truffe. Œufs de caille aux six saveurs. Pigeon
neau au parfum d'épices, abatis en surprise et cuisse laquée.. **Wines** Gaillac, Côtes du
Frontonnais.

🏛🏛🏛 **Michel Sarran,** 21 bd A. Duportal ℰ 05 61 12 32 32, *michelsarran@wanadoo.fr*
🕸 *Fax 05 61 12 32 33,* 🏵 – 🖳. 🖭 🖪   DV m
closed 27 July-28 August, 1 to 10 January, Saturday and Sunday – **Meals** (booking essential)
38,12 b.i./91,50 b.i. and a la carte 60/90
Spec. Soupe tiède de foie gras à l'huître belon. Loup cuit et cru au chorizo. Pigeon er
brochette au sésame et curry.. **Wines** Gaillac, Fronton.

🏛🏛🏛 **Pastel** (Garrigues), 237 road of St-Simon, to the SW : 6 km ⊠ 31100 ℰ 05 62 87 84 30
🕸 *Fax 05 61 44 29 22,* 🏵, 🌿 – 🅿. 🖭 ① 🖪. ⚝
closed 11 to 19 August, Sunday and Monday – **Meals** (booking essential) 27,50 (lunch)
44,50/69 and a la carte 62/82
Spec. Saint-Jacques rôties "Jubilatoires" (10 October-10 April). Poitrine de pigeon, pastilla
et savouries de foie gras (February-September). Assiette de dessert au fruit de saison
Wines Gaillac, Côtes du Marmandais.

🏛🏛🏛 **L'Edelweiss,** 19 r. Castellane ℰ 05 61 62 34 70, *Fax 05 61 62 34 70* – 🖳. 🖭 ① 🖪
🔤   FX
closed 1 to 30 August, Sunday and Monday – **Meals** 26,68 ♀.

🏛🏛 **Depeyre,** 17 rte Revel ⊠ 31400 ℰ 05 61 20 26 56, *depeyre@depeyre.fr*
Fax 05 61 34 83 96 – 🖳. 🖭 ① 🖪   CU
closed 30 July-27 August, 25 February-3 March, Sunday and Monday – **Meals** 38/52 ♀

🏛🏛 **7 Place St-Sernin,** 7 pl. St-Sernin ℰ 05 62 30 05 30, *Fax 05 62 30 04 06,* « Eleganth
furnished "Toulousaine"house » – 🖳. 🖭 🖪   EX
closed 1 to 15 July, 24 December-2 January, Saturday and Sunday – **Meals** 23/49 ♀.

🏛🏛 **Brasserie "Beaux Arts",** 1 quai Daurade ℰ 05 61 21 12 12, *Fax 05 61 21 14 80,* 🏵
– 🖭 ① 🖪   EY
Meals 27,59 b.i..

🏛🏛 **Chez Laurent Orsi "Bouchon Lyonnais",** 13 r. Industrie ℰ 05 61 62 97 43, *or.*
le-bouchon-lyonnais@wanadoo.fr, Fax 05 61 63 00 71, 🏵 – 🖳. 🖭 ① 🖪 🔤   FY
closed Saturday lunch and Sunday – **Meals** 18,50/39 ♀.

🏛🏛 **Émile,** 13 pl. St-Georges ℰ 05 61 21 05 56, *Fax 05 61 21 42 26,* 🏵 – 🖳. 🖭 ① 🖪
closed 22 December-6 January, Monday (except dinner in summer) and Sunday – **Meal**
29/48,80 ♀.   FY

🏛🏛 **Brasserie de l'Opéra,** 1 pl. Capitole ℰ 05 61 21 37 03, *Fax 05 61 23 41 04,* 🏵, bras
serie – 🖳. 🖭 ① 🖪   EY
closed 5 to 28 August – **Meals** 25 ♀.

🏛🏛 **Daurade,** quai de la Daurade ℰ 05 61 22 10 33, *ladaurade@wanadoo.fr*
Fax 05 61 23 08 71, ≤, 🏵, « Converted barge on quayside of river Garonne » – 🖳. 🖪
closed Monday lunch from October-May, Saturday lunch and Sunday – **Meals** 18,30
24,39 ♀.   EY

🏛 **Cosi Fan Tutte** (Donnay), 8 r. Mage ℰ 05 61 53 07 24, *Fax 05 61 52 27 9*
🕸 – 🖪   FZ
closed 5 to 13 May, 28 July-5 September, 22 December-2 January, Sunday and Monda
– **Meals** - Italian rest. - (dinner only)(booking essential) 23 and a la carte 40/55
Spec. Filet de thon séché, oeuf brouillé au parmesan. Épaules de lapin fondantes, jus a
olives et polenta. Charlotte café, chocolat, mascarpone..

🏛 **Au Gré du Vin,** 10 r. Pléau ℰ 05 61 25 03 51, *Fax 05 61 25 03 51* – ① 🖪   FZ
closed August, Christmas-New Year, Saturday, Sunday and Bank Holidays – **Meals** (bookin
essential) 20,58/25,76 ♀.

🏛 **Chais,** 30 r. B. Mulé ℰ 05 61 54 27 20, *Fax 05 61 54 25 15,* 🏵 – 🖳. 🖭 ① 🖪   DV
closed 10 to 25 August, February Holidays, Saturday lunch, Monday and Sunday – **Mea**
20,60/28,20 ♀.

at Blagnac *North-West : 7 km – pop. 20 586 alt. 135 –* ⊠ *31700 :*

Sofitel M, 2 av. Didier Daurat, by road of airport, exit nr 3 ℰ 05 61 71 11 25, *h0565@a ccor-hotels.com*, Fax 05 61 30 02 43, 斎, ⊠, ⚘, ✕ – ♦, ✸ rm, ▤ ⊡ ☎ ☐ – ⚿ 90.
ℿ ⓞ ⒼⒷ ᴊᴄʙ
AS e
Caouec : Meals 27/33 b.i. – ⌧ 15 – **100 rm** 180/190.

Grand Noble, 90 av. Cornebarrieu ℰ 05 34 60 47 47, *hotel.rest.grand.noble@wanad oo.fr*, Fax 05 34 60 47 48, 斎 – ♦, ✸ rm, ▤ ⊡ ☎ & ☐ – ⚿ 50. ℿ ⓞ
ⒼⒷ
AS a
Meals *(closed August, Friday dinner and Saturday)* 15,50/33,50 – ⌧ 8,50 – **44 rm** 64/70.

Le Goulu, r. Bordebasse (north airport area) ℰ 05 61 15 66 66, Fax 05 61 30 43 07, 斎
– ▤ ☐ ℿ ⒼⒷ
AS u
closed lunch Saturday and Sunday – **Meals** 19,51/25,61.

Cercle d'Oc, 6 pl. M. Dassault ℰ 05 62 74 71 71, *cercledoc@wanadoo.fr*, Fax 05 62 74 71 72, 斎, ⚘ – ▤ ☐ ℿ ⓞ ⒼⒷ
AS t
closed 3 to 25 August, 1 to 7 January, Saturday lunch and Sunday – **Meals** 27 b.i. (lunch)/43
♇.

Pré Carré, Toulouse-Blagnac airport (2nd floor) ℰ 05 61 16 70 40, Fax 05 61 16 70 50, ← – ▤. ℿ ⓞ ⒼⒷ ᴊᴄʙ. ✕
AS n
closed 14 July-15 August, Sunday dinner and Saturday – **Meals** 33,50/37 ♇.

Bistrot Gourmand, 1 bd Firmin Pons ℰ 05 61 71 96 95, *bistrot-gourmand@bistro t-gourmand.com*, Fax 05 61 71 96 95, 斎 – ℿ ⓞ ⒼⒷ
AS v
closed 22 July-18 August, 30 December-6 January, Saturday lunch, Sunday and Monday
– **Meals** 10,55 (lunch), 16,90/27,50 ஃ.

Laguiole *12210 Aveyron* 76 ⑬ *– pop. 1 248 alt. 60*
🛈 *Tourist Office pl. du Foirail* ℰ *05 65 44 35 94, Fax 05 65 44 35 76, ot-laguiolewanadoo.fr.*
Toulouse 208.

to the East *6 km by road of Aubrac (D 15)*

Michel Bras M ⯮, ℰ 05 65 51 18 20, *michel.bras@wanadoo.fr*, Fax 05 65 48 47 02, ✳ Landscapes of Aubrac, « At the top of a hill » – ♦, ▤ rest, ⊡ ☎ & ☐ ℿ ⓞ ⒼⒷ.
✳
April-October and closed Monday except July-August – **Meals** *(closed lunch Tuesday and Wednesday except July-August and Monday)* (booking essential) 44,40 (lunch), 80,86/126,84 and a la carte 90/120 – ⌧ 19,02 – **15 rm** 174,40/301,24
Spec. "Gargouillou" de jeunes légumes. Viandes, volailles et gibier de pays. Biscuit de cho-colat "coulant".. **Wines** Marcillac, Gaillac..

Germany

Deutschland

BERLIN – COLOGNE – DRESDEN
DÜSSELDORF – FRANKFURT ON MAIN
HAMBURG – HANOVER – LEIPZIG
MUNICH – STUTTGART

PRACTICAL INFORMATION

LOCAL CURRENCY

1 euro (€) = 0,89 USD ($) (Dec. 2001)

TOURIST INFORMATION

Deutsche Zentrale für Tourismus (DZT):
Beethovenstr. 69, 60325 Frankfurt, ☎ (069) 97 46 40, Fax (069) 75 19 03
National Holiday in Germany: *3 October.*

AIRLINES

DEUTSCHE LUFTHANSA AG: *☎ (01803) 803803*
AIR CANADA: *☎ (069) 27 11 51 11*
AIR FRANCE: *☎ (0180) 5 83 08 30*
AMERICAN AIRLINES: *☎ (01803) 242 324*
BRITISH AIRWAYS: *☎ (01805) 26 65 22*
JAPAN AIRLINES: *☎ (0180) 22 28 700*
AUSTRIAN AIRLINES: *☎ (0180) 300 05 20*

FOREIGN EXCHANGE

In banks, savings banks and at exchange offices.
Hours of opening from Monday to Friday 8.30am to 12.30pm and 2.30pm to 4pm except Thursday 2.30pm to 6pm.

SHOPPING

In the index of street names, those printed in red are where the principal shops are found.

BREAKDOWN SERVICE

ADAC: *for the addresses see text of the towns mentioned*
AvD: *Lyoner Str. 16, 60528 Frankfurt-Niederrad, ☎ (069) 6 60 60, Fax (069) 660 67 89*
In Germany the ADAC (emergency number (01802) 22 22 22), and the AvD (emergency number (0130) 99 09), make a special point of assisting foreign motorists. They have motor patrols covering main roads.

TIPPING

In Germany, prices include service and taxes. You may choose to leave a tip if you wish but there is no obligation to do so.

SPEED LIMITS

The speed limit, generally, in built up areas is 50 km/h - 31 mph and on all other roads it is 100 km/h - 62mph. On motorways and dual carriageways, the recommended speed limit is 130 km/h - 80 mph.

SEAT BELTS

The wearing of seat belts is compulsory for drivers and all passengers.

BERLIN

🅛 Berlin ██████ ██████, *l 23, 24* – pop. 3 500 000 – alt. 40 m.

Frankfurt/Oder 105 – Hamburg 289 – Hannover 288 – Leipzig 183 – Rostock 222.

🛈 *Berlin Tourismus Marketing – Information at Europa-Center (Budapester Straße),*
✉ *10787 ☎ (030) 25 00 25, and information in Brandenburger Tor (side-wing).*

ADAC, Berlin-Wilmersdorf, Bundesallee 29-30.

🛆 🛆 *Berlin-Wannsee, Golfweg 22, ☎ (030) 8 06 70 60 – 🛆 Berlin-Gatow,*
Kladower Damm 182, ☎ (030) 3 65 77 25 – 🛆 Gross Kienitz (South : 23 km),
☎ (033708) 53 70 – 🛆 🛆 Kallin, an der B273 (North-West : 32 km),
☎ (033230) 89 40 – 🛆 Mahlow, Kiefernweg (South : 20 km), ☎ (033379) 37 05 95
🛆 Potsdam, Trommener Landstraße (West : 38 km), ☎ (033233) 8 02 44
– 🛆 🛆 Seddiner See, Zum Weiher 44 (South-West : 37 km), ☎ (033205) 73 20
– 🛆 Stolper Heide, Am Golfplatz 1 (North-West : 20 km), ☎ (03303) 54 92 14.

✈ *Berlin-Tegel EX, ☎ (0180) 5 00 01 86*
✈ *Berlin-Schönefeld (South : 25 km), ☎ (0180) 5 00 01 86*
✈ *Berlin-Tempelhof GZ, ☎ (0180) 5 00 01 86*
Deutsche Lufthansa City Center, Kurfürstendamm 220, ☎ (030) 88 75 33 75.

🚗 *Berlin-Wannsee, Nibelungenstraße.*
Exhibition Centre (Messegelände am Funkturm) BU, ☎ (030) 3 03 80,
Fax (030) 30 38 23 25.

BERLIN

0   1km

● S. Bahn

Bauarbeiten

E

F

A 105

Holländer-

Müller-

str.

SCHILLER

Barfus

PARK

Kurt-Schumacher-Damm

BERLIN-TEGEL

A T11
E 26

r

VOLKSPARK

REHBERGE

Transvaalstraße

Seestr

straße

WEDDING

Hohenzollernkanal

X

Saatwinkler

VOLKSPARK

JUNGFERNHEIDE

SIEMENSSTADT

Damm

See

R

U

651

Berlin - Spandau

Maria Regina

Martyrum

Gedenkstätte

Plötzensee

AB DR
CHARLOTTENBURG

Siemensdamm

628

A 100

WESTHAFEN

Quitzowstr.

Westhafenkanal

Perleberger

Str

Olbersstr.

Sickingenstr.

698   704

FRITZ-
SCHLOSS
PARK

621

SPREE

Huttenstr.

Bessel- str.

a

TIERGARTEN

Turm-

R

Belvedere

SCHLOSS-
GARTEN

Tegeler Weg

Kaiserin- Augusta-Allee

Alt- Moabit

Spandauer

699

a

SCHLOSS
CHARLOTTENBURG

Damm

Otto-

Levetzowstr.

Alt-

S

b

SPREE

str.

Schloß
Bellevue

Westend

637

M13

M

S

Schloßstr.

609

R

616

Landwehrkanal

HANSA-
VIERTEL

des

Suhr- Allee

Damm

699

DEUTSCHE
OPER
BERLIN

U

Straße

Neuer
See

TIERGARTEN

17

713 Kaiser-

Bismarck-

str.

Ernst-
Reuter-Pl.

Hardenberg

U

U

ZOOLOGISCHER
GARTEN

636

FUNKTURM

654

660

Lietzen

Kantstraße

J

625

Leibniz-

str.

Kantstraße

str.

T

str.

642

Lützow

Messe-
gelände

666

See

KURFÜRSTENDAMM

Tauentzienstr.

AB DR
FUNKTURM

A 115

Lietzenburger

str.

Straße

640

Straße

Bül

Koenigs

allee

Hubertus-
see

640

607

Zollern-

damm

WILMERSDORF

Hohenstaufenstr.

Paulsborner

Hohen-

Berliner

Uhland-

Bundes-
allee

Luther-

Grunewaldstr.

SCHÖNEBERG

R

str

straße

Hagenstr.

711

a

Hohenzollerndamm

Forckenbeck

str.

SCHMARGENDORF

R

692

allee

606

VOLKSPARK

Wex-str.

Martin-

612

A 100

3

15

16

17

Wiesbadener Str.

Laubacher Str.

Bundes-

687

R

Haupt-

AB KR
SCHÖNEBERG

Sach

Clay-
allee

Rhienbaben-
allee

708

FRIEDENAU

E

F

G   H

Provinz-str.

Osloer

Str.

684

Pank- str.

d

696

k

Behmstr.

VOLKSPARK HUMBOLDTHAIN

Wollankstr.

Mühlenstr.

PANKOW

Prenzlauer Prom.

Bornholmer Straße

Wisbyer Straße

Wichertstr.

Allee

Berliner Str.

Gustav-

Adolf-

Str.

Str.

Pistorius-

WEISSENSEE

Ostsee-

str.

604

X

Chaussee-

erstr.

str.

Berliner

straße

Brunnen-

Str.

Danziger

Allee

Greifswalder

Storkower

Str.

Straße

EURORA-
SPORT-PARK
BERLIN

Straße

c

Torstraße

Friedrichstraße

MITTE

Lessenstr.

Luisenstr.

Schönhauser Allee

PRENZLAUER

BERG

Prenzlauer

Torstraße

Karl-Liebknecht

Grünen str.

Greifswalder

Str.

Elbinger Str.

Landsberger

Petersburger str.

Allee

Allee

REICHSTAG

61

UNTER DEN LINDEN

BRANDENBURGER
TOR

3

KULTURFORUM

669

Leipziger

FERNSEHTURM

O

ALEXANDERPL.

KARL- 702

MARX-

ALLEE

R

Volkspark
Friedrichshain

Frieden-

Mollstr.

FRANKFURTER
TOR

643

FRIEDRICHSHAIN

Y

Stresemannstr.

Friedrich-

Straße

Gertrauden-

str.

Annen-

Köpenicker

Holzmkt.

str.

Mühlenstr.

Warschauer Straße

Stralauer

Allee

SPREE

Kochstr.

Oranien-

623

645

Straße

622

J

T

655

Berlin- Museum

M

Gitschiner

675

str.

Str.

Skalitzer

Straße

Wiener Str.

Landwehrkanal

710

M8

Yorck-

634

damm

R

KREUZBERG

Gneisenaustraße

Urbanstr.

Hasenheide

Kottbusser Damm

Sonnen-

TREPTOW

Eisen- straße

VIKTORIA-
PARK

Dudenstr.

646

652

Boelcke-

straße

Mehring-

POL

Columbia-

Bergmannstraße

Platz der
Luftbrücke

VOLKSPARK
HASENHEIDE

T

damm

BERLIN-
TEMPELHOF

Tempelhofer Damm

c

Oder-

str.

NEUKÖLLN

Hermannstraße

Karl-

R

Marx-

Str.

allee

a

Z

20

G   H

BERLIN
KURFÜRSTENDAMM ZOO

0 • S.Bahn 400 m

CHARLOTTENBURG

Bismarckstr.

DEUTSCHE OPER BERLIN

Deutsche Oper

Zillestraße

Kaiser-

Schloßstr.

Bismarck-

POL.

Kaiserdamm

Sophie-Ch.-Pl.

Sophie-Charlotte-Pl.

Schillerstr.

Wilmersdorfer

Schillerstr.

SCHILLER-THEATER

Bismarckstra

Fraunho

609

Suhr-

Wynd-

LIETZENSEE PARK

Lietzen

Neue Kantstraße

Amtsgerichts-platz

Suarezstr.

Windscheidstraße

Pestalozzistr.

Kantstraße

Kantstraße

Krumme

Peotalozzis

Leonhardtstr.

705

Straße

CHARLOTTENBURG

Mommsenstr.

Mommsen

Leibnizstr.

Schlüterstr.

SAVIGNYF

Bleibtreu

625

Rönne-straße

Holtzendorff-platz

Gervinusstr.

Dahlmannstr.

Lewishamstr.

Droysenstr.

Damaschke-

Heilbronner Str.

KURFÜRSTENDAMM

Georg-Wilhelm-Straße

Adenauerpl.

Xantener Str.

POL.

600

667

Brandenburgische

Düsseldorfer

Pariser

Str.

Schlüterstr.

Lietzenb

Stral

HALENSEE

Westfälische

Friedrich-

Nestorstraße

Straße

Joachim-

Paulsborner

Straße

Hochmeister-platz

Eisenzahrstraße

Konstanzer Str.

Brandenburgische

Straße

PREUSSEN PARK

Württembergische

Sächsische

Emser

Str

Hohenzollernd

Grieser Pl.

BAB

Stadtring

Seesener Straße

Konstanzer

Straße

Fehrbelliner Platz

Fehrbelliner Pl.

Sigmaringer Str.

Brandenburgische

Paulsborner

Viktoria-

Hohenzollern-

Cunstr.

HOHENZOLLERN-damm

Hohenzollerndamm

Rudolstädter

Straße

R

Bar-

str.

POL.

Berliner

WILMERSDORF

Blisse

Auguste-

Forckenbeckstraße

Cunostraße

EISSTADION STADION

A 100

AB. KR. WILMERSDORF

VOLKSPARK

BAB Abzweig

Mecklenburgische Straße

Bar-

Steglitz

Heidelbg. Pl.

HEIDELBERGER PL.

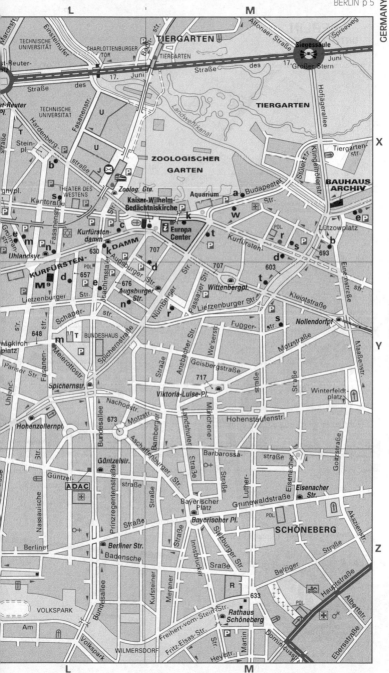

BERLIN
UNTER DEN LINDEN

0 _____ 500 m

● S-bahn   ▨ Bauarbeiten

N **P**

X

Y

Z

WEDDING

Straß

Garten-

Acker-

Bernauer Str.

Bernauer

str.

Brunnen-

Schwartzkopffstr.

Chausseestraße

Scharnhorststr.

Heidestraße

MUSEUM FÜR NATURKUNDE

Zinnowitzer str.

c

NORDBAHNHOF

Invalidenstr.

e MITTE

POL

Straß

Torstra

HAMBURGER BAHNHOF

Straße

a

M

FRIEDRICHSTR.

Torstraße

Invaliden-

CHARITÉ

Oranienburger Tor

ORANIENBURGER STR.

ORANIENBURGER

b

SPIELE KAMMER

DEUTSCHES THEATER

e

LEHRTER STADTBAHNHOF

Willy-Brandt-

Otto-von-Bismarck-Allee

b

Luisen-

683

a

BERLINER ENSEMBLE

MONBIJOU-PARK

M 2

PERGAMON-MUSEUM

M

BUNDES-KANZLER-AMT

PAUL-LÖBE-HAUS

M.-E. LÜDERS-HAUS

BM UMWELT

T

T

Friedrichstr.

n

U

M

Haus der Kulturen der Welt

Straße

SPREE

JAKOB-KAISER-HAUS

M

P

e

U

Neue Wache

De

Platz der Republik

REICHSTAG

Pariser Pl.

b

Friedrichstr.

f

ZEUGHA

Straße

des

17.

Juni

BRANDENBURGER TOR

S

UNTER

DEN

LINDEN

T

a

610

618

St. Hedwig

C n

STAATSOPE

STAATSOPE

TIERGARTEN

Wilhelmstr.

Französ. Str.

d

S

u 618

Friedr.-Werdersc

GENDARMEN-MARKT

Lennéstr.

Mohrenstr.

Stadtmitte

Hausvogteipl.

r

KAMMERMUSIKSAAL

Potsdamer Platz

Leipziger Platz

k

P

FRIEDRICH+

Straße

M 4

T 1

SONY

672

Leipziger

M 7

M

Entlastungs-

P

INFOBOX

POTSDAMER PLATZ

ABGEORDNETENHAUS

Stresemannstr.

a

v

624

P

M 5

J

SPIELBANK BERLIN

MUSICAL THEATER

Koch-

Wilhelmstr.

Kochstr.

Lindenstr.

str.

M

FRIEDRICH

STR.

STAATSBIBLIOTHEK PREUSSICHER KULTURBESITZ

672

c

MARTIN-GROPIUS-BAU

r

e

KREUZBERG

POL

Askanischer Platz

ANHALTER BAHNHOF

N **P**

294

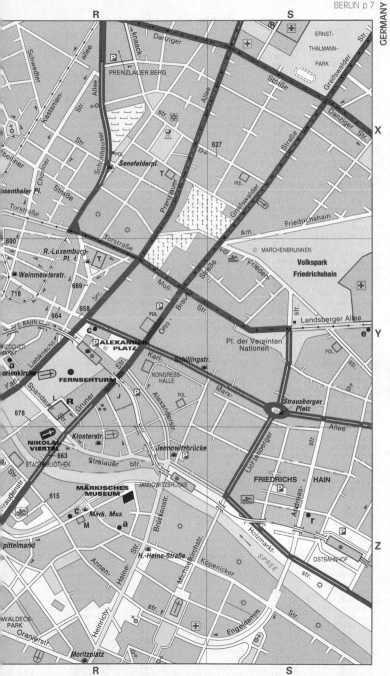

STREET INDEX TO BERLIN TOWN PLANS

STREET INDEX TO BERLIN TOWN PLANS (Concluded)

SIGHTS

MUSEUMS, GALLERIES, COLLECTIONS

Museum Island (Museumsinsel)★★★ PY; *Pergamon-Museum; Collection of Antiquities (Antikensammlung)*★★★, *Altar of Pergamon (Pergamon-Altar)*★★★, *Gate to the Milet market (Markttor von Milet)*★★, *Middle East Museum (Vorderasiatisches Museum)*★, *Processional way and Gate of Ishtar (Prozessionsstraße und Ischtartor)*★★, *Museum of Moslem Art (Museum für Islamische Kunst)*★★ – *National Gallery (Alte Nationalgalerie)*★★ **M**¹ – *Bodemuseum* **M**², *Egyptian Museum (Ägyptisches Museum)*★★ – *Old Museum (Altes Museum)*★★ *(Hildesheim silverware treasure*★★★*)* **M**³ – *Forum of Culture (Kulturforum)*★★★, *Gallery of Paintings (Gemäldegalerie)*★★★ – *Philharmonie*★★★ **T**¹, *Musical Instruments Museum (Musikinstrumenten Museum*★*)* NZ – *Museum of Decorative Arts (Kunstgewerbe-Museum)*★★ NZ **M**⁴, *Guelph Treasure (Welfenschatz)*★★★, *Lüneburg Treasure (Lüneburger Ratssilber)*★★★ – *New National Gallery (Neue Nationalgalerie)*★★ NZ **M**⁵ – *Prussian State Library (Staatsbibliothek Preußischer Kulturbesitz)*★ NZ German Historiy Museum (Deutsches Historisches Museum; Zeughaus)★★ PY – Friedrichswerder Church★ PZ (Schinkel-Museum)★ – Dahlem Museums (Museumszentrum Dahlem) by Clay-Allee EZ – Museum of Ethnography (Museum of Ethnological)★★★, Museum of Indian Art (Museum für indische Kunst)★★, Museum für Ostasiatische Kunst★, Museum für europäischer Kutturen★ – Schloß Charlottenburg★★ EY: Historical Rooms (Historische Räume)★★ Porcelain Room (Porzellan-Kabinett)★★, Chapel (Schloßkapelle)★, The Kronprinz's Silver (Kronprinzensilber)★★ – Neuer Flügel★★ Golden Gallery (Goldene Galerie)★★, Winterkammern★ – Museum of Pre- and Proto-History (Museum für Vor-und Frühgeschichte)★ – Collection Berggruen (Sammlung Berggruen)★★ EY **M**¹³ – Bröhan Museum★ EY **M**¹³ – Egyptian Museum (Ägyptisches Museum)★★★ Bust of Nefertiti (Nofretete)★★★ EY **M**⁶ – Schloßgarten★★ (Schinkel-Pavillon★, Belvedere★, Mausoleum★) – Museum of Contemporary Art (Hamburger Bahnhof – Museum für Gegenwart Berlin)★★ NX – German Museum of Technic (Deutsches Technik Museum Berlin)★★ GZ **M**⁸ – Käthe-Kollwitz Museum★ LXY **M**⁹ – Brücke Museum★ BV **M**³⁶ – March Museum (Märkisches Museum)★ RZ – Bauhaus-Archiv★ MX – Communications Museum (Museum für Kommunikation Berlin)★ PZ

PARKS, GARDENS, LAKES

Tiergarten★★ – *Zoological Park (Zoologischer Garten)*★★★ MX – *Wannsee*★★ *by Clay-Allee* EZ *Volkspark Klein-Glienicke*★★ – *Havel*★★ – *Peacock Island (Pfaueninsel)*★★ *by Clay-Allee* EZ – *Tegeler See*★★ *by Müllerstraße* FX – *Großer Müggelsee*★★ *by Stralauer Allee* HYZ – *Grunewald*★★ *by Clay-Allee* EZ *(Jagdschloß Grunewald*★ **M**²⁸ – *Botanical Gardens (Botanischer Garten)*★★ *by Rheinbabenallee* EZ – *Viktoriapark*★ GZ

HISTORIC BUILDINGS, STREETS, SQUARES

Martin-Gropius-Building★★ NZ – *Brandenburg Gate (Brandenburger Tor)*★★ NZ – *Reichstag*★, *Panoramic platform (Panorama-Plattform)*★★ NY – *Unter den Linden*★★, *State Opera Unter den Linden (Staatsoper Unter den Linden)*★ PZ – *Gendarmenmarkt*★★, PZ *German National Theatre (Schauspielhaus)*★★, *German Cathedral (Deutscher Dom)*★, *French Cathedral (Französischer Dom)*★ – *Arsenal (Zeughaus)*★★ PY – *Berliner Dom*★ – *Interior (Innenraum)*★★ PY – *Alexandersquare (Alexanderplatz)*★ RY, *Fernsehturm*★ – *St-Nicholas District (Nikolaiviertel)*★ RZ – *Friedrichstraße*★ PYZ – *Oranienburger Straße*★★ PY – *Kurfürstendamm*★★ LXY *(Kaiser-Wilhelm-Gedächtniskirche*★*)* – *Olympic Stadium (Olympiastadion)*★ *by Kaiserdamm* AX – *Radio Tower (Funkturm)*★ *by Kaiserdamm* AX – *Spandau, Zitadelle*★ *by Kaiserdamm* JX – *Schloß Tegel*★ *by Chausseestraße* NX

Town Centre : Charlottenburg, Mitte, Schöneberg, Tiergarten, Wilmersdorf

Adlon, Unter den Linden 77, ⌂ 10117, ℰ (030) 2 26 10, adlon@kempinski.com, Fax (030) 22612222, ☆, Massage, ⅙, ⇔, ☒ – ⊠, ⇔ rm, ▤ ⊡ ✆ ⅏ ⇔ – ⚄ 400.
⚏ ⓪ ⓪⓪ 𝚅𝙸𝚂𝙰 𝙹𝙲𝙱. ⅏ rest   NZ s
Meals see **Lorenz Adlon** below – **Hotel-Restaurant** : Meals à la carte 45/64 – **Adlon Stube** (closed 2 weeks January, August, Sunday and Monday) Meals à la carte 21,10/37
– ⊡ 29 – **336 rm** 240/365 – 290/415 – 37 suites.

Four Seasons, Charlottenstr. 49, ⌂ 10117, ℰ (030) 2 03 38, ber.reservation@four seasons.com, Fax (030) 20336166, ☆, Massage, ⅙, ⇔ – ⊠, ⇔ rm, ▤ ⊡ ✆ ⅏ ⇔
– ⚄ 75. ⚏ ⓪ ⓪⓪ 𝚅𝙸𝚂𝙰 𝙹𝙲𝙱. ⅏ rest   PZ n
Seasons: Meals à la carte 44,50/63,50 – ⊡ 24 – **204 rm** 250/310 – 285/345 – 42 suites.

Grand Hyatt, Marlene-Dietrich-Platz 2, ⌂ 10785, ℰ (030) 25 53 12 34, berlin@hya ttintl.com, Fax (030) 25531235, ☆, « Modern interior », Massage, ⅙, ⇔, ☒ – ⊠,
⇔ rm, ▤ ⊡ ✆ ⅏ ⇔ – ⚄ 440. ⚏ ⓪ ⓪⓪ 𝚅𝙸𝚂𝙰 𝙹𝙲𝙱.   NZ a
Vox : Meals 59/64 and à la carte – **Tizian** (Italian) Meals à la carte 29,65/40,39 – ⊡ 20
– **342 rm** 190/305 – 215/345 – 16 suites.

Kempinski Hotel Bristol, Kurfürstendamm 27, ⌂ 10719, ℰ (030) 88 43 40, rese rvations.bristol@kempinski.com, Fax (030) 8836075, ☆, Massage, ⅙, ⇔, ☒ – ⊠,
⇔ rm, ⊡ ✆ ⅏ ⇔ – ⚄ 280. ⚏ ⓪ ⓪⓪ 𝚅𝙸𝚂𝙰 𝙹𝙲𝙱. ⅏ rest   LX n
Kempinski Grill (closed 3 weeks August and Monday) Meals à la carte 46/63,91 – **Kempinski-Eck** : Meals à la carte 26,62/38,34 – ⊡ 20 – **301 rm** 222/310 – 258/346 –
29 suites.

Grand Hotel Esplanade, Lützowufer 15, ⌂ 10785, ℰ (030) 25 47 80, info@espl anade.de, Fax (030) 254788222, (conference boat with own landing stage), « Modern hotel featuring contemporary art », Massage, ⅙, ⇔, ☒ – ⊠, ⇔ rm, ▤ ⊡ ✆ ⅏ ⇔ – ⚄ 260.
⚏ ⓪ ⓪⓪ 𝚅𝙸𝚂𝙰 𝙹𝙲𝙱. ⅏ rest   MX e
Meals see **Harlekin** below – **Eckkneipe** : Meals à la carte 20/38,50 – ⊡ 20 – **386 rm**
225/281 – 250/306 – 23 suites.

Palace, Budapester Str. 45, ⌂ 10787, ℰ (030) 2 50 20, hotel@palace.de, Fax (030) 25021161 – ⊠, ⇔ rm, ▤ ⊡ ✆ ⅏ ⇔ – ⚄ 300. ⚏ ⓪ ⓪⓪ 𝚅𝙸𝚂𝙰. ⅏ rest
Meals see **First Floor** below – **Alt Nürnberg** : Meals à la carte 14,50/27 – ⊡ 20 – **282 rm**
200/295 – 225/320 – 24 suites.   MX k

Swissôtel Ⓜ, Augsburger Str. 44, ⌂ 10789, ℰ (030) 22 01 00, berlin@swissotel.com, Fax (030) 220102222, ⇔ – ⊠, ⇔ rm, ▤ ⊡ ✆ ⅏ ⇔ – ⚄ 200. ⚏ ⓪ ⓪⓪ 𝚅𝙸𝚂𝙰 𝙹𝙲𝙱.
Mosimann's : Meals à la carte 37/51 – **Grande Galerie** : Meals à la carte 34/42 – ⊡ 19
– **316 rm** 240/260 – 260/300.   LX k

The Westin Grand, Friedrichstr. 158, ⌂ 10117, ℰ (030) 2 02 70, info@westin-gr and.com, Fax (030) 20273362, Massage, ⅙, ⇔, ☒ – ⊠, ⇔ rm, ⊡ ✆ ⅏ – ⚄ 90. ⚏
⓪ ⓪⓪ 𝚅𝙸𝚂𝙰 𝙹𝙲𝙱. ⅏ rest   PZ a
Le Grand (closed early October - June Sunday lunch) Meals à la carte 33,50/50,50 –
Stammhaus: Meals à la carte 26/36,50 – ⊡ 20 – **358 rm** 161/340 – 186/365 – 20 suites.

Hilton, Mohrenstr. 30, ⌂ 10117, ℰ (030) 2 02 30, info_berlin@hilton.com, Fax (030) 20234269, ☆, Massage, ⅙, ⇔, ☒ – ⊠, ⇔ rm, ▤ ⊡ ✆ ⅏ ⇔ – ⚄ 300.
⚏ ⓪ ⓪⓪ 𝚅𝙸𝚂𝙰 𝙹𝙲𝙱.   PZ r
Fellini (Italian) (dinner only) Meals à la carte 27.09/45.50 – **Mark Brandenburg** (vegetarian menu available) Meals à la carte 28,63/40,39 – ⊡ 19 – **589 rm** 210/305 – 230/325
– 14 suites.

Inter-Continental, Budapester Str. 2, ⌂ 10787, ℰ (030) 2 60 20, berlin@intercon ti.com, Fax (030) 26022600, ☆, Massage, ⇔, ☒ – ⊠, ⇔ rm, ▤ ⊡ ✆ ⅏ ⇔ ⒫ –
⚄ 860. ⚏ ⓪ ⓪⓪ 𝚅𝙸𝚂𝙰 𝙹𝙲𝙱. ⅏   MX a
Meals see **Zum Hugenotten** below – **L.A. Café** : Meals à la carte 25,60/35,28 – ⊡ 20
– **584 rm** 260/385 – 285/450 – 50 suites.

Dorint Schweizerhof Ⓜ, Budapester Str. 25, ⌂ 10787, ℰ (030) 2 69 60, info.be rsch@dorint.com, Fax (030) 26961000, Massage, ⅙, ⇔, ☒ – ⊠, ⇔ rm, ▤ ⊡ ✆ ⅏
⇔ – ⚄ 460. ⚏ ⓪ ⓪⓪ 𝚅𝙸𝚂𝙰. ⅏ rest   MX w
Meals à la carte 25/40 – ⊡ 19 – **384 rm** 195/235 – 220/260 – 10 suites.

Steigenberger Berlin, Los-Angeles-Platz 1, ⌂ 10789, ℰ (030) 2 12 70, berlin@st eigenberger.de, Fax (030) 2127117, ☆, Massage, ⇔, ☒ – ⊠, ⇔ rm, ▤ ⊡ ✆ ⅏ ⇔
– ⚄ 300. ⚏ ⓪ ⓪⓪ 𝚅𝙸𝚂𝙰. ⅏ rest   MY d
Parkrestaurant (closed 4 weeks July - August, Sunday and Monday) (dinner only) Meals
à la carte 35,80/72,50 – **Berliner Stube** : Meals à la carte 22,50/33,75 – ⊡ 18 – **397 rm**
195/305 – 220/330 – 11 suites.

Brandenburger Hof Ⓜ, Eislebener Str. 14, ⌂ 10789, ℰ (030) 21 40 50, info@br andenburger-hof.com, Fax (030) 21405100, ☆, « Modernized Wilhelminian mansion with Bauhaus furniture », Massage – ⊠, ▤ ⊡ ✆ ⅏ ⇔ – ⚄ 30. ⚏ ⓪ ⓪⓪ 𝚅𝙸𝚂𝙰 𝙹𝙲𝙱   LY n
Meals see **Die Quadriga** below – **Der Wintergarten** : Meals à la carte 34/56 – **82 rm**
⊡ 165/245 – 240/450.

Dorint Am Gendarmenmarkt M, Charlottenstr. 50, ⊠ 10117, ℰ (030) 20 37 50, info.bergen@dorint.com, Fax (030) 20375100, Ⅰ₆, ≘s – ▮, ↔ rm, ≡ ⊡ ✔ ₺ – ₰ 100 ⒶⒺ ⓞ ⓜⓞ 𝓥𝓘𝓢𝓐
PZ s
Aigner : Meals à la carte 30,50/44,50 – � 21 – **92 rm** 197/280 – 218/295.

Berlin M, Lützowplatz 17, ⊠ 10785, ℰ (030) 2 60 50, info@hotel-berlin.de, Fax (030) 26052716, ㄾㄾ, Massage, Ⅰ₆, ≘s – ▮, ↔ rm, ≡ rest, ⊡ ✔ ₰ – ₰ 440 ⒶⒺ ⓞ ⓜⓞ 𝓥𝓘𝓢𝓐 𝓙𝓬𝓫. ※ rest
MX t
Meals à la carte 25,70/36,90 – **701 rm** ⊆ 150/230 – 180/245 – 7 suites.

Maritim proArte M, Friedrichstr. 151, ⊠ 10117, ℰ (030) 2 03 35, info.bpa@maritim.de, Fax (030) 20334209, Ⅰ₆, ≘s, ◸ – ▮, ↔ rm, ≡ ⊡ ✔ ₺ ⇔ – ₰ 700. Ⓐ ⓞ ⓜⓞ 𝓥𝓘𝓢𝓐 𝓙𝓬𝓫. ※ rest
PY
Atelier (dinner only) Meals à la carte 33/46,50 – **Bistro media** : Meals à la carte 24,20/41,70 – ⊆ 18 – **403 rm** 169/205 – 188/218 – 29 suites.

Crowne Plaza M, Nürnberger Str. 65, ⊠ 10787, ℰ (030) 21 00 70, info@cp-berlin.com, Fax (030) 2132009, Massage, ≘s, ◸ – ▮, ↔ rm, ≡ ⊡ ✔ ₺ ⇔ ₰ – ₰ 380 ⒶⒺ ⓞ ⓜⓞ 𝓥𝓘𝓢𝓐 𝓙𝓬𝓫. ※ rest
MX
Meals (closed Saturday lunch, Sunday dinner) à la carte 30/38,50 – ⊆ 17 – **425 rm** 170/355 – 205/390 – 10 suites.

Madison M, Potsdamer Str. 3, ⊠ 10785, ℰ (030) 5 90 05 00 00, welcome@madison-berlin.de, Fax (030) 590050500, ㄾㄾ, Massage, ≘s – ▮, ↔ rm, ⊡ ✔ ⇔ – ₰ 20 ⒶⒺ ⓜⓞ 𝓥𝓘𝓢𝓐. ※
NZ
Facil (closed 2 - 13 January, 20 July - 11 August, Saturday and Sunday) Meals à la carte 45/65 – ⊆ 20 – **169 rm** 140/190 – 175/215 – 17 suites.

Sorat Hotel Spree-Bogen M ⤲, Alt-Moabit 99, ⊠ 10559, ℰ (030) 39 92 00, spree-bogen@sorat-hotels.com, Fax (030) 39920999, ㄾㄾ, ≘s – ▮, ↔ rm, ≡ ⊡ ✔ ₺ ⇔ – ₰ 200. ⒶⒺ ⓞ ⓜⓞ 𝓥𝓘𝓢𝓐 𝓙𝓬𝓫
FY t
Meals à la carte 20,60/34,50 – **221 rm** ⊆ 130/229 – 166/266.

Savoy, Fasanenstr. 9, ⊠ 10623, ℰ (030) 31 10 30, info@hotel-savoy.com, Fax (030) 31103333, ㄾㄾ, Ⅰ₆, ≘s – ▮, ↔ rm, ⊡ ✔ – ₰ 40. ⒶⒺ ⓞ ⓜⓞ 𝓥𝓘𝓢𝓐 𝓙𝓬𝓫
LX
Meals à la carte 25/35 – ⊆ 15 – **125 rm** 142/192 – 192/242 – 18 suites.

Mondial, Kurfürstendamm 47, ⊠ 10707, ℰ (030) 88 41 10, hotel-mondial@t-online.de, Fax (030) 88411150, ㄾㄾ, ≘s, ◸ – ▮, ↔ rm, ⊡ ✔ ₺ ⇔ – ₰ 50. ⒶⒺ ⓞ ⓜⓞ 𝓥𝓘𝓢 𝓙𝓬𝓫
KY t
Meals à la carte 25,05/37,84 – **75 rm** ⊆ 110/210 – 140/245.

Alexander Plaza M, Rosenstr. 1, ⊠ 10178, ℰ (030) 24 00 10, info@alexander-plaza.com, Fax (030) 24001777, ㄾㄾ, Massage, Ⅰ₆, ≘s – ▮, ↔ rm, ≡ ⊡ ✔ ⇔ – ₰ 80 ⒶⒺ ⓞ ⓜⓞ 𝓥𝓘𝓢𝓐 𝓙𝓬𝓫. ※ rest
RY t
Meals à la carte 21,85/36,88 – ⊆ 15 – **92 rm** 140/240 – 150/250.

Astron M, Leipziger Str. 106, ⊠ 10117, ℰ (030) 20 37 60, berlin-mitte@astron-hotels.de, Fax (030) 20376600, ≘s – ▮, ↔ rm, ≡ ⊡ ✔ ₺ ⇔ – ₰ 150. ⒶⒺ ⓞ ⓜⓞ 𝓥𝓘𝓢 𝓙𝓬𝓫. ※ rest
PZ
Meals à la carte 23/37 – **Grissini** (Italian) Meals à la carte 19,50/30,50 – ⊆ 15 – **392 rm** 127/217 – 147/237.

Seehof M, Lietzensee-Ufer 11, ⊠ 14057, ℰ (030) 32 00 20, hotel_seehof_berlin@t-online.de, Fax (030) 32002251, ⩽, « Garden terrace », ≘s, ◸ – ▮, ↔ rm, ⊡ ✔ – ₰ 25. ⒶⒺ ⓜⓞ 𝓥𝓘𝓢𝓐
JX
Meals à la carte 30/45,50 – ⊆ 17 – **77 rm** 120/209 – 159/259.

Alsterhof, Augsburger Str. 5, ⊠ 10789, ℰ (030) 21 24 20, info@alsterhof.com, Fax (030) 2183949, beer garden, Massage, Ⅰ₆, ≘s – ▮, ↔ rm, ⊡ ✔ ⇔ – ₰ 40. ⒶⒺ ⓞ ⓜⓞ 𝓥𝓘𝓢𝓐 𝓙𝓬𝓫. ※ rest
MY
Alsters (closed Sunday dinner) Meals à la carte 21,60/34,50 – **Zum Lit-Fass** (dinner only) Meals à la carte 15,60/27,50 – ⊆ 15 – **200 rm** 102/171 – 118/187.

President, An der Urania 16, ⊠ 10787, ℰ (030) 21 90 30, info@president.bestwestern.de, Fax (030) 2186120, Ⅰ₆, ≘s – ▮, ↔ rm, ≡ ⊡ ✔ ⇔ ₰ – ₰ 75. ⒶⒺ ⓞ ⓜ 𝓥𝓘𝓢𝓐
MY
Meals à la carte 25/31 – **181 rm** ⊆ 134/165 – 164/205.

Art'otel M, Wallstr. 70, ⊠ 10179, ℰ (030) 24 06 20, berlin@artotel.de, Fax (030) 24062222, ㄾㄾ, « Reconstructed nobleman's house with modern hotel wing » – ▮, ≡ rm, ⊡ ✔ ₺ ⇔ – ₰ 35. ⒶⒺ ⓞ ⓜⓞ 𝓥𝓘𝓢𝓐 𝓙𝓬𝓫
RZ t
Ermelerhaus (closed end June - end August, Sunday and Monday) (dinner only) Meals à la carte 37/54 – **Raabe - Diele** : Meals à la carte 22/28 – **109 rm** ⊆ 128/178 – 158/208.

Hollywood Media Hotel M without rest, Kurfürstendamm 202, ⊠ 10719, ℰ (030) 88 91 00, info@hollywood-media-hotel.de, Fax (030) 88910280 – ▮ ↔ ⊡ ✔ ₺ ⇔ ₰ 90. ⒶⒺ ⓞ ⓜⓞ 𝓥𝓘𝓢𝓐 𝓙𝓬𝓫
LY t
185 rm ⊆ 130/180 – 152/202 – 12 suites.

🏠 **Luisenhof**, Köpenicker Str. 92, ☒ 10179, ℘ (030) 2 41 59 06, info@luisenhof.de, Fax (030) 2792983, « Elegant installation » – 🛗 🆃🆅 ✆ – 🔬 30. 🆀🅴 ⓞ 🆀🅾 𝗩𝗜𝗦𝗔 𝗝𝗖𝗕
Meals (closed Sunday) à la carte 14,80/32,20 – **27 rm** ⌸ 120/180 – 150/250. RZ a

🏠 **Berlin Excelsior Hotel**, Hardenbergstr. 14, ☒ 10623, ℘ (030) 3 15 50, info@hot el excelsior.de, Fax (030) 31551002, 🍴 – 🛗, ⇔ rm, 🔳 rest, 🆃🆅 ⇦ 🅿 – 🔬 60. 🆀🅴 ⓞ
🆀🅾 𝗩𝗜𝗦𝗔 𝗝𝗖𝗕 ✼ rest LX b
Meals (closed Sunday and Monday) à la carte 16,36/39 – **317 rm** ⌸ 125/205 – 155/235 – 3 suites.

🏠 **Domicil** 🅼, Kantstr. 111a, ☒ 10627, ℘ (030) 32 90 30, info@hotel-domicil-berlin.de, Fax (030) 32903299, 🍴 – 🛗, ⇔ rm, 🆃🆅 ✆ ♿ – 🔬 50. 🆀🅴 ⓞ 🆀🅾 𝗩𝗜𝗦𝗔 JX v
Meals à la carte 19/26 – **70 rm** ⌸ 102/143 – 133/184 – 8 suites.

🏠 **Hamburg**, Landgrafenstr. 4, ☒ 10787, ℘ (030) 26 47 70, hoham@t-online.de, Fax (030) 2629394, 🍴 – 🛗, ⇔ rm, ⇦ 🅿 – 🔬 60. 🆀🅴 ⓞ 🆀🅾 𝗩𝗜𝗦𝗔 𝗝𝗖𝗕 ✼ rest
Meals à la carte 22,50/38 – **191 rm** ⌸ 115/145 – 144/198. MX s

🏠 **Die Zwölf Apostel**, Hohenzollerndamm 33, ☒ 10713, ℘ (030) 86 88 90, Info@ 12-apost el.de, Fax (030) 86889103, 🍴, « Furnished in Italian period style » – 🛗, ⇔ rm, 🆃🆅 ✆
Meals (Italian) à la carte 19,40/38,85 – **36 rm** ⌸ 95 – 125. KZ b

🏠 **Residenz**, Meinekestr. 9, ☒ 10719, ℘ (030) 88 44 30, info@hotel-residenz.com, Fax (030) 8824726 – 🛗, ⇔ rm, 🆃🆅. 🆀🅴 ⓞ 🆀🅾 𝗩𝗜𝗦𝗔. ✼ rest LY d
Meals à la carte 25,50/53,88 – ⌸ 13 – **81 rm** 120/153 – 140/175 – 4 suites.

🏠 **Bleibtreu-Hotel** 🅼, Bleibtreustr. 31, ☒ 10707, ℘ (030) 88 47 40, info@bleibtreu.c om, Fax (030) 88474444, 🍴, « Modern interior », Massage, ⊑s – 🛗, ⇔ rm, 🆃🆅 ✆ ♿
🅿. 🆀🅴 ⓞ 🆀🅾 𝗩𝗜𝗦𝗔 KY s
Meals à la carte 25/36 – ⌸ 15 – **60 rm** 142/192 – 192/242.

🏠 **Hecker's Hotel**, Grolmanstr. 35, ☒ 10623, ℘ (030) 8 89 00, info@heckers-hotel.com, Fax (030) 8890260 – 🛗, ⇔ rm, 🆃🆅 ✆ ♿ ⇦ 🅿 – 🔬 25. 🆀🅴 ⓞ 🆀🅾 𝗩𝗜𝗦𝗔 𝗝𝗖𝗕 LX e
Cassambalis (closed Sunday) Meals à la carte 30,70/39,20 – ⌸ 15 – **69 rm** 125/200 – 150/200 – 3 suites.

🏠 **Hackescher Markt** without rest, Große Präsidentenstr. 8, ☒ 10178, ℘ (030) 28 00 30, info@hackescher-markt.com, Fax (030) 28003111 – 🛗 ⇔ 🆃🆅 ✆ ⇦. 🆀🅴 ⓞ
🆀🅾 𝗩𝗜𝗦𝗔 𝗝𝗖𝗕 PY c
⌸ 15 – **31 rm** 120/165 – 155/175.

🏠 **Kanthotel** without rest, Kantstr. 111, ☒ 10627, ℘ (030) 32 30 20, info@kanthotel .com, Fax (030) 3240952 – 🛗 ⇔ 🆃🆅 ✆ ♿ ⇦ – 🔬 25. 🆀🅴 ⓞ 🆀🅾 𝗩𝗜𝗦𝗔 𝗝𝗖𝗕 JX e
70 rm ⌸ 135/140 – 145/150.

🏠 **Sorat Art'otel** 🅼 without rest, Joachimstaler Str. 29, ☒ 10719, ℘ (030) 88 44 70, art-otel@sorat-hotels.com, Fax (030) 88447700 – 🛗 ⇔ 🔳 🆃🆅 ✆ ♿ ⇦ – 🔬 65. 🆀🅴
ⓞ 🆀🅾 𝗩𝗜𝗦𝗔 𝗝𝗖𝗕 LY e
133 rm ⌸ 139/189 – 162/219.

🏠 **Kronprinz** without rest, Kronprinzendamm 1, ☒ 10711, ℘ (030) 89 60 30, receptio n@kronprinz-hotel.de, Fax (030) 8931215, (restored 1894 house) – 🛗 ⇔ 🆃🆅 ✆ ♿
🔬 25. 🆀🅴 ⓞ 🆀🅾 𝗩𝗜𝗦𝗔 𝗝𝗖𝗕 JY d
80 rm ⌸ 100/160 – 110/175.

🏠 **Sylter Hof** without rest, Kurfürstenstr. 114, ☒ 10787, ℘ (030) 2 12 00, info@sylt erhof-berlin.de, Fax (030) 2142826 – 🛗 ⇔ 🆃🆅 ✆ 🅿 – 🔬 90. 🆀🅴 ⓞ 🆀🅾 𝗩𝗜𝗦𝗔 MX d
160 rm ⌸ 90/125 – 130/140 – 18 suites.

🏠 **Joachimshof** 🅼, Invalidenstr. 98, ☒ 10115, ℘ (030) 2 03 95 61 00, info@la-vie-ho tels.de, Fax (030) 203956199, ⊑s – 🛗, ⇔ rm, 🆃🆅 ✆ ⇦ – 🔬 15. 🆀🅴 ⓞ 🆀🅾 𝗩𝗜𝗦𝗔
Meals à la carte 24/37 – ⌸ 13 – **39 rm** 105/110 – 130/170 – 3 suites. NX a

🏠 **Concept Hotel**, Grolmanstr. 41, ☒ 10623, ℘ (030) 88 42 60, info@concept-hotel.c om, Fax (030) 88426820, 🍴, Massage, ⊑s – 🛗, ⇔ rm, 🆃🆅 ♿ ⇦ – 🔬 85. 🆀🅴 ⓞ 🆀🅾
𝗩𝗜𝗦𝗔 LX m
Meals à la carte 17/32,70 – **153 rm** ⌸ 115/145 – 145/180 – 5 suites.

🏠 **Holiday Inn Garden Court** without rest, Bleibtreustr. 25, ☒ 10707, ℘ (030) 88 09 30, info@hi-berlin.de, Fax (030) 88093939 – 🛗 ⇔ 🔳 🆃🆅 ✆ 🅿 – 🔬 15. 🆀🅴 ⓞ
🆀🅾 𝗩𝗜𝗦𝗔 𝗝𝗖𝗕 KY g
73 rm ⌸ 110/195 – 130/215.

🏠 **Albrechtshof**, Albrechtstr. 8, ☒ 10117, ℘ (030) 30 88 60, albrechtshof-berlin@ vc h.de, Fax (030) 30886100, 🍴 – 🛗, ⇔ rm, 🆃🆅 ✆ ♿ 🅿 – 🔬 50. 🆀🅴 ⓞ 🆀🅾 𝗩𝗜𝗦𝗔 𝗝𝗖𝗕 ✼ rest
Meals à la carte 17,90/33,23 – **100 rm** ⌸ 113/164 – 144/194. NY a

🏠 **Park Consul** without rest, Alt-Moabit 86a, ☒ 10555, ℘ (030) 39 07 80, pcberlin@ c onsul-hotels.com, Fax (030) 39078900 – 🛗 ⇔ 🆃🆅 ✆ ⇦. 🆀🅴 ⓞ 🆀🅾 𝗩𝗜𝗦𝗔 𝗝𝗖𝗕
52 rm ⌸ 150 – 178. FY s

🏠 **Forum Hotel**, Alexanderplatz, ☒ 10178, ℘ (030) 2 38 90, forumberlin@interconti.c om, Fax (030) 23894305, ⊑s – 🛗, ⇔ rm, 🆃🆅 ✆ ♿ ⇦ – 🔬 320. 🆀🅴 ⓞ 🆀🅾 𝗩𝗜𝗦𝗔 𝗝𝗖𝗕
Meals à la carte 28,50/31,50 – ⌸ 15 – **1006 rm** 125 – 150. RY c

🏠 **Boulevard** without rest, Kurfürstendamm 12, ✉ 10719, ℰ (030) 88 42 50, *info@h
otel-boulevard.com, Fax (030) 88425450* – 🛗 ⬛ 📺 ✆ – 🅰 25. 🆎 ⓞ ⓜⓞ 𝗩𝗜𝗦𝗔   LX c
57 rm ☑ 95/123 – 118/164.

🏠 **Kurfürstendamm am Adenauerplatz** without rest, Kurfürstendamm 68,
✉ 10707, ℰ (030) 88 46 30, *info@ hotel-kurfuerstendamm.de, Fax (030) 8825528* – 🛗
📺 ✆ 🅿 – 🅰 30. 🆎 ⓞ ⓜⓞ 𝗩𝗜𝗦𝗔 ᴊᴄʙ   JY n
34 rm ☑ 94 – 142 – 4 suites.

🏠 **Scandotel Castor** without rest, Fuggerstr. 8, ✉ 10777, ℰ (030) 21 30 30, *scando
tel@ t-online.de, Fax (030) 21303160* – 🛗 ⬛ 📺 ✆. 🆎 ⓞ ⓜⓞ 𝗩𝗜𝗦𝗔 ᴊᴄʙ   MY s
78 rm ☑ 120/128 – 148/163.

🏠 **Fjord Hotel** without rest, Bissingzeile 13, ✉ 10785, ℰ (030) 25 47 20, *fjordhotelbe
rlin@ t-online.de, Fax (030) 25472111* – 🛗 ⬛ 📺 ⟷ 🅿. 🆎 ⓜⓞ 𝗩𝗜𝗦𝗔. 🍴   NZ c
57 rm ☑ 85 – 100.

XXXXX **Lorenz Adlon** - Hotel Adlon, Unter den Linden 77, ✉ 10117, ℰ (030) 22 61 19 60
❄️   *Fax (030) 22612222* – ▦ ⟷. 🆎 ⓞ ⓜⓞ 𝗩𝗜𝗦𝗔 ᴊᴄʙ. 🍴   NZ s
     closed 2 weeks January, August, Sunday and Monday – **Meals** *(dinner only)* 92/128 and
     à la carte
     Spec. Steinpilzsavarin mit eigenem Saft und Wildkräutern. Rehbock mit Brotkruste und
     getrüffelter Gänsestopfleber. Weinbergpfirsich "Haeberlin".

XXXX **Zum Hugenotten** - Hotel Inter-Continental, Budapester Str. 2, ✉ 10787, ℰ (030
❄️   26 02 12 63, *berlin@ interconti.com, Fax (030) 26022600* – ▦ 🅿. 🆎 ⓞ ⓜⓞ 𝗩𝗜𝗦𝗔
     ᴊᴄʙ. 🍴   MX a
     closed 2 weeks early January, 4 weeks July - August and Sunday – **Meals** *(dinner only)*
     (outstanding wine list) 74/100 and à la carte 60/73
     Spec. Fischeintopf mit Olivenbrotcroûtons. Loup de mer mit Papaya, Ananas und Avocado
     Schokoladenvariation.

XXXX **First Floor** - Hotel Palace, Budapester Str. 45, ✉ 10787, ℰ (030) 25 02 10 20, *hote
❄️   l@palace.de, Fax (030) 25021197* – 🆎 ⓞ ⓜⓞ 𝗩𝗜𝗦𝗔. 🍴   MX I
     closed 28 July - 25 August and Saturday lunch – **Meals** 40 *(lunch)* and à la carte 54/7:
     Spec. Salat von bretonischem Hummer mit braisierten Artischocken und Trüffel. St. Jakobs
     muschel und Langostino mit Chili-Koriandersud. Schottischer Lammrücken mit Oliven
     Ciabattakruste.

XXXX **Margaux**, Unter den Linden 78 (entrance Wilhelmstrasse), ✉ 10117, ℰ (030
❄️   22 65 26 11, *info@ margaux-berlin.de, Fax (030) 22652612*, ⌣ – ▦. 🆎 ⓞ ⓜⓞ
     𝗩𝗜𝗦𝗔. 🍴   NZ I
     closed 26 March - 9 April, 16 July - 6 August, Sunday and Monday – **Meals** (outstandin
     wine list) 33 *(lunch)* and à la carte 58/83
     Spec. Cassoulet von Bohnen und Pulpo mit Olivengelée. Poelierter Steinbutt mit Kara
     melzwiebeln und Sardinen. Gebratene Taube mit geschmortem Knollensellerie und Boskop

XXXX **Harlekin** - Grand Hotel Esplanade, Lützowufer 15, ✉ 10785, ℰ (030) 2 54 78 86 30
     info@ esplanade.de, Fax (030) 254788603, ⌣ – ▦. 🆎 ⓞ ⓜⓞ 𝗩𝗜𝗦𝗔 ᴊᴄʙ. 🍴   MX ■
     closed 1 to 10 January, August, Sunday and Monday – **Meals** *(dinner only)* 41/62 an
     à la carte.

XXX **Die Quadriga** - Hotel Brandenburger Hof, Eislebener Str. 14, ✉ 10789, ℰ (030
❄️ 21 40 56 50, *info@ brandenburger-hof.com, Fax (030) 21405100* – 🆎 ⓞ ⓜⓞ 𝗩𝗜𝗦𝗔 ᴊᴄ
    🍴   LY
    closed 1 to 13 January, 15 July - 18 August, Saturday and Sunday – **Meals** *(dinner only*
    à la carte 46/74
    Spec. Gebratene St. Jakobsmuscheln mit Blumenkohl-Kokospüree. Mit Aromaten gebra
    tener Rehrücken und glacierte Äpfel. Topfenkuchen mit Mangosalat und Schokolader
    sorbet.

XXX **Adermann** (1st floor), Oranienburger Str. 27, ✉ 10117, ℰ (030) 28 38 73 71, *rest
❄️ urant@ adermann.de, Fax (030) 28387372* – 🅿. 🆎 ⓞ ⓜⓞ 𝗩𝗜𝗦𝗔 ᴊᴄʙ. 🍴   PY
    closed 1 week early January, 2 weeks July - August, Sunday and Monday – **Meals** *(dinne
    only)* 60/95 and à la carte 54/68
    Spec. Frühlingsrolle vom Ziegenkäse mit sautierten Garnelen. Steinbutt mit St. Jakob:
    muscheln und kleinem Gemüse. Grießsoufflé mit Beeren und Orangen-Estragonsorbet.

XX **VAU**, Jägerstr. 54, ✉ 10117, ℰ (030) 2 02 97 30, *vau@ viehhauser.de
❄️ *Fax (030) 20297311*, ⌣, « Bistro-restaurant with modern interior » – 🆎 ⓞ ⓜ
   𝗩𝗜𝗦𝗔. 🍴   PZ
   closed Sunday – **Meals** 52 *(lunch)*/100 and à la carte 60/76
   Spec. Lauwarm marinierter Hummer mit Erdbeeren und Melone (June). Geräucherter Stö
   mit Imperial Kaviar. Variation vom Müritz Lamm.

XX **Ponte Vecchio**, Spielhagenstr. 3, ✉ 10585, ℰ (030) 3 42 19 99, *Fax (030) 342195
   – ⓞ   JX
   closed 4 weeks July - August and Tuesday – **Meals** *(dinner only)* (Italian) (booking essenti.
   à la carte 33/53.

XX **Ana e Bruno**, Sophie-Charlotten-Str. 101, ✉ 14059, ℘ (030) 3 25 71 10, *info@ana-e-bruno.de, Fax (030) 3226895* – AE. EY s
closed 2 weeks January, 2 weeks July - August, Sunday and Monday – **Meals** *(dinner only)* (Italian) (outstanding Italian wine list) à la carte 57,78/65,95.

XX **Alt Luxemburg**, Windscheidstr. 31, ✉ 10627, ℘ (030) 3 23 87 30, *Fax (030) 3274003* – AE. JX s
closed Sunday – **Meals** *(dinner only)* (booking essential) 67/75 and à la carte 47/60,50.

XX **Kaiserstuben**, Am Kupfergraben 6a, ✉ 10117, ℘ (030) 20 45 29 80, *info@kaiserstuben.de, Fax (030) 20452981*, – AE VISA PY n
closed 1 week January, Sunday and Monday – **Meals** *(dinner only)* (booking essential) à la carte 36,50/45.

XX **IL Sorriso**, Kurfürstenstr. 76, ✉ 10787, ℘ (030) 2 62 13 13, *ilsorriso@t-online.de, Fax (030) 2650277*, – P. AE VISA. MX r
closed 22 December - 5 January and Sunday – **Meals** (Italian) (booking essential for dinner) à la carte 30,67/41,92.

XX **Guy**, Jägerstr. 59 (courtyard), ✉ 10117, ℘ (030) 20 94 26 00, *info@guy-restaurant.de, Fax (030) 20942610*, – AE VISA. rest PZ d
closed Saturday lunch and Sunday – **Meals** 20 *(lunch)* and à la carte 38/47.

XX **Paris-Moskau**, Alt-Moabit 141, ✉ 10557, ℘ (030) 3 94 20 81, *Fax (030) 3942602*,
closed 2 weeks August – **Meals** *(dinner only)* (booking essential) à la carte 32,50/48. GY s

X **Rutz**, Chausseestr. 8, ✉ 10115, ℘ (030) 24 62 87 60, *info@rutz-weinbar.de, Fax (030) 24628761*, – AE VISA NX c
closed Sunday – **Meals** *(dinner only)* (outstanding wine list) à la carte 33/42.

XX **Borchardt**, Französische Str. 47, ✉ 10117, ℘ (030) 20 38 71 10, *veranstaltung@gastart.de, Fax (030) 20387150*, « Courtyard-terrace » – AE VISA PZ c
Meals à la carte 31/44.

X **Maxwell**, Bergstr. 22 (entrance in courtyard), ✉ 10115, ℘ (030) 2 80 71 21, *maxwell.berlin@t-online.de, Fax (030) 28599848*, « Art nouveau facade ; courtyard-terrace » – AE VISA JCB PX e
Meals *(dinner only)* (booking essential) à la carte 35/48.

X **Am Karlsbad**, Am Karlsbad 11, ✉ 10785, ℘ (030) 2 64 53 49, *info@restaurantamkarlsbad.de, Fax (030) 2644240*, (modern restaurant in bistro style) – P. VISA NZ c
closed Saturday lunch, Sunday and Monday – **Meals** à la carte 30/45.

X **Weinstein**, Mittelstr. 1, ✉ 10117, ℘ (030) 20 64 96 69, *Fax (030) 20649699*, – VISA PY f
closed Saturday lunch, Sunday and Bank Holidays – **Meals** à la carte 31,70/37,32.

X **Mario**, Leibnizstr. 43, ✉ 10629, ℘ (030) 3 24 35 16 AE KX e
closed 3 weeks July - August, 23 December - 5 January, Saturday and Sunday lunch – **Meals** (Italian) à la carte 28/38,50.

X **Maothai**, Meierottostr. 1, ✉ 10719, ℘ (030) 8 83 28 23, *maothai@snafu.de, Fax (030) 88756558*, – AE VISA. LY m
Meals *(Monday - Friday dinner only)* (Thai) à la carte 22/40,50.

X **Lutter und Wegner**, Charlottenstr. 56, ✉ 10117, ℘ (030) 2 02 95 40, *Fax (030) 20295425*, « Intimate wine tavern » – AE VISA PZ e
Meals 16 *(lunch)* and à la carte 23/42.

Berlin-Friedrichshain

Inn Side Residence-Hotel M, Lange Str. 31, ✉ 10243, ℘ (030) 29 30 30, *berlin@innside.de, Fax (030) 29303199*, – rm, – 35. AE VISA JCB SZ r
Meals à la carte 22,90/35,70 – 14 – **133 rm** 160/230 – 180/250.

Astron M, Landsberger Allee 26, ✉ 10249, ℘ (030) 4 22 61 30, *berlin-alexanderplatz@astron-hotels.de, Fax (030) 42261300*, – rm, – 160. AE VISA JCB SY e
Meals à la carte 27/41 – 13 – **225 rm** 113/203 – 133/223.

Berlin-Grunewald

The Ritz Carlton Schlosshotel, Brahmsstr. 10, ✉ 14193, ℘ (030) 89 58 40, *purchs@the-ritzcarlton.de, Fax (030) 89584800*, « Former Wilhelminian mansion », Massage, – rm, P – 40. AE VISA JCB. EZ a
Vivaldi *(closed Sunday) (dinner only)* **Meals** à la carte 52,15/72,60 – ***Le Jardin*** : **Meals** à la carte 42,50/57,60 – 20 – **54 rm** 269/356 – 407/509 – 12 suites.

Berlin-Kreuzberg :

Stuttgarter Hof, Anhalter Str. 9, ✉ 10963, ℘ (030) 26 48 30, *info@hotel-stuttgarterhof.de, Fax (030) 26483900*, – rm, – 25. AE VISA JCB
Meals à la carte 28/46 – **110 rm** 136/171 – 151/210. NZ e

at **Berlin-Lichtenberg** East : 5 km, by Karl-Marx-Allee HY :

🏦 **Abacus Tierpark Hotel** Ⓜ, Franz-Mett-Str. 3, ✉ 10319, ✆ (030) 5 16 20, info@a
bacus-hotel.de, Fax (030) 5162400 – 🛗, ✤ rm, 📺 🍸 🖫 – 🔏 250. 🖭 ⑩ ⓜ 🚾
Meals 20 (buffet) and à la carte 19,50/27 – **278 rm** ⬚ 99/119 – 125/145.

at **Berlin-Lichterfelde** Southwest : 7 km, by Boelcke Straße GZ :

🏦 **Villa Toscana** without rest, Bahnhofstr. 19, ✉ 12207, ✆ (030) 7 68 92 70, hotel@v
illa-toscana.de, Fax (030) 7734488, « Garden » – 🛗 📺. 🖭 ⑩ ⓜ 🚾 🚭. ❄
16 rm ⬚ 80/90 – 100.

at **Berlin-Mariendorf** South : 7 km, by Tempelhofer Damm GZ :

🏦 **Landhaus Alpinia**, Säntisstr. 32, ✉ 12107, ✆ (030) 76 17 70 (hotel) 74 19 99 8 (rest.), info
@ alpina-berlin.de, Fax (030) 7419835, « Garden-terrace », ☎ – 🛗, ✤ rm, 📺 🍸 ⇔ –
🔏 20. ⓜ 🚾 – **Villa Rossini** (dinner only) **Meals** à la carte 18/40 – **58 rm** ⬚ 93 – 115

at **Berlin-Neukölln** :

🏨 **Estrel** Ⓜ, Sonnenallee 225, ✉ 12057, ✆ (030) 6 83 10, hotel@estrel.com
Fax (030) 68312345, beer garden, Massage, 🏋, ☎ – 🛗, ✤ rm, 📺 🍸 🖫 🏃 ⇔ –
🔏 2700. 🖭 ⑩ ⓜ 🚾 🚭   HZ a
Sans Souci (closed July - August) **Meals** à la carte 23,52/36,30 – **Portofino** (Italian) **Meals**
à la carte 20,95/31,69 – **Estrel-Stube** (dinner only) **Meals** à la carte 15,59/26,07 – ⬚ 15
– **1125 rm** 123/235 – 133/246 – 70 suites.

🏨 **Mercure**, Hermannstr. 214, ✉ 12049, ✆ (030) 62 78 00, h1894@ accor-hotels.com
Fax (030) 62780111, 🏋, ☎ – 🛗, ✤ rm, 📺 🍸 ⇔ – 🔏 250. 🖭 ⑩ ⓜ 🚾 🚭
❄ rest   HZ d
Meals à la carte 19,43/32,21 – ⬚ 13 – **216 rm** 106 – 121.

at **Berlin Prenzlauer Berg** :

🏦 **Park Plaza** Ⓜ, Storkower Str. 160, ✉ 10407, ✆ (030) 42 18 10, ppberlin@parkpla
aww.com, Fax (030) 42181234 – 🛗, ✤ rm, 📺 🍸 🖫 – 🔏 50. 🖭 ⑩ ⓜ 🚾
Meals à la carte 23/34,26 – **155 rm** ⬚ 114/145 – 135/166.   HY e

at **Berlin-Reinickendorf** :

🏦 **Dorint Airport Hotel**, Gotthardstr. 96, ✉ 13403, ✆ (030) 49 88 40, info-berte
@ dorint.com, Fax (030) 49884555 – 🛗, ✤ rm, 📺 🖫 ⇔ 🖫 – 🔏 70. 🖭 ⑩ ⓜ 🚾
🚭 ❄ rest   FX e
Meals à la carte 21/32 – ⬚ 12 – **303 rm** 90/120 – 102/132.

🏦 **Rheinsberg am See**, Finsterwalder Str. 64, ✉ 13435, ✆ (030) 4 02 10 02, info@hotel-
heinsberg.com, Fax (030) 4035057, « Lakeside garden terrace », Massage, 🏋, ☎, 🏊
🗗, 🖛 – 🛗, ✤ rm, 📺 🍸 🖫 – 🔏 30. ⓜ 🚾
Meals à la carte 17/40 – **81 rm** ⬚ 105/120 – 120/135.
Northwest : 7 km, by Markstraße GX

at **Berlin-Siemensstadt** Northwest : 12 km, by Siemensdamm EX :

🏨 **Holiday Inn Berlin-Esplanade** Ⓜ, Rohrdamm 80, ✉ 13629, ✆ (030) 38 38 90, inf
@ holiday-inn-esplanade.de, Fax (030) 38389900, �, ☎, 🗗 – 🛗, ✤ rm, 📺 🍸 🍸
⇔ – 🔏 170. 🖭 ⑩ ⓜ 🚾 🚭. ❄ rest
Il Faggio (closed dinner Saturday and Sunday) **Meals** à la carte 21,90/28,40 – ⬚ 16
336 rm 143/173 – 163/193 – 4 suites.

🏦 **Novotel**, Ohmstr. 4, ✉ 13629, ✆ (030) 3 80 30, h0483@ accor-hotels.com
Fax (030) 3819403, 🏊 – 🛗, ✤ rm, 📺 🍸 🖫 – 🔏 200. 🖭 ⑩ ⓜ 🚾
Meals à la carte 21/31 – ⬚ 13 – **119 rm** 111/136 – 126/151.

at **Berlin-Steglitz** Southwest : 5 km, by Hauptstraße FZ :

🏨 **Steglitz International**, Albrechtstr. 2 (corner of Schloßstraße) ✉ 12165, ✆ (030
79 00 50, info@steglitz.bestwestern.de, Fax (030) 79005550 – 🛗, ✤ rm, 🍽 rest, 📺 🍸
– 🔏 280. 🖭 ⑩ ⓜ 🚾. ❄ rest
Meals à la carte 22,10/31 – ⬚ 22 – **200 rm** 100/120 – 125/145 – 3 suites.

✗ **Edogawa**, Lepsiusstr. 36, ✉ 12063, ✆ (030) 79 70 62 40, sino.com@ t-online.d
Fax (030) 79706240, 🌇 – 🖭 ⑩ ⓜ 🚾. ❄
closed Monday – **Meals** (Japanese) à la carte 29/59,50.

at **Berlin-Tegel** :

🏦 **Sorat Hotel Humboldt-Mühle** Ⓜ 🐾, An der Mühle 5, ✉ 13507, ✆ (030) 43 90 4
humboldt-muehle@ sorat-hotels.com, Fax (030) 43904444, 🌇 – 🛗, ✤ rm, 🍽
📺 🍸 🖫 ⇔ – 🔏 50. 🖭 ⑩ ⓜ 🚾 🚭 Northwest : 13 km, by Müllerstraße FX
Meals (closed Sunday) à la carte 23,50/38,85 – **120 rm** ⬚ 107/177 – 132/203.

🏦 **Novotel Berlin Airport**, Kurt-Schumacher-Damm 202 (by airport approach
✉ 13405, ✆ (030) 4 10 60, h0791@ accor-hotels.com, Fax (030) 4106700, 🌇, ☎, 🏊
– 🛗, ✤ rm, 📺 🍸 🖫 🖫 – 🔏 150. 🖭 ⑩ ⓜ 🚾 🚭   EX
Meals à la carte 18,92/33,15 – ⬚ 13 – **184 rm** 111 – 126.

at Berlin-Wedding

🏠🏠🏠 **Christiania**, Osloer Str. 116a, ⊠ 13359, ✆ (030) 43 73 70, Fax (030) 43737333 – 📶, ✉ rm, 📺 ✆ ♿ – 🔬 200. 🅰🅴 ⓪ 🆎 💳. ✸ rest   GX k
Meals *(dinner only)* *(residents only)* – **94 rm** ⊇ 110/161 – 146/217 – 5 suites.

COLOGNE (KÖLN) *Nordrhein-Westfalen* 🇩🇪🇮🇼 N 4 – pop. 1 017 700 – alt. 65 m.

See : Cathedral (Dom)✶✶ (Magi's Shrine✶✶✶, Gothic stained glass windows✶ Cross of Gero (Gerokreuz)✶, South chapel (Marienkapelle) : Patrone Saints altar✶✶✶, stalls✶, treasury✶ GY – Roman-Germanic Museum (Römisch-Germanisches Museum)✶✶ (Dionysos Mosaic✶, Roman glassware collection✶✶) GY M1 – Wallraf-Richartz-Museum✶✶ GZ M12 Museum Ludwig✶✶ FV M2 (Photo-Historama Agfa✶) GY M2 – Diocesan Museum (Diözesean Museum)✶ GY M3 – Schnütgen-Museum✶✶ GZ M4 – Museum of Fast-Asian Art (Museum für Ostasiatische Kunst)✶✶ by Hahnenstraßeand Richard Wagner Straße EV – Museum for Applied Art (Museum für Angewandte Kunst)✶ GYZ M6 – St. Maria Lyskirchen (frescoes✶✶) FX – St. Severin (interior✶) FX – St. Pantaleon (rood screen✶) EX – St. Kunibert (chancel : stained glass windows✶) FU – St. Mary the Queen (St. Maria Königin) : wall of glass✶ by Bonnerstraße FX – St. Apostoln (apse✶) EV K – St. Ursula (treasury✶) FU – St. Mary of the Capitol (St. Maria im Kapitol) (romanesque wooden church door✶, trefoil chancel✶) GZ – Imhoff-Stollwerrk-Museum✶ FX – Old Town Hall (Altes Rathaus)✶ GZ – Botanical garden Flora✶ by Konrad-Adenauer-Ufer FU.

🏌 Köln-Marienburg, Schillingsrotterweg (South : 3 km), ✆ (0261) 38 40 53 ; 🏌 Köln-Rogendorf, Parallelweg 1 (by Erftstraße and A 57 : 16 km), ✆ (0221) 78 40 18 ; 🏌 Bergisch-Gladbach-Refrath, Golfplatz 2 (East : 17 km), ✆ (02204) 9 27 60 ; 🏌 Pulheim Gut Lärchenhof (North-West : 19 km), ✆ (022389) 92 39 00.

✈ Köln-Bonn at Wahn (South-East : 17 km) ✆ (02203) 4 01.

🚉 Köln-Deutz, Barmer Straße by Deutzer Brücke FV.

Exhibition Centre (Messegelände) by Deutzer Brücke (FV), ✆ (0221) 82 11, Fax (0221) 8212574 – 🅱 Köln Tourismus (Verkehrsamt), Unter Fettenhennen 19 ⊠ 50667, ✆ (0221) 22 13 33 45, Fax (0221) 22123320.

ADAC, Luxemburger Str. 169.

Düsseldorf 39 – Aachen 69 – Bonn 32 – Essen 68.

Plans on following pages

🏠🏠🏠🏠 **Excelsior Hotel Ernst**, Domplatz, ⊠ 50667, ✆ (0221) 27 01, ehe@excelsiorhotel ernst.de, Fax (0221) 135150 – 📶 ▤ 📺 – 🔬 80. 🅰🅴 ⓪ 🆎 💳. ✸ rest   GY a
Meals see – **Hanse-Stube** below – **Taku** *(closed Sunday lunch and Monday)* Meals à la carte 33/46,15 – **154 rm** ⊇ 210/285 – 280/380 – 25 suites.

🏠🏠🏠 **Maritim** Ⓜ, Heumarkt 20, ⊠ 50667, ✆ (0221) 2 02 70, info.kol@maritim.de, Fax (0221) 2027826, Massage, 🛁, ≘s, 📲 – 📶, ✉ rm, ▤ 📺 ✆ 🚗 – 🔬 1300. 🅰🅴 ⓪ 🆎 💳 🇯🇨🇧   GZ m
Bellevue ✸ « Terrace with ≤ Cologne » Meals 45,50/71,07 – **La Galerie** *(closed 8 July - 27 August, Sunday and Monday)* *(dinner only)* Meals à la carte 21,51/35,29 – ⊇ 30 – **454 rm** 144/294 – 160/319 – 28 suites.

🏠🏠🏠 **Im Wasserturm** ⚘, Kaygasse 2, ⊠ 50676, ✆ (0221) 2 00 80, info@hotel-im-was serturm.de, Fax (0221) 2008888, 🌳, roof garden terrace with ≤ Cologne, « 19C former water tower, elegant modern installation », ≘s – 📶, ✉ rm, ▤ rest, 📺 ✆ 🚗 – 🔬 25. 🅰🅴 ⓪ 🆎 💳 🇯🇨🇧. ✸ rest   FX c
Meals 30 *(lunch)* and à la carte 44/64 – ⊇ 18 – **88 rm** 165/255 – 200/305 – 34 suites.

🏠🏠🏠🏠 **Dom-Hotel** ⚘, Domkloster 2a, ⊠ 50667, ✆ (0221) 2 02 40, sales@dom-hotel.com, Fax (0221) 2024444, « Terrace with ≤ » – 📶, ✉ rm, 📺 ✆ – 🔬 60. 🅰🅴 ⓪ 🆎 💳 🇯🇨🇧
Meals à la carte 36,70/42,95 – ⊇ 18 – **125 rm** 185/310 – 260/435.   GY d

🏠🏠🏠🏠 **Renaissance Köln Hotel**, Magnusstr. 20, ⊠ 50672, ✆ (0221) 2 03 40, rhi.cgnrn.s alcs@renaissancehotels.com, Fax (0221) 2034777, 🌳, Massage, ≘s, 📲 – 📶, ✉ rm, ▤ 📺 ✆ ♿ 🚗 – 🔬 220. 🅰🅴 ⓪ 🆎 💳 🇯🇨🇧
Raffael : Meals à la carte 26/39 – **Valentino** : Meals à la carte 22,50/24 – ⊇ 16 – **236 rm** 168/345 – 193/370.   EV b

🏠🏠🏠 **Jolly Hotel Media Park** Ⓜ, Im Mediapark 8b, ⊠ 50670, ✆ (0221) 2 71 50, Fax (0221) 2715999, 🌳, 🛁, ≘s – 📶, ✉ rm, ▤ 📺 ✆ ♿ 🚗 – 🔬 200. 🅰🅴 ⓪ 🆎 💳
Meals *(Italian)* à la carte 28/44 – **220 rm** ⊇ 165/315 – 200/350.   EU a

🏠🏠🏠 **Dorint Kongress-Hotel**, Helenenstr. 14, ⊠ 50667, ✆ (0221) 27 50, info.cgnjun@d orint.com, Fax (0221) 2751301, Massage, ≘s, 📲 – 📶, ✉ rm, ▤ 📺 ✆ ♿ 🚗 – 🔬 500. 🅰🅴 ⓪ 🆎 💳 🇯🇨🇧. ✸ rest   EV p
closed July - August – Meals 25,10 *(buffet lunch)* and à la carte 30,67/45,50 – **Kabuki** *(Japanese)* *(closed Sunday and Monday lunch)* Meals à la carte 21,47/32,72 – ⊇ 16 – **284 rm** 161 – 12 suites.

🏠🏠🏠 **Savoy** ⚘, Turiner Str. 9, ⊠ 50668, ✆ (0221) 1 62 30, office@hotelsavoy.de, Fax (0221) 1623200, « Savoy-Health-Club », Massage, 🛁, ≘s – 📶, ✉ rm, ▤ rm, 📺 ✆ 🚗 📲 – 🔬 70. 🅰🅴 ⓪ 🆎 💳
Meals *(dinner only)* à la carte 26/41,50 – **103 rm** ⊇ 102 – 187.   FU s

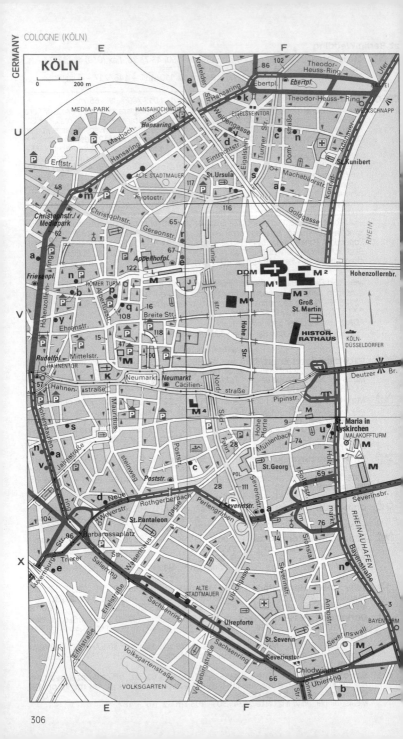

KÖLN

0 — 200 m

MEDIA-PARK

HANSAHOCHHAUS

Theodor-Heuss-Ring

Ebertpl. · Ebertpl.

Theodor-Heuss-Ring

WERKSCHNAPP

EIGELSTEINTOR

Hansaring

Maybach

Hansaring

Erftstr.

Meldengasse

Eintrachtstr.

St. Kunibert

ALTE STADTMAUER

Machabaerstr.

Kyotostr.

St. Ursula

Dom str.

Turiner Str.

Eigelsteinstraße

Konrad

Christophstr./ Mediapark

Christophstr.

Gereonstr.

Goldgasse

RHEIN

Friesenpl.

RÖMER TURM

Appelhofpl.

Tunis str.

Albertusstr.

DOM

Hohenzollernbr.

Hohenzollern- Ring

Ehrenstr.

Breite Str.

M¹ M²

M³

Groß St. Martin

Hohenzollernbr.

Rudolfpl.

Mittelstr.

M⁶

HISTOR- RATHAUS

KÖLN- DÜSSELDORFER

HAHNENTOR

Neumarkt · Neumarkt

Cäcilien-

Hohe Str.

Nord- straße

Deutzer Br.

Hahnen- straße

Mauritius

Pipinstr.

M⁴

Hohe Pforte

St. Maria in Lyskirchen

MALAKOFFTURM

M

Poststr.

Mühlenbach

Jahnstraße

Poststr.

St. Georg

Hölz

Severinstr.

M

Neue

Rothgerberbach

Perlengraben

Severinstr.

Weyerstr.

St. Pantaleon

Severinsbr.

Barbarossaplatz

Severinstr.

Siebstr.

RHEINAUHAFEN

Bayenstraße

Trierer

Salierring

Wäsenhaus

Luxemburger Str.

Eifelstraße

ALTE STADTMAUER

Ulrepforte

Sachsenring

Ulrgasse

Sachsenstraße

BAYENTURM

Eifelstraße

St. Severin

Severins wall

Anhostr.

Volksgartenstraße

Sachsenring

Severinstor

Chlodwigpl.

VOLKSGARTEN

Volksgebirgstraße

Ubierring

Bonner

306

KÖLN

GERMANY

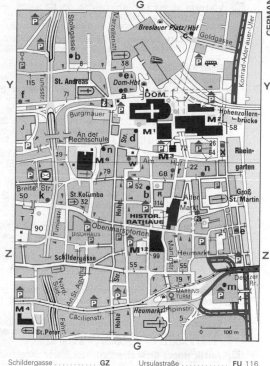

🏨 **Crowne Plaza**, Habsburger Ring 9, ⊠ 50674, ℘ (0221) 22 80, info@ crowncplaza-koeln.de, Fax (0221) 251206, Massage, I₀, ⇌s, 🔲 – 📱, ⇜ rm, 📺 📞 ⇌ – 🔏 220. 🖭 ⓪ ⓪ 🆅🆂🅰 🅹🅲🅱. ⋇ rest   by Hahnenstraße EV
Meals 23 (buffet lunch) **– Die Auster** (closed 4 weeks July - August, Sunday and Monday) (dinner only) Meals à la carte 23/40,50 – ⊑ 16 **– 301 rm** 170/220 – 195/245.

🏨 **Lindner Dom Residence** 🅼, An den Dominikanern 4a (entrance Stolkgasse), ⊠ 50668, ℘ (0221) 1 64 40, info.domresidence@lindner.de, Fax (0221) 1644440, ⇌s, 🔲 – 📱, ⇜ rm, 📺 📺 📞 ⇌ – 🔏 120. 🖭 ⓪ ⓪ 🆅🆂🅰 🅹🅲🅱. ⋇ rest   GY b
La Gazetta : Meals à la carte 24/44 – ⊑ 16 **– 194 rm** 189/262 – 225/298.

🏨 **Dorint**, Friesenstr. 44, ⊠ 50670, ℘ (0221) 1 61 40, cgncol@dorint.com, Fax (0221) 1614100, 🍴 – 📱, ⇜ rm, 📺 📞 ⇌ – 🔏 160. 🖭 ⓪ ⓪ 🆅🆂🅰 🅹🅲🅱. ⋇ rest
Meals (closed 24 to 31 December) à la carte 22,50/34 – ⊑ 13 **– 103 rm** 107/207 – 134/209.   EV n

🏨 **Mercure Severinshof**, Severinstr. 199, ⊠ 50676, ℘ (0221) 2 01 30, h1206@accor-hotels.com, Fax (0221) 2013666, 🍴, I₀, ⇌s – 📱, ⇜ rm, 📺 rm, 📺 📞 ⇌ – 🔏 160. 🖭 ⓪ ⓪ 🆅🆂🅰. ⋇ rest   FX a
Meals à la carte 21,56/32 **– 252 rm** ⊑ 118/175 – 157/222 – 6 suites.

🏨 **Lyskirchen**, Filzengraben 32, ⊠ 50676, ℘ (0221) 2 09 70, info.bwlyskirchen@event hotels.com, Fax (0221) 2097718, ⇌s, 🔲 – 📱, ⇜ rm, 📺 rest, 📺 📞 ⇌ – 🔏 30. 🖭 ⓪ ⓪ 🆅🆂🅰. ⋇ rest   FX u
closed 21 December - 2 January **– Meals** (closed 9 to 21 April, 5 July - 18 August, Saturday, Sunday and Bank Holidays) à la carte 22,50/33,20 **– 103 rm** ⊑ 115 – 150/240.

🏨 **Ascot** without rest, Hohenzollernring 95, ⊠ 50672, ℘ (0221) 9 52 96 50, info@ascot.bestwestern.de, Fax (0221) 952965100, I₀, ⇌s – 📱 ⇜ 📺 📞. 🖭 ⓪ ⓪ 🆅🆂🅰   EV a
closed 22 December - 1 January **– 46 rm** ⊑ 95/106 – 135/167.

🏨 **Viktoria** without rest, Worringer Str. 23, ✉ 50668, ℰ (0221) 9 73 17 20, *hotel@ho* *telviktoria.com, Fax (0221) 727067* – 📶 ✻ 📺 📞 ℙ. 🅰🅴 ① 🆎 *VISA*. ⅍   FU t
closed Easter, 24 December - 1 January – **47 rm** ☑ 90 – 113.

🏨 **Novotel City**, Bayenstr. 51, ✉ 50678, ℰ (0221) 80 14 70, *h3127@accor-hotels.com,* *Fax (0221) 80147148,* 🍴, 🎣, ☎ – 📶, ✻ rm, 📺 📞 ㅎ ↺ – 🔬 150. 🅰🅴 ① 🆎 *VISA* 🆑   FX n
Meals à la carte 29,50/36 – ☑ 13 – **222 rm** 111 – 130.

🏨 **Four Points Hotel Central**, Breslauer Platz 2, ✉ 50668, ℰ (0221) 1 65 10, *info* *@ eurotels.de, Fax (0221) 1651333* – 📶, ✻ rm, ▤ rest, 📺 – 🔬 20. 🅰🅴 ① 🆎 *VISA*
Meals à la carte 17,40/29,15 – **116 rm** ☑ 125 – 155 – 6 suites.   GY c

🏨 **Senats Hotel**, Unter Goldschmied 9, ✉ 50667, ℰ (0221) 2 06 20, *info@ senats-hot* *el.de, Fax (0221) 2062200* – 📶, ✻ rm, 📺 – 🔬 230. 🅰🅴 🆎 *VISA* 🆑   GZ b
closed 23 December - 3 January – **Falstaff** *(closed Saturday lunch, Sunday and Bank* *Holidays)* **Meals** à la carte 23/44 – **59 rm** ☑ 77/90 – 110/120.

🏨 **Cristall** without rest, Ursulaplatz 9, ✉ 50668, ℰ (0221) 1 63 00, *hotelcristall@ t-online.de,* *Fax (0221) 1630333,* « Modern interior » – 📶 ✻ ▤ 📺 ℙ. 🅰🅴 ① 🆎 *VISA* 🆑. ⅍
84 rm ☑ 102 – 133.   FU

🏨 **Coellner Hof**, Hansaring 100, ✉ 50670, ℰ (0221) 1 66 60, *info@ coellnerhof.de,* *Fax (0221) 1666166* – 📶, ✻ rm, ▤ rest, 📺 ↺ – 🔬 30. 🅰🅴 ① 🆎 *VISA*   FU k
Meals *(closed Saturday and Sunday) (dinner only)* à la carte 16,90/37,80 – **70 rm**
☑ 77/150 – 105/200.

🏨 **Euro Garden Cologne** without rest, Domstr. 10, ✉ 50668, ℰ (0221) 1 64 90, *info* *@ eurotels.de, Fax (0221) 1649333,* ☎ – 📶 ✻ 📺 ↺ – 🔬 40. 🅰🅴 ① 🆎 *VISA*
85 rm ☑ 115 – 145.   FU a

🏨 **Mado** Ⓜ without rest, Moselstr. 36, ✉ 50674, ℰ (0221) 92 41 90, *info@ hotelmado.de* *Fax (0221) 92419101,* ☎ – 📶, ✻ rm, 📺 📞 ℙ – 🔬 20. 🅰🅴 ① 🆎 *VISA* 🆑 EX e
51 rm ☑ 85/95 – 102/132.

🏨 **Königshof** without rest, Richartzstr. 14, ✉ 50667, ℰ (0221) 2 57 87 71, *hotel@ ho* *telkoenigshof.com, Fax (0221) 2578762* – 📶 ✻ 📺 📞. 🅰🅴 ① 🆎 *VISA*   GY r
82 rm ☑ 80/115 – 110/166.

🏨 **Esplanade** without rest, Hohenstaufenring 56, ✉ 50674, ℰ (0221) 9 21 55 70, *info* *@ e-splana.de, Fax (0221) 216822* – 📶 ✻ 📺. 🅰🅴 ① 🆎 *VISA* 🆑   EX a
closed 23 December - 2 January – **33 rm** ☑ 80/95 – 105/116.

🏨 **Antik Hotel Bristol** without rest, Kaiser-Wilhelm-Ring 48, ✉ 50672, ℰ (0221
12 01 95, *hotel@ antik-hotel-bristol.de, Fax (0221) 131495,* « Antique furniture » – 📶 ✻
📺 📞 ㅎ. 🅰🅴 ① 🆎 *VISA* 🆑   EU m
closed 21 December - 2 January – **44 rm** ☑ 85/110

🏨 **Classic Hotel Santo** Ⓜ without rest, Dagobertstr. 22, ✉ 50668, ℰ (0221) 9 13 97 70
santo@ classic-hotels.com, Fax (0221) 913977777, « Modern interior » – 📶 ✻ 📺 ㅎ ↺
ℙ. 🅰🅴 ① 🆎 *VISA* 🆑   FU c
69 rm ☑ 113 – 133.

🏨 **Hopper St. Antonius** Ⓜ, Dagobertstr. 32, ✉ 50668, ℰ (0221) 1 66 00(hotel
1 30 00 69(rest.), *st.antonius@ hopper.de, Fax (0221) 1660166,* 🍴, « Modern interior »
– 📶, ✻ rm, 📺 📞 ㅎ ↺ – 🔬 15. 🅰🅴 ① 🆎 *VISA*   FU n
Spitz im Hotel *(closed Saturday lunch)* **Meals** à la carte 23,50/36,80 – **54 rm** ☑ 100/130
– 140/250 – 15 suites.

🏨 **Hopper** Ⓜ, Brüsseler Str. 26, ✉ 50674, ℰ (0221) 92 44 00, *hotel@ hopper.de*
Fax (0221) 924406, 🍴, « Modern hotel in a former monastery », ☎ – 📶, ✻ rm, 📺
📞 ↺. 🅰🅴 ① 🆎 *VISA* 🆑   by Hahnenstraße
closed Easter, Whit Sunday, Whit Monday and 20 December - 1 January **Meals** *(close* *Saturday lunch)* à la carte 23/35 – **49 rm** ☑ 90/100 – 120/130.

🏨 **Astor** without rest, Friesenwall 68, ✉ 50672, ℰ (0221) 20 71 20, *astorhotel@ t-or* *ne.de, Fax (0221) 253106,* ☎ – 📶 ✻ 📺 📞 ℙ. 🅰🅴 🆎 *VISA* 🆑. ⅍   EV
closed 22 December - 6 January – **50 rm** ☑ 94/98 – 115/145.

🏨 **Leonet** without rest, Rubensstr. 33, ✉ 50676, ℰ (0221) 27 23 00, *leonetkoeln@ ne* *cologne.de, Fax (0221) 210893,* ☎ – 📶 ✻ 📺 📞 ℙ – 🔬 20. 🅰🅴 🆎 *VISA* 🆑   EX
78 rm ☑ 85/135 – 115/195.

🏨 **Ibis Barbarossaplatz**, Neue Weyerstr. 4, ✉ 50676, ℰ (0221) 2 09 60, *h1449@a* *cor-hotels.com, Fax (0221) 2096199* – 📶, ✻ rm, ▤ rm, 📺 📞 ㅎ ↺ – 🔬 25. 🅰🅴 ①
🆎 *VISA* 🆑   EX
Meals à la carte 20,71/33,49 – ☑ 8 – **208 rm** 61/95

🏨 **Metropol** without rest, Hansaring 14, ✉ 50670, ℰ (0221) 13 33 77, *Fax (0221) 13830*
– 📶 📺. 🅰🅴 ① 🆎 *VISA*   EU r
closed 22 December - 2 January – **27 rm** ☑ 65 – 98.

XXXX **Hanse Stube** - Excelsior Hotel Ernst, Dompropst-Ketzer-Str. 2, ✉ 50667, ℰ (0221) 2 70 34 02, ehe@excelsiorhotelernst.de, Fax (0221) 135150, 🌤 – 🔳. 🆎 �ⓞ ⓜⓢ 𝗩𝗜𝗦𝗔. �
GY e
Meals 30,17 (lunch) and à la carte 50,13/61,92.

XXX **Börsen-Restaurant Maître** (Schäfer), Unter Sachsenhausen 10, ✉ 50667, ℰ (0221)
🏵 13 30 21, Fax (0221) 133040, 🌤 – 🔳. 🆎 ⓞ ⓜⓢ 𝗩𝗜𝗦𝗔. �
EV r
closed end March - early April, 4 weeks July - August, Saturday lunch, Sunday and Bank Holidays – Meals à la carte 44/59,50 – **Börsen-Stube** (closed Saturday dinner, Sunday and Bank Holidays) Meals à la carte 27,50/40
Spec. Roulade von Seezunge und Basilikum mit Flußkrebsnage. Sisteron-Lammrücken mit gebratener Artischocke und Calamatas-Oliven. Rotwein-Schokoladeneistorte mit warmem Pumpernickelpudding.

XXX **Ambiance**, Komödienstr. 50, ✉ 50667, ℰ (0221) 9 22 76 52 – 🆎 ⓞ
ⓜⓢ 𝗩𝗜𝗦𝗔
GY f
closed 3 weeks August, Saturday, Sunday and Bank Holidays – Meals 33 (lunch)/62 and à la carte 49/53.

XXX **Grande Milano**, Hohenstaufenring 29, ✉ 50674, ℰ (0221) 24 21 21, Fax (0221) 244846, 🌤 – 🔳. 🆎 ⓞ ⓜⓢ 𝗩𝗜𝗦𝗔 ⻊ⓒⒷ
EX v
closed 2 weeks July, Saturday lunch and Sunday – Meals (Italian) à la carte 33,50/54 –
Pinot di Pinot : Meals 12,50 (lunch) and à la carte 17/28.

XXX **Domerie**, Buttermarkt 42, ✉ 50667, ℰ (0221) 2 57 40 44, stefanruessel@netcolog ne.de, Fax (0221) 2574269, « 15 C house » – 🆎 ⓞ ⓜⓢ 𝗩𝗜𝗦𝗔
GZ e
closed 1 to 15 January, carnival, Sunday and Monday, except exhibitions – Meals (dinner only) (dinner only in winter) 40,86/44,43 and à la carte 27,35/40,66.

XX **Fischers**, Hohenstaufenring 53, ✉ 50674, ℰ (0221) 3 10 84 70, fischers.wein@t-on line.de, Fax (0221) 31084789, 🌤 – 🍸 40. ⓜⓢ 𝗩𝗜𝗦𝗔
EX n
closed 27 December - 10 January, Saturday lunch, Sunday and Bank Holidays – Meals à la carte 30,50/42.

XX **Alfredo**, Tunisstr. 3, ✉ 50667, ℰ (0221) 2 57 73 80, info@ristorante-alfredo.com, Fax (0221) 2577380 – 🆎
GZ k
closed 3 weeks July - August, Saturday lunch and Sunday – Meals (booking essential) à la carte 37/51.

XX **Bizim**, Weidengasse 47, ✉ 50668, ℰ (0221) 13 15 81, Fax (0221) 131581 – 🆎 ⓞ ⓜⓢ
𝗩𝗜𝗦𝗔. �
FU d
closed 2 weeks February, 3 weeks July - August, Saturday lunch, Sunday and Monday –
Meals (Turkish) (booking essential for dinner) 29 (lunch) and à la carte 35,50/47,30.

XX **Em Krützche**, Am Frankenturm 1, ✉ 50667, ℰ (0221) 2 58 08 39, info@em-kruez che.de, Fax (0221) 253417, 🌤 – 🆎 ⓞ ⓜⓝ 𝗩𝗜𝗦𝗔
GY x
closed Holy week and Monday – Meals (booking essential for dinner) à la carte 27,50/43,50.

XX **Bosporus**, Weidengasse 36, ✉ 50668, ℰ (0221) 12 52 65, restaurant.bosporus@t-o nline.de, Fax (0221) 9123829, 🌤 – 🆎 ⓞ ⓜⓢ 𝗩𝗜𝗦𝗔
FU v
closed Sunday lunch – Meals (Turkish) à la carte 23,82/36,50.

X **Le Moissonnier**, Krefelder Str. 25, ✉ 50670, ℰ (0221) 72 94 79, Fax (0221) 7325461,
🏵 (typical French bistro)
FU e
closed 1 week Easter, 3 weeks July - August, 1 week Christmas, Sunday and Monday –
Meals (booking essential) à la carte 37/57,50
Spec. Foie gras Maison. Filet d'agneau rôti au four à l'aubergine et à la crème au vin rouge. Pigeonneau rôti en fricassée à la graine de coriandre.

X **Le Domaine Payet**, Alteburger Str. 37, ✉ 50678, ℰ (0221) 32 91 62, Fax (0221) 329162 – ⓜⓢ 𝗩𝗜𝗦𝗔
FX b
closed July – Meals (dinner only) (French) 25,31/40,65 and à la carte.

X **Daitokai**, Kattenbug 2, ✉ 50667, ℰ (0221) 12 00 48, Fax (0221) 1392989 – 🔳. 🆎 ⓞ
ⓜⓢ 𝗩𝗜𝗦𝗔 ⻊ⓒⒷ. �
EV e
closed 2 weeks July, Monday and Tuesday lunch – Meals (Japanese) 38,90/72 and à la carte 30,70/45.

Cologne brewery inns :

X **Peters Brauhaus**, Mühlengasse 1, ✉ 50667, ℰ (0221) 2 57 39 50, peters-brauhau s@netcologne.de, Fax (0221) 2573962, 🌤 – �
GZ n
Meals à la carte 18,40/24,70.

X **Höhn's Dom Brauerei Ausschank**, Goltsteinstr. 83 (Bayenthal), ✉ 50968, ℰ (0221) 3 48 12 93, m.k.hoehn@t-online.de, Fax (0221) 3406456
T v
closed Christmas – Meals à la carte 19,60/32,50.

X **Gaffel-Haus**, Alter Markt 20, ✉ 50667, ℰ (0221) 2 57 76 92, Fax (0221) 253879, 🌤
– 🆎 ⓜⓢ 𝗩𝗜𝗦𝗔 ⻊ⓒⒷ
GZ a
Meals à la carte 16,40/29,70.

✗ **Brauhaus Sion**, Unter Taschenmacher 5, ⊠ 50667, ℰ (0221) 2 57 85 40, *info@br*
⊝ *auhaus-sion.de*, Fax (0221) 2582081, 🍽 – ◍ ◍ 📧 GZ **r**
Meals à la carte 13,25/23,45.

✗ **Früh am Dom**, Am Hof 12, ⊠ 50667, ℰ (0221) 2 61 32 11, Fax (0221) 2613299, beer
garden GY **w**
Meals à la carte 15,24/25,46.

at Cologne-Braunsfeld *West* : *5 km, by Rudolfplatz EV and Aachener Straße :*

🏨 **Regent** without rest, Melatengürtel 15, ⊠ 50933, ℰ (0221) 5 49 90, *hotel@hotelre*
gent.de, Fax (0221) 5499998, 🍽 – 📶 ➚ 🗹 ➪ 📵 – 🅰 80. 📧 ◍ ◍ 📧
closed 24 December - 1 January – ⊐ 14 – **148 rm** 93/144 – 108/144 – 5 suites.

at Cologne-Deutz *East* : *1 km, by Deutzer Brücke FV :*

🏨 **Hyatt Regency**, Kennedy-Ufer 2a, ⊠ 50679, ℰ (0221) 8 28 12 34, *concierge@hya*
tt.com, Fax (0221) 8281370, ≤, beer garden, Massage, 🛌, 🍽, 🔲 – 📶, ➚ rm, 🖩 🗹
➪ 🕭 ➪ 📵 – 🅰 260. 📧 ◍ ◍ 📧 📧 ❀
Graugans (closed lunch Saturday and Sunday) **Meals** 25 (lunch) and à la carte 38/64 –
Glashaus (Italian) **Meals** 27 (buffet lunch) and à la carte 37,66/49 – ⊐ 18 – **288 rm**
165/360 – 190/400 – 17 suites.

🏨 **Dorint An der Messe** Ⓜ, Deutz-Mülheimer-Str. 22, ⊠ 50679, ℰ (0221) 80 19 00,
info.cgnmes@dorint.com, Fax (0221) 80190800, 🍽, 🛌, 🍽, 🔲 – 📶, ➚ rm, 🖩 🗹
🕭 ➪ – 🅰 360. 📧 ◍ ◍ 📧 📧 ❀ rest
Meals à la carte 29/59 – ⊐ 16 – **313 rm** 151/333 – 151/353 – 31 suites.

✗✗ **Der Messeturm**, Kennedy-Ufer (18th floor), ⊠ 50679, ℰ (0221) 88 10 08,
Fax (0221) 818575, ≤ Cologne – 📶 🖩 – 🅰 30. 📧 ◍ ◍ 📧 ❀
closed Saturday lunch – **Meals** 23 *(lunch)* and à la carte 32,70/45,50.

at Cologne-Ehrenfeld *West* : *3 km, by Rudolfplatz EV and Aachener Straße :*

🏨 **Imperial**, Barthelstr. 93, ⊠ 50823, ℰ (0221) 51 70 57, *imperial@hotel-imperial.de*,
Fax (0221) 520993, 🍽 – 📶, ➚ rm, 🖩 rest, 🗹 🕭 ➪ 📵 – 🅰 25. 📧 ◍ ◍ 📧
📧 ❀ rest
Meals *(closed Saturday and Sunday)* à la carte 21,50/37 – **35 rm** ⊐ 102/144 – 153/185

at Cologne-Holweide : *Northeast: 10 km, by Konrad-Adenauer-Ufer FU and Mühlheimer Brücke :*

✗✗✗ **Isenburg**, Johann-Bensberg-Str. 49, off Bergisch-Gladbacher-Straße, ⊠ 51067
ℰ (0221) 69 59 09, *blindert@restaurant-isenburg.de*, Fax (0221) 698703, « Garder
terrace » – 📵. 📧 ◍ ◍ 📧
closed carnival, mid July - mid August, Christmas, Saturday lunch, Sunday and Monday –
Meals *(booking essential)* 35 *(lunch)* and à la carte 40/50.

at Cologne-Junkersdorf *West* : *9 km, by Rudolfplatz EV and Aachener Straße :*

🏨 **Brenner'scher Hof** 🌫, Wilhelm-von-Capitaine-Str. 15, ⊠ 50858, ℰ (0221
9 48 60 00, *hotel@brennerscher-hof.de*, Fax (0221) 94860010, « Country house style
interior » – 📶 🗹 🕭 ➪ – 🅰 25. 📧 ◍ ◍ 📧 ❀ rest
Galloria (closed Monday)(dinner only) **Meals** à la carte 23,50/38,50 – *Pino's Osteria* (Italian)
(dinner only) **Meals** à la carte 16,90/36,40 – **42 rm** ⊐ 133/205 – 161/235 – 6 suites.

🏨 **Dorint Hotel** Ⓜ, Aachener Str. 1059, ⊠ 50858, ℰ (0221) 4 89 80, *info.cgnjun@dorint.*
om, Fax (0221) 48981000 – 📶, ➚ rm, 🖩 🗹 🕭 ➪ – 🅰 80. 📧 ◍ ◍ 📧 📧 📧
Meals à la carte 20/31,50 – ⊐ 12 – **145 rm** 97 – 107.

at Cologne-Lindenthal *West* : *4,5 km, by Rudolfplatz EV and B 264 :*

🏨 **Queens Hotel**, Dürener Str. 287, ⊠ 50935, ℰ (0221) 4 67 60, *reservation.qkoeln@*
ueensgruppe.de, Fax (0221) 433765, « Garden terrace » – 📶, ➚ rm, 🖩 rest, 🗹 🕭 ➪
➪ 📵 – 🅰 250. 📧 ◍ ◍ 📧
Meals à la carte 21,50/34,70 – ⊐ 15 – **147 rm** 115/146 – 146/164.

✗✗ **Bruno Lucchesi**, Dürener Str. 218, ⊠ 50931, ℰ (0221) 40 80 22, Fax (0221) 400989
– 🖩 rest. 📧 ◍ ◍ 📧 ❀
closed 20 July - 5 August and Monday, except exhibitions – **Meals** à la carte 29,50/46,50

at Cologne-Marienburg *South* : *4 km, by Bonner Straße FX :*

🏨 **Marienburger Bonotel**, Bonner Str. 478, ⊠ 50968, ℰ (0221) 3 70 20, *info@bo*
otel.de, Fax (0221) 3702132, 🍽 – 📶, ➚ rm, 🗹 🕭 ➪ – 🅰 40. 📧 ◍ ◍ 📧 📧
Meals *(closed lunch Saturday and Sunday)* à la carte 19/40 – **93 rm** ⊐ 99 – 125 – 4 suite

at Cologne-Marsdorf *West* : *8 km, by Rudolfplatz EV and B 264 :*

🏨 **Novotel Köln-West**, Horbeller Str. 1, ⊠ 50858, ℰ (02234) 51 40, *h0705@accor*
otels.com, Fax (02234) 514106, 🍽, beer garden, 🛌, 🍽, 🖾 (heated), 🔲 – 📶, ➚ rm
🖩 rest, 🗹 🕭 ➪ 📵 – 🅰 120. 📧 ◍ ◍ 📧 📧
Meals à la carte 20,70/33 – **199 rm** ⊐ 114 – 142.

at Cologne-Mülheim North : 8 km, by Konrad-Adenauer-Ufer FU and Mühlheimer Brücke :

🏨🏨 **Park Plaza** M, Clevischer Ring 121, ✉ 51063, ℰ (0221) 9 64 70, ppkoeln@parkplaz aww.com, Fax (0221) 9647100, *ℓ₅*, ⇔s – ⏸, ⇼ rm, ▤ rest, 📺 ❤ ₺ ⇔ – 🛦 140.
🇦🇪 🇴 🇴🇴 🇻🇮🇸🇦 🇯🇨🇧
Meals à la carte 23/39 – **188 rm** ☑ 115/130 – 155/170.

at Cologne-Müngersdorf West : 7 km, by Rudolfplatz EV and B 55 :

XXX **Landhaus Kuckuck**, Olympiaweg 2, ✉ 50933, ℰ (0221) 48 53 60, info@landhaus -kuckuck.de, Fax (0221) 4853636, ㈜ – 🛦 100. 🇦🇪 🇴 🇴🇴 🇻🇮🇸🇦
closed 2 weeks during carnival, Sunday dinner and Monday – **Meals** (booking essential) 23 (lunch) and à la carte 29,65/42,95.

at Cologne-Porz-Grengel Southeast : 16 km, by Severin Brücke, follow signs to airport :

🏨🏨 **Holiday Inn**, Waldstr. 255, near the airport, ✉ 51147, ℰ (02203) 56 10, reservatio n.hikoeln-bonn@queensgruppe.de, Fax (02203) 5619, ㈜ – ⏸, ⇼ rm, ▤ 📺 ₺ 📱 –
🛦 90. 🇦🇪 🇴 🇴🇴 🇻🇮🇸🇦 🇯🇨🇧
Meals à la carte 24,50/40 – ☑ 15 – **177 rm** 150 – 185.

at Cologne-Rodenkirchen South : 8 km, by Bayernstraße 5FX and Agrippina Ufer :

🏨🏨 **Atrium-Rheinhotel** ॐ without rest (with guest house), Karlstr. 2, ✉ 50996, ℰ (0221) 93 57 20, reservierung@atrium-rheinhotel.de, Fax (0221) 93572222, ⇔s – ⏸ 📺 ⇔. 🇦🇪 🇴 🇴🇴 🇻🇮🇸🇦 🇯🇨🇧
closed 24 December - 1 January – **70 rm** ☑ 79/92 – 96.

Bergisch Gladbach Nordrhein-Westfalen 🔢🔢 N 5 – pop. 104 000 – alt. 86 m.
Köln 17.

XXXX **Restaurant Dieter Müller** – Schlosshotel Lerbach, Lerbacher Weg, ✉ 51465,
❀❀❀ ℰ (02202) 20 40, Fax (02202) 204940 – 📱 🇦🇪 🇴 🇴🇴 🇻🇮🇸🇦. ❀
closed 1 to 15 January, 3 weeks July - August, Sunday and Monday – **Meals** (booking essential) 62 (lunch)/118 and à la carte 69/99
Spec. Trilogie von der Gänsestopfleber mit Feigen-Rosmarinbrioche. Roulade von St. Petersfisch mit Champagner-Eisenkrautsauce und Wildreis. Geschmorte Ochsenbacke mit Balsamicojus und Kartoffel-Schneckenravioli.

Neuenahr-Ahrweiler, Bad Rheinland-Pfalz 🔢🔢 O 5 – pop. 28 000 – alt. 92 m.
Köln 63.

at Bad Neuenahr-Ahrweiler-Heppingen East : 5 km :

XXX **Steinheuers Restaurant Zur Alten Post** with rm, Landskroner Str. 110 (entrance
❀❀ Konsumgasse), ✉ 53474, ℰ (02641) 9 48 60, steinheuers.restaurant@t-online.de,
🍴 Fax (02641) 948610, ㈜ – 📺 📱 🇦🇪 🇴 🇴🇴 🇻🇮🇸🇦. ❀ rm
Meals (closed 3 weeks July, Tuesday and Wednesday lunch) 60/101 and à la carte 53/70
– **Landgasthof Poststuben** (closed Tuesday and Wednesday lunch) **Meals** à la carte 24/42 – **11 rm** ☑ 80 - 125
Spec. Gänseleberterrine mit Feigen-Tokayergelée. Steinbutt mit Trüffelkruste und Pete-silienwurzel-Tortellini. Eifeler Reh mit Champignons.

Wittlich Rheinland-Pfalz 🔢🔢 Q 4 – pop. 17 300 alt. 155 m.
Köln 160.

at Dreis Southwest : 8 km :

XXXX **Waldhotel Sonnora** (Thieltges) ॐ with rm, Auf dem Eichelfeld, ✉ 54518, ℰ (06578)
❀❀❀ 9 82 20, info@hotel-sonnora.de, Fax (06578) 1402, ⬿, « Garden » – 📺 📱 🇦🇪 🇴🇴 🇻🇮🇸🇦. ❀
closed January - early February, 2 weeks early July – **Meals** (closed Monday and Tuesday) (booking essential) 85/110 and à la carte 62/73 – **20 rm** ☑ 55/70 – 85/155
Spec. Kleine Torte vom Rinderfilet-Tatar mit Imperiel Kaviar. Steinbutt und Kaisergranat im Pastilla-Teig gebacken mit Estragonsauce. Challans-Blutente mit Gewürzhaut und gla-cierten Nektarinen.

Perl Saarland 🔢🔢 R 3 – pop. 6 500 – alt. 254 m.
Köln 230.

t Perl-Nennig North : 9 km :

XXXX **Gourmetrestaurant Schloss Berg** ॐ with rm, Schloßhof 7, ✉ 66706, ℰ (06866)
❀❀ 7 91 18, christian.bau@victors.de, Fax (06866) 79458, ⬿, ㈜, « Restored 12 C moated castle with elegant-modern installation » – ⏸ ⇼ 📺 📱 🇦🇪 🇴🇴 🇻🇮🇸🇦
closed 3 weeks January, 3 weeks July, Monday and Tuesday – **Meals** 81/101 and à la carte 62/78 – **17 rm** ☑ 99/151 – 165/217
Spec. Feines vom Taschenkrebs mit St. Jakobsmucheln und Avocado. Mille-feuille mit gla-sierten Äpfeln und gebratener Gänseleber. Champagnerkutteln mit Trüffelhachée und gegrilltem Hummerschwanz.

311

DRESDEN 🗺 Sachsen 𝟜𝟙𝟠 M 25 – pop. 450 000 – alt. 105 m.

See : Zwinger★★★ (Wallpavilion★★, Nymphs' Bath★★, Porcelain Collection★★, Mathemati
cal-Physical Salon★★, Armoury★★) AY – Semper Opera★★ AY – Former court church★★
(Hofkirche) BY – Palace (Schloß) : royal houses★ (Fürstenzug-Mosaik), Long Passage★ (Lan
ger Gang) BY – Albertinum : Picture Gallery Old Masters★★★ (Gemäldegalerie Alte Meister)
Picture Gallery New Masters★★★ (Gemäldegalerie Neue Meister), Green Vault★★★ (Grünes
Gewölbe) BY – Prager Straße★ ABZ – Museum of History of Dresden★ (Museum für
Geschichte der Stadt Dresden) BY L – Church of the Cross★ (Kreuzkirche) BY – Japanese
Palace★ (Japanisches Palais)(garden ≤★) ABX – Museum of Folk Art★ (Museum für Volks
kunst) BX M 2 – Great Garden★ (Großer Garten) CDZ – Russian-Orthodox Church★ (Rus
sisch-orthodoxe Kirche) (by Leningrader Str. BZ) – Brühl's Terrace ≤★ (Brühlsche Terrasse
BY – Equestrian statue of Augustus the Strong ★ (Reiterstandbild Augusts des Starken
BX E – Pfunds dairy (Pfunds Molkerei) (interior★) Bautzener Straße 97CX.

Envir. : Schloß (palace) Moritzburg★ (North-West : 14 km by Hansastraße BX) – Schloß
(palace) Pillnitz★ (South-East : 15 km by Bautzener Straße CX) – Saxon Swiss★★★ (Sächsische
Schweiz):Bastei★★★, Festung (fortress) Königstein★★ ≤★★, Großsedlitz : Baroque Garden★

🔟 Possendorf, Ferdinand-von-Schill-Str. 2 (South : 13 km). ℘ (035206) 24 30 ; 🔟 Jagd
schloß Herzogswalde (South-West : 19 km), ℘ (0172) 7 97 09 10 ; 🔟 Ullersdorf, Am Golf
platz 1 (East : 8 km), ℘ (03528) 4 80 60.

✈ Dresden-Klotzsche (North : 13 km), ℘ (0351) 8 81 33 60.

🛈 Tourist-Information, Prager Str. 2a, ✉ 01069, ℘ (0351) 49 19 20, Fax (0351
49192116.

ADAC, Striesener Str. 35.

Berlin 192 – Chemnitz 70 – Görlitz 98 – Leipzig 111 – Praha 152.

Plans on following pages

Kempinski Hotel Taschenbergpalais, Taschenberg 3, ✉ 01067, ℘ (0351
4 91 20, reservation@kempinski-dresden.de, Fax (0351) 4912812, 🍽, « Modern hotel in
18C baroque palace », Massage, 🛏, ⇔, 🔲 – 🕴, ⇄ rm, 🔳 🔟 📞 �%, ⟷ – 🔬 320
🆎 ⓔ 🕠 💳 📇 JCB
Meals à la carte 39,70/51,23 – ☑ 21 – **213 rm** 230/310 – 260/340 – 25 suites.

The Westin Bellevue, Große Meißner Str. 15, ✉ 01097, ℘ (0351) 80 50, hotelin
o@westin-bellevue.com, Fax (0351) 8051609, ≤, beer garden, « Courtyard terraces »
🛏, ⇔, 🔲 – 🕴, ⇄ rm, 🔳 🔟 📞 ☑ 📁 – 🔬 400. 🆎 ⓔ 💳 📇 💳 🌸 rest BX
Meals à la carte 22/40,90 – ☑ 16 – **339 rm** 102/245 – 117/260 – 16 suites.

Radisson SAS Gewandhaus Hotel 🅼, Ringstr. 1, ✉ 01067, ℘ (0351) 4 94 90
info.dresden@radissonsas.com, Fax (0351) 4949490, 🛏, ⇔, 🔲 – 🕴, ⇄ rm, 🔳 🔟
☑ 📁 – 🔬 60. 🆎 ⓔ 💳 💳 📇 BY
Meals à la carte 33,20/43,40 – ☑ 16 – **97 rm** 135/178

Hilton 🅼, An der Frauenkirche 5, ✉ 01067, ℘ (0351) 8 64 20, dresden-hilton@t-o
line.de, Fax (0351) 8642725, 🍽, Massage, 🛏, ⇔, 🔲 – 🕴, ⇄ rm, 🔳 🔟 📞 ☑ ⟷
📁 – 🔬 320. 🆎 ⓔ 💳 💳 📇 BY
Rossini (Italian) **Meals** à la carte 27,20/48,30 – **Wettiner Keller** (closed Sunday and Mon
day) (dinner only) **Meals** à la carte 20/36,40 – **Ogura** (Japanese) (closed Monday) **Meals**
à la carte 16,87/38,34 – ☑ 16 – **333 rm** 150/200 – 165/230 – 4 suites.

Bülow Residenz, Rähnitzgasse 19, ✉ 01097, ℘ (0351) 8 00 30, info@buelow-resi
enz.de, Fax (0351) 8003100, « Courtyard terrace » – 🕴, ⇄ rm, 🔟 📞 ☑ 📁 – 🔬 20. 🆎
ⓔ 💳 💳 BX
Carousel (booking essential) **Meals** à la carte 49/62 – ☑ 15 – **30 rm** 170 – 210
Spec. Komposition vom Kalbskopf mit Wurzelgemüse und Tomatenvinaigrette. Täubche
mit Trüffelrisotto und Selleriepüree. Gebackene Apfeltarte mit Honigbaiser und Calva
dosschaum.

Bayerischer Hof, Antonstr. 33, ✉ 01097, ℘ (0351) 82 93 70, info@bayerischer-
of-dresden.de, Fax (0351) 8014860, 🍽 – 🕴, ⇄ rm, 🔟 ⟷ 📁 – 🔬 40. 🆎 ⓔ 💳 💳
JCB 🌸 rest BX
closed 23 to 27 December – **Meals** (closed Sunday, October - April Saturday and Sunday
(dinner only) à la carte 16/34 – **50 rm** ☑ 95 – 126 – 5 suites.

Park Plaza 🅼, Königsbrückerstr. 121a, ✉ 01099, ℘ (0351) 8 06 30, ppdresden@
arkplazaww.com, Fax (0351) 8063721, beer garden, « 19 C dance hall », ⇔ – 🕴, ⇄ rm
🔟 📞 ⟷ – 🔬 330. 🆎 ⓔ 💳 💳 by Königsbrückerstraße BX
Meals à la carte 19/29 – ☑ 13 – **148 rm** 130 – 140.

Dorint 🅼, Grunaer Str. 14, ✉ 01069, ℘ (0351) 4 91 50, info.drshdd@dorint.com
Fax (0351) 4915100, ⇔, 🔲 – 🕴, ⇄ rm, 🔟 📞 ☑, ⟷ – 🔬 190. 🆎 ⓔ 💳 💳 JC
Meals à la carte 25/38,50 – ☑ 14 – **244 rm** 123/147 – 128/152. CYZ

Astron 🅼, Hansastr. 43, ✉ 01097, ℘ (0351) 8 42 40, dresden@astron-hotels.de
Fax (0351) 8424200, 🍽, 🛏, ⇔ – 🕴, ⇄ rm, 🔳 🔟 📞 ☑, ⟷ – 🔬 220. 🆎 ⓔ 💳
💳 JCB by Hansastraße BX
Meals à la carte 18,10/34,50 – ☑ 12 – **269 rm** 95 – 118.

🏨 **Holiday Inn** Ⓜ, Stauffenbergallee 25a, ✉ 01099, ℰ (0351) 8 15 10, info@holiday-i nn-dresden.de, Fax (0351) 8151333, ₁₆, ⇔, 🔲 – |≇|, ↔ rm, ■ rest, 🔟 ℃ & ℙ - 🏛 120. ℀ ⓪ ⓜ VISA JCB   by Königsbrücker Straße BX
Meals à la carte 23/30 – **120 rm** ⌷ 95/155 – 110/170.

🏨 **Elbflorenz** Ⓜ without rest, Rosenstr. 36, ✉ 01067, ℰ (0351) 8 64 00, info@hotel -elbflorenz.de, Fax (0351) 8640100, ⇔ – |≇| ↔ 🔟 ℃ ⇐ - 🏛 150. ℀ ⓪ ⓜ VISA JCB
227 rm ⌷ 105/125 – 125/146.   AZ v

🏨 **Comfort Hotel** Ⓜ without rest, Buchenstr. 10, ✉ 01097, ℰ (0351) 8 15 15 00, info @comfort-hotel-dresden.de, Fax (0351) 8151555, ⇔ – |≇| ↔ 🔟 ℃ & ⇐ ⇔ - 🏛 15. ℀ ⓪ ⓜ VISA JCB   by Königsbrücker Straße BX
76 rm ⌷ 75/115 – 85/130 – 8 Suites.

🏨 **Art'otel**, Ostra-Allee 33, ✉ 01067, ℰ (0351) 4 92 20, dresden@artotel.de, Fax (0351) 4922776, « Modern interior », ₁₆, ⇔ – |≇|, ↔ rm, ■ 🔟 ℃ & ⇐ - 🏛 250. ℀ ⓪ ⓜ VISA JCB   AY s
Meals à la carte 17/31,50 – ⌷ 15 – **174 rm** 145/185 – 155/185.

🏨 **Am Terrassenufer**, Terrassenufer 12, ✉ 01069, ℰ (0351) 4 40 95 00, hat@hotel-terrassenufer.de, Fax (0351) 4409600, 🔭 – |≇|, ↔ rm, 🔟 ℃ - 🏛 20. ℀ ⓪ ⓜ VISA JCB   CY a
Meals à la carte 14,20/23,70 – **196 rm** ⌷ 125 – 135 – 6 suites.

🏨 **Windsor** without rest, Roßmäßlerstr. 13, ✉ 01139, ℰ (0351) 8 49 01 41, info@hotel-windsor.de, Fax (0351) 8490144 – |≇| ↔ 🔟 ℀ ⓪ ⓜ VISA
25 rm ⌷ 55/65 – 75/90.   by Leipziger Straße AX

🏨 **Golden Tulip Transmar** Ⓜ, Bamberger Str. 14, ✉ 01187, ℰ (0351) 4 66 00, dres den@transmar-hotels.de, Fax (0351) 4660100, 🔭, ⇔ – |≇|, ↔ rm, ■ 🔟 ℃ & ⇐ - 🏛 35. ℀ ⓪ ⓜ VISA JCB. ℀ rest   by Budapester Straße AZ
Meals à la carte 19/29 – ⌷ 13 – **92 rm** 88/110 – 110/126.

🏨 **Mercure Newa**, St. Petersburger Str. 34, ✉ 01069, ℰ (0351) 4 81 41 09, h1577@a ccor-hotels.com, Fax (0351) 4955137, 🔭, ⇔ – |≇|, ↔ rm, ■ 🔟 ⇐ - 🏛 180. ℀ ⓪ ⓜ VISA JCB. ℀ rest   BZ n
Meals à la carte 16,50/28 – ⌷ 13 – **315 rm** 110 – 126.

🏨 **Mercure Albertbrücke** Ⓜ without rest, Melanchthonstr. 2, ✉ 01099, ℰ (0351) 8 06 10, h2824-gm@accor-hotels.com, Fax (0351) 8061444 – |≇| ↔, ■ rm, 🔟 ℃ & ⇐ - 🏛 25. ℀ ⓪ ⓜ VISA   CX a
⌷ 12 – **132 rm** ⌷ 82/100 – 102/107 – 6 suites.

🏨 **Martha Hospiz**, Nieritzstr. 11, ✉ 01097, ℰ (0351) 8 17 60, marthahospiz.dresden @t-online.de, Fax (0351) 8176222 – |≇| 🔟 ℃ & - 🏛 20. ℀ ⓜ VISA JCB. ℀ rm
closed 22 to 27 December – **Kartoffelkeller** (dinner only) **Meals** à la carte 13,50/21,50 – **50 rm** ⌷ 76/89 – 97/118.   BX s

🏨 **Achat** Ⓜ without rest, Budapester Str. 34, ✉ 01069, ℰ (0351) 47 38 00, dresden @achat-hotel.de, Fax (0351) 47380999 – |≇| ↔ 🔟 ℃ ⇐ - 🏛 20. ℀ ⓪ ⓜ VISA JCB
⌷ 11 – **118 rm** 74/129 – 84/139.   AZ e

🏨 **Novalis** Ⓜ, Bärnsdorfer Str. 185, ✉ 01127, ℰ (0351) 8 21 30, novalis.hotel@t-onlin e.de, Fax (0351) 8213180, ⇔ – |≇|, ↔ rm, 🔟 ℃ ℙ - 🏛 40. ℀ ⓪ ⓜ VISA
Meals (dinner only) (residents only) – **85 rm** ⌷ 69/82 – 76/100.by Hansastraße BX

🏨 **Wenotel** without rest, Messering 24, ✉ 01067, ℰ (0351) 4 97 60, info@wenotel.de, Fax (0351) 4976100 – |≇| ↔ 🔟 ℙ - 🏛 20. ℀ ⓪ ⓜ VISA
81 rm ⌷ 59/64 – 72/77.   by Pieschener Allee AX

✕✕ **Italienisches Dörfchen**, Theaterplatz 3, ✉ 01067, ℰ (0351) 49 81 60, gastro.the aterplatz@t-online.de, Fax (0351) 4981688, beer garden, « Terrace with ≤ » - ℀ ⓪ ⓜ VISA   BY n
Bellotto (Italian) **Meals** à la carte 18,15/34,77 – **Weinzimmer** : **Meals** à la carte 16,60/35,28 – **Kurfürstenzimmer** : **Meals** à la carte 16,10/34,26.

✕✕ **Drachen**, Bautzner Str. 72, ✉ 01099, ℰ (0351) 8 04 11 88, info@drachen-dresden.de, Fax (0351) 8036855, 🔭, beer garden – ℙ. ⓪ ⓜ VISA   DX a
closed January – **Meals** 25,05 and à la carte 27/42.

✕✕ **Coselpalais**, An der Frauenkirche 12a, ✉ 01067, ℰ (0351) 4 96 24 44, Fax (0351) 4962445, 🔭 – ↔. ℀ ⓪ ⓜ VISA JCB   BY b
Meals à la carte 17,90/29.

✕✕ **Opernrestaurant**, Theaterplatz 2 (1st floor), ✉ 01067, ℰ (0351) 4 91 15 21, gast ro.theaterplatz@t-online.de, Fax (0351) 4956097 – ℀ ⓪ ⓜ VISA JCB   AY r
closed 15 July - 4 August – **Meals** (weekdays dinner only) à la carte 21/29.

✕✕ **Am Glacis**, Glacisstr. 8, ✉ 01099, ℰ (0351) 8 03 60 33, restaurant@am-glacis.de, Fax (0351) 8036034, 🔭 – ℀ ⓪ ⓜ VISA JCB   CX a
closed Saturday lunch, Sunday and Bank Holidays – **Meals** à la carte 19/45.

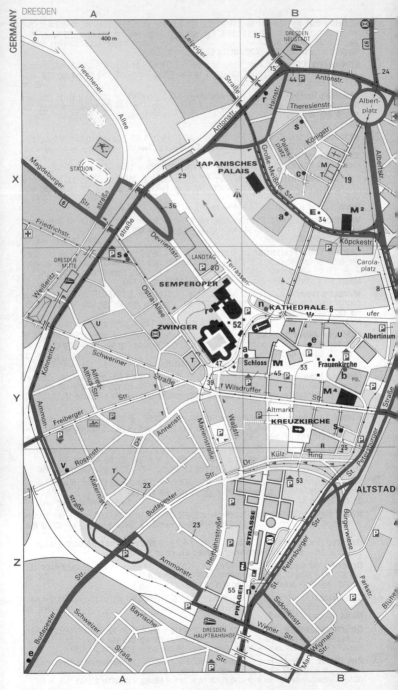

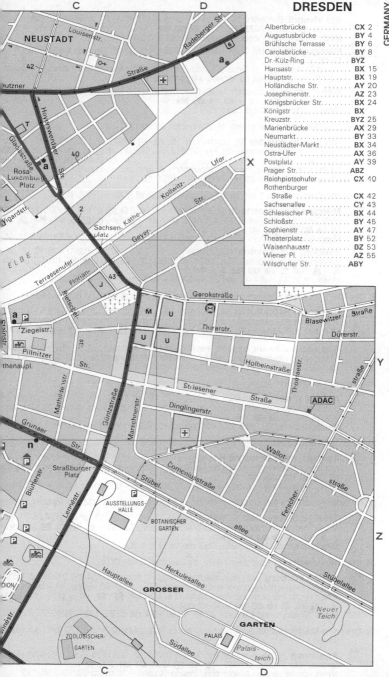

DRESDEN

✗ **Ars Vivendi**, Bürgerstr. 14, ⊠ 01127, ✆ (0351) 8 40 09 69, *arsvivendi-dresden@t-o
nline.de, Fax (0351) 8473473*, 🍴 – AE **MO** *VISA*   by Leipziger Straße   AX
Meals *(dinner only) (booking essential)* 23/45 and à la carte.

✗ **Fischgalerie**, Maxstr. 2, ⊠ 01067, ✆ (0351) 4 90 35 06, *Fax (0351) 4903508*, 🍴 –
AE **MO** *VISA*   AY s
closed 22 December - 5 January, Sunday, lunch Saturday and Monday – Meals *(fish dishes
only) (booking essential for dinner)* à la carte 25/37.

✗ **Alte Meister**, Theaterplatz 1a, ⊠ 01067, ✆ (0351) 4 81 04 26, *info@altemeister.net,
Fax (0351) 4810479*, 🍴 – AE ① **MO** *VISA*. ✀   AY e
Meals 17 *(lunch)* and à la carte 23/37.

at Dresden-Blasewitz *East : 5 km, by Blasewitzer Straße* DY :

🏨 **Am Blauen Wunder** M, Loschwitzer Str. 48, ⊠ 01309, ✆ (0351) 3 36 60, *dresde
n@hotel-am-blauen-wunder.de, Fax (0351) 3366299*, 🍴 – ⊜ 📺 ✆ ⇦ – 🏛 35. AE **MO**
VISA ᴊᴄʙ   by Blasewitzer Straße   DY
La Strada *(Italian) (closed 22 December - 6 June and Sunday) (dinner only)* Meals
à la carte 22,50/34 – **39 rm** ⊑ 88/95 – 105/115.

at Dresden-Cotta *West : 5 km, by Magdeburger Straße (B 6)* AX :

🏨 **Mercure Elbpromenade** M, Hamburger Str. 64 (B 6), ⊠ 01157, ✆ (0351) 4 25 20,
h0479@t-online.de, Fax (0351) 4252420, 🍴, ⊜ – ⊜, ⊁ rm, 📺 ⅋ ⇦ 🅿 – 🏛 60.
AE ① **MO** *VISA* ᴊᴄʙ. ✀ rest
Meals *(closed Saturday - Sunday)* à la carte 19,50/33 – ⊑ 13 – **103 rm** 57/85 – 72/95.

🏨 **Residenz Alt Dresden**, Mobschatzer Str. 29, ⊠ 01157, ✆ (0351) 4 28 10, *residen
zaltdresden@ringhotels.de, Fax (0351) 4281988*, 🍴, 🛁, ⊜ – ⊜, ⊁ rm, 📺 ⅋ ⇦
🅿 – 🏛 100. AE ① **MO** *VISA* ᴊᴄʙ. ✀ rest
Meals 19,50/43 and à la carte 25,50/34,25 – **124 rm** ⊑ 90/97 – 95/112.

In Dresden-Kemnitz *Northwest : 6 km, by Magdeburger Straße* AX *and Bremer Straße* :

🏨🏨 **Romantik Hotel Pattis** M, Merbitzer Str. 53, ⊠ 01157, ✆ (0351) 4 25 50, *pattis
@romantik.de, Fax (0351) 4255255*, 🍴, « Health, fitness and beauty centre ;
small park », Massage, ⊜, ⌖ – ⊜, ⊁ rm, ☰ rest, 📺 ⅋ ⇦ 🅿 – 🏛 80. AE ①
MO *VISA*
Gourmet-Restaurant *(closed 2 weeks January, 2 weeks August, Sunday and Monday,
(dinner only)* Meals à la carte 45/62 – **Vitalis :** Meals à la carte 24,83/34,50 – **47 rm**
⊑ 110/160 – 160/190 – 6 suites.

at Dresden-Klotzsche *Northeast : 9 km, by Königsbrücker Straße* BX :

🏨 **Airport Hotel** M, Karl-Marx-Str. 25, ⊠ 01109, ✆ (0351) 8 83 30, *bestwestern@air
porthoteldresden.com, Fax (0351) 8833333*, 🍴, ⊜ – ⊜, ⊁ rm, ☰ rest, 📺 ⅋ ⇦ ⇦
🅿 – 🏛 50. AE ① **MO** *VISA* ᴊᴄʙ
Meals à la carte 18,60/28,60 – **100 rm** ⊑ 95/105 – 111/125 – 7 suites.

at Dresden-Laubegast *East : 9 km by Striesener Straße* DY :

🏨 **Ramada-Treff Resident Hotel** M, Brünner Str. 11, ⊠ 01279, ✆ (0351) 2 56 20,
resident.dresden@treff-hotels.de, Fax (0351) 2562800 – ⊜, ⊁ rm, 📺 ⅋ ⇦ 🅿 – 🏛 45.
AE ① **MO** *VISA* ᴊᴄʙ. ✀ rest
Meals *(weekdays dinner only)* à la carte 17,39/26,59 – **122 rm** ⊑ 62/77 – 87/122.

at Dresden-Leubnitz-Neuostra *Southeast : 5,5 km, by Parkstraße* BCZ *and Teplitzer Straße*

🏨🏨 **Treff Hotel Dresden** M, Wilhelm-Franke-Str. 90, ⊠ 01219, ✆ (0351) 4 78 20, *info
@treff-hotels-dresden.de, Fax (0351) 4782550*, 🍴, 🛁, ⊜ – ⊜, ⊁ rm, 📺 ⅋ ⇦ 🅿
– 🏛 370. AE ① **MO** *VISA* ᴊᴄʙ
Meals à la carte 20,96/28,89 – **262 rm** ⊑ 89 – 118.

at Dresden-Loschwitz *Northeast : 6 km, by Bautzner Straße* CDX :

🏨🏨 **Schloß Eckberg** (with separate hotel wing), Bautzner Str. 134, ⊠ 01099, ✆ (0351)
8 09 90, *email@hotel-schloss-eckberg.de, Fax (0351) 8099199*, ≤ Dresden and Elbe, 🍴,
« Neo Gothic mansion ; extensive parkland », Massage, 🛁, ⊜, ⌖ – ⊜, ⊁ rm, 📺 ⅋
🅿 – 🏛 70. AE ① **MO** *VISA* ᴊᴄʙ. ✀ rest
Meals 20 *(lunch)* and à la carte 27,20/45,50 – **84 rm** ⊑ 85/180 – 135/235.

at Dresden-Niedersedlitz *Southeast : 10 km by Parkstraße* BZ *and B 172, off Lockwitzta
straße* :

🏨 **Ambiente** ⌂, Meusegaster Str. 23, ⊠ 01259, ✆ (0351) 20 78 80, *info@hotel-amb
iente.de, Fax (0351) 2078836* – ⊜ ⊁ 📺 ⅋ 🅿. **MO** *VISA* ᴊᴄʙ. ✀ rest
Meals *(closed Sunday) (dinner only) (residents only)* – **20 rm** ⊑ 70/98 – 90/125.

at Dresden-Strehlen *South : 4 km, by Parkstraße CZ and B 172, off Casper-David-Friedrich-Straße :*

Four Points Hotel Königshof M, Kreischaer Str. 2, ✉ 01219, ℘ (0351) 8 73 10, *fourpointshotelkoenigshof@arabellasheraton.com, Fax (0351) 8731499* – |♦|, ⇔ rm, TV ☎ ♿ 🚗 – 🏔 180. AE ⊙ MC VISA JCB
Meals à la carte 15,34/30,17 – ☕ 11 – **94 rm** 103/177 – 123/177 – 10 suites.

at Dresden-Weißer Hirsch *Northeast : 8 km, by Bautzner Straße CDX :*

Villa Emma 🐚, Stechgrundstr.2, ✉ 01324, ℘ (0351) 26 48 10, *info@hotel-villaemma.de, Fax (0351) 2648118,* 🏠, « Restored Art Deco villa », ≘s – ⇔ rm, TV P. AE ⊙ MC VISA
Meals *(dinner only)* (booking essential) à la carte 26,85/31,96 – **21 rm** ☕ 80/123 – 159/185.

DÜSSELDORF

L *Nordrhein-Westfalen* 417 *M 4 – pop. 570 000 – alt. 40 m.*

See : *Königsallee★* EZ – *Hofgarten★* DEY *and Schloß Jägerhof (Goethemuseum★* EY **M1**) – *Hetjensmuseum★* DZ **M4** – *Museum of Art (Kunstmuseum)★* DY **M2** – *Collection of Art (Kunstsammlung NRW)★* DY **M3** – *Löbbecke-Museum and Aquazoo★ by Kaiserswerther Straße* AU.

Envir. : *Chateau of Benrath (Schloß Benrath) (Park★) South : 10 km by Siegburger Straße* CX.

⛳9 *Düsseldorf-Grafebberg, Rennbahnstr. 24,* ℘ *(0211) 96 49 50 ,* ⛳18 *Gut Rommeljans (North-East : 12 km),* ℘ *(02102) 8 10 92 ;* ⛳18 *Düsseldorf-Hubbelrath (East : 12 km),* ℘ *(02104) 7 21 78 ;* ⛳9 *Düsseldorf-Hafen, Auf der Lausward,* ℘ *(0211) 39 66 17.*

✈ *Düsseldorf-Lohausen (North : 8 km),* ℘ *(0211) 42 10.*

🚗 *Hauptbahnhof.*

Exhibition Centre (Messegelände), ℘ *(0211) 45 60 01, Fax (0211) 4560668.*

ℹ *Tourist office, Immermannstr. 65b,* ✉ *40210,* ℘ *(0211) 17 20 20, Fax (0211) 161071.*

ADAC, *Himmelgeister Str. 63.*

Berlin 552 – Amsterdam 225 – Essen 31 – Köln 40 – Rotterdam 237.

Plans on following pages

Steigenberger Parkhotel, Corneliusplatz 1, ✉ 40213, ℘ (0211) 1 38 10, *duesseldorf@steigenberger.de, Fax (0211) 1381592,* 🏠 – |♦|, ⇔ rm, ▤ TV ☎ P – 🏔 110. AE ⊙ MC VISA JCB. ✂ rest — EY p
Menuett : **Meals** à la carte 30,50/46 – **133 rm** ☕ 195/320 – 260/380 – 9 suites.

Nikko, Immermannstr. 41, ✉ 40210, ℘ (0211) 83 40, *sales@nikko-hotel.de, Fax (0211) 161216,* ≘s, 🏊 – |♦|, ⇔ rm, ▤ TV ☎ ♿ – 🏔 300. AE ⊙ MC VISA JCB
Benkay (Japanese) **Meals** à la carte 33,23/63,91 – ***Brasserie Nikkolette*** : **Meals** à la carte 23,40/43,50 – ☕ 17 – **301 rm** 185/265 – 216/286 – 6 suites. — BV g

Queens, Ludwig-Erhard-Allee 3, ✉ 40227, ℘ (0211) 7 77 10, *reservation.qduesseldorf@queensgruppe.de, Fax (0211) 7771777,* ≘s – |♦|, ⇔ rm, ▤ TV ☎ ♿ 🚗 – 🏔 50. AE ⊙ MC VISA — BV s
closed 20 December - 5 January – **Meals** à la carte 21,30/35,90 – ☕ 17 – **134 rm** 154/278 – 179/304 – 5 suites.

Holiday Inn, Graf-Adolf-Platz 10, ✉ 40213, ℘ (0211) 3 84 80, *reservation.hiduesseldorf@queensgruppe.de, Fax (0211) 3848390,* ≘s, 🏊 – |♦|, ⇔ rm, ▤ rm, TV ☎ 🚗 – 🏔 140. AE ⊙ MC VISA JCB — EZ t
Meals à la carte 25,83/38,86 – ☕ 18 – **253 rm** 182 – 213 – 4 suites.

Majestic, Cantadorstr. 4, ✉ 40211, ℘ (0211) 36 70 30, *info@hotelmajestic.de, Fax (0211) 3670399,* ≘s – |♦|, ⇔ rm, TV ☎ – 🏔 30. AE ⊙ MC VISA JCB. ✂ — BV a
closed 23 December - 2 January – ***l'Emporio*** (Italian) *(closed Saturday lunch, Sunday and Bank Holidays, except exhibitions)* **Meals** à la carte 23/34 – ☕ 13 – **52 rm** 139/157

Günnewig Hotel Esplanade without rest, Fürstenplatz 17, ✉ 40215, ℘ (0211) 38 68 50, *hotel-esplanade@guennewig.de, Fax (0211) 38685555,* ≘s, 🏊 – |♦| ⇔ TV ☎ 🚗 – 🏔 45. AE ⊙ MC VISA JCB — BX s
80 rm ☕ 89/105 – 116/142.

Madison I without rest, Graf-Adolf-Str. 94, ✉ 40210, ℘ (0211) 1 68 50, *reservierung@madisson1.de, Fax (0211) 1685328,* 🏋, ≘s, 🏊 – |♦| ⇔ TV 🚗 – 🏔 40. AE ⊙ MC VISA — BV n
100 rm ☕ 90/135 – 110/150.

Günnewig Hotel Uebachs without rest, Leopoldstr. 5, ✉ 40211, ℘ (0211) 17 37 10, *hotel.uebachs@guennewig.de, Fax (0211) 17371555* – |♦| ⇔ TV ☎ 🚗 – 🏔 30. AE ⊙ MC VISA JCB — BV r
82 rm ☕ 89/105 – 116/142.

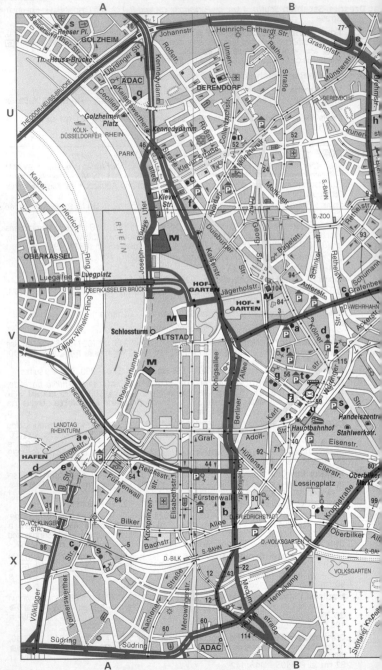

STREET INDEX

DÜSSELDORF

MÖRSENBROICH

GRAFENBERG

FLINGERN

D.-FLINGERN

LIERENFELD

DÜSSELDORF

🏨 **Dorint**, Stresemannplatz 1, ✉ 40210, ℰ (0211) 3 55 40, *info.dusgra@dorint.com*, Fax (0211) 354120 – 🛗, ✻ rm, 🗏 rm, 📺 🕿 – 🛦 50. 🅰🅴 ① 🐵 🚾 🍱 ⅍ rest
Meals *(closed Sunday) (dinner only)* à la carte 24,54/40 – ⌁ 15 – **162 rm** 93/212 – 156/242 – 3 suites.   EZ j

🏨 **Madison II** without rest, Graf-Adolf-Str. 47, ✉ 40210, ℰ (0211) 38 80 30, Fax (0211) 3880388 – 🛗 📺 🅰🅴 ① 🐵 🚾 🍱
closed 20 December - 3 January and July – **24 rm** ⌁ 90/115 – 115/140.   EZ a

🏨 **Burns Art Hotel** 🅼, Bahnstr. 76, ✉ 40210, ℰ (0211) 7 79 29 10, *info@hotel-burns.de, Fax (0211) 77929177*, « Modern interior » – 🛗 ✻ 📺 🕿 🚗. 🅰🅴 ① 🐵
🚾 🍱   EZ e
Silai Thai (Thai) **Meals** à la carte 23/41,50 – **35 rm** ⌁ 125/255 – 145/285 – 4 suites.

🏨 **Rema-Hotel Concorde** without rest, Graf-Adolf-Str. 60, ✉ 40210, ℰ (0211) 36 98 25, *concorde@remahotel.de, Fax (0211) 354604* – 🛗 ✻ 📺 🕿. 🅰🅴 ① 🐵 🚾 🍱
84 rm ⌁ 89/170 – 125/220.   EZ f

🏨 **Carat Hotel** without rest, Benrather Str. 7a, ✉ 40213, ℰ (0211) 1 30 50, *info-d@carat-hotel.de, Fax (0211) 322214*, 🕿 – 🛗 ✻, 🗏 rm, 📺 – 🛦 20. 🅰🅴 ① 🐵 🚾
73 rm ⌁ 122/132 – 147/152.   DZ r

🏨 **Amber** without rest, Corneliusstr. 82, ✉ 40215, ℰ (0211) 38 65 60, *duesseldorf@amber-hotels.de, Fax (0211) 382050* – 🛗 ✻ 📺 🕿 🄿 – 🛦 25. 🅰🅴 ① 🐵 🚾 🍱
52 rm ⌁ 80/100 – 100/110.   BX s

🏨 **Asahi** 🅼 without rest, Kurfürstenstr. 30, ✉ 40211, ℰ (0211) 3 61 20, *hotel.asahi@akzent.de, Fax (0211) 3612345* – 🛗 ✻ 📺 🕿 🕹 🚗. 🅰🅴 ① 🐵 🚾 🍱   BV t
53 rm ⌁ 123/130 – 141.

🏨 **Astoria** without rest, Jahnstr. 72, ✉ 40215, ℰ (0211) 38 51 30, *hotelastoriadus@t-online.de, Fax (0211) 372089* – 🛗 ✻ 📺 🕿 🄿 🅰🅴 ① 🐵 🚾 🍱 ⅍ BX b
closed 22 December - 8 January – **26 rm** ⌁ 83/128 – 102/208 – 4 suites.

🏨 **Windsor** without rest, Grafenberger Allee 36, ✉ 40237, ℰ (0211) 91 46 80, *d.kiermeier@t-online.de, Fax (0211) 9146840*, 🕿 – 📺 🚗. 🅰🅴 ① 🐵 🚾   BV c
18 rm ⌁ 98/115 – 130/248.

🏨 **Orangerie** 🅼 ☞ without rest, Bäckergasse 1, ✉ 40213, ℰ (0211) 86 68 00, *hotel orangerie@t-online.de, Fax (0211) 8668099* – 🛗 ✻ 📺 🕿 – 🛦 30. 🅰🅴 ① 🐵 🚾 ⅍
27 rm ⌁ 100/150 – 126/180.   DZ n

🏨 **An der Kö** without rest, Talstr. 9, ✉ 40217, ℰ (0211) 37 10 48, *hotelanderkoe@t-online.de, Fax (0211) 370835* – 🛗 📺 🄿 🅰🅴 🐵 🚾 🍱
closed Christmas - early January – **45 rm** ⌁ 88 – 124.   EZ n

🏨 **Residenz** without rest, Worringer Str. 88, ✉ 40211, ℰ (0211) 5 50 48 80, *info@residenzhotelduesseldorf.de, Fax (0211) 55048877* – 🛗 ✻ 📺. 🅰🅴 🐵 🚾 🍱 BV z
34 rm ⌁ 81/94 – 97/102.

XXX **Victorian**, Königstr. 3a (1st floor), ✉ 40212, ℰ (0211) 8 65 50 22, Fax (0211) 8655013
– 🗏. 🅰🅴 ① 🐵 🚾 🍱. ⅍   EZ c
closed Sunday and Bank Holidays – **Meals** *(booking essential) (outstanding wine list)* 28 *(lunch)* and à la carte 54/68 – **Bistro im Victorian** : **Meals** à la carte 20,50/30,70.

XX **Weinhaus Tante Anna**, Andreasstr. 2, ✉ 40213, ℰ (0211) 13 11 63, *info@tanteanna.de, Fax (0211) 132974*, (former 16C private chapel), « Antique pictures and furniture » – 🅰🅴 ① 🐵 🚾 🍱   DY c
closed Sunday, except exhibitions – **Meals** *(dinner only) (booking essential) (outstanding wine list)* à la carte 30/44 *(vegetarian menu available).*

XX **La Terrazza**, Königsallee 30 (Kö-Centre, 2nd floor), ✉ 40212, ℰ (0211) 32 75 40, Fax (0211) 320975 – 🛗 🗏. 🅰🅴 ① 🐵 🚾 🍱   EZ v
closed Sunday and Bank Holidays, except exhibitions – **Meals** *(booking essential)* à la carte 37/54.

X **La Lampada**, Hüttenstr. 9, ✉ 40215, ℰ (0211) 37 47 92, *lalampada@lalampada.de, Fax (0211) 377799*, 🗏 – 🅰🅴 ① 🐵 🚾   EZ a
closed Saturday lunch and Sunday – **Meals** à la carte 24/38.

X **Käfer**, Königsallee 60a (Kö-Galerie), ✉ 40212, ℰ (0211) 8 66 26 18, Fax (0211) 8662661, 🍴 – 🗏 – 🛦 40. 🅰🅴 ① 🐵 🚾   EZ z
closed Sunday dinner – **Meals** à la carte 22,50/37,80.

X **Nippon Kan**, Immermannstr. 35, ✉ 40210, ℰ (0211) 1 73 47 10, Fax (0211) 3613625
– 🅰🅴 ① 🐵 🚾 🍱. ⅍   BV g
closed Christmas to New Year – **Meals** *(Japanese) (booking essential)* 40,90/92,03 and à la carte 21,48/47,04.

X **Daitokai**, Mutter-Ey-Str. 1, ✉ 40213, ℰ (0211) 32 50 54, *dus@daitokai.de, Fax (0211) 325056* – 🗏. 🅰🅴 ① 🐵 🚾 🍱. ⅍   DY z
closed 2 weeks July – **Meals** *(dinner only) (Japanese)* à la carte 27,10/55,22.

Brewery-inns :

 ✗ **Zum Schiffchen**, Hafenstr. 5, ⊠ 40213, ℘ (0211) 13 24 21, *schiffchen.stockheim
@t-online.de, Fax (0211) 134596,* ♔ – 🆎 ⓞ 🆎 *VISA*   DZ f
closed 23 December - 2 January, Sunday and Bank Holidays, except exhibitions – **Meals**
à la carte 18,40/36.

at Düsseldorf-Angermund *North : 15 km by Danziger Straße* AU :

 🏨 **Haus Litzbrück**, Bahnhofstr. 33, ⊠ 40489, ℘ (0203) 99 79 60, *hotellitzbrueck@ao
l.com, Fax (0203) 9979653,* « Garden terrace », ⇖s, 🔲, 🌳 – 📺 ⇔ 🅿 – 🔬 30. 🆎
ⓞ 🆎 *VISA* 🎴
Meals *(closed Monday)* à la carte 21,75/40 – **22 rm** ⊇ 89/109 – 148/160.

at Düsseldorf-Derendorf :

 🏨 **Villa Viktoria** without rest, Blumenthalstr. 12, ⊠ 40476, ℘ (0211) 46 90 00, *villa.vi
ktoria@t-online.de, Fax (0211) 46900601,* « Elegant modern installation », ⇖s, 🌳 – 📳
⇔ 📺 🍴 ⇔ – 🔬 15. 🆎 ⓞ 🆎 *VISA*   BU c
closed 20 December - 1 January – ⊇ 16 – **40 suites** 151/266

 🏨 **Lindner Hotel Rhein Residence** Ⓜ, Kaiserswerther Str. 20, ⊠ 40477, ℘ (0211)
4 99 90, *info.rheinresidence@lindner.de, Fax (0211) 4999499,* ♔, Massage, ₤6, ⇖s – 📳
⇔ rm, 📺 🍴 – 🔬 20. 🆎 ⓞ 🆎 *VISA* 🎴   ABU f
Meals à la carte 25/34,70 – ⊇ 15 – **126 rm** 100/180 – 125/205.

 🏨 **Gildors Hotel** without rest (with guest house), Collenbachstr. 51, ⊠ 40476, ℘ (0211)
5 15 85 00, *mail@gildors-hotel.de, Fax (0211) 51585050 –* 📳 ⇔ 📺 ⇔. 🆎 ⓞ
🆎 *VISA*   BU n
50 rm ⊇ 90/150 – 155/180.

 🏨 **Cascade** without rest, Kaiserswerther Str. 59, ⊠ 40477, ℘ (0211) 49 22 00,
info@hotel-cascade.de, Fax (0211) 4922022 – 📳 ⇔ 📺 🍴 ⇔. 🆎 🆎 *VISA*
🎴. 🎴   AU c
closed Christmas - early January – **29 rm** ⊇ 78/85 – 94/110.

at Düsseldorf-Düsseltal :

 🏨 **Haus am Zoo** ⇗ without rest (with guest house), Sybelstr. 21, ⊠ 40239, ℘ (0211)
6 16 96 10, *hotel_haus_am_zoo@t-online.de, Fax (0211) 61696169,* « Garden », ⇖s.
🔲 (heated) – 📳 📺 ⇔. 🆎 🆎 *VISA*   BU h
23 rm ⊇ 97/108 – 128.

at Düsseldorf-Golzheim :

 🏨 **Radisson SAS Hotel**, Karl-Arnold-Platz 5, ⊠ 40474, ℘ (0211) 4 55 30, *reservation
.duesseldorf@radissonsas.com, Fax (0211) 4553110,* ♔, Massage, ₤6, ⇖s, 🔲, 🌳 – 📳
⇔ rm, 🍽 📺 🍴 ⇔ 🅿 – 🔬 450. 🆎 ⓞ 🆎 *VISA* 🎴. 🎴 rest   AU o
Meals à la carte 25,50/49,50 – ⊇ 17 – **309 rm** 169/202 – 169/228 –
16 suites.

 🏨 **Hilton**, Georg-Glock-Str. 20, ⊠ 40474, ℘ (0211) 4 37 70, *sales_duesseldorf@hilton.c
om, Fax (0211) 4377650,* ♔, Massage, ⇖s, 🔲, 🌳 – 📳, ⇔ rm, 🍽 📺 🍴 ₺, ⇔ 🅿
– 🔬 800. 🆎 ⓞ 🆎 *VISA* 🎴. 🎴 rest   AU ■
Meals à la carte 24,50/34,50 – ⊇ 20 – **372 rm** 190/250 – 205/265 – 9 suites.

 ✗✗✗ **Rosati**, Felix-Klein-Str. 1, ⊠ 40474, ℘ (0211) 4 36 05 03, *Fax (0211) 452963,* ♔ – 🅿.
🆎 ⓞ 🆎 *VISA* 🎴. 🎴   AU s
closed Saturday lunch and Sunday, except exhibitions – **Meals** *(Italian)* (booking essential)
à la carte 33/44.

at Düsseldorf-Kaiserswerth *North : 10 km, by Kaiserswerther Straße* AU :

 ✗✗✗✗ **Im Schiffchen** (Bourgueil), Kaiserswerther Markt 9, ⊠ 40489, ℘ (0211) 40 10 50
❀❀❀ *restaurant.imschiffchen@t-online.de, Fax (0211) 403667 –* 🆎. 🎴
closed 3 weeks July, Sunday and Monday – **Meals** *(dinner only)* (booking essential) à la carte
59/83
Spec. Leichte Stör-Velouté mit Koriander. Bastilla von der Gauthier-Taube. Bitter
Moon.

at Düsseldorf-Lörick *West : 6 km, by Luegallee* AV *and Arnulfstraße :*

 🏨 **Fischerhaus** ⇗, Bonifatiusstr. 35, ⊠ 40547, ℘ (0211) 59 79 79, *fischerhaus@ao
com, Fax (0211) 5979759 –* ⇔ rm, 📺 🍴 🅿. 🆎 ⓞ 🆎 *VISA*
closed 23 December - 2 January – **Meals** see *Hummerstübchen* below – ⊇ 8 – **40 rm**
87/138 – 101/179.

DÜSSELDORF

GERMANY

XXX **Hummerstübchen** (Nöthel) - Hotel Fischerhaus, Bonifatiusstr. 35, ⊠ 40547, 𝒫 (0211)
ॐॐ 59 44 02, *fischerhaus@aol.com*, Fax (0211) 5979759 – 🅿. 🆎 ⓪ ⑩ 🆅🆂🅰
closed 27 December - 4 January and Sunday, except exhibitions – **Meals** *(dinner only)*
(booking essential) 91,52/104,82 and à la carte 56,24/68,51
Spec. Hummer-Menu. Hummersuppe mit Champagner. Gebratener Steinbutt mit Zitro-
nengrassauce und marinierten Glasnudeln.

at Düsseldorf-Lohausen *North : 8 km, by Danziger Straße* AU :

🏨 **ArabellaSheraton Airport Hotel**, at the airport, ⊠ 40474, 𝒫 (0211) 4 17 30, *airp
ort.duesseldorf@arabellasheraton.com*, Fax (0211) 4173707 – |自|, 🛌× rm, 📺 ✦ ὲ –
🔬 120. 🆎 ⓪ ⑩ 🆅🆂🅰 🃏. ⋇ rest
Meals à la carte 30/46 – ⏛ 17 – **200 rm** 177/263 – 212/291.

at Düsseldorf-Mörsenbroich :

🏨 **Renaissance**, Nördlicher Zubringer 6, ⊠ 40470, 𝒫 (0211) 6 21 60, *rhi.dusrn.dos@r
enaissancehotels.com*, Fax (0211) 6216666, 🍽, Massage, ≘s, ⊠ – |自|, 🛌× rm, ▤ 📺
✦ ⟵ – 🔬 260. 🆎 ⓪ ⑩ 🆅🆂🅰 🃏   BU e
Meals à la carte 24/44 – ⏛ 17 – **244 rm** 149/164 – 3 suites.

at Düsseldorf-Oberbilk :

🏨 **Astron** 🅼, Kölner Str. 186, ⊠ 40227, 𝒫 (0211) 7 81 10, *duesseldorf@astron-hotels.de*,
Fax (0211) 7811800, 🏋, ≘s – |自|, 🛌× rm, ▤ 📺 ✦ ὲ ⟵ – 🔬 90. 🆎 ⓪ ⑩ 🆅🆂🅰 🃏
⋇ rest   BV b
Meals à la carte 19,50/27,50 – **338 rm** ⏛ 138/298 – 141/311.

at Düsseldorf-Oberkassel *West : 5 km, by Luegallee* AV :

🏨 **Lindner Congress Hotel**, Emanuel-Leutze-Str. 17, ⊠ 40547, 𝒫 (0211) 5 99 70, *info
.congresshotel@lindner.de*, Fax (0211) 59971111, ≘s, ⊠ – |自|, 🛌× rm, ▤ 📺 ✦ ⟵
🅿 – 🔬 240. 🆎 ⓪ ⑩ 🆅🆂🅰 🃏. ⋇ rest
Meals 22 *(buffet lunch)* and à la carte 23,50/37,50 – ⏛ 15 – **254 rm** 130/150 –
140/170.

🏨 **Courtyard by Marriott**, Am Seestern 16, ⊠ 40547, 𝒫 (0211) 59 59 59, *cy.duscy
.dos@marriott.com*, Fax (0211) 593569, ≘s, ⊠ – |自|, 🛌× rm, ▤ 📺 ✦ 🅿 – 🔬 120. 🆎
⓪ ⑩ 🆅🆂🅰 🃏
Meals à la carte 18,90/36,80 – **217 rm** ⏛ 110/120

🏨 **Mercure** 🅼, Fritz-Vomfelde-Str.38, ⊠ 40547, 𝒫 (0221) 53 07 60, *h2199@accor-ho
tels.com*, Fax (0221) 53076444, 🍽, 🏋, ≘s – |自| 🛌× rm ▤ 📺 ✦ ὲ ⟵ – 🔬 120. 🆎 ⓪
⑩ 🆅🆂🅰
Meals *(Italian)* à la carte 24,54/36,55 – **160 rm** ⏛ 128/133 – 153/163.

🏨 **Inn Side Residence** 🅼, Niederkasseler Lohweg 18a, ⊠ 40547, 𝒫 (0211) 52 29 90,
duesseldorf@innside.de, Fax (0211) 52299522, 🍽, « Modern hotel », 🏋, ≘s – |自|,
🛌× rm, ▤ rm, 📺 ✦ ⟵ 🅿. 🆎 ⓪ ⑩ 🆅🆂🅰
Meals *(closed Sunday)* à la carte 21/36 – **126 rm** ⏛ 142/232 – 177/267 – 6 suites.

🏨 **Hanseat** without rest, Belsenstr. 6, ⊠ 40545, 𝒫 (0211) 57 50 69, Fax (0211) 589662,
« Elegant installation » ▤. 🆎 ⓪ ⑩ 🆅🆂🅰
closed Christmas to New Year – **37 rm** ⏛ 95/100 – 130.

XXX **De' Medici**, Amboßstr. 3, ⊠ 40547, 𝒫 (0211) 59 41 51, Fax (0211) 592612 – 🆎 ⓪
⑩ 🆅🆂🅰
closed Saturday lunch, Sunday and Bank Holidays, except exhibitions – **Meals** *(Italian)*
(booking essential) à la carte 27/43.

at Düsseldorf-Pempelfort :

XXX **Rossini**, Kaiserstr. 5, ⊠ 40479, 𝒫 (0211) 49 49 94, *info@restaurant-rossini.de*,
Fax (0211) 4910819, 🍽 – 🆎 ⓪ ⑩ 🆅🆂🅰 🃏. ⋇   EY r
closed Sunday and Bank Holidays, except exhibitions – **Meals** à la carte 43/57.

at Düsseldorf-Unterbilk :

🏨 **Sorat** 🅼, Volmerswerther Str. 35, ⊠ 40221, 𝒫 (0211) 3 02 20, *duesseldorf@sorat-h
otels.com*, Fax (0211) 3022555, ≘s – |自|, 🛌× rm, ▤ 📺 ✦ ⟵ – 🔬 150. 🆎 ⓪
⑩ 🆅🆂🅰   AX c
Meals *(closed Sunday, except exhibitions)* à la carte 24,50/33,50 – **160 rm** ⏛ 115/245
– 165/315.

XXX **Savini**, Stromstr. 47, ⊠ 40221, 𝒫 (0211) 39 39 31, *carlosavini@aol.com*,
Fax (0211) 391719, 🍽 – 🆎 ⑩ 🆅🆂🅰   AX e
closed Sunday, except exhibitions – **Meals** *(booking essential) (outstanding wine list)* à la
carte 40/59.

GERMANY

DÜSSELDORF

XX **Berens am Kai**, Kaistr. 16, ✉ 40221, ✆ (0211) 3 00 67 50, *info@berensamkai.de*, *Fax (0211) 30067515*, 🌫 – 🝳 🟠 🟢 🟦 AX d
closed 1 to 7 January, Saturday lunch and Sunday – **Meals** à la carte 55/66.

XX **Schorn** with rm, Martinstr. 46a, ✉ 40223, ✆ (0211) 3 98 19 72, *Fax (0211) 3981972* – 🝳 ✪ 🌫 rm AX s
closed 1 week Easter and 3 weeks July - August – **Meals** *(closed Sunday and Monday)* *(dinner only)* (booking essential, outstanding wine list) à la carte 33/47 – **4 rm** ☲ 76/105 – 150/185.

XX **Rheinturm Top 180**, Stromstr. 20, ✉ 40221, ✆ (0211) 8 48 58, *rheinturm@gue nnewig.de*, *Fax (0211) 325619*, « Revolving restaurant at 172 m ; 🔆 Düsseldorf and Rhein » (🛗, charge) – 🍴 – 🝳 40. 🝳 🟠 🟢 🟦 🟦 🌫 AV a
Meals à la carte 31,45/47,75.

X **Brunello**, Brückenstr. 12, ✉ 40221, ✆ (0211) 3 08 31 31 – 🝳 🟠 🟢 🟦 AX b
closed Saturday and Sunday dinner – **Meals** à la carte 35/38,60.

at Düsseldorf-Unterrath North : 7 km, by Ulmenstraße BU :

🏨 **Lindner Hotel Airport** 🝳, Unterrather Str. 108, ✉ 40468, ✆ (0211) 9 51 60, *info .airport@lindner.de*, *Fax (0211) 9516516*, 🗠, 🍸 – 🛗, 🌫 rm, 🟦 🟥 ✪ 🚗 🅿 – 🝳 120. 🝳 🟠 🟢 🟦
Meals à la carte 22/33,50 – ☲ 16 – **201 rm** 154/174 – 174/195.

🏨 **Avidon** 🝳 without rest, Unterrather Str. 42, ✉ 40468, ✆ (0211) 95 19 50, *hotel@a vidon.de*, *Fax (0211) 95195333* – 🛗 🌫 🟥 ✪ 🅿 – 🝳 15. 🝳 🟠 🟢 🟦 🟦
closed Christmas to New Year – **33 rm** ☲ 121/189 – 141/189.

at Meerbusch-Büderich Northwest : 7 km, by Luegallee AV and Neusser Straße :

XXX **Landsknecht** with rm, Poststr. 70, ✉ 40667, ✆ (02132) 9 33 90, *Fax (02132) 10978*, 🍽 – 🌫 rm, 🟥 🅿 🝳 🟢 🟦 🌫
Meals *(closed Saturday lunch and Monday)* (outstanding wine list) à la carte 32,20/48 – **10 rm** ☲ 80/110 – 110/160.

XX **Landhaus Mönchenwerth**, Niederlöricker Str. 56 (at the boat landing stage), ✉ 40667, ✆ (02132) 75 76 50, *contact@moenchenwerth.com*, *Fax (02132) 32757638*, ≼, 🍽, beer garden – 🅿 🝳 🟠 🟦
closed Monday – **Meals** à la carte 41/52.

X **Lindenhof**, Dorfstr. 48, ✉ 40667, ✆ (02132) 26 64, *service@lindenhof-restaurant.de*, *Fax (02132) 10196*, 🍽, « Changing exhibition of paintings » – 🝳 🟢 🟦
closed 27 December - 3 January and Monday – **Meals** (booking essential) à la carte 23,70/42,50.

at Meerbusch - Langst-Kirst Northwest : 14 km by Luegallee AV and Neusser Straße :

🏨 **Rheinhotel Vier Jahreszeiten** 🝳 🍷, Zur Rheinfähre 14, ✉ 40668, ✆ (02150) 91 40, *info@rheinhotel-meerbusch.bestwestern.de*, *Fax (02150) 914900*, 🍽, beer garden, 🍸 🌫 rm, 🟦 🟥 ✪ 🅿 – 🝳 120. 🝳 🟠 🟢 🟦 🟦
Bellevue (closed 27 December - 3 January, Sunday and Monday) (dinner only) **Meals** à la carte 36,40/45,95 – **Orangerie** (lunch only) **Meals** 19,43/28,63 (buffet) – **Langster Fährhaus** (closed January and Tuesday) **Meals** à la carte 22,85/32,50 – **75 rm** ☲ 133/153 – 153/173 – 3 suites.

Dortmund Nordrhein-Westfalen 🝳 L 6 – pop. 600 000 – alt. 87 m.
Düsseldorf 78.

at Dortmund-Syburg Southwest : 13 km :

XXXX **La Table**, Hohensyburgstr. 200 (at the casino), ✉ 44265, ✆ (0231) 7 74 07 37, *info @restaurant-latable.de*, *Fax (0231) 774077*, 🍽 – 🅿 🝳 🟠 🟢 🟦 🟦 🌫
🟢🟢 closed 1 to 10 January, 3 weeks July - August, Bank Holidays, Monday and Tuesday – **Meals** (dinner only) (outstanding wine list) 60,33/98,17 and à la carte
Spec. Variation von der Gänsestopfleber. Mosaik von St. Pierre und Lachs mit Tomaten-Algensud. Filet vom Bison mit Currylinsen und Anispflaumen.

Essen Nordrhein-Westfalen 🝳 L 5 – pop. 600 000 – alt. 120 m.
Düsseldorf 31.

at Essen-Kettwig South : 11 km :

XXXX **Résidence** (Bühler) 🍷 with rm, Auf der Forst 1, ✉ 45219, ✆ (02054) 9 55 90, *info @hotel-residence.de*, *Fax (02054) 82501*, 🍽 – 🟥 ✪ 🚗 🅿 🝳 🟠 🟢 🟦
🟢🟢 closed 1 to 10 January and 3 weeks July - August – **Meals** (closed Sunday and Monday) (dinner only) (booking essential, outstanding wine list) à la carte 62/90 – ☲ 13 – **18 rm** 95/125 – 125/192
Spec. Geeiste Suppe von Cavaillon-Melone und Kaisergranat (season). Zander und St. Jakobs muscheln mit Zucchini gebraten. Mosaik von Kaninchen und Gänsestopfleber mit Ölrauke.

324

Grevenbroich *Nordrhein-Westfalen* 🔢 *M 3 – pop. 62 000 – alt. 60 m.*
Düsseldorf 28.

XXXXX   **Zur Traube** (Kaufmann) with rm, Bahnstr. 47, ✉ 41515, 🏠 (02181) 6 87 67, *zurtra*
ube-grevenbroich@t-online.de, Fax (02181) 61122 – 📺 🎬 📞 🍷 🅥🅘🅢🅐. ✨ rm
closed 26 March - 6 April, 16 July - 6 August and 24 December - 16 January – **Meals** *(closed*
Sunday - Monday) (booking essential, outstanding wine list) 48 *(lunch)*/110 and à la carte
66/88 – **6 rm** ⌁ 120/180 – 170/260
Spec. Unsere Gänseleber. Steinbutt mit Kartoffelkruste und Trüffelsud. Crème brûlée von
der Kokosnuß.

FRANKFURT ON MAIN (FRANKFURT AM MAIN) *Hessen* 🔢 *P 10 – pop. 650 000 –*
alt. 40 m.

See : *Zoo*★★★ FX – *Goethe's House (Goethehaus)*★ GZ – *Cathedral (Dom)*★ *(Gothic*
Tower★★*, Choir-stalls*★*, Museum*★*)* HZ – *Tropical Garden (Palmengarten)*★ CV –
Senckenberg-Museum★ *(Palaeontology department*★★*)* CV **M9** – *Städel Museum (Städel-*
sches Museum and Städtische Galerie) ★★ GZ – *Museum of Applied Arts (Museum für*
Kunsthandwerk)★ HZ – *German Cinema Museum*★ GZ **M7** – *Henninger Turm* ※★ FX –
Museum of Modern Art (Museum für moderne Kunst)★ HY **M10.**

🏌 *Frankfurt-Niederrad, Golfstr. 41 (by Kennedy-Allee CDX), 🏠 (069) 6 66 23 18 ;* 🏌 *Frank-*
furt-Niederrad, Schwarzwaldstr. 127 (by Kennedy-Allee CDX), 🏠 (069)96 74 13 53 ; 🏌
Hanau-Wilhelmsbad (East : 12 km by Hanauer Landstraße), 🏠 (06181) 8 20 71 ; 🏌 *Hofgut*
Neuhof (South : 13 km by A 661 and exit Dreieich), 🏠 (06102) 32 70 10.

✈ *Rhein-Main (South-West : 12 km), 🏠 (069) 6 90 25 95.*

🚗 *at Neu-Isenburg (South : 7 km).*

Exhibition Centre (Messegelände) (CX), 🏠 (069) 7 57 50, Fax (069) 75756433.

🛈 *Tourist Information, Main Station (Hauptbahnhof), ✉ (069) 21 23 88 00, Fax (069)*
21237880.

🛈 *Tourist Information, im Römer, ✉ 60311, 🏠 (069) 21 23 88 00, Fax (069) 21237880.*

ADAC, Schumannstr. 4.

ADAC, Schillerstr. 12.

Berlin 537 – Wiesbaden 41 – Bonn 178 – Nürnberg 226 – Stuttgart 204.

Plans on following pages

🏨🏨🏨🏨   **Steigenberger Frankfurter Hof**, Bethmannstr. 33, ✉ 60311, 🏠 (069) 2 15 02,
infoline@frankfurter-hof.steigenberger.de, Fax (069) 215900, 🌫, Massage, ⟺ – 🛗,
✨ rm, 🍴 📺 🍷 & – 🈵 220. 🅐🅔 ① 🍷 🅥🅘🅢🅐   GZ e
Restaurant Français (booking essential) *(closed 17 June - 25 August, Sunday and Mon-*
day) **Meals** à la carte 51,60/61,30 – **Oscar's :** **Meals** à la carte 29,90/41,50 – ⌁ 20 –
332 rm 335/385 – 385/435 – 17 suites.

🏨🏨🏨   **ArabellaSheraton Grand Hotel**, Konrad-Adenauer-Str. 7, ✉ 60313, 🏠 (069)
2 98 10, *grandhotel.frankfurt@arabellasheraton.de, Fax (069) 2981810,* Massage, 🏋,
⟺, 🔲 – 🛗, ✨ rm, 🍴 📺 🍷 🚗 – 🈵 300. 🅐🅔 ① 🍷 🅥🅘🅢🅐 🅙🅒🅑   HY c
Meals à la carte 30,16/42,44 – ⌁ 22 – **378 rm** 280/404 – 317/440 – 12 suites.

🏨🏨🏨   **Hessischer Hof**, Friedrich Ebert Anlage 40, ✉ 60325, 🏠 (069) 7 54 00, *info@hessi*
scher-hof.com, Fax (069) 75402924, « Rest. with collection of Sèvres porcelain » – 🛗,
✨ rm, 🍴 📺 🍷 🚗 🎬 – 🈵 110. 🅐🅔 ① 🍷 🅥🅘🅢🅐 🅙🅒🅑. ✨ rest   CX p
Meals 28 and à la carte 36/55 – ⌁ 19 – **117 rm** 208/292 – 253/326 – 11 suites.

🏨🏨🏨   **Inter-Continental** Ⓜ, Wilhelm-Leuschner-Str. 43, ✉ 60329, 🏠 (069) 2 60 50, *fran*
kfurt@interconti.com, Fax (069) 252467, Massage, 🏋, ⟺, 🔲 – 🛗, ✨ rm, 🍴 📺 🍷
& – 🈵 400. 🅐🅔 ① 🍷 🅥🅘🅢🅐 🅙🅒🅑. ✨ rest   GZ a
Signatures : Meals à la carte 53/59,50 – ⌁ 21 – **770 rm** 250/405 – 275/425 – 35 suites.

🏨🏨🏨   **Hilton** Ⓜ, Hochstr. 4, ✉ 60313, 🏠 (069) 1 33 80 00, *sales_frankfurt@hilton.com,*
Fax (069) 13381338, 🌫, ⟺, 🔲 – 🛗, ✨ rm, 🍴 📺 🍷 🚗 – 🈵 300. 🅐🅔 ① 🍷 🅥🅘🅢🅐
🅙🅒🅑   GY n
Meals 25,05 *(buffet lunch)* and à la carte 29,65/42,12 – ⌁ 20 – **342 rm** 299 – 499 –
3 suites.

🏨🏨🏨   **Maritim** Ⓜ, Theodor-Heuss-Allee 3, ✉ 60486, 🏠 (069) 7 57 80, *info.fra@maritim.de,*
Fax (069) 75781000, Massage, 🏋, ⟺, 🔲 – 🛗, ✨ rm, 🍴 📺 🍷 & 🚗 – 🈵 210. 🅐🅔
① 🍷 🅥🅘🅢🅐 🅙🅒🅑. ✨ rest   CVX c
Classico : Meals à la carte 39,81/46,02 – **SushiSho** (Japanese) *(closed Saturday lunch and*
Sunday) **Meals** à la carte 22,50/36,80 – ⌁ 20 – **543 rm** 225/275 – 250/300 – 24 suites.

🏨🏨🏨   **Marriott** Ⓜ, Hamburger Allee 2, ✉ 60486, 🏠 (069) 7 95 50, *mhrs.fradt@marriott.com,*
Fax (069) 79552432, ≤ Frankfurt, Massage, 🏋, ⟺ – 🛗, ✨ rm, 🍴 📺 🍷 🚗 – 🈵 600.
🅐🅔 ① 🍷 🅥🅘🅢🅐 🅙🅒🅑. ✨ rest   CV a
Meals à la carte 21,99/33,75 – ⌁ 18 – **588 rm** 120 – 365 – 10 suites.

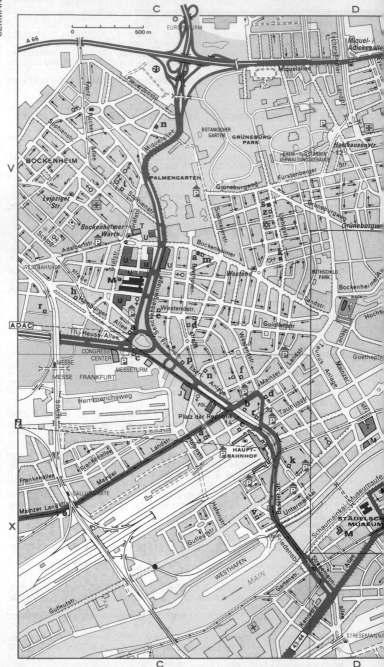

FRANKFURT AM MAIN

FRANKFURT
AM MAIN

Le Méridien Parkhotel, Wiesenhüttenplatz 28, ✉ 60329, ℰ (069) 2 69 70, gm1275@forte-hotels.com, Fax (069) 2697884, 斎, 🔏, ⇘ – |🛗|, ↦ rm, 🗐 🖸 ❤ ⇘
🖳 – 🏄 180. 🖭 ⑩ 🐠 💳 🇯🇨🇧   CX k
Meals à la carte 30/44 – ⌷ 20 – **296 rm** 197/304 – 233/380 – 11 suites.

Alexander am Zoo 🅼 without rest, Waldschmidtstr. 59, ✉ 60316, ℰ (069) 94 96 00, info@alexander.bestwestern.de, Fax (069) 94960720, ⇘ – |🛗| ↦ 🖸 ❤ ⇘ – 🏄 30.
🖭 ⑩ 🐠 💳 🇯🇨🇧 ❀
⌷ 12 – **59 rm** 110 – 120 – 9 suites.   FV c

Palmenhof, Bockenheimer Landstr. 89, ✉ 60325, ℰ (069) 7 53 00 60, info@palme
nhof.com, Fax (069) 75300666 – |🛗| 🖸 ❤ ⇘. 🖭 ⑩ 🐠 💳 🇯🇨🇧   CV m
closed 23 December - 2 January – **Meals** see **L'Artichoc** below – **46 rm** ⌷ 115/140 –
155/170.

An der Messe without rest, Westendstr. 104, ✉ 60325, ℰ (069) 74 79 79, hotel.a
n.der.messe@web.de, Fax (069) 748349 – |🛗| 🖸 ❤ ⇘. 🖭 ⑩ 🐠 💳 🇯🇨🇧   CV e
46 rm ⌷ 123 – 149.

Sofitel, Savignystr. 14, ✉ 60325, ℰ (069) 7 53 30, h1305@accor-hotels.com,
Fax (069) 7533175 – |🛗|, ↦ rm, 🖸 ❤ – 🏄 90. 🖭 ⑩ 🐠 💳 🇯🇨🇧   CX f
Meals à la carte 25,15/38 – ⌷ 17 – **155 rm** 197/258 – 223/284.

Mercure, Voltastr. 29, ✉ 60486, ℰ (069) 7 92 60, h1204@accor-hotels.com,
Fax (069) 79261606, 斎, ⇘ – |🛗|, ↦ rm, 🗐 🖸 ❤ ⇘ – 🏄 🖭 ⑩ 🐠
💳 🇯🇨🇧   by Th.-Heuss-Allee CV
Meals à la carte 20/42 – **346 rm** ⌷ 117/235 – 153/248 – 12 suites.

Villa Orange 🅼 without rest, Hebelstr. 1, ✉ 60318, ℰ (069) 40 58 40, contact@v
illa-orange.de, Fax (069) 40584100, « Elegant modern installation » – |🛗| ↦ 🖸 ❤ – 🏄 25.
🖭 ⑩ 🐠 💳   EV a
38 rm ⌷ 110/130 – 130.

Steigenberger MAXX Hotel 🅼, Lange Str. 5, ✉ 60311, ℰ (069) 21 93 00, fran
kfurt-city@maxx-hotels.de, Fax (069) 21930599 – |🛗|, ↦ rm, 🗐 🖸 ❤ & ⇘ 🖳 – 🏄 165.
🖭 ⑩ 🐠   FX s
Meals à la carte 17,88/39,35 – ⌷ 14 – **150 rm** 140/170 – 170/186.

Imperial, Sophienstr. 40, ✉ 60487, ℰ (069) 7 93 00 30, info@imperial.bestwestern.de,
Fax (069) 79300388, 斎 – |🛗|, ↦ rm, 🗐 🖸 ❤ ⇘. 🖳 🖭 ⑩ 🐠 💳 🇯🇨🇧   CV t
Meals (dinner only) à la carte 18,10/28,35 – **60 rm** ⌷ 114 – 142.

Atlantic 🅼 without rest, Düsseldorfer Str. 20, ✉ 60329, ℰ (069) 27 21 20, info@a
tlantic.pacat.com, Fax (069) 27212100 – |🛗| ↦ 🖸 ❤ ⇘. 🖭 ⑩ 🐠 💳 🇯🇨🇧 ❀
60 rm ⌷ 108/133 – 159.   CX b

Liebig-Hotel without rest, Liebigstr. 45, ✉ 60323, ℰ (069) 72 75 51, hotelliebig@l
-online.de, Fax (069) 727555 – ↦ 🖸. 🖭 ⑩ 🐠 💳 🇯🇨🇧 ❀   CV z
closed 22 December - 2 January – ⌷ 12 – **19 rm** 98/150 – 120/180.

Rema-Hotel Bristol without rest, Ludwigstr. 13, ✉ 60327, ℰ (069) 24 23 90, bris
tol@remahotel.de, Fax (069) 251539 – |🛗| ↦ 🖸 ❤ – 🏄 20. 🖭 ⑩ 🐠 💳 🇯🇨🇧
145 rm ⌷ 92/180 – 130/240.   CX a

InterCityHotel, Poststr. 8, ✉ 60329, ℰ (069) 27 39 10, frankfurt@intercityhotel.de,
Fax (069) 27391999 – |🛗|, ↦ rm, 🖸 ❤ 🖳 – 🏄 80. 🖭 ⑩ 🐠 💳 🇯🇨🇧   CX o
Meals (closed Saturday) à la carte 19/32 – **384 rm** ⌷ 135/185 – 160/240 – 3 suites.

Novotel Frankfurt City West, Lise-Meitner-Str. 2, ✉ 60486, ℰ (069) 79 30 30,
h1049@accor-hotel.com, Fax (069) 79303930, 斎, ⇘ – |🛗|, ↦ rm, 🗐 🖸 ❤ & ⇘
🖳 – 🏄 160. 🖭 ⑩ 🐠 💳. ❀ rest   CV r
Meals à la carte 18,05/32,22 – ⌷ 15 – **235 rm** 100/151 – 128/169.

Plaza 🅼 without rest, Esslinger Str. 8, ✉ 60329, ℰ (069) 2 71 37 80, Info@plaza-fr
ankfurt.bestwestern.de, Fax (069) 237650 – |🛗| ↦ 🖸 ⇘. 🖭 ⑩ 🐠 💳 🇯🇨🇧   CX v
closed Christmas - New Year – **45 rm** ⌷ 92/119 – 127/137.

Metropolitan 🅼 without rest, Münchener Str. 15, ✉ 60329, ℰ (069) 2 42 60 90,
metropolitan-hotel@t-online.de, Fax (069) 24260999 – |🛗| 🖸 ❤ 🖳. 🖭 ⑩ 🐠 💳
42 rm ⌷ 92/102 – 107/143.   GZ s

Miramar 🅼 without rest, Berliner Str. 31, ✉ 60311, ℰ (069) 9 20 39 70, info@mir
amar-frankfurt.de, Fax (069) 92039769 – |🛗| ↦ 🗐 🖸 ❤. 🖭 ⑩ 🐠 💳 🇯🇨🇧   HZ a
closed 23 December - 2 January – **39 rm** ⌷ 110 – 135.

Domicil without rest, Karlstr. 14, ✉ 60329, ℰ (069) 27 11 10, info@domicil-frankfu
rt.bestwestern.de, Fax (069) 253266 – |🛗| ↦ 🖸. 🖭 ⑩ 🐠 💳 🇯🇨🇧   CX d
closed Christmas - New Year – **67 rm** ⌷ 89/110 – 118/128.

Manhattan without rest, Düsseldorfer Str. 10, ✉ 60329, ℰ (069) 2 69 59 70, manh
attan-hotel@t-online.de, Fax (069) 269597777 – |🛗| 🖸 ❤. 🖭 ⑩ 🐠 💳   CX r
60 rm ⌷ 85/95 – 100/175.

🏠 **Atrium** without rest, Beethovenstr. 30, ⊠ 60325, ℘ (069) 97 56 70, info@atrium.p
acat.com, Fax (069) 97567100 – |≢| 📺. 🄰🄴 🄼🄾 🆅🅸🆂🅰 🅹🅲🅱   CV o
closed 21 December - 6 January – **45 rm** ⊑ 115/195 – 165/245.

🏠 **Am Dom** without rest, Kannengießergasse 3, ⊠ 60311, ℘ (069) 1 38 10 30,
Fax (069) 283237 – |≢| 📺. 🄰🄴 🄼🄾 🆅🅸🆂🅰   HZ s
31 rm ⊑ 85/95 – 110/130.

XXX **Tiger-Restaurant**, Heiligkreuzgasse 20, ⊠ 60313, ℘ (069) 92 00 22 25, info@tige
😕 rpalast.com, Fax (069) 92002217, (with variety-theatre) – ▤. 🄰🄴 🄾 🄼🄾
🆅🅸🆂🅰. 🕸   FV s
closed 8 July - 21 August, Sunday and Monday – **Meals** (dinner only) (booking essential)
à la carte 54,19/68,50 – **Tiger-Bistrot** (closed Monday) (dinner only) **Meals** à la carte
32,21/40,64
Spec. Gegrillte Langostinos mit Basmatireis und Zitronen-Ingwerschaum. Glaciertes Rehrückenfilet mit geschmortem Spitzkohl und grüner Pfefferjus. Schokoladensoufflé mit
Banyulseis.

XXX **Opéra**, Opernplatz 1, ⊠ 60313, ℘ (069) 1 34 02 15, info@opera-restauration.de,
Fax (069) 1340239, 🍴, « Former foyer of the "Alte Oper" » – 🄰🄴 🄼🄾 🆅🅸🆂🅰   GY f
closed Saturday lunch – **Meals** 35 and à la carte 35,30/52,50.

XXX **Union Club Restaurant**, Am Leonhardsbrunnen 12, ⊠ 60487, ℘ (069) 70 30 33,
Fax (069) 7073202, 🍴 – 🄰🄴 🄾 🄼🄾 🆅🅸🆂🅰. 🕸   CV n
closed early to mid January, Saturday and Sunday – **Meals** (booking essential) à la carte
37/46.

XX **Aubergine**, Alte Gasse 14, ⊠ 60313, ℘ (069) 9 20 07 80, Fax (069) 9200786 – 🄰🄴 🄾
🄼🄾 🆅🅸🆂🅰   HY b
closed Christmas to New Year, 3 weeks July - August, Saturday lunch, Sunday and Bank
Holidays, except exhibitions – **Meals** (booking essential) (outstanding wine list) 27 (lunch,
à la carte 44/52.

XX **Gallo Nero**, Kaiserhofstr. 7, ⊠ 60313, ℘ (069) 28 48 40, Fax (069) 91396594, 🍴 –
🄰🄴 🄾 🄼🄾 🆅🅸🆂🅰 🅹🅲🅱   GY s
closed 24 December - 2 January, Sunday and Bank Holidays, except exhibitions – **Meals**
(Italian) à la carte 32/53.

XX **La Trattoria**, Fürstenberger Str. 179, ⊠ 60322, ℘ (069) 55 21 30, ristorante_la_tr
attoria@t-online.de, Fax (069) 552130 – 🄰🄴 🄾 🄼🄾 🆅🅸🆂🅰 🅹🅲🅱   DV s
closed 24 December - 2 January, Saturday and Sunday, except exhibitions – **Meals** (Italian)
(booking essential) à la carte 50/54.

XX **L'Artichoc** - Hotel Palmenhof, Bockenheimer Landstr. 91, ⊠ 60325, ℘ (069)
90 74 87 71, info@lartichoc.de, Fax (069) 90748772 – 🄰🄴 🄼🄾 🆅🅸🆂🅰   CV a
closed 24 December - 7 January, Sunday and Bank Holidays – **Meals** 17 (lunch) and à la carte
30,67/48.

X **Gargantua**, Liebigstr. 47, ⊠ 60323, ℘ (069) 72 07 18, gargantua@t-online.de,
Fax (069) 71034695, 🍴 – 🄰🄴 🄾 🄼🄾 🆅🅸🆂🅰   CV s
closed 22 December - 8 January, Saturday lunch, Sunday and Bank Holidays – **Meals**
(booking essential) à la carte 44/59.

X **Ernos Bistro**, Liebigstr. 15, ⊠ 60323, ℘ (069) 72 19 97, Fax (069) 173838, 🍴 – 🄰🄴
😕 🄼🄾 🆅🅸🆂🅰 🅹🅲🅱   CV k
closed 13 July - 4 August, 21 December - 6 January, Saturday and Sunday, except exhi-
bitions – **Meals** (French) (booking essential) 36 (lunch) and à la carte 48/62
Spec. Hausgemachte Gänsestopfleber "à la cuillère". Zanderfilet mit Stampfkartoffeln und
Kalbskopfragoût. Roulade vom Rindenentrecôte mit gebratenen Gurken und Tomaten.

X **Meyer's Restaurant**, Große Bockenheimerstr. 54, ⊠ 60313, ℘ (069) 91 39 70 70,
Fax (069) 91397071, 🍴 – 🄰🄴 🄾 🄼🄾 🆅🅸🆂🅰   GY a
closed 1 to 8 January and Sunday – **Meals** à la carte 34/42.

X **Kabuki**, Kaiserstr. 42, ⊠ 60329, ℘ (069) 23 43 53, Fax (069) 233137 – 🄰🄴 🄾 🄼🄾 🆅🅸🆂🅰.
🕸   GZ v
closed Saturday lunch and Sunday – **Meals** (Japanese) à la carte 28/55.

X **Toan**, Friedberger Anlage 14, ⊠ 60316, ℘ (069) 44 98 44, Fax (069) 432596, 🍴 – 🄰🄴
🄾 🄼🄾 🆅🅸🆂🅰   FV a
closed 2 weeks July, Monday and Saturday lunch – **Meals** (Vietnamese) à la carte
16,50/29,50.

X **Stars und Starlet**, Friedrich-Ebert-Anlage 49, ⊠ 60327, ℘ (069) 7 56 03 00,
Fax (069) 75603044, « Fantasy interior by Jordan Mozer » – 🄰🄴 🄾 🄼🄾 🆅🅸🆂🅰 🅹🅲🅱. 🕸
closed Saturday lunch and Sunday – **Meals** à la carte 28,43/34,10.   CX u

X **Main Tower Restaurant**, Neue Mainzer Str. 52 (53th floor), ⊠ 60297, ℘ (069)
36 50 47 71, Fax (069) 36504871, ≤ Frankfurt – |≢|. 🄰🄴 🄼🄾 🆅🅸🆂🅰. 🕸   GY u
Meals (booking essential) à la carte 23,40/41,50.

Frankfurter Äppelwoilokale *(mainly light meals only)* :

X · ⊕ **Zum Rad**, Leonhardsgasse 2 (Seckbach), ⊠ 60389, ℘ (069) 47 91 28, *info@zum-rad.de*, Fax (069) 472942, 🍴 by Im Prüfling and Seckbacher Landstraße FV
closed 20 December - 15 January, Tuesday and November - March Monday - Tuesday –
Meals *(weekdays open from 5.00 pm, Sunday and Bank Holidays from 3.00 pm)* à la carte 12,80/24,10.

X · ⊕ **Klaane Sachsehäuser**, Neuer Wall 11 (Sachsenhausen), ⊠ 60594, ℘ (069) 61 59 83, Fax (069) 622141, 🍴 FX n
closed Sunday – **Meals** *(open from 4 pm)* à la carte 12/23.

X · ⊕ **Zum gemalten Haus**, Schweizer Str. 67 (Sachsenhausen), ⊠ 60594, ℘ (069) 61 45 59, Fax (069) 6031457, 🍴 EX c
closed 2 weeks July, Monday and Tuesday, except exhibitions – **Meals** à la carte 10,20/12,30.

at Frankfurt-Bergen-Enkheim *East : 8 km, by Wittelsbacherallee FV* :

🏨 **Avalon**, Röntgenstr. 5, ⊠ 60388, ℘ (06109) 37 00, *frankfurt@avalon-hotels.de*, Fax (06109) 370720, 🍴 – 🛗, ⇄ rm, ☰ 📺 📞 & ⇔ 🅿 – 🔬 70. 🆎 ① 🅞 🆅🅸🆂🅰. ※ rest
Meals *(closed 22 December - 7 January, lunch Saturday and Sunday)* à la carte 23,50/35,50 – ⊑ 13 – **160 rm** 128/148 – 132/152.

at Frankfurt-Griesheim *West : 8 km, by Th.-Heuss-Allee CV* :

🏨 **Courtyard by Marriott**, Oeserstr. 180, ⊠ 65933, ℘ (069) 3 90 50, Fax (069) 3808218, 🛋, ⟨| – 🛗, ⇄ rm, ☰ rest, 📺 📞 🅿 – 🔬 240. 🆎 ① 🅞 🆅🅸🆂🅰 🅹🅲🅱. ※ rest
Meals à la carte 22/31 – ⊑ 14 – **236 rm** 99/115

at Frankfurt-Höchst *West : 10 km, by Mainzer Landstraße CX* :

🏨 **Lindner Congress Hotel** Ⓜ, Bolongarostr. 100, ⊠ 65929, ℘ (069) 3 30 02 00, *info.frankfurt@lindner.de*, Fax (069) 33002999, 🛋, ⇄ – 🛗, ⇄ rm, ☰ 📺 📞 & ⇔ – 🔬 160. 🆎 ① 🅞 🆅🅸🆂🅰 🅹🅲🅱
Meals à la carte 29/43,50 – ⊑ 17 – **303 rm** 137/167 – 154/184.

at Frankfurt-Niederrad *Southwest : 6 km, by Kennedy-Allee CDX* :

🏨 **Queens Hotel**, Isenburger Schneise 40, ⊠ 60528, ℘ (069) 6 78 40, *reservation.qfr ankfurt@queensgruppe.de*, Fax (069) 6784190, 🍴, beer garden, Massage, 🛋, ⇄ – 🛗, ⇄ rm, ☰ 📺 📞 🅿 – 🔬 250. 🆎 ① 🅞 🆅🅸🆂🅰 🅹🅲🅱. ※ rest
Meals à la carte 21,10/31,60 – **295 rm** ⊑ 150/260 – 195/315.

🏨 **ArabellaSheraton Congress Hotel**, Lyoner Str. 44, ⊠ 60528, ℘ (069) 6 63 30, *congress@arabellasheraton.com*, Fax (069) 6633667, ⇄, ⟨| – 🛗, ⇄ rm, ☰ 📺 📞 ⇔ 🅿 – 🔬 290. 🆎 ① 🅞 🆅🅸🆂🅰
Meals à la carte 24,54/34,76 – **396 rm** ⊑ 185/305 – 220/340 – 4 suites.

🏨 **Dorint** Ⓜ, Hahnstr. 9, ⊠ 60528, ℘ (069) 66 30 60, *info.frafur@dorint.com*, Fax (069) 66306600, ⇄, ⟨| – 🛗, ⇄ rm, ☰ 📺 📞 & 🅿 – 🔬 180. 🆎 ① 🅞 🆅🅸🆂🅰
Meals à la carte 26,56/45,25 – ⊑ 19 – **191 rm** 192/220 – 238/276.

XX **Weidemann**, Kelsterbacher Str. 66, ⊠ 60528, ℘ (069) 67 59 96, *mail@weidemann -online.de*, Fax (069) 673928, 🍴 – 🅿 🆎 ① 🅞 🆅🅸🆂🅰 by Gartenstraße CX
closed Easter, Saturday lunch, Sunday and Bank Holidays – **Meals** *(booking essential)* 28 *(lunch)* and à la carte 39,50/57.

at Frankfurt-Sachsenhausen :

🏨 **Holiday Inn** Ⓜ, Mailänder Str. 1, ⊠ 60598, ℘ (069) 6 80 20, *info@frankfurt.holida yinn-queens.de*, Fax (069) 6802333, 🛋, ⇄ – 🛗, ⇄ rm, ☰ 📺 📞 ⇔ 🅿 – 🔬 220. 🆎 ① 🅞 🆅🅸🆂🅰 🅹🅲🅱 by Darmstädter Landstraße (B 3) FX
Meals à la carte 23/48 – ⊑ 18 – **436 rm** 175/230 – 210/276.

XX **Maingaustuben**, Schifferstr. 38, ⊠ 60594, ℘ (069) 61 07 52, *maingau@t-online.de*, Fax (069) 61995372 – 🆎 ① 🅞 🆅🅸🆂🅰 🅹🅲🅱 HZ g
closed end July - early August, Saturday lunch, Sunday dinner and Monday – **Meals** 14,30 *(lunch)* and à la carte 32/47,50.

XX **Bistrot 77**, Ziegelhüttenweg 1, ⊠ 60598, ℘ (069) 61 40 40, Fax (069) 615998, 🍴 – 🆎 🅞 🆅🅸🆂🅰 EX a
closed 23 December - 5 January, Saturday lunch and Sunday – **Meals** (French) *(outstanding wine list)* 40/65 and à la carte 43/55.

at Eschborn *Northwest : 12 km by A66 CV* :

🏨 **Novotel**, Philipp-Helfmann-Str. 10, ⊠ 65760, ℘ (06196) 90 10, *h0491@accor-hotels.com*, Fax (06196) 482114, 🍴, ⟂ (heated), 🌳 – 🛗, ⇄ rm, ☰ 📺 & 🅿 – 🔬 200. 🆎 ① 🅞 🆅🅸🆂🅰 🅹🅲🅱 by A 66 CV
Meals à la carte 18,90/35,30 – ⊑ 13 – **224 rm** 99 – 114.

at Neu-Isenburg - Gravenbruch *Southeast : 11 km by Darmstädter Landstraße* FX *and B 459*

🏨🏨🏨 **Kempinski Hotel Gravenbruch**, An der Bundesstraße 459, ✉ 63263, 𝒫 (06102) 50 50, *reservations.gravenbruch@kempinski.com, Fax (06102) 505900,* 🍴, « Park », Massage, ⚛, ⬛ (heated), 🖳, 🖛, 🗞 – 📱, ✦ rm, 🗏 📺 📞 ⟺ 🅿 – 🔏 350. 🆎 ⓞ 🐵 🆅🆂🅰 🅹🅲🅱. 🞕 rest
Meals à la carte 40,40/61,90 – 🖙 22 – **283 rm** 225/320 – 313/418 – 15 suites.

near Rhein-Main airport *Southwest : 12 km by Kennedy-Allee* CX :

🏨🏨🏨 **Sheraton** M, Hugo-Eckener-Ring 15 (terminal 1), ✉ 60549 *Frankfurt,* 𝒫 (069) 6 97 70, *salesfrankfurt@sheraton.com, Fax (069) 69772209,* Massage, 🛁, ⚛, 🖳 – 📱, ✦ rm, 🗏 📺 📞 & – 🔏 700. 🆎 ⓞ 🐵 🆅🆂🅰 🅹🅲🅱. 🞕 rest
Flawors* : Meals** à la carte 33,75/46,50 – ***Taverne *(closed Saturday and Sunday lunch)*
Meals à la carte 30,94/38,90 – 🖙 20 – **1006 rm** 159/440 – 159/455 – 28 suites.

🏨🏨🏨 **Steigenberger Airport Hotel**, Unterschweinstiege 16, ✉ 60549 *Frankfurt,* 𝒫 (069) 6 97 50, *info@airporthotel.steigenberger.de, Fax (069) 69752505,* Massage, 🛁, ⚛, 🖳 – 📱, ✦ rm, 🗏 📺 📞 ⟺ 🅿 – 🔏 300. 🆎 ⓞ 🐵 🆅🆂🅰 🅹🅲🅱
***Waldrestaurant Unterschweinstiege* :** Meals à la carte 27,20/48,60 – 🖙 19 – **421 rm** 170/325 – 190/345 – 10 suites.

🏨 **Steigenberger Esprix Hotel** M, Cargo City Süd, ✉ 60549 *Frankfurt,* 𝒫 (069) 69 70 99, *frankfurt@esprix-hotels.de, Fax (069) 69709444,* 🍴 – 📱, ✦ rm, 📺 📞 & 🅿 – 🔏 65. 🆎 ⓞ 🐵 🆅🆂🅰 🅹🅲🅱
Meals 22 *(buffet)* – 🖙 16 – **360 rm** 89/196

HAMBURG 🅻 *Stadtstaat Hamburg* 🚼🚼 *F 14 – pop. 1 700 000 – alt. 10 m.*

See : *Jungfernstieg* GY – *Außenalster* *(trip by boat* *)* GHXY – *Hagenbeck Zoo (Tierpark Hagenbeck)* *by Schröderstiftstr.* EX – *Television Tower (Fernsehturm)* *(🞕)* EX – *Fine Arts Museum (Kunsthalle)* HY M1 – *St. Michael's church (St. Michaelis)* *(tower 🞕)* EFZ – *Stintfang (≤)* EZ – *Port (Hafen)* EX – *Decorative Arts and Crafts Museum (Museum für Kunst und Gewerbe)* HY M2 – *Historical Museum (Museum für Hamburgische Geschichte)* EYZ M3 – *Post-Museum* FY M4 – *Planten un Blomen Park* EFX – *Museum of Ethnography (Hamburgisches Museum für Völkerkunde)* by Rothenbaumchaussee FX.

Envir. : *Altona : Northern Germany Museum (Norddeutsches Landesmuseum)* *by Reeperbahn* EZ – *Altona Balcony (Altonaer Balkon)* ≤ *by Reeperbahn* EZ – *Elbchaussee* *by Reeperbahn* EZ.

🇹🇹 *Falkenstein, Hamburg-Blankenese, In de Bargen 59 (West : 17 km),* 𝒫 *(040) 81 21 77 ;*
🇹🇹 *Treudelberg, Hamburg-Lehmsahl, Lemsahler Landstr. 45 (North : 16 km),* 𝒫 *(040) 60 82 25 00 ;* 🇹🇹 *Hamburg-Wendlohe, Oldesloer Str. 251 (North : 14 km),* 𝒫 *(040) 5 50 89 66 ;* 🇹🇹 *Wentorf-Reinbek, Golfstr. 2 (South-East : 20 km),* 𝒫 *(040) 72 97 80 66.*

✈ *Hamburg-Fuhlsbüttel (North : 15 km),* 𝒫 *(040) 5 07 50.*

🚂 *Hamburg-Altona, Sternenschanze.*

Exhibition Centre (Messegelände) (EFX), 𝒫 *(040) 3 56 90, Fax (040)35692180.*

🇮 *Tourismus-Zentrale, Steinstr. 7,* ✉ *20095,* 𝒫 *(040) 30 05 13 00, Fax (040) 300051333.*
ADAC, *Amsinckstr. 39.*

Berlin 284 – Bremen 120 – Hannover 151.

Plans on following pages

Town centre :

🏨🏨🏨🏨 **Vier Jahreszeiten**, Neuer Jungfernstieg 9, ✉ 20354, 𝒫 (040) 3 49 40, *vier-jahres zeiten@hvj.de, Fax (040) 34942600,* « ≤ *Binnenalster-side setting* », Massage, 🛁, ⚛ – 📱, ✦ rm, 🗏 rest, 📺 📞 ⟺ – 🔏 80. 🆎 ⓞ 🐵 🆅🆂🅰 🅹🅲🅱. 🞕 GY v
Meals see ***Haerlin*** below – ***Dog Cheng's*** *(Euro-Asian) (closed lunch Saturday and Sunday, Monday)* **Meals** à la carte 27/42 – ***Jahreszeiten Grill* : Meals** à la carte 33/60 – 🖙 22 – **156 rm** 205/275 – 255/325 – 11 suites.

🏨🏨🏨🏨 **Kempinski Hotel Atlantic**, An der Alster 72, ✉ 20099, 𝒫 (040) 2 88 80, *hotel.a tlantic@kempinski.com, Fax (040) 247129,* « ≤ *Außenalster-side setting ; courtyard-terrace* », Massage, ⚛, 🖳 – 📱, ✦ rm, 📺 📞 ⟺ – 🔏 280. 🆎 ⓞ 🐵 🆅🆂🅰 🅹🅲🅱. 🞕 rest HY a
Meals *(closed Sunday lunch)* 28 *(lunch)* and à la carte 46/72 – 🖙 22 – **254 rm** 215/280 – 250/315 – 11 suites.

🏨🏨🏨🏨 **Park Hyatt Hamburg**, Bugenhagenstr. 8, ✉ 20095, 𝒫 (040) 33 32 12 34, *concier ge@hyatt.com, Fax (040) 33321235,* 🍴, Massage, 🛁, ⚛, 🖳 – 📱, ✦ rm, 📺 & ⟺ – 🔏 120. 🆎 ⓞ 🐵 🆅🆂🅰 🅹🅲🅱. 🞕 rest HYZ t
***Apples* : Meals** à la carte 34,80/55,70 – 🖙 20 – **252 rm** 180/315 – 215/355 – 21 suites.

Dorint M, Alter Wall 40, ✉ 20457, ℰ (040) 36 95 00, *info.hamalt@dorint.com*, Fax (040) 36951000, 🛋, Massage, 🔥, 🚌, 🔲 – 🛗 🖂 🗐 📺 📶 🔥 🚗 – 🛦 350. 🆎
⑪ 🅾🅾 VISA JCB. 🛠 rest   FZ g
Ticino *(dinner only)* **Meals** à la carte 33/40 – **Seagull** *(lunch only)* **Meals** 25 (buffet only)
– 🍽 17 – **241 rm** 163/230 – 189/256 – 16 Suites.

Steigenberger Hamburg M, Heiligengeistbrücke 4, ✉ 20459, ℰ (040) 36 80 60, *hamburg@steigenberger.de*, Fax (040) 36806777, 🛋 – 🛗 🖂 rm, 🗐 📺 📶 🚗 –
🛦 180. 🆎 ⑪ 🅾🅾 VISA JCB   FZ s
Calla *(closed 23 December - 10 January, Easter, July - August, Sunday and Monday) (dinner only)* **Meals** à la carte 37/54 – **Bistro am Fleet** : **Meals** à la carte 21/34 – 🍽 17 – **234 rm** 162/202 – 188/228 – 4 suites.

Marriott Hotel M, ABC-Str. 52, ✉ 20354, ℰ (040) 3 50 50, *hamburg.marriott@marriott.com*, Fax (040) 35051777, 🛋, Massage, 🔥, 🚌, 🔲 – 🛗, 🖂 rm, 🗐 📺 📶 🔥
🚗 – 🛦 150. 🆎 ⑪ 🅾🅾 VISA JCB   FY b
Meals 15 *(buffet lunch)* and à la carte 25/46 – 🍽 17 – **277 rm** 166/210 – 5 suites.

Renaissance Hotel, Große Bleichen, ✉ 20354, ℰ (040) 34 91 80, *rhi.hamrn.dom@renaissancehotels.com*, Fax (040) 34918919, Massage, 🚌 – 🛗, 🖂 rm, 🗐 📺 📶 🅿 – 🛦 90.
🆎 ⑪ 🅾🅾 VISA JCB. 🛠 rest   FY e
Meals à la carte 28,60/34,80 – 🍽 16 – **205 rm** 136/251 – 181/251.

SIDE M, Drehbahn 49, ✉ 20354, ℰ (040) 30 99 90, *reservation@side-hamburg.de*, Fax (040) 30999399, Massage, 🔥, 🚌, 🔲 – 🛗, 🖂 rm, 🗐 📺 🔥 🚗 – 🛦 160. 🆎
⑪ 🅾🅾 VISA   FY h
Meals à la carte 29/44 – 🍽 18 – **178 rm** 150/250 – 200/280.

Europäischer Hof M, Kirchenallee 45, ✉ 20099, ℰ (040) 24 82 48, *info@europaeischer-hof.de*, Fax (040) 24824799, 🛋, Massage, 🔥, 🚌, 🔲 Squash – 🛗, 🖂 rm, 🗐 rest, 📺 📶 🚗 – 🛦 200. 🆎 ⑪ 🅾🅾   FY
Meals *(closed Sunday)* à la carte 27,10/35,80 – **Paulaner's** *(closed Sunday) (dinner only)* **Meals** à la carte 15,30/23,20 – **320 rm** 🍽 103/183 – 133/220.

Crowne Plaza, Graumannsweg 10, ✉ 22087, ℰ (040) 22 80 60, *sales.cphamburg@6c.com*, Fax (040) 2208704, 🔥, 🚌, 🔲 – 🛗, 🖂 rm, 🗐 📺 📶 VISA – 🛦 150. 🆎 ⑪ 🅾🅾 VISA   by Lange Reihe HX
Blue Marlin : **Meals** à la carte 30,86/44,05 – **King George Pub** : **Meals** à la carte 18,16/31,45 – 🍽 19 – **285 rm** 176/281

Radisson SAS Hotel, Marseiller Str. 2, ✉ 20355, ℰ (040) 3 50 20, *res@hamza.rdsas.com*, Fax (040) 35023530, ≤ Hamburg, Massage, 🔥, 🚌, 🔲 – 🛗, 🖂 rm, 🗐 📺 📶 🔥 🚗 – 🛦 400. 🆎 ⑪ 🅾🅾 VISA JCB   FX a
Vierländer Stuben : **Meals** à la carte 20,30/42,50 – **Trader Vic's** *(dinner only)* **Meals** à la carte 23,50/56,80 – 🍽 15 – **560 rm** 145/193 – 20 suites.

Maritim Hotel Reichshof, Kirchenallee 34, ✉ 20099, ℰ (040) 24 83 30, *info.ham@maritim.de*, Fax (040) 24833888, 🚌, 🔲 – 🛗, 🖂 rm, 📺 🚗 – 🛦 150. 🆎 ⑪ 🅾🅾 VISA JCB. 🛠 rest   HY d
Meals à la carte 31,45/46,79 – 🍽 13 – **303 rm** 129/226 – 198/226.

Prem, An der Alster 9, ✉ 20099, ℰ (040) 24 83 40 40, *info@hotel-prem.de*, Fax (040) 2803851, « Garden terrace », 🚌 – 🛗 📺 📶 🅿. 🆎 ⑪ 🅾🅾 VISA JCB   HX c
La mer *(closed lunch Saturday and Sunday)* **Meals** 31 *(lunch)* and à la carte 45/56 – **Prem Stüberl** *(closed lunch Saturday and Sunday)* **Meals** à la carte 29/37 – 🍽 15 – **54 rm** 105/200 – 115/200 – 3 suites.

Residenz Hafen Hamburg M, Seewartenstr. 9, ✉ 20459, ℰ (040) 31 11 90, *info@hotel-hamburg.de*, Fax (040) 31119977, ≤ – 🛗, 🖂 rm, 📺 🚗 🅿 – 🛦 220. 🆎 ⑪ 🅾🅾 VISA JCB. 🛠 rest   EZ y
Meals see Hotel **Hafen Hamburg** – 🍽 12 – **125 rm** 110/165

Berlin M, Borgfelder Str. 1, ✉ 20537, ℰ (040) 25 16 40, *hotelberlin.hamburg@t-online.de*, Fax (040) 25164413, 🛋 – 🛗 📺 🚗 🅿 – 🛦 25. 🆎 ⑪ 🅾🅾 VISA. 🛠 rest
Meals à la carte 22,90/36,70 – **93 rm** 🍽 94/110 – 110/123.by Adenauerallee HY

Senator without rest, Lange Reihe 18, ✉ 20099, ℰ (040) 24 12 03, *info@hotel-senator-hamburg.de*, Fax (040) 2803717 – 🛗 🖂 📺 📶 🚗 – 🛦 30. 🆎 ⑪ 🅾🅾 VISA JCB
56 rm 🍽 99/109 – 109/175.   HY u

Novotel City Süd, Amsinckstr. 53, ✉ 20097, ℰ (040) 23 63 80, *h1163@accor-hotels.com*, Fax (040) 234230, 🛋, 🚌 – 🛗, 🖂 rm, 📺 📶 🔥 🚗 🅿 – 🛦 50. 🆎 ⑪ 🅾🅾 VISA JCB   by Amsinckstraße HZ
Meals à la carte 20/29 – 🍽 13 – **185 rm** 99/129 – 115/155.

Hafen Hamburg, Seewartenstr. 9, ✉ 20459, ℰ (040) 31 11 30, *info@hotel-hamburg.de*, Fax (040) 31113755, ≤, 🛋 – 🛗, 🖂 rm, 📺 🔥 🚗 🅿 – 🛦 220. 🆎 ⑪ 🅾🅾 VISA JCB. 🛠 rest   EZ y
Meals à la carte 24/41 – 🍽 12 – **230 rm** 90/115 – 90/125.

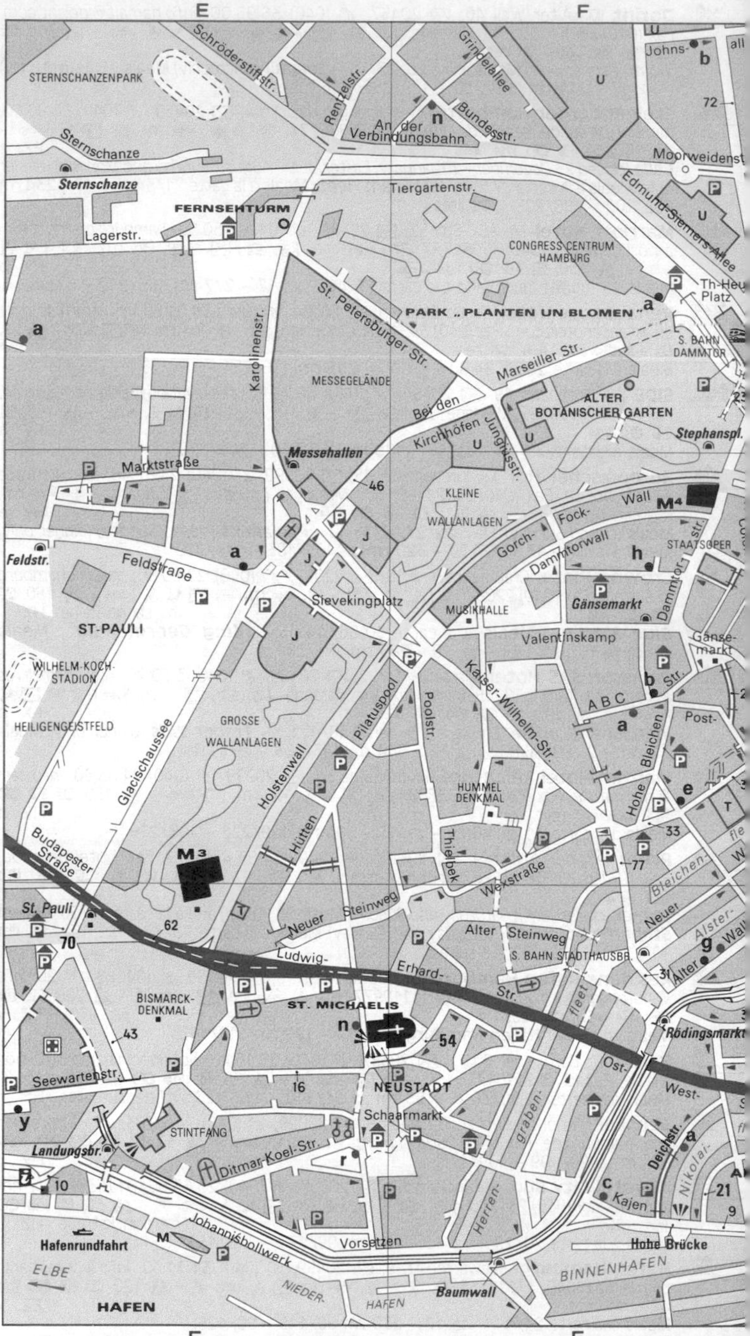
E
F
X
Y
Z
STERNSCHANZENPARK
Schröderstiftstr.
Rentzelstr.
Grindelallee
Bundesstr.
An der Verbindungsbahn
Johns-
Moorweidenst
Sternschanze
Sternschanze
FERNSEHTURM
Tiergartenstr.
Edmund-Siemers-Allee
Lagerstr.
CONGRESS CENTRUM HAMBURG
Th-Heu Platz
St. Petersburger Str.
PARK „ PLANTEN UN BLOMEN "
S. BAHN DAMMTOR
Karolinenstr.
MESSEGELÄNDE
Marseiller Str.
Bei den Kirchhöfen
Jungiusstr.
ALTER BOTANISCHER GARTEN
Stephanspl.
Messehallen
Marktstraße
KLEINE WALLANLAGEN
Gorch-Fock-Wall
STAATSOPER
Feldstr.
Feldstraße
Dammtorwall
Dammtorstr.
Sievekingplatz
MUSIKHALLE
Gänsemarkt
ST-PAULI
Valentinskamp
Gänse-markt
WILHELM-KOCH-STADION
Kaiser-Wilhelm-Str.
ABC Str.
HEILIGENGEISTFELD
GROSSE WALLANLAGEN
Pilatuspool
Poolstr.
Post-
Glacischaussee
Holstenwall
Bleichen
HUMMEL DENKMAL
Hohe Bleichen
Hütten
Thielbek
Budapester Straße
Wexstraße
Neuer Steinweg
St. Pauli
Alter Steinweg
S. BAHN STADTHAUSBR.
Ludwig-Erhard-Str.
Neuer Wall
Alter Wall
BISMARCK-DENKMAL
ST. MICHAELIS
fleet
Rödingsmarkt
Seewartenstr.
NEUSTADT
Ost-West-
Schaarmarkt
STINTFANG
Landungsbr.
Ditmar-Koel-Str.
Herrengraben-
Deichstr.
Nikolai-
Kajen
Hafenrundfahrt
Johannisbollwerk
Vorsetzen
Hohe Brücke
ELBE
NIEDER-HAFEN
Baumwall
BINNENHAFEN
HAFEN

HAMBURG

0   200 m

G

H

X

Y

Z

Heilnh. der Str.
Mittelweg
Fontenay   r
ROTHERBAUM   c
P
Alsterufer

MOORWEIDE
Mittelweg
Narburgstraße
Alsterufer
Alsterglacis

AUSSENALSTER

c
d

b
An   der   Alster   Koppel

Lange   Reihe

V

ST. GEORG

splanade
x
V
Neuer Jungfernstieg
Kennedybrücke
Lombardsbrücke

BINNENALSTER

ALSTERRUNDFAHRT
ANLEGESTELLE
ALSTERPAVILLON

JUNGFERNSTIEG
Jungfernstieg
fleet
71

Rathaus-
markt
R
ÖRSE
34
18
V

Glockengießerwall
Ballindamm
Ferdinandstr.
Hermannstr.
Bergstr.
Mönckeberg
Domstr.
Neß
b

Hauptbf. Nord
39
Kirchenallee
Hauptbf. Süd
Spitalerstr.
Mönckebergstr.
St. Jacobi
Steinstr.
Sppersort
Burchard-
platz
Meßberg
Ost-   West-   Str.
Dovenfleet
Speicherstadt
St. Katharinen
den Mühren
ollkanal

a
Holzdamm
M¹
d
T
e   r
u
Hansa-
platz
Steindamm
Steinstr.
2
P 80
79
M²
Kurt-Schumacher-
Allee
M P
HAMMERBROOK
Steinstr.
a
Deichtorplatz
Amsinckstr.
Hogerdamm
OBERHAFEN

69
76
50
37
88
e
68
NICOLAI-
KIRCHTURM
TADT

Steintorwall
Altmann-
brücke
Klosterwall

STREET INDEX TO HAMBURG TOWN PLAN

Bellevue, An der Alster 14, ✉ 20099, ✆ (040) 28 44 40, *hamburg@relaxa-hotel.de*, Fax (040) 28444222 – |🛗|, ↔ rm, 📺 ⟺ 🅿 – 🔥 40. 🆎 ① 🐵 *VISA*   HX **d**
Meals à la carte 21/32,20 – **93 rm** ⚏ 90/120 – 135/185.

St. Raphael, Adenauerallee 41, ✉ 20097, ✆ (040) 24 82 00, *info@straphael-hamburg.bestwestern.de*, Fax (040) 24820333, ⇌s – |🛗|, ↔ rm, 📺 ✆ 🅿 – 🔥 30. 🆎 ① 🐵 *VISA* 🇯🇨🇧. 🎄 rest   by Adenauerallee HY
Meals *(closed Saturday lunch and Sunday dinner)* à la carte 14,50/26,50 – ⚏ 10 – **125 rm** 102/132 – 118/148.

Quality Hotel Arcadia, Spaldingstr. 70, ✉ 20097, ✆ (040) 23 65 04 00, *arcadia@compuserve.com*, Fax (040) 23650629, ⇌s – |🛗|, ↔ rm, 🖥 📺 ✆ 🚹 ⟺ – 🔥 40. 🆎 ① 🐵 *VISA*   DU **b**
Meals *(closed Sunday)* à la carte 17,40/29 – ⚏ 13 – **98 rm** 90/110

Baseler Hof, Esplanade 11, ✉ 20354, ✆ (040) 35 90 60, *info@baselerhof.de*, Fax (040) 35906918 – |🛗|, ↔ rm, 📺 – 🔥 50. 🆎 ① 🐵 *VISA* 🇯🇨🇧. 🎄   GY **x**
Kleinhuis : Meals 12,50(lunch) and à la carte 23/34 – **150 rm** ⚏ 79/109 – 109/119.

Alster-Hof without rest, Esplanade 12, ✉ 20354, ✆ (040) 35 00 70, *info@alster-hof.de*, Fax (040) 35007514 – |🛗| 📺 🆎 ① 🐵 *VISA* 🇯🇨🇧   GY **x**
closed 22 December - 2 January – **118 rm** ⚏ 75/95 – 113/130 – 3 suites.

Eden without rest, Ellmenreichstr. 20, ✉ 20099, ✆ (040) 24 84 80, Fax (040) 241521 – |🛗| 📺. 🆎 ① 🐵 *VISA* 🇯🇨🇧   HY **r**
63 rm ⚏ 72/93 – 103/119.

Wedina without rest (with guest house), Gurlittstr. 23, ✉ 20099, ✆ (040) 24 30 11, *info@wedina.com*, Fax (040) 2803894 – 📺 🅿. 🆎 ① 🐵 *VISA*   HY **b**
45 rm ⚏ 85/110 – 90/125.

Haerlin - Hotel Vier Jahreszeiten, Neuer Jungfernstieg 9, ✉ 20354, ✆ (040) 34 94 33 10, Fax (040) 34942600, ≤ Binnenalster – 🆎 ① 🐵 *VISA* 🇯🇨🇧. 🎄   GY **v**
closed 1 to 14 January, 29 March - 8 April, 14 July - 12 August, Sunday and Monday – **Meals** *(dinner only)* 89 and à la carte 49/66
Spec. Bretonische Felsenrotbarbe mit Artischocken und Thunfischbutter. Carré vom Lamm mit Kräuterkruste und Bohnen-Perlzwiebelragoût. Zitronenkuchen mit Himbeercoulis und Thymianeis.

XX **il Ristorante**, Große Bleichen 16 (1st floor), ✉ 20354, ℰ (040) 34 33 35,
Fax (040) 345748 – 🍽. ⒶⒺ ⓪ ⓜⓢ   FY c
Meals (Italian) à la carte 28/42.

XX **Josef Viehhauser**, Alter Wall 40, ✉ 20457, ℰ (040) 36 90 18 13, josefviehhauser
@viehhauser.de, Fax (040) 36901836 – ⒶⒺ ⓜⓢ ⓋⒾⓈⒶ   FZ g
closed Sunday – Meals à la carte 25/45.

XX **San Michele**, Englische Planke 8, ✉ 20459, ℰ (040) 37 11 27, Fax (040) 378121 – ⒶⒺ
⓪ ⓜⓢ ⓙⒸⒷ   EZ n
closed 5 to 21 August – Meals (Italian) à la carte 33/47.

XX **Zippelhaus**, Zippelhaus 3, ✉ 20457, ℰ (040) 30 38 02 80, Fax (040) 321777 – ⒶⒺ ⓜⓢ
ⓋⒾⓈⒶ   GZ e
closed Saturday lunch and Sunday – Meals 19,50 (lunch) and à la carte 27/43,50.

XX **Anna**, Bleichenbrücke 2, ✉ 20354, ℰ (040) 36 70 14, Fax (040) 37500736, 🈂 – ⒶⒺ
ⓜⓢ ⓋⒾⓈⒶ   FY v
closed Sunday and Bank Holidays – Meals à la carte 34,50/43.

XX **Deichgraf**, Deichstr. 23, ✉ 20459, ℰ (040) 36 42 08, info@deichgraf-hamburg.de,
Fax (040) 364268, 🈂 – ⒶⒺ ⓪ ⓜⓢ ⓋⒾⓈⒶ ⓙⒸⒷ   FZ a
closed Sunday, October - April Sunday and Staturday lunch – Meals (booking essential) 21
and à la carte 24,40/44,40.

XX **Al Campanile**, Spadenteich 1, ✉ 20099, ℰ (040) 24 67 38, Fax (040) 246738, 🈂 –
ⒶⒺ ⓪ ⓜⓢ ⓋⒾⓈⒶ   HY m
closed 4 weeks July - August, Saturday lunch, Sunday and Monday – Meals (Italian) à la carte
22/42.

XX **Ratsweinkeller**, Große Johannisstr. 2, ✉ 20457, ℰ (040) 36 41 53, ratsweinkeller
@ratsweinkeller.de, Fax (040) 372201, « 1896 Hanseatic rest. » – 🈺 200. ⒶⒺ ⓪ ⓜⓢ ⓋⒾⓈⒶ
ⓙⒸⒷ   GZ R
closed Sunday dinner and Bank Holidays – Meals à la carte 21,68/44,69.

XX **Vero**, Domstr. 17, ✉ 20095, ℰ (040) 33 90 51, Fax (040) 339052 – 🍽. ⒶⒺ ⓜⓢ ⓋⒾⓈⒶ
closed 24 December - 1 January, Saturday lunch, Sunday and Monday – Meals (Italian)
(booking essential) à la carte 34/40.   GZ b

X **Fischmarkt**, Ditmar-Koel-Str. 1, ✉ 20459, ℰ (040) 36 38 09, Fax (040) 362191, 🈂
– ⒶⒺ ⓜⓢ ⓋⒾⓈⒶ   EZ r
closed Saturday lunch – Meals (booking essential) à la carte 24,50/52,45.

X **Fischküche**, Kajen 12, ✉ 20459, ℰ (040) 36 56 31, Fax (040) 36091153, 🈂 – ⒶⒺ ⓪
ⓜⓢ ⓋⒾⓈⒶ   FZ c
Meals (booking essential) à la carte 26/36.

X **Cox**, Lange Reihe 68, ✉ 20099, ℰ (040) 24 94 22, Fax (040) 28050902 – ⒶⒺ   HY v
closed lunch Saturday and Sunday – Meals (booking essential for dinner) à la carte
28/35,80.

X **Ilot**, ABC-Str. 46 (ABC-Forum), ✉ 20354, ℰ (040) 35 71 58 85, Fax (040) 35715887, 🈂
– ⒶⒺ ⓪ ⓜⓢ ⓋⒾⓈⒶ   FY a
closed Sunday, April - September Sunday and Saturday lunch – Meals à la carte 24/42.

X **Le Plat du Jour**, Dornbusch 4, ✉ 20095, ℰ (040) 32 14 14, Fax (040) 4105857 – ⒶⒺ
⓪ ⓜⓢ ⓋⒾⓈⒶ   GZ v
closed 23 December - 7 January, Sunday, July - August Saturday and Sunday – Meals
(booking essential) 25 (dinner) and à la carte 26,80/31,40.

X **Matsumi**, Colonnaden 96, ✉ 20354, ℰ (040) 34 31 25, Fax (040) 344219 – ⒶⒺ ⓪ ⓜⓢ
ⓋⒾⓈⒶ ⓙⒸⒷ   FY r
closed Christmas - New Year and Sunday – Meals (Japanese) à la carte 20/37.

X **Jena Paradies**, Klosterwall 23, ✉ 20095, ℰ (040) 32 70 08, Fax (040) 327598
Meals (booking essential) à la carte 24/34.   HZ a

at Hamburg-Alsterdorf North : 8 km, by Grindelallee FX and Breitenfelder Straße :

🏬 **Alsterkrug-Hotel**, Alsterkrugchaussee 277, ✉ 22297, ℰ (040) 51 30 30, rez@alst
erkrug.bestwestern.de, Fax (040) 51303403, 🈂, 🍴 – 🛗, 🔄 rm, 📺 📞 🚗 🅿 – 🈺 50.
ⒶⒺ ⓜⓢ ⓋⒾⓈⒶ ⓙⒸⒷ. ❄
Meals à la carte 21,90/33 – 🍴 13 – **105 rm** 102/138 – 112/150.

at Hamburg-Altona West : 5 km, by Reeperbahn EZ :

🏨 **Rema-Hotel Domicil** without rest, Stresemannstr. 62, ✉ 22769, ℰ (040) 4 31 60 26,
domicil@remahotel.de, Fax (040) 4397579 – 🛗 🔄 📺 🚗. ⒶⒺ ⓪ ⓜⓢ ⓋⒾⓈⒶ ⓙⒸⒷ
75 rm 89/109 – 125/220.   by Budapester Straße EY

🏨 **InterCityHotel** Ⓜ, Paul-Nevermann-Platz 17, ✉ 22765, ℰ (040) 38 03 40, hambur
g@intercityhotel.de, Fax (040) 38034999 – 🛗, 🔄 rm, 📺 📞 🍴 – 🈺 60. ⒶⒺ ⓪ ⓜⓢ ⓋⒾⓈⒶ
ⓙⒸⒷ
Meals (closed Sunday dinner) à la carte 17,60/30,20 – 🍴 13 – **133 rm** 123/138

XXXX **Landhaus Scherrer**, Elbchaussee 130, ⌧ 22763, ℰ (040) 8 80 13 25, info@landh
   ✿ ausscherrer.de, Fax (040) 8806260 – 🄿. 🄰🄴 ⓞ ⓶⑨ 𝚅𝙸𝚂𝙰
   closed Easter, Whit Sunday, Whit Monday and Sunday – **Meals** (outstanding wine list) à la
   carte 41/82 – **Bistro-Restaurant** (lunch only) **Meals** à la carte 38/44
   Spec. Eintopf von Nordseefischen mit Safran und Sauce Rouille. Kalbskopf und Hummer
   mit Graupengemüse. Quarkknödel aus der Wilster Marsch.

XXX **Le Canard**, Elbchaussee 139, ⌧ 22763, ℰ (040) 8 80 50 57, lecanard@viehhauser.de,
   ✿ Fax (040) 88913259, ≤, 🍽 – 🄿. 🄰🄴 ⓞ ⓶⑨ 𝚅𝙸𝚂𝙰. ✹
   closed Sunday – **Meals** (booking essential) (outstanding wine list) 36 (lunch) and à la carte
   55/70
   Spec. Seesaibling mit weißem Bohnenpüree und Ingwersauce. Krosse Vierländer Ente mit
   Bordeauxsauce. Topfensoufflé mit Champagnersabayon und Rotweineis.

XXX **Fischereihafen-Restaurant**, Große Elbstr. 143, ⌧ 22767, ℰ (040) 38 18 16, info
   @fischereihafen-restaurant-hamburg.de, Fax (040) 3893021, ≤, 🍽 – 🄿. 🄰🄴 ⓞ ⓶⑨ 𝚅𝙸𝚂𝙰
   Meals (seafood only) (booking essential) 20 (lunch) and à la carte 26,80/56,20.

XX **Au Quai**, Grosse Elbstr. 145 b-d, ⌧ 22767, ℰ (040) 38 03 77 30, info@au.quai.com,
   Fax (040) 38037732, ≤, 🍽 – 🄰🄴 ⓶⑨
   closed lunch Saturday and Sunday – **Meals** à la carte 28,12/45,50.

XX **Stocker**, Max-Brauer-Allee 80, ⌧ 22765, ℰ (040) 38 61 50 56, manfred.stocker@t-o
   ✿ nline.de, Fax (040) 38615058, 🍽 – 🄰🄴 ⓞ ⓶⑨ 𝚅𝙸𝚂𝙰
   closed 1 to 15 January, Monday, lunch Saturday and Sunday – **Meals** 17 (lunch) and à la
   carte 25,50/38.

X **Rive Bistro**, Van-der-Smissen-Str. 1 (Kreuzfahrt-Centre), ⌧ 22767, ℰ (040) 3 80 59 19,
   ✿ Fax (040) 3894775, ≤, 🍽 – 🄰🄴
   Meals (booking essential) à la carte 25,60/51.

at Hamburg-Bahrenfeld West : 7 km, by Budapester Straße EY and Stresemannstraße :

🏛 **Gastwerk** 🄼, Beim Alten Gaswerk 3, ⌧ 22761, ℰ (040) 89 06 20, info@gastwerk-h
   otel.de, Fax (040) 8906220, « Hotel with modern interior in a former gas factory », ⇔s
   – 🕴, 🌙 rm, 🄣 💲 🄿 – 🏛 100. 🄰🄴 ⓶⑨ 𝚅𝙸𝚂𝙰
   Meals (closed Saturday lunch and Sunday) à la carte 27,11/39,88 – ⌑ 14 – **100 rm**
   100/195

🏛 **Novotel Hamburg West** 🄼, Albert-Einstein-Ring 2, ⌧ 22761, ℰ (040) 89 95 20,
   h1656@accor-hotels.com, Fax (040) 89952333, ⇔s – 🕴, 🌙 rm, 🗐 🄣 💲 🗲 🗫 🄿 –
   🏛 50. 🄰🄴 ⓞ ⓶⑨ 𝚅𝙸𝚂𝙰
   Meals 14,85 (lunch buffet) and à la carte 16,65/28,10 – ⌑ 13 – **137 rm** 99 – 109 –
   4 suites.

XX **Tafelhaus** (Rach), Holstenkamp 71, ⌧ 22525, ℰ (040) 89 27 60, tafelhaus-hamburg
   ✿ @t-online.de, Fax (040) 8993324, 🍽 – 🄿. 🄰🄴 ⓞ ⓶⑨ 𝚅𝙸𝚂𝙰
   closed 2 weeks January, end July - mid August, Saturday lunch, Sunday and Monday – **Meals**
   (booking essential) 35 (lunch) and à la carte 55/62
   Spec. Gebratener Kräutercrêpe mit Steinbutt und St. Jakobsmuscheln. Kalbsfilet im Salzteig
   gegart (2 people). Holundersüppchen mit Zitronenravioli und Sauerrahmeis.

at Hamburg-Barmbek Northeast : 6 km, by An der Alster HX and Mundsburger Damm :

🏛 **Rema-Hotel Meridian** without rest, Holsteinischer Kamp 59, ⌧ 22081, ℰ (040)
   2 91 80 40, meridian@remahotel.de, Fax (040) 2983336, ⇔s, 🔲 – 🕴 🌙 🄣 💲 🄿 –
   🏛 30. 🄰🄴 ⓞ ⓶⑨ 𝚅𝙸𝚂𝙰 ᴶᶜᴮ
   68 rm ⌑ 89/170 – 125/220.

at Hamburg-Billbrook East : 8 km, by Amsinckstraße HZ and Billstraße :

🏛 **Böttcherhof**, Wöhlerstr. 2, ⌧ 22113, ℰ (040) 73 18 70, info@boettcherhof.com,
   Fax (040) 73187899, 🛌, ⇔s – 🕴, 🌙 rm, 🄣 💲 🗫 🄿 – 🏛 130. 🄰🄴 ⓶⑨ 𝚅𝙸𝚂𝙰. ✹ rest
   Meals à la carte 23/34,25 – ⌑ 12 – **155 rm** 100/128 – 121/149.

at Hamburg-Billstedt : East : 9 km, by Kurt Schumacher-Allee HY and B 5 :

🏛 **Panorama** without rest, Billstedter Hauptstr. 44, ⌧ 22111, ℰ (040) 73 35 90, pano
   rama-billstedt@t-online.de, Fax (040) 73359950, 🔲 – 🕴 🌙 🄣 💲 🗫 🄿 – 🏛 150. 🄰🄴
   ⓞ ⓶⑨ 𝚅𝙸𝚂𝙰
   111 rm ⌑ 90/100 – 105/115 – 7 suites.

at Hamburg-City Nord North : 7,5 km, by Mittelweg GX and Hudtwalckerstraße :

🏛 **Queens Hotel** 🄼, Mexikoring 1, ⌧ 22297, ℰ (040) 63 29 40, reservation.qhambur
   g@queensgruppe.de, Fax (040) 6322472, 🍽, ⇔s – 🕴, 🌙 rm, 🗐 rest, 🄣 🗫 🄿 –
   🏛 120. 🄰🄴 ⓞ ⓶⑨ 𝚅𝙸𝚂𝙰. ✹ rest
   Meals à la carte 24,50/41,70 – ⌑ 14 – **182 rm** 116/156 – 139/169.

at Hamburg-Eimsbüttel West : 3 km, by Schröderstiftstraße EX :

🏨 **Golden Tulip Hotel Norge**, Schäferkampsallee 49, ✉ 20357, ℰ (040) 44 11 50, hotel@ norge.de, Fax (040) 44115577 – |🕸|, ↦ rm, 🍴 rest, 📺 ✆ 🏧 – 🕍 100. 🆎 ⓪ 🐂🐄 💳 Ꞙ🄲🄱
Meals (closed Sunday dinner) à la carte 25,10/32,30 ⚌ 13 – **128 rm** 115/154 – 126/165.

at Hamburg-Eppendorf North : 5 km, by Grindelallee FX and Breitenfelder Straße :

🍽🍽 **Piment** (Nouri), Lehmweg 29, ✉ 20251, ℰ (040) 42 93 77 88, Fax (040) 42937789, 🎍
ॐ – 🐂🐄 💳
closed Sunday – **Meals** (dinner only) à la carte 36,50/48
Spec. Lauwarmer Hummer auf Cous-Coussalat mit drei verschiedenen Pesti. Taube mit Portweinjus und Sellerieschnitzel. Topfenknödel auf glacierten Birnenspalten mit Orangencrisps.

🍽🍽 **Poletto**, Eppendorfer Landstr. 145, ✉ 20251, ℰ (040) 4 80 21 59, Fax (040) 41406993,
🎍 – 🆎 ⓪ 🐂🐄 💳
closed Saturday lunch, Sunday and Bank Holidays – **Meals** 39/58 and à la carte.

🍽🍽 **Sellmer**, Ludolfstr. 50, ✉ 20249, ℰ (040) 47 30 57, Fax (040) 4601569 – 🏧 🆎 🐂🐄 💳
Meals (mainly seafood) à la carte 28,40/51,90.

at Hamburg-Flottbek West : 9 km, by Budapester Straße EY and Stresemannstraße :

🏨 **Landhaus Flottbek**, Baron-Voght-Str. 179, ✉ 22607, ℰ (040) 8 22 74 10, landhau s-flottbek@ t-online.de, Fax (040) 82274151, 🎍, « Hotel in former farmhouses ; elegant rustic installation », 🎋 – 📺 ✆ 🏧 – 🕍 30. 🆎 ⓪ 🐂🐄 💳 Ꞙ🄲🄱. 🍽 rest
Meals (closed Sunday) (dinner only) 38/73 and à la carte 40/56 – **Club-House** : Meals à la carte 26,40/40 – **25 rm** ⚌ 100/115 135/160.

at Hamburg-Fuhlsbüttel North : 8 km, by Grindelallee FX and Breitenfelder Straße :

🏨 **Airport Hotel** Ⓜ, Flughafenstr. 47 (at the airport), ✉ 22415, ℰ (040) 53 10 20, serv ice@ airporthh.com, Fax (040) 53102222, 🏧, 🔲 – |🕸|, ↦ rm, 🍴 rest, 📺 ✆ 🚗 🏧 – 🕍 140. 🆎 ⓪ 🐂🐄 💳
Meals à la carte 26,34/47,55 – ⚌ 15 – **159 rm** 135/205 – 160/230 – 11 suites.

🍽🍽 **top air**, Flughafenstr. 1 (at the airport, terminal 4, level 3), ✉ 22335, ℰ (040) 50 75 33 24, top-air.hamburg@ woellhaf-airport.de, Fax (040) 50751842 – 🏧 🆎 ⓪ 🐂🐄 💳
closed Saturday – **Meals** à la carte 39,88/60,84.

at Hamburg-Harburg South : 15 km by Amsinckstraße HZ and Wilhelmsburger Reichsstraße :

🏨 **Lindtner** Ⓜ 🍸, Heimfelder Str. 123, ✉ 21075, ℰ (040) 79 00 90, Info@ lindtner.com, Fax (040) 79009482, 🎍, « Elegant modern installation ; collection of contemporary art » – |🕸|, ↦ rm, 📺 ✆ 🏧 – 🕍 450. 🆎 ⓪ 🐂🐄 💳 Ꞙ🄲🄱. 🍽 rest
Lilium (closed Sunday) **Meals** à la carte 32,50/43,50 – **Diele** : **Meals** à la carte 29/39 – ⚌ 15 – **115 rm** 120/145 – 145/175 – 7 suites.

🏨 **Panorama Harburg**, Harburger Ring 8, ✉ 21073, ℰ (040) 76 69 50, panoramahh @ aol.com, Fax (040) 76695183 – |🕸|, ↦ rm, 🚗 – 🕍 110. 🆎 ⓪ 🐂🐄 💳 Ꞙ🄲🄱
Meals (closed Sunday) (dinner only) à la carte 16.90/33.40 – **99 rm** ⚌ 97 – 113.

🍽🍽 **Marinas**, Schellerdamm 26, ✉ 21079, ℰ (040) 7 65 38 28, info@ marinas.de, Fax (040) 7651491, 🎍 – 🆎 ⓪ 🐂🐄 💳
closed Saturday lunch and Sunday – **Meals** 24,54 (lunch) and à la carte 31,18/55,74.

at Hamburg-Harvestehude :

🏨 **Inter-Continental**, Fontenay 10, ✉ 20354, ℰ (040) 4 14 20, hamburg@ interconti .com, Fax (040) 41422299, ≼ Hamburg and Alster, 🎍, Massage, 🏧, 🔲 – |🕸|, ↦ rm, 🍴 📺 🚗 🏧 – 🕍 300. 🆎 ⓪ 🐂🐄 💳. 🍽 rest   GX r
Windows : Meals à la carte 43/65 – **Signatures** : Meals à la carte 31/44 – ⚌ 19 – **281 rm** 160/230 – 10 suites.

🏨 **Garden Hotel** Ⓜ 🍸 without rest (with guest houses), Magdalenenstr. 60, ✉ 20148, ℰ (040) 41 40 40, garden@ garden-hotel.de, Fax (040) 4140420, « Elegant modern installation », 🎋 – |🕸| ↦ 📺 ✆ 🚗. 🆎 ⓪ 🐂🐄 💳   by Mittelweg GX
⚌ 12 – **59 rm** 115/155 – 135/280.

🏨 **Abtei** 🍸, Abteistr. 14, ✉ 20149, ℰ (040) 44 29 05, p-lay@ abtei-hotel.de, Fax (040) 449820, 🎍, 🎋 – 🍴 rest, 📺 ✆ 🚗. 🆎 🐂🐄 💳. 🍽 rest
Meals (closed 5 to 11 March, 15 to 22 July, Sunday and Monday) (dinner only) (booking essential) 30/84 – **11 rm** ⚌ 130/180 – 180/255   by Rothenbaumchaussee FX
Spec. Terrine von Fenchel und getrockneten Tomaten mit St. Jakobsmuscheln. Steinbuttfilet mit Artischocken-Langostino-Fondue. Rehrückenfilet im Pfifferling-Crêpe mit Balsamicokirschen.

XXX **Wollenberg**, Alsterufer 35, ✉ 20354, 🅿 (040) 4 50 18 50, wollenberg-hamburg@
❀ -online.de, Fax (040) 45018511, « Alsters-side setting villa with modern elegant interior »
– 🛦 40. 🆎 🅞 🕥 𝘝𝘐𝘚𝘈   GX c
closed Sunday – **Meals** (dinner only) à la carte 40,88/65,44
Spec. Bouillabaisse von Nordseefischen mit Sauce Rouille. Getrüffeltes Kartoffelpüree mit
Hummerfrikassée. Holsteiner Rehrücken mit Walnuß-Pfefferkruste und Spitzkohl.

at Hamburg-Langenhorn North : 8 km by Grindelallee FX and Breitenfelder Straße :

🏰 **Dorint-Hotel-Airport** 🄼, Langenhorner Chaussee 183, ✉ 22415, 🅿 (040) 53 20 90
info.hamburg@dorint.com, Fax (040) 53209600, 🏤, 🚅, 🔲 – 🕸, ✵ rm, 📺 🎣 👌 ⇦
– 🛦 80. 🆎 🅞 🕥 𝘝𝘐𝘚𝘈 𝗝𝗖𝗕
Meals à la carte 24,02/41,93 – ☲ 15 – **146 rm** 140/170 – 160/190.

XX **Zum Wattkorn**, Tangstedter Landstr. 230, ✉ 22417, 🅿 (040) 5 20 37 97, wattko
n@viehhauser.de, Fax (040) 5209044, 🏤 – 🄿.
closed Monday – **Meals** à la carte 34,76/41,92.

at Hamburg-Lemsahl-Mellingstedt Northeast : 16 km, by An der Alster HX and B 1 :

🏰 **Marriott Hotel Treudelberg** 🄼 🦢, Lemsahler Landstr. 45, ✉ 22397, 🅿 (040)
60 82 20, info@treudelberg.com, Fax (040) 60822444, ≤, 🏤, Massage, 🏂, 🚅, 🔲, 🏌
🏌 – 🕸, ✵ rm, 📺 🎣 🄿 – 🛦 150. 🆎 🅞 🕥 𝘝𝘐𝘚𝘈 𝗝𝗖𝗕. ✸ rest
Meals à la carte 32,50/47 – ☲ 15 – **135 rm** 125.

XX **Stock's Fischrestaurant**, An der Alsterschleife 3, ✉ 22399, 🅿 (040) 6 02 00 43
info@stocks.de, Fax (040) 6022826, 🏤 – 🄿. 🆎 🅞 𝘝𝘐𝘚𝘈
Meals (weekdays dinner only) (booking essential) à la carte 29,50/49,90.

at Hamburg-Niendorf : North : 12 km, by Grindelallee FX and Garstedter Weg :

XX **Lutz und König**, König-Heinrich-Weg 200, ✉ 22455, 🅿 (040) 55 59 95 53
🕏 Fax (040) 55599554, 🏤 – 🄿. 🆎 🅞 𝘝𝘐𝘚𝘈
closed Monday – **Meals** (weekdays dinner only) (booking essential) à la carte 25/38.

at Hamburg-Nienstedten West : 13 km by Reeperbahn EZ and Elbchaussee :

🏰 **Louis C. Jacob** 🄼, Elbchaussee 401, ✉ 22609, 🅿 (040) 82 25 50, jacob@hotel-jac
❀ ob.de, Fax (040) 82255444, ≤ Harbour and Elbe, « Elbe-side setting ; lime-tree terrace »
🚅 – 🕸 🔲 📺 🎣 ⇦ – 🛦 120. 🆎 🅞 🕥 𝘝𝘐𝘚𝘈 𝗝𝗖𝗕. ✸ rest
Meals (booking essential) à la carte 44/65 – **Weinwirtschaft Kleines Jacob** (closed 2
weeks early January, 23 July - 20 August and Tuesday) (weekdays dinner only) **Meals**
à la carte 20/34 – ☲ 18 – **85 rm** 180/300 – 220/330 – 8 suites.
Spec. Gebratene St. Jakobsmuscheln mit Brunnenkressesalat. Loup de mer mit Fenchel-
gemüse und Curry-Safranfond. Rücken und Schulter vom Pyrenäen-Lamm mit Aromaten
gebraten.

at Hamburg-Rothenburgsort Southwest : 3 km, by Amsinkstraße HZ :

🏰 **Forum Hotel** 🄼, Billwerder Neuer Deich 14, ✉ 20539, 🅿 (040) 7 88 40, forumham
burg@interconti.com, Fax (040) 78841000, ≤, 🏤, 🏂, 🚅, 🔲 – 🕸 ✵ 📺 🎣 👌 ⇦
🄿 – 🛦 90. 🆎 🅞 🕥 𝘝𝘐𝘚𝘈
Meals à la carte 27/38 – ☲ 13 – **385 rm** 115/145 – 135/165 – 12 suites.

at Hamburg-Rotherbaum :

🏨 **Elysee**, Rothenbaumchaussee 10, ✉ 20148, 🅿 (040) 41 41 20, elysee@elysee-hamb
urg.de, Fax (040) 41412733, 🏤, Massage, 🚅, 🔲 – 🕸, ✵ rm, 📺 🎣 👌 ⇦ – 🛦 320
🆎 🅞 🕥 𝘝𝘐𝘚𝘈 𝗝𝗖𝗕   FX m
Piazza Romana (Italian) **Meals** à la carte 30/42 – **Brasserie :** **Meals** à la carte 20/31 –
☲ 15 – **305 rm** 140/180 – 160/200 – 4 suites.

🏨 **Vorbach** without rest, Johnsallee 63, ✉ 20146, 🅿 (040) 44 18 20, vorbach1@aol.com,
Fax (040) 44182888 – 🕸 ✵ 📺 🎣 ⇦ – 🛦 20. 🆎 🕥 𝘝𝘐𝘚𝘈   FX b
116 rm ☲ 85/130 – 105/145.

at Hamburg-St. Pauli :

🏨 **Astron Suite-Hotel** 🄼 without rest, Feldstr. 53, ✉ 20357, 🅿 (040) 43 23 20, haml
urg@astron-hotels.de, Fax (040) 43232300, 🚅 – 🕸 ✵ 📺 🎣 👌 ⇦ – 🛦 10. 🆎 🅞
🕥 𝘝𝘐𝘚𝘈 𝗝𝗖𝗕   EY a
☲ 14 – **119 rm** 118/220 – 130/230.

XXX **Mertens**, Kampstr. 25, ✉ 20357, 🅿 (040) 43 18 41 44, info@restaurantmertens.com,
❀ Fax (040) 43184145 – 🕥 𝘝𝘐𝘚𝘈 ✸   EX a
closed 24 December - 14 January, 18 July - 7 August, Saturday lunch, Sunday and Monday
– **Meals** (booking essential) 60/111 and à la carte
Spec. Lutscher von Entenstopfleber und Trüffel auf Gänsestopfleber. Rehrücken und das
"Falsche Kotelett à la Royale" mit Pfirsich. "Misslungenes" Küchlein mit Limonencrème.

at Hamburg-Stellingen *Northwest* : *7 km, by Schröderstiftstraße* FX :

🏠 **Holiday Inn** Ⓜ, Kieler Str. 333, ✉ 22525, ℰ (040) 54 74 00, *holiday-inn-hamburg@t -online.de, Fax (040) 54740100,* ⇌ – 🛗, ⇔ rm, 📺 📞 ⇨ 🅿 – ⚕ 25. ⒶⒺ ① ⓄⓈ 🆅🅸🆂🅰
🄹🄲🄱
Meals à la carte 16/33 – ⊑ 13 – **105 rm** 97/128

at Hamburg-Stillhorn *South* : *11 km, by Amsinckstraße* HZ *and A 1* :

🏠🏠🏠 **Le Méridien**, Stillhorner Weg 40, ✉ 21109, ℰ (040) 75 01 50, *lemeridien.hamburg @t-online.de, Fax (040) 75015444,* ⇌ – 🛗, ⇔ rm, ▤ rest, 📺 📞 ⅋ 🅿 – ⚕ 120. ⒶⒺ
① ⓄⓈ 🆅🅸🆂🅰
Meals à la carte 27,75/37,50 – ⊑ 12 – **148 rm** 111/121 – 125/135.

at Hamburg-Uhlenhorst *East* : *5 km, by An der Alster* HX :

🏠 **Nippon**, Hofweg 75, ✉ 22085, ℰ (040) 2 27 11 40, *reservation@nippon-hotel-hh.de, Fax (040) 22711490,* (Japanese installation) – 🛗, ⇔ rm, 📺 📞 ⇨ – ⚕ 20. ⒶⒺ ① ⓄⓈ
🆅🅸🆂🅰 🄹🄲🄱 ⋇
closed 23 December - 1 January – **Meals** (closed Monday) (dinner only) (Japanese) à la carte
27/39 – ⊑ 10 – **42 rm** 95/118 – 113/179.

at Hamburg-Winterhude : *North* : *5 km, by Mittelweg* GX :

🏠🏠 **Allegria**, Hudtwalckerstr. 13, ✉ 22299, ℰ (040) 46 07 28 28, *y.a.tschebull@t-online.de,*
🍴 *Fax (040) 46072607,* 🌤 –
closed Monday – **Meals** (weekdays dinner only) à la carte 25,80/43,32.

HANOVER (HANNOVER) 🇱 *Niedersachsen* 🄰🄸🄶 🄰🄸🄶 🄰🄸🄷 🄰🄸🄶 / 13 – pop. 530 000 – alt. 55 m.
See : *Herrenhausen Gardens (Herrenhäuser Gärten)*★★ *(Großer Garten*★★*, Berggarten*★*)*
CV – *Kestner-Museum*★ DY **M1** – *Market Church (Marktkirche) (Altarpiece*★★*)* DY –
Museum of Lower Saxony (Niedersächsisches Landesmuseum) (Prehistorical department★*)*
EZ **M2.**
🅂 *Garbsen, Am Blauen See (West : 14 km),* ℰ (05137) 7 30 68 ; 2g *Isernhagen, Gut Lohne,*
ℰ (05139) 89 31 85 ; 🅂 *Langenhagen, Hainhaus 22 (North : 12 km),* ℰ (0511) 79 93 00.
🛫 *Hanover-Langenhagen (North : 11 km),* ℰ (0511) 9 77 12 23.
🚆 *Raschplatz (EX)*
Exhibition Centre (Messegelände) (by Bischofsholer Damm FY *and Messe Schnellweg),*
ℰ (0511) 8 90, Fax (0511) 8931216.
🄱 *Tourismus-Service, Ernst-August-Platz 2,* ✉ 30159, ℰ (0511) 16 84 97 00, Fax (0511)
16840707.
ADAC, *Nordmannpassage 4.*
Berlin 289 – Bremen 123 – Hamburg 151.

Plans on following pages

🏠🏠🏠 **Kastens Hotel Luisenhof**, Luisenstr. 1, ✉ 30159, ℰ (0511) 3 04 40, *info@kaste ns-luisenhof.de, Fax (0511) 3044807* – 🛗, ⇔ rm, ▤ rest, 📺 📞 ⇨ 🅿 – ⚕ 90. ⒶⒺ ①
ⓄⓈ 🆅🅸🆂🅰 🄹🄲🄱 ⋇ rest EX b
Meals (closed Sunday July - August) à la carte 28,38/42,95 – **152 rm** ⊑ 165/265 –
220/320 – 7 suites.

🏠🏠🏠 **Maritim Grand Hotel**, Friedrichswall 11, ✉ 30159, ℰ (0511) 3 67 70, *info.hgr@m aritim.de, Fax (0511) 325195,* 🌤 – 🛗, ⇔ rm, 📺 ⅋ – ⚕ 250. ⒶⒺ ① ⓄⓈ 🆅🅸🆂🅰 DY a
L'Adresse - Brasserie : Meals à la carte 27,65/37,30 – **Wilhelm-Busch-Stube** (closed
August, Saturday, Sunday and Bank Holidays) (dinner only) Meals à la carte 18,41/26,08
– ⊑ 15 – **285 rm** 120/140 – 140/160 – 14 suites.

🏠🏠🏠 **Maritim Stadthotel**, Hildesheimer Str. 34, ✉ 30169, ℰ (0511) 9 89 40, *info.hnn @maritim.de, Fax (0511) 9894900,* 🌤 ⇌ 🖼 – 🛗, ⇔ rm, ▤ 📺 ⅋ ⅋ ⇨ 🅿 – ⚕ 350.
ⒶⒺ ① ⓄⓈ 🆅🅸🆂🅰 ⋇ rest EZ b
Meals à la carte 22/36,30 – ⊑ 15 – **291 rm** 115/135 – 135/155.

🏠🏠 **Courtyard by Marriott** Ⓜ, Arthur-Menge-Ufer 3, ✉ 30169, ℰ (0511) 36 60 00, *cy.hajay.asst.fom@marriott.com, Fax (0511) 36600555,* 🌤, beer garden, « Lakeside set- ting terrace », 🏋, ⇌ – 🛗, ⇔ rm, 📺 ⅋ ⅋ 🅿 – ⚕ 190. ⒶⒺ ① ⓄⓈ 🆅🅸🆂🅰 DZ b
Julian's (dinner only) Meals à la carte 25/33 – **Grand Café** : Meals à la carte 20,50/31,25
– ⊑ 14 – **149 rm** 110/220 – 5 suites.

🏠🏠🏠 **Forum Hotel Schweizerhof**, Hinüberstr. 6, ✉ 30175, ℰ (0511) 3 49 50, *hannov er@interconti.com, Fax (0511) 3495123* – 🛗, ⇔ rm, ▤ 📺 ⅋ ⅋ ⇨ – ⚕ 250. ⒶⒺ ①
ⓄⓈ 🆅🅸🆂🅰 🄹🄲🄱 EX d
Gourmet's Buffet : Meals à la carte 25,56/46 – ⊑ 17 – **201 rm** 115/205 – 140/260
– 3 suites.

HANNOVER

343

Mercure, Willy-Brandt-Allee 3, ✉ 30169, ℰ (0511) 8 00 80, *h1016@accor-hotels.com*
Fax (0511) 8093704, 🍴, � – 🛗 ✳, ▤ rm, 📺 📞 ⟸ – 🧖 110. 🄰🄴 🅾 🆇 VISA
Meals *(closed 20 December - 3 January)* à la carte 20,45/38,50 – **145 rm** ⛺ 120 -
141/146. EZ r

Congress-Hotel am Stadtpark 🅼, Clausewitzstr. 6, ✉ 30175, ℰ (0511)
info@congress-hotel-hannover.de, Fax (0511) 814652, 🍴, Massage, 🚖s, 🔾 – 🛗
✳ rm, 📺 📞 ℙ – 🧖 1300. 🄰🄴 🅾 🆇 VISA. ❀ rest   by Hans-Böckler Allee FY
Meals à la carte 18,50/39 – **256 rm** ⛺ 96/136 – 146/166 – 4 suites.

Grand Hotel Mussmann without rest, Ernst-August-Platz 7, ✉ 30159, ℰ (0511
3 65 60, *grandhotel@hannover.de*, 🚖s – 🛗 ✳ 📺 📞 – 🧖 40. 🄰
🅾 🆇 VISA 🄹🄲🄱   EX v
100 rm ⛺ 92/142 – 142/162.

Loccumer Hof, Kurt-Schumacher-Str. 16, ✉ 30159, ℰ (0511) 1 26 40, *loccumerho*
f@compuserve.com, Fax (0511) 131192 – 🛗, ✳ rm, 📺 📞 ⟸ ℙ – 🧖 35. 🄰🄴 🅾 🆇
VISA   DX s
Meals *(closed dinner Saturday and Sunday)* à la carte 22/37 – **87 rm** ⛺ 76/95 – 104/124

Königshof Am Funkturm without rest, Friesenstr. 65, ✉ 30161, ℰ (0511) 3 39 80
info@koenigshof-hannover.de, Fax (0511) 3398111 – 🛗 ✳ 📺 📞 ⟸ – 🧖 30. 🄰🄴 🅾
🆇 VISA   EV c
91 rm ⛺ 68/109 – 99/125.

ANDOR Hotel Plaza 🅼, Fernroder Str. 9, ✉ 30161, ℰ (0511) 3 38 80, *plaza.han*
over@andor-hotels.de, Fax (0511) 3388188, 🕭, 🚖s – 🛗, ✳ rm, 📺 📞 – 🧖 90. 🄰🄴 🅾
🆇 VISA   EX u
Meals à la carte 20/33 – **140 rm** ⛺ 100/115 – 130.

Concorde Hotel am Leineschloß 🅼 without rest, Am Markte 12, ✉ 30159
ℰ (0511) 35 79 10, *leineschloss@concorde-hotels.de*, Fax (0511) 35791100 – 🛗 ✳ 📺
📞 ⟸. 🄰🄴 🅾 🆇 VISA 🄹🄲🄱   DY e
81 rm ⛺ 101 – 136.

Am Rathaus, Friedrichswall 21, ✉ 30159, ℰ (0511) 32 62 68, *info@hotelamrathau*
s.de, Fax (0511) 32626968 – 🛗 📺. 🄰🄴 🅾 🆇 VISA   EY y
Meals *(closed Saturday lunch and Sunday)* à la carte 17,89/32,72 – **43 rm** ⛺ 83 – 120

Savoy, Schloßwender Str. 10, ✉ 30159, ℰ (0511) 1 67 48 70, *savoy-hannover-ml@t*
-online.de, Fax (0511) 16748710, 🚖s – 🛗 📺 📞 ⟸. 🄰🄴 🅾 🆇 VISA   CV e
Meals *(residents only)* à la carte 14,31/16,62 – **18 Z** ⛺ 82/107 – 107/153.

Landhaus Ammann with rm, Hildesheimer Str. 185, ✉ 30173, ℰ (0511) 83 08 18
mail@landhaus-ammann.de, Fax (0511) 8437749, « Elegant installation
courtyard-terrace », 🍴 – 🛗 📺 ⟸ ℙ – 🧖 100. 🄰🄴 🅾 🆇 VISA 🄹🄲🄱 ❀ rest
Meals *(outstanding wine list)* à la carte 43,50/60,84 – **15 rm** ⛺ 131/177 – 187/218.
                                                   by Hildesheimer Straße EFZ

Georgenhof-Stern's Restaurant 🐾 with rm, Herrenhäuser Kirchweg 20,
✉ 30167, ℰ (0511) 70 22 44, *georgenhof@gmx.de*, Fax (0511) 708559, « Lower Saxony
country house in a park ; garden terrace » – 📺 ℙ. 🄰🄴 🅾 🆇 VISA
Meals *(outstanding wine list)* 19 *(lunch)* and à la carte 40,64/70,05 – **14 rm** ⛺ 57/88 –
124/144.   by Engelbosteler Damm CV

Clichy, Weißekreuzstr. 31, ✉ 30161, ℰ (0511) 31 24 47, *clichy@clichy.de*
Fax (0511) 318283 – 🄰🄴 🆇 VISA   EV o
closed Saturday lunch and Sunday – Meals à la carte 37/47,50.

Gattopardo, Hainhölzer Str. 1 / corner of Postkamp, ✉ 30159, ℰ (0511) 1 43 75,
Fax (0511) 318283, 🍴 – 🄰🄴 🆇 VISA   DV f
Meals *(dinner only)* (Italian) à la carte 27/38.

Bierstuben Alt-lila Kranz with rm, Berliner Allee 33, ✉ 30175, ℰ (0511) 85 89 21,
lilakranz@t-online.de, Fax (0511) 854383, 🍴 – 📺 ℙ. 🄰🄴 🅾 🆇 VISA   FX b
Meals *(closed Saturday lunch)* à la carte 20/46 – **5 rm** ⛺ 80/140 – 90/175.

at Hannover-Bemerode *Southeast : 8 km, by Bischofsholer Damm FY :*

Ramada-Treff Hotel Europa, Bergstr. 2, ✉ 30539, ℰ (0511) 9 52 80, *hannover*
@ramada-treff.de, Fax (0511) 9528488, 🍴, 🚖s – 🛗, ✳ rm, 📺 📞 ℙ – 🧖 180. 🄰🄴
🅾 🆇 VISA 🄹🄲🄱
Meals à la carte 20,45/40 – **183 rm** ⛺ 120/150 – 150/180.

at Hannover-Buchholz *Northeast : 7 km, by Bödekerstraße FV and Podbielskistraße :*

Mercure Atrium 🅼, Karl-Wiechert-Allee 68, ✉ 30625, ℰ (0511) 5 40 70, *h1701@a*
ccor-hotels.com, Fax (0511) 5407826, 🍴, 🚖s – 🛗, ✳ rm, 📺 📞 ⟸ ℙ – 🧖 140.
🄰🄴 🅾 🆇 VISA
Meals à la carte 27,10/42,44 – **223 rm** ⛺ 123 – 195 – 7 suites.

XX **Gallo Nero**, Groß Buchholzer Kirchweg 72b, ✉ 30655, ✆ (0511) 5 46 34 34, *mail@g isyvino.de, Fax (0511) 548283,* 🌳, « 18C farmhouse with contemporary interior design ; permanent exhibition of paintings » – 🅿. 🕮 🕮 𝓥𝓘𝓢𝓐 𝐉𝐂𝐁
closed 1 week January, 3 weeks June - July, Saturday lunch, Sunday and Bank Holidays –
Meals (Italian) (outstanding Italian wine and grappa list) (booking essential for dinner) 25 and à la carte 32/43.

at Hanover-Döhren :

XXX **Wichmann**, Hildesheimer Str. 230, ✉ 30519, ✆ (0511) 83 16 71, *gast.wichmann@h tp-tel.de, Fax (0511) 8379811,* « Courtyard » 🅿. 🕮 🕮 𝓥𝓘𝓢𝓐
Meals à la carte 34,50/50.   by Hildesheimer Straße EFZ

XX **Die Insel**, Rudolf-von-Bennigsen-Ufer 81, ✉ 30519, ✆ (0511) 83 12 14, *norbert.sch u@t-online.de, Fax (0511) 831322,* ≤, 🌳 – 🅿. 🕮 🕮 𝓥𝓘𝓢𝓐
closed Monday, except exhibitions – **Meals** (booking essential) (outstanding wine list) 25 *(lunch)* à la carte 30,67/54,19.   by Rudolf von Benningsen-Ufer   EZ

at Hanover-Flughafen (Airport) *North : 11 km, by Vahrenwalder Straße DV :*

🏨 **Maritim Airport Hotel** Ⓜ, Flughafenstr. 5, ✉ 30669, ✆ (0511) 9 73 70, *info.hfl @maritim.de, Fax (0511) 9737590,* ≘, 🔲 – 🛗, ⇄ rm, 📺 ❤ ᵹ, ⇔ – 🔬 980. 🕮 ⓪ 🕮 𝓥𝓘𝓢𝓐 𝐉𝐂𝐁, ⁑ rest
Meals (buffet only) 22 *(lunch)*/24 *(dinner) –* **Bistro Bottaccio** *(closed Sunday and Monday)* **Meals** à la carte 24,54/40,39 – ⌑ 15 – **527 rm** 125/155 – 140/170 – 30 suites.

🏨 **Holiday Inn Airport** Ⓜ, Petzelstr. 60, ✉ 30662, ✆ (0511) 7 70 70, *reservation.hi hannover@ queensgruppe.de, Fax (0511) 737781,* 🌳, ≘, 🔲 – 🛗, ⇄ rm, 🔲 📺 ❤ ᵹ, 🅿 – 🔬 150. 🕮 ⓪ 🕮 𝓥𝓘𝓢𝓐
Meals 20 *(buffet lunch)* and à la carte 28/45 – ⌑ 15 – **209 rm** 135/355 – 155/375.

at Hanover-Kirchrode *Southeast : 8 km, by Hans-Böckler Allee FY :*

🏨 **Queens** ⊛, Tiergartenstr. 117, ✉ 30559, ✆ (0511) 5 10 30, *reservation.quhannove r@queensgruppe.de, Fax (0511) 5103510,* 🌳, 𝑓ᵹ, ≘ – 🛗, ⇄ rm, 📺 ❤ ᵹ, ⇔ 🅿 – 🔬 150. 🕮 ⓪ 🕮 𝓥𝓘𝓢𝓐 𝐉𝐂𝐁
Meals à la carte 22/36 – **178 rm** ⌑ 109/145 – 152/188 – 3 suites.

at Hanover-Kleefeld *East : 4 km, by Hans-Böckler Allee FY :*

🏠 **Kleefelder Hof** without rest, Kleestr. 3a, ✉ 30625, ✆ (0511) 5 30 80, *kleefelderho f-hannover@t-online.de, Fax (0511) 5308333* – 🛗 ⇄ 📺 ❤ ᵹ, ⇔ 🅿 – 🔬 20. 🕮 ⓪ 🕮 𝓥𝓘𝓢𝓐 𝐉𝐂𝐁
⌑ 13 – **86 rm** 77/95 – 95/110.

at Hanover-Lahe *Northeast : 10 km, by Bödekerstraße FV and Podbielskistraße :*

🏠 **Holiday Inn**, Oldenburger Allee 1, ✉ 30659, ✆ (0511) 6 15 50, *Fax (0511) 6155555,* 🌳, ≘ – 🛗, ⇄ rm, 📺 ❤ ᵹ, ⇔ 🅿 – 🔬 280. 🕮 ⓪ 🕮 𝓥𝓘𝓢𝓐 𝐉𝐂𝐁
Meals à la carte 18/33 – ⌑ 12 – **150 rm** 102.

at Hannover-List *Northeast : 5 km, by Bödekerstraße FV :*

🏨 **ArabellaSheraton Pelikan** Ⓜ, Podbielskistr. 145, ✉ 30177, ✆ (0511) 9 09 30, *peli kanhotel@arabellasheraton.com, Fax (0511) 9093555,* 🌳, « Hotel with modern interior in a former factory », 𝑓ᵹ, ≘ – 🛗, ⇄ rm, 📺 ❤ ᵹ, ⇔ 🅿 – 🔬 140. 🕮 ⓪ 🕮 𝓥𝓘𝓢𝓐 𝐉𝐂𝐁
5th Avenue : Meals à la carte 23/38,85 – **Benihana** (Japanese) *(closed Sunday)* **Meals** 48,57/79,25 – ⌑ 16 – **147 rm** 133/280 – 11 suites.

🏠 **Dorint** Ⓜ, Podbielskistr. 21, ✉ 30163, ✆ (0511) 3 90 40, *info.hajhan@dorint.com, Fax (0511) 3904100,* 🌳, ≘ – 🛗, ⇄ rm, 🔲 rm, 📺 ❤ ᵹ, ⇔ – 🔬 200. 🕮 ⓪ 🕮 𝓥𝓘𝓢𝓐 𝐉𝐂𝐁
Meals à la carte 23/35 – ⌑ 15 – **206 rm** 119/139 – 139/169 – 4 suites.

at Hanover-Messe (near Exhibition Centre) *Southeast : 9 km, by Hildesheimer Straße EFZ :*

🏨 **Radisson SAS** Ⓜ, Expo-Plaza 5 (at Exhibitions Centre), ✉ 30539, ✆ (0511) 38 38 30, *infohannover@radissonsas.com, Fax (0511) 383838000,* ≘ – 🛗, ⇄ rm, 🔲 📺 ❤ ᵹ, ⇔ – 🔬 250. 🕮 ⓪ 🕮 𝓥𝓘𝓢𝓐 𝐉𝐂𝐁
Meals à la carte 20,10/33,40 – ⌑ 14 – **250 rm** 110/130 – 110/140.

🏨 **Parkhotel Kronsberg** (with guest house), Laatzener Str. 18 (at Exhibition Centre), ✉ 30539, ✆ (0511) 8 74 00, *parkh@kronsberg.bestwestern.de, Fax (0511) 867112,* 🌳, ≘, 🔲, 🌳 – 🛗, ⇄ rm, 🔲 rest, 📺 ❤ ⇔ 🅿 – 🔬 150. 🕮 ⓪ 🕮 𝓥𝓘𝓢𝓐
Meals *(closed 27 December - 2 January)* à la carte 30,16/35,02 – **200 rm** ⌑ 85/105 – 130/180.

HANOVER (HANNOVER)

at Hanover-Roderbruch *Northeast : 7 km, by Hans-Böckler Allee* FY *and Karl-Wiechert Allee :*

🏨 **Novotel**, Feodor-Lynen-Str. 1, ✉ 30625, ✆ (0511) 9 56 60, *h1631@accor-hotels.com* Fax (0511) 9566333, �, ⊜s, ⬛ (heated) – 🛗, ⇄ rm, 📺 🛳 & 🖭 – 🏛 100. 🆎 ⓪ ⓶⓪ VISA
Meals à la carte 18,50/41 – ⊑ 13 – **112 rm** 65/89 – 84/104.

at Hanover-Vahrenwald *North : 4 km, by Vahrenwalder Straße* DV :

🏨 **Fora**, Großer Kolonnenweg 19, ✉ 30163, ✆ (0511) 6 70 60, *reservation.hannover@ ora.de, Fax (0511) 6706111*, �, ⊜s – 🛗, ⇄ rm, ▦ rest, 📺 🛳 & ⇦ – 🏛 100. 🆎 ⓪ ⓶⓪ VISA JCB
Meals à la carte 18/29,30 – **142 rm** ⊑ 121/141 – 141/162.

at Laatzen *South : 9 km, by Hildesheimer Straße* EFZ :

🏨 **Copthorne** Ⓜ, Würzburger Str. 21, ✉ 30880, ✆ (0511) 9 83 60, *copthorne@hann over.de, Fax (0511) 9836666*, 🌐, ⚕, ⊜s, ⬛ – 🛗, ⇄ rm, ▦ rm, 📺 🛳 & ⇦ 🖭 – 🏛 300. 🆎 ⓪ ⓶⓪ VISA JCB
Meals à la carte 22,95/40,90 – **222 rm** ⊑ 150 – 190.

🏨 **Mercure Messe** Ⓜ, Karlsruher Str. 8a, ✉ 30880, ✆ (0511) 87 57 30, *h2831@acc or-hotels.com, Fax (0511) 87573555* – 🛗, ⇄ rm, ▦ 📺 🛳 & 🖭 – 🏛 130. 🆎 ⓪ ⓶⓪ VISA
Meals à la carte 20,50/34 – ⊑ 14 – **120 rm** 88 – 98.

🏨 **Ramada-Treff Hotel Britannia**, Karlsruher Str. 26, ✉ 30880, ✆ (0511) 8 78 20, *hannover@ramada-treff.de, Fax (0511) 863466*, 🌐, 🍴(indoor) golf simulator – 🛗, ⇄ rm, 📺 & 🖭 – 🏛 120. 🆎 ⓪ ⓶⓪ VISA JCB
Meals 23 *(buffet lunch)* and à la carte 17,50/40 – **100 rm** ⊑ 120/150 – 150/180.

at Langenhagen *North : 10 km, by Vahrenwalder Straße* DV :

🏨 **Allegro** Ⓜ without rest, Walsroder Str. 105, ✉ 30853, ✆ (0511) 7 71 96 10, *info@h otel-allegro.de, Fax (0511) 77196196* – 🛗 ⇄ 📺 🛳 ⇦ – 🏛 200. 🆎 ⓪ ⓶⓪ VISA. 🌺
73 rm ⊑ 95 – 125.

🏨 **Ambiente**, Walsroder Str. 70, ✉ 30853, ✆ (0511) 7 70 60, *hotel@ambiente.com, Fax (0511) 7706111* – 🛗, ⇄ rm, 📺 🛳 ⇦ 🖭 – 🏛 20. 🆎 ⓪ ⓶⓪ VISA
closed 24 December - 2 January – **Meals** *(closed Saturday and Sunday) (dinner only)* à la-carte 17/27 – **67 rm** ⊑ 90 – 115.

at Ronnenberg-Benthe *Southwest : 10 km, by Deisterplatz* CZ *Bornumer Straße and B 65 :*

🏨 **Benther Berg** ⮑, Vogelsangstr. 18, ✉ 30952, ✆ (05108) 6 40 60, *info@hotel-be nther-berg.de, Fax (05108) 640650*, 🌐, « Park », ⊜s, ⬛ – 🛗, ▦ rest, 📺 🖭 – 🏛 60. 🆎 ⓪ ⓶⓪ VISA
Meals à la carte 33,20/47,50 – **70 rm** ⊑ 77/98 – 93/130.

at Isernhagen KB *North : 14 km, by Bödekerstraße* FV *and Podbielskistraße, off Sutelstraße :*

🍴 **Hopfenspeicher** with rm, Dorfstr. 16, ✉ 30916, ✆ (05139) 89 29 15,
🐛 *Fax (05139) 892913*, « Garden terrace » – 📺 🛳 🖭 ⓶⓪ VISA. 🌺
closed 2 weeks January and 2 weeks July – **Meals** *(closed Sunday) (dinner only)* à la carte 38/54 – **18 rm** ⊑ 80/123 – 131/160
Spec. Zitronenspaghettini mit gebratener Gänsestopfleber. Steinbutt und Hummer mit marinierten Artischocken. Dreierlei von der Ziege mit geschmortem Knoblauch und weißem Bohnenragoût.

Nenndorf, Bad *Niedersachsen* 415 416 *I 12 – pop. 10 000 – alt. 70 m.*
Hannover 33.

at Bad Nenndorf-Riepen *Northwest : 4,5 km by B 65 :*

🍴 **La Forge** (Gehrke) - Schmiedegasthaus Gehrke, Riepener Str. 21, ✉ 31542,
🐛 ✆ (05725) 9 44 10, *info@schmiedegasthaus.de, Fax (05725) 944141* – 🖭 🆎 ⓪ VISA. 🌺
closed 2 weeks early January, 2 weeks July - August, Monday and Tuesday – **Meals** *(dinner only) (booking essential)* 58,80/84,40
Spec. Salat von Hummer mit Champagner-Trüffelgelée und Saubohnen. Kaninchen aus dem Ofen mit Paprikagemüse. Ziegenquarksoufflé mit Erdbeer-Basilikummarmelade und Sauerrahmeis.

Deynhausen, Bad *Nordrhein-Westfalen* **417** *J 10 – pop. 52 000 – alt. 71 m.*
Hannover 79.

at Bad Oeynhausen-Lohe *South : 2 km :*

XXX **Die Windmühle** (Lohse), Detmolder Str. 273 (direction Bad Salzuflen), ✉ 32545,
ⓈⓈ 𝒫 (05731) 9 24 62, Fax (05731) 96583, 🏡 – 🅿. ⬛ VISA
closed 2 weeks early February, 2 weeks end September, Sunday and Monday – **Meals**
(booking essential) à la carte 56/86 **– Bistro ô Cêpe : Meals** à la carte 29/42
Spec. Atlantik-Langostinos gefüllt mit geröstetem Lammbries. Biryani vom Lamm mit grünen Tomaten und gelbe Curryjus von Kichererbsen. Rote Wassermelone gefüllt mit Cocos-
Chiboust und Passionsfruchtgelée.

GREEN TOURIST GUIDES
Picturesque scenery, buildings
Attractive routes
Touring programmes
Plans of towns and buildings

LEIPZIG *Sachsen* **418** *L 21 – pop. 450 000 – alt. 118 m.*
See : Old Town Hall★ (Altes Rathaus) BY – Old Stock Exchange★ (Naschmarkt) BY –
Museum of Fine Arts★ (Museum der Bildenden Künste) BZ – Thomaskirche★ BZ – Grassi
Museum (Museum of Fine Art★, Museum of Ethnography★, Musical Instrument Museum★)
CZ.

🐾 Leipzig-Seehausen, Borgweg 10 (North : 8 km by Eutritzscher Straße), 𝒫 (034242)
5 21 74 42 ; 🐾 Markkleeberg, Mühlweg/corner Koburger Straße (South : 11 km by Har-
kortstraße and B 2), 𝒫 (0341) 3 58 26 86 ; 🐾 Noitzsch (Northeast : 29 km by Eutritzscher
Straße and B 2), 𝒫 (034242) 5 03 02.

✈ Leipzig-Halle (Northwest : 13 km by Gerberstraße and Eutritzscher Straße BY),
𝒫 (0341) 22 40.

Exhibition Grounds (Neue Messe), Messe Allee1 (by Eutritzscher Str BY), ✉ 04356,
𝒫 (0341) 67 80, Fax (0341) 6788762.

🛈 Tourist-Information, Richard-Wagner Str. 1, ✉ 04109, 𝒫 (0341) 7 10 42 60, Fax (0341)
7104271 **– ADAC**, Augustusplatz 6.
Berlin 180 – Dresden 109 – Erfurt 126.

Plans on following pages

🏨 **Fürstenhof**, Tröndlinring 8, ✉ 04105, 𝒫 (0341) 14 00, fuerstenhof.leipzig@arabell
asheraton.com, Fax (0341) 1403700, 🏡, « 1770 Patrician palace ; fitness and beauty
centre », Massage, 🛌, �, 🅇 – 🕪, ⇝ rm, ▤ 🅣🆅 📞 & ⇝ – 🕍 60. 🆎 ⓞ ⬛ VISA
JCB ⅏ rest   BY c
Meals à la carte 35/47 – 🖙 19 – **92 rm** 210/280 – 235/305 – 4 suites.

🏨 **Marriott** ℳ, Am Hallischen Tor 1, ✉ 04109, 𝒫 (0341) 9 65 30, leipzig.marriott@ma
rriott.com, Fax (0341) 9653999, 🛌, �, 🅇 – 🕪, ⇝ rm, ▤ 🅣🆅 📞 & ⇝ – 🕍 220.
🆎 ⓞ ⬛ VISA JCB   BY n
Meals à la carte 29,50/38 – **231 rm** 🖙 110/139 – 125/154 – 11 suites.

🏨 **Inter-Continental**, Gerberstr. 15, ✉ 04105, 𝒫 (0341) 98 80, leipzig@interconti.com,
Fax (0341) 9881229, beer garden, Massage, �, 🅇 – 🕪, ⇝ rm, ▤ 🅣🆅 📞 & 🅿 – 🕍 360.
🆎 ⓞ ⬛ VISA JCB ⅏ rest   BY a
Meals à la carte 32/42 **– Yamato** (Japanese) **Meals** 15,33/25,56 and à la carte – 🖙 16
– **447 rm** 130/180 – 150/200 – 21 suites.

🏨 **Renaissance** ℳ, Großer Brockhaus 3, ✉ 04103, 𝒫 (0341) 1 29 20, renaissance.leip
zig@renaissance.com, Fax (0341) 1292800, 🛌, �, 🅇 – 🕪, ⇝ rm, ▤ 🅣🆅 📞 &
– 🕍 360. 🆎 ⓞ ⬛ VISA JCB   DY a
Meals 18 (buffet lunch) and à la carte 27/36,50 – **356 rm** 🖙 100/124 – 114/138.

🏨 **Victor's Residenz** ℳ, Georgiring 13, ✉ 04103, 𝒫 (0341) 6 86 60, info@l.victors.de,
Fax (0341) 6866899, beer garden – 🕪, ⇝ rm, 🅣🆅 & ⇝ 🅿 – 🕍 110. 🆎 ⓞ ⬛
Meals à la carte 21/39,50 – **101 rm** 🖙 90/140 – 105/165.   CY e

🏨 **Dorint** ℳ, Stephanstr. 6, ✉ 04103, 𝒫 (0341) 9 77 90, info.leijlei@dorint.com,
Fax (0341) 9779100, beer garden, � – 🕪, ⇝ rm, 🅣🆅 📞 & ⇝ – 🕍 150. 🆎 ⓞ ⬛
VISA JCB ⅏ rest   DZ n
Meals à la carte 24,60/42 – 🖙 14 – **177 rm** 98/145

🏨 **Seaside Park Hotel** ℳ, Richard-Wagner-Str. 7, ✉ 04109, 𝒫 (0341) 9 85 20, info
@seaside-hotels.de, Fax (0341) 9852750, Massage, � – 🕪, ⇝, ▤ rest, 🅣🆅 📞 &
– 🕍 80. 🆎 ⓞ ⬛ VISA JCB   CY s
Meals (closed mid July - end August and Sunday) à la carte 20,30/40,40 – **288 rm**
🖙 105/125 – 126/140 – 9 suites.

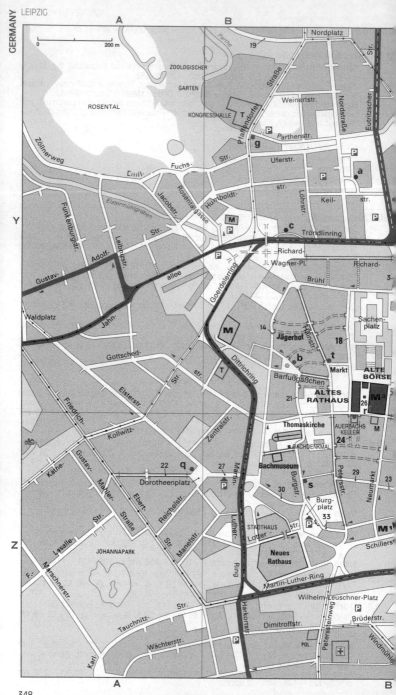

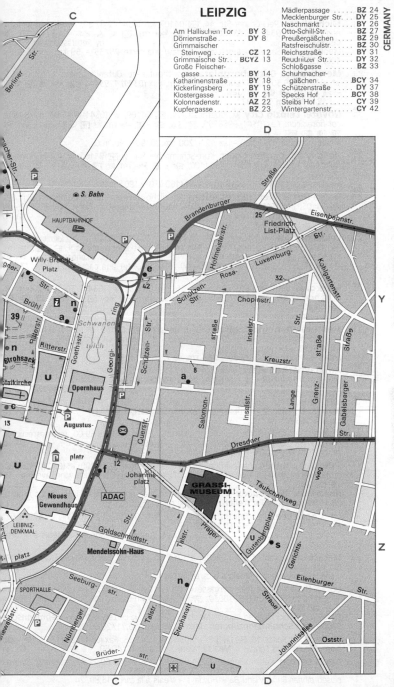

LEIPZIG

GERMANY

Michaelis [M], Paul-Gruner-Str. 44, ✉ 04107, ✆ (0341) 2 67 80, *hotel.michaelis@t-online.de, Fax (0341) 2678100,* – ⦿, ⇔ rm, TV ✆ ♿ – 40. AE ⦿ MC VISA by Peterssteinweg BZ
Meals *(closed Saturday lunch and Sunday)* à la carte 25/35 – **59 rm** ☕ 75/95 – 100/125.

Mercure am Gutenbergplatz [M] without rest, Gutenbergplatz 1, ✉ 04103, ✆ (0341) 1 29 30, *h2837@accor-hotels.com, Fax (0341) 1293444* – ⦿ ⇔ ▤ TV ✆ ♿ – 25. AE ⦿ MC VISA JCB DZ s
☕ 12 – **122 rm** 77 – 87.

Novotel Leipzig City [M], Goethestr. 11, ✉ 04109, ✆ (0341) 9 95 80, *h1784@accor-hotels.com, Fax (0341) 9958200,* , Fб, ≘s – ⦿, ⇔ rm, ▤ TV ✆ ♿ – 150. AE ⦿ MC VISA JCB CY n
Meals à la carte 17/31,50 – ☕ 12 – **200 rm** 80/90 – 90/100.

Holiday Inn Garden Court, Kurt-Schumacher-Str. 3, ✉ 04105, ✆ (0341) 1 25 10, *hileipzig@aol.com, Fax (0341) 1251100,* ≘s – ⦿, ⇔ rm, ▤ TV P – 20. AE ⦿ MC VISA JCB CY g
Meals à la carte 17/27 – **115 rm** ☕ 71/160 – 81/180.

Rema-Hotel Vier Jahreszeiten [M] without rest, Kurt-Schumacher-Str. 23, ✉ 04105, ✆ (0341) 9 85 10, *vier-jahreszeiten@remahotel.de, Fax (0341) 985122* – ⦿ ⇔ TV. AE ⦿ MC VISA JCB CY b
67 rm ☕ 81/130 – 110/190.

Leipziger Hof, Hedwigstr. 1, ✉ 04315, ✆ (0341) 6 97 40, *info@leipziger-hof.de, Fax (0341) 6974150,* beer garden, « Permanent exhibition of paintings », ≘s – ⦿, ⇔ rm, TV ✆ P – 50. AE ⦿ MC VISA by Eisenbahnstraße DY
Meals *(closed Saturday and Sunday) (dinner only)* à la carte 21/28 – **73 rm** ☕ 80 – 113.

Markgraf without rest, Körnerstr. 36, ✉ 04107, ✆ (0341) 30 30 30, *hotel@markgraf-leipzig.de, Fax (0341) 3030399,* ≘s – ⦿ ⇔ TV ✆ . AE ⦿ MC VISA JCB by Peterssteinweg BZ
☕ 9 – **54 rm** 65/75 – 70/75.

Mercure am Augustusplatz, Augustusplatz 5, ✉ 04109, ✆ (0341) 2 14 60, *mercure_leipzig@t-online.de, Fax (0341) 9604916* – ⦿, ⇔ rm, ▤ rest, TV P – 120. AE ⦿ MC VISA JCB CZ f
Meals à la carte 16,60/27,80 – **283 rm** ☕ 72/87 – 105.

Am Bayrischen Platz without rest, Paul-List-Str. 5, ✉ 04103, ✆ (0341) 14 08 60, *Fax (0341) 1408648* – ⦿ ⇔ TV ✆ P. AE ⦿ MC VISA JCB
32 rm ☕ 56/72 – 76/92. by Windmühlenstraße CZ

Ibis without rest, Brühl 69, ✉ 04109, ✆ (0341) 2 18 60, *h1811@accor-hotels.com, Fax (0341) 2186222* – ⦿ ⇔ TV ✆ ♿ . AE ⦿ MC VISA JCB CY a
☕ 8 – **126 rm** 64.

Kaiser Maximilian, Neumarkt 9, ✉ 04105, ✆ (0341) 9 98 69 00, *webmaster@kaiser-maximilian.de, Fax (0341) 9986901,* – AE MC VISA JCB BZ a
closed 1 week January – **Meals** à la carte 29,91/39,11.

Auerbachs Keller, Grimmaische Str. 2 (Mädler-Passage), ✉ 04109, ✆ (0341) 21 61 00, *info@auerbachs-keller-leipzig.de, Fax (0341) 2161011,* « 16C historical wine tavern » – AE ⦿ MC VISA BYZ
Historische Weinstuben *(closed Sunday) (dinner only)* **Meals** 41/61 and à la carte 28,13/40,64 – ***Großer Keller :*** **Meals** à la carte 15,90/31,50.

La Cachette, Pfaffendorfer Str. 26, ✉ 04105, ✆ (0341) 5 62 98 67, *Fax (0341) 5629869,* – AE ⦿ MC VISA. BY g
closed 1 week mid January, 3 weeks August, Sunday and Monday – **Meals** à la carte 35,28/48,20.

Medici, Nikolaikirchhof 5, ✉ 04109, ✆ (0341) 2 11 38 78, *Fax (0341) 9839399* – AE ⦿ MC VISA JCB CY c
closed Sunday lunch – **Meals** à la carte 31/44.

Coffe Baum, Kleine Fleischergasse 4, ✉ 04109, ✆ (0341) 9 61 00 61, *coffe-baum@t-online.de, Fax (0341) 9610030,* , « Historic inn from 1546 ; museum of coffee » – ♿. MC VISA BY b
Lusatia (1st floor) *(closed August)* **Meals** 30/43 and à la carte 27/36,26 – ***Lehmannsche Stube und Schuhmannzimmer :*** **Meals** à la carte 16,71/26,59.

Classico, Nikolaistr. 16, ✉ 04109, ✆ (0341) 2 11 13 55, *Fax (0341) 2111355,* – MC
closed Easter and Sunday – **Meals** (Italian) à la carte 23/40,50. CY n

Apels Garten, Kolonnadenstr. 2, ✉ 04109, ✆ (0341) 9 60 77 77, *mueller@apels-garten.de, Fax (0341) 9607779,* – 30. AE MC VISA AZ q
closed dinner Sunday and Bank Holidays – **Meals** à la carte 13,80/24.

LEIPZIG

GERMANY

※ **Weinstock**, Marktplatz 7, ✉ 04109, ℘ (0341) 14 06 06 06, *Fax (0341) 14060607,* 斎,
« 16C former bank » – AE ➊ ⓜ VISA JCB   BY t
Meals à la carte 18,95/35,75.

※ **Thüringer Hof**, Burgstr. 19, ✉ 04109, ℘ (0341) 9 94 49 99, *reservierung@ thuerin
ger-hof.de, Fax (0341) 9944933,* 斎, « Restored 15C tavern » – AE ⓜ VISA   BZ s
Meals à la carte 15,70/24,30.

※ **Mövenpick**, Naschmarkt 1, ✉ 04109, ℘ (0341) 2 11 77 22, *Fax (0341) 2114810,* 斎
– AE ➊ ⓜ VISA   BY r
Meals à la carte 17,33/30,67.

at Leipzig-Breitenfeld *Northwest : 8 km, by Euritzscher Straße* BX :

🏨 **Breitenfelder Hof** Ⓜ ⚘, Lindenallee 8, ✉ 04466, ℘ (0341) 4 65 10, *info@ breit
enfelderhof.de, Fax (0341) 4651133,* 斎, « Park » – ✳ rm, TV ✆ 🅿 – 🔏 120. AE ➊
ⓜ VISA
closed 22 December - 7 January – *Gustav's (closed Sunday)* **Meals** à la carte 21,05/28
– ☲ 13 – **75 rm** 82/90

at Leipzig-Eutritzsch : *by Eutritzscher Straße* BY :

🏨 **Vivaldi** Ⓜ *without rest,* Wittenberger Str. 87, ✉ 04129, ℘ (0341) 9 03 60, *info@ h
otel-vivaldi.de, Fax (0341) 9036234* – 📶 ✳ TV 🚗 – 🔏 25. AE ➊ ⓜ VISA JCB
107 rm ☲ 60/75 – 70/85.

at Leipzig-Gohlis *North : 2,5 km, by Pfaffendorfer Straße* BY :

🏨 **De Saxe**, Gohliser Str. 25, ✉ 04155, ℘ (0341) 5 93 80, *hoteldesaxe@ aol.com,
Fax (0341) 5938299* – 📶 TV ✆ 🅿. AE ➊ ⓜ VISA
Meals à la carte 14,32/25,05 – **33 rm** ☲ 67 – 82.

at Leipzig-Grosszschocher *Southwest : 7 km, by Käthe-Kollwitz-Straße* AZ *and Erich-Zeigner-
Allee :*

🏨 **Windorf**, Gerhard-Ellrodt-Str. 21, ✉ 04249, ℘ (0341) 4 27 70, *info@ windorf.bestwe
stern.de, Fax (0341) 4277222,* 斎 – 📶, ✳ rm, TV ✆ 🅿 – 🔏 55. AE ➊ ⓜ VISA JCB
Meals à la carte 16,87/26,59 – **91 rm** ☲ 59/75 – 70/84.

at Leipzig-Leutzsch *West : 5,5 km, by Friedrich-Ebert-Straße* AY :

🏨 **Lindner Hotel** Ⓜ, Hans-Driesch-Str. 27, ✉ 04179, ℘ (0341) 4 47 80, *info leipzig@ l
indner.de, Fax (0341) 4478478,* 斎, ☎, 🐎 – 📶, ✳ rm, TV ✆ 🚗 – 🔏 120. AE ➊
ⓜ VISA JCB
closed 27 December - 7 January – **Meals** à la carte 19,94/34,77 – ☲ 14 – **200 rm** 83/151
– 89/137 – 15 suites.

at Leipzig-Lindenau *West : 5 km, by Jahn-Allee* AY :

🏨 **Lindenau**, Georg-Schwarz-Str. 33, ✉ 04177, ℘ (0341) 4 48 03 10, *info@ hotel-linde
nau.de, Fax (0341) 4480300,* ☎ – 📶, ✳ rm, TV ✆ 🅿 – 🔏 25. ⓜ VISA. ⚒ rest
Meals *(closed Saturday and Sunday)* à la carte 15/25 – **50 rm** ☲ 60/70 – 75/90.

at Leipzig-Paunsdorf *East : 5 km, by Dresdner Straße* DZ *and Wurzner Straße :*

🏨 **Ramada Treff Hotel** Ⓜ, Schongauer Str. 39, ✉ 04329, ℘ (0341) 25 40, *leipzig@ r
amada-treff.de, Fax (0341) 2541550,* 斎, Massage, ☎ – 📶, ✳ rm, ▤ TV ✆ 🅿 –
🔏 600. AE ➊ ⓜ VISA JCB
Meals à la carte 19,48/31,89 – **291 rm** ☲ 99 – 125.

at Leipzig-Portitz *Northeast : 10 km, by Berliner Straße* CY :

🏨 **Accento** Ⓜ, Tauchaer Str. 260, ✉ 04349, ℘ (0341) 9 26 20, *welcome@ accento-ho
tel.de, Fax (0341) 9262100,* 斎, ☎ – 📶, ✳ rm, ▤ rest, TV ✆ 🚗 🅿 – 🔏 60. AE ➊
ⓜ VISA
closed 22 December - 6 January – **Meals** à la carte 17,50/28 – ☲ 12 – **114 rm** 72/112

at Leipzig-Reudnitz *Southeast : 3 km, by Dresdner Straße* DZ *and Breite Straße :*

🏨 **Berlin** *without rest,* Riebeckstr. 30, ✉ 04317, ℘ (0341) 2 67 30 00, *hotel-berlin-leipz
ig@ t-online.de, Fax (0341) 2673280* – 📶 ✳ TV – 🔏 20. AE ➊ ⓜ VISA
51 rm ☲ 65/70 – 65/75.

In Leipzig-Seehausen : *North : 8 km, by Eutitzscher Straße* BY *and Theresienstraße :*

🏨 **Im Sachsenpark** Ⓜ, Walter-Köhn-Str. 3, ✉ 04356, ℘ (0341) 5 25 20, *info@ sachs
enparkhotel.de, Fax (0341) 5252528,* 斎, ☎ – 📶, ✳ rm, ▤ rm, TV ✆ 🅿 – 🔏 60.
AE ➊ ⓜ VISA ⚒
Meals à la carte 16,50/29 – **112 rm** ☲ 82/112 – 101/122.

351

at Leipzig-Stötteritz *Southeast : 5 km, by Prager Straße DZ and Stötteritzer Straße :*

🏠🏠 **Holiday Inn Alte Messe** M, Breslauer Str. 33, ✉ 04299, 𝒫 (0341) 8 67 90, *info
@ holiday-inn-leipzig.de, Fax (0341) 8679444,* 🌳, ⇌ – 📶, 🔆 rm, 🍴 rest, 📺 ⚓ 🔥 🚗
– 🏛 25. 🝏 ⓪ ⓪ VISA JCB
Meals à la carte 17,20/30,60 – **126 rm** ⚏ 69/95 – 76/110 – 9 suites.

at Leipzig-Wiederitzsch *North : 7 km, by Eutrizscher Straße BY and Delitzscher Straße :*

🏠🏠🏠 **Astron Hotel** M, Fuggerstr. 2, ✉ 04448, 𝒫 (0341) 5 25 10, *leipzig@ astron-hotels.de*
Fax (0341) 5251300, 🔥, ⇌ – 📶, 🔆 rm, 🍴 📺 ⚓ 🔥 🚗 – 🏛 220. 🝏 ⓪ ⓪ VISA
JCB
U ⤬
Meals à la carte 19/33 – **308 rm** ⚏ 82/100 – 93/111.

at Wachau *Southeast : 8 km, by Prager Straße DZ and Chemnitzer Straße :*

🏠🏠🏠 **Atlanta Hotel** M, Südring 21, ✉ 04445, 𝒫 (034297) 8 40, *info@atlanta-hotel.de*
Fax (034297) 84999, ⇌ – 📶, 🔆 rm, 🍴 📺 ⚓ 🔥 📠 – 🏛 250. 🝏 ⓪ ⓪ VISA
Meals à la carte 20,69/30,86 – **196 rm** ⚏ 60/68 – 75/83 – 6 suites.

MUNICH (MÜNCHEN) 🗺 *Bayern* 🔢🔢🔢🔢 *V 18 – pop. 1 300 000 – alt. 520 m.*

See : Marienplatz★ *KZ* – Church of Our Lady (Frauenkirche)★, (Prunkkenotaph of Bavarian
Emperor Ludwig★, tower ⁂★) *KZ* – Old Pinakothek (Alte Pinakothek)★★★ *KY* – German
Museum (Deutsches Museum)★★★ *LZ* – The Palace (Residenz)★★ (Treasury★★, Residenz
Museum★★, Palace Theatre★) *KY* – Church of Asam Brothers (Asamkirche)★ *KZ* –
Nymphenburg★★ (Castle★, Gallery of Beauties König Ludwig★, Park★, Amalienburg★★
Botanical Garden (Botanischer Garten)★★, Carriage Museum (Marstallmuseum) and China
Collection (Porzellansammlung★) by Arnulfstr. EV – New Pinakothek (Neue Pinakothek)★★
KY – City Historical Museum (Münchener Stadtmuseum)★ (Moorish Dancers★★) *KZ* **M7** –
Villa Lenbach Collections (Städt. Galerie im Lenbachhaus) (Portraits by Lenbach★) *JY* **M4**
– Antique Collections (Staatliche Antikensammlungen)★ *JY* **M3** – Glyptothek★ *JY* **M2** –
St Michael's Church (Michaelskirche)★ *KYZ* – Theatine Church (Theatinerkirche)★ *KY* –
German Hunting Museum (Deutsches Jagdmuseum)★ *KZ* **M1** – Olympic Park (Olympia-Park)
(Olympic Tower ⁂★★★) by Schleißheimer Straße FU – Englich Garden (Englischer Garten)★
(⇐ from Monopteros Temple★) *LY* – Hellabrunn Zoo (Tierpark Hellabrunn)★ by Lind
wurmstraße (B 11) EX.

🏌 München-Daglfing, Graf-Lehndorff Str. 36, 𝒫 (089) 94 50 08 00 ; 🏌 München
Thalkirchen, Zentralländstr. 40, 𝒫 (089) 7 23 13 04 ; 🏌 Straßlach, Tölzer Straße (South
17 km), 𝒫 (08170) 4 50 ; 🏌 Eichenried, Kurfürstenweg 10 (Northwest : 16 km), 𝒫 (08131
56 74 10.

✈ Flughafen Franz-Josef Strauß (North-East : 29 km by Ungererstraße HU), 𝒫 (089
9 75 00, City Air Terminal, Arnulfstraße (Main Station).

🚉 Ostbahnhof, Friedenstraße(HX).

🚢 Exhibition Centre (Messegelände) (by ③), ✉ 81823, 𝒫 (089) 9 49 01, Fax (089) 94909
🛈 Tourist-Office, Bahnhofsplatz, ✉ 80335, 𝒫 (089) 2 33 03 00, Fax (089) 23330233.
ADAC, Sendlinger-Tor-Platz 9.

Berlin 586 – Innsbruck 162 – Nürnberg 165 – Salzburg 140 – Stuttgart 222.

Plans on following pages

🏠🏠🏠🏠 **Bayerischer Hof,** Promenadeplatz 2, ✉ 80333, 𝒫 (089) 2 12 00, *info@ bayerische
rhof.de, Fax (089) 2120906,* 🌳, Massage, ⇌, 🌊 – 📶, 🔆 rm, 🍴 📺 ⚓ 🔥 🚗 –
🏛 1200. 🝏 ⓪ ⓪ VISA JCB
KY ⤬
Garden-Restaurant (booking essential) **Meals** à la carte 39,11/59,31 – **Trader Vic's**
(Polynesian) *(dinner only)* **Meals** à la carte 27,61/48,32 – **Palais Keller** (Bavarian beer inn
Meals à la carte 17,40/27,87 – ⚏ 20 – **399 rm** 145/335 – 232/360 – 47 suites.

🏠🏠🏠🏠 **Mandarin Oriental,** Neuturmstr. 1, ✉ 80331, 𝒫 (089) 29 09 80, *info-momuc@ mc
hg.com, Fax (089) 222539,* « Roof terrace with ⤓ » – 📶 🍴 📺 ⚓ 🚗 – 🏛 40. 🝏 ⓪
⓪ VISA JCB. 🌸 rest
KZ ⤬
Mark's *(closed Sunday and Monday) (dinner only)* **Meals** à la carte 45/61 – **Mark's Corner**
(lunch only Tuesday - Saturday) **Meals** 32 (lunch) and à la carte 29/44 – ⚏ 22 – **73 rm**
270/370 – 320/420 – 6 suites.

🏠🏠🏠 **Königshof,** Karlsplatz 25, ✉ 80335, 𝒫 (089) 55 13 60, *koenigshof-muenchen@geis
❀ el-hotels.de, Fax (089) 55136113,* 🔥, ⇌ – 📶, 🔆 rm, 🍴 📺 ⚓ 🚗 – 🏛 80. 🝏 ⓪
⓪ VISA JCB
JY ⤬
Meals *(closed 2 to 6 January, 5 August - 8 September Sunday) (5 August - 8 September
dinner only) (booking essential) (outstanding wine list)* à la carte 43/72 – ⚏ 18 – **87 rm**
215/245 – 260/350 – 10 suites
Spec. Gänseleberravioli mit Kirschen und altem Portwein (summer). Gegrillte St. Jakobsmuscheln mit Löwenzahnrisotto und wildem Spargel. Geschmorte Milchlammschulter mit
breiten Bohnen und jungem Knoblauch.

🏨 **Park Hilton**, Am Tucherpark 7, ⌂ 80538, 𝒫 (089) 3 84 50, *sales_munich-park@hilt on.com*, Fax (089) 38452588, beer garden, Massage, ⬌, ▨ – ⧈, ↔ rm, 🍽 📺 ⚓ ⬧, ⬅ – 🔏 690. ᴀᴇ ⓞ ⓜⓢ 𝘝𝘐𝘚𝘈 ᴊᴄʙ
HU n
Meals à la carte 33,24/43,45 – **Tse Yang** (Chinese) *(closed Monday)* Meals à la carte 24/44 – ⬩ 19 – **479 rm** 205/345 – 255/395 – 16 suites.

🏨 **Kempinski Hotel Vier Jahreszeiten**, Maximilianstr. 17, ⌂ 80539, 𝒫 (089) 2 12 50, *reservations.vierjahreszeiten@kempinski.com*, Fax (089) 21252000, Massage, ⬌, ▨ – ⧈, ↔ rm, 🍽 📺 ⚓ ⬅ – 🔏 220. ᴀᴇ ⓞ ⓜⓢ 𝘝𝘐𝘚𝘈 ᴊᴄʙ. ⬩ rest
LZ a
Meals à la carte 37/68 – ⬩ 23 – **316 rm** 295/445 – 335/485 – 50 suites.

🏨 **Excelsior**, Schützenstr. 11, ⌂ 80335, 𝒫 (089) 55 13 70, *excelsior-muenchen@geise l-hotels.de*, Fax (089) 55137121 – ⧈, ↔ rm, 📺 ⚓ – 🔏 25. ᴀᴇ ⓞ ⓜⓢ 𝘝𝘐𝘚𝘈 ᴊᴄʙ
JY z
Vinothek : Meals à la carte 27,50/36 – ⬩ 15 – **113 rm** 144/160 – 179/203.

🏨 **Maritim** Ⓜ, Goethestr. 7, ⌂ 80336, 𝒫 (089) 55 23 50, *info.mun@maritim.de*, Fax (089) 55235900, 🏛, ⬌, ▨ – ⧈, ↔ rm, 🍽 📺 ⚓ ⬅ – 🔏 250. ᴀᴇ ⓞ ⓜⓢ 𝘝𝘐𝘚𝘈 ᴊᴄʙ. ⬩ rest
JZ z
Meals 20 *(buffet lunch)* and à la carte 28/37,50 – ⬩ 17 – **347 rm** 150/198 – 172/220 – 10 suites.

🏨 **ArabellaSheraton Westpark**, Garmischer Str. 2, ⌂ 80339, 𝒫 (089) 5 19 60, *west park@arabellasheraton.com*, Fax (089) 51963000, 🏛, ⬌, ▨ – ⧈, ↔ rm, 🍽 rest, 📺 ⚓ ⬧ ⬅ – 🔏 80. ᴀᴇ ⓞ ⓜⓢ 𝘝𝘐𝘚𝘈 ᴊᴄʙ   by Leopoldstraße GU
closed 21 December - 6 January – Meals à la carte 25/39 – ⬩ 16 – **258 rm** 140/165 – 166/191 – 6 suites.

🏨 **Eden-Hotel-Wolff**, Arnulfstr. 4, ⌂ 80335, 𝒫 (089) 55 11 50, *sales@ehw.de*, Fax (089) 55115555 – ⧈, ↔ rm, 📺 ⚓ ⬅ – 🔏 140. ᴀᴇ ⓞ ⓜⓢ 𝘝𝘐𝘚𝘈 ᴊᴄʙ   JY p
Meals à la carte 19,50/29,50 – **210 rm** ⬩ 131/202 – 169/282.

🏨 **King's Hotel** without rest, Dachauer Str. 13, ⌂ 80335, 𝒫 (089) 55 18 70, *first@kin gshotels.de*, Fax (089) 55187300 – ⧈ ↔ 🍽 📺 ⚓ ⬅ 🅿 – 🔏 30. ᴀᴇ ⓞ ⓜⓢ 𝘝𝘐𝘚𝘈 ᴊᴄʙ
86 rm ⬩ 125/145 – 155/170 – 6 suites.   JY f

🏨 **Exquisit** without rest, Pettenkoferstr. 3, ⌂ 80336, 𝒫 (089) 5 51 99 00, *info@hotel cxquisit.com*, Fax (089) 55199499, ⬌ – ⧈ ↔ 📺 ⬧ ⬅ – 🔏 30. ᴀᴇ ⓞ ⓜⓢ 𝘝𝘐𝘚𝘈 ᴊᴄʙ
closed 24 to 27 December – **50 rm** ⬩ 110/155 – 150/185 – 5 suites.   JZ s

🏨 **Platzl**, Sparkassenstr. 10, ⌂ 80331, 𝒫 (089) 23 70 30, *info@plazl.de*, Fax (089) 23703800, 🍴, ⬌ – ⧈, ↔ 📺 ⚓ ⬧ ⬅ – 🔏 30. ᴀᴇ ⓞ ⓜⓢ 𝘝𝘐𝘚𝘈 ᴊᴄʙ
Pfistermühle *(closed Sunday)* Meals à la carte 24,76/36,20 – **Ayingers :** Meals à la carte 16,60/31,20 – **167 rm** ⬩ 105/155 – 168/238.   KZ z

🏨 **Drei Löwen** without rest, Schillerstr. 8, ⌂ 80336, 𝒫 (089) 55 10 40, *hotel-drei-loew en-muc@t-online.de*, Fax (089) 55104905 – ⧈ ↔ 📺 – 🔏 15. ᴀᴇ ⓞ ⓜⓢ 𝘝𝘐𝘚𝘈 ᴊᴄʙ
97 rm ⬩ 105/140 – 140/150 – 3 suites.   JZ m

🏨 **Four Points Hotel München Central** without rest, Schwanthalerstr. 111, ⌂ 80339, 𝒫 (089) 51 08 30, *fourpoints.central@arabellasheraton.com*, Fax (089) 51083800, ⬌ – ⧈ ↔ 📺 ⬅ – 🔏 30. ᴀᴇ ⓞ ⓜⓢ 𝘝𝘐𝘚𝘈 ᴊᴄʙ   EX s
closed 22 December - 6 January – **102 rm** ⬩ 122/152 – 153/184.

🏨 **Stadthotel Asam**, Josephspitalstr. 3, ⌂ 80331, 𝒫 (089) 2 30 97 00, *info@hotel-a sam.de*, Fax (089) 23097097 – ⧈ ↔ 📺 ⬧ ⬅. ᴀᴇ ⓞ ⓜⓢ 𝘝𝘐𝘚𝘈
⬩ 12 – **25 rm** 127/142 – 155/172 – 9 Suites.   JZ a

🏨 **International de Ville** Ⓜ, Schillerstr. 10, ⌂ 80336, 𝒫 (089) 8 90 53 70, Fax (089) 89053737 – ⧈, ↔ rm, 📺 ⬧ – 🔏 60. ᴀᴇ ⓜⓢ 𝘝𝘐𝘚𝘈   JZ g
Meals à la carte 18/31,50 – **89 rm** ⬩ 103/141 – 133/220.

🏨 **Torbräu**, Tal 41, ⌂ 80331, 𝒫 (089) 24 23 40, *info@torbraeu.de*, Fax (089) 24234235 – ⧈, ↔ rm, 📺 ⚓ ⬅ 🅿 – 🔏 30. ᴀᴇ ⓜⓢ 𝘝𝘐𝘚𝘈 ᴊᴄʙ
La Famiglia (Italian) Meals à la carte 31/39,50 – **86 rm** ⬩ 115/151 – 155/189 – 3 suites. LZ g

🏨 **Mercure City**, Senefelder Str. 9, ⌂ 80336, 𝒫 (089) 55 13 20, *h0878@accor-ho tels.com*, Fax (089) 596444, beer garden – ⧈ ↔ 🍽 📺 ⬧ ⬅ – 🔏 50. ᴀᴇ ⓞ ⓜⓢ 𝘝𝘐𝘚𝘈 ᴊᴄʙ
JZ v
Meals à la carte 18,90/28 – **167 rm** ⬩ 118/142 – 148/164.

🏨 **Erzgießerei-Europe**, Erzgießereistr. 15, ⌂ 80335, 𝒫 (089) 12 68 20, *erz1europe@aol.com*, Fax (089) 1236198, 🏛 – ⧈, ↔ rm, 📺 ⚓ ⬅ – 🔏 50. ᴀᴇ ⓞ ⓜⓢ 𝘝𝘐𝘚𝘈 ᴊᴄʙ. ⬩ rest
JY a
Meals *(closed Saturday and Sunday lunch)* à la carte 22,50/31,09 – **106 rm** ⬩ 92 – 113.

🏨 **Ambiente** Ⓜ without rest, Schillerstr. 12, ⌂ 80336, 𝒫 (089) 54 51 70, *info@hotel -ambiente-muenchen.de*, Fax (089) 54517200 – ⧈ ↔ 📺. ᴀᴇ ⓞ ⓜⓢ 𝘝𝘐𝘚𝘈 ᴊᴄʙ JZ g
46 rm ⬩ 80/140 – 90/150.

🏨 **King's Hotel Center** without rest, Marsstr. 15, ⌂ 80335, 𝒫 (089) 51 55 30, *cent er@kingshotels.de*, Fax (089) 51553300 – ⧈ ↔ 📺 ⚓ ⬧ ⬅. ᴀᴇ ⓞ ⓜⓢ 𝘝𝘐𝘚𝘈 ᴊᴄʙ
⬩ 11 – **90 rm** 85/115 – 105/145.   JY b

STREET INDEX

Continued on following pages

354

MÜNCHEN

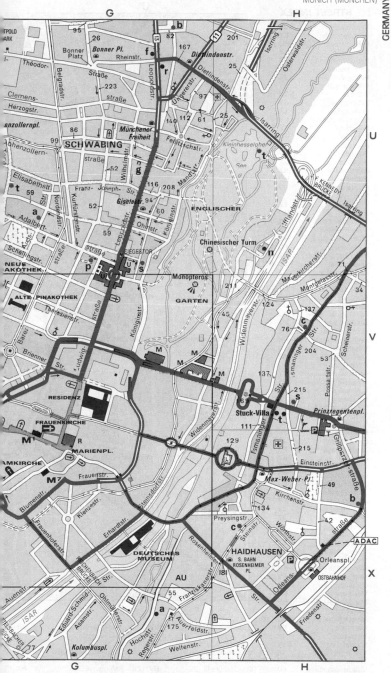

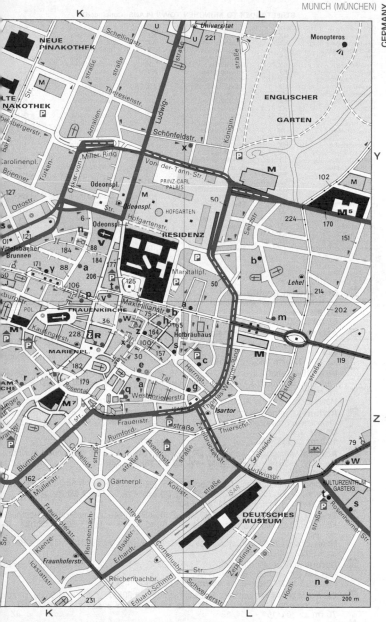

🏢 **Drei Löwen Residenz** without rest, Aldolf-Kolping-Str. 11, ✉ 80336, ✆ (089) 55 10 40, *hotel-drei-loewen-muc@t-online.de*, Fax (089) 55104905 – 📶 ✦ 📺 ✆. 🖭 ⓄⓄ 🆚🆂🅰 𝐽𝐶𝐵
JZ c
63 rm ⇆ 90/115 – 125.

🏢 **Astron Hotel Deutscher Kaiser** Ⓜ without rest, Arnulfstr. 2, ✉ 80335, ✆ (089) 5 45 30, *astroncity@aol.com*, Fax (089) 54532255 – 📶 ✦ 📺 ✆ – 🅰 80. 🖭 Ⓞ ⓄⓄ 🆚🆂🅰 𝐽𝐶𝐵
JY
⇆ 15 – **174 rm** 133/225 – 153/256.

🏢 **Intercity-Hotel**, Bayerstr. 10, ✉ 80335, ✆ (089) 54 55 60, *reservierung@intercity* -hotel.de, Fax (089) 54556610 – 📶, ✦ rm, 📺 ✆ – 🅰 85. 🖭 Ⓞ ⓄⓄ 🆚🆂🅰 𝐽𝐶𝐵 ✂ rest
JY L
Meals (closed 2 weeks August) à la carte 19,19/28,89 – **200 rm** ⇆ 110 – 142 – 4 suites

🏢 **Atrium** Ⓜ without rest, Landwehrstr. 59, ✉ 80336, ✆ (089) 51 41 90, *info@atrium* -muenchen.bestwestern.de, Fax (089) 535066, ☎ – 📶 ✦ 📺 ✆ ☞ – 🅰 25. 🖭 Ⓞ ⓄⓄ 🆚🆂🅰 𝐽𝐶𝐵
JZ k
162 rm ⇆ 135 – 165.

🏢 **Admiral** without rest, Kohlstr. 9, ✉ 80469, ✆ (089) 21 63 50, *info@hotel-admiral.de* Fax (089) 293674 – 📶 ✦ 📺 ✆ ☞. 🖭 Ⓞ ⓄⓄ 🆚🆂🅰
LZ l
33 rm ⇆ 150 – 180.

🏢 **Europa** Ⓜ without rest, Dachauer Str. 115, ✉ 80335, ✆ (089) 54 24 20, *info@hot* el-europa.de, Fax (089) 54242500, ☎ – 📶 📺 ✆ ☞ – 🅰 60. 🖭 Ⓞ ⓄⓄ 🆚🆂🅰 𝐽𝐶𝐵. ✂
– **180 rm** ⇆ 85/108 – 108/118 – 7 suites.
FU c

🏢 **Tryp** Ⓜ, Paul-Heyse-Str. 24, ✉ 80336, ✆ (089) 51 49 00, *tryp.muenchen@t-online.de* Fax (089) 51490701, 🖐, ☎ – 📶, ✦ rm, 📺 ✆ ☞ – 🅰 35. 🖭 Ⓞ ⓄⓄ 🆚🆂🅰 𝐽𝐶𝐵 ✂ rest
JZ c
Meals (closed lunch Saturday, Sunday and Bank Holidays) à la carte 14,80/39,60 – **200 rm** ⇆ 92/122 – 102/138.

🏢 **Domus** without rest, St.-Anna-Str. 31, ✉ 80538, ✆ (089) 22 17 04, Fax (089) 2285355 – 📶 ✦ 📺 ☞. 🖭 Ⓞ ⓄⓄ 🆚🆂🅰
LY b
closed 23 to 28 December – **45 rm** ⇆ 103/128 – 149.

🏢 **Carat-Hotel** Ⓜ without rest, Lindwurmstr. 13, ✉ 80337, ✆ (089) 23 03 80, *carat-m* uc@t-online.de, Fax (089) 23038199 – 📶 ✦ 📺 ✆ ☞ – 🅰 15. 🖭 Ⓞ ⓄⓄ 🆚🆂🅰
JZ
70 rm ⇆ 104/161 – 134/186.

🏢 **Kraft** without rest, Schillerstr. 49, ✉ 80336, ✆ (089) 59 48 23, *kraft.hotel@t-online.de* Fax (089) 5503856 – 📶 ✦ 📺 ✆. 🖭 Ⓞ ⓄⓄ 🆚🆂🅰 𝐽𝐶𝐵
JZ y
closed 23 to 26 December – **33 rm** ⇆ 80 – 95.

🏢 **Concorde** without rest, Herrnstr. 38, ✉ 80539, ✆ (089) 22 45 15, *info@concorde* -muenchen.de, Fax (089) 2283282 – 📶 📺 ✆ ☞. 🖭 Ⓞ ⓄⓄ 🆚🆂🅰 𝐽𝐶𝐵
LZ c
closed Christmas - early January – **71 rm** ⇆ 97 – 128.

🏨 **Cristal** Ⓜ without rest, Schwanthalerstr. 36, ✉ 80336, ℘ (089) 55 11 10, *info@cris tal.bestwestern.de, Fax (089) 55111992* – ⧉ ⇌ 📺 ☎ ⇔ – ⚐ 75. ⚙ 🄷
🟥🟥 🆅🅸🆂🅰 JZ h
100 rm ⊇ 128 – 152.

🏨 **Präsident** Ⓜ without rest, Schwanthalerstr. 20, ✉ 80336, ℘ (089) 5 49 00 60, *hote l.praesident@t-online.de, Fax (089) 54900628* – ⧉ ⇌ 📺 ☎ – ⚐ 15. ⚙ ⓪ 🟥🟥 🆅🅸🆂🅰 🆓🅲🅱
42 rm ⊇ 80/156 – 115/177. JZ q

🏨 **Schlicker** without rest, Tal 8, ✉ 80331, ℘ (089) 2 42 88 70, *schlicker-munich@t-on line.de, Fax (089) 296059* – ⧉ 📺 ☎ 🄿 ⚙ ⓪ 🟥🟥 🆅🅸🆂🅰 KZ a
closed 23 December - 7 January – **69 rm** ⊇ 78/105 – 97/129.

🏨 **Meier** Ⓜ without rest, Schützenstr. 12, ✉ 80335, ℘ (089) 5 49 03 40, *info@hotel -meier-city-muenchen.de, Fax (089) 549034340* – ⧉ ⇌ 📺 ☎ ⚙ ⓪ 🟥🟥 🆅🅸🆂🅰 JY x
closed 23 to 26 December – **50 rm** ⊇ 87/98 – 115.

🏨 **Europäischer Hof** without rest, Bayerstr. 31, ✉ 80335, ℘ (089) 55 15 10, *info@h eh.de, Fax (089) 55151222* – ⧉ ⇌ 📺 ☎ ⇔ 🄿 – ⚐ 20. ⚙ ⓪ 🟥🟥 🆅🅸🆂🅰 🆓🅲🅱 JZ b
148 rm ⊇ 97/147 – 112/167.

🏨 **Astor** without rest, Schillerstr. 24, ✉ 80336, ℘ (089) 54 83 70, *info@hotel-astor.de, Fax (089) 54837666* – ⧉ ⇌ 📺 ☎ ⇔ ⚙ ⓪ 🟥🟥 🆅🅸🆂🅰 🆓🅲🅱 JZ e
46 rm ⊇ 71/112 – 92/143.

🏨 **Olympic** without rest, Hans-Sachs-Str. 4, ✉ 80469, ℘ (089) 23 18 90,
Fax (089) 23189199 – 📺 ⇔ ⚙ ⓪ 🟥🟥 🆅🅸🆂🅰 KZ c
38 rm ⊇ 95/115 – 135.

XXX **Am Marstall**, Maximilianstr. 16, ✉ 80539, ℘ (089) 29 16 55 11, *restaurant_am_ma*
🕸🕸 *rstall@t-online.de, Fax (089) 29165512* – ⚙ ⓪ 🟥🟥 🆅🅸🆂🅰 ✂ KZ b
closed 1 week January, 1 week August, Sunday and Monday – **Meals** à la carte 54/76
Spec. Gänsestopfleber mit Sauternesgelée und Wachteltarte. Variation von Hummer mit
Estragonaromen. Rehbock mit Spätzle und süsser Pfeffersauce.

XX **Ca'Brunello**, Maffeistr. 3a, ✉ 80333, ℘ (089) 20 40 04 91, *Fax (089) 20400492*, 🍴,
« Modern interior » – ▤ KY p
closed Sunday – **Meals** à la carte 33/42.

XX **Boettner's**, Pfisterstr. 9, ✉ 80331, ℘ (089) 22 12 10, *Fax (089) 29162024*, 🍴 – ▤.
⚙ ⓪ 🟥🟥 KZ h
closed 15 April - 15 September Saturday and Sunday, 15 September - 15 April Sunday –
Meals (booking essential) à la carte 36/66.

XX **Halali**, Schönfeldstr. 22, ✉ 80539, ℘ (089) 28 59 09, *Fax (089) 282786*, « Cosy, rustic
installation » – ⚙ 🟥🟥 🆅🅸🆂🅰 LY x
closed 3 weeks August, Saturday lunch, Sunday and Bank Holidays – **Meals** (booking essential) 21,44 *(lunch)* and à la carte 32,16/42,88.

XX **Gasthaus Glockenbach** (Ederer), Kapuzinerstr. 29, ✉ 80337, ℘ (089) 53 40 43,
🕸 *Fax (089) 534043*, (former old Bavarian pub) – ⚙ ⓪ 🟥🟥 🆅🅸🆂🅰 FX e
closed 24 to 31 December, 2 weeks August, Sunday - Monday and Bank Holidays – **Meals**
(booking essential) 25 *(lunch)* and à la carte 40/56
Spec. Steinpilze im Ganzen gebraten mit Geflügelglace und Petersilie. Hummer mit Couscous und Kräuteröl. Ausgelöstes Perlhuhn mit jungen Erbsen und Estragonsauce.

XX **Ederer**, Kardinal-Faulhaber-Str. 10, ✉ 80333, ℘ (089) 24 23 13 10, *Fax (089) 24231312*
– ▤. ⚙ ⓪ 🟥🟥 KY a
closed Sunday and Bank Holidays – **Meals** (booking essential) à la carte 35/51.

XX **Hunsinger's Pacific**, Maximiliansplatz 5, ✉ 80333, ℘ (089) 55 02 97 41,
Fax (089) 55029742 – ▤. ⚙ ⓪ 🟥🟥 🆅🅸🆂🅰 🆓🅲🅱 KY s
closed Bank Holidays, lunch Saturday and Sunday, May - October Sunday – **Meals** (Asiatic-
Pacific) à la carte 23/39.

XX **Austernkeller**, Stollbergstr. 11, ✉ 80539, ℘ (089) 29 87 87, *Fax (089) 223166*,
« Vaulted cellar with collection of china plates » – ⚙ ⓪ 🟥🟥 🆅🅸🆂🅰 🆓🅲🅱 LZ e
closed 23 to 26 December – **Meals** *(dinner only)* (booking essential) à la carte 28,50/47.

XX **Dallmayr**, Dienerstr. 14 (1st floor), ✉ 80331, ℘ (089) 2 13 51 00, *gastrodallmayr@d allmayr.de, Fax (089) 2135443* – ⧉ ⇌ ▤. ⚙ ⓪ 🟥🟥 🆅🅸🆂🅰 KZ w
*closed Monday - Wednesday from 7 pm, Thursday and Friday from 8 pm, Saturday from
4 pm, Sunday and Bank Holidays* – **Meals** à la carte 34/55.

XX **Nymphenburger Hof**, Nymphenburger Str. 24, ✉ 80335, ℘ (089) 1 23 38 30,
Fax (089) 1233852, 🍴 – ⚙ 🟥🟥 🆅🅸🆂🅰. ✂ EV a
closed 23 December - 15 January, Saturday lunch, Sunday, Monday and Bank Holidays –
Meals à la carte 31/57.

XX **Lenbach**, Ottostr. 6, ✉ 80333, ℘ (089) 5 49 13 00, *info@lenbach.de,
Fax (089) 54913075*, 🍴, « Mansion with modern interior » – ⚙ ⓪ 🟥🟥 🆅🅸🆂🅰 JY c
closed Sunday – **Meals** à la carte 34,70/56,50.

XX **Galleria**, Ledererstr. 2/corner of Sparkassenstraße, ⊠ 80331, 𝒫 (089) 29 79 95
Fax (089) 2913653, « Changing exhibition of paintings » – ▤. AE ① ◉◉ VISA   KZ ›
closed 1 to 10 January, 10 to 20 August and Sunday – **Meals** (Italian) (booking essential
à la carte 32/40.

XX **Weinhaus Neuner**, Herzogspitalstr. 8, ⊠ 80331, 𝒫 (089) 2 60 39 54, *weinhaus-ne*
uner@t-online.de, Fax (089) 266933, « 19C wine-restaurant » – AE ◉◉
VISA JCB   JZ e
closed 1 week August, Sunday and Bank Holidays – **Meals** à la carte 24,50/36,50.

X **Dukatz**, Salvatorplatz 1, ⊠ 80333, 𝒫 (089) 2 91 96 00,
🍴 *Fax (089) 29196028*   KY r
closed Sunday dinner – **Meals** (booking essential) à la carte 25,30/37,80.

X **Zum Alten Markt**, Dreifaltigkeitsplatz 3, ⊠ 80331, 𝒫 (089) 29 99 95, *lehner.gast.*
@zumaltenmarkt.de, Fax (089) 2285078, 😤, « Furnished in traditional Alpine
style » –   KZ c
closed Sunday and Bank Holidays – **Meals** (booking essential for dinner) à la carte 22/34,50

Brewery-inns :

X **Spatenhaus an der Oper**, Residenzstr. 12, ⊠ 80333, 𝒫 (089) 2 90 70 60, *spate*
nhaus@kuffler-gastronomie.de, Fax (089) 2913054, 😤, « Furnished in traditional Alpine
style » – AE ◉◉ VISA   KY
Meals à la carte 28,22/39,82.

X **Weisses Bräuhaus**, Tal 7, ⊠ 80331, 𝒫 (089) 29 98 75, Fax (089) 29013815, 😤 ·
🅰 30   KZ e
Meals à la carte 17,87/27,06.

X **Augustiner Gaststätten**, Neuhauser Str. 27, ⊠ 80331, 𝒫 (089) 23 18 32 57
Fax (089) 2605379, « Beer garden » – AE ① ◉◉ VISA JCB   JZ v
Meals à la carte 15/30,10.

X **Altes Hackerhaus**, Sendlinger Str. 14, ⊠ 80331, 𝒫 (089) 2 60 50 26, *hackerhau.*
@aol.com, Fax (089) 2605027, 😤, « Courtyard terrace » – AE ① ◉◉ VISA JCB   KZ
Meals à la carte 17,36/33,18.

X **Zum Franziskaner**, Perusastr. 5, ⊠ 80333, 𝒫 (089) 2 31 81 20, *zum.franziskane*
@t-online.de, Fax (089) 23181244, 😤 – ▤ rest. AE ① ◉◉ VISA JCB   KY
Meals à la carte 16,75/25,40.

X **Bratwurstherzl**, Dreifaltigkeitsplatz 1 (at Viktualienmarkt), ⊠ 80331, 𝒫 (089)
🍴 29 51 13, Fax (089) 29163751, beer garden – AE ◉◉ VISA   KZ c
closed Sunday and Bank Holidays – **Meals** à la carte 13,27/22,46.

at Munich-Allach *Northwest : 12 km, by Arnulfstraße EV and Menzinger Straße* :

🏨 **Lutter** without rest, Eversbuschstr. 109, ⊠ 80999, 𝒫 (089) 8 92 67 80, *hotel-lutte*
@t-online.de, Fax (089) 89267810 – 📳 TV 🅿. ◉◉ VISA
closed 20 December - 7 January – **36 rm** ⊇ 66/77 – 80/107.

at Munich-Bogenhausen :

🏨🏨🏨 **ArabellaSheraton Grand Hotel** 🅼, Arabellastr. 6, ⊠ 81925, 𝒫 (089) 9 26 40, *gra*
dhotel.muenchen@arabellasheraton.com, Fax (089) 92648699, ≤, beer garden
Massage, 🛦, 😊, 🔲 – 📳, 🚭 rm, ▤ TV 🗙 & 🚗 – 🅰 650. AE ① ◉◉ VISA JCB
🍽 rest   by Ismaninger Straße HVU
Die Ente vom Lehel (closed Sunday and Monday) (dinner only) **Meals** à la carte
33,50/52,50 – *Paulaner's* (closed lunch Saturday, Sunday and Bank Holidays) **Meals** à l.
carte 18/30,50 – ⊇ 19 – **644 rm** 310/405 – 380/430 – 14 Suiten.

🏨🏨🏨 **Palace** 🅼, Trogerstr. 21, ⊠ 81675, 𝒫 (089) 41 97 10, *info@hotel-palace-muenchen.de*
Fax (089) 41971819, « Elegant installation with period furniture ; Garden », 🛦, 😊, 🚗
– 📳, 🚭 rm, TV 🗙 🚗 – 🅰 30. AE ① ◉◉ VISA JCB   HV
Meals à la carte 27/45,50 – ⊇ 15 – **71 rm** 115/180 – 200/230 – 6 suites.

🏨🏨 **Prinzregent** without rest, Ismaninger Str. 42, ⊠ 81675, 𝒫 (089) 41 60 50, *contac*
@hotel-prinzregent.de, Fax (089) 41605466, « Furnished in traditional Alpine style », 😊
– 📳 🚭 TV 🗙 🚗 – 🅰 35. AE ① ◉◉ VISA   HV
closed 24 December - 5 January – **64 rm** ⊇ 165/185 – 200/300.

🏨🏨 **Rothof** without rest, Denninger Str. 114, ⊠ 81925, 𝒫 (089) 91 50 61, *rothof@t-online.de*
Fax (089) 915066, 🚗 – 📳 🚭 TV 🚗. AE ① ◉◉ VISA   by Ismaninger Straße HUV
closed 22 December - 6 January – **37 rm** ⊇ 121/161 – 172/212.

XXX **Bogenhauser Hof**, Ismaninger Str. 85, ⊠ 81675, 𝒫 (089) 98 55 86
Fax (089) 9810221, (1825 former hunting lodge), « Garden terrace » – AE ①
◉◉ VISA   HV e
closed 24 December - 8 January, Sunday and Bank Holidays – **Meals** (booking essentia
à la carte 35/56.

XX **Acquarello**, Mühlbaurstr. 36, ✉ 81677, ℰ (089) 4 70 48 48, Fax (089) 476464, 🏠 –
AE OO. 🛇   by Prinzregentenstraße   HV
closed lunch Saturday, Sunday and Bank Holidays – **Meals** 25 (lunch) à la carte 40/55
Spec. Vitello Tonnato mit Sopressa von Tintenfischen. Rinderschmorbraten mit Selleriepüree und Barolosauce. Ricottasoufflé mit Schokoladenravioli.

XX **Käfer Schänke**, Prinzregentenstr. 73, ✉ 81675, ℰ (089) 4 16 82 47, kaeferschaen
ke@feinkost-kaefer.de, Fax (089) 4168623, 🏠, « Several rooms with elegant rustic
installation » – AE OO OO VISA. 🛇   HV s
closed Sunday and Bank Holidays – **Meals** (booking essential) 25 (lunch) and
à la carte 44/61.

t Munich-Denning East : 8 km, by Denninger Straße HV :

XXX **Casale**, Ostpreußenstr. 42, ✉ 81927, ℰ (089) 93 62 68, Fax (089) 9306722, 🏠 – P.
AE OO VISA
Meals (Italian) à la carte 31,20/38,80.

t Munich-Haidhausen .

Hilton City M, Rosenheimer Str. 15, ✉ 81667, ℰ (089) 4 80 40, sales_munich-park
@hilton.com, Fax (089) 48044804, 🏠 – 📶, 🔆 rm, 🔲 📺 💕 ♿ ☎ – 🔏 180. AE OO
OO VISA JCB   LZ s
Meals à la carte 26/34,20 – 🖵 18 – **479 rm** 205/345 – 255/395 – 4 suites.

Preysing without rest, Preysingstr. 1, ✉ 81667, ℰ (089) 45 84 50,
Fax (089) 45845444, ☎, 🔲 – 📶 🔆 ☎ – 🔏 15. AE OO OO VISA JCB LZ w
closed 22 December - 6 January – **76 rm** 🖵 118/153 – 174 – 5 suites.

Forum Hotel, Hochstr. 3, ✉ 81669, ℰ (089) 4 80 30, muchb@interconti.com,
Fax (089) 4488277, ☎, 🔲 – 📶, 🔆 rm, 🔲 📺 💕 – 🔏 400. AE OO OO VISA. 🛇 rest
Meals à la carte 26,08/42,44 – 🖵 17 – **580 rm** 190/295 – 205/310 – 12 suites. LZ t

XXX **Massimiliano**, Rablstr. 10, ✉ 81699, ℰ (089) 4 48 44 77, massimiliano-muenchen@t
-online.de, Fax (089) 4484405, 🏠 – P. OO OO VISA JCB   LZ n
closed Saturday lunch – **Meals** 22 (lunch) and à la carte 41/56.

XX **Al Gallo Nero**, Grillparzerstr. 1, ✉ 81675, ℰ (089) 2 54 25 56, Fax (089) 4701321, 🏠
– AE OO VISA   HX b
closed Saturday lunch and Sunday – **Meals** (Italian) 21,47 (lunch) and à la carte
32,47/42,43.

X **Vinaiolo**, Steinstr. 42, ✉ 81667, ℰ (089) 48 95 03 56, Fax (089) 48997774, « Interior
of a former pharmacy » – OO   HX c
closed Sunday and Monday lunch – **Meals** (Italian) (booking essential for dinner) à la carte
30/40
Spec. Ravioli di Ricotta e Aspargi. Filetto di Rombo con Zucca e Fagiolini. Costata di Manzo
su carciofi.

t Munich-Laim West : 6 km, by Landsberger Straße (B 2) EV :

Park Hotel, Zschokkestr. 55, ✉ 80686, ℰ (089) 57 93 60, park-hotel-laim@t-online.de,
Fax (089) 57930100, ☎ – 📶, 🔆 rm, 📺 ☎ – 🔏 30. AE OO OO VISA JCB
Meals (closed August, Saturday and Sunday) à la carte 16,40/29,15 – **74 rm** 🖵 100 – 125.

t Munich-Neu Perlach Southeast : 10 km, by Rosenheimer Straße HX and Otto-Brunner-
Straße :

Mercure, Karl-Marx-Ring 87, ✉ 81735, ℰ (089) 6 32 70, h1374@accor-hotels.com,
Fax (089) 6327407, 🏠, 🏋, ☎, 🔲 – 📶, 🔆 rm, 🔲 📺 💕 ☎ P – 🔏 130. AE OO
OO VISA
Meals à la carte 19,94/40,39 – **185 rm** 🖵 92/205 – 105/249 – 3 suites.

Villa Waldperlach M without rest, Putzbrunner Str. 250 (Waldperlach), ✉ 81739,
ℰ (089) 6 60 03 00, Fax (089) 66003066 – 📶 🔆 📺 💕 ☎. AE OO OO VISA
21 rm 🖵 80 – 95.

t Munich-Pasing West : 11 km, by Landsberger Straße EV :

XX **Zur Goldenen Gans**, Planegger Str. 31, ✉ 81241, ℰ (089) 83 70 33,
Fax (089) 8204680, 🏠, « Atmospheric Bavarian inn » – P. OO OO VISA
closed Monday – **Meals** 15 (lunch) and à la carte 24,72/32,98.

t Munich-Schwabing :

Marriott-Hotel M, Berliner Str. 93, ✉ 80805, ℰ (089) 36 00 20, mhrs.mucno.sales
.office@marriott.com, Fax (089) 36002200, Massage, 🏋, ☎, 🔲 – 📶, 🔆 rm, 🔲 📺
💕 ♿ – 🔏 320. AE OO OO VISA JCB. 🛇 rest   by Ungererstraße (B 11) HU
Meals à la carte 25,05/36,80 – 🖵 15 – **348 rm** 148/270 – 18 suites.

🏨🏨 **Holiday Inn City Nord**, Leopoldstr. 194, ⊠ 80804, ℰ (089) 38 17 90, *reservati* *.himuenchen@queensgruppe.de, Fax (089) 38179888*, 🍽, Massage, �, ◻ – 📧, 💠 r 📺 💺 🚗 – 🔏 320. 🖭 ⓪ 🐵 🗾 🏧 ❄ rest *by Leopoldstraße* GU
Meals à la carte 25,56/44,48 – 🖙 17 – **365 rm** 175/375 – 195/395.

🏨🏨 **Renaissance Hotel**, Theodor-Dombart-Str. 4 (corner of Berliner Straße), ⊠ 8080C ℰ (089) 36 09 90, *renaissance.munich.mucbr@renaissancehotels.d* *Fax (089) 360996900*, 🍽, � – 📧, 💠 rm, 📺 💺 🚗 – 🔏 40. 🖭 ⓪ 🐵 🗾
Meals à la carte 18,40/33,75 – 🖙 15 – **260 rm** 133 – 87 suites. *by Ungererstraße (B 11)* HU

🏨🏨 **Four Points Hotel München Olympiapark**, Helene-Mayer-Ring 12, ⊠ 8080 ℰ (089) 35 75 10, *fourpoints.olympiapark@arabellasheraton.com, Fax (089) 3575180C* 📧, 💠 rm, 📺 💺 🚗 – 🔏 90. 🖭 ⓪ 🐵 🗾 *by Schleißheimer Straße* FU
closed 21 December - 6 January – **Meals** *(closed Sunday)* à la carte 16,35/34,30 – **105 r** 🖙 92/138 – 124/174.

🏨 **Cosmopolitan** Ⓜ without rest, Hohenzollernstr. 5, ⊠ 80801, ℰ (089) 38 38 10, *cos o@cosmopolitan-hotel.de, Fax (089) 38381111* – 📧 💠 📺 💺 🚗. 🖭 ⓪ 🐵 🗾 🏧 **71 rm** 🖙 95/110 – 110/120. GU

🏨 **Mercure** without rest, Leopoldstr. 120, ⊠ 80802, ℰ (089) 3 89 99 30, *h1104@ac r-hotels.com, Fax (089) 349344* – 📧 💠 ☰ 📺 🚗. 🖭 ⓪ 🐵 🗾 🏧 **65 rm** 🖙 90/118 – 130/140. GU

🏨 **Leopold**, Leopoldstr. 119, ⊠ 80804, ℰ (089) 36 04 30, *hotel-leopold@t-online.d* *Fax (089) 36043150*, 🍽, � – 📧, 💠 rm, 📺 💺 🚗 📧 – 🔏 20. 🖭 ⓪ 🐵 🗾 🏧 *closed 23 to 30 December, 1 to 6 January* – **Meals** à la carte 17,60/33,45 – **75 r** 🖙 95/126 – 126/169.

ꞩꞩꞩꞩ ✕✕✕✕ **Tantris**, Johann-Fichte-Str. 7, ⊠ 80805, ℰ (089) 3 61 95 90, *tantris@t-online.d* ✿✿ *Fax (089) 3618469*, 🍽 – 🗔 📧 🖭 ⓪ 🐵 🗾 ❄ GU
closed 1 week January, Sunday - Monday and Bank Holidays – **Meals** *(booking essenti* 56 *(lunch)*/120 *(dinner)* and à la carte 50/70
Spec. Geräucherte Taubenbrust mit Gänseleber und eingelegten Auberginen. Kabeljau ur Langostinen im Baguette gebacken mit Feldsalat. In der Schale gebratene Banane mit Sch koladenschaum und Sauerrahmeis.

✕✕ **Savoy**, Tengstr. 20, ⊠ 80798, ℰ (089) 2 71 14 45, *Fax (089) 2711445* – 🖭 ⓪ 🐵 🗾 *closed 2 weeks June and Sunday* – **Meals** (Italian) (booking essential for dinne à la carte 29/38. GU

✕✕ **Spago**, Neureutherstr. 15, ⊠ 80799, ℰ (089) 2 71 24 06, *spago@spago.d* *Fax (089) 2780448*, 🍽 – 🖭 ⓪ 🐵 🗾 GU
closed Sunday – **Meals** (Italian) à la carte 25,50/36,80.

✕✕ **Seehaus**, Kleinhesselohe 3, ⊠ 80802, ℰ (089) 3 81 61 30, *seehaus@kuffler-gastro omie.de, Fax (089) 341803*, ≤, beer garden, « Lakeside setting terrace » – 📧. 🖭 🐵 🗾 **Meals** à la carte 17,05/48,10. HU

✕ **Bistro Terrine**, Amalienstr. 89 (Amalien-Passage), ⊠ 80799, ℰ (089) 28 17 80, *te* ✿ *ine.bistro@t-online.de, Fax (089) 2809316*, 🍽 – 🖭 🐵 🗾 GU
closed 1 week early January, Bank Holidays, Sunday, lunch Monday and Saturday – **Mea** (booking essential for dinner) 21,70 *(lunch)* and à la carte 28/41,60
Spec. Seesaibling mit Zuckerschoten und Estragon-Senfsauce. Lammnüsschen mit Zwi belconfit und Gnocchi. Schokoladentarte.

at Munich-Sendling *Southwest : 6 km, by Lindwurmstraße (B 11)* EX :

🏨🏨 **Holiday Inn München-Süd**, Kistlerhofstr. 142, ⊠ 81379, ℰ (089) 78 00 20, *sale .hi.muenchen-sued@t-online.de, Fax (089) 78002672*, beer garden, Massage, 🚶, ◻ – 📧, 💠 rm, ☰ 📺 💺 🚗 – 🔏 90. 🖭 ⓪ 🐵 🗾 🏧 **Meals** à la carte 23,80/30 – 🖙 16 – **320 rm** 212 – 244.

🏨 **Ambassador Parkhotel**, Plinganserstr. 102, ⊠ 81369, ℰ (089) 72 48 90, *cchub r@t-online.de, Fax (089) 72489100*, beer garden – 📧, 💠 rm, 📺 🚗 🖭 ⓪ 🐵 🗾 *closed 24 December - 6 January* – **Meals** *(closed Saturday lunch and Monday)* (Italia à la carte 19,50/38 – **42 rm** 🖙 99/109 – 119.

🏨 **K+K Hotel am Harras** without rest, Albert-Rosshaupter-Str. 4, ⊠ 81369, ℰ (08 74 64 00, *kkhotel@muc.kkhotels.de, Fax (089) 7212820* – 📧 💠 📺 💺 🚗. 🖭 ⓪ 🗾 🏧 **106 rm** 🖙 136/210 – 161/235.

at Munich-Untermenzing *Northwest : 12 km, by Dachauer Straße* EU *and Baldur Straße*

🏨🏨 **Romantik Hotel Insel Mühle**, Von-Kahr-Str. 87, ⊠ 80999, ℰ (089) 8 10 10, *ins l-muehle@t-online.de, Fax (089) 8120571*, 🍽, beer garden, « Converted 16C riversio mill », 🌲 – 📺 🔥 🚗 📧 – 🔏 30. ⓪ 🐵 🗾 🏧 **Meals** *(closed Sunday and Bank Holidays)* 17,64 *(lunch)* and à la carte 30,75/42,45 – **37 r** 🖙 97/199 – 141/199.

Unterhaching *South : 10 km, by Kapuzinerstraße GX and Tegernseer Landstraße :*

🏨 **Schrenkhof** *without rest*, Leonhardsweg 6, ⊠ 82008, ℰ (089) 6 10 09 10, *Fax (089) 61009150*, « Bavarian farmhouse furniture », ⇌s – ⊯ 🗖 ⇐⇒ 🅿 – 🅪 35. ⚏
ⓘ ⓜⓞ 𝖵𝖨𝖲𝖠
closed Christmas - early January and Easter – ⊊ 8 – **25 rm** 90/113 – 110/155.

🏨 **Holiday Inn** Ⓜ, Inselkammer Str. 7, ⊠ 82008, ℰ (089) 66 69 10, *info@holiday-inn -muenchen.de*, *Fax (089) 66691600*, beer garden, 𝕗ᵹ, ⇌s – ⊯, ⤫ rm, 🗖 ⚭ & ⇐⇒ 🅿
– 🅪 220. ⚏ ⓘ ⓜⓞ 𝖵𝖨𝖲𝖠 𝖩𝖢𝖡
Meals à la carte 23,26/36,55 – ⊊ 15 – **271 rm** 123/148 – 148/184 – 6 suites.

🏨 **Astron Suite-Hotel** Ⓜ *without rest*, Leipziger Str.1, ⊠ 82008, ℰ (089) 66 55 20, *muenchen-unterhaching@astron-hotels.de*, *Fax (089) 66552200*, ⇌s – ⊯ ⤫ 🗖 ⚭ ⇐⇒
🅿 ⚏ ⓘ ⓜⓞ 𝖵𝖨𝖲𝖠 𝖩𝖢𝖡
⊊ 14 – **80 rm** 123 – 138.

⏴ Aschheim *Northeast : 13 km, by Prinzregentenstraße HV and Riem :*

🏨 **Schreiberhof** Ⓜ, Erdinger Str. 2, ⊠ 85609, ℰ (089) 90 00 60, *Fax (089) 90006459*,
🏖 ⇧, Massage, 𝕗ᵹ, ⇌s – ⊯, ⤫ rm, 🗖 ⚭ & ⇐⇒ 🅿 – 🅪 90. ⚏ ⓘ ⓜⓞ 𝖵𝖨𝖲𝖠
closed 23 December - 7 January – **Alte Gaststube** : **Meals** à la carte 23/42,50 – **87 rm**
⊊ 116/177 – 156/213.

⏴ Aschheim-Dornach *Northeast : 12 km, by Prinzregentenstraße HV and Riem :*

🏨 **Inn Side Residence-Hotel** Ⓜ, Humboldtstr. 12 (Businesspark-West), ⊠ 85609,
ℰ (089) 94 00 50, *muenchen@innside.de*, *Fax (089) 94005299*, 🏖 , 𝕗ᵹ, ⇌s – ⊯, ⤫ rm,
▤ rest, 🗖 ⚭ ⇐⇒ 🅿 – 🅪 80. ⚏ ⓘ ⓜⓞ 𝖵𝖨𝖲𝖠
Meals *(closed Sunday lunch, dinner Friday and Saturday)* à la carte 22,50/41,96 – ⊊ 14
– **134 rm** 110/132

⏴ Grünwald *South : 13 km by Wittelsbacher Brücke 35GX :*

🏨 **Tannenhof** *without rest*, Marktplatz 3, ⊠ 82031, ℰ (089) 6 41 89 60, *info@tanne nhof-gruenwald.de*, *Fax (089) 6415608*, « Period house with elegant interior » – ⤫ 🗖
🅿 ⚏ ⓘ ⓜⓞ 𝖵𝖨𝖲𝖠 ⚘ – *closed 20 December - 6 January* – **21 rm** ⊊ 85/105 – 105/120.

⏴ airport Franz-Josef-Strauß *Northeast : 37 km by A 9 and A 92 :*

🏨 **Kempinski Airport München** Ⓜ, Terminalstraße/Mitte 20, ⊠ 85356 *München*,
ℰ (089) 9 78 20, *info@kempinski-airport.de*, *Fax (089) 97822610*, 🏖 , 𝕗ᵹ, ⇌s, 🅂 – ⊯,
⤫ rm, ▤ 🗖 ⚭ & ⇐⇒ 🅿 – 🅪 280. ⚏ ⓘ ⓜⓞ 𝖵𝖨𝖲𝖠 𝖩𝖢𝖡
Meals à la carte 30,17/44,90 – ⊊ 22 – **389 rm** 210 – 345 – 46 suites.

XX **Il Mondo**, Terminalstr. Mitte 18 (area R, level 07), ⊠ 85356 *München*, ℰ (089)
97 59 32 22, *info@allresto.de*, *Fax (089) 97593226*, ⇐ – 🅿 ⓘ ⓜⓞ 𝖵𝖨𝖲𝖠 ⚘
Meals (Italian) à la carte 27,09/38,08.

...schau im Chiemgau *Bayern* 𝟜𝟚𝟘 W 20 – *pop. 5 000 – alt. 615 m.*
München 82.

XXXX **Restaurant Heinz Winkler** - Hotel Residenz Heinz Winkler, Kirchplatz 1, ⊠ 83229,
ⓢ ⚘⚘ ℰ (08052) 1 79 90, *info@residenz-heinz-winkler.de*, *Fax (08052) 179966*, 🏖 – 🅿 ⚏ ⓘ
ⓜⓞ 𝖵𝖨𝖲𝖠 𝖩𝖢𝖡 ⚘ – *closed Monday lunch* – **Meals** à la carte 49/01
Spec. Praline von der Entenleber mit Portweingelée. Reh soufliert mit Selleriemousse und
Apfelcrêpes. Schokoladenträne mit Kokosnußeis.

...TUTTGART ⓛ *Baden-Württemberg* 𝟜𝟙𝟡 T 11 – *pop. 565 000 – alt. 245 m.*

See : *Linden Museum* ✶✶ KY **M1** – *Park Wilhelma*✶ HT and *Killesberg-Park*✶ GT – *Television Tower (Fernsehturm)* ⚶✶ HX – *Stuttgart Gallery (Otto-Dix-Collection*✶*)* LY **M4** – *Swabian Brewery Museum (Schwäb. Brauereimuseum)*✶ *by Böblinger Straße* FX – *Old Castle (Altes Schloß) (Renaissance courtyard*✶*)* – *Württemberg Regional Museum*✶ LY **M3** – *State Gallery* ✶ *(Old Masters Collection*✶✶*)* LY **M2** – *Collegiate church (Stiftskirche) (Commemorative monuments of dukes*✶*)* KY **A** – *State Museum of Natural History (Staatl. Museum für Naturkunde)*✶ HT **M5** – *Daimler-Benz Museum*✶ JV **M6** – *Porsche Museum*✶ *by Heilbronner Straße* GT – *Schloß Solitude*✶ *by Rotenwaldstraße* FX.

Envir. : *Bad Cannstatt Spa Park (Kurpark)*✶ *East : 4 km* JT.

⛳ *Kornwestheim, Aldinger Straße* (*North : 11 km),* ℰ (07141) 87 13 19; ⛳ *Mönsheim (North-West : 30 km by A 8)*, ℰ (07044) 9 11 04 10.

✈ *Stuttgart-Echterdingen, by Obere Weinsteige (B 27)* GX, ℰ (0711) 94 80, *City Air Terminal*, *Stuttgart, Lautenschlagerstr. 14* (**LY**), ℰ (0711) 20 12 68.

*Exhibition Centre (Messegelände Killesberg) (*GT*),* ℰ (0711) 2 58 90, *Fax (0711) 2589440.*
🗐 *Tourist-Info, Königstr. 1a,* ⊠ 70173, ℰ (0711) 2 22 82 40, *Fax (0711) 2228253.*
ADAC, *Am Neckartor 2.*
Berlin 630 – Frankfurt am Main 204 – Karlsruhe 88 – München 222 – Strasbourg 156.

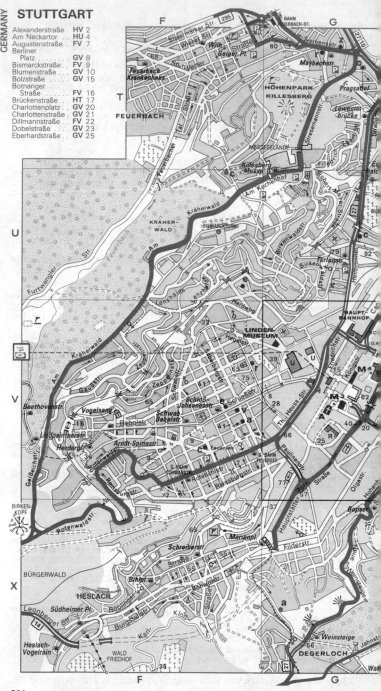

STUTTGART

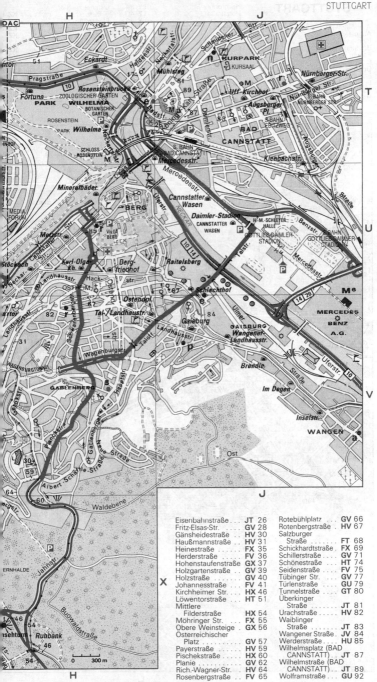

STUTTGART

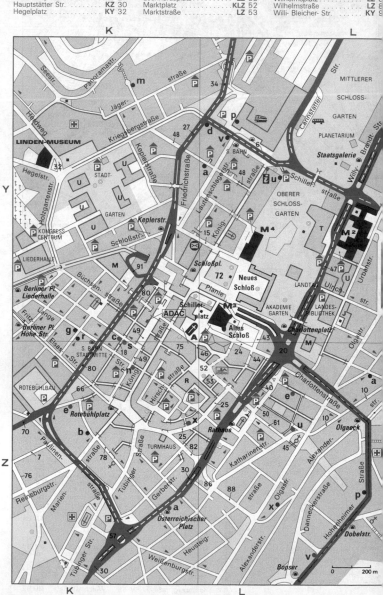

Steigenberger Graf Zeppelin M, Arnulf-Klett-Platz 7, ✉ 70173, ℰ (0711) 2 04 80, stuttgart@steigenberger.de, Fax (0711) 2048542, Massage, ≘s, ☒ – ⧢, ⥺ rm, ☰ ☑ ⚒ ఈ ⇌ – ⚤ 300. ﷼ ① ⦿ 〓 ⊠ ⣿ ⣿ rest
LY v
Graf Zeppelin (Italian) (closed 1 August - 3 September, Sunday, Monday and Bank Holidays)
(dinner only) Meals 55/90 and à la carte 40/61 – **Zeppelin Stuble** (closed Sunday dinner)
Meals à la carte 21,80/35 – *Zeppelino's :* Meals à la carte 24/33 – ⛁ 17 – **195 rm**
195/225 – 220/240.

Am Schloßgarten, Schillerstr. 23, ✉ 70173, ℰ (0711) 2 02 60, info@hotelschloss
garten.com, Fax (0711) 2026888, « Terrace with ≤ » – ⧢, ⥺ rm, ☰ ☑ ⚒ ⇌ – ⚤ 100.
﷼ ① ⦿ 〓 ⊠ ⣿ ⣿ rest
LY u
Meals see *Zirbelstube* below – **Schlossgarten-Restaurant :** Meals à la carte 37/47 –
Vinothek (closed Sunday) Meals 19 and à la carte 30/40 – ⛁ 17 – **116 rm** 155/258 –
229/258 – 4 suites.

Maritim M, Seidenstr. 34, ✉ 70174, ℰ (0711) 94 20, infostu@maritim.de,
Fax (0711) 9421000, Massage, ₤₅, ≘s, ☒ – ⧢, ⥺ rm, ☰ ☑ ⚒ ఈ ⇌ – ⚤ 500 ﷼
① ⦿ 〓 ⊠ ⣿ ⣿ rest
FV r
Meals à la carte 23,01/42,44 – **555 rm** ⛁ 140/105 – 162/198 – 16 suites.

Inter-Continental, Willy-Brandt-Str. 30, ✉ 70173, ℰ (0711) 2 02 00, stuttgart@in
terconti.com, Fax (0711) 20202020, Massage, ₤₅, ≘s, ☒ – ⧢, ⥺ rm, ☰ ☑ ⚒ ఈ
– ⚤ 300. ﷼ ① ⦿ 〓 ⊠ ⣿ ⣿ rest
HV t
Meals à la carte 26/44 – ⛁ 17 – **276 rm** 170/250 – 28 suites.

Dorint City M, Heilbronner Str. 88, ✉ 70191, ℰ (0711) 25 55 80, info.strbud@dor
int.com, Fax (0711) 25558100 – ⧢, ⥺ rm, ☰ ☑ ⚒ ఈ ⇌ – ⚤ 120. ﷼ ① ⦿ 〓 ⊠
⣿
GU c
Meals à la carte 18,70/28 – ⛁ 13 – **174 rm** 100/120 – 110/130.

Royal, Sophienstr. 35, ✉ 70178, ℰ (0711) 6 25 05 00, royalhotel@t-online.de,
Fax (0711) 628809 – ⧢, ⥺ rm, ☰ ☑ ⚒ ☝ – ⚤ 70. ﷼ ① ⦿ 〓 ⊠ ⣿ KZ b
closed 24 to 26 December – Meals (closed Sunday and Bank Holidays) à la carte 21/44
– **100 rm** ⛁ 100/136 – 143/245 – 3 suites.

Kronen-Hotel ⣼, without rest, Kronenstr. 48, ✉ 70174, ℰ (0711) 2 25 10, kronen
hotel@s.netic.de, Fax (0711) 2251404, ≘s – ⧢ ⥺ ☑ ⚒ ⇌ – ⚤ 20. ﷼ ① ⦿ 〓 ⊠
⣿
KY m
closed 22 December - 7 January – **83 rm** ⛁ 99/120 – 133/175.

Parkhotel, Villastr. 21, ✉ 70190, ℰ (0711) 2 80 10, parkhotelamrundfunk@t-online
.de, Fax (0711) 2864353, ☞ – ⧢, ⥺ rm, ☑ ⚒ ⇌ ☝ – ⚤ 60. ﷼ ① ⦿ 〓 ⊠ ⣿
⣿
HU r
Meals (closed Saturday and Sunday) à la carte 26,59/42 – **72 rm** ⛁ 92/107 – 122/148.

Azenberg ⣼, Seestr. 114, ✉ 70174, ℰ (0711) 2 25 50 40, info@hotelazenberg.de,
Fax (0711) 22550499, ≘s, ☒, ☞ – ⧢, ⥺ rm, ☑ ⚒ ⇌ ☝ – ⚤ 20. ﷼ ① ⦿ 〓 ⊠
⣿ ⣿ rest
FU e
Meals (closed Saturday, Sunday and Bank Holidays) (dinner only) (residents only) – **57 rm**
⛁ 79/99 – 109/139.

Bergmeister without rest (with guest house), Rotenbergstr. 16, ✉ 70190, ℰ (0711)
2 68 48 50, hobergmeis@aol.com, Fax (0711) 268485169, ≘s – ⧢ ⥺ ☑ ⇌ ﷼ ①
⦿ 〓
HV r
closed 23 December - 6 January – **46 rm** ⛁ 75/96 – 105.

Unger without rest, Kronenstr. 17, ✉ 70173, ℰ (0711) 2 09 90, info@hotel-unger.de,
Fax (0711) 2099100 – ⧢ ⥺ ☑ ⚒ ⇌ – ⚤ 15. ﷼ ① ⦿ 〓 ⊠ LY a
98 rm ⛁ 92/123 – 143/180.

Rega Hotel, Ludwigstr. 18, ✉ 70176, ℰ (0711) 61 93 40, info@rega-hotel.de,
Fax (0711) 6193477 – ⧢ ☑ ⚒ ⇌ – ⚤ 20. ﷼ ① ⦿ 〓 ⊠ ⣿ FV a
Meals à la carte 17/27 – **60 rm** ⛁ 80/136 – 102/162.

InterCityHotel M without rest, Arnulf-Klett-Platz 2, ✉ 70173, ℰ (0711) 2 25 00, stuttg
art@intercityhotel.de, Fax (0711) 2250499 – ⧢ ⥺ ☑ ⚒ – ⚤ 25. ﷼ ① ⦿ 〓 ⊠ ⣿
112 rm ⛁ 112 – 139.
LY p

Wörtz zur Weinsteige, Hohenheimer Str. 30, ✉ 70184, ℰ (0711) 2 36 70 00, info
@hotel-woertz.de, Fax (0711) 2367007, ☞ – ⥺ rm, ☑ ☝. ﷼ ① ⦿ 〓 ⊠ ⣿ LZ p
Meals (closed 3 weeks January, 3 weeks August, Sunday, Monday and Bank Holidays) (outstanding wine list) à la carte 22/53 – **25 rm** ⛁ 70/100 – 80/140.

Wartburg, Lange Str. 49, ✉ 70174, ℰ (0711) 2 04 50, hotel.wartburg.stgt@gmx.de,
Fax (0711) 2045450 – ⧢, ⥺ rm, ☰ rest, ☑ ☝ – ⚤ 60. ﷼ ① ⦿ 〓 ⊠ ⣿ rest
closed Easter and 22 December - 2 January – Meals (closed Saturday, Sunday and Bank
Holidays) (lunch only) à la carte 15,50/26,50 – **76 rm** ⛁ 82/90 – 135. KY g

Rema-Hotel Astoria without rest, Hospitalstr. 29, ✉ 70174, ℰ (0711) 29 93 01, asto
ria@remahotel.de, Fax (0711) 299307 – ⧢ ⥺ ☑ ☝ – ⚤ 20. ﷼ ① ⦿ 〓 ⊠ ⣿
57 rm ⛁ 92/170 – 125/220.
KY r

🏠 **Abalon** Ⓜ ⌖ without rest, Zimmermannstr. 7 (approach by Olgastr. 79), ✉ 7018
   𝒫 (0711) 2 17 10, info@abalon.de, Fax (0711) 2171217 – 🛗 ≒ 📺 ✆ ⟺. 🅰🅴 ⓞ ◉
   𝘝𝘐𝘚𝘈   LZ
   42 rm ⌿ 71/76 – 96/110.

🏠 **Central Classic** Ⓜ without rest, Hasenbergstr. 49a, ✉ 70176, 𝒫 (0711) 6 15 50 5
   central-classic@gmx.de, Fax (0711) 61550530 – 🛗 📺 ✆. 🅰🅴 ⓞ ◉ 𝘝𝘐𝘚𝘈 ᴊᴄ
   ⌖   FV
   closed 22 December - 6 January – **33 rm** ⌿ 65/79 – 79/95.

🏠 **City-Hotel** without rest, Uhlandstr. 18, ✉ 70182, 𝒫 (0711) 21 08 1
   Fax (0711) 2369772 – 📺 🅿. 🅰🅴 ⓞ ◉ 𝘝𝘐𝘚𝘈 ᴊᴄʙ. ⌖   LZ
   31 rm ⌿ 79/85 – 95/115.

🏠 **Rieker** without rest, Friedrichstr. 3, ✉ 70174, 𝒫 (0711) 22 13 11, info@hotel-rieker.c
   Fax (0711) 293894 – 🛗 ≒ 📺 ⟺. 🅰🅴 ⓞ ◉ 𝘝𝘐𝘚𝘈 ᴊᴄʙ   LY
   66 rm ⌿ 91/101 – 121/131.

🏠 **Ibis am Löwentor** Ⓜ without rest, Presselstr. 15, ✉ 70191, 𝒫 (0711) 25 55 1
   h2202@accor-hotels.com, Fax (0711) 25551150 – 🛗 ≒ 🛗 📺 ✆ ዿ ⟺. 🅰🅴 ⓞ ◉ 𝖵
   ᴊᴄʙ   GT
   ⌿ 9 – **132 rm** 63.

🏠 **Bellevue**, Schurwaldstr. 45, ✉ 70186, 𝒫 (0711) 48 07 60, Fax (0711) 4807631 – [
   ⟺ 🅿. 🅰🅴 ⓞ ◉ 𝘝𝘐𝘚𝘈   JV
   Meals (closed August, Tuesday and Wednesday) à la carte 18/31 ⅋ – **12 rm** ⌿ 45/'
   – 75.

XXXX **Zirbelstube** - Hotel Am Schloßgarten, Schillerstr. 23, ✉ 70173, 𝒫 (0711) 2 02 68 2
   ❀ info@hotelschlossgarten.com, Fax (0711) 2026888, « Terrace with ≤ » – ⟺. 🅰🅴 ⓞ ◉
   𝘝𝘐𝘚𝘈. ⌖   LY
   closed 1 to 15 January, 3 weeks August, Sunday and Monday – **Meals** à la carte 49/72,
   Spec. Variation von der Gänseleber mit Brioche. Lasagne von Felsenrotbarbe mit St. Jakob
   muscheln. Etouffé-Taube aus dem Ofen mit gefülltem Gemüse und Trüffelrisotto.

XX **Kern's Pastetchen**, Hohenheimer Str. 64, ✉ 70184, 𝒫 (0711) 48 48 55, kerns.p
   tetchen@t-online.de, Fax (0711) 487565   LZ
   closed 1 week early January, 3 weeks August, Sunday and Monday – **Meals** (dinner on
   46/54 and à la carte 32/49.

XX **Délice** (Gutscher), Hauptstätter Str. 61, ✉ 70178, 𝒫 (0711) 6 40 32 22, « Vaulted cell
   ❀ with contemporary art » – ⌖   KZ
   closed 24 December - 7 January, Saturday, Sunday and Bank Holidays – **Meals** (dinner on
   (booking essential) (outstanding wine list) 70 and à la carte 40/55
   Spec. Marinierte Spaghettini mit Kaviar. Limousin Lammrücken mit Safran-Couscous. Gra
   mohn-Topfenknödel mit Marillenröster.

XX **La Fenice**, Rotebühlplatz 29, ✉ 70178, 𝒫 (0711) 6 15 11 44, g.vincenzo@t-online.c
   Fax (0711) 6151146, ☂ – 🅰🅴   KZ
   closed 2 weeks August, Sunday and Monday – **Meals** (Italian) à la carte 35/52.

XX **Di Gennaro**, Kronprinzstr. 11, ✉ 70173, 𝒫 (0711) 22 29 60 51, Fax (0211) 2229604
   – 🅰🅴 ⓞ ◉ 𝘝𝘐𝘚𝘈   KZ
   closed Sunday and Bank Holidays – **Meals** (Italian) à la carte 37,30/42,50.

XX **Da Franco**, Calwer Str. 23 (1st floor), ✉ 70173, 𝒫 (0711) 29 15 81, Fax (0711) 29454
   – ▤. 🅰🅴 ◉ 𝘝𝘐𝘚𝘈   KYZ
   closed 4 weeks July - August and Monday – **Meals** (Italian) à la carte 26/38.

XX **La nuova Trattoria da Franco**, Calwer Str. 32, ✉ 70173, 𝒫 (0711) 29 47 4
   Fax (0711) 294549, ☂ – 🅰🅴 ◉ 𝘝𝘐𝘚𝘈   KYZ
   Meals (Italian) à la carte 25,05/41,40.

XX **La Scala**, Friedrichstr. 41 (1st floor, 🛗), ✉ 70174, 𝒫 (0711) 29 06 0'
   ✿ Fax (0711) 2991640 – ▤. 🅰🅴 ⓞ ◉ 𝘝𝘐𝘚𝘈   KY
   closed 2 weeks August, Sunday and Bank Holidays lunch – **Meals** (Italian) à la car
   24/38.

X **Der Zauberlehrling**, Rosenstr. 38, ✉ 70182, 𝒫 (0711) 2 37 77 70, kontakt@zau
   erlehrling.de, Fax (0711) 2377775 – 🅰🅴   LZ
   closed Saturday lunch, Sunday and Bank Holidays – **Meals** à la carte 31,20/49,60.

Swabian wine taverns (Weinstuben) (mainly light meals only) :

X **Weinstube Schellenturm**, Weberstr. 72, ✉ 70182, 𝒫 (0711) 2 36 48 88, juerg
   nwurst@t-online.de, Fax (0711) 2262699, ☂ – 🅰🅴   LZ
   closed Sunday and Bank Holidays – **Meals** (dinner only) à la carte 17,50/27,50.

X **Weinstube Klösterle**, Marktstr. 71 (Bad Cannstatt), ✉ 70372, 𝒫 (0711) 56 89 6
   Fax (0711) 558606, ☂, « 1463 former monastery, rustic interior » – 🅰🅴 ◉   HJT
   closed Sunday and Bank Holidays – **Meals** (open from 5 pm) à la carte 16/28,50.

X **Kachelofen**, Eberhardstr. 10 (entrance Töpferstraße), ⊠ 70173, ℰ (0711) 24 23 78,
Fax (0711) 5299162, ⋒ – 🆎 𝖵𝖨𝖲𝖠   KZ x
closed Sunday – **Meals** (open from 5 pm) à la carte 18/35.

X **Weinstube Klink**, Epplestr. 1 (Degerloch), ⊠ 70597, ℰ (0711) 7 65 32 05,
Fax (0711) 760307, ⋒   by Obere Weinsteige GX
closed mid August - early September, Saturday, Sunday and Bank Holidays – **Meals** (open
from 5 pm) (booking essential) à la carte 25,50/42,95.

X **Weinstube Träuble**, Gablenberger Hauptstr. 66 (entrance Bussenstraße), ⊠ 70186,
ℰ (0711) 46 54 28, Fax (0711) 4207961, ⋒ – 🆗. ⋙   HV s
closed 1 week January, end July - mid August, Sunday and Bank Holidays – **Meals** (open
from 5 pm) (only cold and warm light meals).

X **Weinhaus Stetter**, Rosenstr. 32, ⊠ 70182, ℰ (0711) 24 01 63, Fax (0711) 240193,
⋒   LZ e
closed 24 December - 8 January, Sunday and Bank Holidays – **Meals** (open Monday to
Friday from 3 pm, Saturday 10 am to 3 pm) (outstanding wine list) (only cold and warm light
meals) ⅃.

t **Stuttgart-Büsnau** West : 9 km, by Rotenwaldstraße FX :

🏨 **Relexa Waldhotel Schatten**, Magstadter Straße (Solitudering), ⊠ 70569, ℰ (0711)
6 86 70, stuttgart @ relexa-hotel.de, Fax (0711) 6867999, ⋒, ⇌s – 📲, ⥾ rm, 📺 🌜 ᴧ
⟺ 🅿 – 🔏 90. 🆎 ⓞ 🄼🄾 𝖵𝖨𝖲𝖠 🅹🄲🄱
La Fenêtre (closed Sunday, Monday and Bank Holidays) (dinner only) **Meals** à la carte
30,69/42,42 – **Kaminrestaurant :** Meals à la carte 28,61/40,88 – **136 rm** ⊒ 111/149
– 172/246 – 12 suites.

t **Stuttgart-Bad Cannstatt** :

🏨 **Mercure** 🄼, Teinacher Str. 20, ⊠ 70372, ℰ (0711) 9 54 00, h1704@ accor-hotels.com,
Fax (0711) 9540630, ⋒, ⇌s – 📲, ⥾ rm, 🗐 rest, 📺 🌜 ᴧ ⟺ – 🔏 110. 🆎 ⓞ 🄼🄾
𝖵𝖨𝖲𝖠 🅹🄲🄱   JT n
Meals à la carte 21/42 – **156 rm** ⊒ 105/130 – 135/165 – 5 suites.

XX **Krehl's Linde** with rm, Obere Waiblinger Str. 113, ⊠ 70374, ℰ (0711) 5 20 49 00,
info@ krehlslinde.de, Fax (0711) 52049013, ⋒ – 📺 ⟺. 🆎 🄼🄾 𝖵𝖨𝖲𝖠   JT r
closed 3 weeks August – **Meals** (closed Sunday and Monday) à la carte 30/41 – **18 rm**
⊒ 52/95 – 81/132.

t **Stuttgart-Degerloch** :

XXXX **Wielandshöhe**, Alte Weinsteige 71, ⊠ 70597, ℰ (0711) 6 40 88 48,
Fax (0711) 6409408, ⋒, « Beautiful location with ⪡ Stuttgart » – 🆎 ⓞ 🄼🄾
𝖵𝖨𝖲𝖠 🅹🄲🄱   GX a
closed Sunday and Monday – **Meals** (booking essential) 66/102 and à la carte 44/77.

XXX **Weber's Gourmet im Turm**, Jahnstr. 120, ⊠ 70597, ℰ (0711) 24 89 96 10, rest
⁂ aurant@ fernsehturm-stgt.de, Fax (0711) 24899627, ⁂ Stuttgart and surroundings, (in
TV-tower at 144 m, 📲) – 🗐 🅿. 🆎 🄼🄾 𝖵𝖨𝖲𝖠. ⋙   HX
closed 3 weeks August, 2 weeks January, Sunday and Monday – **Meals** (booking essential
for dinner) à la carte 49/92
Spec. Currysüppchen mit Limetten und Krustentierbällchen. Hummer mit Granny Smith
und Tonkabohnenschaum. Bresse-Taube "Financier" mit Majoran.

XX **Das Fässle**, Löwenstr. 51, ⊠ 70597, ℰ (0711) 76 01 00, info@ faessle.de,
⟿ Fax (0711) 764432, ⋒ – 🗐. 🆎 ⓞ 🄼🄾 𝖵𝖨𝖲𝖠   by Jahnstraße GX
closed Sunday and Monday lunch – **Meals** (booking essential) 30 and à la carte 26,70/39,30.

t **Stuttgart-Fasanenhof** South : 10 km, by Obere Weinsteige GX and B 27 :

🏨 **Mercure** 🄼, Eichwiesenring 1, ⊠ 70567, ℰ (0711) 7 26 60, h1574@ accor-hotel.com,
Fax (0711) 7266444, ⋒, ᶅ, ⇌s – 📲, ⥾ rm, 🗐 📺 🌜 ᴧ ⟺ 🅿 – 🔏 120. 🆎 ⓞ 🄼🄾
𝖵𝖨𝖲𝖠
Meals à la carte 23/38,85 – **148 rm** ⊒ 135/155 – 155/175.

🏨 **Fora Hotel** 🄼, Vor dem Lauch 20, ⊠ 70567, ℰ (0711) 7 25 50, reservation.fasane
nhof@ flora.de, Fax (0711) 7255666, ⋒, ⇌s – 📲, ⥾ rm, 📺 🌜 ⟺ – 🔏 55. 🆎 ⓞ
🄼🄾 𝖵𝖨𝖲𝖠
Meals à la carte 17/29 – **101 rm** ⊒ 115 – 131.

t **Stuttgart-Feuerbach** :

🏨 **Messehotel Europe** 🄼, Siemensstr. 33, ⊠ 70469, ℰ (0711) 81 00 40 (hotel) 8 10
04 23 55 (rest.), europestgt@ aol.com, Fax (0711) 810042555 – 📲, ⥾ rm, 🗐 📺 🌜 ⟺.
🆎 ⓞ 🄼🄾 𝖵𝖨𝖲𝖠   GT r
closed August – **Landhausstuben** (closed Sunday and Monday) (dinner only) Meals à la
carte 18/36 – **114 rm** ⊒ 102 – 128 – 4 suites.

🏨 **Kongresshotel Europe**, Siemensstr. 26, ✉ 70469, ℰ (0711) 81 00 40, *europestgt@ ol.com*, Fax (0711) 810041444, ⌨ – 📶, ≒ rm, ☰ 📺 ✆ ⟵ – 🏋 120. 🅰🅴 ⓞ ⒸⓄ ⓥ
Meals *(closed lunch Saturday and Sunday)* à la carte 18/36 – **145 rm** ⥮ 70/90 – 107/16
– 4 suites.
GT

at Stuttgart-Flughafen (Airport) South : 15 km by Obere Weinsteige GX and B 27 :

🏨 **Mövenpick-Hotel** Ⓜ, Randstr. 7, ✉ 70629, ℰ (0711) 7 90 70, *hotel.stuttgart-ai ort@moevenpick.com*, Fax (0711) 793585, 🌫, ≒ – 📶, ⅍ rm, ☰ 📺 ✆ ⅙ 🄟 – 🏋 4
🅰🅴 ⓞ ⒸⓄ 🆅🅸🆂🅰 🅹🅲🅱
Meals à la carte 22/33,80 – ⥮ 15 – **229 rm** 150/166 – 175/191.

🍴 **TOP AIR**, at the airport (terminal 1, level 4), ✉ 70629, ℰ (0711) 9 48 21 37, *top.a
🏵 *stuttgart@woellhaf-airport.de*, Fax (0711) 7979210 – ☰ 📺 – 🏋 40. 🅰🅴 ⓞ ⒸⓄ 🆅🅸
closed 2 weeks early January, August and Saturday – **Meals** 38,35 *(lunch)*/70,56 and à
carte 37,84/54,20
Spec. Vatiation von der Gänsestopfleber mit Sauternesgelée. Spinatrisotto mit gebratene
Milchferkel und Trüffel. Suprême vom Atlantik Steinbutt mit Hummer-Kaviarsoufflé un
Kartoffelpüree.

at Stuttgart-Hoheheim South : 10 km, by Mittlere Filderstraße HX :

🍴 **Speisemeisterei** (Öxle), Am Schloß Hoheneim, ✉ 70599, ℰ (0711) 4 56 00 3′
🏵🏵 Fax (0711) 4560038 – 🄟 🌫
closed 1 to 15 January, 29 July - 15 August, Monday and Tuesday – **Meals** *(weekdays dinn
only) (booking essential)* 65//110
Spec. St. Jakobsmuschelkrustade mit bretonischen Langostinos. Roulade von Etouff
Taubenbrust mit Gänseleber und Limonen-Ingwerrisotto. Rehrücken im Roggen-Teigbla
mit Trüffelrahmsauce und Sellerie-Walnußflan.

at Stuttgart-Möhringen Southwest : 8 km by Obere Weinsteige GX and B 27 :

🏨 **Copthorne Hotel Stuttgart International** Ⓜ (with 🏨 **SI**), Plieninger Str. 10
✉ 70567, ℰ (0711) 7 21 10 50, *sales.stuttgart@mill-cop.com*, Fax (0711) 7212931, 🌫
beer garden, direct entrance to the recreation centre Schwaben Quelle – 📶, ⅍ rm, ☰
📺 ✆ ⅙ ⟵ – 🏋 650. 🅰🅴 ⓞ ⒸⓄ
Meals *(19 different restaurants, bars and cafes)* à la carte 20/40 – ⥮ 15 – **454 rr
159/199 – 179/219.

🏨 **Fora Hotel** without rest, Filderbahnstr. 43, ✉ 70567, ℰ (0711) 71 60 80, *reserva
on.moehringen@flora.de*, Fax (0711) 7160850 – 📶 ⅍ rm 📺 ⟵. 🅰🅴 ⓞ ⒸⓄ 🆅🅸🆂🅰 🅹🅲🅱
closed end December - early January – **41 rm** ⥮ 61/86 – 77/102.

at Stuttgart-Obertürkheim East : 6 km, by Augsburger Straße JU :

🏨 **Brita Hotel**, Augsburger Str. 671, ✉ 70329, ℰ (0711) 32 02 30, *info@brita-hotel.d
Fax (0711) 324440 – 📶, ⅍ rm, 📺 ✆ ⟵ – 🏋 80. 🅰🅴 ⓞ ⒸⓄ 🆅🅸🆂🅰
closed 24 December - 6 January – **Meals** *(closed Saturday and Sunday)* à la cart
19,50/28,50 – **70 rm** ⥮ 70/91 – 121.

at Stuttgart-Stammheim North : 10 km, by Heilbronner Straße GT :

🏨 **Novotel-Nord**, Korntaler Str. 207, ✉ 70439, ℰ (0711) 98 06 20, *h0501@accor-hc
els.com*, Fax (0711) 98062137, 🌫, ≒, ⚊ *(heated)* – 📶, ⅍ rm, ☰ 📺 ✆ 🄟 – 🏋 20C
🅰🅴 ⓞ ⒸⓄ
Meals à la carte 20/31 – **113 rm** ⥮ 106/126 – 126/149.

at Stuttgart-Vaihingen Southwest : 9,5 km, by Böblinger Straße FX :

🏨 **Dorint Fontana** Ⓜ, Vollmoellerstr. 5, ✉ 70563, ℰ (0711) 73 00, *info.strfon@do
nt.com*, Fax (0711) 7302525, Massage, ♨, 🝔, ≒, ⚊ – 📶, ⅍ rm, ☰ 📺 ✆ ⅙ ⟵
– 🏋 250. 🅰🅴 ⓞ ⒸⓄ 🆅🅸🆂🅰 🅹🅲🅱 🌫 rest
Meals à la carte 28/52 – ⥮ 16 – **252 rm** 158/188 – 173/203.

at Stuttgart-Weilimdorf Northwest : 12 km, by Steiermärker Straße FT and B 295 :

🏨 **Holiday Inn** Ⓜ, Mittlerer Pfad 27, ✉ 70499, ℰ (0711) 98 88 80, *holidayinn.stuttg
rt@t-online.de*, Fax (0711) 988889, beer garden, 🝔, ≒ – 📶, ⅍ rm, 📺 ✆ ⅙ ⟵
🏋 220. 🅰🅴 ⓞ ⒸⓄ 🆅🅸🆂🅰 🅹🅲🅱
Meals à la carte 18,20/37,20 – ⥮ 15 – **325 rm** 153/189 – 158/205 – 4 suites.

at Stuttgart-Zuffenhausen North : 8 km, by Heilbronner Straße GT and B 10 :

🏨 **Golden Leaf Hotel**, Schützenbühlstr. 16, ✉ 70435, ℰ (0711) 8 20 01 00, *reserva
ion.zuffenhausen@flora.de*, Fax (0711) 8200101, 🌫 – 📶, ⅍ rm, 📺 ✆ ⟵. 🅰🅴 ⓞ Ⓜ
🆅🅸🆂🅰 🅹🅲🅱
Meals *(dinner only)* à la carte 13,80/31,20 – **119 rm** ⥮ 105 – 125.

🏨 **Achat** Ⓜ without rest, Wollinstr. 6, ✉ 70439, ℰ (0711) 82 00 80, *stuttgart@acha
-hotel.de*, Fax (0711) 82008999 – 📶 ⅍ 📺 ✆ ⟵. 🅰🅴 ⓞ ⒸⓄ 🆅🅸🆂🅰 🅹🅲🅱
⥮ 11 – **104 rm** 74/114 – 84/124.

Fellbach *Northeast : 8 km, by Nürnberger Straße (B 14)* JT :

🏨 **Classic Congress Hotel**, Tainer Str. 7, ✉ 70734, ℰ (0711) 5 85 90, *info@cch-bw.de*, Fax (0711) 5859304, « Changing exhibition of paintings », 🔥, 🛋 – 🛗, ✻ rm, 📺 📞 🚗 🅿 – 🏛 55. 🄰🄴 ① 🆗🅾 🆅🅸🆂🅰
closed 23 December - 6 January – **Meals** see *Eduard M.* below – **149 rm** 🍽 130/135 – 153.

✕✕ **Eduard M.** - Classic Congress Hotel, Tainer Str. 7 (Schwabenlandhalle), ✉ 70734, ℰ (0711) 5 85 94 11, *restaurant@eduardm.de*, Fax (0711) 5859427, 🍽 – 🍴. 🄰🄴 ① 🆗🅾 🆅🅸🆂🅰
closed 27 to 30 December – **Meals** à la carte 24,50/42,50.

✕✕ **Zum Hirschen** with rm, Hirschstr. 1, ✉ 70734, ℰ (0711) 9 57 93 70, ☺ Fax (0711) 95793710, 🍽, « Modernised 16C timbered house » – 📺 📞. 🆅🅸🆂🅰
Meals *(closed Sunday and Monday) (dinner only)* (booking essential) and à la carte 39/54 – **9 rm** 🍽 60 – 90
Spec. Provenzalische Terrine vom Rochenflügel. Kalbskopf-Tarte mit Rote-Bete und Meerrettichschaum. Taube im Strudelteig mit getrüffelten Saubohnen.

✕✕ **Aldinger's Weinstube Germania**, Schmerstr. 6, ✉ 70734, ℰ (0711) 58 20 37, *aldi* ☻ *nger.germania@t-online.de*, Fax (0711) 582077, 🍽 – 📺. ✻
closed 2 weeks February - March, 3 weeks August, Sunday and Monday – **Meals** (booking essential) à la carte 23/35.

: Gerlingen *West : 12 km, by Rotenwaldstraße* FX :

🏨 **Krone** (with guest house), Hauptstr. 28, ✉ 70839, ℰ (07156) 4 31 10, *info@krone-g erlingen.de*, Fax (07156) 4311100, 🍽, 🛋 – 🛗, ✻ rm, 📺 📞 🚗 🅿 – 🏛 80. 🄰🄴 ① 🆗🅾 🆅🅸🆂🅰
Meals *(closed 30 July - 7 August, Sunday dinner and Monday)* (booking essential) à la carte 22.50/47 – **56 rm** 🍽 75/85 – 105/140.

🏨 **Mercure**, Dieselstr. 2, ✉ 70839, ℰ (07156) 43 13 00, *h2838@accor-hotels.com*, Fax (07156) 431343 – 🛗, ✻ rm, 📺 📞 🚗 🅿 – 🏛 120. 🄰🄴 ① 🆗🅾 🆅🅸🆂🅰
Meals *(closed Monday)* à la carte 16,36/27,50 – **96 rm** 🍽 84/102 – 102.

: Korntal-Münchingen *Northwest : 9 km, by Heilbronner Straße* GT *and B 10 :*

🏨 **Mercure**, Siemensstr. 50, ✉ 70825, ℰ (07150) 1 30, *h0685@accor-hotels.com*, Fax (07150) 13266, 🍽, beer garden, 🛋, 🗏 – 🛗 📺 📞 🛢 🅿 – 🏛 180. 🄰🄴 ① 🆗🅾 🆅🅸🆂🅰
Meals à la carte 28,89/37,32 – **200 rm** 🍽 85/95 – 92/103 – 6 suites.

: Leinfelden-Echterdingen *South : 13 km by Obere Weinsteige* GX *and B 27 :*

🏨 **Am Park** Ⓜ, Lessingstr. 4 (Leinfelden), ✉ 70771, ℰ (0711) 90 31 00, *info@hotelam park-leinfelden.de*, Fax (0711) 9031099, beer garden – 🛗 📺 📞 🅿 – 🏛 20. 🄰🄴 ① 🆗🅾 🆅🅸🆂🅰 🄹🄲🄱
closed 24 December - 10 January – **Meals** *(closed Saturday and Sunday)* à la carte 23,27/37,34 – **42 rm** 🍽 72 – 95.

🏨 **Filderland** without rest, Tübinger Str. 16 (Echterdingen), ✉ 70771, ℰ (0711) 9 49 46, *hote lfilderland@t-online.de*, Fax (0711) 9494888 – 🛗 ✻ 📺 📞 🚗 – 🏛 20. 🄰🄴 ① 🆗🅾 🆅🅸🆂🅰
closed 21 December - 6 January – **48 rm** 🍽 61/74 – 77/92.

aiersbronn *Baden-Württemberg* 🔢 U 9 – *pop. 16 600 – alt. 550 m.*
Stuttgart 100.

✕✕✕✕ **Schwarzwaldstube** - Hotel Traube Tonbach, Tonbachstr. 237, ✉ 72270, ℰ (07442) ৪৪৪ 49 26 65, *traube-tonbach@t-online.de*, Fax (07442) 492692, ≤ – 🍴 🅿. 🄰🄴 ① 🆗🅾 🆅🅸🆂🅰. ✻
closed 7 January - 1 February, 29 July - 27 August, Monday and Tuesday – **Meals** (booking essential) (outstanding wine list) 96/115 and à la carte 55/83
Spec. Heissgeräucherte Wolfsbarschschnitte aus dem Sternanisrauch. St. Jakobsmuscheln mit orientalischen Gemüsen und Krustentiersauce. Gänseleber mit Zitronenconfit im Salzteigmantel gebacken.

✕✕✕✕ **Restaurant Bareiss** - Hotel Bareiss, Gärtenbühlweg 14, ✉ 72270, ℰ (07442) 4 70, ৪৪৪ *info@bareiss.com*, Fax (07442) 47320, ≤, 🍽 – 🍴 🅿. 🄰🄴 ① 🆗🅾 🆅🅸🆂🅰. ✻
closed 14 July - 22 August, 24 November - 24 December, Monday and Tuesday – **Meals** (booking essential) (outstanding wine list) 89/105 and à la carte 56/79
Spec. Rosette von gratinierten St. Jakobsmuscheln mit Imperial Kaviar. Variation vom Rehkitzrücken. Schokoladentarte "Guanaja".

ulzburg *Baden-Württemberg* 🔢 W 7 – *pop. 2 630 – alt. 474 m.*
Stuttgart 229.

✕✕✕ **Hirschen** (Steiner) with rm, Hauptstr. 69, ✉ 79295, ℰ (07634) 82 08, *hirschen-sulzburg@t* ৪৪ *-online.de*, Fax (07634) 6717, (18 C inn), « Antiques and period style furniture »
closed 7 to 24 January and 22 July - 8 August – **Meals** *(closed Monday - Tuesday)* (booking essential) (outstanding wine list) 33,50 *(lunch)* and à la carte 47,50/68 – **9 rm** 🍽 62 – 82/125
Spec. Variation von der Gänseleber mit Brioche. Cassolette von Krebsen mit Gemüserauten und Kalbskopf. Ausgelöste Wachtel mit Trüffel gefüllt und Trüffelsauce.

Greece

Elláda

ATHENS

PRACTICAL INFORMATION

LOCAL CURRENCY

1 euro (€) = 0,89 USD ($) (Dec 2001)

TOURIST INFORMATION

National Tourist Organisation (EOT): *2, Amerikis, ℘ (01) 327 13 00-2. Hotel reservation: Hellenic Chamber of Hotels, 24 Stadiou, ℘ (01) 323 71 93. Fax (01) 322 54 49, also at Athens International Airport ℘ (01) 353 04 45 - Tourist Police: 4 Stadiou ℘ 171.*

National Holidays in Greece: *25 March and 28 October.*

FOREIGN EXCHANGE

Banks are usually open on weekdays from 8am to 2pm. A branch of the National Bank of Greece is open daily from 8am to 2pm (from 9am to 1pm at weekends) at 2 Karageorgi Servias (Sindagma).

AIRLINES

OLYMPIC AIRWAYS: *96 Singrou 117 41 Athens, ℘ (01) 926 73 33/926 91 11-3, 2 Kotopouli (Omonia), ℘ (01) 926 72 16-9, reservations only ℘ (01) 966 66 66.*
AIR FRANCE: *18 Vouliagmenis, Glyfada 166 75 Athens, ℘ (01) 960 11 00.*
BRITISH AIRWAYS: *1 Themistokleous Street 166 74 Glyfada ℘ (01) 890 6666.*
JAPAN AIRLINES: *22 Voulis 105 63 Athens, ℘ (01) 323 03 31.*
LUFTHANSA: *11 Vas. Sofias ℘ (01) 369 22 00.*
SABENA: *41 Vouliagmenis Ave ℘ (01) 960 00 21.*
SWISSAIR: *4 Othonos, (Ist floor) 105 57 Athens, ℘ (01) 337 05 33.*

TRANSPORT IN ATHENS

Taxis: *may be hailed in the street even when already engaged; it is always advisable to pay by the meter (double fare after midnight).*
Bus: *good for sightseeing and practical for short distances: 120 GRD.*
Metro: *Three lines cross the city from North east (Kifissia) to South west (Pireas) : from Northwest (Sepolia) to South (Dafni) and from Syntagma (Parliament Square) to Ethniki Amyna.*

POSTAL SERVICES

General Post Office: *100 Eolou (Omonia) with poste restante, and also at Sindagma.*
Telephone (OTE): *15 Stadiou and 85 Patission (all services).*

SHOPPING IN ATHENS

In summer, shops are usually open from 8am to 1.30pm, and 5.30 to 8.30pm. They close on Sunday, and at 2.30pm on Monday, Wednesday and Saturday. In winter they open from 9am to 5pm on Monday and Wednesday, from 10am to 7pm on Tuesday, Thursday and Friday, from 8.30am to 3.30pm on Saturday. Department Stores in Patission and Eolou are open fron 8.30 am to 8 pm on weekdays and 3 pm on Saturdays. The main shopping streets are to be found in Sindagma, Kolonaki, Monastiraki and Omonia areas. Flea Market (generally open on Sunday) and Greek Handicraft in Plaka and Monastiraki.

TIPPING

Service is generally included in the bills but it is usual to tip employees.

SPEED LIMITS

The speed limit in built up areas is 50 km/h (31 mph); on motorways the maximum permitted speed is 100 km/h (62 mph) and 80 km/h (50 mph) on others roads.

SEAT BELTS

The wearing of seat belts is compulsory for drivers and front seat passengers.

BREAKDOWN SERVICE

The ELPA (Automobile and Touring Club of Greece, ℘ (01) 60 68 800) operate a 24 hour breakdown service: phone 174 for tourist information, 104 for emergency road service.

ATHENS
(ATHÍNA)

Atikí 980 ⑨ *– Pop. 3 076 786 (Athens and Piraeus area).*

Igoumenítsa 581 – Pátra 215 – Thessaloníki 479.

🛈 *Tourist Information (EOT), 2 Amerikis 𝒻 (01) 327 13 00-2, Information center 𝒻 (01) 331 05 65.*
ELPA (Automobile and Touring Club of Greece), 395 Messogion 𝒻 (01) 606 88 00.
🛦 *Glifáda 𝒻 (01) 894 68 20, Fax (01) 894 37 21.*
✈ *F : 35 km, Athens International Airport 𝒻 (01) 369 83 00.*
🚗 *1 Karolou 𝒻 (01) 529 77 77.*

SIGHTS

Views of Athens: Lycabettos (Likavitós) ☀★★★ *DX – Philopappos Hill (Lófos Filopápou)* ≼★★★ *AY.*

ANCIENT ATHENS

Acropolis★★★ (Akrópoli) ABY – Theseion★★ (Thissío) AY and Agora★ (Arhéa Agorá) AY – Theatre of Dionysos★★ (Théatro Dioníssou) BY and Odeon of Herod Atticus★ (Odío Iródou Atikoú) AY – Olympieion★★ (Naós Olimbíou Diós) BY and Hadrian's Arch★ (Píli Adrianoú) BY – Tower of the Winds★ BY A in the Roman Forum (Romaiki Agorá).

OLD ATHENS AND THE TURKISH PERIOD

Pláka★★ : Old Metropolitan★★ BY P¹ – Monastiráki★ (Old Bazaar): Kapnikaréa (Church) BY K, Odós Pandróssou★ BY 29, Monastiráki Square★ BY.

MODERN ATHENS

Sindagma Square★ CY : Greek guard on sentry duty – Academy, University and Library Buildings★ (Akadimía CX, Panepistímio CX, Ethnikí Vivliothíki BX) – National Garden★ (Ethnikós Kípos) CY.

MUSEUMS

National Archaelogical Museum★★★ (Ethnikó Arheologikó Moussío) BX – Acropolis Museum★★★ BY M⁵ – Museum of Cycladic and Ancient Greek Art★★ DY M¹⁰ – Byzantine Museum★★ (Vizandinó Moussío) DY – Benaki Museum★★ (Moussío Benáki, private collection of antiquities and traditional art) CDY – Museum of Traditional Greek Art★ BY M⁷ – National Historical Museum★ BY M² – Jewish Museum of Greece★ BY M³ – National Gallery and Soutzos Museum★ (painting and sculpture) DY M¹.

EXCURSIONS

Cape Sounion★★★ (Soúnio) SE : 71 km BY – Kessariani Monastery★★, E : 9 km DY – Daphne Monastery★★ (Dafni) NW : 10 km AX – Aigina Island★ (Égina) : Temple of Aphaia★★, 3 hours return.

ΛΑΡΙΣΑ
LARISSA
AHARNES
THESSALONIKI
LAM
PAP

Ioulianou

NEOΦ. ΜΕΤΑΞΑ
Neof. Metaxa

28 ΟΚΤΩΒΡΙΟΥ
ΜΕΤΕΟ

ΕΘΝΙΚΟ
ΒΡΗΕΟLO
MOUSSIO

ΙΩΑΝΝΙΝΩΝ
IOANNINON

ΠΕΤΡΑΣ

ΠΕΛΟΠΟΝΗΣΟΣ
PELOPONISSOS

ΛΕΝΟΡΜΑΝ

Deligiani

ΛΙΟΣΙΩΝ
Liossion

ΗΠΕΙΡΟΥ

ΑΧΑΡΝΩΝ

ΣΤΟΥΡΝΑΡΑ

Marni

t

H

ΜΑΡΝΗΣ

ΣΕΠΤΕΜΒΡΙΟΥ (Patission)
Septemvriou

ΠΟΛΙΤΕΗΝΙΟU
POLITEHNIOU

ΧΙΟΥ
ΧΙΟΥ

ΦΑΒΙΕΡΟΥ
FABIEROU

ΠΛΑΤ. ΒΑΘΗΣ
Pl. Vathis

ΠΛΑΤ. ΚΑΝΙΓ
Pl. Kaning

X

ΔΕΛΗΓΙΑΝΝΗ

Metaxourghio
ΜΕΤΑΞΟΥΡΓΕΙΟ

ΚΑΡΟΛΟΥ
Karolou

3 ΟΚΤΩΒΡΙΟΥ
3 Oktovriou

ΘΕΜΙΣΤΟΚΛΕΟ

ΠΛΑΤ.
ΚΑΡΑΙΣΚΑΚΗ
Pl. Karaiskaki

ΜΑΡΝΗ
Marni

ΟΜΟΝΟΙΑ
OMONOIA
Omónia

ΑΧΙΛΛΕΩΣ

ΑΓ. ΚΟΝΣΤΑΝΤΙΝΟΥ
Ag. Konstandinou

T

28 ΟΚΤΩΒΡΙΟΥ

ΑΚΑ

Ahileos

ΟΜΟΝΟΙΑ
Omónia
a
b

ΠΑΝΕΠΙΣΤΗΜΙΟΥ
PANEPISTIMIOU
ΠΑΝΕΠΙΣΤΗΜΙΟΥ

c
DEUT
ARCH. IN

ΜΕΓ. ΘΕΡΜΟΠΥΛΩΝ

ΜΥΛΛΕΡΟΥ

ΚΟΛΟΚΥΝΘΟΥΣ

ΔΕΛΗΓΙΩΡΓΗ

ΜΕΝΑΝΔΡΟΥ

ΑΙΟΛΟΥ

ΣΤΑΔΙΟ

ΕΘΝΙΚΗ
ΧΙΛΙΟΘΗΝΙ

ΜΕΤΑXΟΥΡΓΙΟ
METAXOURGIO

ΚΕΡΑΜΕΙΚΟΥ

ΑΛΕΞΑΝΔΡΑΣ

ΠΛΑΤ. ΚΟΤΖΙΑ
Pl. Kotzia

H

ΤΑΝΕΠΙΣΤΗΜΙU
Panepistimi

ΣΟΦΟΚΛΕΟΥΣ
Sofokleous

ΕΟΛΟΥ

ΠΛΑΤ
ΚΛΑΥΘΜΩΝΟΣ
Pl. Klafthmonos

(ΠΕΙΡΑΙΩΣ)
(Pireos)

ΠΑΝΑΓΗ ΤΣΑΛΔΑΡΗ
Panagi Tsaldari

ΠΛΑΤ.
ΕΛΕΥΘΕΡΙΑΣX
Pl. Eleftherias

ΚΕΝΔΡΙΚΗ ΑΓΟΡΑ
KENDRIKI AGORA

ΑΠΡΟΤΟΘΑΝΟΥΣ

ΕΥΡΙΠΙΔΟΥ
EVRIPIDOU

PIREAS

ΚΡΙΕΖΗ
KRIEZI

ΣΑΡΡΗ
SARRI

ΑΘΗΝΑΣ
Athinas

ΚΕΡΑΜΙΚΟΣ
KERAMIKOS

M

S

M 14

PSIRI

ΕΡΜΟΥ
ERMOU

ΚΟΛΟΚΟΤΡΩΝΗ

M 2

e

ΠΛΑΤ ΜΟΝΑΣΤΗΡΑΚΙ
PL. MONASTIRAKI

ΜΟΝΑΣΤΗΡΑΚΙ
MONASTIRAKI

v

ΜΟΝΑΣΤΗΡΑΚΙ
Monastiraki

a

Mitropoleos

c

K

Ermou

ΘΗΣΕΙΟ
Thissio

b

ΘΗΣΣΙΟ
THISSIO

Αποστόλου
Apostolou

b

ΜΗΤΡΟΠΟΛΕ

P 1

29

ΑΡΗΕΑ ΑΓΟΡΑ
ARHEA AGORA

A

ΝΑΥΑΡΧΟΥ
ΝΑΥΑΡΧΟΥ

NIKO

h

ΠΛΑΚΑ
PLAKA

M 12

ΛΟΦΟΣ ΝΙΜΦΩΝ
LOFOS NIMFON
(Nympheion)

ΑΡΙΟΣ
ΠΑΓΟΣ
ARIOS
PAGOS

ΑΝΑΦΙΩΤΙΚΑ
ANAFIOTIKA

M

16

M 7

Παυλου
Pavlou

ΠΝΙΚΑ
PNIKA
(Pnyx)

ΑΚΡΟΠΟΛΗ
AKROPOLI

ΑΔΡΙΑΝΟΥ

n

ΠΙΛΙ
PILI
ADRIAN

Ag. Dimitrios

ΩΔΙΟ ΙΡΟΔΟΥ
ΑΤΙΚΟΥ
ODIO IRODOU
ATIKOU

M

Διονίσιου
Dionissiou

ΔΙΟΝΥΣΙΟΥ ΘΕΑΤΡΟ ΔΙΟΝΥΣΟΥ
THEATRO DIONISSOU

ΑΡΕΟΑΓΙΤΟΥ

ΝΑΟΣ
ΟΛΙΜΒΙΟ
NAOS
OLIMBIO
DIOS

ΔΙΑΚ

ΛΟΦΟΣ
LOFOS
FILOPAPOU
(Mouseion)

Diomysos
Diomysos

Ρ.Θ. ΓΚΑΛΗ
Aeropagitou

a

30

ΓΚΑΛΗ

Akropoli
ΑΚΡΟΠΟΛΗ

L

M

SYTΓΡΟΥ
Singrou Diakou

ΣΥΓΓΡΟΥ

P

T

36

ΚΑΒΑΛΛΟΤΙ
KAVALLOTI

p

ΧΑΤΖΗΧΡΗΣΤΟΥ

21

r

ΜΑΚΡΙΓΙΑΝΗ
MAKRIGIANI

39

f

d

PIREAS

So

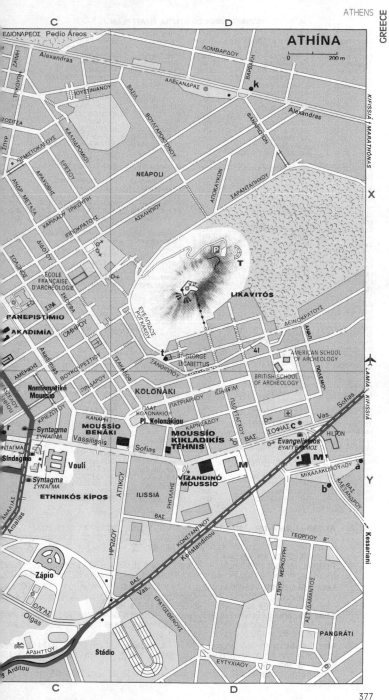

STREET INDEX TO ATHÍNA TOWN PLAN

Athenaeum Inter-Continental Ⓜ, 89-93 Singrou, ✉ 117 45, Southwest : 2 ¾ kr ℰ (01) 9206 000, athens@interconti.com, Fax (01) 9206 500, 🏖, « Première roofto restaurant with ⩽ City and Acropolis », 🛄, ⇌s, 🎠 – 🍴, 🍴 rm, 🖭 📺 🕻 ♿ 🚗 🛢 2000. 🅼🅾 🅰🅴 ⓞ VISA JCB. ✗

Pergola : Meals (buffet lunch) 18/32 and a la carte 26/34 🍴 8.50 – **Première** (9th floor) Meals (dinner only) 42.50/57.20 and a la carte approx. 33.70 – 🖵 22 – **520 rm** 400, 23 suites

Ledra Marriott, 115 Singrou, ✉ 117 45, Southwest : 3 km ℰ (01) 9300 000, mar iott@otenet.gr, Fax (01) 9359 153, « Rooftop terrace with 🎠 and 🌸 Athens », 🛄, ⇌s – 🍴, 🍴 rm, 🖭 📺 🕻 ♿ 🚗 – 🛢 500. 🅼🅾 🅰🅴 ⓞ VISA. ✗

Kona Kai : Meals - Polynesian and Japanese - (closed 4 days Easter and Sunday) (dinne only) 36.68/71.47 and a la carte 40/71 – **Zephyros** : Meals (buffet lunch) 15/35 and la carte 20/35 🍴 10.27 – 🖵 18 – **258 rm** 240/280, 16 suites.

Metropolitan Ⓜ, 385 Singrou, ✉ 175 64, Southwest : 7 km ℰ (01) 9471 000, met opolitan@chandris.gr, Fax (01) 9471 010, 🏖, 🛄, ⇌s, 🎠 – 🍴 rm, 🖭 📺 🕻 🐾 – 🛢 450 🅼🅾 🅰🅴 ⓞ VISA JCB. ✗

Trocadero : Meals (buffet lunch) 18 and a la carte 36/47 – 🖵 17 – **351 rm** 230, 1 suites.

🏨🏨🏨 **NJV Athens Plaza** Ⓜ, 2 Vas. Georgiou A, Sindagma Sq., ✉ 105 64, ☎ (01) 335 2400, *sales njv@grecotel.gr, Fax (01) 323 5856* – 🛗, ⇔ rm, 🗐 📺 ☎ – 🛦 250. 🕮 🖭 ⓞ 𝐕𝐈𝐒𝐀 𝐉𝐂𝐁. ⊁
CY r
The Parliament : Meals a la carte 31/57 ⑂ 15 – ⇌ 20 – **159 rm** 353/440, 23 suites.

🏨🏨🏨 **Divani Caravel**, 2 Vas. Alexandrou, ✉ 161 21, ☎ (01) 7207 000, *divanis@divanicar avel.gr, Fax (01) 7253 770*, « Rooftop ⬜ with ⩽ Athens » – 🛗, ⇔ rm, 🗐 📺 ☎ ⇐ – 🛦 100. 🕮 🖭 ⓞ 𝐕𝐈𝐒𝐀 𝐉𝐂𝐁. ⊁
DY b
Millennium : Meals (dinner only) a la carte 35/50 ⑂ 20 – *Café Constantinople :* Meals (buffet lunch) 26/44 and dinner a la carte 39/52 ⑂ 20 – ⇌ 22 – **423 rm** 405/607, 48 suites.

🏨🏨🏨 **Divani Palace Acropolis**, 19-25 Parthenonos, ✉ 117 42, ☎ (01) 9280 100, *divan is@divaniacropolis.gr, Fax (01) 9214 993*, « Ancient ruins of Themistocles wall in basement », ⬜ – 🛗 🗐 📺 ☎ – 🛦 300. 🕮 🖭 ⓞ 𝐕𝐈𝐒𝐀 𝐉𝐂𝐁. ⊁
BY r
Aspassia : Meals 22/30 and a la carte 30/44 ⑂ 20 – *Roof Garden :* Meals *(closed mid October-mid May and Tuesday)* (live music) (buffet dinner only) 35 – ⇌ 18 – **243 rm** 190, 7 suites.

🏨🏨🏨 **Park H. Athens**, 10 Alexandras Ave, ✉ 106 82, ☎ (01) 8832 711, *park-hotel@ote net.gr, Fax (01) 8238 420*, « Rooftop terrace with ⬜ and ⩽ Athens » – 🛗 🗐 📺 ☎ ⇐ – 🛦 150. 🕮 🖭 ⓞ 𝐕𝐈𝐒𝐀 𝐉𝐂𝐁. ⊁
BX c
Alexandros : Meals a la carte 22/41 ⑂ 16.14 – *Park Café :* Meals a la carte 13/25 ⑂ 16.14 – ⇌ 14.67 – **136 rm** 264.12/352.16, 10 suites.

🏨🏨🏨 **Holiday Inn**, 50 Mihalakopoulou, ✉ 115 28, ☎ (01) 7278 000, *holinn@ath.forthnet.gr, Fax (01) 7278 600*, ⩽, « Rooftop terrace with ⬜ », 🛵, ⇌ – 🛗, ⇔ rm, 🗐 📺 ☎ ⇐ – 🛦 650. 🕮 🖭 ⓞ 𝐕𝐈𝐒𝐀 𝐉𝐂𝐁. ⊁
DY a
Meals 22/26 and a la carte 24/30 ⑂ 13 – ⇌ 20 – **192 rm** 305/580.

🏨🏨🏨 **Zafolia** Ⓜ, 87-89 Alexandras, ✉ 114 74, ☎ (01) 6449 002, *zafoliahotel@compulink.gr, Fax (01) 6442 042*, « Rooftop terrace with ⬜ and ⩽ Athens », 🛵, ⇌ – 🛗 🗐 📺 ☎ ⇐ – 🛦 150. 🕮 🖭 ⓞ 𝐕𝐈𝐒𝐀 𝐉𝐂𝐁. ⊁
DX k
Meals a la carte approx. 19 ⑂ 11.50 – **185 rm** ⇌ 278.50/341, 7 suites.

🏨🏨🏨 **St George Lycabettus**, 2 Kleomenous, ✉ 106 75, ☎ (01) 7290 711, *info@sglyca bettus.gr, Fax (01) 7290 439*, 佘, « ⩽ Athens from rooftop restaurant », ⇌, ⬜ – 🛗 🗐 📺 ☎ ⇐ – 🛦 210. 🕮 🖭 ⓞ 𝐕𝐈𝐒𝐀. ⊁
DX t
Meals 22/34 and a la carte 28/86 ⑂ 21.72 – *Le Grand Balcon :* Meals (dinner only) 44/88 and a la carte 40/65 ⑂ 21.72 – ⇌ 20.25 – **152 rm** 276.10/413.14, 6 suites.

🏨🏨 **Andromeda** Ⓜ ⤸, 22 Timoleontos Vassou St, ✉ 115 21, via Vas. Sofias behind U.S. Embassy ☎ (01) 6415 000, *reservations@andromedaathens.gr, Fax (01) 6466 361*, « Contemporary interior design » – 🛗, ⇔ rm, 🗐 📺 ☎ – 🛦 100. 🕮 🖭 ⓞ 𝐕𝐈𝐒𝐀. ⊁
Etrusco : Meals a la carte 13/19 ⑂ 23.33 – ⇌ 20 – **21 rm** 300/325, 9 suites.

🏨🏨 **Alexandros** Ⓜ ⤸, 8 Timoleontos Vas., ✉ 115 21, via Vas Sofias behind U.S. Embassy ☎ (01) 6430 464, *airotel@otenet.gr, Fax (01) 6441 084* – 🛗 🗐 📺 ☎ ⇐ – 🛦 90. 🕮 🖭 ⓞ 𝐕𝐈𝐒𝐀. ⊁
Meals a la carte 14/41 ⑂ 11.50 – **77 rm** ⇌ 143/158, 3 suites.

🏨🏨 **Omonia Grand** Ⓜ, 2 Pireos, Omonia Sq., ✉ 105 52, ☎ (01) 5235 230, *salesacr@g recotel.gr, Fax (01) 5231 361* – 🛗 🗐 📺 ☎. 🕮 🖭 ⓞ 𝐕𝐈𝐒𝐀. ⊁ rest
BX a
Meals a la carte 21/28 ⑂ 13.50 **115 rm** ⇌ 92/353.

🏨🏨 **Athens Acropol**, 1 Pireos, Omonia Sq., ✉ 105 52, ☎ (01) 5282 100, *sales-acr@gr ecotel.gr, Fax (01) 5282 159* – 🗐 📺 – 🛦 450. 🕮 🖭 ⓞ 𝐕𝐈𝐒𝐀. ⊁ rest
BX b
Meals a la carte 16/27 ⑂ 12 – ⇌ 6100 – **167 rm** ⇌ 92/100, 2 suites.

🏨🏨 Esperia Palace, 22 Stadiou, ✉ 105 64, ☎ (01) 3238 001, *reservations.asds@otenet.gr, Fax (01) 3238 100* – 🛗 🗐 📺
BX d
174 rm, 15 suites.

🏨🏨 **Herodion**, 4 Rovertou Galli, ✉ 117 42, ☎ (01) 9236 832, *herodion@herodion.gr, Fax (01) 9211 650*, « Roof garden with ⩽ Acropolis » – 🛗 🗐 📺 ☎ – 🛦 50. 🕮 ⓞ 𝐕𝐈𝐒𝐀 𝐉𝐂𝐁. ⊁
BY p
Meals 22/25 and a la carte – **90 rm** ⇌ 162/242.

🏨🏨 **Novotel**, 4-6 Mihail Voda, ✉ 104 39, ☎ (01) 8200 700, *h0866@accor-hotels.com, Fax (01) 8200 777*, « Roof terrace with ⬜ and ❀ Athens » – 🛗 🗐 📺 ☎ ⇐ – 🛦 800. 🕮 🖭 ⓞ 𝐕𝐈𝐒𝐀. ⊁ rest
AX t
Meals 18/26 and a la carte – ⇌ 13 – **190 rm** 150/202, 5 suites.

🏨🏨 **Electra Palace** (reopens May 2002), 18 Nikodimou, ✉ 105 57, ☎ (01) 3370 000, *aele ctrapalace@ath.forthnet.gr, Fax (01) 3241 875*, « Terrace with ⬜ and ⩽ Athens » – 🛗, ⇔ rm, 🗐 📺 ☎ ⇐ – 🛦 200. 🕮 🖭 ⓞ 𝐕𝐈𝐒𝐀. ⊁
BY h
Meals 18 and a la carte 16/28 ⑂ 13 – **101 rm** ⇌ 157/190, 5 suites.

🏨🏨 **Electra**, 5 Ermou, ✉ 105 63, ☎ (01) 3223 223, *electrahotels@ath.forthnet.gr, Fax (01) 3220 310* – 🛗, ⇔ rm, 🗐 📺 – 🛦 70. 🕮 🖭 ⓞ 𝐕𝐈𝐒𝐀. ⊁
BY e
Meals 18 and a la carte 16/28 ⑂ 13 – **109 rm** ⇌ 157/239.

🏠 **Plaka** without rest., 7 Kapnikareas and Mitropoleos St, ✉ 105 56, ☏ (01) 3222 09 *plaka@ tourhotel.gr*, Fax *(01) 3222 412*, « Rooftop terrace with ≤ Athens » – 🛗 ▤ 🖪
🕿. ⓜⓞ ⒶⒺ ① 𝗩𝗜𝗦𝗔 ᴊᴄʙ. ⅏ BY
67 rm ⮸ 90/112.

🏠 **Achilleas** without rest., 21 Lekka St, ✉ 105 62, ☏ (01) 3233 197, *achilleas@ tourl tel.gr*, Fax *(01) 3228 531* – 🛗 ▤ 📺. ⓜⓞ ⒶⒺ 𝗩𝗜𝗦𝗔 ᴊᴄʙ. ⅏ BY
34 rm ⮸ 90/112.

🏠 **Philippos** without rest., 3 Mitseon, ✉ 117 42, ☏ (01) 9223 611, *philippos@ herodion.* Fax *(01) 9223 615* – 🛗 ▤ 📺 🕿. ⓜⓞ ① 𝗩𝗜𝗦𝗔. ⅏ BY
48 rm ⮸ 120/162.

🏠 **Jason Inn** without rest., 12 Assomaton St Thission, ✉ 105 53, ☏ (01) 3251 106, *do os@otenet.gr*, Fax *(01) 3243 132* – 🛗 ▤ 📺. ⓜⓞ ⒶⒺ 𝗩𝗜𝗦𝗔. ⅏ AY
57 rm ⮸ 74/96.

ⅩⅩⅩ **Pil-Poul**, 51 Apostolou Pavlou, ✉ 118 51, ☏ (01) 3423 665, Fax *(01) 3413 046*, « Form mansion with ≤ Acropolis and Athens from rooftop terrace » – ⓜⓞ ⒶⒺ 𝗩𝗜𝗦𝗔. ⅏ BY
closed Easter, 25 December and Sunday – **Meals** (dinner only) 53/73 and a la carte 65/7

ⅩⅩⅩ **Boschetto,** Evangelismou, off Vas. Sofias, ✉ 116 76, ☏ (01) 7210 89 Fax *(01) 7223 598*, 斧, « Summerhouse in small park » – ▤. ⒶⒺ 𝗩𝗜𝗦𝗔 DY
closed 25 December – **Meals** - Italian influences - (dinner only) 35/41 and a la carte 48/7
ⅿ 17.61.

ⅩⅩⅩ **Symbosio,** 46 Erehthiou, ✉ 117 42, ☏ (01) 9225 321, Fax *(01) 9232 780*, « Attracti conservatory in winter, terrace in summer » – ⓜⓞ ⒶⒺ ① 𝗩𝗜𝗦𝗔. ⅏ AY
closed 1 week Easter, 4-27 August, 25 December and Sunday – **Meals** (booking essentia (dinner only) a la carte 43/60 ⅿ 29.35.

ⅩⅩ **Diatiriteo,** 28 Kariaikaki, ✉ 105 51, ☏ (01) 3314 601, *info@ cubanita.g* Fax *(01) 3314 604*, 斧, « Modernised 18C former Government building » – ⟸. ⓜⓞ Ⓑ ① 𝗩𝗜𝗦𝗔. ⅏ AY
26 September-14 April – **Meals** *(closed Monday)* (dinner only and Sunday lunch)/dinner la carte 27/30.

ⅩⅩ **Edodi,** 80 Veikou, via Makrigiani ☏ (01) 9213 013, Fax *(01) 9213 013*, « 182 town house » – ⓜⓞ ⒶⒺ ① 𝗩𝗜𝗦𝗔. ⅏
closed 3-6 May, 12-25 August, 1-2 January and Sunday – **Meals** (booking essential) (dinn only) 44/55 and a la carte 47/67.

ⅩⅩ **Sponti,** 5 Pyronos, off Varnava Sq., ✉ 116 36, via Eratosthenous ☏ (01) 7564 02 *info@ spondi.gr*, Fax *(01) 7567 021*, 斧 – ⓜⓞ ⒶⒺ ① 𝗩𝗜𝗦𝗔 ᴊᴄʙ. ⅏
closed 4 days Easter and 1 week in summer – **Meals** (dinner only) a la carte 44/64 ⅿ 17.6

ⅩⅩ **Mezzo Mezzo,** 58 Singrou, ✉ 117 42, ☏ (01) 9242 444, Fax *(01) 9242 71* « Warehouse style conversion, modern art » – ▤ 🄵. ⓜⓞ ⒶⒺ ① 𝗩𝗜𝗦𝗔. ⅏ BY
closed 1-15 May, 1-15 October, 25 December, 1 January and Sunday – **Meals** (dinner on 53/59 and a la carte 43/67.

ⅩⅩ **7 Anemous,** 121 Ermou (17 Astingos), Monastiraki, ✉ 105 55, ☏ (01) 3240 38 Fax *(01) 7010 572* – ▤. ⓜⓞ ⒶⒺ ① 𝗩𝗜𝗦𝗔. ⅏ AY
closed August – **Meals** a la carte 21/30 ⅿ 12.33.

ⅩⅩ **Daphne's,** 4 Lysikratous, Plaka, ✉ 105 58, ☏ (01) 3227 971, Fax *(01) 3227 971*, 斧 « Frescoes depicting ancient Greek myths, attractive inner courtyard » – ▤. ⓜⓞ ⒶⒺ Ⓒ 𝗩𝗜𝗦𝗔. ⅏ BY
Meals (booking essential) (dinner only) a la carte 32/51 ⅿ 20.54.

ⅩⅩ **Ideal,** 46 Panepistimiou, (El. Venizelou), ✉ 106 78, ☏ (01) 3303 000, *idealepe@ ot et.gr*, Fax *(01) 3303 003* – ▤. ⓜⓞ ⒶⒺ ① 𝗩𝗜𝗦𝗔 ᴊᴄʙ. ⅏ BX
closed 2 days Easter, 25-26 December, Mardi Gras, 15 August and Sunday – **Meals** a la carte 22/37 ⅿ 13.21.

Ⅹ **Taverna Strofi,** 25 Rovertou Galli, ✉ 117 42, ☏ (01) 9214 130, 斧, « ≤ Acropo from rooftop terrace » – ⓜⓞ ① 𝗩𝗜𝗦𝗔. ⅏ AY
closed 4-7 May, 24-26 and 31 December-2 January and Sunday – **Meals** (dinner only) la carte 24/29 ⅿ 7.

Ⅹ **Taverna Sigalas,** 2 Monastiraki Sq., ✉ 105 55, ☏ (01) 3213 036, Fax *(01) 3252 44* 斧, « Traditional Greek atmosphere », live music – ⓜⓞ ⒶⒺ 𝗩𝗜𝗦𝗔. ⅏ BY
Meals a la carte 10/13 ⅿ 4.40.

Environs

at Kifissia *Northeast : 15 km by Vas. Sofias* DY :

🏨 **Pentelikon** 🌤, 66 Diligianni, Kefalari, ✉ 145 62, off Harilaou Trikoupi, follow signs Politia ☏ (01) 6230 650, *pentelik@ otenet.gr*, Fax *(01) 8010 314*, 斧, ⅀, 🌳 – 🛗 ▤ 🖪 🄿 – 🔬 150. ⓜⓞ ⒶⒺ ① 𝗩𝗜𝗦𝗔. ⅏
La Terrasse : **Meals** 27 (lunch) and a la carte 29/48 ⅿ 14.09 (see also **Vardis** below)
⮸ 19.50 – **44 rm** 595/705, 6 suites.

🏨 **The Kefalari Suites** without rest., 1 Pentelis and Kolokotroni St, Kefalari, ⊠ 145 62, ℘ (01) 6233 333, info@kefalarisuites.gr, Fax (01) 6233 330, « Contemporary interior, rooftop spa bath » – 📶 🖭 📺 📞 🆖 🅰🅴 ⑩ 𝘝𝘐𝘚𝘈. ✀
12 rm ⊃ 322.82/381.51, 1 suite.

XXXX **Vardis** (at Pentelikon H.), 66 Diligianni, Kefalari, ⊠ 145 62, off Harilaou Trikoupi, follow signs to Politia ℘ (01) 6230 650, Fax (01) 8010 314, � – 🖭. 🆖 🅰🅴 ⑩ 𝘝𝘐𝘚𝘈. ✀
closed 2 weeks August, 25 December, 1 January and Sunday – **Meals** - French - (dinner only) a la carte 69/101
Spec. Ravioli de homard, crème de cèpes. Côte de veau de lait, légumes caramelisés. Millefeuille, crème vanille.

XXX **Beau Brummel,** 9 Ag Dimitriou, ⊠ 145 61, ℘ (01) 6236 780, Fax (01) 6236 981, � – 📶 🖭 🅿 🆖 🅰🅴 ⑩ 𝘝𝘐𝘚𝘈 🅹🅲🄱. ✀
closed August-10 September – **Meals** - French - (lunch by arrangement)/dinner a la carte 66/99 ▯ 30.

t Pireas Southwest : 10 km by Singrou BY :

XX **Varoulko** (Lefteris), 14 Deligiorgi, off Omiridou Skilitsi, ⊠ 185 33, ℘ (01) 4112 043, Fax (01) 4221 283 – 🖭. 🆖 🅰🅴 ⑩ 𝘝𝘐𝘚𝘈. ✀
closed 20 July-30 August, 24-26 and 31 December-2 January and Sunday dinner – **Meals** - Seafood - (booking essential) (dinner only) a la carte 42/70 ▯ 25
Spec. Clams in sweet wine jus. Crab bisque, cuttlefish ink. Baked red snapper with aubergine mousse.

t Vouliagmeni South : 18 km by Singrou BY :

🏩 **Divani Apollon Palace,** 10 Ag. Nicolaou and Iliou St (Kavouri), off Athinas, ⊠ 166 71, ℘ (01) 8911 100, divanis@divaniapollon.gr, Fax (01) 9658 010, ≤ Saronic Gulf, ㎡, ⊥, 🏊, ✗ – 🖭 📺 📞 ☞. 🆖 🅰🅴 ⑩ 𝘝𝘐𝘚𝘈. ✀
Mythos : Meals (closed Sunday) (dinner only) a la carte 38/56 ▯ 24 – **Anemos** : Meals 33/53 and a la carte 30/47 ▯ 14 – ⊃ 22 – **286 rm** 290/1350, 7 suites.

Hungary

Magyarország

BUDAPEST

PRACTICAL INFORMATION

LOCAL CURRENCY

Forint: *100 HUF = 0,40 euro (€) (Dec. 2001)*
National Holidays in Hungary: *15 March, 20 August, and 23 October.*

PRICES

Prices may change if goods and service costs in Hungary are revised and it is therefore always advisable to confirm rates with the hotelier when making a reservation.

FOREIGN EXCHANGE

It is strongly advised against changing money other than in banks, exchange offices or authorised offices such as large hotels, tourist offices, etc... Banks are usually open on weekdays from 8.30am to 4pm.

HOTEL RESERVATIONS

In case of difficulties in finding a room through our hotel selection, it is always possible to apply to TRIBUSZ Hotel Service, Apáczai ut. 1, Budapest 5th ☏ (01) 318 39 25, Fax (01) 317 90 99. This office offers a 24-hour assistance to the visitor.

POSTAL SERVICES

Main Post offices are open from 8am to 7pm on weekdays and 8am to 3pm on Saturdays.
General Post Office: *Városház ut. 18, Budapest 5th, ☏ (01) 318 48 11.*

SHOPPING IN BUDAPEST

In the index of street names, those printed in red are where the principal shops are found. Typical goods to be bought include embroidery, lace, china, leather goods, paprika, salami, Tokay (Tokaij), palinka, foie-gras... Shops are generally open from 10am to 6pm on weekdays (7pm on Thursday) and 9am to 1pm on Saturday.

TIPPING

Hotel, restaurant and café bills often do not include service in the total charge. In these cases it is usual to leave the staff a gratuity which will vary depending upon the service given.

CAR HIRE

The international car hire companies have branches in Budapest. Your hotel porter should be able to give details and help you with your arrangements.

BREAKDOWN SERVICE

A breakdown service is operated by MAGYAR AUTÓKLUB ☏ 188.

SPEED LIMIT

On motorways, the maximum permitted speed is 130 km/h – 80 mph, 100 km/h – 62 mph on main roads, 90 km/h – 55 mph on others roads and 50 km/h – 31 mph in built up areas.

SEAT BELTS

In Hungary, the wearing of seat belts is compulsory for drivers and front seat passengers. On motorways : all passengers.

TRANSPORT

The three metro lines (yellow, red and blue) and the trams and buses make up an extensive public transport network. Tickets must be purchased in advance. Daily, weekly and monthly passes are available.
Airport buses : apply to your hotel porter.

TAXIS

Only use authorised taxis displaying clear signage and yellow number plates.

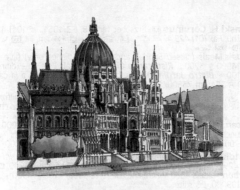

BUDAPEST

Hungary 🄰🄶🄴 D 8 – Pop. 1 909 000.

Munich 678 – Prague 533 – Venice 740 – Vienna 243 – Zagreb 350

🅱 Tourist Office of Budapest, Király Útca 93, ✉ 1077 ☎ (01) 352 14 33, Fax (01) 352 98 04 – IBUSZ Head Office, Ferenciek tér 5, Budapest 5th ☎ (01) 318 68 66.

✈ Ferihegy SE : 16 km by Üllöi DZ, ☎ (01) 296 96 96 (information), Bus to airport : from International Bus station, Erzsébet tér, Station 6 Budapest 5th and Airport Minibus Service I.RI – MALEV, Roosevelt tér 2, Budapest 5th ☎ (01) 267 29 11

Views of Budapest

Citadel (Citadella)★★★ GX – St. Gellert Monument (Szt. Gellért szobor)★★ GX – Liberation Monument (Szabadság szobor)★★ GX – Fishermen's Bastion (Halászbástya) ≼★★ FU.

BUDA

Gellert Thermal Baths (Gellért Gyógyfürdő)★★★ GX – Matthias Church★★ (Mátyástemplom) FU – Attractive Streets★★ (Tancsics Mihaly utca – Fortuna utca – Uri utca) EFU – Royal Palace★★★ (Budavári palota) FV – Hungarian National Gallery★★ – Király Baths (Király Gyógyfürdő)★★ CY.

PEST

Parliament Building★★★ (Országház) GU – Museum of Fine Arts★★★ (Szépművészeti Múzeum) DY M^{13} – Hungarian National Museum★★ (Magyar Nemzeti Múzeum) HVX – Museum of Applied Arts★★ (Iparművészeti Múzeum) CZ M^5 – Széchenyi Thermal Baths★★★ (Széchenyi Gyógyfürdő) DY Q – Hungarian State Opera House★★ (Magyar Állami Operaház) HU – Chain Bridge (Széchenyi Lánchíd)★★ FGV – Liberty Bridge (Szabadság híd)★★ GHX – Ethnographical Museum (Néprajzi Múzeum)★★ GU – Former Post Office Savings Bank (Posta Takarékpénztár)★★ GU – Central Market Hall (Vásárcsarnok)★★ HX – Dohány utca Synagogue (Dohány utcai zsinagóga)★★ HV – Café New York★★ CZ A.

ADDITIONAL SIGHTS

Margaret Island★★ (Margit-sziget) CY – Aquincum Museum★ (Aquincumi Múzéum) N : 12 km by Szentendrei út CY – St. Ann's Church★ (Szent Anna templom) FU.

Envir.: Szentendre★★ N : 20 km – Visegrád N : 42 km : Citadel, view★★★

Kempinski H. Corvinus Ⓜ, Erzsébet tér 7-8, ✉ 1051, ℰ (01) 429 3777, hotel@
empinski.hu, Fax (01) 429 4777, 🍽, ℉⎯, ⇆s, 🔲 – 🛗, ✺ rm, 🖿 📺 🅦 ㅎ ⇐ – 🏛 45
🅜🄾 🄐🄴 🄾 𝗩𝗜𝗦𝗔 🅹🄲🄱
GV
Corvinus : Meals *(closed Sunday and Monday)* (dinner only) (live music) a la cart
11500/14900 🕴 5200 – *Ristorante Giardino* : Meals - Italian - (dinner only) a la car
8200/9100 – *Bistro Jardin* : Meals (buffet lunch) 4600 and a la carte 4800/9200
⇆ 4900 – **354 rm** 73500/124600, 15 suites.

Hilton ♨, Hess András tér 1-3, ✉ 1014, ℰ (01) 488 6600, hiltonhu@ hungary.ne
Fax (01) 488 6644, ≼ Danube and Pest, « Remains of a 13C Dominican church and cellars
℉⎯, ⇆s – 🛗, ✺ rm, 🖿 📺 🅦 ㅎ ⇐ – 🏛 600. 🅜🄾 🄐🄴 🄾 𝗩𝗜𝗦𝗔 🅹🄲🄱
FU
Dominican : Meals (dinner only) (pianist) a la carte 6200/9800 🕴 6000 – *Corvina* : Mea
(buffet lunch) 4750 and a la carte 5500/7000 – *Sushi Bar* : Meals - Japanese - (dinn
only) 10200 and a la carte 7000/9500 – ⇆ 4500 – **295 rm** 51900/63000, 27 suite

Le Meridien, Erzsébet tér 9-10, ✉ 1051, ℰ (01) 429 5500, info@ le-meridien.h
Fax (01) 429 5555, 🍽, ℉⎯, ⇆s, 🔲 – 🛗, ✺ rm, 🖿 📺 🅦 ㅎ – 🏛 200. 🅜🄾 🄐🄴 🄾 𝗩𝗜𝗦𝗔 🅹🄲
Le Bourbon : Meals 4800 (lunch) and a la carte 5050/7100 🕴 4900 – ⇆ 4600 – **192 r**
59100/109000, 26 suites.
GV

Hyatt Regency Ⓜ, Roosevelt tér 2, ✉ 1051, ℰ (01) 266 1234, reservation@ bu☐
pest.hyatt.hu, Fax (01) 266 9101, ≼, ℉⎯, ⇆s, 🔲 – 🛗, ✺ rm, 🖿 📺 🅦 ㅎ ⇐ – 🏛 40
🅜🄾 🄐🄴 🄾 𝗩𝗜𝗦𝗔 🅹🄲🄱 ❀ rest
GV
Atrium Terrace : Meals (buffet lunch) 3900 and a la carte 5000/5700 🕴 4700 – *Foca*
cia : Meals - Mediterranean - a la carte 5050/5950 – ⇆ 4350 – **328 rm** 57800/8800☐
23 suites.

Inter-Continental, Apáczai Csere János útca 12-14, ✉ 1052, ℰ (01) 327 6333, bu☐
pest@interconti.com, Fax (01) 327 6357, ≼ Danube and Buda, 🍽, ℉⎯, ⇆s, 🔲 – |
✺ rm, 🖿 📺 ㅎ ⇐ – 🏛 800. 🅜🄾 🄐🄴 🄾 𝗩𝗜𝗦𝗔 🅹🄲🄱 ❀ rest
GV
Corso : Meals (buffet lunch) 5000 and dinner a la carte 6500/9600 🕴 5200 – ⇆ 475
– **383 rm** 64300/85300, 15 suites.

Marriott, Apáczai Csere János útca 4, ✉ 1052, ℰ (01) 266 7000, marriott.budape
@ pronet.hu, Fax (01) 266 5000, ≼ Danube and Buda, 🍽, ℉⎯, ⇆s, squash – 🛗, ✺ rr
🖿 📺 🅦 ㅎ ⇐ – 🏛 600. 🅜🄾 🄐🄴 🄾 𝗩𝗜𝗦𝗔 🅹🄲🄱 ❀
GV
Csarda : Meals *(closed Sunday)* (dinner only) (gypsy music) 4250 and a la carte – *Dur*
Grill : Meals (buffet) 4250 and a la carte – ⇆ 3850 – **351 rm** 45200/75950, 11 suite

Corinthia Aquincum Ⓜ, Árpád Fejedelem útca 94, ✉ 1036, ℰ (01) 436 4100, c☐
resv@ aqu.hu, Fax (01) 436 4156, ≼, Thermal spa and therapy centre, ℉⎯, ⇆s, 🔲 – |
✺ rm, 🖿 📺 🅦 ㅎ ⇐ 🅿 – 🏛 300. 🅜🄾 🄾 𝗩𝗜𝗦𝗔 🅹🄲🄱 ❀ rest
CY
Apicius : Meals (buffet lunch) 4350 and a la carte 7450/9800 🕴 5200 – **302 r**
⇆ 40600/51100, 8 suites.

Radisson SAS Béke, Teréz körút 43, ✉ 1067, ℰ (01) 301 1600, sales@ budzh.r☐
as.com, Fax (01) 301 1615, ⇆s, 🔲 – 🛗, ✺ rm, 🖿 📺 🅦 ㅎ ⇐ – 🏛 200. 🅜🄾 🄐🄴 ☐
𝗩𝗜𝗦𝗔 🅹🄲🄱 ❀ rest
HU
Szondi Lugas : Meals (buffet lunch) 3200/4500 and a la carte 4410/5300 🕴 2800
⇆ 3700 – **239 rm** 34100/47200, 8 suites.

Danubius Grand H. ♨, Margitsziget, ✉ 1138, ℰ (01) 452 6200, margotel@ hur
ary.net, Fax (01) 452 6262, ≼, 🍽, Direct entrance to thermal spa and therapy centr
℉⎯, ⇆s, 🔲 – 🛗, ✺ rm, 🖿 📺 🅦 ㅎ ⇐ 🅿 – 🏛 130. 🅜🄾 🄐🄴 🄾 𝗩𝗜𝗦𝗔 🅹🄲🄱 ❀ re
Széchenyi : Meals 4750 and a la carte 7500/8900 🕴 4300 – ⇆ 2650 – **154 r**
42200/57400, 10 suites.
CY

Art'otel Ⓜ, Bem Rakpart 16-19, ✉ 1011, ℰ (01) 487 9487, budapest@ artotel.h
Fax (01) 487 9488, ≼, 🍽, « Contemporary interior, Donald Sultan artwork », ℉⎯, ⇆s
🛗, ✺ rm, 🖿 📺 🅦 ㅎ ⇐ – 🏛 160. 🅜🄾 🄐🄴 🄾 𝗩𝗜𝗦𝗔
FU
Chelsea : Meals a la carte approx. 5200 – **159 rm** ⇆ 51800/57000, 6 suites.

Hilton WestEnd Ⓜ, Váci útca 1-3, ✉ 1069, ℰ (01) 288 5500, infobudapest-wes☐
nd@ hilton.com, Fax (01) 288 5588, 🍽, ℉⎯ – 🛗, ✺ rm, 🖿 📺 🅦 ㅎ ⇐ – 🏛 350. ☐
🄐🄴 🄾 𝗩𝗜𝗦𝗔 🅹🄲🄱
CY
Arrabona : Meals (buffet lunch) 4500 and a la carte 6200/7100 – **230 r**
⇆ 51800/75300.

K + K Opera Ⓜ ♨, Révay útca 24, ✉ 1065, ℰ (01) 269 0222, kk.hotel.opera@ ☐
hotels.hu, Fax (01) 269 0230, ℉⎯, ⇆s – 🛗, ✺ rm, 🖿 📺 🅦 ⇐ – 🏛 60. 🅜🄾 🄐🄴 ☐
𝗩𝗜𝗦𝗔 ❀ rest
HU
Meals (light meals in bar) a la carte approx. 3450 🕴 2800 – **203 rm** ⇆ 36600/4440☐
2 suites.

Astoria, Kossuth Lajos útca 19-21, ✉ 1053, ℰ (01) 484 3200, astoria@ hungary.ne
Fax (01) 318 6798, « Art Nouveau decor » – 🛗, ✺ rm, 🖿 rest, 📺 🅦 – 🏛 80. 🅜🄾 ☐
🄾 𝗩𝗜𝗦𝗔 🅹🄲🄱
HV
Empire : Meals 3300 and a la carte 5100/7300 🕴 3400 – ⇆ 2650 – **126 r**
26100/33900, 5 suites.

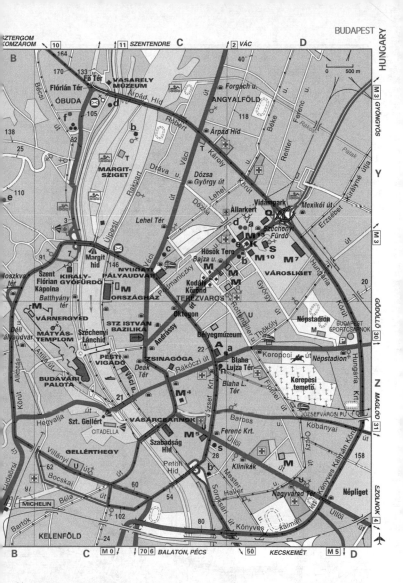

Andrássy, Andrássy útca 111, ✉ 1063, ✆ (01) 321 2000, *welcome@ andrassyhotel. com*, Fax (01) 322 9445, « Contemporary interior », ↳₆, ☎ – 🛗, 쓪 rm, 🔲 ✆ 🄿. 🕮 🕮 ① 𝘝𝘐𝘚𝘈 ⌘ DY b
Meals a la carte approx. 3250 ⅄ 2000 – ☲ 3300 – **65 rm** 28100/38200, 6 suites.

Mercure Nemzeti, József Körút 4, ✉ 1088, ✆ (01) 477 2000, *h1686@accor-hote ls.com*, Fax (01) 477 2001, « Art Nouveau decor » – 🛗, 쓪 rm, 🔲 rm, 📺 ✆ – 🄰 60. 🕮 🕮 🕮 ① 𝘝𝘐𝘚𝘈. 🍽 rest CZ n
Meals a la carte approx. 2450 – ☲ 2000 – **75 rm** 24800, 1 suite.

Mercure Buda, Krisztina körút 41-43, ✉ 1013, ✆ (01) 488 8100, *mercurebuda@p annoniahotels.hu*, Fax (01) 355 6964, ↳₆, ☎, 🗔 – 🛗, 쓪 rm, 🔲 📺 ✆ & ⇔ 🄿 – 🄰 220. 🕮 🕮 ① 𝘝𝘐𝘚𝘈 ⌘. 🍽 rest EV f
Meals a la carte 4300/5000 ⅄ 4200 – ☲ 2000 – **392 rm** 24800/30000, 8 suites.

387

E   F

Csalogány u.

Nagy imre
tér

143 Moszkva

Széna
tér
46

Krisztina

Körút

5

5

Moszkva
tér

Várfok u.

49 128

Batthyány tér

Donáti

Toldy

Bem

SZENT ANNA
TEMPLOM

U

85

Lovas út

Bécsi kapu
tér
Kapisztrán
tér

BÉCSI KAPU

Középkori Zsidó
Imaház

Zenetörténeti
Múzeum

Ferenc

Fő

VIZIVÁROS

utca

DUNA

HADTÖRTÉNETI
MÚZEUM

36 150

Úri

Attila

Várhegy

104

Kereskedelmi és
Vendéglátóipari
Múzeum

Úri utca

Halászbástya

Hess
András tér

t a

Corvin tér

b

c

135

MÁTYÁS-
TEMPLOM

rakpart

d

Tárnok

Városmajor u.

Déli pu.

Krisztina út

DÉLI PU.

Lovas út

136

Patika
Múzeum

VÁRNEGYED

Hunyadi János út

utca

SZÉCHE
LÁNCI

56

95

f

148

Palota

Dísz
tér
P

a

Clark Ádár

P

Lánchíd

Körút

Alagút

75

Krisztina
tér

Ludwig
Múzeum

132

MAGYAR
NEMZETI
GALÉRIA

78

100

Attila

BUDAVÁRI
PALOTA

BUDAPEST
TÖRTÉNETI
MÚZEUM

V

Márvány u.

BUDA

Győri út

Liszt Jenő

Mészáros

Krisztina út

U

Naphegy
tér

Fém

100

Semmelweis
Orvostörténeti
Múzeum

Tigris

Avar

Derék u.

Deső u.

Körút

Kereszt

Tabáni plébá
templ

TABÁN

Csörsz u.

Aladár

Hegyalja út

Sánc út

GELLÉRT-

h

Hegyalja

Mihály

Szirtes út

X

Hegyalja

Budaörsi út

Villányi út

Alsóhegy út

Ménesi út

Somlói út

Kelenhegyi út

Szirtes

BUDAPEST

0   300 m

E   F

G

H

SZÁGHÁZ

NÉPRAJZI MÚZEUM

Kossuth Lajos tér

Alkotmány u.

Homlok

FÖLDMÜVELÉSÜGYI MINISZTERIUM

Báthory

58

Vadász

Bajcsy

Podmaniczky

Lovag

Dessewffy

Szondi u.

Csengery

Teréz

Vörösmarty

Aradi

Jenő

Nagymező

Liszt Ferenc Emlékmúzeum

Hunyadi tér

U

Kossuth tér

b

Vértanúk tere

Szabadság tér

Zoltán

Akadémia

Nádor

Hold

POSTA TAKARÉKPÉNZTAR

b

Mozsár

Hajós

Zichy

Arany János u.

Zrínyi

Bank

Hercegprímás

Sas

Szent István tér

Jókai

Oktogon

tér

Liszt Ferenc tér

MAGYAR ÁLLAMI OPERAHÁZ

Liszt Ferenc Zeneművészeti Főiskola

U

Lázár

Opera

f

Zöldmárty u.

Révay

Ede

Király

T

Kis Diófa

Csányi u.

Dob

Kertész u.

Széchenyi

Arany

János

Október

Szent István tér

SZENT ISTVÁN BAZILIKA

Postamúzeum

Andrássy

Székely M. u.

Kazinczy

Klauzál tér

Nagy Diófa

Klauzál u.

Roosevelt tér

József

Attila

Bajcsy-Zs. út

Paulay

Király

PEST

120

Dorottya

József Nádor tér

Erzsébet tér

Deák Ferenc tér

Wesselényi

ZSINAGÓGA

Dob

Szerecsen-Király u.

V

e

n

Duna

Vörösmarty tér

Deák tér

M

Károly

Dohány

Körút

út

T

PESTI VIGADÓ

Vörösmarty tér

Bécsi

POL

b

H

PEST MEGYEI TANÁCS

k

Rákóczi

Szentkirályi

Vigadó tér

t

VÁCI

4

142

38

Astoria

q

Muzeum

Piskin

U

Sándor

8

T

Kossuth L. u.

Bródy

kaú

r

2

108

116

44

106

c

Petőfi tér

160

Párizsi udvar

Ferences templom

112

e

88

Petőfi Irodalmi Muzeum

MAGYAR NEMZETI MÚZEUM

159

f

90

70

32

a

Ferenciek tere

M

EGYETEMI TEMPLOM

64

r

Múzeum

Körút

Belvárosi plébániatemplom

Erzsébet híd

Belgrád

52

Mohra

Váci

Veres

140

66

t

s

U

U

Szt. Gellért

RUDAS GYÓGYFÜRDŐ

HEGY

Szt.

Gellért

DUNA

rakpart

Párné

Körút

Kálvin Tér

Kálvin tér

Baross

n

Ráday

Üllői u.

X

Citadella

adella

Sétány

Szabadság szobor

Vámház

Csarnok tér

VÁSÁRCSARNOK

U

M

U

ileumi park

GELLÉRTFÜRDŐ

Sziklakápolna

SZABADSÁG HÍD

Szent Gellért tér

Mátyás

Kinizsi

U

Kelenhegyi út

G

H

STREET INDEX TO BUDAPEST TOWN PLAN

🏨 **Novotel** Ⓜ, Alkotás útca 63-67, ✉ 1123, ☎ (01) 372 5700, *h0511@ accor-hotels.com*, Fax (01) 466 5636, 🛐, 🍴, 🏊, 🖿 – ⬚, ✤ rm, 🖿 📺 ✆ 🅿 – 🏛 1750. 🅾 🆎 ⑩ 🆚 🅹🅲🅱 EX h
Meals (buffet lunch) 3300 and a la carte approx. 3470 – 🖵 3500 – **319 rm** 25350.

🏨 **Taverna**, Váci útca 20, ✉ 1052, ☎ (01) 485 3100, *hotel@ hoteltaverna.hu*, Fax (01) 485 3111, 🍴 – 🛗 ✤ 🖿 📺 ⇦ – 🏛 100. 🅾 🆎 ⑩ 🆚 🅹🅲🅱 GV h
Gambrinus : Meals (dinner only) (gypsy music) 8600 and a la carte 9000/12000 – **Holsten Brasserie :** Meals a la carte 6000/8000 – **222 rm** 🖵 30000/40000, 4 suites.

🏨 **Mercure Korona**, Kecskeméti útca 14, ✉ 1053, ☎ (01) 317 4111, *mercurekorona @pannoniahotels.hu*, Fax (01) 318 3867, 🍴, 🖿 – 🛗 ✤ 🖿 📺 ✆ 🅗 ⇦ – 🏛 100. 🅾 🆎 ⑩ 🆚 🅹🅲🅱 HX s
Meals (buffet lunch) 4800 and a la carte 3550/5200 🍷 2500 – **424 rm** 🖵 35700/39100.

🏨 **Mercure Metropol** Ⓜ, Rákóczi útca 58, ✉ 1074, ☎ (01) 462 8100, *h2997@ acco r-hotels.com*, Fax (01) 462 8181 – 🛗, ✤ rm, 🖿 📺 ✆ 🅗 – 🏛 50. 🅾 🆎 ⑩ 🆚 CDZ a
Meals a la carte approx. 3200 🍷 2400 – 🖵 2000 – **130 rm** 24800/32600.

🏨 **Victoria** without rest., Bem Rakpart 11, ✉ 1011, ☎ (01) 457 8080, *victoria@ victoria.hu*, Fax (01) 457 8088, ≤ Danube and Pest, 🍴 – 🛗 🖿 📺 ✆ 🅿. 🅾 🆎 ⑩ 🆚 🅹🅲🅱 FU d
27 rm 🖵 24700/26000.

🏨 **Sissi** without rest., Angyal útca 33, ✉ 1094, ☎ (01) 215 0082, *hsissi@ matavnet.hu*, Fax (01) 216 6063, �იგ – 🛗 ✤ 📺 🅗 ⇦ – 🏛 25. 🅾 🆎 ⑩ 🆚 CZ s
44 rm 🖵 22200/28700.

🏨 **Carlton** without rest., Apor Péter útca 3, ✉ 1011, ☎ (01) 224 0999, *carltonhotel@ m atavnet.hu*, Fax (01) 224 0990 – 🛗 ✤ 🖿 📺 ✆ ⇦ – 🏛 25. 🅾 🆎 ⑩ 🆚 FV a
95 rm 🖵 22200/26100.

🏨 **Corvin**, Angyal útca 31, ✉ 1094, ☎ (01) 218 6566, *corvin@ maildatanct.hu*, Fax (01) 218 6562, 🍴 – 🛗 ✤ rm, 🖿 🅿 – 🏛 30. 🅾 🆎 ⑩ 🆚 ✀ CZ s
Meals a la carte 2900/4100 – **40 rm** 🖵 20900/24800.

🏨 **Mercure Relais Duna** Ⓜ without rest., Soroksári út 12, ✉ 1095, ☎ (01) 455 8300, *h2025@ accor-hotels.com*, Fax (01) 455 8385 – 🛗 ✤ 🖿 📺 🅿 – 🏛 40. 🅾 🆎 ⑩ 🆚
🖵 2000 **124 rm** 19600/26100, 6 suites. CZ b

🏨 **Liget** Ⓜ, Dózsa György útca 106, ✉ 1068, ☎ (01) 269 5300, *hotel@ liget.hu*, Fax (01) 269 5329, 🍴 – 🛗, ✤ rm, 📺 ⇦ 🅿. 🅾 🆎 ⑩ 🆚 🅹🅲🅱 DY e
Meals a la carte approx. 3750 🍷 3200 – **139 rm** 🖵 22250/28800.

🏨 **Ibis Centrum** Ⓜ without rest., Raday útca 6, ✉ 1092, ☎ (01) 215 8585, *ibiscentru m@ pannoniahotels.hu*, Fax (01) 215 8787 – ✤ 🖿 📺 ✆ 🅗 ⇦ 🅾 🆎 ⑩ 🆚 HX n
126 rm 🖵 22450/24300.

🏨 **Art**, Királyi Pál útca 12, ✉ 1053, ☎ (01) 266 2166, *hotelart@ mail.matav.hu*, Fax (01) 266 2170, 🛌, 🍴 – 🛗, ✤ rm, 🖿 📺. 🅾 🆎 ⑩ 🆚 🅹🅲🅱 ✀ rest HX t
Meals a la carte 2580/4880 🍷 1800 – **29 rm** 🖵 20900/33900, 3 suites.

XXXX **Gundel**, Állatkerti útca 2, ✉ 1146, ☎ (01) 468 4040, *info@ gundel.hu*, Fax (01) 363 1917, « Summer terrace », Gypsy and classical music at dinner – 🖿 🅿 🅾 🆎 ⑩ 🆚 DY d
Meals (booking essential) 3800/17500 and a la carte 8150/12460 🍷 7500.

XXX **Vadrózsa**, Pentelei Molnár útca 15, ✉ 1025, via Rómer Flóris útca ☎ (01) 326 5817, *vadrozsa@ hungary.com*, Fax (01) 326 5809, « Summer terrace », Pianist at dinner – 🖿 🅾 🆎 ⑩ 🆚 🅹🅲🅱 BY e
closed 23-26 December – **Meals** 3500/8900 and a la carte 7960/9420 🍷 7200.

XXX **Alabárdos**, Országház útca 2, ✉ 1014, ☎ (01) 356 0851, *alabardos@ matavnet.hu*, Fax (01) 214 3814, 🍴, « Vaulted Gothic interior, covered courtyard » – 🖿. 🅾 🆎 ⑩ 🆚 🅹🅲🅱 ✀ EU c
closed lunch in winter – **Meals** (booking essential) a la carte 4700/8100 🍷 7000.

XXX **Fortuna**, Hess András tér 4, ✉ 1014, ☎ (01) 355 7177, *fortuna@ elender.hu*, Fax (01) 375 6857, 🍴, « 13C Champagne cellar » – ✤ 🖿. 🅾 🆎 🆚 EFU t
Meals a la carte 6000/8600 🍷 6500.

XXX **Légrádi & Tsa**, Magyar útca 23, ✉ 1053, ☎ (01) 318 6804, Vaulted cellar, Gypsy music – 🖿. 🅾 🆎 ⑩ 🆚 HX r
closed July and Sunday – **Meals** (booking essential) (dinner only) a la carte 3900/6400 🍷 4800.

XXX **Légrádi Antique**, Bárczy István útca 3-5 (first floor), ✉ 1052, ☎ (01) 266 4993, « Elegant decor, antiques », Gypsy music at dinner – 🅾 🆎 ⑩ 🆚 GV b
closed 24-26 December, Saturday lunch and Sunday – **Meals** (booking essential) a la carte 8450/12500.

XX **Fausto's**, Dohány útca 5, ✉ 1072, ☎ (01) 269 6806, Fax (01) 269 6806 – 🖿. 🅾 🆎 🆚. ✀ HV k
closed 3 weeks July, 1 week January, 24-26 December and Sunday – **Meals** - Italian - a la carte 4700/7400 🍷 5200.

XX **Kárpátia,** Ferenciek tere 7-8, ⊠ 1053, ℰ (01) 317 3596, *restaurant@karpatia.hu*
Fax (01) 318 0591, « Vaulted Gothic style interior », Gypsy music at dinner – ✦✦. ⓜ③ ᴬᴱ
ⓞ 𝘝𝘐𝘚𝘈   HV ᴇ
Meals a la carte 5200/9600 ⓐ 5400.

XX **Cosmo,** Kristóf tér 7-8 (first floor), ⊠ 1052, ℰ (01) 266 4747, *Fax (01) 266 6818,* 🍴
« Contemporary interior, courtyard terrace » – ✦✦ ▤. ⓜ③ ᴬᴱ ⓞ 𝘝𝘐𝘚𝘈   GV
closed 24 and dinner 31 December and Sunday lunch in winter – **Meals** (booking essential
a la carte 4160/6310 ⓐ 4300.

XX **Bagolyvár,** Allatkertí ut 2, ⊠ 1146, ℰ (01) 468 3110, *bagolyvar@gundel.hu*
Fax (01) 363 1917, 🍴, Music at dinner – ⓜ③ ᴬᴱ ⓞ 𝘝𝘐𝘚𝘈. ⌘   DY ᴄ
Meals 2200 (lunch) and a la carte 3600/4700 ⓐ 2200.

XX **Lou Lou,** Vigyázó Ferenc útca 4, ⊠ 1051, ℰ (01) 312 4505, *Fax (01) 312 4505* – ▤
ⓜ③ ᴬᴱ   GU ᴀ
closed Christmas, Saturday lunch and Sunday – **Meals** a la carte 5800/7300 ⓐ 4100.

XX **Robinson,** Városligeti tó, ⊠ 1146, ℰ (01) 422 0222, *robinson@matavnet.hu*
Fax (01) 422 0224, 🍴, « Lakeside setting », Music at dinner – ▤. ⓜ③ ᴬᴱ ⓞ
𝘝𝘐𝘚𝘈 ᴊᴄʙ   DY ᴀ
closed 25 December and dinner 24 December – **Meals** a la carte 5000/7550 ⓐ 3000.

XX **Fuji Japan,** Csatárka útca 54, Rózsadomb, ⊠ 1025, by Szépvölgyi útca ℰ (01) 325 7111
japanco@mail.datanet.hu, Fax (01) 325 7111 – ▤ 🅿. ⓜ③ ᴬᴱ ⓞ 𝘝𝘐𝘚𝘈 ᴊᴄʙ. ⌘
closed 24 and 31 December – **Meals** - Japanese - 2200/11500 and a la carte 4380/6800
ⓐ 4700.

XX **Múzeum,** Múzeum körút 12, ⊠ 1088, ℰ (01) 338 4221, *Fax (01) 338 4221* – ▤. ⓜ③
ᴬᴱ ⓞ 𝘝𝘐𝘚𝘈   HV ᴇ
Meals a la carte 4600/8400 ⓐ 3200.

XX **Belcanto,** Dalszínház útca 8, ⊠ 1061, ℰ (01) 269 2786, *restaurant@belcanto.hu*
Fax (01) 311 9547, « Classical and operatic recitals » – ✦✦ ▤. ⓜ③ ᴬᴱ ⓞ 𝘝𝘐𝘚𝘈
ᴊᴄʙ   HU
Meals (booking essential) (buffet lunch) 1900 and a la carte 5600/10100 ⓐ 7200.

X **Krizia,** Mozsár útca 12, ⊠ 1066, ℰ (01) 331 8711, *Fax (01) 331 8711* – ▤. ⓜ③
𝘝𝘐𝘚𝘈   HU ʙ
closed 15 days July-August, 10 days January and Sunday – **Meals** - Italian - 2600 (lunch
and a la carte 5100/8800 ⓐ 5000.

X **La Fontaine,** Mérleg útca 10, ⊠ 1051, ℰ (01) 317 3715, *Fax (01) 318 8562* – ⓜ③ ᴬᴱ
ⓞ 𝘝𝘐𝘚𝘈 ᴊᴄʙ   GV ꜱ
closed Saturday lunch and Sunday – **Meals** - French - 2790 (lunch) and a la carte 5020/8460
ⓐ 3380.

X **Cyrano,** Kristóf tér 7-8, ⊠ 1052, ℰ (01) 266 3096, *Fax (01) 266 6818,* 🍴 – ▤. ⓜ③
ᴬᴱ ⓞ   GV
closed 24 December and dinner 31 December – **Meals** (booking essential) a la carte
3980/5080 ⓐ 3700.

X **Chapter One,** Nádur útca 29, ⊠ 1054, ℰ (01) 354 0113, *info@chapterone.hu*
Fax (01) 354 0115, 🍴 – ▤. ⓜ③ ᴬᴱ ⓞ 𝘝𝘐𝘚𝘈   GU ʙ
Meals 1900 (lunch) and a la carte 3870/5410 ⓐ 2800.

LOCAL ATMOSPHERE

X **Náncsi Néni,** Ördögárok útca 80, Hüvösvölgy, ⊠ 1029, Northwest : 10 km by Szilágy
🏡 Erzsébetfasor ℰ (01) 397 2742, *Fax (01) 397 2742,* 🍴, Accordion music at dinner – ⓜ③
ⓞ 𝘝𝘐𝘚𝘈 ᴊᴄʙ
Meals a la carte 3080/4350 ⓐ 1890.

X **Kisbuda Gyöngye,** Kenyeres útca 34, ⊠ 1034, ℰ (01) 368 6402, *remiz@matavne*
🏡 *t.hu, Fax (01) 368 9227,* 🍴, Music at dinner – ▤. ⓜ③ ᴬᴱ ⓞ 𝘝𝘐𝘚𝘈   CY
closed Sunday – **Meals** (booking essential) 5500 and a la carte 3980/5080 ⓐ 5000.

X **Remiz,** Budakeszi útca 5, ⊠ 1021, Northwest : 5 km by Szilágyi Erzsébet ℰ (01) 275 1396
Fax (01) 394 1896, « Terrace » – ⓜ③ ᴬᴱ ⓞ 𝘝𝘐𝘚𝘈
Meals a la carte 2980/4280 ⓐ 2700.

X **Apostolok,** Kígyó útca 4, ⊠ 1052, ℰ (01) 318 3559, *Fax (01) 318 3559,* « Old chapel-
style interior, mosaics of The Twelve Apostles, stained glass window » – ▤. ⓜ③ ᴬᴱ ⓞ
𝘝𝘐𝘚𝘈 ᴊᴄʙ   GV
Meals (booking essential) a la carte 2800/4180 ⓐ 2800.

Republic of
Ireland
Eire

DUBLIN

PRACTICAL INFORMATION

LOCAL CURRENCY

1 euro (€) = 0,89 USD ($) (Dec 2001)

TOURIST INFORMATION

The telephone number and address of the Tourist Information office is given in the text under 🛈.

National Holiday in the Republic of Ireland: *17 March.*

FOREIGN EXCHANGE

Banks are open between 10am and 4pm on weekdays only.
Banks in Dublin stay open to 5pm on Thursdays and banks at Dublin and Shannon airports are open on Saturdays and Sundays.

SHOPPING IN DUBLIN

In the index of street names, those printed in red are where the principal shops are found.

CAR HIRE

The international car hire companies have branches in each major city. Your hotel porter should be able to give details and help you with your arrangements.

TIPPING

Many hotels and restaurants include a service charge but where this is not the case an amount equivalent to between 10 and 15 per cent of the bill is customary. Additionally doormen, baggage porters and cloakroom attendants are generally given a gratuity.
Taxi drivers are tipped between 10 and 15 per cent of the amount shown on the meter in addition to the fare.

SPEED LIMITS

The maximum permitted speed in the Republic is 60 mph (97 km/h) except where a lower speed limit is indicated.

SEAT BELTS

The wearing of seat belts is compulsory if fitted for drivers and front seat passengers. Additionally, children under 12 are not allowed in front seats unless in a suitable safety restraint.

ANIMALS

It is forbidden to bring domestic animals (dogs, cats...) into the Republic of Ireland.

DUBLIN

(Baile Átha Cliath) *Dublin* 🄈🄔🄖 *N 7 – pop. 481 854.*

Belfast 103 – Cork 154 – Londonderry 146.

🄩 *Bord Failte Offices, Baggot Street Bridge ℘ (01) 602 4000 – Suffolk St – Arrivals Hall, Dublin Airport – The Square Shopping Centre, Tallaght.*

🏌₁₈ *Elm Park, Nutley House, Donnybrook ℘ (01) 269 3438 – 🏌₁₈ Milltown, Lower Churchtown Rd, ℘ (01) 497 6090, EV – 🏌₁₈ Royal Dublin, North Bull Island, Dollymount, ℘ (01) 833 6346, NE : by R 105 – 🏌₁₈ Forrest Little, Cloghran ℘ (01) 840 1183 – 🏌₁₈ Lucan, Celbridge Rd, Lucan ℘ (01) 628 0246 – 🏌₁₈ Edmondstown, Rathfarnham ℘ (01) 493 2461 – 🏌₁₈ Coldwinters, Newtown House, St Margaret's ℘ (01) 864 0324.*

✈ *Dublin Airport ℘ (01) 814 1111, N : 5 ½ m. by N 1 – Terminal : Busaras (Central Bus Station) Store St*

⛴ *to Holyhead (Irish Ferries) 2 daily (3 h 15 mn) – to Holyhead (Stena Line) 1-2 daily (3 h 45 mn) – to the Isle of Man (Douglas) (Isle of Man Steam Packet Co Ltd.) (2 h 45 mn) – to Liverpool (Merchant Ferries Ltd) 2 daily (7 h 45 mn) – to Liverpool (P & O Irish Sea) (8 h).*

SIGHTS

See: *City*★★★ *– Trinity College*★★ *JY – Old Library*★★★ *(Treasury*★★★*, Long Room*★★*) – Dublin Castle*★★ *(Chester Beatty Library*★★★*) HY – Christ Church Cathedral*★★ *HY – St Patrick's Cathedral*★★ *HZ – Marsh's Library*★★ *HZ – National Museum*★★ *(The Treasury*★★*) KZ – National Gallery*★★ *KZ – Newman House*★★ *JZ – Bank of Ireland*★★ *JY – Custom House*★★ *KX – Four Courts*★★ *HY – Tailors' Hall*★ *HY – City Hall*★ *HY – Temple Bar*★ *HJY – Liffey Bridge*★ *JY – Merrion Square*★ *KZ – Number Twenty-Nine*★ *KZ D – Grafton Street*★ *JYZ – Powerscourt Centre*★ *JY – Rotunda Hospital Chapel*★ *JX – O'Connell Street*★ *JX – Hugh Lane Municipal Gallery of Modern Art*★ *JX M⁴ – Pro-Cathedral*★ *JX.*

Envir.: *The Ben of Howth*★ *(≤★), NE: 6 m. by R 105 KX.*

Exc.: *Powerscourt*★★ *(Waterfall*★★ *AC), S: 14 m. by N 11 and R 117 EV – Russborough House*★★★*, SW: 22 m. by N 81 DV.*

DUBLIN
SOUTH EAST
BUILT UP AREA

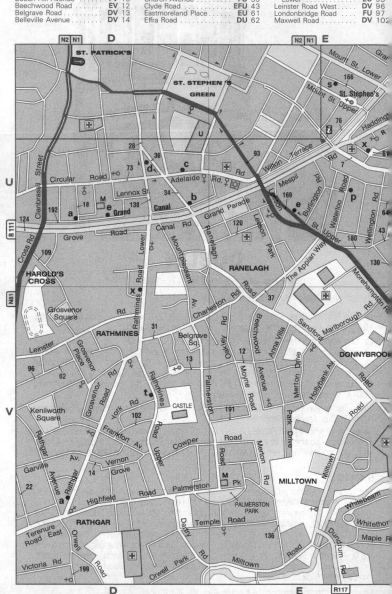

Your recommendation is self-evident if you always walk into a hotel Guide in hand.

IRELAND

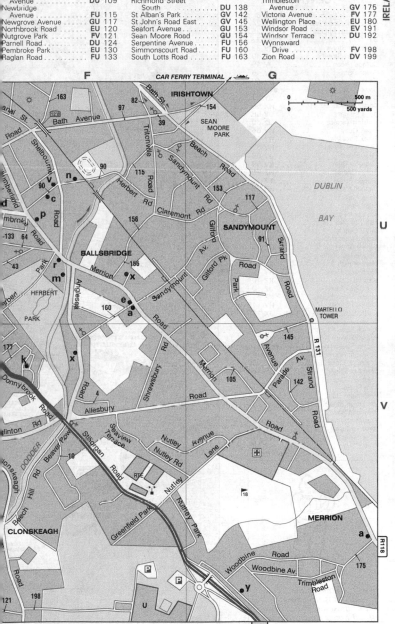

If you find you cannot take up a hotel booking you have made, please let the hotel know immediately.

397

DUBLIN
CENTRE

*Town plans:
roads most used by traffic
and those on which guide-
listed hotels and restaurants
stand are fully drawn;
the beginning only
of lesser roads is indicated.*

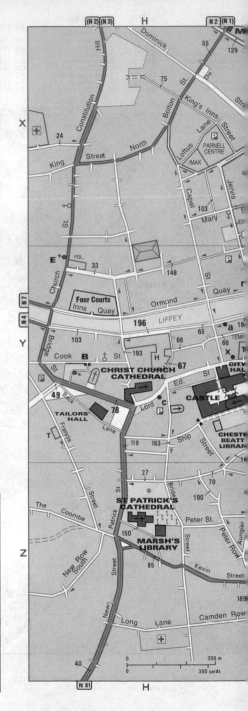

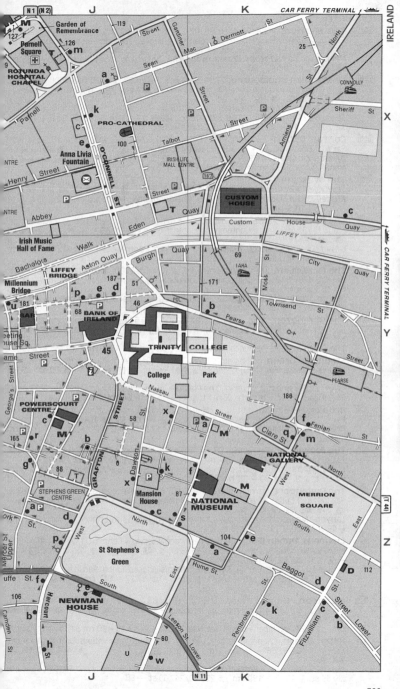

🏠🏠🏠 **The Merrion,** Upper Merrion St, D2, ☎ (01) 603 0600, *info@merrionhotel.com*, Fax (01) 603 0700, « Restored Georgian town houses, collection of contemporary Irish art », ⅃₅, ◌, ⊛ – ⌷, ╳ rm, ▦ ⊡ ⾕ & ⊘ *VISA* ⸨ – ⌀ 50. ⬤ ⅄ ① *VISA* ✆ KZ e
Meals (see *Morningtons Brasserie* and *The Cellar Bar* below) – ⌷ 18.00 – **135 rm** 393.62 t., 10 suites – SB.

🏠🏠🏠 **Le Meridien Shelbourne,** 27 St Stephen's Green, D2, ☎ (01) 663 4500, *shelbourn einfo@lemeridien-hotels.com*, Fax (01) 661 6006, ⅃₅, ⇌s, ◌ – ⌷, ╳ rm, ⊡ ⟿ –
⌀ 400. ⬤ ⅄ ① *VISA* ✆ JZ s
No. 27 The Green : Meals *(closed Saturday lunch)* 24.76/37.47 and a la carte 36.51/62.23 t. ⅄ 20.95 – *The Side Door* : Meals a la carte 33.02/36.05 t. ⅄ 20.96 – ⌷ 20.96 – **168 rm** 315/340 t., 22 suites – SB.

🏠🏠🏠 **Conrad Dublin,** Earlsfort Terr., D2, ☎ (01) 676 5555, *info@conraddublin.com*, Fax (01) 676 5424, ⅃₅ – ⌷, ╳ rm, ▦ ⊡ ⾕ & ⟿ – ⌀ 50. ⬤ ⅄ ① *VISA* ✆
Alexandra : Meals 24.13/30.97 and a la carte 32/38 st. ⅄ 20.32 – *Plurabelle Brasserie* : Meals 24.13/30.97 and a la carte 32/38 st. ⅄ 20.32 – **191 rm** 255/380. JZ w

🏠🏠🏠 **The Westbury,** Grafton St, D2, ☎ (01) 679 1122, *westbury@jurysdoyle.com*, Fax (01) 679 7078, ⅃₅, ╳ rm, ⊡ ⾕ & ⟿ – ⌀ 220. ⬤ ⅄ ① *VISA* ✆
Russell Room : Meals 35/57 t. ⅄ 20 – *The Sandbank* : Meals a la carte 22/33 t. ⅄ 19 – ⌷ 23 – **196 rm** 311/350 t., 8 suites. JY b

🏠🏠 **The Clarence,** 6-8 Wellington Quay, D2, ☎ (01) 407 0800, *reservations@theclarence.ie*, Fax (01) 407 0820, ⩽, « Contemporary interior design » – ⌷ ⊡ ⾕ & ⸨ – ⌀ 60. ⬤ ⅄ ① *VISA* ✆ HY a
closed 25-26 December – Meals (see *The Tea Room* below) – ⌷ 15.00 – **45 rm** 285/305 st., 4 suites.

🏠🏠 **The Fitzwilliam,** St Stephen's Green, D2, ☎ (01) 478 7000, *enq@fitzwilliam-hotel.com*, Fax (01) 478 7878, ⩽, « Contemporary interior » – ⌷, ╳ rm, ▦ rest, ⊡ ⾕ ⟿ – ⌀ 70. ⬤ ⅄ ① *VISA* ✆ JZ d
Mango Toast : Meals a la carte 25/40 st. (see also *Peacock Alley* below) – ⌷ 20 – **128 rm** 275/370 st., 2 suites – SB.

🏠🏠 **The Burlington,** Upper Leeson St, D4, ☎ (01) 660 5222, *burlington@jurysdoyle.com*, Fax (01) 660 8496 – ⌷, ╳ rm, ▦ rest, ⊡ ⾕ & ⸨ – ⌀ 1500. ⬤ ⅄ ① *VISA* ✆ EU e
The Sussex : Meals (bar lunch)/dinner 22 st. ⅄ 19 – ⌷ 20 – **500 rm** 210/235 t., 6 suites.

🏠🏠 **Stephen's Green,** St Stephen's Green, D2, ☎ (01) 607 3600, *stephensgreenres@oc allaghanhotels.ie*, Fax (01) 661 5663, ⅃₅ – ⌷, ╳ rm, ▦ ⊡ ⾕ ⟿ – ⌀ 50. ⬤ ⅄ ① *VISA* ✆ JZ f
closed 24 December-2 January – *The Pie Dish* : Meals (closed lunch Saturday and Sunday) 24/29 and dinner a la carte 36/41 t. ⅄ 19 – ⌷ 20 – **64 rm** 315 t., 11 suites – SB.

🏠🏠 **Brooks,** 59-62 Drury St, D2, ☎ (01) 670 4000, *reservations@brookshotel.ie*, Fax (01) 670 4455 – ⌷, ╳ rm, ▦ ⊡ ⾕ – ⌀ 50. ⬤ ⅄ ① *VISA* ✆ JY r
Francesca's : Meals (dinner only) 25 and a la carte 30/50 t. ⅄ 20 – ⌷ 16.50 – **75 rm** 190.50/260 st.

🏠🏠 **The Alexander,** Merrion Sq, D2, ☎ (01) 607 3700, *alexanderres@ocallaghanhotels.ie*, Fax (01) 661 5663, ⅃₅ – ⌷, ╳ rm, ▦ ⊡ ⾕ ⟿ – ⌀ 400. ⬤ ⅄ ① *VISA* ✆
Caravaggio's : Meals (closed lunch Saturday and Sunday) 24/33 and dinner a la carte 34/52 t. ⅄ 9 – ⌷ 20 – **98 rm** 298 t., 4 suites – SB. KY f

🏠🏠 **The Davenport,** Merrion Sq, D2, ☎ (01) 607 3500, *davenportres@ocallaghanhotels.ie*, Fax (01) 661 5663, « Part Victorian gospel hall », ⅃₅ – ⌷, ╳ rm, ▦ ⊡ ⾕ & ⟿ – ⌀ 275. ⬤ ⅄ ① *VISA* ✆ KY m
Lanyon : Meals (closed Saturday lunch and Sunday) 24/33 and dinner a la carte 35/54 t. ⅄ 19 – ⌷ 20 – **113 rm** 298 t., 2 suites – SB.

🏠🏠 **Clarion H. Dublin IFSC,** International Financial Services Centre, D1, ☎ (01) 433 8800, *info@clarionhotelifsc.com*, Fax (01) 433 8811, ⩽, ⅃₅, ⇌s, ◌ – ⌷, ╳ rm, ▦ ⊡ ⾕ ⟿ – ⌀ 120. ⬤ ⅄ ① *VISA* ✆ ✆
closed 24-26 December – *Sinergie* : Meals (closed lunch Saturday and Sunday) 22.22/25.39 and a la carte 26/47 t. ⅄ 20.95 – ⌷ 17.77 – **147 rm** 203.15/761.84 t. – SB.

🏠🏠 **Morrison,** Ormond Quay, D1, ☎ (01) 887 2400, *info@morrisonhotel.ie*, Fax (01) 878 3185, « Contemporary interior » – ⌷, ╳ rm, ▦ ⊡ ⾕ ⸨ ⬤ ⅄ ① *VISA* ✆ ✆ HY r
closed 24-27 December – Meals (see *Halo* below) – ⌷ 17.15 – **90 rm** 317.50 st., 4 suites.

🏠🏠 **Hilton Dublin,** Charlemont Pl, D2, ☎ (01) 402 9988, *reservationsdublin@hilton.com*, Fax (01) 402 9966 – ⌷, ╳ rm, ▦ rest, ⊡ ⾕ & ⟿ – ⌀ 400. ⬤ ⅄ ① *VISA* ✆ DU b
closed 25 December – *Waterfront* : Meals (closed lunch Saturday and Sunday) a la carte 26/39 st. ⅄ 15.87 – **189 rm** ⌷ 220.20/247.59 st. – SB.

The Gresham, 23 Upper O'Connell St, D1, *℘* (01) 874 6881, *info@gresham-hotels.com,* *Fax (01) 878 7175,* **↧** – |♦| ■ ▥ ❤ ৬ ⬅ 🅿 – 🔬 400. ⓶⬤ 🅐🅔 ⓪ ▨𝘼. 🎀   JX k
The Aberdeen : Meals 15.50/23.50 and a la carte **t.** ▯ 19 – ⌁ 15 – **282 rm** 200 **t.,** 6 suites – SB.

La Stampa H., 35 Dawson St, D2, *℘* (01) 677 4444, *Fax (01) 677 4411* – ■ ▥ ❤. ⓶⬤ 🅐🅔 ⓪ ▨𝘼. 🎀   JZ x
closed 25 December – Meals (see *La Stampa* below) – ⌁ 17.78 – **12 rm** 139.67/209.51, 8 suites – SB.

brownes townhouse, 22 St Stephen's Green, D2, *℘* (01) 638 3939, *info@browne sdublin.com, Fax (01) 638 3900,* « Georgian town house » – |♦| ↤ ■ ▥ ❤ ৬. ⓶⬤ 🅐🅔 ⓪ ▨𝘼. 🎀   JZ c
closed 24 December-4 January – Meals (see *brownes brasserie* below) – **12 rm** ⌁ 159/222 **st.**

Clarion Stephen's Hall, Earlsfort Centre, 14-17 Lower Leeson St, D2, *℘* (01) 638 1111, *stephens@premgroup.com, Fax (01) 638 1122* – |♦| ↤ ▥ ❤ ⬅. ⓶⬤ 🅐🅔 ⓪ ▨𝘼. 🎀   JZ t
Meals *(closed Sunday)* a la carte 17/31 **t.** ▯ 15.87 – ⌁ 13.97 – **3 rm** 184.11 **t., 28 suites** 234.90 **t.**

The Morgan, 10 Fleet St, D2, *℘* (01) 679 3939, *reservations@themorgan.com, Fax (01) 679 3946,* « Contemporary interior design », **↧** – |♦| ↤ rm, ■ rest, ▥ ❤ ⓶⬤ 🅐🅔 ⓪ ▨𝘼. 🎀   JY p
closed 23-26 December – **All Sports Cafe :** Meals (grill rest.) 10.49/17.09 and a la carte **t.** – **59 rm** 171.53/237.51 **st.,** 2 suites.

Mont Clare, Merrion Sq, D2, *℘* (01) 607 3800, *montclareres@ocallaghanhotels.ie, Fax (01) 661 5663* – |♦|, ↤ rm, ■ ▥ ⬅ – 🔬 120. ⓶⬤ 🅐🅔 ⓪ ▨𝘼. 🎀   KY q
Goldsmiths : Meals *(closed lunch Saturday and Sunday)* 28/30 and dinner a la carte 32/38 **t.** ▯ 16.50 – ⌁ 17 – **74 rm** 205 **t.** – SB.

Chief O'Neills, Smithfield Village, Smithfield, D7, *℘* (01) 817 3838, *reservations@chi efoneills.com, Fax (01) 817 3839,* « Contemporary interior, interactive music centre, observation tower » – |♦| ↤ rm, ▥ ❤ ৬ 🅿 – 🔬 120. ⓶⬤ 🅐🅔 ▨𝘼. 🎀
Kelly & Ping : Meals - Asian - 32.95 dinner and a la carte 23/37 **t.** ▯ 16.50 – ⌁ 12.63 – **73 rm** 253.95 **st.**

Cassidys, 6-8 Cavendish Row, Upper O'Connell St, D1, *℘* (01) 878 0555, *rese@cassid ys.iol.ie, Fax (01) 878 0687* – |♦| ↤, ■ rest, ▥ ❤ 🅿 – 🔬 80. ⓶⬤ 🅐🅔 ⓪ ▨𝘼. 🎀   JX m
closed 23-27 December – **Number Six :** Meals (dinner only) a la carte 19/31 **t.** ▯ 16.67 – **87 rm** ⌁ 110/150 **st.,** 1 suite.

Grafton Capital, Stephen's St Lower, D2, *℘* (01) 648 1100, *info@graftoncapital-ho tel.com, Fax (01) 648 1122* – |♦|, ↤ rm, ▥ ❤ ৬. ⓶⬤ 🅐🅔 ⓪ ▨𝘼. 🎀   JZ g
closed 24-26 December – Meals (dinner only) a la carte 23/33 **t.** ▯ 15.17 – ⌁ 12.70 – **75 rm** 158.83/229 **st.**

The Mercer, Mercer Street Lower, D2, *℘* (01) 478 2179, *stay@mercerhotel.ie, Fax (01) 478 0328* – |♦|, ↤ rm, ■ ▥ ৬ ⬅ – 🔬 100. ⓶⬤ 🅐🅔 ▨𝘼. 🎀   JZ a
closed 24-26 December – **Cusack's :** Meals *(closed Sunday dinner)* 19/58 and a la carte 22/34 **ct.** ▯ 15.23 – ⌁ 6.50 – **31 rm** ⌁ 165/203 **st.** – SB.

Trinity Capital, Pearse St, D2, *℘* (01) 648 1000, *info@trinitycapital-hotel.com, Fax (01) 648 1010* – |♦|, ↤ rm, ■ rest, ▥ ❤ ৬ ⬅ – 🔬 40. ⓶⬤ 🅐🅔 ⓪ ▨𝘼. 🎀   KY b
closed 24-26 December – **Siena :** Meals (bar lunch)/dinner a la carte 29/31 **st.** ▯ 17.14 – ⌁ 12.70 – **81 rm** 152.37/222.20 **st.**

Buswells, Molesworth St, D2, *℘* (01) 614 6500, *buswells@quinn-hotels.com, Fax (01) 676 2090* – |♦|, ↤ rm, ■ rest, ▥ ❤ 🅿 – 🔬 80. ⓶⬤ 🅐🅔 ⓪ ▨𝘼. 🎀 KZ f
closed 25-26 December – **Brasserie :** Meals (carving lunch)/dinner a la carte 26.87/39.85 **st.** – **67 rm** ⌁ 146/218 **st.,** 2 suites – SB.

Bewley's, Merrion Rd, D4, *℘* (01) 668 1111, *bb@bewleyshotels.com, Fax (01) 668 1999,* 🍴, « Victorian facade » – ↤ rm, ▥ ❤ ৬. ⓶⬤ 🅐🅔 ⓪ ▨𝘼. 🎀
closed 24-26 December – **O'Connells** *(℘ (01) 647 3400)* **:** Meals 20.32 (lunch) and dinner a la carte 25.97/37.34 **t.** ▯ 20.32 – ⌁ 8.76 – **220 rm** 99 **st.**   FU a

Camden Court, Camden St, D2, *℘* (01) 475 9666, *sales@camdencourthotel.com, Fax (01) 475 9677,* **↧**, ≋s, ⬜ – |♦| ↤, ■ rest, ▥ ❤ ৬ ⬅ – 🔬 125. ⓶⬤ 🅐🅔 ⓪ ▨𝘼. 🎀   DU d
closed 24 December-3 January – **The Court :** Meals (carving lunch Monday-Saturday) 17.78/31.68 and a la carte 22.85/36 **st.** ▯ 19 – **246 rm** ⌁ 205/255 **st.**

Holiday Inn Dublin, 99-107 Pearse St, D2, *℘* (01) 670 3666, *info@holidayinndublin.ie, Fax (01) 670 3636* – |♦| ↤ rm, ■ rest, ▥ ৬ ⬅ – 🔬 100. ⓶⬤ 🅐🅔 ⓪ ▨𝘼. 🎀
The Brasserie : Meals (carvery lunch)/dinner a la carte 28/36 **st.** ▯ 15.17 – ⌁ 9.95 – **92 rm** 163.79/189.19 **st.**

🏨 **Academy,** Findlater Pl, D1, ☏ (01) 878 0666, stay@ academy-hotel.ie, Fax (01) 878 0600 – |劇|, ⇔ rm, ☰ ☑ ❤ 🅿 – 🅐 45. ☒ 🅐🅴 ⓪ 𝘝𝘐𝘚𝘈. ✦   JX a
closed 23 December-2 January – **Oscar's** : Meals (bar lunch Monday-Friday)/dinner 18.41 and a la carte 18/28 **t.** 🍷 11.36 – **96 rm** ☲ 101.57/152.36 **st.**, 2 suites – SB.

🏨 **Temple Bar,** Fleet St, D2, ☏ (01) 677 3333, templeb@ iol.ie, Fax (01) 677 3088 – |劇| ☑ 🕭 🅿 – 🅐 80. ☒ 🅐🅴 ⓪ 𝘝𝘐𝘚𝘈. ✦   JY e
closed 24-27 December – **Citrus** : Meals (bar lunch)/dinner a la carte 20.31/30.47 **st.** 🍷 14.92 – **129 rm** ☲ 139.68/177.76 **st.**

🏨 **Jurys Inn Christchurch,** Christchurch Pl, D8, ☏ (01) 454 0000, jurysinnchristchurch@ jurysdoyle.com, Fax (01) 454 0012 – |劇|, ⇔ rm, ☰ rest, ☑ 🕭. ☒ 𝘝𝘐𝘚𝘈. ✦   HY c
closed 24-26 December – **Arches** : Meals (bar lunch Saturday and Sunday) (carvery lunch)/dinner 21.50 **st.** 🍷 14 – ☲ 8.50 – **182 rm** 96 **st.**

🏨 **Jurys Inn Custom House,** Custom House Quay, D1, ☏ (01) 607 5000, jurysinncustomhouse@ jurysdoyle.com, Fax (01) 829 0400 – |劇|, ⇔ rm, ☑ ❤ 🕭. – 🅐 100. ☒ 🅐🅴 𝘝𝘐𝘚𝘈. ✦   KX c
closed 24-26 December – Meals (closed lunch Saturday and Sunday) (carvery lunch Monday-Friday)/dinner 21.50 and a la carte **st.** 🍷 14 – ☲ 8.50 – **239 rm** 96 **st.**

🏨 **Longfield's,** 10 Lower Fitzwilliam St, D2, ☏ (01) 676 1367, info@ longfields.ie, Fax (01) 676 1542, « Georgian town house » – |劇| ☑ ❤. ☒ 🅐🅴 ⓪ 𝘝𝘐𝘚𝘈. ✦   KZ d
Meals (see **Number Ten** below) – **26 rm** ☲ 133.35/190.50 **t.**

🏨 **Harrington Hall** without rest., 70 Harcourt St, D2, ☏ (01) 475 3497, harringtonhall@ eircom.net, Fax (01) 475 4544, « Georgian town houses » – |劇| ⇔ ☑ ❤ 🅿. ☒ 🅐🅴 𝘝𝘐𝘚𝘈   JZ h
28 rm ☲ 127/165 **st.**

🏨 **Trinity Lodge** without rest., 12 South Frederick St, D2, ☏ (01) 679 5044, trinitylodge@ eircom.net, Fax (01) 679 5223, « Georgian town houses » – ☰ ☑. ☒ 🅐🅴 ⓪ 𝘝𝘐𝘚𝘈 🅹🅲🅱. ✦   JY x
10 rm ☲ 85/220 **st.**, 3 suites.

🏨 **Lynam's** without rest., 63-64 O'Connell St, D1, ☏ (01) 888 0886, lynamhtl@ indigo.ie, Fax (01) 888 0890 – |劇|, ⇔ rm, ☑ ❤. ☒ 🅐🅴 ⓪ 𝘝𝘐𝘚𝘈. ✦   JX e
closed 24-28 December – **42 rm** ☲ 95.23/152.36 **st.**

🏨 **Eliza Lodge,** 23-24 Wellington Quay, D2, ☏ (01) 671 8044, info@ dublinlodge.com, Fax (01) 671 8362, ← – |劇| ☰ ☑. ☒ 🅐🅴 𝘝𝘐𝘚𝘈. ✦   JY u
closed 22-28 December – **Eliza Blues** : Meals 34.28/40.63 (dinner) and a la carte 26.54/33.90 **t.** 🍷 17.71 – **18 rm** ☲ 70/140 **st.**

🏠 **Kilronan House** without rest., 70 Adelaide Rd, D2, ☏ (01) 475 5266, info@ dublinn.com, Fax (01) 478 2841 – ⇔ ☑. ☒ 🅐🅴 𝘝𝘐𝘚𝘈. ✦   DU c
12 rm ☲ 70/140 **st.**

XXXX
😋😋 **Patrick Guilbaud,** 21 Upper Merrion St, D2, ☏ (01) 676 4192, Fax (01) 661 0052, « Georgian town house, contemporary Irish Art collection » – ☰. ☒ 🅐🅴 ⓪ 𝘝𝘐𝘚𝘈   KZ e
closed first week January, Sunday and Monday – Meals 28/50 (lunch) and a la carte 71/122 **st.** 🍷 32.00
Spec. Lobster ravioli with coconut cream and almonds. Roast squab pigeon with fennel marmalade and spiced Madeira sauce. Rum baba.

XXXX
😋 **The Commons,** Newman House, 85-86 St Stephen's Green, D2, ☏ (01) 478 0530, sales@ thecommonsrestaurant.ie, Fax (01) 478 0551, « Contemporary collection of James Joyce inspired Irish Art » – ☰ ☒ 🅐🅴 ⓪ 𝘝𝘐𝘚𝘈   JZ a
closed 2 weeks August, 1 week Christmas, Saturday lunch, Sunday and Bank Holidays – Meals 31.74 (lunch) and a la carte 65/74 **t.** 🍷 25.39
Spec. Brochette of langoustine and asparagus. Roast loin of rabbit, morel risotto and pea purée. Assiette of chocolate.

XXX **Shanahan's,** 119 St Stephen's Green, D2, ☏ (01) 407 0939, info@ shanahans.ie, Fax (01) 407 0940, « Georgian town house » – ⇔ ☰. ☒ 🅐🅴 ⓪ 𝘝𝘐𝘚𝘈   JZ p
closed 2 weeks Christmas and January, and Sunday – Meals (dinner only) a la carte 52/63 **t.** 🍷 38.02.

XXX
😋 **Peacock Alley** (Gallagher) (at The Fitzwilliam H.), 128 St Stephen's Green, D2, ☏ (01) 478 7015, info@ restaurantpeacockalley.com, Fax (01) 478 7043 – ☰ 🚗. ☒ 🅐🅴 ⓪ 𝘝𝘐𝘚𝘈   JZ d
Meals 27.87/69.83 and a la carte 53/76 **t.** 🍷 22.85
Spec. Seared and roasted foie gras, vanilla and orange syrup. Roast turbot, pea purée, carrot and ginger. Chocolate fondant, vanilla ice cream, bitter chocolate sauce.

XXX **L'Ecrivain,** 109 Lower Baggot St, D2, ☏ (01) 661 1919, enquiries@ lecrivain.com, Fax (01) 661 0617, 🍴 – ☰. ☒ 🅐🅴 𝘝𝘐𝘚𝘈   KZ b
closed Saturday lunch, Sunday and Bank Holidays – Meals (booking essential) 21.52/44.10 and dinner a la carte 32/48.50 **t.**

XXX £3£3 **Thornton's,** 1 Portobello Rd, D8, ✆ (01) 454 9067, Fax (01) 453 2947 – ▤. **⬤⬤ AE ⬤**
VISA   DU e
closed 1 week August, 2 weeks Christmas, Sunday and Monday – **Meals** (booking essential)
(dinner only and Friday lunch) 31.74 (lunch) and a la carte 64/70 **t.** ⓧ 22.85
Spec. Sautéed foie gras with scallops and cep jus. Roast suckling pig with stuffed trotter,
poitín sauce. Pyramid of fruit parfait, orange sauce.

XXX **Chapter One,** The Dublin Writers Museum, 18-19 Parnell Sq, D1, ✆ (01) 873 2266,
chapterone@oceanfree.net, Fax (01) 873 2330, « Contemporary Irish art collection » –
▤ **P. ⬤⬤ AE ⬤ VISA**   JX r
closed 25 December-9 January, Sunday, Monday, Saturday lunch and Bank Holidays – **Meals**
25.39 (lunch) and dinner a la carte 37/43 **t.** ⓧ 18.41.

XX **The Tea Room** (at The Clarence H.), 6-8 Wellington Quay, D2, ✆ (01) 670 7766,
Fax (01) 670 7833 – **⬤⬤ AE ⬤ VISA**   HY a
closed lunch Saturday and Sunday – **Meals** (booking essential) 19.05/49.52 and a la carte
29.20/34.28 ⓧ 23.49.

XX **Halo** (at Morrison H.), Ormond Quay, D1, ✆ (01) 887 2421, Fax (01) 887 2499,
« Contemporary interior » – ▤. **⬤⬤ AE ⬤ VISA JCB**   HY r
closed 24-27 December – **Meals** 25/40 (lunch) and dinner a la carte 45/59 **t.** ⓧ 20.95.

XX **brownes brasserie** (at brownes townhouse H.), 22 St Stephen's Green, D2, ✆ (01)
638 3939, info@brownesdublin.ie, Fax (01) 638 3900 – ▤. **⬤⬤ AE ⬤ VISA**   JZ c
Meals (booking essential) 34.65/47.25 and a la carte 34.75/52.50 **t.** ⓧ 18.95.

XX **Morningtons Brasserie** (at The Merrion H.), Upper Merrion St, D2, ✆ (01) 603 0630,
Fax (01) 603 0700 – ▤ 🛋 **⬤⬤ AE ⬤ VISA JCB**   KZ e
closed lunch Saturday and Sunday – **Meals** 20.31/24.12 (lunch) and dinner a la carte
30/42 **t.** ⓧ 22.85.

XX **One Pico,** 5-6 Molesworth Pl, School House Lane, D2, ✆ (01) 676 0300, eamonnoreilly
@ireland.com, Fax (01) 676 0411 – **⬤⬤ AE ⬤ VISA**   JZ k
closed 25-27 December, 1 January and Sunday – **Meals** a la carte 32/44 **t.** ⓧ 19.68.

XX **Les Frères Jacques,** 74 Dame St, D2, ✆ (01) 679 4555, info@lesfreresjacques.com,
Fax (01) 679 4725 – **⬤⬤ VISA**   HY x
closed 24 December-2 January, Saturday lunch and Sunday – **Meals** - French - 19.04/31.74
and a la carte 40/58 **t.** ⓧ 15.87.

XX **Number Ten** (at Longfield's H.), 10 Lower Fitzwilliam St, D2, ✆ (01) 676 1060,
Fax (01) 676 1542 – **VISA**   KZ d
closed lunch Saturday and Sunday) – **Meals** 17.78/36.77 **t.** ⓧ 19.70.

XX **La Stampa** (at La Stampa H.), 35 Dawson St, D2, ✆ (01) 677 8611, lastampa@eircom.net,
Fax (01) 677 336, « Former 19C ballroom, collection of Graham Nuttel paintings » – **⬤⬤**
AE ⬤ VISA   JZ x
Meals (booking essential) (dinner only) 44.44/48.25 and a la carte 30/44 **t.** ⓧ 18.41.

XX **Diep Le Shaker,** 55 Pembroke Lane, D2, ✆ (01) 661 1829, Fax (01) 661 5905 – ▤. **⬤⬤**
AE ⬤ VISA   KZ k
closed 25-26 December, Saturday lunch, Sunday and Bank Holidays – **Meals** - Thai -
31.74/44.44 (dinner) and a la carte 20/60 **t.** ⓧ 18.41.

XX **Saagar,** 16 Harcourt St, D2, ✆ (01) 475 5060, saagar@iol.ie, Fax (01) 475 5741 – **⬤⬤**
AE VISA   JZ b
closed 25 December, 1 January, Saturday and Sunday lunch – **Meals** - Indian - a la carte
20/27 **st.**

XX **Locks,** 1 Windsor Terr, Portobello, D8, ✆ (01) 4543391, Fax (01) 4538352 – **⬤⬤ AE ⬤ VISA**
closed 24 December-7 January, Saturday lunch, Sunday and Bank Holidays – **Meals**
22.80/38.05 and a la carte 41.75/58.65 **t.** ⓧ 17.45.   DU a

XX **Jacobs Ladder,** 4-5 Nassau St, D2, ✆ (01) 670 3865, jaladder@gofree.indigo.ie,
Fax (01) 670 3868 – 🍴 **⬤⬤ AE ⬤ VISA**   KY a
closed 3 weeks Christmas-New Year, 1 week August, 17 March, Sunday and Monday – **Meals**
(booking essential) 31.74 (dinner) and a la carte 32.30/48.20 **st.** ⓧ 16.50.

XX **Bang Café,** 11 Merrion Row, D2, ✆ (01) 676 0898, Fax (01) 676 0899 – ▤. **⬤⬤ AE VISA**
closed 1 week Christmas and Sunday – **Meals** (booking essential) a la carte 25/45.44 **t.**
ⓧ 17.71.   KZ a

X **Dobbin's,** 15 Stephen's Lane, off Lower Mount St, D2, ✆ (01) 676 4679, dobbinswine
bistro@eircom.net, Fax (01) 661 3331, 🌤 – ▤. **⬤⬤ AE ⬤ VISA**   EU s
*closed 1 week Christmas-New Year, Sunday, Monday dinner, Saturday lunch and Bank Holi-
days* – **Meals** - Bistro - (booking essential) 20.95 (lunch) and dinner a la carte 39/50 **t.**
ⓧ 20.95.

X **Eden,** Meeting House Sq, Temple Bar, D2, ✆ (01) 670 5372, Fax (01) 670 3330, 🌤 –
▤. **⬤⬤ AE ⬤ VISA**   HY e
closed 25-28 December and Bank Holidays – **Meals** 20.95 (lunch) and dinner a la carte
24/37 **t.** ⓧ 20.31.

✗ **Cooke's Café**, 14 South William St, D2, ℰ (01) 679 0536, *cookes1@iol.ie*, *Fax (01) 679 0546*, ☆ – ▦, ◍◉ 🜇 ◑ 𝗩𝗜𝗦𝗔   JY c
Meals a la carte 23/40 ⓑ 19.40.

✗ **Moe's**, 112 Lower Baggot St, D2, ℰ (01) 676 7610, *moesdublin@hotmail.com*, *Fax (01) 676 7606* – ◍◉ 𝗩𝗜𝗦𝗔   KZ c
closed 24-25 December, 1 January, Saturday lunch and Sunday – **Meals** a la carte 29/40 **t.** ⓑ 20.12.

✗ **Mermaid Café**, 69-70 Dame St, D2, ℰ (01) 670 8236, *Fax (01) 670 8205* – ▦. ◍◉ 𝗩𝗜𝗦𝗔
𝖺 *closed 24-26 and 31 December, 1 January and Good Friday* – **Meals** (booking essential) a la carte 23/39 **t.** ⓑ 17.07.   HY d

🍽 **The Cellar Bar** (at The Merrion H.), Upper Merrion St, D2, ℰ (01) 603 0631, *info@m errionhotel.com, Fax (01) 603 0700*, « Restored vaulted Georgian cellars » – ☞. ◍◉ 🜇 ◑ 𝗩𝗜𝗦𝗔   KZ e
Meals (live music Sunday brunch) (lunch only) a la carte 20/21 **t.** ⓑ 22.85.

Ballsbridge
Dublin 4.

🏨 **Four Seasons**, Simmonscourt Rd, D4, ℰ (01) 665 4000, *sales.dublin@fourseasons.com*, *Fax (01) 665 4099*, 𝐼ᵴ, ☎, ▨, ☞ – ▮§▮, ❦ rm, ▦ 📺 ❦ ὅ ⇔ 🄿 – 🅰 500. ◍◉ 🜇 ◑ 𝗩𝗜𝗦𝗔   FU e
Seasons : **Meals** 32.69 (lunch) and a la carte 53/70 **t.** ⓑ 31.74 – *The Cafe* : **Meals** a la carte 30/46 **t.** ⓑ 31.74 – ☲ 20.95 – **192 rm** 495 **st.**, 67 suites 635/2100 **st.**

🏨 **The Berkeley Court**, Lansdowne Rd, D4, ℰ (01) 660 1711, *berkeleycourt@jurysdo yle.com, Fax (01) 661 7238*, 𝐼ᵴ – ▮§▮, ❦ rm, ▦ 📺 ❦ ὅ ⇔ 🄿 – 🅰 450. ◍◉ 🜇 ◑ 𝗩𝗜𝗦𝗔. ❦   FU c
Berkeley Room : **Meals** (closed Saturday lunch Sunday dinner) 33 and a la carte 41/95 **t.** ⓑ 20.00 – *Palm Court Café* : **Meals** 18 (lunch) and a la carte 28/42 **t.** ⓑ 18 – ☲ 22 – **183 rm** 300 **t.**, 5 suites.

🏨 **The Towers**, Lansdowne Rd, D4, ℰ (01) 667 0033, *towers@jurysdoyle.com*, *Fax (01) 660 5324*, 𝐼ᵴ, ☎, ⅀ heated – ▮§▮ ❦ ▦ 📺 ❦ ὅ 🄿 – 🅰 100. ◍◉ 𝗩𝗜𝗦𝗔. ❦ FU p
Meals 22 (lunch) and a la carte 28/42 **t.** ⓑ 17 – ☲ 17 – **101 rm** 280/320 **t.**, 4 suites.

🏨 **Jurys**, Pembroke Rd, D4, ℰ (01) 660 5000, *ballsbridge@jurysdoyle.com*, *Fax (01) 660 5540*, 𝐼ᵴ, ☎, ⅀ heated – ▮§▮ ❦, ▦ rest, 📺 ❦ ὅ 🄿 – 🅰 800. ◍◉ 🜇 ◑ 𝗩𝗜𝗦𝗔. ❦   FU p
Raglans : **Meals** 22 (lunch) and a la carte 18/33 **t.** ⓑ 17 – ☲ 17 – **300** 240/270 **t.**, 3 suites.

🏨 **Herbert Park**, D4, ℰ (01) 667 2200, *reservations@herbertparkhotel.ie*, *Fax (01) 667 2595*, ☆, 𝐼ᵴ – ▮§▮ – 🅰 100. ◍◉ 🜇 ◑ 𝗩𝗜𝗦𝗔. ❦
The Pavilion : **Meals** (closed dinner Sunday and Bank Holidays) 23.50/25 (lunch) and dinner a la carte 31.74/45.65 **st.** ⓑ 20 – ☲ 19 – **150 rm** 130/275 **st.**, 3 suites – SB. FU m

🏨 **The Hibernian**, Eastmoreland Pl, D4, ℰ (01) 668 7666, *info@hibernianhotel.ie*, *Fax (01) 660 2655* – ▮§▮ ❦ 📺 ❦ ὅ 🄿 – 🅰 30. ◍◉ 🜇 ◑ 𝗩𝗜𝗦𝗔 𝗝𝗖𝗕. ❦   EU x
closed 24-27 December – *Patrick Kavanagh Room* : **Meals** (closed Saturday and Sunday lunch and Sunday dinner to non-residents) 17.71/22.79 (lunch) and dinner a la carte 31.04/48.82 **t.** ⓑ 20.32 – ☲ 15.24 – **40 rm** ☲ 190.46/241.25 **st.** – SB.

🏨 **The Schoolhouse**, 2-8 Northumberland Rd, D4, ℰ (01) 667 5014, *school@schoolho usehotel.iol.ie, Fax (01) 667 5015*, « Converted Victorian schoolhouse », ☞ – ▮§▮, ❦ rm, ▦ 📺 ❦ ὅ ◍◉ 🜇 ◑ 𝗩𝗜𝗦𝗔. ❦   EU a
closed 24-27 December – *Satchels* : **Meals** (bar lunch Saturday) 9/38 and dinner a la carte 23.50/38 **st.** ⓑ 18 – **31 rm** ☲ 159/204 **st.**

🏨 **Ariel House** without rest., 52 Lansdowne Rd, D4, ℰ (01) 668 5512, *reservations@ar iel-house.com, Fax (01) 668 5845* – ❦ 📺 🄿. ◍◉ 𝗩𝗜𝗦𝗔. ❦   FU n
closed 2 weeks Christmas – ☲ 12.00 – **37 rm** 95.25/228.60 **st.**

🏨 **Bewley's**, 19-20 Fleet St, D2, ℰ (01) 670 8122, *bewleyshotel@eircom.net*, *Fax (01) 670 8103* – ▮§▮, ❦ rm, ▦ 📺. ◍◉ 🜇 ◑ 𝗩𝗜𝗦𝗔. ❦   JY d
closed 24-26 December – *Bewley's Café* : **Meals** (dinner only) 20/25 **st.** ⓑ 16 – ☲ 10 – **70 rm** 115/144 **st.**

🏨 **Butlers Town House**, 44 Lansdowne Rd, D4, ℰ (01) 667 4022, *info@butlers-hotel .com, Fax (01) 667 3960* – ▦ 📺 ❦ 🄿. ◍◉ 🜇 ◑ 𝗩𝗜𝗦𝗔. ❦   FU v
closed 23 December-8 January – **Meals** (room service only) – **19 rm** ☲ 139.67/215.86 **st.**

🏨 **Pembroke Townhouse** without rest., 90 Pembroke Rd, D4, ℰ (01) 660 0277, *info @pembroketownhouse.ie, Fax (01) 660 0291*, « Georgian town house » – ▮§▮ ❦ 📺 ❦ 🄿. ◍◉ 🜇 ◑ 𝗩𝗜𝗦𝗔. ❦   FU d
closed 22 December-3 January – **48 rm** ☲ 129/192 **st.**

🏨 **Waterloo House** without rest., 8-10 Waterloo Rd, D4, ℰ (01) 660 1888, *waterloohouse@e ircom.ie, Fax (01) 667 1955*, « Georgian town house », ☞ – ▮§▮ ❦ 📺 ❦ 🄿. ◍◉ 𝗩𝗜𝗦𝗔. ❦
closed 23 to 28 December – **17 rm** ☲ 95.25/165.10.   EU p

⛫ **Simmonstown House** without rest., Sydenham Rd, off Merrion Rd, D4, ℰ (01) 660 7260, *info@simmonstownhouse.com, Fax (01) 660 7341* – 🚰 📺 🅿, 🆖 🆎 𝗩𝗜𝗦𝗔, ⚡️ *closed 13 December-7 January* – **4 rm** 89/152 **st.**   FU x

✕ **Roly's Bistro**, 7 Ballsbridge Terr., D4, ℰ (01) 668 2611, *Fax (01) 660 8535* – 🔲, 🆖 🆎 ① 𝗩𝗜𝗦𝗔   FU r
  Meals (booking essential) 17.71 (lunch) and a la carte 31/35 **t.** ⓘ 16.44.

Donnybrook
Dublin 4.

✕✕ **Ernie's,** Mulberry Gdns, off Morehampton Rd, D4, ℰ (01) 269 3300, *Fax (01) 269 3260,* « Contemporary Irish Art collection » – 🔲, 🆖 🆎 ① 𝗩𝗜𝗦𝗔   FV k
  closed 22 December-3 January, Sunday, Monday and Saturday lunch – **Meals** 16.44/36.82 and a la carte 50.14/66.01 **st.** ⓘ 17.78.

Drumcondra
Dublin 5.

🏨 **Jurys Skylon,** Upper Drumcondra Rd, D9, North : 2 ½ m. on N 1 ℰ (01) 837 9121, *skylon@jurysdoyle.com, Fax (01) 837 2778* – 📱, 🚰 rm, 📺 📞 ♿ 🅿, 🆖 🆎 𝗩𝗜𝗦𝗔, ⚡️
  The Rendezvous Room : **Meals** 18/26 **t.** ⓘ 14 – ⌑ 10 – **88 rm** 149 **st.**

Merrion
Dublin 6.

🏨 **Jurys Tara,** Merrion Rd, D4, Southeast : 4 m. on R 118 ℰ (01) 269 4666, *tara@jury sdoyle.com, Fax (01) 269 1027* – 📱 📺 📞 ♿ 🅿 – 🔷 300. 🆖 🆎 𝗩𝗜𝗦𝗔, ⚡️   GV a
  Meals a la carte 17.65/24.95 ⓘ 7.00 **The Conservatory :** **Meals** (dinner only and lunch Saturday and Sunday) 18/27 **t.** ⓘ 18 – ⌑ 12 – **113 rm** 149 **st.**

Rathgar
Dublin 6.

✕✕ **Poppadom,** 91A Rathgar Rd, D6, ℰ (01) 490 2383, *Fax (01) 492 3900* – 🔲, 🆖 🆎 𝗩𝗜𝗦𝗔
  closed 25-26 December – **Meals** - Indian - (booking essential) (dinner only) a la carte 25/34 **t.** ⓘ 15.23.   DV a

Rathmines
Dublin 6.

🏨 **Quality Charleville,** Lower Rathmines Rd, D6, ℰ (01) 406 6100, *info@charlevilleho tel.com, Fax (01) 406 6200* – 📱, 🚰 rm, 🔲 rest, 📺 📞 ♿ 🚐, 🆖 🆎 ① 𝗩𝗜𝗦𝗔, ⚡️
  Carmines . **Meals** - Italian - (bar lunch Monday Saturday)/dinner 19.05 **t.** ⓘ – **9 rm** ⌑ 165.07/203.16 **st.**, **43 suites** 203.16 **st.**   DV x

✕✕ **Zen,** 89 Upper Rathmines Rd, D6, ℰ (01) 4979428 – 🔲, 🆖 🆎 ① 𝗩𝗜𝗦𝗔   DV t
  Meals - Chinese (Szechuan) - (dinner only and lunch Thursday, Friday and Sunday) a la carte 22.22/46.98 **t.** ⓘ 16.44.

at Dublin Airport *North : 6 ½ m. by N 1 DU and M 1 –* ✉ *Dublin*

🏨 **Great Southern,** ℰ (01) 844 6000, *dubairport@gsh.ie, Fax (01) 844 6001* – 📱, 🚰 rm, 📺 📞 ♿ 🅿 – 🔷 450. 🆖 🆎 ① 𝗩𝗜𝗦𝗔, ⚡️
  closed 24-26 December – **Potters :** **Meals** (bar lunch Monday-Saturday)/dinner 35 ⓘ 13.97 – **Clancys Bar :** **Meals** (carvery lunch) a la carte 13/17 **st.** ⓘ 13.97 – ⌑ 17 – **147 rm** 190 **st.** – SB.

🏨 **Holiday Inn Dublin Airport,** ℰ (01) 808 0500, *reservations-dublinairport@6c.com, Fax (01) 844 6002* – 🚰 rm, 🔲 rest, 📺 📞 ♿ 🅿 – 🔷 130. 🆖 🆎 ① 𝗩𝗜𝗦𝗔, ⚡️
  closed 24-25 December – **Bistro :** **Meals** *(closed Saturday lunch)* 16.75/26.60 and dinner a la carte 31/37 **t.** ⓘ 6.95 – **Sampan's :** **Meals** - Asian - *(closed Bank Holidays)* (dinner only) a la carte 22/31 **t.** ⓘ 15.17 – ⌑ 16.44 – **249 rm** 177/209 **t.** – SB.

at Clontarf *Northeast : 3 ½ m. by R 105 KX –* ✉ *Dublin*

🏨 **Clontarf Castle,** Castle Ave, D3, ℰ (01) 833 2321, *info@clontarfcastle.ie, Fax (01) 833 0418,* ƒ – 📱, 🚰 rm, 📺 📞 ♿ 🅿 – 🔷 500. 🆖 🆎 ① 𝗩𝗜𝗦𝗔, ⚡️
  closed 24-25 December – **Templars Bistro :** **Meals** (carvery lunch Monday-Saturday)/dinner a la carte 36/44 **t.** ⓘ 19.80 – ⌑ 15.87 – **108 rm** 222/242 **t.**, 3 suites –SB.

at Stillorgan *Southeast : 5 m. on N 11 GV –* ✉ *Dublin*

🏨 **Radisson SAS St Helen's,** Stillorgan Rd, D4, ℰ (01) 218 6000, *info.dublin@radisso nsas.com, Fax (01) 218 6010,* « Part 18C mansion, formal gardens », ƒ⚖ – 📱 🚰 🔲 📺 📞 ♿ 🅿 – 🔷 350. 🆖 🆎 ① 𝗩𝗜𝗦𝗔, ⚡️
  Le Panto : **Meals** *(closed Sunday and Monday)* (dinner only) a la carte 44.44/60.94 **st.** ⓘ 24.13 – **Tolavera :** **Meals** - Italian - 29.50 (lunch) and a la carte 25.39/44.44 ⓘ 19 – ⌑ 19 – **130 rm** 205 **st.**, 21 suites.

🏨 **Stillorgan Park,** Stillorgan Rd, ℘ (01) 288 1621, *sales@stillorganpark.com*, Fax (01) 283 1610 – 📶, ✳ rm, 🔲 📺 ♿ 🅿 – 🔬 600. 🆗 🅰🅴 ⓞ 𝗩𝗜𝗦𝗔. ✳
Purple Sage : Meals (carvery lunch)/dinner a la carte 29.85/42.52 **st.** ⚬ 20.30 – **Turf Club** : Meals 21.54/32.94 **st.** ⚬ 20.30 – **129 rm** ⊆ 170/195 **st.**

🏨 **Jurys Montrose,** Stillorgan Rd, D4, ℘ (01) 269 3311, *montrose@jurysdoyle.com*, Fax (01) 269 1164 – 📶, ✳ rm, 📺 📱 🅿 – 🔬 70. 🆗 🅰🅴 𝗩𝗜𝗦𝗔. ✳   GV y
The Belfield : Meals 17/27 **t.** ⚬ 18 – ⊆ 8.50 – **179 rm** 149 **st.**

at Blackrock Southeast : 5 ½ m. by R 118 GV – ✉ Dublin

🍴🍴 **Dali's,** 63-65 Main St, ℘ (01) 278 0660, Fax (01) 278 0661 – 🔳. 🆗 🅰🅴 ⓞ 𝗩𝗜𝗦𝗔
closed 25-27 and 31 December, Monday and Sunday dinner – **Meals** 13.90/17.71 (lunch) and a la carte 29.12/35.56 **t.** ⚬ 17.14.

🍴 **Blueberry's,** 1st floor (above Jack O'Rourkes pub), 15 Main St, ℘ (01) 278 9000, *blue berrys@clubi.ie*, Fax (01) 278 8903 – 🆗 🅰🅴 𝗩𝗜𝗦𝗔
closed 25-26 December, 1 January, Good Friday, Saturday lunch and Sunday dinner – **Meals** (booking essential) 16.50 (lunch) and dinner a la carte 19.60/28.00 ⚬ 14.50.

at Tallaght Southwest : 7 ½ m. by N 81 DV – ✉ Dublin

🏨 **The Plaza,** Belgard Rd, D24, at junction of N 81 and R 113 ℘ (01) 462 4200, *sales @plazahotel.ie*, Fax (01) 462 4600 – 📶, ✳ rm, 🔲 rest, 📺 📱 ♿ 🅿 – 🔬 300. 🆗 🅰🅴 ⓞ 𝗩𝗜𝗦𝗔. ✳
closed 24-30 September – **The Olive Tree** : Meals (closed Sunday) 35/44 and a la carte 33/44 **st.** ⚬ 16.44 – ⊆ 17.71 – **120 rm** 159 **st.**, 2 suites.

🏨 **Abberley Court,** Belgard Rd, D24, on R 113 ℘ (01) 459 6000, *abberley@iol.ie*, Fax (01) 462 1000 – 📶 📺 📱 ⟵. 🆗 🅰🅴 ⓞ 𝗩𝗜𝗦𝗔. ✳
closed 25-30 December – **The Leaf** : Meals - Chinese - (dinner only and lunch Thursday, Friday and Sunday) a la carte 24.12/31.74 **t.** ⚬ 15.24 – **38 rm** ⊆ 100.30/124.43 **t.**

at Clondalkin Southwest : 8 m. by N 7 HY on R 113 – ✉ Dublin

🏨 **Red Cow Moran,** Naas Rd, D22, Southeast : 2 m. on N 7 at junction with M 50 ℘ (01) 459 3650, *info@morangroup.ie*, Fax (01) 459 1588 – 📶, ✳ rm, 🔲 📺 📱 ♿ 🅿 – 🔬 700. 🆗 🅰🅴 ⓞ 𝗩𝗜𝗦𝗔. ✳
closed 24-26 December – **The Winter Garden** : Meals 19.68/47.29 and dinner a la carte 28.18/47.29 **t.** ⚬ 17.71 – **120 rm** ⊆ 185/250 **t.**, 3 suites – SB.

🏨 **Bewley's H. Newlands Cross,** Newlands Cross, Naas Rd (N7), D22, ℘ (01) 464 0140, *res@bewleyshotels.com*, Fax (01) 464 0900 – 📶, ✳ rm, 🔲 rest, 📺 📱 ♿ 🅿 🆗 🅰🅴 ⓞ 𝗩𝗜𝗦𝗔.
closed 24-26 December – **Meals** (carving lunch) a la carte 15/27 **t.** – ⊆ 9 – **258 rm** 75 **st.**

at Saggart Southwest : 9 ¼ m. off N 7 HY – ✉ Dublin

🏨 **Citywest Conference Centre and Golf Resort,** ℘ (01) 401 0500, *info@city west-hotel.ie*, Fax (01) 458 8565, 🎣, ⇔, 🏊, 🏌 – 📶, ✳ rm, 🔲 rest, 📺 📱 🅿 – 🔬 3800. 🆗 🅰🅴 ⓞ 𝗩𝗜𝗦𝗔. ✳
The Terrace : Meals 16.95/30.95 ⚬ 12.95 – **The Grill Room** : Meals (carvery rest.) a la carte approx. 24.75 ⚬ 12.95 – **317 rm** ⊆ 145/175 **t.**, 13 suites – SB.

🏨 **Quality,** Naas Rd, ℘ (01) 458 7000, *info@qualityhotel.com*, Fax (01) 458 7019, ⚓ – 📶, 🔲 rest, 📺 ♿ 🅿 – 🔬 30. 🆗 🅰🅴 ⓞ 𝗩𝗜𝗦𝗔. ✳
closed 24-27 December – **The Westpark** : Meals a la carte 18/29 **st.** – ⊆ 8.25 – **74 rm** 100.31/113.01 **st.**, **72 suites** 126.97/152.37 **st.** – SB.

Italy

Italia

ROME – FLORENCE – MILAN – NAPLES
PALERMO – TAORMINA – TURIN – VENICE

PRACTICAL INFORMATION

LOCAL CURRENCY
1 euro (€) = 0,89 USD ($) (Dec 2001)

TOURIST INFORMATION
Welcome Office *(Azienda Promozione Turistica):*
– Via Parigi 5 - 00185 ROMA (closed Saturday afternoon and Sunday), ℰ 06 48899208, Fax 06 4819316
– Via Marconi 1 - 20123 MILANO, ℰ 02 72 5241, Fax 02 72 52 43 50
See also telephone number and address of other Tourist Information offices in the text of the towns under ⬛.
American Express:
– Largo Caduti di El Alamein 9 - 00173 ROMA, ℰ 06 722801, Fax 06 67 64 24 99
– Via Brera 3 - 20121 MILANO, ℰ 02 809645, Fax 02 86 10 28
National Holiday in Italy: *25 April.*

AIRLINES
ALITALIA: *Via Bissolati 13 - 00187 ROMA, ℰ 06 65621, Fax 06 656 28 282*
Via Albricci 5 - 20122 MILANO, ℰ 02 24992700, Fax 02 805 67 57
AIR FRANCE: *Via Sardegna 40 - 00187 ROMA, ℰ 848884466, Fax 06 483803*
Piazza Cavour 2 - 20121 MILANO, ℰ 02 760731, Fax 02 760 73 355
DELTA AIRLINES: *via Malpensa 2000 - 20100 MILANO, ℰ 02 58 58 11 23, Fax 02 86 33 74 09*

FOREIGN EXCHANGE
Money can be changed at the Banca d'Italia, other banks and authorised exchange offices (Banks close at 1.30pm and at weekends).

POSTAL SERVICES
Local post offices: *open Monday to Saturday 8.30am to 2.00pm*
General Post Office *(open 24 hours only for telegrams):*
– Viale Europa 190 00144 ROMA – Piazza Cordusio 20123 MILANO

SHOPPING
In the index of street names, those printed in red are where the principal shops are found. In Rome, the main shopping streets are: Via del Babuino, Via Condotti, Via Frattina, Via Vittorio Veneto; in Milan: Via Dante, Via Manzoni, Via Monte Napoleone, Corso Vittorio Emanuele, Via della Spiga.

BREAKDOWN SERVICE
Certain garages in the centre and outskirts of towns operate a 24 hour breakdown service. If you break down the police are usually able to help by indicating the nearest one.
A free car breakdown service (a tax is levied) is operated by the A.C.I. for foreign motorists carrying the fuel card (Carta Carburante).

TIPPING
As well as the service charge, it is the custom to tip employees. The amount can vary depending upon the region and the service given.

SPEED LIMITS
On motorways, the maximum permitted speed is 130 km/h - 80 mph. On other roads, the speed limit is 110 km/h - 68 mph.

ROME
(ROMA)

00100 🔢 *Q 19* 🔢 *– Pop. 2 655 970 – alt. 20.*

Distances from Rome are indicated in the text of the other towns listed in this Guide.

🛈 *via Parigi 5* ✉ *00185* ☎ *06 48 89 92 08, Fax 06 481 93 16 ;*

🛈 *at Fiumicino Airport* ☎ *06 65956074.* 🛈 *Termini Station* ☎ *06 4871270.*

A.C.I. *via Cristoforo Colombo 261* ✉ *00147* ☎ *06 514 971 and via Marsala 8* ✉ *00185*
☎ *06 49981, Fax 06 499 822 34.*

🏌 *Parco de' Medici (closed Tuesday)* ✉ *00148 Roma SW : 4,5 km* ☎ *06 655 34 77 –*
Fax 06 655 33 44.

🏌 *Circolo del Golf di Roma (closed Monday) via Appia Nuova 716/A* ✉ *00178 Roma*
SE : 12 km. ☎ *06 78 34 07, Fax 06 78 34 62 19.*

🏌 *and* 🏌 *Marco Simone at Guidonia Montecelio* ✉ *00012 Roma W : 7 km* ☎ *0774*
366 469, Fax 0774 366 476.

🏌 *and* 🏌 *Arco di Costantino (closed Monday)* ✉ *00188 Roma N : 15 km*
☎ *06 33 62 44 40, Fax 06 33 61 29 19*

🏌 *and* 🏌 *(closed Monday) at Olgiata* ✉ *00123 Roma NW : 19 km* ☎ *06 308 89 141,*
Fax 06 308 89 968.

🏌 *Fioranello (closed Wednesday) at Santa Maria delle Mole* ✉ *00040 Roma SE : 19 km*
☎ *06 713 80 80, Fax 06 713 82 12.*

✈ *Ciampino SW : 15 km* ☎ *794941.*

✈ *Leonardo da Vinci di Fiumicino SE : 26 km* ☎ *06 65631 – Alitalia, via Bissolati 20*
✉ *00187* ☎ *06 65621 and viale Alessandro Marchetti 111* ✉ *00148* ☎ *06 65643.*

SIGHTS

How to make the most of a trip to Rome – some ideas :

Borghese Gallery★★★ – Villa Giulia★★★ DS – Catacombs★★★ – Santa Sabina★★ MZ –
Villa Borghese★★ NOU – Baths of Caracalla★★★ ET – St Lawrence Without the Walls★★
FST **E** *– St Paul Without the Walls★★ – Old Appian Way★★ – National Gallery of Modern*
Art★ DS **M⁷** *– Mausoleum of Caius Cestius★ DT – St Paul's Gate★ DT* **B** *– San'Agnese*
and Santa Costanza★ FS **C** *– Santa Croce in Gerusalemme★ FT* **D** *– San Saba★ ET –*
E.U.R.★ – Museum of Roman Civilisation★★.

ANCIENT ROME

Colosseum★★★ OYZ – Roman Forum★★★ NOY – Basilica of Maxentius★★★ OY **B** *–*
Imperial Fora★★★ NY – Trajan's Column★★★ NY **C** *– Palatine Hill★★★ NOYZ –*
Pantheon★★★ MVX – Largo Argentina Sacred Precinct★★ MY **W** *– Altar of Augustus★★*
LU – Temple of Apollo Sosianus★★ MY **X** *– Theatre of Marcellus★★ MY – Tempio della*
Fortuna Virile★ MZ **Y** *– Tempio di Vesta★ MZ* **Z** *– Isola Tiberina★ MY.*

CHRISTIAN ROME

Gesù Church★★★ MY – *St Mary Major*★★★ PX – *St John Lateran*★★★ FT – *Santa Maria d'Aracoeli*★★ NY **A** – *San Luigi dei Francesi*★★ LV – *Sant'Andrea al Quirinale*★★ OV **F** – *St Charles at the Four Fountains*★★ OV **K** – *St Clement's Basilica*★★ PZ – *Sant'Ignazio*★★ MV **L** – *Santa Maria degli Angeli*★★ PV **N** – *Santa Maria della Vittoria*★★ PV – *Santa Susanna*★★ OV – *Santa Maria in Cosmedin*★★ MNZ – *Basilica of St Mary in Trastevere*★★ KZ **S** – *Santa Maria sopra Minerva*★★ MX **V** – *Santa Maria del Popolo*★★ MU **D** – *New Church*★ KX – *Sant'Agostino*★ LV **G** – *St Peter in Chains*★ OY – *Santa Cecilia*★ MZ – *San Pietro in Montorio*★ JZ ⩽★★★ – *Sant'Andrea della Valle*★★ LY **Q** – *Santa Maria della Pace*★ KV **R**.

PALACES AND MUSEUMS

Conservators' Palace★★★ MNY **M¹** – *New Palace*★★★ *(Capitoline Museum*★★*)* NY **M¹** – *Senate House*★★★ NY **H** – *Castel Sant'Angelo*★★★ JKV – *National Roman Museum*★★★ : *Aula Ottagona*★★★ PV **M⁹**, *Palazzo Massimo alle Terme* PV and *Altemps Palace*★★★ KLV – *Chancery Palace*★★ KX **A** – *Palazzo Farnese*★★ KY – *Quirinal Palace*★★ NOV – *Barberini Palace*★★ OV – *Villa Farnesina*★★ KY – *Palazzo Venezia*★ MY **M³** – *Palazzo Braschi*★ KX **M⁴** – *Palazzo Doria Pamphili*★ MX **M⁵** – *Palazzo Spada*★ KY – *Museo Napoleanico*★ KV.

THE VATICAN

St Peter's Square★★★ HV – *St Peter's Basilica*★★★ *(Dome* ⩽★★★*)* GV – *Vatican Museums*★★★ *(Sistine Chapel*★★★*)* GHUV – *Vatican Gardens*★★★ GV.

PRETTY AREAS

Pincian Hill ⩽★★★ MU – *Capitol Square*★★★ MNY – *Spanish Square*★★★ MNU – *Piazza Navona*★★★ LVX – *Fountain of the Rivers*★★★ LV **E** – *Trevi Fountain*★★★ NV – *Victor Emmanuel II Monument (Vittoriano)* ⩽★★ MNY – *Quirinale Square*★★ NV – *Piazza del Popolo*★★ MU – *Gianicolo*★ JY – *Via dei Coronari*★ KV – *Ponte Sant'Angelo*★ JKV – *Piazza Bocca della Verità*★ MNZ – *Piazza Campo dei Fiori*★ KY **28** – *Piazza Colonna*★ MV **46** – *Porta Maggiore*★ FT – *Piazza Venezia*★ MNY.

STREET INDEX TO ROMA TOWN PLANS

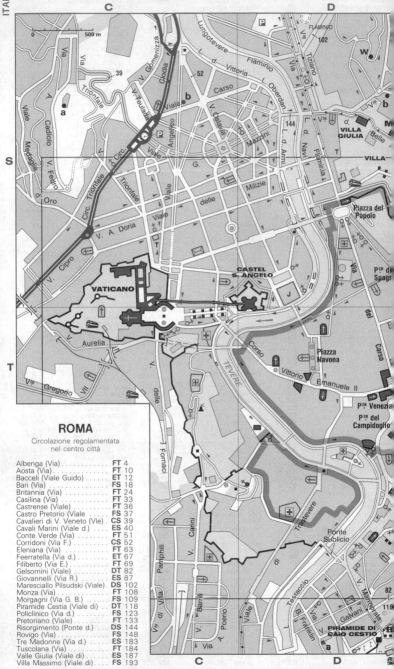

ROMA

Circolazione regolamentata
nel centro città

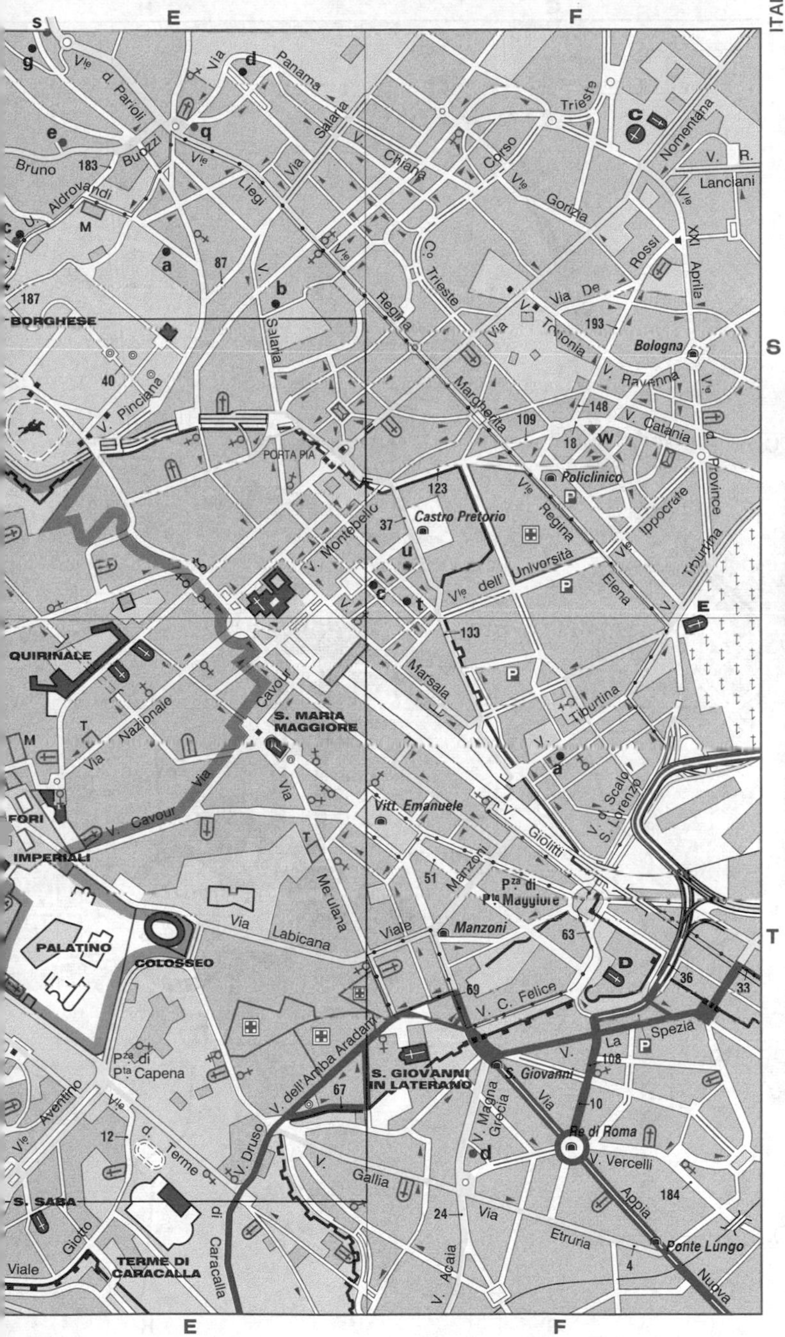

s
g
Vle d Parioli
d
Panama
Trieste
C
V. R.
Nomentana
Lanciani
e
Bruno
183
Bupzzi
q
Vle
Via
Chiana
Corso
Vle
Gorizia
Aldrovandi
Liegi
Via
Regina
C° Trieste
Rossi
Via De
XXI Aprile
c
M
a
87
V.
Salaria
b
Trionfa
193
Bologna
187
Regina
V. Ravenna
Vle
BORGHESE
Margherita
109
146
V. Catania
S
40
V. Pinciana
18
W
Policlinico
Province
PORTA PIA
123
Vle Regina
Vle Ippocrate
Montebello
37
Castro Pretorio
Vle dell' Università
Elena
Tiburtina
QUIRINALE
u
c
t
133
Marsala
E
Via Nazionale
Cavour
S. MARIA
MAGGIORE
Tiburtina
V.
FORI
IMPERIALI
V. Cavour
Via
Via
a
V. di Scalo
V. S. Lorenzo
PALATINO
Vitt. Emanuele
V. Giolitti
COLOSSEO
Me. Jana
Via Labicana
Viale
51
Manzoni
Manzoni
Pza di
Pta Maggiore
63
D
36
33
T
Pza di
Pta Capena
69
V. C. Felice
P
Spezia
Aventino
S. GIOVANNI
IN LATERANO
S. Giovanni
108
10
12
Vle
d
Terme
67
V. dell'Amba Aradam
V. Druso
d
V. Magna Grecia
Via
Re di Roma
V. Vercelli
184
S. SABA
Gallia
24
Via
Etruria
4
Ponte Lungo
Viale
Gioto
di
Caracalla
TERME DI
CARACALLA
Accaia
Nuova
Aggia

E
F

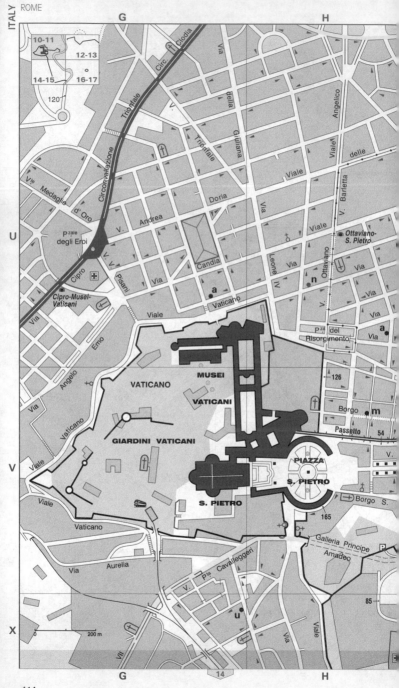

G

H

10-11
12-13
14-15
16-17
120

Circ. Clodia
Via

V. Bella
Via Trionfale
Via Giuliana
Angelico

Triontale
Circonvallazione
Doria
Viale
Viale delle

V.te Medaglie d'Oro
V. Andrea
Viale
V. Barletta

U

P.zale degli Eroi
Candia
Leone IV
V. Ottaviano
Ottaviano-S. Pietro

Cipro
Via Pisani
Viale
Via

Cipro-Musei-Vaticani
Via Emo
Viale Vaticano
a
Via
n
Via

V. Angelo
MUSEI
P.za del Risorgimento
a
Via

Via Vaticano
VATICANO
VATICANI
126

V

GIARDINI VATICANI
PIAZZA S. PIETRO
Borgo
m
Passetto
54
V.

Viale
S. PIETRO
165
Borgo S.

Viale
Vaticano
Galleria Principe
P

Via
Aurelia
P.ta Cavalleggeri
Amadeo

X

0   200 m
V.
u
Viale
85

VII
14

G

H

414

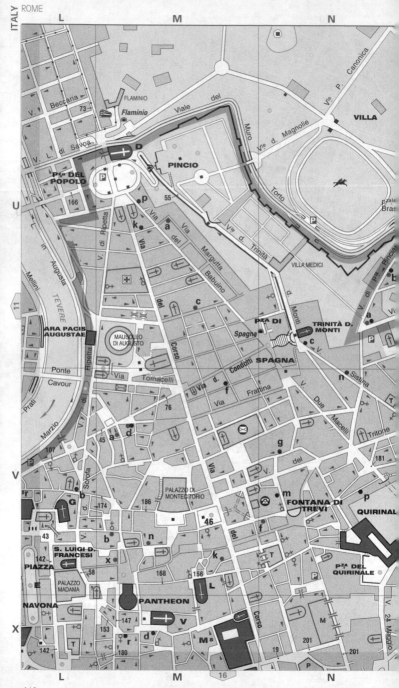

L   M   N

Beccaria

V.

73

FLAMINIO

Flaminio

Viale del

Muro

Vle d. Magnolie

VILLA

V. L. di Savoa

D

PINCIO

P.za DEL POPOLO

166

55

p

Via

k

a

del

Via

Babuino

Margutta

Torto

p.zale
Bras...

Vle d. Trinità

VILLA MEDICI

Mellini

Augusta

TEVERE

11

del

c

Corso

Via

Monti

P.za DI

Spagna

TRINITÀ D.
MONTI

ARA PACIS
AUGUSTAE

MAUSOLEO
DI AUGUSTO

a

c

SPAGNA

Ponte

Cavour

Ripetta

Via

Tomacelli

Condotti

n

Sistina

Via d.

f

Frattina

Via

Due

Macelli

Tritone

Prati

Marzio

V. di

76

Via

del

g

181

V.

V.

45

a

d

Scrofa

107

P

r

b

G

174

186

PALAZZO DI
MONTECITORIO

d

m

FONTANA DI
TREVI

p

QUIRINAL

43

b

n

46

f

S. LUIGI D.
FRANCESI

142

PIAZZA

E

58

PALAZZO
MADAMA

x

168

k

156

L

P.za DEL
QUIRINALE

NAVONA

PANTHEON

L

M

V

T

147

153

r

d

180

142

T

v

19

201

201

M

V. 2...
Maggio...

16

L   M   N

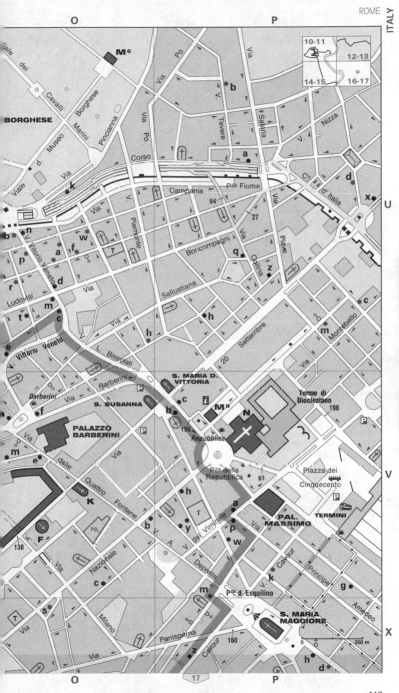

10

G

H

85

X

0 ——— 200 m

Vil

Gregorio

Viale

u

Viale

Via

S. PIETRO

delle

delle

Mura

Aurelie

di Gianicolo

Passeggiata

Y

Fornaci

Via   Aurelia   Antica

S. Pancrazio

VILLA DORIA PAMPHILI

del Vascello

Z

V. di

Vitellia

Vle di

Villa

V. Dezza

Fontejana

Via

Pamphili

Barilli

25

171

10-11

12-13

14-15

16-17

G

H

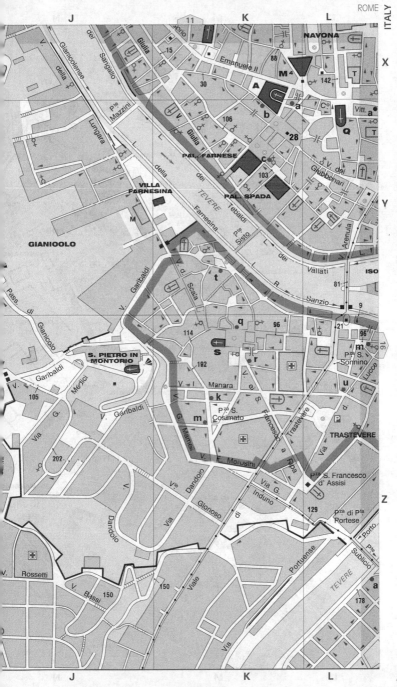

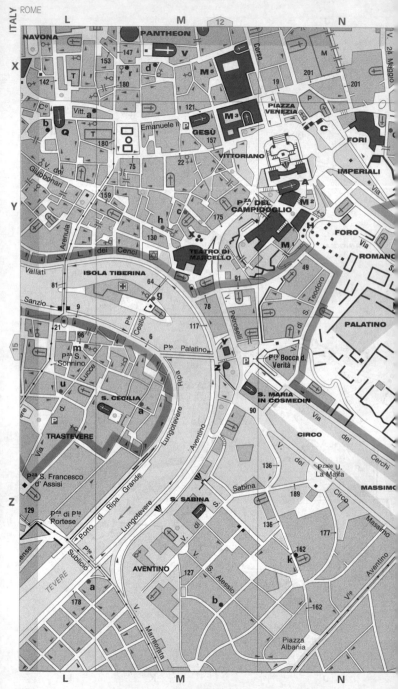

NAVONA
PANTHEON
Corso

147
153
r
d
v
Ms

142
T
Co
180
121
M3
PIAZZA
VENEZIA
201
201

Vitt.
a
b
Q
Emanuele II
GESÙ
157
VITTORIANO
C
FORI

180
75
22
A
M2
IMPERIALI

d. V. dei
Giubbonari
159
P.ZA DEL
CAMPIDOGLIO
175
H
FORO

Arenula
h
c
x
M1
ROMANO

L. dei Cenci
130
TEATRO DI
MARCELLO
49

Vallati
81
ISOLA TIBERINA
64
91
78
di S. Teodoro
PALATINO

Sanzio
9
g
117
Petroselli

21
96
6
Pte Palatino
v
PALATINO

m
P.za S.
Sonnino
Pte Cestio
Ripa
z
P.za Bocca d.
Verità
P

u
Lucee
S. CECILIA
a
90
S. MARIA
IN COSMEDIN

TRASTEVERE
P
Lungotevere
Aventino
CIRCO
del
Cerchi

P.za S. Francesco
d' Assisi
136
p.zale U.
La Malfa
MASSIMO

Z
129
P.za di P.ta
Portese
Sabina
189
Circo
Massimo
177

ense
S. SABINA
S.
Aventino

TEVERE
Sublicio
Pte
Lungotevere
Porto di Ripa Grande
136
k
162

a
178
AVENTINO
127
S. Alessio
b
162
Massimo

Piazza
Albania

420

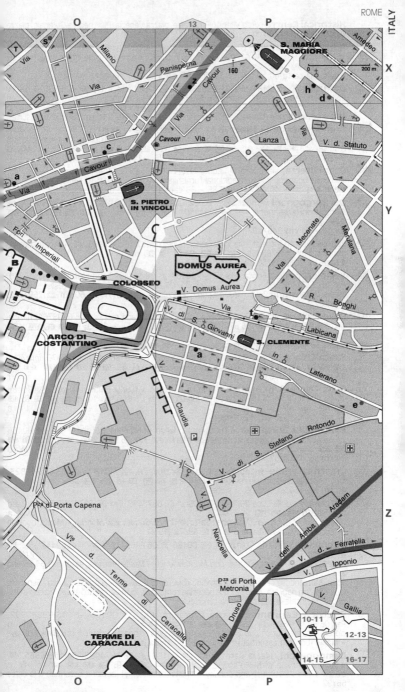

S. MARIA
MAGGIORE

Amedeo

X

Via
Milano

Panisperna

Cavour   160

Via

Cavour   Via   G.   Lanza

h
d

Via

Via

Cavour

c

V. d. Statuto

a

Via

S. PIETRO
IN VINCOLI

Mecenate

Merulana

Imperiali

DOMUS AUREA

B

COLOSSEO

V. Domus Aurea

Via

V.   R   Bonghi

ARCO DI
COSTANTINO

V. di S. Ginvanni

a

S. CLEMENTE

in

Labicana

Laterano

e

Claudia

S. Stefano   Rotondo

V. di S. Stefano

Pza di Porta Capena

V. d. Navicella

Aradam

Amba

V. d. Ferratella

dell'

Ipponio

V.

Pza di Porta
Metronia

Vle   d.   Terme   di   Caracalla

Via   Druso

V.   Gallia

TERME DI
CARACALLA

10-11

12-13

14-15   16-17

Z

200 m

Historical Centre corso Vittorio Emanuele, piazza Venezia, Pantheon e Quirinale, piazza di Spagna, piazza Navona :

🏨🏨🏨🏨 **Hassler Villa Medici**, piazza Trinità dei Monti 6 ⊠ 00187 ℰ 06 699340, *booking @hotelhassler.it*, Fax 06 6789991, « Roof-rest. with ≤ city » – |≢| 🗐 📺 📞 – 🔏 120. ⚿ 🕄 ⓞ ⓜⓞ 𝘝𝘐𝘚𝘈 Jᴄв. 𝒮𝒞
                                                            NU c
Meals a la carte 60/105 – � 39,77 – **85 rm** 513,87/725,62, 15 suites.

🏨🏨🏨🏨 **De Russie** 🅼, via del Babuino 9 ⊠ 00187 ℰ 06 328881 and rest. ℰ 06 32888870, *reserv ations@hotelderussie.it*, Fax 06 32888888, « Restaurant service on shaded terrace-garden », 𝑓ᵦ, ≤s – |≢|, ⤢ rm, 🗐 📺 📞 & – 🔏 85. ⚿ 🕄 ⓞ ⓜⓞ 𝘝𝘐𝘚𝘈. 𝒮𝒞   MU p
Meals *Le Jardin de Russie* Rest. a la carte 50/120 – � 34 – **110 rm** 380/520, 19 suites.

🏨🏨🏨 **Grand Hotel de la Minerve** 🅼, piazza della Minerva 69 ⊠ 00186 ℰ 06 695201, *minerva@hotel-invest.com*, Fax 06 6794165, « Terrace roof garden with summer evening rest. service » – |≢|, ⤢ rm, 🗐 📺 📞 & – 🔏 120. ⚿ 🕄 ⓞ ⓜⓞ 𝘝𝘐𝘚𝘈 Jᴄв. 𝒮𝒞   MX d
Meals *La Cesta* Rest. a la carte 62/103 – � 26 – **115 rm** 350/515, 3 suites.

🏨🏨🏨 **D'Inghilterra**, via Bocca di Leone 14 ⊠ 00187 ℰ 06 699811, Fax 06 69922243, « Former boarding house, traditional furnishings » – |≢| 🗐 📺. ⚿ 🕄 ⓞ ⓜⓞ 𝘝𝘐𝘚𝘈 Jᴄв. 𝒮𝒞
Meals a la carte 40/72 – � 23,86 – **88 rm** 261,33/443,69, 10 suites.   MV f

🏨🏨 **Dei Borgognoni** without rest., via del Bufalo 126 ⊠ 00187 ℰ 06 69941505, *hotel .borgognoni@flashnet.it*, Fax 06 69941501 – |≢| 🗐 📺 ⟷ – 🔏 60. ⚿ 🕄 ⓞ ⓜⓞ 𝘝𝘐𝘚𝘈 Jᴄв. 𝒮𝒞   NV g
� 14 – **51 rm** 245/297.

🏨🏨 **White** 🅼 without rest., via in Arcione 77 ⊠ 00187 ℰ 06 6991242, *white@travelro ma.com*, Fax 06 6788451 – |≢| 🗐 📺. ⚿ 🕄 ⓞ ⓜⓞ 𝘝𝘐𝘚𝘈 Jᴄв. 𝒮𝒞   NV p
41 rm � 206,50/258,20.

🏨🏨 **Valadier**, via della Fontanella 15 ⊠ 00187 ℰ 06 3611998 and rest. ℰ 06 3610880, Fax 06 3201558, ⇪ – |≢| 🗐 📺 – 🔏 35. ⚿ 🕄 ⓞ ⓜⓞ 𝘝𝘐𝘚𝘈 Jᴄв. 𝒮𝒞 rest   MU k
Meals *Il Valentino* Rest. *(closed Sunday lunch)* a la carte 37/48 – **60 rm** � 269/352, 3 suites.

🏨🏨 **Delle Nazioni**, via Poli 7 ⊠ 00187 ℰ 06 6792441 and rest. ℰ 06 6795761, *nazioni @remarhotels.com*, Fax 06 6782400 – |≢| 🗐 📺 & ⟷ – 🔏 50. ⚿ 🕄 ⓞ ⓜⓞ 𝘝𝘐𝘚𝘈 Jᴄв. 𝒮𝒞   NV m
Meals *Le Grondici* Rest. a la carte 40/60 – **83 rm** � 217/300.

🏨 **Santa Chiara** without rest., via Santa Chiara 21 ⊠ 00186 ℰ 06 6872979, *info@alb ergosantachiara.com*, Fax 06 6873144 – |≢| 🗐 📺 – 🔏 40. ⚿ 🕄 ⓞ ⓜⓞ 𝘝𝘐𝘚𝘈 Jᴄв. 𝒮𝒞
93 rm � 170/206,61, 3 suites.   MX r

🏨 **Della Torre Argentina** without rest., corso Vittorio Emanuele 102 ⊠ 00186 ℰ 06 6833886, *info@dellatorreargentina.com*, Fax 06 68801641 – |≢| 🗐 📺. ⚿ 🕄 ⓞ ⓜⓞ 𝘝𝘐𝘚𝘈 Jᴄв. 𝒮𝒞   LY a
57 rm � 134,28/201,42, suite.

🏨 **Fontanella Borghese** without rest., largo Fontanella Borghese 84 ⊠ 00186 ℰ 06 68809504, *fontanellaborghese@interfree.it*, Fax 06 6861295 – 🗐 📺. ⚿ 🕄 ⓞ ⓜⓞ 𝘝𝘐𝘚𝘈 Jᴄв. 𝒮𝒞   MV d
24 rm ⊆ 114/207.

🏨 **Internazionale** without rest., via Sistina 79 ⊠ 00187 ℰ 06 69941823, *info@ hotelinternazionale.com06 784764* – |≢| 🗐 📺. ⚿ 🕄 ⓜⓞ 𝘝𝘐𝘚𝘈 Jᴄв   NV n
40 rm ⊆ 134,27/196,25, 2 suites.

🍴🍴🍴 **El Toulà**, via della Lupa 29/b ⊠ 00186 ℰ 06 6873498, Fax 06 6871115, Elegant rest. – 🗐. ⚿ 🕄 ⓞ ⓜⓞ 𝘝𝘐𝘚𝘈 Jᴄв. 𝒮𝒞   MV a
closed August, 24 to 26 December, Saturday lunch, Sunday and Monday – **Meals** (booking essential) 56,81/67,14 and a la carte 49/72 (15 %).

🍴🍴🍴 **Il Convivio**, vicolo dei Soldati 31 ⊠ 00186 ℰ 06 6869432, Fax 06 6869432 – 🗐. ⚿ ✿   KLV r
closed 9 to 15 August, Sunday and Monday lunch – **Meals** (booking essential) 64,55 and a la carte 58/77
Spec. Mazzancolle croccanti, caponatina di verdure e salsa speziata. Spaghetti "Senatore Cappelli" con pagliata, mentuccia e pecorino romano. Piccione arrostito alla salvia con involtino di radicchio e salsa di acero canadese.

🍴🍴🍴 **Enoteca Capranica**, piazza Capranica 100 ⊠ 00186 ℰ 06 69940992, Fax 06 69940989 – 🗐. ⚿ 🕄 ⓞ ⓜⓞ 𝘝𝘐𝘚𝘈 Jᴄв. 𝒮𝒞   MV n
closed Saturday lunch and Sunday ; in August open dinner, all day on the Bank Holidays – **Meals** (booking essential for dinner) 51,64 and a la carte 40/66.

🍴🍴🍴 **Camponeschi**, piazza Farnese 50 ⊠ 00186 ℰ 06 6874927, Fax 06 6865244, « Summer service with ≤ Farnese palace » – ⤢⤢ 🗐. ⚿ 🕄 ⓞ ⓜⓞ 𝘝𝘐𝘚𝘈. 𝒮𝒞   KY c
closed 13 to 22 August and Sunday – **Meals** (dinner only) (booking essential) a la carte 66/92.

XXX **Ciro,** via Vittoria 22 ⊠ 00186 ℰ 06 3614148, *cirofish@ jumpy.it*, *Fax 06 36092654* – ▤. ◫ 🛉 ⓪ ◍ ❿ ᴊᴄ◉. ⅋
MU c
closed 10 August-8 September, 24 December-4 January and Sunday – **Meals** (dinner only) (booking essential) seafood a la carte 115/147.

XX **Taverna Giulia,** vicolo dell'Oro 23 ⊠ 00186 ℰ 06 6869768, *Fax 06 6893720* – ▤. ◫ 🛉 ⓪ ◍ ❿ ᴊᴄ◉. ⅋
JV r
closed August and Sunday – **Meals** (booking essential for dinner) Ligurian rest. a la carte 28/36.

XX **La Rosetta,** via della Rosetta 9 ⊠ 00187 ℰ 06 6861002, *larosetta@ tin.it*, ⭆ *Fax 06 68215116* – ◫ 🛉 ⓪ ❿ ᴊᴄ◉. ⅋
MV x
closed 8 to 22 August, Saturday lunch and Sunday – **Meals** (booking essential) seafood a la carte 88/160
Spec. Insalata di tonno scottato con salsa agrodolce (April-September). Strozzapreti con calamaretti e gamberi rossi al profumo di limone. Crespelle di scampi con salsa al rabarbaro e limone caramellato.

XX **La Fontanella,** largo della Fontanella Borghese 86 ⊠ 00186 ℰ 06 6871582, *Fax 06 6871092* – ▤. ◫ 🛉 ⓪ ◍ ❿ ᴊᴄ◉. ⅋
MV d
closed Monday – **Meals** (booking essential for dinner) a la carte 42/57 (15 %).

XX **Vecchia Roma,** via della Tribuna di Campitelli 18 ⊠ 00186 ℰ 06 6864604, *Fax 06 6864604,* ⌲ – ▤. ◫ ⓪
MY c
closed 10 to 25 August and Wednesday – **Meals** Roman and seafood rest. a la carte 39/52.

XX **Quinzi Gabrieli,** via delle Coppelle 6 ⊠ 00186 ℰ 06 6879389, *quinzigabrieli@ katam* ⭆ *ail.com, Fax 06 6874940,* ⌲ – ◫ 🛉 ⓪ ◍ ❿ ❿. ⅋
MV b
closed August, Christmas and Sunday – **Meals** (dinner only) (booking essential) seafood a la carte 65/93
Spec. Trionfo di crudo di mare. Spaghetti al sugo di triglia e pomodorino. Ombrina all'acqua di mare al profumo di limone.

XX **Quirino,** via delle Muratte 84 ⊠ 00187 ℰ 06 69922509, *Fax 06 6791888* – ✦⯇ ▤. ◫ 🛉 ⓪ ❿ ᴊᴄ◉. ⅋
NV f
closed August and Sunday – **Meals** Roman and Sicilian rest. a la carte 33/45.

XX **Margutta Vegetariano-RistorArte,** via Margutta 118 ⊠ 00187 ℰ 06 32650577, *Fax 06 36003287,* « Contemporary Art exhibition » – ▤. 🛉 ◍ ❿
MU a
Meals Vegetarian rest. 25,82 and a la carte 26/46.

X **Al Bric,** via del Pellegrino 51 ⊠ 00186 ℰ 06 6879533 – ▤. ⤶ 🛉 ⓪ ❿
KY b
closed Monday and lunch (except Sunday) – **Meals** a la carte 26/43 (10 %).

X **Il Falchetto,** via del Montecatini 12/14 ⊠ 00186 ℰ 06 6791160, Rustic trattoria – ▤. ◫ 🛉 ⓪ ◍ ❿. ⅋
MV k
closed 5 to 20 August and Friday – **Meals** a la carte 25/34.

X **Ditirambo,** piazza della Cancelleria 74 ⊠ 00186 ℰ 06 6871626, *Fax 06 6871626* ▤. ⤶ 🛉 ❿
KY a
closed August and Monday lunch – **Meals** (booking essential) a la carte 29/41.

X **Da Giggetto,** via del Portico d'Ottavia 21/a ⊠ 00186 ℰ 06 6861105, *Fax 06 6832106,* ⌲ – ▤. ◫ 🛉 ⓪ ◍ ❿. ⅋
MY h
closed 25 July-8 August and Monday – **Meals** Typical Roman trattoria a la carte 28/45.

Termini Railway Station via Vittorio Veneto, via Nazionale, Viminale, Santa Maria Maggiore, Porta Pia :

🏨🏨🏨🏨 **The Westin Excelsior,** via Vittorio Veneto 125 ⊠ 00187 ℰ 06 47081, *Fax 06 4826205* – 🛗, ✦⯇ rm, ▤ �📺 – 🕍 600. ◫ 🛉 ⓪ ❿ ᴊᴄ◉. ⅋
OU d
Meals a la carte 61/78 – ⌷ 40 – **318 rm** 450/750, 23 suites.

🏨🏨🏨🏨 **St. Regis Grand,** via Vittorio Emanuele Orlando 3 ⊠ 00185 ℰ 06 47091, *Fax 06 4747307,* 🎿, ⌲ – 🛗 ▤ �📺 – 🕍 300. ◫ 🛉 ⓪ ◍ ❿ ᴊᴄ◉. ⅋
PV c
Meals a la carte 92/108 – ⌷ 43 – **137 rm** 590/840, 25 suites.

🏨🏨🏨🏨 **Eden,** via Ludovisi 49 ⊠ 00187 ℰ 06 478121, *Fax 06 4821584,* ≼, 🎿 – 🛗 ▤ �📺 🎧 – 🕍 100. ◫ 🛉 ⓪ ❿ ᴊᴄ◉. ⅋
NU a
Meals (see rest. **La Terrazza** below) – ⌷ 41,80 – **121 rm** 456,50/786,50, 13 suites.

🏨🏨🏨 **Regina Baglioni,** via Vittorio Veneto 72 ⊠ 00187 ℰ 06 421111, *regina.roma@ bag lionihotels.com, Fax 06 42012130* – 🛗, ✦⯇ rm, ▤ �📺 ⅋ – 🕍 50. ◫ 🛉 ⓪ ◍ ❿ ᴊᴄ◉. ⅋
OU m
Meals (closed Sunday) a la carte 54/76 – **143 rm** ⌷ 350,67/525,23, 7 suites.

🏨🏨🏨 **Majestic,** via Vittorio Veneto 50 ⊠ 00187 ℰ 06 421441, *hotelmajestic@ flashnet.it, Fax 06 4880984* – 🛗 ▤ �📺 🎿, ⅋ – 🕍 150. ◫ 🛉 ⓪ ◍ ❿ ᴊᴄ◉. ⅋
OU e
Meals *La Veranda* Rest. (closed Sunday) a la carte 70/103 and *La Ninfa* Rest.-bistrot a la carte 41/62 – ⌷ 40 – **87 rm** 431,24/568,10, 13 suites.

🏨 **Bernini Bristol,** piazza Barberini 23 ⊠ 00187 ℰ 06 4883051, *bbsina@tin.it,*
Fax 06 4824266, « Roof-garden with ≤ city » – |⧈|, ⇔ rm, ⬛ 📺 ✆ – ⚑ 100. 🆎 🚬
ⓞ ⓂⓈ 𝗩𝗜𝗦𝗔 𝗝𝗖𝗕. ℅   OV
Meals *L'Olimpo* Rest. a la carte 64/111 – ⚌ 28,60 – **110 rm** 380,60/482,90, 10 suites

🏨 **Splendide Royal,** porta Pinciana 14 ⊠ 00187 ℰ 06 421689, *splendide@splendider*
oyale.com, Fax 06 42168800 – |⧈| ⬛ 📺 – ⚑ 150. 🆎 🚬 ⓞ ⓂⓈ 𝗩𝗜𝗦𝗔. ℅   NU b
Meals *(see rest. **Mirabelle** below)* – **68 rm** ⚌ 425/490.

🏨 **Jolly Hotel Vittorio Veneto,** corso d'Italia 1 ⊠ 00198 ℰ 06 8495, *Fax 06 8841104*
– |⧈|, ⇔ rm, ⬛ 📺 ⟵ �ⓜ – ⚑ 380. 🆎 🚬 ⓞ ⓂⓈ 𝗩𝗜𝗦𝗔 𝗝𝗖𝗕. ℅ rest   OU k
Meals a la carte 35/54 – **200 rm** ⚌ 260/290.

🏨 **Grand Hotel Palace,** via Veneto 70 ⊠ 00187 ℰ 06 478719, *reservation@palace.
boscolo.com, Fax 06 47871800* – |⧈|, ⇔ rm, ⬛ 📺 ✆ &. – ⚑ 200. 🆎 🚬 ⓞ ⓂⓈ 𝗩𝗜𝗦𝗔
℅   OU c
Meals *(dinner only)* a la carte 42/62 – **86 rm** ⚌ 284,05/490,63, 3 suites.

🏨 **Mecenate Palace Hotel** Ⓜ without rest., via Carlo Alberto 3 ⊠ 00185
ℰ 06 44702024, *info@mecenatepalace.com, Fax 06 4461354* – |⧈| ⇔ ⬛ 📺 ✆ &. –
⚑ 45. 🆎 🚬 ⓞ 𝗩𝗜𝗦𝗔. ℅   PX h
59 rm ⚌ 258,22/351,19, 3 suites.

🏨 **Artemide,** Ⓜ, via Nazionale 22 ⊠ 00184 ℰ 06 489911, *hotel.artemide@tiscalinet.it,*
Fax 06 48991700 – |⧈|, ⇔ rm, ⬛ 📺 &. – ⚑ 140. 🆎 🚬 ⓞ ⓂⓈ 𝗩𝗜𝗦𝗔 𝗝𝗖𝗕. ℅   OV b
Meals only snacks *(residents only)* – **85 rm** ⚌ 232,40/320,30.

🏨 **Quirinale,** via Nazionale 7 ⊠ 00184 ℰ 06 4707, *info@hotelquirinale.it, Fax 06 4820099,*
« Summer service rest. in the garden » – |⧈| ⬛ 📺 – ⚑ 250. 🆎 🚬 ⓞ ⓂⓈ 𝗩𝗜𝗦𝗔 𝗝𝗖𝗕. ℅
Meals a la carte 36/62 – **210 rm** ⚌ 255/315, 5 suites.   PV h

🏨 **Marriott Gd H. Flora** Ⓜ, via Vittorio Veneto 191 ⊠ 00187 ℰ 06 489929,
Fax 06 4820359 – |⧈|, ⇔ rm, ⬛ 📺 ✆ &. – ⚑ 150. 🆎 🚬 ⓞ ⓂⓈ 𝗩𝗜𝗦𝗔 𝗝𝗖𝗕. ℅
Meals a la carte 34/71 – ⚌ 21 – **139 rm** 300/445, 24 suites.   OU b

🏨 **Starhotel Metropole,** via Principe Amedeo 3 ⊠ 00185 ℰ 06 4774, *metropole.rm.
@starhotels.it, Fax 06 4740413* – |⧈| ⬛ 📺 ✆ &. ⟵ – ⚑ 200. 🆎 🚬 ⓞ ⓂⓈ 𝗩𝗜𝗦𝗔 𝗝𝗖𝗕.
℅   PV p
Meals a la carte 58/66 – **253 rm** ⚌ 253/351.

🏨 **Empire Palace Hotel,** via Aureliana 39 ⊠ 00187 ℰ 06 421281, *gold@empirepala
cehotel.com, Fax 06 421284000,* ⌘ – |⧈|, ⇔ rm, ⬛ 📺 ✆ &. – ⚑ 50. 🆎 🚬 ⓞ ⓂⓈ
𝗩𝗜𝗦𝗔 𝗝𝗖𝗕. ℅   PU h
Meals *(closed Sunday)* a la carte 50/68 – **110 rm** ⚌ 247,50/357,50, 5 suites.

🏨 **Imperiale,** via Vittorio Veneto 24 ⊠ 00187 ℰ 06 4826351, *Fax 06 4742583,* ⌘ – |⧈|,
⇔ rm, ⬛ 📺. 🆎 🚬 ⓞ ⓂⓈ 𝗩𝗜𝗦𝗔. ℅   OV s
Meals 37/54 – **95 rm** ⚌ 201/404.

🏨 **Londra e Cargill,** piazza Sallustio 18 ⊠ 00187 ℰ 06 473871, *info@hotellondrarom
a.com, Fax 06 4746674* – |⧈| ⬛ 📺 ⟵. 🆎 🚬 ⓞ ⓂⓈ 𝗩𝗜𝗦𝗔 𝗝𝗖𝗕. ℅   PU q
Meals a la carte 30/40 – **105 rm** ⚌ 211,75/268,56, suite.

🏨 **Mascagni** without rest., via Vittorio Emanuele Orlando 90 ⊠ 00185 ℰ 06 48904040,
mascagni@venere.it, Fax 06 4817637 – |⧈| ⬛ 📺 ✆. 🆎 🚬 ⓞ ⓂⓈ 𝗩𝗜𝗦𝗔 𝗝𝗖𝗕. ℅
40 rm ⚌ 242,74/309,88.   PV b

🏨 **Rex** without rest., via Torino 149 ⊠ 00184 ℰ 06 4824828, *hotel.rex@alfanet.it,*
Fax 06 4882743 – |⧈| ⇔ ⬛ 📺 – ⚑ 50. 🆎 🚬 ⓞ ⓂⓈ 𝗩𝗜𝗦𝗔 𝗝𝗖𝗕   PV w
46 rm ⚌ 191/258, 2 suites.

🏨 **La Residenza** without rest., via Emilia 22/24 ⊠ 00187 ℰ 06 4880789, *hotel.la.res
denza@venere.it, Fax 06 485721* – |⧈| ⬛ 📺. 🚬 𝗩𝗜𝗦𝗔   OU t
22 rm ⚌ 92,90/191,10.

🏨 **Canada** without rest., via Vicenza 58 ⊠ 00185 ℰ 06 4457770, *info@hotelcanadaro
ma.com, Fax 06 4450749* – |⧈| ⬛ 📺 ✆. 🆎 🚬 ⓞ ⓂⓈ 𝗩𝗜𝗦𝗔 𝗝𝗖𝗕. ℅   FS u
70 rm ⚌ 98/152.

🏨 **Britannia** without rest., via Napoli 64 ⊠ 00184 ℰ 06 4883153, *info@hotelbritannia.it,*
Fax 06 4882343 – |⧈| ⬛ 📺 ✆. 🆎 🚬 ⓞ ⓂⓈ 𝗩𝗜𝗦𝗔 𝗝𝗖𝗕   PV y
32 rm ⚌ 173/233.

🏨 **Barberini** without rest., via Rasella 3 ⊠ 00187 ℰ 06 4814993, *info@hotelbarberini.
com, Fax 06 4815211* – |⧈| ⬛ 📺. 🆎 🚬 ⓞ ⓂⓈ 𝗩𝗜𝗦𝗔 𝗝𝗖𝗕. ℅   OV e
⚌ 15 – **31 rm** 220/290.

🏨 **Virgilio** without rest., via Palermo 30 ⊠ 00184 ℰ 06 4884360, *mail@hotelvirgilio.it,*
Fax 06 4884360 – |⧈| ⬛ 📺 ✆. 🆎 🚬 ⓞ ⓂⓈ 𝗩𝗜𝗦𝗔 𝗝𝗖𝗕. ℅   OV c
33 rm ⚌ 114/180.

🏨 **Ariston** without rest., via Turati 16 ⊠ 00185 ℰ 06 4465399, *hotelariston@hotelari
ston.it, Fax 06 4465396* – |⧈| ⇔ ⬛ 📺 ✆ &. – ⚑ 100. 🆎 🚬 ⓞ ⓂⓈ 𝗩𝗜𝗦𝗔 𝗝𝗖𝗕. ℅
97 rm ⚌ 129,11/216,91.   PV g

Barocco without rest., via della Purificazione 4 angolo piazza Barberini ⊠ 00187 ℰ 06 4872001, hotelbarocco@hotelbarocco.it, Fax 06 485994 – 🛗 🔟 👆. 🖭 🕄 ⓪ 🐠 𝐕𝐈𝐒𝐀 𝐉𝐂𝐁. ⅍
OV a
34 rm ⊑ 196,25/335,70, 3 suites.

Venezia without rest., via Varese 18 ⊠ 00185 ℰ 06 4457101, info@hotelvenezia.com, Fax 06 4957687 – 🛗 🔟. 🖭 🕄 ⓪ 🐠 𝐕𝐈𝐒𝐀 𝐉𝐂𝐁. ⅍
FS t
59 rm ⊑ 106/144.

Marcella without rest., via Flavia 106 ⊠ 00187 ℰ 06 42014591, info@hotelmarcell a.com, Fax 06 4815832, « Breakfast service on roof-garden terrace » – 🛗 🔟. 🖭 🕄 ⓪ 🐠 𝐕𝐈𝐒𝐀 𝐉𝐂𝐁. ⅍
PU z
75 rm ⊑ 129,11/206,58.

De Petris without rest., via Rasella 142 ⊠ 00187 ℰ 06 4819626, hoteldepe@tiscali net.it, Fax 06 4820733 – 🛗 🔟. 🖭 🕄 ⓪ 🐠 𝐕𝐈𝐒𝐀 𝐉𝐂𝐁
OV m
53 rm ⊑ 152,35/216,91.

Turner without rest., via Nomentana 9 ⊠ 00161 ℰ 06 44250077, info@hotelturne r.com, Fax 06 44250165 – 🛗 🔟. 🖭 🕄 ⓪ 🐠 𝐕𝐈𝐒𝐀 𝐉𝐂𝐁. ⅍
PU x
43 rm ⊑ 144/180, 4 suites.

Columbia without rest., via del Viminale 15 ℰ 06 4883509, info@hotelcolumbia.com, Fax 06 4740209, « Terrace roof-garden » – 🛗 🔟 📞. 🖭 🕄 ⓪ 🐠 𝐕𝐈𝐒𝐀 𝐉𝐂𝐁. ⅍
PV a
45 rm ⊑ 130/144.

Invictus without rest., via Quintino Sella 15 ⊠ 00187 ℰ 06 42011433, info@solisin victus.com, Fax 06 42011561 – 🔟. 🖭 🕄 ⓪ 🐠 𝐕𝐈𝐒𝐀. ⅍
PU f
13 rm ⊑ 103,29/170,43.

Astoria Garden without rest., via Bachelet 8/10 ⊠ 00185 ℰ 06 4469908, astoria. garden@flashnet.it, Fax 06 4453329, 🐾 – 🔟. 🖭 🕄 ⓪ 🐠 𝐕𝐈𝐒𝐀 𝐉𝐂𝐁. ⅍
FS c
34 rm ⊑ 130/170,43.

La Terrazza - Hotel Eden, via Ludovisi 49 ⊠ 00187 ℰ 06 478121, Fax 06 4821584, « Roof garden with ≼ city » – 🗐. 🖭 🕄 ⓪ 𝐕𝐈𝐒𝐀 𝐉𝐂𝐁. ⅍
NU a
Meals (booking essential) 75/85 and a la carte 70/91
Spec. Tartelletta di pesce crostacei ed ostriche con fagioli cannellini e pomodori canditi. Stracci di pasta all'astice con pomodori ramati. Trancio di branzino al sale di olive nere con tortino di patate.

Sans Souci, via Sicilia 20/24 ⊠ 00187 ℰ 06 42014510, sanssouci@mllink.it, Fax 06 4821771, Elegant rest. – 🗐. 🖭 🕄 ⓪ 🐠 𝐕𝐈𝐒𝐀 𝐉𝐂𝐁. ⅍
OU a
Meals (dinner only) (booking essential) a la carte 73/91
Spec. Carpaccio di struzzo in citronette con erbe di campo e scaglie di parmigiano. Spaghettelli di grano duro con medaglioni di aragosta e pomodorini ciliegia. Petto di fagiano sautè con foie fras tartufato.

Mirabelle - Hotel Splendide Royal, porta Pinciana 14 ⊠ 00187 ℰ 06 42168838, « Summer service on terrace with ≼ city » – 🗐. 🖭 🕄 ⓪ 🐠 𝐕𝐈𝐒𝐀. ⅍
NU b
Meals (booking essential) a la carte 64/85.

Cucina Italiana, via Aurora 19 ⊠ 00187 ℰ 06 48903764, 🏠 – 🖭 🕄 ⓪ 🐠 𝐕𝐈𝐒𝐀 𝐉𝐂𝐁. ⅍
OU s
Meals (dinner only) a la carte 80/101.

Harry's Bar, via Vittorio Veneto 150 ⊠ 00187 ℰ 06 484643, Fax 06 4883117, 🏠 – 🗐. 🖭 🕄 ⓪ 🐠 𝐕𝐈𝐒𝐀 𝐉𝐂𝐁. ⅍
OU b
closed Sunday – **Meals** (booking essential) a la carte 39/53.

Asador Cafè Veneto, via Vittorio Veneto 116 ⊠ 00187 ℰ 06 4827107, cafeveneto@i nterfree.it, Fax 06 42011240, 🏠, Rest. cocktail bar – 🗐. 🖭 🕄 ⓪ 🐠 𝐕𝐈𝐒𝐀 𝐉𝐂𝐁. ⅍
OU p
closed 10 to 31 August and Monday – **Meals** Classical and Argentinian rest. 25,82/36,15 (lunch only) and a la carte 40/53.

Agata e Romeo, via Carlo Alberto 45 ⊠ 00185 ℰ 06 4466115, agataeromeo@tis calinet.it, Fax 06 4465842 – 🗐. 🖭 🕄 ⓪ 🐠 𝐕𝐈𝐒𝐀 𝐉𝐂𝐁. ⅍
PX d
closed 4 to 19 August, 2 to 15 January, Saturday and Sunday – **Meals** (booking essential) 103,29 and a la carte 48/67
Spec. Sformato di formaggio di fossa con salsa di pere e miele di corbezzolo. Vignarola (specialità romana a base di fave, piselli e carciofi) (spring). Quaglia disossata avvolta in foglie di vite e crema di mais (summer-autumn).

Al Grappolo d'Oro, via Palestro 4/10 ⊠ 00185 ℰ 06 4941441, Fax 06 4452350 – 🗐. 🖭 🕄 𝐕𝐈𝐒𝐀 𝐉𝐂𝐁
PU c
closed August and Sunday – **Meals** a la carte 28/40.

Edoardo, via Lucullo 2 ⊠ 00187 ℰ 06 486428, Fax 06 486428 – 🗐. 🖭 🕄 ⓪ 🐠 𝐕𝐈𝐒𝐀. ⅍
OU h
closed August and Sunday – **Meals** 25,82/56,81 (lunch) 30,99/77,47 (dinner) and a la carte 41/65 (15 %).

425

XX **Girarrosto Fiorentino**, via Sicilia 46 ⌧ 00187 ℰ 06 42880660, *Fax 06 42010078* – 🍽. ⒶⒺ 🕙 ⓞ ⓜⓔ *VISA* ⌡ⒸⒷ. ✸ OU f
Meals a la carte 38/52.

XX **Cicilardone Monte Caruso**, via Farini 12 ⌧ 00185 ℰ 06 483549 – 🍽. ⒶⒺ 🕙 ⓞ ⓜⓔ *VISA*. ✸ PV k
closed August, Sunday and Monday lunch – Meals Lucan rest. a la carte 30/48.

XX **Papà Baccus**, via Toscana 36 ⌧ 00187 ℰ 06 42742808, *papabaccus@papabaccus. com*, *Fax 06 42010005* – ✒ 🍽. ⒶⒺ 🕙 ⓞ ⓜⓔ *VISA* ⌡ⒸⒷ. ✸ OU w
closed 10 to 20 August, Saturday lunch and Sunday – Meals (booking essential) Tuscan and seafood specialities a la carte 38/57.

XX **Giovanni**, via Marche 64 ⌧ 00187 ℰ 06 4821834, *Fax 06 4817366*, Habitués rest. – 🍽. ⒶⒺ 🕙 ⓞ ⓜⓔ *VISA*. ✸ OU a
closed August, Friday dinner and Saturday – Meals a la carte 34/52.

XX **Dai Toscani**, via Forlì 41 ⌧ 00161 ℰ 06 44231302 – 🍽. ⒶⒺ 🕙 ⓞ ⓜⓔ *VISA* ⌡ⒸⒷ. ✸ FS w
closed August and Sunday – Meals Tuscan rest. a la carte 26/42.

XX **Peppone**, via Emilia 60 ⌧ 00187 ℰ 06 483976, *Fax 06 483976*, Traditional rest. – 🍽. ⒶⒺ 🕙 ⓞ ⓜⓔ *VISA* ⌡ⒸⒷ. ✸ OU r
closed Saturday and Sunday in August, only Sunday other months – Meals a la carte 33/43 (15 %).

X **Trimani il Wine Bar**, via Cernaia 37/b ⌧ 00185 ℰ 06 4469630, *info@trimani.com*, *Fax 06 4468351*, Wine bar serving quick meals – 🍽. ⒶⒺ 🕙 ⓞ ⓜⓔ *VISA* ⌡ⒸⒷ PU m
closed 11 to 24 August, Sunday (except December) and Bank Holidays – Meals a la carte 21/37.

Ancient Rome Colosseo, Fori Imperiali, Aventino, Terme di Caracalla, Porta San Paolo, Monte Testaccio :

🏛 **Forum**, via Tor de' Conti 25 ⌧ 00184 ℰ 06 6792446, *Fax 06 6786479*, « Roof garden rest. with ⩽ Imperial Forum » – ✒ 🍽 📺 ✆ ⩽ – 🔬 100. ⒶⒺ 🕙 ⓞ ⓜⓔ *VISA* ⌡ⒸⒷ. ✸ OY a
Meals *(closed Sunday dinner)* a la carte 58/78 – **79 rm** ⌸ 170/310.

🏨 **Borromeo** without rest., via Cavour 117 ⌧ 00184 ℰ 06 485856, *borromeo@travel.it*, *Fax 06 4882541* – ✒ 🍽 📺 ✆ &. ⒶⒺ 🕙 ⓞ ⓜⓔ *VISA* ⌡ⒸⒷ PX z
30 rm ⌸ 232,41/335,70, 3 suites.

🏨 **Cilicia** Ⓜ without rest., via Cilicia 5/7 ⌧ 00179 ℰ 06 7005554, *Fax 06 77250016* – ✒ 🍽 📺 &. 🅿 ⒶⒺ 🕙 ⓞ ⓜⓔ *VISA*. by viale delle Terme di Caracalla OPZ x
62 rm ⌸ 130/180.

🏨 **Villa San Pio** ⏚ without rest., via di Santa Melania 19 ⌧ 00153 ℰ 06 5743547, *info @aventinohotels.com*, *Fax 06 5741112*, ⇝ – ✒ 🍽 📺 & 🅿 – 🔬 25. ⒶⒺ 🕙 ⓞ ⓜⓔ *VISA*. ✸ MZ b
78 rm ⌸ 170,43/180,75.

🏨 **Duca d'Alba** without rest., via Leonina 12/14 ⌧ 00184 ℰ 06 484471, *info@hotel ducalba.com*, *Fax 06 4884040* – ✒ 🍽 📺 ✆. ⒶⒺ 🕙 ⓞ ⓜⓔ *VISA* ⌡ⒸⒷ OY c
⌸ 8 – **27 rm** 120/175.

🏨 **Celio** without rest., via dei Santi Quattro 35/c ℰ 06 70495333, *info@hotelcelio.com*, *Fax 06 7096377* – 🍽 📺. ⒶⒺ 🕙 ⓞ ⓜⓔ *VISA* ⌡ⒸⒷ. ✸ PZ a
19 rm, ⌸ 205/260.

🏨 **Domus Aventina** ⏚ without rest., via Prisca 11/b ⌧ 00153 ℰ 06 5746135, *info@domus-aventina.com*, *Fax 06 57300044* – 🍽 📺. ⒶⒺ 🕙 ⓞ ⓜⓔ *VISA* ⌡ⒸⒷ. ✸ NZ k
26 rm ⌸ 140/230.

🏨 **Mercure Hotel Roma Delta Colosseo** without rest., via Labicana 144 ⌧ 00184 ℰ 06 770021, *mercure.romacolosseo@accor-hotels.it*, *Fax 06 7005781*, « ⏇ on panoramic terrace with ⩽ Colosseum » – ✒ 🍽 📺 ⇜. ⒶⒺ 🕙 ⓞ ⓜⓔ *VISA*. ✸ PYZ t
160 rm ⌸ 155/274.

🏛 **Sant'Anselmo** ⏚ without rest., piazza Sant'Anselmo 2 ⌧ 00153 ℰ 06 5748119, *Fax 06 5783604*, « Art Nouveau style villa with small garden » – 📺. ⒶⒺ 🕙 ⓞ ⓜⓔ *VISA*. ✸ MZ m
44 rm ⌸ 154,94/165,27.

XX **Checchino dal 1887**, via Monte Testaccio 30 ⌧ 00153 ℰ 06 5746318, *checchino _roma@tin.it*, *Fax 06 5743816*, Historical building – ✒. ⒶⒺ 🕙 ⓞ ⓜⓔ *VISA* ⌡ⒸⒷ. ✸ DT a
closed August, 24 December-2 January, Sunday and Monday – Meals (booking essential) Roman rest. 38,74/74,89 and a la carte 32/62.

XX **Maharajah**, via dei Serpenti 124 ⌧ 00184 ℰ 06 4747144, *maharajah@maharajah.it*, *Fax 06 47885393* – 🍽. ⒶⒺ 🕙 ⓞ ⓜⓔ *VISA* ⌡ⒸⒷ OX s
Meals Indian rest. 10,40/15,30 (lunch only) and a la carte 28/39 (10 %).

XX **Papok,** salita del Grillo 6/b ⊠ 00184 𝒫 06 69922183, *info@papok.it*, Fax 06 69922183
– 🗏. 🕮 🕃 ⓞ 🚳 𝘝𝘐𝘚𝘈 NY c
closed 10 to 25 August and Monday – **Meals** a la carte 30/49.

XX **Charly's Sauciere,** via di San Giovanni in Laterano 270 ⊠ 00184 𝒫 06 70495666,
Fax 06 77077483 – 🗏. 🕮 🕃 ⓞ 🚳 𝘝𝘐𝘚𝘈 𝙅𝘊𝘽. ⅏ PZ e
closed 5 to 20 August, Sunday and lunch Saturday-Monday – **Meals** (booking essential)
French-Swiss rest. a la carte 30/38.

St. Peter's Basilica (Vatican City) Gianicolo, Monte Mario, Stadio Olimpico :

🏨 **Cavalieri Hilton** Ⓜ, via Cadlolo 101 ⊠ 00136 𝒫 06 35091, *fom_rome@hilton.com*,
Fax 06 35092241, ≤ city, 🍴, *Private art collection*, « Terrace solarium and park with
🏊 », 🖐, ⊆s, 🏊, ⚲ – 🛗, ≉ rm, 🗏 📺 ⚑ 🕭 ⇌ 🅿 – 🔬 2000. 🕮 🕃 ⓞ 🚳 𝘝𝘐𝘚𝘈
𝙅𝘊𝘽. ⅏ CS a
Meals *Il Giardino dell'Uliveto* Rest. a la carte 62/85 see also rest. **La Pergola** – � 33,57
– **354 rm** 400/645, 17 suites.

🏨 **Dei Mellini** Ⓜ without rest., via Muzio Clementi 81 ⊠ 00193 𝒫 06 324771, *info@h*
otelmellini.com, Fax 06 32477801, « Terrace-solarium » – 🛗, ≉ rm, 🗏 📺 ⚑ 🕭 ⇌
– 🔬 70. 🕮 🕃 ⓞ 🚳 𝘝𝘐𝘚𝘈 𝙅𝘊𝘽. ⅏ KU f
67 rm ⊑ 247,90/273,72, 11 suites.

🏨 **Jolly Hotel Villa Carpegna** Ⓜ, via Pio IV 6 ⊠ 00165 𝒫 06 393731, *roma_villaca*
rpegna@jollyhotels.it, Fax 06 636856, 🏊 – 🛗, ≉ rm, 🗏 📺 ⚑ 🕭 🅿 – 🔬 330. 🕮 🕃
ⓞ 🚳 𝘝𝘐𝘚𝘈 𝙅𝘊𝘽. ⅏ rest by via Cipro CS
Meals a la carte 30/42 – **201 rm** ⊑ 165/233, 2 suites.

🏨 **Visconti Palace** without rest., via Federico Cesi 37 ⊠ 00193 𝒫 06 3684, *viscontip*
alace@italyhotel.com, Fax 06 3200551 – 🛗, ≉ rm, 🗏 📺 ⚑ 🕭 ⇌ – 🔬 150. 🕮 🕃
ⓞ 🚳 𝘝𝘐𝘚𝘈 𝙅𝘊𝘽. ⅏ KU b
234 rm ⊑ 207/259, 13 suites.

🏨 **Atlante Star,** via Vitelleschi 34 ⊠ 00193 𝒫 06 6873233, *atlante.star@atlantehote*
l.com, Fax 06 6872300 – 🛗 🗏 📺 ⇌ – 🔬 50. 🕮 🕃 ⓞ 🚳 𝘝𝘐𝘚𝘈 𝙅𝘊𝘽 JV c
Meals (see rest. **Les Etoiles** below) – **70 rm** ⊑ 232,41/320,20, 3 suites.

🏨 **Giullo Cesare** without rest., via degli Scipioni 287 ⊠ 00192 𝒫 06 3210751,
Fax 06 3211736, ⚘ – 🛗 🗏 📺 ⚑ – 🔬 40. 🕮 🕃 ⓞ 🚳 𝘝𝘐𝘚𝘈 𝙅𝘊𝘽. ⅏ KU d
80 rm ⊑ 257/290.

🏨 **Farnese** without rest., via Alessandro Farnese 30 ⊠ 00192 𝒫 06 3212553, *hotel.fa*
rnese@mclink.it, Fax 06 3215129 – 🛗 🗏 📺 🅿. 🕮 🕃 ⓞ 🚳 𝘝𝘐𝘚𝘈. ⅏ KU e
23 rm ⊑ 180/258.

🏨 **Starhotel Michelangelo,** via Stazione di San Pietro 14 ⊠ 00165 𝒫 06 398739, *mich*
elangelo.rm@starhotels.it, Fax 06 632359 – 🛗, ≉ rm, 🗏 📺 🕭 ⇌ – 🔬 150. 🕮 🕃
ⓞ 🚳 𝘝𝘐𝘚𝘈 𝙅𝘊𝘽. ⅏ GX u
Meals a la carte 50/70 – **170 rm** ⊑ 243/336, 8 suites.

🏨 **Dei Consoli** without rest., via Varrone 2/d ⊠ 00193 𝒫 06 68892972, *info@hoteld*
eiconsoli.com, Fax 06 68212274 – 🛗, ≉ rm, 🗏 📺 ⚑ 🕭. 🕮 🕃 ⓞ 🚳 𝘝𝘐𝘚𝘈
𝙅𝘊𝘽. ⅏ HU a
28 rm ⊑ 185,92/273,73.

🏨 **Sant'Anna** without rest., borgo Pio 133 ⊠ 00193 𝒫 06 68801602, *santanna@travel.it*,
Fax 06 68308717 – 🛗 🗏 📺 ⚑. 🕮 🕃 ⓞ 🚳 𝘝𝘐𝘚𝘈 𝙅𝘊𝘽 HV m
20 rm ⊑ 144,61/201,42.

🏨 **Arcangelo** without rest., via Boezio 15 ⊠ 00192 𝒫 06 6874143, *hotel.arcangelo@t*
ravel.it, Fax 06 6893050, « Terrace-solarium with ≤ St. Peter's Basilica » – 🛗 🗏 📺. 🕮
🕃 ⓞ 🚳 𝘝𝘐𝘚𝘈. ⅏ JU f
33 rm ⊑ 140/206.

🏠 **Alimandi** without rest., via Tunisi 8 ⊠ 00192 𝒫 06 39723948, *Fax alimanditin.it06*
39723943, « Breakfast served on the terrace » – 🗏 📺 ⇌. 🕮 🕃 ⓞ 🚳 𝘝𝘐𝘚𝘈 𝙅𝘊𝘽. ⅏
closed 8 January-1 February – **35 rm** ⊑ 109/145. GU a

XXXXX **La Pergola** - Hotel Cavalieri Hilton, via Cadlolo 101 ⊠ 00136 𝒫 06 35091, *lapergola*
❀❀ *@hilton.com*, Fax 06 35092165, 🍴, « Elegant and refined roof restaurant with panoramic ≤ over the capital » – 🗏 🅿. 🕮 🕃 ⓞ 🚳 𝘝𝘐𝘚𝘈 𝙅𝘊𝘽. ⅏ CS a
closed 11 to 26 August, 1 to 21 January, Sunday and Monday – **Meals** (dinner only) (booking
essential) 110,71/113,75 and a la carte 71/119
Spec. Emincè di astice con salsa di arance e basilico. Capriolo in crosta di sale con pistacchi
(spring-autumn). Variazione di cioccolato.

XXX **Les Etoiles** - Hotel Atlante Star, via dei Bastioni 1 ⊠ 00193 𝒫 06 6893434, *les.eto*
iles@atlantehotels.com, Fax 06 6872300, « Roof garden and summer service on terrace
with ≤ St. Peter's Basilica » – 🗏. 🕮 🕃 ⓞ 🚳 𝘝𝘐𝘚𝘈 𝙅𝘊𝘽. ⅏ JV c
Meals 49,06/77,47 (lunch) 61,97/111,04 (dinner) and a la carte 77/108.

XX **Al Limone,** viale Angelico 66 ⊠ 00195 ℰ 06 3722003, *info@al-limone.com*
Fax 06 37526669 – 🔲 ◼ 🏧 ⑩ 🆚 🅙🅒🅑. CS b
closed 4 to 31 August, 30 December-7 January, Saturday lunch and Sunday – **Meals** a la
carte 39/50.

XX **Il Simposio-di Costantini,** piazza Cavour 16 ⊠ 00193 ℰ 06 3211502
Fax 06 3213210, Wine bar and rest. – ◼ ◎ 🆚 🅙🅒🅑 KU c
closed August, Saturday lunch and Sunday – **Meals** (booking essential) a la carte
36/56.

XX **Taverna Angelica,** piazza Amerigo Capponi 6 ⊠ 00193 ℰ 06 6874514, Post theatre
restaurant, open until late – ◼. ◼ 🏧 🆚 🅙🅒🅑. JV l
closed 10 to 20 August and 31 December-1 January – **Meals** (dinner only) (booking essential) a la carte 26/53.

X **Dal Toscano-al Girarrosto,** via Germanico 58 ⊠ 00192 ℰ 06 39725717
Fax 06 39730748, 🍴, Habitués rest. – ◼. ◼ 🏧 🆚 🅙🅒🅑. HU l
closed 10 August-1 September, 24 December-3 January and Monday – **Meals** Tuscan specialities a la carte 26/39.

X **Da Cesare,** via Crescenzio 13 ⊠ 00193 ℰ 06 6861227, *alessandro_arrigoni@ristor-
ntecesare.it*, Fax 06 68130351 – ◼. ◼ 🏧 ⑩ 🆚 🅙🅒🅑. KUV s
closed Easter, August, Christmas, Sunday dinner and Monday – **Meals** Tuscan and seafood
specialities 30 and a la carte 40/51.

Parioli via Flaminia, Villa Borghese, Villa Glori, via Nomentana, via Salaria :

🏨 **Parco dei Principi,** via Gerolamo Frescobaldi 5 ⊠ 00198 ℰ 06 854421, *principi@p
arcodeiprincipi.com*, Fax 06 8845104, ≤, « Overlooking extensive Villa Borghese park »
🏋, 🏊, – 📶 ◼ 📺 ✆ 🚗 – 🔏 700. ◼ 🏧 ⑩ 🆚 🅥🅘🅢🅐. ⋘ rest ES a
Meals a la carte 46/63 – **140 rm** ⊇ 315/490, 25 suites.

🏨 **Lord Byron** ⋟, via De Notaris 5 ⊠ 00197 ℰ 06 3220404, *info@lordbyronhotel.com*
Fax 06 3220405 – 📶 ◼ 📺 ✆. ◼ 🏧 ⑩ 🆚 🅙🅒🅑. ⋘ DS l
Meals (see rest. **Relais le Jardin** below) – **30 rm** ⊇ 341/462, 5 suites.

🏨 **Aldrovandi Palace,** via Aldrovandi 15 ⊠ 00197 ℰ 06 3223993, *hotel@aldrovand
.com*, Fax 06 3221435, « Small shaded park with 🏊 », 🏋 – 📶 ✆ ◼ 📺 ✆ 🄿 – 🔏 300
◼ 🏧 ⑩ 🆚 🅥🅘🅢🅐 🅙🅒🅑. ES c
Meals (see rest. **Relais La Piscine** below) – ⊇ 22 – **122 rm** 400/500, 13 suites.

🏨 **The Duke Hotel** without rest., via Archimede 87 ⊠ 00197 ℰ 06 367221, *theduke
@thedukehotel.com*, Fax 06 36004104 – 📶 ◼ 📺 ♿ 🚗 – 🔏 60. ◼ 🏧 ⑩ 🆚 🅙🅒🅑
⋘ DS w
64 rm ⊇ 258,22/315,03, 14 suites.

🏨 **Albani** without rest., via Adda 45 ⊠ 00198 ℰ 06 84991, *hotelalbani@flashnet.it
Fax 06 8499399 – 📶 ◼ 📺 🚗 – 🔏 40. ◼ 🏧 ⑩ 🆚 🅙🅒🅑. ⋘ rest ES c
157 rm ⊇ 171/248.

🏨 **Borromini** without rest., via Lisbona 7 ⊠ 00198 ℰ 06 852561, Fax 06 8417550 – 📶
◼ 📺 🚗 – 🔏 100. ◼ 🏧 ⑩ 🆚 🅥🅘🅢🅐 🅙🅒🅑. ⋘ ES c
84 rm ⊇ 222,08/252,03.

🏨 **Degli Aranci,** via Oriani 11 ⊠ 00197 ℰ 06 8070202, *hotel.degliaranci@flashnet.it
Fax 06 8070704 – 📶 ◼ 📺 – 🔏 40. ◼ 🏧 ⑩ 🆚 🅥🅘🅢🅐. ⋘ rest ES g
Meals 24/33 – **52 rm** ⊇ 97,93/191,09, 2 suites.

🏨 **Executive** without rest., via Aniene 3 ⊠ 00198 ℰ 06 8552030, *executive@e-nights.it
Fax 06 8414078, 🍴 – 📶 ◼ 📺 ♿. ◼ 🏧 ⑩ 🆚 🅥🅘🅢🅐 🅙🅒🅑 PU a
54 rm ⊇ 140/207.

XXXX **Relais le Jardin** - Hotel Lord Byron, via De Notaris 5 ⊠ 00197 ℰ 06 3220404, *info
@lordbyronhotel.com*, Fax 06 3220405, Elegant rest. – ◼. ◼ 🏧 ⑩ 🆚 🅥🅘🅢🅐
🅙🅒🅑. ⋘ DS l
closed Sunday – **Meals** (dinner only) (booking essential) a la carte 56/71.

XXX **Relais la Piscine** - Hotel Aldrovandi Palace, via Mangili 6 ⊠ 00197 ℰ 06 3216126
« Outdoor summer service » – ✆ ◼ 🄿 ◼ 🏧 ⑩ 🆚 🅥🅘🅢🅐 🅙🅒🅑. ⋘ ES c
Meals a la carte 62/79.

XX **Al Ceppo,** via Panama 2 ⊠ 00198 ℰ 06 8551379, *alceppo@tiscalinet.it*
Fax 06 85301370 – ◼ 🏧 ⑩ 🆚 🅥🅘🅢🅐. ⋘ ES c
closed 8 to 24 August and Monday – **Meals** (booking essential) a la carte 39/43.

XX **La Scala,** viale dei Parioli 79/d ⊠ 00197 ℰ 06 8083978, Fax 06 8084463, 🍴 – ◼
◼ 🏧 ⑩ 🆚 🅥🅘🅢🅐. ⋘ ES s
closed 6 to 21 August and Wednesday – **Meals** Rest. and evening pizzeria a la carte 25/37

XX **Ambasciata d'Abruzzo,** via Pietro Tacchini 26 ⊠ 00197 ℰ 06 8078256, *info@a
mbasciata-di-abruzzo.it*, Fax 06 8074964, 🍴 – ◼. ◼ 🏧 ⑩ 🆚 🅥🅘🅢🅐 🅙🅒🅑 ES e
closed Sunday – **Meals** a la carte 30/56.

XX **Al Chianti,** via Ancona 17 ✉ 00198 ✆ 06 44291534 – ▤. AE Ⓢ ◉ MC VISA JCB. ⊘ PU d
closed 6 to 22 August and Sunday – **Meals** (booking essential) Typical Tuscan trattoria a la carte 24/31.

XX **Al Fogher,** via Tevere 13/b ✉ 00198 ✆ 06 8417032, *Fax 06 8558097* – ▤. AE Ⓢ ◉ MC VISA JCB. ⊘ PU b
closed August, Saturday lunch and Sunday – **Meals** Rustic rest. with Venetian specialities a la carte 34/47.

XX **Coriolano,** via Ancona 14 ✉ 00198 ✆ 06 44249863, *Fax 06 44249724*, Elegant trattoria – ▤. AE Ⓢ ◉ MC VISA JCB PU d
closed 5 to 30 August – **Meals** (booking essential) a la carte 42/55.

X **Franco l'Abruzzese,** via Anerio 23/25 ✉ 00199 ✆ 06 8600704, *Fax 06 8600704*, Habituès trattoria – AE Ⓢ ◉ MC VISA. ⊘ by corso Trieste FS
closed August and Sunday – **Meals** a la carte 18/31.

Trastevere area (typical district) :

XXX **Alberto Ciarla,** piazza San Cosimato 40 ✉ 00153 ✆ 06 5818668, *alberto@albertociarla.com, Fax 06 5884377*, ☂ – ▤. AE Ⓢ ◉ MC VISA JCB. ⊘ KZ k
closed Sunday – **Meals** (dinner only) (booking essential) seafood 41,32/72,30 and a la carte 45/68.

XX **Corsetti-il Galeone,** piazza San Cosimato 27 ✉ 00153 ✆ 06 5816311, *Fax 06 5896255*, ☂, « Typical atmosphere » – ▤. AE Ⓢ ◉ MC VISA JCB. ⊘ KZ m
closed Wednesday lunch – **Meals** Roman and seafood rest. 25,82/30,99 b.i. and a la carte 26/44.

XX **Sora Lella,** via di Ponte Quattro Capi 16 (Isola Tiberina) ✉ 00186 ✆ 06 6861601, *Fax 06 6861601* – ▤. AE Ⓢ ◉ MC VISA JCB. ⊘ MY g
closed Easter, August, 24 to 26 December, New Year and Sunday – **Meals** Traditional Roman rest. a la carte 41/67.

XX **Galeassi,** piazza di Santa Maria in Trastevere 3 ✉ 00153 ✆ 06 5803775, *Fax 06 5809898*, ☂ – AE Ⓢ ◉ MC VISA JCB. ⊘ KZ q
closed 20 December-January and Monday – **Meals** Roman and seafood rest. a la carte 33/44.

XX **Paris,** piazza San Callisto 7/a ✉ 00153 ✆ 06 5815378, *Fax 06 5815378*, ☂ – ▤. AE Ⓢ ◉ MC VISA JCB. ⊘ KZ r
closed August, Sunday dinner and Monday – **Meals** Roman rest. a la carte 29/49.

XX **Pastarellaro,** via di San Cricogono 33 ✉ 00153 ✆ 06 5810871, *Fax 06 5810871*, Rest. wine bar with live piano music at dinner – ▤. AE Ⓢ ◉ MC VISA. ⊘ LZ u
closed August and Wednesday – **Meals** (dinner only except Sunday) Roman and seafood rest. a la carte 34/46 (12 %).

X ☺ **Asinocotto,** via dei Vascellari 48 ✉ 00153 ✆ 06 5898985, *Fax 06 5898985* – AE Ⓢ ◉ MC VISA MZ a
closed 15 to 31 January and Monday – **Meals** (dinner only except Sunday) (booking essential) a la carte 41/54.

X **Checco er Carettiere,** via Benedetta 10 ✉ 00153 ✆ 06 5817018, *Fax 06 5884282*, ☂ – ▤. AE Ⓢ ◉ MC VISA JCB. ⊘ KY t
closed Sunday dinner – **Meals** Roman and seafood rest. a la carte 39/62.

North-Western area via Flaminia, via Cassia, Balduina, Prima Valle, via Aurelia :

🏨 **Holiday Inn Rome West,** via Aurelia at km 8 ✉ 00163 ✆ 06 66411200, *holidayinn.romewest@alliancealberghi.com, Fax 06 66414437*, ☂, ≈, ⛱ – ⇅, 🚭 rm, ▤ 📺 ☎ P – 👥 140. AE Ⓢ ◉ MC VISA JCB. ⊘ by via Aurelia CT
Meals 25,82 – **204 rm** ☕ 205/230.

🏨 **Colony Flaminio** 𝓢, via Monterosi 18 ✉ 00191 ✆ 06 36301843, *colony@iol.it, Fax 06 36309495*, 🏋 – ⇅ ▤ 📺 P – 👥 90. AE Ⓢ ◉ MC VISA JCB
Meals a la carte 29/45 – **74 rm** ☕ 145, suite. by viale Maresciallo DS

🏨 **Classhotel Roma** Ⓜ 𝓢 without rest., via Fusco 118 ✉ 00136 ✆ 06 35404111, *classrm@tin.it, Fax 06 35420322* – ⇅ 🚭 ▤ 📺 ☎ ♿ 🚗 P – 👥 30. AE Ⓢ ◉ MC VISA. ⊘
54 rm ☕ 73,34/134,28. by via Trionfale CS

🏨 **Sisto V** without rest., via Lardaria 10 ✉ 00168 ✆ 06 35072185, *hotel.sistov@tiscalinet.it, Fax 06 35072186* – ⇅ ▤ 📺 🚗. AE Ⓢ ◉ MC VISA by via Trionfale CS
21 rm ☕ 87,80/170,50.

XX **L'Ortica,** via Flaminia Vecchia 573 ✉ 00191 ✆ 06 3338709, *Fax 06 3338709*, ☂, « Collection of 20C products and objets d'art » – AE Ⓢ ◉ MC VISA JCB by viale Maresciallo Pilsudski DS
closed Sunday – **Meals** (dinner only) Napolitan rest. a la carte 36/49.

North-Eastern area via Salaria, via Nomentana, via Tiburtina :

🏨 **Hotel la Giocca** Ⓜ, via Salaria 1223 ⊠ 00138 ℘ 06 8804411 and rest. ℘ 06 8804503, info@lagiocca.it, Fax 06 8804495, ☒ – 🛗 ☰ 📺 ✆ 🅿 – 🔏 150. 🖭 🕃 ⓪ ⓪ 🚾 🕃
☒ by via Salaria **ES**
Meals *L'Elite* Rest. *(closed Sunday)* Roman and seafood rest. a la carte 29/39 – **88 rm** ⊠ 107,16/129,11, 3 suites.

🏨 **Carlo Magno** without rest., via Sacco Pastore 13 ⊠ 00141 ℘ 06 8603982, Fax 06 8604355 – 🛗 ☰ 📺 – 🔏 50. 🖭 🕃 ⓪ ⓪ 🚾 by via Salaria **ES**
55 rm ⊠ 111,04/160,10.

🏨 **La Pergola** without rest., via dei Prati Fiscali 55 ⊠ 00141 ℘ 06 8107250, Fax 06 8124353, ☞ – 🛗 ☰ 📺 – 🔏 50. 🖭 🕃 ⓪ ⓪ 🚾 by via Salaria **ES**
96 rm ⊠ 103/144.

✗✗ **Gabriele,** via Ottoboni 74 ⊠ 00159 ℘ 06 4393498, Fax 06 43535366 – ☰. 🖭 🕃 ⓪
⓪ 🚾. ☒ by via Tiburtina **FS**
closed August, Saturday, Sunday and Bank Holiday – **Meals** (booking essential) a la carte 31/44.

South-Eastern area via Appia Antica, via Appia Nuova, via Tuscolana, via Casilina :

🏨 **Appia Park Hotel** without rest., via Appia Nuova 934 ⊠ 00178 ℘ 06 7716741, info@appiaparkhotel.it, Fax 06 7182457, ☞ – 🛗 ☰ 📺 ♿ 🚗 🅿 – 🔏 60. 🖭 🕃 ⓪ ⓪
🚾. ☒ by via Appia Nuova **FT**
79 rm ⊠ 108,46/139,44.

✗✗ **Rinaldo all'Acquedotto,** via Gabi 36/38 ⊠ 00183 ℘ 06 77206792, Fax 06 77206792 – ☰. 🖭 🕃 ⓪ 🚾 **FT d**
closed August and Tuesday – **Meals** a la carte 22/26.

✗ **Alfredo a via Gabi,** via Gabi 36/38 ⊠ 00183 ℘ 06 77206792, Fax 06 77206792 – ☰ **FT d**
closed August and Tuesday – **Meals** a la carte 22/26.

✗ **Profumo di Mirto,** viale Amelia 8/a ⊠ 00181 ℘ 06 78395192 – ☰. 🖭 🕃 ⓪ 🚾
☒ by via Merulana **PY**
closed August and Monday – **Meals** Sardinian and seafood specialities a la carte 21/36.

South-Western area via Aurelia Antica, E.U.R., Città Giardino, via della Magliana, Portuense :

🏨 **Sheraton Roma Hotel** Ⓜ, viale del Pattinaggio 100 ⊠ 00144 ℘ 06 54531, res497.sheraton.roma@sheraton.com, Fax 06 5940689, ♨, ☎s, ☒, ✗ – 🛗 ☒ rm, ☰ 📺 ♿ 🚗 🅿 – 🔏 1800. 🖭 🕃 ⓪ ⓪ 🚾 🕃. ☒ by viale Aventino **ES**
Meals a la carte 42/89 – **634 rm** ⊠ 170/455, 13 suites.

🏨 **Crowne Plaza Rome St. Peter's,** via Aurelia Antica 415 ⊠ 00165 ℘ 06 66420, cpstpert@hotel-invest.com, Fax 06 6637190, 🍽, « Garden with ☒ », ☎s, ✗ – 🛗, ☒ rm, ☰ 📺 ✆ ♿ 🅿 – 🔏 240. 🖭 🕃 ⓪ ⓪ 🚾 🕃. ☒
Meals a la carte 35/45 – ☒ 18 – **321 rm** 295/363. by viale Gregorio VII **CT**

🏨 **Villa Pamphili** ☜, via della Nocetta 105 ⊠ 00164 ℘ 06 6602, prenotazioni@hotelvillapamphili.com, Fax 06 66157747, 🍽, ♨, ☎s, ☒ (covered in winter), ☞, ✗ – 🛗, ☒ rm, ☰ 📺 ✆ ♿ 🅿 – 🔏 500. 🖭 🕃 ⓪ ⓪ 🚾 🕃. ☒ rest by viale Gregorio VII **CT**
Meals a la carte 30/45 – **248 rm** ⊠ 181/243, 10 suites.

🏨 **Shangri Là-Corsetti,** viale Algeria 141 ⊠ 00144 ℘ 06 5916441, info@shangrilacorsetti.it, Fax 06 5413813, ☒ heated, ☞ – ☰ 📺 🅿 – 🔏 80. 🖭 🕃 ⓪ ⓪ 🚾.
☒ by viale Aventino **ET**
Meals (see rest. *Shangri Là-Corsetti* below) – **52 rm** ⊠ 170/216.

🏨 **Dei Congressi,** viale Shakespeare 29 ⊠ 00144 ℘ 06 5926021, Fax 06 5911903, 🍽
– 🛗 ☰ 📺 ✆ – 🔏 250. 🖭 🕃 ⓪ ⓪ 🚾. ☒ by viale Aventino **ET**
closed 30 July-30 August – **Meals** *La Glorietta* Rest. *(closed 28 July-25 August and Sunday)* a la carte 27/46 – **104 rm** ⊠ 124/201,42.

✗✗✗ **Shangri-Là Corsetti,** viale Algeria 141 ⊠ 00144 ℘ 06 5918861, Fax 06 5413813, 🍽
– ☰ 🅿. 🖭 🕃 ⓪ ⓪ 🚾 🕃. ☒ by viale Aventino **ET**
closed 10 to 26 August – **Meals** seafood a la carte 30/44.

✗ **Pietro al Forte,** via dei Capasso 56/64 ⊠ 00164 ℘ 06 66158531, Fax 06 66158531, 🍽 – 🖭 🕃 ⓪ ⓪ 🚾 🕃. ☒ by viale Gregorio VII **CT**
closed 15 to 31 August and Monday – **Meals** (dinner only except Bank Holiday)) Rest. and pizzeria a la carte 21/33.

Outskirts of Rome

Fiumicino 00054 Roma 🐘🏛🏬 Q 18.

    ✈ Leonardo da Vinci South-Eastern : 26 km

    Roma 31 – Anzio 52 – Civitavecchia 66 – Latina 78.

🏨🏨 **Hilton Rome Airport** Ⓜ via Arturo Ferrarin ✉ 00054 Fiumicino ☎ 06 65258, sale s_rome_apt@hilton.com, Fax 06 65256525, ⅃₅, ≦ₛ, ◩, ⚒ – 🛗, ⇆ rm, 🔲 📺 📶 🄿 – ᆇ 650. 🄰🄴 🖪 🕦 🆅🆂🄰 🄹🄲🄱. ⋙

    Meals a la carte 42/66 – 🖵 20,65 – **511** 350/405, 6 suites.

Baschi 05023 Terni 🐘🏛 N 18. pop. 2670 alt. 165.

    Roma 118 – Orvieto 10 – Terni 70 – Viterbo 46.

※※※※ **Vissani,** North : 12 km ✉ 05020 Civitella del Lago ☎ 0744 950206, Fax 0744 950186
※※※ – ⇆ 🔲 🄿 🄰🄴 🖪 🕦 🔞 🆅🆂🄰. ⋙

    closed Sunday dinner, Wednesday and Thursday lunch – **Meals** (booking essential) 129,10/154,92 and a la carte 88/160 (15 %)

    Spec. Astice blu in salsa di asparagi bianchi, caffè verde, quenelle di zucca gialla all'amaretto. Lasagne di ostriche, brunoise di peperoni, tartufo nero e foie gras. Teneroni di vitella in salsa di ostriche e mandorle, spinaci al tartufo nero.

When driving through towns
use the plans in the **MICHELIN Red Guide***.*

Features indicated include :
    throughroutes and bypasses,
    traffic junctions and major squares,
    new streets, car parks, pedestrian streets...
All this information is revised annually.

FLORENCE (FIRENZE) 50100 🄿 🐘🏛, 🐘🏛🏬 K 15 G. Tuscan. – pop. 374 501 alt. 49.

    See : Cathedral★★★ (Duomo) Y : east end★★★, dome★★★ (※★★) _ Campanile★★★ Y B : ※★★ _ Baptistry★★★ Y A : doors★★★, mosaics★★★ _ Cathedral Museum★★ Y M5 – Piazza della Signoria★★ Z _ Loggia della Signoria★★ Z K : Perseus★★★ by B. Cellini _ Palazzo Vecchio★★★ Z H _ Uffizi Gallery★★★ EU M – Bargello Palace and Museum★★★ EU M _ San Lorenzo★★★ DU V : Church★★, Laurentian Library★★, Medici Tombs★★★ in Medicee Chapels★★ – Medici-Riccardi Palace★★ EU S : Chapel★★★, Luca Giordano Gallery★★ Church of Santa Maria Novella★★ DU W : frescoes★★★ by Ghirlandaio – Ponte Vecchio★★ Z _ Pitti Palace★★ DV : Palatine Gallery★★★, Silver Museum★★, Works★★ by Macchiaioli in Modern Art Gallery★ – Boboli Garden★ DV : ※★ from the Citadel Belvedere _ Porcelain Museum★ DV _ Monastery and Museum of St. Mark★★ ET : works★★★ by Beato Angelico – Academy Gallery★★ ET : Michelangelo gallery★★★ _ Piazza della Santissima Annunziata★ ET **168** : frescoes★ in the church, portico★★ with corners decorated with terracotta Medallions★★ in the Foundling Hospital★ – Church of Santa Croce★★ EU : Pazzi Chapel★★ _ Excursion to the hills★★ : ※★★★ from Michelangiolo Square ETV, Church of San Miniato al Monte★★ EFV_ Strozzi Palace★★ DU S – Rucellai Palace★★ DU S _ Masaccio's frescoes★★★ in the Chapel Brancacci a Santa Maria del Carmine DUV _ Last Supper of Fuligno★ DT, Last Supper of San Salvi★ BS G _ Orsanmichele★ EU R2 : tabernacle★★ by Orcagna – La Badia EU E : campanile★, delicate relief sculpture in marble★★, tombs★, Madonna appearing to St. Bernard★ by Filippino Lippi – Sassetti Chapel★★ and the Chapel of the Annunciation★ in the Holy Trinity Church DU X _ Church of the Holy Spirit★ DUV – Last Supper★ of Sant'Appollonia ET _ All Saints' Church DU : Last Supper★ by Ghirlandaio _ Davanzati Palace★ Z M _ New Market Loggia★ Z L – Museums : Archaeological★★ (Chimera from Arezzo★★, Françoise Vase★★) ET, Science★ EU M _ Marino Marini Museum★ Z M _ Bardini Museum★ EV _ La Specola Museum★ DV.

    See also : Casa Buonarroti★ EU M _ Semi-precious Stone Workshop★ ET M _ Crucifixion★ by Perugino EU C.

    Envir. : Medicee Villas★ : villa della Petraia★, villa di Castello★, villa di Poggio a Caiano★★ by via P. Toselli CT : 17 km _ Galluzzo Carthusian Monastery★★ by via Senese CV.

    🏌 Dell'Ugolino (closed Monday except March-November), to Grassina ✉ 50015 ☎ 055 2301009, Fax 055 2301141, South : 12 km BS.

    ✈ Amerigo Vespucci North-West : 4 km by via P. Toselli CT ☎ 055 30615, Fax 055 2788400 – Alitalia, vicolo dell'Oro 1, ✉ 50123 ☎ 055 27881, Fax 055 2788400.

    🛈 via Cavour 1 r ✉ 50129 ☎ 055 290832, Fax 055 2760383.

    A.C.I. viale Amendola 36 ✉ 50121 ☎ 055 24861.

    Roma 277 – Bologna 105 – Milano 298.

LIVORNO, GENOVA

LIVORNO, GENOVA

C

D

FORTEZZA DA BASSO

PAL. D. CONGRESSI

PAL. D. AFFARI

pza d. Indipenden

135

PORTA AL PRATO

Cenacolo di Fuligno

pza Vittorio Veneto

P.te d. Vittoria

PISA LIVORNO

Lungarno Amerigo

pza Gaddi

Ognissanti

ARNO

Fonderia L. S. Rosa

PONTE VESPUCCI

Pisana

Borgo S.

Frediano

L. Guicciardini

Piazza del Carmine

S. SPIRITO

PONTE VECCHIO

S. MARIA DEL CARMINE

Piazza S. Spirito

Corridoio Vasariano

pza T. Tasso

Piazza dei Pitti

S. Felicit

Via di Bellosguardo

PALAZZO PITT

MUSEO LA SPECOLA

GIARDINO DI BOBOLI

Forte del Belvedere

PORTA ROMANA

VIOTTOLONE

PIAZZALE D. ISOLOTTO

MUSEO DELL PORCELLAN

PASSEGGIATA AI COL

C

SIENA

SIENA

SIENA

D

Traffic restricte

432

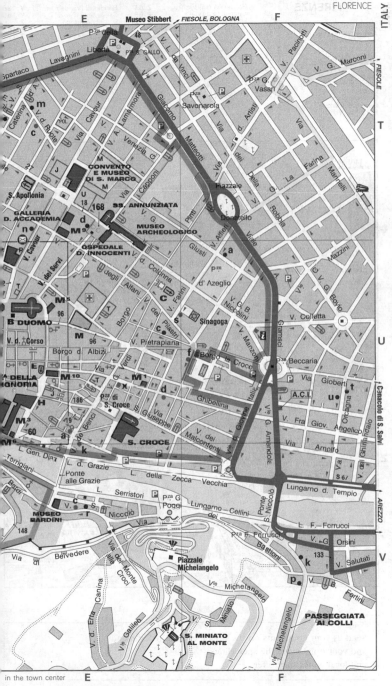

Museo Stibbert — FIESOLE, BOLOGNA

P.za della
Libertà

PTA S. GALLO
48
V. La Vinci

V. G. Pacinotti

V. G. Marconi

Lavagnini

Spartaco

Caterina   V. d. Ricoli

m

c

V. A. Caponi

V. Cavour

V. A. Lamarmora

Via   Venezia G.

J

27

CONVENTO
E MUSEO
DI S. MARCO

Giacinto

P.za G.
Vasari

P.za
Savonarola

Via   dei   Artisti

Via

La   Farina

V. G. Mannelli

Matteotti

Piazzale

99. ANNUNZIATA

S. Apollonia

GALLERIA
D. ACCADEMIA

d

n

18
168

M

MUSEO
ARCHEOLOGICO

Donatello

Robbia   G.

Della

V. G. B. Bovio

Mazzini

V. Cavour

V. dei Servi

OSPEDALE
D. INNOCENTI

V. d. Colonna

Alfani

Giusti   V. d'Alfieri   Viale

a

P.za
d' Azeglio

Via

P

V. Colletta

Borgo

degli

Farini

V. G. B
Niccolini

M

96

B DUOMO

V. d. Corso

M   96

Pinti

Borgo   d.   Albizi

V. Pietrapiana

Sinagoga

V. dei Pilastri

f

Borgo la Croce

P.za Beccaria

Via

Gioberti

A DELLA
IGNORIA

H

M 10

V. Verdi

M 1

d

186

P.za
di
S. Croce

Via
Giuseppe

Ghibellina

V. Manzoni

V. Gramsci

Via

A.C.I.

u

t

Orcagna

Canacolo di S. Salvi

M 3

60

M

x

V. de' Benci

S. CROCE

V. dei
Malcontenti

V. G. Giovine

Via   Italia

V. G. Amendole

V. Fra Giov. Angelico

Via

Arnolfo

Via   G.   Ghirlandaio

S 6/

Torrigiani

L. Gen. Diaz

k

L. d. Grazie

Ponte
alle Grazie

L.   della   Zecca   Vecchia

Lungarno d. Tempio

AREZZO

Bardi

Serristori

P.za G
Poggi

Lungarno   Cellini
dei

Ponte S. Niccolò

L. F.—Ferrucci

MUSEO
BARDINI

V.   c

S.

Niccolò

Via

148

Via   di   Belvedere

Via dei Monte
Via d. Erta Canina
Via delle Croci

Piazzale
Michelangelo

P.za F. Ferrucci

Bastioni

V. G. Orsini

k

133

V. Salutati

p

V.—B.

Fortini

V.le   Michelangelo

S. MINIATO
AL MONTE

V.le   Galileo

V.

S.   Miniato

Via   Michelangelo

PASSEGGIATA
AI COLLI

FIRENZE

Traffic restricted in the town centre

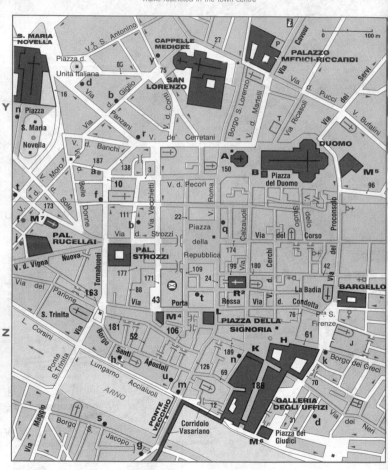

Send us your comments on the restaurants we recommend
and your opinion on the specialities
and local wines they offer.

STREET INDEX TO FIRENZE TOWN PLAN

The Westin Excelsior, piazza Ognissanti 3 ⊠ 50123 ℰ 055 264201, Fax 055 21027. – |✿|, ⇆ rm, ▤ 📺 ⚒ 🍴 ⅙ – 🏛 150. 🆎 🕄 ⓞ 🕦 𝙑𝙄𝙎𝘼 𝙅𝘾𝘽. ⅙⅙   DU |
Meals a la carte 65/100 – ⊇ 40,50 – **152 rm** 575/690, 16 suites.

Grand Hotel, piazza Ognissanti 1 ⊠ 50123 ℰ 055 288781, Fax 055 217400 – |✿| ⇆ rm, ▤ 📺 ⅙ – 🏛 220. 🆎 🕄 ⓞ 🕦 𝙑𝙄𝙎𝘼 𝙅𝘾𝘽. ⅙⅙   DU a
Meals a la carte 65/100 – ⊇ 40,50 – **90 rm** 575/690, 17 suites.

Savoy Ⓜ, piazza della Repubblica 7 ⊠ 50123 ℰ 055 27351, reservations@hotelsavoy.it Fax 055 2735888, ☞ – |✿| ▤ 📺 ⅙ ⅙ – 🏛 80. 🆎 🕄 ⓞ 🕦 𝙑𝙄𝙎𝘼. ⅙⅙   Z |
Meals a la carte 46/78 – ⊇ 23 – **98 rm** 304,71/645, 9 suites.

Grand Hotel Villa Medici, via Il Prato 42 ⊠ 50123 ℰ 055 2381331, villa.medici@ inahotels.it, Fax 055 2381336, ☞, ⅙⅙, ≘s, ⊒, ⅌ – |✿| ▤ 📺 – 🏛 90. 🆎 🕄 ⓞ 🕦 𝙑𝙄𝙎𝘼 𝙅𝘾𝘽.   CT c
Meals a la carte 56/74 – ⊇ 28,60 – **87 rm** 297/484, 14 suites.

Regency, piazza Massimo D'Azeglio 3 ⊠ 50121 ℰ 055 245247, info@regency-hote l.com, Fax 055 2346735, ☞, ⅌ – |✿| ▤ 📺 ⟷. 🆎 🕄 ⓞ 🕦 𝙑𝙄𝙎𝘼. ⅙⅙ rest   FU a
Meals *Relais le Jardin* Rest. (booking essential) a la carte 48/64 – **33 rm** ⊇ 330/462 2 suites.

Helvetia e Bristol, via dei Pescioni 2 ⊠ 50123 ℰ 055 287814, reservation.hbf@ oyaldemeure.com, Fax 055 288353 – |✿| ▤ 📺. 🆎 🕄 ⓞ 🕦 𝙑𝙄𝙎𝘼 𝙅𝘾𝘽. ⅙⅙   Z |
Meals a la carte 37/60 – ⊇ 23 – **45 rm** 214,50/473, 13 suites.

Albani, via Fiume 12 ⊠ 50123 ℰ 055 26030, hotelalbani@firenzealbergo.it Fax 055 211045 – |✿|, ⇆ rm, ▤ 📺 – 🏛 300. 🆎 🕄 ⓞ 🕦 𝙑𝙄𝙎𝘼 𝙅𝘾𝘽. ⅙⅙ rest   DT a
Meals a la carte 34/45 – **99 rm** ⊇ 217/325, 4 suites.

Gd H. Minerva Ⓜ, piazza Santa Maria Novella 16 ⊠ 50123 ℰ 055 27230 Fax 055 268281, ⊒ – |✿| ▤ 📺 – 🏛 90. 🆎 🕄 ⓞ 🕦 𝙑𝙄𝙎𝘼 𝙅𝘾𝘽. ⅙⅙ rest   Y r
Meals a la carte 39/54 – **100 rm** ⊇ 200/361, 6 suites.

Boscolo Astoria-Palazzo Gaddi, via del Giglio 9 ⊠ 50123 ℰ 055 2398095, hote l.astoria@boscolo.com, Fax 055 214632 – |✿| ▤ 📺 ⅙ – 🏛 130. 🆎 🕄 ⓞ 🕦 𝙑𝙄𝙎𝘼 𝙅𝘾𝘽. ⅙⅙ rest   Y b
Meals a la carte 37/52 – **103 rm** ⊇ 237,58/304,71, 6 suites.

Brunelleschi, piazza Santa Elisabetta 3 ⊠ 50122 ℰ 055 27370, info@hotelbrunelle schi.it, Fax 055 219653, ≤, « Small private museum in a Byzantine tower » – |✿|, ⇆ rm ▤ 📺 – 🏛 100. 🆎 🕄 ⓞ 🕦 𝙑𝙄𝙎𝘼 𝙅𝘾𝘽.   Z c
Meals (residents only) (closed Sunday) – **89 rm** ⊇ 216,91/320, 7 suites.

Grand Hotel Baglioni, piazza Unità Italiana 6 ⊠ 50123 ℰ 055 23580, info@hote baglioni.it, Fax 055 23588895, « Roof garden rest. with ≤ city » – |✿| ▤ 📺 – 🏛 200 🆎 🕄 ⓞ 🕦 𝙑𝙄𝙎𝘼 𝙅𝘾𝘽.   Y o
Meals a la carte 42/54 – **193 rm** ⊇ 210/295, 2 suites.

Lungarno, borgo Sant'Jacopo 14 ⊠ 50125 ℰ 055 27261, lungarno@lungarnohote s.com, Fax 055 268437, ≤, « Collection of modern pictures » – |✿| ▤ 📺 ⅙ – 🏛 40. 🆎 🕄 🕦 𝙑𝙄𝙎𝘼 𝙅𝘾𝘽. ⅙⅙ rest   Z s
Meals *(closed August, Sunday and lunch)* a la carte 42/52 – **56 rm** ⊇ 323/363, 5 suites.

Sofitel Ⓜ, via de' Cerretani 10 ⊠ 50123 ℰ 055 2381301, sofitel@tin.it, Fax 055 2381312 – |✿|, ⇆ rm, ▤ 📺 ⅙. 🆎 🕄 ⓞ 🕦 𝙑𝙄𝙎𝘼 𝙅𝘾𝘽. ⅙⅙   Y r
Meals *Il Patio* Rest. a la carte 29/32 – **83 rm** ⊇ 305/352, suite.

Gallery Hotel Art Ⓜ, piazzetta dell'Oro 5 ⊠ 50123 ℰ 06 055 27263, gallery@lur gamohotels.com, Fax 055 268557, « Contemporary design and cosmopolitan art » – |✿|, ⇆ rm, ▤ 📺. 🆎 🕄 ⓞ 🕦 𝙑𝙄𝙎𝘼 𝙅𝘾𝘽   Z u
Meals *The Fusion Bar Shozan Gallery* Rest. a la carte 23/39 – **61 rm** ⊇ 290/392, 4 suites.

Starhotel Michelangelo, viale Fratelli Rosselli 2 ⊠ 50123 ℰ 055 2784, michelang elo.fi@starhotels.it, Fax 055 2382232 – |✿|, ⇆ rm, ▤ 📺 – 🏛 250. 🆎 🕄 ⓞ 🕦 𝙑𝙄𝙎𝘼 𝙅𝘾𝘽. ⅙⅙   CT f
Meals (residents only) a la carte 45/64 – **117 rm** ⊇ 269/372.

De la Ville without rest., piazza Antinori 1 ⊠ 50123 ℰ 055 2381805, delaville@fire nze.net, Fax 055 2381809 – |✿| ▤ 📺 ⅙ – 🏛 60. 🆎 🕄 ⓞ 🕦 𝙑𝙄𝙎𝘼 𝙅𝘾𝘽. ⅙⅙   Y l
71 rm ⊇ 216,91/392,50, 4 suites.

Londra, via Jacopo da Diacceto 18 ⊠ 50123 ℰ 055 27390, info@hotellondra.com, Fax 055 210682, ☞, ⅙⅙, ≘s – |✿|, ⇆ rm, ▤ 📺 ⟷ – 🏛 200. 🆎 🕄 ⓞ 🕦 𝙑𝙄𝙎𝘼 𝙅𝘾𝘽. ⅙⅙ rest   DT h
Meals a la carte 39/50 – **158 rm** ⊇ 190/269.

J and J without rest., via di Mezzo 20 ⊠ 50121 ℰ 055 263121, jandj@dada.it, Fax 055 240282 – ▤ 📺. 🆎 🕄 ⓞ 🕦 𝙑𝙄𝙎𝘼 𝙅𝘾𝘽. ⅙⅙   EU c
15 rm ⊇ 300, 5 suites.

Continental without rest., lungarno Acciaiuoli 2 ⊠ 50123 ℰ 055 27262, *continental@lungarnohotels.com*, Fax 055 283139, « Floral terrace with ≤ » – |≱| ▤ 🆃🆅 ♿ – 🅰 400. 🝳 🖪 ⓪ 🅜🅞 🆅🅘🆂🅐 🅙🅒🅑
closed until April – **47 rm** ⊐ 212/284, suite.   Z m

Montebello Splendid, via Montebello 60 ⊠ 50123 ℰ 055 2398051, *info@montebellosplendid.com*, Fax 055 211867, ☞ – |≱| ▤ 🆃🆅 ♨ – 🅰 100. 🝳 🖪 ⓪ 🅜🅞 🆅🅘🆂🅐
🅙🅒🅑. ⅍ rest   CU e
Meals a la carte 37/56 – ⊐ 18 – **53 rm** 180/310, suite.

Berchielli without rest., lungarno Acciaiuoli 14 ⊠ 50123 ℰ 055 264061, *info@berchielli.it*, Fax 055 218636, ≤ – |≱| ▤ 🆃🆅 – 🅰 100. 🝳 🖪 ⓪ 🅜🅞 🆅🅘🆂🅐 🅙🅒🅑. ⅍   Z h
76 rm ⊐ 217/304.

Pierre without rest., via De' Lamberti 5 ⊠ 50123 ℰ 055 216218, *pierre@remarhotels.com*, Fax 055 2396573 – |≱| ▤ 🆃🆅. 🝳 🖪 ⓪ 🅜🅞 🆅🅘🆂🅐 🅙🅒🅑. ⅍   Z t
44 rm ⊐ 248/335,80.

Rivoli without rest., via della Scala 33 ⊠ 50123 ℰ 055 282853, *hotel.rivoli@firenzealbergo.it*, Fax 055 294041, ☞ – |≱| ▤ 🆃🆅 ♿ – 🅰 100. 🝳 🖪 ⓪ 🅜🅞 🆅🅘🆂🅐 🅙🅒🅑. ⅍
65 rm ⊐ 201/304,50.   DU m

Executive without rest., via Curtatone 5 ⊠ 50123 ℰ 055 217451, *info@hotelexecutive.it*, Fax 055 268346 – |≱| ▤ 🆃🆅 – 🅰 50. 🝳 🖪 ⓪ 🅜🅞 🆅🅘🆂🅐 🅙🅒🅑   CU k
38 rm ⊐ 181/258.

Il Guelfo Bianco without rest., via Cavour 29 ⊠ 50129 ℰ 055 288330, *info@ilguelfobianco.it*, Fax 055 295203 – |≱| ▤ 🆃🆅 ♿. 🝳 🖪 🅜🅞 🆅🅘🆂🅐. ⅍   ET n
30 rm ⊐ 133/208.

Porta Faenza without rest., via Faenza 77 ⊠ 50123 ℰ 055 217975, *info@hotelportafaenza.it*, Fax 055 210101 – |≱| ⅍≒ ▤ 🆃🆅 ♿ 🚗 – 🅰 30. 🝳 🖪 ⓪ 🅜🅞 🆅🅘🆂🅐 🅙🅒🅑
25 rm ⊐ 180/206,58.   DT d

Botticelli without rest., via Taddea 8 ⊠ 50123 ℰ 055 290905, *botticelli@fi.flashnet.it*, Fax 055 294322 – |≱| ▤ 🆃🆅 ♿. 🝳 🖪 ⓪ 🅜🅞 🆅🅘🆂🅐 🅙🅒🅑   ET p
34 rm ⊐ 127/204.

Palazzo Benci without rest., piazza Madonna degli Aldobrandini 3 ⊠ 50123 ℰ 055 2382821, *palazzobenci@iol.it*, Fax 055 288308, ☞ – |≱| ▤ 🆃🆅 – 🅰 30. 🝳 🖪 ⓪ 🅜🅞 🆅🅘🆂🅐 🅙🅒🅑.   Y y
35 rm ⊐ 104/192.

Royal without rest., via delle Ruote 52 ⊠ 50129 ℰ 055 483287, Fax 055 490976, « Garden » – |≱| ▤ 🆃🆅 🅿. 🝳 🖪 ⓪ 🅜🅞 🆅🅘🆂🅐 🅙🅒🅑. ⅍   ET m
39 rm ⊐ 113,62/185,92.

De Rose Palace Hotel without rest., via Solferino 5 ⊠ 50123 ℰ 055 2396818, *info@hotelderose.it*, Fax 055 268249 – |≱| ▤ 🆃🆅. 🝳 🖪 ⓪ 🅜🅞 🆅🅘🆂🅐 🅙🅒🅑   CU c
18 rm ⊐ 135/210.

Loggiato dei Servi without rest., piazza SS. Annunziata 3 ⊠ 50122 ℰ 055 289592, *info@loggiatodeiservitihotel.it*, Fax 055 289595, « 16C building » – |≱| ▤ 🆃🆅. 🝳 🖪 ⓪
🅜🅞 🆅🅘🆂🅐 🅙🅒🅑   ET d
25 rm ⊽ 139,44/201,41, 4 suites.

Malaspina without rest., piazza dell'Indipendenza 24 ⊠ 50129 ℰ 055 489869, *info@malaspinahotel.it*, Fax 055 474809 – |≱| ▤ 🆃🆅 ♿. 🝳 🖪 ⓪ 🅜🅞 🆅🅘🆂🅐. ⅍   ET g
31 rm ⊐ 120/185.

Select without rest., via Giuseppe Galliano 24 ⊠ 50144 ℰ 055 330342, *info@selecthotel.it*, Fax 055 351506 – |≱|, ⅍≒ rm, ▤ – 🅰 25. 🝳 🖪 ⓪ 🅜🅞 🆅🅘🆂🅐   CT t
closed 20 to 27 December – ⊐ 6 – **39 rm** 155/199.

Villa Liberty without rest., viale Michelangiolo 40 ⊠ 50125 ℰ 055 6810581, *info@hotelvillaliberty.com*, Fax 055 6812595, ☞ – |≱| ⅍≒ ▤ 🆃🆅 🅿. 🝳 🖪 ⓪ 🅜🅞 🆅🅘🆂🅐
🅙🅒🅑   FV p
16 rm ⊐ 149,77/185,92, suite.

Ville sull'Arno, Lungarno Colombo 3 ⊠ 50136 ℰ 055 670971, *hotel@villesullarno.it*, Fax 055 678244, ≤, « Small garden with 🛝 » – ▤ 🆃🆅 ♿ 🚗 🅿 – 🅰 25. 🝳 🖪 ⓪ 🅜🅞
🆅🅘🆂🅐. ⅍ rest   by lungarno del Tempio FV
Meals (residents only) a la carte 34/44 – **47 cam** ⊐ 140/220.

Pitti Palace without rest., via Barbadori 2 ⊠ 50125 ℰ 055 2398711, *pittipalace@vivahotels.com*, Fax 055 2398867, « Terrace with ≤ » – |≱| ▤ 🆃🆅. 🝳 🖪 ⓪ 🅜🅞 🆅🅘🆂🅐 🅙🅒🅑.
⅍   Z g
⊐ 12,91 – **71 rm** 123/196, suite.

Rosary Garden without rest., via di Ripoli 169 ℰ 055 6800136, *info@rosarygarden.it*, Fax 055 6800458 – ▤ 🆃🆅 🅿. 🝳 🖪 ⓪ 🅜🅞 🆅🅘🆂🅐. ⅍   by via Salutati FV
14 rm ⊐ 134,28/160,10.

🏠 **Unicorno** without rest., via dei Fossi 27 ⊠ 50123 ℰ 055 287313, hotel.unicorno@u
sa.net, Fax 055 268332 – |$|, ✦ rm, ▤ 🆃🆅, 🅰🅴 🆂 🅾 🅼🅾 𝘝𝘐𝘚𝘈 𝗝𝗖𝗕. ❄
28 rm ⊇ 93/176.

🏠 **Rapallo** without rest., via di Santa Caterina d'Alessandria 7 ⊠ 50129 ℰ 055 472412
rapallo@dinonet.it, Fax 055 470385 – |$| ▤ 🆃🆅, 🅰🅴 🆂 🅾 🅼🅾 𝘝𝘐𝘚𝘈   ET g
⊇ 12,92 – **27 rm** 118,79/180,76.

🏠 **Silla** without rest., via dei Renai 5 ⊠ 50125 ℰ 055 2342888, hotelsilla@tin.it,
Fax 055 2341437 – |$| ▤ 🆃🆅 ◁, 🅰🅴 🆂 🅾 🅼🅾 𝘝𝘐𝘚𝘈   EV r
36 rm ⊇ 140/160.

XXXXX   **Enoteca Pinchiorri**, via Ghibellina 87 ⊠ 50122 ℰ 055 242777, enoteca.pinchiorr
❀❀   @pronet.it, Fax 055 244983, « Summer service in an open courtyard » – ▤. 🅰🅴 🆂 🅼🅾
𝘝𝘐𝘚𝘈 𝗝𝗖𝗕.   EU x
closed August, Christmas, New Year, Sunday, Monday, and Tuesday-Wednesday lunch –
Meals (booking essential) 145/150 (dinner) and a la carte 135/186
Spec. Astice con melanzane caramellate, purea di datteri, salsa corallo e pepe di Sechuan. Trofie
con melanzane alla griglia, pomodoro al basilico e mozarella affumicata. Anatra glassata al
miele di ciliegio, cosce farcite di fegato grasso e bietole, frittelle di ananas e insalata di
indivia e noci.

XXX   **Don Chisciotte**, via Ridolfi 4 r ⊠ 50129 ℰ 055 475430, Fax 055 485305 – ▤. 🅰🅴 🆂
🅾 🅼🅾 𝘝𝘐𝘚𝘈 𝗝𝗖𝗕. ❄   DT x
closed August, Sunday and Monday lunch – **Meals** (booking essential) a la carte 41/55
(10 %).

XXX   **Taverna del Bronzino**, via delle Ruote 25/27 r ⊠ 50129 ℰ 055 495220,
Fax 055 4620076 – ▤. 🅰🅴 🆂 🅾 🅼🅾 𝘝𝘐𝘚𝘈 𝗝𝗖𝗕   ET c
closed Easter, August, Christmas and Sunday – **Meals** (booking essential) a la carte 52/66.

XX   **Cibreo**, via dei Macci 118/r ⊠ 50122 ℰ 055 2341100, cibreo.fi@tin.it, Fax 055 244966
– ▤. 🅰🅴 🆂 🅾 🅼🅾 𝘝𝘐𝘚𝘈 𝗝𝗖𝗕   FU f
closed 26 July-6 September, 31 December-6 January, Sunday and Monday – **Meals** (booking
essential) a la carte 56/65 see also rest. **Vineria Cibreino**.

XX   **Osteria n. 1**, via del Moro 20 r ⊠ 50123 ℰ 055 284897, Fax 055 294318 – ▤. 🅰🅴
🆂 🅾 🅼🅾 𝘝𝘐𝘚𝘈   Z f
closed 3 to 26 August, Sunday and Monday lunch – **Meals** a la carte 40/66.

XX   **Buca Lapi**, vid el Trebbio 1 r ⊠ 50123 ℰ 055 213768, Fax 055 284862 – ▤. 🅰🅴 🆂
🅾 🅼🅾 𝘝𝘐𝘚𝘈 𝗝𝗖𝗕. ❄   Y a
closed August, Sunday and Monday lunch – **Meals** (booking essential for dinner) a la carte
41/55 (10 %).

XX   **Enoteca Pane e Vino**, via di San Niccolò 70 a/r ⊠ 50125 ℰ 055 2476956, pane
evino@yahoo.it, Fax 055 2476956 – ▤. 🅰🅴 🆂 🅾 🅼🅾 𝘝𝘐𝘚𝘈. ❄   EV c
closed 7 to 21 August and Sunday – **Meals** (dinner only) 30 and a la carte 28/38.

XX   **I 4 Amici**, via degli Orti Orticellari 29 ⊠ 50123 ℰ 055 215413, iquattroamici@acca
demiadelgusto.it, Fax 055 289767 – ▤. 🅰🅴 🅾 🅼🅾 𝘝𝘐𝘚𝘈 𝗝𝗖𝗕. ❄   DT e
Meals seafood a la carte 34/72 (12 %).

XX   **Mamma Gina**, borgo Sant'Jacopo 37 r ⊠ 50125 ℰ 055 2396009, info@mammagina.it,
Fax 055 213908 – ▤. 🅰🅴 🆂 🅾 🅼🅾 𝘝𝘐𝘚𝘈 𝗝𝗖𝗕. ❄   Z s
closed 7 to 20 August and Sunday – **Meals** a la carte 37/46.

XX   **La Baraonda**, via Ghibellina 67 r ⊠ 50122 ℰ 055 2341171, labaraonda@tin.it,
Fax 055 2341171 – 🆂 🅾 🅼🅾 𝘝𝘐𝘚𝘈. ❄   EU d
closed August, 3 to 9 January, Sunday and Monday lunch – **Meals** (booking essential) a
la carte 25/39 (10 %).

X   **Vineria Cibreino** - Cibreo Rest., via dei Macci 122/r ⊠ 50122 ℰ 055 2341100 – ▤
⊛   closed 26 July-6 September, 31 December-6 January, Sunday and Monday – **Meals** (few
tables available ; no booking) a la carte 22/27.   FU f

X   **Il Profeta**, borgo Ognissanti 93 r ⊠ 50123 ℰ 055 212265 – ▤. 🅰🅴 🆂 🅾 🅼🅾
𝘝𝘐𝘚𝘈   DU c
closed 15 to 31 August and Sunday – **Meals** à la carte 36/46.

X   **Baldini**, via il Prato 96 r ⊠ 50123 ℰ 055 287663, Fax 055 287663 – ▤. 🅰🅴 🆂 🅾 🅼🅾
𝘝𝘐𝘚𝘈. ❄   CT h
closed 1 to 20 August, 24 December-3 January, Saturday and Sunday dinner, June-July
also Sunday lunch – **Meals** a la carte 23/35.

X   **Del Fagioli**, corso Tintori 47 r ⊠ 50122 ℰ 055 244285, Typical Tuscan trattoria –
⊛   ❄   EV k
closed August, Saturday and Sunday – **Meals** a la carte 22/30.

X   **Del Carmine**, piazza del Carmine 18 r ⊠ 50124 ℰ 055 218601, 🍴 – 🅰🅴 🅾 🅼🅾
𝘝𝘐𝘚𝘈 𝗝𝗖𝗕. ❄   DU k
closed 7 to 21 August and Sunday – **Meals** (booking essential) a la carte 20/28.

✕ **Osteria de' Benci**, via de' Benci 10/13 r ⊠ 50122 ✆ 055 2344923, customers@o
steriadebenci.com, Fax 055 2344932, 😭 – 🗏. ₳ℇ 🖸 ⓞ ⓸ 𝗩𝗜𝗦𝗔   EU a
closed Sunday – **Meals** (booking essential) a la carte 20/39 (10 %).

✕ **Il Latini**, via dei Palchetti 6 r ⊠ 50123 ✆ 055 210916, Fax 055 289794, Typical trattoria
– ₳ℇ 🖸 ⓞ 𝗩𝗜𝗦𝗔 𝗝𝗖𝗕. ⅗   Z j
closed 24 December-5 January and Monday – **Meals** a la carte 25/30.

✕ **Alla Vecchia Bettola**, viale Ludovico Ariosto 32 r ⊠ 50124 ✆ 055 224158,
Fax 055 223061, « Typical atmosphere » – ⅗   CV m
closed August, 23 December-2 January, Sunday and Monday – **Meals** a la carte 25/35.

✕ **Ruth's**, via Farini 2 ⊠ 50121 ✆ 055 2480888 – 🗏   EU s
closed Friday dinner, Saturday lunch and Jewish holidays – **Meals** (booking essential) Jewish
rest. a la carte 20/25.

on the hills South : 3 km :

🏨 **Gd H. Villa Cora** ⅘, viale Machiavelli 18 ⊠ 50125 ✆ 055 2298451, reservations@v
illacora.it, Fax 055 229086, 😭, Shuttle service to city centre, « 19C house in floral park
with ⛱ » – 🛗 🗏 🗏 🆃🆅 🅿 – 🕍 150. ₳ℇ 🖸 ⓞ ⓸ 𝗩𝗜𝗦𝗔 𝗝𝗖𝗕. ⅗ rest   DV b
Meals *Taverna Machiavelli* Rest. a la carte 56/92 – **48 rm** � 270/490, 9 suites.

🏨 **Torre di Bellosguardo** ⅘ without rest., via Roti Michelozzi 2 ⊠ 50124
✆ 055 2298145, torredibellosguardo@dada.it, Fax 055 229008, ⅙ town and hills, « Park
with botanical garden, aviary and ⛱ » – 🛗 🅿. ₳ℇ 🖸 ⓞ ⓸ 𝗩𝗜𝗦𝗔 𝗝𝗖𝗕   CV a
⊠ 20 – **10 rm** 160/280, 7 suites 330/380.

🏨 **Villa Belvedere** ⅘ without rest., via Benedetto Castelli 3 ⊠ 50124 ✆ 055 222501,
Fax 055 223163, ⅙ town and hills, « Garden-park with ⛱ », ⅗ – 🛗 🗏 🆃🆅 🅿. ₳ℇ 🖸 ⓞ
⓸ 𝗩𝗜𝗦𝗔.   by via Senese CV
March-November – **23 rm** ⊠ 130/207, 3 suites.

🏨 **Classic** without rest., viale Machiavelli 25 ⊠ 50125 ✆ 055 229351, info@classichotel.it,
Fax 055 229553, 🌳 – 🛗 🆃🆅 🅿. ₳ℇ 🖸 ⓞ ⓸ 𝗩𝗜𝗦𝗔   DV c
⊠ 8 – **19 rm** 90/177.

at Arcetri South : 5 km

🏨 **Villa Montartino**, via Silvani 151 ✆ 051 223520, info@montartino.com,
Fax 051 223495, ⅙ the hills, countryside and the Certosa, 😭, « Elegant villa on the hills »,
⛱ heated, 🌳 – 🗏 🆃🆅 🅿 – 🕍 40. ₳ℇ 🖸 ⓞ 𝗩𝗜𝗦𝗔. ⅗
Meals (residents only) 41/62 – **7 rm** ⊠ 268/361.

at Candeli East : 7 km – ⊠ 50012 :

🏨 **Villa La Massa** ⅘, via La Massa 24 ✆ 055 62611, info@villalamassa.com,
Fax 055 633102, ⅙, 😭, « 17C mansion decorated and furnished in period style », ⛱,
🌳 – 🛗 🗏 🆃🆅 ⅙ 🅿 – 🕍 60. ₳ℇ 🖸 ⓞ ⓸ 𝗩𝗜𝗦𝗔 𝗝𝗖𝗕. ⅗ rest
March-November – **Meals** *Il Verrocchio* Rest. a la carte 81/124 – **37 rm** ⊠ 380/705,
10 suites.

on the motorway at ring-road A1-A11 Florence North North-West : 10 km :

🏨 **Holiday Inn Firenze Nord**, ⊠ 50013 Campi Bisenzio ✆ 055 4471111, holidayinn.
firenze@alliancealberghi.com, Fax 055 4219015 – 🛗, ⅙× rm, 🗏 🆃🆅 ⅙ 🗏 – 🕍 200. ₳ℇ
🖸 ⓞ ⓸ 𝗩𝗜𝗦𝗔. ⅗ rest
Meals (closed Sunday) a la carte 36/46 – **148 rm** ⊠ 182/207.

close to motorway station A1 Florence South South-East : 6 km :

🏨 Sheraton Firenze Hotel, via Agnelli 33 ⊠ 50126 ✆ 055 64901, sheraton@dada.it,
Fax 055 6490769, ⛱, ⅗ – 🛗, ⅙× rm, 🗏 🆃🆅 ⅙ 🗏 – 🕍 1500
319 rm.

Colle di Val d'Elsa 53034 Siena 𝟒𝟑𝟎 L 15 G. Toscana. – pop. 19 292 alt. 223.
🅑 via Campana 43 ✆ 0577 922791, Fax 0577 922621.
Roma 255 – Arezzo 88 – Firenze 50 – Pisa 87 – Siena 24.

✕✕✕ **Arnolfo** with rm, via XX Settembre 52 ✆ 0577 920549, arnolfo@arnolfo.com,
❀❀ Fax 0577 920549, « Summer evening service on terrace » – 🗏 🆃🆅. ₳ℇ 🖸 ⓞ ⓸ 𝗩𝗜𝗦𝗔.
⅗
closed 1 to 8 August and 10 January-13 February – **Meals** (closed Tuesday, Wednesday,
Christmas dinner and New Year lunch) (booking essential) 62/67 and a la carte 55/73 –
4 rm ⊠ 130/160
Spec. Tortelli di piccione velati al fegato d'oca con brodo ristretto al Chianti (autumn-
winter). Filetto di coniglio profumato al timo con fagioli zolfini di Pratomagno (spring).
Capretto delle crete senesi alle erbe fini con carciofi in casseruola (spring).

San Casciano in Val di Pesa *50026 Firenze* 429, 430 L 15 *G. Toscana. – pop. 16 284 alt. 306.*
Roma 283 – Firenze 17 – Livorno 84 – Siena 53.

a Cerbaia *North-West : 6 km –* ⊠ *50020 :*

XXXX **La Tenda Rossa,** piazza del Monumento 9/14 ℰ 055 826132, *latendarossa@tin.it,*
糸糸糸 Fax 055 825210 – 🞐. 🗚🗎 🚫 🞐 🞐 *VISA* 🞐. 🞐
closed August, Christmas, Sunday and Monday lunch – **Meals** (booking essential) a la carte
61/91
Spec. Carpaccio di code di scampi in extravergine alle erbe aromatiche con "cassata" di pomodoro al basilico (spring-summer). Tortelli di cinta senese in sfoglia di cruschello aromatizzata al finocchio selvatico con petali di cipolla dolce e cubetti di fegato grasso. Petto di piccione farcito sottopelle con fegato grasso e tartufo nero di Norcia in salsa al balsamico (January-April).

San Vincenzo *57027 Livorno* 430 M 13 *G. Toscana. – pop. 6 837 – High Season : 15 June-15 September.*
🞐 *via Beatrice Alliata 2* ℰ *0565 701533, Fax 0565 706914.*
Roma 260 – Firenze 146 – Grosseto 73 – Livorno 60 – Piombino 21 – Siena 109.

XXX **Gambero Rosso,** piazza della Vittoria 13 ℰ 0565 701021, Fax 0565 704542, ≼ – 🞐.
糸糸 🗚🗎 🚫 🞐 🞐 *VISA*
closed 27 October-18 December, Monday and Tuesday – **Meals** (booking essential) 75/90
and a la carte 60/100
Spec. Passatina di ceci con gamberi. Ravioli di cipolle. Coda di rospo con guanciale e capperi.

MILAN (MILANO) *20100* 🄿 428 F 9 *G. Italy. – pop. 1 301 551 alt. 122.*
See : *Cathedral*★★★ *(Duomo)* MZ *– Cathedral Museum*★★ MZ **M** *– Via and Piazza Mercanti*★
MZ **155** _ *La Scala Opera House*★★ MZ _ *Manzoni House*★ MZ **M** _ *Brera Art Gallery*★★★
KV _ *Castle of the Sforza*★★★ JV *– Ambrosian Pinacoteca*★★ MZ : *Raphael's cartoons*★★★
and Basket of fruit★★★ *by Caravaggio – Poldi-Pezzoli Museum*★ KV **M** : *portrait of a woman*★★★ *(in profile) by Pollaiolo – Palazzo Bagatti Valsecchi*★★ KV **L** _ *Natural History Museum*★ LV **M** *– Leonardo da Vinci Museum of Science and Technology*★ HX **M** *– Church of St. Mary of Grace*★ HX : *Leonardo da Vinci's Last Supper*★★★ *– Basilica of St. Ambrose*★★
HJX : *altar front*★★ *– Church of St. Eustorgius*★ JY – *Portinari Chapel*★★ *– General Hospital*★ KXY *– Church of St. Satiro*★ : *dome*★ MZ *– Church of St. Maurice*★★ JX *– Church of St. Lawrence Major*★ JY.
Envir. : *Chiaravalle Abbey*★ *South-East : 7 km by corso Lodi* FGS_ *Motor-Racing circuit at Monza Park North : 20 km* ℰ *039 24821.*
🞐 *(closed Monday) at Monza Park* ⊠ *20052 Monza* ℰ *039 303081, Fax 039 304427, North : 20 km;*
🞐 *Molinetto (closed Monday) at Cernusco sul Naviglio* ⊠ *20063* ℰ *02 92105128, Fax 02 92106635, North-East : 14 km;*
🞐 *Barlassina (closed Monday) at Lentate sul Seveso* ⊠ *20030* ℰ *0362 560621, Fax 0362 560934, North : 26 km;*
🞐 *(closed Monday) at Zoate di Tribiano* ⊠ *20067* ℰ *02 90632183, Fax 02 90631861, South-East : 20 km;*
🞐 *Le Rovedine (closed Monday) at Noverasco di Opera* ⊠ *20090* ℰ *02 57606420, Fax 02 57606405, by via Ripamonti* FS.
🞐 *Forlanini of Linate East : 8 km* ℰ *02 74852200.*
🞐 *Malpensa North-West : 45 km – Alitalia Sede* ℰ *02 24991, corso Como 15* ⊠ *20154* ℰ *02 24992500, Fax 02 24992525 and via Albricci 5* ⊠ *20122* ℰ *02 24992700, Fax 02 8056757.*
🞐 *via Marconi 1* ⊠ *20123* ℰ *02 725241, Fax 02 72524350 –* **Central Station** ⊠ *20124*
ℰ *02 72524360.*
🞐🄰.🄲.🄸 *corso Venezia 43* ⊠ *20121* ℰ *02 77451.*
Roma 572 – Genève 323 – Genova 142 – Torino 140.

Plans on following pages

Historical centre _ Duomo, Scala, Sforza Castle, corso Magenta, via Torino, corso Vittorio Emanuele, via Manzoni

🞐🞐 **Four Seasons,** via Gesù 8 ⊠ 20121 ℰ 02 77088, *milano@fourseasons.com,*
Fax 02 77085000, « In a 15C convent », 🞐, 🞐 – 🞐 🞐 🞐 🞐 🞐 🞐 🞐 – 🞐 280.
🗚🗎 🚫 🞐 🞐 *VISA* 🞐. 🞐 rest   KV a
Meals *Il Teatro* Rest. *(closed August, Sunday and lunch)* a la carte 46/69 and **La Veranda**
Rest. a la carte 40/59 – 🞐 28 – **77 rm** 475/705, 41 suites.

🏨🏨🏨 **Grand Hotel et de Milan**, via Manzoni 29 ✉ 20121 ✆ 02 723141, *infos@grand hoteletdemilan.it*, Fax 02 86460861, *ʄ₆* – 🛗 🔲 📺 ✆ – 🔥 100. 🅰🅴 🆂 ⑩ ⓜ🌑 𝘝𝘐𝘚𝘈
🄹🄲🄱. ✷ rest KV g
Meals *Caruso* Rest. *(closed dinner)* a la carte 49/78 see also rest **Don Carlos** below –
⊠ 28 – **88 rm** 339/493, 8 suites.

🏨🏨🏨 **Carlton Hotel Baglioni**, via Senato 5 ✉ 20121 ✆ 02 77077, *carlton.milano@bagl ionihotels.com*, Fax 02 783300 – 🛗, ✫ rm, 🔲 📺 ⅙ ↞. 🅰🅴 🆂 ⑩ ⓜ🌑 𝘝𝘐𝘚𝘈
🄹🄲🄱 ✷ rest KV b
Meals a la carte 53/73 – ⊠ 15 – **60 rm** 310/465, 2 suites.

🏨🏨🏨 **Grand Hotel Duomo**, via San Raffaele 1 ✉ 20121 ✆ 02 8833, Fax 02 86462027, ≤
Duomo, 🍽 – 🛗, ✫ rm, 🔲 📺 – 🔥 100. 🅰🅴 🆂 ⑩ ⓜ🌑 𝘝𝘐𝘚𝘈 🄹🄲🄱. ✷ MZ u
Meals a la carte 40/59 – ⊠ 12,91 – **142 rm** 227,24/490,63, 17 suites.

🏨🏨🏨 **Jolly Hotel President**, largo Augusto 10 ✉ 20122 ✆ 02 77461, Fax 02 783449 –
🛗, ✫ rm, 🔲 📺 ✆ – 🔥 100 🅰🅴 ⑩ ⓜ🌑 𝘝𝘐𝘚𝘈 🄹🄲🄱. ✷ rest NZ q
Meals a la carte 38/48 – **242 rm** ⊠ 227/330, 18 suite.

🏨🏨🏨 **Starhotel Rosa**, via Pattari 5 ✉ 20122 ✆ 02 8831, *rosa.mi@starhotels.it*,
Fax 02 8057964 – 🛗, ✫ rm, 🔲 📺 ✆ – 🔥 130. 🅰🅴 🆂 ⑩ ⓜ🌑 𝘝𝘐𝘚𝘈. ✷ NZ v
Meals a la carte 30/60 – **250 rm** ⊠ 374/390, 10 suites.

🏨🏨🏨 **Brunelleschi** Ⓜ, via Baracchini 12 ✉ 20123 ✆ 02 88431, Fax 02 804924 – 🛗 🔲 📺
⅙. 🅰🅴 🆂 ⑩ ⓜ🌑 𝘝𝘐𝘚𝘈 🄹🄲🄱. MZ z
Meals a la carte 37/54 – **123 rm** ⊠ 225/275, 5 suites.

🏨🏨🏨 **Sir Edward**, via Mazzini 4 ✉ 20123 ✆ 02 877877, *siredw@infosquare.it*,
Fax 02 877844, ⇌ – 🛗 ✫ 🔲 📺 ✆ ⅙. 🅰🅴 🆂 ⑩ ⓜ🌑 𝘝𝘐𝘚𝘈 🄹🄲🄱. ✷ MZ h
Meals only dinner snack – **38 rm** ⊠ 200/250, suite.

🏨🏨🏨 **Spadari al Duomo** Ⓜ, via Spadari 11 ✉ 20123 ✆ 02 72002371, *reservation@spa darihotel.com*, Fax 02 861184, « Collection of modern art » – 🛗 🔲 📺 ✆. 🅰🅴 🆂 ⑩ ⓜ🌑
𝘝𝘐𝘚𝘈 🄹🄲🄱. ✷ MZ f
Meals only snack – **39 rm** ⊠ 208/268, suite.

🏨🏨🏨 **Una Hotel Cusani**, via Cusani 13 ✉ 20121 ✆ 02 85601, *una.cusani@unahotel.it*,
Fax 02 8693601 – 🛗 🔲 📺 ✆ ↞. 🅰🅴 🆂 ⑩ ⓜ🌑 𝘝𝘐𝘚𝘈 🄹🄲🄱. ✷ JV a
Meals a la carte 51/65 – **87 rm** ⊠ 540, 5 suites.

🏨🏨🏨 **De la Ville** Ⓜ, via Hoepli 6 ✉ 20121 ✆ 02 867651, *delaville@tin.it*, Fax 02 866609,
ʄ₆, ⇌ – 🛗, ✫ rm, 🔲 📺 ✆ ↞ – 🔥 85. 🅰🅴 🆂 ⑩ ⓜ🌑 𝘝𝘐𝘚𝘈 NZ h
Meals a la carte 33/44 – **108 rm** ⊠ 295,90/341, suite.

🏨🏨🏨 **Cavour**, via Fatebenefratelli 21 ✉ 20121 ✆ 02 6572051, *hotel.cavour@traveleurope.it*,
Fax 02 6592263 – 🛗 🔲 📺 ✆ – 🔥 100. 🅰🅴 🆂 ⑩ ⓜ🌑 𝘝𝘐𝘚𝘈 🄹🄲🄱. ✷ KV x
closed August and 24 December-6 January – **Meals** (see rest. **Conte Camillo** below) –
113 rm ⊠ 174/228.

🏨🏨🏨 **Galileo**, corso Europa 9 ✉ 20122 ✆ 02 77431, *galileo4milanhotel.it*, Fax 02 76020584
– 🛗 🔲 📺 – 🔥 30. 🅰🅴 🆂 ⑩ ⓜ🌑 𝘝𝘐𝘚𝘈 🄹🄲🄱. NZ x
Meals a la carte 37/46 – **81 rm** ⊠ 191,09/258,23, 8 suites.

🏨🏨🏨 **Regina** without rest., via Cesare Correnti 13 ✉ 20123 ✆ 02 58106913,
Fax 02 58107033, « 18C building » – 🛗 🔲 📺 ⅙ – 🔥 40. 🅰🅴 🆂 ⑩ ⓜ🌑 𝘝𝘐𝘚𝘈 🄹🄲🄱
closed August and 23 December-7 January – **43 rm** ⊠ 129/238. JY a

🏨🏨🏨 **Dei Cavalieri**, piazza Missori 1 ✉ 20123 ✆ 02 88571, *hl@hoteldeicavalieri.com*,
Fax 02 72021683, « Panoramic terrace » – 🛗 🔲 📺 – 🔥 150. 🅰🅴 🆂 ⑩ ⓜ🌑 𝘝𝘐𝘚𝘈
🄹🄲🄱. ✷ rest MZ m
Meals a la carte 43/70 – **188 rm** ⊠ 237,57/340,86, 7 suites.

🏨🏨🏨 **Carrobbio** without rest., via Medici 3 ✉ 20123 ✆ 02 89010740, *hotelcarrobbio@tr aveleurope.it*, Fax 02 8053334 – 🛗 🔲 📺 ⅙ – 🔥 30. 🅰🅴 🆂 ⑩ ⓜ🌑 𝘝𝘐𝘚𝘈 🄹🄲🄱 JX d
closed August and 22 December-6 January – ⊠ 13 – **56 rm** 180/256.

🏨🏨🏨 **Ascot** without rest., via Lentasio 3/5 ✉ 20122 ✆ 02 58303300, *info4hotelascotmila no.it*, Fax 02 58303203 – 🛗 🔲 📺. 🅰🅴 🆂 ⑩ ⓜ🌑 𝘝𝘐𝘚𝘈. ✷ KY c
closed 23 December-6 January – **64 rm** ⊠ 134/310.

🏨🏨🏨 **Manzoni** without rest., via Santo Spirito 20 ✉ 20121 ✆ 02 76005700, *hotel.manzo ni@tin.it*, Fax 02 784212 – 🛗 🔲 📺 ✆ ↞. 🅰🅴 🆂 ⑩ ⓜ🌑 𝘝𝘐𝘚𝘈 🄹🄲🄱. ✷ KV s
closed 22 July-August and 24 December-4 January – ⊠ 12,91 – **49 rm** 113,62/160,10,
3 suites.

🏨🏨 **Lloyd** without rest., corso di Porta Romana 48 ✉ 20122 ✆ 02 58303332, *info@lloy dhotelmilano.it*, Fax 02 58303365 – 🛗 🔲 📺 – 🔥 100. 🅰🅴 🆂 ⑩ ⓜ🌑 𝘝𝘐𝘚𝘈 KY c
closed 22 December-6 January – **57 rm** ⊠ 134/310, suite.

🏨🏨 **Zurigo** without rest., corso Italia 11/a ✉ 20122 ✆ 02 72022260, *zurigo@brerahotels.it*,
Fax 02 72000013 – 🛗 🔲 📺 ✆. 🅰🅴 🆂 ⑩ ⓜ🌑 𝘝𝘐𝘚𝘈 🄹🄲🄱 KY j
closed 24 December-7 January – **41 rm** ⊠ 123,95/175,60.

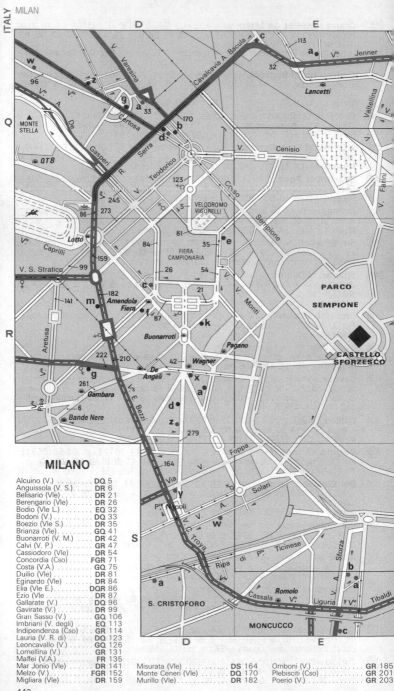

MILANO

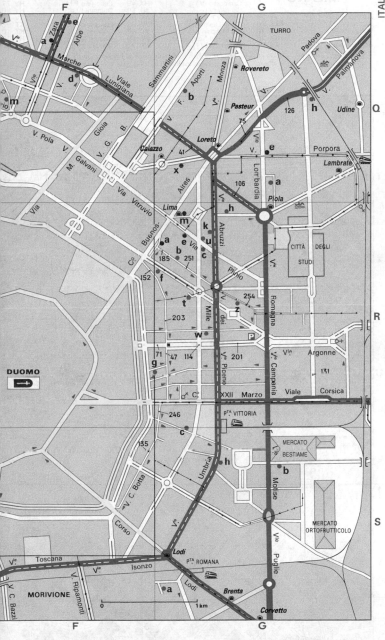

DUOMO

ITALY

MILANO

Within the green shaded area, the city is divided into zones wich are signposted all the way round.
Once entered, it is not possible to drive from one zone into another.

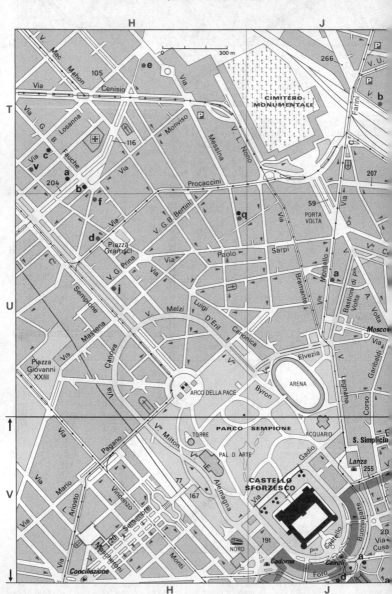

ITALY

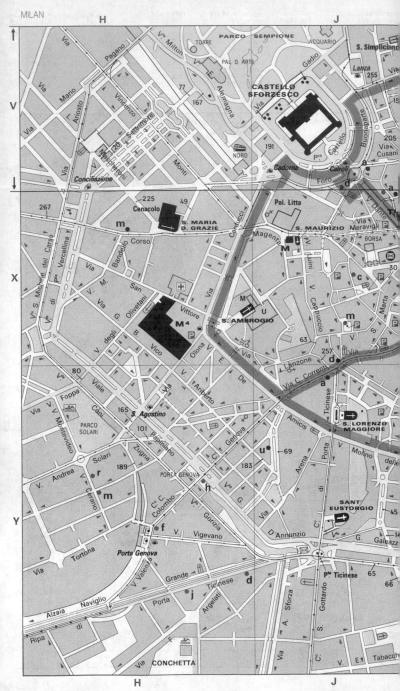

MILAN

446

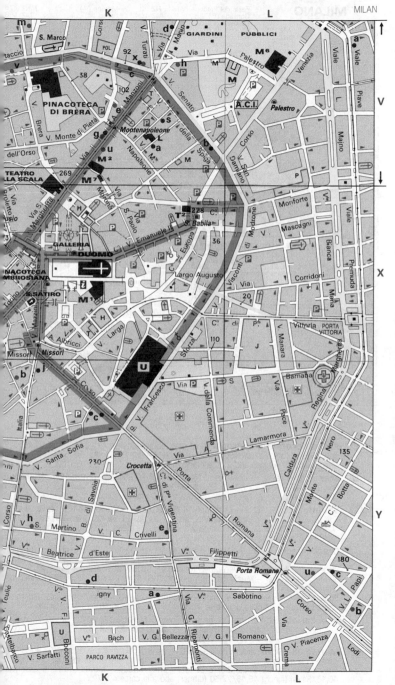

MILANO

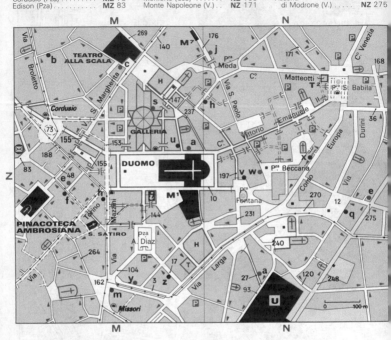

🏠 **Antica Locanda Leonardo** without rest., corso Magenta 78 ⊠ 20123 ℘ 02 463317
desk@leoloc.com, Fax 02 48019012, 🐕 – ≣ 📺. 🆎 🆂 ⓞ 🆚 ✂️   HX m
closed 6 to 19 August and 27 December-1 January – **20 rm** ⊑ 95/180.

🏠 **Star** without rest., via dei Bossi 5 ⊠ 20121 ℘ 02 801501, information@starhotel.it
Fax 02 861787 – 🛗 ≣ 📺. 🆎 🆂 ⓞ 🆚 🆚 ✂️   MZ b
closed August and 24 December-6 january – **30 rm** ⊑ 108,46/154,94.

XXXX **Savini**, galleria Vittorio Emanuele II ⊠ 20121 ℘ 02 72003433, savini@thi.it
Fax 02 72022888, Elegant traditional decor – ≣. 🆎 🆂 ⓞ 🆚 🆚 JCB. ✂️   MZ s
closed 6 to 27 August, 1 to 6 January and Sunday – **Meals** (booking essential) a la carte
62/89 (12 %).

XXXX **Cracco-Peck,** via Victor Hugo 4 ⊠ 20123 ℘ 02 876774, cracco-peck@peck.it
🕃 Fax 02 876774 – ≣. 🆎 🆂 ⓞ 🆚 🆚 JCB. ✂️   MZ e
closed 1 to 21 August, 22 December-10 January, Sunday and Saturday lunch, all day from
June to September – **Meals** (booking essential) 67,15/93 (lunch) 77,50/93 (dinner) and
a la carte 62/103
Spec. Musetto di maiale con scampi e pomodori verdi. Petto di germano reale arrosto con
cosce brasate e timballo di bietole. Tortino di robiola con ristretto al rabarbaro.

XXXX **Don Carlos** - Grand Hotel et de Milan, vicolo Manzoni ⊠ 20121 ℘ 02 72314640
Fax 02 86460861, Late night dinners – ≣. 🆎 🆂 ⓞ 🆚 🆚 JCB   KV g
closed August – **Meals** (dinner only) (booking essential) a la carte 54/88.

XXX **Marino alla Scala**, piazza della Scala 5 (Trussardi palace) ⊠ 20121 ℘ 02 80688201
cafeteria@marinoallascala.it, Fax 02 80688287 – 🛗 ≣. 🆎 🆂 ⓞ 🆚 🆚 JCB MZ c
closed August, 25 December-6 January and Sunday – **Meals** (booking essential)
46,15/51,64 (lunch) 46,48/72,30 (dinner) and a la carte 40/72.

XXX **Conte Camillo** - Hotel Cavour, via Fatebenefratelli 21 (galleria di Piazza Cavour) ✉ 20121 ✆ 02 6570516, *hotel.cavour@traveleurope.It*, Fax 02 6592263 – ▤. 🕮 🕃 ◑
🕦 *VISA* 🕹. ❀
KV x
closed 11 to 24 August, 24 December-6 January and Sunday – **Meals** 39 and a la carte 35/55.

XXX **Antico Ristorante Boeucc,** piazza Belgioioso 2 ✉ 20121 ✆ 02 76020224, Fax 02 796173 – ▤. 🕮. ❀
NZ j
closed 13 to 17 April, August, 24 December-2 January, Saturday and Sunday lunch – **Meals** (booking essential) a la carte 44/57.

XXX **Don Lisander,** via Manzoni 12/a ✉ 20121 ✆ 02 76020130, Fax 02 784573, « Outdoor summer service » – ▤. 🕮 🕃 ◑ 🕦 *VISA* 🕹. ❀
KV u
closed 12 to 22 August, 24 December-10 January and Sunday – **Meals** (booking essential) a la carte 47/60.

XX **Bistrot Duomo,** via San Raffaele 2 ✉ 20121 ✆ 02 877120, Fax 02 877035, 🏠, « Panoramic terrace with < Duomo », 🚡 🛗 ▤. 🕮 🕃 ◑ 🕦 *VISA* 🕹
MZ a
closed 15 to 25 August, Sunday and Monday lunch (booking essential) a la carte 42/63.

XX **Eolieolie,** piazza Mentana 8/10 ✉ 20123 ✆ 02 8692875, Fax 02 86913353 – ▤. 🕃
◑ *VISA*. ❀
JX m
closed August and Sunday – **Meals** 20,66/30,99 and a la carte 31/44.

XX **La Dolce Vita,** via Bergamini 11 ✉ 20122 ✆ 02 58307418 – ▤. 🕮 🕃 🕦 *VISA* 🕹. ❀
closed August, Saturday lunch and Sunday – **Meals** (booking essential for dinner) 13,94/20,66 (lunch only) and a la carte 36/47 (dinner only).
NZ a

XX **Armani/Nobu,** via Pisoni 1 ✉ 20121 ✆ 02 62312645, Fax 02 62312674 – 🍽️ ▤. 🕮
🕃 ◑ 🕦 *VISA* 🕹. ❀
KV e
closed August, 25 December-7 January Sunday and at lunchtime Saturday and Monday – (booking essential) Japanese rest. with South American influences 31,30/80,85 (lunch) 80,70/155,17 (dinner) and a la carte 63/78 (10 %).

XX **4 Mori,** largo Maria Callas 1 (angolo Largo Cairoli) ✉ 20121 ✆ 02 878483, « Outdoor summer service » – 🕮 🕃 ◑ 🕦 *VISA*
JV d
closed 15 to 25 August, 24 December-6 January, Saturday and Sunday – **Meals** a la carte 31/42.

XX **Alla Collina Pistolese,** via Amedei 1 ✉ 20123 ✆ 02 877248, Fax 02 877248, Old Milan atmosphere – ▤. 🕮 🕃 ◑ 🕦 *VISA*
KY b
closed Easter, 10 to 20 August, 24 December-2 January, Friday and Saturday lunch – **Meals** a la carte 36/49.

XX **Nabucco,** via Fiori Chiari 10 ✉ 20121 ✆ 02 860663, Fax 02 8361014 – ▤. 🕮 🕃 ◑
🕦 *VISA* 🕹. ❀
KV v
Meals (booking essential) a la carte 37/46 (10 %).

XX **Da Marino-al Conte Ugolino,** piazza Beccaria 6 ✉ 20122 ✆ 02 876134 – ▤. 🕮
🕃 ◑ 🕦 *VISA*
NZ w
closed 13 to 23 August, Christmas, New Year and Sunday – **Meals** a la carte 32/53 (11 %).

XX **Albric,** via Albricci 3 ✉ 20122 ✆ 02 72004766, *rist.albric@tiscalinet.it,* Fax 02 86461329 – ▤. 🕮 🕃 ◑ 🕦 *VISA* 🕹. ❀
MZ y
closed 8 to 30 August, 25 December-6 January, Saturday lunch and Sunday – **Meals** seafood a la carte 43/56.

XX **La Felicità,** via Rovello 3 ✉ 20121 ✆ 02 865255, Fax 02 865235 – ▤. 🕮 🕃 ◑ 🕦
VISA 🕹. ❀
JX a
Meals Chinese rest. 8,50/18,10 (lunch) 14,50/18,10 (dinner) and a la carte 18,50/29.

X **Hostaria Borromei,** via Borromei 4 ✉ 20123 ✆ 02 86453760, Fax 02 86453760, 🏠
– 🕮 🕃 ◑ 🕦 *VISA*. ❀
JX c
closed 9 August-3 September, 24 December-7 January, Saturday lunch and Sunday – **Meals** (booking essential) Mantuan specialities a la carte 36/47.

X **La Tavernetta-da Elio,** via Fatebenefratelli 30 ✉ 20121 ✆ 02 653441, *tavernetta@enter.it* – ▤. 🕮 🕃 ◑ 🕦 *VISA* 🕹
KV c
closed August, 24 December-2 January, Saturday lunch, Sunday and Bank Holidays – **Meals** Tuscan rest. a la carte 30/41.

X **Taverna Visconti,** via Marziale 11 ✉ 20122 ✆ 02 795821, Fax 02 795821, Rest. and wine bar – ▤. 🕮 🕃 ◑ 🕦 *VISA*
NZ e
closed 4 to 23 August, 22 December-4 January, Saturday lunch and Sunday – **Meals** a la carte 42/72.

Directional centre via della Moscova, via Solferino, via Melchiorre Gioia, viale Zara, via Carlo Farini

🏨 **Golden Tulip Grand Hotel Verdi** Ⓜ, via Melchiorre Gioia 6 ✉ 20124 ✆ 02 62371, *mail@grandhotelverdi.com,* Fax 02 62373050 – 🛗, 🍽️ rm, ▤ 📺 📞 🚗. 🕮 🕃 ◑ 🕦
VISA 🕹. ❀
KU n
closed 11 to 25 August – **Meals** a la carte 31/38 – **100 rm** ⛄ 162,68/281,98, 3 suites.

Una Hotel Tocq Ⓜ, via A. de Tocqueville 7/D ⊠ 20154 ℰ 02 62071, *unatocq@u nahotel.it*, Fax 02 6570780 – |‡| ☰ 📺. 🖭 🚭 ① ⓦⓞ 🖪🖪🖪 🗷🖪🖪. ⋘
KU k
Meals a la carte 22/35 – **109 rm** ⊐ 365, 13 suites.

Four Points Sheraton Milan Center, via Cardano 1 ⊠ 20124 ℰ 02 667461, *book in@fourpointsmilano.it*, Fax 02 6703024 – |‡|, ⋙ rm, ☰ 📺 ⋐ – 🔏 180. 🖭 🚭 ① ⓦⓞ
🖪🖪🖪 🗷🖪🖪. ⋘ rest
KT b
Meals a la carte 36/48 – ⊐ 14 – **205 rm** 195/310, 10 suites.

Sunflower without rest., piazzale Lugano 10 ⊠ 20158 ℰ 02 39314071, *sunflower. hotel@tiscalinet.it*, Fax 02 39320377 – |‡| ☰ 📺 🕭 ⟵ – 🔏 100. 🖭 🚭 ① ⓦⓞ 🖪🖪🖪 🗷🖪🖪.
⋘
EQ c
closed 5 to 27 August and 24 December-6 January – ⊐ 12,91 – **55 rm** 123,95/175,60.

Santini, via San Marco 3 20121 ℰ 02 6555587, Fax 02 6555587 – ☰. 🖭 🚭 ① ⓦⓞ 🖪🖪🖪.
⋘
KV m
closed Saturday lunch and Sunday – **Meals** 36 (lunch only) 62 (dinner only) and a la carte 53/78.

Gianni e Dorina, via Pepe 38 ⊠ 20159 ℰ 02 606340, Fax 02 606340, ⇞ – ☰. 🖭
🚭 ① ⓦⓞ 🖪🖪🖪. ⋘
JT b
closed 31 July-6 September, Christmas, Saturday lunch and Sunday – **Meals** (booking essential) Pontremolesi rest. a la carte 38/49.

Casa Fontana-23 Risotti, piazza Carbonari 5 ⊠ 20125 ℰ 02 6704710, *trattoria @23risotti.it*, Fax 02 66800465 – ☰. 🖭 🚭 ① ⓦⓞ 🖪🖪🖪. ⋘
FQ d
closed Easter, 28 July-27 August, 23 December-8 January, Monday, Saturday lunch and Saturday dinner-Sunday in July – **Meals** (booking essential) risotto specialities a la carte 31/41.

Alla Cucina delle Langhe, corso Como 6 ⊠ 20154 ℰ 02 6554279, Fax 02 29006859
– ☰. 🖭 🚭 ① ⓦⓞ 🖪🖪🖪 🗷🖪🖪. ⋘
KU d
closed August, Sunday and Saturday in July – **Meals** Lombardy and Piedmontese specialities a la carte 39/46.

Antica Osteria il Calessino, via Thaon de Revel 9 ⊠ 20159 ℰ 02 6684935, Fax 02 6684935, Live music and cabaret – ☰. 🖭 🚭 ① ⓦⓞ 🖪🖪🖪. ⋘
FQ m
closed 1 to 10 January and Monday – **Meals** (dinner only) 46 b.i.

Le Petit Prince, viale Monte Grappa 6 ⊠ 20124 ℰ 02 29011439, *lepetitprince.mil ano@libero.it*, Fax 02 29011439 – ⋙ ☰. 🖭 🚭 ① ⓦⓞ 🖪🖪🖪 🗷🖪🖪
KU m
closed 10 to 31 August, 25-26 December, 31 December-7 January and Sunday – **Meals** (dinner only) French rest. a la carte 35/50

Fuji, viale Montello ⊠ 20154 ℰ 02 6552517 – ☰. 🚭 ① ⓦⓞ 🖪🖪🖪 🗷🖪🖪. ⋘
JU a
closed Easter, 1 to 23 August, 24 December-2 January and Sunday – **Meals** (dinner only) (booking essential) Japanese rest. 48/78 and a la carte 38/57.

Central Station corso Buenos Aires, via Vittor Pisani, piazza della Repubblica

Principe di Savoia, piazza della Repubblica 17 ⊠ 20124 ℰ 02 62301, *hotelprincip edisavoia@luxurycollection.com*, Fax 02 6595838, ℉₅, ⇌, ▨ – |‡| ⋙ ☰ 📺 ⋐ – 🔏 700.
🖭 🚭 ① ⓦⓞ 🖪🖪🖪 🗷🖪🖪. ⋘
KU a
Meals *Galleria* Rest. a la carte 73/89 – ⊐ 39,04 – **304 rm** 531,43/667, 132 suites.

The Westin Palace, piazza della Repubblica 20 ⊠ 20124 ℰ 02 63361, Fax 02 654485,
℉₅ – |‡|, ⋙ rm, ☰ 📺 ⋐ & ⟵ ▣ – 🔏 170. 🖭 🚭 ① ⓦⓞ 🖪🖪🖪 🗷🖪🖪. ⋘
LU b
Meals *Casanova Grill* Rest. (closed August) (booking essential) a la carte 76/99 – ⊐ 34,70
– **228 rm** 336/517, 16 suites.

Excelsior Gallia, piazza Duca d'Aosta 9 ⊠ 20124 ℰ 02 67851, *sales@excelsiorgallia.it*, Fax 02 66713239 – |‡|, ⋙ rm, ☰ 📺 ⋐ & – 🔏 700. 🖭 🚭 ① ⓦⓞ 🖪🖪🖪 🗷🖪🖪. ⋘
LT a
Meals a la carte 46/70 – ⊐ 30 – **237 rm** 405/480, 13 suites.

Hilton Milan Ⓜ, via Galvani 12 ⊠ 20124 ℰ 02 69831, *sales_milan@hilton.com*, Fax 02 66710810 – |‡|, ⋙ rm, ☰ 📺 ⋐ & – 🔏 180. 🖭 🚭 ① ⓦⓞ 🖪🖪🖪 🗷🖪🖪. ⋘ rest
LT c
Meals a la carte 45/55 – ⊐ 25 – **317 rm** 260/380, 2 suites.

Starhotel Ritz, via Spallanzani 40 ⊠ 20129 ℰ 02 20551, *ritz.mi@starhotels.it*, Fax 02 29518679 – |‡| ⋙ ☰ 📺 – 🔏 180. 🖭 🚭 ① ⓦⓞ 🖪🖪🖪 🗷🖪🖪. ⋘
GR a
Meals (residents only) a la carte 39/60 – **189 rm** ⊐ 319/367, 6 suites.

Una Hotel Century Ⓜ, via Fabio Filzi 25/b ⊠ 20124 ℰ 02 67504, *una.century@u nahotel.it*, Fax 02 66980602, ℉₅ – |‡|, ⋙ rm, ☰ 📺 ⋐ – 🔏 60. 🖭 🚭 ① ⓦⓞ 🖪🖪🖪 🗷🖪🖪.
⋘
LT f
Meals (closed August) a la carte 37/48 – **144 suites** ⊐ 200/387.

Michelangelo, via Scarlatti 33 ang. piazza Luigi di Savoia ⊠ 20124 ℰ 02 67551, *mich elangelo@milanhotel.it*, Fax 02 6694232 – |‡|, ⋙ rm, ☰ 📺 ⋐ & ⟵ – 🔏 500. 🖭
① ⓦⓞ 🖪🖪🖪 🗷🖪🖪. ⋘ rest
LTU s
Meals a la carte 40/55 – **293 rm** ⊐ 200/245, 7 suites.

Jolly Hotel Touring, via Tarchetti 2 ✉ 20121 ☎ 02 6335, *Fax 02 6592209* – |‡|, ⇌ rm, ▤ TV ☎ ♿ – 🏛 120. AE $ ⓓ ⓜ VISA. ✻ KU f
Meals ***Amadeus*** Rest. a la carte 44/55 – **285 rm** ☕ 198/288, 4 suites.

Sheraton Diana Majestic, viale Piave 42 ✉ 20129 ☎ 02 20581, *sheraton.diana.majestic@starwood.com, Fax 02 20582058,* 🏞, « Shaded garden », Lб – |‡|, ⇌ rm, ▤ TV ☎ – 🏛 80. AE $ ⓓ ⓜ VISA JCB LV a
closed August – **Meals *Il Milanese*** Rest. a la carte 47/68 – ☕ 31,25 – **103 rm** 181,79/279,46, suite.

Jolly Hotel Machiavelli M, via Lazzaretto 5 ✉ 20124 ☎ 02 631141 and rest ☎ 02 63114921, *machiavelli@jollyhotels.it, Fax 02 6599800* – |‡|, ⇌ rm, ▤ TV ☎ ♿ – 🏛 80. AE $ ⓓ ⓜ VISA JCB. ✻ rest LU a
Meals ***Caffè Niccolò*** Rest. a la carte 36/53 – **103 rm** ☕ 172/242.

Doria Grand Hotel, viale Andrea Doria 22 ✉ 20124 ☎ 02 67411411, *doriagrandhotel@traveleurope.it, Fax 02 6696669* – |‡|, ⇌ rm, ▤ TV ♿ – 🏛 120. AE $ ⓓ ⓜ VISA JCB GQ x
Meals *(closed 27 July-23 August, 24 December-6 January)* a la carte 43/65 – **118 rm** ☕ 315/363, 2 suites.

Manin, via Manin 7 ✉ 20121 ☎ 02 6596511, *info@hotelmanin.it, Fax 02 6552160,* « Garden » – |‡| ▤ TV – 🏛 100. AE $ ⓓ ⓜ VISA JCB. ✻ rest KV d
closed 3 to 26 August – **Meals** *(closed Saturday)* a la carte 47/59 – **111 rm** ☕ 139,44/247,90, 7 suites.

Bristol without rest., via Scarlatti 32 ✉ 20124 ☎ 02 6694141, *hotelbristol@comm2000.it, Fax 02 6702942* – |‡| ▤ TV ☎ – 🏛 60. AE $ ⓓ ⓜ VISA. ✻ LT m
closed August and 24 December-2 January – **68 rm** ☕ 129/180.

Sanpi without rest., via Lazzaro Palazzi 18 ✉ 20124 ☎ 02 29513341, *info@hotelsanpimilano.it, Fax 02 29402451,* 🌳 – |‡| ▤ TV ♿ – 🏛 30. AE $ ⓓ ⓜ VISA JCB. ✻
closed 4 to 27 August and 24 December-2 January – **71 rm** ☕ 215/265. LU e

Auriga without rest., via Pirelli 7 ✉ 20124 ☎ 02 66985851, *auriga@auriga-milano.com, Fax 02 66980698* – |‡| ▤ TV – 🏛 25. AE $ ⓓ ⓜ VISA JCB. ✻ LTU k
closed August and 24 December-2 January – **52 rm** ☕ 170/230.

Berna without rest., via Napo Torriani 18 ✉ 20124 ☎ 02 677311, *info@hotelberna.com, Fax 02 6693892* – |‡| ⇌ ▤ TV – 🏛 30. AE $ ⓓ ⓜ VISA JCB. ✻ LU h
115 rm ☕ 150/210.

Mediolanum without rest., via Mauro Macchi 1 ✉ 20124 ☎ 02 6705312, *booking@mediolanumhotel.com, Fax 02 66981921* – |‡| ▤ TV ☎. AE $ ⓓ ⓜ VISA JCB. ✻ LU n
52 rm ☕ 154,94/232,41.

Augustus without rest., via Napo Torriani 29 ✉ 20124 ☎ 02 66988271, *info@augustushotel.it, Fax 02 6703096* – |‡| ▤ TV. AE $ ⓓ ⓜ VISA JCB LU q
closed 30 July-22 August and 23 to 29 December – **56 rm** ☕ 152/201.

Atlantic without rest., via Napo Torriani 24 ✉ 20124 ☎ 02 6691941, *booking@atlantichotel.it, Fax 02 6706533* – |‡| ⇌ ▤ TV ☎ 🚗 – 🏛 25. AE $ ⓓ ⓜ VISA JCB. ✻ LU h
62 rm ☕ 166/248.

Madison without rest., via Gasparotto 8 ✉ 20124 ☎ 02 67074150, *madisonhotel@tin.it, Fax 02 67075059* – |‡| ▤ TV – 🏛 100. AE $ ⓓ ⓜ VISA LT j
92 rm ☕ 180/260.

Galles, piazza Lima ang. corso Buenos Aires ✉ 20124 ☎ 02 204841, *reception@galles.it, Fax 02 2048422* – |‡|, ⇌ rm, ▤ TV ☎ – 🏛 100. AE $ ⓓ ⓜ VISA JCB. ✻ GR m
Meals *(closed Sunday)* a la carte 34/56 – ☕ 12,91 – **150 rm** 105,90/361,52, 3 suites.

Fenice without rest., corso Buenos Aires 2 ✉ 20124 ☎ 02 29525541, *Fax 02 29523942* – |‡| ▤ TV. AE $ ⓓ ⓜ VISA. ✻ LU x
closed 6 to 28 August and 24 December-7 January – **46 rm** ☕ 111/165.

Demidoff without rest., via Plinio 2 ✉ 20129 ☎ 02 29513889, *demidoff@milanohotels.com, Fax 02 29405816* – |‡| ▤ TV ☎. AE $ ⓓ ⓜ VISA. ✻ GR e
closed 2 to 30 August and 24 December-7 January – **40 rm** ☕ 100,71/134,28.

Mini Hotel Aosta without rest., piazza Duca d'Aosta 16 ✉ 20124 ☎ 02 6691951, *aosta@minihotel.it, Fax 02 6696215* – |‡| ▤ TV. AE $ ⓓ ⓜ VISA JCB LT p
63 rm ☕ 57/161.

New York without rest., via Pirelli 5 ✉ 20124 ☎ 02 66985551, *Fax 02 6697267* – |‡| ▤ TV. AE $ ⓓ ⓜ VISA LTU k
closed 1 to 28 August and 24 December-5 January – **69 rm** ☕ 103,30/151,33.

San Carlo without rest., via Napo Torriani 28 ✉ 20124 ☎ 02 6693236, *sh@polohotels.it, Fax 02 6703116* – |‡| ▤ TV – 🏛 30. AE $ ⓓ ⓜ VISA JCB LU u
75 rm ☕ 116,18/220.

🏠 **Sempione,** via Finocchiaro Aprile 11 ⊠ 20124 *ℰ* 02 6570323 and rest *ℰ* 02 6552715, *Fax 02 6575379* – 🛗 🖃 📺 🌐 🗟 🗟 🌐 🗟 🗟 ⚒ rest   LU **r**
closed 13 to 27 August and 23 December-2 January – **Meals *Piazza Repubblica*** Rest.
a la carte 31/46 – **43 rm** ⌑ 110/150.

🏠 **Bolzano** without rest., via Boscovich 21 ⊠ 20124 *ℰ* 02 6691451, *Fax 02 6691455,* 🚗
– 🛗 🖃 📺 🌐 🗟 🌐 🗟 🗟 ⚒   LU **t**
⌑ 7,75 – **35 rm** 90,38/129,11.

XXX **La Terrazza di Via Palestro,** via Palestro 2 ⊠ 20121 *ℰ* 02 76002186, *terrazza milano@tiscalinet.it, Fax 02 76003328*, ≤, « Summer service on terrace » – 🖃 – 🏛 200. 🌐 🗟 🗟 🗟   KV **h**
closed 8 to 24 August, 24 December-12 January, Saturday and Sunday – **Meals** (booking essential) 30/50 (lunch) 50/70 (dinner) and a la carte 45/62.

XX **Piccolo Sogno,** via Stoppani 5 angolo via Zambelletti ⊠ 20129 *ℰ* 02 20241210 – 🖃. 🌐 🗟 🌐 🗟 ⚒ – *closed 10 to 31 August and 26 December-5 January* – **Meals** (booking essential) a la carte 38/64.   GR **b**

XX **Mediterranea,** piazza Cincinnato 4 ⊠ 20124 *ℰ* 02 29522076, *Fax 02 201156* – 🖃. 🌐 🗟 🌐 🗟 🗟 ⚒   LU **d**
closed 5 to 25 August, 1 to 10 January, Sunday and Monday lunch – **Meals** seafood a la carte 34/58.

XX **Joia,** via Panfilo Castaldi 18 ⊠ 20124 *ℰ* 02 29522124, *Fax 02 2049244* – 🍴 🖃 🅿. 🌐
🕃 🗟 🌐 🗟 🌐 🗟   LU **c**
closed Easter, August, 26 December-10 January, Saturday and Sunday – **Meals** (booking essential) Vegetarian and seafood rest. 40/62 a la carte 41/54
Spec. La spirale del gusto. Raviolo rinascimentale con pesto intenso, contrasto di aceto balsamico e fichi. Il pianeta verde va verso il suo centro.

XX **I Malavoglia,** via Lecco 4 ⊠ 20124 *ℰ* 02 29531387, *Fax 02 20402722* – 🖃. 🌐 🗟
🗐 🌐 🗟 🗟. ⚒   LU **g**
closed Easter, 1 May, August, 24 December-4 January, Monday and lunch (except Sunday and Bank Holidays) – **Meals** (booking essential) Sicilian and seafood rest. a la carte 35/48.

XX **Cavallini,** via Mauro Macchi 2 ⊠ 20124 *ℰ* 02 6693174, *Fax 02 6693077*, « Summer service under pergola » – 🌐 🗟 🌐 🗟 🌐 🗟   LU **y**
closed 3 to 23 August, 22 to 26 December, Saturday and Sunday – **Meals** 23,24/41,30 a la carte 32/49.

XX **13 Giugno,** via Goldoni 44 ang. via Uberti ⊠ 20129 *ℰ* 02 719654, *Fax 02 70100311,* 🌴 – 🖃. 🌐 🗟 🌐 🗟 🌐 🗟 ⚒   GR **w**
closed 5 to 26 August, 1 to 6 January and Sunday – **Meals** (booking essential) Sicilian rest. a la carte 45/65.

XX **Le 5 Terre,** via Appiani 9 ⊠ 20121 *ℰ* 02 6575177, *Fax 02 653034* – 🖃. 🌐 🗟 🌐 🌐
🗟 🗟   KU **j**
closed 10 to 27 August, Saturday lunch and Sunday – **Meals** seafood a la carte 33/47.

XX **Giglio Rosso,** piazza Luigi di Savoia 2 ⊠ 20124 *ℰ* 02 6696659, *Fax 02 6694174,* 🌴
– 🖃. 🌐 🗟 🌐 🗟 🌐 🗟. ⚒   LT **p**
closed August, 24 December-6 January, Saturday and Sunday lunch – **Meals** 20,65 and a la carte 26/38 (12 %).

XX **Hana,** via Lecco 15 ⊠ 20124 *ℰ* 02 29523227, *Fax 02 20241362* – 🖃. 🌐 🗟 🌐 🗟 🗟
closed 15 to 26 August, Saturday lunch and Sunday – **Meals** (booking essential for dinner) Korean rest. 10,36/20,73 (lunch) 20,73/36,27 (dinner) and a la carte 34/40 (10 %). LU **m**

XX **Altopascio,** via Gustavo Fara 17 ⊠ 20124 *ℰ* 02 6702458 – 🖃. 🌐 🗟 🌐 🗟 🌐 🗟. ⚒
closed August, Saturday and Sunday lunch – **Meals** Tuscan rest. a la carte 26/38.   KU **n**

X **Centro Ittico,** via Ferrante Aporti 35 ⊠ 20125 *ℰ* 02 26823449, *Fax 02 26143774* – 🖃. 🗟 🌐 🗟 🌐 🗟 ⚒   GQ **b**
closed August, 25 December-7 January, Sunday and Monday lunch – **Meals** (booking essential for dinner) seafood a la carte 35/64.

X **L'Imperiale,** via Plinio 30 ⊠ 20129 *ℰ* 02 29513532 – 🖃. 🌐 🗟 🌐 🗟 🌐 🗟   GR **c**
closed 16 to 20 August and Monday – **Meals** Chinese rest. a la carte 17/21.

X **I 4 Toscani,** via Plinio 33 ⊠ 20129 *ℰ* 02 29518130, *Fax 02 29518130,* 🌴 – 🌐 🗟
🌐 🗟 🗟   GR **u**
closed 12 to 27 August, 2 to 6 January, Sunday dinner and Monday – **Meals** a la carte 26/41.

X **Da Giannino-L'Angolo d'Abruzzo,** via Pilo 20 ⊠ 20129 *ℰ* 02 29406526, *Fax 02 29406526* – 🖃. 🌐 🗟 🌐 🗟 🌐 🗟   GR **t**
closed August, Sunday dinner and Monday – **Meals** (booking essential for dinner) Abruzzi specialities a la carte 23/29.

X **La Tana del Lupo,** viale Vittorio Veneto 30 ⊠ 20124 *ℰ* 02 6599006, *latana.dellup o@libero.it, Fax 02 6572168*, « Typical taverna » – 🖃. 🗟 🌐 🗟 🌐 🗟   KU **q**
closed August, 1 to 7 January and Sunday – **Meals** (dinner only) (booking essential) specialities from mountains of veneto 36,15 b.i..

Romana-Vittoria corso Porta Romana, corso Lodi, corso XXII Marzo, corso Porta Vittoria

Una Hotel Mediterraneo [M], via Muratori 14 ✉ 20135 ✆ 02 550071, *una.medit erraneo@unahotel.it*, Fax 02 550072217 – |‡|, ✦ rm, ▤ ⓣⓥ 🍴 – 🔏 75. 🝩 🕄 ⓞ ⓦⓔ *VISA* *JCB*. ✼ rest — LY c
Meals (residents only) 23,24/25,82 – **93 rm** ⌑ 170/243.

Da Giacomo, via B. Cellini angolo via Sottocorno ✉ 20129 ✆ 02 76023313, *Fax 02 76024505* – ▤. 🝩 🕄 ⓞ ⓦⓔ *VISA*. ✼ — FGR g
closed August, 23 December-7 January, Monday and Tuesday lunch – **Meals** seafood a la carte 47/73.

Isola dei Sapori, via Anfossi 10 ✉ 20135 ✆ 02 54100708, *Fax 02 54100708* – ▤. 🝩 🕄 ⓞ ⓦⓔ *VISA* — GS c
closed August, 26 December-4 January, Saturday lunch and Tuesday – **Meals** (booking essential for dinner) a la carte 29/42.

Masuelli San Marco, viale Umbria 80 ✉ 20135 ✆ 02 55184138, *masuelli.trattoria @tin.it*, Fax 02 55184138, Typical trattoria – ▤. 🝩 🕄 ⓞ ⓦⓔ *VISA* *JCB* — GS h
closed 16 August-10 September, 25 December-6 January, Sunday and Monday lunch – **Meals** (booking essential for dinner) Lombardy-Piedmontese rest. a la carte 35/47.

Dongiò, via Corio 3 ✉ 20135 ✆ 02 5511372, *Fax 02 5401869* – ▤. 🝩 🕄 ⓞ ⓦⓔ *VISA* *JCB*. ✼ — LY u
closed August, Saturday lunch and Sunday – **Meals** (booking essential for dinner) a la carte 23/33.

Al Merluzzo Felice, via Lazzaro Papi 6 ✉ 20135 ✆ 02 5454711 – 🝩 🕄 ⓞ ⓦⓔ *VISA*. ✼ *closed 7 to 31 August, Sunday and Bank Holidays* – **Meals** (booking essential) Sicilian rest. a la carte 25/48. — LY b

Navigli via Solari, Ripa di Porta Ticinese, viale Bligny, piazza XXIV Maggio

D'Este without rest., viale Bligny 23 ✉ 20136 ✆ 02 58321001, *Fax 02 58321136* – |‡| ▤ ⓣⓥ – 🔏 80. 🝩 🕄 ⓞ ⓦⓔ *VISA*. ✼ — KY d
79 rm ⌑ 134,27/165,26.

Crivi's without rest., corso Porta Vigentina 46 ✉ 20122 ✆ 02 582891, *crivis@tin.it*, *Fax 02 58318182* – |‡| ▤ ⓣⓥ 🍴 – 🔏 120. 🝩 🕄 ⓞ ⓦⓔ *VISA* *JCB* — KY e
closed August – **83 rm** ⌑ 135/205, 3 suites.

Liberty without rest., viale Bligny 56 ✉ 20136 ✆ 02 58318562, *Fax 02 58319061* – |‡| ▤ ⓣⓥ. 🝩 🕄 ⓞ ⓦⓔ *VISA*. ✼ — KY a
closed 1 to 24 August – ⌑ 10,33 – **50 rm** 105,87/206,58.

Mercure Relais Milano Corso Genova without rest., via Conca del Naviglio 20 ✉ 20123 ✆ 02 58104141, *mercuremilanocg@metha.com*, Fax 02 89401012 – |‡| ▤ ⓣⓥ 🍴 ☛ 🅿 🝩 🕄 ⓞ ⓦⓔ *VISA* *JCB* — JY u
105 rm ⌑ 72/206.

Sadler, via Ettore Troilo 14 angolo via Conchetta ✉ 20136 ✆ 02 58104451, *sadler @sadler.it*, Fax 02 58112343, ☂ – ▤. 🕄 ⓞ ⓦⓔ *VISA* *JCB* — ES a
closed 8 August-2 September, 1 to 12 January and Sunday – **Meals** (dinner only) (booking essential) 75/87,20 and a la carte 65/95
Spec. Riccioli di sogliola e mozzarella in salsa pizzaiola (spring summer). Cannolloni di stoc cafisso, spinaci novelli all'aglio tostato e crema di polenta (autumn-winter). Costata di tonno con fagioli borlotti in umido (spring).

Al Porto, piazzale Generale Cantore ✉ 20123 ✆ 02 89407026, *alportodimilano@ac ena.it*, Fax 02 8321481 – ▤. 🝩 🕄 ⓞ ⓦⓔ *VISA* — HY h
closed August, 24 December-3 January, Sunday and Monday lunch – **Meals** (booking essential) seafood a la carte 37/53.

Osteria di Porta Cicca, ripa di Porta Ticinese 51 ✉ 20143 ✆ 02 8372763, *Fax 02 8372763* – ▤. 🝩 🕄 ⓞ ⓦⓔ *VISA* *JCB*. ✼ — HY j
closed Saturday lunch and Sunday – **Meals** (booking essential) a la carte 29/42.

Tano Passami l'Olio, via Vigevano 32/9 ✉ 20144 ✆ 02 8394139, *tano@mail.mdsnet.it* – ▤. 🝩 🕄 ⓞ ⓦⓔ *VISA*. ✼ — HY f
closed August, 24 December-6 January and Sunday – **Meals** (dinner only) (booking essential) a la carte 49/70.

Il Torchietto, via Ascanio Sforza 47 ✉ 20136 ✆ 02 8372910, *info@it.torchietto.com*, Fax 02 8372000 – ▤. 🝩 🕄 ⓞ ⓦⓔ *VISA* *JCB*. ✼ — ES b
closed August, 26 December-3 January and Monday – **Meals** Mantuan rest. a la carte 32/43.

Le Buone Cose, via San Martino 8 ✉ 20122 ✆ 02 58310589, *lebuonecose@hotm ail.com*, Fax 02 58310589 – ▤. 🝩 🕄 ⓞ ⓦⓔ *VISA* — KY h
closed August, Saturday lunch and Sunday – **Meals** (booking essential) seafood a la carte 35/56.

Al Capriccio, via Washington 106 ✉ 20146 ☏ 02 48950655 – ▤. AE ⓢ ⓓ ⓜⓒ VISA JCB. ✂ DS y
closed August and Monday – **Meals** (booking essential) seafood a la carte 34/44.

Trattoria Trinacria, via Savona 57 ✉ 20144 ☏ 02 4238250, *trattoria.trinacria@libero.it* – ▤. AE ⓢ ⓓ ⓜⓒ VISA. ✂ DS w
closed Sunday – **Meals** (dinner only) (booking essential) Sicilian rest. a la carte 37/44.

Trattoria Aurora, via Savona 23 ✉ 20144 ☏ 02 89404978, *trattoriaurora@libero.it, Fax 02 89404978,* « Summer service in garden » – AE ⓢ ⓓ ⓜⓒ VISA JCB HY m
Piedmontese rest. 13 b.i. (lunch only) 35 (dinner only).

Trattoria all'Antica, via Montevideo 4 ✉ 20144 ☏ 02 58104860 – ▤. AE ⓢ ⓓ ⓜⓒ VISA JCB. ✂ HY r
closed August, 26 December-7 January, Saturday lunch and Sunday – **Meals** Lombardy rest. 25,82/38,73 (dinner only) and a la carte 24/32.

Ponte Rosso, Ripa di Porta Ticinese 23 ✉ 20143 ☏ 02 8373132, Trattoria-bistrot – ⓢ ⓜⓒ VISA HY d
closed August, Sunday and Wednesday dinner – **Meals** Triestine and Lombardy specialities a la carte 26/31.

Fiera-Sempione corso Sempione, piazzale Carlo Magno, via Monte Rosa, via Washington

Hermitage Ⓜ, via Messina 10 ✉ 20154 ☏ 02 33107700, *hermitage.res@monrifhotels.it, Fax 02 33107399,* – |‡|, ⇸ rm, ▤ TV ☏ ♿ 🚗 – 🏟 200. AE ⓢ ⓓ ⓜⓒ VISA JCB. ✂ HU q
closed August – **Meals** (see rest. ***Il Sambuco*** below) – **119 rm** ☕ 237,50/284, 12 suites.

Milan Marriott Hotel Ⓜ, via Washington 66 ✉ 20146 ☏ 02 48521 and rest ☏ 02 48522834, *Fax 02 4818925* – |‡|, ⇸ rm, ▤ TV 🚗 – 🏟 1200. AE ⓢ ⓓ ⓜⓒ VISA JCB. ✂ DR d
Meals ***La Brasserie de Milan*** Rest. *(closed Monday)* a la carte 47/67 – ☕ 16,50 – **322 rm** 223/388, suite.

Una Hotel Scandinavia Ⓜ, via Fauchè 15 ✉ 20154 ☏ 02 336391, *una.scandinavia@unahotel.it, Fax 02 33104510,* – |‡|, ⇸ rm, ▤ TV ☏ ♿ 🚗 – 🏟 170. AE ⓢ ⓓ ⓜⓒ VISA JCB. ✂ HT c
Meals ***Giardino-Sempione*** Rest. a la carte 39/46 – ☕ 12 – **149 rm** 200/335, suite.

Gd H. Fieramilano, viale Boezio 20 ✉ 20145 ☏ 02 336221, *prenotazioni@grandhotelfieramilano.com, Fax 02 314119* – |‡| ▤ TV ♿ – 🏟 240. AE ⓢ ⓓ ⓜⓒ VISA JCB. ✂ rest
closed August – **Meals** a la carte 20/31 – **238 rm** ☕ 183/222. DR e

Capitol Millennium Ⓜ, via Cimarosa 6 ✉ 20144 ☏ 02 438591, *Fax 02 4694724,* – |‡| ▤ TV ☏ – 🏟 70. AE ⓢ ⓓ ⓜⓒ VISA JCB. ✂ rest DR a
Meals (residents only) (closed 10 to 21 August and lunch) a la carte 30/39 – ☕ 18 – **61 rm** 201/289, 5 suites.

Regency without rest., via Arimondi 12 ✉ 20155 ☏ 02 39216021, *regency@regency-milano.com, Fax 02 39217734,* « In a late 19C mansion with pleasant courtyard » – |‡| ▤ TV ☏ – 🏟 50. AE ⓢ ⓓ ⓜⓒ VISA. ✂ DQ b
closed August and 24 December-5 January – **59 rm** ☕ 145,64/211,75.

Domenichino without rest., via Domenichino 41 ✉ 20149 ☏ 02 48009692, *hd@hoteldomenichino.it, Fax 02 48003953* – |‡| ▤ TV 🚗 – 🏟 50. AE ⓢ ⓓ ⓜⓒ VISA DR f
closed 2 to 25 August and 20 December-6 January – **75 rm** ☕ 115/165, 2 suites.

Mozart without rest., piazza Gerusalemme 6 ✉ 20154 ☏ 02 33104215, *Fax 02 33103231* – |‡| ▤ TV 🚗 – 🏟 40. AE ⓢ ⓓ ⓜⓒ VISA. ✂ HT b
closed August and 22 December-2 January – **116 rm** ☕ 171/222, 3 suites.

Metrò without rest., corso Vercelli 61 ✉ 20144 ☏ 02 4987897, *hotelmetro@tin.it, Fax 02 48010295* – |‡| ▤ TV – 🏟 35. AE ⓢ ⓓ ⓜⓒ VISA DR x
37 rm ☕ 92,96/134,28.

Astoria without rest., viale Murillo 9 ✉ 20149 ☏ 02 40090095, *astoriahotel@tin.it, Fax 02 40074642* – |‡| ▤ TV – 🏟 30. AE ⓢ ⓓ ⓜⓒ VISA DR m
closed 28 July-28 August – **69 rm** ☕ 80/190, suite.

Mini Hotel Tiziano without rest., via Tiziano 6 ✉ 20145 ☏ 02 4699035, *tiziano@minihotel.it, Fax 02 4812153,* « Small park » – |‡| ▤ TV 🚗 P. AE ⓢ ⓓ ⓜⓒ VISA DR k
54 rm ☕ 68/186.

Berlino without rest., via Plana 33 ✉ 20155 ☏ 02 324141, *hotelberlino@traveleurope.it, Fax 02 39210611* – |‡| ▤ TV. AE ⓢ ⓓ ⓜⓒ VISA JCB DQ d
48 rm ☕ 100/170.

Il Sambuco - Hotel Hermitage, via Messina 10 ✉ 20154 ☏ 02 33610333, *info@ilsambuco.it, Fax 02 33611850* – ▤. AE ⓢ ⓓ ⓜⓒ VISA JCB HU q
closed 1 to 20 August, 25 December-3 January, Saturday lunch and Sunday – **Meals** seafood 38,73/49,06 (lunch) and a la carte 46/88.

XX **Alfredo-Gran San Bernardo,** via Borgese 14 ⊠ 20154 ☎ 02 3319000,
Fax 02 29006859 – ⬛. 🜨 🕤 ⓞ ⓶⑧ *VISA* ✂   HT e
closed August, 20 December-7 January, Sunday and Saturday June-July – **Meals** (booking
essential for dinner) Milanese rest. a la carte 44/55.

XX **Arrow's,** via Mantegna 17/19 ⊠ 20162 ☎ 02 341533, Fax 02 341533, 🍽 – ⬛. 🜨
🕤 ⓞ ⓶⑧ *VISA*. ✂ – *closed August, Sunday and Monday lunch* – **Meals** (booking essential)
seafood a la carte 38/64.   HU f

XX **Sadler Wine e Food,** via Monte Bianco 2/A ⊠ 20149 ☎ 02 4814677, *wine.food
@wine.food.it, Fax 02 48109490*, Rest. and wine bar – ⬛. 🜨 🕤 ⓞ ⓶⑧ *VISA* ✂
closed 6 to 27 August and Sunday – **Meals** (booking essential) a la carte 25/47.   DR c

XX **Da Stefano il Marchigiano,** via Arimondi 1 angolo via Plana ⊠ 20155
☎ 02 33001863 – ⬛. 🜨 🕤 ⓞ ⓶⑧ *VISA*. ✂   DQ d
closed August, Friday dinner and Saturday – **Meals** a la carte 26/44.

XX **Montecristo,** corso Sempione angolo via Prina ⊠ 20154 ☎ 02 3495049,
Fax 02 312760 – ⬛. 🕤 ⓞ ⓶⑧ *VISA*. ✂   HT j
closed August, 25 December-2 January, Tuesday and Saturday lunch – **Meals** seafood a
la carte 35/51.

XX **Osteria del Borgo Antico,** via Piero della Francesca 40 ⊠ 20154 ☎ 02 3313641,
osteria@borgoantico.net – ⬛. 🜨 🕤 ⓞ ⓶⑧ *VISA*. ✂   HT v
closed August, Saturday lunch and Sunday – **Meals** seafood a la carte 33/54.

XX **Montina,** via Procaccini 54 ⊠ 20154 ☎ 02 3490498 – ⬛. 🕤 ⓞ ⓶⑧ *VISA*   HU d
closed Sunday and Monday lunch – **Meals** a la carte 29/45.

X **Pace,** via Washington 74 ⊠ 20146 ☎ 02 468567, Fax 02 468567 – ⬛. 🜨 🕤 ⓞ ⓶⑧ *VISA*
closed 14 to 18 April, 1 to 23 August, Christmas, Saturday lunch and Wednesday – **Meals**
a la carte 23/32.

Outskirts of Milan

North-Western area viale Fulvio Testi, Niguarda, viale Fermi, viale Certosa, San Siro,
via Novara

🏨 **Grand Hotel Brun** 📎, via Caldera 21 ⊠ 20153 ☎ 02 452711, *brun.res@monrifhotels.it,
Fax 02 48204746* – 🛗, ✛ rm, ⬛ 📺 ⇔ 🅿 – 🛆 500. 🜨 🕤 ⓞ ⓶⑧ *VISA* 🇯 ✂
closed 23 December-4 January – **Meals** *(closed Sunday)* a la carte 34/55 – **308 rm**
⌷ 223/299, 16 suites.   by via S. Stratico   DR

🏨 **Rubens,** via Rubens 21 ⊠ 20148 ☎ 02 40302, *rubens@antareshotels.com,
Fax 02 48193114*, « Rooms with fresco murals »   🛗, ✛ rm, ⬛ 📺 📞 🅿 – 🛆 35. 🜨
🕤 ⓞ ⓶⑧ *VISA* 🇯 ✂ rest   DR g
Meals (residents only) a la carte 26/44 – **87 rm** ⌷ 81/295.

🏨 **Accademia,** viale Certosa 68 ⊠ 20155 ☎ 02 39211122, *accademia@antareshotels.
com, Fax 02 33103878*, « Rooms with fresco murals » – 🛗 ⬛ 📺 📞 – 🛆 70. 🜨 🕤 ⓞ
⓶⑧ *VISA* 🇯. ✂ rest   DQ g
Meals (residents only) 29/48 – **67 rm** ⌷ 125/265.

🏨 **Blaise e Francisc,** via Butti 9 ⊠ 20158 ☎ 02 66802366, *info@blaisefrancis.it,
Fax 02 66802909* – 🛗, ✛ rm, ⬛ 📺 ♿ ⇔ – 🛆 200. 🜨 🕤 ⓞ ⓶⑧ *VISA*. ✂ rest
Meals (closed Sunday) (residents only) a la carte 27/40 – **110 rm** ⌷ 130/284.   EQ a

🏨 **Novotel Milano Nord,** viale Suzzani 13 ⊠ 20162 ☎ 02 66101861, *novotelmilanon
ord@accor-hotels.it, Fax 02 66101961, ᴵ♨, ☰ – 🛗, ✛ rm, ⬛ 📺 ♿ ⇔ – 🛆 500. 🜨
🕤 ⓞ ⓶⑧ *VISA*. ✂ rest   by viale Zara   FQ
Meals a la carte 29/48 – **172 rm** ⌷ 195/240.

🏨 **Mirage** without rest., via Casella 61 angolo viale Certosa ⊠ 20156 ☎ 02 39210471,
mirage@gruppomirage.it, Fax 02 39210589 – 🛗 ⬛ 📺 – 🛆 50. 🜨 🕤 ⓞ ⓶⑧ *VISA*
50 rm ⌷ 147/200.   DQ z

🏨 **Valganna** without rest., via Varè 32 ⊠ 20158 ☎ 02 39310089, *hotel.valganna@tra
veleurope.it, Fax 02 39312566* – 🛗 ⬛ 📺 ⇔. 🜨 🕤 ⓞ ⓶⑧ *VISA*
40 rm ⌷ 78/104.   by via degli Imbriani   EQ

XXX **Affori,** via Astesani ang. via Novaro ⊠ 20161 ☎ 02 66208629, Fax 02 66280414 – ⬛.
🕤 ⓞ ⓶⑧ *VISA* 🇯   by via degli Imbriani   EQ
closed 13 to 27 August and Monday – **Meals** (booking essential) 31 (lunch) and a la carte
51/66.

XX **Innocenti Evasioni,** via privata della Bindellina ⊠ 20155 ☎ 02 33001882, *innocen
tievasioni@libero.it, Fax 02 33001882*, 🍽 – ⬛. 🜨 🕤 ⓞ *VISA*   DQ a
closed August, 3 to 9 January, Sunday and Monday – **Meals** (dinner only) (booking essential)
31/33 and a la carte 32/40.

XX **La Pobbia 1821,** via Gallarate 92 ⊠ 20151 ☎ 02 38006641, *lapobbia@tin.it,
Fax 02 38000724*, Ancient Milanese rest., « Outdoor summer service » – 🛆 40. 🜨 🕤 ⓞ
⓶⑧ *VISA*. ✂   DQ w
closed August and Sunday – **Meals** a la carte 31/44.

North-Eastern area viale Monza, via Padova, via Porpora, viale Romagna, viale Argonne, viale Forlanini

🏨 **Concorde,** viale Monza 132 ✉ 20125 ℰ 02 26112020, *concorde@ antareshotels.com* Fax 02 26147879 – 🛗 🗏 📺 🚗 – 🅰️ 160. 🅰🅴 🆂 ⓪ 🆖 𝐕𝐈𝐒𝐀 𝐉𝐂𝐁 ⚓
by viale Monza GQ
Meals (dinner only) (residents only) a la carte 26/44 – **120 rm** ☷ 81/285.

🏨 **Starhotel Tourist,** viale Fulvio Testi 300 ✉ 20126 ℰ 02 6437777, *tourist.mi@ sta rhotels.it,* Fax 02 6472516, 🛁 – 🛗, ❧ rm, 🗏 📺 🚗 🄿 – 🅰️ 150. 🅰🅴 🆂 ⓪ 🆖 𝐕𝐈𝐒𝐀 𝐉𝐂𝐁
by viale Zara FQ
Meals a la carte 46/58 – **140 rm** ☷ 185/260.

🏨 **Lombardia,** viale Lombardia 74 ✉ 20131 ℰ 02 2824938, *hotelomb@ tin.it* Fax 02 2893430 – 🛗, ❧ rm, 🗏 📺 🚗 🆖 🄿 – 🅰️ 100. 🅰🅴 🆂 ⓪ 🆖 𝐕𝐈𝐒𝐀. ⚓ GQ e
closed 4 to 19 August – **Meals** (closed Saturday and Sunday) (dinner only) 20,14/30 –
80 rm ☷ 98,13/170,43.

🍴 **L'Altra Scaletta,** viale Zara 116 ✉ 20125 ℰ 02 6888093, Fax 02 6888093, Habituès's rest. – 🗏. 🅰🅴 🆂 ⓪ 🆖 𝐕𝐈𝐒𝐀 𝐉𝐂𝐁. ⚓
FQ e
closed August, 25 December-6 January, Saturday lunch and Sunday – **Meals** 16 and a la carte 29/42.

🍴 **Tre Pini,** via Tullo Morgagni 19 ✉ 20125 ℰ 02 66805413, Fax 02 66801346, « Summer service under pergola » – 🗏. 🅰🅴 🆂 ⓪ 🆖 𝐕𝐈𝐒𝐀
by via Arbe FQ
closed 5 to 31 August, 25 December-4 January and Saturday – **Meals** (booking essential) char-grilled specialities a la carte 32/44.

🍴 **Da Renzo,** piazza Sire Raul 4 ✉ 20131 ℰ 02 2846261, Fax 02 2896634, 🍽 – 🗏. 🅰🅴 🆂 ⓪ 🆖 𝐕𝐈𝐒𝐀. ⚓ GQ h
closed August, 26 December-2 January, Monday dinner and Tuesday – **Meals** a la carte 28/38.

🍴 **Piero e Pia,** piazza Aspari 2 angolo via Vanvitelli ✉ 20129 ℰ 02 718541, Fax 02 718541 🍽 – 🗏. 🅰🅴 🆂 ⓪ 🆖 𝐕𝐈𝐒𝐀 GR z
closed 12 to 26 August and Sunday (except December) – **Meals** (booking essential for dinner) Piacentine specialities a la carte 31/52.

🍴 **Alla Capanna-da Attilio e Maria,** via Donatello 9 ✉ 20131 ℰ 02 29400884, Fax 02 29521491 – 🗏. 🅰🅴 🆂 ⓪ 🆖 𝐕𝐈𝐒𝐀 𝐉𝐂𝐁 GR h
closed August and Saturday – **Meals** a la carte 25/30.

🍴 **Charmant,** via G. Colombo 42 ✉ 20133 ℰ 02 70100136 – 🗏. 🅰🅴 🆂 ⓪ 🆖 𝐕𝐈𝐒𝐀. ⚓ **Meals** (booking essential) seafood a la carte 40/56.
GR k

🍴 **Baia Chia,** via Bazzini 37 ✉ 20131 ℰ 02 2361131, 🍽 – 🗏. 🆂 🆖 𝐕𝐈𝐒𝐀. ⚓ GQ a closed Easter, August, 24 December-2 January, Sunday and Monday lunch – **Meals** (booking essential) Sardinian and seafood rest. a la carte 24/34.

South-Eastern area viale Molise, corso Lodi, via Ripamonti, corso San Gottardo

🏨 **Quark,** via Lampedusa 11/a ✉ 20141 ℰ 02 84431, *commerciale@ quarkhotel.com* Fax 02 8464190, 🛁, 🌊 – 🛗, ❧ rm, 🗏 📺 🚗 🄿 – 🅰️ 1000. 🅰🅴 🆂 ⓪ 🆖 𝐕𝐈𝐒𝐀. ⚓
by via C. Bazzi FS
closed 24 July-22 August – **Meals** a la carte 46/69 – **190 rm** ☷ 139,44/185,92, 92 suites

🏨 **Starhotel Business Palace,** via Gaggia 3 ✉ 20139 ℰ 02 53545, *business.mi@ sta hotels.it,* Fax 02 57307550, 🛁 – 🛗 🗏 📺 🆖 🚗 – 🅰️ 200. 🅰🅴 🆂 ⓪ 🆖 𝐕𝐈𝐒𝐀 𝐉𝐂𝐁
by corso Lodi FGS
Meals (residents only) a la carte 27/47 – **214 rm** ☷ 195/260, 23 suites.

🏨 **Novotel Milano Est Aeroporto,** via Mecenate 121 ✉ 20138 ℰ 02 507261 Fax 02 58011086, 🌊, 🚐 – 🛗, ❧ rm, 🗏 📺 🆖 🄿 – 🅰️ 350. 🅰🅴 🆂 ⓪ 🆖 𝐕𝐈𝐒𝐀. ⚓ rest **Meals** a la carte 28/37 – **206 rm** ☷ 217/269. by viale Corsica GR

🍴 **Antica Trattoria Monluè,** via Monluè 75 ✉ 20138 ℰ 02 7610246, Fax 02 7610246 Country trattoria with summer service – 🗏 🄿. 🅰🅴 🆂 ⓪ 🆖 𝐕𝐈𝐒𝐀 𝐉𝐂𝐁
closed 2 to 14 August, 6 to 25 January, Saturday lunch and Sunday – **Meals** a la carte 38/54. by viale Corsica GR

🍴 **La Plancia,** via Cassinis 13 ✉ 20139 ℰ 02 5390558, Fax 02 5390558 – 🗏. 🅰🅴 🆂 ⓪ 🆖 𝐕𝐈𝐒𝐀. ⚓ by corso Lodi FGS
closed August and Sunday – **Meals** seafood and pizzeria a la carte 31/41.

🍴 **Nuovo Macello,** via Cesare Lombroso 20 ✉ 20137 ℰ 02 45480007, Fax 02 59902122 – 🗏 GS b
closed Saturday lunch and Sunday – **Meals** (booking essential) 19 (lunch only) and a la carte 37/49.

🍴 **Taverna Calabiana,** via Calabiana 3 ✉ 20139 ℰ 02 55213075 – 🗏. 🅰🅴 🆂 ⓪ 𝐕𝐈𝐒𝐀. ⚓ closed Easter, August, 24 December-5 January, Sunday and Monday – **Meals** Rest. and pizzeria a la carte 26/36.
FS a

South-Western area viale Famagosta, viale Liguria, via Lorenteggio, viale Forze Armate, via Novara

ŵŵŵ **Holiday Inn,** via Lorenteggio 278 ⊠ 20152 ℰ 02 413111, *sales.holidayinn-milano.it*, Fax 02 413113, ℔ – ฿ ⇔ ☰ ☑ ✆ & ⇔ – 🛵 85. 🝣 ⑤ ① ⑩ 𝘝𝘐𝘚𝘈 𝘑𝘊𝘣. ❀ rest
Meals *L'Univers Gourmand* Rest. a la carte 31/42 – ⇌ 19 – **119 rm** 241/333.

ХХХ **Il Luogo di Aimo e Nadia,** via Montecuccoli 6 ⊠ 20147 ℰ 02 416886, *info@aim*
❀❀ *oenadia.com*, Fax 02 48302005 – ☰. 🝣 ⑤ ① ⑩ 𝘝𝘐𝘚𝘈. ❀ by via Foppa DES
closed August, 1 to 8 January, Saturday lunch and Sunday – **Meals** (booking essential) a la carte 71/98
Spec. Farfalle di semola e crescione con alici, capperi di Pantelleria e mentuccia fresca (spring-autumn). Stufatino di porcini e pasta di salame di cinta senese con gnocchetti di parmigiano (summer-autumn). Sformato caldo e cuore mordido di cioccolato all'olio extra-vergine di olive nocellara.

ХХХ **L'Ape Piera,** via Lodovico il Moro 11 ⊠ 20143 ℰ 02 8912060, *info@ape-piera.com* –
☰. 🝣 ⑤ ① ⑩ 𝘝𝘐𝘚𝘈 𝘑𝘊𝘣 DS a
closed Sunday – **Meals** (dinner only) (booking essential) a la carte 39/69.

on national road 35-Milanofiori by via Ascanio ES : 10 km :

ŵŵ **Royal Garden Hotel** Ⓜ ❊, via Di Vittorio ⊠ 20090 Assago ℰ 02 457811, *garde n.res@monrifhotels.it*, Fax 02 45702901, ❀ – ฿ ☰ ☑ ✆ & ⇔ 🅿 – 🛵 180. 🝣 ⑤ ① ⑩ 𝘝𝘐𝘚𝘈. ❀
closed 1 to 24 August and 24 December-5 January – **Meals** a la carte 35/58 – **121 rm** ⇌ 197/204, 33 suites.

ŵŵ **Jolly Hotel Milanofiori,** Strada 2 ⊠ 20090 Assago ℰ 02 82221, *milanofiori@jolly hotels.it*, Fax 02 89200946, ℔, ☎, ❀ – ฿, ⇔ rm, ☰ ☑ 🅿 – 🛵 120. 🝣 ⑤ ① ⑩ 𝘝𝘐𝘚𝘈. ❀ rest
closed August and 24 to 30 December – **Meals** a la carte 41/50 – **255 rm** ⇌ 165/232.

at Forlanini Park (West Wide) by viale Corsica GR : 10 km :

ХХ **Osteria i Valtellina,** via Taverna 34 ⊠ 20134 Milano ℰ 02 7561139, Fax 02 7560436, « Summer service under pergola » – 🅿. 🝣 ⑤ ① ⑩ 𝘝𝘐𝘚𝘈. ❀
closed 4 to 24 August, 26 December-7 January and Monday – **Meals** (booking essential) Valtellina rest. 46,48/61,97 (dinner only) and a la carte 44/59.

on national road West-Assago by via Foppa DS : 11 km :

ŵŵ **Holiday Inn Milan Assago,** ⊠ 20094Assago ℰ 02 488601, *holidayinn.assago@allia ncealberghi.com*, Fax 02 48843958, ℔, ⤢ – ฿ ⇔ ☰ ☑ ✆ & 🅿 – 🛵 300. 🝣 ⑤ ① ⑩ 𝘝𝘐𝘚𝘈. ❀ rest
Meals *Alla Bella Italia* Rest. a la carte 28/46 – **203 rm** ⇌ 182/207.

Abbiategrasso 20081 Milano 𝟺𝟸𝟾 F 8. pop. 28 079 alt. 120.
Roma 590 – Alessandria 80 – Milano 24 – Novara 29 – Pavia 33.

at Cassinetta di Lugagnano North : 3 km – ⊠ 20081 :

ХХХ **Antica Osteria del Ponte,** piazza G. Negri 9 ℰ 02 9420034, Fax 02 9420610, ❀
❀❀ – ☰ 🅿. 🝣 ⑤ ① ⑩ 𝘝𝘐𝘚𝘈. ❀
closed August, 25 December-12 January, Sunday and Monday – **Meals** (booking essential) 60,50 (lunch) 100 and a la carte 86/132
Spec. Gamberi di San Remo marinati con cipollotto fresco e caviale Oscetra. Risotto alle zucchine in fiore e zafferano in fili (May-September). Flan di cioccolato amaro in salsa al cioccolato bianco.

Bergamo 24100 🅿 𝟺𝟸𝟾 E 11 G. Italy. – pop. 117 415 alt. 249.
 ⛳ parco dei Colli (closed Monday) ℰ 035 4548811, Fax 035 260444;
 ⛳ Bergamo L'Albenza (closed Monday) at Almenno San Bartolomeo ⊠ 24030 ℰ 035 640028, Fax 035 643066;
 ⛳ La Rossera (closed Tuesday) at Chiuduno ⊠ 24060 ℰ 035 838600, Fax 035 4427047.
 ✈ Orio al Serio ℰ 035 326111, Fax 035 326339.
 🛈 viale Vittorio Emanuele II 20 ⊠ 24121 ℰ 035 210204, Fax 035 230184.
 A.C.I. via Angelo Maj 16 ⊠ 24121 ℰ 035 285985.
Roma 601 – Brescia 52 – Milano 47.

ХХХ **Da Vittorio,** viale Papa Giovanni XXIII 21 ⊠ 24121 ℰ 035 213266, Fax 035 210805 –
❀❀ ⇔ ☰. 🝣 ⑤ ① ⑩ 𝘝𝘐𝘚𝘈. ❀
closed August and Wednesday – **Meals** (booking essential) 41,32 (lunch) 77,47/92,97 (dinner) and a la carte 75/106
Spec. Scampi semicrudi con fagioli zolfini e spuma di zola. Risotto ai crostacei in carpaccio di scampi. Gran fritto misto.

Canneto sull'Oglio 46013 Mantova 👥👥👥 G 13. pop. 4 569 alt. 35.
Roma 493 – Brescia 51 – Cremona 32 – Mantova 38 – Milano 123 – Parma 44.

towards Carzaghetto North-West : 3 km :

XXXX **Dal Pescatore,** ✉ 46013 🖉 0376 723001, dalpescatore@dalpescatore.it
🌸🌸🌸 Fax 0376 70304, Elegant installation, « Outdoor summer dinner service » – 🍴 📮 AE 🄮
🄿 🅭 🅫 VISA JCB. ✸
closed 14 August-8 September, 1 to 20 January, Monday, Tuesday and Wednesday lunch
– **Meals** (booking essential) 110 and a la carte 88/135
Spec. Carciofi e fegato di vitello al burro e rosmarino (November-May). Tortelli di zucca.
Stracotto di cavallo al barbera e polenta gialla.

Concesio 25062 Brescai 👥👥, 👥👥 F 12. pop. 12 793 alt. 218.
Roma 544 – Bergamo 50 – Brescia 10 – Milano 91.

XXX **Miramonti l'Altro,** via Crosette 34, località Costorio 🖉 030 2751063
🌸🌸 Fax 030 2753189 – 🍴 📮 – ⚓ 25. 🄵 🄿 🅫 VISA. ✸
closed 5 to 20 August and Monday – **Meals** (booking essential) 56,81/77,47 and a la carte
50/76
Spec. Sfogliatina di lumache, funghi e pomodori alla curcuma. Risotto ai formaggi dolci di
montagna. Agnello in crosta di erbe aromatiche.

Erbusco 25030 Brescia 👥👥👥 F 11. pop. 6 927 alt. 251.
Roma 578 – Bergamo 35 – Brescia 22 – Milano 69.

XXXX **Gualtiero Marchesi,** via Vittorio Emanuele 11, località Bellavista North : 1,5 km
🌸🌸 🖉 030 7760562, ristorante@marchesi.it, Fax 030 7760379, ≤ lake and mountains, Elegant installation – 🍴 📮 AE 🄵 🄿 🅫 VISA JCB. ✸
closed 7 January-3 February – **Meals** (booking essential) 134,28 and a la carte 70/105
Spec. Insalata di storione con le suo uova. Rombo in crosta di sale con salsa mediterranea.
Tiramisù al panettone.

Soriso 28018 Novara 👥👥 E 7, 👥👥 ⑯. pop. 770 alt. 452.
Roma 654 – Arona 20 – Milano 78 – Novara 40 – Stresa 35 – Torino 114 – Varese 46.

XXXX **Al Sorriso** with rm, via Roma 18 🖉 0322 983228, Fax 0322 983328 – 🍴 rest, 📺 🄐
🌸🌸🌸 🄵 🄿 🅫 VISA JCB. ✸
closed 3 to 26 August and 8 to 25 January – **Meals** (closed Monday and Tuesday lunch
(booking essential) 95/110 and a la carte 80/119 – **8 rm** ⮑ 104/176
Spec. Lasagnetta di patate e zucchine con animelle, seppioline e ragù di finferli (May-
December). Gnocehtti di polenta con cardi gobbi e fegato d'oca in salsa al parmigiano e
tartufo d'Alba (September-February). Petto di piccione su crostone delle sue frattaglie
all'aceto balsamico tradizionale (January-September).

NAPLES (NAPOLI) 80100 **P** **431** E 24 *G. Italy. – pop. 1 000 470 – High Season : April-October.*

See : *National Archaeological Museum*★★★ KY – *New Castle*★★ KZ – *Port of Santa Lucia*★★ BU – ≤★★ *of Vesuvius and bay* – ≤★★★ *at night from via Partenope of the Vomero and Posillipo* FX – *San Carlo Theatre*★ KZ **T** – *Piazza del Plebiscito*★ JKZ – *Royal Palace*★ KZ – *Carthusian Monastery of St. Martin*★★ JZ.

Spaccanapoli and Decumano Maggiore★★ KLY – *Tomb*★★ *of King Robert the Wise and Cloisters*★★ *in Church of Santa Chiara*★ KY _ *Cathedral*★ *(Duomo)* LY – *Sculptures*★ *in Chapel Sansevero* KY – *Arch*★, *Tomb*★ *of Catherine of Austria, apse*★ *in Church of St. Lawrence Major* LY – *Capodimonte Palace and National Gallery*★★.

Mergellina★ – ≤★★ *of the bay* – *Villa Floridiana*★ EVX – ≤★ – *Catacombs of St. Gennaro*★★ – *Church of Santa Maria Donnaregina*★ LY – *Church of St. Giovanni a Carbonara*★ LY – *Capuan Gate*★ LMY – *Cuomo Palace*★ LY – *Sculptures*★ *in the Church of St. Anne of the Lombards* KYZ – *Posillipo*★ – *Marechiaro*★ – ≤★★ *of the bay from Virgiliano Park (or Rimembranza Park).*

Exc. : *Bay of Naples*★★★ _ *Campi Flegrei*★★ _ *Sorrento Penisula*★★ *Island of Capri*★★★ *Island of Ischia*★★★.

☞ *(closed Tuesday) at Arco Felice* ✉ 80078 ℘ 081 660772, Fax 081 660566, West : 19 km.

✈ *Ugo Niutta of Capodichino North-East : 6 km* ℘ 081 7091111 – *Alitalia, via Medina 41* ✉ 80133 ℘ 081 5513188, Fax 081 5513709.

🚢 *to Capri (1 h 15 mn), Ischia (1 h 25 mn) e Procida (1 h), daily – Caremar-Travel and Holidays, molo Beverello* ✉ 80133 ℘ 081 5513882, Fax 081 5522011; *to Cagliari 19 June-14 July Thursday and Saturday, 15 July-11 September Thursday and Tuesday (15 h 45 mn) and Palermo daily (11 h) – Tirrenia Navigazione, Stazione Marittima, molo Angioino* ✉ 80133 ℘ 081 2514740, Fax 081 2514767 ; *to Ischia daily (1 h 20 mn) – Linee Lauro, molo Beverello* ✉ 80133 ℘ 081 5522838, Fax 081 5513236; *to Aeolian Island Wednesday and Friday, 15 June-15 September Monday, Tuesday, Thursday, Friday, Saturday and Sunday (14 h) – Siremar-Genovese Agency, via De Petris 78* ✉ 80133 ℘ 081 5512112, Fax 081 5512114.

⛴ *to Capri (45 mn), Ischia (45 mn) and Procida (35 mn), daily – Caremar-Travel and Holidays, molo Beverello* ✉ 80133 ℘ 081 5513882, Fax 081 5522011; *to Ischia (30 mn) and Capri (40 mn), daily – Alilauro, via Caracciolo 11* ✉ 80122 ℘ 081 7611004, Fax 081 7614250 and Linee Lauro, molo Beverello ✉ 80133 ℘ 081 5522838, Fax 081 5513236; *to Capri daily (40 mn) – Navigazione Libera del Golfo, molo Beverello* ✉ 80133 ℘ 081 5520763, Fax 081 5525589; *to Capri (45 mn), to Aeolian Island June-September (4 h) and Procida-Ischia daily (35 mn) – Aliscafi SNAV, via Caracciolo 10* ✉ 80122 ℘ 081 7612348, Fax 081 7612141.

🛈 *piazza dei Martiri 58* ✉ 80121 ℘ 081 405311 – *piazza del Plebiscito (Royal Palace)* ✉ 80132 ℘ 081 418744, Fax 081 418619 – *Central Station* ✉ 80142 ℘ 081 268779 - *Capodichino Airport* ✉ 80133 ℘ 081 7805761 – *piazza del Gesù Nuovo 7* ✉ 80135 ℘ 081 5523328 - *Stazione Mergellina* ✉ 80122 ℘ 081 7612102.

A.C.I. *piazzale Tecchio 49/d* ✉ 80125 ℘ 081 2394511.

Roma 219 – Bari 261

Plans on following pages

🏨 **Grand Hotel Vesuvio**, via Partenope 45 ✉ 80121 ℘ 081 7640044, info@ vesuvio.it, Fax 081 7644483, ≤ gulf and Castel dell'Ovo, « Roof-garden rest. », ↻, ≘s – ⧈, ↔ rm, ▤ 📺 ℃ ⅚ ☜ – 🕭 400. 🝙 🗓 ⑩ ⑳ 𝗩𝗜𝗦𝗔. ⚘
FX n
Meals *Caruso* Rest. (booking essential) a la carte 68/93 – **146 rm** ⌑ 285/336, 17 suites.

🏨 **Excelsior**, via Partenope 48 ✉ 80121 ℘ 081 7640111, info@ excelsior.it, Fax 081 7649743, « Roof garden solarium with ≤ gulf and Castel dell'Ovo » – ⧈ ▤ 📺 ℃. 🝙 🗓 ⑩ ⑳ 𝗩𝗜𝗦𝗔 𝗝𝗖𝗕. ⚘ rest
GX w
Meals *La Terrazza* Rest. a la carte 39/54 – **121 rm** ⌑ 248/300, 12 suites.

🏨 **Gd H. Parker's**, corso Vittorio Emanuele 135 ✉ 80121 ℘ 081 7612474, ghparker @ tin.it, Fax 081 663527, « Roof garden rest. with ≤ city and gulf » – ⧈, ↔ rm, ▤ 📺 ℃ ☜ – 🕭 250. 🝙 🗓 ⑩ ⑳ 𝗩𝗜𝗦𝗔. ⚘
EX r
Meals *George's* Rest. a la carte 45/57 – **73 rm** ⌑ 212/260,50, 10 suites.

🏨 **Santa Lucia**, via Partenope 46 ✉ 80121 ℘ 081 7640666, reservations@ santalucia.it, Fax 081 7648580, ≤ gulf and Castel dell'Ovo – ⧈, ↔ rm, ▤ 📺 ℃ ⅚ – 🕭 100. 🝙 🗓 ⑩ ⑳ 𝗩𝗜𝗦𝗔. ⚘
GX c
Meals (see rest. *Megaris* below) – **85 rm** ⌑ 239,99/319,99, 11 suites.

🏨 **Starhotel Terminus** Ⓜ, piazza Garibaldi 91 ✉ 80142 ℘ 081 7793111, terminus.n a@ starhotels.it, Fax 081 206689, ↻, ≘s – ⧈, ↔ rm, ▤ 📺 ☜ – 🕭 300. 🝙 🗓 ⑩ ⑳ 𝗩𝗜𝗦𝗔 𝗝𝗖𝗕. ⚘
MY a
Meals (residents only) 33,57 – **168 rm** ⌑ 149,77/206,58.

🏨 **Holiday Inn Napoli** Ⓜ, centro direzionale Isola e/6 ✉ 80143 ℘ 081 2250111, holy nap@ tin.it, Fax 081 5628074, ↻, ≘s – ⧈, ↔ rm, ▤ 📺 ℃ ⅚ ☜ – 🕭 320. 🝙 🗓 ⑩ ⑳ 𝗩𝗜𝗦𝗔 𝗝𝗖𝗕. ⚘
by corso Meridionale MY
Meals *Bistrot Victor* Rest. 25/30,80 and a la carte 30/41 – **298 rm** ⌑ 185/205, 32 suites.

459

NAPOLI

Arena della Sanità (Via) . . **GU** 6
Artisti (Piazza degli) . . . . . . **EV** 9
Bernini (Via G. L.) . . . . **EV** 12

Bonito (Via G.) . . . . **FV** 13
Carducci (Via G.) . . . . **FX** 20
Chiatamone (Via) . . . . **GU** 27
Cirillo (Via D.) . . . . **FX** 25
Colonna (Via Vittoria) . . . . . **FX** 29
Crocelle (Via) . . . . **GU** 35
D'Auria (Via G.) . . . . **FV** 40

Ferraris (Via Galileo) . . . . . . **HV** 54
Gaetani (Via) . . . . **FX** 61
Gen. Pignatelli (Via) . . . . . . **HU** 63
Giordano (Via L.) . . . . **EV** 64
Martini (Via Simone) . . . . . . **EV** 75
Mazzocchi (Via Alessio) . . . **HU** 76
Menzinger (Via G.) . . . . **EV** 77

Traffic restricted in the town centre

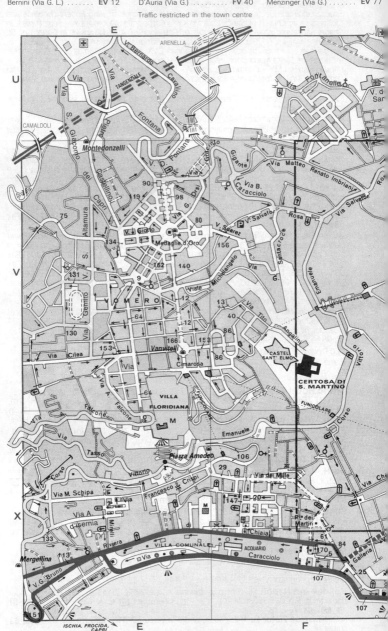

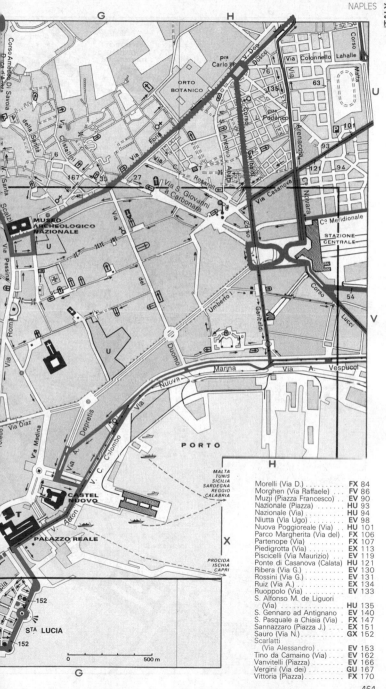

461

NAPOLI

0   300 m

MUSEO ARCHEOLOGICO NAZIONALE

Piazza Cavour

P.za Cavour

V. S. Teresa degli Scalzi

Rosa

88

145

U

Via Pisanelli

V. Salvatore Tommasi

U

32   Via

Sapienza

Via del Sole

S. Paolo Maggiore

S. Maria Maggiore

Francesco Saverio

Salita Pontecorvo

Correra

P.za Bellini

145

148

V. S. Rosa

P.za Mazzini

V. Manica

Via

V. G. Brombeis

P.ta ALBA

123

P.za Miraglia

Sansevero

Emanuele

Via

Ventaglieri

Tarsia

P.za Dante

149

S. Domenico Maggiore

139

P.za del M

Vittorio

67

Salvatore

Via

Montesanto

83

Via

SPACCANAPOLI

B. Croce

Scala Montesanto

STAZIONE CUMANA E FERROVIA CIRCUMFLEGREA

Via Porta Medina

P.za del Gesù Nuovo

S. CHIARA

Via S. Chiara

Mezzoca

Corso

MONTESANTO

V. Forno Vecchio

15

72

136

165

V. P. Scura

V. Pignasecca

82

S. Nicola alla Carità

U

85

S. Anna d. Lombardi

154

Emanuele

Via Francesco Girardi

Piazza d. Carità

Via C. Battisti

Via Monteoliveto

c

154

P.za G.

31

31

P.za G. Matteotti

73

e

CERTOSA DI S. MARTINO

Vittorio

Toledo

Via Cardinale G. Sanfelice

Bovio

Via I.

Diaz

POL

d

Depretis

de Il Gasper

Via Cervantes

Via Medina

Speranzella

V. S. Giacomo

P

b

FUNICOLARE

Corso

V. E. Imbriani

H

Piazza P

T

Via Acton

Via Cris

Via

CENTRALE

Via S. Mattia

138

171

Verdi

Municipio

P

W

Galleria Umberto I

Via

S. Carlo

CASTEL NUOVO

P

Ammiraglio

Nicotera

D

T

P.za Trieste e Trento

P

PALAZZO REALE

MOLO BEVERELLO

57

Via

Chiaia

P

PZA DEL PLEBISCITO

S. Francesco di Paola

POR

Via Chiaia

Monte di Dio

M

GALLERIA DELLA VITTORIA

V. Cesario Console

F. Acton

P.za dei Martiri

J   K

Y

Z

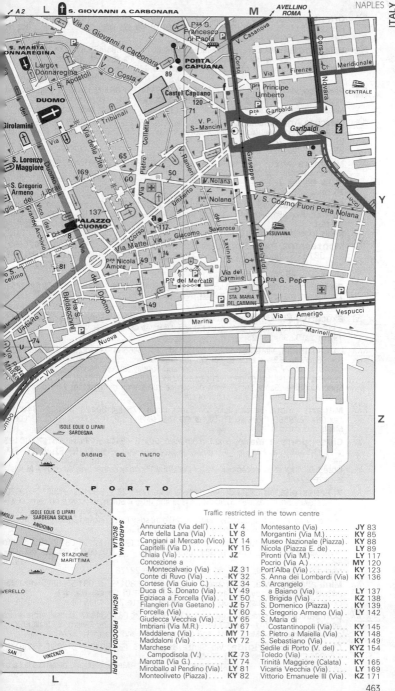

S. GIOVANNI A CARBONARA

PORTA CAPUANA

DUOMO

S. MARIA DONNAREGINA

Girolamini

S. Lorenzo Maggiore

S. Gregorio Armeno

PALAZZO CUOMO

Castel Capuano

P.za S. Francesco di Paola

V. Casanova

AVELLINO ROMA

A2

Pza Principe Umberto

Pza Garibaldi

Garibaldi

CENTRALE

S. Cosmo Fuori Porta Nolana

VESUVIANA

Pza Nolana

Pza Nicola Amore

Pza del Mercato

STA MARIA DEL CARMINE

Pza G. Pepe

Via Amerigo Vespucci

Marina

Marinella

Nuova

PORTO

BACINO DEL PILIERO

ISOLE EOLIE O LIPARI
SARDEGNA

ISOLE EOLIE O LIPARI
SARDEGNA SICILIA

STAZIONE MARITTIMA

VERELLO

SAN VINCENZO

ANGIOINO

SARDEGNA SICILIA

ISCHIA, PROCIDA, CAPRI

Traffic restricted in the town centre

🏨 **Oriente** without rest., via Diaz 44 ✉ 80134 ℰ 081 5512133, *ghorient@tin.it*, *Fax 081 5514915* – 🛗 📺 📺 🍷 – 🔬 300. 🆎 🆂 ⓞ ⓦⓞ 𝚅𝙸𝚂𝙰. ⅍　　　　　　　　　KZ d
129 rm ⌑ 154,90/216,90, 2 suites.

🏨 **Villa Capodimonte** ⌗, via Moiariello 66 ✉ 80131 ℰ 081 459000, *Fax 081 299344*, ≼, 🏡, 🌿, ⚸ – 🛗 🗐 📺 ⟵ 🅿 – 🔬 110. 🆎 🆂 ⓞ ⓦⓞ 𝚅𝙸𝚂𝙰. ⅍ rest
Meals (dinner only) a la carte 27/41 – **57 rm** ⌑ 145/196.
by corso Amedeo di Savoia GU

🏨 **Paradiso,** via Catullo 11 ✉ 80122 ℰ 081 2475111, *Fax 081 7613449*, ≼ gulf, city and Vesuvius, 🏡 – 🗐 📺 📺 – 🔬 80. 🆎 🆂 ⓞ ⓦⓞ 𝚅𝙸𝚂𝙰 ᴊᴄʙ.
Meals a la carte 35/44 – **74 rm** ⌑ 108/191.　　　　by Riviera di Chiaia EFX

🏨 **Mercure Angioino** without rest., via Depretis 123 ✉ 80133 ℰ 081 5529500, *dire zione.mercurenapoliangioino@accor-hotels.it*, *Fax 081 5529509* – 🛗 🗐 📺 – 🔬 30. 🆎 🆂 ⓞ ⓦⓞ 𝚅𝙸𝚂𝙰 ᴊᴄʙ　　　　　　　　　　　　　　　　　　　　　　　　　　KZ b
85 rm ⌑ 122/180.

🏨 **Miramare** without rest., via Nazario Sauro 24 ✉ 80132 ℰ 081 7647589, *info@hot elmiramare.com*, *Fax 081 7640775*, ≼ gulf and Vesuvius, « Roof garden » – 🛗 🗐 📺. 🆎 🆂 ⓞ 𝚅𝙸𝚂𝙰 ᴊᴄʙ. ⅍ rest　　　　　　　　　　　　　　　　　　　　　GX e
30 rm ⌑ 169/282.

🏨 **San Germano,** via Beccadelli 41 ✉ 80125 ℰ 081 5705422, *sangermano.na@bestw estern.it*, *Fax 081 5701546*, 🏊 – 🛗 🗐 📺 ⟵ – 🔬 200. 🆎 🆂 ⓞ ⓦⓞ 𝚅𝙸𝚂𝙰 ᴊᴄʙ.
⅍ rest　　　　　　　　　　　　　　　　　　　　　　　　　by Riviera di Chiaia EFX
Meals (closed 7 to 20 August) a la carte 24/35 – **105 rm** ⌑ 83/130.

🏨 **Montespina Park Hotel,** via San Gennaro 2 ✉ 80125 ℰ 081 7629687, *Fax 081 5702962*, « Park », 🏊 – 🛗 🗐 📺 ♿ 🅿 – 🔬 100. 🆎 🆂 ⓞ ⓦⓞ 𝚅𝙸𝚂𝙰.
⅍　　　　　　　　　　　　　　　　　　　　　　　　　　by Riviera di Chiaia EFX
Meals 20 – **45 rm** ⌑ 95/140.

🏨 **Suite Esedra** without rest., via Cantani 12 ✉ 80133 ℰ 081 287451, *Fax 081 287451*, 🛁 – 🛗 🗐 📺 🍷. 🆎 🆂 ⓞ ⓦⓞ 𝚅𝙸𝚂𝙰 ᴊᴄʙ. ⅍　　　　　　　　　LY a
16 rm ⌑ 92,96/134,28, suite.

🏨 **Executive** without rest., via del Cerriglio 10 ✉ 80134 ℰ 081 5520611, *Fax 081 5520611*, « Roof garden terrace », 🛎 – 🛗 🗐 📺 ⟵. 🆎 🆂 ⓞ ⓦⓞ 𝚅𝙸𝚂𝙰 ᴊᴄʙ. ⅍　　　　KZ c
19 rm ⌑ 92,96/134,28.

🍴🍴🍴 **La Cantinella,** via Cuma 42 ✉ 80132 ℰ 081 7648684, *la.cantinella@lacantinella.it*,
⛶ *Fax 081 7648769* – 🗐. 🆎 🆂 ⓞ ⓦⓞ 𝚅𝙸𝚂𝙰 ᴊᴄʙ. ⅍　　　　　　　　GX v
closed 12 to 27 August, 24-25 December and Sunday (except November-May) – **Meals** (booking essential for dinner) a la carte 37/65
Spec. Linguine "Santa Lucia". Rana pescatrice con crema di crostacei. Filetto di manzo lardellato al fegato d'oca in crosta di sale.

🍴🍴🍴 **Megaris** - Hotel Santa Lucia, via Santa Lucia 175 ✉ 80121 ℰ 081 7640511, *Fax 081 7648580* – ⅍⟵ 🗐. 🆎 🆂 ⓞ ⓦⓞ 𝚅𝙸𝚂𝙰. ⅍　　　　　　　GX c
Meals a la carte 41/54.

🍴🍴 **Giuseppone a Mare,** via Ferdinando Russo 13-Capo Posillipo ✉ 80123 ℰ 081 5756002, *Fax 081 5756002*, ≼ city and gulf – 🗐 🅿. 🆎 🆂 ⓞ ⓦⓞ 𝚅𝙸𝚂𝙰.
⅍　　　　　　　　　　　　　　　　　　　　　　　　by via Caracciolo FX
closed 16 August-3 September, 24-25 December, Sunday dinner and Monday – **Meals** a la carte 22/45.

🍴🍴 **'A Fenestella,** via Calata del Ponticello a Marechiaro 23 ✉ 80123 ℰ 081 7690020, *afenestella@tin.it*, *Fax 081 5750686*, ≼ sea and gulf, « Summer service on terrace » –
🅿 🆎 🆂 ⓦⓞ 𝚅𝙸𝚂𝙰 ᴊᴄʙ　　　　　　　　　　　　　　by via V. G. Bruno EX
closed 14 to 16 August, Sunday dinner and Wednesday lunch, closed Sunday July-August – **Meals** (dinner only in August) a la carte 27/42 (15 %).

🍴🍴 **Rosolino-Il Posto Accanto,** via Nazario Sauro 2 ✉ 80132 ℰ 081 7649873, *info @rosolino-restaurant.com*, *Fax 081 7649870* – 🗐 – 🔬 70. 🆎 🆂 ⓞ ⓦⓞ 𝚅𝙸𝚂𝙰 ᴊᴄʙ.
⅍　　　　　　　　　　　　　　　　　　　　　　　　　　　　　　GX a
closed Sunday – **Meals** Rest. and pizzeria a la carte 22/28.

🍴🍴 **Mimi alla Ferrovia,** via Alfonso d'Aragona 21 ✉ 80139 ℰ 081 5538525, *mimiallf errovia@mimiallaferrovia.it*, *Fax 081 289004* – 🗐. 🆎 🆂 ⓞ ⓦⓞ 𝚅𝙸𝚂𝙰 ᴊᴄʙ　　MY f
closed 13 to 22 August and Sunday – **Meals** a la carte 25/34 (15 %).

🍴🍴 **Don Salvatore,** strada Mergellina 4 A ✉ 80122 ℰ 081 681817, *donsalvatore@virg ilio.it*, *Fax 081 661241* – 🗐. 🆎 🆂 ⓞ ⓦⓞ 𝚅𝙸𝚂𝙰 ᴊᴄʙ　　　by Riviera di Chiaia EFX
closed Wednesday – **Meals** Rest. and pizzeria 26/34 and a la carte 27/42.

🍴🍴 **Ciro a Santa Brigida,** via Santa Brigida 73 ✉ 80132 ℰ 081 5524072, *Fax 081 5528992* – 🗐. 🆎 🆂 ⓞ ⓦⓞ 𝚅𝙸𝚂𝙰　　　　　　　　　　　　　　JZ w
closed 6 to 22 August and Sunday (except December) – **Meals** Rest. and pizzeria a la carte 24/34.

XX **Transatlantico**, via Luculliana-borgo Marinari ⊠ 80132 ℰ 081 7648842,
Fax 081 7649201, « Summer service at Santa Lucia harbour » – 🗚 🛠 ⑩ ⑩⑩ 𝘝𝘐𝘚𝘈.
※ by via Nazario Sauro GX
closed 22 January-5 February and Tuesday – **Meals** a la carte 27/41.

X **La Fazenda**, via Marechiaro 58/a ⊠ 80123 ℰ 081 5757420, *Fax 081 5757420,* ≤ sea
and Capri Island, 🍴 – 🅿. 🗚 🛠 ⑩ 𝘝𝘐𝘚𝘈 by Riviera di Chiaia EFX
closed Sunday dinner and Monday lunch – **Meals** a la carte 20/36 (15 %).

X **Taverna dell'Arte**, rampe San Giovanni Maggiore1/A ⊠ 80134 ℰ 081 5527558,
Fax 081 5527558 – ⇖, 🗐. 🛠 𝘝𝘐𝘚𝘈. ※ LZ a
closed 4 to 25 August and Sunday – **Meals** (booking essential) a la carte 18/30.

X **L'Europeo di Mattozzi**, via Campodisola 4/6/8 ⊠ 801335 ℰ 081 5521323,
Fax 081 5521323 – 🗐. 🗚 🛠 ⑩ ⑩⑩ 𝘝𝘐𝘚𝘈 𝙅𝘾𝘽. ※ KZ e
closed 15 to 31 August, Sunday and dinner (except Thursday, Friday, Saturday and Vigils)
– **Meals** Rest. and pizzeria a la carte 23/34 (12 %).

X **Al Poeta**, piazza Salvatore di Giacomo 134/135 ⊠ 80123 ℰ 081 5756936,
Fax 081 5756936 – 🗐. 🗚 🛠 ⑩ ⑩⑩ 𝘝𝘐𝘚𝘈 KZ a
closed 10 to 25 August and Monday – **Meals** a la carte 22/35 (15 %).

X **Marino**, via Santa Lucia 118/120 ⊠ 80132 ℰ 081 7640280 – 🗐. 🗚 🛠 ⑩⑩ 𝘝𝘐𝘚𝘈 𝙅𝘾𝘽.
※ GX b
closed August and Monday – **Meals** Rest. and pizzeria a la carte 18/31 (15 %)

X **Sbrescia**, rampe Sant'Antonio a Posillipo 109 ⊠ 80122 ℰ 081 669140,
Fax 081 669140, Typical rest.-pizzeria with ≤ city and gulf – 🗚 🛠 ⑩ ⑩⑩ 𝘝𝘐𝘚𝘈. ※
closed Monday – **Meals** a la carte 25/35 (13 %). by Riviera di Chiaia EFX

Island of Capri 80073 Napoli 𝟰𝟯𝟭 F 24 *G. Italy.* – *pop. 13 189 alt.* – *High Season : Easter and June-September.*
The limitation of motor-vehicles' access is regulated by legislative rules.

🏨🏨🏨 **Gd H. Quisisana**, via Camerelle 2 ℰ 081 8370788, *info@quisi.com, Fax 081 8376080,*
≤ sea and Certosa, 🍴, « Garden with ⊅ », 🏋, ≦s, ⬜, ❀ – 🛗 🗐 📺 🍴 – 🏊 550.
🗚 🛠 ⑩ ⑩⑩ 𝘝𝘐𝘚𝘈 𝙅𝘾𝘽.
March-October – **Meals** *Quisi* Rest. *(closed lunch also Sunday June-September)* a la carte
46/80 and *La Colombaia* Rest. *(closed dinner April-May and October)* a la carte 37/63
– **145 rm** ⩝ 190/490, 7 suites.

🏨🏨 **Punta Tragara** ⸾, via Tragara 57 ℰ 081 8370844, *hotel.tragara@capri.it,*
Fax 081 8377790, ≤ Faraglioni and coast, 🍴, « Panoramic terrace with ⊅ heated » –
🛗 🗐 📺. 🗚 🛠 ⑩ ⑩⑩ 𝘝𝘐𝘚𝘈 𝙅𝘾𝘽. ※
Easter-October – **Meals** a la carte 44/64 **35 rm** ⩝ 434, 15 suites.

🏨🏨 **Scalinatella** ⸾ without rest., via Tragara 8 ℰ 081 8370633, *Fax 081 8378291,* ≤ sea
and Certosa, ⊅ heated – 🛗 🗐 📺. 🗚 🛠 ⑩ 𝘝𝘐𝘚𝘈. ※
15 March-5 November – **30 rm** ⩝ 360/500.

🏨 **Luna** ⸾, viale Matteotti 3 ℰ 081 8370433, *luna@capri.it, Fax 081 8377459,* 🍴,
« Terraces with ≤ sea, Faraglioni and Certosa ; big floral garden », ⊅ – 🛗 🗐 📺 🍴. 🗚
🛠 ⑩ ⑩⑩ 𝘝𝘐𝘚𝘈.
Easter-October – **Meals** a la carte 35/44 – **50 rm** ⩝ 210/335, 4 suites.

🏨 **Casa Morgano** ⸾ without rest., via Tragara 6 ℰ 081 8370158, *casamorgano@capri.it,*
Fax 081 8370681, ≤ sea and Certosa, « Floral terraces in pinewood », ⊅ heated – 🛗 🗐
📺. 🗚 🛠 ⑩ ⑩⑩ 𝘝𝘐𝘚𝘈
26 March-5 November – **28 rm** ⩝ 220/410.

🏨 **Villa Brunella** ⸾, via Tragara 24 ℰ 081 8370122, *villabrunella@capri.it,*
Fax 081 8370430, ≤ sea and coast, 🍴, « Floral terraces with ⊅ heated » – 🛗 🗐 📺.
🗚 🛠 ⑩ ⑩⑩ 𝘝𝘐𝘚𝘈. ※
19 March-5 November – **Meals** *Brunella Terrace* Rest. (booking essential) a la carte 29/45
(12 %) – **20 rm** ⩝ 270/300.

🏨 **Syrene**, via Camerelle 51 ℰ 081 8370102, *syrene@capri.it, Fax 081 8370957,* ≤, 🍴,
« Lemon-garden with ⊅ » – 🛗 🗐 📺. 🗚 🛠 ⑩ ⑩⑩ 𝘝𝘐𝘚𝘈. ※
April-October – **Meals** *(closed Tuesday except June to September)* a la carte 29/37 – **34 rm**
⩝ 180,76/278,89.

🏨 **Canasta** without rest., via Campo di Teste 6 ℰ 081 8370561, *canasta@capri.it,*
Fax 081 8376675 – 🗐 📺 🍴. 🗚 🛠 ⑩ ⑩⑩ 𝘝𝘐𝘚𝘈. ※
closed 15 January-15 March – **17 rm** ⩝ 92,96/175,59.

🏨 **Villa Sarah** ⸾ without rest., via Tiberio 3/a ℰ 081 8377817, *info@villasarah.it,*
Fax 081 8377215, ≤, « Shady garden » – 🗐 📺. 🗚 🛠 ⑩ ⑩⑩ 𝘝𝘐𝘚𝘈. ※
Easter-October – **19 rm** ⩝ 124/176, 🗐 18.

🏨 **Villa Krupp** ⸾ without rest., via Matteotti 12 ℰ 081 8370362, *Fax 081 8376489,* ≤
Faraglioni and coast – 🛠 ⑩⑩ 𝘝𝘐𝘚𝘈. ※
20 March-October – **12 rm** ⩝ 75/140.

XX **La Capannina**, via Le Botteghe 12 bis/14 ℘ 081 8370732, capannina@capri.it,
Fax 081 8376990 – ▤, ﹐ 🅰🄴 🄢 ⓞ ⓞⓞ 𝑽𝑰𝑺𝑨. 🎘
10 March-10 November and 27 December-5 January – **Meals** (booking essential for dinner)
a la carte 36/45 (15 %).

XX **Aurora**, via Fuorlovado 18 ℘ 081 8370181, aurora@capri.it, Fax 081 8376533, 🏡 –
🕸. 🅰🄴 🄢 ⓞ ⓞⓞ 𝑽𝑰𝑺𝑨. 🎘
closed January-March – **Meals** Rest. and pizzeria a la carte 28/51 (15 %).

X **Da Tonino**, via Dentecala 12 ℘ 081 8376718, « Summer service on terrace » – 🅰🄴 🄢
ⓞ 𝑽𝑰𝑺𝑨
closed 16 Janury-14 March – **Meals** a la carte 25/34.

X **Verginiello**, via Lo Palazzo 25/a ℘ 081 8370944, Fax 081 8370944, ≤ sea and coast
« Summer service on panoramic terrace » – ▤. 🅰🄴 🄢 ⓞ ⓞⓞ 𝑽𝑰𝑺𝑨 🄹🄲🄱. 🎘
closed 10 to 25 November : – **Meals** Rest. and pizzeria a la carte 19/41.

at Anacapri alt. 275 – ✉ 80071 :

🏨 **Capri Palace Hotel**, via Capodimonte 2 ℘ 081 9780111, info@capri-palace.com,
Fax 081 8373191, ≤, 🏡, Rooms with small private swimming pools, « Floral terraces with
🛌 », 🛏, ≋, 🔲 – 🛗 ▤ 📺 – 🔬 200. 🅰🄴 🄢 ⓞ ⓞⓞ 𝑽𝑰𝑺𝑨 🄹🄲🄱. 🎘
March-November – **Meals** *L'Olivo* Rest. (dinner only) 46,48 and a la carte 61/84 – **85 rm**
⌑ 360/568, 3 suites.

at Marina Piccola – ✉ 80073 Capri :

XX **Canzone del Mare**, via Marina Piccola 93 ℘ 081 8370104, certosella@infinito.it
Fax 081 8377504, ≤ Faraglioni and sea, 🏡, « Bathing establishment with 🛌 » – 🅰🄴 🄢
ⓞ ⓞⓞ 𝑽𝑰𝑺𝑨 🄹🄲🄱. 🎘
Easter-October – **Meals** (lunch only except August) a la carte 39/73.

Sant'Agata sui due Golfi 80064 Napoli 🄴🄸🄸 F 25 G. Italy. – alt. 391 – High Season : April-
September.
Roma 266 – Castellammare di Stabia 28 – Napoli 55 – Salerno 56 – Sorrento 9.

XXX **Don Alfonso 1890** with rm, corso Sant'Agata 11 ℘ 081 8780026, donalfonso@sy
💎💎 rene.it, Fax 081 5330226, 🌳 – 🕸 ▤ 📺 🄿 🅰🄴 🄢 ⓞ ⓞⓞ 𝑽𝑰𝑺𝑨. 🎘
closed 7 January-1 March and 24-25 December – **Meals** (closed Monday and Tuesday lunch
June-September, Monday and Tuesday in other months) (booking essential) 75/98 and a
la carte 63/84 – 5 suites ⌑ 176
Spec. Zeppola di astice in agrodolce con melanzane, porri e zucchine dell'orto su Capri
(summer). Passata di fagioli cannellini con vongole alla brace, polipetti veraci e semi di
finocchio selvatico (winter). Capretto lucano alle erbe fresche mediterranee.

PALERMO (Sicily) 90100 🄿 🄴🄸🄸 M 22 G. Italy. – pop. 679 290.

See : Palace of the Normans★★ : the palatine Chapel★★★, mosaics★★★, Ancient Royal
Apartments★★ AZ – Oratory of St Dominic's Rosary★★★ BY N _ Oratory of St Cita★★★
BY N – Church of St. John of the Hermits★★ : cloister★ AZ – Piazza Pretoria★★ BY – Piazza
Bellini★ BY : Martorana Church★★, Church of St. Cataldo★★ – Abatellis Palace★ : Regional
Gallery of Sicily★★ CY **G** _ Magnolia fig trees★★ in Garibaldi Gardens CY – International
Museum of Marionetes★★ CY **M** – Archaeological Museum★ : metopes from the temples
at Selinus★★, the Ram★★ BY **M** _ Villa Malfitano★★ – Botanical garden★ : magnolia fig
trees★★ CDZ _ Capuchin Catacombs★★ _ Villa Bonanno★ AZ – Cathedral★ AYZ _ Quattro
Canti★ BY _ Gancia, interior★ CY _ Magione : facade★ CZ _ St Francis of Assisi★ CY –
Mirto Palace★ CY _ Chiaramonte Palace★ CY _ St Mary of the chain★ CY **S** _ Gallery of
Modern Art E. Restivo★ AX – Villino Florio★ _ St John of the Lepers★ _ Zisa★ _ Cuba★*.
Envir. : Monreale★★★ by Corso Calatafimi : 8 km AZ – Addura's Caves★ North-East.

✈ Falcone-Borsellino East : 30 km ℘ 091 7020111, Fax 091 7020394 – Alitalia, via
Mazzini 59 ✉ 90139 ℘ 091 6019111, Fax 091 6019346.

🚢 to Genova daily except Sunday (20 h) and to Livorno Tuesday, Thursday and Saturday
(17 h) – Grimaldi-Grandi Navi Veloci, calata Marinai d'Italia ✉ 90133 ℘ 091 587404, Fax
091 6110088; to Napoli daily (11 h), to Genova Monday, Wednesday and Friday and Sunday
18 June-31 December (24 h) and Cagliari Saturday (13 h 30 mn) – Tirrenia Navigazione,
calata Marinai d'Italia ✉ 90133 ℘ 1478 99000, Fax 091 6021221.

⛴ to Aeolian Island June-September daily (1 h 50 mn) – SNAV Barbaro Agency, piazza
Principe di Belmonte 51/55 ✉ 90139 ℘ 091 586533, Fax 091 584830.

🛈 piazza Castelnuovo 34 ✉ 90141 ℘ 091 583847, Fax 091 582788 – Punta Raisi Airport
at Cinisi ℘ 091 591698 – piazza Giulio Cesare (Central Station) ✉ 90127 ℘ 091 6165914
A.C.I. via delle Alpi 6 ✉ 90144 ℘ 091 300468.
Messina 235.

Plans on following pages

🏨 **Villa Igiea Gd H.**, salita Belmonte 43 ⊠ 90142 ℘ 091 6312111, *villa-igea@thi.it*, *Fax 091 547654*, ≤, 🍴, « 19C mansion with seafront terrace », 🏊, ≋, ✗ – 🛗 🖭 🗜 📞 – 🔬 400   by via Crispi BX
111 rm, 5 suites.

🏨 **Astoria Palace Hotel**, via Montepellegrino 62 ⊠ 90142 ℘ 091 6281111, *astoria @tin.it*, *Fax 091 6372178* – 🛗, 💤 rm, 🖭 📞 – 🔬 800. 🖭 🔞 ⓪ 🆖 **VISA**. ✗
                 by via Crispi BX
Meals *Il Cedro* Rest. a la carte 28/42 – **315 rm** ⊇ 113,63/165,26, 14 suites.

🏨 **Centrale Palace Hotel** Ⓜ, corso Vittorio Emanuele 327 ⊠ 90134 ℘ 091 336666, *cphotel@tin.it*, *Fax 091 334881*, « In a 17C building ; rest. service on panoramic terrace » – 🛗 🖭 📺 & 🚗 📞 – 🔬 120. 🖭 🔞 ⓪ 🆖 **VISA** **JCB**. ✗   BY b
Meals a la carte 33/51 – ⊇ 10,33 – **63 rm** 144/206.

🏨 **San Paolo Palace**, via Messina Marine 91 ⊠ 90123 ℘ 091 6211112, *hotel@sanpa olopalace.it*, *Fax 091 6215300*, ≤, « Roof garden rest. », 🏋, ≋, 🏊, ✗ – 🛗 🖭 📺 ✆ & 🚗 📞 – 🔬 1600. 🖭 🔞 ⓪ **VISA**. ✗   by via Ponte di Mare DZ
Meals a la carte 22/33 – **274 rm** ⊇ 98,13/124, 10 suites.

🏨 **Principe di Villafranca**, via G. Turrisi Colonna 4 ⊠ 90141 ℘ 091 6118523, *info @principedivillafranca.it*, *Fax 091 588705*, 🏋 – 🛗 🖭 📺 🚗. 🖭 🔞 ⓪ 🆖 **VISA** **JCB**. ✗   AX d
Meals 23,24 – **34 rm** ⊇ 118,79/170,43.

🏨 **Massimo Plaza Hotel** Ⓜ without rest., via Maqueda 437 ⊠ 90133 ℘ 091 325657, *booking@massimoplazahotel.com*, *Fax 091 325711*, « In a palace of the historic centre » – 🖭 📺 ✆. 🖭 🔞 ⓪ 🆖 **VISA** **JCB**   BY e
15 rm ⊻ 98,13/134,28.

🏨 **Villa d'Amato**, via Messina Marine 180 ⊠ 90123 ℘ 091 6212767, *villadamato@ju mpy.it*, *Fax 091 6212767*, 🍴 – 🛗 🖭 📺 📞 – 🔬 100. 🖭 🔞 ⓪ 🆖 **VISA**. ✗ rest   by via Ponte di Mare DZ
Meals *(closed Sunday lunch)* a la carte 23/31 – **37 rm** ⊇ 67,14/103,29.

🏨 **Holiday Inn Palermo**, viale della Regione Siciliana 2620 ⊠ 90145 ℘ 091 6983111, *holidayinn.palermo@alliancealberghi.com*, *Fax 091 408198* – 🛗 🖭 📺 ✆ 📞 – 🔬 90. 🖭 🔞 ⓪ 🆖 **VISA**. ✗   by via della Libertà AX
Meals a la carte 26/39 – **95 rm** ⊇ 165/190.

🍽️🍽️🍽️ **La Scuderia**, viale del Fante 9 ⊠ 90146 ℘ 091 520323, *la.scuderia@tiscalinet.It*, *Fax 091 520467* – 🖭 🖭 🔞 ⓪ 🆖 **VISA**. ✗   by via C.A. Dalla Chiesa AX
closed 13 to 30 August and Sunday – **Meals** a la carte 35/49.

🍽️🍽️ **Il Ristorantino**, piazza De Gasperi 19 ⊠ 90146 ℘ 091 512861, *Fax 091 6702999*, 🍴 – 🖭. 🖭 🔞 ⓪ 🆖 **VISA**. ✗   by via C.A. Dalla Chiesa AX
closed 10 to 30 August, 1 to 9 January and Monday – **Meals** a la carte 33/44.

🍽️🍽️ **Regine**, via Trapani 4/a ⊠ 90141 ℘ 091 586566, *ristoranteregine@gestelnet.it*, *Fax 091 586566* – 🖭. 🖭 🔞 ⓪ 🆖 **VISA**. ✗   AX e
closed August and Sunday – **Meals** a la carte 34/38.

🍽️🍽️ **Friend's Bar**, via Brunelleschi 138 ⊠ 90145 ℘ 091 201401, *catering@friendsbarsrl .com*, *Fax 091 201066*, 🍴 – 🖭. 🖭 🔞 ⓪ **VISA**. ✗   by via della Libertà AX
closed 10 to 31 August and Monday – **Meals** (booking essential) a la carte 30/57.

🍽️🍽️ **Lo Scudiero**, via Turati 7 ⊠ 90139 ℘ 091 581628, *Fax 091 581628* – 🖭. 🖭 🔞 ⓪ 🆖 **VISA** **JCB**. ✗   AX c
closed 10 to 20 August and Sunday – **Meals** a la carte 25/46.

🍽️🍽️ **Santandrea**, piazza Sant'Andrea 4 ⊠ 90133 ℘ 091 334999, 🍴 – 🖭. 🖭 🔞 ⓪ 🆖 **VISA** **JCB**   BY d
closed January and Tuesday, July-August closed Sunday – **Meals** (booking essential) local dishes a la carte 27/38.

🍽️ **Capricci di Sicilia**, via Istituto Pignatelli 6 angolo piazza Sturzo ⊠ 90139 ℘ 091 327777 – 🖭. 🖭 🔞 ⓪ 🆖 **VISA** **JCB**. ✗   AX f
Meals a la carte 24/40.

at Borgo Molara *West : 3 km –* ⊠ *90046 Palermo :*

🏨 **Baglio Conca d'Oro**, via Aquino 19/d ℘ 091 6406286, *hotelbaglio@libero.it*, *Fax 091 6408742*, 🍴, « In a restored 18C paper-mill » – 🛗 🖭 📺 ✆ & 📞 – 🔬 500. 🖭 🔞 ⓪ 🆖 **VISA**. ✗
Meals (booking essential) a la carte 27/34 – **27 rm** ⊇ 108,45/154,93.

at Sferracavallo *North-West : 12 Km –* ⊠ *90148 Palermo :*

🍽️ **Il Delfino**, via Torretta 80 ℘ 091 530282, *ildelfi@tin.it*, *Fax 091 6914256* – 🖭. 🖭 🔞 ⓪ 🆖 **VISA** **JCB**. ✗
closed Monday – **Meals** seafood 21.

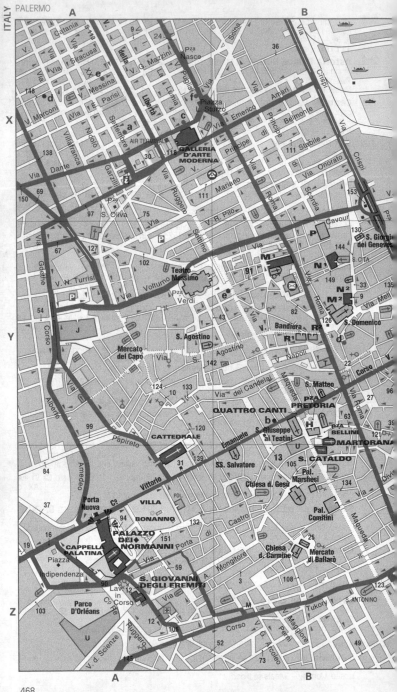

A

B

Catania
S.113
Siracusa
V.
Via
V. Marconi
V. Parisi
V. Messina
V. G. Mazzini
Pza Nasce
Via Puglisi
24
Scinà
36
Crispi
Via
Settembre
XX
Libertà
Via
148
d
e
a
c
f
Piazza
L. Sturzo
Via Emerico
Principe di Belmonte
Amari
Via
Crispi
X
V. Villafranca
Nicolò
Via Garzilli
AIR TERMINAL
30
118
GALLERIA
D'ARTE
MODERNA
Principe
Via Stabile
111
Via Onorato
153
V.
Pza
138
Via Dante
Via
Mariano
Via
Roma
Scordia
Cavour
69
150
i
Pza
Via R. Pilo
Settimo
P
130
S. Giorgio
dei Genovesi
144
S. CITA
97
S. Oliva
75
Via
Via
M1
P
N
67
127
Via
102
Teatro
Massimo
91
M
149
33
135
V. Mell
9
Goethe
V. N. Turrisi
P
Voltumo
Pza
Verdi
e
Via
82
N2
M2
S. Domenico
126
54
Corso
J
43
Bandiera
R2
d
V.
V.
Y
S. Agostino
Via
Agostino
142
V. Napoli
R1
22
Corso
V.
Alberto
Via
Mercato
del Capo
124
10
133
Via dei Candelai
Matteda
S. Matteo
96
27
PZA
PRETORIA
Via Roma
QUATTRO CANTI
b
63
H
39
PZA
BELLINI
121
99
CATTEDRALE
120
Emanuele
S. Giuseppe
ai Teatini
U
MARTORANA
84
Papireto
139
31
SS. Salvatore
13
105
S. CATALDO
134
Amedeo
Vittorio
Chiesa d. Gesù
Pal.
Marshesi
37
Porta
Nuova
C°
VILLA
BONANNO
132
Castro
Via
Pal.
Comitini
16
94
PALAZZO
DEI
Porta
di
25
Mercato
di Ballarò
19
CAPPELLA
PALATINA
NORMANNI
151
59
Chiesa
d. Carmine
123
Piazza
Indipendenza
Via
Mongitore
3
108
S. GIOVANNI
DEGLI EREMITI
Via
Lav.
in Corso
12
M
S. ANTONINO
Z
103
Parco
D'Orléans
U
C° Re
12
106
Tukoty
S. Maggiore
Corso
52
G. Alcoleo
73
49
V. d. Scienze
135
Ruggero

A

B

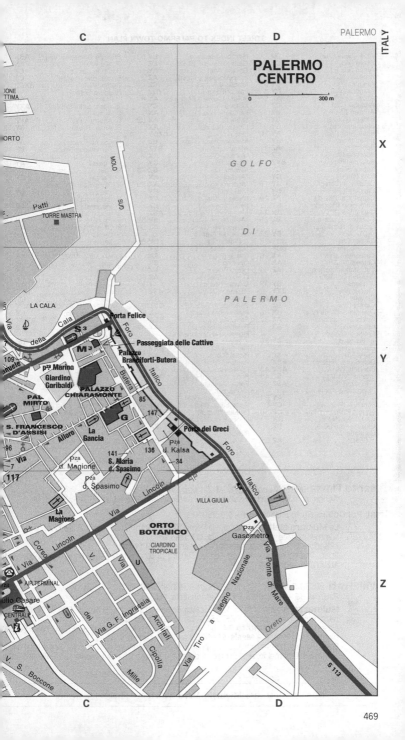

GOLFO

DI

PALERMO

IONE
TTIMA

ORTO

MOLO
SUD

Patti
TORRE MASTRA

LA CALA

della Cala

S 3

M 3

Porta Felice

Foro

Passeggiata delle Cattive

Palazzo
Branciforti-Butera

p.za Marino

Giardino
Garibaldi

PALAZZO
CHIARAMONTE

Butera

Italico

PAL.
MIRTO

85

G

147

Porta dei Greci

Foro

S. FRANCESCO
D'ASSISI

Alloro

La
Gancia

136

Pza
d. Kalsa

96

Via

Pza
d. Magione

141

S. Maria
d. Spasimo

34

7

117

Pza
d. Spasimo

Lincoln

Italico

La
Magione

Via

VILLA GIULIA

ORTO
BOTANICO

Pza
Gasometro

Corso Lincoln

GIARDINO
TROPICALE

Via

Via

U

Via Ponte di Mare

AIR. TERMINAL

del

Via G. F. Ingrassia

Archirafi

Cipolla

Via Tiro a segno Nazionale

ulio Cesare

CENTRALE

Oreto

V. S. Boccone

Mille

S 113

C D

STREET INDEX TO PALERMO TOWN PLAN

Santa Flavia 90017 Palermo 🌐🇮🇹 M 22. pop. 9 950.
Agrigento 130 – Caltanissetta 116 – Catania 197 – Messina 223 – Palermo 18.

at Porticello North-East : 1 km – ⬚ 90010 :

XX **La Muciara-Nello el Greco**, via Roma 103 ℘ 091 957868, Fax 091 957271, « Outdoor
summer service » – 🍴. ⲀⲈ 🇸 ⓞ ⲘⲞ 𝘝𝘐𝘚𝘈. ⲋ⅋
closed Monday – **Meals** seafood a la carte 24/39 (10 %)
Spec. Polpettine di spatola o cernia. Tartara di tonno (May-September). Filetto di pesce
azzurro in agrodolce.

Villafrati 90030 Palermo, 🌐🇮🇹 N 22. pop. 3 394 alt. 450.
Palermo 36 – Agrigento 87 – Caltanissetta 100.

XX **Mulinazzo,** strada statale 121, località Bolognetta North : 9 Km ℘ 091 8724870, mu
nazzo@libero.it, Fax 091 8737533 – 🍴 🅿. ⲀⲈ 🇸 ⓞ ⲘⲞ 𝘝𝘐𝘚𝘈
closed 6 to 26 July, 10 to 24 January, dinner Easter, Christmas and New Year, Sunday
dinner and Monday – **Meals** 31/46,50 and a la carte 33/45
Spec. Fiore di gamberoni all'olio al profumo di mandarini verdi. "Cannolo" di pasta al cacao
con mousse di melanzane. Filetto di dentice con lenticchie di Ustica e salsa alle acciughe

---

Don't get lost, use **Michelin Maps** which are updated annually.

TAORMINA (Sicily) 98039 Messina, 𝟒𝟑𝟐 N 27 G. Italy. – pop. 10 697 alt. 250.

See : Site★★★ – Greek Theatre★★★ ; ≤★★★ BZ – Public garden★★ BZ – ☀★★ from the Square 9 Aprile AZ – Corso Umberto★ ABZ – Castle : ≤★★ AZ.

Exc. : Etna★★★ South-West : for Linguaglossa Mola Castle★ North-West : 5 km Alcantara Gorge★.

🛇 Picciolo (closed Tuesday) via Picciolo ✉ 95030 Castiglione di Sicilia ✆ 0942 986252, Fax 0942 986252, West : 25 km.

🅑 piazza Santa Caterina (Corvaja palace) ✆ 0942 23243, Fax 0942 24941.

Catania 52 ② – Enna 135 ② – Messina 52 ① – Palermo 255 ② – Siracusa 111 ② – Trapani 359 ②

Plans on following pages

🏨🏨🏨 **Grand Hotel Timeo** ≫, via Teatro Greco 59 ✆ 0942 23801, ricevimento. timeo@framon-hotels.it, Fax 0942 628501, ≤ sea, coast and Etna, 🏤, « Extensive park and floral terraces » – 🛗 🖿 📺 🅿 – 🔬 200. 🆎 🕄 ⓞ 🗫 🆅🆂🅰 �🇯🇨🇧. ☀
BZ x
Meals *Il Dito e La Luna* Rest. a la carte 46/73 – **46 rm** ⊇ 253/366, 10 suites.

🏨🏨🏨 **San Domenico Palace** ≫, piazza San Domenico 5 ✆ 0942 613111, san-domenico@thl.it, Fax 0942 625506, 🏤, « 15C monastery with floral garden, ≤ sea, coast and Etna », 🏋, 🏊 heated – 🛗 🖿 📺 🕭 🅿 – 🔬 400. 🆎 🕄 ⓞ 🗫 🆅🆂🅰. ☀
AZ m
Meals a la carte 42/56 – **100 rm** ⊇ 203/423, 8 suites.

🏨🏨🏨 **Villa Diodoro,** via Bagnoli Croci 75 ✆ 0942 23312, diodoro@gaishotels.com, Fax 0942 23391, ≤ sea, coast and Etna, « 🏊 on panoramic terrace », 🏤 – 🛗 🖿 📺 🕭 🅿 – 🔬 400. 🆎 🕄 ⓞ 🆅🆂🅰. ☀
BZ q
Meals a la carte 34/46 – **102 rm** ⊇ 185,92/258,22.

🏨🏨 **Gd H. Miramare,** via Guardiola Vecchia 27 ✆ 0942 23401, Fax 0942 626223, ≤ sea and coast, 🏤, 🏊, 🏤, 🍴 – 🛗 🖿 📺 🅿 🆎 🕄 ⓞ 🗫 🆅🆂🅰. ☀
CZ c
March-October – Meals a la carte 34/40 – **68 rm** ⊇ 123,95/206,58, suite.

🏨🏨 **Villa Fabbiano** without rest., via Pirandello 81 ✆ 0942 626058, info@villafabbiano.com, Fax 0942 23732, ≤ sea and coast, « Roof garden terraces », 🏊, 🏤 – 🛗 🖿 📺 🕹 🅿. 🆎 🕄 ⓞ 🗫 ☀
CZ a
March-October – **26 rm** ⊇ 150/185, 4 suites.

🏨🏨 **Villa Ducale** ≫ without rest., via Leonardo da Vinci 60 ✆ 0942 28153, villaducale@t ao.it, Fax 0942 28710, ≤ sea, coast and Etna – 🖿 📺 🅿. 🆎 🕄 ⓞ 🗫 🆅🆂🅰 🇯🇨🇧. ☀
AZ p
closed until 20 February – **13 rm** ⊇ 175/260.

🏨🏨 **Villa Belvedere** without rest., via Bagnoli Croci 79 ✆ 0942 23791, info@villabelved ere.it, Fax 0942 625830, ≤ gardens, sea and Etna, « Garden with 🏊 » – 🛗 🖿 📺 🅿. 🕄 🗫 🆅🆂🅰
BZ b
closed 26 November-20 December and 10 January-10 March – **49 rm** ⊇ 102,25/161,60.

🏨🏨 **Villa Sirina,** contrada Sirina ✆ 0942 51776, sirina@tao.it, Fax 0942 51671, 🏊, 🏤 – 🖿 📺 🅿. 🆎 🕄 ⓞ 🗫 🆅🆂🅰. ☀   2 km by via Crocifisso   AZ
closed 10 January-20 March – Meals (residents only) (dinner only) – **15 rm** ⊇ 93/130.

🏨 **Andromaco** ≫ without rest., via Fontana Vecchia ✆ 0942 23436, info@andromaco.it, Fax 0942 24985, ≤, 🏊 – 🖿 📺 🅿. 🆎 🕄 ⓞ 🆅🆂🅰   by via Cappuccini   BZ
20 rm ⊇ 82/114.

🍴🍴🍴🍴 **La Giara,** vico La Floresta 1 ✆ 0942 23360, Fax 0942 23233, 🏤, ≤, Rest. and piano bar – 🖿. 🆎 🕄 ⓞ 🆅🆂🅰. ☀
BZ f
closed November, February, March (except Friday-Saturday) and Monday (except July-September) – Meals (dinner only) (booking essential) a la carte 41/55.

🍴🍴🍴 **Casa Grugno,** via Santa Maria de' Greci ✆ 0942 21208, info@casagrugno.it, 🏤 – 🖿. 🆎 🕄 ⓞ 🗫 🆅🆂🅰. ☀
AZ a
closed February and Sunday (except June-September) – Meals a la carte 44/58.

🍴🍴 **Maffei's,** via San Domenico de Guzman 1 ✆ 0942 24055, Fax 0942 24055, 🏤 – 🆎 🕄 ⓞ 🗫
AZ y
closed 10 January-20 February and Tuesday (except Easter to October) – Meals (booking essential) a la carte 36/44.

🍴🍴 **Al Duomo,** vico Ebrei 11 ✆ 0942 625656, info@ristorantealduomo.it, « Summer service on terrace » – 🖿. 🆎 🕄 ⓞ 🗫 🆅🆂🅰. ☀
AZ q
closed February and Wednesday (except April-September) – Meals (booking essential) Sicilian rest. a la carte 27/45.

XX **La Griglia,** corso Umberto 54 ℘ 0942 23980, *Fax 0942 626047* – 🗐. 🖭 🖪 ⓞ 🐠 𝚅𝙸𝚂𝙰
※
BZ c
closed 20 November-20 December and Tuesday – **Meals** a la carte 21/36.

XX **Vicolo Stretto,** via Vicolo Stretto 6 ℘ 0942 23849, *vicolostretto@tao.it*, ≤, 😤 – 🗐
🖭 🖪 ⓞ 𝚅𝙸𝚂𝙰. ※
BZ h
closed 9 to 20 December, 8 January-12 February and Monday (except 15 June-15 September) – **Meals** (booking essential) a la carte 26/44.

X **Il Baccanale,** piazzetta Filea 1 ℘ 0942 625390, *Fax 0942 625390,* 😤 – 🗐. 🖪 🐠 𝚅𝙸𝚂𝙰
※
BZ e
closed Thursday except April-September – **Meals** a la carte 21/35.

at Capo Taormina *South : 4 Km –* ⊠ *98030 Mazzarò :*

🏨 **Grande Albergo Capotaormina** 🦢, via Nazionale 105 ℘ 0942 572111, *prenotazioni@capotaorminahotel.com, Fax 0942 625467,* ≤ sea and coast, « Garden terrace on cliffs, lifts to beach », 𝐅𝐚, ≘s, 🏊 sea water – 📶, ✦ rm, 🗐 📺 📞 🚗 🅿 – 🔬 450.
🖭 🖪 ⓞ 🐠 𝚅𝙸𝚂𝙰 𝙹𝙲𝙱. ※
CZ g
April-October – **Meals** a la carte 27/40 – **200 rm** ⊊ 252/360, 4 suites.

at Mazzarò *East : 5,5 km CZ –* ⊠ *98030 :*

🏨 **Grand Hotel Mazzarò Sea Palace** Ⓜ, via Nazionale 147 ℘ 0942 612111, *info@mazzaroseapalace.it, Fax 0942 626237,* ≤ small bay, 😤, « Solarium terrace with 🏊 », 𝐅𝐚, 🐾ₛ – 📶, ✦ rm, 🗐 📺 📞 – 🔬 100. 🖭 🖪 ⓞ 🐠 𝚅𝙸𝚂𝙰 𝙹𝙲𝙱.
※
CZ b
April-October – **Meals** 47 – **79 rm** ⊊ 196/388, 9 suites.

🏨 **Villa Sant'Andrea,** via Nazionale 137 ℘ 0942 23125, *ricevimento.vsa@framon-hotels.it, Fax 0942 24838,* ≤ small bay, « Park with floral terraces overlooking the sea », 🐾ₛ
😤 – 📶 🗐 📺 – 🔬 200. 🖭 🖪 ⓞ 🐠 𝚅𝙸𝚂𝙰. ※
CZ d
Meals a la carte 32/48 – **67 rm** ⊊ 216/308.

472

TAORMINA

Traffic restricted
in the town centre

at Lido di Spisone *North-East : 1,5 km* – ⊠ 98030 *Mazzarò :*

🏨 **Hotel Caparena,** via Nazionale 189 ℘ 0942 652033, *caparena@gaishotels.com,*
Fax 0942 36915, ≤, « Extensive flower garden with outdoor rest. summer service », ⊒,
🏖 – 🕽 🗏 📺 ⅗ 🅿 – 🛦 200. 🖭 🕄 ① 🚳 *VISA*. ✸
Meals a la carte 34/47 – **88 rm** ⊇ 165,26/247,89.

at Castelmola *North-West : 5 km AZ. alt. 550* – ⊠ 98030 :

🏨 **Villa Sonia** ⑤, via Porta Mola 9 ℘ 0942 28082, *intelisano@tao.it,* Fax 0942 28083, ≤
Etna, 😤, « Antiques and regional handicraft collectibles », ⇔, 😤 – 🕽 🗏 📺 ⅗ 🚗
🅿 – 🛦 110. 🖭 🕄 🚳 *VISA*. ✸
Meals a la carte 26/42 – **35 rm** ⊇ 108,46/171,43, 3 suites.

Pleasant hotels and restaurants
are shown in the Guide by a red sign.
Please send us the names
of any where you have enjoyed your stay.
Your **Michelin Guide** will be even better.

🏨🏨🏨 ... 🏠

✗✗✗✗✗ ... ✗

TURIN (TORINO) 10100 🅿 🄸🄸🄸 G 5 *G. Italy. – pop. 900 987 alt. 239.*

See : Piazza San Carlo★★ CXY – Egyptian Museum★★★, Sabauda Gallery★★ in Academ: of Science CX **M1** – Cathedral★ VX : relic of the Holy Shroud★★★ – Mole Antonelliana★ ☀★★ DX – Madama Palace★ : museum of Ancient Art★ – CX **A** – Royal Palace★ : Roy. Armoury★ CDVX – Risorgimento Museum★ in Carignano Palace★★ CX **M2** – Carlo Bi: caretti di Ruffia Motor Museum★★ – Model medieval village★ in the Valentino Park CD:

Envir. : Basilica di Superga★ : ≤★★★ – Sacra di San Michele ★★★ – Tour to the pass, Col. della Maddalena★ : ≤★★ of the city from the route Superga-Pino Torinese, ≤★ of th city from the route Colle della Maddalena-Cavoretto _ Palazzina di Caccia di Stupinigi ★

🖙, I Roveri (closed Monday) at La Mandria ⊠ 10070 Fiano Torinese 0119235719, Fa 0119235669, North : 18 km;

🖙, 🖙 Torino (closed Monday, January and February), at Fiano Torinese ⊠ 1007 𝒫 0119235440, Fax 0119235886, North : 20 km;

🖙 Le Fronde (closed Tuesday, January and February) at Avigliana ⊠ 1005 𝒫 0119328053, Fax 0119320928, West : 24 km;

🖙 Stupinigi (closed Monday), at Stupinigi ⊠ 10040 𝒫 0113472640, Fax 011397803৪

🖙 Vinovo (closed Monday and 20 December-10 January) at Vinovo ⊠ 1004 𝒫 0119653880, Fax 0110623740.

✈ Turin Airport of Caselle North : 15 km 𝒫 0115676361 – Alitalia, via Lagrange 3 ⊠ 10123 𝒫 01157691, Fax 0115769220.

🛈 piazza Castello 161 ⊠ 10122 𝒫 011535901, Fax 011530070 – Porta Nuova Railwa Station ⊠ 10125 𝒫 011531327, Fax 0115617095.

A.C.I. via Giovanni Giolitti 15 ⊠ 10123 𝒫 01157791.

Roma 669 – Briançon 108 – Chambéry 209 – Genève 252 – Genova 170 – Grenoble 224 – Milano 140 – Nice 220.

Plans on following pages

🏨🏨 **Turin Palace Hotel,** via Sacchi 8 ⊠ 10128 𝒫 011 5625511, palace@thi.it Fax 011 5612187 – |‡| 🗏 🆃🆅 ᯤ – 🛳 200. 🆔 🆂 ⓞ 🆖🆖 🆅🆂🅰 🆓🅱. ⅏ rest   CY ፣ Meals **Vigna Reale** Rest. (closed August, Saturday and Sunday lunch) a la carte 36/6(– **121 rm** ⊇ 219/268, suite.

🏨🏨 **Le Meridien Lingotto** 🄼, via Nizza 262 ⊠ 10126 𝒫 011 6642000 and res 𝒫 011 6642714, reservations@lemeridien-lingotto.it, Fax 011 6642001, « Tropica garden » – |‡|, ⅏ rm, 🗏 🆃🆅 ᯤ ᯤ ᯤ 🄿 – 🛳 67. 🆔 🆂 ⓞ 🆖🆖 🆅🆂🅰 🆓🅱. ⅏   by via Nizza CZ Meals **Torpedo** Rest. (closed Monday) a la carte 49/67 – **227 rm** ⊇ 256, 13 suites.

🏨🏨 **Jolly Hotel Principi di Piemonte,** via Gobetti 15 ⊠ 10123 𝒫 011 5577111, tor no_principidipiemonte@jollyhotels.it, Fax 011 5620270 – |‡|, ⅏ rm, 🗏 🆃🆅 – 🛳 250. 🆔 🆂 ⓞ 🆖🆖 🆅🆂🅰 🆓🅱. ⅏   CY ፣ Meals **L' Gentilom** Rest. a la carte 37/54 – **89 rm** ⊇ 181/271, 8 suites.

🏨🏨 **Gd H. Sitea,** via Carlo Alberto 35 ⊠ 10123 𝒫 011 5170171, sitea@thi.it Fax 011 548090 – |‡| 🗏 🆃🆅 ᯤ – 🛳 100. 🆔 🆂 ⓞ 🆖🆖 🆅🆂🅰 🆓🅱. ⅏ rest   CY Meals **Carignano** Rest. (closed August, Saturday and Sunday lunch) a la carte 39/51 – **116 rm** ⊇ 175,50/234, 2 suites.

🏨🏨 **Starhotel Majestic,** corso Vittorio Emanuele II 54 ⊠ 10123 𝒫 011 539153, maje stic.to@starhotels.it, Fax 011 534963 – |‡|, ⅏ rm, 🗏 🆃🆅 ᯤ – 🛳 500. 🆔 🆂 ⓞ 🆖🆖 🆅🆂🅰 🆓🅱. ⅏   CY € Meals **le Regine** Rest. (closed August and lunch) a la carte 39/60 – **160 rm** ⊇ 254/357 2 suites.

🏨🏨 **Jolly Hotel Ambasciatori,** corso Vittorio Emanuele II 104 ⊠ 10121 𝒫 011 5752 torino-ambasciatori@jollyhotels.it, Fax 011 544978 – |‡|, ⅏ rm, 🗏 🆃🆅 – 🛳 400. 🆔 🆂 ⓞ 🆖🆖 🆅🆂🅰. ⅏ rest   BX ε Meals **Il Diplomatico** Rest. a la carte 35/57 – **199 rm** ⊇ 167,85/206,58, 4 suites.

🏨🏨 **Jolly Hotel Ligure** 🄼, piazza Carlo Felice 85 ⊠ 10123 𝒫 011 55641, torino_ligur e@jollyhotels.it, Fax 011 535438 – |‡|, ⅏ rm, 🗏 🆃🆅 – 🛳 200. 🆔 🆂 ⓞ 🆖🆖 🆅🆂🅰. ⅏ rest Meals (dinner only) a la carte 37/52 – **167 rm** ⊇ 181/212, 2 suites.   CY b

🏨🏨 **Villa Sassi** 🌭, strada al Traforo del Pino 47 ⊠ 10132 𝒫 011 8980556, info@villas assi.com, Fax 011 8980095, 🍴, « 18C country house in extensive parkland » – |‡| 🗏 🆃🆅 🄿 – 🛳 200. 🆔 🆂 ⓞ 🆖🆖 🆅🆂🅰. ⅏ rest   by corso Casale DY closed August – Meals (closed August and Sunday) a la carte 44/57 – **16 rm** ⊇ 170,43/216,91.

🏨🏨 **Concord,** via Lagrange 47 ⊠ 10123 𝒫 011 5176756, prenotazioni@hotelconcord.com Fax 011 5176305 – |‡| 🗏 🆃🆅 ᯤ – 🛳 200. 🆔 🆂 ⓞ 🆖🆖 🆅🆂🅰 🆓🅱. ⅏ rest   CY s Meals a la carte 29/45 – **135 rm** ⊇ 195/230, 4 suites.

🏨🏨 **Boston** without rest., via Massena 70 ⊠ 10128 𝒫 011 500359, hotel.boston@hotels.it Fax 011 599358, 🍴 – |‡|, ⅏ rm, 🗏 🆃🆅 ᯤ ᯤ – 🛳 50. 🆔 🆂 ⓞ 🆖🆖 🆅🆂🅰   BZ c **82 rm** ⊇ 135/185, 5 suites.

🏨🏨🏨 **Victoria** without rest., via Nino Costa 4 ⊠ 10123 ℰ 011 5611909, *reservation@ho telvictoria-torino.com*, Fax 011 5611806, « Elegant and intimate ambience » – |♦| 🔟
AE 🕄 ⓞ ⓜⓞ 𝘝𝘐𝘚𝘈. ⬚⬚ CY v
108 rm ⬚ 97/157.

🏨🏨🏨 **Diplomatic,** via Cernaia 42 ⊠ 10122 ℰ 011 5612444, *info@hotel-diplomatic.it*, Fax 011 540472 – |♦|, ⬚⬚ rm, ☰ 🔟 ⬚ – ⬚ 180. AE 🕄 ⓞ ⓜⓞ 𝘝𝘐𝘚𝘈. ⬚⬚ rest BX g
Meals (residents only) (closed Saturday and Sunday) – **123 rm** ⬚ 150/260, 3 suites.

🏨🏨🏨 **City** without rest., via Juvarra 25 ⊠ 10122 ℰ 011 540546, *city.hotel@iol.it*, Fax 011 548188 – |♦| ☰ 🔟 ⬚⬚ – ⬚ 60. AE 🕄 ⓞ ⓜⓞ 𝘝𝘐𝘚𝘈. ⬚⬚ BV e
57 rm ⬚ 113,62/258,23.

🏨🏨🏨 **Holiday Inn Turin City Centre** Ⓜ, via Assietta 3 ⊠ 10128 ℰ 011 5167111, Fax 011 5167699 – |♦|, ⬚⬚ rm, ☰ 🔟 ⬚ ⬚ ⬚⬚ – ⬚ 40. AE 🕄 ⓞ ⓜⓞ 𝘝𝘐𝘚𝘈.
⬚⬚ CY a
Meals (dinner only) a la carte 26/41 – ⬚ 15,49 – **57 rm** 157,52/209,17.

🏨🏨🏨 **Genio** without rest., corso Vittorio Emanuele II 47 ⊠ 10125 ℰ 011 6505771, *hotel.g enio@hotelres.it*, Fax 011 6508264 – |♦|, ⬚⬚ rm, ☰ 🔟 – ⬚ 25. AE 🕄 ⓞ ⓜⓞ 𝘝𝘐𝘚𝘈 JCB
117 rm ⬚ 135/185, 3 suites. CYZ w

🏨🏨🏨 **Royal,** corso Regina Margherita 249 ⊠ 10144 ℰ 011 4376777, Fax 011 4376393 – |♦|
☰ 🔟 ⬚ ⬚⬚ P. – ⬚ 600. AE 🕄 ⓞ ⓜⓞ 𝘝𝘐𝘚𝘈 JCB BV u
Meals (closed Saturday and Sunday lunch) a la carte 26/36 – **75 rm** ⬚ 100/140.

🏨🏨 **Genova e Stazione** without rest., via Sacchi 14/b ⊠ 10128 ℰ 011 5629400, *hote l.genova@hotelres.it*, Fax 011 5629896 – |♦| ☰ 🔟 ⬚ – ⬚ 70. AE 🕄 ⓞ ⓜⓞ 𝘝𝘐𝘚𝘈.
⬚⬚ CZ b
59 rm ⬚ 113,60/134,30, 4 suites.

🏨🏨 **Giotto** without rest., via Giotto 27 ⊠ 10126 ℰ 011 6637172, *giottohotel@libero.it*, Fax 011 6637173 – |♦| ☰ 🔟 – ⬚ 50. AE 🕄 ⓞ ⓜⓞ 𝘝𝘐𝘚𝘈 JCB CZ c
50 rm ⬚ 85/139.

🏨🏨 **Lancaster** without rest., corso Filippo Turati 8 ⊠ 10128 ℰ 011 5681982, *hotel.lanc aster@contacta.it*, Fax 011 5683019 – |♦| ☰ 🔟 ⬚ – ⬚ 40. AE 🕄 ⓞ ⓜⓞ 𝘝𝘐𝘚𝘈 BZ r
closed 5 to 20 August – **77 rm** ⬚ 92,96/129,11.

🏨🏨 **Crimea** without rest., via Mentana 3 ⊠ 10133 ℰ 011 6604700, *hotel.crimea@hotel res.it*, Fax 011 6604912 – |♦| 🔟 ⬚ ⬚⬚ – ⬚ 35. AE 🕄 ⓞ ⓜⓞ 𝘝𝘐𝘚𝘈 JCB. ⬚⬚ DZ e
48 rm ⬚ 103/145, suite.

🏨🏨 **Gran Mogol** without rest., via Guarini 2 ⊠ 10123 ℰ 011 5612120, *hotel.gmogol@h otelres.it*, Fax 011 5623160 – |♦|, ⬚⬚ rm, ☰ 🔟. AE 🕄 ⓞ ⓜⓞ 𝘝𝘐𝘚𝘈 JCB CY r
closed August and 23 December-1 January – **45 rm** ⬚ 115/150.

🏨🏨 **Piemontese** without rest., via Berthollet 21 ⊠ 10125 ℰ 011 6698101, *info@hotel piemontese.it*, Fax 011 6690571 – |♦| ⬚⬚ ☰ 🔟 P. AE 🕄 ⓞ ⓜⓞ 𝘝𝘐𝘚𝘈. ⬚⬚ CZ x
39 rm ⬚ 92,96/118,79.

🏨🏨 **Amadeus** without rest., via Principe Amedeo 41 bis ⊠ 10123 ℰ 011 8174951, Fax 011 8174953 – ☰ 🔟. AE 🕄 ⓞ ⓜⓞ 𝘝𝘐𝘚𝘈 JCB DY v
closed August – ⬚ 10,33 – **28 rm** 67,14/129,12, 2 suites.

🏨🏨 **Cairo** without rest., via La Loggia 6 ⊠ 10134 ℰ 011 3171555, *hcairo@ipsnet.it*, Fax 011 3172027 – |♦| ☰ 🔟 P. AE 🕄 ⓞ ⓜⓞ 𝘝𝘐𝘚𝘈. ⬚⬚ by corso Unione Sovietica BZ
closed 1 to 28 August – ⬚ 15 – **50 rm** 100/140.

🏨🏨 **Due Mondi,** via Saluzzo 3 ⊠ 10125 ℰ 011 6698981, Fax 011 6699383 – |♦| ☰ 🔟.
AE 🕄 ⓞ ⓜⓞ 𝘝𝘐𝘚𝘈 JCB. ⬚⬚ CZ k
closed 10 to 20 August – **Meals** a la carte 23/38 – ⬚ 10,33 – **42 rm** 56/134.

🏨🏨 **Liberty,** via Pietro Micca 15 ⊠ 10121 ℰ 011 5628801, *hotelliberty@tiscalinet.it*, Fax 011 5628163 – |♦| 🔟. AE 🕄 ⓞ ⓜⓞ 𝘝𝘐𝘚𝘈. ⬚⬚ rest CX f
Meals a la carte 20/24 – **34 rm** ⬚ 90/124.

🏨🏨 **President**, via Cecchi 67 ⊠ 10152 ℰ 011 859555, *info@hotelpresident.to.it*, Fax 011 2480465 – |♦| ☰ 🔟 ⬚ AE 🕄 ⓞ ⓜⓞ 𝘝𝘐𝘚𝘈 JCB. ⬚⬚ CV s
Meals (closed August) (residents only) a la carte 24/43 – **72 rm** ⬚ 69,72/92,96.

XXXX **Del Cambio,** piazza Carignano 2 ⊠ 10123 ℰ 011 543760, Fax 011 535282, Historic traditional restaurant, « 19C decor » – ☰. AE 🕄 ⓞ ⓜⓞ 𝘝𝘐𝘚𝘈. ⬚⬚ CX a
closed 3 to 31 August and Sunday – **Meals** (booking essential) 59,39/67,14 and a la carte 46/60 (15 %).

XXX **Balbo,** via Andrea Doria 11 ⊠ 10123 ℰ 011 8395775, *balbodoria@libero.it*, ❀ Fax 011 8151042 – ☰. AE 🕄 ⓞ ⓜⓞ 𝘝𝘐𝘚𝘈. ⬚⬚ CY n
closed 25 July-20 August and Monday – **Meals** (booking essential) 57/67 and a la carte 77/103
Spec. Code di scampi con porri croccanti. Schiena di coniglio farcita con salsa di peperone rosso dolce (summer-autumn). Piccione di nido farcito con fegato d'oca e salsa di miele di timo.

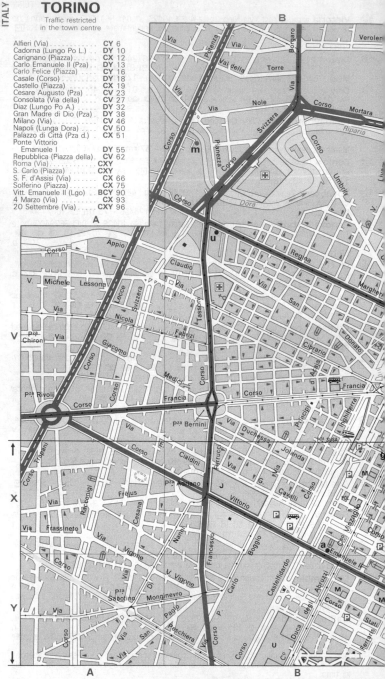

ITALY

TORINO

Traffic restricted
in the town centre

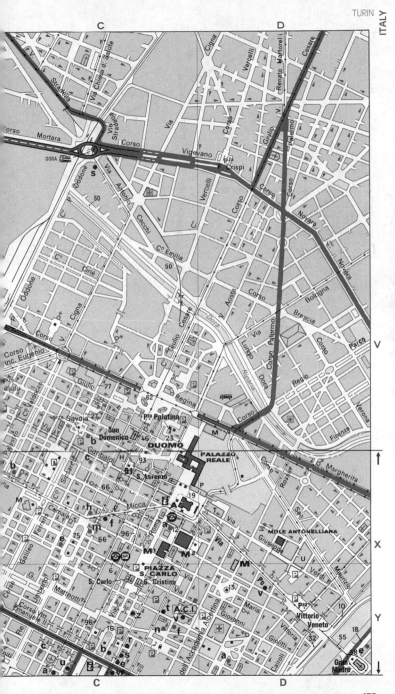

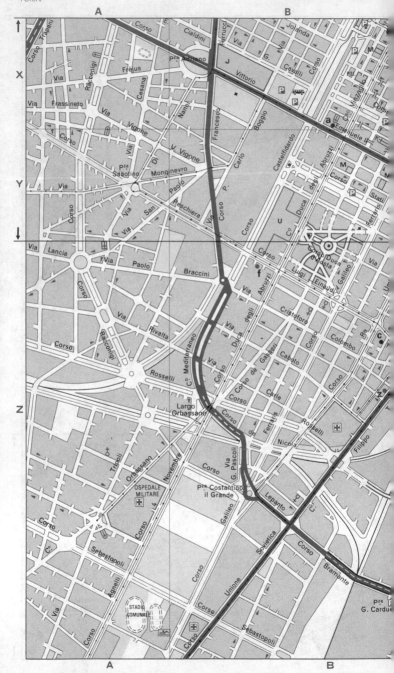

TORINO

Traffic restricted
in the town centre

XXX **Vintage 1997,** piazza Solferino 16/h ⊠ 10121 ℰ 011 535948, *info@vintage1997.
com, Fax 011 535948* – 🔄 ▤. AE 🆂 ① ⑩ VISA   CX
closed 6 to 31 August, Saturday lunch and Sunday – **Meals** (booking essential) a la carte
34/52.

XXX **Norman,** via Pietro Micca 22 ⊠ 10122 ℰ 011 540854, *Fax 011 5113838* – ▤. 🆂 ⑩
VISA JCB. ⌘   CX
closed Sunday – **Meals** 25,82/36,15 (lunch) 56,81/61,97 (dinner) and a la carte 46/72.

XXX **La Prima Smarrita,** corso Unione Sovietica 244 ⊠ 10134 ℰ 011 3179657, *prima
marrita@libero.it, Fax 011 3179191* – ▤. AE 🆂 ① ⑩ VISA JCB.   GU
closed 10 to 26 August – **Meals** (booking essential) a la carte 38/51.

XXX **Villa Somis,** strada Val Pattonera 138 ⊠ 10133 ℰ 011 6614626, *villasomis@coms
ls.com, Fax 011 6614626*, ≤, « 18C house with summer service in park under a pergola »
– 🅿. AE 🆂 ⑩ ⑩ VISA   HU
closed 26 December-10 January and Monday – **Meals** (booking essential) a la carte 34/50.

XXX **La Cloche,** strada al Traforo del Pino 106 ⊠ 10132 ℰ 011 8994213, *info@lacloche.it,
Fax 011 8981522* – ▤ 🅿 – 🔬 100. AE 🆂 ① ⑩ VISA JCB. ⌘
closed Sunday dinner, Monday and lunch in August – **Meals** 25,36/36,15 and a la carte
38/75.   by corso Moncalieri CDZ

XXX **Marco Polo,** via Marco Polo 38 ⊠ 10129 ℰ 011 500096, *Fax 011 599900 ristoran
emarcopolo@libero.it,* – ▤. AE 🆂 ① ⑩ VISA JCB   BZ
closed lunch (except Sunday) – **Meals** (booking essential) seafood 46,48 and a la carte
41/70.

XXX **La Barrique,** corso Dante 53 ⊠ 10126 ℰ 011 657900, *Fax 011 657995* – ▤. AE 🆂
① ⑩ VISA   CZ
closed Monday, Saturday and Sunday lunch – **Meals** (booking essential) 15,50/18,07 (only
lunch) a la carte 33/56.

XX **Hosteria la Vallée,** via Provana 3 b ⊠ 10123 ℰ 011 8121788, *Fax 011 8121788* –
▤. 🆂 ⑩ VISA   DY
closed lunch in July and Sunday in August – **Meals** (booking essential) 25,82/36,15 (lunch)
36,15/51,65 (dinner) and a la carte 38/57.

XX **Al Garamond,** via Pomba 14 ⊠ 10123 ℰ 011 8122781 – ▤. AE 🆂 ⑩ VISA.
⌘   CY
closed Saturday lunch and Sunday – **Meals** (booking essential) 36,15 and a la carte 31/49.

XX **Del Grappolo,** via Cigliano 38 ⊠ 10135 ℰ 011 8154227, *Fax 011 2484544* – ▤. AE
🆂 ① ⑩ VISA JCB   by corso Moncalieri DZ
closed August and Sunday (except November-April) – **Meals** 15/30 (lunch) 20/35 (dinner)
and a la carte 25/42.

XX **Locanda Mongreno,** strada Mongreno 50 ⊠ 10132 ℰ 011 8980417, �ұ – 🆂 ⑩
VISA   by corso Moncalieri DZ
*closed 12 to 16 August, 2 to 8 September, 1 to 15 January, Monday and lunch (except
Sunday)* – **Meals** (booking essential) 30,98/51,65 and a la carte 37/49.

XX **Al Gatto Nero,** corso Filippo Turati 14 ⊠ 10128 ℰ 011 590414, *Fax 011 502245* –
▤. AE 🆂 ① ⑩ VISA. ⌘   BZ z
closed August and Sunday – **Meals** a la carte 38/50.

XX **Savoia,** via Corte d'Appello 13 ⊠ 10122 ℰ 011 4362288, *savoia97@libero.it* – ▤. AE
🆂 ① ⑩ VISA   CV b
closed Saturday lunch and Sunday – **Meals** 18,59 (lunch only) 30,98/43,89 and a la carte
32/53.

XX **Trait d'Union,** via degli Stampatori 4 ⊠ 10122 ℰ 011 5612506, *Fax 011 5633896,*
🌱 – ▤. AE 🆂 ① ⑩ VISA JCB. ⌘   CX c
closed August, Saturday lunch and Sunday – **Meals** (booking essential for dinner) a la carte
31/44.

XX **Galante,** corso Palestro 15 ⊠ 10122 ℰ 011 537757, *011 32163* – ▤. AE 🆂 ① ⑩
VISA JCB   CX b
closed August, Saturday lunch and Sunday – **Meals** a la carte 32/50.

XX **Porta Rossa,** via Passalacqua 3/b ⊠ 10122 ℰ 011 530816, *Fax 011 530816* – ▤. AE
🆂 ① ⑩ VISA. ⌘   CV a
closed 14 to 22 April, August, 26 December-10 January, Saturday lunch and Sunday –
Meals (booking essential) 26 (lunch only) and a la carte 31/60.

XX **Al Bue Rosso,** corso Casale 10 ⊠ 10131 ℰ 011 8191393, *Fax 011 8191393* – ▤. AE
🆂 ① ⑩ VISA. ⌘   DY e
closed August, Saturday lunch and Monday – **Meals** a la carte 34/44 (10 %).

XX **Perbacco,** via Mazzini 31 ⊠ 10123 ℰ 011 882110 – ▤. AE 🆂 ① VISA   DZ x
closed August and Sunday – **Meals** (dinner only) (booking essential) 25,82/30.

XX **Il 58,** via San Secondo 58 ⊠ 10128 ℰ 011 505566, Fax 011 505566 – 🍽. 🆎 🟦 🔘
     🚫🟩 VISA. ❄️   CZ a
     closed September and Monday – **Meals** seafood 30,98 and a la carte 33/43.

X   **Taverna delle Rose,** via Massena 24 ⊠ 10128 ℰ 011 538345, Fax 011 538345,
     « Typical atmosphere » – 🍽. 🆎 🔘 🚫🟩 VISA. ❄️   CZ r
     closed August, Saturday lunch and Sunday – **Meals** a la carte 25/43.

X   **Ristorantino Tefy,** corso Belgio 26 ⊠ 10153 ℰ 011 837332, Fax 011 837332 – 🍽.
     🆎 🟦 🔘 🚫🟩 VISA JCB. ❄️   by corso Novara DV
     closed August, 1 to 15 December and Sunday – **Meals** (booking essential) Umbrian rest.
     20,66 (lunch) 31 and a la carte 26/43.

X   **C'era una Volta,** corso Vittorio Emanuele II 41 ⊠ 10125 ℰ 011 6504589,
     Fax 011 6505774 – 🍽. 🆎 🟦 🔘 🚫🟩 VISA JCB   CZ k
     closed 1 to 27 August and Sunday – **Meals** (dinner only) Piedmontese rest. 23,24 and a
     la carte 23/39.

X   **Da Toci,** corso Moncalieri 190 ⊠ 10133 ℰ 011 6614809, 🌳 – 🍽. 🟦 🚫🟩 VISA   CZ q
     closed 16 August-5 September, Sunday and Monday lunch – **Meals** seafood a la carte
     21/35.

X   **Anaconda,** via Angiolino 16 (corso Potenza) ⊠ 10143 ℰ 011 752903, Fax 011 752903,
     Rustic trattoria, « Outdoor summer service » – 🅿. 🆎 🟦 🔘 🚫🟩 VISA JCB   BV m
     closed August, Friday dinner and Saturday – **Meals** 28 b.i..

X   **Le Maschere,** via Fidia 28 ang. via Vandalino ⊠ 10141 ℰ 011 728928 – 🍽. 🆎 🟦 🔘
     🚫🟩 VISA   by corso Francia ABV
     closed Sunday and Wednesday dinner – **Meals** (booking essential) a la carte 17/31.

───

VENICE (VENEZIA) 30100 🅿 🏣🏣🏣 F 19 G. Venice. – pop. 275.368.

     See : St. Marks Square★★★ KZ : Basilica★★★ LZ – Doges Palace★★★ LZ – Campanile★★ :
     ✳★★ KLZ Q – Correr Museum★★ KZ M – Bridge of Sighs★★ LZ.
     Santa Maria della Salute★★ DV – St. Giorgio Maggiore★ : ✳★★★ from campanile FV – St.
     Zanipolo★★ LX – Santa Maria Gloriosa dei Frari★★★ BTU – St. Zaccaria★★ LY – Interior
     decoration★★ by Veronese in the Church of St. Sebastiano BV – Ceiling★ of the Church
     of St. Pantaleone BU – Santa Maria dei Miracoli★ KLX – St. Francesco della Vigna★ FT –
     Ghetto★★ BT.
     Scuola di St. Rocco★★★ BU – Scuola di St. Giorgio degli Schiavoni★★★ FU – Scuola dei
     Carmini★ BV – Scuola di St. Marco★ LX – Palazzo Labia★★ BT – Murano★★ : Glass Museum★,
     Church of Santi Maria e Donato★★ – Burano★★ – Torcello★★ : mosaics★★ in the basilica
     of Santa Maria Assunta.
     Grand Canal★★★ : Rialto Bridge★★ KY – Ca' d'Oro★★ JX – Academy of Fine Arts★★★ BV
     – Ca' Rezzonico★★ BV – Ca' Dario★ DV – Grassi Palace★ BV – Peggy Guggenheim
     Collection★★ in Palace Venier dei Leoni DV M1 – Ca' Pesaro★ JX.

     🏌 (closed Monday) at Lido Alberoni ⊠ 30011 ℰ 041 731333, Fax 041 731339, 15 mn
     by boat and 9 km;
     🏌 et 🏌 Cà della Nave (closed Tuesday) at Martellago ⊠ 30030 ℰ 041 5401555, Fax
     041 5401926, North-West : 12 km;
     🏌 Villa Condulmer (closed Monday), at Zerman di Mogliano Veneto ⊠ 31020
     ℰ 041 457062, Fax 041 457202, North : 17 km.
     ✈ Marco Polo of Tessera, North-East : 13 km ℰ 041 2606111 – Alitalia, via Sansovino
     7 Mestre-Venezia ⊠ 30173 ℰ 041 2581111, Fax 041 2581246.
     🚢 to Lido-San Nicolò from piazzale Roma (Tronchetto) daily (35 mn); to island of Pel-
     lestrina-Santa Maria del Mare from Lido Alberoni daily (15 mn).
     🚤 to Punta Sabbioni from Riva degli Schiavoni daily (40 mn) , to islands of Burano (30 mn),
     Torcello (40 mn), Murano (1 h 10 mn) from Punta Sabbioni daily ; to islands of Murano
     (10 mn), Burano (50 mn), Torcello (50 mn) from Fondamenta Nuove daily; to Treporti-
     Cavallino from Fondamenta Nuove daily (1 h 10 mn); to Venezia-Fondamenta Nuove from
     Treporti-Cavallino (1 h 10 mn), to islands of Murano (1 h), Burano (20 mn), Torcello (25 mn)
     daily – Information : ACTV-Venetian Trasport Union, piazzale Roma ⊠ 30135
     ℰ 041 5287886, Fax 041 5207135.
     🅱 calle Ascensione-San Marco 71/f ⊠ 30124 ℰ 041 5297811, Fax 041 5230399 – Santa
     Lucia Railway station ⊠ 30121 ℰ 041 5298727, Fax 041 2581246.
     Roma 528 ① – Bologna 152 ① – Milano 267 ① – Trieste 158 ①

───
Plans on following pages
───

🏨🏨🏨 **Cipriani** 🐦, isola della Giudecca 10 ⊠ 30133 ℰ 041 5207744, info@hotelcipriani.it,
     Fax 041 5203930, ≤, 🌳, « Floral garden with heated 🏊 », 🧖, ≦s, ✂️ – 📶 🟰 📺 –
     🦽 80. 🆎 🟦 🔘 🚫🟩 VISA. ❄️   FV h
     15 March-15 November – **Meals** a la carte 77/103 see also rest. **Cip's Club** – **84 rm**
     ⚏ 1040/1180, 7 suites.

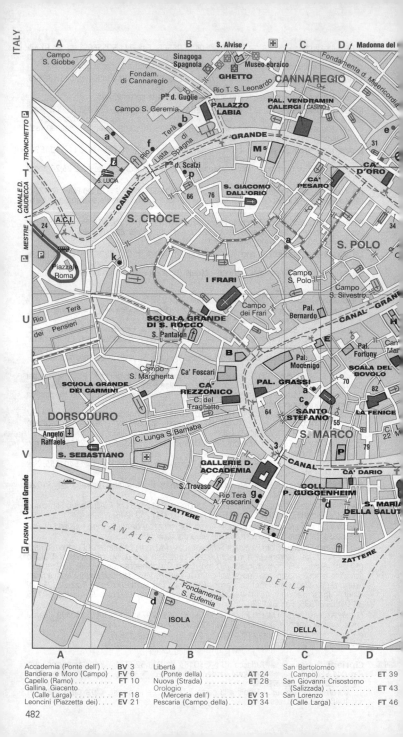

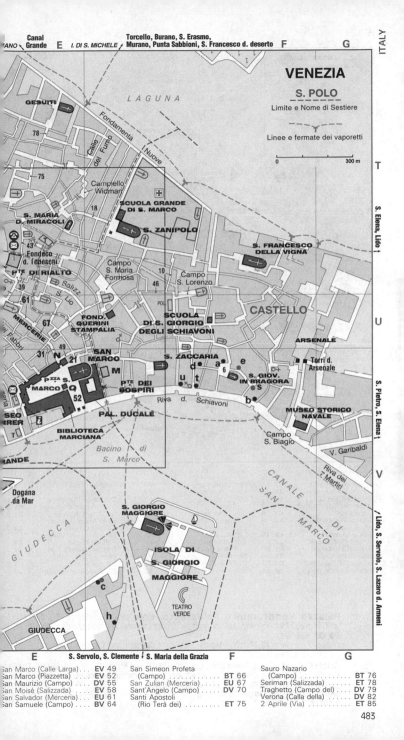

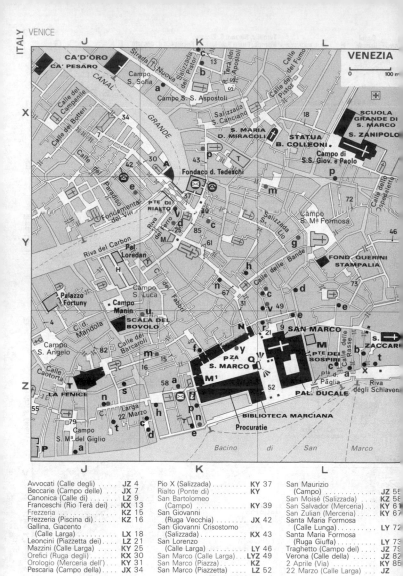

VENEZIA

0   100 m

Palazzo Vendramin e Palazzetto, isola della Giudecca 10 ✉ 30133
☎ 041 5207744, *info@hotelcipriani.it*, ← Giudecca canal and San Marco – 🔲 📺 🄰🄴 🔢
🄾 🄼🄾 𝘝𝘐𝘚𝘈 ⌧   FV c
closed 7 January-15 March – **Meals** (see hotel **Cipriani** and **Cip's Club** below) – **10 rm**
⊇ 767, 5 suites 2300/3727.

🏨🏨🏨 **Gritti Palace,** campo Santa Maria del Giglio 2467, San Marco ✉ 30124 ☎ 041 794611
Fax 041 5200942, ← Grand Canal, « Outdoor rest. summer service on the Grand Canal »
🛗 – 🛗, ⇚ rm, 🔲 📺 🗫 🄰🄴 🔢 🄾 🄼🄾 𝘝𝘐𝘚𝘈 ᴊᴄʙ ⌧   JZ a
Meals *Club del Doge* Rest. a la carte 102/151 – ⊇ 48 – **82 rm** 365/780
9 suites.

🏨🏨🏨 **Danieli,** riva degli Schiavoni 4196, Castello ✉ 30122 ✆ 041 5226480, reso72.danieli @starwoodhotels.com, Fax 041 5200208, < San Marco Canal, « Hall in a small Venetian style courtyard and summer rest. service on terrace with panoramic view », 🔟 – 📶 ☼
🖭 📺 ✆ – 🏋 150. 🆎 🅱 ① ⓜ🅾 𝗩𝗜𝗦𝗔 𝗝𝗖𝗕. ☼   LZ a
Meals a la carte 86/124 – ☲ 48 – **233 rm** 320,98/735,95, 11 suites.

🏨🏨🏨 **Bauer e Il Palazzo,** campo San Moisè 1459, San Marco ✉ 30124 ✆ 041 5207022, booking@bauervenezia.it, Fax 041 5207557, « Summer rest. service on terrace with <
Grand Canal », 🎐, ☲ – 📶 – 📺 – 🏋 150. 🆎 🅱 ① ⓜ🅾 𝗩𝗜𝗦𝗔 𝗝𝗖𝗕.   KZ h
Meals a la carte 65/87 – ☲ 33 – **138 rm** 500/600, 59 suites.

🏨🏨🏨 **Luna Hotel Baglioni,** calle larga dell'Ascensione 1243, San Marco ✉ 30124
✆ 041 5289840, Fax 041 5287160 « 18C hall with frescoes attributed to Tiepolo's school », 🔟 – 📶 ☼ 🖭 📺 – 🏋 150. 🆎 🅱 ① ⓜ🅾 𝗩𝗜𝗦𝗔 𝗝𝗖𝗕.   KZ p
Meals *Canova* Rest. a la carte 50/65 – ☲ 15,49 – **106 rm** 295/597, 9 suites.

🏨🏨🏨 **Londra Palace,** riva degli Schiavoni 4171 ✉ 30122 ✆ 041 5200533, info@hotelon dra.it, Fax 041 5225032, < San Marco Canal, ☕ – 📶 🖭 📺 ✆. 🆎 🅱 ① ⓜ🅾 𝗩𝗜𝗦𝗔
☼   LZ t
Meals *Do Leoni* Rest (Elegant rest., booking essential) a la carte 62/99 – **53 rm**
☲ 320/593.

🏨🏨🏨 **The Westin Europa e Regina,** corte Barozzi 2159, San Marco ✉ 30124
✆ 041 2400001, res075.europaregina@westin.com, Fax 041 5231533, < Grand Canal, « Outdoor rest. summer service on the Grand Canal », 🔟 – 📶, ☼ rm, 🖭 📺 – 🏋 120.
🆎 🅱 ① ⓜ🅾 𝗩𝗜𝗦𝗔 𝗝𝗖𝗕. ☼ rest   KZ d
Meals *La Cusina* Rest. a la carte 73/114 – ☲ 48 – **175 rm** 380/800, 10 suites.

🏨🏨🏨 **Grand Hotel dei Dogi,** Fondamenta Madonna dell'Orto 3500, Cannaregio ✉ 30121
✆ 041 2208111, reservation@deidogi.boscolo.com, Fax 041 722278, ☕, « Ancient Venetian palace in a secular park », 🔟 – 📶 🖭 📺 – 🏋 50. 🆎 🅱 ① 𝗩𝗜𝗦𝗔 𝗝𝗖𝗕. ☼
Meals *La Zola* Rest. a la carte 50/74 – **68 rm** ☲ 335,70/413,17, 5 suites.
                                                            by Madonna dell'Orto DT

🏨🏨🏨 **Metropole,** riva degli Schiavoni 4149, Castello ✉ 30122 ✆ 041 5205044, venice@h otelmetropole.com, Fax 041 5223679, < San Marco Canal, ☕, « Collection of period bric-a-brac », ☞, 🔟 – 📶 🖭 📺 ㅎ. – 🏋 100. 🆎 🅱 ① ⓜ🅾 𝗩𝗜𝗦𝗔 𝗝𝗖𝗕. ☼   FV t
Meals *Buffet* Rest. 23/32 (lunch) and 37,20 (dinner) – **65 rm** ☲ 300/465, 4 suites.

🏨🏨🏨 **Monaco e Grand Canal,** calle Vallaresso 1325, San Marco ✉ 30124 ✆ 041 5200211, mailbox@hotelmonaco.it, Fax 041 5200501, < Grand Canal and Santa Maria della Salute Church, « Outdoor rest. summer service on the Grand Canal » – 📶 🖭 📺. 🆎 🅱 ① ⓜ🅾
𝗩𝗜𝗦𝗔 𝗝𝗖𝗕.   KZ e
Meals *Grand Canal* Rest. a la carte 66/87 – **71 rm** ☲ 290/506, 7 suites.

🏨🏨🏨 **Sofitel,** Fondamenta Condulmer 245, Santa Croce ✉ 30135 ✆ 041 710400, sofitel.v enezia@accor-hotels.it, Fax 041 710394, « Service rest. in pleasant winter garden », 🔟 – 📶, ☼ rm, 🖭 📺 – 🏋 50. 🆎 🅱 ① ⓜ🅾 𝗩𝗜𝗦𝗔   BT k
Meals a la carte 44/73 – **97 rm** ☲ 340,86/392,51.

🏨🏨 **Ca' Pisani** [M], rio terà Foscarini 979/a, Dorsoduro ✉ 30123 ✆ 041 240141 and rest
✆ 041 2401425, info@capisanihotel.it, Fax 041 2771061, solarium altana, « Futurist design and furniture in the style of the Forties » – 📶, ☼ rm, 🖭 📺 ✆ ㅎ. 🆎 🅱 ① ⓜ🅾
𝗩𝗜𝗦𝗔 𝗝𝗖𝗕. ☼   BV q
closed 6 to 20 August and 8 to 23 January – **Meals** *La Rivista* Rest. (closed Wednesday) a la carte 33/42 – **29 rm** ☲ 324/375.

🏨🏨 **Starhotel Splendid-Suisse,** Mercerie 760, San Marco ✉ 30124 ✆ 041 5200755, splendidsuisse.ve@starhotels.it, Fax 041 5286498 – 📶 ☼ 🖭 📺 ✆. 🆎 🅱 ① ⓜ🅾 𝗩𝗜𝗦𝗔
𝗝𝗖𝗕. ☼   KY n
Meals (residents only) 25,82/41,32 – **151 rm** ☲ 400/550, 13 suites.

🏨🏨 **Colombina** without rest., calle del Remedio 4416, Castello ✉ 30122 ✆ 041 2770525, hotelco@tin.it, Fax 041 2776044, 🔟 – 📶, ☼ rm, 🖭 📺 ✆ – 🏋 20. 🆎 🅱 ① ⓜ🅾 𝗩𝗜𝗦𝗔 𝗝𝗖𝗕.
☼   LY d
32 rm ☲ 130/382.

🏨🏨 **Cavalletto** without rest., calle del Cavalletto 1107, San Marco ✉ 30124
✆ 041 5200955, cavalletto@tin.it, Fax 041 5238184, <, 🔟 – 📶 🖭 📺. 🆎 🅱 ① ⓜ🅾 𝗩𝗜𝗦𝗔
𝗝𝗖𝗕. ☼   KZ f
107 rm ☲ 232/387.

🏨🏨 **Saturnia e International,** calle larga 22 Marzo 2398, San Marco ✉ 30124
✆ 041 5208377, info@hotelsaturnia.it, Fax 041 5207131, « 14C nobleman's town house » – 📶 🖭 📺 – 🏋 60. 🆎 🅱 ① ⓜ🅾 𝗩𝗜𝗦𝗔 𝗝𝗖𝗕.   JZ n
Meals (see rest. *La Caravella* below) – **91 rm** ☲ 260/414.

🏨🏨 **Giorgione,** calle Larga dei Proverbi 4587, Cannareggio ✉ 30131 ✆ 041 5225810, gior gione@hotelgiorgione.com, Fax 041 5239092, « Floral courtyard » – 📶 🖭 📺. 🆎 🅱 ①
ⓜ🅾 𝗩𝗜𝗦𝗔. ☼   KX b
Meals (see rest. *Osteria Giorgi* below) – **64 rm** ☲ 135/250, 2 suites.

🏛 **Bellini** without rest., lista di Spagna 116, Cannaregio ⊠ 30121 ℰ 041 5242488, res
rvation@bellini.boscolo.com, Fax 041 715193 – ▮ ▤ ▥ ℀ ▤ ▤ ⓞ ▥　BT
100 rm ⊇ 227,24/335,70.

🏛 **Locanda Vivaldi** without rest., riva degli Schiavoni 4150/52, Castello ⊠ 3012
ℰ 041 2770477, info@locandavivaldi.it, Fax 041 2770489, ⩽ San Giorgio Island an
lagoon, « Small panoramic terrace », ⅃ – ▮ ▤ ▥ ▥ ♿ ▤ ▤ ⓞ ▥ ᴊᴄʙ　FV
22 rm ⊇ 310/439.

🏛 **Concordia** without rest., calle larga San Marco 367 ⊠ 30124 ℰ 041 5206866
Fax 041 5206775, ⩽ – ▮ ▤ ▥ ▤ ▤ ⓞ ▥ ▥　LZ
59 rm ⊇ 237,57/361,50.

🏛 **Gabrielli Sandwirth**, riva degli Schiavoni 4110, Castello ⊠ 30122 ℰ 041 5231580
hotelgabrielli@libero.it, Fax 041 5209455, 㑊, « Small courtyard-garden and solarium ter
race with ⩽ San Marco Canal », ⅃ – ▮ ▤ ▥. ▤ ▤ ⓞ ▥ ᴊᴄʙ. ℀ rest FV
closed 24 November-20 February – **Meals** 29/44 – **100 rm** ⊇ 250/420.

🏛 **Rialto**, riva del Ferro 5149, San Marco ⊠ 30124 ℰ 041 5209166, hotelrialto@ve.n
ttuno.it, Fax 041 5238958, ⩽ Rialto bridge, 㑊 – ▮ ▤ ▥. ▤ ▤ ⓞ ▥ ᴊᴄʙ. ℀
Meals (closed until April) a la carte 31/43 (12 %) – **79 rm** ⊇ 206,58/335,70. KY

🏛 **Amadeus** without rest., lista di Spagna 227, Cannaregio ⊠ 30121 ℰ 041 2206000 an
rest ℰ 041 715610, htlamadeus@gardenahotels.it, Fax 041 2204040, « Garden » – ▮
▤ ▥ – ⌂ 120. ▤ ▤ ⓞ ▥ ▥ ᴊᴄʙ. ℀　BT
⊇ 20,66 – **63 rm** 227,24/320,20.

🏛 **Bisanzio** ⌂ without rest., calle della Pietà 3651, Castello ⊠ 30122 ℰ 041 5203100
email@bisanzio.com, Fax 041 5204114, ⅃ – ▮ ▤ ▥ ▤ ▤ ⓞ ▥　FV
46 rm ⊇ 130/290.

🏛 **Montecarlo,** calle dei Specchieri 463, San Marco ⊠ 30124 ℰ 041 5207144, mail@
enicehotelmontecarlo.com, Fax 041 5207789 – ▮ ▤ ▥. ▤ ▤ ⓞ ▥ ▥ ᴊᴄʙ　LY
Meals (see rest. **Antico Pignolo** below) – **48 rm** ⊇ 180/361,50.

🏛 **Savoia e Jolanda,** riva degli Schiavoni 4187, Castello ⊠ 30122 ℰ 041 5206644, sav
ia.ve.san@iol.it, Fax 041 5207494, ⩽ San Marco Canal, 㑊 – ▮ ▤ ▥ ▤ ▤ ⓞ ▥
℀　LZ
Meals a la carte 48/58 (12 %) – **73 rm** ⊇ 250/475, suite.

🏠 **Al Ponte dei Sospiri** without rest., calle larga San Marco 381 ⊠ 3012
ℰ 041 2411160, info@alpontedeisospiri.it, Fax 041 2410268 – ▮ ▤ ▥ ℀. ▤ ▤ ⓞ ▥
▥　LZ
8 rm ⊇ 420/619.

🏠 **Kette** without rest., piscina San Moisè 2053, San Marco ⊠ 30124 ℰ 041 5207766
info@hotelkette.com, Fax 041 5228964, ⅃ – ▮ ▤ ▥ ▤ ▤ ⓞ ▥ ᴊᴄʙ. ℀
63 rm ⊇ 250/335.　JZ

🏠 **Belle Arti** without rest., rio terà Foscarini 912/A, Dorsoduro ⊠ 30123 ℰ 041 5226230
info@hotelbellearti.com, Fax 041 5280043, 㑊 – ▮ ▤ ▥ ♿. ▤ ▤ ⓞ ▥. ℀
67 rm ⊇ 144,60/196,25.　BV

🏠 **Tre Archi** without rest., fondamenta di Cannareggio 923, Cannaregio ⊠ 3012
ℰ 041 5244356, info@hotelarchi.com, Fax 041 5244356, 㑊 – ▤ ▥ ♿. ▤ ▤ ⓞ ▥
▥　BT
24 rm ⊇ 217/260.

🏠 **Ai Due Fanali** without rest., Campo San Simeon Grande 946, Santa Croce ⊠ 3013
ℰ 041 718490, request@aiduefanali.com, Fax 041 718344, « Roof-terrace solarium » –
▮ ▤ ▥. ▤ ▤ ⓞ ▥ ▥. ℀　BT
16 rm ⊇ 149,77/196,25.

🏠 **Firenze** without rest., Salizada San Moisè 1490, San Marco ⊠ 30124 ℰ 041 5222858
info@hotel-firenze.com, Fax 041 5202668 – ▮ ▤ ▥. ▤ ▤ ⓞ ▥ ▥ ᴊᴄʙ. ℀
25 rm ⊇ 180,80/232,45.　KZ

🏠 **Panada** without rest., San Marco-calle dei Specchieri 646 ⊠ 30124 ℰ 041 5209088
info@hotelpanada.com, Fax 041 5209619 – ▮ ▤ ▥. ▤ ▤ ⓞ ▥ ▥　LY
48 rm ⊇ 258,50/310.

🏠 **Flora** without rest., calle larga 22 Marzo 2283/a, San Marco ⊠ 30124 ℰ 041 5205844
info@hotelflora.it, Fax 041 5228217, « Small floral garden » – ▮ ▤ ▥. ▤ ▤ ⓞ ▥ ▥
ᴊᴄʙ　JZ
44 rm ⊇ 180/235.

🏠 **Abbazia** without rest., calle Priuli dei Cavalletti 68, Cannaregio ⊠ 30121 ℰ 041 717333
abbazia@iol.it, Fax 041 717949, « In an old monastery », 㑊 – ▤ ▥. ▤ ▤ ⓞ ▥ ▥
ᴊᴄʙ. ℀
closed 7 to 31 January – **39 rm** ⊇ 196/212.　BT

🏠 **Ca' d'Oro** without rest., corte Barbaro 4604, Cannaregio ⊠ 30131 ℰ 041 2411212,
info@hotelcadoro.it, Fax 041 2414385 – ▮ 㑊 ▤ ▥ ♿. ▤ ▤ ⓞ ▥ ▥ ᴊᴄʙ. ℀
17 rm ⊇ 95/220.　KX

🏠 **Anastasia** ♨ without rest., corte Barozzi 2141, San Marco ✉ 30124 ℰ 041 2770776,
hotel.anastasia@tin.it, Fax 041 2777049 – 📶 🗎 📺 📞. 𝔸𝔼 🕙 𝕄𝕆 𝕍𝕀𝕊𝔸. ✺   KZ c
17 rm 🖭 165/244.

🏠 **La Calcina** without rest., fondamenta zattere ai Gesuati 780, Dorsoduro ✉ 30123
ℰ 041 5206466, *la.calcina@libero.it, Fax 041 5227045,* ≤ canal and Giudecca island,
« Covered roof-terrace with view over the Giudecca canal » – 🗎. 𝔸𝔼 🕙 ⓪ 𝕄𝕆 𝕍𝕀𝕊𝔸 𝙹𝙲𝙱.
✺   BV f
29 rm 🖭 77/176.

🏠 **Campiello** without rest., calle del Vin 4647, Castello ✉ 30122 ℰ 041 5239682,
Fax campiellohcampiello.it041 5205798 – 🗎 📺. 𝔸𝔼 🕙 ⓪ 𝕄𝕆 𝕍𝕀𝕊𝔸. ✺   LZ b
16 rm 🖭 134/170.

🏠 **Santo Stefano,** campo Santo Stefano 2957, San Marco ✉ 30124 ℰ 041 5200166,
info_htl.sstefano@tin.it, Fax 041 5224460 – 📶 🗎 📺. 𝔸𝔼 🕙 ⓪ 𝕄𝕆 𝕍𝕀𝕊𝔸   CV c
11 rm 🖭 197/248.

🏠 **Locanda la Corte** without rest., calle Bressana 6317, Castello ✉ 30122
ℰ 041 2411300, *info@locandalacorte.it, Fax 041 2415982* – ✺ 🗎 📺 📞 ♿. 𝔸𝔼 🕙 𝕍𝕀𝕊𝔸
16 rm 🖭 78/165.   LY p

XXXX **Caffè Quadri,** piazza San Marco 120 ✉ 30124 ℰ 041 5222105, *quadri@quadriveni
ce.com, Fax 041 5208041,* ≤ – ✺ 🗎. 𝔸𝔼 🕙 ⓪ 𝕄𝕆 𝕍𝕀𝕊𝔸 𝙹𝙲𝙱. ✺   KZ y
closed Monday November-March – **Meals** (booking essential) a la carte 68/112.

XXX **Harry's Bar,** calle Vallaresso 1323, San Marco ✉ 30124 ℰ 041 5285777, *harry@gp
net.it, Fax 041 5208822,* American bar rest. – 🗎. 𝔸𝔼 🕙 ⓪ 𝕄𝕆 𝕍𝕀𝕊𝔸   KZ n
Meals (booking essential) a la carte 90/108 (15 %).

XXX **Osteria da Fiore,** calle del Scaleter 2202/A, San Polo ✉ 30125 ℰ 041 721308,
❀ *Fax 041 721343* – 🗎. 𝔸𝔼 🕙 ⓪ 𝕄𝕆 𝕍𝕀𝕊𝔸 𝙹𝙲𝙱. ✺   CI a
closed August, 25 December-15 January, Sunday and Monday – **Meals** (booking essential)
seafood a la carte 73/114
Spec. Alghe di mare ai molluschi (March-November). Misto crudo di branzino, calamaretti,
scampi e triglie. Tagliata di tonno al rosmarino.

XXX **La Caravella** - Hotel Saturnia e International, calle Larga 22 Marzo 2397, San Marco
✉ 30124 ℰ 041 5208901, *caravella@hotelsaturnia.it,* 🌣, Typical rest., *Summer service
in the small courtyard,* « Solarium terrace » – 🗎. 𝔸𝔼 🕙 ⓪ 𝕍𝕀𝕊𝔸 𝙹𝙲𝙱. ✺   JZ n
Meals (booking essential) a la carte 57/77.

XXX **La Colomba,** piscina di Frezzeria 1665, San Marco ✉ 30124 ℰ 041 5221175,
Fax 041 5221468, 🌣, « Collection of contemporary art » – ✺ 🗎 – 🔬 60. 𝔸𝔼 🕙 ⓪
𝕄𝕆 𝕍𝕀𝕊𝔸 𝙹𝙲𝙱. ✺   KZ m
closed Wednesday and Thursday lunch except May-Ocotber – **Meals** a la carte 62/90
(15 %).

XX **Do Forni,** calle dei Specchieri 457/468, San Marco ✉ 30124 ℰ 041 5237729, *info4d
oforni.it, Fax 041 5288132* – 🗎. 𝔸𝔼 🕙 ⓪ 𝕄𝕆 𝕍𝕀𝕊𝔸 𝙹𝙲𝙱   LY c
Meals (booking essential) a la carte 51/69 (12 %).

XX **Antico Pignolo,** calle dei Specchieri 451, San Marco ✉ 30124 ℰ 041 5228123, *anti
copignolo@libero.it, Fax 041 5209007,* 🌣 – ✺ 🗎. 𝔸𝔼 🕙 ⓪ 𝕄𝕆 𝕍𝕀𝕊𝔸 𝙹𝙲𝙱. ✺   LY v
Meals a la carte 70/99 (12 %).

XX **Harry's Dolci,** fondamenta San Biagio 773, Giudecca ✉ 30133 ℰ 041 5224844, *harr
ys@pop.gnet.it, Fax 041 5222322,* Rest. and cafeteria, « Outdoor summer service on the
Giudecca canal » – 🗎. 𝔸𝔼 🕙 ⓪ 𝕄𝕆 𝕍𝕀𝕊𝔸   BV d
26 March-7 November, closed Tuesday – **Meals** 49,06 (12 %) and a la carte 54/77 (12 %).

XX **Al Graspo de Ua,** calle dei Bombaseri 5094/A, San Marco ✉ 30124 ℰ 041 5200150,
graspo.deua@flashnet.it, Fax 041 5209389 – 🗎. 𝔸𝔼 🕙 ⓪ 𝕄𝕆 𝕍𝕀𝕊𝔸 𝙹𝙲𝙱   KY d
closed Monday – **Meals** (booking essential) a la carte 60/93 (12 %).

XX **Cip's Club** - Hotel Cipriani, fondamenta de le Zitelle 10, Giudecca ✉ 30133
ℰ 041 5207744, *Fax 041 2408519,* « Outdoor summer service on the Giudecca canal »
– 🗎. 𝔸𝔼 🕙 ⓪ 𝕄𝕆 𝕍𝕀𝕊𝔸. ✺   FV c
closed 7 January-15 March – **Meals** a la carte 68/93.

XX **Al Covo,** campiello della Pescaria 3968, Castello ✉ 30122 ℰ 041 5223812,
Fax 041 5223812, 🌣 – ✺   FV s
closed August, 15 December-15 January, Wednesday and Thursday – **Meals** a la carte
60/76.

XX **Fiaschetteria Toscana,** San Giovanni Grisostomo 5719, Cannaregio ✉ 30121
ℰ 041 5285281, *Fax 041 5285521,* 🌣 – 🗎. 𝔸𝔼 🕙 ⓪ 𝕄𝕆 𝕍𝕀𝕊𝔸 𝙹𝙲𝙱. ✺   KX p
closed 24 July-13 August, Monday lunch and Tuesday – **Meals** a la carte 38/50.

XX **Ai Mercanti,** corte Coppo 4346/A, San Marco ✉ 30124 ℰ 041 5238269,
Fax 041 5238269, 🌣 – 🗎. 𝔸𝔼 🕙 ⓪ 𝕄𝕆 𝕍𝕀𝕊𝔸. ✺   KZ u
closed Sunday and Monday lunch – **Meals** a la carte 48/72.

XX **Ai Gondolieri**, fondamenta de l'Ospedaleto 366, Dorsoduro ⊠ 30123 ℰ 041 528639
aigond@gpnet.it, Fax 041 5210075 – 🆎 🕄 ⑩ 🚳 VISA. ❄
DV
closed Tuesday – **Meals** (booking essential for dinner) beef dishes only a la carte 50/7

XX **Da Mario-alla Fava**, calle Stagneri 5242 e Gallazzo 5265, San Marco ⊠ 3012
ℰ 041 5285147, Fax 041 2443520, 🍴 – 🆎 🕄 ⑩ 🚳 VISA
KY
closed 7 to 20 January – **Meals** a la carte 39/55 (12 %).

X **L'Osteria di Santa Marina**, campo Santa Marina 5911, Castello ⊠ 3012
ℰ 041 5285239, Fax 041 5285239 – ▤. 🕄 🚳 VISA. ❄
LY r
closed 18 August-4 September, 7 to 25 January, Sunday and Monday lunch – **Mea**
seafood a la carte 40/54.

X **Vini da Gigio**, fondamenta San Felice 3628/a, Cannaregio ⊠ 30131 ℰ 041 528514₀
Fax 041 5228597, Inn serving food – 🆎 🕄 ⑩ 🚳 VISA
DT
closed 15 to 31 August, 15 to 31 January and Monday – **Meals** (booking essential) a
carte 32/47.

X **Hostaria da Franz**, fondamenta Sant epo 754, Castello ⊠ 30122 ℰ 041 522086₁
Fax 041 2419278, 🍴 – ▤. 🕄 🚳 VISA. ❄   by riva dei 7 Martiri
closed 12 to 18 August, January and Tuesday – **Meals** a la carte 50/66.

X **Trattoria alla Madonna**, calle della Madonna 594, San Polo ⊠ 3012
ℰ 041 5223824, Fax 041 5210167, Venetian trattoria – 🆎 🕄 🚳 VISA JCB. ❄   JY
closed 4 to 17 August, 24 December-January and Wednesday – **Meals** a la carte 27/3
(12 %).

X **Alle Testiere**, calle del Mondo Novo 5801, Castello ⊠ 30122 ℰ 041 522722₀
Fax 041 5227220, Inn serving food – ❄❄. 🕄 🚳 VISA
LY
closed 25 July-25 August, 24 December-12 January, Sunday and Monday – **Meals** (bookin
essential) seafood a la carte 40/55.

in Lido : 15 mn by boat from San Marco KZ – ⊠ 30126 Venezia Lido.
Car access throughout the year from Piazzale Roma.
🛈 Gran Viale S. M. Elisabetta 6 ℰ 0415265721 :

🏨🏨🏨🏨 **The Westin Excelsior**, lungomare Marconi 41 ℰ 041 5260201, Fax 041 5267276, ≤
🍴, 🏊, ▲ₒ, 🎱 – 🔋, ❄❄ rm, ▤ 📺 ᴋ, 🚗 🅿. – 🏧 600. 🆎 🕄 ⑩ 🚳 VISA JCB. ❄
15 March-20 November – **Meals** a la carte 78/121 – **193 rm** ☑ 569/620, 3 suites.

🏨🏨🏨 **Des Bains**, lungomare Marconi 17 ℰ 041 5265921, Fax 041 5260113, ≤, 🍴, « Flora
park with heated 🏊 and ❄❄ », 🏋₀, ⇌, ▲ₒ – 🔋▤ 📺 🅿 – 🏧 380. 🆎 🕄 ⑩ 🚳 VISA. ❄
March-November – **Meals** a la carte 77/126 and **Pagoda** Rest. (June-September) a la carte
28/42 – **191 rm** ☑ 513/554, suite.

🏨🏨🏨 **Villa Mabapa**, riviera San Nicolò 16 ℰ 041 5260590, info@villamabapa.com
Fax 041 5269441, « Summer rest. service in garden », 🎱 – 🔋 ▤ 📺 – 🏧 60. 🆎 🕄 ⑩
🚳 VISA JCB. ❄ rest
Meals (closed lunch except 15 May-October) a la carte 38/53 – **68 rm** ☑ 178/284.

🏨🏨🏨 **Quattro Fontane** 🔊, via 4 Fontane 16 ℰ 041 5260227, quafonve@tin.it
Fax 041 5260726, « Summer rest. service in garden », ❄❄ – ▤ 📺 🅿 – 🏧 40. 🆎 🕄 ⑩
🚳 VISA. ❄ rest
28 March-10 November – **Meals** a la carte 71/93 – **59 rm** ☑ 300/320.

🏨🏨 **Le Boulevard** without rest., Gran Viale S. M. Elisabetta 41 ℰ 041 5261990
Fax 041 5261917 – 🔋 ▤ 📺 🅿. 🆎 🕄 ⑩ 🚳 VISA JCB
45 rm ☑ 154,94/284,05.

🏨🏨 **Ca' del Borgo** 🔊 without rest., piazza delle Erbe 8, località Malamocco South : 6 km
ℰ 041 770749, Fax 041 770744, ≤, « 16C mansion », ❄ – ▤ 📺. 🆎 🕄 ⑩ 🚳 VISA JCB
8 rm ☑ 155/259.

🏨🏨 **Villa Tiziana** 🔊 without rest., via Andrea Gritti 3 ℰ 041 5261152, reservation@h₀
teltiziana.com, Fax 041 5262145 – ▤ 📺. 🆎 🕄 ⑩ 🚳 VISA JCB. ❄
closed until 7 February – **16 rm** ☑ 206,59/247,90.

🏨🏨 **La Meridiana** without rest., via Lepanto 45 ℰ 041 5260343, info@lameridiana.com
Fax 041 5269240, ❄ – 🔋 ▤ 📺. 🆎 🕄 ⑩ 🚳 VISA
15 March-5 November and Carnival – **33 rm** ☑ 145/186.

🏨🏨 **Petit Palais** without rest., lungomare Marconi 54 ℰ 041 5265993, info@petitpalais.net
Fax 041 5260781, ≤ – 🔋 ▤ 📺. 🆎 🕄 ⑩ 🚳 VISA JCB
closed 11 November-January – **26 rm** ☑ 160/207.

X **Trattoria Favorita**, via Francesco Duodo 33 ℰ 041 5261626, Fax 041 5261626,
« Outdoor summer service » – 🆎 🕄 ⑩ 🚳 VISA JCB
closed 15 January-15 February, Monday and Tuesday lunch – **Meals** a la carte 37/50.

X **Al Vecio Cantier**, via della Droma 76, località Alberoni South : 10 km ⊠ 30011 Alberoni
ℰ 041 5268130, Fax 041 5268130, 🍴 – 🆎 🕄 ⑩ 🚳 VISA JCB
closed November, January, Monday and Tuesday, June-September open Tuesday dinner-
Meals (booking essential) seafood a la carte 29/54.

Murano *10 mn by boat from Fondamenta Nuove* EFT *and 1 h 10 mn by boat from Punta Sabbioni*
– ⊠ 30141 :

X **Ai Frati,** Fondamenta Venier 4 *℘* 041 736694, Fax 041 739346, « Outdoor terrace summer service on the canal » – 🕃 🚗 *VISA*
closed February and Thursday – **Meals** seafood trattoria a la carte 26/42 (12 %).

Burano *50 mn by boat from Fondamenta Nuove* EFT *and 32 mn by boat from Punta Sabbioni*
– ⊠ 30012 :

X **Da Romano,** via Galuppi 221 *℘* 041 730030, Fax 041 735217, 余, « Collection of contemporary art » – 🗏, 🖭 🕃 🚗 *VISA*
closed 15 December-15 February, Sunday dinner and Tuesday – **Meals** a la carte 33/48 (12 %).

X **Al Gatto Nero-da Ruggero,** Fondamenta della Giudecca 88 *℘* 041 730120, Fax 041 735570, 余, Typical trattoria – 🖭 🕃 ⓞ *VISA*
closed 15 to 30 November, 15 to 31 January and Monday – **Meals** a la carte 30/56.

Torcello *45 mn by boat from Fondamenta Nuove* EFT *and 37 mn by boat from Punta Sabbioni*
– ⊠ 30012 *Burano* :

XX **Locanda Cipriani,** piazza Santa Fosca 29 *℘* 041 730150, *info@locandacipriani.com*, Fax 041 735433, « Summer service in garden » – 🗏 🖭 🕃 ⓞ 🚗 *VISA*
closed January-15 February and Tuesday – **Meals** 39/43 (lunch) 46/670 (dinner) and a la carte 60/70.

Isola Rizza 37050 Verona 🔢🔢🔢 G 12. *pop. 2799.*
Roma 487 – Ferrara 91 – Mantova 55 – Padova 84 – Verona 27.

XXX **Perbellini,** via Muselle 11 *℘* 045 7135352, *pperbel@netbusiness.it*, Fax 045 7135899
😋😋 – 🗏 🖲 🖭 🕃 ⓞ 🚗 *VISA*
closed 4 to 28 August, 6 to 16 January, Sunday dinner and Monday, July-August also Sunday lunch – **Meals** (booking essential) 46,50 (lunch) 73/81 (dinner) and a la carte 64/85
Spec. Colori e sapori del mare. Risotto mantecato alle seppie nere con pomodori confit e olio al basilico (spring-summer). Controfiletto d'agnello su purè di cavolfiori con ragù di scampi.

Pieve d'Alpago 32010 Belluno 🔢🔢🔢 D 19. *pop. 2048 alt. 690.*
Roma 608 – Belluno 17 – Cortina d'Ampezzo 72 – Milano 346 – Treviso 67 – Venezia 96.

XXX **Dolada** 🏠 *with rm,* via Dolada 21, località Plois *℘* 0437 479141, *dolada@tin.it*, 😋😋 Fax 0437 478068, ≤, 余 – 🖭 🖲 🕃 ⓞ JCB
(closed Monday and Tuesday lunch except July-August) (booking essential) a la carte 41/70
🛏 12 **6 rm** 77/103, suite
Spec. Terrina di fegatini alle erbe, tartufo nero, vinaigrette all'olio di nocciole. Ravioli agli "antichi sapori". Piccione in casseruola farcito con la peverada e gnocchetti di farina.

Rubano 35030 🔢🔢🔢 F 17. *pop. 13611 alt. 18.*
Roma 490 – Padova 8 – Venezia 49 – Verona 72 – Vicenza 27.

XXX **Le Calandre,** strada statale 11, località Sarmeola *℘* 049 630303, *alajmo@calandre.com*, 😋😋 Fax 049 633000 – 🗏 🖭 🕃 ⓞ 🚗 *VISA*. 🍴
closed 8 to 27 August, 1 to 14 January, Sunday and Monday – **Meals** (booking essential) 88/103 and a la carte 54/101
Spec. Cannelloni croccanti di ricotta e mozzarella di bufala con passata di pomodoro e basilico (spring-summer). Rombo ai vapori di verbena con purea aspra di patate. Spumone di cioccolato al cardamomo con gelatina di ciliege e lamponi.

Verona 37100 🅿 🔢🔢🔢, 🔢🔢🔢 F 14 *G. Italy.* – *pop. 257477 alt. 59.*
🛫 *Verona (closed Tuesday) at Sommacampagna* ⊠ 37066 *℘* 045 510060, Fax 045 510242, West : 13 km.
🏌 *of Villafranca South-East : 14 km ℘* 045 8095666, Fax 045 8095706.
🖪 *via degli Alpini 9 ℘* 045 8095666, Fax 045 8095706 – *Porta Nuova Railway station ℘* 045 8000861 – *Villafranca Airport ℘* 045 8619163.
A.C.I. *via della Valverde 34* ⊠ 37122 *℘* 045 595333.
Roma 503 – Milano 157 – Venezia 114.

XXXX **Il Desco,** via Dietro San Sebastiano 7 ⊠ 37121 *℘* 045 595358, Fax 045 590236 – 🗏.
😋😋 🖭 🕃 ⓞ 🚗 *VISA*. 🍴
closed Easter, 15 to 30 June, 25 December-10 January, Sunday and Monday, only Sunday July-August and December – **Meals** (booking essential) 100 and a la carte 66/92
Spec. Tortino di patate e basilico in zuppetta di frutti di mare. Ravioli di catalogna con fave e bresaola fritta. Filetto di San Pietro con asparagi, carciofi e salsa di pistacchi.

489

490

Norway

Norge

OSLO

PRACTICAL INFORMATION

LOCAL CURRENCY

Norwegian Kroner: *100 NOK = 12,50 euro (€) (Dec. 2001)*

TOURIST INFORMATION

The telephone number and address of the Tourist Information office is given in the text under 🖪.

National Holiday in Norway: *17 May.*

FOREIGN EXCHANGE

In the Oslo area banks are usually open between 8.15am and 3.30pm but in summertime, 15/5 - 31/8, they close at 3pm. Saturdays and Sundays closed.
Most large hotels, main airports and Tourist information office have exchange facilities. At Oslo Airport the bank is open from 6.30am to 8pm (weekdays), 6.30am to 6pm (Saturday), 7am to 8pm (Sunday), all year round.

MEALS

At lunchtime, follow the custom of the country and try the typical buffets of Scandinavian specialities.
At dinner, the a la carte and set menus will offer you more conventional cooking.

SHOPPING IN OSLO

Knitware, silverware, pewter and glassware.

Your hotel porter should be able to help you with information.

CAR HIRE

The international car hire companies have branches in each major city. Your hotel porter should be able to give details and help you with your arrangements. Cars can also be hired from the Tourist Information Office.

TIPPING IN NORWAY

A service charge is included in hotel and restaurant bills and it is up to the customer to give something in addition if he wants to.
The cloakroom is sometimes included in the bill, sometimes an extra charge is made.
Taxi drivers don't expect to be tipped. It is up to you if you want to give a gratuity.

SPEED LIMITS

The maximum permitted speed within built-up areas is 50 km/h - 31mph. Outside these areas it is 80 km/h - 50mph. Where there are other speed limits (lower or higher) they are signposted.

SEAT BELTS

The wearing of seat belts in Norway is compulsory for drivers and all passengers.

OSLO

Norge 985 M 7 – *pop. 507 467.*

Hamburg 888 – København 583 – Stockholm 522.

🛈 The Tourist Information Centre in Oslo, Drynjulf Bulls plass 1 ℰ 23 11 78 80, Fax 22 83 81 50 – KNA (Kongelig Norsk Automobilklub) Royal Norwegian Automobile Club, Drammensveien 20C ℰ 22 56 19 00 – NAF (Norges Automobil Forbund), Storg. 2 ℰ 22 34 14 00.

🏌 Oslo Golfklubb ℰ 22 51 05 60.
✈ Oslo-Gardermoen NE: 45 km ℰ 64 81 20 00 – SAS Head Office: Oslo City, Stenersg. 1 a ℰ 22 17 41 60 – Air Terminal: Galleri Oslo, Schweigaards gate 6.
🚢 Copenhagen, Frederikshavn, Kiel, Hirtshals : contact tourist information centre (see above).

See: Bygdøy ABZ Viking Ship Museum★★★ (Vikingskipshuset) ; Folk Museum★★★ (Norsk Folkemuseum) ; Fram Museum★★ (Frammuseet) ; Kon-Tiki Museum★★ (Kon-Tiki Museet) ; Maritime Museum★★ (Norsk Sjøfartsmuseum) – Munch Museum★★ (Munch-Museet) DY – National Gallery★★★ (Nasjonalgalleriet) CY **M**[1] – Vigelandsanlegget★ (Vigeland sculptures and museum) AX – Akershus Castle★ (Akershus Festning : Resistance Museum★) CZ **M**[2] – Oslo Cathedral (Domkirke: views★★ from steeple) CY – Ibsen-museet★ BY **M**[4].

Outskirts: Holmenkollen★ (NW: 10 km): view from ski-jump tower and ski museum BX – Sonia Henie-Onstad Art Centre★★ (Sonia Henie-Onstad Kunstsenter) (W: 12 km) AY.

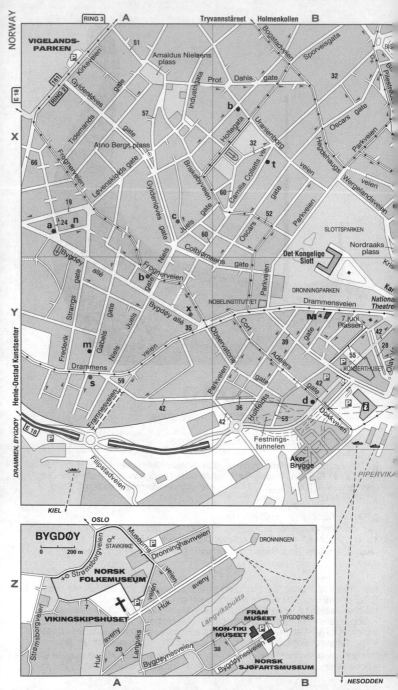

OSLO

FREDRIKSHAVN, KIEL   C   KØBENHAVN   D   E 18 ASKIM   E 6

STREET INDEX TO OSLO TOWN PLAN

Grand Hotel, Karl Johans Gate 31, ✉ 0101, ℰ 23 21 20 00, grand@rica.nc
Fax 23 21 21 00, 🛎s, ⬚ – 🛗, ✤ rm, 🔲 📺 ⟵ – 🛗 300. 🏧 ⒶⒺ ⓪ 𝘝𝘐𝘚𝘈. ✵ res
Julius Fritzner : Meals (dinner only) 495 and a la carte 555/705 ⓘ 395 – **Grand Café**
Meals 285/345 and a la carte approx. 435 – **282 rm** 🖙 1805/2990, 7 suites.

Continental, Stortingsgaten 24-26, ✉ 0117, ℰ 22 82 40 00, booking@hotel-continer
al.no, Fax 22 42 09 89 – 🛗, ✤ rm, 🔲 📺 ⟵ – 🛗 200. 🏧 ⒶⒺ ⓪ 𝘝𝘐𝘚𝘈 𝗝𝗖𝗕. ✵
closed 23 December-2 January – Meals (dinner only) 400/515 and a la carte 335/570 (se
also **Annen Etage** and **Theatercaféen** below) – 151 rm 🖙 1890/2700, 8 suites.   CY

Radisson SAS Scandinavia Ⓜ, Holbergsgate 30, ✉ 0166, ℰ 23 29 30 00, gues
@oslza.rdsas.com, Fax 23 29 30 01, ≼ Oslo and Fjord, 🛌, 🛎s, ⬚ – 🛗, ✤ rm, 🔲 📺
🍴 ᵭ ⟵ – 🛗 720. 🏧 ⒶⒺ ⓪ 𝘝𝘐𝘚𝘈 𝗝𝗖𝗕.   CX
Holberg : Meals (buffet lunch) 250/450 and dinner a la carte – **476 rm** 🖙 1930/2130
12 suites.

Bristol, Kristian IV's Gate 7, ✉ 0164, ℰ 22 82 60 00, booking@bristol.nc
Fax 22 82 60 01, 🛌, 🛎s – 🛗, ✤ rm, 🔲 📺 🍴 – 🛗 450. 🏧 ⒶⒺ ⓪ 𝘝𝘐𝘚𝘈. ✵   CY
Meals (closed Saturday and Sunday lunch) 225 (lunch) and a la carte 455/545 ⓘ 370
243 rm 🖙 1350/1960, 9 suites.

Clarion Royal Christiania Ⓜ, Biskop Gunnerus' Gate 3, ✉ 0106, ℰ 23 10 80 0(
christiania@clarion.choicehotels.no, Fax 23 10 80 80, 🛌, 🛎s, ⬚ – 🛗, ✤ rm, 🔲 📺 🍴
ᵭ ⟵ – 🛗 450. 🏧 ⒶⒺ ⓪ 𝘝𝘐𝘚𝘈 𝗝𝗖𝗕. ✵   DY
closed 21 December-1 January – Meals (buffet lunch) 240/400 and a la carte 255/45
ⓘ 295 – **433 rm** 🖙 1795/1995, 70 suites.

St Olav, St Olavs Plass 1, ✉ 0165, ℰ 23 15 56 00, stolav@scandic-hotels.con
Fax 23 15 56 11, 🛌, 🛎s – 🔲 🍴 – 🛗 100. 🏧 ⒶⒺ ⓪ 𝘝𝘐𝘚𝘈. ✵ rest   CX
closed 22 March-1 April and 20 December-1 January – Meals a la carte 200/285 – **241 rr**
🖙 1150/1395.

Radisson SAS Plaza Ⓜ, Sonja Henies Plass 3, ✉ 0134, ℰ 22 05 80 00, sales@ro
as.com, Fax 22 05 80 10, ≼ Oslo and Fjord, 🛎s, ⬚ – 🛗, ✤ rm, 🔲 📺 🍴 ᵭ ⟵ – 🛗 95(
🏧 ⒶⒺ ⓪ 𝘝𝘐𝘚𝘈 𝗝𝗖𝗕. ✵ rest   DY
Abelone : Meals (buffet lunch) 195/350 and dinner a la carte 375/415 ⓘ 300 – **655 rn**
🖙 1720/1920, 19 suites.

Opera, Christian Frederiks plass 5, ✉ 0103, ℰ 24 10 30 00, opera@rainbow-hotels.nc
Fax 24 10 30 10, 🛌, 🛎s – 🔳. 🏧 ⒶⒺ ⓪ 𝘝𝘐𝘚𝘈 𝗝𝗖𝗕. ✵   DZ
Meals (closed Sunday lunch) (buffet lunch) 215/600 and a la carte approx. 430 – **432 rr**
🖙 1520/1820, 2 suites.

Rica Oslo Ⓜ, Karl Johans Gate 3, ✉ 0105, ℰ 23 10 42 00, rica.oslo.hotel@rica.nc
Fax 23 10 42 10, 🛌, 🛎s – 🛗, ✤ rm, 🔲 📺 ᵭ – 🛗 60. 🏧 ⒶⒺ ⓪ 𝘝𝘐𝘚𝘈 𝗝𝗖𝗕. ✵ res
Bjørvigen : Meals (closed Sunday) (buffet lunch) 195/325 and a la carte 340/420 ⓘ 14(
– **172 rm** 🖙 1195/1595, 2 suites.   DY (

Rica Victoria Ⓜ, Rosenkrantzgate 13, ✉ 0121, ℰ 22 14 70 00, rica.victoria.hotel@
ica.no, Fax 24 14 70 01 – 🛗, ✤ rm, 🔲 📺 ᵭ ⟵ – 🛗 50. 🏧 ⒶⒺ ⓪ 𝘝𝘐𝘚𝘈 𝗝𝗖𝗕. ✵
closed 21-27 December – Meals (closed Sunday) (buffet lunch) 155 and dinner a la cart
230/325 ⓘ 225 – **194 rm** 🖙 1250/1440, 5 suites.   CY

Noble House Ⓜ without rest., Kongens Gate 5, ✉ 0153, ℰ 23 10 72 00, receptio
.oslnob@firsthotels.no, Fax 23 10 72 10, 🛌, 🛎s – 🛗 ✤ 📺 ⟵. 🏧 ⒶⒺ ⓪ 𝘝𝘐𝘚𝘈
53 rm 🖙 1355/1605, 16 suites.   CZ

Rica H. Bygdøy Allé, Bygdøy Allé 53, ✉ 0207, ℰ 23 08 58 00, rica.hotel.bygdoey
alle@rica.no, Fax 23 08 58 08 – 🛗, ✤ rm, 📺 🍴 – 🛗 40. 🏧 ⒶⒺ ⓪ 𝘝𝘐𝘚𝘈. ✵   AX
closed 23 March-1 April and 23 December-2 January – **Magma :** Meals (brunch Saturda
and Sunday) a la carte 360/500 – **57 rm** 🖙 985/1700.

NORWAY

🏨 **Bastion** Ⓜ without rest., Skippergaten 7, ⊠ 0152, ℰ 22 47 77 00, *booking@hotelb astion.no, Fax 22 33 11 80*, 🛱, ⚏ – 🛗 ✑ 📺 📠 🐠 🖭 ⑩ 𝗩𝗜𝗦𝗔 CZ x
closed 28 March-2 April, 21-31 December and 1-5 January – **93 rm** � 1200/1500, 6 suites.

🏨 **Stefan** Ⓜ, Rosenkrantzgate 1, ⊠ 0159, ℰ 23 31 55 00, *stefan@rainbow-hotels.no, Fax 23 31 55 55* – 🛗 ✑ 📺 📺 🐠 🖭 ⑩ 𝗩𝗜𝗦𝗔 𝗝𝗖𝗕 CY r
closed Easter and 22 December-2 January – **Meals** *(closed Sunday)* (buffet lunch) a la carte approx. 200 – **139 rm** ⊇ 1170/1470.

🏨 **Gabelshus** ⍝ without rest., Gabelsgate 16, ⊠ 0272, ℰ 23 27 65 00, *resepsion@g abelshus.no, Fax 23 27 65 60* – 🛗 ✑ 📺 📠 – ♨ 60. 🐠 🖭 ⑩ 𝗩𝗜𝗦𝗔. ✜ AY m
closed Easter and Christmas – **43 rm** ⊇ 1295/1790.

🏨 **Ambassadeur** without rest., Camilla Colletts Vei 15, ⊠ 0258, ℰ 23 27 23 00, *post @hotelambassadeur.no, Fax 22 44 47 91* – 🛗 ✑ 📺 🐠 🖭 ⑩ 𝗩𝗜𝗦𝗔 𝗝𝗖𝗕 BX t
33 rm ⊇ 1175/1375, 8 suites.

🏨 **Millennium** Ⓜ, Tollbugaten 25, ⊠ 0157, ℰ 21 02 28 00, *millennium@firsthotels.no, Fax 21 02 28 30* – 🛗, ✑ rm, 📺 🛆. 🐠 🖭 ⑩ 𝗩𝗜𝗦𝗔 CY s
Meals *(closed Sunday)* (coffee shop) a la carte 215/365 – **102 rm** ⊇ 1105/1355, 10 suites.

🏨 **Børsparken** without rest., Tollbugaten 4, ⊠ 0152, ℰ 22 47 17 17, *booking.boerspa rken@comfort.choicehotels.no, Fax 22 47 17 18* – 🛗 ✑ 📺 🛆 – ♨ 50. 🐠 🖭 ⑩ 𝗩𝗜𝗦𝗔. ✜ CDZ s
closed Easter and 24 December-2 January – **198 rm** ⊇ 1095/1295.

🏨 **Sjølyst** Ⓜ without rest., Sjølyst plass 5, ⊠ 0212, West : 2 km by Bygdøy Allé and Sjølyst Allé ℰ 23 15 51 00, *sjolyst@scandic-hotels.com, Fax 23 15 51 11* – 🛗, ✑ rm, 📺 ✔ 🛆 ⇔, 🐠 🖭 ⑩ 𝗩𝗜𝗦𝗔
closed 22 March-2 April and 20 December-2 January – **193 rm** ⊇ 1195/1395.

🏨 **Byporten** Ⓜ without rest., Jernbanetorget 6, ⊠ 0154, ℰ 23 15 55 00, *byporten@s candic-hotels.com, Fax 23 15 55 11* – 🛗 ✑ 📺 🛆. 🐠 🖭 ⑩ 𝗩𝗜𝗦𝗔 DY n
236 rm ⊇ 1045/1495, 4 suites.

🏠 **Norlandia Saga** without rest., Eilert Sundtsgt. 39, ⊠ 0259, ℰ 22 43 04 85, *saga@n orlandia.no, Fax 22 44 08 63* – ✑ 📺 📠 – ♨ 25. 🐠 🖭 ⑩ 𝗩𝗜𝗦𝗔 𝗝𝗖𝗕 BX b
closed 20 December-2 January – **37 rm** ⊇ 925/1075.

🏠 **Spectrum** Ⓜ without rest., Brugate 7, ⊠ 0186, ℰ 23 36 27 00, *Fax 23 36 27 50* – 🛗 ✑ 📺 🛆. 🐠 🖭 ⑩ 𝗩𝗜𝗦𝗔 𝗝𝗖𝗕. ✜ DY a
151 rm ⊇ 995/1760.

🏠 **Vika Atrium** Ⓜ, Munkedamsveien 45, ⊠ 0121, ℰ 22 83 33 00, *vika.atrium@rainbow-ho tels.no, Fax 22 83 09 57*, 🛱, ⚏ – 🛗, ✑ rm, 📺 📠 – ♨ 240. 🐠 🖭 ⑩ 𝗩𝗜𝗦𝗔 𝗝𝗖𝗕. ✜
Meals *(closed Friday-Sunday and Bank Holidays)* (buffet lunch) 165/170 and dinner a la carte 130/205 ⋒ 225 – **91 rm** ⊇ 1220/1720. BY d

🏠 **Norrøna,** Grensen 19, ⊠ 0159, ℰ 23 31 80 00, *hotelln@online.no, Fax 23 31 80 01* – ✑ rm, ■ – ♨ 50. 🐠 🖭 ⑩ 𝗩𝗜𝗦𝗔 𝗝𝗖𝗕. ✜ CY e
closed 21 December-2 January – **Meals** *(closed Sunday)* (buffet lunch) 120 and a la carte 180/300 – **93 rm** ⊇ 1040/1290.

🏵🏵 **Annen Etage** (at Continental H.), Stortingsgaten 24-26, ⊠ 0117, ℰ 22 82 40 00, *book ing@hotel.continental.no, Fax 22 42 09 89* – ■. 🐠 🖭 ⑩ 𝗩𝗜𝗦𝗔 𝗝𝗖𝗕. ✜ CY n
closed Easter, July, Christmas and Sunday – **Meals** (dinner only) a la carte 510/710 ⋒ 300
Spec. Sautéed scallops with chicken liver purée. Suckling pig with apple compote. Passion fruit soufflé.

🏵🏵 **Bagatelle** (Hellstrøm), Bygdøy Allé 3, ⊠ 0257, ℰ 22 12 14 40, *bagatelle@bagatelle.no, Fax 22 43 64 20*, « Contemporary decor » – ■. 🐠 🖭 ⑩ 𝗩𝗜𝗦𝗔 𝗝𝗖𝗕. ✜ AY x
closed 1 week Easter, 3 weeks July-August, 1 week Christmas and Sunday – **Meals** (booking essential) (dinner only) 650/1150 and a la carte 650/920 ⋒ 460
Spec. Millefeuille with scallops and shallots. Whiting with caviar and lemon sauce. Game in season.

🏵 **Statholdergaarden** (Stiansen), Rådhusgate 11, (entrance by Kirkegate) 1st floor, ⊠ 0151, ℰ 22 41 88 00, *post@statholdergaarden.no, Fax 22 41 22 24*, « Elegant atmosphere in 17C house » – ■. 🐠 🖭 ⑩ 𝗩𝗜𝗦𝗔. ✜ CZ f
closed 25 March-2 April, 15 July-4 August, 22 December-2 January and Sunday – **Meals** (booking essential) (dinner only) 695/825 and a la carte 585/630 ⋒ 350 – **Statholderens Krostue :** **Meals** *(closed Monday)* 150/485 and a la carte 410/470
Spec. Grilled scallops and pumpkin roulade. Fillet of reindeer with artichoke purée. Quince and ginger soufflé with tea sorbet.

🏵 **Le Canard,** President Harbitz Gate 4, ⊠ 0259, ℰ 22 54 34 00, *lecanard@lecanard.no, Fax 22 54 34 10*, 😊, « Tastefully decorated 1900 villa » – ■. 🐠 🖭 ⑩ 𝗩𝗜𝗦𝗔. ✜
closed Easter, Christmas and Sunday – **Meals** (dinner only) 495/550 and a la carte 695/875 ⋒ 300 AX c
Spec. Grilled scallops with foie gras and orange syrup. Roast duck in two servings. "After Eight" soufflé with orange salad.

XXX 🕸🕸 **Spisestedet Feinschmecker,** Balchensgate 5, ✉ 0265, ℰ 22 12 93 80, konta
            @feinschmecker.no, Fax 22 12 93 88, « Tasteful decor » – 🗐. 🐱🐱 AE ① VISA. ❀
            closed 1 week Easter, 3 weeks in summer and Sunday – **Meals** (booking essential) (dinne
            only) 495/625 and a la carte 615/685 🍴 285   AX
            Spec. Terrine of foie gras, marinated fruits. Fillet of veal with herb risotto. Chocolat
            savarin.

XXX 🕸🕸 **Oro** (Ness), Tordenskioldsgate 6A, ✉ 0160, ℰ 23 01 02 40, terje.ness.bocuse99@c2
            net, Fax 23 01 02 48 – 🗐 rest.. 🐱🐱 AE ① VISA. ❀   CY
            closed Easter, last 2 weeks July-first week August, 22 December-7 January, Sunday ar
            lunch Saturday and Monday – **Meals** 225/925 and a la carte 520/755 🍴 650
            Spec. Guinea fowl with truffles and foie gras. Grilled scallops with potato and vanilla. Panr
            cotta.

XX **Det Gamle Raadhus,** Nedre Slottsgate 1, ✉ 0157, ℰ 22 42 01 07, raadhus@start.ne
            Fax 22 42 04 90, 🎨 – 🐱🐱 AE ① VISA JCB. ❀   CZ
            closed 1 week Easter, 3 weeks July, 1 week Christmas and Sunday – **Meals** (dinner onl
            395/570 and a la carte 360/530.

XX **Theatercaféen** (at Continental H.), Stortingsgaten 24-26, ✉ 0117, ℰ 22 82 40 5(
            Fax 22 41 20 94 – 🐱🐱 AE ① VISA JCB. ❀   CY
            closed Sunday lunch – **Meals** 395/655 (dinner) and a la carte 380/860.

XX **Mares,** Frognesveien 12B, ✉ 0263, ℰ 22 54 89 80, lu-mares@frisurf.no
            Fax 22 54 89 85 – 🐱🐱 AE ① VISA JCB. ❀   AY
            closed 28 March-2 April, July and 22 December-2 January – **Meals** - Seafood - (bookir
            essential) (dinner only) 315/435 and a la carte 365/585 🍴 285.

XX **Babette's Gjestehus**, 1 Rådhuspassagen, Fridtjof Nansens Pl. 2, ✉ 016(
            ℰ 22 41 64 64, Fax 22 41 64 63, « Attractive decor » – 🗐. 🐱🐱 AE ① VISA   BY
            closed 24-26 December and Sunday – **Meals** (booking essential) (dinner only) 436 and
            la carte 463/562.

X **Brasserie Hansken,** Akersgata 2, ✉ 0158, ℰ 22 42 60 88, Fax 22 42 24 03 – 🗐. 🐱
            AE ① VISA JCB. ❀   CY
            closed 1 week Easter, 1 week Christmas and Sunday – **Meals** (booking essential) 270/58
            and a la carte 370/555.

X **A Touch of France,** Øvre Slottsgate 16, ✉ 0157, ℰ 23 10 01 65, dartagnan@c
            rtagnan.no, Fax 23 10 01 61, 🎨 – 🗐. 🐱🐱 AE ① VISA JCB. ❀   CY
            closed 24 December-1 January – **Meals** (dinner only) 370 and a la carte 295/450 🍴 29(

X **Hos Thea,** Gabelsgate 11, ✉ 0272, ℰ 22 44 68 74, Fax 22 44 68 74 – 🐱🐱 AE ① VIS
            JCB. ❀   AY
            closed 4 days Easter and 25 December – **Meals** (dinner only) 350/450 and a la cart
            310/500 🍴 235.

at Sandvika Southwest : 14 km by E 18 AY exit E 16 :

🏨 **Oslofjord** Ⓜ, Sandviksveien 184, ✉ 1300 Sandvika, ℰ 67 55 66 00, oslofjord@ra.
            bow-hotels.no, Fax 67 55 66 88, 🗜, 🚗 – 🛗, 🔑 rm, 🗐 📺 🕭 🗕 🖪 – 🔏 350. 🐱🐱 A
            ① VISA. ❀ rest
            closed 27 March-2 April and Christmas - **Fontaine** : **Meals** (buffet lunch) 235 and a la cart
            approx. 345 – **242 rm** 😑 1270/1570, 4 suites.

at Holmenkollen Northwest : 10 km by Bogstadveien BX Sørkedalsveien and Holmenkollveien

🏨 **Holmenkollen Park** Ⓜ 🏔, Kongeveien 26, ✉ 0390, ℰ 22 92 20 00, holmenkoll
            n.park.hotel.rica@rica.no, Fax 22 14 61 92, ≤ Oslo and Fjord, 🗜, 🚗, 🔲 – 🛗, 🔑 rm
            🗐 📺 🕭 🗕 🖪 – 🔏 350. 🐱🐱 AE ① VISA. ❀ rest
            closed December-3 January – **De Fem Stuer** : **Meals** (dinner only) 415/595 and a
            carte 400/615 🍴 415 – **Galleriet** : **Meals** (buffet lunch) 265 and a la carte 275/505
            210 rm 😑 1595/1995, 11 suites.

at Oslo Airport Northeast : 45 km by E 6 DZ at Gardermoen :

🏨 **Radisson SAS Airport** Ⓜ, ✉ 2061, ℰ 63 93 30 00, sales@oslzr.rdsas.com
            Fax 63 93 30 30, 🗜, 🚗 – 🛗, 🔑 rm, 🗐 📺 🕭 🖪 – 🔏 220. 🐱🐱 AE ① VISA. ❀ res
            Meals (buffet lunch) 200/650 and a la carte 310/540 🍴 300 – **347 rm** 😑 1775/2225
            3 suites.

🏨 **Clarion Oslo Airport** Ⓜ, West : 6 km, ✉ 2060, ℰ 63 94 94 94, oslo.airport@cla
            on.choicehotels.no, Fax 63 94 94 95, 🚗, 🔲 – 🛗, 🔑 rm, 📺 🕭 🖪 – 🔏 450. 🐱🐱 AE ①
            VISA JCB. ❀ rest
            Meals (buffet lunch) 250/300 and dinner a la carte 🍴 295 – **343 rm** 😑 1395/1495, 1 suite.

🏨 **Quality Airport,** Gardermoen Naeringspark, ✉ 2050 Jessheim, Southeast : 7 kr
            ℰ 63 92 61 00, resepsjonen@quality.choicehotels.no, Fax 63 92 61 01, 🕭 – 🛗, 🔑 rm
            📺 🕭 🖪 – 🔏 400. 🐱🐱 AE ① VISA JCB. ❀
            Meals (buffet lunch) 250/275 and a la carte 370/410 🍴 250 – **203 rm** 😑 1295/1395
            3 suites.

Poland

Polska

PRACTICAL INFORMATION

LOCAL CURRENCY

Zloty : *100 PLN = 27,62 euro (€) (Dec. 2001)*
National Holidays in Poland: *1 and 3 May and 11 November.*

PRICES

Prices may change if goods and service costs in Poland are revised and it is therefore always advisable to confirm rates with the hotelier when making a reservation.

FOREIGN EXCHANGE

It is strongly advised against changing money other than in banks, exchange offices or authorised offices such as large hotels and Kantor. Banks are usually open on weekdays from 8am to 6pm.

HOTEL RESERVATIONS

In case of difficulties in finding a room through our hotel selection, it is always possible to apply to the Tourist Office, ☎ 94 31, Fax (022) 629 07 50, open on weekdays from 8am to 7pm.

POSTAL SERVICES

Post offices are open from 8am to 8pm on weekdays.
The **General Post Office** *is open 7 days a week and 24 hours a day : Poczta Glówna, Świetokrzyska 31/33.*

SHOPPING IN WARSAW

In the index of street names, those printed in red are where the principal shops are found. They are generally open from 10am to 7pm on weekdays and Saturday.

THEATRE BOOKING

Your hotel porter will be able to make your arrangements or direct you to a theatre booking office: Kasy ZASP, Al Jerozolimskie 25 ☎ (022) 621 93 83, open from 11am to 2pm and 2.30pm to 6pm.

TIPPING

Hotel, restaurant and café bills often do not include service in the total charge. In these cases it is usual to leave the staff a gratuity which will vary depending upon the service given.

CAR HIRE

The international car hire companies have branches in Warsaw. Your hotel porter should be able to give details and help you with your arrangements.

BREAKDOWN SERVICE

A 24 hour breakdown service is operated calling ☎ 981.

SPEED LIMIT

On motorways, the maximum permitted speed is 110 km/h – 68 mph, 90 km/h – 56 mph on other roads and 60 km/h – 37 mph in built up areas. In Warsaw the maximum speed limit is 31 mph, 50 km/h.

SEAT BELTS

In Poland, the wearing of seat belts is compulsory for drivers and all passengers.

WARSAW
(WARSAWA)

Polska 974 *E 13 – Pop. 1 700 000.*

Berlin 591 – Budapest 670 – Gdansk 345 – Kiev 795 – Moscow 1253 – Zagreb 993.

🛈 *Warsaw Tourist Information Centre, Rynek Starego Miasta 28-42, ☏ 94-31, Fax (022) 524 11 43, Al. Jerozolimskie 54 (in railway station) ☏ 94-31, Al. Jerozolimskie 144, ☏ 94-31, Warsaw Airport (Arrivals Hall), ☏ 94-31.*

🛈 *First Warsaw Golf Club and Country Club, Rajszew 70, 05-110 Jabłonna ☏ (022) 782 45 55.*

✈ *Okęcie (Warsaw Airport) SW 10 km, by Żwirki i Wigury ☏ 952 or 953.*
Bus to airport: from major hotels in the town centre (ask the reception).
Polish Airlines (LOT) Al Jerozolimskie 65/79, Warsaw ☏ 952 or 953.

SIGHTS

OLD TOWN★★★ (STARE MIASTO) BX

Castle Square★ (Plac Zamkowy) BX **33** *– Royal Palace★★ (Zamek Królewski) BX – Beer Street (Ulica Piwna) BX – Ulica Świętojańska BX* **57** *– St John's Cathedral★ (Katedra Sw. Jana) BX – Old Town Marketplace★★★ (Rynek Starego Miasta) BX* **54** *– Warsaw History Museum★ (Muzeum Historyczne Warsawy) BX* **M¹** *– Barbakan BX* **A**.

NEW TOWN★ (NOWE MIASTO) ABX

New Town Marketplace (Rynek Nowego Miasta) ABX **36** *– Memorial to the Warsaw Uprising (Pomnik Powstania Warzszawskiego) AX* **D**.

ROYAL WAY★ (TRAKT KRÓLEWSKI)

St Anne's Church (Kościół Św. Anny) BX – Krakow's District Street (Krakowskie Przedmieście) BXY – New World Street (Nowy Świat) BYZ – Holy Cross Church (Św. Krzyża) BY – National Museum★★ (Muzeum Narodowe) CZ.

ŁAZIENKI PARK★★★ (PARK ŁAZIENKOWSKI) FUV

Chopin Memorial (Pomnik Chopina) – Palace-on-the-Water★★ (Pałac na Wodzie) – Belvedere Palace (Belweder).

WILANÓW★★★ GV

ADDITIONAL SIGHTS

John Paul II Collection★★ (Muzeum Kolekcji im. Jana Pawła II) AY – Palace of Culture and Science (Pałac Kultury i Nauki): view★★ from panoramic gallery AZ.

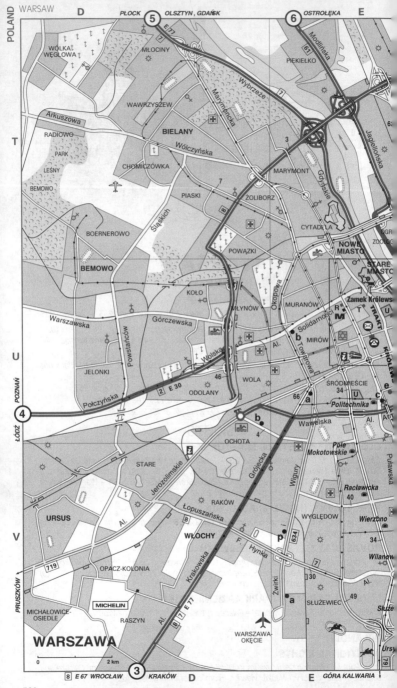

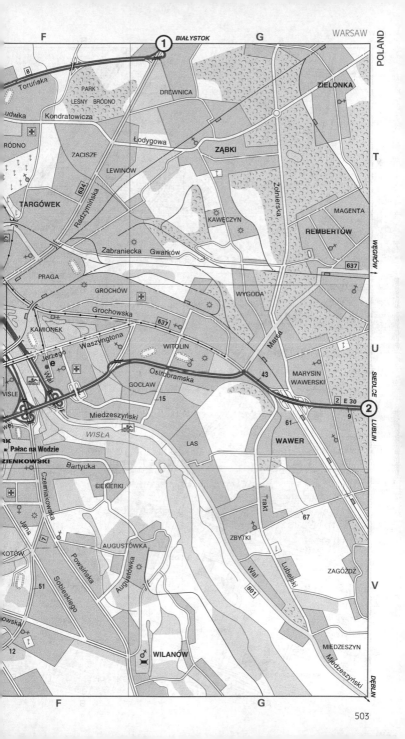

F

G

BIAŁYSTOK

8

Toruńska

PARK
LEŚNY BRÓDNO

DREWNICA

ZIELONKA

Ludwika

Kondratowicza

RÓDNO

ZACISZE

Łodygowa

ZĄBKI

T

LEWINÓW

Radzymińska

624

Żołnierska

MAGENTA

TARGÓWEK

KAWĘCZYN

REMBERTÓW

WĘGRÓW

Zabraniecka Gwarków

637

PRAGA

GROCHÓW

WYGODA

Grochowska

637

Masła

KAMIONEK

Waszyngtona

WITOLIN

U

SIEDLCE

Jerzego

e

Ostrobramska

43

**MARYSIN
WAWERSKI**

LUBLIN

GOCŁAW

2 E 30

2

WISLE

15

61

9

Miedzeszyński

LAS

WAWER

WISŁA

Pałac na Wodzie

ZIENKOWSKI

Bartycka

Czerniakowska

CIEKIERKI

Trakt

67

Jana

AUGUSTÓWKA

ZBYTKI

ZAGÓŹDŹ

KOTÓW

Powsińska

Augustówka

Wał

Lubelski

51

Sobieskiego

801

V

owska

12

WILANÓW

MIEDZESZYN

Miedzeszyński

DĘBLIN

F

G

503

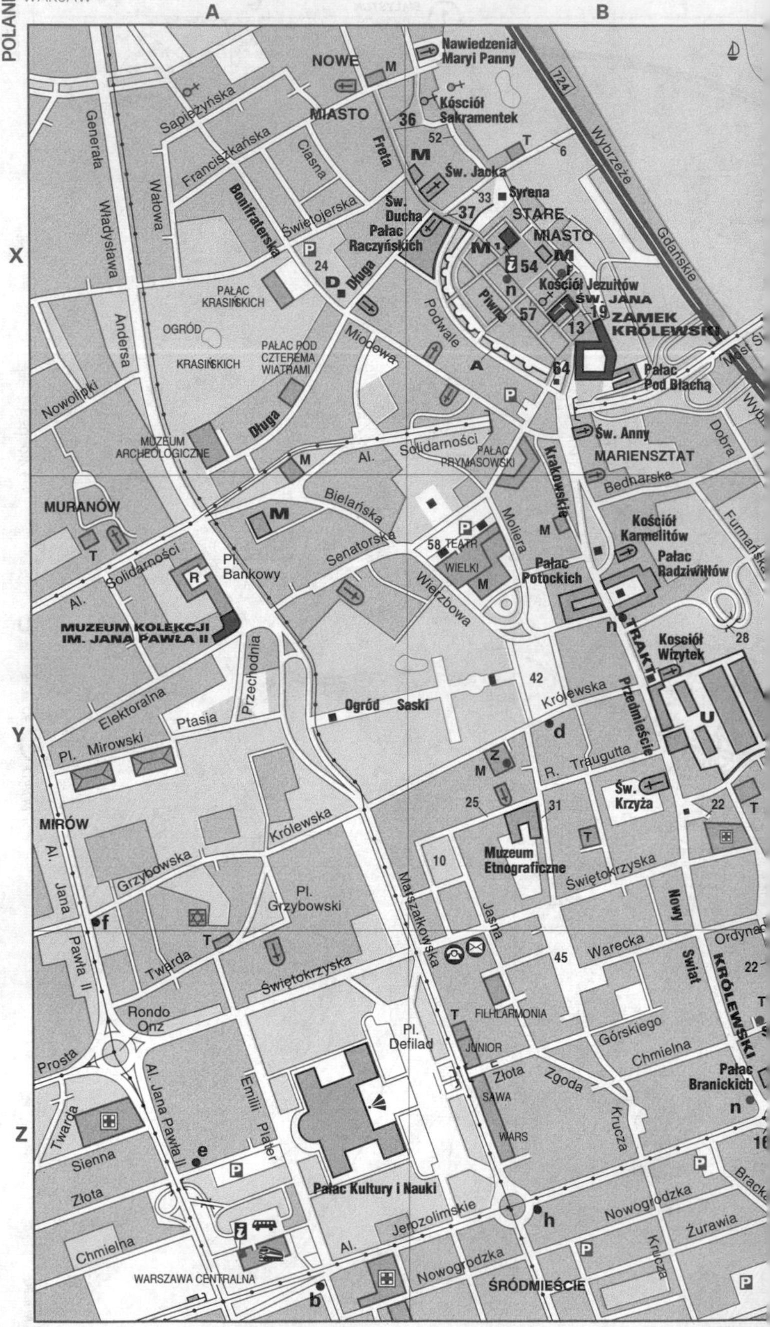

A
B
X
Y
Z
NOWE
MIASTO
Nawiedzenia Maryi Panny
Kościół Sakramentek
Sapieżyńska
Franciszkańska
Generała Władysława Andersa
Wałowa
Bonifraterska
Ciasna
Freta
Świętojerska
Św. Jacka
Syrena
Św. Ducha
Pałac Raczyńskich
STARE MIASTO
Kościół Jezuitów
ŚW. JANA
ZAMEK KRÓLEWSKI
Wybrzeże Gdańskie
724
Długa
PAŁAC KRASIŃSKICH
OGRÓD KRASIŃSKICH
PAŁAC POD CZTEREMA WIATRAMI
Miodowa
Podwale
Piwna
Pałac Pod Blachą
Most Śl
Nowolipki
MUZEUM ARCHEOLOGICZNE
Al. Solidarności
PAŁAC PRYMASOWSKI
Krakowskie
Św. Anny
MARIENSZTAT
Dobra
Bednarska
MURANÓW
Bielańska
Senatorska
Moliera
TEATR WIELKI
Kościół Karmelitów
Pałac Radziwiłłów
Furmańska
Pl. Bankowy
Pałac Potockich
Wierzbowa
MUZEUM KOLEKCJI IM. JANA PAWŁA II
TRAKT
Kościół Wizytek
Przechodnia
Ogród Saski
Królewska
Przedmieście
Elektoralna
Ptasia
Pl. Mirowski
R. Traugutta
Św. Krzyża
MIRÓW
Królewska
Muzeum Etnograficzne
Grzybowska
Pl. Grzybowski
Świętokrzyska
Nowy Świat
Al. Jana Pawła II
Jasna
Marszałkowska
Warecka
Ordynacka
KRÓLEWSKI
Twarda
Świętokrzyska
FILHARMONIA
Rondo Onz
Pl. Defilad
JUNIOR
Górskiego
Chmielna
Prosta
Emilii Plater
Złota
Zgoda
SAWA
Pałac Branickich
Twarda
Sienna
WARS
Krucza
Bracka
Złota
Pałac Kultury i Nauki
Al. Jerozolimskie
Nowogrodzka
Żurawia
Chmielna
WARSZAWA CENTRALNA
Nowogrodzka
ŚRÓDMIEŚCIE
Krucza

STREET INDEX TO WARSZAWA TOWN PLANS

WARSZAWA

0   300 m

PARK PRASKI

Solidarności

Helskie Al.

Wybrzeże

PRAGA

P

Szczecińskie

WISŁA

Lipowa

Kościuszkowskie

27

POWIŚLE

Topiel

Tamka

Dobra

Solec

L. Kruczkowskiego

Pałac Ostrogskich

WARSZAWA POWIŚLE

Al. Jerozolimskie

MUZEUM WOJSKA POLSKIEGO

Kruczkowskiego

MUZEUM NARODOWE

Książęca

Rozbrat

PAŁACYK BRANICKICH

Krzyży

T

C

-60

C

For maximum information from town plans: consult the conventional signs key.

Le Royal Meridien Bristol, Krakowskie Przedmieście 42-44, ✉ 00 325, ℰ (02 551 10 00, *bristol@it.com.pl, Fax (022) 625 25 77*, ☞, « Late 19C facade, partly dec rated in Art Nouveau style », ₲, ⇌, ◻ – ❘, ↝ rm, ❖ ❤ ⅙ – ⚗ 150. ⓌⒷ ⒼⒹ ⓪ 𝘝𝘐𝘚𝘈 ᴊᴄʙ. ⅌ rest   BY
Marconi : Meals - Mediterranean - (buffet lunch) 130/140 and a la carte 145/210 ▯ 14 (see also *Malinowa* below) – ⊆ 90 – **175 rm** 1500/1620, 30 suites.

Sheraton Ⓜ, Ul. B. Prusa 2, ✉ 00 493, ℰ (022) 657 61 00, *res201.warsaw@sher. on.com, Fax (022) 657 62 00*, ₲, ⇌ – ❘, ↝ rm, ❒ 𝘵𝘷 ❤ ⅙ ⇌ – ⚗ 550. ⓌⒷ ⓪ 𝘝𝘐𝘚𝘈 ᴊᴄʙ. ⅌ rest   CZ
The Oriental : Meals - Oriental - (buffet lunch) 145/155 and a la carte 100/215 ▯ 9 – *Lalka* : Meals (buffet lunch) 90/200 and a la carte 70/200 ▯ 90 – **333 rm** ⊆ 1215/1395, 19 suites.

Marriott Ⓜ, Al. Jerozolimskie 65-79, ✉ 00 697, ℰ (022) 630 63 06, *salesoffice@ arriott.com.pl, Fax (022) 830 03 11*, ≼ City, ₲, ⇌, ◻ – ❘ ↝ ❒ 𝘵𝘷 ❤ ⅙ – ⚗ 60 ⓌⒷ ⓪ 𝘝𝘐𝘚𝘈 ᴊᴄʙ. ⅌ rest   AZ
Chicago Grill : Meals *(closed Sunday)* (buffet lunch) 110/230 and dinner a la cart 140/380 ▯ 85 – *Parmizzano's* : Meals - Italian - 140/200 (lunch) and a la carte 125/22 – *Lila Weneda* : Meals 85/95 and a la carte 75/110 – ⊆ 80 – **500 rm** 1035/1155, 2 suites.

Victoria Inter-Continental Ⓜ, Ul. Krȯlewska 11, ✉ 00 065, ℰ (022) 657 80 1 *sofitel@victoria.orbis.pl, Fax (022) 657 80 57*, ₲, ⇌, ◻ – ❘, ↝ rm, ❒ 𝘵𝘷 ❤ ⅙ ⇌ – ⚗ 700. ⓌⒷ ⒶⒺ ⓪ 𝘝𝘐𝘚𝘈 ᴊᴄʙ. ⅌ rest   BY
Canaletto : Meals a la carte 100/125 ▯ 100 – *Hetmańska* : Meals a la carte 90/15 – ⊆ 60 – **329 rm** 910/990, 11 suites.

Jan III Sobieski Ⓜ, Plac Artura Zawiszy 1, ✉ 02 025, ℰ (022) 579 10 00, *hotel@ obieski.com.pl, Fax (022) 658 13 66*, ₲, ☞ – ❘, ↝ rm, ❒ 𝘵𝘷 ❤ ⅙ ⇌ – ⚗ 180. ⓌⒷ ⒶⒺ ⓪ 𝘝𝘐𝘚𝘈 ᴊᴄʙ   EU
Meals a la carte 105/175 ▯ 60 – **420 rm** ⊆ 540/635, 35 suites.

Holiday Inn Ⓜ, Ul. Złota 48-54, ✉ 00 120, ℰ (022) 697 39 99, *holiday@orbis. Fax (022) 697 38 99*, ₲, ⇌ – ❘, ↝ rm, ❒ 𝘵𝘷 ❤ ⅙ ⇌ Ⓟ – ⚗ 200. ⓌⒷ ⒶⒺ ⓪ 𝘝𝘐𝘚 ᴊᴄʙ. ⅌ rest   AZ
Symfonia : Meals a la carte 105/215 ▯ 50 – *Brasserie* : Meals (buffet only) 90 ⊆ 60 – **326 rm** 770/970, 10 suites.

Mercure Fryderyk Chopin Ⓜ, Al. Jana Pawła II 22, ✉ 00 133, ℰ (022) 620 02 0 *h1597-s61@accor-hotels.com, Fax (022) 620 87 79*, ₲, ⇌ – ❘, ↝ rm, ❒ 𝘵𝘷 ❤ ⇌ Ⓟ – ⚗ 250. ⓌⒷ ⒶⒺ ⓪ 𝘝𝘐𝘚𝘈. ⅌ rest   AY
Balzac : Meals - French - a la carte approx. 150 ▯ 35 – *Stanislas* : Meals 65 (lunch) ar a la carte approx. 90 ▯ 35 – **250 rm** ⊆ 735/1010.

Forum, Ul. Nowogrodzka 24-26, ✉ 00 511, ℰ (022) 621 02 71, *waforum@orbis. Fax (022) 625 04 76* – ❘, ↝ rm, ❒ 𝘵𝘷 ⅙ – ⚗ 450. ⓌⒷ ⒶⒺ ⓪ 𝘝𝘐𝘚𝘈. ⅌ rest   BZ
Soplica : Meals a la carte 65/90 ▯ 65 – *Maryla* : Meals (buffet only) 65/125 – **723 rm** ⊆ 500/570, 10 suites.

MDM without rest., Pl. Konstytucji 1, ✉ 00 647, ℰ (022) 621 62 11, *hotel.mdm@sy ena.com.pl, Fax (022) 621 41 73* – ❘ ↝ 𝘵𝘷 ⅙ – ⚗ 65. ⓌⒷ ⒶⒺ ⓪ 𝘝𝘐𝘚𝘈 ᴊᴄʙ   EU
126 rm ⊆ 400/585, 5 suites.

Vera, Ul. Bitwy Warszawskiej 1920 roku 16, ✉ 02 366, ℰ (022) 822 74 21, *vera@orbis. Fax (022) 823 65 56*, ₲ – ❘, ↝ rm, ❒ rest, 𝘵𝘷 ⅙ Ⓟ – ⚗ 155. ⓌⒷ ⒶⒺ ⓪ 𝘝𝘐𝘚 ᴊᴄ ⅌ rest   DU
Meals 35/60 and a la carte 45/80 ▯ 55 – **154 rm** ⊆ 445/485, 7 suites.

Belwederski, Ul. Sulkiewicza 11, ✉ 00 758, ℰ (022) 840 40 11, *info@hot belwederski.pl, Fax (022) 840 08 47* – ❘ ❒ 𝘵𝘷 ❤ – ⚗ 100. ⓌⒷ ⒶⒺ 𝘝𝘐𝘚 ᴊᴄʙ. ⅌   FU
Meals (buffet lunch) 80/100 and a la carte 42/60 ▯ 65 – **40 rm** ⊆ 390/440, 10 suite

Reytan Ⓜ, Ul. Rejtana 6, ✉ 02 516, ℰ (022) 646 31 66, *hotel@reytan.p Fax (022) 646 29 89* – ❘ 𝘵𝘷 ❤ ⅙ Ⓟ – ⚗ 30. ⓌⒷ ⒶⒺ 𝘝𝘐𝘚𝘈   EU
Meals (residents only) a la carte approx. 80 ▯ 30 – **84 rm** ⊆ 440/500, 2 suites.

Ibis Centrum Ⓜ, Al. Solidarności 165, ✉ 00 876, ℰ (022) 520 30 00, *h3129@acc r-hotels.com, Fax (022) 520 30 30* – ❘, ↝ rm, ❒ 𝘵𝘷 ❤ ⅙ ⇌ – ⚗ 40. ⓌⒷ ⒶⒺ ⓪ ⅌ rest   EU
Meals a la carte approx. 55 – ⊆ 25 – **190 rm** 360/420.

Malinowa (at Le Royal Meridien Bristol H.), Krakowskie Przedmieście 42-44, ✉ 00 32 ℰ (022) 551 18 33, *Fax (022) 625 25 77* – ↝ ❒. ⓌⒷ ⒶⒺ ⓪ 𝘝𝘐𝘚𝘈 ᴊᴄʙ. ⅌   BY
Meals - French - (dinner only) 150 and a la carte 185/285.

Dom Polski, Ul. Francuska 11, ✉ 03 906, ℰ (022) 616 24 32, *Fax (022) 616 24 8* « Elegant house, terrace-garden » – ↝ ❒. ⓌⒷ ⒶⒺ ⓪ 𝘝𝘐𝘚𝘈 ᴊᴄʙ. ⅌   FU
Meals a la carte 60/145 ▯ 70.

XX **Belvedere,** Ul. Agrykoli 1A, ⊠ 00 460, ℘ (022) 841 22 50, *restauracja@belvedere.c om.pl, Fax (022) 841 71 35*, ≤, 🍴, « Late 19C orangery in Łazienkowski park » – 🅿. ⓪ AE ⓪ VISA JCB. ⅍ FU d
closed 24 December-5 January – **Meals** a la carte 140/260 ⓵ 90.

XX **Casa Valdemar,** Ul. Piękna 7-9, ⊠ 00 539, ℘ (022) 628 81 40, *Fax (022) 622 88 96*, 🍴, « Elegant Spanish style installation » – ☷. ⓪ AE ⓪ VISA JCB. ⅍ EU e
Meals - Spanish - a la carte 80/265.

XX **Flik,** Ul. Puławska 43, ⊠ 02 508, ℘ (022) 849 44 34, *Fax (022) 849 44 34,* 🍴, Collection of paintings – ☷. ⓪ AE ⓪ VISA JCB EV h
Meals (buffet lunch) 65 and a la carte 70/115.

XX **U Fukiera,** Rynek Starego Miasta 27, ⊠ 00 272, ℘ (022) 831 10 13, *ufukiera@ufuk iera.pl, Fax (022) 831 58 08,* « Traditional Polish decor, patio terrace » – ✦. ⓪ AE ⓪ VISA. ⅍ BX n
closed 24, 25 and 31 December – **Meals** a la carte 105/195 ⓵ 100.

XX Zacheta, Pl. Małachowskiego 3, (in the basement of the Zacheta Art Gallery) ℘ (022) 828 05 84, *Fax (022) 827 85 02.* 🍴 – ☷ BY 7

XX **Świętoszek,** Ul. Jezuicka 6-8, ⊠ 00 281, ℘ (022) 831 56 34, *Fax (022) 635 59 47,* « Vaulted cellar » – ⓪ AE ⓪ VISA JCB. ⅍ BX r
Meals 45/50 (lunch) and a la carte 65/210 ⓵ 85.

XX **Restauracja Polska,** Ul. Nowy Świat 21 (in the basement of the Polish Sculptors Union's Gallery), ⊠ 00 029, ℘ (022) 826 38 77, *Fax (022) 828 31 32,* 🍴 – ☷ 🅿. ⓪ AE ⓪ VISA JCB. ⅍ BZ n
Meals 25/70 and a la carte 65/135 ⓵ 70.

XX Montmartre, Ul. Nowy Świat 7, ⊠ 00 496, ℘ (022) 628 63 15, *Fax (022) 816 13 28* BZ x

XX **Tsubame,** Ul. Foksal 16, ⊠ 00 372, ℘ (022) 826 51 27, *rezerwacja@tsubame.com.pl, Fax (022) 826 48 51,* Japanese decor – ☷. ⓪ AE ⓪ VISA JCB. ⅍ BZ s
Meals - Japanese - (buffet lunch) 30/85 and a la carte 60/150 ⓵ 50.

to the Southwest :

🏨 **Novotel,** Ul. Sierpnia 1, ⊠ 02 134, 6 km on airport rd ℘ (022) 575 60 00, *nov.airpo rt@orbis.pl, Fax (022) 575 69 99,* 🌱 – |≋|, ✦ rm, ☷ 📺 ఉ, 🅿 – 🔏 300. ⓪ AE ⓪ VISA JCB. ⅍ EV p
Meals a la carte 55/130 ⓵ 65 – **270 rm** ⌖ 505/550.

🏨 **Gromada,** Ul. Stycznia 32, ⊠ 02 148, 9 km on airport rd ℘ (022) 609 96 60, *airpor t@gromada.pl, Fax (022) 846 15 80* – |≋|, ✦ rm, 📺 🅿 – 🔏 200. ⓪ AE ⓪ VISA JCB
Meals a la carte 40/55 ⓵ 50 – **146 rm** ⌖ 340/445, 12 suites. EV a

Portugal

LISBON

PRACTICAL INFORMATION

LOCAL CURRENCY

1 euro (€) = 0,89 USD ($) (Dec 2001)
National Holiday in Portugal: *10 June.*

FOREIGN EXCHANGE

Hotels, restaurants and shops do not always accept foreign currencies and the tourist is therefore advised to change cheques and currency at banks, saving banks and exchange offices. The general opening times are as follows: banks 8.30am to 3pm (closed on Saturdays, Sundays, and Bank Holidays), money changers 9.30am to 6pm (usually closed on Sundays and Bank Holidays).

TRANSPORT

Taxis may be hailed when showing the green light or "Livre" sign on the windscreen. Metro (subway) network. In each station complete information and plans will be found.

SHOPPING IN LISBON

Shops and boutiques are generally open from 9am to 7pm. In Lisbon, the main shopping streets are: Rua Augusta, Rua do Carmo, Rua Garrett (Chiado), Rua do Ouro, Rua da Prata, Av. de Roma, Av. da Liberdade, Shopping Center Amoreiras, Shopping Center Colombo.

TIPPING

Hotels, restaurants and café bills always include service in the total charge. Nevertheless it is usual to leave the staff a small gratuity which may vary depending upon the district and the service given. Doormen, porters and taxi-drivers are used to being tipped.

SPEED LIMITS

The speed limit on motorways is 120 km/h - 74 mph, on other roads 90 km/h - 56 mph and in built up areas 50 km/h - 37 mph.

SEAT BELTS

The wearing of seat belts is compulsory for drivers and all passengers.

THE FADO

The Lisbon Fado (songs) can be heard in restaurants in old parts of the town such as the Alfama, the Bairro Alto and the Mouraria. A selection of fado cabarets will be found at the end of the Lisbon restaurant list.

LISBON
(LISBOA)

(LISBOA) 🅿 940 P 2 – Pop. 662 782 – alt. 111.

Paris 1785 – Madrid 624 – Bilbao 902 – Porto 310 – Sevilla 402.

🖪 Palácio Foz, Praça dos Restauradores ✉ 1250-187 ✆ 21 343 36 72, Fax 21 346 87 72 – Santa Apolónia Station (International Arrivals), ✉ 1100-105, ✆ 21 882 16 04, and airport ✉ 1700-111, ✆ 21 844 64 73, Fax 21 848 50 74 – A.C.P. Rua Rosa Araújo 24, ✉ 1250-195, ✆ 21 318 01 00, Fax 21 318 02 27.

🔝₁₈ , 🔝₉ Estoril W : 25 km ✆ 21 468 01 76, Fax 21 468 27 96 – 🔝₁₈ Lisbon Sports Club NW : 20 km ✆ 21 431 00 77 – 🔝₁₈ Club de Campo da Aroeira S : 15 km ✆ 21 297 91 10 Aroeira, Charneca da Caparica.

✈ Lisbon Airport N : 8 km from city centre ✆ 21 841 37 00 – T.A.P., Av. de Berlim (Edifício Garbo Orient), ✉ 1800-033, ✆ 21 317 91 00 – Portugalia, Rua C – Edifício 70. ✉ 1704-801, ✆ 21 842 55 00 and airport ✆ 21 841 50 00.

Santa Apolónia 🚗 ✆ 21 888 50 92 MX.

🚢 to Madeira : E.N.M., Rua de São Julião 5-1°, ✉ 1100-524, ✆ 21 887 01 22.

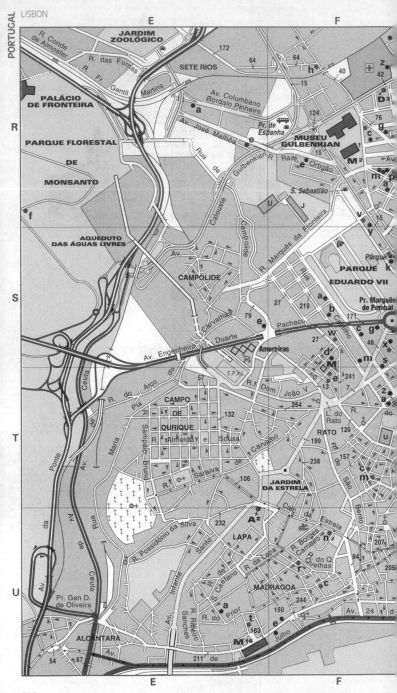

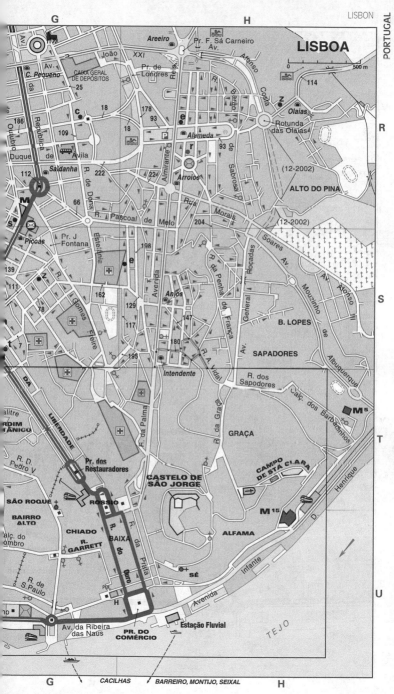

LISBOA

0   500 m

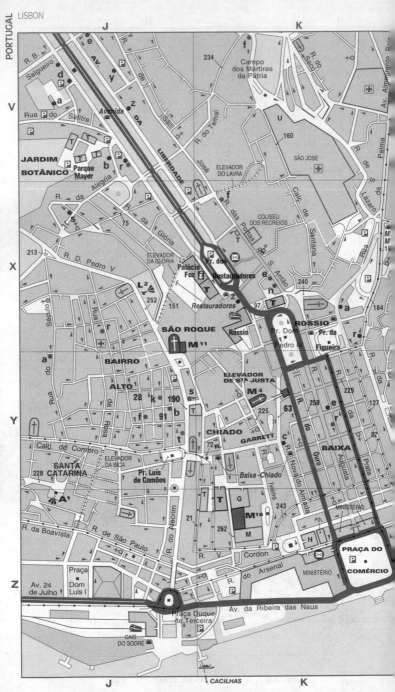

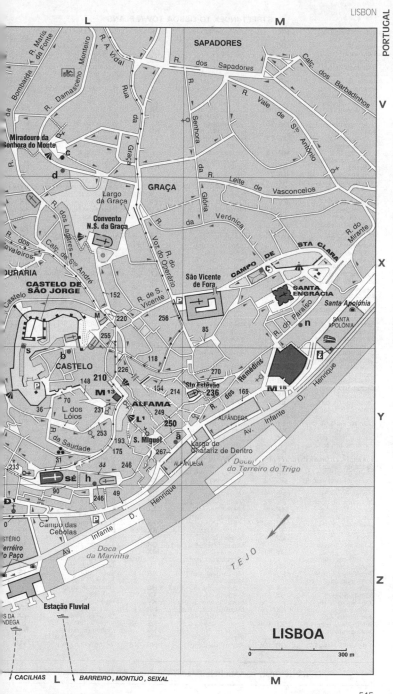

LISBOA

STREET INDEX TO LISBOA TOWN PLANS

Don't get lost, use **Michelin Maps** which are updated annually.

SIGHTS

VIEWS OVER LISBON

≤★★ *from the Suspension Bridge (Ponte 25 de Abril*★*)* **S**: *by Av. da Ponte* EU – ☀★★ *from Christ in Majesty (Cristo Rei)* **S**: *by Av. da Ponte* EU – *St. Georges Castle*★★ *(Castelo de São Jorge:* ≤★★★*)* LX – *Santa Luzia Belvedere*★ *(Miradouro de Santa Luzia):* ≤★★ LY **L¹** – *Santa Justa Lift*★ *(Elevador de Santa Justa):* ≤★ KY – *São Pedro de Alcântara Belvedere*★ *(Miradouro de São Pedro de Alcátara):* ≤★★ JX **L²** – *Alto de Santa Catarina Belvedere*) JZ **A¹** – *Senhora do Monte Belvedere (Miradouro da Senhora do Monte):* ☀★★★ LV – *Largo das Portas do Sol*★*:* ≤★★ LY – *Church & Convent of Our Lady of Grace Belvedere (Igreja e Convento de Nossa Senhora da Graça, Miradouro*★*)* LX

MUSEUMS

Museum of Ancient Art★★★ *(Museum Nacional de Arte Antiga; polyptych da Adoração de São Vicente*★★★*, Tentação de Santo Antão*★★★*, Japanese folding screens*★★*, Twelve' Apostles*★*, Anunciação*★*, Chapel*★*)* EU **M¹⁶** – *Gulbenkian Foundation (Calouste Gulbenkian Museum*★★★ FR, *Modern Art Centre*★ FR **M²**) – *Maritime Museum*★★ *(Museu de Marinha: model boats*★★★*)* W: *by Av. 24 de Julho* EU – *Azulejo Museum*★★ *(Madre de Deus Convent: Church*★★*, chapter house*★*)* NE: *by Av. Infante D. Henrique* MX – *Water Museum EPAL*★ *(Museu da Água da EPAL)* HT **M⁵** – *Costume Museum*★ *(Museu Nacional do Traje)* N: *by Av. da República* GR – *Theatre Museum*★ *(Museu Nacional do Teatro)* N: *by Av. da República* GR – *Military Museum (Museu Militar; cellings*★*)* MY **M¹⁵** – *Museum of Decorative Arts*★★ *(Museu de Artes Decorativas: Fundação Ricardo do Espírito Santo Silva)* LY **M¹³** – *Archaeological Museum (Igreja do Carmo*★*)* KY **M⁴** – *São Roque Arte Sacra Museum*★ *(vestments*★*)* JKX **M¹¹** – *Chiado Museum*★ *(Museu Nacional do Chiado)* KZ **M¹⁸** – *Music Museum*★ *(Museu da Música)* N: *by Av. da República* GR – *Rafael Bordalo Pinheiro Museum (ceramics*★*)* N: *by Av. da República* GR.

CHURCHES AND MONASTERIES

Cathedral★★ *(Sé: gothic tombs*★*, grille*★*, tresor*★*)* LY – *Hieronymite Monastery*★★★ *(Monasteiro dos Jerónimos): Santa Maria Church*★★★ *(vaulting*★★*, cloister*★★★; *Archaeological Museum: treasury*★*)* W: *by Av. 24 de Julho* EU – *São Roque Church*★ *(São João Baptista Chapel*★★*, interior*★*)* JX – *São Vicente de Fora Church (azulejos*★*)* MX – *Our Lady of Fátima Church (Igreja de Nossa Senhora de Fátima: windows*★*)* FR **D²** – *Estrela Basilica*★ *(garden*★*)* EU **A²** – *Old Conception Church (Igreja da Conceição Velha: south front*★*)* LZ **D¹** – *Santa Engracia Church*★ MX.

HISTORIC QUARTERS

Belém★★ *(Culture Centre*★*)* W: *by Av. 24 de Julho* EU – *The Baixa*★★ JKXYZ – *Alfama*★★ LY – *Chiado and Bairro Alto*★ JKY.

PLACES OF INTEREST

Praça do Comércio★★ *(or Terreiro do Paço)* KZ – *Belém Tower*★★★ *(Torre de Belém)* W: *by Av. 24 de Julho* EU – *Marquis Fronteira Palace*★★ *(Palácio dos Marqueses de Fronteira: azulejos*★★*)* ER – *Rossio*★ *(station: neo-manuelina façade*★*)* KX – *Do Carmo st. and Garrett st. (Rua do Carmo and Rua Garrett)* KY – *Liberdade Ave*★ *(Avenida da Liberdade)* JV – *Edward VII Park*★ *(Parque Eduardo VII:* ≤★*, greenhouse*★*)* FS – *Zoological Garden*★★ *(Jardim Zoológico)* ER – *Águas Livres Aqueduct*★ *(Aqueduto das Águas Livres)* ES – *Botanic Garden*★ *(Jardim Botánico)* JV – *Monsanto Park*★ *(Parque Florestal de Monsanto: Miradouro:* ☀★*)* ER – *Campo de Santa Clara*★ MX – *Santo Estêvão stairway and terrace*★ *(*≤★*)* MY – *Ajuda Palace*★ *(Palacio da Ajuda)* W: *by Av. 24 de Julho* EU – *Arpad Szenes-Vieira da Silva Foundation*★ EFS – *Boat trip on the river Tagus*★ *(*≤★★*)* – *Vasco da Gama bridge*★★ **NE**: *by Av. Infante D. Henrique* MX – *Lisbon oceanarium*★★ **NE**: *by Av. Infante D. Henrique* MX – *East Station*★ *(Estação de Oriente)* **NE**: *by Av. Infante D. Henrique* MX.

517

Centre : Av. da Liberdade, Praça dos Restauradores, Praça Dom Pedro IV (Rossio), Praça do Comércio, Rua Dom Pedro V, Rua de Santa Catarina, Campo de Santa Clara, Rua dos Sapadores

🏨🏨🏨 **Tivoli Lisboa,** Av. da Liberdade 185, ⊠ 1269-050, ℰ 21 319 89 00, htlisboa@mail. elepac.pt, Fax 21 319 89 50, 🎢, « Terrace with ≤ town », 🔲 heated, 🎾 – 📳 🗏 ⬛ 🕹 ⟵ – 🔬 40/200. 🆀 ⓞ 🗺. 🕸 JV
Grill Terraço : Meals a la carte 39,90/51,87 – 🖵 12,47 – **300 rm** 209,50/229,45 – 29 suites.

🏨🏨 **Sofitel Lisboa,** Av. da Liberdade 127, ⊠ 1269-038, ℰ 21 322 83 00, h1319@accor-ho els.com, Fax 21 322 83 60 – 📳 🗏 ⬛ 🕹 ⟵ – 🔬 25/300. 🆀 ⓞ 🗺 🗺. 🕸 JV
Meals (see rest. **Brasserie Avenue** below) – 🖵 14,96 – **165 rm** 160/215 – 5 suites

🏨🏨 **Lisboa Plaza,** Travessa do Salitre 7, ⊠ 1269-066, ℰ 21 321 82 18, plaza.hotels@ eritage.pt, Fax 21 347 16 30 – 📳 🗏 ⬛ – 🔬 25/140. 🆀 ⓞ 🗺 🗺 🗺. 🕸 JV
Meals 23 – 🖵 12 – **94 rm** 183/198 – 12 suites.

🏨🏨 **Mundial,** Rua D. Duarte 4, ⊠ 1100-198, ℰ 21 884 20 00, mundial.hot@mail.telepac.pt Fax 21 884 21 10, ≤ – 📳 🗏 ⬛ 🕹 ⟵ – 🔬 25/120. 🆀 ⓞ 🗺 🗺 🗺. 🕸 KX
Meals 18,70 - **Varanda de Lisboa :** Meals a la carte 21,20/39,90 – **252 rm** 🖵 33,10/43,50.

🏨🏨 **Tivoli Jardim,** Rua Julio Cesar Machado 7, ⊠ 1250-135, ℰ 21 353 99 71, htjardim @mail.telepac.pt, Fax 21 355 65 66, 🔲 heated, 🎾 – 📳 🗏 ⬛ 🕹 ⟵ 🅿 – 🔬 25/40. 🆀 ⓞ 🗺 🗺. 🕸 JV
Meals 19,95 – 🖵 7,48 – **119 rm** 137,17/159,62.

🏨🏨 **Lisboa Regency Chiado,** Rua Nova do Almada 114, ⊠ 1200-290, ℰ 21 325 61 00, regencychiado@madeiraregency.pt, Fax 21 325 61 61 – 📳 🗏 ⬛ ⟵. 🆀 ⓞ 🗺 🗺. 🕸 KY
Meals 30 – **40 rm** 🖵 120/130.

🏨🏨 **Lisboa** coffee shop only, Rua Barata Salgueiro 5, ⊠ 1166-069, ℰ 21 355 41 31, hotel is@ip.pt, Fax 21 355 41 39 – 📳 🗏 ⬛ ⟵. 🆀 ⓞ 🗺 🗺. 🕸 JV
55 rm 🖵 124,70/149,64 – 6 suites.

🏨🏨 **Avenida Palace** without rest, Rua 1º de Dezembro 123, ⊠ 1200-359, ℰ 21 346 01 51 hotel.av.palace@mail.telepac.pt, Fax 21 342 28 84 – 📳 🗏 ⬛ – 🔬 25/100. 🆀 ⓞ 🗺 🗺. 🕸 KX
64 rm 🖵 170/190 – 18 suites.

🏨🏨 **Britânia** without rest, Rua Rodrigues Sampaio 17, ⊠ 1150-278, ℰ 21 315 50 16, brit ania.hotel@heritage.pt, Fax 21 315 50 21 – 📳 🗏 ⬛. 🆀 ⓞ 🗺 🗺 🗺. 🕸 JV
🖵 12 – **30 rm** 183/198.

🏨🏨 **NH Liberdade,** Av. da Liberdade 180-B, ⊠ 1250-146, ℰ 21 351 40 60, nhliberdao @nh-hoteles.es, Fax 21 314 36 74, 🔲 – 📳 🗏 ⬛ ⟵ – 🔬 25/35. 🆀 ⓞ 🗺 🗺. 🕸 JV
Meals 30 – **83 rm** 🖵 179/190.

🏨🏨 **Veneza** without rest, Av. da Liberdade 189, ⊠ 1250-141, ℰ 21 352 26 18, comercial@ al@3khoteis.com, Fax 21 352 66 78, « Old palace » – 📳 🗏 ⬛ 🅿. 🆀 ⓞ 🗺 🗺 🗺. 🕸 JV
37 rm 🖵 104,75/129,69.

🏠 **Albergaria Senhora do Monte** without rest, Calçada do Monte 39, ⊠ 1170-250 ℰ 21 886 60 02, Fax 21 887 77 83, ≤ São Jorge castle, town and river Tagus – 📳 🗏 ⬛ 🆀 ⓞ 🗺 🗺. 🕸 LV
28 rm 🖵 99,75/149,63.

🏠 **Lisboa Tejo** without rest, Poço do Borratém 4, ⊠ 1100-408, ℰ 21 886 61 82, hlt eservas@mail.telepac.pt, Fax 21 886 51 63 – 📳 🗏 ⬛. 🆀 ⓞ 🗺 🗺 🗺. 🕸 KX
58 rm 🖵 86,04/97,26.

🏠 **Botánico** without rest, Rua Mãe de Água 16, ⊠ 1250-156, ℰ 21 342 03 92 Fax 21 342 01 25 – 📳 🗏 ⬛. 🆀 ⓞ 🗺 🗺 🗺. 🕸 JX
30 rm 🖵 80/100.

🏠 **Insulana** without rest, Rua da Assunção 52, ⊠ 1100-044, ℰ 21 342 76 25 Fax 21 342 89 24 – 📳 🗏 ⬛. 🆀 ⓞ 🗺 🗺. 🕸 KY
32 rm 🖵 50/60.

XXXX **Clara,** Campo dos Mártires da Pátria 49, ⊠ 1150-225, ℰ 21 885 30 53, clararestaurant@ ail.telepac.pt, Fax 21 885 20 82, 🎢, « Garden terrace » – 🗏. 🆀 ⓞ 🗺 🗺. 🕸
closed 1 to 15 August, Saturday lunch and Sunday – **Meals** a la carte 23,21/26,21. KV

XXXX **Tavares,** Rua da Misericórdia 37, ⊠ 1200-270, ℰ 21 342 11 12, Fax 21 347 81 25, « Late 19C decor » – 🗏. 🆀 ⓞ 🗺 🗺. 🕸 JY
Meals a la carte 36,90/53,70.

XXX **Bachus,** Largo da Trindade 9, ⊠ 1200-466, ℰ 21 342 28 28, Fax 21 342 12 60 – 🗏 🆀 ⓞ 🗺 🗺. 🕸 JY
closed Sunday – **Meals** a la carte 33/41.

XXX **Gambrinus,** Rua das Portas de Santo Antão 25, ⊠ 1150-264, ℰ 21 342 14 66 Fax 21 346 50 32 – 🗏. 🆀 ⓞ 🗺 🗺. 🕸 KX
Meals a la carte 65/80.

XXX **Brasserie Avenue** - Hotel Sofitel Lisboa with buffet, Av. da Liberdade 127 A/B, ✉ 1269-038, ✆ 21 322 83 50, h1319-fb@accor-hotels.com, Fax 21 322 83 60, ☆ – ▤ 🖘. ℀ ① ◐ VISA. ℀ rest JV r
Meals a la carte 23,44/29,68.

XXX **Consenso,** Rua da Académia das Ciências 1-A, ✉ 1200-003, ✆ 21 343 13 13, reserv as@restauranteconsenso.com, Fax 21 343 13 12, « Modern decor in rustic surroundings » – ▤. ℀ ① ◐ VISA JCB JY a
closed Saturday lunch, Sunday lunch and Bank Holidays lunch – **Meals** a la carte 16,50/30,95.

XXX **Escorial,** Rua das Portas de Santo Antão 47, ✉ 1150-160, ✆ 21 346 44 29, Fax 21 346 37 58, ☆ – ▤. ℀ ① ◐ VISA JCB. ℀ KX e
Meals a la carte approx. 54,92.

XXX **Casa do Leão,** Castelo de São Jorge, ✉ 1100-129, ✆ 21 887 59 62, guest@pousa das.pt, Fax 21 887 63 29, ⩽, ☆ – ▤. ℀ ① ◐ VISA. ℀ LXY s
Meals a la carte 29,18/41,65.

XX **Via Graça,** Rua Damasceno Monteiro 9-B, ✉ 1170-108, ✆ 21 887 08 30, Fax 21 887 03 05, ⩽ São Jorge castle, town and river Tagus – ▤. ℀ ① ◐ VISA JCB. ℀ LV d
closed 26 to 31 August, Saturday lunch and Sunday – **Meals** a la carte 16,95/28,43.

XX **O Faz Figura,** Rua do Paraíso 15-B, ✉ 1100-396, ✆ 21 886 89 81, Fax 21 886 89 81, ⩽, ☆ – ▤. ℀ ① ◐ VISA JCB. ℀ MX n
closed Saturday lunch and Sunday – **Meals** a la carte 20,22/30,94

XX **Solar dos Presuntos,** Rua das Portas de Santo Antão 150, ✉ 1150-269, ✆ 21 342 42 53, spresuntos@ip.pt, Fax 21 346 84 68 – ▤. ℀ ① ◐ VISA. ℀ KX b
closed August and Sunday – **Meals** a la carte 18/38.

X **O Múni,** Rua dos Correeiros 115, ✉ 1100-163, ✆ 21 342 89 82 – ▤. ℀ ① ◐ VISA. ℀ KY r
closed September, Saturday and Sunday – **Meals** a la carte 21,20/29,93.

X **Mercado de Santa Clara,** Campo de Santa Clara (at market), ✉ 1170, ✆ 21 887 39 86, Fax 21 887 39 86 – ▤. ℀ ① ◐ VISA MX c
closed 15 August-15 September, Sunday dinner and Monday – **Meals** a la carte 20,22/23,68.

East : Praça Marquês de Pombal, Av. da Liberdade, Av. Almirante Reis, Av. João XXI, Av. da República, Av. Estados Unidos de América, Av. de Berlim

🏨 **Radisson SAS,** Av. Marechal Craveiro Lopes 390, ✉ 1749-009, ✆ 21 759 96 39, Fax 21 758 66 05, 🏋 – 🕴 ▤ 📺 ☆ 🖘 – 🔏 25/200. ℀ ① ◐ VISA. ℀
Meals 24 – ☲ 11 – 205 rm 200/220 – 16 suites. North : by Av. da República GR

🏨 **Altis Park H.,** Av. Engenheiro Arantes e Oliveira 9, ✉ 1900-221, ✆ 21 843 42 00, indiv.reservations@altisparkhotel.com, Fax 21 846 08 38 – 🕴 ▤ 📺 ☆ 🖘 – 🔏 25/600. ℀ ① ◐ VISA. ℀ rest HR z
Meals 20 – 285 rm ☲ 134,80/149,80 – 15 suites.

🏨 **Meliá Confort Lisboa,** Av. Duque de Loulé 45, ✉ 1050-086, ✆ 21 351 04 80, h.me lia.lis.reservas@sapo.pt, Fax 21 353 18 65, ⬙ – 🕴 ▤ 📺 ☆ 🖘 – 🔏 25/50. ℀ ① ◐ VISA JCB. ℀
Meals (closed Sunday) a la carte 18,95/29,93 – **80 rm** ☲ 155/165 – 4 suites. GS z

🏨 **Holiday Inn Lisboa,** Av. António José de Almeida 28-A, ✉ 1000-044, ✆ 21 793 52 22, Fax 21 793 66 72, 🏋 – 🕴 ▤ 📺 ☆ 🖘 – 🔏 25/300. ℀ ① ◐ VISA. ℀ GR c
Meals 20,60 – ☲ 9,48 – **161 rm** 175/187 – 8 suites.

🏨 **Roma,** Av. de Roma 33, ✉ 1749-074, ✆ 21 796 77 61, info@hotelroma.pt, Fax 21 793 29 81, ⩽, 🏋, ⬙ – 🕴 ▤ 📺 ☆ – 🔏 25/230. ℀ ① ◐ VISA JCB. ℀
Meals 14,95 – **263 rm** ☲ 80/125. North : by Av. Almirante Reis HR

🏨 **Dom Carlos** coffee shop only, Av. Duque de Loulé 121, ✉ 1050-089, ✆ 21 351 25 90, hdcarlos@mail.telepac.pt, Fax 21 352 07 28 – 🕴 ▤ 📺 – 🔏 25/40. ℀ ① ◐ VISA JCB. ℀ GS n
76 rm ☲ 94/113.

🏨 **Presidente** without rest, Rua Alexandre Herculano 13, ✉ 1150-005, ✆ 21 317 35 70, hpresidente@mail.telepac.pt, Fax 21 352 02 72 – 🕴 ▤ 📺 – 🔏 25/40. ℀ ① ◐ VISA JCB. ℀ GS t
59 rm ☲ 88/102.

🏨 **A.S. Lisboa** without rest, Av. Almirante Reis 188, ✉ 1000-055, ✆ 21 842 93 60, info @hotel-aslisboa.com, Fax 21 842 93 74 – 🕴 ▤ 📺 – 🔏 25/80. ℀ ① ◐ VISA. ℀ HR e
75 rm ☲ 67,34/77,31.

🏨 **Dom João** without rest, Rua José Estêvão 43, ✉ 1150-200, ✆ 21 314 41 71, Fax 21 352 45 69 – 🕴 ▤ 📺. ℀ ① ◐ VISA. ℀ HS e
18 rm ☲ 37,50/43.

O Nobre, Marina Expo-Edifício Nau-F 18, ✉ 1990-182, ✆ 21 893 16 00 *Fax 21 896 99 88*, ≤, 余 – ■. ᴀᴇ ⓞ ⓜⓞ 𝚅𝙸𝚂𝙰
Meals a la carte 32,11/41,59. North-East : by Av. Infante D. Henrique MX

Panorâmico, Torre Vasco da Gama, ✉ 1990-173, ✆ 21 893 95 50, *Fax 21 895 60 50* « In Parque das Nações with ≤ river Tagus and city » – 🍴 ■. ᴀᴇ ⓞ ⓜⓞ 𝚅𝙸𝚂𝙰 ᴊᴄʙ. 🏶 North-East : by Av. Infante D. Henrique MX
closed Monday – **Meals** a la carte 30,38/39,48.

D'Avis, Rua do Grilo 98, ✉ 1900-707, ✆ 21 868 13 54, *Fax 21 868 13 54*, « Typical rest. » – ■. ᴀᴇ ⓜⓞ 𝚅𝙸𝚂𝙰 East : by Av. Infante D. Henrique MX
closed Sunday – **Meals** - Alentejo rest - a la carte 12,12/16,20.

West : Av. da Liberdade, Av. 24 de Julho, Av. da India, Largo de Alcántara, Av. da India, Av. Infante Santo, Praça Marquês de Pombal, Av. António Augusto de Aguiar, Av. de Berna, Praça de Espahna

Four Seasons H. The Ritz Lisbon, Rua Rodrigo da Fonseca 88, ✉ 1099-039, ✆ 21 381 14 00, *ritzfourseasons@mail.telepac.pt, Fax 21 383 17 83*, ≤, 余, ƒδ – 🍴 ■, ᴛᴠ & ⇔ 🅿 – 🔬 25/500. ᴀᴇ ⓞ ⓜⓞ 𝚅𝙸𝚂𝙰 ᴊᴄʙ. 🏶 FS b
Varanda : **Meals** a la carte 51,80/64 – ⊑ 19,50 – **264 rm** 315/340 – 20 suites.

Sheraton Lisboa H. & Towers, Rua Latino Coelho 1, ✉ 1069-025, ✆ 21 312 00 00, *lisboasheraton@sheraton.com, Fax 21 354 71 64*, ≤, ƒδ, 🔲 heated – 🍴 ■ ᴛᴠ & ⇔ – 🔬 25/550. ᴀᴇ ⓞ ⓜⓞ 𝚅𝙸𝚂𝙰 ᴊᴄʙ. 🏶 GR s
Alfama : **Meals** a la carte 43,90/51 - *Caravela :* **Meals** a la carte 31,92/37,41 – ⊑ 14,96 – **374 rm** 214,48/229,45 – 7 suites.

Lapa Palace 🦢, Rua do Pau de Bandeira 4, ✉ 1249-021, ✆ 21 394 94 94, *info@hotelapa.com, Fax 21 395 06 65*, ≤, 余, « Park with waterfall and 🔲 », ƒδ, 🔲 – 🍴 ■ ᴛᴠ & ⇔ 🅿 – 🔬 25/250. ᴀᴇ ⓞ ⓜⓞ 𝚅𝙸𝚂𝙰 ᴊᴄʙ. 🏶 EU a
Hotel Cipriani : **Meals** *(Italian rest)* a la carte 54/66 – ⊑ 20 – **101 rm** 350/375 – 8 suites.

Carlton Palace H. 🦢, Rua Jau 54, ✉ 1300-314, ✆ 21 361 56 00, *carlton.palac.@pestana.com, Fax 21 361 56 25*, ƒδ, 🔲, 🛋 – 🍴 ■ ᴛᴠ & ⇔ – 🔬 25/520. ᴀᴇ ⓞ ⓜⓞ 𝚅𝙸𝚂𝙰 ᴊᴄʙ. 🏶 West : by Av. 24 de Julho EU
Valle Flor : **Meals** a la carte 31,50/56,50 – ⊑ 16 – **173 rm** 325/350 – 17 suites.

Dom Pedro Lisboa, Av. Engenheiro Duarte Pacheco 24, ✉ 1070-109, ✆ 21 389 66 00, *dp.lisboa@dompedro-hotels.com, Fax 21 389 66 01*, ≤, 余 – 🍴 ■ ᴛᴠ ⇔ – 🔬 25/500. ᴀᴇ ⓞ ⓜⓞ 𝚅𝙸𝚂𝙰 ᴊᴄʙ. 🏶 ES a
Il Gattopardo *(Italian rest)* **Meals** a la carte 26,94 a 37,31 – ⊑ 16 – **254 rm** 400/425 – 9 suites.

Le Meridien Park Atlantic Lisboa, Rua Castilho 149, ✉ 1099-034, ✆ 21 381 87 00, *reservas.lisboa@lemeridien.lisboa, Fax 21 389 05 05*, ≤ – 🍴 ■ ᴛᴠ & ⇔ – 🔬 25/550. ᴀᴇ ⓞ ⓜⓞ 𝚅𝙸𝚂𝙰 ᴊᴄʙ. 🏶 rest FS a
L'Appart : **Meals** a la carte 34,73/54,03 – ⊑ 13,97 – **313 rm** 225,21/251,39 – 17 suites.

Altis, Rua Castilho 11, ✉ 1269-072, ✆ 21 310 60 00, *reservations@hotel-altis.pt, Fax 21 310 62 62*, ƒδ, 🔲 – 🍴 ■ ᴛᴠ & ⇔ – 🔬 25/700. ᴀᴇ ⓞ ⓜⓞ 𝚅𝙸𝚂𝙰 ᴊᴄʙ. 🏶
Girassol *(lunch only except Sunday)* **Meals** a la carte 26,39/32,37 - *Grill Dom Fernando* *(closed Sunday)* **Meals** a la carte 28,88/33,86 – **290 rm** ⊑ 180/200 – 53 suites. FT x

Corinthia Alfa H., Av. Columbano Bordalo Pinheiro, ✉ 1099-031, ✆ 21 723 63 63, *alfa.hotel@mail.telepac.pt, Fax 21 723 63 64*, ≤, ƒδ, 🔲 – 🍴 ■ ᴛᴠ ⇔ – 🔬 25/700. ᴀᴇ ⓞ ⓜⓞ 𝚅𝙸𝚂𝙰. 🏶 ER a
A Aldeia : **Meals** a la carte 29/37 – **434 rm** ⊑ 240/255 – 7 suites.

Holiday Inn Lisboa-Continental, Rua Laura Alves 9, ✉ 1069-169, ✆ 21 793 50 05, *vcordeiro@grupo-continental.com, Fax 21 797 36 69* – 🍴 ■ ᴛᴠ & ⇔ – 🔬 25/180. ᴀᴇ ⓞ ⓜⓞ 𝚅𝙸𝚂𝙰 ᴊᴄʙ. 🏶 FR a
Meals 23 – ⊑ 8,98 – **210 rm** 160/184 – 10 suites.

Real Parque, Av. Luís Bívar 67, ✉ 1069-146, ✆ 21 319 90 00, *info@hoteisreal.com, Fax 21 357 07 50* – 🍴 ■ ᴛᴠ & ⇔ – 🔬 25/100. ᴀᴇ ⓞ ⓜⓞ 𝚅𝙸𝚂𝙰 ᴊᴄʙ. 🏶 FR a
Cozinha do Real : **Meals** a la carte 24/33 – **147 rm** ⊑ 139,66/159,62 – 6 suites.

Metropolitan Lisboa H., Rua Soeiro Pereira Gomes-parcela 2, ✉ 1600-198, ✆ 21 798 25 00, *comer@metropolitan-lisboa-hotel.pt, Fax 21 795 08 64* – 🍴 ■ ᴛᴠ ⇔ – 🔬 25/250. ᴀᴇ ⓞ ⓜⓞ 𝚅𝙸𝚂𝙰. 🏶 North : by Av. da República GR
Meals 20 – **315 rm** ⊑ 124,70/149,64.

Fénix, Praça Marquês de Pombal 8, ✉ 1269-133, ✆ 21 386 21 21, *h.fenix@ip.pt, Fax 21 386 01 31* – 🍴 ■ ᴛᴠ ⇔ – 🔬 25/100. ᴀᴇ ⓞ ⓜⓞ 𝚅𝙸𝚂𝙰. 🏶 FS
Bodegón : **Meals** a la carte 19,95/34,17 – **119 rm** ⊑ 124,70/149,64 – 4 suites.

Marquês de Pombal coffee shop only, Av. da Liberdade 243, ✉ 1250-143, ✆ 21 319 79 00, *info@hotel-marquesdepombal.pt, Fax 21 319 79 90* – 🍴 ■ ᴛᴠ & ⇔ – 🔬 25/120. ᴀᴇ ⓞ ⓜⓞ 𝚅𝙸𝚂𝙰. 🏶 FS
123 rm ⊑ 150/160.

Sana Classic Reno H. without rest, Av. Duque d'Ávila 195-197, ✉ 1050-082, ℘ 21 313 50 00, sanaclassicreno@sanchotels.com, Fax 21 313 50 01, ⚒ – 🛗 🗏 📺 ♿ 🚗 – 🏛 25/115. 🖭 ⓪ ⓜ 🆚   FR m
89 rm ⚏ 109,74/119,71 – 3 suites.

Zurique, Rua Ivone Silva 18, ✉ 1050-124, ℘ 21 781 40 00, hotelzurique@viphotels.com, Fax 21 793 72 90, ⚒ – 🛗 🗏 📺 🚗 – 🏛 25/250. 🖭 ⓪ ⓜ 🆚 🚉   FR s
Meals 15 – ⚏ 7 – **248 rm** 64/74 – 4 suites.

Diplomático, Rua Castilho 74, ✉ 1250-071, ℘ 21 383 90 20, reservas@hotel-diplomatico.mailpac.pt, Fax 21 386 21 55 – 🛗 🗏 📺 📇 – 🏛 25/80. 🖭 ⓪ ⓜ 🆚 🚉 ✂ rest
Meals (closed Saturday, Sunday and Bank Holidays) a la carte approx. 22 – **90 rm**   FS c
⚏ 120/125.

Barcelona without rest, Rua Laura Alves 10, ✉ 1050-138, ℘ 21 795 42 73, reservas@3khoteis.com, Fax 21 795 42 81 – 🛗 🗏 📺 ♿ 🚗 – 🏛 25/230. 🖭 ⓪ ⓜ 🆚 🚉   FR z
120 rm ⚏ 124,70/149,64 – 5 suites.

Quality H., Campo Grande 7, ✉ 1700-087, ℘ 21 791 76 00, quality.lisboa@mail.telepac.pt, Fax 21 795 75 00, 🏋 – 🛗 🗏 📺 ♿ 🚗 – 🏛 25/70. 🖭 ⓪ ⓜ 🆚 ✂
Meals 18,75 – **80 rm** ⚏ 159,62/179,57 – 2 suites.North : by Av. da República GR

Amazónia Jamor, Av. Tomás Ribeiro 129 Queijas, ✉ 2795-891 Linda-A-Pastora, ℘ 21 417 56 38, Fax 21 417 56 30, ⟨, 🏋, ⚒, 🏊, ✂ – 🛗 🗏 📺 ♿ 🚗 📇 – 🏛 25/200. 🖭 ⓪ ⓜ 🆚   West : 10 km by Av. Engenheiro Duarte Pacheco ES
Meals 18,85 – **93 rm** ⚏ 89,78/99,76 – 4 suites.

Flórida without rest, Rua Duque de Palmela 34, ✉ 1250-098, ℘ 21 357 61 45, florida@mail.telepac.pt, Fax 21 354 35 84 – 🛗 🗏 📺 – 🏛 25/100. 🖭 ⓪ ⓜ 🆚 🚉 ✂
72 rm ⚏ 118/142.   FS x

Amazónia Lisboa without rest, Travessa Fábrica dos Pentes 12, ✉ 1250-106, ℘ 21 387 70 06, amazoniahoteis@reetcabo.pt, Fax 21 387 90 90, ⚒ heated – 🛗 🗏 📺 ♿ 🚗 – 🏛 25/200. 🖭 ⓪ ⓜ 🆚 ✂   FS d
192 rm ⚏ 89,78/99,76.

Dom Rodrigo Lisboa coffee shop only, Rua Rodrigo da Fonseca 44, ✉ 1250-193, ℘ 21 386 38 00, htdrodrigo@mail.telepac.pt, Fax 21 386 30 00, ⚒ – 🛗 🗏 📺 🚗. 🖭 ⓪ ⓜ 🆚 🚉 ✂   FS m
⚏ 6 – **57 suites** 93.

York House, Rua das Janelas Verdes 32, ✉ 1200-691, ℘ 21 396 25 44, yorkhouse@hlcmm.pt, Fax 21 397 27 93, ✿, « 16C former convent, Portuguese decor » – 📺 – 🏛 25/90. 🖭 ⓪ ⓜ 🆚 🚉 ✂   FU e
Meals a la carte 35,91/53,87 – ⚏ 13,97 – **34 rm** 176,57/199,52.

Novotel Lisboa, Av. José Malhoa 1642, ✉ 1099-051, ℘ 21 724 48 00, ho784@accor-hotels.com, Fax 21 724 48 01, ⟨, ✿, ⚒ – 🛗 🗏 📺 ♿ 🚗 – 🏛 25/300. 🖭 ⓪ ⓜ 🆚 ✂ rest   ER e
Meals 16,46 – ⚏ 6,48 – **246 rm** 64,84/72,82.

Dom Manuel I without rest, Av. Duque d'Ávila 189, ✉ 1050-082, ℘ 21 359 30 00, dmanuel@hoteldmanuel.pt, Fax 21 357 69 85 – 🛗 🗏 📺. 🖭 ⓪ ⓜ 🆚 ✂   FR p
64 rm ⚏ 90/100.

Sana Classic Executive H. without rest, Av. Conde Valbom 56, ✉ 1050-069, ℘ 21 795 11 57, sanaclassic.executive@sanahotels.cem, Fax 21 795 11 66 – 🛗 🗏 📺 ♿ 🚗 – 🏛 25/55. 🖭 ⓪ ⓜ 🆚 ✂   FR g
72 rm ⚏ 100/110.

Miraparque, Av. Sidónio Pais 12, ✉ 1050-214, ℘ 21 352 42 86, miraparque@esoterica.pt, Fax 21 357 89 20 – 🛗 🗏 📺. 🖭 ⓪ ⓜ 🆚 ✂   FS k
Meals 16 – **101 rm** ⚏ 75/80.

Eduardo VII, Av. Fontes Pereira de Melo 5, ✉ 1069-114, ℘ 21 356 88 22, sales@hoteleduardovii.pt, Fax 21 356 88 33, ⟨ – 🛗 🗏 📺 – 🏛 25/100. 🖭 ⓪ ⓜ 🆚 ✂
Varanda : Meals a la carte 19/30 – **137 rm** ⚏ 89/101,50 – 1 suite.   FS p

Marquês de Sá, Av. Miguel Bombarda 130, ✉ 1050-167, ℘ 21 791 10 14, marquessahotel@mail.telepac.pt, Fax 21 793 69 86 – 🛗 🗏 📺 🚗 – 🏛 25/150. 🖭 ⓪ ⓜ 🆚 ✂   FR c
Meals 15,46 – **164 rm** ⚏ 89,78/99,76.

As Janelas Verdes without rest, Rua das Janelas Verdes 47, ✉ 1200-690, ℘ 21 396 81 43, jverdes@heritage.pt, Fax 21 396 81 44, « Late 18C house with attractive courtyard » – 🛗 🗏 📺. 🖭 ⓪ ⓜ 🆚 🚉 ✂   FU e
⚏ 12 – **29 rm** 198/215.

Nacional without rest, Rua Castilho 34, ✉ 1250-070, ℘ 21 355 44 33, hotelnacional@mail.telepac.pt, Fax 21 356 11 22 – 🛗 🗏 📺 ♿ 🚗. 🖭 ⓪ ⓜ 🆚 ✂   FST s
59 rm ⚏ 72,82/82,80 – 2 suites.

🏨🏨 **Sana Classic Rex H.,** Rua Castilho 169, ✉ 1070-050, ✆ 21 388 21 61, *sanaclassic rex@sanahotels.com*, Fax 21 388 75 81 – 🔋 ☰ 📺 – 🔏 25/50. 🗚 ① ⑩ 𝓥𝓘𝓢𝓐. ✀
Meals 18 – **68 rm** ⛳ 110/120. FS a

🏨🏨 **Da Torre,** Rua dos Jerónimos 8, ✉ 1400-211, ✆ 21 361 69 40, *hoteldatorre.belen @mail.telepac.pt*, Fax 21 361 69 46 – 🔋 ☰ 📺 – 🔏 25/50. 🗚 ① ⑩ 𝓥𝓘𝓢𝓐 𝓙𝓒𝓑. ✀
Meals (see rest. *São Jerónimo* below) – **59 rm** ⛳ 69,83/83,30.
West : by Av. 24 de Julho EU

🏨🏨 **Berna** without rest, Av. António Serpa 13, ✉ 1069-199, ✆ 21 781 43 00, *hotelbern a@viphotels.com*, Fax 21 793 62 78 – 🔋 ☰ 📺 ☞ – 🔏 25/180. 🗚 ① ⑩ 𝓥𝓘𝓢𝓐. ✀
⛳ 6 – **240 rm** 59/69. GR a

🏨🏨 **Real Residência,** Rua Ramalho Ortigão 41, ✉ 1070-228, ✆ 21 382 29 00, *info@ho teisreal.com*, Fax 21 382 29 30 – 🔋 ☰ 📺 🅿. – 🔏 25/70. 🗚 ① ⑩ 𝓥𝓘𝓢𝓐 𝓙𝓒𝓑. ✀
Meals a la carte 11,23/21,47 – ⛳ 6 – **24 suites** 139,66/159,62. FR e

🏨 **Ibis Lisboa Liberdade** without rest, Rua Barata Salgueiro 53, ✉ 1250-043
✆ 21 330 06 30, *h3137@accor-hotels.com*, Fax 21 330 06 31 – 🔋 ☰ 📺 ⛴ ☞. 🗚 ①
⑩ 𝓥𝓘𝓢𝓐 FT a
⛳ 4 – **70 rm** 53,37.

🏨 **Nazareth** without rest, Av. António Augusto de Aguiar 25-4°, ✉ 1050-012
✆ 21 354 20 16, Fax 21 356 08 36 – 🔋 ☰ 📺. 🗚 ① ⑩ 𝓥𝓘𝓢𝓐. ✀ FRS y
32 rm ⛳ 42,50/59.

🍴🍴🍴 **Casa da Comida,** Travessa das Amoreiras 1, ✉ 1250-025, ✆ 21 388 53 76, *reser as@casadacomida.pt*, Fax 21 387 51 32, « Patio with plants » – ☰. 🗚 ① ⑩ 𝓥𝓘𝓢𝓐 𝓙𝓒𝓑.
✀ FT c
closed Saturday lunch and Sunday – **Meals** a la carte 49/66.

🍴🍴🍴 **Pabe,** Rua Duque de Palmela 27-A, ✉ 1250-097, ✆ 21 353 74 84, Fax 21 353 64 37
« English pub style » – ☰. 🗚 ① ⑩ 𝓥𝓘𝓢𝓐. ✀ FS z
Meals a la carte 37,90/43,39.

🍴🍴🍴 **Conventual,** Praça das Flores 45, ✉ 1200-192, ✆ 21 390 91 96, Fax 21 390 91 96
☰. 🗚 ① ⑩ 𝓥𝓘𝓢𝓐 FT n
closed Saturday lunch, Sunday, Bank Holidays lunch and Monday lunch – **Meals** a la cart
22,48/39,50.

🍴🍴🍴 **São Jerónimo** - *Hotel Da Torre*, Rua dos Jerónimos 12, ✉ 1400-211, ✆ 21 364 87 97
Fax 21 363 26 92, « Modern decor » – ☰. 🗚 ① ⑩ 𝓥𝓘𝓢𝓐 𝓙𝓒𝓑. ✀
closed Saturday lunch and Sunday – **Meals** a la carte 29,68/37,16.
West : by Av. 24 de Julho EU

🍴🍴🍴 **T Clube,** Av. de Brasília, ✉ 1400-038, ✆ 21 301 66 52, Fax 21 301 58 81 – ☰. 🗚 ①
⑩ 𝓥𝓘𝓢𝓐. ✀ West : by Av. 24 de Julho EU
closed Saturday lunch and Sunday – **Meals** a la carte approx. 37,41.

🍴🍴 **Chester,** Rua Rodrigo da Fonseca 87-D ✆ 21 385 73 47, Fax 21 388 78 11 – ☰. 🗚 ①
⑩ 𝓥𝓘𝓢𝓐 𝓙𝓒𝓑. ✀ FS v
closed Saturday lunch and Sunday – **Meals** a la carte 24,71/33.

🍴🍴 **XL,** Calçada da Estrela 57, ✉ 1200-661, ✆ 21 395 61 18, Fax 21 395 85 12 – ☰. 🗚 ⑩
𝓥𝓘𝓢𝓐. ✀ FU r
closed 3 weeks in August and Sunday – **Meals** - dinner only, booking essential - a la cart
24,60/32,43.

🍴🍴 **Saraiva's,** Rua Engenheiro Canto Resende 3, ✉ 1050-104, ✆ 21 354 06 09
Fax 21 353 19 87, « Modern decor » – ☰. 🗚 ① ⑩ 𝓥𝓘𝓢𝓐. ✀ FR s
closed Saturday and Bank Holidays – **Meals** a la carte 14,77/38,79.

🍴🍴 **Estufa Real,** Jardim Botânico da Ajuda - Calçada do Galvão, ✉ 1400, ✆ 21 361 90 21
Fax 21 361 90 18, « Old greenhouse in a botanic garden » – ☰ 🅿. 🗚 ① ⑩
𝓥𝓘𝓢𝓐. ✀ West : by Av. 24 de Julho EU
closed 29 July-18 August and Saturday – **Meals** - lunch only - a la carte 24,84/36,91

🍴🍴 **Adega Tia Matilde,** Rua da Beneficéncia 77, ✉ 1600-017, ✆ 21 797 21 72
Fax 21 797 21 72 – ☰ ☞. 🗚 ① ⑩ 𝓥𝓘𝓢𝓐. ✀ FR a
closed Saturday dinner and Sunday – **Meals** a la carte approx. 23,94.

🍴🍴 **Varanda da União,** Rua Castilho 14 C-7°, ✉ 1250-069, ✆ 21 314 10 45
Fax 21 314 10 46, « Balcony with ≤ over the rooftops » – 🔋 ☰. 🗚 ① ⑩ 𝓥𝓘𝓢
𝓙𝓒𝓑. ✀ FT q
closed Saturday lunch, Sunday and Bank Holidays lunch – **Meals** a la carte 25,44/35,1

🍴🍴 **Umpontocinco,** Rua Marcos Portugal 5, ✉ 1200-256, ✆ 21 396 48 95
Fax 21 390 56 37 – ☰. 🗚 ⑩ 𝓥𝓘𝓢𝓐. ✀ FT c
closed August, Saturday lunch and Sunday – **Meals** a la carte 18/27.

🍴🍴 **O Polícia,** Rua Marquês Sá da Bandeira 112, ✉ 1050-150, ✆ 21 796 35 05
Fax 21 796 97 91 – ☰. 🗚 ⑩ 𝓥𝓘𝓢𝓐. ✀ FR c
closed 15 days in August, Saturday dinner and Sunday – **Meals** a la carte 22,21/28.

✗ **Sua Excelência,** Rua do Conde 34, ⊠ 1200-367, ✆ 21 390 36 14, *sua xcelencia@m ail.telepac.pt, Fax 21 396 75 85,* 🍴 – 🍽. AE ⓂⓈ VISA JCB EU t
closed September and Wednesday – **Meals** a la carte 24,20/36,91.

✗ **O Mercado do Peixe,** Estrada do Casal Pedro Teixeira-Caramão da Ajuda, ⊠ 1400-047, ✆ 21 361 60 70, *mercadodopeixe@clix.pt, Fax 21 362 30 23* – 🍽 ℗. AE Ⓞ ⓂⓈ VISA. 🍴
West : by Av. Engenheiro Duarte Pacheco ES
closed Sunday dinner and Monday – **Meals** - Seafood - a la carte approx. 40.

✗ **A Travessa,** Travessa das Inglesinhas 28 (Madragoa), ⊠ 1200-687, ✆ 21 390 20 34, *Fax 21 397 03 68* – 🍽. AE Ⓞ ⓂⓈ VISA. 🍴 FU c
closed Sunday – **Meals** - French rest - a la carte 20,95/24,94.

✗ **Caseiro,** Rua de Belém 35, ⊠ 1300-354, ✆ 21 363 88 03, *Fax 21 364 23 39* – 🍽. AE Ⓞ ⓂⓈ VISA. 🍴 West : by Av. 24 de Julho EU
closed August and Sunday – **Meals** a la carte 22,24/31,02.

The fado restaurants :

✗✗ **O Faia,** Rua da Barroca 56, ⊠ 1200-050, ✆ 21 342 67 42, *Fax 21 342 19 23* – 🍽. AE Ⓞ ⓂⓈ VISA JCB. 🍴 JY f
closed Sunday – **Meals** - dinner only - a la carte 38,41/48,89.

✗✗ **Clube de Fado,** São João da Praça 94, ⊠ 1100-521, ✆ 21 885 27 04, *info@clube -de-fado.com, Fax 21 888 26 94* – 🍽. AE Ⓞ ⓂⓈ VISA JCB. 🍴 LYZ h
Meals - dinner only - a la carte 45,50/52,75.

✗✗ **Sr. Vinho,** Rua do Meio-à-Lapa 18, ⊠ 1200 723, ✆ 21 397 26 01, *restsrvinho@tele pac.pt, Fax 21 395 20 72* – 🍽. AE Ⓞ ⓂⓈ VISA. 🍴 FU r
closed Sunday – **Meals** - dinner only - a la carte 30,13/44,19.

✗✗ **Taverna do Embuçado,** Beco dos Cortumes 10, ⊠ 1100-172, ✆ 21 886 50 88, *embucado@tavernaembucado.com, Fax 21 886 50 78* – 🍽. AE Ⓞ ⓂⓈ VISA JCB. 🍴 LY a
closed 3 to 17 January, 4 to 14 August and Sunday – **Meals** - dinner only - a la carte 31/40.

✗✗ **A Severa,** Rua das Gáveas 51, ⊠ 1200-206, ✆ 21 342 83 14, *Fax 21 346 40 06* – 🍽. AE Ⓞ ⓂⓈ VISA JCB. 🍴 JY b
closed Thursday – **Meals** a la carte 31,91/46,39.

✗ **Adega Machado,** Rua do Norte 91, ⊠ 1200-284, ✆ 21 322 46 40, *Fax 21 346 75 07* – 🍽. AE Ⓞ ⓂⓈ VISA JCB. 🍴 JY k
closed 10 to 25 December and Monday – **Meals** - dinner only - a la carte 45/55.

Spain

España

MADRID – BARCELONA – BILBAO
MÁLAGA – SEVILLE – VALENCIA

PRACTICAL INFORMATION

LOCAL CURRENCY

1 euro (€) = 0,89 USD ($) (Dec 2001)
National Holiday in Spain: *12 October*

TOURIST INFORMATION

The telephone number and address of the Tourist Information offices is given in the text of the towns under 🛈.

FOREIGN EXCHANGE

Banks are usually open fron 8.30am to 2pm (closed on Saturdays and Sundays in summer).
Exchange offices in Sevilla and Valencia airports open from 9am to 2pm, in Barcelona airport from 9am to 2pm and 7 to 11pm. In Madrid and Málaga airports, offices operate a 24-hour service.

TRANSPORT

Taxis may be hailed when showing the green light or "Libre" sign on the windscreen. Madrid, Barcelona, Bilbao and Valencia have a Metro (subway) network. In each station complete information and plans will be found.

SHOPPING

In the index of street names, those printed in red are where the principal shops are found.
The big stores are easy to find in town centres; they are open from 10am to 9.30pm. Exclusive shops and boutiques are open from 10am to 2pm and 5 to 8pm. In Madrid they will be found in Serrano, Princesa and the Centre; in Barcelona, Passeig de Gràcia, Diagonal and the Rambla de Catalunya.
Second-hand goods and antiques: El Rastro (Flea Market), Las Cortes, Serrano in Madrid; in Barcelona, Les Encantes (Flea Market), Gothic Quarter.

TIPPING

Hotel, restaurant and café bills always include service in the total charge. Nevertheless it is usual to leave the staff a small gratuity which may vary depending upon the district and the service given. Doormen, porters and taxi-drivers are used to being tipped.

SPEED LIMITS

The maximum permitted speed on motorways is 120 km/h - 74 mph, and 90 km/h - 56 mph on other roads.

SEAT BELTS

The wearing of seat belts is compulsory for drivers and all passengers.

"TAPAS"

Bars serving "tapas" (typical Spanish food to be eaten with a glass of wine or an aperitif) will usually be found in central, busy or old quarters of the following selected cities.

MADRID

Madrid 28000 🅿 **444** *K 19 – Pop. 3 084 673 – alt. 646.*

Paris (by Irún) 1276 – Barcelona 617 – Bilbao 395 – A Coruña/La Coruña 684 – Lisboa 625 – Málaga 494 – Porto 609 – Sevilla 531 – València 352 – Zaragoza 322.

🛈 *Duque de Medinaceli 2,* ✉ *28014,* ☎ *91 429 49 51, turismo@comadrid.es, Fax 91 429 37 05, Pl. Mayor 3,* ✉ *28012,* ☎ *91 588 16 36, inforturismo@munimadrid.es, Fax 91 366 54 77, Puerta de Toledo Market,* ✉ *28005,* ☎ *91 364 18 76, turismo@comadrid.es, Fax 91 364 24 32, Estación de Atocha,* ✉ *28014,* ☎ *91 528 46 30, turismo@comadrid.es, Chamartín Station,* ✉ *28036,* ☎ *91 315 99 76 turismo@comadrid.es, Fax 91 323 79 51 and Madrid-Barajas airport* ✉ *28042,* ☎ *91 305 86 56, turismo@comadrid.es, Fax 91 301 00 33 – R.A.C.E. Isaac Newton – Parque Technológico de Madrid (PTM),* ✉ *28760 Tres Cantos (Madrid),* ☎ *91 594 74 00, Fax 91 594 73 88.*

🏌🏌🏌 *Club de Campo-Villa de Madrid, North-west by Av. de la Victoria* ☎ *91 550 20 10 DU*

🏌🏌 *La Moraleja, North : 11 km by Pas. de la Castellana* ☎ *91 650 07 00 GR–* 🏌 *Club Barberán, South-west : 10 km by Av. de Portugal* ☎ *91 509 11 40 DX*

🏌🏌 *Las Lomas – El Bosque, South-west : 18 km by Av. de Portugal and detour to Boadilla del Monte* ☎ *91 616 75 00 DX*

🏌 *Real Automóvil Club de España, North : 28 km by Pas. de la Castellana* ☎ *91 657 00 11 GR*

🏌 *Nuevo Club de Madrid, Las Matas, West : 26 km by Av. de la Victoria* ☎ *91 630 08 20 DU*

🏌 *Somosaguas, West : 10 km by Puente del Rey* ☎ *91 352 16 47 DX*

🏌 *Club Olivar de la Hinojosa, North-east by Av. de América and detour to M 40* ☎ *91 721 18 89 JT*

🏌 *La Dehesa, Villanueva de la Cañada, West : 28 km by Av. de la Victoria and detour to El Escorial* ☎ *91 815 70 22 DU*

🏌🏌 *Real Sociedad Hípica Española Club de Campo, North : 28 km by Pas. de la Castellana* ☎ *91 657 10 18 GR.*

✈ *Madrid-Barajas E : 12 km* ☎ *91 393 60 00 – Iberia : Velázquez 130,* ✉ *28006,* ☎ *91 587 87 87 HUV, Santa Cruz de Marcenado 2,* ✉ *28015,* ☎ *902 400 500 EV and at airport,* ✉ *28042,* ☎ *91 587 87 87.*

Chamartín 🚇 ☎ *91 733 11 22 HR.*

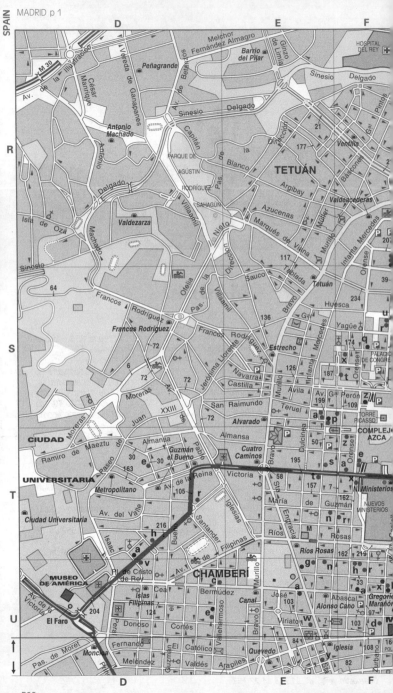

MADRID

Cercanías

0   500 m

G   H   J   R

S

T

U

.165

LADIO DE
OSICIONES

178
Burgos
M·30
Av. de
Av. de
Arturo
San
Luis

171
CHAMARTIN
P
P
Hiedra

89

a
e
3
Inurria
POL.
IXII

z
u
Mateo

Duque de
Pastrana
XII
34
d
Sta. María Magdalena
la Paz
M·30
Añastro
Gran Vía
de Hortaleza
Hoyos

11 106
Pl. de
Castilla
94
Francisco Suárez
Jerez
Pío XII
Soria
Asura

73 c
CHAMARTIN
102
Padre
P
237   76
Alfonso
Av. de

v
Av. 127
S de Alberto Alcocer
202
Costa
P Rica
XII
Av. de la Paz
Arturo Soria
31

Cuzco a k
183
v c Colombia
Serrano
Arturo Soria

t
f
253 h
Uruguay
c
José Silva

190
m
Asilo de
San Rafael
(06-02)
a
r
Serrano
Víctor
Ramón
y Cajal
Av. de la Paz

ESTADIO
S. BERNABÉU
135
Concha
Espina Av.
XIII
f

Santiago
Bernabéu
b
Av. de Conche Espina
t
PARQUE
DE
BERLÍN
Hoyos
M·30

Paseo
Pl. de
Cataluña
132
z
184
Alfonso XIII
y w

h
Joaquín
c
Dr. Arce
AUDITORIO NAC.
DE MÚSICA
M
López
Rey
de María

201
República
Argentina
R.T.V.E.
Vergara
Canillas
P

Cruz del
Rayo
Hoyos
Prosperidad
Clara
Corazón de María
América

b
Serrano
Costa
Castillo
Cartagena
TORRES
BLANCAS
Avenida
Bruselas
t
Puente
de la Paz

M
López
138
Cartagena
Parque
de
las Avenidas
P

q
María
de Molina
Av. de América
Cartagena
b
a

M
130
Velázquez
169
c
z
Francisco
Brasilia
Av. de

u
a s
n
Arcona
17
PLAZA
MONUMENTAL
DE LAS VENTAS

en
d
X
Juan
Bravo
67
POL.
Diego de León
156
El Carmen

G   H   J

Fernando
El
Guzmán
Católico
Quevedo
Iglesia
108
16
POL.
Pas. de Moret
Moncloa
Meléndez
Valdés
Arapiles
84
Zurbano
82
Pas. de Pinto
Pincosa
Argüelles
San Bernardo
Englacia
e
k
b
e
Ferraz
Alberto Aguilera
b
Lochana
40
a
PARQUE
150
Rosales
Princesa
Z
c
208
Carranza
166
25
DEL
OESTE
TELEFÉRICO
Ferraz
San Bernardo
Fuencarral
Sagasta
Génova
La Rosaleda
e
San Antonio
de la Florida
h
Rosales
M
Templo de
Debod
Pl. de
España
Gran
Vía
CENTRO
Hortaleza
15
M 30
100
Príncipe Pío
Vicente
Torija
Gran
Vía
Gran
Vía
PL. DE
CIBELES
147
CASA
DE
CAMPO
18
Cuesta de S.
PALACIO
REAL
Teatro Real
de la Opera
Montera
Alcalá
PASEO
Puente
del Rey
M 1
CAMPO
DEL
MORO
Bailén
Arenal
Pl. de la
Puerta del Sol
M
Av.
de
Portugal
Mayor
PLAZA
MAYOR
Prado
DEL
MUSEO
DEL PRADO
Pte de
Segovia
H
Huertas
PRADO
93
M 30
Segovia
Segovia
Atocha
1
258
Bailén
Gran Vía de
S. Francisco
Ribera
de
Curtidores
Embajadores
Lavapiés
Sta. Isabel
Atocha
M
Y
Toledo
Pas. del Santo
Ermita
de la
Pas. de los Melancólicos
Manzanares
Pas.
de
Segovia
Gta de Puerta
de Toledo
v
Puerta
de Toledo
i
CASINO
DE LA REINA
242
22
Embajadores
243
Puente de
San Isidro
181
181
235
85
Toledo
Pirámides
Acacias
172
n
Pas. de
la
Cabeza
Palos de
la Frontera
Imperial
r
Acacias
87
ESTADIO
V. CALDERÓN
Pirámides
las
Pas. del Dr.
Vallejo Nágera
Embajadores
Ferrocarril
228
Pas.
de
la
Delicias
M
Av.
del
Manzanares
87
Pas.
de
e
15
PARQUE
DE LA
ARGANZUELA
Yeserías
Pas. del Quince de Mayo
Z
Marqués
de Vadillo
Antonio
M 30
ARGANZUELA
121
Manzanares
v
P
28
Urgel
General
Ricardos
Jacinto Verdaguer
u
2
del
Pas.
Legazpi
240
Mercedes
Arteaga
Laya
0
500 m
Antonio
Pas. de San
López
PALACIO
DE CRISTAL
Pte de
Legaz
14

G   H   J

U

Castellan

Serrano

e
Velá
Juan
Vergara
67
POL
Diego de León   156
Azcona
PLAZA
MONUMENTAL
DE LAS VENTAS
El Carmen
a

d
r
w
N. de Balboa
Bravo
y
Av. de los
Toreros
129
Ventas
Alcalá
a

48
130
f
169
SALAMANCA
k
t
Alcalá
6
63

José
Ortega
148
Lista
de
Gasset
75
Pl. de Manuel
Becerra

a
Ayala
75
N. de Balboa
Ayala
4
Manuel Becerra
V

u
k
169
s
Hermosilla
Conde
Alcalá
Hormosilla
151
Parque de la
Quinta
Fuente del Berro

Serrano
48
Velázquez
Goya
c
Goya
P
r
210
PALACIO
DE LOS
DEPORTES
Jorge Juan
O'Donnell
Baranda

Jorge
Juan
130
e
Alcalá
Jorge
Juan
X
Juan
TORRE
ESPAÑA
R.T.V.E.

h
t
Pl. de
Vergara
96
O'Donnell
O'Donnell

UERTA
ALCALA
Retiro
O'Donnell
70

Alfonso
XII
Estanque
EL PARTERRE
Menéndez
Ibiza
Ibiza
Salix
PARQUE
DE
ROMA

VI
Alfonso
Alfonso XII
s
Alcalde
Juan Espandiú
7
4

XII
XII
Alfonso
Alfonso XII
PARQUE
DEL BUEN RETIRO
Palacio
de Cristal
POL
69
Sáinz de
Baranda
RETIRO
x

LA CHOPERA
OBSERVATORIO
ASTRONOMICO
Pelayo
180
de Nazaret
Astros
175
90
55
37

Pl. de Mariano
de Cavia
a
198
PANTEON
Pelayo
Conde de Casal
90
Estrella
19
55
Pl. Corregidor
Alonso de Aguilar

Atocha Renfe
ATOCHA
P
Av. de
Menéndez
Pelayo
Valderibas
Av. Menéndez
Avenida
Cavaniles
Izquierdo
Pl. Conde
de Casal
a
del
3
A 3
Mediterráneo

Alvaro
stamante
Comercial
la
Ciudad
Doctor
Valderribas
Barcelona
Pacífico
139
Camino
de
Valderribas
Sierra

PARQUE
DE LAS
DELICIAS
P
P
PLANETARIO
Méndez
Pedro
Méndez
Alvaro
Méndez
Alvaro
M
CINE IMAX
Bosch
de
M 30
Av. de la Paz
P. de Vallecas
193
Igueldo
Monte
155
de
Av.
Nueva Numancia
Arroyo del Olivar
Albufera
Perdido
POL
Portazgo

G   H   J

531

K
L

a
m
T
Bilbao
Sagas
Montserrat
Divino
Glorieta
de Bilbao
159
Princesa
t
Palacio de Liria
Conde
Duque
Amaniel
Palma
Pastor
Apodaca
Pl. Dos
de Mayo
Fuencarral
Bardeló
V. Rodríguez
d
CENTRO CULTURAL
CLARA DEL REY
Palma
M 10
M
V
250
TORRE
DE MADRID
Princesa
Espiritu
MALASAÑA
San Bernardo
Santo
Tribunal
San Mateo
22
EDIFICIO
ESPAÑA
211
Noviciado
San
Pez
Pablo
MUSEO
CERRALBO
s
Reyes
123
Madera
Colón
Ferraz
r
Pl. Luna
f
z
Pizarro
Baja
246
Plaza
Gran Via
POL
g
Corredera
Puebla
Fuencarral
24
de España
v
c
Gran Via
133
238
Barco
Hortaleza
Cuesta
de San Vicente
PALACIO DEL
SENADO
Leganitos
y
T
n
a
Santo Domingo
e
Gran Via
Gran Via
Infantas
Jardines de
Sabatini
Bailén
Torija
p
r
Bola
k
231
z
36
Calleo
Carmen
d
c
T
Jardines
256
PALACIO REAL
LA ENCARNACIÓN
18
h
Teatro Real
de la Opera
LAS DESCALZAS
REALES
v
t
f
Montera
P
M 2
Pl. de
Isabel II
186
v
Pl. de
Oriente
W
Ópera
Alcalá
Se
252
e
Arenal
x
232
Pl. de
Canal
g
Mayor
116
r
Sol
Pl. de la
Puerta del Sol
21
Catedral N. S. de
la Almudena
PL. DE LA
VILLA
32
POL
88
Cruz
24
u
188
Bailén
Mayor
45
PLAZA
MAYOR
Pl. de
la Provincia
168
T
s
P
Arco de
Cuchilleros
SAN
MIGUEL
60
d
Pl. de
Benavente
Carretas
Atocha
Huertas
Sacramento
Segovia
H
S
54
San Pedro
220
191
52
53
T
Jardines
Pl. de la
Paja
Capilla
del Obispo
c
V
r
43
S. Isidro
Colegiata
Magdalena
Anton M.
de las
Vistillas
e
y
42
Toledo
91
Pl. de Tirso
de Molina
78
Jesús
María
Lavapiés
Olivar
a
Don Pedro
192
T
La Latina
225
San Francisco
el Grande
214
Pl. de
Cascorro
Mesón
de
Paredes
Embajadores
Z
Pl. de la
Cebada
Calatrava
112
Ave María
Gran Vía de
San Francisco
Toledo
el Rastro
Ribera de Curtidores
Lavapiés
Argu
Valencia

0   200 m
Cercanías

K
L

MADRID

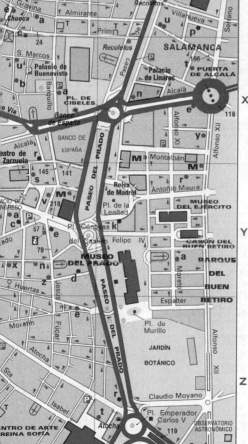

Michelin
pone sus mapas
constantemente al día.
Llévelos en su coche
y no tendrà Vd. sorpresas
desagradables
en caretera.

STREET INDEX TO

MADRID TOWN PLAN

SIGHTS

VIEW OVER MADRID

Moncloa Beacon (Faro de Madrid): ☀★★ DU.

MUSEUMS

Prado-Museum★★★ NY – *Thyssen Bornemisza Museum*★★★ MY **M⁶** – *Royal Palace*★★ *(Palacio Real)* KXY *(Palace*★*: Throne Room*★*, Royal Armoury*★★*, Royal Carriage Museum*★ DX **M¹**) – *National Archaeological Museum*★★ *(Dama de Elche*★★★*)* NV – *Lázaro Galdiano Museum*★★ *(collection of enamels and ivories*★★★*)* GU **M⁴** – *Casón del Buen Retiro*★ *(annexe to the Prado)* NY – *Reina Sofía Art Museum*★ *(Picasso's Guernica*★★★*)* MZ – *Army Museum*★ *(Museo del Ejército)* NY – *Museum of the Americas*★ *(Museo de América; Treasure of Los Quimbayas*★*, Cortesano Manuscript*★★★*),* DU – *San Fernando Royal Fine Arts Academy*★ *(Real Academia de Bellas Artes de San Fernando)* LX **M²** – *Cerralbo Museum*★ KV – *Sorolla Museum*★ FU **M⁵** – *City Museum (Museo de la Ciudad : models*★*)* HT **M⁷** – *Naval Museum (ship models*★*, map of Juan de la Cosa*★★*)* NXY **M³** – *National Museum of Decorative Arts (embossed leather*★*)* NX **M⁸** – *Municipal Museum (facade*★★*, model of Madrid*★*)* LV **M¹⁰** – *National Museum of Science and Technology (ballestilla*★★*)* FZ **M⁹**.

CHURCHES AND MONASTERIES

Descalzas Reales Monastery★★ KLX – *San Francisco el Grande Church (stall*★ *in chancel and sacristy)* KZ – *Royal Convent of the Incarnation*★ *(Real Monasterio de la Encarnación: shrine*★*)* KX – *San Antonio de la Florida Chapel (frescoes*★★*)* DV – *Saint Michael Church*★ KY

THE OLD TOWN

Eastern Quarter★★ *(Barrio de Oriente)* KVXY – *Bourbon Madrid*★★ MNXYZ – *Old Madrid*★ KYZ

PLACES OF INTEREST

Plaza Mayor★★ KY – *Buen Retiro Park*★★ HY – *Zoo-Aquarium*★★ West : by Casa de Campo Park*★ DX – *Plaza de la Villa*★ KY – *Vistillas Gardens (*☀★*)* KYZ – *Campo del Moro Winter Garden*★ DX – *University City*★ *(Ciudad Universitaria)* DT – *Casa de Campo (Park)*★ DX – *Plaza de Cibeles*★ MNX – *Paseo del Prado*★ MNXYZ – *Alcalá Arch*★ *(Puerta de Alcalá)* NX – *Bullring*★ *(Plaza Monumental de las Ventas)* JUV – *West Park*★ *(Parque del Oeste)* DV

Centre : Paseo del Prado, Puerta del Sol, Gran Vía, Alcalá, Paseo de Recoletos, Plaza Mayor

🏨🏨🏨🏨 **The Westin Palace,** pl. de las Cortes 7, ⊠ 28014, ℰ 91 360 80 00, Fax 91 360 81 00, 𝄙 – ⁅ 🗍 📺 ⅙ ⟵⟶ – 🏄 25/500. 🆎 ⓞ ⓜⓞ 𝐕𝐈𝐒𝐀 𝐉𝐂𝐁. ❄ rest   MY e
Meals 41,17 - *La Cupola* (dinner only, closed August, Sunday and Monday) **Meals** a la carte 54,46/68,72 – ⌑ 25 – **417 rm** 350/376, 48 suites.

🏨🏨🏨 **Villa Real,** pl. de las Cortes 10, ⊠ 28014, ℰ 91 420 37 67, villareal@derbyhotels.es, Fax 91 420 25 47, « Tastefully decorated with antique works of art » – ⁅ 🗍 📺 ⟵⟶ – 🏄 35/220. 🆎 ⓞ ⓜⓞ 𝐕𝐈𝐒𝐀 𝐉𝐂𝐁. ❄ rest   MY c
Europa : **Meals** a la carte 30,48/48,03 – ⌑ 16,23 – **96 rm** 267,45/300,51 – 19 suites.

🏨🏨🏨 **Crowne Plaza Madrid City Centre,** pl. de España, ⊠ 28013, ℰ 91 454 85 00, reservas@crowneplazamadrid.com, Fax 91 548 23 89, ≼, 𝄙 – ⁅ 🗍 📺 ⅙ – 🏄 25/220. 🆎 ⓞ ⓜⓞ 𝐕𝐈𝐒𝐀 𝐉𝐂𝐁.   KV s
Meals a la carte approx. 33 – ⌑ 18 – **295 rm** 258/280 – 11 suites.

🏨🏨🏨 **Tryp Ambassador,** Cuesta de Santo Domingo 5, ⊠ 28013, ℰ 91 541 67 00, amba sador@trypnet.com, Fax 91 559 10 40 – ⁅ 🗍 📺 – 🏄 25/280. 🆎 ⓞ ⓜⓞ 𝐕𝐈𝐒𝐀 𝐉𝐂𝐁. ❄ **Meals** a la carte 27,95/36,06 – ⌑ 13,52 – **159 rm** 172,76/218,51 – 23 suites.   KX k

🏨🏨 **NH Nacional,** paseo del Prado 48, ⊠ 28014, ℰ 91 429 66 29, nh@nh-hoteles.es, Fax 91 369 15 64 – ⁅ 🗍 📺 ⅙ ⟵⟶ – 🏄 25/150. 🆎 ⓞ ⓜⓞ 𝐕𝐈𝐒𝐀 𝐉𝐂𝐁. ❄ rest   NZ r
Meals (closed August) a la carte 52,88/58,36 – ⌑ 15,43 – **213 rm** 168,28/210,35 – 1 suite.

🏨🏨 **Llabeny,** Salud 3, ⊠ 28013, ℰ 91 531 90 00, liabeny@apunte.es, Fax 91 532 74 21 – ⁅ 🗍 📺 ⟵⟶ – 🏄 25/125. 🆎 ⓞ ⓜⓞ 𝐕𝐈𝐒𝐀. ❄   LX c
Meals 18 – ⌑ 11,40 – **222 rm** 99,25/134,25.

🏨🏨 **Emperador** without rest, Gran Vía 53, ⊠ 28013, ℰ 91 547 28 00, hemperador@sei.cs, Fax 91 547 28 17, 𝄙, ⅃ – ⁅ 🗍 📺 – 🏄 25/150. 🆎 ⓞ ⓜⓞ 𝐕𝐈𝐒𝐀. ❄   KX n
⌑ 15,02 – **230 rm** 152,05/189,91 – 2 suites.

🏨🏨 **Santo Domingo,** pl. de Santo Domingo 13, ⊠ 28013, ℰ 91 547 98 00, reserva@h otelsantodomingo.com, Fax 91 547 59 95 – ⁅ 🗍 📺 – 🏄 25/70. 🆎 ⓞ ⓜⓞ 𝐕𝐈𝐒𝐀. ❄ **Meals** 28,55 – ⌑ 10,52 – **120 rm** 153,26/202,84.   KX a

🏨🏨 **Palacio San Martín,** pl. San Martín 5, ⊠ 28013, ℰ 91 701 50 00, sanmartin@intu r.com, Fax 91 701 50 10 – ⁅ 🗍 📺 – 🏄 25. 🆎 ⓞ ⓜⓞ 𝐕𝐈𝐒𝐀. ❄   KX t
Meals 22,54 – ⌣ 13 – **93 rm** 144,24/192,32 – 1 suite.

🏨🏨 **Arosa** coffee shop only, Salud 21, ⊠ 28013, ℰ 91 532 16 00, arosa@hotelarosa.com, Fax 91 531 31 27 – ⁅ 🗍 📺 ⟵⟶ – 🏄 25/45. 🆎 ⓞ ⓜⓞ 𝐕𝐈𝐒𝐀 𝐉𝐂𝐁.   LX q
⌑ 12,02 – **134 rm** 104,73/161,97.

🏨🏨 **Mayorazgo,** Flor Baja 3, ⊠ 28013, ℰ 91 547 26 00, comercial@hotelmayorazgo.com, Fax 91 541 24 85 – ⁅ 🗍 📺 ⟵⟶ – 🏄 25/200. 🆎 ⓞ ⓜⓞ 𝐕𝐈𝐒𝐀 𝐉𝐂𝐁.   KV c
Meals 24 – ⌣ 12 – **200 rm** 120/156.

🏨🏨 **Gaudí,** Gran Vía 9, ⊠ 28013, ℰ 91 531 22 22, gaudi@hoteles-catalonia.es, Fax 91 531 54 69, 𝄙 – ⁅ 🗍 📺 ⅙ – 🏄 25/120. 🆎 ⓞ ⓜⓞ 𝐕𝐈𝐒𝐀. ❄   LX s
Meals 16,83 – ⌑ 12,03 – **185 rm** 171,28/204,38.

🏨🏨 **G.H. Reina Victoria,** pl. de Santa Ana 14, ⊠ 28012, ℰ 91 531 45 00, rvasvic@try pnet.com, Fax 91 522 03 07 – ⁅ 🗍 📺 ⟵⟶ – 🏄 25/350. 🆎 ⓞ ⓜⓞ 𝐕𝐈𝐒𝐀 𝐉𝐂𝐁. ❄ **Meals** 21,03 – ⌑ 13,52   **195 rm** 164,50/208,10 – 6 suites.   LY s

🏨🏨 El Coloso, Leganitos 13, ⊠ 28013, ℰ 91 548 76 40, hotelelcoloso@cestein.es, Fax 91 547 49 68 – ⁅ 🗍 📺 ⟵⟶ – **84 rm.**   KX y

🏨🏨 **Lope de Vega,** Lope de Vega 49, ⊠ 28014, ℰ 91 360 00 11, lopedevega@gree n-hoteles.com, Fax 91 429 23 91 – ⁅ 🗍 📺 ⟵⟶ – 🏄 25/50. 🆎 ⓞ ⓜⓞ 𝐕𝐈𝐒𝐀 𝐉𝐂𝐁   MY d
⌑ 11 – **60 rm** 150.

🏨🏨 **Suecia,** Marqués de Casa Riera 4, ⊠ 28014, ℰ 91 531 69 00, bookings@hotelsuecia. com, Fax 91 521 71 41 – ⁅ 🗍 📺 – 🏄 25/150. 🆎 ⓞ ⓜⓞ 𝐕𝐈𝐒𝐀 𝐉𝐂𝐁. ❄   MX r
Meals 22 – ⌑ 13 – **119 rm** 132/165 – 9 suites.

🏨🏨 **Tryp Cibeles** without rest, Mesonero Romanos 13, ⊠ 28004, ℰ 91 532 15 52, Fax 91 532 65 70 – ⁅ 🗍 📺 – 🏄 25. 🆎 ⓞ ⓜⓞ 𝐕𝐈𝐒𝐀 𝐉𝐂𝐁. ❄   LX n
⌑ 12,02 – **132 rm** 164,52/208,10.

🏨🏨 **Atlántico** without rest, Gran Vía 38, ⊠ 28013, ℰ 91 522 64 80, informacion@hote latlantico.es, Fax 91 531 02 10 – ⁅ 🗍 📺. 🆎 ⓞ ⓜⓞ 𝐕𝐈𝐒𝐀. ❄   LX e
78 rm ⌑ 108,07/150,87.

🏨🏨 **Regina** without rest, Alcalá 19, ⊠ 28014, ℰ 91 521 47 25, Fax 91 522 40 88 – ⁅ 🗍 📺. 🆎 ⓞ ⓜⓞ 𝐕𝐈𝐒𝐀. ❄   LX v
142 rm ⌑ 125.

🏨🏨 **Casón del Tormes** without rest, Río 7, ⊠ 28013, ℰ 91 541 97 46, hotormes@inf onegocio.com, Fax 91 541 18 52 – ⁅ 🗍 📺. 🆎 ⓞ ⓜⓞ 𝐕𝐈𝐒𝐀. ❄   KV v
⌑ 5 – **63 rm** 71/89.

🏨 **El Prado** without rest, Prado 11, ⊠ 28014, 𝒫 91 369 02 34, prado@green-hoteles
com, Fax 91 429 28 29 – 🔄 🗐 📺 – 🕍 25/50. 🆎 ⓪ ⓒ ⓪ VISA JCB. ✂   LY a
⊐ 4 – **47 rm** 113/141.

🏨 **Tryp Gran Vía** without rest, Gran Vía 25, ⊠ 28013, 𝒫 91 522 11 21, granvía@
rypnet.com, Fax 91 521 24 24 – 🔄 🗐 📺 ᴃ – 🕍 25/50. 🆎 ⓪ ⓒ ⓪ VISA JCB. ✂   LX z
⊐ 10 – **175 rm** 123/154.

🏨 **Carlos V** without rest, Maestro Vitoria 5, ⊠ 28013, 𝒫 91 531 41 00, recepcion@hc
telcarlosv.com, Fax 91 531 37 61 – 🔄 🗐 📺. 🆎 ⓪ ⓒ ⓪ VISA JCB. ✂   LX
67 rm ⊐ 90,04/113,31.

🏨 **Los Condes** without rest, Los Libreros 7, ⊠ 28004, 𝒫 91 521 54 55, hcondes@ve
ial.es, Fax 91 521 78 82 – 🔄 🗐 📺. 🆎 ⓪ ⓒ ⓪ VISA JCB. ✂   KLV g
68 rm ⊐ 82/125.

🏨 **Alexandra** without rest, San Bernardo 29, ⊠ 28015, 𝒫 91 542 04 00, alexhot@te
eline.es, Fax 91 559 28 25 – 🔄 🗐 📺 – 🕍 25/90. 🆎 ⓪ ⓒ ⓪ VISA JCB. ✂   KV z
⊐ 6,51 – **68 rm** 66/82,75.

🏨 **California** without rest, Gran Vía 38-1º, ⊠ 28013, 𝒫 91 522 47 03, Fax 91 531 61 0ʹ
– 🔄 🗐 📺. 🆎 ⓪ ⓒ ⓪ VISA. ✂   LX e
26 rm ⊐ 69/96.

🍽️🍽️🍽️🍽️ **Teatro Real,** Felipe V-2º, ⊠ 28013, 𝒫 91 516 06 70, Fax 91 559 96 29, « Within the
Teatro Real » – 🗐. 🆎 ⓪ ⓒ ⓪ VISA. ✂   KX h
closed August – **Meals** - dinner only - a la carte 38,46/46,87.

🍽️🍽️🍽️🍽️ **La Terraza** (Madrid Casino), Alcalá 15-3º, ⊠ 28014, 𝒫 91 521 87 00, jmartinf@cas
✿ nomadrid.org, Fax 91 523 44 36, 🌤️, « Elegant 19C setting in Madrid Casino, terrace »
– 🔄 🗐. 🆎 ⓪ ⓒ ⓪ VISA. ✂   LX v
closed August, Saturday lunch and Sunday – **Meals** 77,92 and a la carte 58,08/66,74
Spec. Carpaccio de ceps con pasta fresca en vinagreta de piñones y aceitunas. Cabracho
en salmorejo con puré de patata y aceite de oliva. Sablé de chocolate con helado de hier
babuena.

🍽️🍽️🍽️ **Paradis Madrid,** Marqués de Cubas 14, ⊠ 28014, 𝒫 91 429 73 03, paradis-madric
@ paradis.es, Fax 91 429 32 95 – 🗐. 🆎 ⓪ ⓒ ⓪ VISA. ✂   MY v
closed Saturday lunch, Sunday and Bank Holidays – **Meals** a la carte 33,06/43,28.

🍽️🍽️🍽️ **Café de Oriente,** pl. de Oriente 2, ⊠ 28013, 𝒫 91 541 39 74, cafeoriente@grupc
lezama.com, Fax 91 547 77 07, « In a bodega » – 🗐. 🆎 ⓪ ⓒ ⓪ VISA. ✂   KXY w
Meals a la carte approx. 40,27.

🍽️🍽️🍽️ **Moaña,** Hileras 4, ⊠ 28013, 𝒫 91 548 29 14, Fax 91 541 65 98 – 🔄 🗐 🍴. 🆎 ⓪
ⓒ ⓪ VISA JCB. ✂   KY i
closed Sunday dinner – **Meals** - Galician rest - a la carte 22,96/39,52.

🍽️🍽️🍽️ **I,** Barquillo 10, ⊠ 28004, 𝒫 91 522 82 26, Fax 91 523 02 77 – 🗐. 🆎 ⓪ ⓒ ⓪ VISA. ✂
closed 6 to 23 August and Sunday – **Meals** a la carte 21,17/30,05.   MX a

🍽️🍽️🍽️ **Bajamar,** Gran Vía 78, ⊠ 28013, 𝒫 91 548 48 18, rtebajamar@jazzfree.com
Fax 91 559 13 26 – 🗐. 🆎 ⓪ ⓒ ⓪ VISA JCB. ✂   KV
Meals - Seafood - a la carte 33,66/40,88.

🍽️🍽️ **Errota-Zar,** Jovellanos 3-1º, ⊠ 28014, 𝒫 91 531 25 64, errota@ errota-zar.com
Fax 91 531 25 64 – 🗐. 🆎 ⓪ ⓒ ⓪ VISA. ✂   MY s
closed August and Sunday – **Meals** - Basque rest - a la carte 37,20/39,50.

🍽️🍽️ **El Asador de Aranda,** Preciados 44, ⊠ 28013, 𝒫 91 547 21 56, Fax 91 556 62 02ʹ
« Castilian decor » – 🗐. 🆎 ⓪ ⓒ ⓪ VISA. ✂   KX z
closed 22 July-14 August and Monday dinner – **Meals** - Roast lamb - a la carte approx
27,95.

🍽️🍽️ **Arce,** Augusto Figueroa 32, ⊠ 28004, 𝒫 91 522 04 40, Fax 91 522 59 13 – 🗐. 🆎 ⓪
ⓒ ⓪ VISA JCB. ✂   MV c
closed Holy Week, 16 to 31 August, Saturday lunch and Sunday – **Meals** a la carte
31,91/44,87.

🍽️🍽️ **El Mentidero de la Villa,** Santo Tomé 6, ⊠ 28004, 𝒫 91 308 12 85, « Original
decor » – 🗐. 🆎 ⓪ ⓒ ⓪ VISA. ✂   MV b
closed August, Saturday lunch and Sunday – **Meals** a la carte 29,40/34,50.

🍽️🍽️ **Julián de Tolosa,** Cava Baja 18, ⊠ 28005, 𝒫 91 365 82 10, Fax 91 366 33 08
« Neorustic decor » – 🗐. 🆎 ⓪ ⓒ ⓪ VISA JCB. ✂   KZ c
closed Sunday dinner – **Meals** - Braised meat specialities - a la carte 28,56/37,56.

🍽️🍽️ **Maestro Villa,** Cava de San Miguel 8, ⊠ 28005, 𝒫 91 364 20 36, Fax 91 366 35 4
– 🗐. 🆎 ⓪ ⓒ ⓪ VISA. ✂   KY r
Meals a la carte 28/36.

🍽️🍽️ **La Ópera de Madrid,** Amnistía 5, ⊠ 28013, 𝒫 91 559 50 92, Fax 91 559 50 92
« Welcoming ambience » – 🗐. 🆎 ⓪ ⓒ ⓪ VISA JCB. ✂   KY g
closed August and Sunday – **Meals** a la carte 27/32.

XX **Pinocchio Bel Canto,** Sánchez Bustillo 5, ⊠ 28012, ℘ 91 468 73 73, *restauran te@pinocchio.es*, Fax 91 662 18 65, Lively evening meals – ⬛. 𝐀𝐄 ⓞ ⓒⓞ 𝘝𝘐𝘚𝘈. ⋙ NZ t
closed August, Saturday lunch and Sunday – **Meals** a la carte 20,92/23,44.

XX **El Landó,** pl. Cabriel Miró 8, ⊠ 28005, ℘ 91 366 76 81, *ellandomadrid@hotmail.com*,
Fax 91 366 76 81 – ⬛. 𝐀𝐄 ⓞ 𝘝𝘐𝘚𝘈. ⋙ KZ a
closed Holy Week, August and Sunday – **Meals** a la carte approx. 40,87.

XX **Romesco,** Gravina 18, ⊠ 28004, ℘ 91 531 09 49, *restauranteromesco@hotmail.com*,
Fax 91 531 09 49 – ⬛. 𝐀𝐄 ⓞ ⓒⓞ 𝘝𝘐𝘚𝘈. ⋙ MV a
closed Sunday and Bank Holidays – **Meals** a la carte approx. 29,15.

XX **Casa Gallega,** pl. de San Miguel 8, ⊠ 28005, ℘ 91 547 30 55 – ⬛. 𝐀𝐄 ⓞ ⓒⓞ 𝘝𝘐𝘚𝘈 𝐉𝐂𝐁.
⋙ KY c
closed Monday – **Meals** - Galician rest - a la carte 29,20/40,23.

XX **El Rincón de Esteban,** Santa Catalina 3, ⊠ 28014, ℘ 91 429 92 89, Fax 91 365 87 70
– ⬛. 𝐀𝐄 ⓞ ⓒⓞ 𝘝𝘐𝘚𝘈. ⋰⋙ MY a
closed August and Sunday – **Meals** a la carte 29,45/37,86.

XX **Casa Parrondo,** Trujillos 4, ⊠ 28013, ℘ 91 522 62 34, Fax 91 542 31 47 – ⬛. 𝐀𝐄 ⓞ
ⓒⓞ 𝘝𝘐𝘚𝘈. ⋙ KX v
closed Sunday dinner – **Meals** - Asturian rest. - a la carte 28,86/46,88.

XX **La Cava del Faraón,** Segovia 8, ⊠ 28005, ℘ 91 542 52 54, Fax 91 457 45 30 – ⬛.
𝐀𝐄 ⓞ ⓒⓞ 𝘝𝘐𝘚𝘈. ⋙ KY s
closed Monday – **Meals** - Egyptian rest, dinner only - a la carte 19,85/24,94.

XX **La Gastroteca de Stéphane y Arturo,** pl. de Chueca 8, ⊠ 28004, ℘ 91 532 25 64,
Fax 91 522 88 04 – ⬛. 𝐀𝐄 ⓞ ⓒⓞ 𝘝𝘐𝘚𝘈 MV e
closed Holy Week, August, Saturday lunch and Sunday – **Meals** a la carte 30,60/40,80.

X **La Barraca,** Reina 29, ⊠ 28004, ℘ 91 532 71 54, *Ibarraca@eresmas.com*,
Fax 91 523 82 73 – ⬛. 𝐀𝐄 ⓞ ⓒⓞ 𝘝𝘐𝘚𝘈 𝐉𝐂𝐁. ⋙ LX a
Meals - Rice dishes - a la carte approx. 28.

X **Plaza Marina,** pl. de la Marina Española 4, ⊠ 28013, ℘ 91 542 38 95, Fax 91 372 94 87
– ⬛. 𝐀𝐄 ⓞ 𝘝𝘐𝘚𝘈 𝐉𝐂𝐁. ⋙ KX p
closed August and Sunday dinner – **Meals** a la carte 20,43/24,64.

X **Robata,** Reina 31, ⊠ 28004, ℘ 91 521 85 28, Fax 91 531 30 63 – ⬛. 𝐀𝐄 ⓞ 𝘝𝘐𝘚𝘈. ⋙
closed Tuesday – **Meals** - Japanese rest - a la carte approx. 27,05. LX a

X **La Vaca Verónica,** Moratín 38, ⊠ 28014, ℘ 91 429 78 27 – ⬛. 𝐀𝐄 ⓞ ⓒⓞ 𝘝𝘐𝘚𝘈 𝐉𝐂𝐁.
⊛ ⋙ MZ e
closed Saturday lunch – **Meals** a la carte 22,70/26,90.

X **Casa Vallejo,** San Lorenzo 9, ⊠ 28004, ℘ 91 308 61 58 – ⬛. ⓒⓞ 𝘝𝘐𝘚𝘈 𝐉𝐂𝐁. ⋙
⊛ *closed Holy Week, August, Sunday, Monday dinner and Bank Holidays* – **Meals** a la carte
16,53/26,15. LV f

X **La Bola,** Bola 5, ⊠ 28013, ℘ 91 547 69 30, Fax 91 541 71 64 – ⬛. ⋙ KX r
⊛ *closed Saturday dinner, Sunday in July-August and Sunday dinner the rest of the year* –
Meals - Madrid style stew - a la carte 22/30.

X **La Esquina del Real,** Amnistía 2, ⊠ 28013, ℘ 91 559 43 09 – ⬛. 𝐀𝐄 ⓒⓞ 𝘝𝘐𝘚𝘈.
⋙ KY e
closed 13 August-11 September, Saturday lunch and Sunday – **Meals** a la carte 32,50/37.

X **Taberna Carmencita,** Libertad 16, ⊠ 28004, ℘ 91 531 66 12, *carmencita@imfo
⊛ blue.com*, « Typical taverna » – ⬛. 𝐀𝐄 ⓞ ⓒⓞ 𝘝𝘐𝘚𝘈. ⋙ MX u
closed August, Saturday lunch and Sunday – **Meals** a la carte 12,62/23,44.

𝖸/ **La Botillería,** pl. de Oriente 4, ⊠ 28013, ℘ 91 548 46 20, *cafeoriente@grupolezam
a.com*, Fax 91 547 77 07, ☟ – ⬛. 𝐀𝐄 ⓞ ⓒⓞ 𝘝𝘐𝘚𝘈. ⋙ KX w
Tapa 2,70 **Ración** approx. 12.

𝖸/ **Prada a Tope,** Príncipe 11, ⊠ 28012, ℘ 91 429 59 21 – ⬛. ⓞ ⓒⓞ 𝘝𝘐𝘚𝘈 𝐉𝐂𝐁. ⋙ LY u
closed August and Monday – **Tapa** 4,20 **Ración** - Dishes from El Bierzo - approx. 6.

𝖸/ **La Cava de Don Pedro,** Don Pedro 4, ⊠ 28005, ℘ 91 366 78 04 – ⬛. 𝘝𝘐𝘚𝘈. ⋙ KZ e
closed 15 to 31 August, Monday and Tuesday lunch – **Tapa** 1,50 **Ración** approx. 5,41.

𝖸/ **Taberna Almendro 13,** Almendro 13, ⊠ 28005, ℘ 91 365 42 52 – ⬛. ⋙ KZ r
Tapa 1,60 **Ración** approx. 5,41.

𝖸/ **Taberna de San Bernardo,** San Bernardo 85, ⊠ 28015, ℘ 91 445 41 70 – ⬛
Tapa 1,20 **Ración** approx. 4,60. LV m

𝖸/ **Desahogo Taberna,** pl. de San Miguel, ⊠ 28005, ℘ 91 559 08 97 – 𝐀𝐄 ⓞ ⓒⓞ 𝘝𝘐𝘚𝘈
closed Sunday dinner and Monday – **Tapa** 2,40 **Ración** (dinner only July-August)
approx. 9,62. KY c

𝖸/ **Taberna de Dolores,** pl. de Jesús 4, ⊠ 28014, ℘ 91 429 22 43 – ⬛. ⋙ MY z
Tapa 1,50 **Ración** approx. 7,21.

¶/ **Bocaito,** Libertad 6, ✉ 28004, ☎ 91 532 12 19, *bocaito@bocaito.com*
Fax 91 522 56 29 – ▤. ① ⓌⓈ *VISA*. ✻ MX ⊦
closed August, Saturday lunch and Sunday – **Tapa** 1,80 **Ración** approx. 9,02.

¶/ **La Taurina,** Carrera de San Jerónimo 5, ✉ 28014, ☎ 91 531 39 69, « Bullfighting
theme » – ▤. ⓌⓈ *VISA*. ✻ LY ⊢
Tapa 2,10 **Ración** approx. 5,41.

Typical atmosphere :

XX **Posada de la Villa,** Cava Baja 9, ✉ 28005, ☎ 91 366 18 60, *povisa@posadadela-
lla.com, Fax 91 366 18 80*, « Old Spanish style inn » – ▤. ① ⓌⓈ *VISA*. ✻ KZ ⊬
closed August and Sunday dinner – **Meals** a la carte 20,89/33,96.

XX **Botín,** Cuchilleros 17, ✉ 28005, ☎ 91 366 42 17, *Fax 91 366 84 94*, « Old Madrid decor
typical bodega » – ▤. 🆎 ① ⓌⓈ *VISA* ᴊᴄʙ. ✻ KY ⊢
Meals a la carte 24,20/30,70.

X Casa Lucio, Cava Baja 35, ✉ 28005, ☎ 91 365 32 52, *Fax 91 366 48 66*, « Castilian
decor » – ▤ KZ ⊬

X **Zerain,** Quevedo 3, ✉ 28014, ☎ 91 429 79 09, *Fax 91 429 17 20*, Basque cider pros-
🍴 – ▤. 🆎 ① ⓌⓈ *VISA*. ✻ MY ⊬
closed Christmas, Holy Week August and Sunday – **Meals** a la carte 24/30,20.

X **Taberna del Alabardero,** Felipe V-6, ✉ 28013, ☎ 91 547 25 77, *Fax 91 541 73 98*
« Typical taverna » – ▤. ⓌⓈ *VISA* ᴊᴄʙ. ✻ KX ⊦
Meals a la carte 35,54/39,71.

Retiro, Salamanca, Ciudad Lineal : Paseo de la Castellana, Velázquez, Serrano, Goya
Príncipe de Vergara, Narváez, Don Ramón de la Cruz

🏨🏨🏨 **Ritz,** pl. de la Lealtad 5, ✉ 28014, ☎ 91 701 67 67, *reservas@ritz.es, Fax 91 701 67 76*
🍽️, ♨ – 🛗 ▤ 📺 – 🅰 25/280. 🆎 ① ⓌⓈ *VISA* ᴊᴄʙ. ✻ rest NY ⊦
Meals a la carte 45,08/60,10 – ☲ 24,64 – **130 rm** 510/570 – 29 suites.

🏨🏨🏨 **Villa Magna,** paseo de la Castellana 22, ✉ 28046, ☎ 91 587 12 34, *hotel@villamag-
na.es, Fax 91 431 22 86*, 🍽️, ♨ – 🛗 ▤ 📺 🚗 – 🅰 25/440. 🆎 ① ⓌⓈ *VISA* ᴊᴄʙ. ✻
Meals 33,06 - *Le Divellec* *(closed Sunday)* **Meals** a la carte 43,06/58,29 - *Tsé Yang* *(Chinese
rest)* **Meals** a la carte 28/41,50 – ☲ 24 – **164 rm** 420,71/475,72 – 18 suites. GV ⊢

🏨🏨🏨 **Wellington,** Velázquez 8, ✉ 28001, ☎ 91 575 44 00, *wellington@hotel-wellington.com*
Fax 91 576 41 64, ☲ – 🛗 ▤ 📺 🚗 – 🅰 25/300. 🆎 ① ⓌⓈ *VISA*. ✻ HX ⊦
Meals - see rest. *Goizeko Wellington* below - - ☲ 16,50 – **198 rm** 215/270 – 25 suites.

🏨🏨🏨 **Foxá M-30,** Serrano Galvache 14, ✉ 28033, ☎ 91 384 04 00, *foxam30@foxa.com*
Fax 91 384 04 02, « Elegant decor with period furniture », ♨, ☲, 🧊 – 🛗 ▤ 📺 & 🚗
– 🅰 25/650. 🆎 ① ⓌⓈ *VISA*. ✻ JR ⊦
Meals 48 – **73 rm** ☲ 160 – 2 suites.

🏨🏨 **Adler,** Velázquez 33, ✉ 28001, ☎ 91 426 32 20, *hoteladler@iova-sa.com*
Fax 91 426 32 21, « Welcoming atmosphere » – 🛗 ▤ 📺 🚗. 🆎 ① ⓌⓈ *VISA*. ✻ HV ⊢
Meals a la carte 34,71/43,18 – ☲ 19,23 – **45 rm** 258,45/321,55.

🏨🏨 **Meliá Galgos,** Claudio Coello 139, ✉ 28006, ☎ 91 562 66 00, *melia.galgos@solmelia.es*
Fax 91 561 76 62 – 🛗 ▤ 📺 🚗 – 🅰 25/300. 🆎 ① ⓌⓈ *VISA* ᴊᴄʙ. ✻ GU ⊢
Diábolo : **Meals** a la carte 24,19/37,12 – ☲ 16 – **357 rm** 137,50/281,90.

🏨🏨 **Gran Meliá Fénix,** Hermosilla 2, ✉ 28001, ☎ 91 431 67 00, *Fax 91 576 06 61* – 🛗
▤ 📺 🚗 – 🅰 25/100. 🆎 ① ⓌⓈ *VISA* ᴊᴄʙ. ✻ NV ⊢
Meals a la carte approx. 39,07 – ☲ 18 – **213 rm** 289/346 – 13 suites.

🏨🏨 **Meliá Avenida América,** Juan Ignacio Luca de Tena 36, ✉ 28027, ☎ 91 423 24 00
melia.avenida.america@solmelia.es, Fax 91 320 14 40, ♨, ☲, 🧊 – 🛗 ▤ 📺 & 🚗
🅰 25/1500. 🆎 ① ⓌⓈ *VISA* ᴊᴄʙ. ✻ North-East : by Av. de América JT ⊢
Meals 28 – ☲ 13,52 – **322 rm** 158/198 – 18 suites.

🏨🏨 **Sofitel Madrid Aeropuerto,** Av. Capital de España, Madrid 10, ✉ 28042
☎ 91 721 00 70, *h1606@accor-hotels.com, Fax 91 721 05 15*, ☲ – 🛗 ▤ 📺 & 🚗
🅰 50/120. 🆎 ① ⓌⓈ *VISA*. ✻ rest North-East : by Av. de América JT ⊢
Meals 25,24 – ☲ 15 – **178 rm** 248/258 – 3 suites.

🏨🏨 **NH Príncipe de Vergara,** Príncipe de Vergara 92, ✉ 28006, ☎ 91 563 26 95, *nhp-
incipe@nh-hoteles.es, Fax 91 563 72 53*, ♨ – 🛗 ▤ 📺 🚗 – 🅰 25/200. 🆎 ① ⓌⓈ *VISA*.
✻ HU ⊢
Meals a la carte 27,05/36,06 – ☲ 16 – **170 rm** 201 – 3 suites.

🏨🏨 **Emperatriz,** López de Hoyos 4, ✉ 28006, ☎ 91 563 80 88, *comercial@hotel-emp-
ratriz.com, Fax 91 563 98 04* – 🛗 ▤ 📺 – 🅰 25/150. 🆎 ① ⓌⓈ *VISA*. ✻ GU ⊢
Meals 24,04 – ☲ 13,22 – **155 rm** 156,26/186,31 – 3 suites.

🏨🏨 **NH Sanvy,** Goya 3, ✉ 28001, ☎ 91 576 08 00, *nhsanvy@nh-hoteles.es*
Fax 91 575 24 43 – 🛗 ▤ 📺 – 🅰 25/150. 🆎 ① ⓌⓈ *VISA* ᴊᴄʙ. ✻ rest NV ⊢
Meals (see rest. *Sorolla* below) – ☲ 15,62 – **139 rm** 171,65/195,63 – 10 suites.

Bauzá, Goya 79, ⊠ 28001, ✆ 91 435 75 45, info@hotelbauza.com, Fax 91 431 09 43, ↳ – 🛗 ≡ 📺 🚗 – 🏄 25/425. 🝙 ⓪ ⓪ 🝙. ⅏   HV c
Meals 36,06 – � 11,72 – **169 rm** 150,25/210,35 – 8 suites.

Agumar coffee shop only, paseo Reina Cristina 7, ⊠ 28014, ✆ 91 552 69 00, hotel agumar@h-santos.es, Fax 91 433 60 95 – 🛗 ≡ 📺 🚗 – 🏄 25/150. 🝙 ⓪ ⓪ 🝙 🝙. ⅏   HY a
⊡ 12,62 – **239 rm** 138,23/174,29 – 6 suites.

Novotel Madrid Puente de La Paz, Albacete 1, ⊠ 28027, ✆ 91 724 76 00, h0843@accor-hotels.com, Fax 91 724 76 10, 🛒 – 🛗 ≡ 📺 🖕 🚗 🄿 – 🏄 25/250. 🝙 ⓪ 🝙. ⅏ rest   JT t
Meals 21,80 – ⊡ 11 – **236 rm** 110/120.

Zenit Conde de Orgaz, Moscatelar 24, ⊠ 28043, ✆ 91 748 97 60, condeorgaz@z enithoteles.com, Fax 91 388 00 09 – 🛗 ≡ 📺 🚗 – 🏄 25/140. 🝙 ⓪ ⓪ 🝙. ⅏   North-East : by José Silva   JS
Meals a la carte 24,02/43,86 – ⊡ 10,90 – **90 rm** 129,90/157,01.

NH Parque Avenidas, Biarritz 2, ⊠ 28028, ✆ 91 361 02 88, nhparque@nh-hotel es.es, Fax 91 361 21 38, 🛒 – 🛗 ≡ 📺 🖕 🚗 – 🏄 25/400. 🝙 ⓪ ⓪ 🝙. ⅏
Meals a la carte 27,05/36,06 – ⊡ 14 – **198 rm** 173 – 1 suite.   JU a

Rafael Ventas, Alcalá 269, ⊠ 28027, ✆ 91 326 16 20, rafaelventas@rafaelhoteles .com, Fax 91 326 18 19 – 🛗 ≡ 📺 🚗 – 🏄 25/80. 🝙 ⓪ ⓪ 🝙. ⅏   JV a
Meals a la carte 33,70/38,60 – ⊡ 9,50 – **110 rm** 124/145 – 1 suite.

NH Alcalá, Alcalá 66, ⊠ 28009, ✆ 91 435 10 60, nhalcala@nh-hoteles.es, Fax 91 435 11 05 – 🛗 ≡ 📺 🚗 – 🏄 25/100. 🝙 ⓪ ⓪ 🝙. ⅏   HX w
Meals (closed Christmas, Holy Week, August, Saturday, Sunday and Bank Holidays) 15,02 – ⊡ 13,99 – **146 rm** 159/192.

AC Avenida de América coffee shop dinner only, Cartagena 83, ⊠ 28028, ✆ 91 724 42 40, acamerica@ac-hoteles.com, Fax 91 724 42 41 – 🛗 ≡ 📺 🚗. 🝙 ⓪ ⓪ 🝙. ⅏   JU b
⊡ 9,02 – **145 rm** 156.

Jardín de Recoletos, Gil de Santivañes 6, ⊠ 28001, ✆ 91 781 16 40, Fax 91 781 16 41, 🍸, « Terrace » – 🛗 ≡ 📺 🚗. 🝙 ⓪ ⓪ 🝙. ⅏   NV p
Meals 21,04 – **43 rm** ⊡ 159,27/177,30.

El Madroño, General Díaz Porlier 101, ⊠ 28006, ✆ 91 562 52 92, Fax 91 563 06 97 – 🛗 ≡ 📺 🚗 – 🏄 25/300. 🝙 ⓪ ⓪ 🝙. ⅏   HU z
Meals (closed August and Sunday) 15,03 – ⊡ 6,61 – **66 rm** 124,11/155,05.

NH Lagasca, Lagasca 64, ⊠ 28001, ✆ 91 575 46 06, nhlagasca@nh-hoteles.es, Fax 91 575 16 94 – 🛗 ≡ 📺 – 🏄 25/45. 🝙 ⓪ ⓪ 🝙. ⅏   GHV k
Meals (closed August, Saturday and Sunday) a la carte 27,05/30,06 – ⊡ 14 – **100 rm** 192.

G.H. Colón, Pez Volador 1-11, ⊠ 28007, ✆ 91 573 59 00, fiesta-colon@eurociber.es, Fax 91 573 08 09, ↳, 🍸 – 🛗 ≡ 📺 🚗 – 🏄 25/250. 🝙 ⓪ ⓪ 🝙 🝙. ⅏   JY x
Meals 13,20 – ⊡ 9,60 – **359 rm** 123,40/148,10.

Novotel Madrid Campo de las Naciones, Amsterdan 3, ⊠ 28042, ✆ 91 721 18 18, h1636@accor-hotels.com, Fax 91 721 11 22, 🍸, 🛒 – 🛗 ≡ 📺 🖕 🚗 – 🏄 25/400. 🝙 ⓪ 🝙. ⅏ rest   North-East : by Av. de América   JT
Meals 15,63 – ⊡ 11 – **240 rm** 116/130 – 6 suites.

NH Balboa, Núñez de Balboa 112, ⊠ 28006, ✆ 91 563 03 24, nhbalboa@nh-hoteles.es, Fax 91 562 69 80 – 🛗 ≡ 📺 – 🏄 25/30. 🝙 ⓪ ⓪ 🝙 🝙. ⅏   HU n
Meals (closed August) a la carte 30,17/33,64 – ⊡ 12,02 – **120 rm** 155/226.

Zenit Abeba without rest, Alcántara 63, ⊠ 28006, ✆ 91 401 16 50, abeba@zenith oteles.com, Fax 91 402 75 91 – 🛗 ≡ 📺 🚗. 🝙 ⓪ ⓪ 🝙 🝙. ⅏   JV k
⊡ 9,61 – **90 rm** 126,21/158,06.

NH Sur without rest, paseo Infanta Isabel 9, ⊠ 28014, ✆ 91 539 94 00, nhsur@nh-h oteles.es, Fax 91 467 09 96 – 🛗 ≡ 📺 – 🏄 25/30. 🝙 ⓪ ⓪ 🝙 🝙. ⅏   NZ a
⊡ 10,20 – **68 rm** 127,25/186,30.

Horcher, Alfonso XII-6, ⊠ 28014, ✆ 91 522 07 31, Fax 91 523 34 90, « Tasteful decor » – ≡. 🝙 ⓪ ⓪ 🝙. ⅏   NX y
closed August, Holy Week, Saturday lunch and Sunday – **Meals** a la carte 60,10/66,20.

Club 31, Alcalá 58, ⊠ 28014, ✆ 91 531 00 92, club31@club31.net, Fax 91 531 00 92 – ≡. 🝙 ⓪ ⓪ 🝙 🝙. ⅏   NX e
closed August – **Meals** a la carte 31,55/48,38.

El Amparo, Puigcerdá 8, ⊠ 28001, ✆ 91 431 64 56, Fax 91 575 54 91, « Original decor » – ≡. 🝙 ⓪ ⓪ 🝙. ⅏   HX h
closed Saturday lunch and Sunday – **Meals** a la carte 57,99/61,60.

XXX **Combarro,** José Ortega y Gasset 40, ⊠ 28006, ✆ 91 577 82 72, combarro@comba
rro.com, Fax 91 435 95 12 – 🗏. 🝰 ⓞ 🝰 𝘝𝘐𝘚𝘈 𝘫𝘤𝘣. ※   HV e
closed August and Sunday dinner – **Meals** - Seafood - a la carte 37,56/47,18.

XXX **Pedro Larumbe,** Serrano 61-ático 2nd floor, ⊠ 28006, ✆ 91 575 11 12, info@lar
umbe.com, Fax 91 576 60 19 – ⎟⎟ 🗏. 🝰 ⓞ 🝰 𝘝𝘐𝘚𝘈 𝘫𝘤𝘣. ※   GV a
closed Holy Week, 15 days in August, Saturday lunch, Sunday and Bank Holidays – **Meals**
a la carte 34,35/54,69.

XXX **Goizeko Wellington** - *Hotel Wellington,* Villanueva 34, ⊠ 28001, ✆ 91 577 01 38,
goizeko@goizekowellington.com – 🗏. 🝰 ⓞ 🝰 𝘝𝘐𝘚𝘈. ※   HX t
closed Sunday dinner – **Meals** a la carte 41/55.

XXX **Sorolla** - *Hotel Sanvy,* Hermosilla 4-1º, ⊠ 28001, ✆ 91 431 27 15, Fax 91 431 83 75
– 🗏. 🝰 ⓞ 🝰 𝘝𝘐𝘚𝘈. ※   NV r
closed August – **Meals** a la carte 24,04/36,06.

XXX **Suntory,** paseo de la Castellana 36, ⊠ 28046, ✆ 91 577 37 34, rsmad@nova.es,
Fax 91 577 44 55 – 🗏 ⇦. 🝰 ⓞ 🝰 𝘝𝘐𝘚𝘈 𝘫𝘤𝘣. ※   GU d
closed Holy Week, Sunday and Bank Holidays – **Meals** - Japanese rest - a la carte
32,50/53,53.

XXX **Balzac,** Moreto 7, ⊠ 28014, ✆ 91 420 01 77, balzac@burosoft.com, Fax 91 429 83 70
– 🗏. 🝰 ⓞ 🝰 𝘝𝘐𝘚𝘈. ※   NY a
closed 15 days in August, Saturday lunch and Sunday – **Meals** a la carte 31,97/48,05.

XXX **Ponteareas,** Claudio Coello 96, ⊠ 28006, ✆ 91 575 58 73, Fax 91 431 99 57 – 🗏 ⇦.
🝰 ⓞ 🝰 𝘝𝘐𝘚𝘈 𝘫𝘤𝘣. ※   GV w
closed 20 days in August and Sunday – **Meals** - Galician rest - a la carte 24,17/42,80.

XXX **Paradis Casa América,** paseo de Recoletos 2, ⊠ 28001, ✆ 91 575 45 40, casa-a
merica@paradis.es, Fax 91 576 02 15, 🌳, « Within the Palacio de Linares » – 🗏. 🝰 ⓞ
𝘝𝘐𝘚𝘈. ※   NX n
closed Saturday lunch, Sunday and Bank Holidays – **Meals** a la carte approx. 39,07.

XXX **Castelló 9,** Castelló 9, ⊠ 28001, ✆ 91 435 00 67, Fax 91 435 91 34 – 🗏. 🝰 ⓞ 🝰
𝘝𝘐𝘚𝘈. ※   HX e
closed Holy Week, August, Sunday and Bank Holidays – **Meals** a la carte 37,14/41,36.

XX **La Paloma,** Jorge Juan 39, ⊠ 28001, ✆ 91 576 86 92, Fax 91 575 51 41 – 🗏. 🝰 ⓞ
🝰 𝘝𝘐𝘚𝘈. ※   HX g
closed Christmas, Holy Week, August, Sunday and Bank Holidays – **Meals** 51,09 and a la
carte 32,90/44,93
Spec. Raviolis rellenos de colas de cigalas. Cordero caramelizado a la miel de romero y ajos.
Milhojas de hojaldre con pera Williams caramelizada.

XX **Viridiana,** Juan de Mena 14, ⊠ 28014, ✆ 91 523 44 78, Fax 91 532 42 74 – 🗏. 🝰 🝰
𝘝𝘐𝘚𝘈   NY r
closed Sunday – **Meals** a la carte 45,09/60,11.

XX **Al Mounia,** Recoletos 5, ⊠ 28001, ✆ 91 435 08 28, Fax 91 575 01 73, « Oriental
atmosphere » – 🗏. 🝰 ⓞ 🝰 𝘝𝘐𝘚𝘈. ※   NV u
closed Holy Week, August, Sunday and Monday – **Meals** - North African rest - a la carte
approx. 26.

XX **Teatriz,** Hermosilla 15, ⊠ 28001, ✆ 91 577 53 79, Fax 91 431 69 10, « Housed in an
old theatre » – 🗏. 🝰 ⓞ 🝰 𝘝𝘐𝘚𝘈. ※   GV u
Meals a la carte 25,23/28,23.

XX **La Miel,** Maldonado 14, ⊠ 28006, ✆ 91 435 50 45 – 🗏. 🝰 ⓞ 🝰 𝘝𝘐𝘚𝘈. ※ HU x
closed Holy Week, 4 to 25 August and Sunday – **Meals** a la carte 28,20/34,20.

XX **El Chiscón de Castelló,** Castelló 3, ⊠ 28001, ✆ 91 575 56 62, Fax 91 575 56 05,
« Welcoming ambience » – 🗏. 🝰 ⓞ 🝰 𝘝𝘐𝘚𝘈. ※   HX e
closed August, Sunday and Bank Holidays – **Meals** a la carte 23,50/28.

XX **Rafa,** Narváez 68, ⊠ 28009, ✆ 91 573 10 87, casarafa@jazzfree.com,
Fax 91 573 82 98, 🌳 – 🗏 ⇦. 🝰 ⓞ 🝰 𝘝𝘐𝘚𝘈. ※   HX s
closed Monday dinner – **Meals** a la carte 28,90/43,40.

XX **El Asador de Aranda,** Diego de León 9, ⊠ 28006, ✆ 91 563 02 46, Fax 91 556 62 02
– 🗏. 🝰 ⓞ 🝰 𝘝𝘐𝘚𝘈. ※   HU s
closed 5 August-3 September and Sunday dinner – **Meals** - Roast lamb - a la carte approx.
27,95.

XX **Guisando,** Núñez de Balboa 75, ⊠ 28006, ✆ 91 575 10 10, Fax 91 575 09 00 – 🗏. 🝰
ⓞ 🝰 𝘝𝘐𝘚𝘈. ※   HV f
closed Holy Week, August, Saturday lunch and Sunday – **Meals** a la carte 19,24/20,44.

XX **Nicolás,** Villalar 4, ⊠ 28001, ✆ 91 431 77 37, jam@mail.ddnet.es, Fax 91 577 86 65 –
🗏. 🝰 ⓞ 🝰 𝘝𝘐𝘚𝘈. ※   NX t
closed Holy Week, August, Sunday and Monday – **Meals** a la carte 24,52/30,94.

% ⚙ **Casa d'a Troya,** Emiliano Barral 14, ⊠ 28043, ☎ 91 416 44 55, *Fax 91 416 42 80 –*
▤. ① ◎◎ *VISA*. ⋘
JS f
closed 24 December-2 January, 15 July-1 September, Sunday and Bank Holidays – **Meals**
- Galician rest, seafood - a la carte 20,44/34,56
Spec. Pulpo a la gallega. Merluza a la gallega. Tarta de Santiago.

% **La Giralda IV,** Claudio Coello 24, ⊠ 28001, ☎ 91 576 40 69 – ▤
GX h
Meals - Andalusian rest.

% **Asador Velate,** Jorge Juan 91, ⊠ 28009, ☎ 91 435 10 24, *catering@asadorvelate
.com, Fax 91 576 12 40 –* ▤. ▦ ① ◎◎ *VISA* ᴊᴄʙ. ⋘
JX x
closed 3 to 18 August and Sunday – **Meals** - Basque rest - a la carte 26,75/40,72.

% **Pelotari,** Recoletos 3, ⊠ 28001, ☎ 91 578 24 97, *informacion@asados-pelotari.com,
Fax 91 431 60 04 –* ▤. ▦ ① ◎◎ *VISA*. ⋘
NV u
closed 15 days in August and Sunday – **Meals** a la carte 24,42/38,40.

% **La Trainera,** Lagasca 60, ⊠ 28001, ☎ 91 576 05 75, *Fax 91 575 06 31 –* ▤, ▦ ①
◎◎ *VISA* ᴊᴄʙ. ⋘
GHV k
closed August and Sunday – **Meals** - Seafood - a la carte 28,83/42,06.

% **El Pescador,** José Ortega y Gasset 75, ⊠ 28006, ☎ 91 402 12 90, *Fax 91 401 30 26
–* ▤. ▦ *VISA*. ⋘
JV t
closed Holy Week, August and Sunday – **Meals** - Seafood - a la carte 30,35/57,50.

% **La Castela,** Doctor Castelo 22, ⊠ 28009, ☎ 91 574 00 15 – ▤. ▦ ① ◎◎ *VISA* ᴊᴄʙ.
⋘
HX r
Meals a la carte approx. 27,94.

⚏/ **José Luis,** General Oráa 5, ⊠ 28006, ☎ 91 561 64 13, 🍴 – ▤. ▦ ① ◎◎ *VISA*. ⋘
Tapa 2,10 **Ración** approx. 9,62.
GU z

⚏/ **Mesón Cinco Jotas,** Puigcerdá, ⊠ 28001, ☎ 91 575 41 25, *jgarcia@osborne.es,
Fax 91 575 56 35,* 🍴 – ▤. ▦ ① ◎◎ *VISA*. ⋘
GX v
Tapa 1,90 **Ración** - Ham specialities - approx. 9.

⚏/ **Tasca La Farmacia,** Diego de León 9, ⊠ 28006, ☎ 91 564 86 52, *Fax 91 556 62 02
–* ▤. ▦ ① ◎◎ *VISA*
GHU s
closed 23 July-20 August and Sunday – **Tapa** 2,10 **Ración** - Cod specialities - approx. 4.

⚏/ **Mesón Cinco Jotas,** Serrano 118, ⊠ 28006, ☎ 91 563 27 10, *jgarcia@osborne.es,
Fax 91 561 32 84,* 🍴 – ▤. ▦ ① ◎◎ *VISA*. ⋘
GU a
Tapa 1,90 **Ración** - Ham specialities - approx. 9.

⚏/ **El Barril,** Goya 86, ⊠ 28009, ☎ 91 578 39 98 – ▤. ▦ ① ◎◎ *VISA*. ⋘
JVX r
closed Sunday dinner – **Tapa** 1,80 **Ración** - Shellfish specialities - approx. 15.

⚏/ **José Luis,** Serrano 89, ⊠ 28006, ☎ 91 563 09 58, *joseluis@nexo.es, Fax 91 563 31 02,*
🍴 – ▤. ▦ ① ◎◎ *VISA*. ⋘
GU u
Tapa 1,50 **Ración** approx. 10,82.

⚏/ **Taberna de la Daniela,** General Pardiñas 21, ⊠ 28001, ☎ 91 575 23 29,
Fax 91 409 07 11 – ▤. ▦ ◎◎ *VISA*. ⋘
HV s
Tapa 1,35 **Ración** approx. 5,70.

⚏/ **El Barril,** Don Ramón de la Cruz 91, ⊠ 28006, ☎ 91 401 33 05 – ▤. ▦ ① ◎◎ *VISA*.
⋘
JV n
closed 16 to 31 August – **Tapa** 2 **Ración** - Shellfish - approx. 7.

⚏/ **Jurucha,** Ayala 19, ⊠ 28001, ☎ 91 575 00 98 – ▤. ⋘
GV a
closed Holy Week, August, Sunday and Bank Holidays – **Tapa** 1,20 **Ración** approx. 3.

⚏/ **El Cantábrico,** Padilla 39, ⊠ 28006, ☎ 91 402 50 42 – ▤. ▦ ① ◎◎ *VISA*. ⋘
HV r
closed August – **Ración** - Shellfish - approx. 15,03.

Arganzuela, Carabanchel, Villaverde : Antonio López, Paseo de Las Delicias, Paseo
Santa María de la Cabeza

🏨 **Rafael Atocha,** Méndez Álvaro 30, ⊠ 28045, ☎ 91 468 81 00, *rafaelatocha@rafa
elhoteles.com, Fax 91 468 81 20 –* ▤ ▤ ▦ ⅏ & ⇔ – ▵ 25/450. ▦ ① ◎◎ *VISA*. ⋘
GZ t
Meals 18,03 – � 9,32 – **245 rm** 150/185.

🏨 **Rafael Pirámides,** paseo de las Acacias 40, ⊠ 28005, ☎ 91 517 18 28, *rafaelpi
ramides@rafaelhoteles.com, Fax 91 517 00 90 –* ▤ ▤ ▦ & ⇔. ▦ ① ◎◎ *VISA*
DZ r
Meals 9,92 – ⊊ 8,41 – **84 rm** 110/130 – 9 suites.

🏨 **Carlton,** paseo de las Delicias 26, ⊠ 28045, ☎ 91 539 71 00, *carlton@hotelcarlton.com,
Fax 91 527 85 10 –* ▤ ▤ ▦ ▦ ① ◎◎ *VISA* ᴊᴄʙ. ⋘
FZ n
Meals 24,34 – ⊊ 11,27 – **105 rm** 138,83/173,54 – 7 suites.

🏨 **Praga** coffee shop only, Antonio López 65, ⊠ 28019, ☎ 91 469 06 00, *hotelpraga@h
-santos.es, Fax 91 469 83 25 –* ▤ ▤ ▦ ⇔ – ▵ 25/350. ▦ ① ◎◎ *VISA* ᴊᴄʙ. ⋘
DZ u
⊊ 10,22 – **420 rm** 120,20/150,25.

🏨🏨 **Aramo,** paseo Santa María de la Cabeza 73, ✉ 28045, ✆ 91 473 91 11, *aramo@ab...* *ahoteles.com, Fax 91 473 92 14* – 📶 🖵 📺 🚗, 🝙 ⓞ 🝙 🝙 ※   EZ e
Meals 14,15 – ⚏ 10,20 – **108 rm** 109/120.

🏨 **Puerta de Toledo,** without rest, glorieta Puerta de Toledo 4, ✉ 28005 ✆ 91 474 71 00, *hpto@hotel-puertadetoledo.es, Fax 91 474 07 47* – 📶 🖵 📺 🚗 – 🝙 25/30. 🝙 ⓞ 🝙 🝙 🝙 ※   DY v
⚏ 8 – **152 rm** 60/100.

✗✗ **Hontoria,** pl. del General Maroto 2, ✉ 28045, ✆ 91 473 04 25 – 🖵. 🝙 ⓞ 🝙 🝙 ※   EZ v
closed Holy Week, August, Sunday and Bank Holidays – **Meals** a la carte 24,04/34,11.

Moncloa : Princesa, Paseo del Pintor Rosales, Paseo de la Florida, Casa de Campo

🏨🏨🏨 **Meliá Madrid Princesa,** Princesa 27, ✉ 28008, ✆ 91 541 82 00, *melia.madrid@s... olmelia.es, Fax 91 541 19 88,* 🝙 – 📶 🖵 📺 – 🝙 25/200. 🝙 ⓞ 🝙 🝙 🝙 ※   KV t
Meals a la carte 36,31/52,53 – ⚏ 17,12 – **253 rm** 234,72/266,87 – 23 suites.

🏨🏨🏨 **Husa Princesa,** Princesa 40, ✉ 28008, ✆ 91 542 21 00, *husaprincesa@ husa.es, Fax 91 542 73 28,* 🝙, 🝙 – 📶 🖵 📺 🝙 🚗 – 🝙 25/500. 🝙 ⓞ 🝙 🝙 🝙 ※ rest   DV z
Meals a la carte 34/43 – ⚏ 17 – **263 rm** 240/300 – 12 suites.

🏨🏨 **Tryp Monte Real** 🝙, Arroyofresno 17, ✉ 28035, ✆ 91 316 21 40, *montereal@t rypnet.com, Fax 91 316 39 34,* « Garden », 🝙 – 📶 🖵 📺 🚗 🝙 – 🝙 25/250. 🝙 ⓞ 🝙 🝙 🝙 ※   North-West : by Av. de la Victoria DU
Meals 33 – ⚏ 13,52 – **76 rm** 120/150 – 4 suites.

🏨🏨 **Sofitel Madrid Plaza de España** without rest, Tutor 1, ✉ 28008, ✆ 91 541 98 80, *h1320@ accor-hotels.com, Fax 91 542 57 36* – 📶 🖵 📺 🝙 – 🝙 25/30. 🝙 ⓞ 🝙   KV d
⚏ 15,60 – **97 rm** 245/263.

🏨🏨 **Moncloa Garden** without rest, Serrano Jover 1, ✉ 28015, ✆ 91 542 45 82, *comercial @ moncloagarden.com, Fax 91 542 71 69* – 📶 🖵 📺 – 🝙 25/60. 🝙 ⓞ 🝙 🝙 🝙 ※ – ⚏ 8,41 – **113 rm** 136,43/150,25 – 15 suites.   DV c

✗✗ **Sal Gorda,** Beatriz de Bobadilla 9, ✉ 28040, ✆ 91 553 95 06 – 🖵. 🝙 ⓞ 🝙 🝙 ※   DT e
closed August and Sunday – **Meals** a la carte 22,24/26,45.

✗✗ **El Molino de los Porches,** paseo Pintor Rosales 1, ✉ 28008, ✆ 91 548 13 36, *Fax 91 547 97 61,* 🝙, « Situated in Parque del Oeste with pleasant terrace » – 🖵. 🝙 ⓞ 🝙 🝙 ※   DV e
Meals - Roast specialities - a la carte 29,75/60,70.

✗✗ **Chantarella,** Luisa Fernanda 27, ✉ 28008, ✆ 91 541 80 03 – 🖵. 🝙 ⓞ 🝙 🝙 ※   DV h
closed 1 to 28 August, Saturday lunch and Sunday – **Meals** a la carte 25,10/30,95.

✗ **Currito,** Casa de Campo-Pabellón de Vizcaya, ✉ 28011, ✆ 91 464 57 04, *Fax 91 479 72 54,* 🝙 – 🖵 🝙. 🝙 ⓞ 🝙 🝙 ※   West : by Av. de Portugal DX
closed Sunday dinner – **Meals** - Basque rest - a la carte 33,66/40,88.

Chamberí : San Bernardo, Fuencarral, Alberto Aguilera, Santa Engracia

🏨🏨🏨 **AC Santo Mauro,** Zurbano 36, ✉ 28010, ✆ 91 319 69 00, *santo-mauro@ ac-hotel es.com, Fax 91 308 54 77,* 🝙, « Elegant palace with garden », 🝙 – 📶 🖵 📺 🚗 – 🝙 25. 🝙 ⓞ 🝙 🝙 🝙 ※   FV e
Santo Mauro : **Meals** a la carte 47,46/59,48 – ⚏ 17 – **33 rm** 329,46 – 4 suites.

🏨🏨🏨 **Miguel Ángel,** Miguel Ángel 31, ✉ 28010, ✆ 91 442 00 22, *hma@ occidental-hotel es.com, Fax 91 442 53 20,* 🝙, 🝙 – 📶 🖵 📺 🚗 – 🝙 25/300. 🝙 ⓞ 🝙 🝙 🝙 ※   FU c
Arco : **Meals** a la carte 21,02/33,34 – ⚏ 16,53 – **251 rm** 240/299 – 20 suites.

🏨🏨🏨 **Hesperia Madrid,** paseo de la Castellana 57, ✉ 28046, ✆ 91 210 88 00, *hotel@ h esperia-madrid.com, Fax 91 210 88 99* – 📶 🖵 📺 – 🝙 25/300. 🝙 ⓞ 🝙 🝙 🝙 ※   FU b
Meals - see also rest. **Santceloni** below - 21,04 – ⚏ 16,23 – **139 rm** 270,46/315,53, 32 suites.

🏨🏨🏨 **Castellana Inter-Continental,** paseo de la Castellana 49, ✉ 28046, ✆ 91 700 73 00, *madrid@ interconti.com, Fax 91 308 54 23,* 🝙, « Garden », 🝙 – 📶 🖵 📺 🚗 – 🝙 25/550. 🝙 ⓞ 🝙 🝙 🝙 ※   GU v
Meals a la carte 34,86/41,47 – ⚏ 21,04 – **281 rm** 320/355 – 27 suites.

🏨🏨🏨 **Orfila,** Orfila 6, ✉ 28010, ✆ 91 702 77 70, *inforeservas@ hotelorfila.com, Fax 91 702 77 72,* 🝙, « Small, elegantly furnished 19C palace » – 📶 🖵 📺 🚗 – 🝙 25/80. 🝙 ⓞ 🝙 🝙 ※   NV d
Meals a la carte 40/56 – ⚏ 18 – **28 rm** 271/331 – 4 suites.

🏨🏨🏨 **Mindanao,** paseo de San Francisco de Sales 15, ✉ 28003, ✆ 91 549 55 00, *recepci on@ hotel-mindanao.es, Fax 91 544 55 96,* 🝙, 🝙 – 📶 🖵 📺 🝙 🚗 – 🝙 25/250. 🝙 ⓞ 🝙 🝙 🝙 ※   DT a
Meals 33,06 - **El Candelabro** *(closed August and Sunday)* **Meals** a la carte 33,06/36,66 – ⚏ 12,92 – **272 rm** 116,75/142 – 9 suites.

🏠🏠🏠 **NH Abascal,** José Abascal 47, ✉ 28003, ✆ 91 441 00 15, *Fax 91 442 22 11,* 🛏 – 🛗
🖭 📺 ⅙ 🚗 – 🏊 25/180. 🆎 ⓪ 🆖 𝖵𝖨𝖲𝖠 ᴊᴄʙ. ఘ rest   FU a
Meals *(closed August)* 27 – ☕ 16 – **181 rm** 202/222 – 3 suites.

🏠🏠🏠 **NH Zurbano,** Zurbano 79-81, ✉ 28003, ✆ 91 441 45 00, *nhzurbano@ nh-hoteles.es,*
Fax 91 441 32 24 – 🛗 🖭 📺 ⅙ 🚗 – 🏊 25/200. 🆎 ⓪ 🆖 𝖵𝖨𝖲𝖠. ఘ   FU x
Meals 21,03 – ☕ 13,22 – **255 rm** 148,75/168,58 – 11 suites.

🏠🏠🏠 **NH Embajada,** Santa Engracia 5, ✉ 28010, ✆ 91 594 02 13, *nhembajada@ nh-hote-
les.es, Fax 91 447 33 12,* « Spanish style building » – 🛗 🖭 📺 – 🏊 25/60. 🆎 ⓪ 🆖
𝖵𝖨𝖲𝖠.   MV r
Meals *(closed August, Saturday and Sunday)* a la carte 27,05/36,06 – ☕ 13 – **101 rm**
178.

🏠🏠🏠 **NH Alberto Aguilera,** Alberto Aguilera 18, ✉ 28015, ✆ 91 446 09 00,
Fax 91 446 09 04 – 🛗 🖭 📺 ⅙ 🚗 – 🏊 25/100. 🆎 ⓪ 🆖 𝖵𝖨𝖲𝖠. ఘ   DV b
Meals *(closed August, Saturday and Sunday)* a la carte 27,05/36,06 – ☕ 14 – **148 rm**
173 – 5 suites.

🏠🏠🏠 **NH Prisma,** Santa Engracia 120, ✉ 28003, ✆ 91 441 93 77, *nhprisma@ nhhoteles.es,*
Fax 91 442 58 51 – 🛗 🖭 📺 – 🏊 25/70. 🆎 ⓪ 🆖 𝖵𝖨𝖲𝖠 ᴊᴄʙ.   EU g
Meals *(closed August)* a la carte 21,31/36,94 – ☕ 12 – **103 suites** 210 – 7 rm.

🏠🏠 **NH Argüelles** coffee shop dinner only, Vallehermoso 65, ✉ 28015,
✆ 91 593 97 77, *nharguelles@ nh-hoteles.es, Fax 91 594 27 39* – 🛗 🖭 📺 🚗. 🆎 ⓪
🆖 𝖵𝖨𝖲𝖠.   DU e
☕ 12 – **75 rm** 162.

🏠🏠 **Sol Inn Alondras** coffee shop only, José Abascal 8, ✉ 28003, ✆ 91 447 40 00, *sol
inn.alondras@ solmelia.com, Fax 91 593 88 00* – 🛗 🖭 📺. 🆎 ⓪ 🆖 𝖵𝖨𝖲𝖠 ᴊᴄʙ. ఘ
☕ 10,52 – **72 rm** 136,73/190,64.   EU a

🍴🍴🍴🍴 **Santceloni** - *Hotel Hesperia Madrid,* paseo de la Castellana 57, ✉ 28046,
❀❀ ✆ 91 210 88 40, *santceloni@ hesperia-madrid.com, Fax 91 210 88 99* – 🖭. 🆎 ⓪ 🆖
ᴊᴄʙ.   FU b
closed 6 August-3 September, Saturday lunch, Sunday and Bank Holidays – **Meals** 62,35
and a la carte 54,99/86,24
Spec. Raviolis de gambas al aceite de ceps. Lubina con alcachofas al vino tinto. Canapé de
plátano con helado de turrón.

🍴🍴🍴🍴 Jockey, Amador de los Ríos 6, ✉ 28010, ✆ 91 319 24 35, *Fax 91 319 24 35* – 🖭
NV k

🍴🍴🍴 **La Broche,** Miguel Ángel 29, ✉ 28010, ✆ 91 399 34 37, *labroche@ teleline.es,*
❀❀❀ *Fax 91 399 37 78* – 🖭. 🆎 ⓪ 🆖 𝖵𝖨𝖲𝖠. ఘ   GS t
closed Holy Week, August, Saturday and Sunday – **Meals** 63,71 and a la carte 50,52/64,92
Spec. Sardinas marinadas rellenas de huevas de arenque y verduras. Lomo de bacalao con
sanfaina y una crema ligera al pil pil y aceite de salvia. Arroz Basmati guisado con pichón
de Navaz aromatizado al aceite de brasas (Season).

🍴🍴🍴 **Las Cuatro Estaciones,** General Ibáñez de Íbero 5, ✉ 28003, ✆ 91 553 63 05,
Fax 91 553 32 98 – 🖭. 🆎 ⓪ 🆖 𝖵𝖨𝖲𝖠 ᴊᴄʙ. ఘ   DT r
closed Holy Week, August, Saturday lunch and Sunday – **Meals** a la carte 35,46/55,30.

🍴🍴🍴 **Annapurna,** Zurbano 5, ✉ 28010, ✆ 91 319 87 16, *Fax 91 308 32 49* – 🖭. 🆎 ⓪ 𝖵𝖨𝖲𝖠.
ఘ   MV w
closed Saturday lunch, Sunday and Bank Holidays – **Meals** - Indian rest - a la carte
21,67/27,92.

🍴🍴🍴 Lur Maitea, Fernando el Santo 4, ✉ 28010, ✆ 91 308 03 50, *Fax 91 308 62 25* – 🖭
Meals - Basque rest.   MV u

🍴🍴🍴 **Solchaga,** pl. Alonso Martínez 2, ✉ 28010, ✆ 91 447 14 96, *webmanager@ mail.tod
oesp.es, Fax 91 593 22 23* – 🖭. 🆎 ⓪ 🆖 𝖵𝖨𝖲𝖠. ఘ   MV x
closed August, Sunday dinner and Bank Holidays dinner – **Meals** a la carte 22,84/30,95.

🍴🍴 **La Cava Real,** Espronceda 34, ✉ 28003, ✆ 91 442 54 32, *cavareal@ navegalia.com,*
Fax 91 442 34 04, Wine-cellar – 🖭. 🆎 ⓪ 🆖 𝖵𝖨𝖲𝖠. ఘ   FU h
closed August, Sunday and Bank Holidays – **Meals** a la carte 30,81/36,06.

🍴🍴 **Escolástico,** Santa Engracia 24, ✉ 28010, ✆ 91 594 04 67 – 🖭. 🆎 🆖 𝖵𝖨𝖲𝖠. ఘ
closed August and Sunday – **Meals** a la carte 32,50/37,50.   FV b

🍴🍴 **La Vendimia,** pl. del Conde del Valle de Suchil 7, ✉ 28015, ✆ 91 445 73 77,
Fax 91 448 86 72 – 🖭. 🆎 ⓪ 𝖵𝖨𝖲𝖠. ఘ   DV b
closed Sunday dinner – **Meals** a la carte 24,04/30,05.

🍴🍴 **Soroa,** Modesto Lafuente 88, ✉ 28003, ✆ 91 553 17 95, *Fax 91 553 17 98* – 🖭. 🆎
⓪ 🆖 𝖵𝖨𝖲𝖠. ఘ   FT x
closed August, Sunday, Monday and Bank Holidays – **Meals** a la carte 32,78/34,20.

🍴🍴 **Kulixka,** Fuencarral 124, ✉ 28010, ✆ 91 447 25 38 – 🖭. 🆎 ⓪ 🆖 𝖵𝖨𝖲𝖠. ఘ   EV v
closed Holy Week, August and Sunday – **Meals** - Seafood - a la carte 24/30.

XX **Odriozola,** Zurbano 13, ⊠ 28010, ℰ 91 319 31 50 – 🍴. 🆎 ⓪ ⓶ *VISA* JCB. ✦
closed 1 to 7 January, 21 days in August, Saturday lunch and Sunday – **Meals** a la carte
36/39.
MV d

XX **Tsunami,** Caracas 10, ⊠ 28010, ℰ 91 308 05 69, Fax 91 308 05 69 – 🍴. 🆎 ⓶ *VISA*
✦
FV a
closed 15 days in August, Saturday lunch, Sunday and Bank Holidays – **Meals** - Japanese
rest - a la carte 24,04/36,06.

XXX **Polizón,** Viriato 39, ⊠ 28010, ℰ 91 593 39 19 – 🍴. 🆎 ⓪ ⓶ *VISA* JCB. ✦
closed August and Sunday dinner – **Meals** - Seafood - a la carte 24/26.
EU w

XX **La Plaza de Chamberí,** pl. de Chamberí 10, ⊠ 28010, ℰ 91 446 06 97,
Fax 91 594 21 20 – 🍴. 🆎 ⓪ ⓶ *VISA* JCB. ✦
FV k
Meals a la carte 25,71/26,65.

XX **Gala,** Espronceda 14, ⊠ 28003, ℰ 91 442 22 44 – 🍴. 🆎 ⓶ *VISA*. ✦
EU n
closed the 2nd week in August and Sunday – **Meals** a la carte 25,85/33,24.

XX **Doña,** Zurbano 59, ⊠ 28010, ℰ 91 319 25 51, Fax 91 441 90 20 – 🍴. 🆎 ⓪ *VISA*. ✦
closed 15 to 31 August and Sunday dinner – **Meals** a la carte 19,08/31,55.
FU d

XX **Alborán,** Ponzano 39-41, ⊠ 28003, ℰ 91 399 21 50, alboran@alboran-rest.com,
Fax 91 399 21 50 – 🍴. 🆎 ⓪ ⓶ *VISA*. ✦
EU g
closed Sunday dinner – **Meals** a la carte 21,64/35,47.

X **Villa de Foz,** Gonzálo de Córdoba 10, ⊠ 28010, ℰ 91 446 89 93 – 🍴. 🆎 *VISA*. ✦
closed August and Sunday – **Meals** - Galician rest - a la carte 20,10/27,90.
EV e

X **Pinocchio Orfila,** Orfila 2, ⊠ 28010, ℰ 91 308 16 47, restaurante@pinocchio.es,
Fax 91 662 18 65 – 🍴. 🆎 ⓪ *VISA*. ✦
NV d
closed August, Saturday lunch, Sunday and Bank Holidays – **Meals** - Italian rest - a la carte
18,06/24,97.

X **Balear,** Sagunto 18, ⊠ 28010, ℰ 91 447 91 15, Fax 91 445 19 97 – 🍴. 🆎 ⓶
VISA. ✦
EU y
closed Sunday dinner and Monday dinner – **Meals** - Rice dishes - a la carte 24,60/45.

X **La Despensa,** Cardenal Cisneros 6, ⊠ 28010, ℰ 91 446 17 94 – 🍴. 🆎 ⓪ ⓶ *VISA*
⊛ ✦
EV p
closed 20 August-13 September, Sunday dinner and Monday – **Meals** a la carte
16,52/19,24.

♈/ **Triclinivm,** Ponzano 99, ⊠ 28003, ℰ 91 536 05 67 – 🍴. *VISA*. ✦
ET t
closed 5 to 26 August – **Tapa** 1,50 **Ración** approx. 13,82.

♈/ **Mesón Cinco Jotas,** paseo de San Francisco de Sales 27, ⊠ 28003, ℰ 91 544 01 89,
jgarcia@osboire..es, Fax 91 549 06 51, 🍴 – 🍴. 🆎 ⓪ ⓶ *VISA*. ✦
DT h
Tapa 1,90 **Ración** - Ham specialities - approx. 9.

♈/ **José Luis,** paseo de San Francisco de Sales 14, ⊠ 28003, ℰ 91 442 67 40, 🍴 – 🍴.
🆎 ⓪ ⓶ *VISA*. ✦
DU v
Tapa 2,10 **Ración** approx. 9,62.

♈/ **Asturianos,** Vallehermoso 94, ⊠ 28003, ℰ 91 533 59 47, Fax 91 533 59 47, 🍴 – 🍴.
🆎 ⓶ *VISA*
DU c
closed July and Saturday – **Tapa** 2,72 **Ración** approx. 6,58.

♈/ Zubia, Espronceda 28, ⊠ 28003, ℰ 91 441 04 32, zubiarestaurante@eresmas.com,
Fax 91 441 10 43 – 🍴
FU h

♈/ **La Taberna de Don Alonso,** Alonso Cano 64, ⊠ 28003, ℰ 91 533 52 49 – 🍴. ✦
closed Holy Week, August, Sunday and Bank Holidays dinner – **Tapa** 1,60 **Ración**
approx. 9,10.
EFT r

♈/ **Taberna El Maño,** Vallehermoso 59, ⊠ 28015, ℰ 91 448 40 35, 🍴, Bullfighting
theme – ⓶ *VISA*
DU e
closed August, Sunday dinner and Monday – **Tapa** 2,40 **Ración** approx. 7,81.

Chamartín, Tetuán : Paseo de la Castellana, Capitán Haya, Orense, Alberto Alcocer,
Paseo de la Habana

🏨🏨🏨 **Meliá Castilla,** Capitán Haya 43, ⊠ 28020, ℰ 91 567 50 00, melia.castilla@solmelia.
com, Fax 91 567 50 51, 🏊 – 🛗 🍴 📺 🕭 🚗 – 🔬 25/800. 🆎 ⓪ ⓶ *VISA* JCB.
✦
FR c
Meals (see rest. **L'Albufera** and rest. **La Fragata** below) – 🍴 17 – **891 rm** 233/241,
14 suites.

🏨🏨 **NH Eurobuilding,** Padre Damián 23, ⊠ 28036, ℰ 91 345 45 00, nheurobuilding@n
h-hoteles.es, Fax 91 345 45 76, « Garden and terrace with 🏊 », 🏋 – 🛗 🍴 📺 🕭 🚗
– 🔬 25/900. 🆎 ⓪ ⓶ *VISA*. ✦ rest
GS a
Magerit (closed August) **Meals** a la carte 29,43/36,34 – 🍴 16,22 – **416 rm** 192,32,
84 suites.

Holiday Inn Madrid, pl. Carlos Trías Beltrán 4 (entrance by por Orense 22-24), ✉ 28020, ℰ 91 456 80 00, Fax 91 456 80 01, ⅃₅, ⊥ – 🕸 ▤ 📺 ♨ – ⅍ 25/400. 🖭 ① ⑩ 𝘝𝘐𝘚𝘈 ⱼ꜀ʙ
FS z
Meals - Buffet - 13,62 - *Big Blue* : Meals (closed 15 July-August) Meals a la carte 20,98/33,03 – ⌑ 17 – **282 rm** 283/500 – 31 suites.

Cuzco coffee shop only, paseo de la Castellana 133, ✉ 28046, ℰ 91 556 06 00, hote lcuzco@mundivia.es, Fax 91 556 03 72, ⅃₅ – 🕸 ▤ 📺 ⇌ 🅿 – ⅍ 25/450. 🖭 ① ⑩ 𝘝𝘐𝘚𝘈. ⅏
FS a
⌑ 11 – **322 rm** 164/205 – 8 suites.

Chamartín, Chamartín railway station, ✉ 28036, ℰ 91 334 49 00, chamartin@husa.es, Fax 91 733 02 14 – 🕸 ▤ 📺 ⇌ – ⅍ 25/600. 🖭 ① ⑩ 𝘝𝘐𝘚𝘈 ⱼ꜀ʙ
HR
Meals (see rest. *Cota 13* below) – ⌑ 10,20 – **360 rm** 135,70/157,70 – 18 suites.

Confortel Madrid, López de Hoyos 143, ✉ 28002, ℰ 91 744 50 00, com.conforte l@once.es, Fax 91 415 30 73 – 🕸 ▤ 📺 ⇌ – ⅍ 25/40. 🖭 ① ⑩ 𝘝𝘐𝘚𝘈
JT y
Meals (closed August, Saturday and Sunday) 21,03 – ⌑ 10,21 – **120 suites** 129.81/162,27.

AC Aitana, paseo de la Castellana 152, ✉ 28046, ℰ 91 458 49 70, aitana@ac-hote les.com, Fax 91 458 49 71 – 🕸 ▤ 📺 ♨. 🖭 ① ⑩ 𝘝𝘐𝘚𝘈. ⅏
GS c
Meals 21,04 – ⌑ 11,12 – **110 rm** 214 – 2 suites.

NH La Habana, paseo de la Habana 73, ✉ 28036, ℰ 91 345 82 84, Fax 91 457 75 79 – 🕸 ▤ 📺 ⇌ – ⅍ 25/250. 🖭 ① ⑩ 𝘝𝘐𝘚𝘈 ⱼ꜀ʙ. ⅏ rest
HS f
Meals 50 – ⌑ 14 – **156 rm** 157/178.

Orense, Pedro Teixeira 5, ✉ 28020, ℰ 91 597 15 68, comercial@hotelorense.com, Fax 91 597 12 95 – 🕸 ▤ 📺. 🖭 ① ⑩ 𝘝𝘐𝘚𝘈 ⱼ꜀ʙ. ⅏
FS q
Meals 16,88 – ⌑ 10,82 – **140 rm** 147,04/174,17.

Foxá 32, Agustín de Foxá 32, ✉ 28036, ℰ 91 733 10 60, foxa32@foxa.com, Fax 91 314 11 65 – 🕸 ▤ 📺 ⇌ – ⅍ 25/250. 🖭 ① ⑩ 𝘝𝘐𝘚𝘈. ⅏
GR u
Meals 10,82 – ⌑ 10 – **63 rm** 150/167 – 98 suites.

Foxá 25, Agustín de Foxá 25, ✉ 28036, ℰ 91 323 11 19, foxa25@foxa.com, Fax 91 314 53 11 – 🕸 ▤ 📺 ⇌. 🖭 ① ⑩ 𝘝𝘐𝘚𝘈. ⅏
GR a
Meals 10,82 – ⌑ 10 – **121 suites** 150/167.

Puerta Castilla, paseo de la Castellana 191, ✉ 28046, ℰ 91 453 19 00, comercial @puertacastilla.com, Fax 91 453 19 05, ⅃₅ – 🕸 ▤ 📺 ⇌ – ⅍ 25/150. 🖭 ① ⑩ 𝘝𝘐𝘚𝘈. ⅏
GR z
Meals (closed August) 21 – ⌑ 14,50 – **234 rm** 183,31/201,34 – 28 suites.

Castilla Plaza, paseo de la Castellana 220, ✉ 28046, ℰ 91 567 43 00, castilla-plaza@ab hahoteles.com, Fax 91 315 54 06 – 🕸 ▤ 📺 ⇌ – ⅍ 25/150. 🖭 ① ⑩ 𝘝𝘐𝘚𝘈. ⅏
GR u
Meals 21,64 – ⌑ 13,25 – **139 rm** 162/202,50.

Don Pío without rest, av. Pío XII-25, ✉ 28016, ℰ 91 353 07 80, Fax 91 353 07 81 – 🕸 ▤ 📺 🅿. 🖭 ⑩ 𝘝𝘐𝘚𝘈. ⅏
HR s
⌑ 9,02 – **40 rm** 129,22/144,24.

El Gran Atlanta without rest, Comandante Zorita 34, ✉ 28020, ℰ 91 553 59 00, hatlan ta@arrakis.es, Fax 91 533 08 58, ⅃₅ – 🕸 ▤ 📺 ⇌ – ⅍ 25/120. 🖭 ① ⑩ 𝘝𝘐𝘚𝘈. ⅏
ES p
⌑ 8,41 – **180 rm** 84,14/127,80.

Aristos, av. Pío XII-34, ✉ 28016, ℰ 91 345 04 50, hotelaristos@elchaflan.com, Fax 91 345 10 23 – 🕸 ▤ 📺. 🖭 ① ⑩ 𝘝𝘐𝘚𝘈. ⅏
JR d
Meals (see rest. *El Chaflán* below) – ⌑ 11,41 – **22 rm** 106,10/144,13 – 1 suite.

La Residencia de El Viso ⏃, Nervión 8, ✉ 28002, ℰ 91 564 03 70, reservas@r esidenciadelviso.com, Fax 91 564 19 65, ⇞ – 🕸 ▤ 📺 ⇌. 🖭 ① ⑩ 𝘝𝘐𝘚𝘈. ⅏
HT c
Meals 16 – ⌑ 8 – **12 rm** 72/118.

XXXXX **Zalacaín**, Álvarez de Baena 4, ✉ 28006, ℰ 91 561 48 40, Fax 91 561 47 32 – ▤. 🖭 ㊂ ① ⑩ 𝘝𝘐𝘚𝘈 ⱼ꜀ʙ. ⅏
GU b
closed Holy Week, August, Saturday lunch, Sunday and Bank Holidays – Meals 81,14 and a la carte 44,32/58,15
Spec. Cazoleta de carabineros con corazones de alcachofa al coriandro. Albondigón de pato confitado y cordero lechal con hortalizas. Sopa de piña con crema de anís.

XXXX **Príncipe y Serrano**, Serrano 240, ✉ 28016, ℰ 91 458 62 31, Fax 91 458 62 31 – ▤. 🖭 ① ⑩ 𝘝𝘐𝘚𝘈. ⅏
HS a
closed August, Saturday lunch, and Sunday – Meals a la carte 32,76/46,58.

XXXX **El Bodegón**, Pinar 15, ✉ 28006, ℰ 91 562 31 37, Fax 91 562 97 25 – ▤. 🖭 ① ⑩ 𝘝𝘐𝘚𝘈. ⅏
GU q
closed August, Saturday lunch, Sunday and Bank Holidays – Meals a la carte 41,16/50,18.

XXXX **Príncipe de Viana**, Manuel de Falla 5, ✉ 28036, ℰ 91 457 15 49, p.viana@teleline.es, Fax 91 457 52 83 – ▤. 🖭 ① ⑩ 𝘝𝘐𝘚𝘈 ⱼ꜀ʙ. ⅏
GS c
closed Holy Week, August, Saturday lunch and Sunday – Meals - Basque rest - a la carte 40,80/48,20.

XXX **L'Albufera** - *Hotel Meliá Castilla*, Capitán Haya 45, ✉ 28020, ℰ 91 567 51 97,
Fax 91 567 50 51 – ☰ ⇦. AE ① ◍◐ VISA JCB. ✀   FR
Meals - Rice dishes - a la carte approx. 40,57.

XXX **La Fragata** - *Hotel Meliá Castilla*, Capitán Haya 45, ✉ 28020, ℰ 91 567 51 96,
Fax 91 567 50 51 – ☰ ⇦. AE ① ◍◐ VISA JCB. ✀   FR
closed August and Bank Holidays – **Meals** a la carte 37,28/50.

XXX **Combarro**, Reina Mercedes 12, ✉ 28020, ℰ 91 554 77 84, combarro@combarro.com,
Fax 91 534 25 01 – ☰. AE ① ◍◐ VISA JCB. ✀   ES
closed August and Sunday dinner – **Meals** - Seafood - a la carte 37,56/47,18.

XXX **El Chaflán** - *Hotel Aristos*, av. Pío XII-34, ✉ 28016, ℰ 91 350 61 93, restaurante@
✿ lchaflan.com, Fax 91 345 10 23, ☂ – ☰. AE ① ◍◐ VISA. ✀   JR
closed 21 days in August, Saturday lunch, Sunday and Bank Holidays – **Meals** a la carte
36,04/52,43
Spec. Foie con salteado de tubérculos y espuma de boniato. Besugo con judías y chopitos.
Sopa de pera con helado de vainilla y mousse de chocolate.

XXX **José Luis,** Rafael Salgado 11, ✉ 28036, ℰ 91 457 50 36, Fax 91 344 10 46 – ☰. A
① ◍◐ VISA. ✀   GS
closed August and Sunday – **Meals** a la carte 33,36/40,27.

XXX **Goizeko Kabi,** Comandante Zorita 37, ✉ 28020, ℰ 91 533 01 85, Fax 91 533 02 14
✿ – ☰. AE ① VISA. ✀   ES
closed Sunday – **Meals** - Basque rest - a la carte 47,50/57
Spec. Marinada de atún con tapenade de olivas (15 May-October). Ligero suquet de langostinos. Becada asada al viejo brandy (15 November-February).

XXX **El Olivo,** General Gallegos 1, ✉ 28036, ℰ 91 359 15 35, elolivojpv@yahoo.com,
Fax 91 345 91 83 – ☰. AE ① ◍◐ VISA JCB. ✀   GR
closed 15 to 31 August, Sunday and Monday – **Meals** a la carte 37/42,35.

XXX **Cabo Mayor,** Juan Ramón Jiménez 37, ✉ 28036, ℰ 91 350 87 76, cabomayor@te-
eline.es, Fax 91 359 16 21, « Marine theme » – ☰. AE ① ◍◐ VISA. ✀   GS
closed Sunday – **Meals** a la carte 35,46/63,09.

XXX **Aldaba,** av. de Alberto Alcocer 5, ✉ 28036, ℰ 91 345 21 93 – ☰. AE ① ◍◐ VISA. ✀
closed August, Saturday lunch and Sunday – **Meals** a la carte 28,10/39,06.   GS

XXX **El Foque,** Suero de Quiñones 22, ✉ 28002, ℰ 91 519 25 72, Fax 91 561 07 99 – ☰.
AE ① ◍◐ VISA. ✀   HT
closed Sunday – **Meals** - Cod dishes specialities - a la carte 32,10/38,70.

XXX **Castelló 9,** Corazón de María 78, ✉ 28002, ℰ 91 519 34 15, castello9@castello9.com,
Fax 91 519 37 23 – ☰. AE ① ◍◐ VISA. ✀   JT
closed August and Sunday – **Meals** a la carte 27,64/33,21.

XX **De Vinis,** paseo de la Castellana 123, ✉ 28046, ℰ 91 556 40 33, devinis@wanadoo.es,
Fax 91 556 08 58 – ☰. AE ① VISA. ✀   GS
closed Holy Week, 15 days in August, Saturday lunch, Sunday and Bank Holidays – **Meals**
a la carte approx. 51,09.

XX Teitu, Capitán Haya 20, ✉ 28020, ℰ 91 556 21 14, Fax 91 556 22 60 – ☰   FS

XX **La Tahona,** Capitán Haya 21 (side), ✉ 28020, ℰ 91 555 04 41, Fax 91 556 62 02,
« Castilian medieval decor » – ☰. AE ① ◍◐ VISA. ✀   FS
closed 12 August-11 September and Sunday dinner – **Meals** - Roast lamb - a la carte approx.
27,95.

XX **La Misión,** Comandante Zorita 6, ✉ 28020, ℰ 91 533 27 57, lamision@lamision.es,
Fax 91 534 50 90 – ☰. AE ① ◍◐ VISA. ✀   ET
closed Saturday lunch and Sunday – **Meals** a la carte 27,34/28,84.

XX **O'Pazo,** Reina Mercedes 20, ✉ 28020, ℰ 91 553 23 33, Fax 91 554 90 72 – ☰. ◍◐ VISA. ✀
closed Holy Week, August and Sunday – **Meals** - Seafood - a la carte 36,96/42,37. EFS

XX **Carta Marina,** Padre Damián 40, ✉ 28036, ℰ 91 458 68 26, Fax 91 458 68 26 – ☰.
AE ① ◍◐ VISA JCB. ✀   HS
closed August and Sunday – **Meals** - Galician rest - a la carte 35/39.

XX **Pedralbes,** Basílica 15, ✉ 28020, ℰ 91 555 30 27, Fax 91 570 95 30, ☂ – ☰. AE ①
◍◐ VISA. ✀   FT
closed Sunday dinner – **Meals** - Catalonian rest - a la carte 20/28,50.

XX **El Telégrafo,** Padre Damián 44, ✉ 28036, ℰ 91 350 61 19, Fax 91 401 34 43, ☂,
« Resembles the inside of a boat » – ☰. AE ① VISA. ✀   GS
Meals - Seafood - a la carte 26/35.

XX **Gaztelupe,** Comandante Zorita 32, ✉ 28020, ℰ 91 534 90 28, Fax 91 554 65 66 – ☰.
AE ① VISA. ✀   ES
closed Sunday (July-15 September) and Sunday dinner the rest of the year – **Meals** -
Basque rest - a la carte 39/46.

XX **Rianxo,** Oruro 11, ⊠ 28016, ℘ 91 457 10 06, Fax 91 457 22 04 – ≣. ◭ ⓞ ⓜⓞ 𝘝𝘐𝘚𝘈. ⅏
Meals - Galician rest - a la carte 34,27/46,58.   HS h

XX **El Comité,** pl. de San Amaro 8, ⊠ 28020, ℘ 91 571 87 11, Fax 91 435 43 27, Bistro
– ≣. ◭ ⓞ ⓜⓞ 𝘝𝘐𝘚𝘈. ⅏   FS x
closed 1 week in August, Saturday lunch and Sunday – Meals a la carte 30,63/33,64.

XX **Cota 13** - Hotel Chamartín, Chamartín railway station, ⊠ 28036, ℘ 91 334 49 00, cham
artin@husa.es, Fax 91 733 02 14 – ≣. ◭ ⓞ ⓜⓞ 𝘝𝘐𝘚𝘈 𝗝𝗖𝗕. ⅏   HR
closed August – Meals a la carte 21,80/30,80.

XX **De Funy,** Serrano 213, ⊠ 28016, ℘ 91 457 69 15, defuny@eresmas.es,
Fax 91 457 45 30 – ≣. ◭ ⓞ ⓜⓞ 𝘝𝘐𝘚𝘈 𝗝𝗖𝗕. ⅏   HS z
Meals - Lebanese rest - a la carte 27,95/31,55.

XX **La Ancha,** Príncipe de Vergara 204, ⊠ 28002, ℘ 91 563 89 77, Fax 91 563 89 77, ☞
– ≣. ◭ ⓞ 𝘝𝘐𝘚𝘈. ⅏   HT z
closed 15 days in Christmas, Holy Week, Sunday and Bank Holidays – Meals a la carte
25,24/28,85.

XX **Fass,** Rodríguez Marín 84, ⊠ 28002, ℘ 91 563 60 83, fass@wanadoo.es,
Fax 91 563 74 53, « Bavarian style decor » – ≣. ◭ ⓞ ⓜⓞ 𝘝𝘐𝘚𝘈. ⅏   HS t
Meals - German rest - a la carte 17,10/26,10.

X **El Asador de Aranda,** pl. de Castilla 3, ⊠ 28046, ℘ 91 733 87 02, Fax 91 556 62 02,
« Castilian decor » – ≣. ◭ ⓞ ⓜⓞ 𝘝𝘐𝘚𝘈. ⅏   GR b
closed 12 August-10 September and Sunday dinner – Meals - Roast lamb - a la carte approx.
27.

X **Kabuki,** av. Presidente Carmona 2, ⊠ 28020, ℘ 91 417 64 15, Fax 91 556 02 32, ☞
– ≣. ◭ ⓞ ⓜⓞ 𝘝𝘐𝘚𝘈 𝗝𝗖𝗕. ⅏   FS t
closed August, Saturday lunch, Sunday and Bank Holidays – Meals a la carte 24/30,20.

Ⴘ **Tasca La Farmacia,** Capitán Haya 19, ⊠ 28020, ℘ 91 555 81 46, Fax 91 556 62 02
– ≣. ◭ ⓞ ⓜⓞ 𝘝𝘐𝘚𝘈   FS r
closed 13 August-10 September and Sunday – Tapa 2,10 Ración - Cod specialities - approx. 4.

Ⴘ **José Luis,** paseo de la Habana 4, ⊠ 28036, ℘ 91 562 75 96, joseluis@nexo.es,
Fax 91 562 31 18 – ≣. ◭ ⓞ ⓜⓞ 𝘝𝘐𝘚𝘈. ⅏   GT h
Tapa 1,50 Ración approx. 10,82.

Ⴘ **Mesón Cinco Jotas,** Padre Damián 42, ⊠ 28036, ℘ 91 350 31 73, jgarcia@osboire.es,
Fax 91 345 79 51 – ≣. ◭ ⓞ ⓜⓞ 𝘝𝘐𝘚𝘈. ⅏   GS s
Tapa 1,90 Ración approx. 9.

Ⴘ **Madrid Jabugo I,** Capitán Haya 54, ⊠ 28020, ℘ 91 570 33 78 – ≣. ◭ ⓜⓞ 𝘝𝘐𝘚𝘈. ⅏
closed August and Sunday – Tapa 2,30 Ración - Hams and cured pork specialities -
approx. 16,10.   FR k

Environs

by motorway N II :

🏨 **Tryp Barajas,** av. de Logroño 305 - N II and detour to Barajas city, North-East : 15 km,
⊠ 28042, ℘ 91 747 77 00, hotel.barajas@intelideas.com, Fax 91 747 87 17, ☞, ℉б, ⊿,
☞ – 🛗 ≣ ⓣⓥ ℗ – 🅰 25/675. ◭ ⓞ ⓜⓞ 𝘝𝘐𝘚𝘈 𝗝𝗖𝗕. ⅏ rest
Meals a la carte 23,75/33,36 – ⊡ 13,52 – **218 rm** 164,53/208,10 – 12 suites.

🏨 **Tryp Alameda,** av. de Logroño 100 - N II and detour to Barajas city, North-East : 15
km, ⊠ 28042, ℘ 91 747 48 00, hotel.alameda@intelideas.com, Fax 91 747 89 28, ☒ –
🛗 ≣ ⓣⓥ ℗ – 🅰 25/280. ◭ ⓞ ⓜⓞ 𝘝𝘐𝘚𝘈. ⅏
Meals 24 – ⊡ 11 – **136 rm** 155/193 – 9 suites.

🏨 **Aparthotel Convención Barajas** sin rest, Noray 10 - N II, detour to Barajas city and
Industrial Zone, North-East : 10 km, ⊠ 28042, ℘ 91 371 74 10, comercial@hotel.conv
encion.com, Fax 91 371 79 01 – 🛗 ≣ ⓣⓥ ⟵ – 🅰 25. ◭ ⓞ ⓜⓞ 𝘝𝘐𝘚𝘈. ⅏
⊡ 9 – **95 suites** 125/155.

🏨 **Tryp Diana,** Galeón 27 - N II, detour to Barajas city and airport by service road, North-
East : 13 km, ⊠ 28042, ℘ 91 747 13 55, diana@trypnet.com, Fax 91 747 97 97, ⊿ –
🛗 ≣ ⓣⓥ – 🅰 25/220. ◭ ⓞ ⓜⓞ 𝘝𝘐𝘚𝘈. ⅏
Asador Duque de Osuna (closed Sunday and Bank Holidays) Meals a la carte 23/31 –
⊡ 11 – **227 rm** 155/193 – 39 suites.

🏨 **Express Barajas** coffee shop only except August and weekends, Catamarán 1 - N II,
detour to Barajas city and Industrial Zone, North-East : 10 km, ⊠ 28042, ℘ 91 742 02 00,
exbarajas@nh-hoteles.es, Fax 91 741 11 00 – 🛗 ≣ ⓣⓥ ⟵. ◭ ⓞ ⓜⓞ 𝘝𝘐𝘚𝘈. ⅏
⊡ 6 – **80 rm** 78.

by motorway N VI :

🏨 **AC Aravaca,** Camino de la Zarzuela 3 - Aravaca, North-West : 10,2 km - exit 10 motorway,
⊠ 28023, ℘ 91 740 06 80, acaravaca@ac-hoteles.com, Fax 91 740 06 81, ℉б – 🛗 ≣
ⓣⓥ 🕭 ⟵ – 🅰 25/35. ◭ ⓞ ⓜⓞ 𝘝𝘐𝘚𝘈. ⅏
⊡ 9,02 – **110 rm** 130,42.

🏠 **Concordy** coffee shop only, cruce N VI con M-40 - El Plantío, North-West : 11,7 km
✉ 28023, ✆ 91 307 65 54, Fax 91 372 81 95 – |🍴| 🗐 📺 📮. 🕕🕐 VISA. ⚡
🛏 2,25 – **22 rm** 54,69/60,77.

🟡🟡 **Gaztelubide,** Gopelana 13 - La Florida, North-West : 12,8 km, ✉ 28023, ✆ 91 372 85 44
gaztelubide@teleline.es, Fax 91 372 84 19, 🍽 – |🍴| 🗐 📮. 🔼 🕕 🕐🕐 VISA. ⚡
closed Sunday dinner – **Meals** - Basque rest - a la carte 32,45/37,26.

🟡🟡 **Los Remos,** La Florida, North-West : 13 km, ✉ 28023, ✆ 91 307 72 30
Fax 91 372 84 35 – 🗐 📮. 🔼 🕕 🕐🕐 VISA. ⚡
Meals - Seafood - a la carte 24/28.

by motorway N I North : 13 km :

🏨 **La Moraleja** without rest, av. de Europa 17 - Parque Empresarial La Moraleja, ✉ 28108
✆ 91 661 80 55, h.lamora@intelideas.com, Fax 91 661 21 88, 🛁, 🏊 – |🍴| 🗐 📺 🚗 📮.
🔼 🕕 🕐🕐 VISA. ⚡ – 🛏 13 – **37 suites** 197.

Moralzarzal 28411 Madrid 444 J 18. – pop. 2 248 alt. 979.
Madrid 44.

🟡🟡🟡 **El Cenador de Salvador** 🌿 with rm, av. de España 30 ✆ 91 857 77 22, cenado
🌸 0@teleline.es, Fax 91 857 77 80, 🍽, « Elegant villa with landscaped terrace » – 🗐 📺
📮. 🔼 🕕 🕐🕐 VISA. ⚡
Meals (closed Sunday dinner and Monday) 69,42 and a la carte 34,18/47,66 – 🛏 15,03
– **7 rm** 210,35
Spec. Salmorejo de remolacha y smetana. Risotto de carabineros y boletus edulis. Milhojas
de pistacho y merengue de pera Williams.

BARCELONA 08000 🅿 443 H 36. – pop. 1 681 132.

See : Gothic Quarter★★ (Barri Gòtic : Ardiaca House★ MXA, Cathedral★ MX, No 10 Carrer
Paradis (Roman columns★) MX135, Plaça del Rei★★ MX149, Museum of the City's History★
(The Roman City★★) MXM1, Santa Àgata Chapel★ (Altarpiece of the Constable★★) MXF, Re
Martí Belvedere ≤★★ MXK – Frederic Marès Museum★ MXM2, La Rambla★★ : Barcelona Con-
temporary Art Museum★ (MACBA) (building★★) HXM10, Barcelona Contemporary Culture
Centre (CCCB) : patio★ HXR, (Former) Hospital of Santa Creu (Gothic patio★) LY, Santa Maria
del Pi Church★ LX, Virreina Palace★ LX, Güell Palace★★ LY, Plaça Reial★★ MY – The Sea
Front★ : Shipyards (Drassanes) and Maritime Museum★★ MY, Old Harbour★ (Port Vell)
Aquarium★ NY, Mercè Basilica★ NY, La Llotja★ (Gothic Hall★★) NX, França Station★ NVX,
Ciutadella Park★ NV, KX (Three Dragons Pavilion★★ NVM7, Zoology Museum★ NVM7, Zoo★
KX) – La Barceloneta★ KXY, Museum of the Catalonian History★ KYM9, Vila Olímpica★
(marina★★, twin towers ☀★★★) East : by Av. d'Icària KX, Carrer de Montcada★ : Picasso
Museum★ NV, Santa Maria del Mar Church★★ (rose window★) NX – Montjuïc★ (≤★ from
castle terraces) South : by Av. de la Reina Maria Cristina GY : Mies van der Rohe Pavilion★★,
National Museum of Catalonian Art★★★, Spanish Village★ (Poble Espanyol), Anella Olímpica★
(Olympic Stadium★, Sant Jordi Sports Centre★★) – Joan Miró Foundation★★★, Greek
Theatre★, Archaeological Museum★ – Eixample District★★ : La Sagrada Familia Church★★★
(East or Nativity Façade★★, ≤★★ from east spire) JU, Hospital Sant Pau★ North : by Padilla
JU, Passeig de Gràcia★★ HV (Lleó Morera House★ HVY, Amatller House★ HVY, Batlló
House★★ HVY, La Pedrera or Milà House★★★ HVP) – Terrades House (Les Punxes★) HVQ, Güell
Park★★ (rolling bench★★) North : by Padilla JU – Catalonian Concert Hall★★ (Palau de la Música
Catalana : façade★, inverted cupola★★) MV - Antoni Tàpies Foundation★★ HVS.
Additional sights : Santa Maria de Pedralbes Monastery★★ (Church★, Cloister★, Sant
Miquel Chapel frescoes★★★, Thyssen Bornemisza Collection★) West : by Av. de Pedralbes
EX – Pedralbes Palace (Decorative Arst Museum★ EX, Güell Stables★ (Pabellones) EX, Sant
Pau del Camp Church (Cloister★) LY, Science Museum★ North-West : by Balmes FU, Nati-
onal Theatre of Catalonia★ KUT.

🛫, 🛫 Prat, South-West : 16 km ✆ 93 379 02 78 – 🛫 Sant Cugat, North-West : 20 km
✆ 93 674 39 08 Fax 93 675 51 52.

✈ Barcelona, South-West : 18 km ✆ 93 298 38 38 – Iberia : Diputació 258, ✉ 08007,
✆ 93 401 33 81 HV.

🚂 Sants ✆ 902 240 202.

⛴ . to the Balearic Islands : Cía. Trasmediterránea, Moll de Sant Beltrà - Estació Marítima,
✉ 08039, ✆ 93 295 91 00, Fax 93 295 91 34.

🛈 pl. de Catalunya 17-S ✉ 08002 ✆ 906 301 282 telturf@barcelonaturisme.com Fax
93 304 31 55 passeig de Gràcia 107 (Palau Robert) ✉ 08008 ✆ 93 238 40 00 Fax
93 238 40 10, Sants Estació ✉ 08014 ✆ 906 30 12 82 teltur@barcelonaturisme.com and
at Airport ✆ 93 478 47 04 (Terminal A) and ✆ 93 478 05 65 (Terminal B) - R.A.C.E. Muntaner 81-bajo, ✉ 08011 ✆ 93 451 15 51 Fax 93 451 22 57.

Madrid 627 – Bilbao 607 – Lleida/Lérida 169 – Perpignan 187 – Tarragona 109 – Toulouse
388 – València 361 – Zaragoza 307.

Plans on following pages

Old Town and the Gothic Quarter : Ramblas, Pl. de Catalunya, Via Laietana, Pl. St. Jaume, Passeig de Colom, Passeig de Joan Borbó Comte de Barcelona

Le Méridien Barcelona, La Rambla 111, ⊠ 08002, ℰ 93 318 62 00, *lemeridien@m eridienbarcelona.com*, Fax 93 301 77 76 – 🛗 🗏 📺 🕹 🚗 – 🛦 25/200. 🖭 ⓞ 🐠 𝘝𝘐𝘚𝘈 ᴊᴄʙ.
LX b
Meals a la carte 27/45 – ⊑ 17 – **197 rm** 300/330 – 7 suites.

Colón, av. de la Catedral 7, ⊠ 08002, ℰ 93 301 14 04, *info@hotelcolon.es*, Fax 93 317 29 15 – 🛗 🗏 📺 – 🛦 25/120.
MV e
Meals 15,75 – ⊑ 13,25 – **138 rm** 142/205 – 9 suites.

Rivoli Rambla, La Rambla 128, ⊠ 08002, ℰ 93 481 76 76, *rivoli@alba-mssl.es*, Fax 93 317 20 38, *ₗ₅* – 🛗 🗏 📺 – 🛦 25/180. 🖭 ⓞ 🐠 𝘝𝘐𝘚𝘈 ᴊᴄʙ. ⅍
LX r
Meals 22 – ⊑ 16,50 – **81 rm** 193/228,30 – 9 suites.

Royal coffee shop only, La Rambla 117, ⊠ 08002, ℰ 93 301 94 00, *hotelroyal@h royal.com*, Fax 93 317 31 79 – 🛗 🗏 📺 🚗 – 🛦 25/100. 🖭 ⓞ 🐠 𝘝𝘐𝘚𝘈 ᴊᴄʙ.
LX e
⊑ 12 – **108 rm** 165/195.

Ambassador, Pintor Fortuny 13, ⊠ 08001, ℰ 93 342 61 80, *reservasambassador @vivolihotels.com*, Fax 93 317 20 38, *ₗ₅*, ⊒ – 🛗 🗏 📺 🕹 🚗 – 🛦 25/200. 🖭 ⓞ 🐠 𝘝𝘐𝘚𝘈 ᴊᴄʙ. ⅍
LX v
Meals a la carte 25,04/34,04 – ⊑ 17,68 – **96 rm** 209/250 – 9 suites.

Catalonia Duques de Bergara, Bergara 11, ⊠ 08002, ℰ 93 301 51 51, *duques @hoteles-catalonia.es*, Fax 93 317 34 42, ⊒ – 🛗 🗏 📺 🕹 – 🛦 25/400. 🖭 ⓞ 🐠 𝘝𝘐𝘚𝘈 ᴊᴄʙ. ⅍
LV f
Meals 16,83 – ⊑ 12,03 – **148 rm** 217,56/250,67.

Montecarlo without rest, La Rambla 124, ⊠ 08002, ℰ 93 412 04 04, *hotel@mont ecarlobcn.com*, Fax 93 318 73 23 – 🛗 🗏 📺 🚗. 🖭 ⓞ 🐠 𝘝𝘐𝘚𝘈. ⅍
LX r
⊑ 12,02 – **57 rm** 114,19/300,51 – 2 suites.

G.H. Barcino without rest, Jaume I-6, ⊠ 08002, ℰ 93 302 20 12, *reserve@gargallo -hotels.com*, Fax 93 301 42 42 – 🛗 🗏 📺 🕹. 🖭 ⓞ 𝘝𝘐𝘚𝘈 ᴊᴄʙ
MX r
⊑ 13 – **53 rm** 162/196.

Meliá Confort Apolo coffee shop only, av. del Paral.lel 57, ⊠ 08004, ℰ 93 443 11 22, *meliaconfort.apolo@solmelia.es*, Fax 93 443 00 59 – 🛗 🗏 📺 🕹 🚗 – 🛦 25/500. 🖭 ⓞ 🐠 𝘝𝘐𝘚𝘈 ᴊᴄʙ. ⅍
LY e
⊑ 13 – **314 rm** 158/189.

Barcelona Universal, av. del Paral.lel 76-78, ⊠ 08001, ℰ 93 567 74 47, *bcnunive rsal@nnhotels.es*, Fax 93 567 74 40 – 🛗 🗏 📺 🕹 🚗 – 🛦 25/100. 🖭 ⓞ 🐠 𝘝𝘐𝘚𝘈 ᴊᴄʙ. ⅍
LY a
Meals 18,60 – ⊑ 12 – **164 rm** 100/177   3 suites.

Laietana Palace without rest, Via Laietana 17, ⊠ 08003, ℰ 93 268 79 40, *reserva s@laietanapalace.com*, Fax 93 319 02 45 – 🛗 🗏 📺 🕹. 🖭 ⓞ 🐠 𝘝𝘐𝘚𝘈 ᴊᴄʙ
MX g
⊑ 13,22 – **62 rm** 181,81/208,25.

Montblanc without rest, Via Laietana 61, ⊠ 08003, ℰ 93 343 55 55, *montblanc @hcchotels.com*, Fax 93 343 55 58 – 🛗 🗏 📺 🕹 – 🛦 25/85. 🖭 ⓞ 🐠 𝘝𝘐𝘚𝘈 ᴊᴄʙ. ⅍
LV c
⊑ 14 – **79 rm** 156/195.

Catalonia Albinoni without rest, av. Portal de l'Àngel 17, ⊠ 08002, ℰ 93 318 41 41, *cataloni@hoteles-catalonia.es*, Fax 93 301 26 31, « In the ancient Rocamora palace » – 🛗 🗏 📺 🕹. 🖭 ⓞ 🐠 𝘝𝘐𝘚𝘈 ᴊᴄʙ. ⅍
LV a
⊑ 12,03 – **74 rm** 164,67/177,93.

Reding, Gravina 5, ⊠ 08001, ℰ 93 412 10 97, *reding@occidental-hotels.com*, Fax 93 268 34 82 – 🛗 🗏 📺 🕹 – 🛦 25/150. 🖭 🐠 𝘝𝘐𝘚𝘈 ᴊᴄʙ. ⅍
HX d
Meals (closed Sunday) 7,81 – ⊑ 8,11 – **44 rm** 135,23/159,27.

Lleó coffee shop only, Pelai 22, ⊠ 08001, ℰ 93 318 13 12, *reserva@hotel-lleo.es*, Fax 93 412 26 57 – 🛗 🗏 📺 🕹 – 🛦 25/150. 🖭 🐠 𝘝𝘐𝘚𝘈 ᴊᴄʙ. ⅍
HX a
⊑ 9 – **89 rm** 99/132.

Regina coffee shop only, Bergara 2, ⊠ 08002, ℰ 93 301 32 32, *reservas@reginaho tel.com*, Fax 93 318 23 26 – 🛗 🗏 📺. 🖭 ⓞ 🐠 𝘝𝘐𝘚𝘈 ᴊᴄʙ. ⅍
LV r
⊑ 12,50 – **102 rm** 156,26/216,36.

Atlantis without rest, Pelai 20, ⊠ 08001, ℰ 93 318 90 12, *hotelatlantis@retemail.es*, Fax 93 412 09 14 – 🛗 🗏 📺. 🖭 ⓞ 🐠 𝘝𝘐𝘚𝘈. ⅍
HX a
⊑ 7,21 – **42 rm** 120,20/150,25.

Catalunya Plaza coffee shop lunch only, pl. de Catalunya 7, ⊠ 08002, ℰ 93 317 71 71, *catalunya@city-hoteles.es*, Fax 93 317 78 55 – 🛗 🗏 📺 – 🛦 25. 🖭 ⓞ 🐠 𝘝𝘐𝘚𝘈. ⅍
LV g
⊑ 12,62 – **46 rm** 225/255.

Park H., av. Marquès de l'Argentera 11, ⊠ 08003, ℰ 93 319 60 00, *parkhotel@park hotelbarcelona.com*, Fax 93 319 45 19 – 🛗 🗏 📺 🕹. 🖭 ⓞ 🐠 𝘝𝘐𝘚𝘈. ⅍
NX e
Meals - see rest. *Àbac* below – **91 rm** ⊑ 103/135.

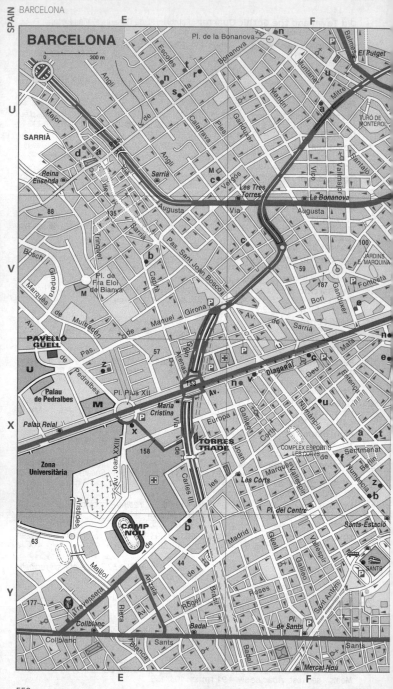

G   H

U

V

X

Y

SANTS

Pl. Molina
Fontana
GRÀCIA
Lesseps
Joanic
Muntaner
Pl. Francesc Macià
Gràcia
St. Gervasi
Diagonal
Pl. Joan Carles I
Pas. de Gràcia
Provença
Pl. Doctor Letamendi
Hospital Clínic
Universitat
Urgell
Sant Antoni
PARC JOAN MIRÓ
Pl. d'Espanya
Espanya FIRA
PALAU DEL CINQUANTENARI
Hostafrancs
Poble Sec
Paral. lel
Ronda de Sant Pau
Ronda de Sant Antoni Abat
Av. del Paral. lel

G   TARRAGONA   H

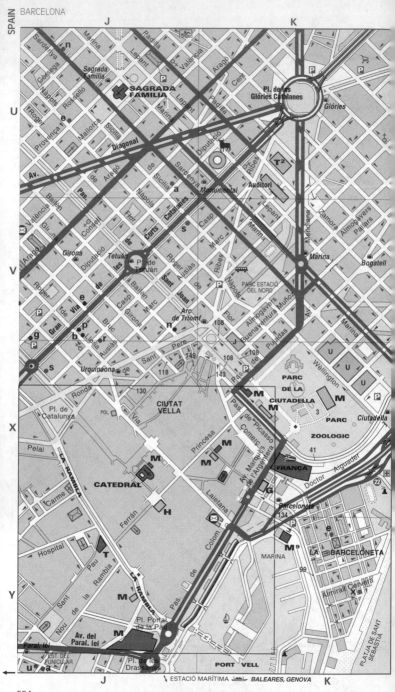

STREET INDEX TO BARCELONA TOWN PLAN

In addition to establishments indicated by XXXXX ... X,
many hotels possess good class restaurants.

BARCELONA

We suggest:

*For a successful tour,
that you prepare it
in advance.
Michelin maps and **guides**
will give you much
useful information
on route planning,
places of interest,
accommodation, prices, etc.*

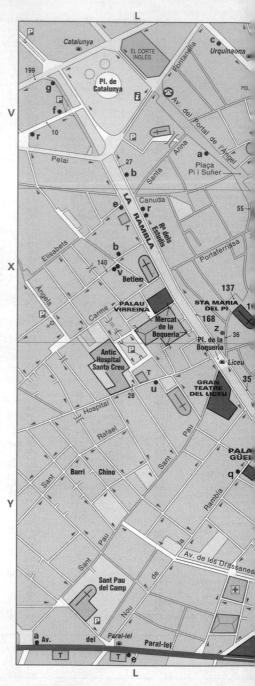

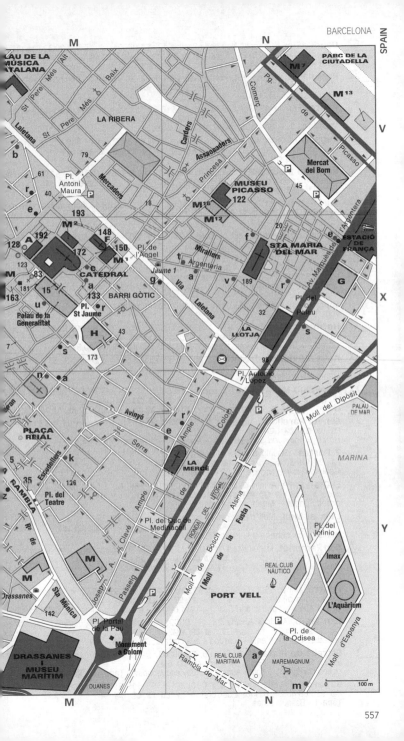

PALAU DE LA
MÚSICA
CATALANA

M

N

PARC DE LA
CIUTADELLA

M 7

M 13

V

LA RIBERA

Carders

Pq.

Comerç

de

Picasso

Assaonadors

Princesa

Laietana

St. Pere Més Alt

St. Pere Més Baix

Mercaders

b

61

79

Pl.
Antoni
Maura
P

r

40

e

193

Mercaders

18

MUSEU
PICASSO
122

Mercat
del Born

45

P

M 2

M 16

M 12

20

Av. Marques de l'Argentera

A 192

128

148
F
150

172

M

Pl. de
l'Angel

Miraliers

t

Argenteria

a

STA MARIA
DEL MAR

f

e

ESTACIÓ
DE
FRANÇA

V

123

83

e

CATEDRAL

Jaume 1

g

189

r

G

X

181

15

M

a

133

BARRI GÒTIC

Via

v

Pl. del
Palau

163

u

Pl.
St Jaume

r

Laietana

32

Palau de la
Generalitat

H

43

LA
LLOTJA

s

7

s

173

98

n

a

Pl. Antonio
López

Moll del Dipòsit

PALAU
DE MAR

P

Avinyó

Colom

r

P

MARINA

PLAÇA
REIAL

e

Ample

Serra

LA
MERCÉ

5

k

Escudellers

126

Pl. del
Teatre

Ample

de

RONDA DEL LITORAL

Alsina

Pl. del
Jofinio

Y

z

RAMBLA

Re

de

Pl. del Duc de
Medinaceli

A. Clavé

Josepn

Passeig

(Moll

de

Bosch

de

la

Fusta)

Imax

M

REAL CLUB
NÁUTICO

M

Drassanes

Sta. Mónica

142

PORT VELL

L'Aquàrium

P

Pl. de
la Odisea

Moll d'Espanya

Pl. Portal
de la Pau

Monument
a Colom

REAL CLUB
MARITIMA

a

DRASSANES
i
MUSEU
MARÍTIM

DUANES

Rambla de Mar

MAREMAGNUM

m

0   100 m

M

N

Moll del Dipòsit

Gaudí coffee shop only, Nou de la Rambla 12, ✉ 08001, ☎ 93 317 90 32, *gaudi@ telgaudi.es, Fax 93 412 26 36,* ⓕ – 🛗 🔲 📺 🚗 – 🏛 25. 🆎 ① 🅾🅾 💳 🃏   LY
⇄ 8 – **73 rm** 92/117.

Ramblas H. without rest, Rambles 33, ✉ 08002, ☎ 93 301 57 00, *info@ramblash eles.com, Fax 93 412 25 07* – 🛗 🔲 📺. 🆎 🅾🅾 💳   MY
77 rm ⇄ 135,23/144,24.

Rialto, Ferran 42, ✉ 08002, ☎ 93 318 52 12, *reserve@gargallo-hoteles.cor Fax 93 318 53 12* – 🛗 📺. 🆎 ① 🅾🅾 💳 🃏. ✀ rest   MX
Meals 14 – ⇄ 11 – **199 rm** 97/117 – 2 suites.

Regencia Colón without rest, Sagristans 13, ✉ 08002, ☎ 93 318 98 58, *info@ho elregenciacolon.com, Fax 93 317 28 22* – 🛗 🔲 📺. 🆎 ① 🅾🅾 💳 🃏. ✀   MV
⇄ 8,55 – **55 rm** 85,19/129,36.

Hesperia Metropol without rest, Ample 31, ✉ 08002, ☎ 93 310 51 00, *hotel@ esperia-metropol.com, Fax 93 319 12 76* – 🛗 🔲 📺 – 🏛 25. 🆎 ① 🅾🅾 💳. ✀   NY
⇄ 8,41 – **68 rm** 123,51/136,13.

Turín without rest, Pintor Fortuny 9, ✉ 08001, ☎ 93 302 48 12, *hotelturin@ teleline.e Fax 93 302 10 05* – 🛗 🔲 📺 ⓕ 🚗. 🆎 ① 🅾🅾 💳. ✀   LX
⇄ 9 – **60 rm** 90/132.

Continental without rest, Rambles 138-2°, ✉ 08002, ☎ 93 301 25 70, *ramblas@ otelcontinental.com, Fax 93 302 73 60* – 🛗 📺. 🆎 ① 🅾🅾 💳   LV
⇄ 3,80 – **35 rm** 61,30/89,55.

Àbac, Rec 79-89, ✉ 08003, ☎ 93 319 66 00, *restabac@infonegocio.com Fax 93 319 45 19* – 🔲 🚗. 🆎 ① 🅾🅾 💳. ✀   NX
closed 6 to 13 January, 3 weeks in August, Sunday and Monday lunch – **Meals** 55 and la carte 42,07/57
Spec. Foie gras al vapor de bambú. Arroz caldoso de ñoras y gambas. Conguito helado yogurt ácido.

Hofmann, Argenteria 74-78 (1°), ✉ 08003, ☎ 93 319 58 89, *hofmann@ ysi.es Fax 93 319 58 89,* « Pleasant setting amongst plants » – 🔲. 🆎 ① 🅾🅾 💳. ✀   NX
closed August, Saturday and Sunday – **Meals** a la carte 30,64/40,87.

Agut d'Avignon, Trinitat 3, ✉ 08002, ☎ 93 302 60 34, Fax 93 302 53 18 – 🔲. 🆎 ① 🅾🅾 💳 🃏. ✀   MY
Meals a la carte 24,25/36,78.

Reial Club Marítim, Moll d'Espanya, ✉ 08039, ☎ 93 221 71 43, Fax 93 221 44 12 ≤, 🌳, « At the pleasure harbour » – 🔲. 🆎 ① 🅾🅾 💳 🃏. ✀   NY
closed 3 weeks in August and Sunday dinner – **Meals** a la carte 22,69/32,75.

Senyor Parellada, Argenteria 37, ✉ 08003, ☎ 93 310 50 94, Fax 93 268 31 57 – 🔲 🆎 ① 🅾🅾 💳 🃏. ✀   NX
closed Sunday and Bank Holidays – **Meals** a la carte approx. 21,04.

7 Portes, passeig d'Isabel II-14, ✉ 08003, ☎ 93 319 30 33, *info@7portes.com Fax 93 319 30 46* – 🔲. 🆎 ① 🅾🅾 💳 🃏. ✀   NX
Meals a la carte approx. 27,80.

El Gran Café, Avinyó 9, ✉ 08002, ☎ 93 318 79 86, Fax 93 412 07 42, « 1900 style decor » – 🆎 ① 🅾🅾 💳. ✀   MY
closed Sunday – **Meals** a la carte 19/29,06.

L'Elx al Moll, Moll d'Espanya-Maremagnun, Local 9, ✉ 08039, ☎ 93 225 81 17, Fax 93 225 81 20, ≤, 🌳, « At the pleasure harbour » – 🔲. 🆎 🅾🅾 💳   NY
Meals - Rice dishes - a la carte 17,44/24,64.

Can Ramonet, Maquinista 17, ✉ 08003, ☎ 93 319 30 64, *canramonet@ eresmas.com, Fax 93 319 70 14,* 🌳 – 🔲. 🆎 ① 🅾🅾 💳 🃏. ✀   KY
closed 7 to 22 January, 17 to 31 August and Sunday dinner – **Meals** - Seafood - a la carte 21,60/33,30.

Pitarra, Avinyó 56, ✉ 08002, ☎ 93 301 16 47, Fax 93 301 85 62, « Period decor and memorabilia of the poet Pitarra » – 🔲. 🆎 ① 🅾🅾 💳 🃏   NY
closed August, Sunday and Bank Holidays dinner – **Meals** a la carte 16,16/24,41.

Can Majó, Almirall Aixada 23, ✉ 08003, ☎ 93 221 54 55, *canmajo@ terra.es, Fax 93 221 54 55,* 🌳 – 🔲. 🆎 🅾🅾 💳. ✀   KY
closed Monday – **Meals** - Seafood - a la carte 25,24/31,85.

Estrella de Plata, pl. del Palau 9, ✉ 08003, ☎ 93 319 60 07, *tapas@ estrella-de-pl ata.es, Fax 93 310 38 50,* 🌳 – 🔲. 🆎 ① 🅾🅾 💳   NX
closed Christmas, 1 to 15 August, Sunday and Monday – **Tapa** 5,11 **Ración** approx. 8,40.

Sagardi, Argenteria 62, ✉ 08003, ☎ 93 319 99 93, *sagardi@ sagardi.es, Fax 93 268 48 86,* Basque cider press – 🔲. 🆎 ① 🅾🅾 💳. ✀   NX
Tapa 1 - Basque tapas.

℣/ **Irati,** Cardenal Casanyes 17, ⊠ 08002, ℰ 93 302 30 84, *sagardi@sagardi.es*, Fax 93 412 73 76 – ▤. ﷼ ⓞ ⓜⓞ 𝘝𝘐𝘚𝘈. ﷼ LX z
closed Christmas, 3 weeks in August, Sunday dinner and Monday – **Tapa** 1 - Basque tapas.

℣/ **El Xampanyet,** Montcada 22, ⊠ 08003, ℰ 93 319 70 03 – ⓞ ⓜⓞ. ﷼ NX f
closed August, Sunday dinner and Monday – **Tapa** 2 **Ración** - Preserves and salted foods - approx. 4,50.

South of Av. Diagonal : Gran Via de les Corts Catalanes, Passeig de Gràcia, Balmes, Muntaner, Aragó

🏨🏨🏨🏨 **Arts** ⟨⟩, Marina 19, ⊠ 08005, ℰ 93 221 10 00, *info@harts.es*, Fax 93 221 10 70, ≤, ☞, « Superb location by the Olympic Port overlooking the city and surrounding area », ₤ₐ, ⤓ – ▯▯ 🍴 ✆ – 🕿 25/900. ﷼ ⓞ ⓜⓞ 𝘝𝘐𝘚𝘈 𝗝𝗰𝗯. ﷼
Meals 69 - **Newport Room** : **Meals** a la carte 58/70,75 – ⊊ 21,60 – **397 rm** 421, 86 suites. East : by Av. d'Icària KX

🏨🏨🏨🏨 **Rey Juan Carlos I** ⟨⟩, av. Diagonal 661, ⊠ 08028, ℰ 93 364 40 40, *Fax 93 364 42 32*, ≤ *city*, ☞, « Modern installation overlooking the city and surrounding area, park with lake and ⤓ », ₤ₐ, ⊠, ⚞ – ▯▯ ▤ 🖵 🍴 ✆ 🅿 🕿 25/1000 ﷼ ⓞ ⓜⓞ 𝘝𝘐𝘚𝘈. ﷼ West : by Av. Diagonal EX
Chez Vous (closed 27 December-10 January and Sunday) **Meals** a la carte 33,60/47,42 - *Café Polo* (buffet) **Meals** 27,04 – ⊊ 18,90 – **375 rm** 241/300 – 37 suites.

🏨🏨🏨🏨 **Ritz,** Gran Via de les Corts Catalanes 668, ⊠ 08010, ℰ 93 318 52 00, *ritz@ritzbcn.com*, Fax 93 318 01 48 – ▯▯ ▤ 🖵 🍴 – 🕿 25/280. ﷼ ⓞ ⓜⓞ 𝘝𝘐𝘚𝘈 𝗝𝗰𝗯. ﷼ JV p
Meals a la carte 47/52 – ⊊ 20 – **119 rm** 337/561 – 6 suites.

🏨🏨🏨 **Claris** ⟨⟩, Pau Claris 150, ⊠ 08009, ℰ 93 487 62 62, *claris@derbyhotels.es*, Fax 93 215 79 70, « Modern facilities with antiques, archaeological museum », ₤ₐ, ⤓ – ▯▯ ▤ 🖵 ☎ – 🕿 25/120. ﷼ ⓞ ⓜⓞ 𝘝𝘐𝘚𝘈. ﷼ rest HV w
East 47 (closed August and Monday) **Meals** a la carte 40/50 – ⊊ 18 – **80 rm** 328/365, 40 suites.

🏨🏨🏨 **Majestic,** passeig de Gràcia 68, ⊠ 08007, ℰ 93 488 17 17, *recepcion@hotelmajesti c.es*, Fax 93 488 18 80, ₤ₐ, ⤓ – ▯▯ ▤ 🖵 🍴 ☎ – 🕿 25/400. ﷼ ⓞ ⓜⓞ 𝘝𝘐𝘚𝘈 𝗝𝗰𝗯. ﷼
Meals - see rest. **Drolma** below - 22 – ⊊ 18 – **273 rm** 228/284 – 30 suites. HV f

🏨🏨🏨 **Fira Palace,** av. Rius i Taulet 1, ⊠ 08004, ℰ 93 426 22 23, *sales@fira-palacc.com*, Fax 93 424 86 79, ₤ₐ, ⤓ – ▯▯ ▤ 🖵 🍴 ☎ – 🕿 25/1300. ﷼ ⓞ ⓜⓞ 𝘝𝘐𝘚𝘈 𝗝𝗰𝗯. ﷼
Meals 21,04 - **El Mall** : **Meals** a la carte 23,50/30,96 – ⊊ 13,22 – **258 rm** 204,34/240,40, 18 suites. South : by Lleida HY

🏨🏨🏨 **G.H. Havana,** Gran Via de les Corts Catalanes 647, ⊠ 08010, ℰ 93 412 11 15, *hote lhavanasilkcn@hoteles-silken.com*, Fax 93 412 26 11 – ▯▯ ▤ 🖵 🍴 ☎ – 🕿 25/150. ﷼ ⓞ ⓜⓞ 𝘝𝘐𝘚𝘈 𝗝𝗰𝗯. ﷼ rest JV e
Meals a la carte 24,40/39 – ⊊ 14,12 – **141 rm** 156,26/174,29 – 4 suites.

🏨🏨🏨 **Meliá Barcelona,** av. de Sarrià 50, ⊠ 08029, ℰ 93 410 60 60, *melia.barcelona@so lmelia.com*, Fax 93 321 51 79, ≤, ₤ₐ – ▯▯ ▤ 🖵 ☎ – 🕿 25/500. ﷼ ⓞ ⓜⓞ 𝘝𝘐𝘚𝘈 𝗝𝗰𝗯. ﷼ FV n
Meals 25,25/46 – ⊊ 17 – **299 rm** 195/222 – 15 suites.

🏨🏨🏨 **Princesa Sofía Inter-Continental,** pl. Pius XII-4, ⊠ 08028, ℰ 93 508 10 00, *barc elona@interconti.com*, Fax 93 508 10 01, ≤, ₤ₐ, ⊠, ⚞ – ▯▯ ▤ 🖵 🍴 ☎ 🕿 25/1200. ﷼ ⓞ ⓜⓞ 𝘝𝘐𝘚𝘈 𝗝𝗰𝗯. ﷼ EX x
Meals 23,20 – ⊊ 20 – **475 rm** 319/349 – 25 suites.

🏨🏨🏨 **Hilton Barcelona,** av. Diagonal 589, ⊠ 08014, ℰ 93 495 77 77, *barcelona@hilton. com*, Fax 93 495 77 00, ☞, ₤ₐ – ▯▯ ▤ 🖵 🍴 ☎ 🅿 – 🕿 25/600. ﷼ ⓞ ⓜⓞ 𝘝𝘐𝘚𝘈 𝗝𝗰𝗯. ﷼ FX v
Meals a la carte 35/43 – ⊊ 17,43 – **287 rm** 270/300 – 2 suites.

🏨🏨🏨 **AC Diplomatic,** Pau Claris 122, ⊠ 08009, ℰ 93 272 38 10, Fax 93 272 38 11, ₤ₐ – ▯▯ ▤ 🖵 🍴 ☎ – 🕿 25/70. ﷼ ⓞ ⓜⓞ 𝘝𝘐𝘚𝘈 𝗝𝗰𝗯. ﷼ HV g
Meals 19,23 – ⊊ 11,12 – **209 rm** 232,23 – 2 suites.

🏨🏨🏨 **NH Calderón,** Rambla de Catalunya 26, ⊠ 08007, ℰ 93 301 00 00, *nhcalderon@nh-hot eles.es*, Fax 93 412 01 20, ₤ₐ, ⤓, ⊠ – ▯▯ ▤ 🖵 ☎ – 🕿 25/200. ﷼ ⓞ ⓜⓞ 𝘝𝘐𝘚𝘈. ﷼
Meals a la carte 27,05/36,06 – ⊊ 17 – **224 rm** 213 – 29 suites. HX t

🏨🏨🏨 **Catalonia Barcelona Plaza,** pl. d'Espanya 6, ⊠ 08014, ℰ 93 426 26 00, *plaza@h oteles-catalonia.es*, Fax 93 426 04 00, ₤ₐ, ⤓ heated – ▯▯ ▤ 🖵 🍴 ☎ – 🕿 25/600. ﷼ ⓞ ⓜⓞ 𝘝𝘐𝘚𝘈 𝗝𝗰𝗯. ﷼ GY r
Gourmet Plaza : **Meals** a la carte approx. 27,05 – ⊊ 12,03 – **338 rm** 217,56/250,67, 9 suites.

🏨🏨🏨 **Barceló H. Sants,** pl. dels Països Catalans, ⊠ 08014, ℰ 93 490 95 95, *hotelbcsant s@barceloclavel.com*, Fax 93 490 60 45, ≤, « At Sants railway station, overlooking the city and surrounding area », ₤ₐ – ▯▯ ▤ 🖵 🍴 🅿 – 🕿 25/1500. ﷼ ⓞ ⓜⓞ 𝘝𝘐𝘚𝘈 𝗝𝗰𝗯. ﷼
Meals 42,07 – ⊊ 13,82 – **364 rm** 150,25/210,35 – 13 suites. FY

🏨🏨🏨🏨 **Condes de Barcelona** *(Monument and Centre)*, passeig de Gràcia 75, ✉ 08008, ℰ 93 467 47 80, reservas@condesdebarcelona.com, Fax 93 467 47 85 – 📶 🗏 📺 & ⇦
– 🛗 25/200. 🆎 ⓞ ⓜⓞ 𝑽𝑰𝑺𝑨 𝐉𝐂𝐁. ❤️
Thalassa : Meals a la carte 28/33 – ☲ 15,02 – **181 rm** 270,45 – 2 suites.
HV n

🏨🏨🏨 **G.H. Catalonia**, Balmes 142, ✉ 08008, ℰ 93 415 90 90, cataloni@hoteles-catalonia.es,
Fax 93 415 22 09 – 📶 🗏 📺 & ⇦ – 🛗 50/230. 🆎 ⓞ ⓜⓞ 𝑽𝑰𝑺𝑨 𝐉𝐂𝐁. ❤️
Meals 18,03 – ☲ 12,03 – **84 rm** 217,56/250,67.
HV l

🏨🏨🏨 **Avenida Palace**, Gran Via de les Corts Catalanes 605, ✉ 08007, ℰ 93 301 96 00,
avpalace@husa.es, Fax 93 318 12 34 – 📶 🗏 📺 – 🛗 25/350. 🆎 ⓞ ⓜⓞ 𝑽𝑰𝑺𝑨 𝐉𝐂𝐁.
❤️ rest
HX
Meals 30,70 – ☲ 12,70 – **146 rm** 142,70/205,70 – 14 suites.

🏨🏨🏨 **L'Illa**, av. Diagonal 555, ✉ 08029, ℰ 93 410 33 00, Fax 93 410 88 92 – 📶 🗏 📺 &
🛗 25/100. 🆎 ⓞ ⓜⓞ 𝑽𝑰𝑺𝑨. ❤️
FX c
Meals *(closed August, Saturday and Sunday)* 15,70 – ☲ 12 – **93 rm** 183,70/222,70 –
10 suites.

🏛🏛🏛 **Abba Sants**, Numància 32, ✉ 08029, ℰ 93 600 31 00, abba-sants@abbahoteles.com,
Fax 93 600 31 01 – 📶 🗏 📺 & ⇦ – 🛗 25/200. 🆎 ⓞ ⓜⓞ 𝑽𝑰𝑺𝑨 𝐉𝐂𝐁. ❤️
FX l
Amalur : Meals a la carte 33,06/42,21 – ☲ 13,22 – **140 rm** 133/145.

🏛🏛🏛 **Ritz Roger de Llúria**, Roger de Llúria 28, ✉ 08010, ℰ 93 343 60 80, hotelritz-rog
erdelluria@rogerdelluria.com, Fax 93 343 60 81 – 📶 🗏 📺 & – 🛗 25/60. 🆎 ⓞ ⓜⓞ 𝑽𝑰𝑺𝑨
❤️
JV b
Meals 36 – ☲ 15 – **46 rm** 171,89/193,77 – 2 suites.

🏛🏛🏛 **Rafael Diagonal Port**, Lope de Vega 4, ✉ 08005, ℰ 93 230 20 00, diagonalport
@rafaelhoteles.com, Fax 93 230 20 10 – 📶 🗏 📺 & ⇦ – 🛗 25/175. 🆎 ⓞ ⓜⓞ 𝑽𝑰𝑺𝑨
❤️
East : by Av. d'Icària KX
Meals 15,63 – ☲ 10,22 – **115 rm** 142,44/154,46.

🏛🏛🏛 **AC Front Marítim**, passeig García Faria 69, ✉ 08019, ℰ 93 303 44 40, acfmaritim
@ac-hoteles.com, Fax 93 303 44 41, 🛁 – 📶 🗏 📺 & ⇦ – 🛗 25/160. 🆎 ⓞ ⓜⓞ 𝑽𝑰𝑺𝑨
❤️
East : by Av. d'Icària KX
Meals - dinner only, residents only - 12 – ☲ 9,02 – **177 rm** 156.

🏛🏛🏛 **Gallery H.**, Rosselló 249, ✉ 08008, ℰ 93 415 99 11, email@galleryhotel.com,
Fax 93 415 91 84, 🍽, 🛁 – 📶 🗏 📺 & ⇦ – 🛗 25/200. 🆎 ⓞ ⓜⓞ 𝑽𝑰𝑺𝑨 𝐉𝐂𝐁.
❤️
HV d
Meals a la carte 28,31/38,54 – ☲ 15,03 – **108 rm** 222,37/258,44 – 5 suites.

🏛🏛🏛 **St. Moritz**, Diputació 264, ✉ 08007, ℰ 93 412 15 00, j.martinez@hccotels.com,
Fax 93 412 12 36 – 📶 🗏 📺 & ⇦ – 🛗 25/200. 🆎 ⓞ ⓜⓞ 𝑽𝑰𝑺𝑨 𝐉𝐂𝐁. ❤️
JV g
Meals 20 – ☲ 18 – **92 rm** 200/240.

🏛🏛🏛 Gran Derby without rest, Loreto 28, ✉ 08029, ℰ 93 322 20 62, info@derbyhotels.es,
Fax 93 419 68 20, 🛋 – 📶 🗏 📺 ⇦ – 🛗 25/100
GX g
29 rm, 12 suites.

🏛🏛🏛 **City Park H.**, Nicaragua 47, ✉ 08029, ℰ 93 363 74 74, cityparkhotel@logiccontrol.es,
Fax 93 419 71 63 – 📶 🗏 📺 & ⇦ – 🛗 25/75. 🆎 ⓞ ⓜⓞ 𝑽𝑰𝑺𝑨. ❤️ rest
FX z
Meals 15,02 – ☲ 12,62 – **80 rm** 168,28/192,32.

🏛🏛🏛 **NH Podium**, Bailén 4, ✉ 08010, ℰ 93 265 02 02, nhpodium@nh-hoteles.es,
Fax 93 265 05 06, 🛁, 🛋 – 📶 🗏 📺 & ⇦ – 🛗 25/240. 🆎 ⓞ ⓜⓞ 𝑽𝑰𝑺𝑨 𝐉𝐂𝐁.
❤️
JV n
Corella : Meals a la carte 22,62/28,71 – ☲ 13,22 – **140 rm** 141,30/171,30 – 5 suites.

🏛🏛🏛 **Balmes**, Mallorca 216, ✉ 08008, ℰ 93 451 19 14, balmes@derbyhotels.es,
Fax 93 451 00 49, « Terrace with 🛋 » – 📶 🗏 📺 ⇦ – 🛗 25/30. 🆎 ⓞ ⓜⓞ 𝑽𝑰𝑺𝑨 𝐉𝐂𝐁.
❤️ rest
HV v
Meals 16,82 – **92 rm** ☲ 153/181 – 8 suites.

🏛🏛🏛 Derby coffee shop only, Loreto 21, ✉ 08029, ℰ 93 322 32 15, info@derbyhotels.es,
Fax 93 410 08 62 – 📶 🗏 📺 ⇦ – 🛗 25/60 – **107 rm**, 4 suites.
FX e

🏛🏛🏛 **Alexandra**, Mallorca 251, ✉ 08008, ℰ 93 467 71 66, informacion@hotel-alexandra.
com, Fax 93 488 02 58 – 📶 🗏 📺 & ⇦ – 🛗 25/100. 🆎 ⓞ ⓜⓞ 𝑽𝑰𝑺𝑨. ❤️
HV v
Meals 13,22 – ☲ **99 rm** 192,32/228,38 – 8 suites.

🏛🏛🏛 **NH Master**, València 105, ✉ 08011, ℰ 93 323 62 15, nhmaster@nhhoteles.es,
Fax 93 323 43 89 – 📶 🗏 📺 ⇦ – 🛗 25/100. 🆎 ⓞ ⓜⓞ 𝑽𝑰𝑺𝑨 𝐉𝐂𝐁. ❤️ rest HX n
Meals *(closed August, Saturday and Sunday)* 15,06 – ☲ 11,74 – **80 rm** 138/180 – 1 suite.

🏛🏛🏛 **Cristal Palace**, Diputació 257, ✉ 08007, ℰ 93 487 87 78, reservas@hotelcristalp
alace.com, Fax 93 487 90 30 – 📶 🗏 📺 & ⇦ – 🛗 25/100. 🆎 ⓞ ⓜⓞ 𝑽𝑰𝑺𝑨 𝐉𝐂𝐁. ❤️
Meals 21,03 – ☲ 13,22 – **147 rm** 181,80/208,25 – 1 suite.
HX t

🏛🏛🏛 **NH Numància**, Numància 74, ✉ 08029, ℰ 93 322 44 51, nhnumancia@nh-hoteles.es,
Fax 93 410 76 42 – 📶 🗏 📺 ⇦ – 🛗 25/70. 🆎 ⓞ ⓜⓞ 𝑽𝑰𝑺𝑨. ❤️
FX f
Meals a la carte 27,05/36,06 – ☲ 12 – **140 rm** 159.

🏠 **NH Sant Angelo** coffe shop dinner only, Consell de Cent 74, ✉ 08015,
𝒫 93 423 46 47, nhangelo@nh-hoteles.es, Fax 93 423 88 40 – 🛗 🖭 📺 🕭 ⚞ – 🏛 25.
🝙 ⓞ 🝙 𝓥𝓘𝓢𝓐. ⚞   GY f
🖵 12 – **50 rm** 159.

🏠 **Núñez Urgell**, Comte d'Urgell 232, ✉ 08036, 𝒫 93 322 41 53, nunezurgell@nnhot
els.es, Fax 93 419 01 06 – 🛗 🖭 📺 ⚞ – 🏛 25/150. 🝙 ⓞ 🝙 𝓥𝓘𝓢𝓐. ⚞ rest GX a
Meals (closed August, Saturday and Sunday) 18 – 🖵 12 – **106 rm** 102/200 – 2 suites.

🏠 **Barcelona Mar**, Provençals 10, ✉ 08019, 𝒫 93 266 52 00, barcelonamar@husa.es,
Fax 93 266 52 07, ⤲ – 🛗 🖭 📺 𝓥𝓘𝓢𝓐. ⚞
Meals (closed Sunday) a la carte approx. 25,70 – 🖵 10,70 – **75 rm** 126,70/159,70.
           East : by Av. d'Icària KX

🏠 **Capital,** Arquitectura 1, ✉ 08908 L'Hospitalet de Llobregat, 𝒫 93 298 05 30, info@h
otelcapital.com, Fax 93 298 05 31 – 🛗 🖭 📺 🕭 ⚞ – 🏛 26/60. 🝙 ⓞ 🝙 𝓥𝓘𝓢𝓐. ⚞
Meals 11 – 🖵 9 – **103 rm** 121/133.
      South : by Gran Via de les Corts Catalanes GY

🏠 **Expo H. Barcelona,** Mallorca 1, ✉ 08014, 𝒫 93 600 30 20, comercialbcn@expogr
upo.com, Fax 93 292 79 60, ⤲ – 🛗 🖭 📺 ⚞ – 🏛 25/300. 🝙 ⓞ 🝙 𝓥𝓘𝓢𝓐 𝓙𝓒𝓑. ⚞
Meals 15,03 – 🖵 10,52 – **435 rm** 96,16/102,17.   GY m

🏠 **Regente** without rest, Rambla de Catalunya 76, ✉ 08008, 𝒫 93 487 59 89, regente
@hcchotels.com, Fax 93 487 32 27, ⤲ – 🛗 🖭 📺 ⚞ – 🏛 25/120. 🝙 ⓞ 🝙 𝓥𝓘𝓢𝓐 𝓙𝓒𝓑. ⚞
🖵 17 – **79 rm** 185/225.   HV t

🏠 **NH Forum,** Ecuador 20, ✉ 08029, 𝒫 93 419 36 36, nhforum@nh-hoteles.es,
Fax 93 419 89 10 – 🛗 🖭 📺 ⚞ – 🏛 25/50. 🝙 ⓞ 🝙 𝓥𝓘𝓢𝓐 𝓙𝓒𝓑. ⚞ rest FX t
Meals (closed Christmas, August and Sunday lunch) 24,04 – 🖵 11,42 – **47 rm** 150,25,
1 suite.

🏠 **NH Rallye,** Travessera de les Corts 150, ✉ 08028, 𝒫 93 339 90 50, nhrallye@nh-h
oteles.es, Fax 93 411 07 90, 🛋, ⤲ – 🛗 🖭 📺 🕭 ⚞ – 🏛 25/300. 🝙 ⓞ 🝙 𝓥𝓘𝓢𝓐 𝓙𝓒𝓑.
⚞ rest   EY b
Meals 21,03 – 🖵 12,02 – **105 rm** 162,27/168,28 – 1 suite.

🏠 **NH Les Corts** coffee shop dinner only, Travessera de les Corts 292, ✉ 08029,
𝒫 93 322 08 11, nhcorts@nh-hoteles.es, Fax 93 322 09 08 – 🛗 🖭 📺 🕭 ⚞ –
🏛 25/80. 🝙 ⓞ 🝙 𝓥𝓘𝓢𝓐 𝓙𝓒𝓑.   FX u
🖵 12 – **80 rm** 120,20/144,25 – 1 suite.

🏠 **Onix** without rest, Llançà 30, ✉ 08015, 𝒫 93 426 00 87, hotelonix@icyesa.es,
Fax 93 426 19 81, ⤲ – 🛗 🖭 📺 🕭 ⚞ – 🏛 25/70. 🝙 ⓞ 🝙 𝓥𝓘𝓢𝓐. ⚞ GY n
🖵 9 – **80 rm** 119/149.

🏠 **Astoria**, París 205, ✉ 08036, 𝒫 93 209 83 11, info@derbyhotels, Fax 93 202 30 08
– 🛗 🖭 📺 ⚞ – 🏛 25/30. 🝙 ⓞ 🝙 𝓥𝓘𝓢𝓐 𝓙𝓒𝓑. ⚞ rest   HV a
Meals - lunch only - 16,83 – **114 rm** 🖵 170,06/197,32 – 3 suites.

🏠 **Abbot** without rest, av. de Roma 23, ✉ 08029, 𝒫 93 430 04 05, informacion@h
otel-abbot.com, Fax 93 419 57 41 – 🛗 🖭 📺 🕭 ⚞ – 🏛 25/80. 🝙 ⓞ 🝙 𝓥𝓘𝓢𝓐. ⚞
🖵 10,50 – **35 rm** 117,50/146 – 4 suites.   GXY e

🍴🍴🍴🍴 **La Dama,** av. Diagonal 423, ✉ 08036, 𝒫 93 202 06 86, Fax 93 200 72 99, « Housed
in a modernist style building » – 🍴, 🝙 ⓞ 🝙 𝓥𝓘𝓢𝓐. ⚞   HV a
Meals a la carte 37/50,55
Spec. Tartar de salmón envuelto en salmón ahumado. Filetes de lenguado con gambas al
perfume de estragón. Carro de pastelería de elaboración propia.

🍴🍴🍴🍴 **Drolma** - Hotel Majestic, passeig de Gràcia 68, ✉ 08007, 𝒫 93 496 77 10, drolma@h
otelmajestic.es, Fax 93 488 18 80 – 🛗 🖭 ⚞ – 🝙 ⓞ 🝙 𝓥𝓘𝓢𝓐 𝓙𝓒𝓑. ⚞ HV f
closed August and Sunday – **Meals** a la carte 68,60/78,80.

🍴🍴🍴🍴 **Beltxenea,** Mallorca 275, ✉ 08008, 𝒫 93 215 30 24, Fax 93 487 00 81, �ு, « Early
20C manor house » – 🍴. 🝙 ⓞ 🝙 𝓥𝓘𝓢𝓐. ⚞   HV h
closed August, Christmas, Saturday lunch and Sunday – **Meals** a la carte 42/51.

🍴🍴🍴 **Casa Calvet,** Casp 48, ✉ 08010, 𝒫 93 412 40 12, Fax 93 412 43 36 – 🍴. 🝙 ⓞ 🝙
𝓥𝓘𝓢𝓐. ⚞   JVX r
closed 11 to 29 August, Sunday and Bank Holidays – **Meals** a la carte 35,76/46,27.

🍴🍴🍴 **Jaume de Provença,** Provença 88, ✉ 08029, 𝒫 93 430 00 29, Fax 93 439 29 50 –
🍴. 🝙 ⓞ 🝙 𝓥𝓘𝓢𝓐 𝓙𝓒𝓑. ⚞   GX h
closed Christmas, Holy Week, August, Sunday dinner and Monday – **Meals** a la carte
38,75/42.

🍴🍴🍴 **Windsor,** Còrsega 286, ✉ 08008, 𝒫 93 415 84 83, windsor@minorisa.es,
Fax 93 217 42 65 – 🍴. 🝙 ⓞ 🝙 𝓥𝓘𝓢𝓐 𝓙𝓒𝓑. ⚞   HV b
closed Holy Week, August, Saturday lunch and Sunday – **Meals** a la carte 25,98/38,96.

🍴🍴🍴 **Oliver y Hardy,** av. Diagonal 593, ✉ 08014, 𝒫 93 419 31 81, oliveryhardy@interm
ail.es, Fax 93 419 18 99, 🌂 – 🍴. 🝙 ⓞ 🝙 𝓥𝓘𝓢𝓐. ⚞   FX n
closed Holy Week, Saturday lunch and Sunday – **Meals** a la carte 33,06/42,97.

XXX **Talaia Mar,** Marina 16, ✉ 08005, ✆ 93 221 90 90, *talaia@talaia-mar.e*
Fax 93 221 89 89, ≤ – 🍴 ⇔. 🖭 ⓪ ⓿ *VISA*. ✄   East : by Av. d'Icària KX
Meals a la carte approx. 42,07.

XXX **Maria Cristina,** Provença 271, ✉ 08008, ✆ 93 215 32 37, *Fax 93 215 83 23* – 🍴. 🖭
⓪ *VISA* JCB. ✄   HV
closed Saturday lunch and Sunday – **Meals** a la carte 37/50.

XX **Orotava,** Consell de Cent 335, ✉ 08007, ✆ 93 487 73 74, *orotavabcn@terra.es*
Fax 93 488 26 50 – 🍴. 🖭 ⓪ ⓿ *VISA* JCB   HX
closed Sunday – **Meals** a la carte 33,67/47,10.

XX **Els Pescadors,** pl. Prim 1, ✉ 08005, ✆ 93 225 20 18, *elspescadors@retemail.es*
Fax 93 224 00 04, 🏠 – 🖭 ⓪ ⓿ *VISA* JCB   East : by Av. d'Icària KX
closed Holy Week – **Meals** a la carte 28,50/37,60.

XX **El Asador de Aranda,** Londres 94, ✉ 08036, ✆ 93 414 67 90, *Fax 93 414 67 90* -
🍴. 🖭 ⓪ ⓿ *VISA*. ✄   GV
closed Sunday dinner – **Meals** - Roast lamb - a la carte 24,10/31,60.

XX **Rías de Galicia,** Lleida 7, ✉ 08004, ✆ 93 424 81 52, *info@riasdegalicia.com*
Fax 93 426 13 07 – 🍴. 🖭 ⓪ ⓿ *VISA*. ✄   HY
Meals - Seafood - a la carte 31,70/38,15.

XX **La Provença,** Provença 242, ✉ 08008, ✆ 93 323 23 67, *Fax 93 451 23 89* – 🍴. 🖭
🌀 ⓪ ⓿ *VISA*   HV
Meals a la carte 17,85/22,66.

XX **Vinya Rosa-Magí,** av. de Sarrià 17, ✉ 08029, ✆ 93 430 00 03, *Fax 93 430 00 41* -
🍴. 🖭 ⓪ ⓿ *VISA*   GX
closed Saturday lunch and Sunday – **Meals** a la carte 28,34/36,96.

XX **Gorría,** Diputació 421, ✉ 08013, ✆ 93 245 11 64, *Fax 93 232 78 57* – 🍴. 🖭 ⓪ ⓿
VISA JCB. ✄   JU
closed Holy Week, August, Sunday and Bank Holidays dinner – **Meals** - Basque rest - a la
carte 32,46/37,26.

XX **La Llotja,** Aribau 55, ✉ 08011, ✆ 93 453 89 58, *Fax 93 453 34 13* – 🍴. 🖭 ⓪ ⓿ *VISA*
🌀 JCB. ✄   HX
closed Sunday dinner – **Meals** - Meat, braised fish and cod specialities - a la carte
21,03/24,03.

XX **Casa Darío,** Consell de Cent 256, ✉ 08011, ✆ 93 453 31 35, *Fax 93 451 33 95* – 🍴.
🖭 ⓪ ⓿ *VISA* JCB. ✄   HX
closed August and Sunday – **Meals** a la carte 29,98/38,77.

XX **Anfiteatro,** av. Litoral (Parc del Port Olímpic), ✉ 08005, ✆ 659 69 53 45,
Fax 93 457 14 19, 🏠 – 🍴. 🖭 ⓿ *VISA*. ✄   East : by Av. d'Icària KX
closed Sunday dinner and Monday – **Meals** a la carte 34,86/44,78.

XX **El Túnel del Port,** Moll de Gregal 12 (Port Olímpic), ✉ 08005, ✆ 93 221 03 21,
Fax 93 221 35 86, ≤, 🏠 – 🍴. 🖭 ⓪ ⓿ *VISA* JCB   East : by Av. d'Icària KX
closed Sunday dinner and Monday – **Meals** a la carte 27,80/35,60.

X **Nervión,** Còrsega 232, ✉ 08036, ✆ 93 218 06 27 – 🍴. 🖭 ⓪ ⓿ *VISA* JCB.
✄   HV
closed Holy Week, August, Sunday and Bank Holidays – **Meals** - Basque rest - a la carte
16,83/45,38.

X **Chicoa,** Aribau 73, ✉ 08036, ✆ 93 453 11 23, « Rustic decor » – 🍴. 🖭 ⓿ *VISA*.
✄   HX
closed August, Sunday, Monday dinner and Bank Holidays – **Meals** a la carte 21,52/29,57.

X **Elche,** Vila i Vilà 71, ✉ 08004, ✆ 93 441 30 89, *Fax 93 329 40 12* – 🍴. 🖭 ⓿ *VISA*.
✄   JY
Meals - Rice dishes - a la carte 17,38/23,61.

X **Cañota,** Lleida 7, ✉ 08004, ✆ 93 325 91 71, *info@riasdegalicia.com*, *Fax 93 426 13 07*,
🏠 – 🍴. 🖭 ⓪ ⓿ *VISA*. ✄   HY
Meals - Braised meat specialities - a la carte 19,21/27,03.

❢/ **Mesón Cinco Jotas,** Rambla de Cataluña 91-93, ✉ 08008, ✆ 93 487 89 42, *meso*
n5j02@airtel.net, *Fax 93 487 91 21*, 🏠 – 🖭 ⓪ ⓿ *VISA*. ✄   HV
Tapa 1,90 **Ración** - Ham specialities - approx. 9.

❢/ **ba-ba-reeba,** passeig de Gràcia 28, ✉ 08007, ✆ 93 301 43 02, *btap01@retemail.es*,
Fax 93 342 55 39, 🏠 – 🍴. 🖭 ⓪ ⓿ *VISA*. ✄   JX
Tapa 1,35 **Ración** approx. 4,96.

❢/ **El Trobador,** Enric Granados 122, ✉ 08008, ✆ 93 416 00 57, *Fax 93 301 35 74* – 🍴.
🖭 ⓪ ⓿ *VISA* JCB. ✄   HV
Tapa 1,95 **Ración** approx. 3,61.

Y/ **Txapela,** passeig de Gràcia 8-10, ✉ 08007, ☎ 93 412 02 89, *Fax 93 412 24 78*, ☂ – ▤ ΑΕ ⓪ ⓦⓞ VISA ᴊᴄʙ JV s
Tapa 1 - Basque tapas.

Y/ **Cervecería Catalana,** Mallorca 236, ✉ 08008, ☎ 93 216 03 68, *jahumada@62onl ine.com, Fax 93 488 17 97,* ☂ – ▤ ΑΕ ⓪ ⓦⓞ VISA HV e
Tapa 1,80 **Ración** approx. 4,80.

North of Av. Diagonal : Via Augusta, Capità Arenas, Ronda General Mitre, Passeig de la Bonanova, Av. de Pedralbes

🏛 Alimara, Berruguete 126, ✉ 08035, ☎ 93 427 00 00, *hotel.alimara@cett.es, Fax 93 427 92 92* – |⌘| ▤ TV ঙ ⇦ – 🅰 25/470   North : by Padilla JU
156 rm.

🏛 **Tryp Presidente,** av. Diagonal 570, ✉ 08021, ☎ 93 200 21 11, *presidente@trypn et.com, Fax 93 209 51 06* – |⌘| ▤ TV – 🅰 25/420. ΑΕ ⓪ ⓦⓞ VISA ᴊᴄʙ. ⌖ GV u
Meals 12,02 – ☲ 12,02 – **155 rm** 175/219.

🏛 **Sansi Pedralbes,** av. Pearson 1-3, ✉ 08034, ☎ 93 206 38 80, *sansihotels@iws.es, Fax 93 206 58 81* – |⌘| ▤ TV ⇦ – 🅰 25/00. ΑΕ ⓪ ⓦⓞ VISA. ⌖ rest
Meals *(closed Saturday and Sunday)* a la carte approx. 28,85 – ☲ 11,85 – **70 rm** 139,74/159,87.   West : by Av. de Pedralbes EV

🏛 **Hesperia Sarrià,** Vergós 20, ✉ 08017, ☎ 93 204 55 51, *hotel@hesperia-sarria.com, Fax 93 204 43 92* – |⌘| ▤ TV ⇦ – 🅰 25/300. ΑΕ ⓪ ⓦⓞ VISA. ⌖ EU c
Meals 13 – ☲ 13 – **134 rm** 168,28/198,33.

🏛 **Córcega,** Còrsega 368, ✉ 08037, ☎ 93 208 19 19, *corcega@hoteles-catalonia.es, Fax 93 208 08 57* – |⌘| ▤ TV ঙ. ΑΕ ⓪ ⓦⓞ VISA ᴊᴄʙ. ⌖ HU x
Meals 12,02 – ☲ 12,03 – **77 rm** 164,67/177,93 – 2 suites.

🏛 **Balmoral** coffee shop only, Via Augusta 5, ✉ 08006, ☎ 93 217 87 00, *info@hot elbalmoral.com, Fax 93 415 14 21* – |⌘| ▤ TV ⇦ – 🅰 25/200. ΑΕ ⓪ ⓦⓞ VISA. ⌖
☲ 11,72 – **106 rm** 123,21/153,26.   HV n

🏛 **Catalonia Suite,** Muntaner 505, ✉ 08022, ☎ 93 212 80 12, *cataloni@hoteles-ca talonia.es, Fax 93 211 23 17* – |⌘| ▤ TV – 🅰 25/90. ΑΕ ⓪ ⓦⓞ VISA ᴊᴄʙ. ⌖ FU a
Meals 15,03 – ☲ 12,03 – **77 suites** 164,67/177,93.

🏢 **Turó de Vilana** coffee shop lunch only, Vilana 7, ✉ 08017, ☎ 93 434 03 63, *hotel @turodevilana.com, Fax 93 418 89 03* – |⌘| ▤ TV ⇦ – 🅰 25/40. ΑΕ ⓪ ⓦⓞ VISA. ⌖
☲ 9,62 – **20 rm** 132,22/150,25.   EU r

🏢 **NH Cóndor,** Via Augusta 1, ✉ 08006, ☎ 93 209 45 11, *nhcondor@nh-hoteles.es, Fax 93 202 27 13* – |⌘| ▤ TV – 🅰 25/50. ΑΕ ⓪ ⓦⓞ VISA. ⌖ GU z
Meals *(closed August, Saturday and Sunday)* 20.10 – ☲ 12 – **66 rm** 122/150 – 12 suites.

🏢 **NH Belagua** coffee shop dinner only, Via Augusta 89, ✉ 08006, ☎ 93 237 39 40, *nhbe lagua@nh-hoteles.es, Fax 93 415 30 62* – |⌘| ▤ TV – 🅰 25/70. ΑΕ ⓪ ⓦⓞ VISA. ⌖
☲ 12 – **72 rm** 159.   GU s

🏢 **St. Gervasi,** Sant Gervasi de Cassoles 26, ✉ 08022, ☎ 93 253 17 40, *stgervasi.booking@h oteles-silken.com, Fax 93 253 17 41* – |⌘| ▤ TV ঙ ⇦ – 🅰 25/50. ΑΕ ⓪ ⓦⓞ VISA. ⌖
Meals 15 – ☲ 9,60 – **51 rm** 103/135.   GU e

🏢 **NH Pedralbes** coffee shop dinner only, Fontcuberta 4, ✉ 08034, ☎ 93 203 71 12, *nhpedralbes@nh-hoteles.es, Fax 93 205 70 65* – |⌘| ▤ TV – 🅰 25. ΑΕ ⓪ ⓦⓞ VISA. ⌖
☲ 11 – **31 rm** 148.   EV b

🏢 **Victoria H. Suites,** Beltrán i Rózpide 7-9, ✉ 08034, ☎ 93 206 99 00, *victoria@ho telvictoriabarcelona.com, Fax 93 280 52 67,* ⌦ – |⌘| ▤ TV ⇦. ΑΕ ⓪ ⓦⓞ VISA. ⌖
Meals *(closed August, Saturday, Sunday and Bank Holidays)* 11,71 – **67 rm** ☲ 151,45/175,49 – 7 suites.   EX z

🏢 **Catalonia Park Putxet,** Putxet 68, ✉ 08023, ☎ 93 212 51 58, *cataloni@hoteles -catalonia.es, Fax 93 418 58 17* – |⌘| ▤ TV ঙ ⇦ – 🅰 25/200. ΑΕ ⓪ ⓦⓞ VISA ᴊᴄʙ. ⌖
Meals 12,02 – ☲ 9,02 – **141 rm** 125,01/144,87.   GU a

🏢 **Covadonga** without rest, av. Diagonal 596, ✉ 08021, ☎ 93 209 55 11, *covadonga @hchotels.com, Fax 93 209 58 33* – |⌘| ▤ TV. ΑΕ ⓪ ⓦⓞ VISA ᴊᴄʙ. ⌖ GV v
☲ 14 – **85 rm** 156/195.

🏢 **Condado** without rest, Aribau 201, ✉ 08021, ☎ 93 200 23 11, *hotelcondado@hote lcondado.es, Fax 93 200 25 86* – |⌘| ▤ TV ঙ. ΑΕ ⓪ ⓦⓞ VISA ᴊᴄʙ. GV g
☲ 9 – **81 rm** 101/127.

🏢 **Catalonia Albéniz** coffee shop dinner only, Aragó 591, ✉ 08026, ☎ 93 265 26 26, *cataloni@hoteles-catalonia.es, Fax 93 265 40 07* – |⌘| ▤ TV ঙ – 🅰 25/40. ΑΕ ⓪ ⓦⓞ VISA ᴊᴄʙ. ⌖   North-East : by Gran Via de les Corts Catalanes HX
☲ 9,02 – **47 rm** 125,01/144,87.

🏠 **Colors** without rest, Campoamor 79, ✉ 08031, ☎ 93 274 99 20, *gruptravi@hotelco lors.com, Fax 93 427 42 20* – |⌘| ▤ TV. ΑΕ ⓪ ⓦⓞ VISA. ⌖   North : by Padilla JU
25 rm ☲ 71,38/96,46.

XXXX **Neichel,** Beltran i Rózpide 1, ⊠ 08034, ℰ 93 203 84 08, *neichel@relaischateaux.con*
ξξξ *Fax 93 205 63 69 –* ≡. ⒶⒺ ① ⓂⒸ 𝗩𝗜𝗦𝗔. ⅏ EX
closed August, Sunday and Monday – **Meals** 51,68 and a la carte 43,86/55,88
Spec. Arroz integral de Pals salteado con corintos, verduritas y gambas de Palamós
jengibre. Lubina rellena con couscous de bogavante, jugo/emulsión de hinojo fresco
aceite de oliva a la trufa. Menú de sabores y aromas del Mediterráneo en degustación

XXXX **Via Veneto,** Ganduxer 10, ⊠ 08021, ℰ 93 200 72 44, *pmonje@adam.es*
ξξ *Fax 93 201 60 95,* « Early 20C style » – ≡. ⒶⒺ ① ⓂⒸ 𝗩𝗜𝗦𝗔. ⅏ FV
closed 1 to 20 August, Saturday lunch and Sunday – **Meals** a la carte 40,15/51,99
Spec. Salmonetes dorados con jugo de verduras, muselina de berenjenas y aceitunas ne
gras. Pato asado en su jugo con cebollitas y tomate relleno de higos. Helado de lech
merengada con tocinillo de cielo y salsa toffee.

XXXX **Jean Luc Figueras,** Santa Teresa 10, ⊠ 08012, ℰ 93 415 28 77, *jlfigueras@ret*
ξξ *mail.es, Fax 93 218 92 62,* « Tasteful decor » – ≡. ⒶⒺ ① ⓂⒸ 𝗩𝗜𝗦𝗔. ⅏ HV
closed 1 to 8 January, Holy Week, 11 to 26 August, Saturday lunch and Sunday – **Meal**
35,76 and a la carte 42,09/67,01
Spec. Tarta fina de butifarra del perol, patatas ratte y trufa (November-June). Canelone
de cigala con provenzal de tomate y olivas negras. Cochinillo confitado con miel de melo
cotón y queso de cabra.

XXXX **Reno,** Tuset 27, ⊠ 08006, ℰ 93 200 91 29, *reno@paradis.es, Fax 93 414 41 14 –* ≡
ⒶⒺ ① ⓂⒸ 𝗩𝗜𝗦𝗔 ⒿⒸⒷ. ⅏ GV
closed Saturday lunch – **Meals** a la carte 33,60/48,09.

XXX **Gaig,** passeig de Maragall 402, ⊠ 08031, ℰ 93 429 10 17, *RTGAIG@teleline.es*
ξξ *Fax 93 429 70 02,* ⇱ – ≡. ⒶⒺ ① ⓂⒸ 𝗩𝗜𝗦𝗔 ⒿⒸⒷ
closed Holy Week, 3 weeks in August, Monday and Bank Holidays dinner – **Meals** a la carte
31,71/45,53 North : by Travessera de Gràcia HU
Spec. Arroz bomba del Delta con pichón y setas de Burdeos. Rape asado a la catalana con
patatas a la brotesca. La innovación de la crema catalana.

XXX **Botafumeiro,** Gran de Gràcia 81, ⊠ 08012, ℰ 93 218 42 30, *info@botafumeiro.es,*
Fax 93 415 58 48 – ≡. ⒶⒺ ① ⓂⒸ 𝗩𝗜𝗦𝗔 ⒿⒸⒷ. ⅏ HU v
closed 3 weeks in August – **Meals** - Seafood - a la carte 35,46/53,49.

XX **El Racó d'en Freixa,** Sant Elíes 22, ⊠ 08006, ℰ 93 209 75 59, *freixa@chi.es,*
ξξ *Fax 93 209 79 18 –* ≡. ⒶⒺ ① ⓂⒸ 𝗩𝗜𝗦𝗔. ⅏ GU h
closed Holy Week, August, Monday and Bank Holidays dinner – **Meals** 50,82 and a la carte
39,70/54,73
Spec. Sopa de perejil con cangrejos de mar y de río con helado de algas. Pichón castellano
con coca de maíz y setas a la pimienta larga (autumn). Líquido, helado y caliente de cho-
colates a las especies.

XX **Celler Can Mateo,** passeig de Sant Joan 149, ⊠ 08037, ℰ 93 457 60 54,
Fax 93 457 60 54 – ≡. ⒶⒺ ① ⓂⒸ 𝗩𝗜𝗦𝗔. ⅏ HU e
closed 7 to 27 August, Saturday and Sunday – **Meals** a la carte 59,31/76,43.

XX **El Trapío,** Esperanza 25, ⊠ 08017, ℰ 93 211 58 17, *Fax 93 417 10 37,* ⇱,
« Terrace » – ≡. ⒶⒺ ① ⓂⒸ 𝗩𝗜𝗦𝗔. ⅏ EU t
closed Saturday lunch and Sunday in July-August and Sunday dinner the rest of the year
– **Meals** a la carte 18,28/26,75.

XX **Can Cortada,** av. de l'Estatut de Catalunya, ⊠ 08035, ℰ 93 427 23 15, *gruptravi*
@cancortada.com, Fax 93 427 02 94, ⇱, « 16C farm » – |≢| ≡ ℙ. ⒶⒺ ① ⓂⒸ 𝗩𝗜𝗦𝗔 ⒿⒸⒷ
Meals a la carte approx. 24,64. North : by Padilla JU

XX **El Asador de Aranda,** av. del Tibidabo 31, ⊠ 08022, ℰ 93 417 01 15,
Fax 93 212 24 82, ⇱, « Former palace » – ≡ ℙ. ⒶⒺ ① ⓂⒸ 𝗩𝗜𝗦𝗔. ⅏
closed Sunday dinner – **Meals** - Roast lamb - a la carte 24,10/31,60.

North-West : by Balmes FU

XX **Roig Robí,** Sèneca 20, ⊠ 08006, ℰ 93 218 92 22, *roigrobi@inicia.es, Fax 93 415 78 42,*
⇱, « Garden terrace » – ≡ ⇩. ⒶⒺ ① ⓂⒸ 𝗩𝗜𝗦𝗔 ⒿⒸⒷ. ⅏ HV c
closed 3 weeks in August, Saturday lunch and Sunday – **Meals** a la carte 35/52.

XX **Tram-Tram,** Major de Sarrià 121, ⊠ 08017, ℰ 93 204 85 18, ⇱ – ≡. ⒶⒺ ⓂⒸ 𝗩𝗜𝗦𝗔.
⅏ EU d
closed 23 to 31 December, Holy Week, 15 days in August, Saturday lunch and Sunday –
Meals a la carte 29,67/45,92.

XX **St. Rémy,** Iradier 12, ⊠ 08017, ℰ 93 418 75 04, *Fax 93 434 04 34 –* ≡. ⒶⒺ ① ⓂⒸ
𝗩𝗜𝗦𝗔 EU n
closed Sunday dinner – **Meals** a la carte 19,42/24,46.

XX **Laurak,** La Granada del Penedès 14-16, ⊠ 08006, ℰ 93 218 71 65, *Fax 93 218 98 67*
– ≡. ⒶⒺ ① ⓂⒸ 𝗩𝗜𝗦𝗔. ⅏ HV e
closed 23 December-2 January, 6 to 27 August and Sunday – **Meals** - Basque rest - a la
carte approx. 35.

XX **Le Quattro Stagioni,** Dr. Roux 37, ✉ 08017, ℘ 93 205 22 79, susana@4stagioni.
com, Fax 93 205 78 65, ☆, « Patio-terrace » – ▤. ᴀᴇ ① ◑◐ ᴠɪsᴀ. ❄   FV c
closed Holy Week, Sunday and Monday lunch (July-August), Sunday dinner and Monday the
rest of the year – **Meals** - Italian rest - a la carte 22,69/30,35.

XX **La Petite Marmite,** Madrazo 68, ✉ 08006, ℘ 93 201 48 79, Fax 93 202 23 43 – ▤
⇌. ᴀᴇ ① ◑◐ ᴠɪsᴀ. ❄   GU f
closed Holy Week, August, Saturday (June-September), Sunday and Bank Holidays – **Meals**
a la carte 19,20/26,50.

X **Vivanda,** Major de Sarrià 134, ✉ 08017, ℘ 93 205 47 17, Fax 93 434 05 48, ☆ – ▤.
⊛ ① ◑◐ ᴠɪsᴀ. ❄   EU a
closed Sunday and Monday lunch – **Meals** a la carte 23,56/30.

X **OT,** Torres 25, ✉ 08012, ℘ 93 284 77 52, olage13@hotmail.com, Fax 93 284 77 52 –
▤. ᴀᴇ ① ◑◐ ᴠɪsᴀ   HU f
closed 24 December-6 January, 15 to 31 August, Saturday lunch, Sunday and Bank Holidays
- **Meals** - Set monthly menu - 36,74

X **L'Oliana,** Santaló 54, ✉ 08021, ℘ 93 201 32 82, Fax 93 414 44 17 – ▤. ᴀᴇ ◑◐ ᴠɪsᴀ.
❄   GV e
closed Sunday dinner – **Meals** a la carte 20,59/32,10.

X **La Venta,** pl. Dr. Andreu, ✉ 08035, ℘ 93 212 64 55, Fax 93 212 51 44, ☆, « Former
cafe » – ▤. ᴀᴇ ① ◑◐ ᴠɪsᴀ   North-West : by Balmes   FU
closed Sunday – **Meals** a la carte 23,89/32,76.

X **Sal i Pebre,** Alfambra 14, ✉ 08034, ℘ 93 205 36 58, Fax 93 205 56 72 – ▤. ᴀᴇ ①
⊛ ◑◐ ᴠɪsᴀ. ᴊᴄʙ. ❄   West : by Pas. de Manuel Girona   EX
Meals a la carte 12,91/18,17.

X **La Taula,** Sant Màrius 8-12, ✉ 08022, ℘ 93 417 28 48, Fax 93 434 01 27 – ▤. ᴀᴇ ①
⊛ ◑◐ ᴠɪsᴀ. ❄   FU u
closed August, Saturday lunch, Sunday and Bank Holidays – **Meals** a la carte 15,62/22,24.

X **La Yaya Amelia,** Sardenya 364, ✉ 08025, ℘ 93 456 45 73 – ▤. ᴀᴇ ① ◑◐ ᴠɪsᴀ
⊛ ᴊᴄʙ   JU n
closed Holy Week, 3 weeks in August and Sunday – **Meals** a la carte 21,13/30,01.

Y/ **José Luis,** av. Diagonal 520, ✉ 08006, ℘ 93 200 83 12, Fax 93 200 83 12, ☆ – ▤.
ᴀᴇ ① ◑◐ ᴠɪsᴀ. ❄   HV s
Tapa 2,10 **Ración** approx. 9,62.

Y/ **Casa Pepe,** pl de la Bonanova 4 ℘ 93 418 00 87, Fax 93 418 95 53 – ▤. ◑◐ ᴠɪsᴀ.
❄   FU n
closed 6 to 27 August and Monday – **Tapa** 7,22 **Ración** approx. 13,83.

Y/ **Casa Pepe,** Balmes 377, ✉ 08022, ℘ 93 417 11 76, Fax 93 418 95 53 – ▤. ᴀᴇ ◑◐ ᴠɪsᴀ.
❄   GU u
closed 13 to 19 August and Monday – **Tapa** 7,22 **Ración** approx. 13,83.

Typical atmosphere :

XX **La Bona Cuina,** Pietat 12, ✉ 08002, ℘ 93 268 23 94, Fax 93 315 08 12 – ▤. ᴀᴇ ①
◑◐ ᴠɪsᴀ. ❄   MX e
Meals a la carte approx. 42,07.

X **Can Culleretes,** Quintana 5, ✉ 08002, ℘ 93 317 64 85, Fax 93 412 59 92, « Typical
rest » – ▤. ◑◐ ᴠɪsᴀ. ᴊᴄʙ. ❄   MY c
closed July, Sunday dinner and Monday – **Meals** a la carte 15/22.

X **Los Caracoles,** Escudellers 14, ✉ 08002, ℘ 93 302 31 85, caracoles@versin.com,
Fax 93 302 07 43, « Typical rest, rustic regional decor » – ▤. ᴀᴇ ① ◑◐ ᴠɪsᴀ ᴊᴄʙ.
❄   MY k
Meals a la carte 21,17/34,01.

Environs

at Esplugues de Llobregat West : 5 km :

XXX **La Masía,** av. Països Catalans 58-60, ✉ 08950 Esplugues de Llobregat, ℘ 93 371 00 09,
lamasia@lamasia-rte.com, Fax 93 372 84 00, ☆, « Terrace under pine trees » – ▤ ℙ.
ᴀᴇ ① ◑◐ ᴠɪsᴀ ᴊᴄʙ. ❄
closed Sunday dinner – **Meals** a la carte 25,50/37,50.

at Sant Just Desvern West : 6 km :

⛫ **Hesperia Sant Just,** Frederic Mompou 1, ✉ 08960 Sant Just Desvern,
℘ 93 473 25 17, hotel@hesperia-santjust.com, Fax 93 473 24 50, ≤, ₤₅ – ⁙ ▤ ᴛᴠ ⇌
– 🔏 25/450. ᴀᴇ ① ◑◐ ᴠɪsᴀ. ❄
Meals 20,83 - **Alambí :** Meals a la carte 30,91/33 – ☲ 11 – **144 rm** 170/201,90,
6 suites.

XX **El Mirador de Sant Just,** av. Indústria 12, ⌧ 08960 Sant Just Desver
℘ 93 499 03 42, elmirador@elmirador.org, Fax 93 499 04 41, ≤, « Hanging in the ch
mney of an old factory » – ▤. 𝔸𝔼 ⓞ ⓜⓞ 𝕍𝕀𝕊𝔸
closed 15 to 31 August and Sunday dinner – **Meals** a la carte 25,36/38,33.

at Sant Joan Despí West : 7 km :

🏨 **Hesperia Sant Joan** coffee shop only, Josep Trueta 2, ⌧ 08970 Sant Joan Desp
℘ 93 477 30 03, hotel@hesperia-santjoansuites.com, Fax 93 477 33 88, ⌘, ⤳, – ⚑ ▤
📺 & ⟺ – 🛗 25/90. 𝔸𝔼 ⓞ ⓜⓞ 𝕍𝕀𝕊𝔸
⊟ 8,41 – **128 rm** 145,44/171,29.

at Sant Cugat del Vallès North-West : 18 km :

🏛 **Novotel Barcelona Sant Cugat,** pl. Xavier Cugat, ⌧ 08190, ℘ 93 589 41 41
h1167@accor-hotels.com, Fax 93 589 30 31, ≤, ㄡ, ⤳ – ⚑ ▤ 📺 & ⟺ 🅿 ·
🛗 25/300. 𝔸𝔼 ⓞ 𝕍𝕀𝕊𝔸 ⋇ rest
Meals 21 – ⊟ 11 – **146 rm** 98/113, 4 suites.

Girona or **Gerona** 17000 Girona ⁴⁴³ G 38. – pop. 70 409 alt. 70.
See : The Old town (Força Vella)★★ – Cathedral★ (nave★★, main altar★, Tresor★★
Beatus★★, Tapestry of the Creation★★★, Cloister★) – Museum of Art★★ : Beam Cruilles★
Púbol Altar★, Sant Miquel of Cruilles alatar★★ – Collegiate Church of Sant Feliu : tomb★
tomb decorated with lion hunt scene★ – Sant Pere of Galligants Monastery★ : Archae
ological Museum (Season'stomb)★ – Moorish Baths★.
Envir. : Pùbol (Castell Gala Dalí House Museum★) East : 16 km by C 255.
🏌 Girona, Sant Julià de Ramis - North : 4 km ℘ 972 17 16 41 Fax 972 17 16 82.
✈ of Girona, by ② : 13 km ℘ 972 18 66 00.
🛈 Rambla de la Llibertat 1 ⌧ 17004 ℘ 972 22 65 75 Fax 972 22 66 12 – R.A.C.C. carret
de Barcelona 22 ⌧ 17002 ℘ 972 22 36 62 Fax 972 22 15 57.
Madrid 708 – Barcelona 97.

XXX **El Celler de Can Roca,** carret. Taialà 40, North-West : 2 km, ⌧ 17007
⛬⛬ ℘ 972 22 21 57, Fax 972 48 52 59 – ▤ 🅿. 𝔸𝔼 ⓞ ⓜⓞ 𝕍𝕀𝕊𝔸 𝕁ℂ𝔹. ⋇
closed 23 December-8 January, 1 to 15 July, Sunday and Monday – **Meals** 45,08 and a
la carte 34,85/47,10
Spec. Tartar de bonito con helado de anchoa y caramelo de aceitunas negras (summer)
Salmonetes con naranja y coliflor. Pies de cerdo con espardenyes, alcachofas y aceite de
picada.

Roses or **Rosas** 17480 Girona ⁴⁴³ F 39. – pop. 10 303 – Seaside resort.
See : City★ – Ciudadela★.
🛈 Av. de Rhode 101 ℘ 972 25 73 31 otroses@ddgi.es Fax 972 15 11 50.
Madrid 763 – Barcelona 153 – Girona/Gerona 56.

at Cala Montjoi South-East : 7 km :

XXX **El Bulli,** ⌧ 17480 apartado 30 Roses, ℘ 972 15 04 57, bulli@elbulli.com,
⛬⛬⛬ Fax 972 15 07 17, ㄡ, « Pleasant rustic villa overlooking a creek » – ▤ 🅿. 𝔸𝔼 ⓞ ⓜⓞ 𝕍𝕀𝕊𝔸. ⋇
April-October – **Meals** (closed Monday and Tuesday except july-September) - dinner only
- 115 and a la carte 73/93
Spec. Raviolis de sepia y coco a la soja y jengibre. Civet de conejo. Espardenyes en agridulce.

Sant Celoni 08470 Barcelona ⁴⁴³ G 37. – pop. 11 937 alt. 152.
Envir. : North-West : Sierra de Montseny★ : itinerary★★ from San Celoni to Santa Fé del
Montseny - Road★ from San Celoni to Tona by Montseny.
Madrid 662 – Barcelona 51 – Girona/Gerona 54.

XXXX **Can Fabes,** Sant Joan 6 ℘ 93 867 28 51, racocanfabes@troc.es, Fax 93 867 38 61,
⛬⛬⛬ « Rustic decor » – ▤ ⟺. 𝔸𝔼 ⓞ ⓜⓞ 𝕍𝕀𝕊𝔸 𝕁ℂ𝔹
closed 28 January-February, 24 June-8 July, Sunday dinner and Monday – **Meals** 107 and
a la carte 78/96
Spec. Langostinos con sofrito y pimienta. Pichón mar y montaña. Festival de chocolate.

Sant Pol de Mar 08395 Barcelona ⁴⁴³ H 37. – pop. 2 383 – Seaside resort.
Madrid 679 – Barcelona 46 – Girona/Gerona 53.

XXX **Sant Pau,** Nou 10 ℘ 93 760 06 62, santpaurest@eresmas.com, Fax 93 760 09 50 – ▤
⛬⛬ 🅿. 𝔸𝔼 ⓞ ⓜⓞ 𝕍𝕀𝕊𝔸. ⋇
closed 6 to 22 May, 4 to 20 November, Sunday dinner, Monday and Thursday lunch – **Meals**
a la carte 55,50/74
Spec. Bacalao confitado, yema rellena, crema de patatas, membrillo y pasas (January-May).
Salmonete relleno de verduras dos salsas. Estudio sobre una manzana reineta al horno, en
texturas y temperaturas (December-April).

ILBAO 48000 🅿 Bizkaia 🄫🄫🄫 C 20. – pop. 372054.

See : Guggenheim Bilbao Museum★★★ DX – Fine Arts Museum★ (Museo de Bellas Artes : Antique Art Collection★★) DYM.

🄸🄸 Laukariz, urb. Monte Berriaga-carret de Munguía, North-East by railway BI 631 FYZ
𝒫 94 674 04 62.

✈ de Bilbao, Sondica, North-East : 11 km by railway BI 631 𝒫 94 486 96 64 – Iberia :
Ercilla 20 ⊠ 48009 𝒫 94 424 19 35 DY.

🚢 Abando 𝒫 94 423 06 17.

⚓ Cía Trasmediterránea, Colón de Larreátegui 30 ⊠ 48009 𝒫 94 423 43 00 Telex 32056 Fax 94 424 74 59 EY.

🛈 paseo del Arenal 1 ⊠ 48005 𝒫 94 479 57 60 bit@ayto.bilbao.net Fax 94 479 57 61 –
R.A.C.V.N. (R.A.C. Vasco Navarro) Rodríguez Arias 59 bis ⊠ 48013 𝒫 94 442 58 08 Fax 94 441 27 12.

Madrid 393 – Barcelona 613 – A Coruña/La Coruña 567 – Lisboa 899 – Donostia-San Sebastián 102 – Santander 103 – Toulouse 449 – València 600 – Zaragoza 305.

Plans on following pages

🏨🏨🏨 **López de Haro**, Obispo Orueta 2, ⊠ 48009, 𝒫 94 423 55 00, lh@hotellopezdeharo
.com, Fax 94 423 45 00 – 🛗 🔲 📺 ⟷ – 🔬 25/40. 🆎 ⓞ ⓞⓞ 𝚅𝙸𝚂𝙰. ❄️ EY r
Club Náutico (closed 15 July-15 August, Saturday lunch and Sunday) **Meals** a la carte
35,74/42,08 – ☖ 10,75 – **49 rm** 169,95/232,65 – 4 suites.

🏨🏨🏨 **Carlton**, pl. de Federico Moyúa 2, ⊠ 48009, 𝒫 94 416 22 00, hcarlton@hcarlton.tsai.es,
Fax 94 416 46 28 – 🛗 🔲 📺 ⟷ – 🔬 25/200. 🆎 ⓞ ⓞⓞ 𝚅𝙸𝚂𝙰 𝙹𝙲𝙱. ❄️ DY x
Meals a la carte 23,81/34,01 – ☖ 13,50 – **141 rm** 134/168 – 7 suites.

🏨🏨🏨 **Indautxu**, pl. Bombero Etxaniz 2, ⊠ 48010, 𝒫 94 421 11 98, reservas@hotelindaut
xu.com, Fax 94 422 13 31 – 🛗 🔲 📺 & ⟷ – 🔬 25/400. 🆎 ⓞ ⓞⓞ 𝚅𝙸𝚂𝙰 𝙹𝙲𝙱.
❄️ DZ b
Meals (see rest. **Etxaniz** below) – ☖ 10,82 – **181 rm** 112,99/138,83 – 3 suites.

🏨🏨🏨 **Ercilla**, Ercilla 37, ⊠ 48011, 𝒫 94 470 57 00, ercilla@hotelercilla.es, Fax 94 443 93 35
– 🛗 🔲 📺 ⟷ – 🔬 25/400. 🆎 ⓞ ⓞⓞ 𝚅𝙸𝚂𝙰. ❄️ rest DY a
Meals (see rest. **Bermeo** below) – **338 rm** ☖ 136,15/178,70 – 8 suites.

🏨🏨🏨 **NH Villa de Bilbao**, Gran Vía de Don Diego López de Haro 87, ⊠ 48011,
𝒫 94 441 60 00, nhbilbao@nh-hoteles.es, Fax 94 441 65 29 – 🛗 🔲 📺 ⟷ – 🔬 25/250.
🆎 ⓞ ⓞⓞ 𝚅𝙸𝚂𝙰 𝙹𝙲𝙱. ❄️ CY n
Meals 21 - **La Pérgola :** Meals a la carte 23,70/28,50 – ☖ 10,80 – **139 rm** 145 – 3 suites.

🏨🏨🏨 **Abando**, Colón de Larreátegui 9, ⊠ 48001, 𝒫 94 423 62 00, habando@habando.tsai.es,
Fax 94 424 55 20 – 🛗 🔲 📺 ⟷ – 🔬 25/150. 🆎 ⓞ ⓞⓞ 𝚅𝙸𝚂𝙰. ❄️ EY b
Meals (closed Sunday and Bank Holidays) a la carte 30,05/39,07 – ☖ 9,62 – **142 rm**
75,13/126,21 – 3 suites.

🏨🏨 **Hesperia Zubialde**, Camino de la Ventosa 34, ⊠ 48013, 𝒫 94 400 81 00, hotel@h
esperia-zubialde.com, Fax 94 400 81 10 – 🛗 🔲 📺 & 🄿 – 🔬 25/300. 🆎 ⓞ ⓞⓞ 𝚅𝙸𝚂𝙰 𝙹𝙲𝙱.
❄️ West : by Juan Antonio Zunzunegui CY
El Botxo : Meals a la carte 27,35/40,57 – ☖ 10,22 – **82 rm** 139,43.

🏨🏨 **Barceló H Avenida**, av. Zumalacárregui 40, ⊠ 48006, 𝒫 94 412 43 00, hotelbcav
enida@barcelovel.com, Fax 94 411 40 17 🛗 🔲 📺 & ⟷ 🄿 – 🔬 25/800. 🆎 ⓞ
ⓞⓞ 𝚅𝙸𝚂𝙰 𝙹𝙲𝙱. ❄️ FZ a
Meals 16,80 – ☖ 10,50 – **140 rm** 60/98 – 3 suites.

🏨🏨 **Barceló H. Nervión**, paseo Campo de Volantín 11, ⊠ 48007, 𝒫 94 445 47 00, hote
lbcnervion@barceloclavel.com, Fax 94 445 56 08 – 🛗 🔲 📺 & ⟷ – 🔬 25/350. 🆎 ⓞ
ⓞⓞ 𝚅𝙸𝚂𝙰 𝙹𝙲𝙱. ❄️ rest EX m
Meals 15 – ☖ 10 – **324 rm** 84/105 – 24 suites.

🏨🏨 **NH de Deusto** coffee shop only except weekends, Francisco Maciá 9, ⊠ 48014,
𝒫 94 476 00 06, hoteldedeusto@teleline.es, Fax 94 476 21 99 – 🛗 🔲 📺 ⟷ –
🔬 25/90. 🆎 ⓞ ⓞⓞ 𝚅𝙸𝚂𝙰. ❄️ CX f
☖ 10 – **70 rm** 142.

🏨🏨 **Tryp Arenal**, Fueros 2, ⊠ 48005, 𝒫 94 415 31 00, adolfo.arribas@solmelia.com,
Fax 94 415 63 95 – 🛗 🔲 📺 – 🔬 25/75. 🆎 ⓞ ⓞⓞ 𝚅𝙸𝚂𝙰. ❄️ EYZ m
Meals 21,04 – ☖ 9,02 – **40 rm** 105,18/133,22.

🏨 **Iturrienea** 🌿 without rest, Santa María 14, ⊠ 48005, 𝒫 94 416 15 00,
Fax 94 415 89 29 – 📺. ⓞ ⓞⓞ 𝚅𝙸𝚂𝙰. ❄️ EZ e
☖ 3 – **21 rm** 52/58.

🏨 **Vista Alegre** without rest, Pablo Picasso 13, ⊠ 48012, 𝒫 94 443 14 50, info@hot
elvistaalegre.com, Fax 94 443 14 54 – 📺 ⟷. ⓞⓞ 𝚅𝙸𝚂𝙰. ❄️ DZ t
☖ 4 – **35 rm** 45,01/60.

🏨 **Zabálburu** without rest, Pedro Martínez Artola 8, ⊠ 48012, 𝒫 94 443 71 00,
Fax 94 410 00 73 – 📺 ⟷. 🆎 ⓞⓞ 𝚅𝙸𝚂𝙰. ❄️ DZ d
☖ 5 – **38 rm** 43/57.

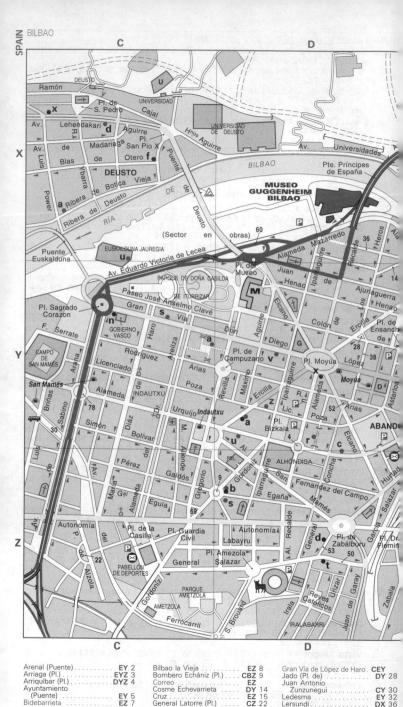

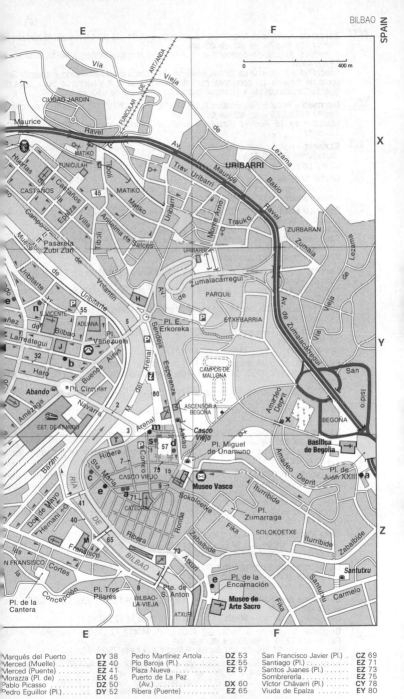

XXXX
ঠ
Zortziko, Alameda de Mazarredo 17, ✉ 48001, ℰ 94 423 97 43, *zortziko@zortziko.e*
Fax 94 423 56 87 – 🍽. 🆎 ① 🆚 *VISA*. ✛   EY
closed 16 August-16 September, Sunday and Monday dinner – **Meals** a la cart
39,67/49,88
Spec. Foie a la plancha en terrina, gelée de vino blanco al anís estrellado y rosas de Siri
Lomo de merluza dos cocciones, puré de guisantes, almejas y harina de espárragos tr
gueros. Caneton asado y su muslo deshuesado a la miel de encinas.

XXXX
Bermeo - *Hotel Ercilla,* Ercilla 37, ✉ 48011, ℰ 94 470 57 00, *ercilla@hotelercilla.e*
Fax 94 443 93 35 – 🍽. 🆎 ① 🆚 *VISA*.   DY
closed 1 to 15 August, Saturday lunch and Sunday dinner – **Meals** a la cart
31,75/42.

XXX
Etxaniz - *Hotel Indautxu,* Gordoniz 15, ✉ 48010, ℰ 94 421 11 98, *reservas@hotel*
dautxu.com, Fax 94 422 13 31 – 🍽. 🆎 ① 🆚 *VISA*. ✛   DZ
closed Holy Week, 1 to 15 August and Sunday – **Meals** a la carte 28,85/40,27.

XXX
Guria, Gran Vía de Don Diego López de Haro 66, ✉ 48011, ℰ 94 441 57 80, *restgu*
ia@euskalnet.net, Fax 94 441 85 64 – 🍽. 🆎 ① 🆚 *VISA*. 🕬. ✛   CY
closed Sunday dinner – **Meals** a la carte 57,81/51,69.

XXX
ঠ
Goizeko Kabi, Particular de Estraunza 4, ✉ 48011, ℰ 94 442 11 29, *goizekokabi@*
qua.com, Fax 94 441 50 04 – 🍽. 🆎 ① 🆚 *VISA*. ✛   CDY
closed 15 July-18 August and Sunday – **Meals** 36,10 and a la carte 37,05/43,30
Spec. Templado de bogavante en crema de calabacín y teja de queso. Lomos de lenguad
con cigalas empanadas y espárragos naturales (April-July). Jamoncito de gallo de corral co
ninfas del bosque y pasta fresca.

XXX
ঠ
Gorrotxa, Alameda Urquijo 30 (arcade), ✉ 48008, ℰ 94 443 49 37, *Fax 94 422 05 3*
– 🍽. 🆎 ① 🆚 *VISA* 🇯🇨🇧. ✛   DY
closed 28 March-1 April, 25 August-16 September and Sunday – **Meals** 38 and a la cart
38/47
Spec. Ensalada de bogavante con verdura templada. Escalopines de rape en salsa Colbert
Pato a la naranja.

XXX
Matxinbenta, Ledesma 26, ✉ 48001, ℰ 94 424 84 95, *Fax 94 423 84 03* – 🍽. 🆎 ①
🆚 *VISA* 🇯🇨🇧. ✛   EY
closed Sunday dinner – **Meals** a la carte 31,85/39,07.

XX
ঠ
Etxanobe, av. de Abandoibarra 4-3°, ✉ 48009, ℰ 94 442 10 71, *etxanobe@abafo*
um.es, Fax 94 442 10 23, 🌿, « Within the Euskalduna palace » – 🛗 🍽. 🆎 ① 🆚 *VISA*
✛   CXY
closed 1 to 20 August, Sunday and Bank Holidays dinner – **Meals** a la carte 35,30/
43,50
Spec. Arroz cremoso con hongos y manitas. Rape asado con sofrito de chipirones y bacon
Pastel fluido de almendra.

XX
Víctor, pl. Nueva 2-1°, ✉ 48005, ℰ 94 415 16 78, *victor@cyl.com, Fax 94 415 06 1*
– 🍽. 🆎 ① 🆚 *VISA* 🇯🇨🇧. ✛   EZ
closed Holy Week, 1 to 15 August, 1 to 15 September and Sunday except May – **Meals**
a la carte 28,23/41,15.

XX
Guggenheim Bilbao, av. de Abandoibarra 2 ℰ 94 423 93 33, *restguggen@bezerc*
ak.euskaltel.es, Fax 94 424 25 60, Modern decor, « Within the Guggenheim Bilba
Museum » – 🍽. 🆎 ① 🆚 *VISA*.   DX
closed 25 December-1 January, Sunday dinner, Monday dinner, Tuesday dinner (July)
August) and Sunday dinner, Monday and Tuesday dinner the rest of the year – **Meals**
la carte 43,56/45,98.

XX
Casa Vasca, av. Lehendakari Aguirre 13, ✉ 48014, ℰ 94 448 39 80, *casavasca@ca*
savasca.com, Fax 94 476 14 87 – 🍽 🚗. 🆎 ① 🆚 *VISA*. ✛   CX
closed Sunday dinner and Bank Holidays dinner – **Meals** a la carte 23,59/30,34.

XX
La Cuchara de Euskalduna, Ribera de Botica Vieja 27, ✉ 48014, ℰ 94 476 15 59
Fax 94 448 01 24 – 🍽. 🆎 🆚 *VISA*. ✛   CX
closed Sunday – **Meals** a la carte 34/44.

XX
El Asador de Aranda, Egaña 27, ✉ 48010, ℰ 94 443 06 64, *Fax 94 443 06 64* – 🍽
🆎 ① 🆚 *VISA*. ✛   DZ
closed Sunday dinner – **Meals** - Roast lamb - a la carte 22,54/30.

XX
Begoña, Virgen de Begoña, ✉ 48006, ℰ 94 412 72 57, *rest-begoña-@jet.es,*
Fax 94 412 72 57 – 🍽. 🆎 ① 🆚 *VISA*. ✛   FY
closed 15 July-14 August and Sunday – **Meals** a la carte 25,25/36,11.

XX
🍴
Rogelio, carret. de Basurto a Castrejana 7, ✉ 48002, ℰ 94 427 30 21, *pegusa@inf*
onegocio.com, Fax 94 427 17 78 – 🍽. 🆎 ① 🆚 *VISA*. ✛
closed Holy Week, 21 July-1 September and Sunday – **Meals** a la carte
24/30.   *West : by Av. Autonomía CZ*

X **Serantes,** Licenciado Poza 16, ✉ 48011, ℘ 94 421 21 29, Fax 94 444 59 79 – 🗐. 📧
① 🐠 *VISA*. 🦐   DY z
closed 1 to 20 September – **Meals** - Seafood - a la carte 35,15/ 38,77.

℘/ **Colmado Ibérico,** Alameda de Urquijo 20, ✉ 48008, ℘ 94 443 60 01, colmadoiber
ico@infonegocio.com, Fax 94 470 30 39 – 🗐. 📧 ① 🐠 *VISA*. 🦐   DYZ c
Tapa 1,02 **Ración** - Ham specialities - approx. 8.

℘/ **El Viandar de Sota,** Gran Vía de Don Diego López de Haro 45, ✉ 48011,
℘ 94 415 25 00, Fax 94 415 25 00 – 🗐. 🐠 *VISA*. 🦐   DY v
Tapa 1,20 **Ración** approx. 12.

℘/ **Gatz,** Santa María 10, ✉ 48005, ℘ 94 415 48 61 – 🗐. 🦐   EZ c
closed 16 to 30 September and Sunday dinner – **Tapa** 1,10 **Ración** approx. 5,50.

℘/ **Xukela,** El Perro 2, ✉ 48005, ℘ 94 415 97 72 – 🗐. 🐠 *VISA*. 🦐   EZ a
Tapa 1,20 **Ración** - Cheeses and patés - approx. 6.

℘/ **Víctor Montes,** pl. Nueva 8, ✉ 48005, ℘ 94 415 70 67, victormontes.sl@terra.es,
Fax 94 415 95 10, 🍽 – 🗐. 📧 ① 🐠 *VISA*. 🦐   EZ d
closed Holy Week, 1 to 15 August and Sunday dinner – **Tapa** 1,50.

℘/ **Rio-Oja,** El Perro 4, ✉ 48005, ℘ 94 415 08 71 – 🗐. ① 🐠 *VISA*. 🦐   EZ a
closed Holy Week, 24 days in September and Monday – **Ración** approx. 5,90.

Donostia-San Sebastián 20000 🅿 Gipuzkoa 🟦🟦🟦 C 24. – pop. 176 019 – Seaside resort.
See : Location and bay★★★ – Monte Igueldo ⩽★★★ – Monte Urgull ⩽★★ – Aquarium-
Palacio del Mar★.

Envir. : Monte Ulía ⩽★ North-East : 7 km by N I.

🏌 of San Sebastián Jaizkibel, East : 14 km by N I ℘ 943 61 68 45.

✈ of San Sebastián, Fuenterrabía, North-East : 20 km ℘ 943 66 85 00 – Iberia : Ben-
goetxea 3 ✉ 20004 ℘ 943 42 35 86 and airport ℘ 943 66 85 19.

🅱 Erregina Erregentearen 8 ✉ 20003 ℘ 943 48 11 66 cat@donostia.org Fax
943 48 11 72 – R.A.C.V.N. (R.A.C. Vasco Navarro) Foruen pasealekua 4 ✉ 20005
℘ 943 43 08 00 Fax 943 42 91 50.

Madrid 453 – Bayonne 54 – Bilbao 102 – Iruña/Pamplona 79 – Vitoria-Gasteiz 95.

🏨🏨🏨 **María Cristina,** Okendo 1, ✉ 20004, ℘ 943 43 76 00, hmc@westin.com,
Fax 943 43 76 76, ⩽ – 🛗 🗐 📺 – 🛎 25/300. 📧 ① 🐠 *VISA* *JCB*. 🦐 rest
Easo : Meals a la carte 31,26/49,28 – ☲ 19,23 – **108 rm** 337,17/509,06,
28 suites.

XXXX **Arzak,** alto de Miracruz 21, ✉ 20015, ℘ 943 27 84 65, arzak@jet.es, Fax 943 27 27 53
❀❀❀ – 🗐 🅿. 📧 ① 🐠 *VISA*. 🦐
closed 16 June-4 July, 3 to 27 November, Sunday dinner and Monday – **Meals** 75,10 and
a la carte 67,30/79,92
Spec. Acordeón de patata con marisco. Lenguado con gelatina inesperada e infusión de
cocido. Pan de chocolate con helado de levadura y cáscara de mango.

XXXX **Akelaŕe,** paseo del Padre Orcolaga 56 (barrio de Igueldo) : 7,5 km, ✉ 20008,
❀❀ ℘ 943 31 12 09, restaurante@akelarre.net, Fax 943 21 92 68, « Stunning hillside location
overlooking the sea » – 🗐 🅿. 📧 ① 🐠 *VISA*. 🦐
closed February, 1 to 15 October, Sunday dinner and Monday except Bank Holiday weekends – **Meals** 72,12 and a la carte 48,98/77,53
Spec. Irlandés de lentejas y sisas con germen y ficoïde glacial. Lenguado a la parrilla
con cítricos y espárragos frescos. Nueces, limón y canela en crujiente equi-
librio.

℘/ **Ganbara,** San Jerónimo 21, ✉ 20003, ℘ 943 42 25 75, Fax 943 42 25 75 – 🗐. 📧 ①
🐠 *VISA*. 🦐
closed 15 to 30 June, 15 to 30 November, Sunday dinner in winter, Tuesday lunch and
Monday – **Tapa** 1,35 **Ración** approx. 9,02.

℘/ **Martínez,** Abutzuaren 31-13, ✉ 20003, ℘ 943 42 49 65 – 🗐. 🦐
closed 16 to 31 January, June, Thursday and Friday lunch – **Tapa** 1,35 **Ración**
approx. 7,81.

℘/ **Txepetxa,** Arrandegui 5, ✉ 20003, ℘ 943 42 22 27, txepetxa1@clientes.euskaltel.es
– 🗐. 🦐
closed 15 days in June, 15 days in October, Monday and Tuesday lunch in August – **Tapa**
1,50 **Ración** approx. 5,41.

℘/ **Tamboril,** Arrandegui 2, ✉ 20003, ℘ 943 42 35 07, tamboril@teleline.es,
Fax 943 43 17 63, 🍽 – 🗐. 🐠 *VISA*. 🦐
closed 1 to 15 March and 1 to 21 November – **Tapa** 1,35 **Ración** approx. 7.

🍴 **Aloña Berri,** Bermingham 24 (Gros), ✉ 20001, ✆ 943 29 08 18 – 🍽. **⓪ ⓥⓢ**. ⚡
closed 15 days in Holy Week, 1 to 15 November, Sunday dinner and Monday – **Tapa**
1,60 **Ración** approx. 6.

🍴 **Bergara,** General Arteche 8 (Gros), ✉ 20002, ✆ 943 27 50 26, *tapasbarbergar.*
@ eresmas.com – 🍽
closed October – **Tapa** 1,50 **Ración** approx. 5,50.

Lasarte-Oria 20160 Gipuzkoa ⓿⓿⓿ C 23. – pop. 18 165 alt. 42.
Madrid 491 – Bilbao 98 – Donostia-San Sebastián 8.

🏮🏮🏮🏮 **Martín Berasategui,** Loidi 4 ✆ 943 36 64 71, *martin@ martinberasategui.com*
🕸🕸🕸 Fax 943 36 61 07, ≼, 🌳 – 🍽 **Ⓟ. ⒶⒺ ⓪ ⓪ⓥ ⓥⓢ**. ⚡
closed 15 December-15 January, Saturday lunch, Sunday dinner, Monday and Tuesday –
Meals 70,92 and a la carte 51,02/59,95
Spec. Gelatina caliente de frutos de mar con sopa de anís y sorbete de hinojo. Taco de
foie gras asado con crema de rúcula y vinagreta de su jugo de cocción. La sorpresa de
chocolate y canela con granizado de vino tinto.

Oiartzun or **Oyarzun** 20180 Gipuzkoa ⓿⓿⓿ C 24. – pop. 8 393 alt. 81.
Madrid 481 – Bilbao 113 – Donostia-San Sebastián 11.

🏮🏮🏮 **Zuberoa,** barrio Iturriotz 8 ✆ 943 49 12 28, Fax 943 49 26 79, 🌳, « Stylish traditional
🕸🕸 restaurant in a 15C manor house with pleasant terrace and ≼ » – 🍽 **Ⓟ. ⒶⒺ ⓪ ⓪ⓥ ⓥⓢ**
⚡
closed 1 to 15 January, 1 to 15 April, 15 October-1 November, Sunday and Monday – **Meals**
72,12 and a la carte 44,18/60,71
Spec. Yema de huevo escalfada sobre crema de coliflor, gelatina de caviar de trucha y
coral de cigalas. Bacalao confitado con porrusalda glaseada y aceites de perejil y pimentón.
Raviolis de poularda y trufa al Royal de foie.

When driving through towns
use the plans in the MICHELIN Red Guide.

Features indicated include :
*   throughroutes and bypasses,*
*   traffic junctions and major squares,*
*   new streets, car parks, pedestrian streets...*
All this information is revised annually.

MÁLAGA 29000 ⓿⓿⓿ V 16. – pop. 534 683 – Seaside resort.
See : Gibralfaro : ≼★★ DY – Alcazaba★★ ≼★ (Archaeological Museum★) DY – Cathedral★
CZ – El Sagrario Church (marienista altarpiece★) CY – Sanctuary of the Virgin of Victory★
North : by Victoria st. EY.
Envir. : Finca de la Concepción★ North : 7 km – The Retiro★ West : 15 km by Av. de
Andalucía CZ.
🛫 Málaga, South-West : 9 km ✆ 95 237 66 77 Fax 95 237 66 12 – ⛳ El Candado, East :
5 km ✆ 95 229 93 40 Fax 95 229 48 12.
✈ Málaga, South-West : 9 km ✆ 95 204 88 44 – Iberia : Molina Larios 13, ✉ 29015,
✆ 95 213 61 48 CY.
🚗 ✆ 95 212 82 25.
⛴. to Melilla : Cía Trasmediterránea, Estación Marítima, Local E-1 ✉ 29016 CZ,
✆ 95 206 12 06 Fax 95 206 12 21.
🛈 Pasaje de Chinitas 4 ✉ 29015 ✆ 95 221 34 45 otmalaga@turismo-andaluz.com Fax
95 222 94 21 and av. Cervantes 1 ✉ 29016 ✆ 95 260 44 10 info@malagaturismo.com
Fax 95 221 41 20 – R.A.C.E. Córdoba 17 (bajo) ✉ 29001 ✆ 95 222 98 36 Fax 95 260 83 83.
Madrid 494 – Algeciras 133 – Córdoba 175 – Sevilla 217 – València 651.

Plans on following pages

🏨🏨 **Parador de Málaga-Gibralfaro** ⚜, Castillo de Gibralfaro, ✉ 29016,
✆ 95 222 19 02, Fax 95 222 19 04, « Magnificent setting with ≼ Málaga and sea », 🏊
– 📶 🍽 📺 ৬ Ⓟ – 🅰 25/60. ⒶⒺ ⓪ ⓪ⓥ ⓥⓢ ⒿⒸⒷ. ⚡   DY a
Meals 24,04 – 🍴 8,71 – **38 rm** 93,18/116,48.

🏨🏨 **AC Málaga Palacio,** Cortina del Muelle 1, ✉ 29015, ✆ 95 221 51 85, *malaga@ac*
-hoteles.com, Fax 95 222 51 00, ≼, 🏊 – 📶 🍽 📺 ৬ – 🅰 25/60. ⒶⒺ ⓪ ⓪ⓥ
ⓥⓢ. ⚡   DZ n
Meals 22,23 – 🍴 10,81 – **197 rm** 158,19 – 17 suites.

🏨 **NH Málaga** ⚓, av. Río Guadalmedina, ✉ 29007, ✆ 95 207 13 23, *nhmalaga@nhho teles.es*, Fax *95 239 38 62*, 🛗 – ≣ 📺 ⚓ – ⚐ 25/900. 🆎 ① 🐷 💳
🍴 rest   CZ y
Meals 36,06 – ⊑ 10,22 – **129 rm** 150,25 – 4 suites.

🏨 **Tryp Alameda** without rest, av. de la Aurora (C.C. Larios), ✉ 29002, ✆ 95 236 80 20, *alameda@trypnet.com*, Fax *95 236 81 28* – ≣ 📺. 🆎 ① 🐷 💳. 🍴
⊑ 10,22 – **130 rm** 129,37/160,92 – 2 suites.   West : by Av. de Andalucía CZ

🏨 **Larios**, Marqués de Larios 2, ✉ 29005, ✆ 95 222 22 00, *info@hotel-larios.com*,
Fax *95 222 24 07* – ≣ 📺 – ⚐ 25/150. 🆎 ① 🐷 💳. 🍴   DY s
Meals 25,84 – ⊑ 9,01 – **40 rm** 150,25/360,60.

🏨 **Don Curro** coffee shop only, Sancha de Lara 7, ✉ 29015, ✆ 95 222 72 00, *hoteldo ncurro@infonegocio.com*, Fax *95 221 59 46* – ≣ 📺 – ⚐ 25/60. 🆎 ① 🐷 💳 💳
⊑ 4,50 – **118 rm** 65/95.   DZ e

🏨 **Los Naranjos** without rest, paseo de Sancha 35, ✉ 29016, ✆ 95 222 43 19, *reser @hotel-losnaranjos.com*, Fax *95 222 59 75* – 🛗 ≣ 📺 ⚓. 🆎 ① 🐷
💳. 🍴   East : by Paseo de Reding FY
⊑ 6,01 – **40 rm** 67,43/97,36 – 1 suite.

🏨 **California** without rest, paseo de Sancha 17, ✉ 29016, ✆ 95 221 51 64, *hcalifornia @spa.es*, Fax *95 222 68 86* – 🛗 ≣ 📺. 🆎 ① 🐷 💳. 🍴
⊑ 4,80 – **25 rm** 66,11.   East : by Paseo de Reding FY

🏨 **Don Paco** without rest, no ⊑, Salitre 53, ✉ 29002, ✆ 95 231 90 08, *recepcion@h otel-donpaco.com*, Fax *95 231 90 62* – 🛗 ≣ 📺. 🐷 💳. 🍴
25 rm 48,20/60,25.   South-West : by Av. Manuel Agustín Heredia DZ

XXX **Café de París**, Vélez Málaga 8, ✉ 29016, ✆ 95 222 50 43, *cafedeparis@mixmail.com*,
Fax *95 260 38 64* – ≣ ⚓. 🆎 ① 🐷 💳 💳. 🍴   FZ x
closed Holy Week, 15 to 31 July, Sunday and Monday dinner – Meals 41,92 and a la carte 25,84/38,92
Spec. Carpaccio de langostinos con pie de cerdo y curry. Lubina con maíz y verduras al dente. Coulant de avellanas fluido.

XX **Adolfo**, paseo Marítimo Pablo Ruiz Picasso 12, ✉ 29016, ✆ 95 260 19 14,
Fax *95 260 19 14* – ≣. 🆎 ① 🐷 💳 💳. 🍴   East:by Paseo Cánovas del Castillo FZ
closed Sunday – Meals a la carte 24,62/29,94.

XX **La Ménsula**, Maestranza 18, ✉ 29016, ✆ 95 222 50 30 – ≣. 🆎 ①
💳. 🍴   FZ b
closed 16 to 31 July and Sunday – Meals a la carte approx. 30,05.

XX **Doña Pepa**, Vélez Málaga 6, ✉ 29016, ✆ 95 260 34 89, *donapepa@infhosteleria.com*,
Fax *95 260 34 89* – ≣. 🆎 🐷 💳. 🍴   FZ a
closed September and Sunday – Meals a la carte 21/32.

X **Figón de Juan**, pasaje Esperanto 1, ✉ 29007, ✆ 95 228 75 47 – ≣. 🆎 🐷
💳. 🍴   West : by Av. de Andalucía CZ
closed August and Sunday – Meals a la carte 18,03/25,22.

🍴 **El Trillo**, Don Juan Díaz 4, ✉ 29015, ✆ 95 260 39 20, Fax *952 60 23 82*, 🍽 – ≣. 🆎
💳. 🍴   DZ r
closed Sunday – Tapa 1,80 Ración approx. 4,81

🍴 **La Posada**, Granada 33, ✉ 29015, ✆ 95 221 70 69, « Typical decor » – ≣. 🆎 🐷 💳.
🍴   DY n
Tapa 1,20 Ración - Meat specialities - approx. 4,21.

🍴 **La Casa del Piyayo**, Granada 36, ✉ 29015, ✆ 95 222 00 96, « In the style of a fishing boat » – ≣. 🆎 🐷 💳. 🍴   DY d
closed Monday – Tapa 1,20 Ración - Seafood - approx. 4,81.

at Club de Campo South-West : 9 km :

🏨 **Parador de Málaga del Golf**, at the golf course - 5 km, ✉ 29080 apartado 324 Málaga, ✆ 95 238 12 55, *malaga@parador.es*, Fax *95 238 89 63*, ≤, 🍽, « Overlooking the golf course », 🏊, 🍽, 🏌 – ≣ 📺 ⚓ 🅿 – ⚐ 25/70. 🆎 ① 🐷
💳. 🍴
Meals 22,84 – ⊑ 8,71 – **56 rm** 85,82/107,28 – 4 suites.

at Urbanización Mijas Golf South-West : 30 km by N 340 :

🏨 **Byblos Andaluz** ⚓, ✉ 29640, ✆ 95 246 02 50, *byblos@spa.es*, Fax *95 247 67 83*, ≤ *golf course and mountains*, 🍽, Thalassotherapy facilities, « Tasteful Andalusian style situated between two golf courses », 🛁, 🏊, 🏊, ⚓, 🍽, 🏌 🏌 – 🛗 ≣ 📺 🅿 – ⚐ 20/170.
🆎 ① 🐷 💳 💳. 🍴 rest
Le Nailhac (dinner only, closed January and Wednesday) Meals a la carte 49,88/54,69 -
Byblos Andaluz (dinner only) Meals a la carte 37,26/42,67 – ⊑ 18 – **108 rm** 256/380, 36 suites.

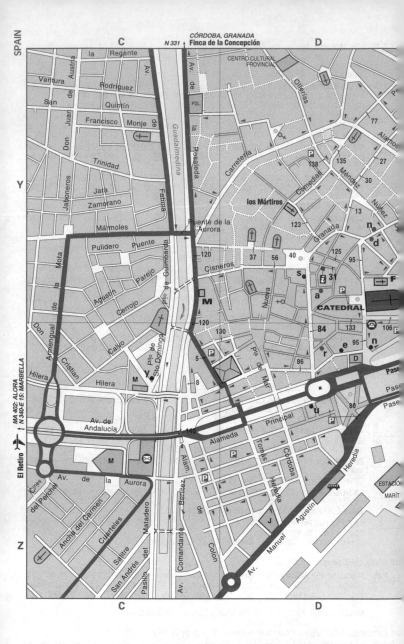

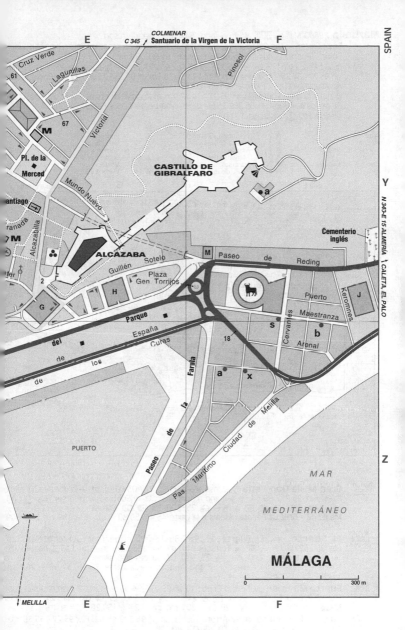

SPAIN

MÁLAGA

Marbella 29600 Málaga 446 W 15. – pop. 84 410 – Seaside resort.

See : City★★ – The Old town★ – Naranjos Square★ – Contemporary Spain Print Museum★
Envir. : Puerto Banús (Pleasure harbour★★) by ② : 8 km.

Río Real, by ① : 5 km 95 276 57 33 Fax 95 277 21 40 – Los Naranjos, by ② : 7 km
95 281 24 28 – Aloha, urb. Aloha by ② : 8 km 95 281 23 88 – Las Brisas, Nuev.
Andalucía by ② : 11 km, 95 281 08 75.

Glorieta de la Fontanilla 95 277 14 42 turismomarbella@ctv.es Fax 95 277 94 57 and
Pl. de los Naranjos 95 282 35 50 turismomarbella@ctv.es Fax 95 277 36 21.
Madrid 602 ① – Málaga 59 ①

Alameda	A 2	Fontanilla (Glorieta)	A 10	Pedraza		A 17
Ancha	A 3	Huerta Chica	A 12	Portada		B 18
Carlos Mackintosch	A 4	Mar (Av. del)	A 14	Ramón y Cajal (Av.)		AB 20
Chorrón	A 5	Marítimo (Pas.)	A 15	Santo Cristo (Pl.)		A 21
Enrique del Castillo	AB 8	Naranjos		Valdés		A 24
Estación	A 9	(Pl. de los)	A 16	Victoria (Pl.)		A 26

N 340-E 15 COIN

Gran Meliá Don Pepe, José Meliá 95 277 03 00, gran.melia.don.pepe@solme
lia.es, Fax 95 277 99 54, ≤ sea and mountains, « Subtropical plants », heated,
– Meals 44 - Grill La Farola : Meals a la carte 45,44/59,80 – 18 - 199 rm 275/309,
3 suites. by ②

El Fuerte, av. El Fuerte 95 286 15 00, elfuerte@fuertehoteles.com,
Fax 95 282 44 11, ≤, « Terraces with garden and palm trees », heated,
– Meals - dinner only except July and August - a la carte 28,55/37,56 – 261 rm
102,17/150,25 – 2 suites. B e

Fuerte Miramar, av. Severo Ochoa 10 95 276 84 00, elfuerte@fuertehoteles.com,
Fax 95 276 84 14, – Meals - buffet dinner only - 28,25 – 201 rm 102,17/150,25 – 25 suites. B v

Sultán Club Marbella, av. Arturo Rubinstein 95 277 15 62, Fax 95 277 55 58,
– Monarque : Meals a la carte 30/42 – 9 – 76 suites 213/258. by ②

Marbella Inn coffee shop only, Jacinto Benavente - bloque 6 95 282 54 87, marb
ella@xpress.es, Fax 95 282 54 87, heated – 4 – 24 rm 90 – 32 suites. A x

Lima without rest, av. Antonio Belón 2 95 277 05 00, Fax 95 286 30 91 –
4,50 – 64 rm 69,55/86,94. A h

576

XXX **Santiago**, av. Duque de Ahumada 5 🖉 95 277 43 39, *reservas@restaurantesantiago. com*, Fax 95 282 45 03, � – ▤. ᴬᴱ ① ᴹˢ ᴠᴵˢᴬ ᴶᶜᴮ. ✸
A b
closed November – **Meals** - Seafood - a la carte 27,65/33,06.

XX **Cenicienta**, av. Cánovas del Castillo 52 (bypass) 🖉 95 277 43 18, � – ᴬᴱ ①
ᴹˢ ᴠᴵˢᴬ
by ②
closed 15 January-15 February and Sunday – **Meals** - dinner only - a la carte
34/40.

X **El Balcón de la Virgen**, Remedios 2 🖉 95 277 60 92, Fax 95 277 60 92, �, « 16C
building » – ᴬᴱ ① ᴹˢ ᴠᴵˢᴬ
A u
closed 15 December-January and Sunday – **Meals** - dinner only - a la carte approx. 21,55.

y the motorway to Málaga ① :

🏨🏨🏨 **Don Carlos** 🌊, exit Elviria : 10 km, ⊠ 29600, 🖉 95 283 11 40, *resa@hotel-doncar los.com*, Fax 95 283 34 29, ≼, �, « Extensive gardens », Ⅼ₅, ⅀ heated, ✸ – ⧚ ▤ ᴛᴠ ₼ ₧ – 🏛 25/1200. ᴬᴱ ① ᴹˢ ᴠᴵˢᴬ. ✸
Los Naranjos : Meals a la carte 33,36/48,68 – ☷ 15,62 – **225 rm** 228,38/267,45,
14 suites.

🏨🏨🏨 **Le Méridien Los Monteros** 🌊, 5,5 km, ⊠ 29600, 🖉 95 277 17 00, *hotel@mon teros.com*, Fax 95 277 08 46, ≼, �, « Subtropical garden with ⅀ », 🐎, ✸ – ⧚ ▤ ᴛᴠ ₼ ₧ – 🏛 25/400. ᴬᴱ ① ᴹˢ ᴠᴵˢᴬ. ✸
El Corzo (dinner only) **Meals** a la carte 42,28/60,52 – **34 rm** ☷ 222,37/296,59 –
134 suites.

🏨🏨 **Artola** without rest, 12,5 km, ⊠ 29600, 🖉 95 283 13 90, *hotelartola@inves.es*, Fax 95 283 04 50, ≼, « On a golf course », ⅀, 🐎, Ⅰ₅ – ⧚ ᴛᴠ ⇦ ₧. ᴬᴱ ᴹˢ ᴠᴵˢᴬ
29 rm ☷ 73,85/113,74 – 2 suites.

XXX **La Hacienda**, exit Las Chapas : 11,5 km and detour 1,5 km, ⊠ 29600, 🖉 95 283 12 67, *lahacienda@vnet.es*, Fax 95 283 33 28, �, « Rustic decor, patio-terrace » – ₧. ᴬᴱ ① ᴹˢ ᴠᴵˢᴬ. ✸
closed 15 November-20 December, Monday (except August) and Tuesday (except July-August) – **Meals** - dinner only in July and August - a la carte 37,56/48,39.

XX **Le Chêne Liège**, exit Elviria - La Mairena : 10 km and detour 5,5 km, ⊠ 29600, 🖉 95 285 20 50, *mairena@mairena.com*, Fax 95 283 62 23, � – ▤. ᴬᴱ ① ᴹˢ ᴠᴵˢᴬ
Meals - dinner only - a la carte 29,45/37,26.

XX **Las Banderas**, urb. El Lido-Las Chapas : 9,5 km and detour 0,5 km, ⊠ 29600, 🖉 95 283 18 19, � – ᴹˢ ᴠᴵˢᴬ. ✸
closed Monday – **Meals** a la carte 22,83/29,46.

y the motorway to Cádiz ② :

🏨🏨🏨 **Marbella Club** 🌊, Bulevar Príncipe Alfonso von Hohenlohe : 3 km, ⊠ 29600, 🖉 95 282 22 11, *hotel@marbellaclub.com*, Fax 95 282 98 84, �, Ⅰ₅, ⅀ heated, 🐎, 🌇, ✸ – ▤ ᴛᴠ ₧ – 🏛 25/180. ᴬᴱ ① ᴹˢ ᴠᴵˢᴬ. ✸
Meals a la carte 51,70/64,92 – ☷ 20,58 – **84 rm** 353,70/508,04 – 48 suites.

🏨🏨🏨 **Puente Romano** 🌊, 3,5 km, ⊠ 29600, 🖉 95 282 09 00, *hotel@puenteromano.com*, Fax 95 277 57 66, �, « Elegant Andalusian complex in attractive gardens », Ⅰ₅, ⅀ heated, 🐎, ✸ – ⧚ ▤ ᴛᴠ ₧ – 🏛 25/170. ᴬᴱ ① ᴹˢ ᴠᴵˢᴬ ᴶᶜᴮ. ✸ rest
Roberto : **Meals** a la carte 34,86/49,88 – ☷ 18,03 – **145 rm** 270,46/342,58,
89 suites.

🏨🏨🏨 **Coral Beach**, 5 km, ⊠ 29600, 🖉 95 282 45 00, *reservas@hotelcoralbeach.com*, Fax 95 282 62 57, Ⅰ₅, ⅀, 🐎 – ⧚ ▤ ᴛᴠ ₼ ⇦ ₧ – 🏛 25/200. ᴬᴱ ① ᴹˢ ᴠᴵˢᴬ. ✸
15 March-October - *Florencia* (dinner only) **Meals** a la carte 27,05/39,67 – ☷ 13,82 –
148 rm 198,33/225,38 – 22 suites.

🏨🏨 **Riu Rincón Andaluz** 🌊, 8 km, ⊠ 29660 Nueva Andalucía, 🖉 95 281 15 17, Fax 95 281 41 80, « In the style of an Andalusian village », ⅀ heated, 🐎, 🌇 – ▤ ᴛᴠ ₧ – 🏛 25/100. ᴬᴱ ① ᴹˢ ᴠᴵˢᴬ. ✸
Meals 18,03 – **227 rm** ☷ 157,80/197,25.

🏨🏨 **Meliá Marbella Dinamar**, 6 km, ⊠ 29660 Nueva Andalucía, 🖉 95 281 05 00, *dina mar@trypnet.com*, Fax 95 281 23 46, �, ⧉, ✸ – ⧚ ▤ ᴛᴠ ₧ – 🏛 25/150. ᴬᴱ ① ᴹˢ ᴠᴵˢᴬ. ✸
Meals 30,35 – ☷ 13,52 – **116 rm** 165,28/206,45.

XXXX **La Meridiana**, camino de la Cruz : 3,5 km, ⊠ 29600, 🖉 95 277 61 90, Fax 95 282 60 24, ≼, �, « Garden terrace » – ▤ ₧. ᴬᴱ ① ᴹˢ ᴠᴵˢᴬ
closed 9 January-10 February – **Meals** - dinner only - a la carte 43,56/50,48.

XXX **Villa Tiberio**, 2,5 km, ✉ 29600, 🖉 95 277 17 99, Fax 95 282 47 72, 斎, « Garde
terrace » – 🗜. 🗚 ① ⯁🅾 VISA. ✺
closed Sunday – **Meals** - dinner only - a la carte approx. 39,70.

XXX **El Portalón**, 3 km, ✉ 29600, 🖉 95 282 78 80, Fax 95 277 71 04 – 🍽 🗜. 🗚 ① ◍
VISA. ✺
closed Sunday – **Meals** a la carte approx. 52,90.

at Puerto Banús *West : 8 km :*

XXX **Cipriano**, av. Playas del Duque - edificio Sevilla, ✉ 29660 Nueva Andalucí
🖉 95 281 10 77, *rtecipriano@infonegocio.com*, Fax 95 281 10 77, 斎 – 🍽 🗜. 🗚 ① ◍
VISA. ✺
closed 7 January-7 February – **Meals** a la carte 34,26/40,27.

SEVILLE (SEVILLA) 41000 ℙ 𝟒𝟒𝟔 T 11 y 12. – pop. 704 857 alt. 12.

See : *La Giralda*★★★ (✳★★) BX – *Cathedral*★★★ (*Capilla Mayor altarpiece*★★★, *Capil
Real*★★) BX – *Real Alcázar*★★★ BXY (*Admiral Apartment : Virgin of the Mareante
altarpiece*★ ; *Pedro el Cruel Palace*★★★ : *Ambassadors room vault*★★★ ; *Carlos V Palace
tapestries*★★, *gardens*★ : *grutesco gallery*★) – *Santa Cruz Quarter*★★★ BCX (*Venerable
Hospital*★) – *Fine Arts Museum*★★ (*room V*★★★, *room X*★★) AV – *Pilate's House*★
(*Azulejos*★★, *staircase*★★ : *dome*★) CX – *Maria Luisa Park*★★ (*España Square*★, *Archae
logical Museum*★ : *Carambolo tresor*★, *roman collection*★) *South : by Paseo de las Delicia
BY.

Other curiosities : *Charity Hospital*★ (*church*★★) BY - *Santa Paula Convent*★ CV (*front
church*) – *Salvador Church*★ BX (*baroque altarpieces*★, *Lebrija Countess Palace*★ BV)
San José Chappel★ BX – *Town Hall (Ayuntamiento) : east front*★ BX – *Santa María la Blanc
Church*★ CX - *Isla Mágica*★ *North : by Torneo AV.*

🔟 *Pineda, South-East : 3 km* 🖉 95 461 14 00.

⍿ *Sevilla-San Pablo, North-East : 14 km* 🖉 95 444 90 00 – *Iberia : Av. de la Buhaira
(edificio Cecofar)* ✉ 41018, 🖉 95 498 82 08. – 🚂 *Santa Justa* 🖉 902 240 202.

🄱 *Av. de la Constitución 21-B* ✉ 41001 🖉 95 422 14 04 *otsevilla@andalucia.org Fa
95 422 97 53 and Paseo de las Delicias 9* ✉ 41012 🖉 95 423 44 65 – *R.A.C.E. Av. Eduard
Dato 22,* ✉ 41018 🖉 95 463 13 50, Fax 95 465 96 04.

Madrid 531 – A Coruña/La Coruña 917 – Lisboa 410 – Málaga 211 – València 659.

Plans on following pages

🅷🅾🅷🅷 **Alfonso XIII**, San Fernando 2, ✉ 41004, 🖉 95 491 70 00, Fax 95 491 70 99, 斎
« Magnificent Andalusian building », ⚒, ⫽ – 🛗 🍽 📺 ⟺ – 🔏 25/500. 🗚 ① ◍ VIS.
JCB. ✺
BY ⓒ
San Fernando : **Meals** a la carte 39,66/55,30 – 🖵 19,83 – **127 rm** 300,50/390,65
19 suites.

🅷🅰🅰🅷 **Barceló G.H. Renacimiento** ⑄, Isla de la Cartuja, ✉ 41092, 🖉 95 446 22 22, *ren
cimiento@barcelo.com*, Fax 95 446 04 28, ⚒ – 🛗 🍽 📺 ⟺ – 🔏 25/650. 🗚 ① ◍
VISA. ✺
North : by Torneo AV
Meals 17,43 – 🖵 12,92 – **288 rm** 179,10/221,17 – 7 suites.

🅷🅰🅰🅷 **Meliá Colón**, Canalejas 1, ✉ 41001, 🖉 95 422 29 00, *colon@trypnet.com*
Fax 95 422 09 38, 🖪 – 🛗 🍽 📺 & ⟺ – 🔏 25/200. 🗚 ① ◍ ◍ VISA JCB
✺
AX ⓢ
Meals (see rest. *El Burladero* below) – 🖵 15,03 – **204 rm** 186,43/260 – 14 suites.

🅷🅰🅰🅷 **Hesperia Sevilla**, av. Eduardo Dato 49, ✉ 41018, 🖉 95 454 83 00, *hotel@hesper
a-sevilla.com*, Fax 95 453 23 42, ⚒ – 🛗 🍽 📺 & 🗜. – 🔏 25/600. 🗚 ① ◍
VISA. ✺
East : by Demetrio de los Ríos CXY
Meals (*closed August*) a la carte approx. 27,44 – 🖵 11 – **242 rm** 170/215 – 2 suites

🅷🅰🅰🅷 **Meliá Sevilla**, Doctor Pedro de Castro 1, ✉ 41004, 🖉 95 442 15 11, *melia.sevilla@s
olmelia.es*, Fax 95 442 29 77, 🖪, ⚒ – 🛗 🍽 📺 ⟺ – 🔏 25/1000. 🗚 ① ◍ ◍ VISA
JCB. ✺
South-East : by Av. de Portugal CY
closed July-August – *La Albufera :* **Meals** a la carte approx. 33,34 – 🖵 13,52 – **359 rm**
222,37/250,02 – 5 suites.

🅷🅰🅰🅷 **Meliá Lebreros**, Luis Morales 2, ✉ 41018, 🖉 95 457 94 00, *melia.lebreros@solmel
a.es*, Fax 95 458 23 09, ⚒ – 🛗 🍽 📺 & 🗜. – 🔏 25/600. 🗚 ① ◍ ◍ VISA
JCB. ✺
East : by La Florida CX
Meals (see rest. *La Dehesa* below) – 🖵 14,18 – **431 rm** 233,49/262,52 – 6 suites.

🅷🅰🅰🅷 **Meliá Confort Macarena**, San Juan de Ribera 2, ✉ 41009, 🖉 95 437 58 00, *mel
a.confort.macarena@solmelia.es*, Fax 95 438 18 03, ⚒ – 🛗 🍽 📺 & – 🔏 25/700. ⚒
① ◍ VISA JCB. ✺
North : by María Auxiliadora CV
Meals 20 – 🖵 11,25 – **321 rm** 130,75/147,25 – 10 suites.

Occidental Sevilla coffee shop only, av. Kansas City, ⊠ 41018, 𝒫 95 491 97 97, *rese rvas-sevilla@occidental-hoteles.com, Fax 95 458 46 15*, ⅃ – |‡| ▤ 📺 👌 – 🏛 25/450. ⚿ ⓐ ⓜⓐ 𝘝𝘐𝘚𝘈 ᴊᴄʙ. ⁂   East : by La Florida   CX
⇌ 11 – **228 rm** 120/140 – 14 suites.

Inglaterra, pl. Nueva 7, ⊠ 41001, 𝒫 95 422 49 70, *hotelinglaterra@retemail.es, Fax 95 456 13 36* – |‡| ▤ 📺 ⟵⟶ – 🏛 25. ⚿ ⓐ ⓜⓐ 𝘝𝘐𝘚𝘈 ᴊᴄʙ. ⁂ rest   AX r
Meals 21,04 – ⇌ 9,62 – **105 rm** 111,18/148,30 – 4 suites.

Los Seises, Segovias 6, ⊠ 41004, 𝒫 95 422 94 95, *seises@jet.es, Fax 95 422 43 34*, « On the 3rd patio of the Archbishop's palace », ⅃ – |‡| ▤ 📺 – 🏛 25/100. ⚿ ⓐ ⓜⓐ 𝘝𝘐𝘚𝘈   BX f
Meals *(closed Saturday and Sunday in July-August)* 27,05 – ⇌ 15,03 – **42 rm** 132,22/180,30.

AC Ciudad de Sevilla, av. Manuel Siurot 25, ⊠ 41013, 𝒫 95 423 05 05, *csevilla@a c-hoteles.com, Fax 95 423 85 39*, ↻, ⅃ – |‡| ▤ 📺 ⟵⟶ – 🏛 25/150. ⚿ ⓐ ⓜⓐ 𝘝𝘐𝘚𝘈. ⁂ rest   South-East : by Paseo de las Delicias   BY
Meals 22,83 – ⇌ 11 – **91 rm** 149 – 3 suites.

NH Viapol, Balbino Marrón, ⊠ 41018, 𝒫 95 464 52 54, *nhviapol@nh-hoteles.es, Fax 95 464 66 68* – |‡| ▤ 📺 👌 ⟵⟶ – 🏛 25/250. ⚿ ⓐ ⓜⓐ 𝘝𝘐𝘚𝘈 ᴊᴄʙ. ⁂ rest   East : by Av. de Carlos V   CY
Meals 24 – ⇌ 10,25 – **90 rm** 132,50/138,25 – 6 suites.

NH Plaza de Armas, av. Marqués de Paradas, ⊠ 41001, 𝒫 95 490 19 92, *nhplaza @nh-hoteles.es, Fax 95 490 12 32*, ⅃ – |‡| ▤ 📺 👌 – 🏛 25/250. ⚿ ⓐ ⓜⓐ 𝘝𝘐𝘚𝘈 ᴊᴄʙ. ⁂   AV c
Meals 16,53 – ⇌ 10,22 – **260 rm** 168,28/216,36 – 2 suites.

Casa Imperial without rest, Imperial 29, ⊠ 41003, 𝒫 95 450 03 00, *info@casaimp erial.com, Fax 95 450 03 30*, « Manor house with Andalusian style patios » – ▤ 📺. ⚿ ⓐ ⓜⓐ 𝘝𝘐𝘚𝘈 ᴊᴄʙ. ⁂   CX r
18 rm ⇌ 198/215 – 7 suites.

Bécquer coffee shop only, Reyes Católicos 4, ⊠ 41001, 𝒫 95 422 89 00, *becquer@h otelbecquer.com, Fax 95 421 44 00* – |‡| ▤ 📺 ⟵⟶ – 🏛 25/45. ⚿ ⓐ ⓜⓐ 𝘝𝘐𝘚𝘈. ⁂   AX v
⇌ 7,21 – **137 rm** 108/132 – 2 suites.

Sevilla Congresos, av. Alcalde Luis Uruñuela, ⊠ 41020, 𝒫 95 425 90 00, *sevillac@a rrakis.es, Fax 95 425 95 00*, ↻, ⅃ – |‡| ▤ 📺 ⟵⟶ – 🏛 25/150. ⚿ ⓐ ⓜⓐ 𝘝𝘐𝘚𝘈. ⁂   North-East : by La Florida   CX
Meals a la carte approx. 24,04 – ⇌ 8,86 – **217 rm** 145,99/182,47 – 1 suite.

Isla Cartuja ⑤, Isla de la Cartuja - Estadio Olímpico, ⊠ 41092, 𝒫 95 408 17 00, *rese rvas@hotelslacartuja.com, Fax 95 408 17 79*, « In the Olympic Stadium with ≤ » – |‡| ▤ 📺 👌 🅿. – 🏛 25/150. ⚿ ⓐ ⓜⓐ 𝘝𝘐𝘚𝘈. ⁂   North : by Torneo   AV
Meals 18,03 – ⇌ 10,80 – **72 rm** 150/180.

San Gil without rest, Parras 28, ⊠ 41002, 𝒫 95 490 68 11, *hsangil@arrakis.es, Fax 95 490 69 39*, « Early 20C partially converted typical Sevilian building, patio with garden », ⅃ ▤ 📺 ⚿ ⓐ ⓜⓐ 𝘝𝘐𝘚𝘈. ⁂   North : by María Auxiliadora   CV
48 rm ⇌ 110/138 – 13 suites.

Las Casas del Rey de Baeza ⑤ without rest, Santiago (pl. Jesús de la Redención 2), ⊠ 41003, 𝒫 95 456 14 96, *baeza@zoom.es, Fax 95 456 14 41*, « On the site of an old cattle yard », ⅃ – |‡| ▤ 📺 ⟵⟶. ⚿ ⓐ ⓜⓐ 𝘝𝘐𝘚𝘈. ⁂   CV s
⇌ 10,82 – **41 rm** 103,37/129,22.

Al-Andalus Palace ⑤, av. de la Palmera, ⊠ 41012, 𝒫 95 423 06 00, *Fax 95 423 02 00*, ⁜, ↻, ⅃ – |‡| ▤ 📺 ⟵⟶ – 🏛 25/1100. ⚿ ⓐ ⓜⓐ 𝘝𝘐𝘚𝘈 ᴊᴄʙ. ⁂ **Meals** 42,07 - *El Patio :* **Meals** a la carte 31,26/42,07 – ⇌ 11,12 - **327 rm** 111,19/135,23, 1 suite.   South-East : by Paseo de las Delicias   BY

Las Casas de los Mercaderes without rest, Álvarez Quintero 9, ⊠ 41004, 𝒫 95 422 58 58, *mercaderes@zoom.es, Fax 95 422 98 84* – |‡| ▤ 📺 ⟵⟶. ⚿ ⓐ ⓜⓐ 𝘝𝘐𝘚𝘈. ⁂   BX e
⇌ 10 – **47 rm** 81/117.

G.H. Lar, pl. Carmen Benítez 3, ⊠ 41003, 𝒫 95 441 03 61, *larhotel@interbook.net., Fax 95 441 04 52* – |‡| ▤ 📺 ⟵⟶ – 🏛 25/300. ⚿ ⓐ ⓜⓐ 𝘝𝘐𝘚𝘈. ⁂   CX f
Meals 18,03 – ⇌ 7,81 – **129 rm** 84,14/120,20 – 8 suites.

Zenit Sevilla ⑤, Pagés del Corro 90, ⊠ 41010, 𝒫 95 434 74 34, *sevilla@zenithot eles.com, Fax 95 434 27 07* – |‡| ▤ 📺 ⟵⟶ – 🏛 25/220. ⚿ ⓐ ⓜⓐ 𝘝𝘐𝘚𝘈. ⁂   AY a
Meals 27 – ⇌ 10,22 – **114 rm** 124,29/155,36 – 14 suites.

Doña María without rest, Don Remondo 19, ⊠ 41004, 𝒫 95 422 49 90, *Fax 95 421 95 46*, « Terrace with ⅃ and ≤ » – |‡| ▤ 📺. ⚿ ⓐ ⓜⓐ 𝘝𝘐𝘚𝘈 ᴊᴄʙ. ⁂
⇌ 9,61 – **66 rm** 93,16/162,27 – 2 suites.   BX u

SEVILLA

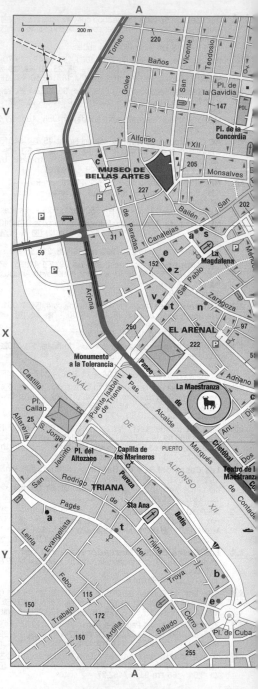

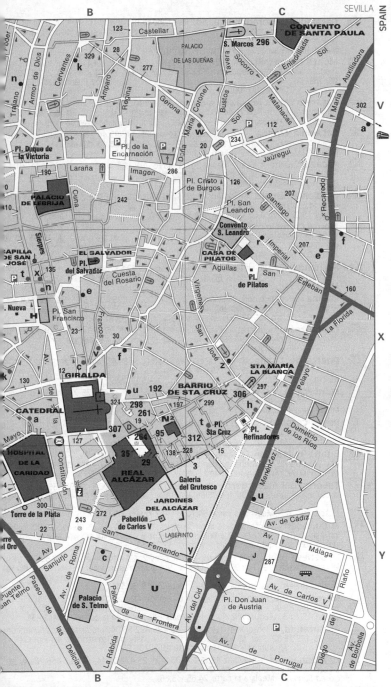

B

C

123 — Castellar

S. Marcos **296**

CONVENTO DE SANTA PAULA

329

28

k

PALACIO DE LAS DUEÑAS

Enladrillada

Sol

n

Cervantes

Armor de Dios

Amparo

277

Regina

Gerona

Doña María Coronel

Sol

Bustos Tavera

Socorro

Matahacas

María Auxiliadora

302

V

a

Trajano

Pl. Duque de la Victoria

Laraña

190

Cuna

Pl. de la Encarnación

w

20

234

112

Jauregui

X Recaredo

PALACIO DE LEBRIJA

Imagen

286

Pl. Cristo de Burgos

126

Pl. San Leandro

Santiago

207

207

f

242

Convento S. Leandro

Imperial

e

CAPILLA DE SAN JOSÉ

Sierpes

EL SALVADOR

135

Pl. del Salvador

Cuesta del Rosario

CASA DE PILATOS

Aguilas

Pl. de Pilatos

San

Esteban

r

160

t

x

n

e

Nueva

H

Pl. San Francisco

23

30

Frenos

San José

Virgenes

La Florida

X

c

v

f

GIRALDA

12

130

de

z

STA MARÍA LA BLANCA

297

Pelayo

u

192

BARRIO DE STA CRUZ

306

CATEDRAL

a

la

324

298

261

197

299

h

k

307

19

Mayo

127

264

95

N

t

Pl. Sta Cruz

312

Demetrio de los Ríos

Pl. Refinadores

HOSPITAL DE LA CARIDAD

35

29

138

228

3

15

REAL ALCÁZAR

Galería del Grutesco

42

u

Menéndez

Constitución

300

4

Torre de la Plata

22

272

243

JARDINES DEL ALCÁZAR

Pabellón de Carlos V

LABERINTO

Av. de Cádiz

torre del Oro

Sanjurjo

San

Fernando

y

Av.

Málaga

Riaño

Paseo

Av. de Roma

c

J

287

Paseo San Telmo

Palos

U

Av. de Carlos V

Diego

de

Puente San Telmo

de

Palacio de S. Telmo

de la Frontera

Pl. Don Juan de Austria

P

Av. de Bohollo

Paseo de las Delicias

La Rábida

Av.

de

Portugal

B

C

581

Catalonia Emperador Trajano, José Laguillo 8, ✉ 41003, ✆ 95 441 11 11, *cat-loni@hoteles-catalonia.es., Fax 95 453 57 02* – 🛗 ▤ 📺 🚗 – 🏃 25/150. AE ⓓ ⓜ VISA JCB. ✂ CV
Meals 16,83 – ☕ 9,02 – **76 rm** 171,88/197,77.

Monte Triana coffee shop only, Clara de Jesús Montero 24, ✉ 41010, ✆ 95 434 31 1 *montetriana@hotelesmonte.com, Fax 95 434 33 28* – 🛗 ▤ 📺 🚗 – 🏃 25/40. AE ⓓ ⓜ VISA. ✂ West : by Puente Isabel II AX
☕ 7,50 – **117 rm** 94/100.

Pasarela without rest, av. de la Borbolla 11, ✉ 41004, ✆ 95 441 55 11, *pasarela-hotel@byprojet.com, Fax 95 442 07 27,* 🏋 – 🛗 ▤ 📺 – 🏃 25. AE ⓓ ⓜ VISA. ✂
☕ 9,62 – **77 rm** 96,16/168,28 – 5 suites. South-East : by Av. de Portugal CY

Catalonia Giralda, Sierra Nevada 3, ✉ 41003, ✆ 95 441 66 61, *cataloni@hoteles-catalonia.es, Fax 95 441 93 52* – 🛗 ▤ 📺 – 🏃 25/250. AE ⓓ ⓜ VISA JCB. ✂ CX
Meals 12,02 – ☕ 9,02 – **98 rm** 171,88/197,77.

Alcázar without rest, Menéndez Pelayo 10, ✉ 41004, ✆ 95 441 20 11 *Fax 95 442 16 59* – 🛗 ▤ 📺 🚗. ⓓ ⓜ VISA. ✂ CY
93 rm ☕ 110,30/136,45.

Catalonia Hispalis, av. de Andalucía 52, ✉ 41006, ✆ 95 452 94 33, *cataloni@hoteles-catalonia.es, Fax 95 467 53 13* – 🛗 ▤ 📺 🅿 – 🏃 25/50. AE ⓓ ⓜ VISA JCB. ✂
Meals 13,22 – ☕ 9,02 – **99 rm** 171,88/197,77. East : by La Florida CX

Monte Carmelo coffee shop only, Virgen de la Victoria 7, ✉ 41011, ✆ 95 427 90 00 *montecarmelo@hotelmonte.com, Fax 95 427 10 04* – 🛗 ▤ 📺 🚗 – 🏃 25/35. AE ⓓ ⓜ VISA. ✂ South : by Pl. de Cuba AY
☕ 6,50 – **68 rm** 68/93.

Fernando III, San José 21, ✉ 41004, ✆ 95 421 77 08, *fernandoiii@altur.com, Fax 95 422 02 46,* 🏊 – 🛗 ▤ 📺 ♿ 🚗 – 🏃 25/250. AE ⓓ ⓜ VISA. ✂ rest CX
Meals 15,25 – ☕ 9,62 – **156 rm** 106,40/133 – 1 suite.

Regina coffee shop only, San Vicente 97, ✉ 41002, ✆ 95 490 75 75, *Fax 95 490 75 6.* – 🛗 ▤ 📺 🚗. AE ⓓ ⓜ VISA. ✂ North : by San Vicente AV
☕ 8,41 – **68 rm** 165,27/204,94 – 4 suites.

Cervantes without rest, Cervantes 10, ✉ 41003, ✆ 95 490 02 80, *hotelcervantes@infonegocio.com, Fax 95 490 05 36* – 🛗 ▤ 📺 🚗. AE ⓓ ⓜ VISA. ✂ BV
☕ 7,21 – **48 rm** 72,88/104,13.

Puerta de Triana without rest, Reyes Católicos 5, ✉ 41001, ✆ 95 421 54 04 *Fax 95 421 54 01* – 🛗 ▤ 📺. AE ⓓ ⓜ VISA JCB. ✂ AX
65 rm ☕ 51/75.

Montecarlo (annexe 🏨), Gravina 51, ✉ 41001, ✆ 95 421 75 03, *info@hotel-montecarlo.net, Fax 95 421 68 25* – 🛗 ▤ 📺. AE ⓓ ⓜ VISA. ✂ AX
Meals *(closed Sunday)* 11,72 – ☕ 5,10 – **51 rm** 60,10/120,20.

Reyes Católicos without rest, no ☕, Gravina 57, ✉ 41001, ✆ 95 421 12 00, *info@hotel-reyescatolicos.com, Fax 95 421 63 12* – 🛗 ▤ 📺. AE ⓓ ⓜ VISA. ✂ AX
27 rm 60,10/120,20.

Egaña Oriza, San Fernando 41, ✉ 41004, ✆ 95 422 72 54, *oriza@jet.es, Fax 95 450 27 27,* « Winter garden beside the old city walls » – ▤. AE ⓓ ⓜ VISA. ✂
closed August, Saturday lunch and Sunday – **Meals** a la carte 42/66. CY

Taberna del Alabardero with rm, Zaragoza 20, ✉ 41001, ✆ 95 456 06 37, *rest.alabardero@esh.es, Fax 95 456 36 66,* « Former palace » – 🛗 ▤ 📺 🚗. AE ⓓ ⓜ VISA JCB. ✂ AX
closed August – **Meals** a la carte 34,70/47 – **7 rm** ☕ 108,50/135.

El Burladero - *Hotel Melia Colón,* Canalejas 1, ✉ 41001, ✆ 95 422 29 00, *trypcolon@sei.es, Fax 95 422 09 38,* « Bullfighting theme » – ▤. AE ⓓ ⓜ VISA JCB. ✂ AX
closed July and August – **Meals** a la carte 32,76/38,46.

La Dehesa - *Hotel Meliá Lebreros,* Luis Morales 2, ✉ 41018, ✆ 95 457 62 04, *melia.lebreros@solmelia.es, Fax 95 458 23 09,* « Typical Andalusian decor » – ▤. AE ⓓ ⓜ VISA JCB. ✂ East : by La Florida CX
Meals - Braised meat specialities - a la carte 20,43/30,33.

Marea Grande, Diego Angulo Íñiguez 16 - edificio Alcázar, ✉ 41018, ✆ 95 453 80 00, *Fax 95 453 80 00* – ▤. AE ⓓ ⓜ VISA. ✂ East : by Demetrio de los Ríos CXY
closed 15 to 31 August and Sunday – **Meals** - Seafood - a la carte 26,74/36,51.

Al-Mutamid, Alfonso XI-1, ✉ 41005, ✆ 95 492 55 04, *modesto@andalunet.com, Fax 95 492 25 02* – ▤. AE ⓓ ⓜ VISA. ✂ East : by Demetrio de los Ríos CXY
closed 15 to 31 August – **Meals** a la carte 19,80/36,96.

La Albahaca, pl. Santa Cruz 12, ✉ 41004, ✆ 95 422 07 14, *Fax 95 456 12 04,* 🏡, « Former manor house » – ▤. AE ⓓ ⓜ VISA JCB. ✂ CX
closed Sunday – **Meals** a la carte 24,65/33,66.

XX **La Isla,** Arfe 25, ✉ 41001, ℘ 95 421 26 31, *laisla@restaurantelaisla.com,*
Fax 95 456 22 19 – 🗏, 🝙 ⓘ ⑩ *VISA*. 🍴   BX a
Meals a la carte 35,46/42,37.

XX **El Asador de Aranda,** Luis Montoto 150, ✉ 41005, ℘ 95 457 81 41,
Fax 95 457 81 41, 🍴, « Housed in an old small palace » – 🗏 🅿. 🝙 ⓘ ⑩
VISA. 🍴   East : by La Florida CX
closed August and Sunday dinner – **Meals** - Roast lamb - a la carte 19,53/
30,80.

XX **Ox's,** Betis 61, ✉ 41010, ℘ 95 427 95 85, *Fax 95 427 84 65* – 🗏. 🝙 ⓘ ⑩ *VISA* ⌷⌷.
🍴   AY b
closed July, Sunday dinner and Monday – **Meals** - Basque rest - a la carte 26,44/
36,06.

XX **Casa Robles,** Álvarez Quintero 58, ✉ 41004, ℘ 95 456 32 72, *casa-robles@andalun*
et.com, Fax 95 456 44 79 – 🗏. 🝙 ⓘ ⑩ *VISA* ⌷⌷. 🍴   BX c
Meals a la carte approx. 31,25.

X **Rincón de Casana,** Santo Domingo de la Calzada 15, ✉ 41010, ℘ 95 453 17 10,
casana@caymasa.es, Fax 95 453 78 37, « Regional decor » – 🗏. 🝙 ⓘ ⑩
VISA. 🍴   East : by Demetrio de los Ríos CXY
closed August and Sunday dinner – **Meals** a la carte approx. 33,04.

X **Horacio,** Antonia Díaz 9, ✉ 41001, ℘ 95 422 53 85, *Fax 95 421 79 27* – 🗏. 🝙 ⓘ ⑩
VISA ⌷⌷. 🍴   AX c
closed 12 to 29 August – **Meals** a la carte 21,02/25,84.

♈/ **Sol y Sombra,** Castilla 149 151, ✉ 41010, ℘ 95 433 39 35, « Bullfighting theme » –
🗏. ⑩ *VISA*. 🍴   West : by Puente Isabel II AX
closed August, Monday and Tuesday lunch – **Tapa** 1,65 **Ración** approx. 10.

♈/ **El Rinconcillo,** Gerona 40, ✉ 41003, ℘ 95 422 31 83, *yojama@eurociber.es,* « Typical
decor in an old taverna » – 🗏. ⓘ ⑩ *VISA*. 🍴   CV w
closed Wednesday – **Tapa** 1,50 **Ración** approx. 7.

♈/ **Mesón Cinco Jotas,** Albareda 15, ✉ 41001, ℘ 954 21 05 21, *narias-b@airtel.net,*
Fax 954 56 41 44 – 🗏. 🝙 ⓘ ⑩ *VISA*. 🍴   BX t
Tapa 1,90 **Ración** - Ham specialities - approx. 9.

♈/ **Modesto,** Cano y Cueto 5, ✉ 41005, ℘ 95 441 68 11, *modesto@andalunet.com,*
Fax 95 492 25 02, 🍴 – 🗏. 🝙 ⓘ ⑩ *VISA*. 🍴   CX h
Tapa 2,10 **Ración** - Seafood - approx. 9.

♈/ **España,** San Fernando 41, ✉ 41004, ℘ 95 422 72 11, *oriza@jet.es, Fax 95 450 27 27,*
🍴 – 🗏. 🝙 ⓘ ⑩ *VISA*. 🍴   CY y
closed August – **Tapa** 2 **Ración** approx. 9.

♈/ **José Luis,** pl. de Cuba 3, ✉ 41011, ℘ 95 427 20 17, *Fax 95 427 64 80,* 🍴 – 🗏. 🝙
ⓘ ⑩ *VISA*. 🍴   AY e
Tapa 1,20 **Ración** approx. 8,41.

♈/ **Bodeguita Romero,** Harinas 10, ✉ 41001, ℘ 95 421 41 78, *sabenye@hotmail.com*
– 🗏. 🝙 ⓘ ⑩ *VISA* ⌷⌷. 🍴   BX k
closed August and Monday – **Tapa** 1,60 **Ración** approx. 7,05.

♈/ **El Portón,** General Polavieja 20, ✉ 41004, ℘ 95 421 40 72, 🍴 – 🗏. 🝙 ⓘ ⑩ *VISA*.
🍴   BX n
Tapa 1,50 **Ración** approx. 5,86.

♈/ **Albahaca,** Pagés del Corro 119, ✉ 41010, ℘ 95 427 41 63, *Fax 95 427 41 63,* 🍴 –
🗏. ⓘ ⑩ *VISA*. 🍴   AY t
closed August and Sunday – **Tapa** 1,62 **Ración** approx. 7,45.

♈/ **Casa La Viuda,** Albareda 2, ✉ 41001, ℘ 95 421 54 20, *Fax 95 450 10 64,* 🍴 – 🗏.
⑩ *VISA*. 🍴   BX x
closed Sunday in July-August – **Tapa** 1,50 **Ración** approx. 6,61.

♈/ **Mesón Cinco Jotas,** Castelar 1, ✉ 41001, ℘ 95 421 58 62, *narias-b@airtel.net,*
Fax 95 421 27 86, 🍴 – 🗏. 🝙 ⓘ ⑩ *VISA*. 🍴   BX z
Tapa 1,90 **Ración** - Ham specialities - approx. 9.

♈/ **Robles,** Placentines 2, ✉ 41004, ℘ 95 421 31 62, *Fax 95 456 44 79,* 🍴 – 🗏. 🝙 ⓘ
⑩ *VISA* ⌷⌷. 🍴   BX v
Tapa 2,10 **Ración** approx. 10.

at Castilleja de la Cuesta *West* : 7 km :

🏛 **Hacienda San Ygnacio,** Real 190 ℘ 954 16 92 90, *reservas@haciendasanygnacio.*
com, Fax 95 416 14 37, 🍴, « In an old hacienda », 🏊, 🎾 – 🗏 📺 🅿 – 🔏 25/200. 🝙
ⓘ ⑩ *VISA* ⌷⌷. 🍴
Almazara : **Meals** a la carte 22/26 – ☷ 8 – **16 rm** 102/135.

at Benacazón West : 20 km :

🏨 **Andalusi Park H.,** autopista A 49 - exit 6 *ℰ* 95 570 56 00, info@hotelandalusipar
.com, Fax 95 570 50 79, « Arabic style building set in gardens inspired by the Alhambr
palace », ⅃ᵟ, ⅃, – 🛗 🍽 📺 ᶳ 🅿 – 🏦 25/500. 🆎 ⓞ ⓜⓞ 𝘝𝘐𝘚𝘈. ᎒᎒
Meals 27,05 – ⚏ 10,52 – **189 rm** 96,16/120,20 – 11 suites.

at Sanlúcar la Mayor West : 18 km :

🏨 **Hacienda Benazuza** ᎒, Virgen de las Nieves *ℰ* 95 570 33 44, hbenazuza@arrakis.es
Fax 95 570 34 10, ≼, « In a 10C Arabian farmhouse », ⅃, 🐎, ᎒᎒ – 🛗 🍽 📺 🅿 -
🏦 25/400. 🆎 ⓞ ⓜⓞ 𝘝𝘐𝘚𝘈. ᎒᎒
closed 7 January-7 February - **La Alquería** (dinner only in spring-summer, closed Sunda
and Monday) **Meals** a la carte 50,48/69,12 – ⚏ 18,63 – **26 rm** 294,50/366,62 – 18 suites

---

VALÈNCIA 46000 🅿 𝟦𝟦𝟧 N 28 y 29. – pop. 777 427 alt. 13.

See : The Old town★ : Cathedral★ (El Miguelete★, Capilla del Santo Cáliz★) EX – Palaci
de la Generalidad★ (golden room : ceiling★) EXD – Lonja★ (silkhall★★) DY.

Other curiosities : Ceramic Museum★★ (Palacio del Marqués de Dos Aguas★★) EYM1 – Fin
Arts San Pío V Museum★ (valencian primitifs★★) FX – Patriarch College or of the Corpu
Christi★ (Passion triptych★) EYN – Serranos Towers★ EX.

🏌 Club de Golf Manises, East : 12 km, *ℰ* 96 153 40 69 – 🏌 Club Escorpión, North-West
19 km by road to Liria *ℰ* 96 160 12 11 – 🏌 El Saler-Parador de El Saler, South-East : 1
km *ℰ* 96 161 03 84.

✈ Valencia-Manises, East : 11 km *ℰ* 96 159 85 00 – Iberia : Paz 14, ✉ 46003
ℰ 902 400 500 EFY.

⛴ . To the Balearic Islands : Cía Trasmediterránea, Estación Marítima ✉ 46024
ℰ 96 367 75 80 Fax 96 367 06 44 by Av. Regne de València FZ.

🛈 Pl. del Ayuntamiento 1, ✉ 46002 *ℰ* 96 351 04 17 turistinfo
aytovalencia@turisme.m400.gva.es Fax 96 352 58 12, Paz 48 *ℰ* 46003 *ℰ* 96 398 64 22
turistinfo.valencia@turisme.m400.gva.es Fax 96 398 64 21 Xàtiva 24 (North Station) ✉
46007 *ℰ* 96 352 85 73 turistinfo.renfe@turisme.m400.gva.es Fax 96 352 85 73 and Poet
Querol ✉ 46002 *ℰ* 96 351 49 07 turistinfo.dipuvalencia@turisme.m400.gva.es Fa
96 351 99 27 – R.A.C.E. (R.A.C. de València) Av. Regne de València 64, ✉ 46005
ℰ 96 374 94 05 Fax 96 373 71 06.

Madrid 352 – Albacete 183 – Alacant/Alicante (by coast) 174 – Barcelona 355 – Bilbac
600 – Castelló de la Plana/Castellón de la Plana 75 – Málaga 608 – Sevilla 659 – Zaragoz
318.

Plans on following pages

🏨 **Meliá Valencia Palace** ᎒, paseo de la Alameda 32, ✉ 46023, *ℰ* 96 337 50 37,
melia.valencia.palace@solmelia.es, Fax 96 337 55 32, ≼, ⅃ᵟ, ⅃ – 🛗 🍽 📺 ᶳ – 🏦 25/800
🆎 ⓞ ⓜⓞ 𝘝𝘐𝘚𝘈 ᴶᶜᴮ. ᎒᎒　　　　　　　　　　East : by Puente de Aragón FZ
Meals 25 – ⚏ 12 – **243 rm** 172/210 – 5 suites.

🏨 **Astoria Palace,** pl. Rodrigo Botet 5, ✉ 46002, *ℰ* 96 398 10 00, info@hotel-astor
a-palace.com, Fax 96 398 10 10, ⅃ᵟ – 🛗 🍽 📺 ᶳ – 🏦 25/500. 🆎 ⓞ ⓜⓞ 𝘝𝘐𝘚𝘈 ᴶᶜᴮ. ᎒᎒
Meals - see rest. **Vinatea** below – ⚏ 10,52 – **196 rm** 163,48/206,15 – 8 suites. EY p

🏨 **Meliá Rey Don Jaime,** av. Baleares 2, ✉ 46023, *ℰ* 96 337 50 30, hotel.melia.rey.d
on.jaime@solmelia.es, Fax 96 337 15 72, ⅃ – 🛗 🍽 📺 ᶳ ⇔ 🅿 – 🏦 25/250. 🆎 ⓞ
ⓜⓞ 𝘝𝘐𝘚𝘈. ᎒᎒　　　　　　　　　　East : by Puente de Aragón FZ
Meals a la carte 33,06/39,07 – ⚏ 10,82 – **317 rm** 126,21/150,25 – 1 suite.

🏨 **NH Las Artes,** av. Instituto Obrero 28, ✉ 46013, *ℰ* 96 335 13 10, nhlasartes@nh-h
oteles.es, Fax 96 374 86 22, ⅃ᵟ, ⅃ – 🛗 🍽 📺 ⇔ – 🏦 25/250. 🆎 ⓞ ⓜⓞ 𝘝𝘐𝘚𝘈 ᴶᶜᴮ.
᎒᎒　　　　　　　　　　South : by Av. Regne de València FZ
Meals a la carte approx. 24,63 – ⚏ 10,22 – **172 rm** 129,22/162,27 – 2 suites.

🏨 **Hesperia Parque Central,** pl. Manuel Sanchís Guarner, ✉ 46006, *ℰ* 96 303 91 00,
hotel@hesperia-parquecentral.com, Fax 96 303 91 30, ⅃ᵟ – 🛗 🍽 📺 ⇔ – 🏦 25/250.
🆎 ⓞ ⓜⓞ 𝘝𝘐𝘚𝘈. ᎒᎒　　　　　　　　　　South : by Alicante EZ
Meals 17,42 – ⚏ 8,41 – **178 rm** 126,21/159,27 – 14 suites.

🏛 **Meliá Plaza,** pl. del Ayuntamiento 4, ✉ 46002, *ℰ* 96 352 06 12, melia.plaza@solme
lia.com, Fax 96 352 04 26, ⅃ᵟ – 🛗 🍽 📺 ᶳ – 🏦 25/80. 🆎 ⓞ ⓜⓞ 𝘝𝘐𝘚𝘈 ᴶᶜᴮ. ᎒᎒ EY d
Meals 17,43 – ⚏ 8,41 – **100 rm** 127,41/161,07 – 1 suite.

🏛 **Abba Acteón** coffee shop only, Vicente Beltrán Grimal 2, ✉ 46023, *ℰ* 96 331 07 07,
acteon@acteon.com, Fax 96 330 22 30, ⅃ᵟ ⇔ – 🏦 25/400. 🆎 ⓞ ⓜⓞ
𝘝𝘐𝘚𝘈. ᎒᎒　　　　　　　　　　East : by Av. Regne de València FZ
⚏ 10,22 – **182 rm** 120/150 – 5 suites.

NH Center, Ricardo Micó 1, ✉ 46009, ℘ 96 347 50 00, *nhcenter@nh-hoteles.es, Fax 96 347 62 52*, heated, – ▯ – 25/400. AE ◑ MC VISA JCB. North : by Gran Vía Fernando el Católico DY
Meals 21,04 – ☕ 10,22 – **190 rm** 129,22 – 3 suites.

Holiday Inn Valencia, paseo de la Alameda 38, ✉ 46023, ℘ 96 303 21 00, *maria.escudero@basshotels.com, Fax 96 303 21 26*, – – 25/55. AE ◑ MC VISA. rest East : by Puente de Aragón FZ
Meals 21,04 – ☕ 10,50 – **200 rm** 185/225.

Jardín Botánico without rest, peset Cervera 6, ✉ 46008, ℘ 96 315 40 12, *inf-reservas@hoteljardinbotanico.com, Fax 96 315 34 08* – ▯. AE MC VISA.
☕ 9 – **16 rm** 93,16/99,17. West : by Gran Vía Fernando el Católico DY

Conqueridor, Cervantes 9, ✉ 46007, ℘ 96 352 29 10, *hconquer@infonegocio.com, Fax 96 352 28 83* – – 25/80. AE ◑ MC VISA JCB. DZ b
Meals 19 – ☕ 10 – **55 rm** 100/160 – 4 suites.

Meliá Confort Inglés, Marqués de Dos Aguas 6, ✉ 46002, ℘ 96 351 64 26, *melia.confort.ingles@solmelia.es, Fax 96 394 02 51*, « Housed in the Duke of Cardona's 18C palace » – – 25/60. AE ◑ MC VISA JCB. EY e
Meals 14 – ☕ 8 – **63 rm** 110/139.

Dimar coffee shop only, Gran Vía Marqués del Turia 80, ✉ 46005, ℘ 96 395 10 30, *dimar@mx2.redestb.es, Fax 96 395 19 26* – – 25/50. AE ◑ MC VISA.
☕ 9 – **103 rm** 72,70/119,70 – 1 suite. FZ q

Reina Victoria, Barcas 4, ✉ 46002, ℘ 96 352 04 87, *hreinavictoriavalencia@husa.es, Fax 96 352 27 21* – – 25/75. AE ◑ MC VISA. EY s
Meals 13,70 – ☕ 8,70 – **94 rm** 87,70/131,70 – 3 suites.

NH Ciudad de Valencia, av. del Puerto 214, ✉ 46023, ℘ 96 330 75 00, *nhc-valencia@nh-hoteles.es, Fax 96 330 98 64* – – 30/80. AE ◑ MC VISA JCB. East : by Puente de Aragón FZ
Meals 15,03 – ☕ 8,42 – **147 rm** 95,59 – 2 suites.

Excelsior without rest, Barcelonina 5, ✉ 46002, ℘ 96 351 46 12, *Fax 96 352 34 78* – . AE ◑ MC VISA. EY a
☕ 9,02 – **81 rm** 131,62/164,71.

Turia, Profesor Beltrán Baguena 2, ✉ 46009, ℘ 96 347 00 00, *hoteltur@infonegocio.com, Fax 96 347 32 44* – – 25/300. AE MC VISA. North-West : by Gran Vía Fernando el Católico DY
Meals - dinner only - 18,03 – ☕ 8,41 – **160 rm** 108,18 – 10 suites.

Cónsul del Mar, av. del Puerto 39, ✉ 46021, ℘ 96 362 54 32, *reservas@hotelconsuldelmar.com, Fax 96 362 16 25*, « Old manor house », – P – 25/50. AE ◑ MC VISA East : by Puente de Aragón FZ
Meals 8,71 – ☕ 5,41 – **45 rm** 81,14/87,15.

NH Abashiri, av. Ausias March 59, ✉ 46013, ℘ 96 373 28 52, *Fax 96 373 49 66* – – 30/250. AE ◑ MC VISA JCB.
Meals 17,43 – ☕ 8,41 – **168 rm** 78,13/102,17. South : by Av. Regne de València FZ

NH Villacarlos without rest, av. del Puerto 60, ✉ 46023, ℘ 96 337 50 25, *nhvillacarlos@nhhoteles.es, Fax 96 337 50 74* – . AE ◑ MC VISA.
☕ 9 – **51 rm** 126,60. East : by Puente de Aragón FZ

Ad-Hoc, Boix 4, ✉ 46003, ℘ 96 391 91 40, *adhoc@nexo.net, Fax 96 391 36 67*, « Attractive 19C building » – . AE ◑ MC VISA. rest FX a
Meals *(closed Saturday lunch and Sunday)* 18,60 – ☕ 6,01 – **28 rm** 105/131.

Express Las Artes without rest, av. Instituto Obrero 26, ✉ 46013, ℘ 96 335 60 62, *exlasartes@nh-hoteles.es, Fax 96 333 46 83* – . AE ◑ MC VISA JCB. South : by Av. Regne de València FZ
☕ 8 – **121 rm** 81,33.

Renasa coffee shop only, av. de Cataluña 5, ✉ 46010, ℘ 96 369 24 50, *hotel-renasa@conexion2000.com, Fax 96 393 18 24* – – 25/75. AE ◑ MC VISA.
69 rm ☕ 66,11/108,18 – 4 suites. East : by Puente del Real FX

Sorolla without rest, Convento de Santa Clara 5, ✉ 46002, ℘ 96 352 33 92, *hsorolla@infonegocio.com, Fax 96 352 14 65* – . AE ◑ MC VISA JCB. EZ z
☕ 7 – **50 rm** 72/105.

XXX **Rías Gallegas,** Cirilo Amorós 4, ✉ 46004, ℘ 96 352 51 11, *Fax 96 351 99 10* – P. AE ◑ MC VISA EZ r
closed August and Sunday – **Meals** a la carte 26,45/50,48.

XXX **Eladio,** Chiva 40, ✉ 46018, ℘ 96 384 22 44, *michel@resteladio.com, Fax 96 384 64 21* – . AE ◑ MC VISA. West : by Ángel Guimerá DY
closed August and Sunday – **Meals** a la carte 24,34/32,76.

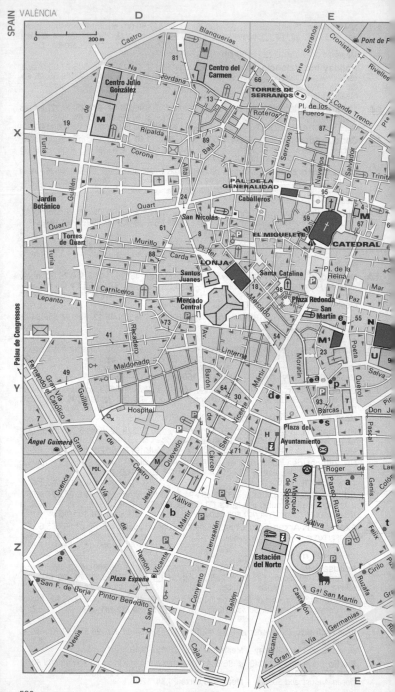

VALÈNCIA

We suggest:
For a successful tour,
that you prepare it
in advance.
Michelin maps
and **guides**
will give you much
useful information
on route planning,
places of interest,
accommodation,
prices, etc.

XXX **Óscar Torrijos,** Dr. Sumsi 4, ✉ 46005, ☎ 96 373 29 49, Fax 96 373 29 49 – 🗏. **A**
🕸 ⓞ ⲱ VISA. ✗
closed 15 August-15 September and Sunday – **Meals** 51,09 and a la carte 36,06/48,08
Spec. Taco de bacalao con carpaccio de pies de cerdo y salsa de miel. Vieiras con patata
(October-April). Tatin de manzanas con helado de vainilla.

XXX **Albacar,** Sorní 35, ✉ 46004, ☎ 96 395 10 05, Fax 96 395 60 55 – 🗏. **AE** ⓞ ⲱ VISA
FY s
closed Holy Week, August, Saturday lunch, Sunday and Bank Holidays – **Meals** a la carte
27,23/33,04.

XXX **La Sucursal,** av. Navarro Reverter 16, ✉ 46004, ☎ 96 374 66 65, Fax 96 374 66 6.
– 🗏. **AE** ⓞ ⲱ VISA. ✗ FY n
closed August, Saturday lunch and Sunday – **Meals** a la carte 25,24/33,96.

XXX **Vinatea** - Hotel Astoria Palace, Vilaragut 4, ✉ 46002, ☎ 96 398 10 00
Fax 96 398 10 10 – 🗏. **AE** ⓞ VISA JCB. ✗ EY p
Meals a la carte 21,64/38,32.

XX **Kailuze,** Gregorio Mayáns 5, ✉ 46005, ☎ 96 335 45 39, Fax 96 335 48 93 – 🗏. **AE** ⲱ
VISA. ✗ FZ c
closed Holy Week and August – **Meals** - Basque rest - a la carte 30,05/35,46.

XX **El Gastrónomo,** av. Primado Reig 149, ✉ 46020, ☎ 96 369 70 36 – 🗏 ⇦⇨. **AE** ⲱ
VISA. ✗ North-East : by Puente del Real FX
closed 1 to 7 January, Holy Week, August, Sunday and Monday dinner – **Meals** a la carte
23,40/30,50.

XX **El Ángel Azul,** Conde de Altea 33, ✉ 46005, ☎ 96 374 56 56, cocinarte@terra.es
Fax 96 374 56 56 – 🗏. **AE** ⓞ ⲱ VISA JCB. ✗ FZ e
closed August, Sunday and Monday – **Meals** a la carte 28,50/49,50.

XX **Joaquín Schmidt,** Visitación 7, ✉ 46009, ☎ 96 340 17 10, Fax 96 340 17 10, 🛋
« In an old house with patio » – 🗏. ⓞ ⲱ VISA. ✗
closed 15 days in Holy Week, 15 days in August, Sunday and Monday lunch – **Meals** a la
carte 33,06/54,09. North : by Cronista Rivelles EX

XX **Civera,** Lérida 11, ✉ 46009, ☎ 96 347 59 17, civera@ole.com, Fax 96 346 50 50 – 🗏
AE ⓞ ⲱ VISA. ✗ North : by Cronista Rivelles EX
closed Holy Week, August, Sunday dinner and Monday – **Meals** - Seafood - a la carte approx
32,45.

XX **Civera Centro,** Mosén Femades 10, ✉ 46002, ☎ 96 352 97 64, civera@ole.com,
Fax 96 346 50 50, 🛋 – 🗏. **AE** ⓞ ⲱ VISA. ✗ EZ a
closed Holy Week and 15 June- 15 July – **Meals** - Seafood - a la carte 26,44/28,25.

XX **Ca'Sento,** Méndez Núñez 17, ✉ 46024, ☎ 96 330 17 75 – 🗏. **AE** ⲱ VISA. ✗
🕸 *closed August, Sunday and Monday dinner* – **Meals** - booking essential - 60,10 and a la
carte 35,03/39,66 East : by Puente de Aragón FZ
Spec. Canelones de trufa y queso. Ventresca de atún fresco con aceite de jengibre (May-
November). Arroz meloso marinero.

XX **El Gourmet,** Martí 3, ✉ 46005, ☎ 96 395 25 09 – 🗏. **AE** ⓞ ⲱ VISA
🍷 JCB. ✗ FZ b
closed Holy Week, August and Monday – **Meals** a la carte approx. 21,04.

XX **Chust Godoy,** Boix 6, ✉ 46003, ☎ 96 391 38 15, Fax 96 391 38 15 – 🗏. ⓞ ⲱ
VISA. ✗ FX a
closed Holy Week, August, Saturday lunch and Sunday – **Meals** a la carte 25,84/
36,06.

XX **El Cabanyal,** Reina 128, ✉ 46011, ☎ 96 356 15 03, Fax 96 355 29 00 – 🗏. **AE** ⓞ ⲱ
VISA. ✗ East : by Puente de Aragón FZ
closed 15 August-15 September and Sunday – **Meals** a la carte 26,15/37,57.

XX **José Mari,** Estación Marítima 1º, ✉ 46024, ☎ 96 367 27 15, ≤ – 🗏. **AE** ⓞ ⲱ VISA.
✗ South-East : by Puente de Aragón FZ
closed August – **Meals** - Basque rest - a la carte 20,43/31,85.

X **Montes,** pl. Obispo Amigó 5, ✉ 46007, ☎ 96 385 50 25 – 🗏. **AE** ⓞ
🍷 VISA. ✗ DZ v
closed Holy Week, August, Sunday dinner and Monday – **Meals** a la carte 18,34/30.

X **Mey Mey,** Historiador Diago 19, ✉ 46007, ☎ 96 384 07 47 – 🗏. **AE** ⓞ ⲱ
VISA. ✗ DZ e
closed Holy Week and the last three weeks in August – **Meals** - Chinese rest - a la carte
16,52/21,85.

X **Eguzki,** av. Baleares 1, ✉ 46023, ☎ 96 337 50 33 – 🗏. ⲱ VISA. ✗
closed August and Sunday – **Meals** - Basque rest - a la carte 21,34/26,45.
East : by Puente de Aragón FZ

X **Palace Fesol,** Hernán Cortés 7, ✉ 46004, ☏ 96 352 93 23, Fax 96 352 93 23, Regional
decor – 🍽, 🆑 ① ⓜⓞ 𝘝𝘐𝘚𝘈, ✑   FZ s
closed Holy Week, 15 days in August, Saturday and Sunday in summer, and Monday the
rest of the year – **Meals** a la carte 20/30.

X **Bazterretxe,** Maestro Gozalbo 25, ✉ 46005, ☏ 96 395 18 94 – 🍽, 🆑
🍴 𝘝𝘐𝘚𝘈,   FZ a
closed August and Sunday dinner – **Meals** - Basque rest - a la carte 16,53/22,54.

X **El Romeral,** Gran Vía Marqués del Turia 62, ✉ 46005, ☏ 96 395 15 17 – 🍽. 🆑 ①
🍴 ⓜⓞ 𝘝𝘐𝘚𝘈, ✑   FZ z
closed Holy Week, August and Monday – **Meals** a la carte 18,03/22,84.

y road C 234 North-West : 8,5 km :

🏨 **NH Jardines del Turia,** Pintor Velázquez, ✉ 46100 Burjassot, ☏ 96 390 54 60, nhja
rdinturia@nh-hoteles.es, Fax 96 364 63 61 – 🛗 🍽 📺 🚗 – 🔏 25/100. 🆑 ① ⓜⓞ 𝘝𝘐𝘚𝘈.
✑   North-West : by Gran Vía Fernando el Católico   DY
Meals a la carte 27,05/36,06 – 🍷 9 – **97 suites** 119 – 15 rm.

t Almàssera North-East : 9 km :

XX **Lluna de València,** Camí del Mar 56, ✉ 46132 Almàssera, ☏ 96 185 10 86,
Fax 96 185 10 06, « Old farmhouse » – 🍽 🅿. 🆑 ① ⓜⓞ 𝘝𝘐𝘚𝘈. ✑
closed Holy Week, Saturday lunch and Sunday – **Meals** a la carte 18,18/24,49.
                                                                    by Puente del Real   FX

t El Saler South : 12 km :

🏨 **Sidi Saler** ⏝, playa - 3 km, ✉ 46012 València, ☏ 96 161 04 11, sidisaler@ctv.es,
Fax 96 161 08 38, ≤, 🌲, 𝑓ₛ, 𝒥, 🏊, 🏖, ✖ – 🛗 🍽 📺 ♿ 🅿 – 🔏 25/300. 🆑 ① ⓜⓞ
𝘝𝘐𝘚𝘈, ✑ rest
Meals 27 - **Les Dunes** (dinner only) **Meals** a la carte 33,43/45,08 - **Brasserie Le Jardin**
(lunch only) **Meals** a la carte 33,06/39,07 – 🍷 12 – **260 rm** 160/220 – 16 suites.

🏨 **Parador de El Saler** ⏝, 7 km, ✉ 46012 València, ☏ 96 161 11 86, Fax 96 162 70 16,
≤, « In the middle of the golf course », 𝑓ₛ, 𝒥, 𝑓ₛ – 🛗 🍽 📺 🅿 – 🔏 25/200. 🆑 ①
ⓜⓞ 𝘝𝘐𝘚𝘈. ✑
Meals 24,04 – 🍷 8,71 – **58 rm** 95,63/119,54.

t Manises on the airport road - East : 9,5 km :

🏨 Meliá Confort Azafata, autopista del aeropuerto 15 ☏ 96 154 61 00, melia.confort.aza
fata@solmelia.com, Fax 96 153 20 19, 𝑓ₛ – 🛗 🍽 📺 🚗 🅿 – 🔏 25/300
124 rm, 4 suites.

t Puçol North : 23 km by motorway A 7 :

🏨 **Monte Picayo** ⏝, urb. Monte Picayo ☏ 96 142 01 00, Fax 96 142 21 68, 🌲, « On
a hillside with ≤ », 🌲, 🏖, ✖ – 🛗 🍽 📺 🅿 – 🔏 25/500. 🆑 ① ⓜⓞ 𝘝𝘐𝘚𝘈, 𝘑𝘊𝘉. ✑
Meals 18 – **79 rm** 🍷 138,23/162,27 – 3 suites.

Sweden

Sverige

STOCKHOLM – GOTHENBURG

PRACTICAL INFORMATION

LOCAL CURRENCY

Swedish Kronor: *100 SEK = 10,59 euro (€) (Dec. 2001)*

TOURIST INFORMATION

In Stockholm, the Tourist Centre is situated in Sweden House, entrance from Kungsträdgården at Hamngatan. Open Mon-Fri 9am-6pm. Sat. and Sun. 9am-3pm. Telephone weekdays (08) 789 24 00, weekends to Excursion Shop and Tourist Centre (08) 789 24 15. For Gothenburg, see information in the text of the town under 🛈.

National Holiday in Sweden: *6 June.*

FOREIGN EXCHANGE

Banks are open between 9.30am and 3pm on weekdays only. Some banks in the centre of the city are usually open weekdays 9am to 6pm. Most large hotels and the Tourist Centre have exchange facilities. Arlanda airport has banking facilities between 7am to 10pm seven days a week.

MEALS

At lunchtime, follow the custom of the country and try the typical buffets of Scandinavian specialities (Smörgåsbord), or try the lunch of the day.
At dinner, the a la carte and set menus will offer you more conventional cooking.

SHOPPING

In the index of street names, those printed in red are where the principal shops are found.
The main shopping streets in the centre of Stockholm are: Hamngatan, Biblioteksgatan, Drottninggatan, Sturegallerian.
In the Old Town mainly Västerlånggatan.

THEATRE BOOKINGS

Your hotel porter will be able to make your arrangements or direct you to Theatre Booking Agents.

CAR HIRE

The international car hire companies have branches in Stockholm, Gothenburg, Arlanda and Landvetter airports. Your hotel porter should be able to give details and help you with your arrangements.

TIPPING

Hotels and restaurants normally include a service charge of 15 per cent. Additionally cloakroom attendants are normally tipped 10 SEK. Doormen, baggage porters etc. are generally given a gratuity.
Taxis include 10 % tip in the amount shown on the meter.

SPEED LIMITS - SEAT BELTS

The maximum permitted speed on motorways and dual carriageways is 110 km/h - 68 mph, 90 km/h - 56 mph on other roads except where a lower speed limit is indicated and in built up areas 50 km/h - 31 mph.
The wearing of seat belts is compulsory for drivers and all passengers.
In Sweden, drivers must not drink alcoholic beverages at all.

BREAKDOWN SERVICE

A 24 hour breakdown service is operated ☎ 112.

STOCKHOLM

Sverige 985 M 15 – *pop. 674 459 Greater Stockholm 1 491 726.*

Hamburg 935 – Copenhagen 630 – Oslo 522.

🖪 *Stockholm Information Service, Tourist Centre, Sverigehuset, Hamngatan 27* ℰ *(08) 789 24 00 – Motormännens Riksförbund* ℰ *(08) 690 38 00 – Kungliga. Automobilklubben (Royal Automobile Club) Gyllenstiernsgatan 4* ℰ *(08) 678 00 55.*

🖿 *Svenska Golfförbundet (Swedish Golf Federation)* ℰ *(08) 622 15 00.*

✈ *Stockholm-Arlanda NW : 40 km* ℰ *(08) 797 61 00 – SAS : Flygcity, Stureplan 8* ℰ *(08) 797 41 75, Reservations (020) 727 727 – Air-Terminal : opposite main railway station – Arlanda Express rail link : departs Central Station every 15 mins – journey time 20 mins.*

🚃 *Motorail for Southern Europe : Ticket Travel-Agency, Kungsgatan 60* ℰ *(08) 24 00 90.*
🚢 *To Finland : contact Silja Line* ℰ *(08) 22 21 40 or Viking Line* ℰ *(08) 452 40 00 – Excursions by boat : contact Stockholm Information Service (see below).*

See: *Old Town★★★ (Gamla Stan) AZ – Vasa Museum★★★ (Vasamuseet) DY – Skansen Open-Air Museum★★★ DY.*
*Royal Palace★★ (Kungliga Slottet) AZ ; Royal Apartments★★ ; Royal Armoury★ ; Royal Treasury★★ – Stockholm Cathedral★★ (Storkyrkan) AZ – City Hall★★ (Stadhuset) : Blue Hall★★★, Golden Hall★★★ ; * ⚹ *★★★ BY H – Prins Eugens Waldemarsudde★★ (house and gallery) DY – Thiel Gallery★★ (Thielska Galleriet) DZ.*
House of the Nobility★ (Riddarhuset) AZ R – Riddarholmen Church★ (Riddarholmskyrkan) AZ K¹ – Österlånggatan★ AZ.
Kaknäs TV Tower (Kaknästornet) ⚹ *★★★ DY – Stigberget : Fjällgatan* ⚹ *★ DZ – Skinnerviksberget :* ⚹ *★ BZ.*

Museums: *National Art Gallery★★ (Nationalmuseum) DY M⁵ – Nordic Museum★★ (Nordiska Museet) DY – Museum of National Antiquities★★ (Historiska Museet) DY – Museum of Medieval Stockholm★★ (Stockholms Medeltidsmuseet) CY M¹ – Museum of Far Eastern Antiquities★ (Östasiatiska Museet) DY M⁶ – Hallwyl Collection★ (Hallwylska Museet) CY M³ – Museum of Modern Art (Moderna Museet) (collections★★) DY M⁴ – Strindberg Museum★ (Strindbergsmuseet) BX M² – Junibacken★ DY.*

Outskirts : *Drottningholm Palace★★★ (Drottningholm Slott) W : 12 km BY – Stockholm Archipelago★★★ – Millesgården★★ (house and gallery) E : 4 km BX – Skogskyrkogården (UNESCO World Heritage Site).*

Excursions : *Gripsholms Slott★★ – Skokloster★★ – Ulriksdal★ – Birka★ – Strängnas★ – Sigtuna★ – Uppsala★★.*

STOCKHOLM

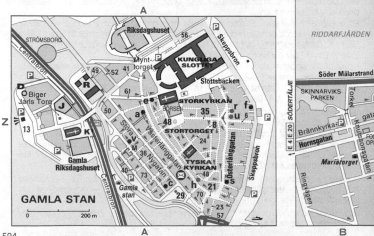

E 20 Naturhistoriska
Riksmuseet C D VÄRTAHAMNEN Millesgården (LIDINGÖ)

TEKNISKA
HÖGSKOLAN

Ödengatan
Valhallavägen
Tekniska
Högskolan
Östermalms-
Lill-Jans
Plan
STADION
Lidingövägen
E 20
Erik Dahlbergsgatan
Gärdet

Engelbrektsgatan
gatan
Valhallavägen
a
TESSIN-
PARKEN
Värtavägen
X

stensgatan
b
Z
Karlavägen
Stadion
18
Sturegatan
gatan
Nybrogatan
Östermalms-
gatan
t
HUMLEGÅRDEN
Stadion
18
Karlavägen
Karlaplan
Karlaplan
Valhallavägen

rgatan
n
KUNGLIGA
BIBLIOTEKET
ÖSTERMALM
Linnégatan
Artillerigatan
Narvavägen
Birgergatan
G. ADOLFS-
PARKEN
Karlavägen

Regeringsgatan
e
Humlegårdsgatan
a
Sture-
gallerian
76
Hedvig Eleonora Kyrka
p
Karlavägen
Linnégatan
HISTORISKA
MUSEET
Sjöhistoriska Museet
Kaknästornet

Hötorget
M
d
k
n
m
m
18
t
3
Östermalmstorg
44
2
28
v
Hamngatan
M
M
M
Styrmansgatan
Storgatan
Strandvägen
r
Nobel-
Parken

NORRMALM
53
10
Regerings-
u
M
T
2
b
32
45
m
Strandvägen
9
Y

Centralen
54
STADSTEATERN
Kungs-
trädgården
Nybrokajen
x
s
BLASIEHOLMEN
NYBROKAJEN
JUNIBACKEN
P
Lejon-
slätten

Kulturhuset
28
14
3
K
19
M
OPERAN
59
f
66
62
63
M
NORDISKA
MUSEET
SKANSEN
VASAMUSEET
a

P
10
f
x
16
M
1
HELGEANDS-
HOLMEN
Skeppsholms-
bron
M
6
K
4
M
4
M
M
e
Djurgården

DAR-
LMEN
GAMLA STAN
AF CHAPMAN
SKEPPSHOLMEN
P
M
Dju rgårdsvägen

Söder
Mälarstrand
Slussen
KASTELL-
HOLMEN
SALTSJÖN
Gröna
Lunds
Tivoli
BECK-
HOLMEN

stugatan
e
Katarinahissen
Stadsgården
Z

orgsgatan
M
64
Slussen
a
74
39
Katarinavägen
gatan
Stadsgården

ria
M
get
Mariatorget
Högbergs-
Götgatan
42
Katarina
Kyrka
60
Fjällgatan
55
Renstiernas Gata
Folkungagatan
P
222
NACKA

SÖDERMALM
Högbergs-
Medborgar-
platsen
r
Medborgarplatsen
Folkungagatan
0   300 m

C NYNÄSHAMN 73 D

Grand Hôtel, Södra Blasieholmshamnen 8, ⊠ S-103 27, ℰ (08) 679 35 00, *info@grandhotel.se*, Fax (08) 611 86 86, « Late 19C hotel on the waterfront ≼ Royal Palace and Old Town », ₤₅, ⇌s – |≢|, ⥽ rm, ▤ rest, ▥ ℋ ᴴ ᴳᴳᴳ – ⩜ 600. ⨾⦿ ᴬᴱ ⦿ ⱽᴵˢᴬ ᴶᶜᴮ. ⤶
CY c
Verandan (ℰ (08) 679 35 86) : **Meals** (buffet lunch) 295/395 and a la carte 315/520 ⫪ 300 (see also **Franska Matsalen** below) – ⌷ 185 – **289 rm** 2795/3995, 21 suites.

Sheraton Stockholm H. and Towers ⓜ, Tegelbacken 6, ⊠ S-101 23, ℰ (08) 412 34 00, *sheraton.stockholm@sheraton.com*, Fax (08) 412 34 09, ≼, ⇌s – |≢|, ⥽ rm ▤ ▥ ℋ ᴳᴳᴳ ᴾ. – ⩜ 380. ⨾⦿ ᴬᴱ ⦿ ⱽᴵˢᴬ ᴶᶜᴮ. ⤶ rest
CY a
Liberty Kitchen : **Meals** (buffet lunch) 160 and a la carte 345/535 ⫪ 240 – **Die Ecke**. **Meals** - German Bierstub - (closed Sunday) a la carte 320/440 ⫪ 240 – ⌷ 170 – **449 rm** 2820/3920, 13 suites.

Radisson SAS Royal Viking ⓜ, Vasagatan 1, ⊠ S-101 24, ℰ (08) 506 540 00, *sales.royal.stockholm@radissonsas.com*, Fax (08) 506 540 01, « Panoramic Sky Bar on 9th floor with ≼ Stockholm », ₤₅, ⇌s, ▨ – |≢|, ⥽ rm, ▤ ▥ ℋ ᴳᴳᴳ ᴳᴳᴳ – ⩜ 140. ⨾⦿ ᴬᴱ ⦿ ⱽᴵˢᴬ ᴶᶜᴮ. ⤶
BY f
Stockholm Fisk : **Meals** - Seafood - 310 (dinner) and a la carte 240/570 ⫪ 245 – **325 rm** ⌷ 2030/3000, 20 suites.

Radisson SAS Strand ⓜ, Nybrokajen 9, ⊠ S-103 27, ℰ (08) 506 640 00, *sales.strand.stockholm@radissonsas.com*, Fax (08) 506 640 01, « Attractive old-world architecture, overlooking the harbour », ⇌s – |≢|, ⥽ rm, ▤ ▥ ℋ – ⩜ 90. ⨾⦿ ᴬᴱ ⦿ ⱽᴵˢᴬ ᴶᶜᴮ. ⤶
CDY x
closed Christmas and New Year – **Meals** a la carte 205/520 ⫪ 220 – ⌷ 165 – **131 rm** 2995, 18 suites.

Diplomat, Strandvägen 7c, ⊠ S-104 40, ℰ (08) 459 68 00, *info@diplomathotel.com*, Fax (08) 459 68 20, « Art Nouveau style former diplomatic lodgings, overlooking the harbour », ⇌s – |≢|, ⥽ rm, ▥ ℋ – ⩜ 30. ⨾⦿ ᴬᴱ ⦿ ⱽᴵˢᴬ. ⤶
DY m
closed 23-26 December – **Meals** a la carte 275/410 ⫪ 250 – **125 rm** ⌷ 1895/2795, 3 suites.

Elite H. Stockholm Plaza, Birger Jarlsgatan 29, ⊠ S-103 95, ℰ (08) 566 220 00, *info@stoplaza.elite.se*, Fax (08) 566 220 20, ⟴, ⇌s – |≢|, ⥽ rm, ▥ ℋ – ⩜ 45. ⨾⦿ ᴬᴱ ⦿ ⱽᴵˢᴬ. ⤶
CX e
closed 21-27 December – **Meals** (dinner only in July) a la carte 370/425 ⫪ 260 – **147 rm** ⌷ 1745/2045, 4 suites.

Scandic H. Park ⓜ, Karlavägen 43, ⊠ S-102 46, ℰ (08) 517 348 00, *park@scandic-hotels.com*, Fax (08) 517 348 11, ⟴, ⇌s – |≢|, ⥽ rm, ▤ ▥ ℋ ᴳᴳᴳ – ⩜ 100. ⨾⦿ ᴬᴱ ⦿ ⱽᴵˢᴬ ᴶᶜᴮ. ⤶ rest
CX t
Park Village : **Meals** (closed Bank Holidays) 80/95 (lunch) and a la carte 245/395 ⫪ 200 – **195 rm** ⌷ 1735/2785, 3 suites.

Nordic Sea ⓜ, Vasaplan, ⊠ S-101 37, ℰ (08) 505 630 00, *info@nordichotels.se*, Fax (08) 505 630 90, ₤₅, ⇌s – ▤ ▥ ᴳᴳᴳ – ⩜ 100. ⨾⦿ ᴬᴱ ⦿ ⱽᴵˢᴬ ᴶᶜᴮ. ⤶ rest
BY a
Meals (see **Nordic Light** below) – **343 rm** ⌷ 2000/2400, 24 suites.

Birger Jarl ⓜ, Tulegatan 8, ⊠ S-104 32, ℰ (08) 674 18 00, *info@birgerjarl.se*, Fax (08) 673 73 66, ₤₅, ⇌s – |≢|, ⥽ rm, ▥ ℋ ᴳᴳᴳ – ⩜ 150. ⨾⦿ ᴬᴱ ⦿ ⱽᴵˢᴬ. ⤶
CX z
closed 20 December-2 January – **Meals** (closed Saturday and Sunday lunch) a la carte 235/340 ⫪ 215 – **230 rm** ⌷ 1520/2450, 5 suites.

Nordic Light ⓜ, Vasaplan, ⊠ S-101 37, ℰ (08) 505 630 00, *info@nordiclight.se*, Fax (08) 505 630 30, ₤₅, ⇌s – ▤ ▥ ᴳᴳᴳ – ⩜ 100. ⨾⦿ ᴬᴱ ⦿ ⱽᴵˢᴬ ᴶᶜᴮ. ⤶ rest
BY b
Meals a la carte 315/495 ⫪ 220 – **160 rm** ⌷ 2200/2600, 15 suites.

First H. Amaranten, Kungsholmsgatan 31, ⊠ S-104 20, ℰ (08) 692 52 00, *amaranten@firsthotels.se*, Fax (08) 652 62 48, ⇌s – |≢|, ⥽ rm, ▤ rest, ▥ ℋ ᴳᴳᴳ – ⩜ 85. ⨾⦿ ᴬᴱ ⦿ ⱽᴵˢᴬ ᴶᶜᴮ. ⤶ rest
BY c
Primo Ciao-Ciao (ℰ (08) 651 28 30) : **Meals** (closed Christmas and New Year) (restricted lunch)/dinner a la carte 230/350 – **422 rm** ⌷ 1555/2205, 1 suite.

Berns, Näckströmsgatan 8, Berzelii Park, ⊠ S-111 47, ℰ (08) 566 322 00, *hotel.berns@berns.se*, Fax (08) 566 322 01 – |≢|, ⥽ rm, ▥ ℋ – ⩜ 180. ⨾⦿ ᴬᴱ ⦿ ⱽᴵˢᴬ. ⤶
closed Christmas-New Year – **Meals** (see **Berns Restaurant** below) – **61 rm** ⌷ 2050/3650, 4 suites.
CY b

Rica City H. Stockholm, Slöjdgatan 7, Hötorget, ⊠ S-111 57, ℰ (08) 723 72 00, *info.stockholm@rica.se*, Fax (08) 723 72 09, ⇌s – |≢|, ⥽ rm, ▤ rest, ▥ ℋ – ⩜ 70. ⨾⦿ ᴬᴱ ⦿ ⱽᴵˢᴬ. ⤶
CY c
Meals (closed Saturday and Sunday) (unlicensed) (lunch only) 70/75 and a la carte approx. 200 – **292 rm** ⌷ 1550/1800.

Comfort Home H. Tapto without rest., Jungfrugatan 57, ⊠ S-115 31, ℰ (08) 664 50 00, *tapto@comfort.choicehotels.se*, Fax (08) 664 07 00, « Military exhibits depicting the history of the Swedish army », ⇌s – |≢| ⥽ ▥ ℋ. ⨾⦿ ᴬᴱ ⦿ ⱽᴵˢᴬ
DX a
restricted opening Christmas-1 January – **86 rm** ⌷ (dinner included) 1440/1580.

🏠 **Wellington** without rest., Storgatan 6, ✉ S-114 51, ☎ (08) 667 09 10, *info.wellingt*
on@swedenhotels.se, Fax (08) 667 12 54, ☎ – 🛗 📺 ⚙, 🆎 ⓪ 𝘝𝘐𝘚𝘈, ⚭ DY p
closed 23-26 December – **58 rm** ⚏ 1645/2095, 2 suites.

🏠 **Lydmar**, Sturegatan 10, ✉ S-114 36, ☎ (08) 566 113 03, *info@lydmar.se*,
Fax (08) 566 113 01 – ⚙ 🆎 ⓪ 𝘝𝘐𝘚𝘈   CX a
Meals a la carte approx. 290 ₰ 210 – **61 rm** ⚏ 1900/2500, 1 suite.

🏠 **Freys**, Bryggargatan 12, ✉ S-101 31, ☎ (08) 50 62 13 00, *freys@freyshotels.com*,
Fax (08) 50 62 13 13 – 🛗, ✉ rm, 📺 ⚙, ⚙ 🆎 ⓪ 𝘝𝘐𝘚𝘈, ⚭ rest   BY u
closed Christmas – **Meals** *(closed Saturday and Sunday lunch)* (light lunch)/dinner a la carte
285/350 ₰ 220 – **114 rm** ⚏ 1595/2200, 1 suite.

🏠 **Lilla Rådmannen** without rest., Rådmansgatan 67, ✉ S-113 60, ☎ (08) 506 215 00,
radmannen@freyshotels.com, Fax (08) 506 215 15 – 🛗 ✉ 📺, ⚙ 🆎 ⓪ 𝘝𝘐𝘚𝘈 ⚭
closed 1 week Christmas – **36 rm** ⚏ 1295/1690.   BX a

XXXXX
&3 **Operakällaren**, Operahuset, Karl XII's Torg, ✉ S-111 86, ☎ (08) 676 58 01, *info@o*
perakallaren.se, Fax (08) 676 58 72, ⪕, « Historic late 19C restaurant situated in the Opera
House, baroque decor » – ▤, ⚙ 🆎 ⓪ 𝘝𝘐𝘚𝘈 𝙅𝘊𝘽, ⚭   CY d
closed July and 24 December 6 January – **Meals** (dinner only) 550/1500 and a la carte
820/915 ₰ 405
Spec. Smoked whitefish with roe. Knuckle of veal with red wine and figs. Chocolate globe
and sorbet.

XXXX **Franska Matsalen** (at Grand Hôtel), Södra Blasieholmshamnen 8, ✉ S-103 27, ☎ (08)
679 35 84, *franska@mbox301.swipnet.se*, Fax (00) 611 86 86, « Jacobean style dining
room, ⪕ Royal Palace and Old Town » – ▤, ⚙ 🆎 ⓪ 𝘝𝘐𝘚𝘈, ⚭   CY r
closed July, Saturday and Sunday – **Meals** (dinner only) a la carte 465/1070 ₰ 300.

XXX
&3 **Bon Lloc** (Dahlgren), Regeringsgatan 111, ✉ S-111 39, ☎ (08) 660 60 60, *bonlloc@t*
elia.com, Fax (08) 10 76 35 – ▤, ⚙ 🆎 ⓪ 𝘝𝘐𝘚𝘈, ⚭   CX n
closed 1 July-11 August, Christmas, Sunday and Bank Holidays – **Meals** (booking essential)
(dinner only) a la carte 475/710 ₰ 300
Spec. Mushroom cappuccino. Monkfish with paella and salsa verde. Terrine of pears, ginger
sabayon.

XX
&3 **Fredsgatan 12** (Andersson), Fredsgatan 12, ✉ S-111 52, ☎ (08) 24 80 52, *info@f*
redsgatan12.com, Fax (08) 23 76 05, « Contemporary interior design » – ⚙ 🆎 ⓪
𝘝𝘐𝘚𝘈, ⚭   CY f
closed July, 1 week Christmas, Sunday and Saturday lunch – **Meals** (booking essential) (light
lunch)/dinner a la carte 505/735 ₰ 310
Spec. Selection of antipasto. Bleakroe "tacos". Venison "B-B-Q".

XX **Café Opera**, Operahuset, Karl XII's Torg, ✉ S-111 86, ☎ (08) 676 58 07, *info@cafe*
opera.se, Fax (08) 676 58 71, ⪕ – ▤, ⚙ 🆎 ⓪ 𝘝𝘐𝘚𝘈 𝙅𝘊𝘽, ⚭   CY x
closed 24 December – **Meals** (booking essential) (dinner only) (music and dancing after
11pm) a la carte 350/515 ₰ 240.

XX **Riche**, Birger Jarlsgatan 4, ✉ S-114 34, ☎ (08) 545 035 65, *riche@riche.se*,
Fax (08) 545 035 69 – ▤, ⚙ 🆎 ⓪ 𝘝𝘐𝘚𝘈, ⚭   CY v
closed July, Sunday, Saturday lunch and Bank Holidays – **Meals** 325/1000 (dinner) and a
la carte 490/950 ₰ 300 – ***Teatergrillen*** : **Meals** 525 and a la carte 225/760 ₰ 300.

XX **Paul and Norbert**, Strandvägen 9, ✉ S-114 56, ☎ (08) 663 81 83, *restaurang.pau*
l.norbert@telia.com, Fax (08) 661 72 36 – ⚙ 🆎 ⓪ 𝘝𝘐𝘚𝘈, ⚭   DY m
closed 23 December-6 January, Sunday and lunch July-August, Monday, Saturday and Bank
Holidays – **Meals** (booking essential) 350 (lunch) and a la carte 630/870 ₰ 400.

XX
&3 **Wedholms Fisk**, Nybrokajen 17, ✉ S-111 48, ☎ (08) 611 78 74, Fax (08) 678 60 11
– ▤, ⚙ 🆎 ⓪ 𝘝𝘐𝘚𝘈 𝙅𝘊𝘽, ⚭   CY s
closed Sunday and Saturday lunch – **Meals** - Seafood - (light lunch) a la carte 570/790
₰ 280
Spec. Fricassee of sole, turbot, lobster and scallops with Champagne sauce. Boiled turbot
with butter and horseradish. Tartare of salmon and roe.

X **Clas På Hörnet**, Surbrunnsgatan 20, ✉ S-113 48, ☎ (08) 16 51 30, *hotel@claspah*
ornet.com, Fax (08) 612 53 15, ⚮, « Characterful part 18C inn » – 🛗, ⚙ 🆎 ⓪ 𝘝𝘐𝘚𝘈
closed Christmas, 1 January and lunch Saturday and Sunday – **Meals** 95/250 and a la carte
205/460 ₰ 190.   CX f

X **Vassa Eggen**, Kungstensgatan 9, ✉ S-114 25, ☎ (08) 21 61 69, *vassa.eggen@swip*
net.se, Fax (08) 20 34 46 – ⚙ 🆎 ⓪ 𝘝𝘐𝘚𝘈 𝙅𝘊𝘽, ⚭   CX b
closed July, 2 weeks Christmas-New Year, Sunday and Monday – **Meals** (dinner only)
575/625 and a la carte 405/635 ₰ 235.

X **Restaurangen**, Oxtorgsgatan 14, ✉ S-111 57, ☎ (08) 22 09 52, *restaurangen.tm*
@telia.com, Fax (08) 22 09 54, « Contemporary interior » – ⚙ 🆎 ⓪ 𝘝𝘐𝘚𝘈, ⚭   CY d
closed July, 1 week Christmas, Saturday lunch and Sunday – **Meals** (booking essential) (light
lunch) 200/400 ₰ 350.

BRASSERIES AND BISTRO

XX **Berns Restaurant** (at Berns H.), Berzelii Park, ⊠ S-111 47, ℰ (08) 566 322 22
Fax (08) 566 323 23, « Restored 19C rococo style ballroom » – 🐠 ﹩ ⓞ
𝗩𝗜𝗦𝗔. ﹩ CY t
Meals 255/295 (lunch) and a la carte 420/565 ⅃ 260.

X **Prinsen,** Mäster Samuelsgatan 4, ⊠ S-111 44, ℰ (08) 611 13 31, matsalen@restau.
angprinsen.se, Fax (08) 611 70 79, 🏡 – 🐠 ﹩ ⓞ 𝗩𝗜𝗦𝗔 jcв. ﹩ CY ⅃
closed Sunday – **Meals** (booking essential) a la carte 310/545 ⅃ 350.

X **Sturehof,** Stureplan 2-4, ⊠ S-114 46, ℰ (08) 440 57 30, info@sturehof.com
Fax (08) 678 11 01, 🏡 – 🐠 ﹩ ⓞ 𝗩𝗜𝗦𝗔 jcв. ﹩ CY r
Meals a la carte 350/605 ⅃ 220.

X **KB,** Smålandsgatan 7, ⊠ S-111 46, ℰ (08) 679 60 32, konstbaren@swipnet.se
Fax (08) 611 82 83, « 19C architecture, modern art display » – 🐠 ﹩ ⓞ
⊜ 𝗩𝗜𝗦𝗔. ﹩ CY u
closed June-August, Saturday lunch and Sunday – **Meals** 455 (dinner) and a la carte
320/655 ⅃ 275.

X **Eriks Bakficka,** Fredrikshovsgatan 4, ⊠ S-115 23, ℰ (08) 660 15 99, info@bakfick
an@eriks.se, Fax (08) 663 25 67, 🏡 – ▤. 🐠 ﹩ ⓞ 𝗩𝗜𝗦𝗔. ﹩ DY ⅃
closed 23-26 and 31 December, 1 January and lunch Saturday and Sunday – **Meals** a la
carte 400/525 ⅃ 195.

X **Grodan,** Grev Turegatan 16, ⊠ S-114 46, ℰ (08) 679 61 00, grevture@grodan.se,
Fax (08) 679 61 10 – 🐠 ﹩ ⓞ 𝗩𝗜𝗦𝗔 jcв CY m
closed midsummer, 24, 25 and 31 December, 1 January and Sunday – **Meals** 95/230 anc
a la carte 225/425 ⅃ 230.

X **Bistro Jarl,** Birger Jarlsgatan 7, ⊠ S-111 45, ℰ (08) 611 76 30, bistrojarl@swipnet.se
Fax (08) 611 07 90, 🏡 – 🐠 ﹩ ⓞ 𝗩𝗜𝗦𝗔 CY z
closed Sunday – **Meals** (booking essential) (restricted lunch) a la carte 315/41C
⅃ 240.

X **Norrlands Bar & Grill,** Norrlandsgatan 24, ⊠ S-111 43, ℰ (08) 611 88 10, norrlar
⊜ ds@swipnet.se, Fax (08) 611 88 30, 🏡 – 🐠 ﹩ ⓞ 𝗩𝗜𝗦𝗔. ﹩ CY k
closed Easter, July, 2 weeks August, Christmas, New Year, Sunday, Monday dinner anc
Saturday lunch – **Meals** a la carte 330/590 ⅃ 235.

at Gamla Stan (Old Stockholm) :

🏨 **First H. Reisen,** Skeppsbron 12, ⊠ S-111 30, ℰ (08) 22 32 60, reisen@firsthotels.se,
Fax (08) 20 15 59, ≤, « 18C hotel on waterfront with original maritime decor », 🚉 – 📶,
🖐 rm, 📺 ﹠. 🐠 ﹩ ⓞ 𝗩𝗜𝗦𝗔. ﹩ rest AZ f
closed 23-26 December – **Primo Ciao-Ciao :** Meals (closed Sunday) a la carte 320/405
⅃ 200 – **137 rm** ⊑ 1895/3095, 7 suites.

🏨 **Victory,** Lilla Nygatan 5, ⊠ S-111 28, ℰ (08) 506 400 00, info@victory-hotel.se,
Fax (08) 506 400 10, « 17C house with Swedish rural furnishings and maritime antiques »,
🚉 – 📶, 🖐 rm, 📺 ﹨ – 🍴 80. 🐠 ﹩ ⓞ 𝗩𝗜𝗦𝗔. ﹩ AZ v
closed 22 December-7 January – **Meals** (see **Leijontornet** below) – **42 rm** ⊑ 2190/2490,
3 suites.

🏨 **Lady Hamilton** without rest., Storkyrkobrinken 5, ⊠ S-111 28, ℰ (08) 506 401 00,
info@lady-hamilton.se, Fax (08) 506 401 10, « 15C house, Swedish rural antiques », 🚉
– 📶 🖐 📺. 🐠 ﹩ ⓞ 𝗩𝗜𝗦𝗔 jcв. ﹩ AZ e
34 rm ⊑ 1990/2350.

🏨 **Lord Nelson** without rest., Västerlånggatan 22, ⊠ S-111 29, ℰ (08) 506 401 20, info
@lord-nelson.se, Fax (08) 506 401 30, « Late 17C house with ship style interior and maritime antiques », 🚉 – 📶 🖐 📺. 🐠 ﹩ ⓞ 𝗩𝗜𝗦𝗔 jcв. ﹩ AZ a
closed 22 December-7 January – **29 rm** ⊑ 1590/1990.

🏨 **Rica City H. Gamla Stan** without rest., Lilla Nygatan 25, ⊠ S-111 28, ℰ (08)
723 72 50, info.gamlastan@rica.se, Fax (08) 723 72 59, « 17C house » – 📶 🖐 📺 –
🍴 25. 🐠 ﹩ ⓞ 𝗩𝗜𝗦𝗔 AZ c
50 rm ⊑ 1590/1990, 1 suite.

XXX **Pontus in the Green House,** Österlånggatan 17, ⊠ S-111 31, ℰ (08) 23 85 00,
info@pontusigamlastan.se, Fax (08) 796 60 69, « 15C house » – 🐠 ﹩ ⓞ 𝗩𝗜𝗦𝗔 AZ u
closed lunch in summer and Sunday – **Meals** (booking essential) 525/675 (lunch) and a la
carte 885/1125 ⅃ 225.

XX **Leijontornet** (at Victory H.), Lilla Nygatan 5, ⊠ S-111 28, ℰ (08) 14 23 55, info@l
eijontornet.se, Fax (08) 406 08 14, « Remains of a 14C fortified tower in the dining room »
– 🐠 ﹩ ⓞ 𝗩𝗜𝗦𝗔 jcв. ﹩ AZ v
closed Sunday – **Meals** (booking essential) (dinner only) 420/650 and a la carte 385/540
⅃ 240.

XX **Den Gyldene Freden**, Österlånggatan 51, ✉ S-103 17, ✐ (08) 24 97 60, *info@ gylden efreden.se, Fax (08) 21 38 70,* « Early 18C inn with vaulted cellars » – ❸ 🅐🅔 ① 𝑽𝑰𝑺𝑨, ❄️, *closed 24-25 December and Sunday* – Meals *(dinner only and Saturday lunch)/dinner 470 and a la carte 330/740* ♦ 400.
AZ s

X **Fem Små Hus**, Nygränd 10, ✉ S-111 30, ✐ (08) 10 04 82, *info@femsmahus.se, Fax (08) 14 96 95,* « 17C cellars, antiques » – ❸ 🅐🅔 ① 𝑽𝑰𝑺𝑨 𝗝𝗖𝗕
AZ r
Meals *(dinner only) 395/470 and a la carte 410/610* ♦ 265.

at Djurgården :

🏛 **Scandic H. Hasselbacken** Ⓜ, Hazeliusbacken 20, ✉ S-100 55, ✐ (08) 517 343 00, *hasselbacken@ scandic-hotels.com, Fax (08) 517 343 11,* ☂, « Historic summer restaurant in former royal park », ☎ – 🛗, ⤢ rm, 🖭 📺 ♿ 🍽 🅿 – ⚿ 100. ❸ 🅐🅔 ① 𝑽𝑰𝑺𝑨. ❄️ rest
DZ e
Meals *(booking essential) (dinner only) 375 and a la carte 375/485* ♦ 280 – **110 rm** ⌂ 1510/2165, 2 suites.

XX **Ulla Winbladh**, Rosendalsvägen 8, ✉ S-115 21, ✐ (08) 663 05 71, *ulla.winbladh@ ul lawinbladh.se, Fax (08) 663 05 73,* ☂, « Late 19C pavilion in former royal hunting ground » – ❸ 🅐🅔 ① 𝑽𝑰𝑺𝑨. ❄️
DY a
Meals *(booking essential) a la carte 170/470* ♦ 225.

at Södermalm :

🏛 **Scandic H. Slussen** Ⓜ, Guldgränd 8, ✉ S-104 65, ✐ (08) 517 353 00, *slussen@ sc andic-hotels.com, Fax (08) 517 353 66,* ≼, ☂, 🛏, ☎, 🔲 – 🛗, ⤢ rm, 🖭 📺 ♿ ♿ ⤢ – ⚿ 300. ❸ 🅐🅔 ① 𝑽𝑰𝑺𝑨. ❄️ rest
CZ e
Eken : Meals *(closed Sunday lunch)* (light lunch) 300 (dinner) and a la carte 315/395 ♦ 280 – **281 rm** ⌂ 2365/2800, 11 suites.

🏛 **Scandic Malmen**, Götgatan 49-51, ✉ S-102 66, ✐ (08) 517 347 00, *malmen@ sca ndic-hotels.com, Fax (08) 517 347 11* – 🛗, ⤢ rm, 🖭 📺 ♿ ♿, ❸ 🅐🅔 ① 𝑽𝑰𝑺𝑨. ❄️ rest
Meals *(dinner only) 275/340 and a la carte approx. 285* ♦ 150 – **270 rm** ⌂ 1410/2030, 13 suites.
CZ r

XX **Eriks Gondolen**, Stadsgården 6 (11th floor), ✉ S-104 56, ✐ (08) 641 70 90, *info @ eriks.se, Fax (08) 641 11 40,* « Glass enclosed passageway with nautical decor, ❅ Stockholm and water » – 🖭 – ⚿ 25. ❸ 🅐🅔 ① 𝑽𝑰𝑺𝑨. ❄️
CZ a
closed 24-26 December, 1 January, 1 April and Sunday – Meals *295/475 and a la carte 425/570* ♦ 235.

XX **Gässlingen**, Brännkyrkagatan 93, ✉ S-117 26, ✐ (08) 669 54 95, *Fax (08) 84 89 90,* « Rustic décor » – ❸ 🅐🅔 ① 𝑽𝑰𝑺𝑨. ❄️
BZ
closed 1 week Easter, 21 June-24 August, 22 December-7 January, Sunday, Monday and Bank Holidays – Meals *(booking essential) (dinner only) 750/895 and a la carte 490/740* ♦ 295.

to the North :

🏛 **Stallmästaregården** Ⓜ ⏚, Norrtull, ✉ S-113 47, North : 2 km by Sveavägen (at beginning of E 4) ✐ (08) 610 13 00, *info@ stallmastaregarden.se, Fax (08) 610 13 40,* ≼, ☂, « Waterside setting », 🍽 – 🛗, 🛗 ⤢ 📺 ♿ 🅿 ❸ 🅐🅔 ① 𝑽𝑰𝑺𝑨. ❄️ rest
Meals *(see below)* – **36 rm** ⌂ 2100/2650, 13 suites.

XX **Stallmästaregården** (at Stallmästaregården H.), Norrtull, ✉ S-113 47, North : 2 km by Sveavägen (at beginning of E 4) ✐ (08) 610 13 00, *info@ stallmastaregarden.se, Fax (08) 610 13 40,* ≼, ☂, « Part 17C inn, waterside setting », 🍽 –, 🛗 🅿 ❸ 🅐🅔 ① 𝑽𝑰𝑺𝑨. ❄️
Meals *425 (dinner) and a la carte 385/585* ♦ 260.

to the East :

at Ladugårdsgärdet :

XX **Villa Källhagen** ⏚ with rm, Djurgårdsbrunnsvägen 10, ✉ S-115 27, East : 3 km by Strandvägen ✐ (08) 665 03 00, *villa@ kallhagen.se, Fax (08) 665 03 99,* ≼, ☂, « Waterside setting, Swedish contemporary interior design », ☎, 🍽 – 🛗, 🛗, ⤢ rm, 📺 🅿 – ⚿ 55. ❸ 🅐🅔 ① 𝑽𝑰𝑺𝑨. ❄️ rest
Meals *a la carte 335/505* ♦ 250 – **18 rm** ⌂ 1900/2700, 2 suites.

at Fjäderholmarna Island *25 mn by boat, departure every hour (½ hour in season) from Nybrokajen* CY :

XX **Fjäderholmarnas Krog**, Stora Fjäderholmen, ✉ S-100 05, ✐ (08) 718 33 55, *fjad erholmarna@ atv.se, Fax (08) 716 39 89,* ☂, « Waterside setting on archipelago island with ≼ neighbouring islands and sea » – ❸ 🅐🅔 ① 𝑽𝑰𝑺𝑨 𝗝𝗖𝗕. ❄️
2 May-22 December except November and lunch October – Meals *385/555 and a la carte 240/555* ♦ 270.

to the Southeast :

at Nacka Strand *Southeast : 10 km by Stadsgården DZ or by boat from Nybrokajen :*

🏨 **Hotel J** M ⌫, Ellensviksvägen 1, ✉ S-131 27, ℰ (08) 601 30 00, *info@hotelj.com*
Fax (08) 601 30 09, ⩽ sea, « Contemporary interior design » – ⊞ ✦ 🖵 🖵 ✓ & P. ⊕
AE ⓪ VISA. ✾ rest
closed Christmas – **Meals** (see **Restaurant J** below) – **43 rm** ⚏ 1595/2395
2 suites.

❌❌ **Restaurant J** (at Hotel J), Augustendalsvägen 52, ✉ S-131 27, ℰ (08) 601 30 00,
info@restaurantj.com, Fax (08) 601 30 09, ⩧ – ⊟. ⊕ AE ⓪ VISA. ✾
closed Christmas – **Meals** a la carte 245/470 ⧪ 245.

to the South :

at Johanneshov (Globen City) :

🏨 **Globe** M, Arenaslingan 7, ✉ S-121 26, South : 1 ½ km by Rd 73 ℰ (08) 686 63 00,
globe@quality.choicehotels.se, Fax (08) 686 63 01, ⩧, ⌫ – ⊞, ✦ rm, ⊟ 🖵 & ⇌
– 🛏 220. ⊕ AE ⓪ VISA. ✾ rest
closed 20 December-2 January – **Tabac :** Meals 160/325 and a la carte 245/325 – **287 rm**
⚏ 1395/1595.

to the West :

at Bromma *West : 5 ½ km by Norr Mälarstrand BY and Drottningholmsvägen :*

❌❌ **Sjöpaviljongen,** Tranebergs Strand 4, Alvik, ✉ 167 40, East : 1 ½ km ℰ (08) 704 04 24,
info@paviljongen.se, Fax (08) 704 82 40, ⩽, ⩧, « Modern pavilion, waterside setting »
– 🗗, ⊕ AE ⓪ VISA JCB.
closed 23 December-6 January, Saturday lunch, Sunday and Bank Holidays – **Meals** (booking
essential) 140/265 (dinner) and a la carte 405/495 ⧪ 230 – **Bistro !** ⩧ **Meals** (bookings
not accepted) 120 (lunch) and dinner a la carte 200/300 ⧪ 230.

to the Northwest :

🏨 **Radisson SAS Royal Park** M ⌫, Frösundaviks Allé 15, ✉ S-169 03, Northwest : 5 km
by Sveavägen and E 4, Exit Frösunda and Frösundavik rd ℰ (08) 624 55 00, *reception*
@royalpark.se, Fax (08) 85 85 66, ⩽, ⩧, « Situated in Royal Park on shores of Brunnsvik
Bay », ⨍ₒ, ⌫, 🖩, ⌀ – ⊞, 🗗, ✦ rm, 🖵 & ⇌ P. – 🛏 280. ⊕ AE ⓪ VISA.
✾ rest
closed 20 December-6 January – **Meals** a la carte 310/455 ⧪ 240 – **187 rm**
⚏ 2040/2440, 6 suites.

❌❌❌ **Ulriksdals Wärdshus,** ✉ 170 79 Solna, Northwest : 8 km by Sveavägen and E 18
towards Norrtälje, taking first junction for Ulriksdals Slott ℰ (08) 85 08 15, *info@ulrik*
sdalswardshus.se, Fax (08) 85 08 58, ⩽, ⩧, « 17C former inn in Royal Park », ⨝ – P.
⊕ AE ⓪ VISA JCB
closed 24-26 December – **Meals** 450 (dinner) and a la carte 450/660 ⧪ 240.

at Sollentuna *Northwest : 15 km by Sveavägen BX and E 4 (exit Sollentuna c) :*

❌❌❌❌ **Edsbacka Krog** (Lingström), Sollentunavägen 220, ✉ 191 35, ℰ (08) 96 33 00, *info*
❀❀ *@edsbackakrog.se, Fax (08) 96 40 19*, « Stylishly decorated 17C inn », ⨝ – P. ⊕ AE ⓪
VISA JCB. ✾
*closed 8 July-2 August, 23 December-3 January, Good Friday, midsummer and Sunday and
Monday except May, June and December* – **Meals** 620 (dinner) and a la carte 545/770
⧪ 275
Spec. Salmon with anchovy and sweet pepper. Saddle of roe deer with blackcurrant sauce.
White chocolate mousse with cherry and cinnamon.

at Arlanda Airport *Northwest : 40 km by Sveavägen BX and E 4 –* ✉ *Arlanda :*

🏨 **Radisson SAS Sky City** M, at Terminals 4-5, 2nd floor above street level, ✉ 190 45
Stockholm-Arlanda, Sky City ℰ (08) 506 740 00, *sales@stozr.rdsas.com, Fax (08) 506 740*
01, ⨍ₒ, ⌫ – ⊞, ✦ rm, ⊟ 🖵 ✓ &. ⊕ AE ⓪ VISA. ✾
Meals 220 (lunch) and a la carte approx. 395 ⧪ 270 – **229 rm** ⚏ 2295/2595,
1 suite.

GOTHENBURG (GÖTEBORG) *Sverige* 985 O 8 – *pop. 437313.*

See : *Art Gallery*★★ *(Göteborgs Konstmuseet)* CX **M1** – *Castle Park*★★ *(Slottsskogen)* AX
– *Botanical Gardens*★★ *(Botaniska Trädgården)* AX – *East India House*★★ *(Ostindiska Huset :
Göteborgs stadmuseum)* BU **M2** *Museum of Arts and Crafts*★★ *(Röhsska Konstlojdmuseet)*
BV **M3** – *Liseberg Amusement Park*★★ *(Liseberg Nöjespark)* DX *Horticultural Gardens*★★
(Trädgårdsföreningen) CU – *Natural History Museum*★ *(Naturhistoriska museet)* AX – *Mari-
time Museum*★ *(Sjöfartsmuseet)* AV – *Kungsportsavenyn*★ BCVX **22** – *Götaplatsen (Carl
Milles Poseidon*★★*)* CX – *Seaman's Tower (Sjömanstornet)* (✳★★*)* AV *Göteborgs-Utkiken*
(✳★★*)* BT – *Masthugg Church (Masthuggskyrkan) (interior*★*)* AV.

Envir. : *Öckerö Archipelago*★ *by boat or by car :* N : *17 km by E 6 and road 155 –
New Älvsborg Fortress*★ *(Nya Älvsborgs Fästning)* AU – *Bohuslan*★★ *(The Golden
Coast)* N : *- Halland coast to the south : Åskhult Open-Air Museum*★ *; Tjölöholms Slott*★
AX.

⛳ *Albatross, Lillhagsvägen Hisings Backa* ℘ *(031) 55 19 01* – ⛳ *Delsjö, Kallebäck* ℘ *(031)
40 69 59* – ⛳ *Göteborgs, Golfbanevägen, Hovås* ℘ *(031) 28 24 44.*

✈ *Scandinavian Airlines System : Svenska Mässan (vid Korsvägen)* ℘ *(031) 94 20 00
Landvetter Airport :* ℘* *(031) 94 10 00.*

⚓ *To Denmark : contact Stena Line A/B* ℘ *(031) 775 00 00, Fax (031) 85 85 95* – *To
Continent : contact Scandinavian Seaways* ℘ *(031) 65 06 50, Fax (031) 53 23 09.* ·

🛈 *Kungsportplatsen 2* ℘ *(031) 61 25 00, Fax (031) 61 25 01.*

Copenhagen 279 – *Oslo 322* – *Stockholm 500.*

Plans on following pages

🏨🏨🏨 **Radisson SAS Scandinavia** Ⓜ, Södra Hamngatan 59-65, ⊠ S-401 24, ℘ (031)
758 50 00, *reservations.scandinavia.gothenburg@radissonsas.com,* Fax (031) 758 50 01,
« Atrium courtyard », ₤ᵭ, ⇆s, ⬚ – ∣≡∣, ⇥ rm, ⬚ ⊤⊽ 🗡 & ⟲ – ▲ 450. 🆖 🆒 🅰🅴 🆔
VISA. ⚘ rest   BU b
Atrium Bar & Restaurant *: Meals (closed Saturday lunch and Sunday)* (buffet
lunch) 90/190 and dinner a la carte ₰ 110 – ⚏ 125 – **333 rm** 1950/2210,
14 suites.

🏨🏨 **Elite Plaza,** Västra Hamngatan 3, ⊠ S-404 22, ℘ (031) 720 40 00, *info@gbgplaza.e
lite.se, Fax (031) 720 40 10,* « Stylishly converted late 19C insurance company » – ⇥ rm,
⊤⊽ 🗡 & – ▲ 50. 🆒 🅰🅴 🆔 *VISA*. ⚘   BU s
closed 24-27 December – **Meals** (see *Swea Hof* below) – **141 rm** ⚏ 1625/2600,
2 suites.

🏨🏨 **Gothia Towers,** Mässans Gata 24, ⊠ S-402 26, ℘ (031) 750 88 00, *info@gothiato
wers.com, Fax (031) 750 88 85,* ⇐. « Panoramic restaurant on 23rd floor », ⇐s – ∣≡∣,
⇥ rm, ⬚ ⊤⊽ & ⟲ – ▲ 1500. 🆖 🆒 🅰🅴 🆔 *VISA*. ⚘ rest   DX k
Heaven 23 : **Meals** (buffet lunch) 90/490 and a la carte 315/490 ₰ 195 – **693 rm**
⚏ 1590/2290, 11 suites.

🏨🏨 **Scandic H. Europa,** Köpmansgatan 38, ⊠ S-404 29, ℘ (031) 751 65 00, *europa@s
candic-hotels.com, Fax (031) 751 65 11,* ⇐s, ⬚ – ∣≡∣, ⇥ rm, ⬚ ⊤⊽ & ⟲ – ▲ 60. 🆖
🅰🅴 🆔 *VISA* 🎫 ⚘ rest   BU a
Meals (in bar Sunday) (buffet lunch) 95 and a la carte 235/430 ₰ 200 – **447 rm**
⚏ 1495/2145, 5 suites.

🏨🏨 **Scandic H. Crown,** Polhemsplatsen 3, ⊠ S-411 11, ℘ (031) 751 51 00, *crown@sc
andic-hotels.com, Fax (031) 751 51 11,* ₤ᵭ, ⇐s – ∣≡∣, ⇥ rm, ⬚ ⊤⊽ 🗡 & ⟲ – ▲ 225.
🆖 🅰🅴 🆔 *VISA* ⚘ rest   CU d
Meals (in bar Saturday lunch and Sunday) (buffet lunch) 145 and a la carte 240/410 ₰ 185
– **328 rm** ⚏ 1850/2585, 5 suites.

🏨🏨 **Riverton,** Stora Badhusgatan 26, ⊠ S-411 21, ℘ (031) 750 10 00, *riverton@riverto
n.se, Fax (031) 750 10 01,* « 12th floor restaurant with ⇐ Göta Älv river and docks », ⇐s
– ∣≡∣, ⇥ rm, ⬚ rest, ⊤⊽ & 🄿 – ▲ 300. 🆖 🆒 🅰🅴 🆔 *VISA*. ⚘   AV c
Meals *(closed Sunday)* (dinner only) a la carte 360/420 ₰ 195 – **187 rm** ⚏ 1230/1540,
4 suites.

🏨🏨 **Scandic H. Opalen,** Engelbrektsgatan 73, ⊠ S-402 23, ℘ (031) 751 53 00, *opalen
@scandic-hotels.com, Fax (031) 751 53 11,* ⇐s – ∣≡∣, ⇥ rm, ⬚ rest, ⊤⊽ 🗡 & ⟲ 🄿 –
▲ 180. 🆖 🆒 🅰🅴 🆔 *VISA*. ⚘ rest   DV u
Meals (in bar Sunday and Bank Holidays) (dancing Thursday-Saturday evenings except mid
June-mid August) (buffet lunch) 190 and a la carte 240/425 ₰ 280 – **238 rm**
⚏ 1295/2250, 4 suites.

🏨🏨 **Radisson SAS Park Avenue,** Kungsportsavenyn 36-38, ⊠ S-400 16, ℘ (031)
758 40 00, *reservations.parkavenue.gothenburg@radissonsas.com, Fax (031) 758 40 01,*
🍴, ₤ᵭ, ⇐s – ∣≡∣, ⇥ rm, ⬚ rest, ⊤⊽ ⟲ – ▲ 550. 🆖 🆒 🅰🅴 🆔 *VISA*
🎫 ⚘   CX f
Parkbaren *: Meals (closed Sunday dinner)* 305 (dinner) and a la carte 290/420 ₰ 200 –
⚏ 125 – **301 rm** 1800/2060, 17 suites.

GÖTEBORG

0   500 m

E 6   OSLO

GÖTA   ÄLV

Götaälvbron

BARKEN VIKING

Göteborgs-Utkiken

Lilla Bommens Hamn   Hamntorget

53

FRIHAMNEN

Göteborgs Operan

Göteborgs Maritima Centrum

LUNDBYVASSEN

P   16   29

Trädgårdn

52   Östra

P 33   Nils Ericsons plats

NORDSTADEN   51   Nordstads-torget

Stenpiren   M   39

23   35   a   e

Stora

35   23   G. Adolfs Torg   H

M   Hamn   kanalen

b   60   f   60

54   Lilla Torget   S   Astra   Korsgatan   gatan   12 P   55

M 4   Drottning-   Haringatan

Skeppsbron   Magasins   Kyrko-   gatan   Kungsportsplatsen

INOM VALLGRAVEN   DOMKYRKAN   Kungsgatan   Kungsports-platsen

Masthuggskajen   Kungsgatan   Haringatan   Kungstorget

STENA-TERMINALEN   P   Stora Teatern

2   20   Feskekörka   45   KUNGSPARKEN   Allén

32   34   Rosenlunds-   17   Nya   gatan

59   Järn-torget   kanalen   Park-   56

Första Långg.   Södra   Allegatan   PUSTERVIK   34

b   Haga   Nygata   Viktor   56   U   Vasagatan

25   HAGA   Vasagatan   Jaschebergs   M 3

SKANSENPARKEN   U   Haga   VASASTADEN   VASAPARKEN

Skansen Kronan   P   Spångkullg.   Kyrkogatan   gatan

7   31   Utsikts-platsen   U   Engelbrekts-

a   44   Sveagatan   U   gatan

Limhamnsgatan   Övre   Brunnsgatan   Föreningsgatan

E 6-E 20   158   Slottsskogen, Botaniska Trädgården   Naturhistoriska museet

Älvsborgsbron. Sjömanstornet   Masthuggskyrkan. Sjöfartsmuseet

VINGA   Nya Älvsborgs Fästning

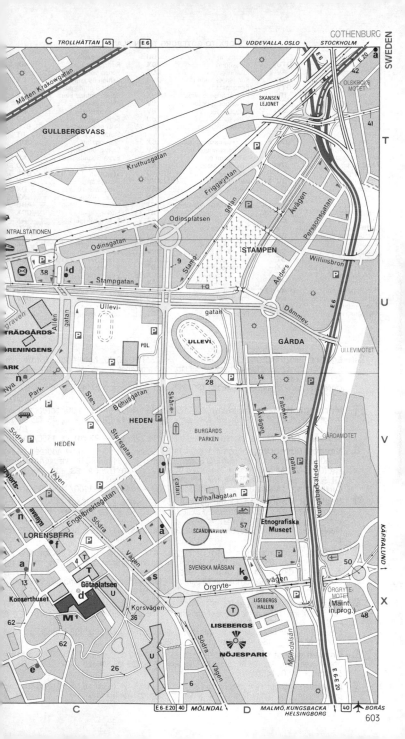

E6

E 20

a

OLSKROKS MOTET

42

T

41

GULLBERGSVASS

Kruthusgatan

SKANSEN LEJONET

Friggagatan

gatan

Avägen

Perssonsgatan

Odinsplatsen

Willinsbron

NTRALSTATIONEN

Odinsgatan

STAMPEN

Anders

9 Stamp

38 d

Stampgatan

gatan

Dämmev.

E6

Ullevi-

U

graven

Allén

TRÄDGÅRDS-

gatan

ULLEVIMOTET

ULLEVI

GÅRDA

RENINGENS

ARK

n

Park-

PÖL

28

14

Sten

Bohusgatan

Skåre-

Fabriks-

GÅRDAMOTET

HEDEN

HEDEN

Sveagatan

BURGÅRDS PARKEN

Avägen

V

Nya

Södra

Park-

gatan

Kungsbackaleden

Vägen

u

catan

Valhallagatan

KÅRRALUND

Engelbrektsgatan

n

57

Etnografiska Museet

avenyn

Södra

4

a

SCANDINAVIUM

k

50

LORENSBERG

f

7

s

SVENSKA MÄSSAN

a

4

Vägen

vägen

ÖRGRYTE-

a

13

T

Örgryte-

MOTET

48

Götaplatsen

(Maint. in prog.)

Konserthuset

d

U

Korsvägen

LISEBERGS HALLEN

X

62

M

36

T

LISEBERGS

62

e

U

26

NÖJESPARK

Mölndalsån

6

Södra

E 6·E 20

STREET INDEX TO GÖTEBORG TOWN PLAN

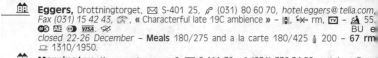

Eggers, Drottningtorget, ⊠ S-401 25, ℘ (031) 80 60 70, *hotel.eggers@telia.com*, *Fax (031) 15 42 43*, 🍴, « Characterful late 19C ambience » – |𝄐|, ½≈ rm, 📺 – 🏛 55. ⚫🅜 🆎 ⓪ 𝘷𝘪𝘴𝘢. ⏦
BU e
closed 22-26 December – **Meals** 180/275 and a la carte 180/425 ⏦ 200 – **67 rm** ⏦ 1310/1950.

Mornington, Kungsportsavenyn 6, ⊠ S-411 36, ℘ (031) 736 34 00, *goteborg@mo rnington.se, Fax (031) 711 34 39*, 🍴, 🆑 – |𝄐|, ½≈ rm, 📱 📺 🌐 – 🏛 45. ⚫🅜 🆎 ⓪ 𝘷𝘪𝘴𝘢 🆑🅱. ⏦ rest
BV e
Brasserie Lipp : **Meals** *(closed Sunday)* a la carte 275/375 – **92 rm** ⏦ 1350/2100.

Novotel Göteborg, Klippan 1, ⊠ S-414 51, Southwest : 3 ½ km by Andréeg taking Kiel-Klippan Ö exit, or boat from Lilla Bommens Hamn ℘ (031) 14 90 00, *info@novotel.se, Fax (031) 42 22 32,* ≤, 🍴, « Converted brewery on waterfront », 🆑 – |𝄐|, ½≈ rm, 📱 📺 ⅙ 🄿 – 🏛 120. ⚫🅜 🆎 ⓪ 𝘷𝘪𝘴𝘢
Carnegie Kaj : **Meals** a la carte 280/350 ⏦ 200 – **143 rm** ⏦ 1160/1450, 5 suites.

Quality H. Panorama, Eklandagatan 51-53, ⊠ S-400 22, ℘ (031) 767 70 00, *info. panorama@quality.choicehotels.se, Fax (031) 767 70 70,* ≤, 🆑 – |𝄐|, ½≈ rm, 📱 📺 ⅙ 🌐 – 🏛 120. ⚫🅜 🆎 ⓪ 𝘷𝘪𝘴𝘢 ⏦ rest
DX
Meals *(closed Sunday, Saturday lunch and Bank Holidays)* a la carte approx. 300 – **339 rm** ⏦ 1350/1550.

Victors, Skeppsbroplatsen 1 (4th floor), ⊠ S-411 18, ℘ (031) 17 41 80, *info@victor s-hotel.com, Fax (031) 13 96 10,* ≤ Göta Älv river and harbour, 🆑 – |𝄐|, ½≈ rm, 📱 📺 ⅙ – 🏛 40. ⚫🅜 🆎 ⓪ 𝘷𝘪𝘴𝘢 🆑🅱. ⏦ rest
AU b
closed 24-26 and 31 December and 1 January – **Meals** *(closed Friday-Sunday)* (dinner only) a la carte 280/395 ⏦ 180 – **35 rm** ⏦ 1250/1650, 9 suites.

Tidbloms, Olskroksgatan 23, ⊠ S-416 66, Northeast : 2 ½ km by E 20 ℘ (031) 707 50 00, *info.tidbloms@swedenhotels.se, Fax (031) 707 50 99,* 🆑 – |𝄐|, ½≈ rm, 📺 🄿. – 🏛 70. ⚫🅜 🆎 ⓪ 𝘷𝘪𝘴𝘢 ⏦ rest
DT a
closed 20 December-8 January – **Meals** *(closed lunch in July)* 100/195 (dinner) and a la carte 290/440 ⏦ 180 – **42 rm** ⏦ 1140/1450.

Onyxen without rest., Sten Sturegatan 23, ⊠ S-412 52, ℘ (031) 81 08 45, *info@h otelonyxen.com, Fax (031) 16 56 72* – |𝄐| ½≈ 📺 🄿. ⚫🅜 🆎 ⓪ 𝘷𝘪𝘴𝘢 🆑🅱
DX a
34 rm ⏦ 1150/1450.

Poseidon without rest., Storgatan 33, ⊠ S-411 33, ℘ (031) 10 05 50, *info@hotelp oseidon.com, Fax (031) 13 83 91* – |𝄐| ½≈ 📺. ⚫🅜 🆎 ⓪ 𝘷𝘪𝘴𝘢 🆑🅱. ⏦
BV a
48 rm ⏦ 980/1250.

XXX
☆ **Sjömagasinet,** Klippans Kulturreservat 5, ✉ S-414 51, Southwest : 3 ½ km by Andréeg taking Kiel-Klippan O exit, or boat from Lilla Bommens Hamn 𝄢 (031) 775 59 20, *info @ sjomagasinet.se*, Fax (031) 24 55 39, ≤, 🍽, « Reconstructed 18C former East India Company warehouse on waterfront » – 🅿. 🕮 🄰🄴 ⑩ 𝘝𝘐𝘚𝘈. ❀
closed 1 week Christmas-New Year and Saturday lunch – **Meals** - Seafood - 395/595 and a la carte 595/690 ₰ 310
Spec. Classic herring platter with Vika crispbread and mature cheese. Baked cod with grilled crayfish and scallops. "Cloudberry creation".

XXX
Swea Hof (at Elite Plaza H.), Västra Hamngatan 3, ✉ S-404 22, 𝄢 (031) 720 40 40, Fax (031) 720 40 10 – 🖭. 🕮 🄰🄴 ⑩ 𝘝𝘐𝘚𝘈. ❀   BU s
closed Sunday and Bank Holidays – **Meals** 465 (dinner) and a la carte 355/640 ₰ 255.

XX
Fiskekrogen, Lilla Torget 1, ✉ S-411 18, 𝄢 (031) 10 10 05, *info@ fiskekrogen.com,* Fax (031) 10 10 06, « 1920's restaurant with contemporary Scandic decor » – 🍽 🖭. 🕮 🄰🄴 ⑩ 𝘝𝘐𝘚𝘈. ❀   AU f
closed 7 July-7 August and 22 December-3 January – **Meals** - Seafood - (buffet lunch) 185 and a la carte approx. 545 ₰ 295.

XX
Thörnströms Kök, Teknologgatan 3, ✉ 411 32, 𝄢 (031) 16 20 66, *info@ thornstr omskok.com,* Fax (031) 16 05 70 – 🖭. 🕮 🄰🄴 ⑩ 𝘑𝘊𝘉. ❀   CX e
closed July, 25 December-1 January, Sunday, Monday and Bank Holidays – **Meals** (booking essential) (dinner only) 400/600 and a la carte 355/665 ₰ 245.

XX
☆ **28 +** (Lyxell), Götabergsgatan 28, ✉ S-411 34, 𝄢 (031) 20 21 61, *28plus@ telia.com,* Fax (031) 81 97 57, « Cellar » – 🕮 🄰🄴 ⑩ 𝘝𝘐𝘚𝘈 𝘑𝘊𝘉. ❀   BX n
closed July-14 August, 22-26 and 30 December-2 January and Sunday – **Meals** (dinner only) a la carte 360/665 ₰ 300.
Spec. Tapas with lobster. Roe deer in two servings. Raspberry soufflé with vanilla ice cream.

XX
Linnéa, Södra Vägen 32, ✉ S-412 54, 𝄢 (031) 16 11 83, *restaurang.linnea@ swipnet.se,* Fax (031) 18 12 92 – 🕮 🄰🄴 ⑩ 𝘝𝘐𝘚𝘈. ❀   CX s
closed 7 July-7 August, 22 December-7 January, Saturday lunch and Sunday – **Meals** 495 (dinner) and a la carte 490/630 ₰ 295.

XX
☟ **Le Village,** Tredje Långgatan 13, ✉ S-413 03, 𝄢 (031) 24 20 03, *ferb@one.se,* Fax (031) 24 20 69, « Antique shop » – 🕮 🄰🄴 ⑩ 𝘝𝘐𝘚𝘈   AX b
closed July, 1 week Christmas and Sunday – **Meals** (dinner only April-September) 235/345 and a la carte.

XX
Kungstorget, Kungstorget 14, ✉ S-411 10, 𝄢 (031) 711 00 22, *info@ kungstorget .com,* Fax (031) 711 00 44 – 🕮 🄰🄴 ⑩ 𝘝𝘐𝘚𝘈   BV r
closed Saturday lunch and Sunday mid June-early August – **Meals** 115/290 and a la carte.

X
Hos Pelle, Djupedalsgatan 2, ✉ S-413 07, 𝄢 (031) 12 10 31, *hos.pelle@ swipnet.se,* Fax (031) 775 38 32 – 🕮 🄰🄴 ⑩ 𝘝𝘐𝘚𝘈. ❀   AX a
closed July, 24, 25 and 31 December and 1 January – **Meals** (dinner only) 455/495 and a la carte 425/535 ₰ 220.

X
Steak, Arkivgatan 7, ✉ S-411 34, 𝄢 (031) 18 50 15, *info@steak.se,* Fax (031) 778 38 85, 🍽 – 🕮 🄰🄴 ⑩ 𝘝𝘐𝘚𝘈 𝘑𝘊𝘉. ❀   CX a
closed Sunday – **Meals** (dinner only) 285/610 and a la carte 285/515 ₰ 310.

X
☆ **Fond,** Götaplatsen, ✉ 412 56, 𝄢 (031) 81 25 80, *fond@ fondrestaurang.com,* Fax (031) 18 37 90, 🍽 – 🍽 🖭. 🕮 🄰🄴 ⑩ 𝘝𝘐𝘚𝘈. ❀   CX d
closed July, 2 weeks Christmas, Sunday, Saturday lunch and Bank Holidays – **Meals** (buffet lunch) 240/765 and a la carte 450/585 ₰ 250
Spec. Smoked salmon with artichoke mousse. Fillet of lamb with root vegetables. Cinnamon crème brûlée.

X
Basement, Götabergsgatan 28, ✉ S-411 34, 𝄢 (031) 28 27 29, *bokning@ restbase ment.com,* Fax (031) 28 27 37 – 🕮 🄰🄴 ⑩ 𝘝𝘐𝘚𝘈. ❀   BX n
closed Christmas-New Year, Sunday and Saturday lunch – **Meals** 660 (dinner) and a la carte 330/420 ₰ 295.

X
Trädgår'n, Nya Allén, ✉ S-411 38, 𝄢 (031) 10 20 90, *info@ tradgarn.se,* Fax (031) 10 20 89, 🍽 – 🕮 🄰🄴 ⑩ 𝘝𝘐𝘚𝘈 𝘑𝘊𝘉. ❀   CV n
closed lunch Saturday and Sunday – **Meals** 225/235 and a la carte approx. 360 ₰ 280.

BRASSERIE

X
☟ **Tvåkanten,** Kungsportsavenyn 27, ✉ S-411 36, 𝄢 (031) 18 21 15, *restaurang.tvak anten@ swipnet.se,* Fax (031) 81 11 98 – 🍽 🖭. 🕮 🄰🄴 ⑩ 𝘝𝘐𝘚𝘈. ❀   CX n
closed 23 December-1 January, 21-22 June and Sunday lunch – **Meals** 295/495 and a la carte 345/555 ₰ 210.

GOTHENBURG

at Eriksberg *West : 6 km by Götaälvbron BT and Lundbyleden, or boat from Lilla Bommens Hamr*

🏨 **Quality Hotel 11** Ⓜ, Maskingatan 11, ✉ S-417 64, ☎ (031) 779 11 11, *info.hote 11@quality.choicehotels.se*, Fax *(031) 779 11 10*, ≤, « Former shipbuilding warehouse modern interior design » – 🛗, ⇄ rm, 🔳 📺 ✆ 🅿 – 🔥 1000. 🆎 ⒶⒺ ⓄⒹ 𝘝𝘐𝘚𝘈. ❄ rest *closed 20 December-2 January* – *Kök & Bar 67 :* **Meals** *(closed lunch Saturday and Sunday* (dinner only) a la carte 290/360 ⓘ 195 – **177 rm** ☷ 1400/1625, 7 suites.

🍴🍴 **Ahlströms,** Ahlströms Pir, ✉ S-417 64, ☎ (031) 51 00 00, *info@ahlstromspir.com* Fax *(031) 51 00 01*, ≤ Göta Älv river and harbour traffic – 🆎 ⒶⒺ ⓄⒹ 𝘝𝘐𝘚𝘈. ❄ *closed 1 week after Christmas* – **Meals** 240/545 and a la carte 455/625 ⓘ 275.

at Landvetter Airport *East : 30 km by Rd 40 DX* – ✉ *S-438 13 Landvetter :*

🏨 **Landvetter Airport H.,** ✉ S-438 13, ☎ (031) 97 75 50, *info@landvetterairporth otel.se*, Fax *(031) 94 64 70*, 🍽, ☎s – 🛗, ⇄ rm, 📺 ⚹ 🅿. 🆎 ⒶⒺ ⓄⒹ 𝘝𝘐𝘚𝘈. ❄ *closed 24, 25 and 31 December* – **Meals** a la carte 140/240 ⓘ 190 – **105 rm** ☷ 1245/1350, 1 suite.

Switzerland

Suisse
Schweiz
Svizzera

BERN – BASLE – GENEVA – ZÜRICH

PRACTICAL INFORMATION

LOCAL CURRENCY – PRICES

Swiss Franc: *100 CHF = 67,86 euro (€) (December 2001)*
National Holiday in Switzerland: *1st August.*

LANGUAGES SPOKEN

German, French and Italian are usually spoken in all administrative departments, shops, hotels and restaurants.

AIRLINES

SWISSAIR: *Genève-Airport, 1215 Genève 15, ℰ 0844 000 955, Fax 0227 993 138. Hirschengraben 84, 8001 Zürich, ℰ 0848 800 700, Fax 012 583 440.*

AIR FRANCE: *15 rte de l'Aéroport, 1215 Genève 15, ℰ 0228 278 787, Fax 0228 278 781. Kanalstr. 31, 8152 Glattbrugg, ℰ 014 391 818.*

ALITALIA: *Genève-Airport, 1215 Genève 15, ℰ 0227 982 080, Fax 0227 885 630. Neugutstr. 66, 8600 Dübendorf, ℰ 018 244 545, Fax 018 244 510.*

AMERICAN AIRLINES: *Hirschengraben 82, 8001 Zürich, ℰ 016 545 256, Fax 016 545 259.*

BRITISH AIRWAYS: *Chantepoulet 13, 1201 Genève, ℰ 0848 801 010, Fax 0229 080 188. Löwenstr. 29, 8001 Zürich, ℰ 0848 845 845, Fax 0848 845 849.*

LUFTHANSA: *Chantepoulet 1-3, 1201 Genève, ℰ 0229 080 180, Fax 0229 080 188. Gutenbergstr. 10, 8002 Zürich, ℰ 014 479 966, Fax 012 867 205.*

POSTAL SERVICES

In large towns, post offices are open from 7.30am to noon and 1.45pm to 6pm, and Saturdays until 11am. The telephone system is fully automatic.
Many public phones are equipped with phone card or credit card facilities. Prepaid phone cards are available from post offices, railway stations and tobacconist's shops.

SHOPPING

Department stores are generally open from 8.30am to 6.30pm, except on Saturdays when they close at 4 or 5pm. They are closed on Monday mornings.
In the index of street names, those printed in red are where the principal shops are found.

TIPPING

In hotels, restaurants and cafés the service charge is generally included in the prices.

SPEED LIMITS – MOTORWAYS

The speed limit on motorways is 120 km/h - 74 mph, on other roads 80 km/h - 50 mph, and in built up areas 50 km/h - 31 mph.
Driving on Swiss motorways is subject to the purchase of a single rate annual road tax (vignette) obtainable from border posts, tourist offices and post offices.

SEAT BELTS

The wearing of seat belts is compulsory in all Swiss cantons for drivers and all passengers.

BERN

3000 Bern 927 ④, 217 ⑥ – pop. 122 686 – alt. 548.

Basle 100 – Lyons 315 – Munich 435 – Paris 556 – Strasbourg 235 – Turin 311.

🛈 *Tourist Office, Railway Station ℘ 0313 281 212, info-res@bernetourism.ch, Fax 0313 121 233 – Tourist Center, Am Bärengraben – T.C.S., Thunstr. 63, ℘ 0313 522 222, Fax 0313 522 229 – A.C.S., Theaterplatz 13, ℘ 0313 113 828, Fax 0313 112 637 and Wasserwerkgasse 39, ℘ 0313 283 111, Fax 0313 110 310.*

🛇 *Blumisberg, ✉ 3184 Wünnewil (mid March-mid November), ℘ 0264 963 438, Fax 0264 963 523, Southwest : 18 km.*
🛇 *at Oberburg, ✉ 3414 (March-November), ℘ 0344 241 030, Fax 0344 241 034, NE : 20 km.*
✈ *Bern-Belp, ℘ 0319 602 111, Fax 0319 602 212.*

See: *Old Bern*★★ : *Marktgasse*★ DZ ; *Clock Tower*★ EZ **C** ; *Kramgasse*★ EZ ; *views*★ from the Nydegg Bridge FY ; *Bear Pit*★ FZ ; *Cathedral of St Vincent*★ EZ : *tympanum*★★, *panorama*★★ from the tower EZ – *Rosengarden* FY : *view*★ of the Old Bern – *Botanical Garden*★ DY – *Dählhölzli Zoo*★ – *Church of St Nicholas*★.

Museums: *Fine Arts Museum*★★ : *Paul Klee Collection*★ DY – *Natural History Museum*★★ EZ – *Bernese Historical Museum*★★ EZ – *Alpine Museum*★★ EZ – *Communication Museum*★ EZ.

Excursions: *The Gurten*★★.

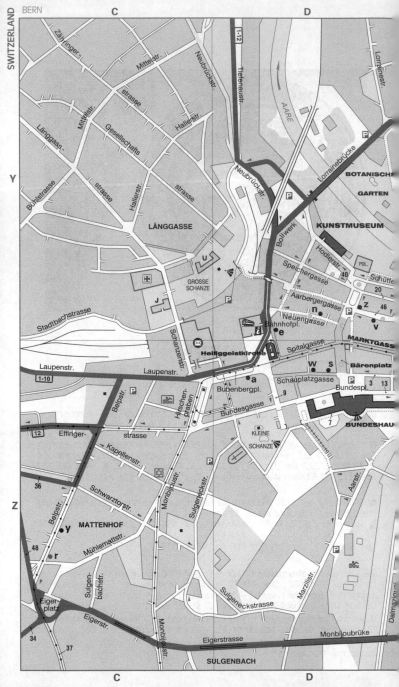

C

D

1-12

Zähringer-

Mittelstr.

Neubrückstr.

Tiefenaustr.

Lorrainestr.

Mittelstr.

strasse

Hallerstr.

AARE

Gesellschafts-

Länggass-

Hallerstr.

strasse

Y

Bühlstrasse

strasse

Neubrückstr.

Lorrainebrücke

P

BOTANISCH

GARTEN

Bollwerk

KUNSTMUSEUM

LÄNGGASSE

Hodlerstr.

POL.

Speichergasse

Schütte

GROSSE
SCHANZE

Aarbergergasse

20

P

Z

46

n

Stadtbachstrasse

Neuengasse

V

Schanzenstr.

Bahnhofpl.

MARKTGASS

i

e

Heiliggeistkirche

Spitalgasse

Laupenstr.

Laupenstr.

W

S

Bärenplatz

1-10

a

Schauplatzgasse

P

3

13

Bubenbergpl.

Bundespl.

Belpstr.

P

9

Bundesgasse

Hirschen-
graben

7

BUNDESHAU

12

Effinger-

strasse

KLEINE
SCHANZE

Aarstr.

Kapellenstr.

P

36

Belpstr.

Z

Schwarztorstr.

Monbijoustr.

Sulgeneckstr.

MATTENHOF

y

48

Mühlemattstr.

r

Sulgen-
bachstr.

Sulgeneckstrasse

Marzilistr.

P

Eiger-
platz

Dalmaziqu

34

Eigerstr.

Monbijoubrüke

37

Eigerstrasse

Monbijoustr.

SULGENBACH

C

D

BERN

SWITZERLAND

0   200 m

Breitenrainstr.

Nordring

Greyerzstr.

Moserstr.

Waldhöheweg

Beundenfeldstr.

Kasernenstrasse

strasse

toriarain

Viktoriapl.

Viktoria-

Schänzli-

Str.

KURSAAL
SCHÄNZLI

a

Spitalackerstr.

Blumenberg

strasse

Papiermühle

Laubeggstr.

Aargauerstalden

Rosengarten

Y

6

nbergrain

Altenbergstr.

Kornhausbrücke

Brunngasshalde

T

M.

6   h

Kornhauspl.

28

30

KRAMGASSE

c

X

m   f

Casinopl.   16   18

CASINO

Aarstr.

Postgasshalde

P   Postgasse

H   Postgasse

15

MÜNSTER

Gerechtigkeitsgasse

Junkerngasse

Erlacherhof

PLATTFORM

Schiffaube

39

NYDEGGKIRCHE

u

22

Gerberngasse

Münstaldep

Mühlenpl.

NYDEGGBRÜCKE

BÄRENGRABEN

Gr.

AARE

Muristalden

Kirchenfeldbrücke

SCHWEIZERISCHES ALPINES
MUSEUM

10

e

Thunstr.

BERNISCHES
HISTORISCHES
MUSEUM

MUSEUM FÜR
KOMMUNIKATION

NATURHISTORISCHES
MUSEUM

Aegertenstr.

Helvetia

Str.

12

Marienstr.

Luisenstrasse

str.

Dufour-

Thunstr.

Jungfraustr.

KIRCHENFELD

strasse

Muristrasse

33

e

Z

Sechinar-

Ensingerstr.

Thunstr.

10

Eliasstr.

Kirchenfeldstr.

Kirchenfeldstr.

E

F

STREET INDEX TO BERN TOWN PLAN

Schweizerhof, Bahnhofplatz 11, ⌂ 3011, ℰ 0313 268 080, info@schweizerhof-bern.ch, Fax 0313 268 090 – |⋕|, ⥲ rm, ☰ rm, ⊡ ⌖ – 🅰 15/120. 🄰🄴 ⓞ ⓦⓢ 🆅🅸🆂🅰 ᴊᴄʙ
Meals see **Schultheissenstube** and **Jack's Brasserie** below – **78 rm** ⚏ 305/480
6 suites.
DY e

Allegro Ⓜ, Kornhausstr. 3, ⌂ 3013, ℰ 0313 395 500, allegro@kursaal-bern.ch,
Fax 0313 395 510, ⩽, « Terrace ⩽ Bern and mountain », 🗜, ⌗ – |⋕|, ⥲ rm, ⌖ &,
🄿 🄿 – 🅰 15/1500. 🄰🄴 ⓞ ⓦⓢ 🆅🅸🆂🅰 ᴊᴄʙ
EY a
Eurasia (closed Sunday, Monday and Bank Holidays) Meals 79 (dinner) and a la carte
57/106 – **Allegretto** : Meals a la carte 39/79 – **Bistro** : (closed Bank Holidays) Meals
45 and a la carte 33/83 – ⚏ 24 – **163 rm** 215/340.

Innere Enge ⌂, Engestr. 54, ⌂ 3012, ℰ 0313 096 111, info@zghotels.ch,
Fax 0313 096 112, ☞, ⌖ – |⋕|, ⥲ rm, ⊡ ⌖ &, 🄿 – 🅰 20. 🄰🄴 ⓞ ⓦⓢ
🆅🅸🆂🅰 ᴊᴄʙ
by Tiefenaustrasse DY
Meals 48 (lunch)/68 and a la carte 44/95 – ⚏ 20 – **26 rm** 210/310.

Savoy without rest, Neuengasse 26, ⌂ 3011, ℰ 0313 114 405, info@zghotels.ch,
Fax 0313 121 978 – |⋕| ⥲ ⊡ ⌖. 🄰🄴 ⓞ ⓦⓢ 🆅🅸🆂🅰 ᴊᴄʙ
DY n
⚏ 20 – **56 rm** 195/295.

Bären Ⓜ without rest, Schauplatzgasse 4, ⌂ 3011, ℰ 0313 113 367, reception@bärenbern.ch, Fax 0313 116 983, ⥲ – |⋕| ⥲ ⊡ ⌖. 🄰🄴 ⓞ ⓦⓢ 🆅🅸🆂🅰 ᴊᴄʙ
DZ s
57 rm ⚏ 190/300.

Bristol Ⓜ without rest, Schauplatzgasse 10, ⌂ 3011, ℰ 0313 110 101, reception@bristolbern.ch, Fax 0313 119 479, ⥲ – |⋕| ⥲ ⊡ ⌖. 🄰🄴 ⓞ ⓦⓢ 🆅🅸🆂🅰 ᴊᴄʙ
DZ w
92 rm ⚏ 190/300.

Belle Epoque, Gerechtigkeitsgasse 18, ⌂ 3011, ℰ 0313 114 336, info@belle-epoque.ch, Fax 0313 113 936, « Belle Epoque decor and furnishings » – |⋕| ⥲ ⊡ ⌖. 🄰🄴 ⓞ
ⓦⓢ 🆅🅸🆂🅰 ᴊᴄʙ
EY u
closed Christmas – **Meals** (only dinner) (closed Sunday and Monday) a la carte 51/92 –
⚏ 15 – **17 rm** 200/350.

Bern, Zeughausgasse 9, ⌂ 3011, ℰ 0313 292 222, hotelbern@hotelbern.ch,
Fax 0313 292 299, ☞ – |⋕|, ⥲ rm, ⊡ ⌖ &, – 🅰 15/120. 🄰🄴 ⓞ ⓦⓢ 🆅🅸🆂🅰 ᴊᴄʙ EY b
Kurierstube (closed July and Sunday) Meals 50/68 and a la carte 45/107 – **7 Stube** :
Meals a la carte 32/93 – **100 rm** ⚏ 230/310.

City Ⓜ without rest, Bubenbergplatz 7, ⌂ 3011, ℰ 0313 115 377, city-ab@fassbind-hotels.ch, Fax 0313 110 636 – |⋕| ⊡. 🄰🄴 ⓞ ⓦⓢ 🆅🅸🆂🅰 ᴊᴄʙ
DZ a
⚏ 18 – **58 rm** 123/198.

Kreuz, Zeughausgasse 41, ✉ 3011, ☎ 0313 299 595, *hotelkreuz@swissonline.ch, Fax 0313 299 596* – |♦| TV ☏ – 🏛 15/130. AE ⓓ MC VISA JCB DY v
closed 4. January - 28. February (only Hotel) – **Meals** *(closed 6 July - 15 August, 18 December - 15 January, Saturday and Sunday)* a la carte 29/66 – **103 rm** ☐ 139/200.

La Pergola without rest, Belpstr. 43, ✉ 3007, ☎ 0313 819 146, *info@hotel-lapergola.ch, Fax 0313 815 054* – |♦| TV. AE MC VISA CZ y
closed Easter, 9 to 12 May, Pentecost and 22 December - 6 January – **55 rm** ☐ 130/180.

Waldhorn without rest, Waldhöheweg 2, ✉ 3013, ☎ 0313 322 343, *hotel@waldhorn.ch, Fax 0313 321 869* – |♦| TV 🚗. AE ⓓ MC VISA. ✂ EY d
46 rm ☐ 120/175.

Bellevue Grill / Bellevue Terrasse - Hotel Bellevue Palace, Kochergasse 3, ✉ 3001, ☎ 0313 204 545, *direktion@bellevue-palace.ch, Fax 0313 114 743,* 🏠, « Terrace with views over the Aare » – ▤. AE ⓓ MC VISA JCB. ✂ EZ p
Grill : closed summer and lunch ; Terrace : closed dinner in winter – **Meals** 66/119 and a la carte 72/123.

Schultheissenstube - Hotel Schweizerhof, Bahnhofplatz 11 (1st floor), ✉ 3011, ☎ 0313 268 080, *info@schweizerhof-bern.ch, Fax 0313 268 090* – AE ⓓ MC VISA JCB. ✂ DY e
closed mid July - mid August and Sunday – **Meals** 75/140 and a la carte 74/146.

Jack's Brasserie - Hotel Schweizerhof, Bahnhofplatz 11, ✉ 3011, ☎ 0313 268 080, *info@schweizerhof-bern.ch, Fax 0313 268 090* – ▤. AE ⓓ MC VISA JCB DY e
Meals 54 and a la carte 56/128.

Ermitage, Amthausgasse 10, ✉ 3011, ☎ 0313 113 541, *Fax 0313 113 542* – MC VISA EZ g
closed 8 July - 7 August, Saturday and Sunday – **Meals** 25 (lunch)/72 and a la carte 52/98.

Kirchenfeld, Thunstr. 5, ✉ 3005, ☎ 0313 510 278, *Fax 0313 518 416,* 🏠 – AE ⓓ MC VISA EZ e
closed Sunday and Monday – **Meals** 45 (lunch)/58 and a la carte 47/88.

Wein und Sein (Blum), Münstergasse 50, ✉ 3011, ☎ 0313 119 844, *blum@weinundsein.ch,* Renovated Bernese cellar – MC VISA. ✂ EZ f
closed mid-July - beginning August, Sunday and Monday – **Meals** *(only dinner)* (booking essential)(only menu) 78
Spec. Rauchlachsterrine mit Melone. Zitronengrassuppe kalt serviert. Sommerbockfilet mit Gemüsetartar und Rösti (Summer).

Zimmermania, Brunngasse 19, ✉ 3011, ☎ 0313 111 542, *zimmermania@swissonline.ch, Fax 0313 122 822,* Old Bernese bistro – AE MC VISA EY h
closed 8 July - 5 August, Sunday, Monday and Bank Holidays – **Meals** (booking essential) 39 (lunch) and a la carte 46/87.

Frohegg, Belpstr. 51, ✉ 3007, ☎ 0313 822 524, *Fax 0313 822 527,* 🏠 – AE ⓓ MC VISA CZ r
closed Sunday – **Meals** (booking essential) 48 (lunch)/54 and a la carte 42/91.

Frohsinn, Münstergasse 54, ✉ 3011, ☎ 0313 113 768, *frohsinn-bern@bluewin.ch,* 🏠 – AE ⓓ MC VISA JCB EZ m
closed 14 July - 11 August, Sunday and Monday – **Meals** 28 (lunch)/78 and a la carte 40/90.

Schosshalde, Kleiner Muristalden 40, ✉ 3006, ☎ 0313 524 523, *Fax 0313 521 091,* 🏠 – AE ⓓ MC VISA FZ e
closed 15 July - 11 August, 24 December - 6 January, Saturday lunch and Sunday – **Meals** - Italian rest. - 59 and a la carte 42/88.

at Muri *Southeast : 3,5 km by Thunstrasse – alt. 560 – ✉ 3074 Muri bei Bern :*

Sternen, Thunstr. 80, ☎ 0319 507 111, *info@sternenmuri.ch, Fax 0319 507 100* – |♦| ✂ TV 🚗 P – 🏛 15/120. AE ⓓ MC VISA
Läubli : **Meals** 35 (lunch) and a la carte 53/94 – ***Gaststube :*** **Meals** a la carte 35/68 – **44 rm** ☐ 160/230.

at Liebefeld *Southwest : 3 km direction Schwarzenburg – alt. 563 – ✉ 3097 Liebefeld :*

Landhaus, Schwarzenburgstr. 134, ☎ 0319 710 758, *Fax 0319 720 249,* 🏠, « Rustic decor » – P. AE ⓓ MC VISA
closed Sunday and Bank Holidays – (booking essential) ***Rôtisserie :*** **Meals** 56 (lunch)/128 and a la carte 67/118 – ***Taverne Alsacienne :*** **Meals** a la carte 48/83.

In addition to establishments indicated by XXXXX ... X, many hotels possess good class restaurants.

SWITZERLAND

BASLE (BASEL) 927 ④, 216 ④, 66 ⑨ ⑩ – pop. 166 678 – alt. 277 – ☺ Basle and environs from France 0041, from this year, Swiss area codes will be incorporated into the main number.

See : Old town* : Cathedral** (Münster): ≤* "Pfalz" terrace CY – Fish Market Fountain* (Fischmarktbrunnen) BY – Old Streets* BY – Zoological Garden*** AZ – The Port (Hafen, ✳*, "From Basle to the High Seas"* Exhibition – City hall* BY H.

Museums : Fine Arts*** (Kunstmuseum) CY – Historical** (Historisches Museum) BY – Ethnographic* (Museum der Kulturen) BY M¹ – Antiquities* (Antikenmuseum) CY – Paper Museum* (Basler Papiermühle) DY M⁶ – Haus zum Kirschgarten* BZ – Jean Tinguely Museum*.

Envir. : ✳* from Bruderholz Water Tower South : 3,5 km – Chapel of St.-Chrischona* Northeast : 8 km – Augst Roman Ruins** Southeast : 11 km – Beyeler Foundation** Northwest : 6 km at Riehen.

₆ at Hagenthal-le-Bas, ✉ F-68220 (March - November), Southwest : 10 km, t° (0033) 389 68 50 91, Fax (0033) 389 68 55 66.

✈ Euro-Airport, ℘ 0613 253 111, Basle (Switzerland) by Flughafenstrasse 8 km and – at Saint-Louis (France), ℘ (0033) 389 90 31 11.

🛈 Tourist Office, Schifflände 5, ℘ 0612 686 868, office@baseltourismus.ch, Fax 0612 686 870 – T.C.S., Steinentorstr. 13, ℘ 0612 059 999, Fax 0612 059 970 – A.C.S., Birsigstr. 4, ℘ 0612 723 933, Fax 0612 813 657.

Bern 100 – Freiburg im Breisgau 72 – Lyons 401 – Mulhouse 35 – Paris 554 – Strasbourg 145.

Plans on following pages

Drei Könige, Blumenrain 8, ✉ 4001, ℘ 0612 605 050, info@drei-koenige-basel.ch, Fax 0612 605 060, ≤, 🍽, – 📶, ⇄ rm, 🍴 rm, 📺 ✓ – 🛗 15/50. 🗚 ⓪ ⓪⓪ 𝘝𝘐𝘚𝘈 𝘑𝘊𝘉
Rôtisserie des Rois : Meals 52 (lunch)/132 and a la carte 88/152 – **Königsbrasserie :** Meals 23 (lunch) and a la carte 45/111 – 🖵 32 – **82 rm** 320/690, 6 suites. BY a

Swissôtel Basel M, Messeplatz 25, ✉ 4021, ℘ 0615 553 333, reservations.basel@swissotel.com, Fax 0615 553 970, ⇄, 🍴, – 📶, ⇄ rm, 🍴 📺 ✓ & 🚗 – 🛗 15/35. 🗚 ⓪ ⓪⓪ 𝘝𝘐𝘚𝘈 𝘑𝘊𝘉 DX r
Meals 26 (lunch)/80 and a la carte 45/89 – 🖵 30 – **230 rm** 520/570, 8 suites.

Hilton M, Aeschengraben 31, ✉ 4002, ℘ 0612 756 600, basel@hilton.ch, Fax 0612 756 650, ⇄, 🍴 – 📶 ⇄ 🍴 📺 ✓ & 🄿 – 🛗 15/300. 🗚 ⓪ ⓪⓪ 𝘝𝘐𝘚𝘈 𝘑𝘊𝘉
Wettstein : Meals 45 (lunch)/58 and a la carte 59/112 – 🖵 24 – **204 rm** 350/640, 10 suites. CZ d

Radisson SAS, Steinentorstr. 25, ✉ 4001, ℘ 0612 272 727, info.basel@radissonsas.com, Fax 0612 272 828, 🎴, ⇄, 🍴 – 📶, ⇄ rm, 🍴 📺 ✓ & 🚗 – 🛗 15/150. 🗚 ⓪ ⓪⓪ 𝘝𝘐𝘚𝘈 𝘑𝘊𝘉 BZ b
Steinenpick (Brasserie) Meals 25 (lunch) and a la carte 46/92 – 🖵 29 – **205 rm** 520/660.

Europe M, Clarastr. 43, ✉ 4005, ℘ 0616 908 080, hotel-europe@balehotels.ch, Fax 0616 908 880 – 📶, ⇄ rm, 🍴 📺 ✓ 🚗 – 🛗 15/150. 🗚 ⓪ ⓪⓪ 𝘝𝘐𝘚𝘈 𝘑𝘊𝘉 CX k
Meals see **Les Quatre Saisons** below – **Bajazzo** (Brasserie) Meals a la carte 43/76 – 166 rm 🖵 330/410.

Victoria M, Centralbahnplatz 3, ✉ 4002, ℘ 0612 707 070, hotel-victoria@balehotels.ch, Fax 0612 707 077, 🎴 – 📶 ⇄ 🍴 📺 video ✓ 🚗 – 🛗 15/80. 🗚 ⓪ ⓪⓪ 𝘝𝘐𝘚𝘈 𝘑𝘊𝘉 BZ d
Le Train Bleu : Meals 45 (lunch)/75 and a la carte 48/85 – 🖵 20 – **107 rm** 330/430.

Basel M, Münzgasse 12, ✉ 4001, ℘ 0612 646 800, reception@hotel-basel.ch, Fax 0612 646 811, 🍽, « Cellar restaurant » – 📶, ⇄ rm, 🍴 📺 ✓ 🄿 – 🛗 25. 🗚 ⓪ ⓪⓪ 𝘝𝘐𝘚𝘈 𝘑𝘊𝘉 BY x
Basler Keller (closed 29 June - 11 August, Saturday lunch and Sunday) Meals 68/98 (dinner) and a la carte 58/112 – **Brasserie Steiger :** Meals a la carte 37/65 – 🖵 14 – **72 rm** 255/420.

Palazzo M without rest, Grenzacherstr. 6, ✉ 4058, ℘ 0616 906 464, hotel-palazzo@bluewin.ch, Fax 0616 906 410, 🎴 – 📶 ⇄ 🍴 📺 ✓ 🚗. 🗚 ⓪ ⓪⓪ 𝘝𝘐𝘚𝘈 ✂ DY e
30 rm 🖵 240/340.

St. Gotthard M without rest, Centralbahnstr. 13, ✉ 4002, ℘ 0612 251 313, reception@st-gotthard.ch, Fax 0612 251 314 – 📶 ⇄ 📺 ✓. 🗚 ⓪ ⓪⓪ 𝘝𝘐𝘚𝘈 𝘑𝘊𝘉 BZ f
103 rm 🖵 223/406.

Der Teufelhof M, Leonhardsgraben 47, ✉ 4051, ℘ 0612 611 010, info@teufelhof.com, Fax 0612 611 004, « Temporary exhibitions » – 📶. 🗚 ⓪ ⓪⓪ 𝘝𝘐𝘚𝘈 BY g
closed 24 December - 5 January – Meals see **Der Teufelhof** below – 29 rm 🖵 190/450, 4 suites.

Merian, Rheingasse 2, ✉ 4005, ℘ 0616 851 111, kontakt@merian-hotel.ch, Fax 0616 851 101, ≤, 🍽 – 📶 📺 ✓ 🚗 – 🛗 15/80. 🗚 ⓪ ⓪⓪ 𝘝𝘐𝘚𝘈 𝘑𝘊𝘉 BY b
Café Spitz Fish specialities Meals 54/81 and a la carte 51/93 – **63 rm** 🖵 220/310.

614

🏠 **Wettstein** without rest, Grenzacherstr. 8, ✉ 4058, 𝄐 0616 906 969, *hotel-wettstei
n@bluewin.ch, Fax 0616 910 545* – 🛗 🍴 📺 📞 🅰🅴 ⑩ 🅼🅾 𝘝𝘐𝘚𝘈   DY q
40 rm ⬚ 210/310.

🏠 **Steinenschanze** without rest, Steinengraben 69, ✉ 4051, 𝄐 0612 725 353, *steine
nschanze@datacomm.ch, Fax 0612 724 573*, 🌿 – 🛗 📺 📞 🅰🅴 ⑩ 🅼🅾 𝘝𝘐𝘚𝘈   BY s
54 rm ⬚ 180/250.

🏠 **Au Violon,** im Lohnhof 4, ✉ 4051, 𝄐 0612 698 711, *auviolon@iprolink.ch,
🍴 Fax 0612 698 712*, �, Former remand prison of Basle – 🛗 🅰🅴 🅼🅾 𝘝𝘐𝘚𝘈   BY v
*Hotel : closed 13 December - 10 January ; Rest : closed 1 to 9 July, 22 December -8 January,
Sunday, Monday and Bank Holidays* – **Meals** a la carte 40/79 – ⬚ 14 – **20 rm**
90/180.

XXXX **Bruderholz,** Bruderholzallee 42, ✉ 4059, 𝄐 0613 618 222, *bruderholz@bluewin.ch,
🕸🕸 Fax 0613 618 203*, �, « Flowered garden », 🌿 – 🅿. 🅰🅴 ⑩ 🅼🅾 𝘝𝘐𝘚𝘈
                                                           South by Margarethenstrasse   BZ
closed 9 to 23 February, Sunday and Monday (except fairs) – **Meals** 68 (lunch)/190 and
a la carte 135/195
Spec. Nage de homard aux pistils de safran, fenouil et basilic. Canard cuit rosé au miel et
gingembre. Soufflé au fromage blanc au coulis de fruits.

XXX **Les Quatre Saisons** - Hotel Europe, Clarastr. 43 (1st floor), ✉ 4005, 𝄐 0616 908 720,
🕸 *hotel-europe@balehotels.ch, Fax 0616 908 880* 📧 🅰🅴 ⑩ 🅼🅾 𝘝𝘐𝘚𝘈 𝘫𝘤𝘣
🕸   CX k
closed 22 July - 10 August and Sunday (except fairs) – **Meals** 58 (lunch)/170 and a la carte
82/145
Spec. Foie d'oie grillé sur compote d'oignon et la poire glacée. Pintade poêlée au curry
vert et légumes frits. Gâteau de leckerli fondant aux cerises glacées à l'aceto
balsamico.

XXX **Der Teufelhof** - Hotel Der Teufelhof, Leonhardsgraben 47, ✉ 4051, 𝄐 0612 611 010,
🕸 *info@teufelhof.com, Fax 0612 611 004*, 🌿, « Vinothek in the old city walls » – 🍴 🅰🅴
⑩ 🅼🅾 𝘝𝘐𝘚𝘈   BY g
Bel Etage *(Sunday and Monday except fairs and Saturday lunch)* **Meals** 75 (lunch)/180
and a la carte 89/165 – **Weinstube :** *(closed 24 December - 5 January)* **Meals** 70 and
a la carte 64/105
Spec. Steinbutt-Lachscarpaccio mit Estragon-Vinaigrette. Sommerbocknüsschen mit Tan-
nenwipfeljus (Summer). Kaltes Erdbeerensüppchen mit Zitronenfeuilleté und Erdbeer-
Rahmeis (Spring-Summer).

XX **Schlüsselzunft,** Freie Strasse 25, ✉ 4001, 𝄐 0612 612 046, *info@schluesselzunft.ch,
Fax 0612 612 056*, « 15C guildhall with attractive tiled stove » – 🅰🅴 🅼🅾 𝘝𝘐𝘚𝘈   BY r
closed Sunday and Bank Holidays – **Meals** 65 and a la carte 47/103 – **Höfli :** Meals a la
carte 42/75.

XX **Charon,** Schützengraben 62, ✉ 4051, 𝄐 0612 619 980, *Fax 0612 619 909*, Bistro
atmosphere – 🅰🅴 ⑩ 🅼🅾 𝘝𝘐𝘚𝘈 𝘫𝘤𝘣   AY s
*closed Easter, 1 July - 4 August, Christmas, Sunday - Monday from October - April, Saturday
- Sunday from May - September and Bank Holidays* – **Meals** 95 (dinner) and a la carte
65/104

XX **Hong Kong,** Riehenring 91, 𝄐 0616 918 814, *info@restaurant-hongkong.ch,
Fax 0616 918 836* – 🅰🅴 ⑩ 🅼🅾 𝘝𝘐𝘚𝘈 𝘫𝘤𝘣   CX w
closed Easter, July and Christmas – **Meals** - Chinese rest. - 50 (lunch)/86 and a la carte
51/91.

X **St. Alban-Stübli,** St. Alban-Vorstadt 74, ✉ 4052, 𝄐 0612 725 415, *Fax 0612 740 488*,
🌿 – 🅰🅴 ⑩ 🅼🅾 𝘝𝘐𝘚𝘈   DY a
closed 27 July - 5 August, 23 December - 9 January, Saturday lunch and Sunday –
Meals (at lunch only little carte) (booking essential) 47 (lunch)/78 and a la carte
55/102.

X **Sakura,** Centralbahnstr. 14, ✉ 4051, 𝄐 0612 720 505, *Fax 0612 953 988*, Japanese
rest. – 📧 🅰🅴 ⑩ 🅼🅾 𝘝𝘐𝘚𝘈   BZ k
closed July - August, Saturday lunch, Sunday and Bank Holidays – **Teppanyaki :** Meals
64/114 and a la carte 37/85 and a la carte 52/90.

X **Toscano,** Bachlettenstr. 1, ✉ 4054, 𝄐 0612 813 220, *Fax 0612 813 221* – 🅰🅴 ⑩ 🅼🅾
𝘝𝘐𝘚𝘈.   AZ u
closed Saturday lunch – **Meals** - Italian rest. - 39 and a la carte 42/90.

at Riehen by ② : 5 km – alt. 288 – ✉ 4125 Riehen :

XX **Schürmann's,** Äussere Baselstr. 159, 𝄐 0616 431 210, *Fax 0616 431 211*, 🌿 – 🅰🅴 ⑩
🕸 🅼🅾 𝘝𝘐𝘚𝘈
*closed 18 to 23 February, 9 to 21 September, Saturday lunch, Sunday and Monday lunch
(also Monday dinner in Summer)* – **Meals** 55 (lunch)/120 and a la carte 77/131
Spec. Jamon Iberico Bellota mit Olivenbrickblättern. Kartoffeltriangoli mit weissem Alba-
trüffel (November-December). In Chianti geschmorter Rindschulterspitz mit fritiertem Sellerie (Winter).

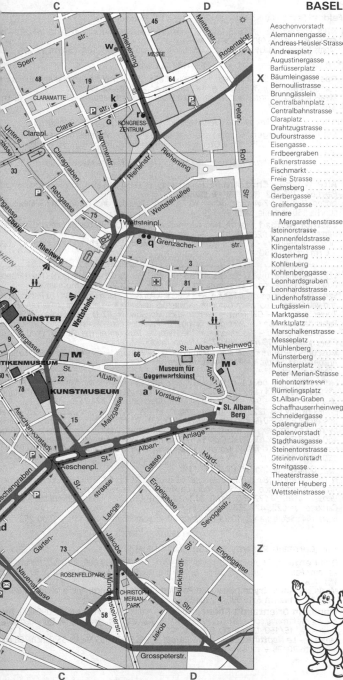

BASEL

at Birsfelden *East by* ④ : *3 km – alt. 260 –* ✉ *4127 Birsfelden :*

🏛 **Alfa,** Hauptstr. 15, ℘ 0613 156 262, alfa.birsfelden@bluewin.ch, Fax 0613 156 263 – 📞
📺 ❤ 📞 – 🏌 15/80. 🖭 ⓪ 🐼 𝘝𝘐𝘚𝘈
Meals (closed Sunday and Monday) 23 (lunch) and a la carte 38/101 – **54 rm** ⊆ 105/200

at Muttenz *by* ⑤ : *4,5 km – alt. 271 –* ✉ *4132 Muttenz :*

🏨 **Baslertor** Ⓜ, St. Jakobsstr. 1, ℘ 0614 655 555, hotel-baslertor@balehotels.ch
Fax 0614 655 550, 🍴, 🖙 – 🛗, 🌬 rm, 📺 ❤ ➡. 🖭 ⓪ 🐼 𝘝𝘐𝘚𝘈
Meals (closed Saturday and Sunday) (dinner only) a la carte approx. 45 – ⊆ 10 – **43 rm**
270/330, 4 suites.

at Binningen *South :* 2 km by Oberwilerstrasse AZ *– alt. 284 –* ✉ *4102 Binningen :*

🏛🏛🏛 **Schloss Binningen,** Schlossgasse 5, ℘ 0614 212 055, wdamman@schloss-binningen
.ch, Fax 0614 210 635, 🍴, « Old mansion, antique furniture, park », 🐎 – 📞 🖭 ⓪ 🐼
𝘝𝘐𝘚𝘈 𝘫𝘤𝘣
closed 9 to 25 February, Sunday and Monday (except fairs) – **Meals** 48 (lunch)/98 and
a la carte 69/135.

🏛🏛🏛 **Alte Waage - Chez Armin,** Hauptstr. 1, ℘ 0614 215 500, info@chez-armin.ch
Fax 0614 215 502, 🍴 – 🖭 ⓪ 🐼 𝘝𝘐𝘚𝘈
closed 18 July - 7 August, 14 to 20 February, Tuesday and Wednesday – **Meals** 49
(lunch)/130 and a la carte 79/129.

🏛🏛 **Gasthof Neubad** with rm, Neubadrain 4, ℘ 0613 020 705, gasthof.neubad@datacc
mm.ch, Fax 0613 028 116, 🍴 – 🌬 rm, 📺 📞 🖭 🐼 𝘝𝘐𝘚𝘈
closed 16 February - 2 March and Wednesday – **Meals** 50 (lunch) and a la carte 41/124
– **6 rm** ⊆ 100/190.

GENEVA 🔟⃝ 🄚 ⑩ ⑪, 🔢 ⑪, 🔢 ⑥ – *pop. 173 519 – alt. 375 –* ❀ *Geneva, environs : from France
0041 - from this year, Swiss area codes will be incorporated into the number.*
See : *The Shores of the lake*★★ *:* ⬅★★★ *FGY – Parks*★★ *: Mon Repos GX, La Perle du Lac
and Villa Barton – Botanical Garden*★ *: alpine rock-garden*★★ *– Cathedral St-Pierre*★ *: north
Tower* ☀★★ *FZ – Old Town*★ *: Reformation Monument*★ *FZ* **D** *; Archaeological Site*★ *–
Palais des Nations*★★ *– Parc de la Grange*★ *– Parc des Eaux-Vives*★ *– Nave*★ *of Church
of Christ the King – Woodwork*★ *in the Historical Museum of the Swiss Abroad – Baur
Collection*★ *(in 19C mansion) GZ – Maison Tavel*★ *FZ.*
Museums : *Ariana*★★ *– Art and History*★★ *GZ – Natural History*★★ *GZ – International
Automobile Museum*★ *– Petit Palais : Modern Art*★★ *GZ – International Red Cross and Red
Crescent Museum*★★.
Excursions : *by boat on the lake, Information :* Cie Gén. de Nav., Jardin Anglais
℘ 0223 125 223, Fax 0223 125 225- Mouettes genevoises, 8 quai Mont-Blanc,
℘ 0227 322 944 - Swiss Boat, 4 quai Mont-Blanc, ℘ 0227 324 747.
🏌 *at* Cologny ✉ *1223 (March - December),* ℘ 0227 074 800, Fax 0227 074 820 ; 🏌 *at*
Bossey ✉ *F-74160 (March - December),* ℘ (0033) 450 43 95 50, Fax (0033) 450 95 32 57
by road to Troinex : 🏌 *at* Esery ✉ *F-74930 Reignier (March - December),* ℘ (0033)
450 36 58 70, Fax (0033) 450 36 57 62, Southeast : 15 km ; 🏌 Maison Blanche at Eche-
nevex-Gex ✉ *F-01170 (1 March - 15 December),* ℘ (0033) 450 42 44 42, Fax (0033)
450 42 44 43, Northwest : 17 km.
🛫 Genève-Cointrin, ℘ 0227 177 111.
🛈 Tourist Office, *18 r. du Mont Blanc,* ℘ 0229 097 070, Fax 0229 097 075, GenèveAirport,
Arrival, c/o Amdaco – T.C.S., 8 cours de Rive, 1204 Genève, 4 ch. de Blandonnet, 1214
Vernier, ℘ 0224 172 030, Fax 0224 172 042 – A.C.S., 21 r. de la Fontenette ✉ *1227
Carouge,* ℘ 0223 422 233, Fax 0223 013 711.
Bern 164 – Bourg-en-B. 101 – Lausanne 60 – Lyons 151 – Paris 538 – Turin 252.

Plans on following pages

Right Bank (Cornavin Railway Station - Les Quais) :

🏨🏨🏨 **Des Bergues,** 33 quai des Bergues, ✉ *1201,* ℘ 0229 087 000, info@hoteldesbergu
es.com, Fax 0229 087 090, 🍴 – 🛗, 🌬 rm, 🍽 📺 ❤ 🔩 – 🏌 15/190. 🖭 ⓪ 🐼
𝘝𝘐𝘚𝘈 𝘫𝘤𝘣
FY **k**
Meals see **Amphitryon** below – **Le Pavillon :** Meals 49 (lunch) and a la carte 73/113
– ⊆ 39 – **112 rm** 570/990, 10 suites.

🏨🏨🏨 **Mandarin Oriental du Rhône,** 1 quai Turrettini, ✉ *1201,* ℘ 0229 090 000, rese
rve-morga@mohg.com, Fax 0229 090 010, ≼, 🖙, 🍷 – 🛗, 🌬 rm, 🍽 📺 video ❤ 🔩
➡ – 🏌 15/150. 🖭 ⓪ 🐼 𝘝𝘐𝘚𝘈 𝘫𝘤𝘣. 🍴
FY **r**
Meals see **Le Neptune** below – **Café Rafael** ℘ 0229 090 005 Meals 55 (lunch)/68 and
a la carte 70/98 – ⊆ 35 – **180 rm** 580/780, 12 suites.

🏛️🏛️🏛️ **Le Richemond,** 8 - 10 r. Adhémar-Fabri, ⊠ 1201, 𝒫 0227 157 000, *reservation@r ichemond.ch*, Fax 0227 157 001, ≤, 🎇, 𝕝₆ – 🕸 ▤ 📺 video 🐾 🚗 – 🏦 15/200. FY u
⓿ 🌑 VISA JCB
Le Gentilhomme – Lebanese rest. – **Meals** 38 (lunch)/95 and a la carte 52/76 – *Le Jardin :* Meals 48/119 et à la carte 66/140 – ⊒ 37 – **86 rm** 450/790, 12 suites.

🏛️🏛️🏛️ **Président Wilson,** 47 quai Wilson, ⊠ 1201, 𝒫 0229 066 666, *resa@hotelpwilson.c om*, Fax 0229 066 667, ≤, 𝕝₆, ⇌, 🏊, – 🕸, ✼ rm, ▤ 📺 video 🐾 🚗 – 🏦 15/600.
🄰🄴 ⓿ 🌑 VISA JCB 🛇 GX d
L'Arabesque – Lebanese rest. – **Meals** 65/95 and à la carte 47/74 – *Le Spice's Café :* Meals 50(lunch)/95 and à la carte 69/125 – *Pool Garden* (May - September) Meals 55 (lunch)/65 and a la carte 69/109 – ⊒ 35 – **227 rm** 550/680, 9 suites.

🏛️🏛️🏛️ **Noga Hilton,** 19 quai du Mont-Blanc, ⊠ 1201, 𝒫 0229 089 081, Fax 0229 089 090, ≤, 🎇, 𝕝₆, ⇌, 🏊 – 🕸 ✼ rm, ▤ 📺 video 🐾 🕭 – 🏦 15/440. 🄰🄴 ⓿ 🌑 VISA JCB
Meals see *Le Cygne* below – *La Grignotière :* Meals a la carte 50/103 – ⊒ 36 – **399 rm** 465/750, 11 suites. GY y

🏛️🏛️ **Beau-Rivage,** 13 quai du Mont-Blanc, ⊠ 1201, 𝒫 0227 166 666, *info@beau-rivage.ch*, Fax 0227 166 060, ≤, 🎇 – 🕸, ✼ rm, ▤ 📺 video 🐾 🚗 – 🏦 15/250. 🄰🄴 ⓿ 🌑
VISA JCB FY d
Rest. *Le Patara :* closed 29 March - 1 April, 22 December - 6 January, Saturday and Sunday lunch – **Meals** see *Le Chat Botté* below – *Le Patara* 𝒫 0227 315 566 – Thai rest. – **Meals** 85 and a la carte 61/106 ⊒ 37 – **91 rm** 395/830, 6 suites.

🏛️🏛️ **Angleterre** Ⓜ, 17 quai du Mont-Blanc, ⊠ 1201, 𝒫 0229 065 555, *hotel_angleterre @gve.ch*, Fax 0229 065 556, ≤, « Atmosphere of a fine English residence », 𝕝₆, ⇌ –
🕸 ▤ 📺 video 🐾 🚗 – 🏦 15/35. 🄰🄴 ⓿ 🌑 VISA FGY n
Tea Roux : Meals a la carte 54/103 – ⊒ 37 – **45 rm** 580/890.

🏛️🏛️ **Novotel Genève Centre,** 19 r. de Zürich, ⊠ 1201, 𝒫 0229 099 000, *novotel@gv e.ch*, Fax 0229 099 001 – 🕸, ✼ rm, ▤ 📺 video 🐾 🚗 – 🏦 15/80. 🄰🄴 ⓿ 🌑
VISA JCB FX s
Meals 31 (lunch)/46 and a la carte 51/75 – ⊒ 25 – **193 rm** 250/450, 12 suites.

🏛️🏛️ **Sofitel,** 18 r. du Cendrier, ⊠ 1201, 𝒫 0229 088 080, *h1322@accor-hotels.com*, Fax 0229 088 081, 🎇, « Beautiful antique furniture » – 🕸, ✼ rm, ▤ 📺 🐾. 🄰🄴 ⓿ 🌑
VISA JCB ✼ rest FY t
Meals (closed 23 December - 2 January) 39 and a la carte 57/111 – ⊒ 34 – **95 rm** 410/520.

🏛️🏛️ **Bristol,** 10 r. du Mont-Blanc, ⊠ 1201, 𝒫 0227 165 700, *bristol@bristol.ch*, Fax 0227 389 039, 𝕝₆, ⇌ – 🕸 ▤ 📺 🐾 – 🏦 15/90. 🄰🄴 ⓿ 🌑 VISA JCB. ✼ rest
Meals 44 and a la carte 45/99 – ⊒ 30 – **95 rm** 555/490, 5 suites. FY w

🏛️🏛️ **Warwick,** 14 r. de Lausanne, ⊠ 1201, 𝒫 0227 168 000, *sales.geneva@warwickhotel s.com*, Fax 0227 168 001 – 🕸, ✼ rm, ▤ 📺 video 🐾 🕭 – 🏦 15/140. 🄰🄴 ⓿ 🌑 VISA JCB
Les 4 Saisons (closed 1 to 21 July, 14 to 30 December, Saturday lunch and Sunday) **Meals** 62 and a la carte 74/121 – *La Bonne Brasserie :* Meals 29 and a la carte 39/81 – ⊒ 22 – **167 rm** 320/525. FY c

🏛️🏛️ **Cornavin** Ⓜ without rest, place de la Gare, ⊠ 1201, 𝒫 0227 161 212, *cornavin@f assbind-hotels.ch*, Fax 0227 161 200, « Hall with the world's largest clock » – 🕸 ✼ ▤
📺 video 🐾 – 🏦 60. 🄰🄴 ⓿ 🌑 VISA JCB FY a
⊒ 18 – **162 rm** 227/400.

🏛️🏛️ **Grand Pré** without rest, 35 r. du Grand-Pré, ⊠ 1202, 𝒫 0229 181 111, *info@grand pre.ch*, Fax 0227 347 691 – 🕸 ▤ 📺 🐾 – 🏦 25. 🄰🄴 ⓿ 🌑 VISA JCB
closed 22 December - 5 January – **89 rm** ⊒ 250/350. by rue du Fort-Barreau FX

🏛️🏛️ **Edelweiss,** 2 pl. Navigation, ⊠ 1201, 𝒫 0225 445 151, *edelweiss@manotel.com*, Fax 0225 445 199, « Chalet style » – 🕸, ✼ rm, ▤ 📺 🐾. 🄰🄴 ⓿ 🌑 VISA JCB FX a
Meals (closed January and for lunch) 40/67 and a la carte 39/89 – **42 rm** ⊒ 205/250.

🏛️🏛️ **Eden,** 135 r. de Lausanne, ⊠ 1202, 𝒫 0227 163 700, *eden@eden.ch*, Fax 0227 315 260 – 🕸 ▤ 📺 video 🐾. 🄰🄴 ⓿ 🌑 VISA JCB in the North FX
Meals (closed 21 December - 6 January, Saturday and Sunday) 32 and a la carte 34/66 – **54 rm** ⊒ 200/270.

🏛️ **du Midi,** 4 pl. Chevelu, ⊠ 1201, 𝒫 0225 441 500, *midihotl@iprolink.ch*, Fax 0225 441 520, 🎇 – 🕸, ▤ rm, 📺 🐾 🕭. 🄰🄴 ⓿ 🌑 VISA FY v
Meals (closed Saturday and Sunday) 42 and a la carte 44/78 – ⊒ 20 – **89 rm** 210/300.

🏛️ **Strasbourg** without rest, 10 r. Pradier, ⊠ 1201, 𝒫 0229 065 800, *info@hotel-stras bourg-geneva.ch*, Fax 0227 384 208 – 🕸 📺 🐾. 🄰🄴 ⓿ 🌑 VISA. ✼ FY q
51 rm ⊒ 190/260.

🏛️ **Ibis** Ⓜ without rest, 10 rue Voltaire, ⊠ 1201, 𝒫 0223 382 020, *h2154@accor-hotel s.com*, Fax 0223 382 030 – 🕸 ✼ ▤ 📺 🐾. 🄰🄴 ⓿ 🌑 VISA in the West FY
⊒ 14 – **65 rm** 129.

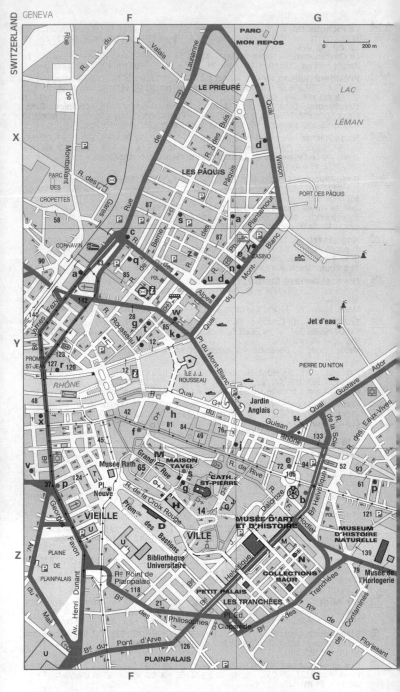

F G

PARC
MON REPOS

LAC

LÉMAN

LE PRIEURÉ

X

PARC
DES
CROPETTES

58

CORNAVIN

90

a

140

142

Y

PROM.
ST-JEAN

RHÔNE

48

x

v

37 p 124

VIEILLE

PLAINE
DE
PLAINPALAIS

Z

U

Musée Rath

Bibliothèque
Universitaire

Rd Point de
Plainpalais

118

21

126

PLAINPALAIS

LES PÂQUIS

PORT DES PÂQUIS

d

87 s P a

c

43 q z

85 POL

28 w

g t 85 k

v 12

123 12

127 r 120

42 h

45 f 81 84 49 76

M MAISON
TAVEL

65 Grand s R. de Rive

Rue CATH.
ST-PIERRE

g H

Rte de la Croix Rouge 14 g

D VILLE

Prom. des Bastions

Jet d'eau

PIERRE DU NITON

Jardin
Anglais

94

Guisan Rhône 133

j

72 94 52 93

e 105 61 p

b POL 121

MUSÉE D'ART
ET D'HISTOIRE M MUSEUM
D'HISTOIRE
NATURELLE

N 139

COLLECTIONS
BAUR 79 Musée de
l'Horlogerie

PETIT PALAIS

LES TRANCHÉES

Pl. Éd.
Claparède

Pont d'Arve

Casino

Jardin

0 200 m

620

STREET INDEX TO GENÈVE TOWN PLAN

XXXX **Le Chat Botté** - Hôtel Beau-Rivage, 13 quai du Mont-Blanc, ⊠ 1201, ℰ 0227 166 920, info@beau-rivage.ch, Fax 0227 166 060, 😭 – ▤. ⚠ ⓪ ⓪ ☑ ⅉ_{CB}
FY d
closed Saturday and Sunday – **Meals** 60 (lunch)/145 and a la carte 79/145.

XXXX **Le Cygne** - Hôtel Noga Hilton, 19 quai du Mont-Blanc, ⊠ 1201, ℰ 0229 089 085, Fax 0229 089 090, ≤ – ▤. ⚠ ⓪ ⓪ ☑ ⅉ_{CB}
GY y
closed 1 week Easter, 3 weeks July and 1 week beginning January – **Meals** 61 (lunch)/139 and a la carte 70/160
Spec. Homard breton juste poêlé, douceur de carottes nouvelles à la coriandre. Turbotin sauvage aux aromates, salicornes à l'huile d'amande douce. Souris d'agneau confite au parfum de mélisse, fleur de courgette en surprise.

XXXX **Le Neptune** - Hôtel Mandarin Oriental du Rhône, 1 quai Turrettini, ⊠ 1201, ℰ 0229 090 006, reserve-mogra@mohg.com, Fax 0229 090 010 – ▤. ⚠ ⓪ ⓪ ☑ ⅉ_{CB}. 🌣
FY r
closed 3 to 25 August, 22 December - 6 January, Saturday, Sunday and Bank Holidays – **Meals** 68 (lunch)/98 and a la carte 104/158
Spec. Thon rouge croustillant, chou-fleur et brocoli en carpaccio à la vinaigrette de tamarin (Summer). Pavé de bar croustillant, pommes écrasées à l'huile d'olive, jus de poulet aux aromates (Summer). Tarte au chocolat, glace à la vanille bourbon (Summer).

XXXX **Amphitryon** - Hotel Des Bergues, 33 quai des Bergues, ⊠ 1201, ℰ 0229 087 000, info@hoteldesbergues.com, Fax 0229 087 090 – ▤. ⚠ ⓪ ⓪ ☑ ⅉ_{CB}
FY k
closed 2 July - 28 August, 24 December - 8 January, Saturday, Sunday and Bank Holidays – **Meals** 67 (lunch)/115 and a la carte 60/141.

XXX **Tsé Yang** - 19 quai du Mont-Blanc, ⊠ 1201, ℰ 0227 325 081, Fax 0227 310 582, ≤, « Elegant installation » – ▤. ⚠ ⓪ ⓪ ☑. 🌣
GY e
Meals - Chinese rest. - 45 (lunch)/135 and a la carte 68/162.

XXX **La Perle du Lac**, 126 r. de Lausanne, ⊠ 1202, ℰ 0229 091 020, info@perledulac.ch, Fax 0229 091 030, 😭, « Chalet in a park with ≤ lake », 💺 – 🅿. ⚠ ⓪ ⓪ ☑. 🌣
in the North FX
closed 23 December - 21 January and Monday – **Meals** 58 (lunch)/115 and a la carte 89/147.

XX **Mövenpick Cendrier**, 17 r. du Cendrier, ⊠ 1201, ℰ 0227 325 030, restaurant.cendrier@moevenpick.com, Fax 0227 319 341 – ⇔ ▤. ⚠ ⓪ ⓪ ☑ ⅉ_{CB}
FY g
Meals a la carte 36/74.

XX **Thai Phuket**, 33 av. de France, ⊠ 1202, ℰ 0227 344 100, Fax 0227 344 240 – ⇔. ⚠ ⓪ ☑
in the North FX
closed Saturday lunch – **Meals** - Thai rest. - 35 (lunch)/90 and a la carte 40/91.

X **Bistrot du Bœuf Rouge**, 17 r. Alfred-Vincent, ⊠ 1201, ℰ 0227 327 537, Fax 0227 314 684 – ⚠ ⓪ ⓪ ☑ ⅉ_{CB}
FY z
closed Saturday and Sunday – **Meals** - Specialities of Lyons - 37 (lunch)/52 and a la carte 54/92.

X **Sagano**, 86 r. de Montbrillant, ⊠ 1202, ℰ 0227 331 150, Fax 0227 332 755 – ⚠ ⓪
☑ ⅉ_{CB}
in the North FX
closed Saturday lunch and Sunday – **Meals** - Japanese rest. - 42 (lunch)/90 and a la carte 48/130.

Left Bank (Commercial Centre) :

🏨🏨 **Swissôtel Genève Métropole,** 34 quai Général-Guisan, ⊠ 1204, ℰ 0223 183 200
reservations.geneva@swissotel.com, Fax 0223 183 300, ≤, 🏤 – 📳 📺 video 📞
🏊 15/120. AE ① 🚳 VISA JCB   GY
Le Grand Quai : Meals a la carte 50/131 – ⊡ 33 – **122 rm** 420/750, 6 suites.

🏨🏨 **La Cigogne,** 17 pl. Longemalle, ⊠ 1204, ℰ 0228 184 040, *cigogne@bluewin.ch*
Fax 0228 184 050, « Tastefully decorated and furnished » – 📳 📺 video 📞 – 🏊 20
AE ① 🚳 VISA 🍴 rest   FGY
Meals *(closed Saturday and Sunday from July - August)* 62 (lunch)/115 and a la carte
80/132 – **47 rm** ⊡ 340/550, 5 suites.

🏨🏨 **Les Armures** 📎, 1 r. du Puits-Saint-Pierre, ⊠ 1204, ℰ 0223 109 172, *armures@*
pan.ch, Fax 0223 109 846, 🏤, « Attractive rustic furnishings in a 17C house » – 📳
📺 video 📞. AE ① 🚳 VISA JCB   FZ
Meals *(closed Easter, Christmas and New Year)* 50 and a la carte 41/88 – **28 rm**
⊡ 315/465.

🏨🏨 **Century** without rest, 24 av. de Frontenex, ⊠ 1207, ℰ 0225 928 888, *hotelcentury*
@bluewin.ch, Fax 0225 928 878 – 📳 ⇔ 📺 📺 P. AE ① 🚳 VISA JCB   GZ
124 rm ⊡ 314/417, 15 suites.

🏨 **Tiffany** Ⓜ, 1 r. des Marbriers, ⊠ 1204, ℰ 0227 081 616, *info@hotel-tiffany.ch*
Fax 0227 081 617, « Belle Epoque decor » – 📳, 📺 rm, 📺 video 📞. AE ① 🚳
VISA JCB   FZ
Meals *(closed Easter, Christmas and New Year)* a la carte 54/92 – **46 rm** ⊡ 215/330

🏨 **Churchill** without rest, 15 r. du Simplon, ⊠ 1207, ℰ 0225 918 888, *Fax 0225 918 878*
– 📳 ⇔ 📺 video 📞. AE ① 🚳 VISA   by quai Gustave Ador GY
35 rm ⊡ 218/278.

XXX **Le Béarn** (Goddard), 4 quai de la Poste, ⊠ 1204, ℰ 0223 210 028, *Fax 0227 813 115*
❀ – ▤. AE ① 🚳 VISA   FY
*closed 15 July - 25 August, 11 to 17 February, Saturday (except dinner from October
May) and Sunday* – **Meals** 65 (lunch)/185 and a la carte 106/168
Spec. Gaspacho de homard bleu à l'avocat, langoustines en fleur de courgette, crème aux
fines épices (Summer). St Pierre rôti à la feuille de laurier et mignonnette de poivre (Spring).
Bécasse sur risotto à l'italienne (Autumn).

XXX **Baron** (Basement, **Mövenpick Fusterie),** 40 r. du Rhône, ⊠ 1204, ℰ 0223 116 947
restaurant.fusterie@moevenpick.com, Fax 0223 109 322 – ▤. AE ① 🚳 VISA JCB
🍴 rest   FY
closed July, August, Saturday, Sunday and for dinner – **Meals** 68 and a la carte 62/130

XX **Roberto,** 10 r. Pierre-Fatio, ⊠ 1204, ℰ 0223 118 033, *Fax 0223 118 466* – ▤. AE
closed Saturday dinner and Sunday – **Meals** - Italian rest. - a la carte 62/124. GZ

XX **Le Patio,** 19 bd Helvétique, ⊠ 1207, ℰ 0227 366 675, *Fax 0227 864 074* – AE ①
🚳 VISA   GZ
closed 21 December - 3 January, Saturday and Sunday – **Meals** a la carte 61/103.

X **Buffet de la Gare des Eaux-Vives,** 7 av. de la Gare des Eaux-Vives, ⊠ 1207,
ℰ 0228 404 430, *catchall@lebuffet.ch, Fax 0228 404 431,* 🏤, « Modern setting, railway
mural » – 🚳 VISA   East direction Annemasse
closed 27 July - 12 August, 22 December - 7 January, Saturday and Sunday – **Meals** 48
(lunch)/95 and a la carte 72/97.

X **La Favola,** 15 r. Jean-Calvin, ⊠ 1204, ℰ 0223 117 437, *ristorante@lafavola.com,*
Fax 0223 491 569, 17C house – 🍴   FZ
closed 28 July - 18 August, Saturday lunch and Sunday – **Meals** - Italian rest. - (number
of covers limited - booking essential) a la carte 74/96.

X **Brasserie Lipp,** 8 r. de la Confédération (2nd floor), ⊠ 1204, ℰ 0223 111 011, *lipp*
@swissonline.ch, Fax 0223 120 104, 🏤 – ⇔ ▤. AE ① 🚳 VISA   FY
closed Christmas – **Meals** a la carte 49/93.

X **Brasserie Victoria,** 2 r. Bovy Lysberg, pl. du Cirque, ⊠ 1204, ℰ 0228 071 199,
🐝 *Fax 0228 071 198* – ▤. AE ① 🚳 VISA   FZ
closed mid July to mid August, Saturday and Sunday from June to September – **Meals**
(booking essential) a la carte 49/94.

Environs
to the North :

Palais des Nations : *by quai Wilson* FGX :

🏨🏨 **Intercontinental,** 7 ch. du Petit-Saconnex, ⊠ 1209, ℰ 0229 193 939, *geneva@in*
terconti.com, Fax 0229 193 838, ≤, 🏤, 🎱, ≤s, ⊒ – 📳 ▤ 📺 📞 🛁 ⇔ P. – 🏊 15/400.
AE ① 🚳 VISA JCB 🍴 rest
Meals see **Les Continents** below – **La Pergola :** ℰ 0229 193 360 Meals 47 (lunch) and
a la carte 61/96 – ⊡ 26 – **285 rm** 430/800, 60 suites.

XXXX **Les Continents** - Hotel Intercontinental, 7 ch. du Petit-Saconnex, ⊠ 1209,
🕸 ℰ 0229 193 350, *geneva@interconti.com, Fax 0229 193 838* – ▤ **P.** **AE** **①** **M⊙** **VISA**
JCB. ⁂
closed 22 December - 2 January, Saturday and Sunday – **Meals** 59 (lunch)/95 and a la carte
84/134
Spec. Mikado de langoustines rôties, fine purée de carottes de sable, beurre à la livèche.
"Crumble" de pigeon de Racan rôti aux pommes, jus au cidre fermier. Pêche pochée à la
verveine, crème légère au sirop d'orgeat.

t Chambésy *5 km -* CT *– alt. 389 –* ⊠ *1292 Chambésy :*

X **Relais de Chambésy,** 8 pl. de Chambésy, ℰ 0227 581 105, *Fax 0227 580 230,* 🌧
🍴 – **AE** **①** **M⊙** **VISA** **JCB**
closed 22 December - 13 January, Saturday and Sunday – **Meals** 34 (lunch)/80 and a la
carte 52/94.

to the East by road to Evian :

t Cologny : *by Quai Gustave Ador* GY *: 3,5 km - alt. 432 –* ⊠ *1223 Cologny :*

XXXX **Auberge du Lion d'Or** (Byrne/Dupont), 5 pl. Pierre-Gautier, ℰ 0227 364 432, *liond*
🕸 *or@maxess.ch, Fax 0227 867 462,* 🌧, « Overlooking the lake and Geneva » – **AE** **①**
M⊙ **VISA**
closed 24 March - 7 April, 21 December - 8 January, Saturday and Sunday – **Meals**
68 (lunch)/160 and a la carte 98/151 – **Meals** (see ***Bistro de Cologny***
below)
Spec. Raviole de tourteau et langoustine à la citronnelle et gingembre. Loup de mer rôti
à l'écaille, sauce niçoise. Les truffes blanches et noires (Winter).

X **Le Bistro de Cologny** - Auberge du Lion d'Or, 5 pl. Pierre-Gautier, ℰ 0227 365 780,
🍴 *liondor@maxess.ch, Fax 0227 867 462,* 🌧 – **AE** **①** **M⊙** **VISA**
closed 24 March - 7 April, 21 December - 8 January, Saturday and Sunday – **Meals** 42 (lunch)
and a la carte 58/96.

t Anières : *by road to Hermance : 7 km - alt. 410 –* ⊠ *1247 Anières :*

XXX **Auberge de Floris** (Legras), 287 rte d'Hermance, ℰ 0227 512 020, *contact@auber*
🕸 *ge-de-floris.com, Fax 0227 512 250,* ⩽ lake, 🌧 – **P.** **AE** **M⊙** **VISA**
closed 7 to 22 April, 24 December - 8 January, Sunday and Monday – **Meals** 56 (lunch)/130
and a la carte 81/143 – **Meals** (see ***Le Bistrot*** below)
Spec. Bouillabaisse à la façon du chef. Nougat de foie gras de canard aux mendiants.
Coussinet d'omble du lac à la crème de marjolaine.

X **Le Bistrot** - Auberge de Floris, 287 rte d'Hermance, ℰ 0227 512 020, *contact@aub*
🍴 *erge-de-floris.com, Fax 0227 512 250,* 🌧 – **P.** **AE** **M⊙** **VISA**
closed 7 to 22 April, 23 December - 7 January, Sunday and Monday – **Meals** (booking
essential) 37 and a la carte 44/84.

to the East by road to Annemasse :

t Thônex : *by rte de Chêne* GZ *: 5 km - alt. 414 –* ⊠ *1226 Thônex :*

XX **Le Cigalon** (Bessire), 39 rte d'Ambilly, at the customs border of Pierre-à-Bochet,
🕸 ℰ 0223 499 733, *jmbessire@le-cigalon.ch, Fax 0223 499 739,* 🌧 – **P.** **AE** **①**
M⊙ **VISA**
closed 15 July - 7 August, 23 to 27 December, 10 to 18 February, Sunday and Monday
– **Meals** 44/99 and a la carte 69/119
Spec. Joue de veau glacée au four, jus corsé à la citronnelle. Filet de St Pierre
rôti sur peau, mousseline de pommes de terre douces. Menu à la truffe noire
(Season).

to the South :

t Conches *Southeast : 5 km - alt. 419 –* ⊠ *1231 Conches :*

X **Le Vallon,** 182 rte de Florissant, ℰ 0223 471 104, *Fax 0223 476 381,* 🌧, « Bistro
style » – **P.** **M⊙** **VISA**
closed 29 March - 7 April, 21 June - 14 July, 21 December - 1 January, Saturday and Sunday
– **Meals** a la carte 58/96.

at Vessy : *by road to Veyrier : 4 km - alt. 419 –* ⊠ *1234 Vessy :*

XX **Alain Lavergnat,** 130 rte de Veyrier, ℰ 0227 842 626, *Fax 0227 841 334,* 🌧 – **P.**
AE **①** **M⊙** **VISA**
closed 29 March - 7 April, 21 July - 4 August, 22 December - 7 January, Sunday and Monday
– **Meals** 50 (lunch)/93 (dinner) and a la carte 75/132 – ***Le Bistrot de la Guinguette* :**
Meals 50 (lunch) and a la carte 53/95.

at Carouge : *by Av. Henri-Dunant* FZ : *3 km – alt. 382 –* ✉ *1227 Carouge :*

XX **Auberge de Pinchat** with rm, 33 ch. de Pinchat, ℰ 0223 423 077, Fax 0223 002 215
🍴 – 📺 📵 AE 🅌 VISA
closed 23 March - 2 April, 11 August - 2 September, 22 December - 4 January – **Meal**
(closed Sunday and Monday) 40 (lunch)/96 and a la carte 72/124 – **5 rm** � 120/145

XX **L'Olivier de Provence**, 13 r. Jacques-Dalphin, ℰ 0223 420 450, Fax 0223 428 880
🍴 – AE ① 🅌 VISA JCB
closed 23 December - 6 January, Saturday except dinner from September - June, Sunda
and Bank Holidays – **Meals** 43 (lunch)/98 and a la carte 77/106 – **Le Bistrot :** Meals 2
(lunch)/34 and a la carte 41/78.

at Petit-Lancy : *by Av. Henri-Dunant* FZ : *3 km – alt. 426 –* ✉ *1213 Petit-Lancy :*

🏨 **Hostellerie de la Vendée**, 28 ch. de la Vendée, ℰ 0227 920 411, info@ vendee.ch
❀ Fax 0227 920 546, 🍴, Winter garden – 📶 🖥 📺 ⚒ 🚗 – 🛏 15/60. AE ① 🅌 VIS
closed Easter and 23 December - 5 January *(closed Saturday lunch, Sunday an*
Bank Holidays) 54 (lunch)/150 and a la carte 64/128 – **Meals** (see **Bistro** below) – **34 rm**
☐ 170/300
Spec. Eventail de fleur de courgette au caviar d'aubergines, coulis de tomate au basili
(Summer). Carré d'agneau de lait des Pyrénées rôti au thym (Spring). Moelleux au chocola
noir des Caraïbes, crème glacée aux noix caramélisées (Autumn).

X **Bistro** - Hostellerie de la Vendée, 28 ch. de la Vendée, ℰ 0227 920 411, info@ vendee.ch
🚗 Fax 0227 920 546, 🍴 – AE ① 🅌 VISA
closed Easter, 23 December - 5 January, Saturday lunch, Sunday and Bank Holidays – **Meal**
38/48 and a la carte 44/76.

à Lully *South-West : 8 km by road to Bernex – alt. 430 –* ✉ *1233 Bernex :*

XX **La Colombière** (Lonati), 122 rte de Soral, ℰ 0227 571 027, Fax 0227 576 549, 🍴 -
❀ 📵 AE ① 🅌 VISA
closed 25 August - 23 September, 21 December - 14 January, Saturday and Sunday – **Meal**
(number of covers limited - booking essential) 45 (lunch)/120 and a la carte 77/103
Spec. Gnocchi au beurre blanc, jus de légumes, truffe noire et gros sel. Tournedos de ba
de ligne au naturel, pommes quenelles à l'huile d'olive. Filet de canette aux cinq parfums
pot-au-feu de chou et foie gras.

to the West :

at Peney-Dessus *by road to Satigny and private lane : 10 km –* ✉ *1242 Satigny :*

XXXX **Domaine de Châteauvieux** (Chevrier) 🛏 with rm, ℰ 0227 531 511, chateauvie
❀❀ x@ bluewin.ch, Fax 0227 531 924, ≤, 🍴, « Beautiful country inn, in a former farm » -
📺 ⚒ 🖥 – 🛏 15. AE ① 🅌 VISA
closed 28 July - 12 August, 23 December - 7 January and 10 to 18 February – **Meals** *(close*
Sunday and Monday) 78 (lunch)/220 and a la carte 156/224 – **18 rm** ☐ 175/395
Spec. Barre de ligne cuit en croûte de sel et épices parfumé au lemon grass (except Winter)
Canette de Bresse rôtie au poivre de Szechuan et au citron vert confit (Summer - Autumn)
Gibier (end September - beginning January).

at Cointrin : *by road to Lyons : 4 km – alt. 428 –* ✉ *1216 Cointrin :*

🏨 **Mövenpick Genève**, 20 rte Pré-Bois, ℰ 0227 987 575, hotel.geneva@ moevenpick
com, Fax 0227 910 284, ≤, 🍴 – 📶, ↔ rm, 🖥 📺 ⚒ & 📵 – 🛏 15/250. AE ① 🅌
VISA JCB
La Brasserie : Meals 42 (lunch) and a la carte 46/99 – **Kamome** – Japanese rest. – *(closed*
August, Saturday lunch, Monday lunch and Sunday) Meals 42 (lunch)/110 and a la carte
45/95 – ☐ 26 – **350 rm** 420/540.

🏨 **Forum Park**, 75 av. Louis-Casaï, ℰ 0227 103 000, resa@ forumparkhotel.ch
Fax 0227 103 100, 🏋, 🏊 – 📶, ↔ rm, 🖥 📺 ⚒ & 🚗 – 🛏 15/600. AE ① 🅌 VISA
JCB, 🍽 rest
La Récolte : Meals 31 and a la carte 42/96 – ☐ 27 – **302 rm** 400/430, 6 suites.

XX **Canonica**, 2nd floor at the airport, ℰ 0227 177 676, restaurant@ canonica.com
Fax 0227 987 768, ≤, Restaurants arranged around an aircraft cabin – 🖥. AE ① 🅌 VISA
Plein Ciel *(closed Sunday except lunch in Winter and Saturday)* Meals 51 (lunch)/99 and
a la carte 71/127 – **Café Bréguet** *(closed Monday dinner)* Meals 32 (lunch) and a la carte
51/83.

at Palais des Expositions : *by quai Wilson* FGX : *5 km – alt. 452 –* ✉ *1218 Grand-Saconnex*

🏨 **Crowne Plaza**, 26 voie de Moëns, ℰ 0227 470 202, sales@ crowneplazageneva.ch
Fax 0227 470 301, 🏋, 🏊, 🔲 – 📶, ↔ rm, 🖥 📺 ⚒ & 🚗 – 🛏 15/140. AE ① 🅌
VISA JCB
L'Intervista – Italian rest. – *(closed Saturday lunch)* Meals a la carte 53/93 – ☐ 30 –
305 rm 350/500.

ufflens-le-Château 1134 Vaud 🗾🗾🗾 ⑪, 🗾🗾🗾 ⑫ – 593 – alt. 471.

Bern 118 – Geneva 53 – Lausanne 14 – Morges 3 – Pontarlier 72 – Yverdon-les-Bains 41.

XXXX 🕷🕷🕷 **L'Ermitage** (Ravet) 🦐 with rm, 26 rte du village, 🖉 0218 046 868, ermitagebr@swi
ssonline.ch, Fax 0218 022 240, « Beautiful residence in a garden, pond » – 📺 🔌 📠 🎴 💳
⑩ 🔳 💳

closed 4 to 28 August, 23 December - 10 January, Sunday and Monday – **Meals** 160/225
and a la carte 151/210 – **9 rm** ⚏ 380/400

Spec. Dinette des quatre foies gras d'oie et de canard apprêtés différemment. La pêche
du lac et ses amusettes (April - September). Jarret de veau doré sur l'os à la broche, jus
au vieux madère.

ossonay 1304 Vaud 🗾🗾🗾 ⑪ 🗾🗾🗾 ③ – 2308 – alt. 565.

Bern 107 – Lausanne 16 – Fribourg 78 – Geneva 62 – Yverdon-les-Bains 28.

XXX 🕷🕷 **Cerf** (Crisci), 10 r. du Temple, 🖉 0218 612 608, Fax 0218 612 627, « 16C house » – 🎴
🔳 💳

closed 6 July - 1 August, 22 December - 3 January, Sunday and Monday – **Meals** (see **La
Fleur de Sel** below) 68 (lunch)/205 and a la carte 105/175

Spec. Foie gras de canard à la broche (Autumn). Dorade royale en velours de tussilage et
violets. Côte de veau en croûte de sel parfumée à la flouve.

X 🍴 **La Fleur de Sel** - Cerf, 10 r. du Temple, 🖉 0218 612 608, Fax 0218 612 627 🎴 🔳
💳

closed 6 July - 1 August, 22 December - 3 January, Sunday and Monday – **Meals** 49 and
a la carte 50/99.

rissier 1023 Vaud 🗾🗾🗾 ⑪ 🗾🗾🗾 ③ – 5756 – alt. 470.

Bern 112 – Geneva 71 – Lausanne 6 – Montreux 40 – Nyon 50 – Pontarlier 64.

XXXX 🕷🕷🕷 **Hôtel de Ville** (Rochat), 1 r. d'Yverdon, 🖉 0216 340 505, Fax 0216 342 464, « Elegant
decor » – 🎴 ⑩ 🔳 💳

closed 28 July - 19 August, 24 December - 7 January, Sunday and Monday – **Meals** 220/245
and a la carte 140/218

Spec. Dodine de cèpes et chanterelles aux févettes, flûtes croustillantes à la farine
de châtaignes (Summer). Truite du lac Léman juste cuite à la livèche au jus de persil (Summer). Côte de boeuf du Simmental au poivre et à l'échalote, sauce au vin rouge et grosses
frites croustillantes (Summer).

ully 1096 Vaud 🗾🗾🗾 ⑫ 🗾🗾🗾 ⑬ – 1758 – alt. 391.

Bern 93 – Geneva 77 – Lausanne 8 – Montreux 15 – Pontarlier 77 – Yverdon-les-Bains 45.

XXX 🕷🕷🕷 **Le Raisin** (Blokbergen) with rm, 1 pl. de l'Hôtel de Ville, 🖉 0217 992 131, raisin@relai
schateaux.com, Fax 0217 992 501, 🍴 – ⬛, 🍴 rest, 📺 🔌 🎴 ⑩ 🔳 💳
Meals 85 (lunch) and a la carte 98/162 – **La Pinte** : **Meals** 45 and a la carte 59/112
– **10 rm** ⚏ 180/320

Spec. Ecrevisses poêlées sur lit de poireaux au vino santo. Dos de turbot à la méditer-
ranéenne. Vapeur de suprême de pigeon fourré au foie gras.

rent Vaud 🗾🗾🗾 ⑫ 🗾🗾🗾 ⑭ – alt. 569.

Bern 85 – Geneva 89 – Lausanne 25 – Martigny 47 – Montreux 5.

XXX 🕷🕷🕷 **Le Pont de Brent** (Rabaey), 🖉 0219 645 230, rabaey@bluewin.ch, Fax 0219 645 530,
« Elegant decor » – ⬛ 🎴 🎴 🔳 💳

closed 14 July - 5 August, 23 December - 7 January, Sunday and Monday – **Meals** 90
(lunch)/220 and a la carte 117/204

Spec. Truite du lac aux pois frais et chanterelles, jus au thym citron. Cuisse de lapin fermier
farcie de son foie, sauce moutarde. Pêche rôtie au miel de romarin, glace amarena (Summer).

*When driving through towns
use the plans in the **MICHELIN Red Guide**.*

Features indicated include :
throughroutes and bypasses,
traffic junctions and major squares,
new streets, car parks, pedestrian streets...
All this information is revised annually.

ZÜRICH 🆘 ⑥, 🆘 ⑱ – pop. 336 822 – alt. 409.

See : *The Quays*★★ : ≤★ FZ ; *Mythenquai* : ≤★ CX – *Fraumünster cloisters*★ (*Alter Kreuz gang des Fraumünsters*), *windows*★ EZ – *Church of SS. Felix and Regula*★ – *Cathedral*★ (*Grossmünster*) FZ – *Fine Arts Museum*★★ (*Kunsthaus*) FZ – *Zoological Gardens*★ (*Zo-Zürich*) – *Bührle Collection*★★ (*Sammlung Bührle*).

Museums : *Swiss National Museum*★★★ (*Schweizerisches Landesmuseum*) EY – *Rietberg Museum*★★ CX M².

Envir : *Uetliberg*★★ *South-West* : by rail – *Albis Pass Road*★ *Southwest by the Bederstrass* – *Former Abbey of Kappel*★ *Southwest* : 22 km – *Eglisau* : *site*★ *North* : 27 km.

Excursions : *Boat Trips, Information* : Zürichsee-Schiffahrtsgesellschaft, Mythenquai 333, ✆ 014 871 333, Fax 014 871 320.

🏌 Dolder (April- mid November), ✆ 012 615 045, Fax 012 615 302 ; 🏌₁₈ at Zumikon ✉ 8126 (April-October), ✆ 019 180 050, Fax 019 180 037, SE : 9 km ; 🏌₁₈ at Hittnau ✉ 8335 (April-October), ✆ 019 502 442, Fax 019 510 166 E : 33 km, 🏌₁₈ at Breitenloo ✉ 8309 Nürensdorf (April-October), ✆ 018 364 080, Fax 018 371 085 N : 22 km.

✈ unique zurich airport, ✆ 018 162 211.

🏢 *Tourist Office, im Hauptbahnhof*, ✆ 012 154 000, *information@zurichtourism.ch* Fax 012 154 044 – T.C.S., Alfred Escher-Str. 38, ✆ 012 868 686, Fax 012 868 687 – A.C.S. Forchstr. 95, ✆ 014 221 500, Fax 014 221 537.

Bern 125 – Basle 109 – Geneva 278 – Innsbruck 288 – Milan 304.

Plans on following pages

On the right bank of the river Limmat (University, Fine Arts Museum) :

🏨🏨🏨🏨 **Dolder Grand Hotel** ⑤, Kurhausstr. 65, ✉ 8032, ✆ 012 693 000, *info@dolderg and.ch*, Fax 012 693 001, 😊, 🏌₉, « Overlooking Zurich lake, town and mountains », 🍴 ⛱ – 🖣 🗏 📺 🚫 ⟸ – 🔬 15/180. 🆔 ⓪ ⓪❸ 𝘝𝘐𝘚𝘈 🍴 rest by Gloriastrasse *La Rotonde* : Meals 96/130 and a la carte 68/174 – **152 rm** 🖾 420/620, 11 suites.

🏨🏨🏨 **Zürich Marriott**, Neumühlequai 42, ✉ 8006, ✆ 013 607 070, *marriott.zurich@ma riott.com*, Fax 013 607 777, ≤, 🛁, ⛺, 🗏 – 🖣, ⛱ rm, 🗏 rm, 📺 🚫 ⟸ – 🔬 15/250 🆔 ⓪ ⓪❸ 𝘝𝘐𝘚𝘈 𝘑𝘊𝘉 EY c *White Elephant* – Thai rest. – *(only dinner)* Meals 38 and a la carte 54/87 – *La Brasserie* Meals 32 (lunch) and a la carte 47/88 – 🖾 30 – **251 rm** 345/405, 9 suites.

🏨🏨🏨 **Eden au Lac**, Utoquai 45, ✉ 8008, ✆ 012 662 525, *info@edenaulac.ch* Fax 012 662 500, ≤, ⛺ – 🖣 🗏 📺 🚫 🅿 – 🔬 20. 🆔 ⓪ ⓪❸ 𝘝𝘐𝘚𝘈 𝘑𝘊𝘉 🍴 rest DX a Meals a la carte 71/146 – **48 rm** 🖾 390/640, 5 suites.

🏨🏨🏨 **Steigenberger Bellerive au Lac** Ⓜ, Utoquai 47, ✉ 8008, ✆ 012 544 000, *belle rive@steigenberger.ch*, Fax 012 544 001, ≤, « Elegant, modern 1920's style furniture » 🛁, ⛺ – 🖣, ⛱ rm, 🗏 📺 🚫 🅿 – 🔬 15/25. 🆔 ⓪ ⓪❸ 𝘝𝘐𝘚𝘈 DX e Meals 53 (lunch) and a la carte 49/111 – **51 rm** 🖾 330/510.

🏨🏨🏨 **Dolder Waldhaus** ⑤, Kurhausstr. 20, ✉ 8030, ✆ 012 691 000, *reservations@do derwaldhaus.ch*, Fax 012 691 001, ≤ Zürich and lake, 😊, 🏌₉, ⛺, 🗏, 🍴 – 🖣, 🗏 rest 📺 🚫 ⟸ 🅿 – 🔬 15/30. 🆔 ⓪ ⓪❸ 𝘝𝘐𝘚𝘈 𝘑𝘊𝘉 by Gloriastrasse DV Meals a la carte 51/106 – 🖾 20 – **70 rm** 240/460.

🏨🏨🏨 **Sofitel**, Stampfenbachstr. 60, ✉ 8006, ✆ 013 606 060, *h1196@accor-hotels.com* Fax 013 606 061 – 🖣, ⛱ rm, 🗏 📺 🚫 ⟸ – 🔬 15/30. 🆔 ⓪ ⓪❸ 𝘝𝘐𝘚𝘈 𝘑𝘊𝘉 FY b *Diff* (*closed Saturday lunch and Sunday lunch*) Meals 38 and a la carte 45/113 – 🖾 32 – **149 rm** 380/520, 4 suites.

🏨🏨🏨 **Central Plaza** Ⓜ, Central 1, ✉ 8001, ✆ 012 515 555, *info@central.ch* Fax 012 518 535 – 🖣, ⛱ rm, 🗏 rm, 📺 video 🚫 🆔 ⓪ ⓪❸ 𝘝𝘐𝘚𝘈 𝘑𝘊𝘉 FY z *King's Cave* – Grill room – Meals a la carte 41/92 – **94 rm** 🖾 350/375, 6 suites.

🏨🏨 **Florhof** ⑤, Florhofgasse 4, ✉ 8001, ✆ 012 614 470, *info@florhof.ch*, Fax 012 614 611, 😊, « Tastefully furnished 16C townhouse » – 🖣, ⛱ rm, 📺 🚫 🆔 ⓪ ⓪❸ 𝘝𝘐𝘚𝘈 FZ k Meals (*closed Christmas - New Year, Saturday, Sunday and Bank Holidays*) 41 (lunch)/85 and a la carte 68/120 – **35 rm** 🖾 240/360.

🏨🏨 **Tiefenau**, Steinwiesstr. 8, ✉ 8032, ✆ 012 678 787, *info@tiefenau.ch* Fax 012 512 476, 😊 – 🖣 📺 🚫 🅿 🆔 ⓪ ⓪❸ 𝘝𝘐𝘚𝘈 𝘑𝘊𝘉 FZ h *closed 26 November - 13 January* – Meals (*closed Sunday*) a la carte 46/88 – 🖾 24 – **31 rm** 270/420.

🏨🏨 **Ambassador**, Falkenstr. 6, ✉ 8008, ✆ 012 589 898, *mail@ambassadorhotel.ch* Fax 012 589 800 – 🖣, ⛱ rm, 🗏 🚫 🆔 ⓪ ⓪❸ 𝘝𝘐𝘚𝘈 𝘑𝘊𝘉 FZ a Meals a la carte 41/117 – **45 rm** 🖾 210/460.

🏨🏨 **Krone Unterstrass**, Schaffhauserstr. 1, ✉ 8006, ✆ 013 605 656, *info@hotel-kron e.ch*, Fax 013 605 600 – 🖣, 🗏 rm, 📺 🚫 🅿 – 🔬 15/75. 🆔 ⓪ ⓪❸ 𝘝𝘐𝘚𝘈 CV b Meals 38 and a la carte 30/111 – **57 rm** 🖾 178/260.

🏨 **Opera** without rest, Dufourstr. 5, ⊠ 8008, ✆ 012 589 999, mail@operahotel.ch, Fax 012 589 900 – 🛗 ✙ ☰ 📺 ✦ 🄰🄴 ① 🄼🄾 *VISA* 🄹🄲🄱   FZ b
62 rm ☷ 260/360.

🏨 **Europe,** Dufourstr. 4, ⊠ 8008, ✆ 012 611 030, info@hoteleurope-zuerich.ch, Fax 012 510 367, 🏛 – 🛗 📺 ✦ 🄰🄴 ① 🄼🄾 *VISA*   FZ u
Quaglinos : Meals a la carte 50/94 – ☷ 21 – **40 rm** 210/310.

🏨 **Wellenberg** Ⓜ without rest, Niederdorfstr. 10, ⊠ 8001, ✆ 012 624 300, reservatio n@hotel-wellenberg.ch, Fax 012 513 130 – 🛗 ✙ 📺 ✦ 🄰🄴 ① 🄼🄾 *VISA* 🄹🄲🄱   FZ s
45 rm ☷ 290/390.

🏨 **Rigihof** Ⓜ, Universitätstr. 101, ⊠ 8006, ✆ 013 611 685, info@hotel-rigihof.ch, Fax 013 611 617, 🏛 – 🛗, ✙ rm, 📺 ✦ 🕭 🄿 🄰🄴 ① 🄼🄾 *VISA* 🄹🄲🄱   DV c
Bauhaus : Meals 64 and a la carte 44/91 – **66 rm** ☷ 275/390.

🏨 **Seefeld** Ⓜ without rest, Seefeldstr. 63, ✆ 013 874 141, info@hotel-seefeld.ch, Fax 013 874 151, 🛁 – 🛗, ✙ rm, ✦ 🕭 🄿 🄰🄵 ① 🄼🄾 *VISA*   DX k
64 rm ☷ 170/340.

🏨 **Adler** Ⓜ, Rosengasse 10, at Hirschplatz, ⊠ 8001, ✆ 012 669 696, info@hotel-adler.ch, Fax 012 669 669, Wall paintings of Zürich by Heinz Blum, in the rooms – 🛗, ✙ rm, 📺 ✦ 🄰🄴 ① 🄼🄾 *VISA* 🄹🄲🄱   FZ w
Swiss Chuchi : Meals a la carte 44/79 – **52 rm** ☷ 170/290.

🏨 **Helmhaus** without rest, Schifflände 30, ⊠ 8001, ✆ 012 518 810, hotel@helmhaus.ch, Fax 012 510 430 – 🛗 ✙ ☰ 📺 ✦ 🄰🄴 ① 🄼🄾 *VISA* 🄹🄲🄱. ✀   FZ v
24 rm ☷ 220/340.

🏨 **Lady's First** Ⓜ without rest, women only, Mainaustr. 24, ✆ 013 808 010, info@lady sfirst.ch, Fax 013 808 020, « Sauna with roof terrace », 🛋 – 🛗 📺 ✦ 🕭 🄰🄴 ① 🄼🄾 *VISA*. ✀   DX n
☷ 18 – **28 Zim** 230/320.

🏨 **Seegarten,** Seegartenstr. 14, ⊠ 8008, ✆ 013 883 737, seegarten@bluewin.ch, Fax 013 833 738, 🏛 – 🛗 📺 ✦ 🄰🄴 ① 🄼🄾 *VISA* 🄹🄲🄱   DX b
Latino – Italian rest. – (closed Saturday lunch and Sunday lunch) Meals a la carte 45/86
28 rm ☷ 179/299.

🏨 **Rex** Ⓜ, Weinbergstr. 92, ⊠ 8006, ✆ 013 602 525, hotelrex@swissonline.ch, Fax 013 602 552, 🏛 – 🛗, ✙ rm, 📺 ✦ 🕭 🄿 🄰🄴 ① 🄼🄾 *VISA*   DV a
Blauer Apfel (closed Saturday and Sunday) Meals a la carte 31/88 – **40 rm** ☷ 140/300.

🏨 **Rütli** without rest, Zähringerstr. 43, ⊠ 8001, ✆ 012 545 800, info@rutli.ch, Fax 012 545 801 – 🛗 ✙ 📺 ✦ 🄰🄴 ① 🄼🄾 *VISA*   FY a
62 rm ☷ 190/290.

🍴🍴🍴 **Sonnenberg,** Hitziweg 15, ⊠ 8032, ✆ 012 669 797, restaurant@sonnenberg-zh.ch, Fax 012 669 798, ≤ Zürich and lake, 🏛 – ☰ 🄿 🄰🄴 ① 🄼🄾 *VISA*   by Gloriastrasse   DV
Meals - veal and beef specialities - (booking essential) a la carte 66/164.

🍴🍴 **Wirtschaft Flühgass,** Zollikerstr. 214, ⊠ 8008, ✆ 013 811 215, Fax 014 227 532, « 16C former wine tavern » – 🄿 🄰🄴 🄼🄾 *VISA*   by Zollikerstrasse   DX
closed 20 July - 18 August, 22 December - 2 January, Saturday (except dinner from November - December) and Sunday – Meals (booking essential) 42 (lunch)/130 and a la carte 52/120.

🍴🍴 **Kronenhalle,** Rämistr. 4, ⊠ 8001, ✆ 012 516 669, Fax 012 516 681, « Collection of exceptional works of art » – ☰. 🄰🄴 ① 🄼🄾 *VISA*   FZ t
Meals (booking essential) a la carte 83/154.

🍴🍴 **Zunfthaus zur Schmiden,** Marktgasse 20, ⊠ 8001, ✆ 012 505 848, schmiden@d inner.ch, Fax 012 505 849, « 15C blacksmith's guild house » – ☰. 🄰🄴 ①
🄼🄾 *VISA*   FZ x
closed 13 July - 18 August, Sunday (except dinner from October - June) and Bank Holidays
– Meals a la carte 56/106.

🍴🍴 **Haus zum Rüden,** Limmatquai 42 (1st floor), ⊠ 8001, ✆ 012 619 566, info@haus zumrueden.ch, Fax 012 611 804, « 13C guild house » – 🛗 ☰. 🄰🄴 ① 🄼🄾 *VISA* 🄹🄲🄱   FZ c
closed Saturday and Sunday – Meals 58 (lunch)/105 and a la carte 75/131.

🍴🍴 **Zunfthaus zur Zimmerleuten,** Limmatquai 40, ⊠ 8001, ✆ 012 505 363, zimme rleuten-zurich@bluewin.ch, Fax 012 505 364, 🏛, « 18C guild house » – ☰. 🄰🄴 ① 🄼🄾 *VISA*   FZ z
closed 28 July - 11 August and Sunday – **Restaurant** (1st floor) : Meals a la carte 55/107
– **Küferstube** : Meals 55/93 and a la carte 35/77.

🍴🍴 **Riesbächli,** Zollikerstr. 157, ⊠ 8008, ✆ 014 222 324, Fax 014 222 941, « Outstanding wine cellar » – 🄰🄴 ① 🄼🄾 *VISA* 🄹🄲🄱   by Zollikerstrasse   DX
closed 27 July - 18 August, 23 December - 2 January, Saturday (except dinner from November - March) and Sunday – Meals 55 (lunch)/160 and a la carte 78/139.

ZÜRICH

SWITZERLAND

36

Sihlquai

Limmatstr.

f

40

k

Zollstr.

Sihl

LIMMAT

Neumühlequai

c

81

b

88

Wenberg.

52

21

Sonneggstrasse

19

Walche-
brücke

c

79

SCHWEIZERISCHES
LANDESMUSEUM

49

Museumstr.

Leonhard-

strasse

103

Leonhard-

P

81

19

Universitätsstr.

U

U

EIDG.

TFCHN.

HOCHSCHULE

K.Schmider

91

Y

Bahnhof
pl.

HAUPTBAHNHOF

e

a

Gessnerallee

Gessner-
br.

Gessner-

strasse

Bahnhof-
brücke

a

Perlisscher-

str.

Bahnhof-

str.

Löwenpl.

100

Werdmühlestr.

Urania-

str.

Rudolf Brun-
Brücke

POL.

Niederdorf-

str.

Mühleg.

Künstler-

gasse

Gloria-
str.

Rämistr.

U

PREDIGER-KIRCHE

Löwen-

str.

Uraniastr.

Schanzengraben

P

Oetenbachg.

63

Limmat-

quai

W

Hirschen-
Platz

Hirschen-

graben

54

k

39

Sihl-

str.

Lindenhof

Bahnhof-

St. Anna

b

P

Nüschelerstr.

9

V

z

c

e

V

y

Weinpl.

60

r

S

64

x

n

46

Münsterg.

J

P

W

90

Tal-

strasse

10

u

85

Bahnhof-

H

c

z. Zwinglipl.

Kirchg.

Heimpl.

Hottinger-
str.

x

48

M

Münsterbr.

KUNSTHAUS

Wohnmuseum

r

58

Fraumünster

M

GROSSMÜNSTER

Zeltweg

h

Paradeplatz

Wasserkirche

Wasserkirche

m

v

Oberdorfstr.

Rämistr.

P

Z

Bleicherweg

12

f

28

Stadthausquai

STADTHAUS-
ANLAGE

Limmat-

quai

Utoquai

Stocker-

str.

Dreikönigstr.

18

a

Bürklipl.

Quaibrücke

t

e

Bellevuepl.

78

STADELHOFEN

Kreuzbühlstr.

Gotthardstr.

KONGRESSGEB.

m

Quai

Guisan-

G.

ZÜRICHSEE

Sechseläuten-
platz

93

Stadelhoferpl.

P

Utoquai

OPERNHAUS

Falkenstr.

v

a

b

u

Seefeldstr.

0   200 m

XX **Conti-da Bianca,** Dufourstr. 1, ⊠ 8008, ℰ 012 510 666, Fax 012 510 686 – 𝔸𝔼 ⓞ
🕮𝕆 𝕍𝕀𝕊𝔸   FZ
closed mid July - mid August, Monday in Spring and Autumn, Saturday lunch and Sunda
– **Meals** - Italian rest. - a la carte 72/130.

XX **Vorderer Sternen,** Theaterstr. 22 (1st floor), ⊠ 8001, ℰ 012 514 949, rosenber
🍴 er@tic.ch, Fax 012 529 063, ⇔ – 𝔸𝔼 ⓞ 🕮𝕆 𝕍𝕀𝕊𝔸   FZ
closed 20 July - 18 August and Christmas – **Meals** a la carte 44/89.

XX **Casa Ferlin,** Stampfenbachstr. 38, ⊠ 8006, ℰ 013 623 509, casaferlin@swissonline.ch
Fax 013 623 534 – ▤. 𝔸𝔼 ⓞ 🕮𝕆 𝕍𝕀𝕊𝔸   FY
closed mid July - mid August, Christmas - New Year, Saturday and Sunday – **Meals** - Italia
rest. - (booking essential) 48 (lunch)/120 and a la carte 66/116.

XX **Blue Monkey Cocostin,** Stüssihofstatt 3, ⊠ 8001, ℰ 012 617 618, koenigstuhl@.
luewin.ch, Fax 012 627 123, ⇔ – 𝔸𝔼 ⓞ 🕮𝕆 𝕍𝕀𝕊𝔸   FZ
Meals - Thai rest. - 50 and a la carte 58/121.

X **Oepfelchammer,** Rindermarkt 12 (1st floor), ⊠ 8001, ℰ 012 512 336
🍴 Fax 012 627 533, ⇔, « 14C inn with original wine bar » – 𝔸𝔼 ⓞ 🕮𝕆 𝕍𝕀𝕊𝔸   FZ r
closed 15 July - 13 August and 24 December - 8 January – **Meals** 105 and a la carte 52/93

X **Blaue Ente,** Seefeldstr. 223 (mill Tiefenbrunnen), ⊠ 8008, ℰ 013 886 840, info@
aue-ente.ch, Fax 014 227 741, ⇔ – 𝔸𝔼 ⓞ 🕮𝕆 𝕍𝕀𝕊𝔸   by Zollikerstrasse DX
closed 21 July - 14 August and 24 December - 4 January – **Meals** (booking essential)
la carte 49/97.

X **Rosaly's,** Freieckgasse 7, ⊠ 8001, ℰ 012 614 430, rosenberger@tic.ch
🍴 Fax 012 614 413, ⇔ – 𝔸𝔼 ⓞ 🕮𝕆 𝕍𝕀𝕊𝔸   FZ
closed Saturday lunch, Sunday lunch and Christmas – **Meals** a la carte 39/80.

On the left bank of the river Limmat (Main railway station, Business centre)

🏨🏨🏨🏨 **Baur au Lac,** Talstr. 1, ⊠ 8001, ℰ 012 205 020, info@bauraulac.ch, Fax 012 205 044
⇔, « Garden and terrace », 𝕃₆, 🏊 – |❦|, ▤ rm, 📺 ℰ 🚬 – 🛎 15/60. 𝔸𝔼 ⓞ 🕮
𝕍𝕀𝕊𝔸 🄹🄲🄱. ⅏   EZ z
Pavillon/Le Français : Meals a la carte 84/163 – **Rive Gauche** (closed 3 weeks July
August, Sunday and Bank Holidays) **Meals** a la carte 63/139 – ⊋ 38 – **103 rm** 460/680
22 suites.

🏨🏨🏨 **Savoy Baur en Ville** Ⓜ, am Paradeplatz, ⊠ 8001, ℰ 012 152 525, contact@savo
y-baurenville.ch, Fax 012 152 500, « Elegant modern decor » – |❦|, ▤ rm, 📺 video ℰ 🚬
– 🛎 15/70. 𝔸𝔼 ⓞ 🕮𝕆 𝕍𝕀𝕊𝔸 🄹🄲🄱. ⅏   EZ
Savoy (1st floor) **Meals** 64 (lunch) and a la carte 70/138 – **Orsini** in front of the cathedra
– Italian rest. (booking essential) **Meals** 59 (lunch) and a la carte 62/138 – **104 rm**
⊋ 450/700, 8 suites.

🏨🏨🏨 **Widder** Ⓜ, Rennweg 7, ⊠ 8001, ℰ 012 242 526, home@widderhotel.com
Fax 012 242 424, ⇔, « Restored old town houses with contemporary interiors » – |❦| ▤
📺 ℰ 🚬 🚬 – 🛎 15/160. 𝔸𝔼 ⓞ 🕮𝕆 𝕍𝕀𝕊𝔸 🄹🄲🄱. ⅏ rest   EZ v
Meals 57 (lunch)/88 and a la carte 64/115 – **42 rm** ⊋ 410/710, 7 suites.

🏨🏨🏨 **Schweizerhof** Ⓜ, Bahnhofplatz 7, ⊠ 8001, ℰ 012 188 888, info@hotelschweizerh
of.com, Fax 012 188 181, « Modern-elegant decor » – |❦|, ⇔ rm, ▤ 📺 ℰ – 🛎 15/40
𝔸𝔼 ⓞ 🕮𝕆 𝕍𝕀𝕊𝔸 🄹🄲🄱. ⅏ rest   EY a
La Soupière (1st floor) closed 22 December - 6 January, Saturday lunch, Sunday and Bank
Holidays **Meals** 70/92 and a la carte 76/134 – **115 rm** ⊋ 410/660.

🏨🏨🏨 **Ascot** Ⓜ, Tessinerplatz 9, ⊠ 8002, ℰ 012 081 414, info@ascot.ch, Fax 012 081 420.
⇔, « Stylish decor » – |❦|, ⇔ rm, ▤ 📺 ℰ 🚬 – 🛎 15/50. 𝔸𝔼 ⓞ 🕮𝕆 𝕍𝕀𝕊𝔸 🄹🄲🄱
Lawrence : Meals 58 (lunch)/86 and a la carte 67/126 – **Fujiya of Japan** ℰ 012 081 555
- Japanese rest. (Teppanyaki) (closed Sunday and Monday) **Meals** 48 (lunch)/95 and a la
carte 57/111 – **74 rm** ⊋ 370/540.   CX a

🏨🏨🏨 **Zum Storchen** Ⓜ, Weinplatz 2, ⊠ 8001, ℰ 012 272 727, info@storchen.ch.
Fax 012 272 700, ⇐ River Limmat and City, ⇔, « Riverside setting, elegant decor » – |❦|
⇔ rm, ▤ rm, 📺 ℰ – 🛎 25. 𝔸𝔼 ⓞ 🕮𝕆 𝕍𝕀𝕊𝔸 🄹🄲🄱. ⅏ rest   EZ u
Rôtisserie (1st floor) **Meals** 65 (lunch)/85 and a la carte 73/114 – **73 rm** ⊋ 325/650.

🏨🏨🏨 **ArabellaSheraton Neues Schloss** Ⓜ, Stockerstr. 17, ⊠ 8002, ℰ 012 869 400,
neuesschloss@arabellasheraton.com, Fax 012 869 445 – |❦|, ⇔ rm, ▤ 📺 ℰ – 🛎 20.
𝔸𝔼 ⓞ 🕮𝕆 𝕍𝕀𝕊𝔸 🄹🄲🄱. ⅏ rest   EZ m
Le Jardin (closed Saturday lunch and Sunday except for residents) **Meals** 52 (lunch)/85
and a la carte 70/116 – ⊋ 28 – **60 rm** 420/490.

🏨🏨🏨 **Splügenschloss,** Splügenstr. 2 / Genferstrasse, ⊠ 8002, ℰ 012 899 999, hotel@s
plugenschloss.ch, Fax 012 899 998 – |❦|, ⇔ rm, ▤ 📺 ℰ 📞 – 🛎 20. 𝔸𝔼 ⓞ 🕮
𝕍𝕀𝕊𝔸 🄹🄲🄱   CX e
Meals 68 (lunch)/110 and a la carte 80/153 – **50 rm** ⊋ 295/580.

Inter-Continental Zürich, Badenerstr. 420, ✉ 8003, ☎ 014 044 444, *zurich@int erconti.com*, *Fax 014 044 440*, 🏨, *Fa*, ≘s, ⛫ - 🛗, ⊬ rm, ▤ 📺 📞 ♿ 🚗 - 🏛 15/300. AE ⓓ ⓜⓒ VISA JCB by Badenerstrasse CV
Relais des Arts : **Meals** 44 (lunch) and a la carte 54/98 - ☕ 28 - **364 rm** 420/540.

Stoller, Badenerstr. 357, ✉ 8003, ☎ 014 054 747, *info@stoller.ch*, *Fax 014 054 848*, 🏨 - 🛗 ⊬ 📺 📞 - 🏛 15/25. AE ⓓ ⓜⓒ VISA JCB by Badenerstrasse CV
Meals 50 and a la carte 42/92 - **79 rm** ☕ 280/450.

Glärnischhof Ⓜ, Claridenstr. 30, ✉ 8002, ☎ 012 862 222, *info@glaernischerhof.com*, *Fax 012 862 286* - 🛗, ⊬ rm, ▤ rest, 📺 📞 🅿 - 🏛 25. AE ⓓ ⓜⓒ VISA JCB EZ f
Le Poisson - Fish specialities - *(closed Saturday and Sunday)* **Meals** 56 (lunch)/78 and a la carte 65/109 - ***Vivace*** - Italian rest. - **Meals** a la carte 44/83 - **62 rm** ☕ 320/480.

ArabellaSheraton Atlantis 🐚, Döltschiweg 234, ✉ 8055, ☎ 014 545 454, *atlan tishotel@arabellasheraton.com*, *Fax 014 545 400*, <, 🏨, *Fa*, ≘s, 🐎 - 🛗, ⊬ rm, 📺 📞 🚗 🅿 - 🏛 15/150. AE ⓓ ⓜⓒ VISA JCB. ⊁ rest by Zweierstrasse CX
Quatre Saisons *(closed Saturday and Sunday)* **Meals** 55 (lunch)/69 and a la carte 54/110 - ***Döltschistube*** : **Meals** a la carte 43/75 - ☕ 32 - **161 rm** 355/490.

Glockenhof, Sihlstr. 31, ✉ 8001, ☎ 012 259 191, *info@glockenhof.ch*, *Fax 012 259 292*, 🏨 - 🛗, ⊬ rm, ▤ rest, 📺 📞 ♿ - 🏛 15/50. AE ⓓ ⓜⓒ VISA JCB
Meals a la carte 46/86 - **106 rm** ☕ 250/400. EZ b

Engimatt, Engimattstr. 14, ✉ 8002, ☎ 012 841 616, *info@engimatt.ch*, *Fax 012 012 516*, 🏨, ⚘ - 🛗, ⊬ rm, 📺 📞 🚗 🅿 - 🏛 25. AE ⓓ ⓜⓒ VISA JCB
Meals 43 (lunch)/79 and a la carte 36/101 - **80 rm** ☕ 240/320. CX d

Novotel Zürich Technopark Ⓜ, Schiffbaustr. 13, ✉ 8005, ☎ 012 762 222, *H2731@accor-hotels.com*, *Fax 012 762 323*, 🏨, *Fa*, ⛫ - 🛗, ⊬ rm, 📺 📞 ♿ 🚗 - 🏛 15/120. AE ⓓ ⓜⓒ VISA by Seebahn-, Hard- and Pfingstweidstrasse CV
Meals a la carte 31/86 - **142 rm** ☕ 182/265.

Walhalla Ⓜ without rest, Limmatstr. 5, ✉ 8005, ☎ 014 465 400, *walhalla-hotel@bl uewin.ch*, *Fax 014 465 454* - 🛗 ⊬ 📺 - 🏛 15/20. AE ⓓ ⓜⓒ VISA JCB EY r
☕ 15 - **48 rm** 150/200.

Kindli, Pfalzgasse 1, ✉ 8001, ☎ 012 115 917, *hotelkindli@compuserve.com*, *Fax 012 116 528*, 🏨, « English country house style installation » - 🛗 📺. AE ⓓ ⓜⓒ VISA. ⊁ rm EZ z
closed Christmas - ***Opus*** ☎ 012 114 182 *(closed Saturday, Sunday and Bank Holidays)* **Meals** a la carte 52/95 - **20 rm** ☕ 220/340.

Montana, Konradstr. 39, ✉ 8005, ☎ 012 716 900, *reservation@hotelmontana.ch*, *Fax 012 723 070* - 🛗, ⊬ rm, 📺 📞 ♿ 🅿. AE ⓓ ⓜⓒ VISA JCB EY f
Bistro le Lyonnais *(closed Saturday lunch and Sunday)* **Meals** a la carte 40/97 - **74 rm** ☕ 235/310.

Ibis, Schiffbaustr. 11, ✉ 8005, ☎ 012 762 100, *h2942@accor-hotels.com*, *Fax 012 762 101*, 🏨 - 🛗, ⊬ rm, 📺 📞 ♿ 🚗. AE ⓓ ⓜⓒ VISA
Meals a la carte 32/59 - ☕ 14 - **155 rm** 129.
by Seebahn-, Hard- and Pfingstweidstrasse CV

Sukhothai, Erlachstr. 46, ✉ 8003, ☎ 014 626 622, *heymann@sukhothai.ch*, *Fax 014 626 654* - ▤. AE ⓓ ⓜⓒ VISA. ⊁ CX h
closed Easter, 7 July - 4 August, 23 December - 2 January, Sunday and Monday - **Meals** - Thai rest. - *(from May - September dinner only)* (booking essential) 165 and a la carte 111/187.

Luca's Giangrossi, Rebgasse 8, ✉ 8004, ☎ 012 412 064, *Fax 012 412 084*, 🏨 - 🅿. AE ⓓ ⓜⓒ VISA CV e
closed Saturday lunch (from mid July - end August also dinner) and Sunday - **Meals** - Italian rest. - 38 (lunch)/75 and a la carte 65/103.

Kaiser's Reblaube, Glockengasse 7, ✉ 8001, ☎ 012 212 120, *rest.reblaube@bluew in.ch*, *Fax 012 212 155*, 🏨 - AE ⓓ ⓜⓒ VISA. ⊁ EZ y
closed 21 July - 12 August, Saturday lunch, Monday dinner and Sunday - ***Goethe-Stübli*** (1st floor) *(booking essential)* **Meals** 56 (lunch)/135 - ***Weinstube*** : **Meals** a la carte 47/116.

Piccoli Accademia, Rotwandstr. 48, ✉ 8004, ☎ 012 414 202, *vinos-accademia@b luewin.ch*, *Fax 012 416 243* - ▤. AE ⓓ ⓜⓒ VISA. ⊁ CV n
closed Saturday (except dinner from October - May) and Sunday - **Meals** - Italian rest. - a la carte 54/134.

Zunfthaus zur Waag, Münsterhof 8 (1st floor), ✉ 8001, ☎ 012 169 966, *zunfth aus-zur-waag@bluewin.ch*, *Fax 012 169 967*, 🏨, Linen weaver's and hatter's guildhall - AE ⓓ ⓜⓒ VISA JCB EZ x
Meals a la carte 62/145.

SWITZERLAND

XX **Carlton,** Bahnhofstr. 41, Nüschelerstr. 6, ⌧ 8001, ℰ 012 271 919, *info@carlton-zu rich.ch, Fax 012 271 927*, 🍴 – ▤. 🆎 ① 🆎 *VISA*   EZ v
closed Sunday and Bank Holidays – **Meals** 48 (lunch) and a la carte 47/99.

XX **Casa Aurelio,** Langstr. 209, ⌧ 8005, ℰ 012 727 744, *Fax 012 727 724*, 🍴 – ▤. 🅰
① 🆎 *VISA*. 🛇   CV
closed 3 weeks August, 22 December - 6 January and Sunday – **Meals** 95 and a la carte
70/106.

XX **Sala of Tokyo,** Limmatstr. 29, ⌧ 8005, ℰ 012 715 290, *sala@active.ch
Fax 012 717 807*, 🍴 – 🆎 ① 🆎 *VISA* 🄹🄲🄱   EY k
*closed Easter, 21 July - 12 August, 23 December - 7 January, Saturday lunch, Sunday and
Monday* – **Meals** - Japanese rest. - 67/120 and a la carte 49/122.

XX **Il Giglio,** Weberstr. 14, ⌧ 8004, ℰ 012 428 597, *Fax 012 910 183* – 🆎 ①
🆎 *VISA*   CX c
closed 20 July - 5 August, 24 December - 2 January, Saturday (except dinner from Sep tember - May), Sunday and Bank Holidays – **Meals** - Italian rest. - 45 (lunch)/83 and a la
carte 53/103.

XX **da Bernasconi,** Lavaterstr. 87, ⌧ 8002, ℰ 012 011 613, *Fax 012 011 649* – 🆎 ①
🆎 *VISA*   CX b
closed Christmas – **Meals** - Italian rest. - (booking essential) a la carte 53/91.

X **Camino "Chez Bertrand",** Freischützgasse 4, ⌧ 8004, ℰ 012 419 436, *chezbert. and@hotmail.com, Fax 012 419 435*, 🍴 – 🆎 ① 🆎 *VISA*   CV k
closed 14 July - 11 August, Saturday (except dinner from September - May) and Sunday
– **Meals** 35 (lunch)/82 and a la carte 47/100.

X **Cantinetta Antinori,** Augustinergasse 25, ⌧ 8001, ℰ 012 117 210, *cantinetta-an tinori@swissonline.ch, Fax 012 211 613*, 🍴 – 🆎 ① 🆎 *VISA*   EZ c
Meals - Italian rest. - 90 and a la carte 60/119.

X **Barometer,** Glockengasse 16, ⌧ 8001, ℰ 012 115 665, *barometer@glockengasse.ch
Fax 012 115 663*, 🍴 – 🆎 ① 🆎 *VISA*   EZ e
🚗 *closed 22 December - 6 January, Saturday and Sunday* – **Meals** a la carte 51/90.

X **Caduff's Wine Loft,** Kanzleistr. 126, ⌧ 8004, ℰ 012 402 255, *caduff@wineloft.ch
Fax 012 402 256* – 🆎 ① 🆎 *VISA*   CV d
🚗 *closed 24 December - 3 January, Saturday lunch and Sunday* – **Meals** (booking essential)
a la carte 40/118.

at Zürich-Oerlikon : *North : by Universitätstrasse DV : 5 km – alt. 442 –* ⌧ *8050 Zürich-
Oerlikon :*

🏨 **Swissôtel Zürich** Ⓜ, Am Marktplatz, ℰ 013 173 111, *reservations.zurich@swissote
l.com, Fax 013 124 468*, ≤, 🍴, 🏋, 🆒, 🖼 – 🛗, ▤ rm, 📺 🗝 & 🅿 – 🎗 15/400. 🆎
① 🆎 *VISA* 🄹🄲🄱. 🛇
Szenario : **Meals** 55 (lunch) and a la carte 43/117 – ⌒ 28 – **337 rm** 350/380,
10 suites.

at Zürich-Seebach : *North : by Schaffenhauserstrasse CV – alt. 442 –* ⌧ *8052 Zürich-
Seebach :*

🏠 **Landhus,** Katzenbachstr. 10, ℰ 013 083 400, *info@landhus-zuerich.ch,
Fax 013 083 451*, 🍴 – 🛗 📺 🅿 – 🎗 15/300. 🆎 ① 🆎 *VISA*
Meals a la carte 43/81 – **28 rm** ⌒ 120/150.

at Glattbrugg : *North : by Universitätstrasse DV : 8 km – alt. 432 –* ⌧ *8152 Glattbrugg :*

🏨 **Renaissance Zürich** Ⓜ, Talackerstr. 1, ℰ 018 745 000, *renaissance.zurich@renaiss
ancehotels.com, Fax 018 745 001*, 🍴, ≅s, 🆒, 🖼 – 🛗 ✂ ▤ 📺 🗝 & 🛌 – 🎗 15/300.
🆎 ① 🆎 *VISA* 🄹🄲🄱. 🛇 rest
Asian Place – Asian rest. – *(closed July, August, Saturday lunch and Sunday lunch)* **Meals**
27 (lunch) and a la carte 49/128 – **Brasserie la Noblesse :** **Meals** a la carte 48/88 – ⌒ 29
– **196 rm** 340/380, 8 suites.

🏨 **Hilton** Ⓜ, Hohenbühlstr. 10, ℰ 018 285 050, *zurich@hilton.ch, Fax 018 285 151*, 🍴
– 🛗, ✂ rm, ▤ 📺 🗝 🅿 – 🎗 15/280. 🆎 ① 🆎 *VISA* 🄹🄲🄱. 🛇 rest
Meals *(Restaurant undergoing renovation until April 2002)* – ⌒ 33 – **310 rm** 350/665,
13 suites.

🏨 **Mövenpick** Ⓜ, Walter Mittelholzerstr. 8, ℰ 018 088 888, *hotel@movenpick-zurich-a
irport.ch, Fax 018 088 877* – 🛗, ✂ rm, ▤ 📺 🗝 & 🅿 – 🎗 15/220. 🆎 ① 🆎
VISA 🄹🄲🄱
Appenzeller Stube *(closed 28 July - 16 August and Saturday lunch)* **Meals** 42 (lunch)/70
and a la carte 59/110 – **Mövenpick Rest. :** **Meals** a la carte 40/70 – **Dim Sum** – Chinese
rest. – *(closed 1 to 19 July, Saturday lunch and Sunday lunch)* **Meals** a la carte 43/97 –
⌒ 28 – **335 rm** 280/400.

Novotel Zürich Airport Messe, Talackerstr. 21, ☎ 018 299 000, *h0884@accor-hotels.com, Fax 018 299 999,* – |‡|, ▤ rm, TV ☎ ♿ 🚗 P – 🏫 15/150. AE ◑ MC VISA
Meals a la carte 35/93 – ☕ 26 – **257 rm** 205/240.

Airport, Oberhauserstr. 30, ☎ 018 094 747, *hotelairport@bluewin.ch, Fax 018 094 774,* – |‡|, ⇆ rm, ▤ rm, TV ☎ P. AE ◑ MC VISA JCB. ✂
Edo Garden : **Meals** 35 (lunch)/79 and a la carte 52/94 – ***Fujiya of Japan*** – Japanese rest. – *(closed Saturday lunch and Sunday lunch)* **Meals** 84/119 and a la carte 58/96 – **44 rm** ☕ 175/255.

t Nürensdorf : *Northeast by Universitätstrasse and road to Bassersdorf : 19 km – alt. 505 – ✉ 8309 Nürensdorf :*

Zum Bären with rm, Alte Winterthurerstr. 45, ☎ 018 383 636, *Fax 018 383 646,* – TV 🚗 P. AE ◑ MC VISA
closed 21 July - 13 August, 23 December - 4 January, Saturday lunch (except Beizli), Sunday and Monday – **Meals** 58 (lunch)/135 and a la carte 73/135 – ***Beizli :*** **Meals** 48 (dinner) and a la carte 52/94 – **14 rm** ☕ 150/215
Spec. Scampi auf kleinem Glasnudelwok mit roter Curryschaumsauce. Gebratene Entenleber auf Mango-Chutney mit Confit de Vin-cuit. Variation von Ormalinger Jungschwein an Tannenhonig-Jus.

at Kloten : *North : by Universitätstrasse* DV *: 12 km – alt. 447 – ✉ 8302 Kloten :*

Allegra Ⓜ without rest, Hamelirainstr. 3, ☎ 018 044 444, *reservation@hotel-allegra.ch, Fax 018 044 141* – |‡| ⇆ TV ☎ ♿ P – 🏫 15/30. AE ◑ MC VISA
132 rm ☕ 175/220.

Fly Away Ⓜ, Marktgasse 19, ☎ 018 044 455, *hotel@hotel-flyaway.ch, Fax 018 044 450,* – |‡|, ⇆ rm, ▤ rm, TV ☎ ♿ 🚗 P. AE ◑ MC VISA
closed 22 December - 2 January (Hotel only) – **Meals** - Italian rest. - a la carte 40/83 – ☕ 14 – **42 rm** 167/196.

Rias, Gerbegasse 6, ☎ 018 142 652, *Fax 018 135 504,* – AE MC VISA
closed Saturday dinner, Sunday and Bank Holidays – **Meals** 44 (lunch)/95 and a la carte 48/113.

at Küsnacht : *Southeast : by Bellerivestrasse* DX *: 8 km – alt. 415 – ✉ 8700 Küsnacht :*

Ermitage am See Ⓜ with rm, Seestr. 80, ☎ 019 144 242, *info@ermitage.ch, Fax 019 144 243,* ≤ Zurich lake, , « Lakeside setting, terrace and garden », , ⚓ – |‡| TV ☎ P. AE ◑ MC VISA. ✂ rest
Meals 65 (lunch)/175 and a la carte 111/170 – **22 rm** ☕ 195/410, 4 suites
Spec. Hummersalat mit Artischocken, Zitronen und Basilikum. Kalamares gefüllt mit Waldpilzen, Bouillabaisse-Jus. Wolfsbarschfilet nach Nizza-Art, Zucchini und deren Blüte im Backteig.

Petermann's Kunststuben, Seestr. 160, ☎ 019 100 715, *petermannskunstuben@bluewin.ch, Fax 019 100 495,* – ▤ P. AE ◑ MC VISA. ✂
closed 25 August - 17 September, 10 to 26 February, Sunday and Monday – **Meals** (dinner : booking essential) 78 (lunch)/195 and a la carte 107/207
Spec. Noix de St-Jacques au confit d'endives et jus de pommes vertes à la vanille (October-March). Poussin aux écrevisses "Pattes rouges" sur un ragoût de blettes aux truffes noires (May-September). Carré de selle de chevreuil aux dattes et noix grillées (October-December).

at Gattikon *South by motorway A3* CX *: 11 km – alt. 510 – ✉ 8136 Gattikon :*

Sihlhalde (Smolinsky), Sihlhaldenstr. 70, ☎ 017 200 927, *Fax 017 200 925,* – P. AE MC VISA
closed 20 July - 12 August, 23 December - 7 January, Sunday and Monday – **Meals** (booking essential) 115 and a la carte 76/119
Spec. St. Petersfisch vom Grill an milder Senfsauce und roten Linsen. Wachtelbrüstchen glaciert im Portwein mit Vanille-Nicola Püree. Rehrückenlende aus der Sommerjagd mit Pilzen (May - September).

at Uetikon am See : *Southeast by Bellerivestrasse : 18 km – alt. 414 – ✉ 8707 Uetikon am See :*

Wirtschaft zum Wiesengrund (Hussong), Kleindorfstr. 61, ☎ 019 206 360, *hussong@wiesengrund.ch, Fax 019 211 709,* – P. AE ◑ MC VISA. ✂
closed 27 July - 19 August, 27 January - 19 February, Sunday and Monday – **Meals** (booking essential) 65 (lunch)/156 and a la carte 99/166
Spec. Millefeuille von Tomate und Kabeljau an Aceto balsamico (Summer). Miéralente mit Zitrone gefüllt im Ofen gebraten (Autumn). Milchlamm an Thymianjus (Spring).

United Kingdom

LONDON – BIRMINGHAM – EDINBURGH
GLASGOW – LEEDS – LIVERPOOL
MANCHESTER

PRACTICAL INFORMATION

LOCAL CURRENCY

Pound Sterling: *1 GBP = 1,60 euro (€) (Dec. 2001)*

TOURIST INFORMATION

Tourist information offices exist in each city included in the Guide. The telephone number and address is given in each text under 🛈

FOREIGN EXCHANGE

Banks are usually open between 9.00am and 4.30pm on weekdays only and some open on Saturdays. Most large hotels have exchange facilities. Heathrow and Gatwick Airports have 24-hour banking facilities.

SHOPPING

In London: *Oxford St/Regent St (department stores, exclusive shops) Bond St (exclusive shops, antiques)*
Knightsbridge area (department stores, exclusive shops, boutiques)
For other towns see the index of street names; those printed in red are where the principal shops are found.

THEATRE BOOKINGS IN LONDON

Your hotel porter will be able to make your arrangements or direct you to Theatre Booking Agents.
In addition there is a kiosk in Leicester Square selling tickets for the same day's performances at half price plus a booking fee. It is open 12 noon-6.30pm.

CAR HIRE

The international car hire companies have branches in each major city. Your hotel porter should be able to give details and help you with your arrangements.

TIPPING

Many hotels and restaurants include a service charge but where this is not the case an amount equivalent to between 10 and 15 per cent of the bill is customary. Additionally doormen, baggage porters and cloakroom attendants are generally given a gratuity.
Taxi drivers are customarily tipped between 10 and 15 per cent of the amount shown on the meter in addition to the fare.

SPEED LIMITS

The maximum permitted speed on motorways and dual carriageways is 70 mph (113 km/h.) and 60 mph (97 km/h.) on other roads except where a lower speed limit is indicated.

SEAT BELTS

The wearing of seat belts in the United Kingdom is compulsory for drivers, front seat passengers and rear seat passengers where seat belts are fitted. It is illegal for front seat passengers to carry children on their lap.

LONDON

404 folds ㊷ to ㊹ – pop. 6 679 699

B *Britain Visitor Centre, 1 Regent Street, W1.*

*Heathrow, ℰ 08700 000123 – **Terminal** : Airbus (A1) from Victoria, Airbus (A2) from Paddington – Underground (Piccadilly line) frequent service daily.*

*Gatwick, ℰ 08700 002468, by A 23 and M 23 – **Terminal** : Coach service from Victoria Coach Station (Flightline 777, hourly service) – Railink (Gatwick Express) from Victoria (24 h service).*

London City Airport, ℰ (020) 7646 0000.

Stansted, at Bishop's Stortford, ℰ 08700 000303, NE : 34 m. by M 11 and A 120.
British Airways, Victoria Air Terminal : *115 Buckingham Palace Rd., SW1, ℰ (020) 7707 4750, p. 16.*

SIGHTS

HISTORIC BUILDINGS AND MONUMENTS

Palace of Westminster★★★ *p. 10* LY – *Tower of London*★★★ *p. 11* PVX – *British Airways London Eye (views*★★★*)* – *Banqueting House*★★ *p. 10* LX – *Buckingham Palace*★★ *p. 16* BVX – *Kensington Palace*★★ *p. 8* FX – *Lincoln's Inn*★★ *p. 17* EV – *Lloyds Building*★★ *p. 7* PV – *Royal Hospital Chelsea*★★ *p. 15* FU – *St. James's Palace*★★ *p. 13* EP – *Somerset House*★★ *p. 17* EXY – *South Bank Arts Centre*★★ *p. 10* MX – *Spencer House*★★ *p. 13* DP – *The Temple*★★ *p. 6* MV – *Tower Bridge*★★ *p. 11* PX – *London Bridge*★ *p. 11* PVX – *Albert Memorial*★ *p. 14* CQ – *Apsley House*★ *p. 12* BP – *George Inn*★, *Southwark p. 11* PX – *Guildhall*★ *p. 7* OU – *International Shakespeare Globe Centre*★ *p. 11* OX T – *Dr Johnson's House*★ *p. 6* NUV **A** – *Leighton House*★ *p. 8* EY – *The Monument*★ *(*❅★*) p. 7* PV **G** – *Royal Albert Hall*★ *p. 14* CQ – *Royal Opera Arcade*★ *p. 13* FGN – *Staple Inn*★ *p. 6* MU **Y** – *Theatre Royal*★ *(Haymarket) p. 13* GM – *Westminster Bridge*★ *p. 10* LY.

CHURCHES

The City Churches – *St. Paul's Cathedral*★★★ *(Dome* ≤★★★*) p. 7* NOV – *St. Bartholomew the Great*★★ *p. 7* OU **K** – *St. Mary-at-Hill*★★ *p. 7* PV **B** – *Temple Church*★★ *p. 6* MV – *All Hallows-by-the-Tower (font cover*★★, *brasses*★*) p. 7* PV **Y** – *St. Bride*★ *(steeple*★★*) p. 7* NV **J** – *St. Giles Cripplegate*★ *p. 7* OU **N** – *St. Helen Bishopsgate*★ *(monuments*★★*) p. 7* PUV **R** – *St. James Garlickhythe (tower and spire*★, *sword rests*★*) p. 7* OV **R** – *St. Margaret Lothbury*★ *p. 7* PU **S** – *St. Margaret Pattens (spire*★, *woodwork*★*) p. 7* PV **N** – *St. Mary Abchurch*★ *p. 7* PV **X** – *St. Mary-le-Bow (tower and steeple*★★*) p. 7* OV **G** – *St. Michael Paternoster Royal (tower and spire*★*) p. 7* OV **D** – *St. Olave*★ *p. 7* PV **S**.

Other Churches – *Westminster Abbey*★★★ *p. 10* LY – *Southwark Cathedral*★★ *p. 11* PX – *Queen's Chapel*★ *p. 13* EP – *St. Clement Danes*★ *p. 17* EX – *St. James's*★ *p. 13* EM – *St. Margaret's*★ *p. 10* LY **A** – *St. Martin in-the-Fields*★ *p. 17* DY – *St. Paul's*★ *(Covent Garden) p. 17* DX – *Westminster Roman Catholic Cathedral*★ *p. 10* KY **B**.

STREETS – SQUARES – PARKS

The City★★★ *p. 7* NV – *Regent's Park*★★★ *(Terraces*★★, *Zoo*★★*) p. 5* HIST – *Belgrave Square*★★ *p. 16* AVX – *Burlington Arcade*★★ *p. 13* DM – *Covent Garden*★★ *(The Piazza*★★*) p. 17* DX – *Hyde Park*★★ *pp. 8 and 9* GHVX – *The Mall*★★ *p. 13* FP – *St. James's Park*★★ *p. 10* KXY – *Trafalgar Square*★★ *p. 17* DY – *Whitehall*★★ *(Horse Guards*★*) p. 10* LX – *Barbican*★ *p. 7* OU – *Bloomsbury*★ *p. 6* LMU – *Bond Street*★ *pp. 12-13* CK-DM – *Cheyne Walk*★ *p. 9* GHZ – *Jermyn Street*★ *p. 13* EN – *Leicester Square*★ *p. 13* GM – *Neal's Yard*★ *p. 17* DV – *Piccadilly Arcade*★ *p. 13* DEN – *Piccadilly Circus*★ *p. 13* FM – *Queen Anne's Gate*★ *p. 10* KY – *Regent Street*★ *p. 13* EM – *St. James's Square*★ *p. 13* FN – *St. James's Street*★ *p. 13* EN – *Shepherd Market*★ *p. 12* CN – *Soho*★ *p. 13* – *Strand*★ *p. 17* DY – *Victoria Embankment gardens*★ *p. 17* DEXY – *Waterloo Place*★ *p. 13* FN.

MUSEUMS

British Museum★★★ *p. 6* LU – *National Gallery*★★★ *p. 13* GM – *Science Museum*★★★ *p. 14* CR – *Tate Britain*★★★ *p. 10* LZ – *Victoria and Albert Museum*★★★ *p. 15* DR – *Wallace Collection*★★★ *p. 12* AH – *Courtauld Institute of Art*★★ *(Somerset House) p. 17* EXY – *Gilbert Collection*★★ *(Somerset House) p. 10* MV – *Museum of London*★★ *p. 7* OU **M** – *National Portrait Gallery*★★ *p. 13* GM – *Natural History Museum*★★ *p. 14* CS – *Sir John Soane's Museum*★★ *p. 6* MU **M** – *Tate Modern*★★ *(views*★★★ *from top floors) p. 11* OX **M** – *Imperial War Museum*★ *p. 10* NY – *London's Transport Museum*★ *p. 17* DX – *Madame Tussaud's*★ *p. 5* IU **M** – *Planetarium*★ *p. 5* IU **M** – *Wellington Museum*★ *(Apsley House) p. 12* BP.

LONDON CENTRE

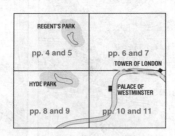

REGENT'S PARK

pp. 4 and 5

pp. 6 and 7

TOWER OF LONDON

HYDE PARK

PALACE OF
WESTMINSTER

pp. 8 and 9

pp. 10 and 11

STREET INDEX TO LONDON CENTRE TOWN PLANS

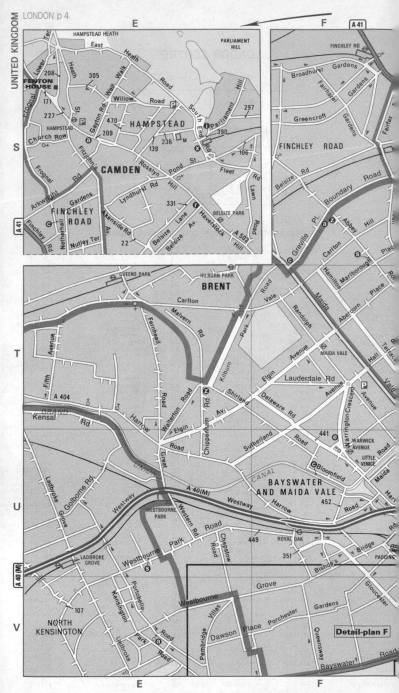

HAMPSTEAD HEATH

PARLIAMENT HILL

FENTON HOUSE

208
305
17
227
470
209
139
236
297
390
106
331
22

HAMPSTEAD

CAMDEN

BELSIZE PARK

FINCHLEY ROAD

A 41

Broadhurst Gardens
Fairhazel
Greencroft
Gardens
FINCHLEY ROAD
Belsize Rd
Boundary Road
Fairfax
Greville Pl.
Abbey Hill
Carlton
Hamilton
Marlborough Place

BRENT
QUEENS PARK
HILBURN PARK
Carlton
Malvern Rd
Fernhead
Kilburn Park Vale
Randolph
Avenue
MAIDA VALE
Avenue
Lauderdale Rd
Elgin
Shirland
Delaware Rd
Warrington Crescent
441
Sutherland Road
WARWICK AVENUE
LITTLE VENICE
Bloomfield
BAYSWATER AND MAIDA VALE
452

Fifth Avenue
A 404
GRAND Kensal Rd
UNION
Harlow Road
Great Western Road
Walterton Road
Chippenham Av.
Elgin

CANAL
A 40(M)
Westway
WESTBOURNE PARK
Harrow
449
ROYAL OAK
351
Bisnde's
PADDINGTON
Bridge

Ladbroke Grove
Golborne Rd.
Westbourne
Park Road
Chepstow Road
Grove
Gloucester

LADBROKE GROVE
Portobello
Kensington Park Road
Westbourne
Villas
Pembridge
Dawson Place
Porchester
Gardens
Queensway
Bayswater Road

NORTH KENSINGTON
107

Detail-plan F

A 40 (M)

A 41

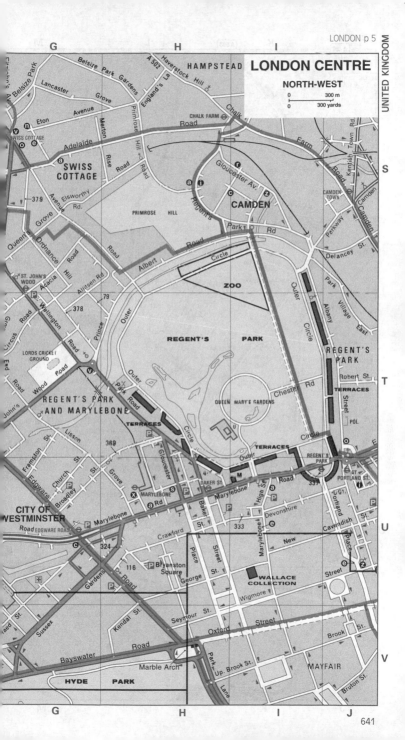

A1 N

N O P

LONDON CENTRE

NORTH-EAST

| 0 | 300 m |
| 0 | 300 yards |

BURY
LINGTON
A1

St. Paul's Road

Road

Road

S

Canonbury Square

Upper H St. POL

EngRlefield Road

De Beauvoir Road

×DALSTON
Rd.

A 10

Richmond Rd

Canonbury Rd

ESSEX RD

Halliford St.

Downham

S

INGTON a
Liverpool
Upper Street
St. Peter's St.
70
c n

Essex Rd

Essex

New North Rd

Road

Street

Nuttall St.

Whiston Rd

464

235

343
350

Kingsland Road

Hackney Rd

ANGEL
St. John
T
293
398
296 U
SBURY Percival St.
110
13

City Road

Goswell Road

Central Street

Lever Street

Eagle Wharf Road

Wharf Road

Shepherdess

City Road

Bath Street

New

North Road

East Road

Pitfield Street

Hoxton Street

HACKNEY

M

T

OLD ST.
192 126
Old St.
TOWER HAMLETS
384 32

J 16

Virginia Rd

Clerkenwell
Z
M
CHARTERHOUSE
113
83 S
454
264
292
178
e Rd
270
81
166
141
Whitecross Street

A 5201

Goswell Street

Old Street

Bunhill Row

Beech Street

BARBICAN
RARBICAN CENTRE
N
M
BARBICAN
Worship Street
Sun Street
5
Wilson Street
BROADGATE
LIVERPOOL STREET
391
MOORGATE
Brushfield St.
398
Commercial

U

372
168
518
Holborn Viaduct
A 40
J Newgate St.
376
Y
ST. PAUL'S CATHEDRAL
301
CITY OF LONDON
BLACKFRIARS
38
291
395

London Wall
GUILDHALL
Gresham St.
247 380
ST. PAUL'S
Cheapside 352
304 Cannon
Queen Victoria MANSION HOUSE
431
THAMES

Moorgate

London Wall
273 S
BANK OF ENGLAND
357
365
BANK
St.
250
268
CANNON STREET
MONUMENT
431
278

Liverpool St.
319
472
417 a
f
P

Houndsditch
36
71
34
260
187
Fenchurch
154
197
62

ALDGATE EAST
456
ALDGATE
145
Aldgate High St.
282
Minories
TOWER
TOWER OF LONDON

A 11
A 13

V

O P

643

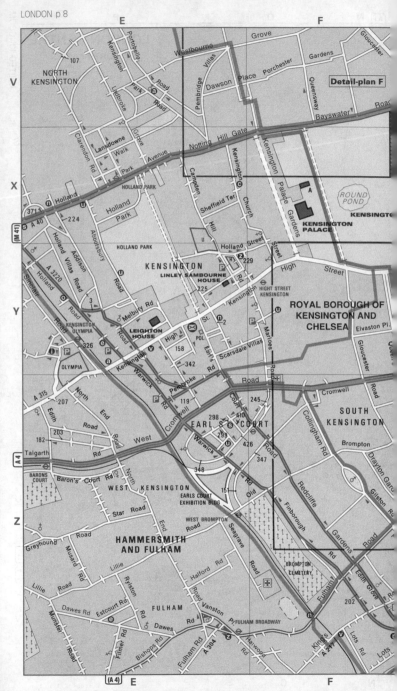

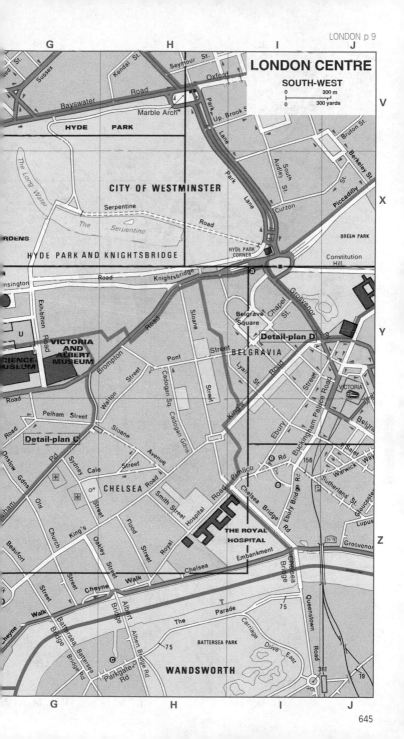

LONDON CENTRE

SOUTH-WEST

0   300 m
0   300 yards

G   H   I   J   V

Seymour St.
Oxford
Kendal St.
Sussex
Bayswater   Road
Marble Arch
Up. Brook S
Park
Lane
Bruton St.

HYDE   PARK   X
South
Audley
St.
Berkeley St.

The Long Water
CITY OF WESTMINSTER
Curzon
Piccadilly

Serpentine
Road
GREEN PARK

The   Serpentine
GARDENS
HYDE PARK CORNER
Constitution
Hill.

HYDE PARK AND KNIGHTSBRIDGE
ensington   Road   Knightsbridge
ⓐ
Grosvenor
Y

Exhibition Road
Sloane
Belgrave
Square
Chapel
St.

VICTORIA AND ALBERT MUSEUM
Detail-plan D

SCIENCE MUSEUM
U
Brompton
Pont
Street
BELGRAVIA
VICTORIA
Road

Road
Walton
Cadogan Sq
Cadogan Gdns
Lyall
St.
Street
Buckingham Palace Road
Belgr

Pelham Street
Sloane
King's
Ebury

Detail-plan C
Onslow Gdns
Sydney
Cale
Street
Avenue
Street
Rd   156
Warwick Way
Sutherland St.
Gloucester

ham
Old
Church
CHELSEA   Road
Smith Street
Pimlico
Road   Lupus
Z

Beaufort
King's
Oakley
Flood
Royal
Street
Street
Hospital   Chelsea Bridge   Rd
THE ROYAL HOSPITAL
Grosvenor

Street
Walk
Cheyne
Chelsea   Embankment
Chelsea
Bridge
Queenstown

Cheyne
Walk
Battersea
Bridge
Albert Bridge
The   Parade   75
Carriage   Drive   East
Road

Bridge Rd
Parkgate
Rd
BATTERSEA PARK
361
19

WANDSWORTH

G   H   I   J

645

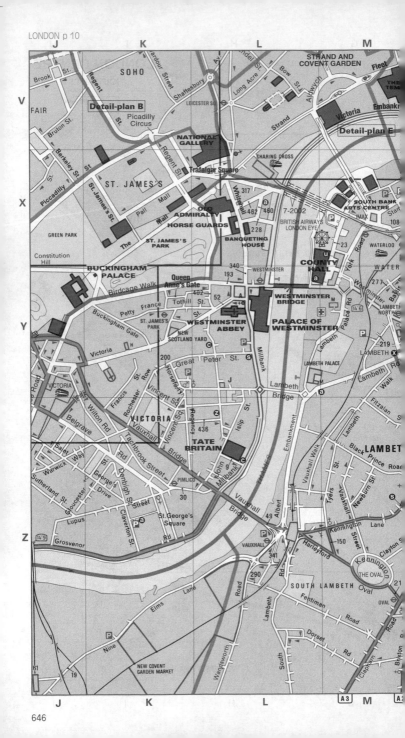

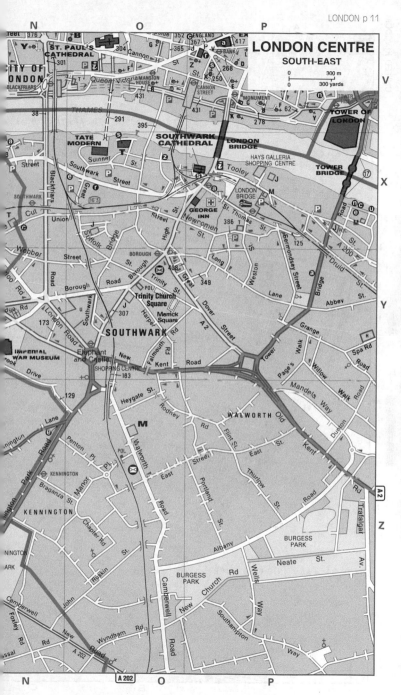

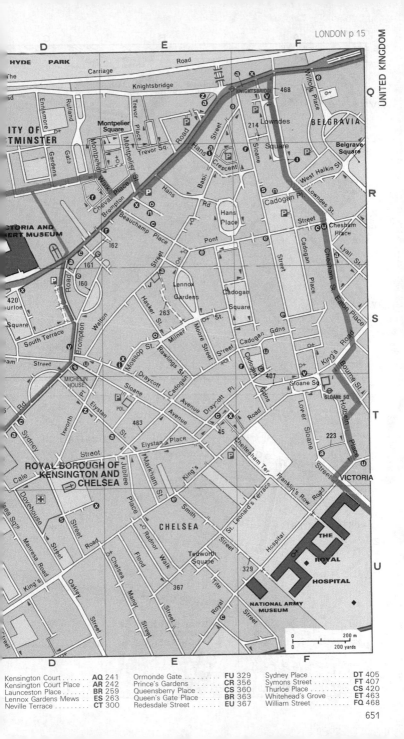

HYDE PARK

Carriage Road

Knightsbridge

CITY OF
WESTMINSTER

Montpelier
Square

BELGRAVIA

Belgrave
Square

Lowndes
Square

214

468

Knightsbridge

Trevor Place

Montpelier St.

Montpelier Walk

Trevor Sq.

Cheval Place

Brompton

Hans Crescent

Hans

Basil St.

Sloane Street

West Halkin St.

Lowndes St.

Cadogan Pl

VICTORIA AND
ALBERT MUSEUM

Beauchamp Place

162

161

160

Road

Hans Rd

Hans Place

Pont Street

Cadogan Place

Street

Chesham Place

Chesham St.

Eaton Place

Lyall St.

South Terrace

420
Thurloe
Square

Walton Street

Hasker St.

283

Lennox
Gardens

Milner St.

Moore Street

Cadogan Street

Cadogan Square

Cadogan Gdns

King's Road

Bourne St.

Brompton Road

Street

Mossop St.

Rawlings St.

MICHELIN
HOUSE

Draycott

Sloane

Cadogan

Avenue Draycott Pl.

Cadogan Gdns

407

Sloane Sq

SLOANE SQ

Lower Sloane Street

POL.

Elystan Street

463

Avenue

45

223

VICTORIA

ROYAL BOROUGH OF
KENSINGTON AND
CHELSEA

Sydney

Ixworth

Elystan Place

Markham St.

Jubilee Place

King's Road

Cheltenham Ter.

Franklin's Row

St. Leonard's Terrace

THE
ROYAL
HOSPITAL

Cale

Dovehouse

Chelsea Sq

Manresa Road

Oakley

Street

CHELSEA

Smith Street

Radnor Walk

Flood Street

Chelsea Mang?

Tedworth
Square

367

329

Tite Street

Royal Hospital Road

NATIONAL ARMY
MUSEUM

King's

0   200 m
0   200 yards

651

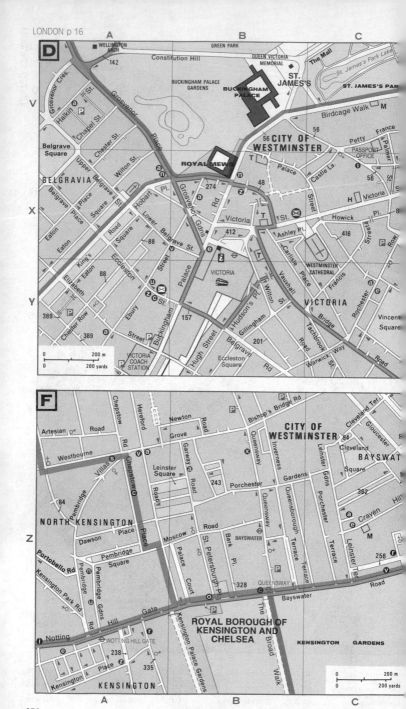

Map D (top)

WELLINGTON ARCH
GREEN PARK
Constitution Hill
142
QUEEN VICTORIA MEMORIAL
The Mall
St. James's Park Lake
ST. JAMES'S
ST. JAMES'S PAR
BUCKINGHAM PALACE GARDENS
BUCKINGHAM PALACE
Grosvenor Cres.
Halkin St.
Chapel St.
Grosvenor Place
Birdcage Walk
M
V
Chester St.
Belgrave Square
56
CITY OF WESTMINSTER
Petty France
Palmer
PASSPORT OFFICE
56
BELGRAVIA
Upper Belgrave
Wilton St.
ROYAL MEWS
Palace
Castle La.
Belgrave Place
Hobart Pl.
Grosvenor Gdns
274
48
Street
H Victoria
56
X
Eaton Place
Lower Belgrave St.
Rd
Victoria
412
Howick Pl.
8
Ashley Pl.
416
Row
King's
Eccleston
Eaton Square
88
Palace
VICTORIA
Carlisle Place
WESTMINSTER CATHEDRAL
Francis
Street
Elizabeth
Eaton
88
Ebury
St.
Hudson's Pl.
Gillingham
Vauxhall
Rochester
VICTORIA
Y
389
Chester Row
389
Street
Buckingham
157
Belgrave
201
Warwick St.
Bridge
Tachbrook
Way
Road
Vincent Square
Hugh Street
Eccleston Square
Rd

0   200 m
0   200 yards

VICTORIA COACH STATION

Map F (bottom)

F
Artesian Road
Chepstow Rd
Hereford
Newton Road
Bishop's Bridge Rd
Cleveland Ter.
Gloucester
CITY OF WESTMINSTER
94
Cleveland
Westbourne
Chepstow Villas
Grove
Garway
Queensway
Inverness
Leinster Gdns
Square
BAYSWAT
84
Pembridge
Chepstow Place
Leinster Square
Road
243
Porchester
Gardens
Queensborough
Porchester
352
NORTH KENSINGTON
Dawson Place
Moscow Road
St. Petersburgh Pl.
Bark
Queensway
Terrace
Terrace
Craven
Z
Portobello Rd
Pembridge Square
Palace Court
BAYSWATER
Terrace
M
Pembridge Gdns
Terrace
256
Kensington Park Rd
Pembridge
328
QUEENSWAY
Leinster
Road
Pembridge
Gate
Hill
Bayswater
The
Broad
Kensington Palace Gardens
Walk
Notting
NOTTING HILL GATE
ROYAL BOROUGH OF KENSINGTON AND CHELSEA
KENSINGTON GARDENS
238
335
Kensington Place
KENSINGTON

0   200 m
0   200 yards

A   B   C

652

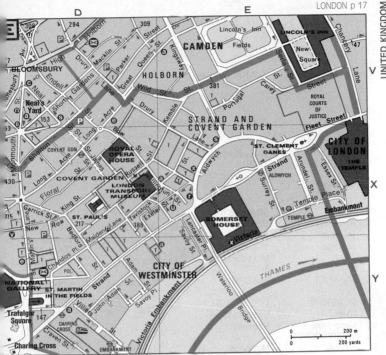

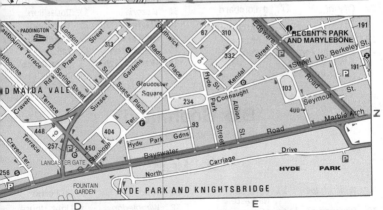

Starred establishments in London

❀❀❀

| 32 | *Chelsea* | XXXX | Gordon Ramsay |

❀❀

31	*Chelsea*	🏛	Capital		45	*Mayfair*	XXXX	Le Gavroche
49	*Regent's Park & Marylebone*	XXXXX	John Burton-Race		43	*Belgravia*	XXXX	La Tante Claire
					46	*Mayfair*	XXX	The Square

❀

44	*Mayfair*	🏛	Connaught		50	*St James's*	XXX	Pétrus
42	*Belgravia*	🏛	Nahm		40	*Putney*	XXX	Putney Bridge
45	*Mayfair*	XXXXX	Cheznico		54	*Victoria*	XXX	Rhodes in the Square
45	*Mayfair*	XXXXX	The Oak Room Marco Pierre White		27	*City of London*	XX	Club Gascon
32	*Chelsea*	XXX	Aubergine		47	*Mayfair*	XX	Nobu
27	*City of London*	XXX	City Rhodes		24	*Bloomsbury*	XX	Pied à Terre
51	*Soho*	XXX	L'Escargot		51	*Soho*	XX	Richard Corrigan at Lindsay House
49	*Hyde Park & Knightsbridge*	XXX	Foliage					
46	*Mayfair*	XXX	Mirabelle		28	*Hammersmith*	XX	River Café
27	*City of London*	XXX	1 Lombard Street (Restaurant)		54	*Victoria*	XX	Roussillon
					46	*Mayfair*	XX	Tamarind
50	*St. James's*	XXX	L'Oranger		43	*Belgravia*	XX	Zafferano
49	*Regent's Park & Marylebone*	XXX	Orrery		35	*Kensington*	XX	Zaika
					41	*Wandsworth*	X	Chez Bruce

"Bib Gourmand"

Good food at moderate prices

😊 Meals

40	*Whitechapel*	XX	Cafe Spice Namaste		52	*Soho*	X	(Il) Forno
30	*Islington*	XX	Metrogusto		38	*Wimbledon*	X	Light House
42	*Bayswater & Maida Vale*	X	L'Accento		35	*Kensington*	X	Malabar
51	*St James's*	X	Al Duca		40	*Battersea*	X	Metrogusto
39	*Southwark*	X	Cantina Vinopolis (Brasserie)		29	*Archway*	X	The Parsee
					40	*Putney*	X	(The) Phoenix
33	*Chelsea*	X	(I) Cardi		41	*Southfields*	X	Sarkhel's
50	*Regent's Park & Marylebone*	X	Chada Chada		42	*Bayswater & Maida Vale*	X	The Vale

Restaurants classified according to type

Bangladeshi

42	Bayswater & Maida Vale	※	Ginger

Chinese

5	Mayfair	※※※※	The Oriental	28	Fulham	※※ Mao Tai
5	Mayfair	※※※	Kai	35	Kensington	※※ Memories of China
0	St James's	※※※	Orient	43	Hyde Park & Knightsbridge	※※ Mr Chow
5	Chelsea	※※	Good Earth			
5	Bloomsbury	※※	Hakkasan	42	Bayswater & Maida Vale	※※ Poons
3	City of London	※※	Imperial City	25	Hampstead	※※ ZeNW3
5	Victoria	※※	Ken Lo's Memories of China	51	St James's	※ China House
5	Chelsea	※※	Mao Tai	52	Soho	※ Fung Shing

Danish

37	South Kensington	※※	Lundum's

Eastern Mediterranean

49	Regent's Park & Marylebone	※※	Levant

English

45	Mayfair	※※※※	Grill Room	53	Strand & Covent Garden	※※ Rules
54	Victoria	※※※	Shepherd's			

French

49	Regent's Park & Marylebone	※※※※※	❀❀ John Burton-Race	33	Chelsea	※※ Brasserie St Quentin
45	Mayfair	※※※※	❀❀ (Le) Gavroche	27	City of London	※※ ❀ Club Gascon
43	Belgravia	※※※※	❀❀ (La) Tante Claire	33	Chelsea	※※ (Le) Colombier
				24	Bloomsbury	※※ Mon Plaisir
35	North Kensington	※※※	Chez Moi	33	Chelsea	※※ Parisienne Chophouse
42	Bayswater & Maida Vale	※※	Amandier	33	Chelsea	※※ Poissonnerie de l'Avenue
49	Regent's Park & Marylebone	※※	(L')Aventure	43	Belgravia	※※ Vong (French-Thai)
				55	Victoria	※ (La) Poule au Pot

UNITED KINGDOM

Indian & Pakistani

38	Bermondsey	XXX	Bengal Clipper
37	South Kensington	XXX	Bombay Brasserie
32	Chelsea	XXX	Chutney Mary
54	Victoria	XXX	(The) Cinnamon Club
	Mayfair	XXX	✿ Tamarind
54	Victoria	XXX	Quilon
40	Spitalfields	XX	Bengal Trader
51	Soho	XX	Café Lazeez
37	South Kensington	XX	Café Lazeez
40	Battersea	XX	Cafe Spice Namaste
40	Whitechapel	XX	✿ Cafe Spice Namaste
47	Mayfair	XX	Chor Bizarre
37	South Kensington	XX	Khan's of Kensington
25	Bloomsbury	XX	Malabar Junction
37	South Kensington	XX	Memories of India
49	Regent's Park & Marylebone	XX	(La) Porte des Indes
28	Hammersmith	XX	Rafique
49	Regent's Park & Marylebone	XX	Rasa Samudra
41	Southfields	XX	✿ Sarkhel's
33	Chelsea	XX	Vama
47	Mayfair	XX	Yatra
35	Kensington	XX	✿ Zaika
41	Wandsworth	X	Bombay Bicycle Club
30	Finsbury	X	Café Lazeez Ci...
35	Kensington	X	✿ Malabar
29	Archway	X	✿ (The) Pars...
52	Soho	X	Soho Spice
33	Chelsea	X	Zaika Bazaar

Italian

46	Mayfair	XXX	Cecconi's
32	Chelsea	XXX	Floriana
54	Victoria	XXX	(L') Incontro
43	Hyde Park & Knightsbridge	XXX	Isola
54	Victoria	XXX	Santini
46	Mayfair	XXX	Sartoria
32	Chelsea	XXX	Toto's
47	Mayfair	XX	Alloro
42	Bayswater & Maida Vale	XX	Al San Vincenzo
35	Kensington	XX	(The) Ark
49	Regent's Park & Marylebone	XX	Bertorelli's
49	Regent's Park & Marylebone	XX	Caldesi
33	Chelsea	XX	Caraffini
55	Victoria	XX	(Il) Convivio
30	Islington	XX	✿ Metrogusto
32	Chelsea	XX	Montes
25	Bloomsbury	XX	Neal Street
33	Chelsea	XX	Pellicano
28	Hammersmith	XX	✿ River Café
49	Regent's Park & Marylebone	XX	Rosmarino
47	Mayfair	XX	Teca
38	Bermondsey	XX	Tentazioni
43	Belgravia	XX	✿ Zafferano
42	Bayswater & Maida Vale	X	✿ (L') Accent
51	St James's	X	✿ Al Duca
42	Bayswater & Maida Vale	X	Assaggi
52	Soho	X	Bertorelli
26	Primrose Hill	X	Black Truffle
39	Bermondsey	X	Cantina Del Ponte
33	Chelsea	X	✿ (I) Cardi
35	Kensington	X	Cibo
52	Soho	X	✿ (Il) Forno
40	Battersea	X	✿ Metrogusto
55	Victoria	X	Olivo
25	Bloomsbury	X	Passione
52	Soho	X	Vasco and Piero's Pavillion

Japanese

50	St James's	XXX	Suntory
27	City of London	XXX	Tatsuso
33	Chelsea	XX	Benihana
27	Swiss Cottage	XX	Benihana
51	St James's	XX	Matsuri
47	Mayfair	XX	✿ Nobu
47	Mayfair	XX	Shogun
40	Canary Wharf	XX	Ubon by Nobu
52	Soho	X	Itsu
29	Shepherd's Bush	X	Onami

Lebanese

43	Belgravia	XX	Noura Brasserie
35	Kensington	XX	Phoenicia

Moroccan

47	Mayfair	XX	Momo
37	South Kensington	XX	Pasha

North African

29	Hammersmith	X	Azou

Pubs

3	Chelsea		Admiral Codrington
9	Hammersmith		Anglesea Arms
9	Clerkenwell		(The) Bear
4	Chelsea		Builders Arms
5	Dartmouth Park		Bull & Last
9	Islington		Centuria
3	Chelsea		Chelsea Ram
2	Bayswater & Maida Vale		(The) Chepstow
0	Putney		Coat and Badge
0	Islington		(The) Crown
0	Battersea		Duke of Cambridge
6	Primrose Hill		(The) Engineer
8	Wimbledon		(The) Fire Stables
29	Shepherd's Bush		Havelock Tavern
26	Primrose Hill		(The) Lansdowne
25	Dartmouth Park		Lord Palmerston
26	Hampstead		(The) Magdala
30	Islington		(The) Northgate
30	Finsbury		(The) Peasant
26	Primrose Hill		(The) Queens
29	Archway		St John's
28	Hammersmith & Fulham		(The) Salisbury Tavern
50	Regent's Park & Marylebone		(The) Salt House
34	Chelsea		Swag and Tails
29	Hammersmith		Thatched House

Russian

36	Mayfair	XXX	Firebird

Scottish

55	Victoria	XX	Boisdale

Seafood

32	Chelsea	XXXX	One-O-One	33	Chelsea	XX	Poissonnerie de l'Avenue (French)
46	Mayfair	XXXX	Scotts	49	Regent's Park & Marylebone	XX	Rasa Samudra (Indian)
47	Mayfair	XX	Bentley's	37	South Kensington	XX	The Restaurant at One Ninety
42	Bayswater & Maida Vale	XX	Jason's	53	Strand & Covent Garden	X	Livebait
53	Strand & Covent Garden	XX	J. Sheekey				

South East Asian

46	Mayfair	XX	Cassia Oriental	28	City of London	XX	Pacific Oriental

Spanish

37	South Kensington	XX	Cambio de Tercio	29	Clerkenwell	XX	Gaudi

Thai

42	Belgravia	♠♠♠ ✿	Nahm	28	City of London	XX	Sri Siam City
28	Fulham	XX	Blue Elephant	43	Belgravia	XX	Vong (French-Thai)
40	Battersea	XX	Chada	50	Regent's Park & Marylebone	X ✿	Chada Chada
	Belgravia	XX	Mango Tree	52	Soho	X	Sri Siam
42	Bayswater & Maida Vale	XX	Nipa				

Turkish

49	Regent's Park & Marylebone	XX	Ozer

Vegetarian

49	Regent's Park & Marylebone	XX	Rasa Samudra (Indian)

Vietnamese

52	Soho	X	Saigon

UNITED KINGDOM

Greater London is divided, for administrative purposes, into 32 boroughs plus the City; thes sub-divide naturally into minor areas, usually grouped around former villages or quarters, whic often maintain a distinctive character.

© *of Greater London:* **020.**

LONDON AIRPORTS

Heathrow *Middx. West : 17 m. by A 4, M 4* **Underground** *Piccadilly line direct.*
✈ ☞ *(020) 8759 4321* – **Terminal :** *Airbus (A 1) from Victoria, Airbus (A 2) from Pad dington.*
🖪 *Terminals 1, 2 and 3, Underground Station Concourse, Heathrow Airport ☞ (0839 123456.*

Radisson Edwardian, 140 Bath Rd, Hayes, UB3 5AW, ☞ (020) 8759 6311, *busct @ radissonedwardian.com*, Fax (020) 8759 4559, *Ⅰ₆, ⇌s, ◪ – ⧫, ⇆ rm, ▤ ⓣⓥ ⓦ ⒫. – ▵ 550.* ⓒⓞ ⒜⒠ ⓞ *VISA* ⒿⒸⒷ. ⅌
Henleys : Meals 25.00 and a la carte 33.00/43.00 **st.** ⓐ 15.25 – *Brasserie :* Meals a l carte approx. 24.00 **st.** ⓐ 15.25 – ⌧ 15.00 – **442 rm** 199.00/219.00 **s.**, 17 suites.

Crowne Plaza London Heathrow, Stockley Rd, West Drayton, UB7 9NA, ☞ (01895 445555, *cpsales3 @ netscape.co.uk*, Fax (01895) 445122, *Ⅰ₆, ⇌s, ◪, ⅃₆ – ⧫, ⇆ rm, ▤ ⓣⓥ ⓦ ⓖ ⒫. – ▵ 200.* ⓒⓞ ⒜⒠ ⓞ *VISA* ⒿⒸⒷ. ⅌
Concha Grill : Meals 18.50/23.50 and a la carte 21.95/43.95 **t.** ⓐ 11.95 (see also *Simply Nico Heathrow* below) – ⌧ 16.50 – **457 rm** 195.00 **st.**, 1 suite.

Sheraton Skyline, Bath Rd, Hayes, UB3 5BP, ☞ (020) 8759 2535, *res268skyline@ heraton.com*, Fax (020) 8750 9150, *Ⅰ₆, ◪ – ⧫, ⇆ rm, ▤ ⓣⓥ ⓦ ⒫. – ▵ 500.* ⓒⓞ ⓞ *VISA* ⒿⒸⒷ. ⅌
Sage : Meals (dinner only) a la carte 22.00/39.00 ⓐ 18.50 – ⌧ 17.00 – **349 rm** 174.00 **st.** 3 suites.

Hilton London Heathrow Airport, Terminal 4, TW6 3AF, ☞ (020) 8759 7755, *gmhe athrow@ hilton.com*, Fax (020) 8759 7579, *Ⅰ₆, ⇌s, ◪ – ⧫, ⇆ rm, ▤ ⓣⓥ ⓦ ⓖ ⒫. – ▵ 240.* ⓒⓞ ⒜⒠ ⓞ *VISA* ⒿⒸⒷ. ⅌
Brasserie : Meals 23.50/29.50 and a la carte 13.40/28.50 **st.** ⓐ 15.90 – *Zen Oriental* . Meals - Chinese - 28.80/38.50 and a la carte 25.50/30.00 **t.** ⓐ 28.00 – ⌧ 17.50 – **390 rm** 148.00/195.00 **s.**, 5 suites – SB.

London Heathrow Marriott, Bath Rd, Hayes, UB3 5AN, ☞ (020) 8990 1100, Fax (020) 8990 1110, *Ⅰ₆, ⇌s, ◪ – ⧫, ⇆ rm, ▤ ⓣⓥ ⓦ ⓖ ⒫. – ▵ 540.* ⓒⓞ ⒜⒠ ⓞ *VISA* ⒿⒸⒷ. ⅌
Tuscany : Meals - Italian -*(closed Sunday)* (dinner only) a la carte 24.50/37.00 **t.** ⓐ 20.00 – *Allie's grille :* Meals a la carte 21.25/31.20 **t.** ⓐ 13.95 – ⌧ 16.45 – **388 rm** 190.00/215.00 **st.**, 2 suites.

Le Méridien Heathrow, Bath Rd, West Drayton, UB7 0DU, ☞ (020) 8759 6611, *exce lsior@ lemeridien.co.uk*, Fax (020) 8759 3421, *Ⅰ₆, ⇌s, ◪ – ⧫, ⇆ rm, ▤ ⓣⓥ ⓖ ⒫. – ▵ 700.* ⓒⓞ ⒜⒠ ⓞ *VISA* ⒿⒸⒷ. ⅌
Meals *(closed Saturday lunch)* (carvery) 22.95 **t.** ⓐ 17.95 – *Snappers :* Meals *(closed Saturday and Sunday lunch and Bank Holidays)* 15.50/39.50 and a la carte 36.10/53.40 **t.** ⓐ 17.95 – ⌧ 14.95 – **525 rm** 125.00 **s.**, 10 suites – SB.

Holiday Inn London Heathrow, Sipson Rd, West Drayton, UB7 0JU, ☞ (0870) 4008595, Fax (020) 8897 8659 – ⧫, ⇆ rm, ▤ ⓣⓥ ⓖ ⒫. – ▵ 140. ⓒⓞ ⒜⒠ ⓞ *VISA* ⒿⒸⒷ. ⅌
Sampans : Meals - Chinese - (dinner only) 18.95/29.95 and a la carte 18.35/27.95 **t.** ⓐ 12.55 – *Rotisserie :* Meals *(closed Saturday lunch)* 19.50 and a la carte 20.35/30.15 **st.** ⓐ 11.95 – ⌧ 14.95 – **604 rm** 169.00, 6 suites – SB.

Renaissance London Heathrow, Bath Rd, TW6 2AQ, ☞ (020) 8897 6363, *106047. 3556@ compuserve.com*, Fax (020) 8897 1113, *Ⅰ₆, ⇌s – ⧫, ⇆ rm, ▤ ⓣⓥ ⓦ ⓖ ⒫. – ▵ 550.* ⓒⓞ ⒜⒠ ⓞ *VISA* ⒿⒸⒷ. ⅌
Meals 18.50/21.50 and a la carte 18.00/37.25 **st.** ⓐ 18.00 – ⌧ 13.95 – **643 rm** 189.00 **st.**, 5 suites.

Sheraton Heathrow, Colnbrook bypass, West Drayton, UB7 0HJ, ☞ (020) 8759 2424, *res29heathrow@ sheraton.com*, Fax (020) 8759 2091, *Ⅰ₆ – ⧫, ⇆ rm, ▤ ⓣⓥ ⓦ ⒫. – ▵ 70.* ⓒⓞ ⒜⒠ ⓞ *VISA* ⒿⒸⒷ. ⅌
Meals 21.50 and a la carte 21.75/33.95 **st.** ⓐ 24.00 – ⌧ 14.25 – **426 rm** 199.00/225.00 **st.**, 5 suites.

Posthouse Heathrow, 118 Bath Rd, Hayes, UB3 5AJ, ☎ (0870) 400 9040, *reserva tions-heathrow@posthouse-hotels.com*, Fax (020) 8564 9265 – 🛗, ⇔ rm, ▤ rest, 📺 🅿 – 🛦 55. 🐵 🝙 ⓪ 𝘝𝘐𝘚𝘈 🃏
Meals *(closed Saturday lunch)* (bar lunch Saturday) (buffet lunch) 13.95 (lunch) and a la carte 23.00/28.00 t. ∦ 13.00 – ⌑ 13.95 – **186 rm** 109.00/189.00 **st.**   SB.

Simply Nico Heathrow (at Crowne Plaza London Heathrow H.), Stockley Rd, West Drayton, UB7 9NA, ☎ (01895) 437564, *heathrow@simplynico.co.uk*, Fax (01895) 437565 – ▤ 📺 🅿 🐵 🝙 ⓪ 𝘝𝘐𝘚𝘈
closed 25-26 December, Saturday lunch, Sunday and Bank Holidays – **Meals** 10.00/12.95 (lunch) and a la carte 26.00/36.50 t. ∦ 13.00.

atwick *W. Sussex South : 28 m. by A 23 and M 23* - **Train** *from Victoria : Gatwick Express* 🯬🯭🯭
T 30 – ✉ *Crawley.*
      ✈ ☎ (01293) 535353.

Hilton London Gatwick Airport, South Terminal, RH6 0LL, ☎ (01293) 518080, *gath itwsal@hilton.com*, Fax (01293) 528980, 🛴, ⇌, 🔲 – 🛗, ⇔ rm, ▤ 📺 ⌗ & 🅿 – 🛦 500. 🐵 🝙 ⓪ 𝘝𝘐𝘚𝘈 🃏. 🛞
Meals a la carte approx. 37.00 t. ∦ 15.00 – ⌑ 14.95 – **565 rm** 190.00/340.00.

Le Meridien London Gatwick, Gatwick Airport (North Terminal), RH6 0PH, ☎ (0870) 4008494, *sales.gatwick@lemeridien-hotels.com*, Fax (01293) 567759, 🛴, ⇌, 🔲 – 🛗, ⇔ rm, ▤ 📺 ⌗ & 🅿 – 🛦 300. 🐵 🝙 ⓪ 𝘝𝘐𝘚𝘈 🃏. 🛞
Gatwick Oriental : Meals - Asian - 17.00/27.00 and a la carte 15.30/29.90 t. ∦ 16.00 – **Brasserie : Meals** *(closed lunch Saturday and Sunday)* (buffet lunch) 19.95 and a la carte 28.95/38.50 t. ∦ 16.00 – ⌑ 13.95 – **488 rm** 179.00 **st.**, 6 suites.

Renaissance London Gatwick, Povey Cross Rd, RH6 0BE, ☎ (01293) 820169, *alex .holmes@renaissancehotels.com*, Fax (01293) 820259, 🛴, ⇌, 🔲, squash – 🛗, ⇔ rm, ▤ 📺 & 🅿 – 🛦 180. 🐵 🝙 ⓪ 𝘝𝘐𝘚𝘈
Meals *(closed Sunday lunch)* 16.50/18.50 and a la carte 19.00/29.00 t. ∦ 12.95 – ⌑ 12.50 – **253 rm** 135.00/150.00 **st.**, 2 suites – SB.

Holiday Inn Gatwick, Povey Cross Rd, RH6 0BA, ☎ (0870) 400 9030, *gm1090@forte-h otels.com*, Fax (01293) 771054 – 🛗, ⇔ rm, ▤ rest, 📺 🅿 – 🛦 300. 🐵 🝙 ⓪ 𝘝𝘐𝘚𝘈 🃏
Meals *(closed Saturday and Sunday lunch)* 14.75/15.00-28.45 and a la carte 14.75/28.45 t. ∦ 11.95 – ⌑ 13.95 – **210 rm** 120.00 **st.** – SB.

Gatwick Moat House, Longbridge Roundabout, Povey Cross Rd, RH6 0AB, ☎ (01293) 899988, *revgat@queensmoat.co.uk*, Fax (01293) 785991, 🛴 – ⇔ rm, 📺 & 🅿 – 🛦 150. 🐵 🝙 ⓪ 𝘝𝘐𝘚𝘈 🃏
Meals (bar lunch)/dinner a la carte 16.60/28.00 ∦ 11.95 – ⌑ 10.50 – **124 rm** 99.00/119.00.

Travel Inn Metro, Longbridge Way, Gatwick Airport (North Terminal), RH6 0NX, ☎ (01293) 568158, *Fax (01293) 568278* – 🛗, ⇔ rm, ▤ rest, 📺 & 🅿 🐵 🝙 ⓪ 𝘝𝘐𝘚𝘈. 🛞
Meals (grill rest.) (dinner only) – **219 rm** 49.95 t.

Premier Lodge, London Rd, Lowfield Heath, RH10 2ST, ☎ (0870) 7001388, Fax (0870) 7001389, « Part 15C manor house », 🎋 – 🛗, ⇔ rm, 📺 & 🅿 – 🛦 220. 🐵 🝙 ⓪ 𝘝𝘐𝘚𝘈. 🛞
Meals a la carte approx. 16.95 t. ∦ 8.75 – **100 rm** 49.95 t.

Travelodge, Church Rd, Lowfield Heath, RH11 0PQ, ☎ (01293) 533441, Fax (01293) 535369 – 🛗, ⇔ rm, ▤ rest, 📺 & 🅿 – 🛦 40. 🐵 🝙 ⓪ 𝘝𝘐𝘚𝘈 🃏. 🛞
Meals (grill rest.) – **186 rm** 49.95 t.

CAMDEN

Bloomsbury – ✉ *NW1/W1/WC1.*

Russell, Russell Sq, WC1B 5BE, ☎ (020) 7837 6470, *reservations.russell@principalhote ls.co.uk*, Fax (020) 7837 2857 – 🛗, ⇔ rm, ▤ 📺 🕰 – 🛦 400. 🐵 🝙 ⓪ 𝘝𝘐𝘚𝘈 🃏. 🛞
Fitzroy Doll's : Meals 15.95 **st.** ∦ 15.95 – **Virginia Woolf's : Meals** a la carte approx. 18.00 **st.** ∦ 15.00 – **378 rm** 190.00/205.00 **st.**, 2 suites.   p. 6   LU o

Holiday Inn Kings Cross, 1 Kings Cross Rd, WC1X 9HX, ☎ (020) 7833 3900, *sales @holidayinnlondon.demon.co.uk*, Fax (020) 7917 6163, 🛴, ⇌, 🔲 – 🛗, ⇔ rm, ▤ 📺 🕰 & – 🛦 220. 🐵 🝙 ⓪ 𝘝𝘐𝘚𝘈 🃏. 🛞   p. 6   MT a
Simply Spice : Meals - Indian - *(closed Saturday lunch)* a la carte 10.00/23.00 – **Carriages : Meals** a la carte 10.00/25.00 – ⌑ 12.50 – **403 rm** 190.00 **st.**, 2 suites.

Marlborough, 9-14 Bloomsbury St, WC1B 3QD, ☎ (020) 7636 5601, *resmarl@radiss on.com*, Fax (020) 7240 0532 – 🛗, ⇔ rm, ▤ rest, 📺 🕰 & – 🛦 200. 🐵 🝙 ⓪ 𝘝𝘐𝘚𝘈 🃏. 🛞   p. 6   LU i
Glass : Meals 19.50 and a la carte 17.00/27.50 **st.** ∦ 15.75 – ⌑ 15.00 – **171 rm** 195.00/222.00 **s.**, 2 suites.

Mountbatten, 20 Monmouth St, WC2H 9HD, ℰ (020) 7836 4300, *Fax (020) 7240 354.* ₲ – |≡|, rm, 📺 – ⚷ 90. 🆚 AE ⓪ VISA JCB. ℅   p. 17 DV
Dial : Meals 25.00 and a la carte approx. 33.00 **st.** ⏐ 15.75 – ⊆ 15.00 – **121 r** 257.00/285.00 s., 7 suites.

Covent Garden, 10 Monmouth St, WC2H 9HB, ℰ (020) 7806 1000, *covent@firm. le.com, Fax (020) 7806 1100,* ₲ – |≡| 📺 ⚷ – ⚷ 50. 🆚 AE VISA. ℅
Brasserie Max : Meals (booking essential) a la carte 27.40/40.45 **t.** ⏐ 16.50 – ⊆ 16.5 **– 56 rm** 190.00/325.00, 2 suites.   p. 17 DV

Grafton, 130 Tottenham Court Rd, W1P 9HP, ℰ (020) 7388 4131, *resgraf@radisso .com, Fax (020) 7387 7394,* ₲ – |≡|, rm, ≡ rest, 📺 ⚷ – ⚷ 100. 🆚 AE ⓪ VISA JC ℅   p. 6 KU
Aston's : Meals 19.95 and a la carte approx. 22.00 **st.** ⏐ 14.00 – ⊆ 12.00 – **320 rm** 172.00/199.00 s., 4 suites.

Kenilworth, 97 Great Russell St, WC1B 3LB, ℰ (020) 7637 3477, *resmarl@radisso com, Fax (020) 7631 3133* – |≡|, rm, ≡ 📺 ⚷ – ⚷ 65. 🆚 AE ⓪ VISA JC ℅   p. 6 LU
Meals 19.50/35.00 **st.** ⏐ 13.75 – ⊆ 12.00 – **187 rm** 195.00/222.00 s.

Grange Holborn, 50-60 Southampton Row, WC1B 4AR, ℰ (020) 7242 1800, *holbo n@grangehotels.co.uk, Fax (020) 7404 1641,* ₲, ≋, 🏊, 🏋 – |≡| rm ≡ 📺 ⚷ key ⚷ 180. 🆚 AE ⓪ VISA JCB. ℅   p. 6 LU
Constellations : Meals *(closed Saturday, Sunday and Bank Holidays)* (dinner only) 26.5 and a la carte 26.85/35.45 **st.** – **Koto** : Meals - Sushi - 10.50/15.50 and a la cart 11.50/20.50 **st.** ⏐ 12.15 – ⊆ 16.50 – **200 rm** 280.00/400.00 st.

Jurys Gt Russell St, 16-22 Gt Russell St, WC1B 3NN, ℰ (020) 7347 1000 *Fax (020) 7347 1001* – |≡|, rm, ≡ 📺 ⚷ key – ⚷ 220. 🆚 AE ⓪ VISA JC ℅   p. 6 LU
Lutyens : Meals (bar lunch)/dinner 23.50 and a la carte 20.00/31.00 **st.** ⏐ 14.00 ⊆ 16.00 – **168 rm** 215.00 **st.**, 1 suite – SB.

Montague, 15 Montague St, WC1B 5BJ, ℰ (020) 7637 1001, *bookmt@rchmail.con Fax (020) 7637 2516,* ☕, ₲, ≋, 🌳 – |≡|, rm, ≡ 📺 ⚷ key – ⚷ 120. 🆚 AE ⓪ VISA JCB. ℅   p. 6 LU
Blue Door Bistro : Meals a la carte 23.15/29.40 **t.** ⏐ 15.50 – ⊆ 11.50 – **98 rm** 165.00/190.00 s., 6 suites.

Thistle Bloomsbury, Bloomsbury Way, WC1A 2SD, ℰ (020) 7242 5881, *bloomsbu y@thistle.co.uk, Fax (020) 7831 0225* – |≡|, rm, ≡ rest, 📺 key – ⚷ 100. 🆚 AE ⓪ VISA JCB. ℅   p. 6 LU
Meals *(closed lunch Saturday, Sunday and Bank Holidays)* 16.50 and a la cart 18.50/29.25 **st.** ⏐ 12.50 – ⊆ 11.95 – **138 rm** 167.00/312.00 st.

Holiday Inn London Bloomsbury, Coram St, WC1N 1HT, ℰ (0870) 4009222, *re. rvations-bloomsbury@6c.com, Fax (020) 7837 5374* – |≡|, rm, ≡ 📺 ⚷ key – ⚷ 300 🆚 AE ⓪ VISA JCB.   p. 6 LT
Meals *(closed Saturday and Sunday dinner and Bank Holiday lunch)* 13.00/15.00 and dinner a la carte 22.65/29.00 **st.** ⏐ 12.95 – ⊆ 14.95 – **312 rm** 179.00 **st.** – SB.

Blooms, 7 Montague St, WC1B 5BP, ℰ (020) 7323 1717, *blooms@mermaid.co.uk Fax (020) 7636 6498,* 🌳 – |≡| 📺 🆚 AE ⓪ VISA JCB   p. 6 LU
Meals a la carte 19.50/26.50 **st.** ⏐ 15.00 – ⊆ 10.00 – **27 rm** 135.00/205.00 **st.** – SB

Myhotel, 11-13 Bayley St, Bedford Sq, WC1B 3HD, ℰ (020) 7667 6000, *guest-servic es@myhotels.co.uk, Fax (020) 7667 6001,* « Contemporary interior », ₲ – |≡| key ≡ 📺 ⚷ – ⚷ 40. 🆚 AE ⓪ VISA   p. 6 KU
Yoë Sushi : Meals - Japanese - a la carte 16.00/24.40 **t.** ⏐ 12.50 – ⊆ 16.00 – **76 rm** 170.00/355.00 s.

Bonnington in Bloomsbury, 92 Southampton Row, WC1B 4BH, ℰ (020) 7242 2828, *sales@bonnington.com, Fax (020) 7831 9170* – |≡|, rm, ≡ 📺 ⚷ key – ⚷ 250. 🆚 AE ⓪ VISA   p. 6 LU
Meals *(closed Sunday and Bank Holiday Mondays)* (bar lunch)/dinner 19.75 **t.** ⏐ 12.00 – **215 rm** ⊆ 117.00/149.00 **t.** – SB.

Conrad Gallagher Shaftesbury Avenue, 179 Shaftesbury Ave, W1D 7EA, ℰ (020) 7836 3111, *info@conradgallagher.co.uk, Fax (020) 7836 3888* – ≡. 🆚 AE ⓪ VISA   p. 17 DV
closed 25 December – Meals 18.75/23.75 (lunch) and a la carte 33.50/50.00 **t.** ⏐ 20.00.

Pied à Terre, 34 Charlotte St, W1P 1HJ, ℰ (020) 7636 1178, *p-a-t@dircon.co.uk,* ❀ *Fax (020) 7916 1171* – ≡. 🆚 AE ⓪ VISA JCB   p. 6 KU
closed 2 weeks Christmas-New Year, Saturday lunch and Sunday – Meals 23.00/65.00 **t.** ⏐ 18.00
Spec. Scallop ceviche, avocado and crème fraîche. Poached foie gras, Sauternes consommé. Venison fillet, juniper boudin, celeriac purée.

XX **Incognico,** 117 Shaftesbury Ave, WC2H 8AD, ℘ (020) 7836 8866, *Fax (020) 7240 9525*
– ☰. ⓦⓢ ⒶⒺ ⓞ *VISA* p. 13 GK a
closed 4 days Easter, 10 days Christmas, Sunday and Bank Holidays – **Meals** 12.50 (lunch)
and a la carte 27.50/41.50 **t.** ⚏ 12.50.

XX **Neal Street,** 26 Neal St, WC2H 9QW, ℘ (020) 7836 8368, *Fax (020) 7240 3964* – ⓦⓢ
ⒶⒺ ⓞ *VISA* p. 17 DV s
closed 1 week Christmas-New Year, Sunday and Bank Holidays – **Meals** - Italian - a la carte
30.00/45.00 **t.** ⚏ 15.00.

XX **Hakkasan,** 8 Hanway Pl, W1P 9DH, ℘ (020) 7927 7000, *mail@hakkasan.com,*
Fax (020) 7907 1889 – ☰. ⓦⓢ ⒶⒺ *VISA* p. 6 KU o
closed 24-26 December – **Meals** - Chinese (Canton) - a la carte 18.70/57.90 **t.** ⚏ 18.50.

XX **Mon Plaisir,** 21 Monmouth St, WC2H 9DD, ℘ (020) 7836 7243, *eatafrog@mail.com,*
Fax (020) 7240 4774 – ⓦⓢ ⒶⒺ ⓞ *VISA* ⓙⒸⒷ p. 17 DV a
closed Christmas-New Year, Saturday lunch, Sunday and Bank Holidays – **Meals** - French
- 13.95/15.95 (lunch) and a la carte 21.70/34.50 **t.** ⚏ 10.50.

XX **Archipelago,** 110 Whitfield St, W1T 5EA, ℘ (020) 7383 3346, *Fax (020) 7383 7181* –
ⓦⓢ ⒶⒺ *VISA* p. 6 KU c
closed Christmas-New Year, Saturday lunch and Sunday – **Meals** 20.50/38.50 **t.** ⚏ 18.50.

XX **Malabar Junction,** 107 Great Russell St, WC1B 3NA, ℘ (020) 7580 5230,
Fax (020) 7436 9942 – ☰. ⓦⓢ ⒶⒺ *VISA* p. 6 LU x
closed 25-26 December – **Meals** - South Indian - a la carte 25.00/30.00 **t.**

X **Passione,** 10 Charlotte St, W1P 1HE, ℘ (020) 7636 2833, *lizprzybylski@lineone.net,*
Fax (020) 7636 2889 – ⓦⓢ ⒶⒺ ⓞ *VISA* ⓙⒸⒷ p. 6 KU u
closed Christmas-New Year, Saturday lunch, Sunday and Bank Holidays – **Meals** - Italian -
(booking essential) a la carte 22.80/31.50 **t.** ⚏ 11.50.

X **Alfred,** 245 Shaftesbury Ave, WC2H 8EH, ℘ (020) 7240 2566, *Fax (020) 7497 0672,* ⌦
– ☰. ⓦⓢ ⒶⒺ ⓞ *VISA* ⓙⒸⒷ p. 17 DV u
closed Saturday lunch, Sunday and Bank Holidays – **Meals** 13.90/17.00 and a la carte
20.45/25.45 **t.** ⚏ 12.65.

Dartmouth Park – ⊠ NW5.

🏠 **Bull & Last,** 168 Highgate Rd, NW5 1QS, ℘ (020) 7267 3641, *Fax (020) 7482 6366* –
ⓦⓢ *VISA* p. 4 EU n
closed 25 December – **Meals** a la carte 15.00/22.00 **t.** ⚏ 10.00.

🏠 **Lord Palmerston,** 33 Dartmouth Park Hill, NW5 1HU, ℘ (020) 7485 1578 – ⓦⓢ *VISA*
Meals (bookings not accepted) a la carte approx. 17.00 ⚏ 8.90. p. 4 EU x

Euston – ⊠ WC1.

🏨 **Shaw Park Plaza,** 100-110 Euston Rd, NW1 2AJ, ℘ (020) 7666 9000, *sppres@par*
kplazahotels.co.uk, Fax (020) 7666 9100, 🔗, ☎ – ▯, ✸ rm, ☰ ▥ ☏ ⅏ – 🔏 450. ⓦⓢ
ⒶⒺ ⓞ *VISA* ⓙⒸⒷ. ⌦ p. 6 LT r
Meals 23.95 and a la carte 26.00/33.00 **t.** ⚏ 17.00 – ⌸ 14.50 – **312 rm** 180.00 **st.**

🏨 **Euston Plaza,** 17-18 Upper Woburn Pl, WC1H 0HT, ℘ (020) 7943 4500, *eustonplaza*
@euston-plaza-hotel.co.uk, Fax (020) 7943 4501, 🔗, ☎ – ▯, ✸ rm, ☰ ▥ ☏ ⅏ –
🔏 150. ⓦⓢ ⒶⒺ ⓞ *VISA* ⓙⒸⒷ. ⌦ p. 6 KLT e
Three Crowns : **Meals** 18.95/19.95 and dinner a la carte 28.85/33.90 **t.** ⚏ 13.95 – *Ter-*
race : **Meals** (*closed Saturday lunch and Sunday dinner*) a la carte 14.60/16.85 **t.** ⚏ 13.95
– ⌸ 12.95 – **150 rm** 179.00/199.00 **st.**

🏠 **London Euston Travel Inn Capital,** 141 Euston Rd, NW1 2AU, ℘ (020) 7554 3400,
Fax (020) 7554 3419 – ▯, ✸ rm, ☰ rest, ▥ ⅏. ⓦⓢ ⒶⒺ ⓞ *VISA.* ⌦ p. 6 LT s
Meals (grill rest.) (dinner only) – **220 rm** 74.95 **t.**

Hampstead – ⊠ NW3.

🇫 Winnington Rd, Hampstead ℘ (020) 8455 0203.

🏨 **Posthouse Hampstead,** 215 Haverstock Hill, NW3 4RB, ℘ (0870) 4009037,
Fax (020) 7435 5586 – ▯, ✸ rm ▥ ℗. – 🔏 30. ⓦⓢ ⒶⒺ ⓞ *VISA* ⌦ p. 4 ES r
Meals (see *MPW Brasserie* below) – ⌸ 13.95 – **140 rm** 99.00/159.00 – SB.

🏠 **Langorf** without rest., 20 Frognal, NW3 6AG, ℘ (020) 7794 4483, *langorf@aol.com,*
Fax (020) 7435 9055 – ▯ ▥. ⓦⓢ ⒶⒺ ⓞ *VISA.* ⌦ p. 4 ES c
31 rm ⌸ 82.00/98.00 **st.**, 5 suites.

XX **ZeNW3,** 83-84 Hampstead High St, NW3 1RE, ℘ (020) 7794 7863, *Fax (020) 7794 6956*
– ☰. ⓦⓢ *VISA* p. 4 ES a
closed 24-25 December – **Meals** - Chinese - 13.80/33.50 and a la carte 22.40/34.20 **t.**
⚏ 12.50.

XX **MPW Brasserie** (at Posthouse Hampstead H.), 215 Haverstock Hill, NW3 4RB, ℰ (02 7435 6080, *Fax (020) 7435 5586*, 😊 – ▤. 🕦🕦 🕮 🕦 *VISA* 🕦   p. 4 ES
Meals 13.50 and a la carte **st.** ⓘ 12.95.

X **Cucina**, 45a South End Rd, NW3 2QB, ℰ (020) 7435 7814, *enquiries@cucina.uk.cor Fax (020) 7435 7815* – ▤. 🕦🕦 🕮 *VISA*   p. 4 ES
closed 4 days Christmas and Sunday dinner – **Meals** a la carte 20.00/24.00 **t.** ⓘ 11.9

X **Base**, 71 Hampstead High St, NW3 1QP, ℰ (020) 7431 2224, *Fax (020) 7433 1262* – ▤ 🕦🕦 🕮 🕦 *VISA*   p. 4 ES
Meals - North African specialities - a la carte 12.00/21.00 **t.**

🍴 **The Magdala**, 2A South Hill Park, NW3 2SB, ℰ (020) 7435 2503, *Fax (020) 7435 616* – 🕦🕦 *VISA*   p. 4 ES
closed 25 December – **Meals** a la carte 17.50/24.95 **t.** ⓘ 9.95.

Hatton Garden – ✉ EC1.

XX **Bleeding Heart**, Bleeding Heart Yard, EC1N 8SJ, off Greville St ℰ (020) 7242 2056 *bookings@bleedingheart.co.uk, Fax (020) 7831 1402*, 😊 – 🕦🕦 🕮 🕦 *VISA* 🕦
closed Christmas-New Year, Saturday, Sunday and Bank Holidays – **Meals** a la cart 21.60/52.15 **t.** ⓘ 12.95.   p. 7 NU

Holborn – ✉ WC2.

🏨 **Renaissance London Chancery Court**, 252 High Holborn, WC1V 7EN, ℰ (02 7829 9888, *sales.chancerycourt@renaissancehotels.com, Fax (020) 7829 9889*, ℔ – ⓼ ✻ rm, ▤ 📺 ✆ ₺ – 🔏 450. 🕦🕦 🕮 🕦 *VISA*   p. 6 MU ⓪
QC : **Meals** a la carte 23.70/47.90 **st.** ⓘ 21.00 – ☲ 16.95 – **357 rm** 275.00/395.00 s

🏨 **Kingsway Hall**, Great Queen St, WC2B 5BX, ℰ (020) 7309 0909, *kingswayhall@cor puserve.com, Fax (020) 7309 9696*, ℔, 😊 – ⓼, ✻ rm, ▤ 📺 ✆ ₺ – 🔏 150. 🕦🕦 🕮 🕦 *VISA* 🕦 🕸   p. 17 EV ⓥ
Harlequin : **Meals** 18.50/22.00 and a la carte 27.75/36.25 **t.** ⓘ 13.50 – ☲ 15.25 – **168 rm** 180.00/190.00 **st.**, 2 suites.

Primrose Hill – ✉ NW1.

XX **Odette's**, 130 Regent's Park Rd, NW1 8XL, ℰ (020) 7586 5486, *Fax (020) 7586 257:* – 🕦🕦 🕮 🕦 *VISA*   p. 5 HS
closed 1 week Christmas and Sunday dinner – **Meals** 12.50 (lunch) and a la carte 25.00/33.50 **t.** ⓘ 12.50 (see also *Odette's Wine Bar* below).

X **Black Truffle**, 40 Chalcot Rd, NW1 8LS, ℰ (020) 7483 0077, *Fax (020) 7483 0088* – ▤. 🕦🕦 🕮 *VISA*   p. 5 HIS ⓒ
closed Sunday – **Meals** - Italian - (dinner only) 15.00/19.00 and a la carte 18.00/27.50 **t** ⓘ 11.50.

X **Odette's Wine Bar** (at Odette's), 130 Regent's Park Rd, NW1 8XL, ℰ (020) 7586 5486 *Fax (020) 7586 2575* – 🕦🕦 🕮 🕦 *VISA*   p. 5 HS
closed 1 week Christmas and Sunday dinner – **Meals** (booking essential) 12.50 (lunch) anc a la carte 16.50/22.00 **t.** ⓘ 12.50.

🍴 **The Queens**, 49 Regent's Park Rd, NW1 8XD, ℰ (020) 7586 0408, *Fax (020) 7586 5677* 😊 – 🕦🕦 *VISA*   p. 5 HS a
Meals a la carte 14.85/22.35 **t.** ⓘ 9.90.

🍴 **The Engineer**, 65 Gloucester Ave, NW1 8JH, ℰ (020) 7722 0950, *info@the-eng.com,* *Fax (020) 7483 0592*, 😊 – 🕦🕦 *VISA* 🕦   p. 5 IS z
closed 25-26 December – **Meals** a la carte 23.50/30.50 **t.** ⓘ 11.50.

🍴 **The Lansdowne**, 90 Gloucester Ave, NW1 8HX, ℰ (020) 7483 0409, *Fax (020) 7586 1723* – 🕦🕦 *VISA*   p. 5 IS r
closed Monday – **Meals** (dinner only and Sunday lunch) a la carte 16.50/22.50 **t.**

Regent's Park – ✉ NW1.

🏨 **Meliá White House**, Albany St, NW1 3UP, ℰ (020) 7387 1200, *melia.whitehouse@s olmelia.com, Fax (020) 7388 0091*, ℔, 😊 – ⓼, ✻ rm, ▤ rest, 📺 ₺ – 🔏 120. 🕦🕦 🕮 🕦 *VISA*, 🕸   p. 5 JT o
The Restaurant : **Meals** *(closed Sunday and Bank Holidays)* 19.50/24.50 and dinner a la carte 27.95/37.00 **t.** ⓘ 15.00 – *Garden Cafe :* **Meals** 12.95/14.95 and a la carte 22.50/29.00 **t.** ⓘ 14.95 – ☲ 16.95 – **580 rm** 243.00 **st.**, 2 suites.

Swiss Cottage – ✉ NW3.

🏨 **Marriott Regents Park**, 128 King Henry's Rd, NW3 3ST, ℰ (020) 7722 7711, *Fax (020) 7586 5822*, ℔, 😊, ▣ – ⓼, ✻ rm, ▤ 📺 ✆ ₺ 🄿 – 🔏 300. 🕦🕦 🕮 🕦 *VISA*. 🕸   p. 5 GS a
Meals *(closed Saturday lunch)* 18.95 (lunch) and a la carte 19.00/30.50 **st.** ⓘ 13.75 – ☲ 16.45 – **298 rm** 175.00 **s.**, 5 suites.

🏨 **Swiss Cottage** without rest., 4 Adamson Rd, NW3 3HP, ✆ (020) 7722 2281, *reservations @ swisscottagehotel.co.uk, Fax (020) 7483 1588* – 🛗 📺 – 🅰️ 35, 🆖 🆎 ⓞ 𝑉𝐼𝑆𝐴 𝐽𝐶𝐵. ✁
53 rm ⊡ 97.50/115.00 **st.**, 6 suites. p. 5 GS n

🍴 **Bradley's,** 25 Winchester Rd, NW3 3NR, ✆ (020) 7722 3457, *Fax (020) 7435 1392* – ☰.
🆖 🆎 𝑉𝐼𝑆𝐴 𝐽𝐶𝐵 p. 5 GS e
closed 1 week Christmas-New Year, Saturday lunch and Bank Holidays – **Meals**
14.00/27.00 **t.**

🍴 **Benihana,** 100 Avenue Rd, NW3 3HF, ✆ (020) 7586 9508, *benihana @ dircon.co.uk, Fax (020) 7586 6740* – ☰. 🆖 🆎 ⓞ 𝑉𝐼𝑆𝐴 𝐽𝐶𝐵 p. 5 GS o
closed 25 December – **Meals** - Japanese (Teppan-Yaki) - 10.00/60.00 and a la carte
24.00/40.00 **t.** 🍷 12.00.

TY OF LONDON

🏯 **Great Eastern,** Liverpool St, EC2M 7QN, ✆ (020) 7618 5000, *sales @ great-eastern-h otel.co.uk, Fax (020) 7618 5011,* 🏋️ – 🛗, ≒ rm, ☰ 📺 📞 & – 🅰️ 250. 🆖 🆎 ⓞ 𝑉𝐼𝑆𝐴
Fishmarket : **Meals** - Seafood - *(closed Saturday lunch and Sunday)* a la carte
27.00/53.00 **t.** – **Miyabi** : **Meals** - Japanese - *(closed Saturday, Sunday and Bank Holidays)*
a la carte 20.50/42.50 **t.** 🍷 12.95 (see also **Aurora** below) – ⊡ 19.00 – **264 rm**
225.00/285.00, 3 suites – SB. p. 7 PU o

🏨 **Novotel London Tower Bridge,** 10 Pepys St, EC3N 2NR, ✆ (020) 7265 6000,
h3107 @ accor-hotels.com, Fax (020) 7265 6060, 🏋️ 🏊 – 🛗, ≒ rm, ☰ rest, 📺 📞 &
– 🅰️ 80. 🆖 🆎 ⓞ 𝑉𝐼𝑆𝐴 p. 7 PV n
The Garden Brasserie : **Meals** 12.00 (lunch) and a la carte 13.50/24.00 **st.** 🍷 12.50 –
⊡ 12.00 – **199 rm** 155.00/175.00 **st.**, 4 suites.

🏠 **Travelodge** without rest., 1 Harrow Pl, E1 7DB, ✆ (020) 7626 1142,
Fax (020) 7626 1105 – 🛗 ≒ 📺 📞 &. 🆖 🆎 ⓞ 𝑉𝐼𝑆𝐴 𝐽𝐶𝐵. ✁ p. 7 PU s
142 rm 79.95 **t.**

🍴🍴🍴 **Aurora** (at Great Eastern H.), Liverpool St, EC2M 7QN, ✆ (020) 7618 7000, *restauran ts @ great-eastern-hotel.co.uk, Fax (020) 7618 7001* – ☰. 🆖 🆎 ⓞ 𝑉𝐼𝑆𝐴 p. 7 PU o
closed Saturday, Sunday and Bank Holidays – **Meals** a la carte 40.00/48.50 **t.** 🍷 19.95.

🍴🍴🍴 **City Rhodes,** 1 New Street Sq, EC4A 3BF, ✆ (020) 7583 1313, *Fax (020) 7353 1662*
❀ – ☰. 🆖 🆎 ⓞ 𝑉𝐼𝑆𝐴 p. 7 NU u
closed 25 and 31 December, 1 January, Saturday, Sunday and Bank Holidays – **Meals** a
la carte 33.00/52.50 **t.** 🍷 16.50
Spec. Steamed langoustine salad, truffle dressing. Rack of lamb with artichoke and coriander barigoule. Bread and butter pudding.

🍴🍴🍴 **Coq d'Argent,** No 1 Poultry, EC2R 8EJ, ✆ (020) 7395 5000, *Fax (020) 7395 5050,* 🌳,
« Rooftop terrace » – 🛗 ☰. 🆖 🆎 𝑉𝐼𝑆𝐴 𝐽𝐶𝐵 p. 7 PV c
closed 25 December, Saturday lunch, Sunday dinner and Bank Holidays – **Meals** (booking
essential) a la carte 32.50/41.00 **t.** 🍷 13.50.

🍴🍴🍴 **Twentyfour,** 24th floor, Tower 42, 25 Old Broad St, EC2N 1HQ, ✆ (020) 7877 2424,
Fax (020) 7877 7788, ✳️ London – 🛗 ☰. 🆖 🆎 ⓞ 𝑉𝐼𝑆𝐴 𝐽𝐶𝐵 p. 7 PU v
closed Saturday, Sunday and Bank Holidays – **Meals** (booking essential) 28.00 (lunch) and
a la carte 32.50/44.20 **t.** 🍷 13.95.

🍴🍴🍴 **Tatsuso,** 32 Broadgate Circle, EC2M 2QS, ✆ (020) 7638 5863, *Fax (020) 7638 5864* –
☰. 🆖 🆎 ⓞ 𝑉𝐼𝑆𝐴 𝐽𝐶𝐵 p. 7 PU u
closed 25 December, Saturday, Sunday and Bank Holidays – **Meals** - Japanese - (booking
essential) 28.00/36.00 and a la carte approx. 40.00 **t.** 🍷 14.50.

🍴🍴🍴 **1 Lombard Street (Restaurant),** 1 Lombard St, EC2V 9AA, ✆ (020) 7929 6611,
❀ *hb @ 1lombardstreet.com, Fax (020) 7929 6622* – ☰. 🆖 🆎 ⓞ 𝑉𝐼𝑆𝐴 𝐽𝐶𝐵 p. 7 PV r
closed 1 week Christmas, Saturday, Sunday and Bank Holidays – **Meals** (lunch booking
essential) 28.00/38.00 and a la carte 40.00/56.00 **t.** (see also **1 Lombard Street (Brasserie)** below)
Spec. Feuilleté of smoked haddock with quail eggs, mustard sauce. Suprême and fricassee
of chicken with young leeks. Chocolate, whisky and coffee praline "Lombardo".

🍴🍴🍴 **Prism,** 147 Leadenhall, EC3V 4QT, ✆ (020) 7256 3875, *Fax (020) 7256 3876* – ☰. 🆖
🆎 ⓞ 𝑉𝐼𝑆𝐴 𝐽𝐶𝐵 p. 7 PV u
closed 25-26 December, Saturday, Sunday and Bank Holidays – **Meals** a la carte
35.00/61.00 **t.** 🍷 13.80.

🍴🍴 **Club Gascon** (Aussignac), 57 West Smithfield, EC1A 9DS, ✆ (020) 7796 0600,
❀ *Fax (020) 7796 0601* – ☰. 🆖 🆎 𝑉𝐼𝑆𝐴 p. 7 OU z
closed 21 December-6 January, Sunday, Saturday lunch and Bank Holidays – **Meals** - French
(Gascony specialities) - (booking essential) 30.00/50.00 and a la carte 20.60/40.50 **t.**
🍷 12.50
Spec. Tatin of foie gras, truffle and turnips. Crispy veal fillet, sorrel and courgette. Prune
and Armagnac parfait.

UNITED KINGDOM

XX **Searcy's at The Barbican,** Level 2, The Barbican, Silk St, EC2Y 8DS, ✆ (0:
7588 3008, *searcys@barbican.org.uk, Fax (028) 7382 7247* – 🖃. 🜂 AE ⓪ VISA
closed 24-25 December, Saturday lunch and Sunday – **Meals** 22.50 and a la carte appr
37.50 **t.** 🍸 15.40. p. 7 OU

XX **The Don,** The Courtyard, 20 St Swithins Lane, EC4N 8AD, ✆ (020) 7626 2606, *bo
ngs@thedonrestaurant.co.uk, Fax (020) 7626 2616* – 🖃. 🜂 AE ⓪ VISA p. 7 PV
closed 23 December-2 January, Saturday, Sunday and Bank Holidays – **Meals** (lunch booki
essential) 14.95/17.95 (dinner) and a la carte 23.10/32.95 **t.** 🍸 14.25.

XX **1 Lombard Street (Brasserie),** 1 Lombard St, EC2V 9AA, ✆ (020) 7929 66'
Fax (020) 7929 6622 – 🖃. 🜂 AE ⓪ VISA JCB p. 7 PV
closed Saturday, Sunday and Bank Holidays – **Meals** (lunch booking essential) a la car
26.50/35.80 **t.** 🍸 15.00.

XX **Brasserie Rocque,** 37 Broadgate Circle, EC2M 2QS, ✆ (020) 7638 791
Fax (020) 7628 5899, 🌣 – 🖃. 🜂 AE VISA p. 7 PU
closed Saturday, Sunday and Bank Holidays – **Meals** (booking essential) (lunch only) a
carte 21.65/36.35 **t.** 🍸 10.50.

XX **Pacific Oriental,** first floor, 1 Bishopsgate, EC2N 3AB, ✆ (020) 7621 9988, *enqui
s@orgplc.co.uk, Fax (020) 7621 9911* – 🖃. 🜂 AE ⓪ VISA p. 7 PV
closed 25-26 December, 1 January, Saturday, Sunday and Bank Holidays – **Meals** - Sou
East Asian influences - a la carte 25.75/37.75 **t.** 🍸 15.00.

XX **Imperial City,** Royal Exchange, Cornhill, EC3V 3LL, ✆ (020) 7626 3437, *enquiries@
rgplc.co.uk, Fax (020) 7338 0125* – 🖃. 🜂 AE ⓪ VISA p. 7 PV
closed 25-26 December, Saturday, Sunday and Bank Holidays – **Meals** - Chinese
20.00/40.00 and a la carte 16.50/32.80 **t.** 🍸 12.50.

XX **Sri Siam City,** 85 London Wall, EC2M 7AD, ✆ (020) 7628 5772, *enquiries@cvgplc.co.t
Fax (020) 7628 3395* – 🖃. 🜂 AE ⓪ VISA p. 7 PU
closed 25-26 December, 1 January, Saturday, Sunday and Bank Holidays – **Meals** - Th
- (booking essential) 16.95/27.95 and a la carte approx. 20.25 **t.** 🍸 16.50.

HAMMERSMITH AND FULHAM

Fulham – ✉ SW6.

🏨 **London Putney Bridge Travel Inn Capital,** 3 Putney Bridge Approach, SW6 3JI
✆ (020) 7471 8300, *Fax (020) 7471 8315* – 🛗, ✦✦ rm, 🖃 rest, 📺 🜂. 🜂 AE ⓪ VS
✦✦
Meals (grill rest.) (dinner only) – **154 rm** 74.95 **t.**

XX **Le Potiron Sauvage,** 755 Fulham Rd, SW6 5UU, ✆ (020) 7371 075!
Fax (020) 7371 0695 – 🜂 AE VISA JCB
closed 25-29 December, 1-7 January, Sunday dinner and Monday – **Meals** (dinner only ar
Sunday lunch except August)/dinner 26.00 **t.** 🍸 15.00.

XX **Blue Elephant,** 4-6 Fulham Broadway, SW6 1AA, ✆ (020) 7385 6595, *london@blu
elephant.com, Fax (020) 7386 7665* – 🖃. 🜂 AE ⓪ VISA p. 8 EZ
closed Christmas and Saturday lunch – **Meals** - Thai - (booking essential) 10.00/36.00 an
a la carte 18.50/32.00 **t.** 🍸 14.00.

XX **Mao Tai,** 58 New Kings Rd, Parsons Green, SW6 4LS, ✆ (020) 7225 2500, *mbmaot
@aol.com, Fax (020) 7471 8992* – 🖃. 🜂 AE ⓪ VISA
closed 25-26 December – **Meals** - Chinese (Szechuan) - 24.70 and a la carte 27.70/36.00 **t**
🍸 14.50.

🍴 **The Salisbury Tavern,** 21 Sherbrooke Rd, SW6 7HX, ✆ (020) 7381 4005, *longshc
@dial.pipex.com, Fax (020) 7381 1002* – 🖃. 🜂 AE VISA p. 8 EZ
closed 25-26 December – **Meals** (live jazz Monday evening) a la carte 19.15/25.90 **t**
🍸 11.00.

Hammersmith – ✉ W6/W12/W14.

XX **River Café** (Ruth Rogers/Rose Gray), Thames Wharf, Rainville Rd, W6 9HA, ✆ (02C
☸ 7386 4200, *info@rivercafe.co.uk, Fax (020) 7386 4201,* 🌣 – 🜂 AE ⓪ VISA
closed Christmas-New Year, Sunday dinner and Bank Holidays – **Meals** - Italian - (bookin
essential) a la carte 42.00/48.00 **t.** 🍸 10.50
Spec. Chargrilled squid with red chilli and rocket. Bollito misto. "Chocolate nemesis".

XX **Rafique,** 291 King St, W6 9NH, ✆ (020) 8748 7345, *Fax (020) 8563 9679* – 🖃. 🜂 AE
⓪ VISA JCB
closed Monday lunch – **Meals** - Indian - 9.50 (lunch) and a la carte 18.95/23.85.

X **Snows on the Green,** 166 Shepherd's Bush Rd, Brook Green, W6 7PB, ✆ (020'
7603 2142, *Fax (020) 7602 7553* – 🖃. 🜂 AE ⓪ VISA
closed 1 week Christmas, Saturday lunch and Sunday dinner – **Meals** 13.50/16.00 (lunch)
and a la carte 22.50/28.50 **t.** 🍸 11.00.

✗ **The Brackenbury,** 129-131 Brackenbury Rd, W6 0BQ, ✆ (020) 8748 0107,
Fax (020) 8/41 0905, ☞ – ◍ AE ◑ VISA
closed 24-26 December, Saturday lunch and Sunday dinner – **Meals** 12.50 (lunch) and a
la carte 19.50/29.30 **t.** ◊ 11.00.

✗ **Azou,** 375 King St, W6 9NJ, ✆ (020) 8536 7266, *Fax (020) 8748 1009* – ▤. ◍ ◑ VISA
closed 25 December and 1 January – **Meals** - North African - (lunch booking essential) a
la carte 14.85/21.75 **t.** ◊ 9.70.

▯❒ **Thatched House,** 115 Dalling Rd, W6 0ET, ✆ (020) 8748 6174, *thatchedhouse@es
tablishment.co.uk, Fax (020) 8563 2735* – ◍ VISA JCB
closed 25 December – **Meals** a la carte 15.85/22.85 **t.** ◊ 10.95.

▯❒ **Anglesea Arms,** 35 Wingate Rd, W6 0UR, ✆ (020) 8749 1291, *fievans@aol.com,
Fax (020) 8749 1254* – ◍ VISA
closed 24-31 December – **Meals** (bookings not accepted) a la carte 18.45/20.65 **t.** ◊ 10.25.

ympia – ✉ W14.

✗✗ **Cotto,** 44 Blythe Rd, W14 0HA, ✆ (020) 7602 9333, *bookings@cottorestaurant.co.uk,
Fax (020) 7602 5003* – ▤. ◍ AE VISA JCB   p. 8 EZ i
closed 1 week Christmas, Saturday lunch, Sunday and Bank Holidays – **Meals** 15.50/18.00
(lunch) and a la carte 22.25/31.70 **t.** ◊ 12.50.

epherd's Bush – ✉ W14.

✗✗ **Chinon,** 23 Richmond Way, W14 0AS, ✆ (020) 7602 5968, *johnchinon@hotmail.com,
Fax (020) 7602 4082* – ▤. ◍ AE ◑ VISA JCB
closed Christmas, Easter and Sunday – **Meals** (dinner only) 25.00 **t.** ◊ 16.00.

✗ **Onami,** 236 Blythe Rd, W14 0HJ, ✆ (020) 7603 7267
Meals - Japanese - a la carte approx. 15.00 **t.** ◊ 10.50.

▯❒ **Havelock Tavern,** 57 Masbro Rd, W14 0LS, ✆ (020) 7603 5374, *Fax (020) 7602 1163,*
☞, ☞ –
closed 23-26 December – **Meals** (bookings not accepted) a la carte 18.50/24.00 **st.** ◊ 9.50.

SLINGTON

rchway – ✉ N19.

✗ **The Parsee,** 34 Highgate Hill, N19 5NL, ✆ (020) 7272 9091, *dining@theparsee.co.uk,*
☸   *Fax (020) 768/ 1139* – ▤. ◍ AE VISA
closed 25 December, Good Friday and Monday – **Meals** - Indian (Parsee) - (dinner only and
Sunday lunch) 20.00/30.00 and a la carte 14.70/23.95 **t** ◊ 11.90.

▯❒ **St John's,** 91 Junction Rd, N19 5QU, ✆ (020) 7272 1587, *stjohnsarchway@virgin.net,
Fax (020) 7272 8023* – ◍ VISA
closed Monday lunch – **Meals** a la carte 16.50/24.50 **t.** ◊ 11.00.

anonbury – ✉ N1.

▯❒ **Centuria,** 100 St Paul's Rd, N1 2QP, ✆ (020) 7704 2345 – ◍ VISA
closed lunch Monday-Friday – **Meals** a la carte 15.70/22.70 **t.** ◊ 11.70.

lerkenwell – ✉ EC1.

✗✗ **Maison Novelli,** 29 Clerkenwell Green, EC1R 0DU, ✆ (020) 7251 6606, *jcnovelli@ws
Irestaurants.co.uk, Fax (020) 7490 1083* – ◍ AE ◑ VISA   p.7 NU a
closed Sunday, Saturday lunch and Bank Holidays – **Meals** a la carte 29.95/48.95 **t.** ◊ 14.95.

✗✗ **Smiths of Smithfield,** Top Floor, 67-77 Charterhouse St, EC1M 6HJ, ✆ (020)
7236 6666, *smiths@smithfield.co.uk, Fax (020) 7236 5666,* ≤, ☞ – ☖ ▤. ◍ AE
◑ VISA   p.7 NU s
closed 25-26 December and Saturday lunch – **Meals** a la carte 27.50/37.50 **t.** ◊ 10.00 –
The Dining Room : **Meals** *(closed Sunday)* a la carte 19.25/20.25 **t.** ◊ 10.00.

✗✗ **Gaudi,** 63 Clerkenwell Rd, EC1M 5PT, ✆ (020) 7608 3220, *gaudi@turnmills.co.uk,
Fax (020) 7250 1057* – ▤. ◍ AE ◑ VISA JCB   p.7 NU z
*closed 24 December-3 January, Good Friday, Saturday lunch, Sunday and Bank Holiday
Monday* – **Meals** - Spanish - 15.00 (lunch) and a la carte 32.50/36.50 **t.** ◊ 11.50.

✗ **St John,** 26 St John St, EC1M 4AY, ✆ (020) 7251 0848, *reservations@stjohnrestaurant.co.
uk, Fax (020) 7251 4090,* « *19C converted former smokehouse* » – ▤. ◍ AE ◑ VISA JCB
closed Christmas-New Year, Easter weekend, Saturday lunch and Sunday – **Meals** a la carte
21.50/31.10 **t.** ◊ 11.50.   p.7 OU c

▯❒ **The Bear,** No 2 St Johns Sq, EC1M 4DE, ✆ (020) 7608 2117, *Fax (020) 7608 2116* – ▤.
◍ VISA   p.7 NU c
closed 25-26 December, Saturday, Sunday and Bank Holidays – **Meals** a la carte
11.90/17.40 **t.** ◊ 9.80.

UNITED KINGDOM

Finsbury – ⊠ EC1.

XX **Simply Nico,** 7 Goswell Rd, EC1M 7AH, ✆ (020) 7336 7677, barbican@ simplynico.co
Fax (020) 7336 7690 – ▤, 🅼🅲 🅰🅴 ⓪ 🆅🅸🆂🅰 🅹🅲🅱 p. 7 OUT
closed 22 December-6 January, Sunday and Saturday lunch – **Meals** 12.50 and a la ca
19.50/29.60 **t.** 🍴 12.95.

X **Café Lazeez City,** 88 St John St, EC1M 4EH, ✆ (020) 7253 2224, lazclerkwell@ cs.c
Fax (020) 7253 2112 – ▤, 🅼🅲 🅰🅴 ⓪ 🆅🅸🆂🅰 🅹🅲🅱 p. 7 OU
closed 22 December-1 January, Saturday lunch, Sunday and Bank Holidays – **Meals** - No
Indian - 12.95/25.00 and a la carte 15.50/27.75 **t.** 🍴 9.95.

X **Quality Chop House,** 94 Farringdon Rd, EC1R 3EA, ✆ (020) 7837 5093, qualityc
phouse@ clara.net, Fax (020) 7833 8748 – ✦⃫. 🅼🅲 🆅🅸🆂🅰 p. 6 MT
closed 23 December-3 January and Saturday lunch – **Meals** a la carte 19.00/34.00
🍴 11.00.

X **Moro,** 34-36 Exmouth Market, EC1R 4QE, ✆ (020) 7833 8336, info@ moro.co.
Fax (020) 7833 9338 – ▤, 🅼🅲 🅰🅴 ⓪ 🆅🅸🆂🅰 p. 7 NT
closed 23 December-1 January, Saturday lunch, Sunday and Bank Holidays – **Meals** a
carte 19.00/28.50 **t.** 🍴 10.50.

🍴▯ **The Peasant,** 240 St John St, EC1V 4PH, ✆ (020) 7336 7726, Fax (020) 7490 108
🅼🅲 🅰🅴 ⓪ 🆅🅸🆂🅰 p. 7 NT
closed 24 December-2 January, Saturday lunch and Sunday – **Meals** a la car
10.70/22.10 **t.** 🍴 10.50.

Islington – ⊠ N1.

🏛 **Hilton London Islington,** 53 Upper St, N1 0UY, ✆ (020) 7354 770
Fax (020) 7354 7711, 🍴, 🛵, 🈺 – 🛗, ✦⃫ rm, ▤ 📺 ✆ 🔥 – 🔒 35. 🅼🅲 🅰🅴 ⓪ 🆅🅸🆂🅰 🅹🅲
🏵 p. 7 NS
Meals 17.50/22.50 and dinner a la carte 18.00/28.50 **t.** 🍴 15.90 – 🛏 16.00 – **178 r**
144.00 **s.**, 6 suites – SB.

🏛 **Jurys Inn London,** 60 Pentonville Rd, N1 9LA, ✆ (020) 7282 5500, jurysinnlond
@ jurysdoyle.com, Fax (020) 7282 5511 – 🛗, ✦⃫ rm, ▤ 📺 ✆ 🔥 – 🔒 40. 🅼🅲 🅰🅴 🆅
🏵 p. 6 MT
closed 24-26 December – **Meals** (bar lunch)/dinner a la carte 16.00 **st.** 🍴 9.95 – 🛏 9.
– **229 rm** 94.00 **st.**

XX **Frederick's,** Camden Passage, N1 8EG, ✆ (020) 7359 2888, eat@ fredericks.co.u
Fax (020) 7359 5173, 🍴, 🌳 – ▤. 🅼🅲 🅰🅴 ⓪ 🆅🅸🆂🅰 🅹🅲🅱 p. 7 NS
closed Christmas, Sunday and Bank Holidays – **Meals** 15.50 (lunch) and a la car
20.00/36.00 🍴 10.95.

XX **Lola's,** Mall Building, 359 Upper St, N1 0PD, ✆ (020) 7359 1932, lolasreatuk@ btinte
et.com, Fax (020) 7359 2209, « Converted tram shed » – ▤. 🅼🅲 🅰🅴 ⓪ 🆅🅸🆂🅰
closed lunch Bank Holidays – **Meals** 15.00 (lunch) and a la carte 25.00/28.75
🍴 10.75. p. 7 NS

XX **La Margherita,** 297 Upper St, N1 2TU, ✆ (020) 7359 3533, Fax (020) 7359 3533 – ▤
🅼🅲 🅰🅴 ⓪ 🆅🅸🆂🅰 🅹🅲🅱 p. 7 NS
Meals (dinner only and lunch Saturday and Sunday)/dinner a la carte 16.50/24.50
🍴 10.50.

XX **Metrogusto,** 13 Theberton St, N1 0RY, ✆ (020) 7226 9400, Fax (020) 7226 9400 – ▤
🐾 🅼🅲 🆅🅸🆂🅰 🅹🅲🅱 p. 7 NS
closed 2 weeks August, 12 days Christmas, New Year and Monday – **Meals** - Italian - a
carte 21.00/26.75 **t.** 🍴 12.50.

🍴▯ **The Crown,** 116 Cloudesley Rd, N1 0EB, ✆ (020) 7837 7107, thecrown@ fullers.co.u
Fax (020) 7833 1084, 🍴 – 🅼🅲 🅰🅴 🆅🅸🆂🅰 p. 7 NS
closed Sunday dinner – **Meals** a la carte 12.50/23.80 **st.** 🍴 11.00.

🍴▯ **The Northgate,** 113 Southgate Rd, N1 3JS, ✆ (020) 7359 7392, Fax (020) 7359 739
🍴 – 🅼🅲 🆅🅸🆂🅰 🅹🅲🅱 p. 7 PS
closed 24-26 December and 1 January – **Meals** (dinner only and lunch Saturday and Sunday
a la carte 19.00/23.50 **t.** 🍴 11.00.

KENSINGTON and CHELSEA (Royal Borough of).

Chelsea – ⊠ SW1/SW3/SW10 –.

🏛🏛 **Carlton Tower,** Cadogan Pl, SW1X 9PY, ✆ (020) 7235 1234, reservations@ hytlon
on.co.uk, Fax (020) 7235 9129, ≤, 🛵, 🈺, ▦, 🌳, ✗ – 🛗, ✦⃫ rm, ▤ 📺 ✆ 🚗 –
🔒 400. 🅼🅲 🅰🅴 ⓪ 🆅🅸🆂🅰 🅹🅲🅱. 🏵 p. 15 FR
Rib Room : Meals 23.00/33.00 and a la carte 30.00/62.00 **t.** 🍴 18.00 – **Grissini :** Meal
- Italian - (closed Saturday lunch and Sunday dinner) 16.00/21.00 (lunch) and a la carte
20.00/37.00 **t.** 🍴 18.00 – 🛏 19.50 – **191 rm** 295.00/360.00, 29 suites – SB.

Conrad London, Chelsea Harbour, SW10 0XG, ℰ (020) 7823 3000, *lonch-rm@hilton .com, Fax (020) 7351 6525,* ≤, ʃ₆, ≘, ▣ – ▮, ⁀☓ rm, ▤ ▣ ❦ ☷ ⌁ – 益 200. 🆎 🆎 ⓞ VISA JCB
Meals (see *Aquasia* below) – ☐ 18.50, **160 suites** 350.00/410.00.

Sheraton Park Tower, 101 Knightsbridge, SW1X 7RN, ℰ (020) 7235 8050, *reserv ationscentrallondon@sheraton.com, Fax (020) 7235 8231,* ≤ – ▮, ⁀☓ rm, ▤ ▣ ❦ ⌁ – 益 100. 🆎 🆎 ⓞ VISA JCB. p. 15 FQ v
Meals (see *One-O-One* below) – ☐ 20.75 – **258 rm** 335.00/355.00, 22 suites.

Capital, 22-24 Basil St, SW3 1AT, ℰ (020) 7589 5171, *reservations@capitalhotel.co.uk, Fax (020) 7225 0011* – ▮ ▤ ▣ ❦ ⌁ – 益 25. 🆎 🆎 ⓞ VISA. ⁒ p. 15 ER a
Meals (booking essential) 26.50/53.00 t. ⌁ 14.50 – ☐ 16.50 – **49 rm** 190.00/315.00.
Spec. Sautéed scallops and boudin noir. Saddle of rabbit with calamari "à la provençale". Coconut and passion fruit fusion.

The Cadogan, 75 Sloane St, SW1X 9SG, ℰ (020) 7235 7141, *info@cadogan.com, Fax (020) 7245 0994,* ☞, ⁒ – ▮, ⁀☓ rm, ▤ rest, ▣ ❦ – 益 40. 🆎 🆎 VISA
Meals (*closed Saturday lunch*) 15.90/28.50 and a la carte 35.00/48.00 **st.** ⌁ 14.00 – ☐ 16.50 – **61 rm** 190.00/240.00 **s.,** 4 suites. p. 15 FR e

Chelsea Village, Fulham Rd, SW6 1HS, ℰ (020) 7565 1400, *reservations@chelseavil lage.com, Fax (020) 7565 1450,* « Adjacent to Chelsea Football Club » – ▮, ⁀☓ rm, ▤ ▣ ❦ ⌁ 🄿 – 益 300. 🆎 🆎 ⓞ VISA. p. 8 FZ n
Arkles : **Meals** - Irish - (*closed Monday and dinner Sunday*) a la carte 23.25/31.75 **t.** ⌁ 13.95 – *Kings brasserie :* **Meals** a la carte 17.00/29.00 **t.** ⌁ 13.95 – *Fishnets :* **Meals** - Seafood - (*closed Sunday and lunch Monday*) (live music Friday evening) a la carte 17.75/25.25 **t.** ⌁ 13.95 – ☐ 14.00 – **288 rm** 155.00/175.00 **st.,** 3 suites.

Durley House, 115 Sloane St, SW1X 9PJ, ℰ (020) 7235 5537, *durley@firmdale.com, Fax (020) 7259 6977,* ☞, ⁒ – ▮ ▣ ❦. 🆎 🆎 VISA. ⁒ p. 15 FS e
Meals (room service only) – ☐ 18.50, **11 suites** 295.00/550.00.

Cliveden Town House, 26 Cadogan Gdns, SW3 2RP, ℰ (020) 7730 6466, *reservat ions@clivedentownhouse.co.uk, Fax (020) 7730 0236,* ☞ – ▮, ⁀☓ rm, ▤ rm, ▣ ❦. 🆎 ⓞ VISA p. 15 FS c
Meals (room service only) – ☐ 18.50 – **31 rm** 160.00/310.00 **s.,** 4 suites.

Millennium Knightsbridge, 17-25 Sloane St, SW1X 9NU, ℰ (020) 7235 4377, *sale s-knightsbridge@mill-cop.com, Fax (020) 7235 3705* – ▮ ⁀☓ ▤ ▣ ❦ – 益 120. 🆎 🆎 ⓞ VISA. ⁒ p. 15 FR r
Mju : **Meals** - French-Japanese - (*closed Saturday, Sunday dinner and Bank Holidays*) (set menu only) 50.00 **st.** ⌁ 15.00 – **218 rm** 230.00/260.00 **s.,** 4 suites.

Franklin, 22 28 Egerton Gdns, SW3 2DB, ℰ (020) 7584 5533, *bookings@franklinhot el.co.uk, Fax (020) 7584 5449,* « Tastefully furnished Victorian town house », ☞ – ▮ ▤ ▣ ❦. 🆎 🆎 ⓞ VISA. ⁒ p. 15 DS e
Meals (room service only) a la carte 23.50/31.00 **t.** – ☐ 16.00 – **47 rm** 160.00/325.00.

Basil Street, 8 Basil St, SW3 1AH, ℰ (020) 7581 3311, *info@thebasil.com, Fax (020) 7581 3693* – ▮, ⁀☓ rm, ▣ ❦ – 益 30. 🆎 🆎 VISA. ⁒ p. 15 FQ o
Meals 15.50/25.00 **t.** ⌁ 14.50 – ☐ 15.00 – **80 rm** 138.00/198.00 **t.**

The London Outpost of the Carnegie Club without rest., 69 Cadogan Gdns, SW3 2RR, ℰ (020) 7589 7333, *londonoutpost@dial.pipex.com, Fax (020) 7581 4958,* ☞ – ▮ ⁀☓ ▤ ▣. 🆎 🆎 ⓞ VISA p. 15 FS r
closed 24-28 December – ☐ 16.95 – **11 rm** 160.00/270.00 **s.**

The Sloane, 29 Draycott Pl, SW3 2SH, ℰ (020) 7581 5757, *reservations@sloanehot el.com, Fax (020) 7584 1348,* « Victorian town house, antiques » ▮ ▤ ▣. 🆎 🆎 VISA JCB. ⁒ p. 15 ET c
Meals (room service) – ☐ 12.00 – **22 rm** 150.00/240.00 **s.**

Eleven Cadogan Gardens, 11 Cadogan Gdns, SW3 2RJ, ℰ (020) 7730 7000, *rese rvations@number-eleven.co.uk, Fax (020) 7730 5217,* ʃ₆, ≘, ☞ – ▮ ▣. 🆎 🆎 ⓞ VISA JCB. ⁒ p. 15 FS u
Meals (room service) – ☐ 13.00 – **56 rm** 165.00/295.00 **t.,** 4 suites.

Egerton House, 17-19 Egerton Terr, SW3 2BX, ℰ (020) 7589 2412, *bookings@ege rtonhousehotel.co.uk, Fax (020) 7584 6540,* « Tastefully furnished Victorian town house » – ▮ ▤ ▣ ❦. 🆎 🆎 ⓞ VISA JCB. p. 15 DR e
Meals (room service only) – ☐ 16.00 – **29 rm** 160.00/250.00 **s.**

Sydney without rest., 9-11 Sydney St, SW3 6PU, ℰ (020) 7376 7711, *sh@zoohotels. com, Fax (020) 7376 4233* – ▮ ▣ ❦. 🆎 🆎 ⓞ VISA JCB. ⁒ p. 15 DT a
☐ 5.00 – **21 rm** 175.00/270.00 **s.**

Chelsea Green without rest., 35 Ixworth Pl, SW3 3QX, ℰ (020) 7225 7500, *cghotel @dircon.co.uk, Fax (020) 7225 7555* – ▮ ⁀☓ ▤ ▣ ❦ – 益 80. 🆎 🆎 ⓞ VISA JCB. ⁒ ☐ 12.00 – **42 rm** 176.00/212.00 **st.,** 4 suites. p. 15 DT z

🏠 **Beaufort** without rest., 33 Beaufort Gdns, SW3 1PP, ℘ (020) 7584 5252, _enquir_
@ thebeaufort.co.uk, Fax (020) 7589 2834, « English floral watercolour collection » –
▤ 📺 📶 📵 ⒶⒺ ⑩ 𝚅𝙸𝚂𝙰 ᴊᴄʙ. ❀   p. 15 ER
28 rm 155.00/295.00 **s.**

🏠 **Parkes** without rest., 41 Beaufort Gdns, SW3 1PW, ℘ (020) 7581 9944, _reception@_
arkeshotel.com, Fax (020) 7581 1999 – 📶 ▤ 📺 📶 📵 ⒶⒺ ⑩ 𝚅𝙸𝚂𝙰 ᴊᴄʙ ❀
🍽 10.00 – **19 rm** 195.00/290.00 **s.**, 14 suites 325.00/415.00 **s.**   p. 15 ER

🏠 **57 Pont Street** without rest., 57 Pont St, SW1X 0BD, ℘ (020) 7590 1090, _sgrec_
y@no57.com, Fax (020) 7590 1099 – 📶 ▤ 📺 📶 📵 ⒶⒺ ⑩ 𝚅𝙸𝚂𝙰 ᴊᴄʙ ❀
🍽 15.00 – **22 rm** 125.00/350.00 **s.**   p. 15 ER

🏠 **L'Hotel,** 28 Basil St, SW3 1AS, ℘ (020) 7589 6286, _reservations@lhotel.co.u_
Fax (020) 7823 7826 – 📶, ▤ rest, 📺 ⇔, 📵 ⒶⒺ ⑩ 𝚅𝙸𝚂𝙰. ❀   p. 15 ER
closed Christmas – **Le Metro** : Meals (closed 25 December, Sunday and Bank Holidays)
la carte approx. 17.75 **t.** ⓐ 12.95 – **12 rm** 135.00/155.00 **s.**

🏠 **Sloane Square Moat House,** Sloane Sq, SW1W 8EG, ℘ (020) 7896 9988, _reserv_
tions@ queensmoat.co.uk, Fax (020) 7824 8381 – 📶 ❀ 📺 📶 – 🏋 40. 📵 ⒶⒺ ⑩ 𝚅𝙸𝚂
ᴊᴄʙ   p 15 EST
Meals (see **Simply Nico** below) – 🍽 8.50 – **105 rm** 163.00/236.00 **st.**

🏠 **Claverley** without rest., 13-14 Beaufort Gdns, SW3 1PS, ℘ (020) 7589 8541, _reser_
ations@claverleyhotel.co.uk, Fax (020) 7584 3410 – 📶 📺. 📵 ⒶⒺ ⑩ 𝚅𝙸𝚂𝙰
❀   p. 15 ER
30 rm 🍽 110.00/195.00 **t.**

🕸🕸🕸🕸
❀❀❀ **Gordon Ramsay,** 68-69 Royal Hospital Rd, SW3 4HP, ℘ (020) 7352 4441
Fax (020) 7352 3334 – ▤. 📵 ⒶⒺ ⑩ 𝚅𝙸𝚂𝙰 ᴊᴄʙ   p. 15 EU
closed 1 week Christmas, Saturday, Sunday and Bank Holidays – **Meals** (booking essentia
35.00/80.00 ⓐ 18.00
Spec. Carpaccio of pigeon with creamed truffle sauce. Fillet of sea bass wrapped in basi
crème fraîche and caviar sauce. Pineapple ravioli with summer fruits.

🕸🕸🕸
❀ **Aubergine,** 11 Park Walk, SW10 0AJ, ℘ (020) 7352 3449, _Fax (020) 7351 1770_ – ▤
📵 ⒶⒺ ⑩ 𝚅𝙸𝚂𝙰   p. 14 CU
closed 2 weeks August, 2 weeks Christmas, Saturday lunch, Sunday and Bank Holidays
Meals (booking essential) 25.00/65.00 **t.** ⓐ 20.00
Spec. Warm salad of quail, foie gras and sweetbreads. Roast sea bass with baby artichoke
and sweet pepper sauce. Roasted peaches with almond ice cream.

🕸🕸🕸 **Drones,** 1 Pont St, SW1X 9EJ, ℘ (020) 7235 9555, _Fax (020) 7235 9566_ – ▤. 📵 Ⓐ
⑩ 𝚅𝙸𝚂𝙰   p. 15 FR (
Meals a la carte 28.50/52.50 **t.** ⓐ 16.50.

🕸🕸🕸 **Bibendum,** Michelin House, 81 Fulham Rd, SW3 6RD, ℘ (020) 7581 5817, _manage_
@ bibendum.co.uk, Fax (020) 7823 7925 – ▤. 📵 ⒶⒺ ⑩ 𝚅𝙸𝚂𝙰   p. 15 DS s
closed 25-26 December – **Meals** 27.00 (lunch) and dinner a la carte 40.00/50.00 **t.**

🕸🕸🕸 **Floriana,** 15 Beauchamp Pl, SW3 1NQ, ℘ (020) 7838 1500, _Fax (020) 7584 1464_ – ▤
📵 ⒶⒺ ⑩ 𝚅𝙸𝚂𝙰 ᴊᴄʙ   p. 15 ER (
Meals - Italian - 15.50/19.50 (lunch) and a la carte approx. 44.50 **t.** ⓐ 19.00.

🕸🕸🕸 **The Fifth Floor** (at Harvey Nichols), Knightsbridge, SW1X 7RJ, ℘ (020) 7235 5250
Fax (020) 7823 2207 – 📶 ▤. 📵 ⒶⒺ ⑩ 𝚅𝙸𝚂𝙰 ᴊᴄʙ   p. 15 FQ a
closed 25-26 December and Sunday dinner – **Meals** 18.50 (lunch) and dinner a la carte
36.00/50.00 **t.** ⓐ 13.50.

🕸🕸🕸 **One-O-One** (at Sheraton Park Tower H.), William St, SW1X 7RN, ℘ (020) 7290 7101,
Fax (020) 7235 6196 – ▤. 📵 ⒶⒺ ⑩ 𝚅𝙸𝚂𝙰   p. 15 FQ v
Meals - Seafood - 19.50 (lunch) and a la carte 35.00/51.00 **t.** ⓐ 23.00.

🕸🕸🕸 **Toto's,** Walton House, Walton St, SW3 2JH, ℘ (020) 7589 0075, _Fax (020) 7581 9668,_
🌡 – 📵 ⒶⒺ ⑩ 𝚅𝙸𝚂𝙰 ᴊᴄʙ   p. 15 ES a
closed 25-27 December – **Meals** - Italian - 20.50 (lunch) and a la carte 30.00/42.00 **st.**
ⓐ 17.00.

🕸🕸🕸 **Chutney Mary,** 535 King's Rd, SW10 0SZ, ℘ (020) 7351 3113, _action@realindianfo_
od.com, Fax (020) 7351 7694 – ▤. 📵 ⒶⒺ ⑩ 𝚅𝙸𝚂𝙰 ᴊᴄʙ   p. 8 FZ v
closed dinner 25 December – **Meals** - Indian - 14.00 (lunch) and a la carte 21.50/28.50 **t.**
ⓐ 11.75.

🕸🕸 **Montes,** 164 Sloane St, SW1X 9QB, ℘ (020) 7245 0896, _Fax (020) 7235 3456_ – ▤.
ⒶⒺ ⑩ 𝚅𝙸𝚂𝙰   p. 15 FR s
closed Sunday and Bank Holidays – **Meals** - Italian - (booking essential) (lunch only) 23.00
and a la carte 30.00/40.00 **t.** ⓐ 19.00.

🕸🕸 **Aquasia** (at Conrad London H.), Chelsea Harbour, SW10 0XG, ℘ (020) 7300 8443,
Fax (020) 7351 6525, ≤, 🌡, « Harbourside setting » – ▤ 📵 ⒶⒺ ⑩ 𝚅𝙸𝚂𝙰 ᴊᴄʙ
Meals 12.00/21.00 and a la carte 24.00/33.00 **t.** ⓐ 13.00.

XX **Bluebird,** 350 King's Rd, SW3 5UU, ✆ (020) 7559 1000, Fax (020) 7559 1111 – 🔓 ▣.
🍷 AE ⑩ VISA JCB   p. 14 CU e
Meals 16.50 (lunch) and dinner a la carte 28.00/39.50 **t.** ⓖ 12.75.

XX **Poissonnerie de l'Avenue,** 82 Sloane Ave, SW3 3DZ, ✆ (020) 7589 2457, info@p
oissonnerie.co.uk, Fax (020) 7581 3360 – ▣. 🍷 AE ⑩ VISA JCB   p. 15 DS u
closed 24 December-3 January, Sunday and Bank Holidays – **Meals** – French Seafood - 18.95
(lunch) and a la carte 31.50/43.50 **t.** ⓖ 14.00.

XX **English Garden,** 10 Lincoln St, SW3 2TS, ✆ (020) 7584 7272, english.garden@ukga
teway.net, Fax (020) 7584 1961 – ▣. 🍷 AE ⑩ VISA JCB   p. 15 ET x
closed 2 weeks August, Christmas and Monday lunch – **Meals** 19.50/27.50 **t.** ⓖ 14.50.

XX **Mao Tai,** 96 Draycott Ave, SW3 3AD, ✆ (020) 7225 2500, mbmaotai@aol.com,
Fax (020) 7471 8992 – ▣. 🍷 AE ⑩ VISA   p. 15 ES i
closed 25-26 December – **Meals** - Chinese (Szechuan) - 24.70 and a la carte 20.50/43.00 **t.**
ⓖ 14.50.

XX **The House,** 3 Milner St, SW3 2QA, ✆ (020) 7584 3002, Fax (020) 7581 2848 – 🍷 AE
⑩ VISA JCB   p. 15 ES o
closed last 2 weeks August, Saturday lunch and Sunday – **Meals** 14.50/27.00 **st.** ⓖ 13.50.

XX **Parisienne Chophouse,** 3 Yeoman's Row, SW3 3AL, ✆ (020) 7590 9999, sales@w
hitestarline.org.uk, Fax (020) 7590 9900 – ▣. 🍷 AE ⑩ VISA   p. 15 ER r
Meals - French - 12.95 and a la carte 18.00/33.00 **t.** ⓖ 12.50.

XX **Pellicano,** 19-21 Elystan St, SW3 3NT, ✆ (020) 7589 3718, Fax (020) 7584 1789, 🌿
– ▣. 🍷 AE VISA   p. 15 ET a
closed 23 December-2 January – **Meals** - Italian - 13.50 (lunch) and a la carte 18.50/29.50 **t.**
ⓖ 12.00.

XX **Brasserie St Quentin,** 243 Brompton Rd, SW3 2EP, ✆ (020) 7589 8005,
Fax (020) 7584 6064 – ▣. 🍷 AE ⑩ VISA   p. 15 DR a
closed 25 December – **Meals** - French - a la carte 13.90/24.85 **st.** ⓖ 10.00.

XX **Benihana,** 77 King's Rd, SW3 4NX, ✆ (020) 7376 7799, benihana@dircon.co.uk,
Fax (020) 7376 7377 – ▣. 🍷 AE ⑩ VISA JCB   p. 15 EU e
closed 25 December – **Meals** - Japanese (Teppan-Yaki) - 8.50/14.00 and a la carte approx.
40.00 **t.**

XX **Caraffini,** 61-63 Lower Sloane St, SW1W 8DH, ✆ (020) 7259 0235, info@caraffini.co.uk,
Fax (020) 7259 0236, 🌿 – ▣. 🍷 AE VISA   p. 15 FT a
closed Sunday and Bank Holidays – **Meals** - Italian - a la carte 19.65/32.25 **t.** ⓖ 10.25.

XX **Vama,** 438 King's Rd, SW10 0LJ, ✆ (020) 7351 4118, vamaoffice@aol.com,
Fax (020) 7565 8501 – 🍷 AE ⑩ VISA   p. 9 GZ e
Meals - Indian - (booking essential) 7.95/9.95 (lunch) and a la carte 16.50/51.25 **t.** ⓖ 12.95.

XX **Le Colombier,** 145 Dovehouse St, SW3 6LB, ✆ (020) 7351 1155, colombier@compu
serve.com, Fax (020) 7351 0077, 🌿 – 🍷 AE ⑩ VISA   p. 15 DT e
Meals - French - 16.90 (lunch) and a la carte 20.80/36.30 **t.** ⓖ 12.90.

XX **The Collection,** 264 Brompton Rd, SW3 2AS, ✆ (020) 7225 1212, collection.office
@belgo-restaurants.co.uk, Fax (020) 7225 1050 – ▣. 🍷 AE ⑩ VISA
JCB   p. 15 DS v
closed 25-26 December, 1 January and Bank Holidays – **Meals** (dinner only) a la carte
28.00/39.25 **t.** ⓖ 12.95.

XX **Good Earth,** 233 Brompton Rd, SW3 2EP, ✆ (020) 7584 3658, goodearthgroup@ao
l.com, Fax (020) 7823 8769 – ▣. 🍷 AE VISA JCB   p. 15 DR c
closed 22-30 December – **Meals** - Chinese - 7.95/29.50 and a la carte 14.60/23.30 **t.**

XX **Dan's,** 119 Sydney St, SW3 6NR, ✆ (020) 7352 2718, Fax (020) 7352 3265, 🌿 – 🍷
AE VISA JCB   p. 15 DU s
closed 24 December-New Year, Easter, Saturday lunch and Sunday and Bank Holidays – **Meals**
17.50 (lunch) and a la carte 24.00/30.50 **t.** ⓖ 12.50.

X **I Cardi,** 351 Fulham Rd, SW10 9TW, ✆ (020) 7351 2939, Fax (020) 7376 4619 – ▣. 🍷
AE VISA   p. 14 BU z
Meals - Italian - a la carte 15.00/25.00 ⓖ 12.50.

X **Zaika Bazaar,** 2a Pond Pl, SW3 6QU, ✆ (020) 7584 6655, info@zaika-bazaar.co.uk,
Fax (020) 7584 6755 – ▣. 🍷 AE VISA   p. 15 DT c
closed Sunday, Saturday lunch and Bank Holidays – **Meals** - Indian - a la carte 20.85/27.00 **t.**

🍺 **Admiral Codrington,** 17 Mossop St, SW3 2LY, ✆ (020) 7581 0005, londshot@dial.
pipex.com, Fax (020) 7589 2452 – 🍷 AE VISA   p. 15 ES x
closed 25-26 December – **Meals** a la carte 20.95/28.45 **t.** ⓖ 11.00.

🍺 **Chelsea Ram,** 32 Burnaby St, SW10 0PL, ✆ (020) 7351 4008, pint@chelsearam.com,
Fax (020) 7349 0885 – 🍷 AE VISA   p. 8 FZ r
closed 25 December – **Meals** (bookings not accepted) a la carte 14.35/22.85 **t.** ⓖ 9.95.

🏠 **Swag and Tails,** 10-11 Fairholt St, SW7 1EG, ℘ (020) 7584 6926, swagandtails@
way.com, Fax (020) 7581 9935 – ⓂⓈ ᴬᴱ 𝓥𝓘𝓢𝓐 ᴶᶜᴮ
p. 15 DR
closed Christmas, Saturday, Sunday and Bank Holidays – **Meals** a la carte 16.20/23.20
🛅 10.95.

🏠 **Builders Arms,** 13 Britten St, SW3 3TY, ℘ (020) 7349 9040, Fax (020) 7357 3181
▣. ⓂⓈ ᴬᴱ ⓸ 𝓥𝓘𝓢𝓐
p. 15 DU
closed 25 December – **Meals** (bookings not accepted) a la carte 15.35/22.85 **s.** 🛅 9.8

Earl's Court – ✉ SW5 –.

🏨 **K + K George,** 1-15 Templeton Pl, SW5 9NB, ℘ (020) 7598 8700, hotelgeorge@k
otels.co.uk, Fax (020) 7370 2285, 🌤 – ▯ ᴙ ▤ 📺 ✆ 🄿 – ⅍ 30. ⓂⓈ ᴬᴱ ⓸ 𝓥
ᴶᶜᴮ
p. 8 EZ
Meals (in bar) a la carte 13.50/19.50 **st.** 🛅 10.50 – **154 rm** ⊇ 165.00/195.00 **st.**

🏠 **Twenty Nevern Square,** Nevern Sq, SW5 9PD, ℘ (020) 7565 9555, hotel@twe.
ynevernsquare.co.uk, Fax (020) 7565 9444 – ▯ 📺 ✆ 🄿 ⅍ 𝓥𝓘𝓢𝓐 ᴶᶜᴮ. 🌤
Meals (closed Sunday and Monday) (residents only) (dinner only) a la carte 26.00/40.0
🛅 11.70 – ⊇ 9.00 – **19 rm** 140.00/275.00 **st.** – SB.
p. 8 EZ

🍴🍴 **Langan's Coq d'Or,** 254-260 Old Brompton Rd, SW5 9HR, ℘ (020) 7259 2599, adr
n@langansrestaurant.co.uk, Fax (020) 7370 7735, 🍽 – ▣. ⓂⓈ ᴬᴱ ⓸ 𝓥𝓘𝓢𝓐 ᴶᶜᴮ
closed Monday and Bank Holidays – **Meals** 16.50 (lunch) and a la carte 19.50/26.00
🛅 12.50.
p. 14 AU

Kensington – ✉ SW7/W8/W11/W14 –.

🏨🏨 **Royal Garden,** 2-24 Kensington High St, W8 4PT, ℘ (020) 7937 8000, sales@roya
arden.co.uk, Fax (020) 7361 1991, ≼, 🛵, 🈺 – ▯, 🍽 rm, ▤ 📺 ✆ ⅍ 🄿 – ⅍ 600. Ⓜ
ᴬᴱ ⓸ 𝓥𝓘𝓢𝓐 ᴶᶜᴮ. 🌤
p. 14 AQ
Park Terrace : **Meals** 9.50/14.75 (lunch) and a la carte 24.15/32.75 **st.** (see also **Th
Tenth** below) – ⊇ 18.00 – **381 rm** 235.00/295.00 **st.**, 15 suites – SB.

🏨🏨 **Copthorne Tara,** Scarsdale Pl, W8 5SR, ℘ (020) 7937 7211, sales.tara@mill-cop.con
Fax (020) 7872 7100 – ▯, 🍽 rm, ▤ 📺 ✆ ⅍ 🄿 – ⅍ 400. ⓂⓈ ᴬᴱ ⓸ 𝓥𝓘𝓢𝓐 ᴶᶜᵢ
🌤
p. 8 FY
Jerome K. Jerome : **Meals** a la carte 17.90/32.00 **t.** 🛅 19.00 – **Brasserie :** **Meals** 19.0
and a la carte approx. 26.00 **t.** 🛅 19.00 – ⊇ 15.00 – **827 rm** 215.00 **st.**, 7 suites.

🏨🏨 **Halcyon,** 81 Holland Park, W11 3RZ, ℘ (020) 7727 7288, reservations@thehalcyon.com
Fax (020) 7229 8516 – ▯ ▤ ▤ 📺 ✆ 🄿. ⓂⓈ ᴬᴱ ⓸ 𝓥𝓘𝓢𝓐
p. 8 EX
Meals (see **Aix en Provence** below) – ⊇ 17.95 – **39 rm** 173.00/213.00 **t.**, 3 suites
SB.

🏨🏨 **Hilton London Kensington,** 179-199 Holland Park Ave, W11 4UL, ℘ (020)
7603 3355, saleskensington@hilton.com, Fax (020) 7602 9397 – ▯, 🍽 rm, ▤ 📺 ✆
🄿 – ⅍ 300. ⓂⓈ ᴬᴱ ⓸ 𝓥𝓘𝓢𝓐 ᴶᶜᴮ. 🌤
p. 8 EX
Market : **Meals** (closed lunch Saturday and Sunday) 22.00 **t.** 🛅 16.50 – **Hiroko :** **Meal**
- Japanese - 16.00/35.00 and a la carte 21.00/39.00 **t.** 🛅 16.50 – ⊇ 15.00 – **603 rm**
149.00 **s.** – SB.

🏨🏨 **Hilton London Olympia,** 380 Kensington High St, W14 8NL, ℘ (020) 7603 3333
rmolympia@hilton.com, Fax (020) 7603 4846 – ▯, 🍽 rm, ▤ 📺 ✆ ⅍ 🄿 – ⅍ 250. Ⓜ
ᴬᴱ ⓸ 𝓥𝓘𝓢𝓐 ᴶᶜᴮ
p. 8 EY a
Meals a la carte 18.00/29.00 **st.** 🛅 18.00 – ⊇ 16.50 – **395 rm** 179.00/209.00, 10 suites

🏨🏨 **Thistle Kensington Park,** 16-32 De Vere Gdns, W8 5AG, ℘ (020) 7937 8080, sale
s.kensington@thistle.co.uk, Fax (020) 7937 7616 – ▯, 🍽 rm, ▤ 📺 ✆ – ⅍ 120. ⓂⓈ ᴬᴱ
⓸ 𝓥𝓘𝓢𝓐 ᴶᶜᴮ. 🌤
p. 14 BQ e
Meals (dinner only) a la carte 19.90/27.95 **st.** 🛅 13.95 – ⊇ 13.95 – **346 rm**
165.00/245.00 **st.**, 6 suites.

🏨🏨 **The Milestone,** 1-2 Kensington Court, W8 5DL, ℘ (020) 7917 1000, reservations@m
ilestone.redcarnationhotels.com, Fax (020) 7917 1010, 🛵, 🈺 – ▯, 🍽 rm, ▤ 📺 ✆. Ⓜ©
ᴬᴱ ⓸ 𝓥𝓘𝓢𝓐
p. 14 AQ u
Meals a la carte 36.50/50.50 **t.** 🛅 18.50 – ⊇ 17.50 – **52 rm** 250.00/400.00 **s.**, 5 suites.

🏠 **Holland Court** without rest., 31-33 Holland Rd, W14 8HJ, ℘ (020) 7371 1133, reser
vations@hollandcourt.com, Fax (020) 7602 9114, 🌤 – ▯ 🍽 📺. ⓂⓈ ᴬᴱ ⓸ 𝓥𝓘𝓢𝓐. 🌤
22 rm ⊇ 100.00/130.00 **st.**
p. 8 EY e

🍴🍴🍴 **The Tenth** (at Royal Garden H.), 2-24 Kensington High St, W8 4PT, ℘ (020) 7361 1910,
Fax (020) 7361 1921, ≼ Kensington Palace and Gardens – ▤ 🄿. ⓂⓈ ᴬᴱ ⓸ 𝓥𝓘𝓢𝓐 ᴶᶜᴮ
closed Sunday and lunch Saturday – **Meals** (live music Saturday) 21.00 (lunch) and a la carte
30.25/41.75 **st.** 🛅 25.00.
p. 14 AQ e

🍴🍴🍴 **Belvedere,** Holland House, off Abbotsbury Rd, W8 6LU, ℘ (020) 7602 1238, sales@w
hitestarline.org.uk, Fax (020) 7610 4382, 🍽, « 19C orangery in Holland Park » – ▣. Ⓜ©
ᴬᴱ ⓸ 𝓥𝓘𝓢𝓐
p. 8 EY u
Meals 17.95/42.50 and a la carte 30.50/48.00 **t.** 🛅 20.00.

XX **Clarke's,** 124 Kensington Church St, W8 4BH, ☏ (020) 7221 9225, *restaurant@sallyc larke.com, Fax (020) 7229 4564* – ✖ 🖃. 🐼 🖭 ⓞ *VISA* ᴊᴄʙ　　　　　p. 8　EX　c
closed 2 weeks August, 10 days Christmas-New Year, Saturday and Sunday – **Meals** (set menu only at dinner) 28.50/44.00 **st.** 👤 14.00.

XX **Aix en Provence** (at Halcyon H.), 129 Holland Park Ave, W11 3UT, ☏ (020) 7727 7288, *Fax (020) 7229 8516*, 🍽 – 🐼 🖭 ⓞ *VISA* ᴊᴄʙ　　　　　p. 8　EX　u
Meals 15.00 (lunch) and a la carte 33.00/38.75 **t.** 👤 17.95.

XX **Launceston Place,** 1a Launceston Pl, W8 5RL, ☏ (020) 7937 6912, *Fax (020) 7938 2412* – 🖃. 🐼 🖭 ⓞ *VISA*　　　　　p. 14　BR　a
closed 25-26 December, Easter, Saturday lunch, Sunday dinner and Bank Holidays – **Meals** 18.50 (lunch) and a la carte 28.50/36.50 **st.** 👤 14.50.

XX **Zaika,** 1 Kensington High St, W8 5NP, ☏ (020) 7351 7823, *info@zaika-restaurant.co.uk, Fax (020) 7376 4971* – 🖃. *VISA*　　　　　p. 14　AQ　r
🐝 *closed Christmas-New Year, Saturday lunch and Bank Holidays* – **Meals** - Indian - 14.95 (lunch) and a la carte 21.90/40.85 **t.** 👤 14.50
Spec. Dhungar machli tikka (tandoori smoked salmon). Gilafi dum biryani (lamb cooked with aromatic spices). Chocolate samosas.

XX **Memories of China,** 353 Kensington High St, W8 6NW, ☏ (020) 7603 6951, *Fax (020) 7603 0848* – 🖃. 🐼 🖭 ⓞ *VISA* ᴊᴄʙ　　　　　p. 8　EY　v
closed Christmas and Sunday lunch – **Meals** - Chinese - (booking essential) 14.50/32.50 and a la carte 19.25/28.40 **t.** 👤 13.50.

XX **The Terrace,** 33c Holland St, W8 4LX, ☏ (020) 7937 3224, *Fax (020) 7937 3323*, 🍽 – 🖃. 🐼 🖭 ⓞ *VISA*　　　　　p. 8　EY　z
closed 24 December-3 January and Sunday dinner – **Meals** (booking essential) 14.50/17.50 (lunch) and a la carte 28.50/36.00 **t.** 👤 11.50.

XX **The Ark,** 122 Palace Gardens Terr, W8 4RT, ☏ (020) 7229 4024, *Fax (020) 7792 8787*, 🍽 – 🖃. 🐼 🖭 *VISA* ᴊᴄʙ　　　　　p. 16　AZ　r
closed 25-26 December, Sunday dinner and Monday lunch – **Meals** - Italian - 12.50 (lunch) and a la carte 25.00/30.00 **t.** 👤 12.50.

XX **Phoenicia,** 11-13 Abingdon Rd, W8 6AH, ☏ (020) 7937 0120, *Fax (020) 7937 7668* – 🖃. 🐼 🖭 ⓞ *VISA* ᴊᴄʙ　　　　　p. 8　EY　n
closed 25-26 December – **Meals** - Lebanese - 11.95/30.95 and a la carte 20.65/26.80 **t.** 👤 10.90.

X **Kensington Place,** 201 Kensington Church St, W8 7LX, ☏ (020) 7727 3184, *kpr@p lacerestaurants.co.uk, Fax (020) 7229 2025* – 🖃. 🐼 🖭 ⓞ *VISA*　　　　　p. 16　AZ　z
closed 24-26 December and 1 January – **Meals** (booking essential) a la carte 24.50/36.00 **t.** 👤 14.50.

X **Cibo,** 3 Russell Gdns, W14 8EZ, ☏ (020) 7371 6271, *Fax (020) 7602 1371* – 🐼 🖭 ⓞ *VISA* ᴊᴄʙ　　　　　p. 8　EY　o
closed 24 December-2 January, Saturday lunch and Sunday dinner – **Meals** - Italian - a la carte 18.50/40.25 **t.** 👤 11.50.

X **Malabar,** 27 Uxbridge St, W8 7TQ, ☏ (020) 7727 8800, *feedback@malabar-restaurant.co.uk* – 🐼 *VISA*　　　　　p. 16　AZ　e
🍴 **Meals** - Indian - (booking essential) (buffet lunch Sunday) a la carte 16.45/24.95 **st.** 👤 9.25.

North Kensington – ✉ W2/W10/W11 –.

🏠 **Westbourne** without rest., 165 Westbourne Grove, W11 2RS, ☏ (020) 7243 6008, *wh@zoohotels.com, Fax (020) 7229 7201* – ✖ 🖃 📺 ✆. 🐼 🖭 *VISA* ᴊᴄʙ. 🍸　　p. 16　AZ　s
☕ 5.00 **20 rm** 175.00 **st.**

🏠 **Pembridge Court** without rest., 34 Pembridge Gdns, W2 4DX, ☏ (020) 7229 9977, *reservations@pemct.co.uk, Fax (020) 7727 4982*, « Collection of antique clothing » – 🛗 🖃 📺 ✆. 🐼 🖭 ⓞ *VISA*　　　　　p. 16　AZ　n
20 rm ☕ 130.00/200.00 **st.**

🏠 **Abbey Court** without rest., 20 Pembridge Gdns, W2 4DU, ☏ (020) 7221 7518, *info @abbeycourthotel.co.uk, Fax (020) 7792 0858*, « Victorian town house » – ✖ 📺. 🐼 🖭 ⓞ *VISA* ᴊᴄʙ. 🍸　　　　　p. 16　AZ　u
22 rm ☕ 105.00/210.00 **st.**

XXX **Chez Moi,** 1 Addison Ave, Holland Park, W11 4QS, ☏ (020) 7603 8267, *chezmoires@h otmail.com, Fax (020) 7603 3898* – 🖃. 🐼 🖭 ⓞ *VISA*　　　　　p. 8　EX　n
closed Sunday, Saturday and Monday lunch and Bank Holidays – **Meals** - French - 15.00 (lunch) and a la carte 26.75/34.50 **t.** 👤 10.75.

XX **Pharmacy,** 150 Notting Hill Gate, W11 3QG, ☏ (020) 7221 2442, *mail@pharmacylon don.com, Fax (020) 7243 2345* – 🖃. 🐼 🖭 ⓞ *VISA*　　　　　p. 16　AZ　a
closed 25-26 December – **Meals** 17.00 (lunch) and a la carte 23.00/35.50 **t.** 👤 14.00.

XX **Notting Hill Brasserie,** 92 Kensington Park Rd, W11 2PN, ℘ (020) 7229 4481, *no inghill@ firmdale.com,* Fax (020) 7221 1246 – ■. **MO AE VISA** p. 8 EV *closed 24-25 December* – **Meals** 14.00/19.95 (lunch) and a la carte 25.00/33.00 ₪ 15.00.

X **Manor,** 6-8 All Saints Rd, W11 1HH, ℘ (020) 7243 6363, *mail@manorw11.cor* Fax (020) 7243 6360 – ■. **MO AE VISA** p. 4 EU **Meals** (dinner only and lunch Saturday and Sunday) a la carte 21.50/33.00 **t.** ₪ 12.50

South Kensington – ✉ SW5/SW7/W8 –.

🏨 **Millennium Gloucester,** 4-18 Harrington Gdns, SW7 4LH, ℘ (020) 7373 6030, *glo cester@ mill-cop.com,* Fax (020) 7373 0409, **ᵴ** – ⫯, ≒ rm, ■ **TV** ☎ ᵶ, **P** – **ẕ** 650 p. 14 BS *SW7 :* **Meals** - Italian - *(closed Sunday)* (dinner only) a la carte approx. 19.45 – **Bugis Street Meals** - Singaporean - a la carte 7.50/15.97 – ☲ 15.00 – **604 rm** 250.00 **t.,** 6 suites SB.

🏨 **The Pelham,** 15 Cromwell Pl, SW7 2LA, ℘ (020) 7589 8288, *pelham@ firmdale.con* Fax (020) 7584 8444, « Tastefully furnished Victorian town house » – ⫯, ≒ rm, ■ **TV** ☎ **MO AE VISA.** ⚇ p. 14 CS **Kemps :** **Meals** *(closed lunch Saturday and Sunday)* 15.00/20.00 and a la carte 25.00/33.20 **t.** ₪ 13.00 – ☲ 15.50 – **48 rm** 150.00/250.00, 3 suites.

🏨 **Blakes,** 33 Roland Gdns, SW7 3PF, ℘ (020) 7370 6701, *blakes@ easynet.co.uk* Fax (020) 7373 0442, ⚘, « Antique oriental furnishings » – ⫯, ■ rest, **TV** ☎, **MO AE ➀ VISA JCB.** p. 14 BU **Meals** a la carte 51.00/65.00 **t.** ₪ 21.50 – ☲ 23.00 – **40 rm** 165.00/325.00, 5 suites

🏨 **Vanderbilt,** 68-86 Cromwell Rd, SW7 5BT, ℘ (020) 7761 9000, *resvand@ radisson.com* Fax (020) 7761 9003 – ⫯, ≒ rm, ■ **TV** ☎ – **ẕ** 120. **MO AE ➀ VISA JCB.** ⚇ **Meals** 19.50 and a la carte approx. 21.00 **st.** ₪ 15.50 – ☲ 12.00 – **215 rm** 183.00/222.00 **s.** p. 14 BS

🏨 **Harrington Hall,** 5-25 Harrington Gdns, SW7 4JW, ℘ (020) 7396 9696, *harrington ales@ compuserve.com,* Fax (020) 7396 9090, **ᵴ,** ⪪ᵴ – ⫯, ≒ rm, ■ **TV** ☎ – **ẕ** 260 **MO AE VISA JCB.** ⚇ p. 14 BST **Wetherby's :** **Meals** a la carte 23.95/32.20 **st.** ₪ 16.00 – ☲ 14.50 – **200 rm** 185.00/215.00 **st.**

🏨 **Millennium Bailey's,** 140 Gloucester Rd, SW7 4QH, ℘ (020) 7373 6000, *baileys@ m ill-cop.com,* Fax (020) 7370 3760 – ⫯, ≒ rm, ■ **TV** ☎ – **ẕ** 460. **MO AE ➀ VISA JCB.** ⚇ p. 14 BS **Olives :** **Meals** (bar lunch)/dinner a la carte 20.95/30.70 **t.** ₪ 14.75 – ☲ 13.00 – **212 rm** 125.00/723.00 **t.**

🏨 **Rembrandt,** 11 Thurloe Pl, SW7 2RS, ℘ (020) 7589 8100, *rembrandt@ sarova.co.uk,* Fax (020) 7225 3476, **ᵴ,** ⪪ᵴ, ⊠ – ⫯, ≒ rm, ■ rest, **TV** – **ẕ** 200. **MO AE ➀ VISA JCB.** ⚇ p. 15 DS x **Meals** (carving lunch)/dinner a la carte 17.85/25.85 **st.** ₪ 15.00 – ☲ 14.95 – **195 rm** 195.00/240.00 **st.**

🏨 **Jurys Kensington,** 109-113 Queen's Gate, SW7 5LR, ℘ (020) 7589 6300, *kensingto n@ jurydoyle.com,* Fax (020) 7581 1492 – ⫯, ≒ rm, ■ **TV** ☎ – **ẕ** 80. **MO AE ➀ VISA.** ⚇ p. 14 CT i *closed 24-26 December* – **Meals** (bar lunch)/dinner 17.50 **st.** ₪ 12.50 – ☲ 15.00 – **173 rm** 200.00 **st.**

🏨 **Regency,** 100 Queen's Gate, SW7 5AG, ℘ (020) 7373 7878, *info@ regency-london.co.uk,* Fax (020) 7370 5555, **ᵴ,** ⪪ᵴ – ⫯, ≒ rm, ■ **TV** ☎ – **ẕ** 100. **MO AE ➀ VISA JCB.** ⚇ **Meals** *(closed lunch Saturday and Sunday)* (carvery lunch) a la carte 15.00/26.00 **st.** ₪ 12.00 – ☲ 13.00 – **204 rm** 160.00 **s.,** 6 suites. p. 14 CT e

🏨 **Holiday Inn Kensington,** 100 Cromwell Rd, SW7 4ER, ℘ (020) 7373 2222, *info@ h ik.co.uk,* Fax (020) 7373 0559, **ᵴ,** ⪪ᵴ, ⚘ – ⫯, ≒ rm, ■ **TV** ☎ ᵶ – **ẕ** 200. **MO AE ➀ VISA.** ⚇ p. 14 BS e **Meals** *(closed dinner 25 December and Sunday lunch)* a la carte 16.40/30.00 **t.** ₪ 11.95 – ☲ 12.75 – **143 rm** 205.00/225.00 **t.,** 19 suites.

🏨 **Gore,** 189 Queen's Gate, SW7 5EX, ℘ (020) 7584 6601, *sales@ gorehotel.co.uk,* Fax (020) 7589 8127, « Antiques » – ⫯, ≒ rm, **TV** ☎. **MO AE ➀ VISA JCB.** ⚇ **Bistrot 190 :** **Meals** *(closed 24-25 December)* (booking essential) a la carte 19.45/25.20 **t.** ₪ 13.50 (see also **The Restaurant at One Ninety** below) – ☲ 9.50 – **53 rm** 147.00/278.00 **s.** p. 14 BR n

🏨 **John Howard,** 4 Queen's Gate, SW7 5EH, ℘ (020) 7808 8400, *info@ johnhowardhot el.co.uk,* Fax (020) 7808 8402 – ⫯ ■ **TV** ☎. **MO AE ➀ VISA JCB.** ⚇ p. 14 BQ V **Meals** *(closed Sunday)* (dinner only) 15.00 and a la carte 15.25/19.50 **st.** ₪ 6.00 – ☲ 12.50 – **45 rm** 129.00/159.00 **st.,** 7 suites.

🏛 **The Cranley,** 10-12 Bina Gdns, SW5 0LA, ✆ (020) 7373 0123, info@ thecranley.com, Fax (020) 7373 9497, « Antiques » – ▦ 📺 📷 ✆. 📷📷 📧 ⓘ 💳 💳 💳.
Meals (room service only) – ☕ 9.95 – **35 rm** 170.00/242.00 s., 3 suites. p. 14 BT c

🏛 **The Gallery** without rest., 8-10 Queensberry Pl, SW7 2EA, ✆ (020) 7915 0000, gallery@ eeh.co.uk, Fax (020) 7915 4400 – ▦ 📺 ✆. 📷📷 📧 ⓘ 💳 💳 💳. ✎   p.14 CS r
36 rm ☕ 120.00/250.00 s.

🏛 **The Gainsborough** without rest., 7-11 Queensberry Pl, SW7 2DL, ✆ (020) 7957 0000, gainsborough@ eeh.co.uk, Fax (020) 7957 0001 – ▦ 📺. 📷📷 📧 ⓘ 💳 💳 💳. ✎   p. 14 CS s
46 rm ☕ 67.00/145.00 s., 3 suites.

🏠 **Five Sumner Place** without rest., 5 Sumner Pl, SW7 3EE, ✆ (020) 7584 7586, reservations@ sumnerplace.com, Fax (020) 7823 9962 – ▦ ✖ 📺. 📷📷 📧 💳 💳 💳. ✎   p. 14 CT u
13 rm ☕ 99.00/152.00 t.

🏠 **Aster House** without rest., 3 Sumner Pl, SW7 3EE, ✆ (020) 7581 5888, asterhouse@ btinternet.com, Fax (020) 7584 4925, 🌲 – ✖ ▦ 📺 ✆. 📷📷 💳 💳 💳. ✎   p. 14 CT u
14 rm ☕ 99.00/180.00 st.

XXX **Bombay Brasserie,** Courtfield Rd, SW7 4QH, ✆ (020) 7370 4040, bombaybrasserie@ aol.com, Fax (020) 7835 1669, « Raj-style decor, conservatory » – ▦. 📷📷 📧 ⓘ 💳   p. 14 BS a
closed 25-26 December – **Meals** - Indian - (buffet lunch) 16.95 and a la carte 26.50/31.00 t. 🍴 13.25.

XX **The Restaurant at One Ninety** (at Gore H.), 190 Queen's Gate, SW7 5EU, ✆ (020) 7581 5666, Fax (020) 7581 8172 – ▦. 📷📷 📧 ⓘ 💳   p. 14 BR n
closed 24-25 December, Sunday and Monday – **Meals** - Seafood - (booking essential) (dinner only) a la carte 22.85/26.15 t. 🍴 13.50.

XX **Chives,** 204 Fulham Rd, SW10 9PG, ✆ (020) 7551 4747, Fax (020) 7351 7646, 🌲 – 📷📷 📧 ⓘ 💳
Meals (dinner only) a la carte 24.00/27.50 t. 🍴 13.50.   p. 14 BU u

XX **Lundum's,** 119 Old Brompton Rd, SW7 3RN, ✆ (020) 7373 7774, Fax (020) 7373 4472, 🌲 – ▦. 📷📷 📧 ⓘ 💳   p. 14 BT o
closed 23 December-4 January, last 2 weeks August and Sunday dinner – **Meals** - Danish - 15.50/21.50 and a la carte 14.00/33.00 t.

XX **Café Lazeez,** First Floor, 93-95 Old Brompton Rd, SW7 3LD, ✆ (020) 7581 9993, cafe lazeez@ compuserve.com.uk, Fax (020) 7581 8200 – ▦. 📷📷 📧 ⓘ 💳 💳 💳
Meals - North Indian - a la carte 18.75/35.40 t. 🍴 9.95.   p. 14 CT a

XX **Khan's of Kensington,** 3 Harrington Rd, SW7 3ES, ✆ (020) 7581 2900, Fax (020) 7581 2900 – ▦. 📷📷 📧 ⓘ 💳   p. 14 CS e
Meals - Indian - 8.95/18.50 and a la carte 13.95/22.35 🍴 8.50.

XX **Cambio de Tercio,** 163 Old Brompton Rd, SW5 0LJ, ✆ (020) 7244 8970, Fax (020) 7373 8817 – 📷📷 📧 💳   p. 14 BT z
closed 2 weeks Christmas – **Meals** - Spanish - a la carte 24.40/32.00 t. 🍴 14.50.

XX **Pasha,** 1 Gloucester Rd, SW7 4PP, ✆ (020) 7589 7969, Fax (020) 7581 9996 – ▦. 📷📷 📧 ⓘ 💳   p. 14 BR i
closed 24-26 December and Sunday lunch – **Meals** - Moroccan - a la carte 23.25/31.25 t. 🍴 13.50.

XX **Memories of India,** 18 Gloucester Rd, SW7 4RB, ✆ (020) 7589 6450, Fax (020) 7584 4438 – ▦. 📷📷 📧 ⓘ 💳 💳   p. 14 BR s
closed 25 December – **Meals** - Indian - a la carte 13.70/15.85 t. 🍴 9.95.

LAMBETH

Kennington – ✉ SE11.

XX **Kennington Lane,** 205-209 Kennington Lane, SE11 5QS, ✆ (020) 7793 8313, Fax (020) 7793 8323, 🌲 – ▦. 📷📷 📧 ⓘ 💳 💳   p. 10 MZ s
Meals 14.75 and a la carte 20.00/25.00 st. 🍴 14.00.

Lambeth – ✉ SE1.

🏛 **Novotel London Waterloo,** 113 Lambeth Rd, SE1 7LS, ✆ (020) 7793 1010, h1785@ accor-hotels.com, Fax (020) 7793 0202, 🍴, 🏋 – ▦, ✖ rm, ▦ 📺 ✆ ♿ ⛟ – 🔧 40. 📷📷 📧 ⓘ 💳
Meals (bar lunch Saturday and Sunday) 19.95 and a la carte 22.00/34.50 st. 🍴 11.25 – ☕ 12.00 – **185 rm** 135.00/155.00 s., 2 suites – SB.   p. 10 LMY a

Waterloo – ⊠ SE1.

Channel Tunnel : Eurostar information and reservations ℘ (08705) 186186.

London Marriott H. County Hall, SE1 7PB, ℘ (020) 7928 5200, *salesadmin.coun tyhall@marriotthotels.co.uk, Fax (020) 7928 5300,* ≤, ₤₅, ⇌s, ⊠, ⬜ – |⊟|, ⋇ rm, ▤ ⊡ ◖ ♦ – ⚿ 70. ⓦⓈ ⒶⒺ ⓞ 𝘝𝘐𝘚𝘈 𝗝𝗖𝗕. ⋇   p. 10 LY a
County Hall : **Meals** 23.50 (lunch) and a la carte 33.75/37.50 **st.** ₰ 18.00 – ⌁ 18.95 –
195 rm 255.00/385.00 **s.,** 5 suites – SB.

London County Hall Travel Inn Capital, Belvedere Rd, SE1 7PB, ℘ (020) 7902 1600, *Fax (020) 7902 1619* – |⊟| ⋇, ▤ rest, ⊡ ♦. ⓦⓈ ⒶⒺ ⓞ 𝘝𝘐𝘚𝘈. ⋇
Meals (grill rest.) (dinner only) – **313 rm** 74.95 **t.**   p. 10 MX u

Days Inn without rest., 54 Kennington Rd, SE1 7BJ, ℘ (020) 7922 1331, Reservations (Freephone) 0800 0280400, *waterloo@daysinn.co.uk, Fax (020) 7922 1441* – |⊟| ⋇ ⊡ ◖ ♦ – ⚿ 35. ⓦⓈ ⒶⒺ ⓞ 𝘝𝘐𝘚𝘈 𝗝𝗖𝗕. ⋇   p. 10 MY x
162 rm 85.00.

MERTON

Wimbledon – ⊠ SW19.

Cannizaro House ⧖, West Side, Wimbledon Common, SW19 4UE, ℘ (020) 8879 1464 *cannizaro.house@thistle.co.uk, Fax (0870) 3339224,* ≤, « Part 18C country house in Can-nizaro Park », ☞ – |⊟|, ⋇ rm, ⊡ ◖ ▣ – ⚿ 60. ⓦⓈ ⒶⒺ ⓞ 𝘝𝘐𝘚𝘈. ⋇
Meals 27.75/32.75 and a la carte 36.20/48.25 **st.** ₰ 16.00 – ⌁ 15.00 – **43 rm** 200.00/390.00 **st.,** 2 suites – SB.

Light House, 75-77 Ridgway, SW19 4ST, ℘ (020) 8944 6338, *lightrest@aol.com,* *Fax (020) 8946 4440* – ⓦⓈ ⒶⒺ 𝘝𝘐𝘚𝘈
closed Easter and 25-26 December – **Meals** - Italian influences - a la carte 21.45/31.75 **t.** ₰ 11.50.

The Fire Stables, 27-29 Church Rd, SW19 5DQ, ℘ (020) 8946 3197, *thefirestables @punchgroup.co.uk, Fax (020) 8946 1101* – ▤. ⓦⓈ ⒶⒺ ⓞ 𝘝𝘐𝘚𝘈 𝗝𝗖𝗕
closed 25 December – **Meals** a la carte 19.50/25.50 **t.** ₰ 11.00.

SOUTHWARK

Bermondsey – ⊠ SE1.

London Bridge, 8-18 London Bridge St, SE1 9SG, ℘ (020) 7855 2200, *sales@londo n-bridge-hotel.co.uk, Fax (020) 7855 2233,* ₤₅ – |⊟|, ⋇ rm, ▤ ⊡ ◖ ♦ – ⚿ 85. ⓦⓈ ⒶⒺ ⓞ 𝘝𝘐𝘚𝘈 𝗝𝗖𝗕. ⋇   p. 11 PX a
Meals (see *Simply Nico* below) – ⌁ 13.95 – **138 rm** 185.00/195.00 **st.,** 3 suites.

London Tower Bridge Travel Inn Capital, 159 Tower Bridge Rd, SE1 ⊠, ℘ (020) 7940 3700, *Fax (020) 7940 3719* – |⊟|, ⋇ rest, ⊡ ♦ ▣. ⓦⓈ ⒶⒺ ⓞ 𝘝𝘐𝘚𝘈 ⋇
Meals (grill rest.) (dinner only) – **195 rm** 74.95 **t.**   p. 11 PY a

Le Pont de la Tour, 36d Shad Thames, Butlers Wharf, SE1 2YE, ℘ (020) 7403 8403 *Fax (020) 7403 0267,* ≤, ⛱, « Thames-side setting » – ⓦⓈ ⒶⒺ ⓞ 𝘝𝘐𝘚𝘈 𝗝𝗖𝗕   p. 11 PX c
closed 25 December and Saturday lunch – **Meals** 28.50 (lunch) and dinner a la carte approx 57.75 **t.** ₰ 12.95.

Bengal Clipper, Cardamom Building, Shad Thames, Butlers Wharf, SE1 2YR, ℘ (020 7357 9001, *clipper@bengalrestaurants.co.uk, Fax (020) 7357 9002* – ▤. ⓦⓈ ⒶⒺ ⓞ 𝘝𝘐𝘚𝘈 𝗝𝗖𝗕   p. 11 PX e
closed Christmas – **Meals** - Indian - a la carte 19.10/28.45.

Tentazioni, 2 Mill St, Lloyds Wharf, SE1 2BD, ℘ (020) 7237 1100, *tentazioni@aol.com Fax (020) 7237 1100* – ⓦⓈ ⒶⒺ ⓞ 𝘝𝘐𝘚𝘈 𝗝𝗖𝗕
closed first week January, last week August, Sunday and lunch Saturday and Monday and Bank Holidays – **Meals** - Italian - 15.00/19.00 (lunch) and a la carte 25.00/35.00 **t.** ₰ 12.50

Simply Nico (at London Bridge H.), 8-18 London Bridge St, SE1 9SG, ℘ (020) 7407 4536 *simplynico@trpplc.com, Fax (020) 7407 4554* – ▤. ⓦⓈ ⒶⒺ ⓞ 𝘝𝘐𝘚𝘈 𝗝𝗖𝗕   p. 11 PX a
closed Christmas-New Year, lunch Saturday and Sunday and Bank Holidays – **Meals** 14.95 and a la carte 24.00/29.00 **t.** ₰ 12.95.

Blue Print Café, Design Museum, Shad Thames, Butlers Wharf, SE1 2YD, ℘ (020) 7378 7031, *Fax (020) 7357 8810,* ⛱, « Thames-side setting, ≤ Tower Bridge » – ⓦⓈ ⒶⒺ ⓞ 𝘝𝘐𝘚𝘈 𝗝𝗖𝗕   p. 11 PX u
closed 25 December and Sunday dinner – **Meals** 22.50 (lunch) and dinner a la carte 25.00/36.50 **t.** ₰ 15.00.

X **Butlers Wharf Chop House,** 36e Shad Thames, Butlers Wharf, SE1 2YE, ✆ (020) 7403 3403, Fax (020) 7403 3414, 余, « Thames-side setting, ≤ Tower Bridge » – **MO** **AE** **O** **VISA** **JCB** p. 11 PX n
closed Sunday dinner and Saturday lunch – **Meals** 23.75 (lunch) and dinner a la carte 25.25/55.50 **t.**

X **Cantina Del Ponte,** 36c Shad Thames, Butlers Wharf, SE1 2YE, ✆ (020) 7403 5403, Fax (020) 7403 4432, ≤, 余, « Thames-side setting » – **MO** **AE** **O** **VISA** **JCB**
closed 25 December – **Meals** - Italian - 12.50 (lunch) and a la carte 20.65/31.10 **t.** 🖐 13.95. p. 11 PX c

Dulwich – ⊠ SE19.

XX **Belair House,** Gallery Rd, Dulwich Village, SE21 7AB, ✆ (020) 8299 9788, Fax (020) 8299 6793, 余, « Georgian summer house », 🌺 – **P.** **MO** **AE** **O** **VISA**
closed Monday and dinner Sunday – **Meals** 21.95/29.95 **t.** 🖐 16.00.

Rotherhithe – ⊠ SE16.

🏨 **Hilton London Nelson Dock,** 265 Rotherhithe St, Nelson Dock, SE16 5HW, ✆ (020) 7231 1001, Fax (020) 7231 0599, ≤, 余, « Thames-side setting », 🎱, ≘s, 🖳 – 🛗, ¥¤ rm, ■ rest, 📺 📞 🕭 🖪 – 🖾 350 **MO** **AE** **O** **VISA**
closed 21-30 December – **Three Crowns** : **Meals** (dinner only) a la carte 27.95/33.75 **t.** 🖐 13.95 – **Columbia's** : **Meals** - Chinese - (closed Sunday) (dinner only) a la carte approx. 16.95 **st.** 🖐 13.95 – ☲ 13.00 – **364 rm** 165.00 **st.,** 4 suites.

Southwark – ⊠ SE1.

🏨 **Mercure,** 75-79 Southwark St, SE1 0JA, ✆ (020) 7902 0800, h2814@accor-hotels.com, Fax (020) 7902 0810, 🎱 – 🛗 ¥¤ 📺 🕭 🖪 – 🖾 35. **MO** **AE** **O** **VISA** **JCB**
The Loft : **Meals** 18.00/21.00 and a la carte 25.00/28.50 **st.** 🖐 13.00 – ☲ 12.00 – **144 rm** 140.00/170.00 **st.** – SB. p. 11 OX r

🏨 **Express by Holiday Inn** without rest., 103-109 Southwark St, SE1 0JQ, ✆ (020) 7401 2525, stay@expresssouthwark.co.uk, Fax (020) 7401 3322 – 🛗 ¥¤ 📺 📞 🕭 🖪 **MO** **AE** **O** **VISA** ⟁
88 rm 99.00 **st.** p. 11 OX e

XXX **Neat (Restaurant),** (2nd Floor), Oxo Tower Wharf, Barge House St, SE1 9PH, ✆ (020) 7928 5533, eat@neatrestaurant.co.uk, Fax (020) 7928 8644 – 🛗. **MO** **AE** **O** **VISA**
closed 11-25 August, 2 weeks Christmas-New Year, Saturday lunch, Sunday and Bank Holidays – **Meals** 29.00/49.00 **t.** 🖐 19.95. p. 11 NX a

XXX **Oxo Tower,** (8th floor), Oxo Tower Wharf, Barge House St, SE1 9PH, ✆ (020) 7803 3888, oxo.reservations@harveynichols.co.uk, Fax (020) 7803 3838, ≤ London skyline and River Thames, 余 – 🛗 ■. **MO** **AE** **O** **VISA** **JCB** p. 11 NX a
closed 25-26 December and lunch Saturday – **Meals** 28.50 (lunch) and a la carte 25.50/50.00 **t.** 🖐 13.50 (see also **Oxo Tower Brasserie** below).

XX **Neat Brasserie,** (2nd Floor), Oxo Tower Wharf, Barge House St, SE1 9PH, ✆ (020) 7928 4433, eat@neatrestaurant.co.uk, Fax (020) 7928 8644 – **MO** **AE** **O** **VISA**
closed Easter Sunday and Monday, 25-26 December and 1 January – **Meals** 16.95 (lunch) and a la carte approx. 29.50 **t.** 🖐 13.45. p. 11 NX a

X **Oxo Tower Brasserie,** (8th floor), Oxo Tower Wharf, Barge House St, SE1 9PH, ✆ (020) 7803 3888, Fax (020) 7803 3838, ≤ London skyline and River Thames, 余 – 🛗 ■. **MO** **AE** **O** **VISA** **JCB**
closed 25-26 December – **Meals** 25.00 (lunch) and a la carte 27.50/36.00 **t.** 🖐 13.50. p. 11 NX a

X **Cantina Vinopolis (Brasserie),** No 1 Bank End, SE1 9BU, ✆ (020) 7940 8333, cantina@vinopolis.co.uk, Fax (020) 7940 8334 – **MO** **AE** **O** **VISA** p. 11 OX z
closed Sunday dinner and Bank Holidays – **Meals** 26.50 and a la carte 16.85/28.25 **t.** 🖐 14.00.

X **Tate Cafe (7th Floor),** Tate Modern, Bankside, SE1 9TE, ✆ (020) 7401 5020, Fax (020) 7401 5171, ≤ London skyline and River Thames – **MO** **AE** **O** **VISA**
closed 24-26 December – **Meals** (lunch only and dinner Friday-Saturday) a la carte 15.10/21.50 **t.** 🖐 11.95. p. 11 OX s

TOWER HAMLETS

Canary Wharf – ⊠ E14.

🏨 **Four Seasons,** Westferry Circus, E14 8RS, ✆ (020) 7510 1999, caw.reservations@fourseasons.com, Fax (020) 7510 1998, ≤, 余, 🎱, ≘s, 🖳 – 🛗 ¥¤ rm, ■ 📺 📞 🕭 ⟷ – 🖾 200. **MO** **AE** **O** **VISA** **JCB**
Quadrato : **Meals** - Italian - 22.50/35.00 and a la carte **t.** – ☲ 18.50 – **128 rm** 260.00/310.00 **s.,** 14 suites.

UNITED KINGDOM

Circus Apartments without rest., 39 Westferry Circus, E14 8RW, ℰ (020) 7719 7000, res@circusapartments.co.uk, Fax (020) 7719 7001, 🛌, 🈺, 🖾 – 📳 🌿 🗏 🖵 ✆ 🚗.
🖸🖸 🆎 ① VISA. ❄
49 suites 240.00/290.00 s.

Ubon by Nobu, 34 Westferry Circus, E14 8RR, ℰ (020) 7719 7800, Fax (020) 7719 7801, ≼ River Thames and city skyline – 📳 🗏 🖳 🖸🖸 🆎 ① VISA JCB
closed Christmas-New Year, Bank Holidays, Sunday and Saturday lunch – **Meals** - New style Japanese - 19.50/100.00 and a la carte **t**.

East India Docks – ✉ E14.

Travelodge, A 13 Coriander Ave, off East India Dock Rd, E14 2AA, off East India Dock Rd ℰ (020) 7531 9705, Fax (020) 7515 9178, ≼ – 📳, 🌿 rm, 🗏 rest, 🖵 🕭 🖳 🖸🖸 🆎 ① VISA. ❄
Meals (grill rest.) – **232 rm** 79.95 **t**.

Spitalfields – ✉ E1.

Bengal Trader, 44 Artillery Lane, E1 7NA, ℰ (020) 7375 0072, trader@bengalresta urant.com, Fax (020) 7247 1002 – 🗏. 🖸🖸 🆎 ① VISA   p. 7 PU **x**
closed Saturday, Sunday and Bank Holidays – **Meals** - Indian - a la carte 14.25/26.50 **t**. 🛢 8.95.

Whitechapel – ✉ E1.

Cafe Spice Namaste, 16 Prescot St, E1 8AZ, ℰ (020) 7488 9242, Fax (020) 7481 0508 – 🗏. 🖸🖸 🆎 ① VISA JCB
closed 1 week Christmas, Sunday, Saturday lunch and Bank Holidays – **Meals** - Indian - 22.00 and a la carte 21.95/28.45 **t**. 🛢 11.90.

Wapping – ✉ E1.

Wapping Food, Wapping Wall, E1W 3ST, ℰ (020) 7680 2080, wappingfood@wappi ng-wpt.com, Fax (020) 7680 2081, 🍴, « Converted hydraulic power station » – 🖳 🖸🖸 🆎 ① VISA
closed 25-26 December, Good Friday and Sunday dinner – **Meals** a la carte 21.50/27.50 🛢 14.00.

WANDSWORTH

Battersea – ✉ SW8/SW11.

Travelodge without rest., 200 York Rd, SW11 3SA, ℰ (020) 7228 5508, Fax (020) 7978 5898 – 📳 🌿 🖵 🕭 🖳 🖸🖸 🆎 ① VISA JCB. ❄
87 rm 69.95 **t**.

Cafe Spice Namaste, 247 Lavender Hill, SW11 1JW, ℰ (020) 7738 1717, Fax (020) 7738 1666 – 🗏 rest,. 🖸🖸 🆎 ① VISA JCB
closed 25-26 December, 1 January, Monday and Bank Holidays – **Meals** - Indian - (dinner only and buffet Sunday lunch)/dinner 18.00/25.00 and a la carte 19.25/26.25 **t**. 🛢 11.90.

Chada, 208-210 Battersea Park Rd, SW11 4ND, ℰ (020) 7622 2209, Fax (020) 7924 2178 – 🗏. 🖸🖸 🆎 ① VISA JCB – closed Sunday and Bank Holidays – **Meals** - Thai - (dinner only) a la carte 11.55/24.00 **t**. 🛢 11.95.

Metrogusto, 153 Battersea Park Rd, SW8 4BX, ℰ (020) 7720 0204, Fax (020) 7720 0888 – 🖸🖸 VISA JCB
closed 4 days Christmas, Sunday dinner and Bank Holidays – **Meals** - Italian - 19.50 (lunch) and a la carte 22.50/27.00 **t**. 🛢 12.50.

Duke of Cambridge, 228 Battersea Bridge Rd, SW11 3AA, ℰ (020) 7223 5662, Fax (020) 7801 9684, 🍴 – 🖸🖸 VISA
Meals a la carte 14.85/22.35 **t**. 🛢 9.90.

Putney – ✉ SW15.

Putney Bridge, Lower Richmond Rd, SW15 1LB, ℰ (020) 8780 1811, Fax (020) 8780 1211, ≼, « Thames-side setting » – 🗏. 🖸🖸 ① VISA JCB
closed Christmas-New Year, Sunday dinner, Monday and Bank Holidays – **Meals** 22.50/45.00 **t**.
Spec. Trelough duck with turnips, confit of leg and young leaf salad. Scottish lobster roasted with spices and squid ink polenta. Chocolate moelleux.

The Phoenix, Pentlow St, SW15 1LY, ℰ (020) 8780 3131, Fax (020) 8780 1114, 🍴 – 🗏. 🖸🖸 🆎 ① VISA
closed Bank Holidays – **Meals** 12.00/18.50 (lunch) and a la carte 20.50/29.50 **t**. 🛢 10.95.

Coat and Badge, 8 Lacy Rd, SW15 1NL, ℰ (020) 8788 4900, Fax (020) 8780 5733, 🍴 – 🖸🖸 VISA
Meals (bookings not accepted) a la carte 13.85/18.85 **t**. 🛢 9.80.

Southfields – ⊠ SW18.

XX　**Sarkhel's,** 199 Replingham Rd, SW18 5LY, ✆ (020) 8870 1483, *veronica@sarkhels.co.uk,*
　　Fax (020) 8874 6603 – ▤. **MC AE VISA**
　　closed 25-26 December and Monday – **Meals** - Indian - 9.95 (lunch) and a la carte
　　18.35/25.90 **t.** ▯ 10.90.

Wandsworth – ⊠ SW12/SW17/SW18.

X　**Chez Bruce** (Poole), 2 Bellevue Rd, SW17 7EG, ✆ (020) 8672 0114, *Fax (020) 8767 6648*
❀　– ▤. **MC AE VISA JCB**
　　closed 24-26 December and Sunday dinner – **Meals** (booking essential) 21.50/30.00 **t.**
　　Spec. Salad paysanne with deep-fried calves brains. Pot-roast rabbit with pappardelle and
　　creamed wild mushrooms. Glazed plum and almond tart, Jersey cream.

X　**Bombay Bicycle Club,** 95 Nightingale Lane, SW12 8NX, ✆ (020) 8673 6217,
　　Fax (020) 8673 9100 – **MC AE ① VISA**
　　closed 1 week Christmas and Sunday – **Meals** - Indian - (dinner only) a la carte
　　22.00/28.50 **t.** ▯ 11.00.

X　**Ditto,** 55-57 East Hill, SW18 2QE, ✆ (020) 8877 0110, *christian-gilles@ditto1.fsnet.co.uk,*
　　Fax (020) 8875 0110 – **MC VISA JCB**
　　closed 25-26 December, 1 January and Saturday lunch – **Meals** 14.50/18.50 and a la carte
　　19.00/28.45 **t.**

WESTMINSTER (City of)

Bayswater and Maida Vale – ⊠ W2/W9 –.

🏨🏨🏨🏨　**Royal Lancaster,** Lancaster Terr, W2 2TY, ✆ (020) 7262 6737, *sales@royallancaste
　　r.com, Fax (020) 7724 3191,* ≼ – |韓|, 垈 rm, ▤ 🎬 ✆ & 🗗 – 🔏 1400. **MC AE ① VISA**
　　JCB. ❀　　　　　　　　　　　　　　　　　　　　　　　　　　　　　　p. 17 DZ e
　　Park : Meals *(closed Sunday, Saturday lunch and Bank Holidays)* 25.90 **t.** ▯ 20.00 – **Pave-
　　ment Cafe :** Meals a la carte 20.15/18.10 **t.** ▯ 11.90 (see also **Nipa** below) – 🖵 15.00
　　– **394 rm** 230.00/305.00 **s.,** 22 suites.

🏨🏨🏨　**Hilton London Metropole,** Edgware Rd, W2 1JU, ✆ (020) 7402 4141,
　　Fax (020) 7724 8866, ≼, *L₆,* 🛆, 🗔 – |韓|, 垈 rm, ▤ 🎬 ✆ 🗗 – 🔏 2000. **MC AE ①**
　　VISA JCB. ❀　　　　　　　　　　　　　　　　　　　　　　　　　　　p. 5 GU c
　　Meals a la carte 20.00/30.00 **t.** ▯ 16.50 (see also **Aspects** below) – 🖵 17.95 – **1033 rm**
　　220.00/240.00 **s.,** 25 suites – SB.

🏨🏨🏨　**Marriott,** Plaza Parade, NW6 5RP, ✆ (020) 7543 6000, *marriottmaidavale@btinterne
　　t.com, Fax (020) 7543 2100, L₆,* 🛆, 🗔 – |韓|, 垈 rm, ▤ 🎬 ✆ & 🚗 – 🔏 200. **MC**
　　AE ① VISA　　　　　　　　　　　　　　　　　　　　　　　　　　p. 4 FS c
　　Fratelli : Meals - Italian - (dinner only) a la carte 17.00/32.00 **st.** ▯ 15.00 – 🖵 13.50 –
　　207 rm 99.00/145.00 **st.,** 16 suites.

🏨🏨🏨　**The Hempel** 🦢, 31-35 Craven Hill Gdns, W2 3EA, ✆ (020) 7298 9000, *hotel@the-h
　　empel.co.uk, Fax (020) 7402 4666,* « Minimalist », 🖛 – |韓| ▤ 🎬 ✆ & **MC AE ① VISA JCB**.
　　❀　　　　　　　　　　　　　　　　　　　　　　　　　　　　　　　p. 16 CZ a
　　I-Thai : Meals - Thai-Italian - 22.50/45.00 and dinner a la carte 43.00/53.00 **t.** ▯ 18.00
　　– 🖵 15.00 – **41 rm** 265.00/505.00 **s.,** 6 suites.

🏨🏨🏨　**Thistle Hyde Park,** Bayswater Rd, 90-92 Lancaster Gate, W2 3NR, ✆ (020) 7262 2711,
　　Fax (020) 7262 2147 – |韓| 垈 ▤ 🎬 ✆ 🗗 – 🔏 30. **MC AE ① VISA JCB**. ❀p. 16 CZ v
　　Meals (bar lunch Saturday) a la carte 18.95/30.95 **t.** ▯ 15.95 – 🖵 14.95 – **52 rm**
　　160.00/210.00 **st.,** 2 suites – SB.

🏨🏨　**Hilton London Hyde Park,** 129 Bayswater Rd, W2 4RJ, ✆ (020) 7221 2217,
　　Fax (020) 7229 0557 – |韓| 垈 ▤ rest, 🎬 ✆ – 🔏 100. **MC AE ① VISA JCB**. ❀
　　Meals (bar lunch)/dinner 19.95 and a la carte approx. 25.00 **st.** – 🖵 12.95 – **128 rm**
　　130.00/150.00 **s.,** 1 suite – SB.　　　　　　　　　　　　　　　　p. 16 BZ c

🏨🏨　**Ramada Jarvis Hyde Park,** 150 Bayswater Rd, W2 4RT, ✆ (020) 7229 1212, *jihy
　　depark@jarvis.co.uk, Fax (020) 7229 2623* – |韓|, 垈 rm, ▤ 🎬 ✆ – 🔏 100. **MC AE ① VISA**
　　Meals a la carte 17.65/26.50 **t.** ▯ 12.95 – 🖵 10.50 – **212 rm** 155.00/175.00 **st.,** 1 suite
　　– SB.　　　　　　　　　　　　　　　　　　　　　　　　　　　　p. 16 BZ o

🏨🏨　**Mornington** without rest., 12 Lancaster Gate, W2 3LG, ✆ (020) 7262 7361, *london
　　@mornington.co.uk, Fax (020) 7706 1028* – |韓| 垈 🎬 ▤ 🎬 ✆ **MC AE ① VISA JCB**. ❀
　　closed 23-27 December – **66 rm** 🖵 120.00/160.00 **st.**　　　　　p. 17 DZ s

🏨🏨　**Colonnade Town House** without rest., 2 Warrington Cres, W9 1ER, ✆ (020)
　　7286 1052, *rescolonnade@etontownhouse.com, Fax (020) 7286 1057,* « Victorian
　　town house » – |韓| 垈 ▤ 🎬 ✆. **MC AE ① VISA JCB**　　　　　　　　p. 4 FU e
　　closed 23-27 December – **40 rm** 🖵 147.00/179.00 **s.,** 3 suites.

UNITED KINGDOM

🏨 **Commodore,** 50 Lancaster Gate, W2 3NA, ℰ (020) 7402 5291, *reservations@comm odore-hotel.com, Fax (020) 7262 1088* – |‡|, ❧ rm, 📺 ✆ ⓂⒸ ᴀᴇ ① VISA ᴊᴄʙ 쏗
Meals a la carte 16.50/24.00 **st.** ⓐ 9.00 – 🖙 12.50 – **76 rm** 115.00/150.00 **st.**,
3 suites.   p. 16 CZ r

🏨 **Miller's** without rest., 111A Westbourne Grove, W2 4UW, ℰ (020) 7243 1024, *enquir ies@millersuk.com, Fax (020) 7243 1064,* « Antique furnishings » – 📺 ✆ ⓂⒸ ᴀᴇ ① VISA
ᴊᴄʙ 쏗   p. 16 AZ a
🖙 12.50 **6 rm** 160.00/188.00 **s.**

XX **Aspects** (at Hilton London Metropole H.), Edgware Rd, W2 1JU, ℰ (020) 7402 4141,
Fax (020) 7724 8866, ≼ London – 🔳, ⓂⒸ ᴀᴇ ① VISA ᴊᴄʙ   p. 5 GU c
closed Sunday dinner – **Meals** a la carte 30.00/50.00 **t.**

XX **Amandier,** 26 Sussex Pl, W2 2TH, ℰ (020) 7262 6073, *Fax (020) 7723 8395* – 🔳, ⓂⒸ
ᴀᴇ ① VISA ᴊᴄʙ   p. 17 DZ r
closed 26 December-3 January, Sunday, Saturday lunch and Bank Holidays – **Meals** - French
- 25.50/31.50 **t.** ⓐ 12.95 (see also ***Bistro Daniel*** below).

XX **Nipa** (at Royal Lancaster H.), Lancaster Terr., W2 2TY, ℰ (020) 7262 6737,
Fax (020) 7724 3191 – 🔳 📭, ⓂⒸ ᴀᴇ ① VISA ᴊᴄʙ   p. 17 DZ e
Meals - Thai - 24.50/27.70 and a la carte 23.80/36.10 **t.** ⓐ 20.00.

XX **Al San Vincenzo,** 30 Connaught St, W2 2AF, ℰ (020) 7262 9623 – ⓂⒸ VISA
closed Saturday lunch and Sunday – **Meals** - Italian - (booking essential) 27.50/33.50 **t.**
ⓐ 15.00.   p. 17 EZ o

XX **Poons,** Unit 205, Whiteleys, Queensway, W2 4YN, ℰ (020) 7792 2884,
Fax (020) 8458 0968 – 🔳, ⓂⒸ ᴀᴇ ① VISA ᴊᴄʙ   p. 16 BZ x
closed 24-26 December – **Meals** - Chinese - 16.00/22.00 and a la carte 22.00/43.00 **t.**
ⓐ 11.00.

XX **Jason's,** Blomfield Rd, Little Venice, W9 2PD, ℰ (020) 7286 6752, *enquiries@jasons.co.uk,
Fax (020) 7266 4332,* 🞉, « Canalside setting » – ⓂⒸ ᴀᴇ ① VISA ᴊᴄʙ   p. 4 FU c
closed 25 December-1 January and Sunday dinner – **Meals** - Seafood - 21.50 and a la carte
24.15/50.45 **t.** ⓐ 11.50.

X **Assaggi,** 39 Chepstow Pl, (above Chepstow pub), W2 4TS, ℰ (020) 7792 5501 – ⓂⒸ ᴀᴇ
① VISA ᴊᴄʙ   p. 16 AZ c
closed 2 weeks Christmas, Sunday and Bank Holidays – **Meals** - Italian - a la carte
29.45/35.65 **t.** ⓐ 10.95.

X **The Vale,** 99 Chippenham Rd, W9 2AB, ℰ (020) 7266 0990, *Fax (020) 7286 7224* – 🔳
🖴 ⓂⒸ ① VISA ᴊᴄʙ   p. 4 ET z
closed Christmas and lunch Monday and Saturday – **Meals** 12.00/15.00 and a la carte
19.25/23.00 **t.** ⓐ 10.50.

X **Ginger,** 115 Westbourne Grove, W2 4UP, ℰ (020) 7908 1990, *info@gingerrestaurar.
t.co.uk, Fax (020) 7908 1991* – 🔳, ⓂⒸ ᴀᴇ VISA ᴊᴄʙ   p. 16 AZ v
closed 25-26 December – **Meals** - Bangladeshi - a la carte 18.50/22.50 **t.** ⓐ 12.00.

X **L'Accento,** 16 Garway Rd, W2 4NH, ℰ (020) 7243 2201, *laccentorest@aol.com,
Fax (020) 7243 2201,* 🞉 – ⓂⒸ VISA ᴊᴄʙ   p. 16 BZ a
closed 25 December and lunch Sunday – **Meals** - Italian - 12.50 and a la carte 21.50/28.00 **t.**
ⓐ 10.50.

🍴 **The Chepstow,** 39 Chepstow Pl, W2 4TS, ℰ (020) 7229 0323, *Fax (020) 7229 0323*
– ⓂⒸ ① VISA   p. 16 AZ
Meals a la carte 25.25/31.45 **st.** ⓐ 11.50.

Belgravia – ✉ SW1 -.

🏨 **The Lanesborough,** Hyde Park Corner, SW1X 7TA, ℰ (020) 7259 5599, *reservatio
ns@lanesborough.co.uk, Fax (020) 7259 5606,* 🇮ᴃ – |‡|, ❧ rm, 🔳 📺 ✆ ♿ 📭 – 🏛 90.
ⓂⒸ ᴀᴇ ① VISA ᴊᴄʙ 쏗   p. 9 IY a
The Conservatory : Meals 15.00/44.00 and a la carte 39.50/59.50 **st.** ⓐ 19.50 –
🖙 23.50 – **86 rm** 275.00/460.00 **s.**, 9 suites.

🏨 **The Berkeley,** Wilton Pl, SW1X 7RL, ℰ (020) 7235 6000, *info@the-berkeley.co.uk,
Fax (020) 7235 4330,* « Rooftop 🏊 », 🇮ᴃ, ≋ – |‡|, ❧ rm, 🔳 📺 ✆ ⇦ – 🏛 220. ⓂⒸ
ᴀᴇ ① VISA ᴊᴄʙ 쏗   p. 15 FQ e
Meals (see ***La Tante Claire*** and ***Vong*** below) – 🖙 21.50 – **140 rm** 320.00/540.00 **st.**,
28 suites.

🏨 **The Halkin,** 5 Halkin St, SW1X 7DJ, ℰ (020) 7333 1000, *res@halkin.co.uk,
Fax (020) 7333 1100,* « Contemporary interior design » – |‡|, ❧ rm, 🔳 📺 ✆ 📭 ⓂⒸ ᴀᴇ
① VISA ᴊᴄʙ 쏗   p. 16 AV a
***Nahm* : Meals** - Thai - *(closed lunch Saturday and Sunday)* (booking essential)
25.00/55.00 **t.** ⓐ 18.00 – 🖙 18.00 – **37 rm** 295.00 **s.**, 4 suites
Spec. Geng jeut gradtai (rabbit and mushroom soup). Pla ling wua tort (lemon sole). Geng
gari bpet (duck curry).

678

Sheraton Belgravia, 20 Chesham Pl, SW1X 8HQ, ℰ (020) 7235 6040, *reservations centrallondon@sheraton.com*, Fax (020) 7201 1926 – |≡|, ⇔ rm, 🖾 📺 📞 ₺ 🖪 – 🔬 25. 🕮 🖎 🕮 ⓪ 𝘝𝘐𝘚𝘈 🖎.
p. 15 FR u
The Mulberry : Meals 15.00/25.00 and a la carte 27.95/36.00 **t.** ₰ 18.00 – ⊊ 17.50 – 82 rm 280.00/300.00 s., 7 suites.

The Lowndes, 21 Lowndes St, SW1X 9ES, ℰ (020) 7823 1234, *lowndes@hyattintl.com*, Fax (020) 7235 1154, ⇬ – |≡|, ⇔ rm, 🖾 📺 📞 🖪 – 🔬 25. 🕮 🖎 🕮 ⓪ 𝘝𝘐𝘚𝘈 🖎.
Brasserie 21 : Meals 16.50/20.00 and a la carte 25.00/39.00 **st.** ₰ 17.50 – ⊊ 16.50 – 77 rm 250.00/280.00 s., 1 suite.
p. 15 FR i

Diplomat without rest., 2 Chesham St, SW1X 8DT, ℰ (020) 7235 1544, *diplomat.hotel@btinternet.co.uk*, Fax (020) 7259 6153 – |≡| 📺. 🕮 🖎 🕮 ⓪ 𝘝𝘐𝘚𝘈 🖎.
26 rm ⊊ 95.00/170.00 **st.**
p. 15 FR a

La Tante Claire (Koffmann) (at The Berkeley H.), Wilton Pl, SW1X 7RL, ℰ (020) 7823 2003, Fax (020) 7823 2001 – 🖾. 🕮 🖎 🕮 ⓪ 𝘝𝘐𝘚𝘈 🖎.
p. 15 FQ e
closed 22 December - 6 January, Saturday lunch, Sunday and Bank Holidays – **Meals** - French - (booking essential) 28.00 (lunch) and a la carte 62.00/77.00 **t.** ₰ 21.00
Spec. Foie gras poêlé, sauce cappuccino. Pied de cochon. Soufflé à la pistache.

Zafferano, 15 Lowndes St, SW1X 9EY, ℰ (020) 7235 5800, Fax (020) 7235 1971 – 🖾. 🕮 🖎 𝘝𝘐𝘚𝘈
p. 15 FR i
Meals - Italian - 21.50/35.50 **t.** ₰ 12.50
Spec. Pan-fried sea bass with sun-dried tomato crust. Rabbit with polenta and Parma ham. Pasta ribbons with broad beans and rocket.

Vong (at The Berkeley H.), Wilton Pl, SW1X 7RL, ℰ (020) 7235 1010, Fax (020) 7235 1011 – 🖾. 🕮 🖎 🕮 ⓪ 𝘝𝘐𝘚𝘈 🖎.
p. 15 FQ e
closed Christmas and Bank Holidays – **Meals** - French-Thai - (booking essential) 20.00 (lunch) and a la carte 20.00/70.00 **t.**

Mango Tree, 46 Grosvenor Pl, SW1X 7EQ, ℰ (020) 7823 1888, Fax (020) 7838 9275 – 🖾. 🕮 🖎 𝘝𝘐𝘚𝘈
p. 16 AX a
closed 25-26 December and Saturday lunch – **Meals** - Thai - 28.00/38.00 and a la carte 26.00/34.00 **t.** ₰ 15.00.

Noura Brasserie, 16 Hobart Pl, SW1W 0HH, ℰ (020) 7235 9444, Fax (020) 7235 9244 – 🖾. 🕮 🖎 🕮 ⓪ 𝘝𝘐𝘚𝘈
p. 16 AX n
Meals - Lebanese - 12.50/28.50 and a la carte 20.50/26.25 **t.**

Hyde Park and Knightsbridge – ⊠ SW1/SW7 –.

Mandarin Oriental Hyde Park, 66 Knightsbridge, SW1X 7LA, ℰ (020) 7235 2000, Fax (020) 7235 4552, ≤, 𝘓𝘴, ⇌ – |≡|, ⇔ rm, 🖾 📺 📞 ₺ – 🔬 220. 🕮 🖎 🕮 ⓪ 𝘝𝘐𝘚𝘈 🖎. ⚘
p. 15 FQ x
The Park : Meals 19.00 (lunch) and a la carte 25.00/42.50 **t.** ₰ 18.50 (see also **Foliage** below) – ⊊ 19.00 – 175 rm 255.00/495.00, 25 suites – SB.

Knightsbridge Green without rest., 159 Knightsbridge, SW1X 7PD, ℰ (020) 7584 6274, *thekghotel@aol.com*, Fax (020) 7225 1635 – |≡| ⇔ 🖾 📺. 🕮 🖎 🕮 ⓪ 𝘝𝘐𝘚𝘈. ⚘
⊊ 10.50 – 16 rm 110.00/145.00 **st.**, 12 suites 170.00 **st.**
p. 15 EQ z

Foliage (at Mandarin Oriental Hyde Park H.), 66 Knightsbridge, SW1X 7LA, ℰ (020) 7201 3723, Fax (020) 7235 4552 – 🖾. 🕮 🖎 🕮 ⓪ 𝘝𝘐𝘚𝘈
p. 15 FQ x
Meals 24.00/42.50 **t.** ₰ 17.50
Spec. Poached lobster, crab vinaigrette and caviar dressing. Bresse pigeon, braised cabbage, celeriac bouillon. Iced coconut parfait, bitter chocolate sorbet.

Isola, 145 Knightsbridge, SW1X 7PA, ℰ (020) 7838 1044, Fax (020) 7838 1099 – 🖾. 🕮 🖎 𝘝𝘐𝘚𝘈
p. 15 EQ a
Meals - Italian - 19.50 (lunch) and a la carte 29.00/39.00 **t.** ₰ 13.50.

Mr Chow, 151 Knightsbridge, SW1X 7PA, ℰ (020) 7589 7347, Fax (020) 7584 5780 – 🖾. 🕮 🖎 🕮 ⓪ 𝘝𝘐𝘚𝘈 🖎.
p. 15 EQ a
closed 24-26 December, 1 January and Easter Monday – **Meals** - Chinese - 15.00 (lunch) and a la carte 34.00/40.00 **t.** ₰ 13.50.

Mayfair – ⊠ W1 –.

Dorchester, Park Lane, W1A 2HJ, ℰ (020) 7629 8888, *reservations@dorchesterhotel.com*, Fax (020) 7409 0114, 𝘓𝘴, ⇌ – |≡|, ⇔ rm, 🖾 📺 📞 ₺ ⇌ – 🔬 550. 🕮 🖎 ⓪ 𝘝𝘐𝘚𝘈 🖎.
p. 12 BN a
Meals (see **The Oriental** and **Grill Room** below) – ⊊ 23.00 – 201 rm 305.00/375.00 s., 49 suites – SB.

Claridge's, Brook St, W1A 2JQ, ℰ (020) 7629 8860, *info@claridges.co.uk*, Fax (020) 7499 2210, « Art Deco », 𝘓𝘴 – |≡|, ⇔ rm, 🖾 📺 📞 ₺ – 🔬 200. 🕮 🖎 🕮 ⓪ 𝘝𝘐𝘚𝘈 🖎.
p. 12 BL c
Gordon Ramsay at Claridge's (ℰ (020) 7499 0099) : Meals (booking essential) 21.00/38.00 **t.** – 143 rm 345.00/420.00, 60 suites.

679

Le Meridien Piccadilly, 21 Piccadilly, W1V 0BH, ✆ (0870) 400 8400, *Impiccres@le meridien-hotels.com*, Fax (020) 7437 3574, *f͞ŏ*, ⇄s, 🔲, squash – |𝄐|, ↝ rm, 🔲 📺 ✆ 😓 – 🛴 250. 🔞 🖭 ⓪ *VISA* J͞C͞B. ⸼
p. 13 EM a
Meals (see *The Oak Room Marco Pierre White* and *Terrace* below) – ⊆ 18.50 – **248 rm** 295.00/315.00, 18 suites.

Le Meridien Grosvenor House, Park Lane, W1A 3AA, ✆ (020) 7499 6363, *grosv enor.reservations@ forte-hotels.com*, Fax (020) 7493 3341, *f͞ŏ*, ⇄s, 🔲 – |𝄐|, ↝ rm, 🔲 📺 ✆ 😓 😓 ⇌ 🛴 1500. 🔞 🖭 ⓪ *VISA* J͞C͞B. ⸼
p. 12 AM a
La Terrazza : Meals - Italian influences - a la carte 34.00/45.50 t. ꭚ 18.50 (see also *chez-nico* below) – ⊆ 18.50 – **373 rm** 396.00/417.00 s., 74 suites.

Four Seasons, Hamilton Pl, Park Lane, W1A 1AZ, ✆ (020) 7499 0888, *fsn.london@f ourseasons.com*, Fax (020) 7493 1895, *f͞ŏ* – |𝄐|, ↝ rm, 🔲 📺 ✆ 😓 ⇌ 🛴 500. 🔞 🖭 ⓪ *VISA* J͞C͞B. ⸼
p. 12 BP a
Lanes : Meals 36.00/33.50 and a la carte 33.75/49.75 st. ꭚ 16.00 – ⊆ 21.00 – **185 rm** 285.00/340.00 s., 35 suites.

London Hilton, 22 Park Lane, W1Y 4BE, ✆ (020) 7493 8000, *reservations@ hilton.com*, Fax (020) 7208 4146, « Panoramic ≼ of London », *f͞ŏ*, ⇄s – |𝄐|, ↝ rm, 🔲 📺 ✆ 😓 – 🛴 1000. 🔞 🖭 ⓪ *VISA* J͞C͞B. ⸼
p. 12 BP a
Trader Vics (✆ (020) 7208 4113) : Meals (dinner only) 30.00 and a la carte 24.50/45.50 t. ꭚ 21.00 – *Park Brasserie* : Meals 23.50/26.50 and a la carte 25.00/44.50 t. ꭚ 17.50 (see also *Windows* below) – ⊆ 24.50 – **396 rm** 325.00 s., 53 suites – SB.

Connaught, Carlos Pl, W1K 2AL, ✆ (020) 7499 7070, *info@ theconnaught.co.uk*, ✿ Fax (020) 7495 3262, *f͞ŏ* – |𝄐| 🔲 📺 ✆ 😓 🔞 🖭 ⓪ *VISA*. ⸼
p. 12 BM e
The Restaurant : Meals (booking essential) 28.50/58.00 and a la carte 45.00/80.00 t. ꭚ 23.00 – *Grill Room* : Meals (closed Sunday and Monday) (booking essential) 28.50/58.00 and a la carte 45.00/80.00 t. – ⊆ 23.00 – **68 rm** 345.00/425.00 s., 23 suites – SB
Spec. Terrine Connaught. Homard d'Ecosse, "Reine Elizabeth". Sole jubilee.

Brown's, Albemarle St, W1S 4BP, ✆ (020) 7493 6020, *brownshotel@ brownshotel.com*, Fax (020) 7493 9381, *f͞ŏ* – |𝄐|, ↝ rm, 🔲 📺 ✆ – 🛴 70. 🔞 🖭 ⓪ *VISA* J͞C͞B. ⸼
p. 13 DM e
Meals (see *1837* below) – ⊆ 20.00 – **112 rm** 290.00/320.00, 6 suites.

Inter-Continental, 1 Hamilton Pl, Hyde Park Corner, W1J 7QY, ✆ (020) 7409 3131 *london@ interconti.com*, Fax (020) 7493 3476, ≼, *f͞ŏ*, ⇄s – |𝄐|, ↝ rm, 🔲 📺 ✆ 😓 ⇌ – 🛴 1000. 🔞 🖭 ⓪ *VISA* J͞C͞B. ⸼
p. 12 BP c
Meals 25.10/29.50 and a la carte ꭚ 13.00 (see also *Le Soufflé* below) – ⊆ 22.00 – **418 rm** 370.00 s., 40 suites.

Millennium Mayfair, Grosvenor Sq, W1K 2HP, ✆ (020) 7629 9400, *sales.mayfair@ m ill-cop.com*, Fax (020) 7629 7736, *f͞ŏ* – |𝄐|, ↝ rm, 🔲 📺 ✆ 😓 – 🛴 770. 🔞 🖭 ⓪ *VISA* J͞C͞B. ⸼
p. 12 BM x
Meals (closed Saturday lunch) 18.50/21.50 and a la carte 28.50/39.50 t. ꭚ 24.50 (see also *Shogun* below) – ⊆ 17.50 – **342 rm** 190.00/275.00 s., 6 suites.

May Fair Inter-Continental, Stratton St, W1A 2AN, ✆ (020) 7629 7777, *mayfai @ interconti.com*, Fax (020) 7629 1459, *f͞ŏ*, ⇄s, 🔲 – |𝄐|, ↝ rm, 🔲 📺 ✆ 😓 – 🛴 300. 🔞 🖭 ⓪ *VISA* J͞C͞B. ⸼
p. 13 DN a
Opus 70 : Meals (closed lunch August, Saturday and Bank Holidays) 20.00 (lunch) and a la carte 24.00/38.50 t. ꭚ 18.00 – *May Fair Café* (✆ (020) 7915 2842) : Meals (lunch only) 17.00 and a la carte 17.50/20.50 t. ꭚ 17.00 – ⊆ 19.50 – **278 rm** 315.00/375.00, 12 suite – SB.

Park Lane, Piccadilly, W1Y 8BX, ✆ (020) 7499 6321, *reservationscentrallondon@ sh raton.com*, Fax (020) 7499 1965, *f͞ŏ* – |𝄐|, ↝ rm, 🔲 📺 ✆ 😓 ⇌ – 🛴 300. 🔞 🖭 ⓪ *VISA* J͞C͞B. ⸼
p. 12 CP e
Citrus (✆ (020) 7290 7364) : Meals 15.00/24.00 and a la carte 22.75/29.00 st. ꭚ 15.00 – ⊆ 19.95 – **287 rm** 260.00/280.00 s., 20 suites.

47 Park Street, 47 Park St, W1K 7EB, ✆ (020) 7491 7282, *reservations@ 47parks reet.com*, Fax (020) 7491 7281 – |𝄐| 🔲 📺 ✆ 😓 🔞 🖭 ⓪ *VISA* J͞C͞B. ⸼ p. 12 AM
Meals (room service) (see also *Le Gavroche* below) – ⊆ 24.50, **52 suite** 300.00/655.00 s.

Westbury, Bond St, W1S 2YF, ✆ (020) 7629 7755, *westburyhotel@ compuserve.com* Fax (020) 7495 1163 – |𝄐|, ↝ rm, 🔲 📺 ✆ 😓 – 🛴 120. 🔞 🖭 ⓪ *VISA* J͞C͞B. ⸼
Meals 16.50/21.50 and a la carte st. ꭚ 16.00 – ⊆ 16.75 – **233 rm** 225.00/290.00 s., 2 suites – SB. p. 13 DM

The Metropolitan, Old Park Lane, W1Y 4LB, ✆ (020) 7447 1000, *sales@ metropol an.co.uk*, Fax (020) 7447 1100, ≼, « Contemporary interior design », *f͞ŏ* – ↝ rm, 🔲 📺 ✆ ⇌. 🔞 🖭 ⓪ *VISA* J͞C͞B. ⸼
p. 12 BP
Meals (see *Nobu* below) – ⊆ 20.00 – **152 rm** 240.00/545.00 s., 3 suites.

🏛 **Athenaeum,** 116 Piccadilly, W15 7BS, ☎ (020) 7499 3464, *foxs@athenaeumhotel.com*, Fax *(020) 7493 1860*, ₤₅, ⇔ – |‡|, ⬥ rm, ▤ TV ✆ – ⚿ 55. ⬀ ⬀ AE ① VISA ⬥
Bulloch's at 116 : Meals *(closed lunch Saturday and Sunday)* 17.00 (lunch) and a la carte approx. 33.40 **st.** ⓐ 17.00 – ☲ 18.50 – **124 rm** 265.00/340.00 **s.**, 33 suites.
p. 12 CP s

🏛 **London Marriott Grosvenor Square,** Duke St, Grosvenor Sq, W1K 6JP, ☎ (020) 7493 1232, *reservations@londonmarriott.co.uk*, Fax *(020) 7491 3201*, ₤₅ – |‡|, ⬥ rm, ▤ TV ✆ – ⚿ 600. ⬀ ⬀ AE ① VISA ⬥
p. 12 BL a
Diplomat : Meals *(closed lunch Saturday and Bank Holidays)* a la carte 23.10/32.00 **st.** ⓐ 17.50 – ☲ 15.95 – **209 rm** 180.00/230.00, 12 suites.

🏛 **Washington Mayfair,** 5-7 Curzon St, W1J 5HE, ☎ (020) 7499 7000, *sales@washin gton-mayfair.co.uk*, Fax *(020) 7495 6172* – |‡|, ⬥ rm, ▤ TV ✆ – ⚿ 90. ⬀ ⬀ AE ① VISA ⬅⬀ⓑ. ⬥
p. 12 CN s
Meals 14.95 and a la carte 22.90/40.85 ⓐ 12.95 – ☲ 13.95 – **168 rm** 195.00/220.00 **s.**, 5 suites.

🏛 **Chesterfield,** 35 Charles St, W1J 5EB, ☎ (020) 7491 2622, *reservations@chesterfie ld.redcarnationhotels.com*, Fax *(020) 7491 4793* – |‡|, ⬥ rm, ▤ TV ✆ – ⚿ 110. ⬀ ⬀ AE ① VISA ⬅⬀ⓑ
p. 12 CN c
Meals *(closed Saturday lunch)* 15.50 and a la carte 25.90/37.95 **t.** ⓐ 15.50 – ☲ 16.50 – **106 rm** 195.00/250.00 **s.**, 4 suites.

🏛 **Holiday Inn Mayfair,** 3 Berkeley St, W1J 8NE, ☎ (020) 7493 8282, *himayfair@holi dayinnmayfair.co.uk*, Fax *(020) 7629 2827*, ₤₅ – |‡|, ⬥ rm, ▤ TV ✆ – ⚿ 60. ⬀ ⬀ AE ① VISA ⬥
p. 13 DN r
Meals a la carte 23.00/37.75 **st.** ⓐ 12.95 – ☲ 14.95 – **184 rm** 249.00 **st.**, 2 suites.

🏨 **Flemings,** Half Moon St, W1J 7BB, ☎ (020) 7499 2964, *reservations@flemings-mayf air.co.uk*, Fax *(020) 7629 4063* – |‡|, ⬥ rm, ▤ TV ✆ – ⚿ 55. ⬀ ⬀ AE ① VISA ⬅⬀ⓑ. ⬥
Meals 15.00/26.50 and a la carte 22.50/31.50 **st.** ⓐ 18.00 – ☲ 17.00 – **120 rm** 169.00/199.00 **s.**, 10 suites.
p. 12 CN z

🏨 **No 5 Maddox St** without rest., 5 Maddox St, W1S 2QD, ☎ (020) 7647 0200, *no5m addoxst@living-rooms.co.uk*, Fax *(020) 7647 0300*, « Contemporary interior » – ▤ TV ✆. ☲ 12.00 **s.**, **12 suites** 230.00/575.00.
p. 13 DK a

🏨 **Hilton London Green Park,** Half Moon St, W1Y 8BP, ☎ (020) 7629 7522, *grccnp arkhotel@btinternet.com*, Fax *(020) 7491 8971* – |‡| ⬥, ▤ rest, TV – ⚿ 130. ⬀ ⬀ AE ① VISA ⬅⬀ⓑ
p. 12 CN a
Meals *(closed Sunday lunch)* a la carte 30.95/38.25 **st.** ⓐ 15.90 – ☲ 16.50 – **161 rm** 160.00/210.00 **s.** – SB.

🏨 **Hilton London Mews,** 2 Stanhope Row, W1Y 7HE, ☎ (020) 7493 7222, *lonmwtw @hilton.com*, Fax *(020) 7629 9423* – |‡| ⬥ ▤ TV – ⚿ 50. ⬀ ⬀ AE ① VISA
Meals *(dinner only)* a la carte 21.70/25.40 **st.** ⓐ 15.90 – ☲ 14.00 – **71 rm** 155.00/175.00 **s.** – SB.
p. 12 BP u

XXXXX ✿ **The Oak Room Marco Pierre White** (at Le Meridien Piccadilly H.), 21 Piccadilly, W1V 0BH, ☎ (020) 7437 0202, Fax *(020) 7851 3141* – ▤. ⬀ ⬀ AE ① VISA ⬅⬀ⓑ *closed Christmas-New Year, Saturday lunch and Sunday* – **Meals** *(booking essential)* 15.00//75.00 **t.** ⓐ 20.00
p. 13 EM a
Spec. Panaché of langoustine and pork belly. Grilled sea bass on the bone with beurre noisette. Feuillantine of raspberries.

XXXXX ✿ **cheznico** (at Le Meridien Grosvenor House H.), 90 Park Lane, W1K 7TN, ☎ (020) 7409 1290, *cheznico@globalnet.co.uk*, Fax *(020) 7355 4877* – ▤. ⬀ ⬀ AE ① VISA *closed 10 days Christmas, 4 days Easter, Sunday, Saturday lunch and Bank Holidays* – **Meals** *(booking essential)* 43.00/70.00 **t.** ⓐ 20.00
p. 12 AM z
Spec. Seared foie gras with brioche and oranges. John Dory with provençal vegetables. Chocolate tart with pistachio sauce.

XXXX ✿✿ **Le Gavroche** (Roux), 43 Upper Brook St, W1K 7QR, ☎ (020) 7408 0881, *gavroche@c wcom.net*, Fax *(020) 7409 0939* – ▤. ⬀ ⬀ AE ① VISA ⬅⬀ⓑ
p. 12 AM c
closed Christmas-New Year, Sunday, Saturday lunch and Bank Holidays – **Meals** - French - *(booking essential)* 40.00 (lunch) and a la carte 56.50/94.20 **t.** ⓐ 25.00
Spec. Foie gras chaud et pastilla de canard à la cannelle. Râble de lapin et galette au parmesan. Le palet au chocolat amer et praline croustillant.

XXXX **The Oriental** (at Dorchester H.), Park Lane, W1A 2HJ, ☎ (020) 7317 6328, Fax *(020) 7317 6464* – ▤. ⬀ ⬀ AE ① VISA ⬅⬀ⓑ
p. 12 BN a
closed August, 25 December, Saturday lunch and Sunday – **Meals** - Chinese (Canton) - 25.00/43.00 and a la carte 43.50/66.00 **st.** ⓐ 23.50.

XXXX **Grill Room** (at Dorchester H.), Park Lane, W1A 2HJ, ☎ (020) 7317 6336, Fax *(020) 7317 6464* – ▤. ⬀ ⬀ AE ① VISA ⬅⬀ⓑ
p. 12 BN a
Meals - English - 29.50/39.50 and a la carte 41.00/62.00 **st.** ⓐ 23.50.

XXXX **1837** (at Brown's H.), Albemarle St, W1S 4BP, ℰ (020) 7408 1837, *brownshotel@ukb usiness.com*, Fax *(020) 7493 9381* – 🖃. ⬛⬤ AE ⬤ VISA JCB   p. 13 DM **e**
closed Saturday lunch and Sunday – **Meals** 25.00/37.00 and a la carte 35.50/50.50 **t.**
🍸 19.00.

XXXX **Windows** (at London Hilton H.), 22 Park Lane, W1Y 4BE, ℰ (020) 7208 4021, Fax *(020) 7208 4147*, « ✳ London » – 🖃. ⬛⬤ AE ⬤ VISA JCB   p. 12 BP **e**
closed Saturday lunch and Sunday dinner – **Meals** 42.50 (lunch) and dinner a la carte 43.00/64.00 **t.** 🍸 21.00.

XXX **The Square** (Howard), 6-10 Bruton St, W1J 6PU, ℰ (020) 7495 7100, *squarethe@a ol.com*, Fax *(020) 7495 7150* – 🖃. ⬛⬤ AE ⬤ VISA JCB   p. 12 CM **v**
🏵🏵 *closed 25-26 December, 1 January, lunch Saturday, Sunday and Bank Holidays* – **Meals** 25.00/50.00 **t.** 🍸 18.50
Spec. Lasagne of crab with langoustine cappuccino. Herb crusted saddle of lamb, shallot purée and rosemary. Roast foie gras, endive and Muscat grape tart.

XXX **Mirabelle,** 56 Curzon St, W1J 8PA, ℰ (020) 7499 4636, *sales@whitestarline.org.uk*, Fax *(020) 7499 5449*, 🍽 – 🖃. ⬛⬤ AE ⬤ VISA   p. 12 CN **x**
🏵 **Meals** 19.95 (lunch) and a la carte 33.40/53.40 **t.** 🍸 20.00
Spec. Grilled scallops with chives and ginger. Bresse pigeon with foie gras en chou vert. Raspberry soufflé "Mirabelle"

XXX **Terrace** (at Le Meridien Piccadilly H.), 21 Piccadilly, W1V 0BH, ℰ (020) 7851 3085, Fax *(020) 7851 3090*, 🍽 – 🖃. ⬛⬤ AE ⬤ VISA JCB   p. 13 EM **a**
Meals a la carte 24.50/42.00 🍸 21.00.

XXX **Cecconi's,** 5a Burlington Gdns, W1X 1LE, ℰ (020) 7434 1500, Fax *(020) 7434 2440* –
🖃. ⬛⬤ AE ⬤ VISA   p. 13 DM **c**
closed 25 December – **Meals** - Italian - a la carte 27.00/37.00 **t.**

XXX **Tamarind,** 20 Queen St, W1X 7PJ, ℰ (020) 7629 3561, *tamarind.restaurant@virgin.net*, Fax *(020) 7499 5034* – 🖃. ⬛⬤ AE ⬤ VISA   p. 12 CN **e**
🏵 *closed 25-26 December, lunch Saturday and Bank Holidays* – **Meals** - Indian - 14.50 (lunch) and a la carte 24.50/30.00 **t.** 🍸 14.50
Spec. Murg kaleji masala (chicken livers). Changezi champen (lamb cutlets). Hara cholia te paneer (cottage cheese with ginger).

XXX **Sartoria,** 20 Savile Row, W1X 1AE, ℰ (020) 7534 7000, *sartoriareservations@conran -restaurants.co.uk*, Fax *(020) 7534 7070* – 🖃. ⬛⬤ AE ⬤ VISA JCB   p. 13 DL **c**
closed 25-26 December, and Sunday lunch – **Meals** - Italian - a la carte 28.50/33.50 **st.**
🍸 15.00.

XXX **Firebird,** 23 Conduit St, W1S 2XS, ℰ (020) 7493 7000, *sales@firebirdrestaurants.co.uk*, Fax *(020) 7493 7088* – 🖃. ⬛⬤ AE ⬤ VISA   p. 13 DL **x**
closed Easter Sunday, 25 December, 1 January, Saturday lunch, Sunday and Bank Holidays – **Meals** - Tsarist Russian - 19.95 (lunch) and a la carte 36.00/144.00 **t.** 🍸 19.50.

XXX **Scotts,** 20 Mount St, W1Y 6HE, ℰ (020) 7629 5248, Fax *(020) 7499 8246* – 🖃. ⬛⬤ AE
⬤ VISA   p. 12 BM **a**
closed 25 December – **Meals** - Seafood - 26.50 (lunch) and a la carte 26.50/34.50 **st.**
🍸 12.50.

XXX **Greenhouse,** 27a Hay's Mews, W1J 7RJ, ℰ (020) 7499 3331, *reservations@greenho userestaurant.co.uk*, Fax *(020) 7499 5368* – 🖃. ⬛⬤ AE ⬤ VISA JCB   p. 12 BN **x**
closed 25 December and Saturday lunch – **Meals** 25.00 (lunch) and a la carte approx. 43.50 **t.** 🍸 14.00.

XXX **Morton's - The Restaurant,** 28 Berkeley Sq, W1X 5HA, ℰ (020) 7493 7171, *rece ption@mortonsclub.co.uk*, Fax *(020) 7495 3160* – ⬛⬤ AE ⬤ VISA   p. 12 CM **a**
closed 1 week Christmas, Sunday and Saturday lunch – **Meals** a la carte 28.75/40.50 **st.**
🍸 15.00.

XXX **Le Soufflé** (at Inter-Continental H.), 1 Hamilton Pl, Hyde Park Corner, W1V 0QY, ℰ (020) 7318 8577, Fax *(020) 7409 7460* – 🖃 ⬛⬤ AE ⬤ VISA   p. 12 BP **o**
closed Monday, Saturday lunch and Sunday dinner – **Meals** (dancing Saturday evening) a la carte 30.50/41.00 🍸 13.00.

XXX **Kaspia,** 18-18A Bruton Pl, W1X 7AA, ℰ (020) 7493 2612, Fax *(020) 7408 1627* – 🖃. ⬛⬤
AE ⬤ VISA   p. 12 CM **i**
closed Sunday and Bank Holidays – **Meals** - Caviar specialities - 39.90 and a la carte 32.50/46.70 **st.** 🍸 16.00.

XXX **Kai,** 65 South Audley St, W1Y 5FD, ℰ (020) 7493 8988, *kai@kaimayfair.co.uk*, Fax *(020) 7493 1456* – 🖃. ⬛⬤ AE ⬤ VISA JCB   p. 12 BM **c**
closed 25-26 December and 1 January – **Meals** - Chinese - a la carte 27.00/50.00 **t.** 🍸 19.00.

XX **Cassia Oriental,** 12 Berkeley Sq, W1X 5HG, ℰ (020) 7629 8886, Fax *(020) 7491 8883* – 🖃. ⬛⬤ AE ⬤ VISA   p. 12 CM **z**
closed 25-26 December, 1 January, Sunday and Bank Holidays – **Meals** - South East Asian - 23.80 (dinner) and a la carte 18.50/28.50.

XX **Noble Rot,** 3-5 Mill St, W1R 9TF, ℰ (020) 7629 8877, noble@noblerot.com, Fax (020) 7629 8878 – ■. ⓄⓈ ⒶⒺ Ⓞ 𝑉𝐼𝑆𝐴 ⒿⒸⒷ   p. 13 DL r
closed 25-26 December, 1 January, Saturday lunch and Sunday – **Meals** a la carte 24.00/43.00 **t.** ⓐ 14.50.

XX **Alloro,** 19-20 Dover St, W1S 4LU, ℰ (020) 7495 4768, Fax (020) 7629 5348 – ■. ⓄⓈ ⒶⒺ Ⓞ 𝑉𝐼𝑆𝐴   p. 13 DM r
closed 23 December-2 January, Sunday and Bank Holidays – **Meals** - Italian - 23.00/28.00 **t.** ⓐ 16.50.

XX **Nobu** (at The Metropolitan H.), 19 Old Park Lane, W1Y 4LB, ℰ (020) 7447 4747, ✿ Fax (020) 7447 4749, ≼ – ■. ⓄⓈ ⒶⒺ Ⓞ 𝑉𝐼𝑆𝐴 ⒿⒸⒷ   p. 12 BP c
closed 25-26 December and Saturday and Sunday lunch – **Meals** - New style Japanese with South American influences - (booking essential) 24.50 (lunch) and a la carte 55.00/85.00 **t.** ⓐ 18.00
Spec. Tiradito. Black cod with miso. Chocolate bento box.

XX **Chor Bizarre,** 16 Albemarle St, W1S 4HW, ℰ (020) 7629 9802, chorbizarrelondon@oldworldhosptials.com, Fax (020) 7493 7756, « Authentic Indian decor and furnishings » – ■. ⓄⓈ ⒶⒺ Ⓞ 𝑉𝐼𝑆𝐴 ⒿⒸⒷ   p. 13 DM s
Meals - Indian - a la carte 27.00/29.50 **t.** ⓐ 14.50.

XX **Yatra,** 34 Dover St, W1S 4NG, ℰ (020) 7493 0200, yatra@lineone.net, Fax (020) 7493 4228 – ■. ⓄⓈ ⒶⒺ Ⓞ 𝑉𝐼𝑆𝐴 ⒿⒸⒷ   p. 13 DM o
closed 25 December, Sunday, Saturday lunch and Bank Holidays – **Meals** - Indian - 17.50 (lunch) and a la carte 22.75/27.75 **t.** ⓐ 14.00.

XX **L'Odéon,** 65 Regent St, W1R 7HH, ℰ (020) 7287 1400, Fax (020) 7287 1300 – ■. ⓄⓈ ⒶⒺ Ⓞ 𝑉𝐼𝑆𝐴   p. 13 EM r
closed Christmas, Sunday and Bank Holidays – **Meals** 18.50 and a la carte 25.50/57.00 **t.** ⓐ 12.50.

XX **Bentley's,** 11-15 Swallow St, W1B 4DG, ℰ (020) 7734 4756, Fax (020) 7287 2972 – ■. ⓄⓈ ⒶⒺ Ⓞ 𝑉𝐼𝑆𝐴 ⒿⒸⒷ   p. 13 EM i
closed 25-26 December – **Meals** - Seafood - a la carte 21.40/38.45 **t.** ⓐ 18.95.

XX **Langan's Brasserie,** Stratton St, W1J 8LB, ℰ (020) 7491 8822, admin@langansrestaurants.co.uk, Fax (020) 7493 8309 – ■. ⓄⓈ ⒶⒺ Ⓞ 𝑉𝐼𝑆𝐴 ⒿⒸⒷ   p. 13 DN e
closed Christmas, Easter, Sunday, Saturday lunch and Bank Holidays – **Meals** a la carte 23.00/32.95 **t.** ⓐ 13.00.

XX **Teca,** 54 Brooks Mews, W1Y 2NY, ℰ (020) 7495 4774, Fax (020) 7491 3545 – ⓄⓈ ⒶⒺ 𝑉𝐼𝑆𝐴
closed 23 December-3 January, Sunday, Saturday lunch and Bank Holidays – **Meals** - Italian - 24.50/29.50 **t.** ⓐ 15.00.   p. 12 CL a

XX **Hush,** 8 Lancashire Court, Brook St, W1S 1EY, ℰ (020) 7659 1500, steamroller@hush.co.uk, Fax (020) 7659 1501 – |≣| ■. ⓄⓈ ⒶⒺ 𝑉𝐼𝑆𝐴 ⒿⒸⒷ   p. 12 CL v
closed Sunday and Bank Holidays – **hush down** 🍴 : Meals a la carte 24.50/38.50 **t.** ⓐ 13.50 – **hush up** : Meals (closed Saturday lunch and Sunday) (booking essential) 26.50 (lunch) and dinner a la carte 33.50/47.50 **t.** ⓐ 13.50.

XX **Shogun** (at Millennium Mayfair H.), Adams Row, W1Y 5DF, ℰ (020) 7493 1255, britannia.res@millcop, Fax (020) 7493 1255 – ■. ⓄⓈ ⒶⒺ Ⓞ 𝑉𝐼𝑆𝐴 ⒿⒸⒷ   p. 12 BM x
closed 10 days summer, 10 days December and Monday – **Meals** - Japanese - (dinner only) 42.00 **t.** ⓐ 12.50.

XX **Momo,** 25 Heddon St, W1B 4BH, ℰ (020) 7434 4040, momoresto@aol.com, Fax (020) 7287 0404 – ■. ⓄⓈ ⒶⒺ Ⓞ 𝑉𝐼𝑆𝐴   p. 13 EM n
Meals - Moroccan - 17.00 (lunch) and a la carte 25.00/42.00 **t.** ⓐ 12.00.

XX **Nicole's** (at Nicole Farhi), 158 New Bond St, W1Y 9PA, ℰ (020) 7499 8408, Fax (020) 7409 0381 – ■. ⓄⓈ ⒶⒺ Ⓞ 𝑉𝐼𝑆𝐴 ⒿⒸⒷ   p. 13 DM n
closed 25 December, Saturday dinner, Sunday and Bank Holidays – **Meals** (booking essential) a la carte 26.20/36.40 **t.** ⓐ 12.50.

Regent's Park and Marylebone – ✉ NW1/NW6/NW8/W1 –.

🏨 **Landmark London,** 222 Marylebone Rd, NW1 6JQ, ℰ (020) 7631 8000, reservations@thelandmark.co.uk, Fax (020) 7631 8080, « Victorian Gothic architecture, atrium and winter garden », 𝟙𝟞, ≘s, ☒ – |≣|, ↮ rm, ■ 📺 ℰ & ⇔ – 🔏 350. ⓄⓈ ⒶⒺ Ⓞ 𝑉𝐼𝑆𝐴 ℀
     p. 5 HU a
Winter Garden : Meals 23.00 and a la carte 30.00/41.00 **t.** ⓐ 19.50 (see also **John Burton-Race** below) – ⌑ 18.50 – **290 rm** 305.00/330.00, 9 suites – SB.

🏨 **Langham Hilton,** 1c Portland Pl, Regent St, W1N 4JA, ℰ (020) 7636 1000, langham@hilton.com, Fax (020) 7323 2340, 𝟙𝟞, ≘s, ☒ – |≣|, ↮ rm, ■ 📺 ℰ & – 🔏 250. ⓄⓈ ⒶⒺ Ⓞ 𝑉𝐼𝑆𝐴   p. 5 JU e
Memories : Meals 24.50 (lunch) and a la carte 29.50/53.75 **t.** ⓐ 19.00 – **Tsar's** : Meals (closed 1 week Easter and Sunday) a la carte 24.00/31.00 **t.** ⓐ 19.00 – ⌑ 21.50 – **419 rm** 250.00 **s.**, 20 suites.

Churchill Inter-Continental London, 30 Portman Sq, W1A 4ZX, ℰ (020) 7486 5800, churchill@interconti.com, Fax (020) 7486 1255, *L₅*, ⇌s, ✗ – |☆|, ✲ rm, ≣ 📺 ✆ ᶑ – 🔬 300. ⍟ ᴁ ⓞ 𝘝𝘐𝘚𝘈 ᴊᴄʙ. ※　　　　　　p. 12 AJ ✗
Terrace on Portman Square : Meals 26.50 (lunch) and a la carte 33.15/39.70 **t.** ᶑ 17.50 – ⌂ 20.75 – **405 rm** 340.00, 40 suites.

Selfridge Thistle, Orchard St, W1H 6JS, ℰ (020) 7408 2080, selfridge@thistle.co.uk, Fax (020) 7409 2295 – |☆|, ✲ rm, ≣ 📺 – 🔬 250. ⍟ ᴁ ⓞ 𝘝𝘐𝘚𝘈 ᴊᴄʙ. ※
Fletchers : Meals (dinner only) 19.00 and a la carte 25.20/32.00 **t.** ᶑ 12.10 – **Orchard Terrace :** Meals (lunch only) 14.50 **t.** ᶑ 13.50 – ⌂ 15.95 – **290 rm** 202.00/247.00 **t.**, 4 suites – SB.　　　　　　p. 12 AK e

Charlotte Street, 15 Charlotte St, W1P 1HB, ℰ (020) 7806 2000, charlotte@firmdale.com, Fax (020) 7806 2002, « Modern English interior », *L₅* – |☆| ≣ 📺 ✆ ᶑ – 🔬 65 ⍟ ᴁ 𝘝𝘐𝘚𝘈. ※　　　　　　p. 6 KU v
Meals (see *Oscar* below) – ⌂ 16.50 – **44 rm** 175.00/280.00, 8 suites.

Sanderson, 50 Berners St, W1P 3NG, ℰ (020) 7300 1400, sanderson@ianschragerhotels.com, Fax (020) 7300 1401, ☂, « Contemporary interior », *L₅* – |☆|, ✲ rm, ≣ 📺 ✆, ⍟ ᴁ ⓞ 𝘝𝘐𝘚𝘈. ※　　　　　　n 13 F,l c
Spoon+ : Meals 25.00 (lunch) and a la carte 45.00/70.00 **t.** ᶑ 30.00 – ⌂ 19.00 – **150 rm** 340.00/365.00.

The Leonard, 15 Seymour St, W1H 7JW, ℰ (020) 7935 2010, theleonard@dial.pipex.com, Fax (020) 7935 6700, « Attractively furnished Georgian town houses », *L₅* – |☆| ≣ 📺 ✆, ⍟ ᴁ ⓞ 𝘝𝘐𝘚𝘈 ᴊᴄʙ. ※　　　　　　p. 12 AK n
Meals (room service only) – ⌂ 18.50 – **9 rm** 200.00/220.00 **s.**, **20 suites** 280.00/550.00 **s.**

Radisson SAS Portman, 22 Portman Sq, W1H 7BG, ℰ (020) 7208 6000, sales@lonza.rdsas.com, Fax (020) 7208 6001, *L₅*, ⇌s, ✗ – |☆|, ✲ rm, ≣ 📺 ✆ – 🔬 650. ⍟ ᴁ ⓞ 𝘝𝘐𝘚𝘈 ᴊᴄʙ. ※　　　　　　p. 12 AJ c
Portman Corner : Meals (buffet lunch)/dinner a la carte 23.00/35.00 **t.** ᶑ 16.00 – ⌂ 17.50 – **265 rm** 195.00/205.00 **s.**, 7 suites.

Montcalm, Great Cumberland Pl, W1A 2LF, ℰ (020) 7402 4288, montcalm@montcalm.co.uk, Fax (020) 7724 9180 – |☆|, ✲ rm, ≣ 📺 ✆ – 🔬 80. ⍟ ᴁ ⓞ 𝘝𝘐𝘚𝘈 ᴊᴄʙ　　　　　　p. 17 EZ x
Meals (see *The Crescent* below) – ⌂ 17.95 – **110 rm** 230.00/250.00, 10 suites – SB.

Ramada Plaza London, 18 Lodge Rd, NW8 7JT, ℰ (020) 7722 7722, regentspark@jarvis.co.uk, Fax (020) 7483 2408 – |☆|, ✲ rm, ≣ 📺 ℗ – 🔬 150. ⍟ ᴁ ⓞ 𝘝𝘐𝘚𝘈 ᴊᴄʙ ※　　　　　　p. 5 GT v
Minsky's : Meals 19.50/20.95 and a la carte 24.05/32.20 **t.** ᶑ 14.95 – *Kashinoki :* Meals - Japanese - (closed Sunday and Monday) 18.00/32.00 and a la carte 19.60/37.80 **t.** ᶑ 11.00 – ⌂ 15.50 – **376 rm** 209.00 **st.**, 1 suite.

Jurys Clifton Ford, 47 Welbeck St, W1M 8DN, ℰ (020) 7486 6600, clifton@jurysdoyle.com, Fax (020) 7486 7492, *L₅*, ⇌s, ▣ – |☆| ≣ 📺 ✆ ᶑ ⟺ – 🔬 230. ⍟ ᴁ ⓞ 𝘝𝘐𝘚𝘈. ※　　　　　　p. 12 BH a
closed 25-26 December – Meals (closed lunch Saturday and Sunday) a la carte approx 25.00 **st.** ᶑ 15.00 – ⌂ 16.00 – **253 rm** 200.00 **st.**, 2 suites.

Berners, 10 Berners St, W1A 3BE, ℰ (020) 7666 2000, berners@berners.co.uk, Fax (020) 7666 2001 – |☆|, ✲ rm, ≣ rest, 📺 ✆ ᶑ – 🔬 160. ⍟ ᴁ ⓞ 𝘝𝘐𝘚𝘈 ᴊᴄʙ. ※
Meals (carving lunch) 16.95 (lunch) and a la carte 22.00/27.50 **t.** ᶑ 14.50 – ⌂ 15.95 – **213 rm** 190.00/260.00 **st.**, 3 suites.　　　　　　p. 13 EJ r

Holiday Inn Regent's Park, Carburton St, W1W 5EE, ℰ (0870) 400 9111, Fax (020) 7387 2806 – |☆|, ✲ rm, ≣ rest, 📺 ✆ – 🔬 350. ⍟ ᴁ ⓞ 𝘝𝘐𝘚𝘈 ᴊᴄʙ ※　　　　　　p. 5 JU v
Meals a la carte 21.85/29.15 **t.** ᶑ 12.95 – ⌂ 13.95 – **333 rm** 179.00 **st.** – SB.

London Marriott Marble Arch, 134 George St, W1H 6DN, ℰ (020) 7723 1277, salesadmin.marblearch@marriott.co.uk, Fax (020) 7402 0666, *L₅*, ⇌s, ▣ – |☆|, ✲ rm, ≣ 📺 ✆ ᶑ ℗ – 🔬 150. ⍟ ᴁ ⓞ 𝘝𝘐𝘚𝘈 ᴊᴄʙ. ※　　　　　　p. 17 EZ t
Meals (closed Saturday lunch) a la carte 17.20/26.65 **st.** – ⌂ 18.95 – **240 rm** 215.00 **s.**

Berkshire, 350 Oxford St, W1N 0BY, ℰ (020) 7629 7474, resberk@radisson.com, Fax (020) 7629 8156 – |☆|, ✲ rm, ≣ 📺 ✆ – 🔬 40. ⍟ ᴁ ⓞ 𝘝𝘐𝘚𝘈 ᴊᴄʙ. ※　　　　　　p. 12 BK n
Ascots : Meals 25.00 **st.** ᶑ 15.25 – ⌂ 15.00 – **145 rm** 247.00/285.00 **s.**, 2 suites.

Durrants, 26-32 George St, W1H 5BJ, ℰ (020) 7935 8131, enquiries@durrantshotel.co.uk, Fax (020) 7487 3510, « Converted Georgian houses with Regency façade » – |☆| ≣ rest, 📺 ✆ – 🔬 55. ⍟ ᴁ 𝘝𝘐𝘚𝘈. ※　　　　　　p. 12 AH e
Meals 19.50 and a la carte 24.95/41.95 **t.** ᶑ 14.50 – ⌂ 13.50 – **88 rm** 110.00/165.00, 4 suites.

🏠 **Dorset Square,** 39-40 Dorset Sq, NW1 6QN, *℘* (020) 7723 7874, *dorset@firmdale.com*, Fax (020) 7724 3328, « Attractively furnished Regency town houses », 🚗 – 🛗 🔳 📺 📞. 🐶 🆎 🚺 🌠
p. 5 HU s
The Potting Shed : Meals *(closed Sunday)* (booking essential) (live jazz Tuesday and Saturday dinner) 17.95/23.50 and a la carte 24.45/28.30 **t.** 🍷 13.95 – � 14.00 – **38 rm** 98.00/240.00.

🏠 **10 Manchester Street** without rest., 10 Manchester St, W1U 4DG, *℘* (020) 7486 6669, *stay@10manchesterstreet.fsnet.co.uk*, Fax (020) 7224 0348 – 🛗 📺. 🐶 🆎 🚺. 🌠
☍ 4.00 **37 rm** 120.00/150.00 **st.**, 9 suites.
p. 12 AH c

🏠 **Ramada Jarvis Marylebone,** Harewood Row, NW1 6SE, *℘* (020) 7262 2707, *107g m@jarvis.co.uk*, Fax (020) 7262 2975 – 🛗, ✳ rm, 🔳 rest, 📺 📞. 🐶 🆎 🚺 🌠
Meals *(closed Saturday and Sunday lunch)* 9.00 and a la carte approx. 18.90 **st.** 🍷 11.95 – ☍ 11.95 – **92 rm** 125.00/165.00 **st.**
p. 5 HU x

🏵🏵 **John Burton-Race** (at Landmark London H.), 222 Marylebone Rd, NW1 6JQ, *℘* (020) 7723 7800, *jbrthelandmark@btconnect.co.uk*, Fax (020) 7723 4700 – 🔳 ⇔. 🐶 🆎 🚺
🚺
p. 5 HU a
closed first week January, Saturday lunch, Sunday and Bank Holidays – **Meals** - French - 29.50/70.00 **t.** 🍷 15.00
Spec. Ravioli of langoustine, truffle scented potato, Madeira jus. Roast poussin with foie gras, baby spinach and Sauternes sauce. Plate of chocolate desserts.

🏵 **Orrery,** 55 Marylebone High St, W1M 3AE, *℘* (020) 7616 8000, Fax (020) 7616 8080, « Converted 19C stables, contemporary interior » – 🛗. 🐶 🆎 🚺 🌠 🚺
closed 1-3 January and 25 December – **Meals** (booking essential) 23.50 *(lunch)* and a la carte 31.50/50.50 **t.** 🍷 12.00
p. 5 IU a
Spec. Cannelloni of Dorset crab. Fillet of beef, foie gras, spinach and Madeira jus. Chocolate fondant, iced crème fraîche.

🍴🍴 **Oscar** (at Charlotte Street H.), 15 Charlotte St, W1T 1RJ, *℘* (020) 7907 4005, *charlot te@firmdale.com*, Fax (020) 7806 2002 – 🔳. 🐶 🆎 🚺
p. 6 KU v
closed Sunday – **Meals** (booking essential) a la carte 31.00/39.00 **t.** 🍷 16.50.

🍴🍴 **The Crescent** (at Montcalm H.), Great Cumberland Pl, W1A 2LF, *℘* (020) 7402 4288, *rese rvations@montcalm.co.uk*, Fax (020) 7724 9180 – 🔳. 🐶 🆎 🚺 🌠 🚺
p. 17 EZ x
closed lunch Saturday, Sunday and Bank Holidays – **Meals** 25.00 **t.** 🍷 17.00.

🍴🍴 **The Providores,** 109 Marylebone High St, W1U 4RX, *℘* (020) 7431 3319, *anyone@t heprovidores.co.uk*, Fax (020) 7431 6877 – ⇔. 🐶 🆎 🚺
p. 12 BH s
Meals a la carte 23.60/33.60 **t.**

🍴🍴 **Ozer,** 4-5 Langham Pl, Regent St, W1B 3DG, *℘* (020) 7323 0505, *info@sofra.co.uk*, Fax (020) 7323 0111 – 🔳. 🐶 🆎 🚺 🌠
p. 5 JU z
Meals - Turkish - 13.95 and a la carte 16.40/32.50 **t.** 🍷 12.50.

🍴🍴 **Rasa Samudra,** 5 Charlotte St, W1P 1HD, *℘* (020) 7637 0222, Fax (020) 7637 0224 – ⇔. 🐶 🆎 🚺 🌠 🚺
p. 6 KU r
closed 24-31 December – **Meals** - Indian Seafood and Vegetarian - a la carte 12.75/23.95 🍷 10.50.

🍴🍴 **La Porte des Indes,** 32 Bryanston St, W1H 7EG, *℘* (020) 7224 0055, *pilondon@ao l.com*, Fax (020) 7224 1144 – 🔳. 🐶 🆎 🚺 🌠 🚺
p. 12 AK r
closed 25-26 December, 1 January and Saturday lunch – **Meals** - Indian - 30.00/54.00 and a la carte 22.30/45.10 **t.** 🍷 6.25.

🍴🍴 **Rosmarino,** 1 Blenheim Terr, NW8 0EH, *℘* (020) 7328 5014, Fax (020) 7625 2639, 🌿 – 🔳. 🐶 🆎 🚺
p. 4 FS s
closed 23 December-3 January and Bank Holidays – **Meals** - Italian - 27.00 (dinner) and lunch a la carte 19.00/24.00 **t.** 🍷 16.50.

🍴🍴 **Levant,** Jason Court, 76 Wigmore St, W1H 9DQ, *℘* (020) 7224 1111, Fax (020) 7486 1216 – 🔳. 🐶 🆎 🚺 🌠
p. 12 BJ c
closed lunch Saturday and Sunday – **Meals** - Eastern Mediterranean - 8.50/19.50 and a la carte 22.70/28.75 **t.** 🍷 13.50.

🍴🍴 **Caldesi,** 15-17 Marylebone Lane, W1V 2NE, *℘* (020) 7935 9226, Fax (020) 7935 9228 – 🔳. 🐶 🆎 🚺 🌠 🚺
p. 12 BJ e
closed 25 December, Saturday lunch, Sunday and Bank Holidays – **Meals** - Italian - a la carte 19.50/29.50 **t.** 🍷 13.50.

🍴🍴 **Bertorelli's,** (First Floor), 19-23 Charlotte St, W1P 1HP, *℘* (020) 7636 4174, Fax (020) 7467 8902 – 🔳. 🐶 🆎 🚺 🌠
p. 6 KU v
closed 25 December – **Meals** - Italian - a la carte 17.85/23.95 **t.** 🍷 10.00.

🍴🍴 **L'Aventure,** 3 Blenheim Terr, NW8 0EH, *℘* (020) 7624 6232, Fax (020) 7625 5548, 🌿 – 🐶 🆎 🚺
p. 4 FS s
closed 1-15 January, Easter, Sunday, Saturday lunch and Bank Holidays – **Meals** - French - 18.50/28.50 **t.** 🍷 15.25.

※ **Mash,** 19-21 Great Portland St, W1N 5DB, ℘ (020) 7637 5555, Fax (020) 7637 7333 –
🔲 🔜 AE ① VISA   p. 13 DJ a
closed Sunday and Bank Holidays – **Meals** (booking essential) a la carte 17.50/27.00 **t.**
🍷 13.00.

※ **Chada Chada,** 16-17 Picton Pl, W1M 5DE, ℘ (020) 7935 8212, Fax (020) 7924 2178
⊛ – 🔲 🔜 AE ① VISA JCB
closed Sunday and Bank Holidays – **Meals** - Thai - a la carte 10.75/23.20 **t.** 🍷 11.95.

🍴 **The Salt House,** 63 Abbey Rd, NW8 0AE, ℘ (020) 7328 6626, enquiries@thesalthc
use.fsnet.co.uk, Fax (020) 7625 9168, ⛱ – 🔲 🔜 AE ① VISA   p. 4 FS z
Meals (booking essential) 11.95 (lunch) and a la carte 21.50/27.50 **t.**

St James's – ✉ W1/SW1/WC2 –.

🏨🏨🏨🏨 **Ritz,** 150 Piccadilly, W1J 9BR, ℘ (020) 7493 8181, enquire@theritzlondon.com,
Fax (020) 7493 2687, 🛁 – 🛗 ≒ rm, 🔲 TV ✆ – 🔺 50. 🔜 AE ① VISA JCB.
❀   p. 13 DN a
Meals (see **The Restaurant** below) – �() 23.50 – **116 rm** 305.00/425.00, 17 suites – SB

🏨🏨🏨 **Dukes** ♨, 35 St James's Pl, SW1A 1NY, ℘ (020) 7491 4040, enquiries@dukeshotel.co.uk,
Fax (020) 7493 1264, 🛁 – 🛗 ≒ rest, 🔲 TV ✆ – 🔺 50. 🔜 AE ① VISA JCB. ❀
Meals (closed Saturday lunch and Bank Holidays) (residents only) 20.00/40.00 and a la carte
24.00/43.00 **t.** 🍷 26.00 – ⊙ 14.75 – **82 rm** 195.00/260.00, 7 suites.   p. 13 EP x

🏨🏨🏨 **The Trafalgar,** 2 Spring Gdns, SW1A 2TS, ℘ (020) 7870 2900, lontshirm@hilton.com,
Fax (020) 7870 2911 – 🛗 ≒ rm, 🔲 TV ✆ ♿ – 🔺 50. 🔜 AE ① VISA JCB. ❀
Jago : **Meals** 19.50 (lunch) and a la carte 25.50/32.00 **t.** 🍷 16.00 – ⊙ 18.50 – **127 rm**
270.00 **s.**, 2 suites.   p. 13 GN a

🏨🏨🏨 **Stafford** ♨, 16-18 St James's Pl, SW1A 1NJ, ℘ (020) 7493 0111, info@thestaffor
dhotel.co.uk, Fax (020) 7493 7121 – 🛗 🔲 TV ✆ – 🔺 40. 🔜 AE ① VISA
Meals (closed Saturday lunch) 27.00/32.50 and a la carte 42.50/54.50 **st.** 🍷 19.50 –
⊙ 16.00 – **75 rm** 220.00/290.00 **s.**, 6 suites.   p. 13 DN u

🏨🏨🏨 **Cavendish,** 81 Jermyn St, SW1Y 6JF, ℘ (020) 7930 2111, cavendish.reservations@c
evere-hotels.com, Fax (020) 7839 2125 – 🛗 ≒ rm, 🔲 rest, TV ⇔ – 🔺 80. 🔜 AE
① VISA JCB. ❀   p. 13 EN
Meals (closed lunch Saturday, Sunday and Bnak Holidays) 24.50 and a la carte
24.50/36.50 **t.** 🍷 13.50 – ⊙ 16.95 – **249 rm** 235.00/265.00 **st.**, 2 suites – SB.

🏨🏨 **22 Jermyn Street,** 22 Jermyn St, SW1Y 6HL, ℘ (020) 7734 2353, office@22jerm
yn.com, Fax (020) 7734 0750 – 🛗 🔲 TV ✆. 🔜 AE ① VISA JCB. ❀   p. 13 FM e
Meals (room service only) – ⊙ 17.00 – **5 rm** 210.00 **s.**, **13 suites** 295.00/335.00 **s.**

🏨🏨 **Thistle Piccadilly** without rest., 39 Coventry St, W1V 7FH, ℘ (020) 7930 4033, picc
adilly@thistle.co.uk, Fax (020) 7925 2586 – 🛗 ≒ 🔲 TV ✆. 🔜 AE ① VISA. ❀
⊙ 14.50 – **92 rm** 181.00/295.00 **st.**   p. 13 FGM a

🏨🏨 **Thistle Trafalgar Square,** Whitcomb St, WC2H 7HG, ℘ (020) 7930 4477, trafalgarsqu
are@thistle.co.uk, Fax (020) 7925 2149 – 🛗 ≒ rm, 🔲 rest, TV ✆. 🔜 AE ① VISA. ❀
Meals 14.50/20.50 and a la carte 12.80/31.00 **t.** 🍷 11.50 – ⊙ 14.50 – **116 rm**
152.00/185.00 **s.** – SB.   p. 13 GM r

XXXXX **The Restaurant** (at Ritz H.), 150 Piccadilly, W1V 9DG, ℘ (020) 7493 8181,
Fax (020) 7493 2687, ⛱, « Elegant restaurant in Louis XVI style » – 🔲. 🔜 AE ① VISA JCB
Meals (dancing Friday and Saturday evenings) 35.00/59.00 and a la carte 41.50/65.00 **st.**
🍷 22.00.   p. 13 DN a

XXX **Pétrus,** 33 St James's St, SW1A 1HD, ℘ (020) 7930 4272, Fax (020) 7930 9702 – 🔲.
❀ 🔜 AE ① VISA JCB   p. 13 EN v
closed 1 week Christmas, Sunday, Saturday lunch and Bank Holidays – **Meals** (booking
essential) 26.00/60.00 **t.** 🍷 18.00
Spec. Fricassee of frog's legs, ceps, spinach and foie gras. Braised turbot with oyster ravioli,
morels and white asparagus. Prune and vanilla soufflé, prune and Armagnac ice cream.

XXX **L'Oranger,** 5 St James's St, SW1A 1EF, ℘ (020) 7839 3774, Fax (020) 7839 4330 – 🔲.
❀ 🔜 AE ① VISA   p. 13 EP a
closed Christmas, 2 weeks August, Saturday lunch and Sunday – **Meals** 23.50/39.50 **t.**
🍷 26.00
Spec. Pot-au-feu of pork belly and black truffle. Braised calves cheeks, mozzarella cheese.
Chocolate fondant, vanilla and nougatine ice cream.

XXX **Orient,** 160 Piccadilly (1st floor), W1V 9DF, ℘ (020) 7499 6888, Fax (020) 7659 9300
– 🛗 🔲. 🔜 AE VISA   p. 13 DN i
closed Saturday lunch and Sunday – **Meals** - Chinese - a la carte 30.00/65.00.

XXX **Suntory,** 72-73 St James's St, SW1A 1PH, ℘ (020) 7409 0201, Fax (020) 7499 0208 –
🔲. 🔜 AE ① VISA JCB   p. 13 EP z
closed Easter, Christmas-New Year and Sunday lunch – **Meals** - Japanese - 17.00/53.00
and a la carte 38.00/87.00 **st.** 🍷 19.00.

XX **Quaglino's,** 16 Bury St, SW1Y 6AL, ✆ (020) 7930 6767, *Fax (020) 7839 2866* – ▤. MC AE DI VISA p. 13 EN r
closed 25 December – **Meals** (booking essential) 15.00 (lunch) and a la carte 23.95/49.00 **t.** 🍷 13.50.

XX **Criterion Brasserie Marco Pierre White,** 224 Piccadilly, W1J 9HP, ✆ (020) 7930 0488, *Fax (020) 7930 8380*, « 19C neo-Byzantine decor » – ▤. MC AE DI VISA JCB
closed 25-26 December and Sunday lunch – **Meals** 17.95 (lunch) and a la carte 27.95/51.50 **t.** 🍷 15.00. p. 13 FM c

XX **Le Caprice,** Arlington House, Arlington St, SW1A 1RT, ✆ (020) 7629 2239, *Fax (020) 7493 9040* – ▤. MC AE DI VISA JCB p. 13 DN c
closed 25-26 December, 1 January and August Bank Holiday – **Meals** a la carte 25.50/56.00 **t.** 🍷 11.50.

XX **Café de Nikolaj,** 161 Piccadilly, W1V 9DF, ✆ (020) 7409 0445, *jp.esmilaire@talk21.com*, *Fax (020) 7493 1667* – ▤. MC AE DI VISA JCB p. 13 DN s
closed 1 January-14 February – **Meals** - Caviar specialities - 22.50 (lunch) and a la carte 27.50/66.50 **st.** 🍷 12.00.

XX **Che,** 23 St James's St, SW1A 1HE, ✆ (020) 7747 9380, *Fax (020) 7747 9389* – |‡| ▤. MC AE DI VISA p. 13 EN o
closed 25 December and Bank Holidays – **Meals** 15.50 (lunch) and a la carte 21.50/55.50 **t.** 🍷 11.50.

XX **The Avenue,** 7-9 St James's St, SW1A 1EE, ✆ (020) 7321 2111, *Fax (020) 7321 2500* – ▤. MC AE DI VISA p. 13 EP e
closed 25-26 December and 1 January – **Meals** 17.50 (lunch) and dinner a la carte 27.75/33.75 **t.** 🍷 14.50.

XX **Matsuri,** 15 Bury St, SW1Y 6AL, ✆ (020) 7839 1101, *Fax (020) 7930 7010* – ▤. MC AE DI VISA JCB p. 13 EN r
closed Sunday and Bank Holidays – **Meals** - Japanese (Teppan-Yaki, Sushi) - 35.00 (dinner) and a la carte 24.00/35.75 **t.** 🍷 18.00.

X **Al Duca,** 4-5 Duke of York St, SW1Y 6LA, ✆ (020) 7839 3090, *Fax (020) 7839 4050* – ▤. MC AE VISA p. 13 EN o
closed Christmas-New Year, Sunday lunch and Bank Holidays – **Meals** - Italian - 19.50/22.00 **t.** 🍷 14.00.

X **China House,** 160 Piccadilly, W1V 9DF, ✆ (020) 7499 6996, *chinahouse@chinahouse.co.uk*, *Fax (020) 7499 7779*, « Former bank » – MC AE VISA p. 13 DN i
closed 25 December, 1 January, Sunday and Bank Holidays – **Meals** - Chinese - a la carte 15.00/16.50 **t.** 🍷 12.50.

Soho – ✉ *W1/WC2 – pp. 12 and 13.*

Hampshire, Leicester Sq, WC2H 7LH, ✆ (020) 7839 9399, *reshamp@radisson.com*, *Fax (020) 7930 8122*, ⛲, 🚲 – |‡|, ⇹ rm, ▤ TV ✆ – 🏊 100. MC AE DI VISA JCB. ⛔
The Apex **: Meals** 25.00/30.00 **st.** 🍷 15.25 – ☕ 16.00 – **119 rm** 329.00/363.00 **s.**, 5 suites. p. 13 GM s

Hazlitt's without rest., 6 Frith St, W1D 3JA, ✆ (020) 7434 1771, *reservations@hazlitts.co.uk*, *Fax (020) 7439 1524*, « Early 18C town houses, antiques » – TV ✆. MC AE DI VISA
22 rm 160.00/205.00, 1 suite. p. 13 FK u

XXX **L'Escargot,** 48 Greek St, W1D 5EF, ✆ (020) 7437 2679, *Fax (020) 7437 0790* – ▤. MC AE DI VISA JCB p. 13 GK e
Ground Floor **: Meals** *(closed 25-26 December, 1 January, Sunday and Saturday lunch)* 17.95 (lunch) and a la carte 22.65/31.65 🍷 17.50 – ***Picasso Room*** « Collection of limited edition Picasso art » **: Meals** *(closed 25-26 December, 1 January, August, Sunday, Monday, Saturday lunch and Bank Holidays)* 25.50/55.00 **t.** 🍷 18.50
Spec. Lobster ravioli, fennel bouillon. Pigeon "en cocotte" with wild mushroom ravioli. Coconut crème brûlée.

XXX **Quo Vadis,** 26-29 Dean St, W1V 6LL, ✆ (020) 7437 9585, *Fax (020) 7734 7593* – ▤. MC AE DI VISA JCB p. 13 FK v
closed 25-26 December, 1 January, Sunday and Saturday lunch – **Meals** 17.95 (lunch) and a la carte 20.70/39.45 **t.** 🍷 14.50.

XX **Richard Corrigan at Lindsay House,** 21 Romilly St, W1V 5TG, ✆ (020) 7439 0450, *Fax (020) 7437 7349* – ▤. MC AE DI VISA JCB p. 13 GL i
closed 1 week Christmas, last week August, first week September, Sunday and Saturday lunch – **Meals** 23.00/44.00 **t.** 🍷 17.00
Spec. Sardines with salt cod, langoustine and tomato butter. Red mullet, barigoule cream, artichoke vinaigrette. Rhubarb compote, vanilla cream.

XX **Café Lazeez,** 21 Dean St, W1V 5AH, ✆ (020) 7434 9393, *soho@cafelazeez.com*, *Fax (020) 7434 0022* – ▤. MC AE DI VISA JCB p. 13 FJ a
closed Saturday lunch and Sunday – **Meals** - North Indian - a la carte 18.75/35.40 **t.** 🍷 9.95.

XX **Teatro,** 93-107 Shaftesbury Ave, W1D 5DY, ℰ (020) 7494 3040, Fax (020) 7494 305
– ▤. 🅼🅾 🅰🅴 ➀ *VISA* 🇯🇨🇧   p. 13 GL
closed 25-31 December, Sunday, Saturday lunch and Bank Holidays – **Meals** 14.00 (lunch
and a la carte 29.50/42.50 **t**. ⅄ 13.50.

XX **The Sugar Club,** 21 Warwick St, W1R 5RB, ℰ (020) 7437 7776, Fax (020) 7437 777
– ⅀. 🅼🅾 *VISA*   p. 13 EL
closed 25-26 December – **Meals** a la carte 26.80/31.70 **t**. ⅄ 24.00.

XX **Circus,** 1 Upper James St, W1F 4DF, ℰ (020) 7534 4000, circus@egami.co.uk
Fax (020) 7534 4010 – ▤. 🅼🅾 🅰🅴 ➀ *VISA*   p. 13 EL
closed 24-26 December, 1-2 January, Sunday and lunch Saturday – **Meals** 19.50 (lunch
and dinner a la carte 20.50/32.40 **t**. ⅄ 14.50.

XX **Mezzo,** Lower Ground Floor, 100 Wardour St, W1F 0TN, ℰ (020) 7314 4000
Fax (020) 7314 4040 – ▤. 🅼🅾 🅰🅴 ➀ *VISA* 🇯🇨🇧   p. 13 FK
closed 24-25 December and lunch Monday, Tuesday and Saturday – **Meals** 12.50 (lunch
and a la carte 22.50/49.50 **t**. ⅄ 13.50.

X **Bertorelli,** First Floor, 11-13 Frith St, W1D 4RB, ℰ (020) 7494 3491
Fax (020) 7437 3091, 🍴 – ▤. 🅰🅴 ➀ *VISA*   p. 13 FK
closed 25 December – **Meals** - Italian - a la carte 17.85/23.95 **t**. ⅄ 10.00.

X **Il Forno,** 63-64 Frith St, W1V 5TA, ℰ (020) 7734 4545, info@ilforno-restaurant.co.uk
🍷 Fax (020) 7287 8624 – ▤. 🅼🅾 🅰🅴 *VISA* 🇯🇨🇧   p. 13 FJK
closed lunch Saturday and Sunday and Bank Holidays – **Meals** - Italian - a la carte
15.25/29.75 **t**. ⅄ 12.50.

X **Alastair Little,** 49 Frith St, W1D 5SG, ℰ (020) 7734 5183, Fax (020) 7734 5206 – ▤
🅼🅾 🅰🅴 ➀ *VISA* 🇯🇨🇧   p. 13 FK
closed Sunday, Saturday lunch and Bank Holidays – **Meals** (booking essential
27.00/35.00 **t**. ⅄ 14.00.

X **Vasco and Piero's Pavilion,** 15 Poland St, W1V 3DE, ℰ (020) 7437 8774
Fax (020) 7437 0467 – ▤. 🅼🅾 🅰🅴 *VISA* 🇯🇨🇧   p. 13 EJK
closed Sunday, Saturday lunch and Bank Holidays – **Meals** - Italian - (lunch booking essential
18.50 (dinner) and lunch a la carte 28.00/32.00 **t**. ⅄ 11.50.

X **itsu,** 103 Wardour St, W1V 3TD, ℰ (020) 7479 4794, glenn.edwards@itsu.co.uk
Fax (020) 7479 4795 – ▤. 🅼🅾 🅰🅴 *VISA* 🇯🇨🇧   p. 13 FK
closed 25 December-3 January – **Meals** - Japanese - (bookings not accepted) a la carte
10.00/20.00 **t**. ⅄ 10.50.

X **Sri Siam Soho,** 16 Old Compton St, W1V 5PE, ℰ (020) 7434 3544, Fax (020) 7287 131
– ▤. 🅼🅾 🅰🅴 *VISA*   p. 13 GK
closed 25-26 December, 1 January and Sunday lunch – **Meals** - Thai - 14.95 and a la carte
30.00/50.00 **t**. ⅄ 10.95.

X **Aurora,** 49 Lexington St, W1F 9AP, ℰ (020) 7494 0514, aurora-restaurant@yahoo.
o.uk, Fax (020) 7494 4357, 🍴 – ▤ *VISA*   p. 13 EK
closed 25 December-3 January, Sunday and Bank Holidays – **Meals** (booking essential)
la carte 19.20/25.40 **t**.

X **Soho Spice,** 124-126 Wardour St, W1V 3LA, ℰ (020) 7434 0808, info@sohospice.co.uk
Fax (020) 7434 0799 – ⅀. 🅼🅾 🅰🅴 ➀ *VISA* 🇯🇨🇧   p. 13 FJ
Meals - Indian - (bookings not accepted) 16.95/27.95 and a la carte 15.45/25.70 **t**.

X **Fung Shing,** 15 Lisle St, WC2H 7BE, ℰ (020) 7437 1539, Fax (020) 7734 0284 – ▤. 🅼🅾
🅰🅴 ➀ *VISA*   p. 13 GL
closed 24-26 December and lunch Bank Holidays – **Meals** - Chinese (Canton) - a la carte
19.70/25.65 **t**. ⅄ 13.50.

X **Saigon,** 45 Frith St, W1V 5TE, ℰ (020) 7437 7109, Fax (020) 7734 1668 – ▤. 🅼🅾 🅰🅴 ➀ *VISA*
closed Easter, 25-26 December, Sunday and Bank Holidays – **Meals** - Vietnamese - a la carte
approx. 16.25 **t**. ⅄ 10.90.   p. 13 FGK

Strand and Covent Garden – ✉ WC2 –.

🏨🏨🏨 **Savoy,** Strand, WC2R 0EU, ℰ (020) 7836 4343, info@the-savoy.co.uk
Fax (020) 7240 6040, 🎱, ⥮, 🖼 – 🛗, ⤮ rm, ▤ 📺 🕭 🚗 – 🔏 500. 🅼🅾 🅰🅴 ➀ *VISA* ⤮
River : Meals 29.75/44.50 and a la carte 44.00/63.00 **t**. ⅄ 20.50 – **Grill :** Meals (closed
August, Sunday, Saturday lunch and Bank Holidays) a la carte 37.50/62.00 **t**. ⅄ 24.50 -
⟲ 23.50 – **159 rm** 290.00/370.00 **s.**, 48 suites.   p. 17 DEY

🏨🏨 **Le Meridien Waldorf,** Aldwych, WC2B 4DD, ℰ (0870) 400 8484, f?etb.waldorf@le
meridien-hotels.com, Fax (020) 7836 7244, 🎱, ⥮, 🖼 – 🛗, ⤮ rm, ▤ rm, 📺 🕭
🔏 200. 🅼🅾 🅰🅴 ➀ *VISA* 🇯🇨🇧. ⤮   p. 13 EX
Palm Court : Meals (closed Saturday lunch) 18.50 and a la carte 27.70/37.00 **t**. ⅄ 21.00
– **Matinée :** Meals a la carte 15.50/24.20 **t**. ⅄ 21.00 – ⟲ 18.00 – **286 rm** 280.00/290.00
6 suites.

Swissôtel London, The Howard, Temple Pl, WC2R 2PR, ℰ (020) 7836 3555, *reservations.london@swissotel.com, Fax (020) 7379 4547*, ≼, 龠 – |≢|, ✎ rm, ▤ 🏧 ✆ ⇔ – 🛣 150. ⚙ ℗ ⓪ 𝓥𝓘𝓢𝓐 .   p. 13 EX e
The Restaurant : Meals *(closed Saturday lunch)* 23.00/29.00 and a la carte 37.00/44.00 **st.** 🍷 21.00 – ☲ 23.50 – **148 rm** 295.00 **s.**, 8 suites.

One Aldwych, 1 Aldwych, WC2B 4RH, ℰ (020) 7300 1000, *reservations@onealdwych.co.uk, Fax (020) 7300 1001*, « Contemporary interior », 𝑓𝑎, ⇌, ▨ – |≢|, ✎ rm, ▤ 🏧 ✆ ⅙ – 🛣 50. ⚙ ℗ ⓪ 𝓥𝓘𝓢𝓐 𝓙𝓒𝓑. 🍴   p. 13 EX r
Indigo : Meals a la carte 30.00/35.00 **t.** 🍷 19.50 *(see also Axis below)* – ☲ 18.75 – **96 rm** 280.00/375.00 **s.**, 9 suites.

St Martins Lane, 45 St Martin's Lane, WC2N 4HX, ℰ (020) 7300 5500, *sml@ianschragerhotels.com, Fax (020) 7300 5501*, 龠, « Contemporary interior », 𝑓𝑎 – |≢|, ✎ rm, ▤ 🏧 ✆ – 🛣 40. ⚙ ℗ ⓪ 𝓥𝓘𝓢𝓐 .   p. 17 DY e
Asia de Cuba : Meals - Asian - 22.50/37.50 and a la carte 50.00/100.00 **t.** 🍷 30.00 –
Tuscan Steak : Meals *(closed Sunday dinner)* 22.50/37.50 and a la carte 50.00/75.00 **t.** 🍷 25.00 – ☲ 18.50 – **200 rm** 265.00/285.00, 4 suites.

Thistle Charing Cross, Strand, WC2N 5HX, ℰ (020) 7839 7282, *charingcross@thistle.co.uk, Fax (020) 7839 3933* – |≢|, ✎ rm, ▤ 🏧 ✆ ⅙ – 🛣 140. ⚙ ℗ ⓪ 𝓥𝓘𝓢𝓐 𝓙𝓒𝓑. 🍴   p. 17 DY a
The Strand Terrace : Meals 22.95 **t.** 🍷 14.95 – ☲ 16.50 – **238 rm** 223.00 **s.** – SB.

Ivy, 1 West St, WC2H 9NG, ℰ (020) 7836 4751, *Fax (020) 7240 9333* – ▤. ⚙ ℗ ⓪ 𝓥𝓘𝓢𝓐 𝓙𝓒𝓑
                                                                        p. 13 GK z
closed dinner 24-26 and 31 December, 1 January and August Bank Holiday – Meals a la carte 23.25/64.25 **t.** 🍷 11.50.

Axis, 1 Aldwych, WC2B 4BZ, ℰ (020) 7300 0300, *sales@onealdwych.co.uk, Fax (020) 7300 0301* – ▤. ⚙ ℗ ⓪ 𝓥𝓘𝓢𝓐 𝓙𝓒𝓑   p. 17 EX r
closed Sunday and Saturday lunch – Meals 24.75 (lunch) and a la carte 30.90/34.80 **t.** 🍷 19.95.

J.Sheekey, 28-32 St Martin's Court, WC2N 4AL, ℰ (020) 7240 2565, *Fax (020) 7240 8114* – ▤. ⚙ ℗ ⓪ 𝓥𝓘𝓢𝓐 𝓙𝓒𝓑   p. 17 DX v
closed dinner 24 December-2 January and Bank Holidays – Meals - Seafood - (booking essential) a la carte 21.25/53.25 **t.** 🍷 11.50.

Rules, 35 Maiden Lane, WC2E 7LB, ℰ (020) 7836 5314, *info@rules.co.uk, Fax (020) 7497 1081*, « London's oldest restaurant with collection of antique cartoons, drawings and paintings » – ✎ ▤. ⚙ ℗ ⓪ 𝓥𝓘𝓢𝓐 𝓙𝓒𝓑   p. 17 DX n
closed 5 days Christmas – Meals - English - (booking essential) a la carte 30.65/37.65 **t.** 🍷 13.95.

The Admiralty, Somerset House, The Strand, WC2R 1LA, ℰ (020) 7845 4646, *Fax (020) 7845 4647*, « Sited within magnificent 18C palace, former Naval headquarters » – ✎. ⚙ ℗ ⓪ 𝓥𝓘𝓢𝓐   p. 17 EY x
closed Sunday dinner – Meals 28.00 (lunch) and a la carte 34.50/47.50 **t.** 🍷 12.90.

Bank, 1 Kingsway, Aldwych, WC2B 6XF, ℰ (020) 7379 9797, *aldres@bankrestaurants.com, Fax (020) 7379 5070* – ▤. ⚙ ℗ ⓪ 𝓥𝓘𝓢𝓐   p. 17 EX s
closed 25 December, 1 January and Bank Holidays – Meals a la carte 27.45/38.50 **t.** 🍷 12.90.

Le Deuxième, 65a Long Acre, WC2E 9JH, ℰ (020) 7379 0033, *Fax (020) 7379 0066* – ▤. ⚙ ℗ ⓪ 𝓥𝓘𝓢𝓐   p. 17 DV e
closed 24-25 December – Meals 13.50 (lunch) and a la carte 21.00/28.00 **t.** 🍷 11.00.

Le Café du Jardin, 28 Wellington St, WC2E 7BD, ℰ (020) 7836 8769, *Fax (020) 7836 4123* – ▤. ⚙ ℗ ⓪ 𝓥𝓘𝓢𝓐   p. 17 EX a
closed 24-25 December – Meals 13.50 (lunch) and a la carte 21.00/28.00 **t.** 🍷 9.75.

Livebait, 21 Wellington St, WC2E 7DN, ℰ (020) 7836 7161, *Fax (020) 7836 7141* – ⚙ ℗ ⓪ 𝓥𝓘𝓢𝓐   p. 17 EX u
closed 25 December – Meals - Seafood - 15.50 (lunch) and a la carte 22.45/34.65 **st.**

Victoria – ✉ SW1 –.
🛈 Victoria Station Forecourt ℰ (0839) 123456.

Royal Horseguards, 2 Whitehall Court, SW1A 2EJ, ℰ (020) 7839 3400, *royal.horseguards@thistle.co.uk, Fax (020) 7925 2263*, 龠, 𝑓𝑎 – |≢| ✎ ▤ 🏧 ✆ – 🛣 180. ⚙ ℗ ⓪ 𝓥𝓘𝓢𝓐 𝓙𝓒𝓑. 🍴   p. 10 LX a
One Twenty One Two : Meals *(closed Saturday and Sunday lunch)* 19.50/24.50 and dinner a la carte **st.** 🍷 18.50 – ☲ 16.50 – **276 rm** 277.00/300.00 **st.**, 4 suites – SB.

Crowne Plaza London St James, 45 Buckingham Gate, SW1E 6AF, ℰ (020) 7834 6655, *sales@cplonsjco.uk, Fax (020) 7630 7587*, 𝑓𝑎, ⇌ – |≢|, ✎ rm, ▤ 🏧 ✆ – 🛣 180. ⚙ ℗ ⓪ 𝓥𝓘𝓢𝓐 𝓙𝓒𝓑. 🍴   p. 16 CX i
Café Mediterranée : Meals *(closed Sunday)* a la carte 20.00/32.50 **t.** 🍷 12.00 *(see also Quilon and Bank below)* – ☲ 16.00 – **323 rm** 245.00/295.00 **s.**, 19 suites.

The Goring, 15 Beeston Pl, Grosvenor Gdns, SW1W 0JW, ℘ (020) 7396 9000, *reception@goringhotel.co.uk, Fax (020) 7834 4393*, ✿ – |$| 🔲 📺 ❤ – 🅰 50. 🝙 🆚 🔳 🆚 🆚.
p. 16 BX a
Meals 25.00/40.00 **st.** 🍴 10.50 – ⚌ 16.50 – **68 rm** 195.00/240.00 **s.,** 6 suites.

41, 41 Buckingham Palace Rd, SW1W 0PS, ℘ (020) 7300 0041, *book41@rchmail.com, Fax (020) 7300 0141* – |$| 🔲 📺 🆚 🔳 🆚 🆚.
p. 16 BX n
Meals (residents only) – **16 rm** (fully inclusive) 295.00 **s.,** 4 suites.

The Rubens at The Palace, 39 Buckingham Palace Rd, SW1W 0PS, ℘ (020) 7834 6600, *reservations@rubens.redcarnationhotels.com, Fax (020) 7828 5401* – |$|, ✿ rm, 🔲 📺 🔳 🆚 🆚. ✿
p. 16 BX n
Meals *(closed lunch Saturday, Sunday and Bank Holidays)* (carving lunch) 16.95 (lunch) and a la carte approx. 18.00 **t.** 🍴 14.50 – **The Library :** **Meals** (dinner only) a la carte 31.00/47.00 **t.** 🍴 14.50 – ⚌ 15.00 – **171 rm** 180.00/210.00 **s.,** 2 suites.

Dolphin Square, Dolphin Sq, Chichester St, SW1V 3LX, ℘ (020) 7834 3800, *reservations@dolphinsquarehotel.co.uk, Fax (020) 7798 8735*, ♨, ⚌, 🔳, ✿, ✾, squash – |$| ✿, 🔲 rest, 📺 ✿ – 🅰 50. 🝙 🆚 🔳 🆚. ✿
p. 10 KZ a
The Brasserie · **Meals** 14.50 and a la carte approx. 18.65 **st.** 🍴 11.00 (see also **Rhodes in the Square** below) – ⚌ 12.95 – **48 rm** 155.00/190.00 **st.,** **117 suites** 190.00/400.00 **st** – SB.

Jolly St Ermin's, Caxton St, SW1H 0QW, ℘ (020) 7222 7888, *Fax (020) 7222 6914* – |$| ✿ rm, 📺 🆚 – 🅰 110. 🝙 🆚 🔳 🆚 🆚. ✿
p. 16 CX a
Cloisters Brasserie : **Meals** (buffet lunch) 19.75 and a la carte 20.00/35.00 **t.** 🍴 14.50 – ⚌ 15.95 – **283 rm** 175.00/215.00 **s.,** 8 suites – SB.

Thistle Victoria, 101 Buckingham Palace Rd, SW1W 0SJ, ℘ (020) 7834 9494, *victoria@thistle.co.uk, Fax (020) 7630 1978* – |$|, ✿ rm, 📺 🆚 – 🅰 200. 🝙 🆚 🔳 🆚. ✿
p. 16 BX e
Meals (see **Christopher's** below) – ⚌ 13.95 – **361 rm** 176.00/247.00 **st.,** 3 suites – SB.

Thistle Westminster, 49 Buckingham Palace Rd, SW1W 0QT, ℘ (020) 7834 1821, *westminster@thistle.co.uk, Fax (020) 7931 7542* – |$|, ✿ rm, 🔲 📺 🆚 – 🅰 150. 🝙 🆚 🔳 🆚. ✿
p. 16 BX z
Meals 14.75 and a la carte approx. 23.35 🍴 11.95 – ⚌ 10.95 – **134 rm** 215.00/242.00 **s.** – SB.

Grange Rochester, 69 Vincent Sq, SW1P 2PA, ℘ (020) 7828 6611, *rochester@grangehotels.co.uk, Fax (020) 7233 6724* – |$| ✿, 🔲 rest, 📺 – 🅰 70. 🝙 🆚 🔳 🆚 🆚.
The Pavilion : **Meals** (bar lunch Saturday, Sunday and Bank Holidays) 24.50 and a la carte 17.55/27.85 **st.** 🍴 12.15 – ⚌ 15.00 – **76 rm** 170.00/190.00 **st.**   p. 16 CY e

Rhodes in the Square (at Dolphin Square H.), Dolphin Sq, Chichester St, SW1V 3LX, ℘ (020) 7798 6767, *Fax (020) 7798 5685* – 🝙 🆚 🔳 🆚   p. 10 KZ a
closed Saturday lunch, Sunday and Monday – **Meals** 19.80/36.50 **st.** 🍴 16.50
Spec. Lobster omelette thermidor. Milk-poached pork, broad beans and sage cream. Grand Marnier baba, compote of kumquats.

The Cinnamon Club, Great Smith St, SW1P 3BU, ℘ (020) 7222 2555, *info@cinnamonclub.com, Fax (020) 7222 1333*, « Former public library » – 🔲 🄿. 🝙 🆚 🔳 🆚. ✿
closed Saturday lunch and Sunday dinner – **Meals** - Indian - 18.00 (lunch) and a la carte 23.50/32.50 **t.** 🍴 13.00.   p. 10 LY c

Quilon (at Crowne Plaza London St James H.), 45 Buckingham Gate, SW1 6AF, ℘ (020) 7821 1899, *Fax (020) 7828 5802* – 🔲. 🝙 🆚 🔳 🆚   p. 16 CX i
closed Sunday and Saturday lunch – **Meals** - Indian - 12.95/15.95 (lunch) and dinner a la carte 21.00/28.00.

L'Incontro, 87 Pimlico Rd, SW1W 8PH, ℘ (020) 7730 6327, *Fax (020) 7730 5062* – 🔲. 🝙 🆚 🔳 🆚   p. 15 FT u
closed Easter, 25-26 December and lunch Saturday and Sunday – **Meals** - Italian - 19.50 (lunch) and a la carte 29.50/49.00 **t.** 🍴 15.75.

Santini, 29 Ebury St, SW1W 0NZ, ℘ (020) 7730 4094, *Fax (020) 7730 0544* – 🔲. 🝙 🆚 🔳 🆚   p. 16 ABX v
closed Easter Sunday, 25-26 December and lunch Saturday and Sunday – **Meals** - Italian - 19.75 (lunch) and a la carte 26.50/43.00 **t.** 🍴 11.00.

Shepherd's, Marsham Court, Marsham St, SW1P 4LA, ℘ (020) 7834 9552, *admin@langansrestaurants.co.uk, Fax (020) 7233 6047* – 🔲. 🝙 🆚 🔳 🆚 🆚   p. 10 LZ z
closed Saturday, Sunday and Bank Holidays – **Meals** - English - (booking essential) 27.00 **t.** 🍴 13.00.

Roussillon, 16 St Barnabas St, SW1W 8PB, ℘ (020) 7730 5550, *alexis@roussillon.co.uk, Fax (020) 7824 8617* – 🔲. 🝙 🆚 🆚 🆚   p. 9 IZ c
closed last 2 weeks August, Sunday, Saturday lunch and Bank Holidays – **Meals** 18.00/50.00 **t.** 🍴 13.50
Spec. Blue Bembridge lobster salad. Fricassee of chicken and crayfish with morels and chervil. Spicy goose egg soufflé, maple infusion and gingerbread fingers.

XX **Il Convivio,** 143 Ebury St, SW1W 9QN, ℰ (020) 7730 4099, Fax (020) 7730 4103, ⌂ – ▤. ◍⊚ Æ ⓪ ᴠɪꜱᴀ ᴊᴄʙ p. 16 AY a
closed 1 week Christmas, Sunday and Bank Holidays – **Meals** - Italian - 20.00/35.50 **t.**
Å 14.50.

XX **Simply Nico,** 48a Rochester Row, SW1P 1JU, ℰ (020) 7630 8061, Fax (020) 7828 8541 – ▤. ◍⊚ Æ ⓪ ᴠɪꜱᴀ ᴊᴄʙ p.16 CY a
closed Easter, 25-26 December, Saturday lunch, Sunday and Bank Holidays – **Meals** (booking essential) a la carte 21.90/33.95 **t.** Å 12.95.

XX **Bank,** 45 Buckingham Gate, SW1E 6BS, ℰ (020) 7379 9797, westres@bankrestaurant s.co.uk, Fax (020) 7379 5070, ⌂ – ▤. ◍⊚ Æ ⓪ ᴠɪꜱᴀ p. 16 CX i
closed 25-26 December – **Meals** 15.50 (lunch) and a la carte 23.80/36.25 **t.** Å 12.90.

XX **Boisdale,** 15 Eccleston St, SW1W 9LX, ℰ (020) 7730 6922, katarina@boisdale.co.uk, Fax (020) 7730 0548, ⌂ – ▤. ◍⊚ Æ ⓪ ᴠɪꜱᴀ p. 16 AY c
closed 25 December-1 January, Bank Holidays, Sunday and Saturday lunch – **Meals** - Scottish - (live jazz at dinner) 17.45 and a la carte 22.45/47.40 **t.** Å 14.00.

XX **Christopher's,** 101 Buckingham Palace Rd, SW1W 0SJ, ℰ (020) 7976 5522, info@christophers.net, Fax (020) 7976 5521 – ▤. ◍⊚ Æ ⓪ ᴠɪꜱᴀ p. 16 BX e
Meals - American Grill - 16.50 (lunch) and a la carte 30.00 **t.** Å 15.50.

XX **Tate Britain,** Tate Gallery, Millbank, SW1P 4RG, ℰ (020) 7887 8825, tate.restaurant @tate.org.uk, Fax (020) 7887 8902, « Rex Whistler murals » – ▤. ◍⊚ Æ ⓪ ᴠɪꜱᴀ p. 10 LZ c
Meals (booking essential) (lunch only) 16.75/19.50 and a la carte 20.95/31.50 **t.** Å 20.00.

XX **Ken Lo's Memories of China,** 67-69 Ebury St, SW1W 0NZ, ℰ (020) 7730 7734, Fax (020) 7730 2992 – ▤. ◍⊚ Æ ⓪ ᴠɪꜱᴀ p. 16 AY u
closed 24 December-1 January, Easter Sunday-Monday, Sunday lunch and Bank Holidays – **Meals** - Chinese - 19.00/28.50 and a la carte 22.00/36.70 **t.** Å 13.50.

XX **The Atrium,** 4 Millbank (lower ground floor), SW1P 3JA, ℰ (020) 7233 0032, Fax (020) 7233 0010 – ▤. ◍⊚ Æ ⓪ ᴠɪꜱᴀ ᴊᴄʙ p. 10 LY s
closed Christmas, Saturday, Sunday and Bank Holidays – **Meals** a la carte 20.25/27.70 **t.**

X **Olivo,** 21 Eccleston St, SW1W 9LX, ℰ (020) 7730 2505 – ▤. ◍⊚ Æ ᴠɪꜱᴀ p. 16 AY z
closed lunch Saturday and Sunday and Bank Holidays – **Meals** - Italian - 17.00 (lunch) and dinner a la carte 24.50/32.50 **t.** Å 13.50.

X **La Poule au Pot,** 231 Ebury St, SW1W 8UT, ℰ (020) 7730 7763, Fax (020) 7259 9651, ⌂ – ▤. ◍⊚ Æ ⓪ ᴠɪꜱᴀ ᴊᴄʙ p. 9 IZ e
Meals - French - 14.50 (lunch) and a la carte 24.75/36.75 **t.** Å 11.50.

---

ray-on-Thames Windsor & Maidenhead ▦▦ R 29 – pop. 8121 – ✉ Maidenhead.
London 34 – Reading 13.

XXXX **Waterside Inn** (Roux) with rm, Ferry Rd, SL6 2AT, ℰ (01628) 620691, reservations
⊛⊛⊛ @waterside-inn.co.uk, Fax (01628) 784710, « ≤ Thames-side setting » –, 🅹 ▤ ᴛᴠ 🅿. ◍⊚ Æ ⓪ ᴠɪꜱᴀ ᴊᴄʙ. ⌂
closed 26 December-31 January and 3-4 April – **Meals** - French - (closed Tuesday except dinner June-August and Monday) 33.50/74.00 and a la carte 67.00/99.50 **t.** Å 26.00 –
8 rm 160.00/185.00 **st.,** 1 suite
Spec. Tronçonnettes de homard poêlées minute au Porto blanc. Filets de lapereau grillés aux marrons glacés. Soufflé chaud aux framboises.

XXX **Fat Duck** (Blumenthal), High St, SL6 2AQ, ℰ (01628) 580333, Fax (01628) 776188, ⌂
⊛⊛ – ◍⊚ Æ ⓪ ᴠɪꜱᴀ ᴊᴄʙ
closed 24 December-8 January, Sunday dinner and Monday – **Meals** 25.75/58.00 and a la carte 58.00/75.00 **t.** Å 16.00
Spec. Crab biscuit, roast foie gras, marinated salmon and oyster vinaigrette. Saddle of lamb, lamb tongue and onion purée. Chocolate fondant, avocado risotto, coconut sorbet.

---

xford Oxon. ▦▦ ▦▦ Q 28 – pop. 118 795.
🅑 The Old School, Gloucester Green ℰ (01865) 726871.
London 59 – Birmingham 63 – Bristol 73.

▦▦ **Le Manoir aux Quat' Saisons** (Blanc) ⌘, Church Rd, OX44 7PD, ℰ (01844) 278881,
⊛⊛ lemanoir@blanc.co.uk, Fax (01844) 278847, ≤, « Part 15C and 16C manor house, gardens », 🅰 – ↬ rest, ▤ rest, ᴛᴠ ℰ 🅿. ⏚ 50. ◍⊚ Æ ⓪ ᴠɪꜱᴀ ᴊᴄʙ. ⌘
Meals - French - 45.00 (lunch weekdays only) and a la carte 70.00/77.00 **st.** Å 25.00 –
25 rm ☷ 245.00/375.00 **st.,** 7 suites 395.00/650.00 **st.** – SB
Spec. Confit of wild salmon, horseradish sauce. Macaroni in truffle butter with langoustines. Braised rabbit shoulder and roasted loin in tarragon mustard jus.

BIRMINGHAM *W. Mids.* 403 404 O 26 *Great Britain G. – pop. 965 928.*

See : *City★ – Museum and Art Gallery★★* JZ **M2** *– Barber Institute of Fine Arts★★ (at Birmingham University)* EX *– Cathedral of St. Philip (stained glass portrayals★)* KYZ.

Envir. : *Aston Hall★★* FV **M.**

Exc. : *Black Country Museum★, Dudley, NW : 10 m. by A 456 and A 4123 – Bourneville★ SW : 4 m. on A 38 and A 441.*

18 Edgbaston, Church Rd ☎ (0121) 454 1736 FX *– 18 Hilltop, Park Lane, Handsworth ☎ (0121) 554 4463 – 18 Hatchford Brook, Coventry Rd, Sheldon (0121) 743 9821* HX *– 18 Brand Hall, Heron Rd, Oldbury, Warley ☎ (0121) 552 2195 – 18 Harborne Church Farm Vicarage Rd, Harborne (0121) 427 1204* EX.

Birmingham International Airport : ☎ (0121) 767 5511, E : 6 ½ m. by A 45.

Convention & Visitor Bureau, 2 City Arcade ☎ (0121) 643 2514, Fax (0121) 616 1038 – Convention & Visitor Bureau, National Exhibition Centre ☎ (0121) 780 4321 – Birmingham Airport, Information Desk ☎ (0121) 767 7145/7146 130 Colmore Row ☎ (0121) 693 6300.

London 122 – Bristol 91 – Liverpool 103 – Manchester 86 – Nottingham 50.

Plans on following pages

Hyatt Regency, 2 Bridge St, B1 2JZ, ☎ (0121) 643 1234, *hrbirm@hrb.co.uk Fax (0121) 616 2323,* ≤, Fб, ≘s, ⊡ – |‡|, ⇹ rm, ▤ TV ♿ – 🅰 250. MC AE ◑ VISA JCB. ⚮ JZ a
Meals 13.50 (lunch) and a la carte 18.00/28.75 **st.** 14.50 – ☐ 13.25 – **315 rm** 175.00 **st.** 4 suites.

Birmingham Marriott, 12 Hagley Rd, B16 8SJ, ☎ (0121) 452 1144 *Fax (0121) 456 3442,* Fб, ⊡ – |‡|, ⇹ rm, ▤ TV ♿ P – 🅰 30. MC AE ◑ VISA JCB FX c
Langtrys **: Meals** *(closed Sunday lunch)* 16.50 (lunch) and a la carte 23.50/32.00 **t.** 12.00 (see also ***Sir Edward Elgar's*** below) – ☐ 14.45 – **94 rm** 149.00/195.00 **st.**, 4 suites – SB.

Hotel Du Vin, 25 Church St, B3 2NR, ☎ (0121) 236 0559, *info@birmingham.hoteldu vin.com, Fax (0121) 236 0889,* « Converted Victorian hospital, contemporary wine themed interior », Fб, ≘s – |‡|, ⇹ rm, TV ♿ – 🅰 85. MC AE ◑ VISA. ⚮ JY e
Bistro **:** **Meals** a la carte 26.25/31.25 **t.** 11.50 – ☐ 11.50 – **66 rm** 110.00/175.00 **t.**

Crowne Plaza Birmingham, Central Sq, B1 1HH, ☎ (0121) 631 2000 *Fax (0121) 643 9018,* Fб, ≘s, ⊡ – |‡|, ⇹ rm, ▤ TV ♿ P – 🅰 150. MC AE ◑ VISA JZ z
closed 24-26 December – **Meals** *(closed Saturday lunch)* (carvery) 12.95/19.95 and a la carte 22.45/27.95 **st.** – ☐ 13.95 – **281 rm** 139.00/149.00 **st.**, 3 suites.

The Burlington, Burlington Arcade, 126 New St, B2 4JQ, ☎ (0121) 643 9191, *ma @burlingtonhotel.com, Fax (0121) 643 5075,* Fб, ≘s – |‡|, ⇹ rm, ▤ rest, TV – 🅰 400 MC AE ◑ VISA KZ a
closed 24-30 December – ***Berlioz*** **: Meals** 18.00/22.00 and a la carte 22.00/40.00 **t** 13.50 – ☐ 13.50 – **107 rm** 135.00/145.00 **st.**, 5 suites.

Copthorne, Paradise Circus, B3 3HJ, ☎ (0121) 200 2727, *sales.birmingham@mill-cop .com, Fax (0121) 200 1197,* Fб, ≘s, ⊡ – |‡|, ⇹ rm, ▤ rest, TV ♿ P – 🅰 180. MC AE ◑ VISA. ⚮ JZ e
Goldsmiths **: Meals** (dinner only) a la carte 24.70/33.95 **t.** – ***Goldies*** **: Meals** 15.00 and a la carte 18.35/27.15 **t.** 13.50 – ☐ 13.95 – **209 rm** 150.00/170.00 **st.**, 3 suites – SB.

Jonathan's, 16-24 Wolverhampton Rd, Oldbury, B68 0LH, West : 4 m. by A 456 ☎ (0121) 429 3757, *sales@jonathans.co.uk, Fax (0121) 434 3107,* « Authentic Victorian furnishing and memorabilia » – ⇹, ▤ rest, TV P – 🅰 100. MC AE ◑ VISA. ⚮
Victorian Restaurant **: Meals** - English - *(closed Saturday lunch and 1 January)* (booking essential) 15.90 (lunch) and a la carte 32.50/35.00 **t.** 12.90 – ***Secret Garden*** **: Meals** *(closed Saturday and Sunday lunch, 1 January and Bank Holidays)* 9.50 (lunch) and a la carte 9.40/14.80 **t.** 12.00 – **46 rm** ☐ 98.00/125.00 **st.**, 2 suites – SB.

Birmingham Grand Moat House, Colmore Row, B3 2DA, ☎ (0121) 607 9988, *rev gd@queensmoat.co.uk, Fax (0121) 233 1465* – |‡|, ⇹ rm, ▤ rest, TV – 🅰 500. MC AE ◑ VISA JKY c
Hugo's **: Meals** a la carte 13.40/23.40 **st.** 11.95 – ☐ 11.50 – **170 rm** 120.00/140.00 **st.** 3 suites – SB.

Posthouse Birmingham City, Smallbrook, Queensway, B5 4EW, ☎ (0870) 4009008 *gm1841@forte-hotels.com, Fax (0121) 631 2528* – |‡|, ⇹ rm, TV P – 🅰 630. MC AE VISA KZ c
Meals *(closed Saturday lunch)* (carvery rest.) 10.00/18.00 **st.** 11.95 – ☐ 13.95 – **280 rm** 129.00 **st.** – SB.

City Inn, 1 Brunswick Sq, Brindley Pl, B1 2HW, ☎ (0121) 643 1003, *birmingham.rese vations@cityinn.com, Fax (0121) 643 1005,* ☂, Fб – |‡| ⇹ ▤ TV ♿ – 🅰 105. MC AE ◑ VISA. ⚮ FV a
closed 24-31 December – ***City Café*** **: Meals** 12.80/15.95 and a la carte 20.20/32.20 **st** 11.25 – ☐ 10.50 – **238 rm** 89.00 **st.**

Novotel, 70 Broad St, B1 2HT, ℰ (0121) 643 2000, *hlo77@accor-hotels.com,* Fax (0121) 643 9796, ₤₅, ≋ – ⧉, ⅙ rm, ▤ rest, 𝕋 ✆ ⅙ ⇔ – 🔬 300. 🐵 🌐 ⓞ ▮☒◭ 🖈
FV e
Meals 10.00/25.00 and a la carte 14.00/28.00 **st.** ⅟ 12.00 – ⌐ 11.00 **148 rm** 99.00 **st.** – SB.

Jurys Inn, 245 Broad St, B1 2HQ, ℰ (0121) 626 0626, *info@chamberlain.co.uk,* Fax (0121) 626 0627 – ⧉ ⅙, ▤ rest, 𝕋 ✆ ⅙ ⇔ – 🔬 400. 🐵 🌐 ⓞ ▮☒◭ 🖈 FV z
Meals (carvery) 10.00/12.00 ⅟ 8.00 – ⌐ 6.00 – **445 rm** 59.00 **st.**

Paragon, Alcester St, B12 0PJ, ℰ (0121) 627 0627, *info@chamberlain.co.uk,* Fax (0121) 627 0628 – ⧉ ⅙, ▤ rest, 𝕋 ✆ ⅙ ⇔ – 🔬 400. 🐵 🌐 ⓞ ▮☒◭ 🖈 FX r
Meals (carving rest.) 10.00 ⅟ 3.75 – **250 rm** ⌐ 49.00/59.00.

Sir Edward Elgar's (at Birmingham Marriott H.), 12 Hagley Rd, B16 8SJ, ℰ (0121) 452 1144, Fax (0121) 456 3442 – ▤ 🄿 ▮☒◭ 🐵 🌐 ⓞ ▮☒◭ 🖈 FX c
closed Monday – **Meals** (dinner only and Sunday lunch)/dinner 32.50 and a la carte 29.75/39.95 **t.** ⅟ 13.95.

Bank, 4 Brindleyplace, B1 2JB, ℰ (0121) 633 4466, Fax (0121) 633 4465, ☞ – ▤. 🐵 ▮☒◭ 🌐 ⓞ ▮☒◭
FV u
closed 26 December and 1 January – **Meals** 12.50 (lunch) and a la carte 23.50/34.65 **t.** ⅟ 11.00.

La Toque D'Or, 27 Warstone Lane, Hockley, B18 6JQ, ℰ (0121) 233 3655, *didier@latoquedor.co.uk,* Fax (01562) 754957, « Former rolling mill » – 🐵 🌐 ▮☒◭ FV r
closed 1 week Easter, 2 weeks August, Christmas, New Year, Sunday, Monday, Tuesday after Bank Holidays and Saturday lunch – **Meals** - French - 15.50/23.50 **t.** ⅟ 12.50.

Metro Bar and Grill, 73 Cornwall St, B3 2DF, ℰ (0121) 200 1911, Fax (0121) 200 1611 – ▤. 🐵 🌐 ▮☒◭
JY n
closed Sunday – **Meals** (booking essential) a la carte 18.90/27.85 **t.** ⅟ 10.95.

Henry's, 27 St Paul's Sq, B3 1RB, ℰ (0121) 200 1136, Fax (0121) 200 1190 – ▤. 🐵 ▮☒◭ ⓞ ▮☒◭
JY a
closed 25-26 December and Bank Holiday Monday – **Meals** - Chinese (Canton) - 16.50/38.00 and a la carte 16.20/36.80 **t.** ⅟ 8.80.

Le Petit Blanc, Nine Brindleyplace, B1 2HS, ℰ (0121) 633 7333, *birmingham@lepetitblanc.co.uk,* Fax (0121) 633 7444 – ⅙ ▤. 🐵 ▮☒◭ ⓞ ▮☒◭ FV x
closed 25 December – **Meals** 15.00 (lunch) and a la carte 24.70/29.90 **t.** ⅟ 11.00.

at Hall Green Southeast : 5 ¾ m. by A 41 on A 34 – ✉ Birmingham :

Mizan, 1347 Stratford Rd, B28 9HW, ℰ (0121) 777 3185 – ▤. 🐵 ▮☒◭ ▮☒◭ 🖈 GX a
Meals - Indian - (dinner only and Thursday lunch)/dinner a la carte 9.90/16.45 **t.** ⅟ 7.50.

at Birmingham Airport Southeast : 9 m. by A 45 HX – ✉ Birmingham :

Holiday Inn Birmingham Airport, Coventry Rd, B26 3QW, on A 45 ℰ (0870) 4009007, *gm1029@forte-hotels.com,* Fax (0121) 782 2476 – ⅙ 𝕋 ✆ ⅙ 🄿 – 🔬 130. 🐵 ▮☒◭ ⓞ ▮☒◭ 🖈
Meals (closed Saturday and Sunday lunch) 13.00/15.00 and dinner a la carte 21.85/30.40 **st.** ⅟ 19.95 – ⌐ 14.95 – **141 rm** 149.00 **st.**

Novotel, Passenger Terminal, B26 5QL, ℰ (0121) 782 7000, *H1158@accor-hotels.com,* Fax (0121) 782 0445 – ⧉, ⅙ rm, 𝕋 ✆ ⅙ – 🔬 35. 🐵 ▮☒◭ ⓞ ▮☒◭
Meals (closed lunch Saturday, Sunday and Bank Holidays) 14.50/20.00 and a la carte 16.50/27.40 **st.** ⅟ 11.25 – ⌐ 11.50 – **195 rm** 107.00 **st.**

at National Exhibition Centre Southeast : 9 ½ m. on A 45 HX – ✉ Birmingham :

Hilton Birmingham Metropole, Bickenhill, B40 1PP, ℰ (0121) 780 4242, Fax (0121) 780 3923, ₤₅, ≋, ☒ – ⧉, ⅙ rm, ▤ 𝕋 ⅙ 🄿 – 🔬 2000. 🐵 ▮☒◭ ⓞ ▮☒◭
Meals (closed Saturday lunch) (carvery) 18.00/28.50 **t.** ⅟ 18.00 – **Primavera :** Meals - Italian - (dinner only) 31.95 and a la carte 32.15/43.95 **st.** ⅟ 18.00 – ⌐ 14.00 – **779 rm** 235.00/315.00 **st.,** 15 suites – SB.

at Acocks Green Southwest : 5 m. by A 41 – ✉ Birmingham

Westley, Westley Rd, B13 9YZ, ℰ (0121) 706 4312, *reservations@westley-hotel.co.uk,* Fax (0121) 706 2824 – 𝕋 🄿 – 🔬 200. 🐵 ▮☒◭ ⓞ ▮☒◭ GX c
accommodation closed 24-25 December – **Meals** (bar lunch Monday-Saturday)/dinner 14.95 and a la carte **st.** ⅟ 10.50 – ⌐ 9.00 – **35 rm** 75.00/86.00 **st.,** 1 suite.

at Great Barr Northwest : 6 m. on A 34 FV – ✉ Birmingham :

Holiday Inn Birmingham, Chapel Lane, B43 7BG, ℰ (0870) 4009009, *gm1030@forte-hotels.com,* Fax (0121) 357 7503, ₤₅, ≋, ☒ – ⅙ rm, 𝕋 🄿 – 🔬 120. 🐵 ▮☒◭ ⓞ ▮☒◭ 🖈
Meals 13.00/15.00 and dinner a la carte 16.15/29.00 **st.** ⅟ 11.95 – ⌐ 13.95 – **192 rm** 129.00 **st.**

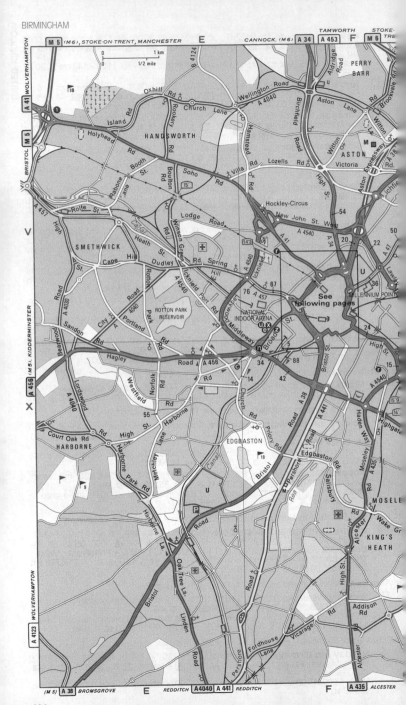

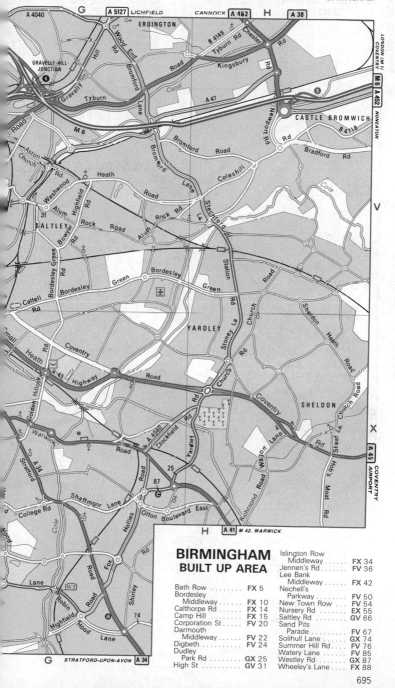

BIRMINGHAM
BUILT UP AREA

BIRMINGHAM
CENTRE

GREEN TOURIST GUIDES

Picturesque scenery, buildings
Attractive route
Touring programmes
Plans of towns and buildings.

STREET INDEX TO BIRMINGHAM TOWN PLANS

Don't get lost, use **Michelin Maps** which are updated annually.

at West Bromwich Northwest : 6 m. on A 41 EV – ⊠ Birmingham :

🏨 **Moat House Birmingham,** Birmingham Rd, B70 6RS, ℰ (0121) 609 9988, revbw.
@ queensmoat.co.uk, Fax (0121) 525 7403, ↳, ⇔, ☒ – ⧉, ⇔ rm, ▤ rest, 📺 ℙ.
⚿ 180. ⓦ ⒶⒺ ⓪ 𝘝𝘐𝘚𝘈 𝘑𝘊𝘉
Meals (closed Saturday lunch) a la carte 13.45/27.85 **t.** ⓵ 11.95 – ⚌ 11.50 – **168 rm**
118.00/135.00 **st.** – SB.

Cheltenham Glos. ⁴⁰³ ⁴⁰⁴ N 28 – pop. 91301.
🛈 77 Promenade ℰ (01242) 522878.
London 99 – Birmingham 48 – Bristol 40 – Oxford 43.

XX **Le Champignon Sauvage** (Everitt-Matthias), 24-26 Suffolk Rd, GL50 2AQ, ℰ (01242
🕸🕸 573449, Fax (01242) 254365 – ⓦ ⒶⒺ ⓪ 𝘝𝘐𝘚𝘈 𝘑𝘊𝘉
closed 3 weeks June, 10 days Christmas-New Year, Sunday and Monday – **Meals**
19.95/39.00 **t.** ⓵ 10.95
Spec. Pan-fried foie gras with walnuts and quince, Banyuls sauce. Fillet of pork, chou farc
and black pudding. Feuillantine of mango, Thai spiced cream and red wine syrup.

Bath Bath & North East Somerset ⁴⁰³ ⁴⁰⁴ M 29 – pop. 85202.
🛈 Abbey Chambers, Abbey Churchyard ℰ (01225) 477101.
London 119 – Birmingham 98.

XX **Blinis** (Blunos), 16 Argyle St, BA2 4BJ, ℰ (01225) 422510, Fax (01225) 421764 – ⇔
🕸🕸 ⓦ ⒶⒺ ⓪ 𝘝𝘐𝘚𝘈
closed Sunday, Monday and lunch Tuesday – **Meals** 25.00/47.50 **t.** ⓵ 22.00
Spec. Scrambled duck egg with Sevruga caviar, blinis and iced vodka. Tortellini of fresh
eel with deep fried elvers. Slow braised honey-glazed belly of pork.

Chagford Devon ⁴⁰³ I 31 – pop. 1417.
London 218 – Bath 102 – Birmingham 186.

🏨 **Gidleigh Park** ⬎, TQ13 8HH, Northwest : 2 m. by Gidleigh Rd ℰ (01647) 432367,
🕸🕸 gidleighpark@gidleigh.co.uk, Fax (01647) 432574, ≼ Teign Valley, woodland and Meldon
Hill, « Timbered country house, water garden », ⬎, ⚘, ✗ – ⇔ rest, 📺 ℙ. ⓦ ⓪ 𝘝𝘐𝘚𝘈
𝘑𝘊𝘉
Meals (booking essential) 33.00/72.50 **st.** ⓵ 20.00 – **12 rm** ⚌ (dinner included)
260.00/500.00 **st.**, 3 suites
Spec. Ravioli of lobster with cabbage and girolles. John Dory with aubergine galette, lemon
thyme sauce. Poached cherries, cherry and kirsch ice cream.

EDINBURGH Edinburgh City ⁴⁰¹ K 16 Scotland G. – pop. 418914.
See : City★★★ Edinburgh International Festival★★★ (August) – National Gallery of
Scotland★★ DY **M4** Royal Botanic Garden★★★ The Castle★★ AC DYZ : Site★★★ – Palace
Block (Honours of Scotland★★★) St. Margaret's Chapel (⚜ ★★★) Great Hall (Hammerbeam
Roof★★) ≼★★ from Argyle and Mill's Mount DZ – Abbey and Palace of Holyroodhouse★★
AC (Plasterwork Ceilings★★★, ⚜ ★★ from Arthur's Seat) – Royal Mile★★ : St. Giles'
Cathedral★★ (Crown Spire★★★) EYZ Gladstone's Land★ AC EYZ **A** – Canongate Talbooth★
EY **B** – New Town★★ (Charlotte Square★★★ CY **14** Royal Museum of Scotland★★ EZ **M2**
– The Georgian House ★ AC CY **D** Scottish National Portrait Gallery★ EY **M3** Dundas House★
EY **E**) – Scottish National Gallery of Modern Art★ Victoria Street★ EZ **84** Scott Monument★
(≼★) AC EY **F** – Craigmillar Castle★ AC Calton Hill (⚜ ★★★ AC from Nelson's Monument)
EY.
Envir. : Edinburgh Zoo★★ AC – Hill End Ski Centre (⚜ ★★) AC, S : 5 ½ m. by A 702 – The
Royal Observatory (West Tower ≼★) AC – Ingleston, Scottish Agricultural Museum★, W :
6 ½m. by A 8.
Exc. : Rosslyn Chapel★★ AC (Apprentice Pillar★★★) S : 7 ½ m. by A 701 and B 7006 – Forth
Bridges★★, NW : 9 ½ m. by A 90 – Hopetoun House★★ AC, NW : 11 ½ m. by A 90 and
A 904 – Dalmeny★ (Dalmeny House★ AC, St. Cuthbert's Church★ - Norman South
Doorway★★) NW : 7 m. by A 90 – Crichton Castle (Italianate courtyard range★) AC, SE :
10 m. by A 7 and B 6372.
🏌, 🏌 Braid Hills, Braid Hills Rd ℰ (0131) 447 6666 – 🏌 Craigmillar Park, 1 Observatory
Rd ℰ (0131) 667 2837 – 🏌 Carrick Knowe, Glendevon Park ℰ (0131) 337 1096 – 🏌
Duddingston Road West ℰ (0131) 661 1005 – 🏌 Silverknowes, Parkway ℰ (0131)
336 3843 – 🏌 Liberton, 297 Gilmerton Rd ℰ (0131) 664 3009 🏌, 🏌 Dalmahoy Hotel C.C.,
Kirknewton ℰ (0131) 333 4105 – 🏌 Portobello, Stanley St. ℰ (0131) 669 4361.
✈ Edinburgh Airport : ℰ (0131) 333 1000, W : 6 m. by A 8 – **Terminal :** Waverley Bridge.
🛈 Edinburgh & Scotland Information Centre, 3 Princes St. ℰ (0131) 473 3800 – Edinburgh
Airport, Tourist Information Desk ℰ (0131) 333 2167.
Glasgow 46 – Newcastle upon Tyne 105.

EDINBURGH

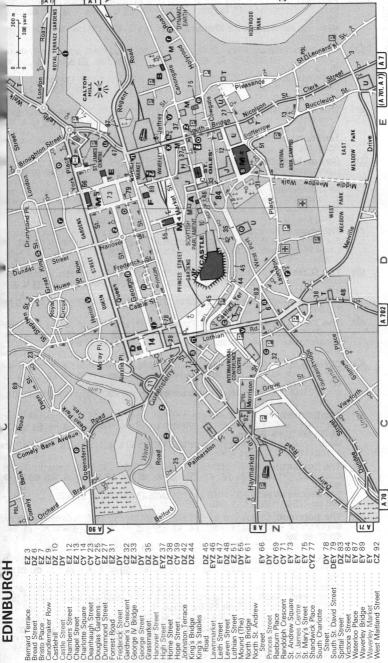

Balmoral, 1 Princes St, EH2 2EQ, *℘* (0131) 556 2414, *reservations@ thebalmoralho l.com, Fax (0131) 557 3747,* ↕↓, ⇌, ⊠ – ⊫ ↤ ▤ TV ✆ & ⟺ – 🔥 400. **◯◯** 🆎 **◯**
VISA JCB EY
Meals (see *Number One* and *Hadrian's* below) – ⊒ 16.75 – **167 rm** 184.00/268.00 st 21 suites.

Caledonian Hilton, Princes St, EH1 2AB, *℘* (0131) 222 8888, *ednchhirm@ hilton.c m.net, Fax (0131) 222 8889,* ↕↓, ⇌, ⊠ – ⊫, ↤ rm, ▤ rest, TV ✆ & 🄿 – 🔥 250. **◯◯**
🆎 **◯** **VISA**. ✁ CY
La Pompadour : Meals 15.50/18.50 (lunch) and a la carte 13.25/31.95 **st.** ⏶ 18.50
Chisholms : Meals a la carte 16.50/30.50 **st.** ⏶ 15.50 – ⊒ 14.95 – **236 rm** 190.00/380.00 **st.**, 13 suites – SB.

Sheraton Grand, 1 Festival Sq, EH3 9SR, *℘* (0131) 229 9131, *grandedinburgh.sher ton@sheraton.com, Fax (0131) 229 6254,* ↕↓, ⇌, ⊠ – ⊫, ↤ rm, ▤ TV ✆ & 🄿.
🔥 500. **◯◯** 🆎 **◯** **VISA JCB**. ✁ CDZ
Terrace : Meals (buffet only) 19.95 and a la carte 15.75/23.00 **t.** ⏶ 19.00 (see also *Gr Room* below) – ⊒ 15.95 – **243 rm** 192.00/272.00 **t.**, 17 suites – SB.

George Inter-Continental, 19 21 George St, EH2 2PB, *℘* (0131) 225 1251, *edin urgh@interconti.com, Fax (0131) 226 5644* – ⊫, ↤ rm, TV ✆ – 🔥 200. **◯◯** 🆎 **◯** **VIS JCB**. ✁ DY
Le Chambertin (*℘* (0131) 240 7178) : Meals *(closed Saturday lunch and Sunday* 15.50 and a la carte 31.00/39.00 **st.** ⏶ 13.50 – *Carvers* (*℘* (0131) 459 2305) : Meal 19.00 and a la carte 26.50/32.00 **st.** ⏶ 13.50 – ⊒ 16.50 – **192 rm** 180.00/230.00 st 3 suites.

The Howard, 34 Great King St, EH3 6QH, *℘* (0131) 557 3500, *reserve@ thehoward.com Fax (0131) 557 6515,* « Georgian town houses » – ⊫ TV 🄿 – 🔥 30. **◯◯** 🆎 **◯** **VISA**. ✁ *closed 23-27 December* – Meals (room service only) – **13 rm** ⊒ 175.00/295.00, 5 suite – SB. DY s

The Scotsman, 20 North Bridge, EH1 1YT, *℘* (0131) 556 5565, *reservations@ the cotsmanhotel.co.uk, Fax (0131) 652 3652,* ↕↓, ⇌, ⊠ – ⊫, ↤ rm, ▤ rest, TV ✆ & 🄿 – 🔥 80. **◯◯** 🆎 **◯** **VISA JCB** EY x
North Bridge Brasserie : Meals a la carte 18.25/27.00 **st.** ⏶ 14.00 – ⊒ 15.50 – **56 rm** 175.00/350.00 **st.**, 12 suites.

The Edinburgh Residence, 7 Rothesay Terr, EH3 7RY, *℘* (0131) 226 3380 *Fax (0131) 226 3381,* ⇐, « Georgian town houses » – ⊫ TV ✆ & 🄿. **◯◯** 🆎 **VISA JCB**. ✁ *closed one week January* – Meals (room service only) – ⊒ 9.65 – **21 rm** 175.00/525.00 st 8 suites. CY x

Channings, 12-16 South Learmonth Gdns, EH4 1EZ, *℘* (0131) 315 2226, *reserve@ c hannings.co.uk, Fax (0131) 332 9631,* « Edwardian town houses » – ⊫ ↤ TV ✆ – 🔥 35 **◯◯** 🆎 **◯** **VISA**. ✁ CY e
closed 23-27 December – Meals (see *Channings* below) – **43 rm** ⊒ 140.00/210.00 **t.** 3 suites – SB.

The Bonham, 35 Drumsheugh Gdns, EH3 7RN, *℘* (0131) 226 6050, *reserve@ thebc nham.com, Fax (0131) 226 6080,* « Contemporary interior design » – ⊫ ↤ TV ✆ & – 🔥 50. **◯◯** 🆎 **◯** **VISA**. ✁ CY z
Meals 12.50/15.00 (lunch) and a la carte 22.20/28.60 **t.** ⏶ 14.50 – ⊒ 7.50 – **46 rm** 135.00/240.00 **t.**, 2 suites – SB.

The Roxburghe, 38 Charlotte Sq, EH2 4HG, *℘* (0131) 240 5500, *roxburghe@ csinn. co.uk, Fax (0131) 240 5555,* ↕↓, ⇌, ⊠ – ⊫ ↤, ▤ rest, TV ✆ & – 🔥 400. **◯◯** 🆎 **◯** **VISA**. ✁ DY i
The Melrose : Meals 10.00/20.00 and a la carte 19.15/32.40 **t.** ⏶ 14.25 – ⊒ 12.50 – **196 rm** 145.00/195.00 **t.**, 1 suite – SB.

The Holyrood, 81 Holyrood Rd, EH8 6AE, *℘* (0131) 550 4500, *holyrood@ macdonal d-hotels.co.uk, Fax (0131) 550 4545,* ↕↓, ⇌, ⊠ – ⊫ ↤ ▤ TV ✆ & ⟺ 🄿 – 🔥 180. **◯◯** 🆎 **◯** **VISA** EY a
Flints : Meals a la carte 25.00/34.00 **st.** – **157 rm** 138.00/305.00 **st.** – SB.

Holiday Inn Edinburgh, Corstorphine Rd, EH12 6UA, West : 3 m. on A 8 *℘* (0870) 4009026, *Fax (0131) 334 9237* – ⊫, ↤ rm, ▤ rest, TV ✆ & 🄿 – 🔥 120. **◯◯** 🆎 **◯** **VISA JCB**. ✁
Sampans : Meals - Asian - (dinner only) 18.50/22.95 and a la carte 17.95/25.40 **t.** ⏶ 11.95 – *Rotisserie* : Meals *(closed Saturday lunch)* (carvery rest.) a la carte 18.85/30.15 **t.** ⏶ 11.95 – ⊒ 13.95 – **303 rm** 140.00/165.00 **st.** – SB.

Crowne Plaza, 80 High St, EH1 1TH, *℘* (0131) 557 9797, *rescpedinburgh@ allianceu k.com, Fax (0131) 557 9789,* ↕↓, ⇌, ⊠ – ⊫, ↤ rm, TV ✆ & ⟺ – 🔥 250. **◯◯** 🆎 **◯** **VISA JCB**. ✁ EY z
closed 24 to 27 December – Meals 18.95 and a la carte 20.85/38.65 **st.** ⏶ 14.50 – ⊒ 13.50 – **229 rm** 85.00/230.00 **st.**, 9 suites – SB.

Prestonfield House ⅏, Priestfield Rd, EH16 5UT, ℰ (0131) 668 3346, *info@pres tonfieldhouse.com, Fax (0131) 668 3976*, ≼, « Part 17C country house, collection of paintings », ㎏, ⚗, 𝄐 – ㎧, ⇆ rm, 🖵 ⚒ – 🍴 500. ⓪ ⅏ ⑤ ꝟ꜡꜠
The Old Dining Room : Meals a la carte 21.75/29.25 **t.** ⅃ 14.50 – **31 rm**
⚏ 185.00/450.00 **t.** – SB.

Point, 34 Bread St, EH3 9AF, ℰ (0131) 221 5555, *info@point-hotel.co.uk, Fax (0131) 221 9929*, « Contemporary interior » – ㎧, ⇆ rm, 🖵 – 🍴 100. ⓪ ⅏ ⑤ ꝟ꜡꜠
DZ a
closed 25-27 December – **Meals** *(closed lunch Saturday and Sunday)* 9.90/14.90 **t.** ⅃ 10.95
– ⚏ 10.00 – **136 rm** 120.00/160.00 **st.**, 4 suites.

Le Meridien Edinburgh, 18 Royal Terr, EH7 5AQ, ℰ (0131) 557 3222, *Fax (0131) 557 5334*, « Georgian town houses », ㎏, ⚗, 🖳, ⚘ – ㎧, ⇆ rest, 🖵 ⚒
– 🍴 80. ⓪ ⅏ ⑤ ꝟ꜡꜠
EY i
Meals *(light lunch)/dinner* 25.00 and a la carte 16.50/24.50 **st.** ⅃ 12.50 – ⚏ 10.50 –
104 rm 120.00/170.00, 4 suites – SB.

Thistle Edinburgh, 107 Leith St, EH1 3SW, ℰ (0131) 556 0111, *Fax (0131) 557 5333*
– ㎧ ⇆ rm ⚒ ⅋ ⚗ ⚒ – 🍴 250. ⓪ ⅏ ⑤ ꝟ꜡꜠
EY u
Craig's : **Meals** *(closed Bank Holidays) (dinner only)* 10.00/19.00 ⅃ 12.10 – ⚏ 12.50 –
139 rm 131.00/151.00 **st.**, 4 suites – SB.

Edinburgh Marriott, 111 Glasgow Rd, EH12 8NF, West : 4 ½ m. on A 8 ℰ (0131)
334 9191, *edinburgh@marriotthotels.com, Fax (0131) 316 4507*, ㎏, ⚗, 🖳 – ㎧, ⇆ rm,
▤ rest, 🖵 ℗ – 🍴 300. ⓪ ⅏ ⑤ ꝟ꜡꜠
Meals *(closed Saturday lunch)* 14.00/23.00 and a la carte 25.00/32.00 **t.** ⅃ 12.95 –
⚏ 12.95 – **245 rm** 125.00/145.00 **st.** – SB.

The Carlton, North Bridge St, EH1 1SD, ℰ (0131) 472 3000, *carlton@paramount-ho tels.co.uk, Fax (0131) 556 2691*, ㎏, ⚗, 🖳, squash – ㎧, ⇆ rm, ▤ rest, 🖵 ⅋ ℗ –
🍴 250. ⓪ ⅏ ⑤ ꝟ꜡꜠. ⚘
EY s
Meals 14.95/20.00 and lunch a la carte 14.85/23.85 **s.** ⅃ 11.95 – ⚏ 12.50 – **184 rm**
155.00/225.00 **t.**, 5 suites – SB.

Hilton Edinburgh Grosvenor, Grosvenor St, EH12 5EF, ℰ (0131) 226 6001, *rese rvations@edinburgh.stakis.co.uk, Fax (0131) 220 2387* – ㎧, ⇆ rm, 🖵 – 🍴 300. ⓪ ⅏
⑤ ꝟ꜡꜠. ⚘
CZ a
Meals 8.50 *(lunch)* and a la carte 14.70/23.95 **st.** ⅃ 12.95 – ⚏ 12.75 – **187 rm**
160.00/180.00 **st.**, 2 suites – SB.

Holyrood Aparthotel without rest., 1 Nether Bakehouse (via Gentles entry), EH8 8PE,
ℰ (0131) 524 3200, *reservations@holyroodaparthotel.com, Fax (0131) 524 3210*, ㎏ –
㎧ ⇆ 🖵 ⅋ ⇐, ⓪ ⅏ ⑤ ꝟ꜡꜠ ⚘
EY r
41 suites 145.00/170.00 **st.**

Best Western Simpson, 79 Lauriston Pl, EH3 9HZ, ℰ (0131) 622 7979, *rez@simp sons.hotel.com, Fax (0131) 622 7900* – ㎧ ⇆ 🖵 ⅋ ⅋ ⓪ ⅏ ⑤ ꝟ꜡꜠. ⚘
DZ r
Meals *(closed 25-26 December)* 7.50/15.00 *(lunch)* and a la carte 16.50/27.50 **st.** ⅃ 13.00
– ⚏ 6.50 – **52 rm** ⚏ 95.00/165.00 **st.**, 1 suite – SB.

Frederick House, 42 Frederick St, EH2 1EX, ℰ (0131) 226 1999, *frederickhouse@c dnet.co.uk, Fax (0131) 624 7064* – ㎧ 🖵 ⅋ ⓪ ⅏ ⑤ ꝟ꜡꜠ ⚒ ⚘
DY a
Meals 12.50/18.00 **t.** ⅃ 10.95 – **44 rm** ⚏ 55.00/95.00 **t.**, 1 suite.

Apex International, 31-35 Grassmarket, EH1 2HS, ℰ (0131) 300 3456, *internation al@apexhotels.co.uk, Fax (0131) 220 5345* – ㎧, ⇆ rm, ▤ rest, 🖵 ⅋ ℗ – 🍴 225. ⓪
⅏ ⑤ ꝟ꜡꜠ ⚘
DZ e
Meals *(bar lunch)/dinner* 12.00/20.00 and a la carte 12.00/29.00 **st.** ⅃ 9.95 – ⚏ 9.50
175 rm 130.00/160.00 **t.**

Jurys Inn Edinburgh, 43 Jeffrey St, EH1 1DG, ℰ (0131) 200 3300, *jurysinnedinbu rgh@jurydoyle.com, Fax (0131) 200 0400* – ㎧, ⇆ rm, 🖵 ⅋ ⅋ ℗ – 🍴 50. ⓪ ⅏ ꝟ꜡꜠.
⚘
EY v
closed 24-25 December – **Meals** *(bar lunch)/dinner* 16.00 and a la carte 15.50/20.00 **st.**
⅃ 12.00 – ⚏ 8.00 – **186 rm** 90.00 **st.**

Holiday Inn Edinburgh North, 107 Queensferry Rd, EH4 3HL, ℰ (0131) 332 2442,
Fax (0131) 332 3408, ≼, ㎏, ⚗ – ㎧, ⇆ rm, 🖵 ⅋ ⅋ ℗ – 🍴 200. ⓪ ⅏ ⑤ ꝟ꜡꜠
Meals *(bar lunch)/dinner* 15.95 and a la carte 16.85/18.85 **st.** ⅃ 10.95 – ⚏ 11.25 – **102 rm**
146.00 **st.** – SB.

Maitland, 23-33 Shandwick Pl, EH2 4RG, ℰ (0131) 229 1467, *maitland@ecosse.ie.co.uk, Fax (0131) 229 7549* – ㎧ ⇆ 🖵 ⅋ ⓪ ⅏ ⑤ ꝟ꜡꜠. ⚘
CY a
closed 24-27 December – **Meals** *(dinner only)* 14.95 **st.** ⅃ 9.95 – ⚏ 9.75 – **65 rm**
90.00/110.00 **st.** – SB.

Ibis without rest., 6 Hunter Sq, EH1 1QW, ℰ (0131) 240 7000, *h2039@accor.hotels.com, Fax (0131) 240 7007* – ㎧ ⇆ 🖵 ⅋ ⅋ ⓪ ⅏ ⑤ ꝟ꜡꜠
EZ o
99 rm 55.00/70.00 **st.**

↑ **27 Heriot Row** without rest., 27 Heriot Row, EH3 6EN, ℰ (0131) 225 9474, t.a@blueyo
der.co.uk, Fax (0131) 220 1699, « Georgian town house », ☞ – ⇌ TV, ☎ VISA, ⅏
3 rm ☑ 60.00/100.00.   DY

↑ **17 Abercromby Place** without rest., 17 Abercromby Pl, EH3 6LB, ℰ (0131) 557 8036
irlys.lloyd@virgin.net, Fax (0131) 558 3453, « Georgian town house » – ⇌ TV ⅏ ℙ, ☎
VISA, ⅏   DY
10 rm ☑ 50.00/120.00 **st.**

XXXX **Number One** (at Balmoral H.), 1 Princes St, EH2 2EQ, ℰ (0131) 622 8831
Fax (0131) 557 8740 – ▤, ☎ AE ① VISA   EY
Meals 12.50/35.00 and a la carte 36.75/44.50 **st.** ⅃ 24.00.

XXX **Grill Room** (at Sheraton Grand H.), 1 Festival Sq, EH3 9SR, ℰ (0131) 221 6422
Fax (0131) 229 6254 – ▤ ℙ, ☎ AE ① VISA JCB   CDZ
closed Saturday lunch and Sunday – **Meals** 27.50/29.00 and a la carte 31.50/44.00 **t.**

XX **Atrium**, 10 Cambridge St, EH1 2ED, ℰ (0131) 228 8882, Fax (0131) 228 8808 – ▤
🍴 AE VISA   DZ
closed 24-25 December, Sunday and Saturday lunch except during Edinburgh Festival –
Meals 25.00 (dinner) and a la carte 24.50/54.00 **t.** ⅃ 14.00.

XX **Duck's at Le Marche Noir**, 2-4 Eyre Pl, EH3 5EP, ℰ (0131) 558 1608, bookings@
ucks.co.uk, Fax (0131) 556 0798 – ⇌, ☎ AE ① VISA JCB
closed 25-26 December, lunch Saturday and Sunday – **Meals** 15.00 (lunch) and a la carte
28.30/34.00 **t.** ⅃ 9.50.

XX **The Marque**, 19-21 Causewayside, EH9 1QF, ℰ (0131) 466 6660, themarque@clara
mail.com, Fax (0131) 466 6661 – ⇌, ☎ AE ① VISA   by A 701   EZ
closed Christmas, New Year and Monday – **Meals** 11.50/14.00 (lunch) and dinner a la carte
23.50/28.65 **t.** ⅃ 12.95.

XX **Channings** (at Channings H.), 12-16 South Learmonth Gdns, EH4 1EZ, ℰ (0131)
315 2225, Fax (0131) 332 9631, 🌲 – ⇌, ☎ AE ① VISA   CY
closed Sunday lunch – **Meals** 12.00/26.00 **t.**

XX **Martins**, 70 Rose St, North Lane, EH2 3DX, ℰ (0131) 225 3106, martinirons@fsbdial.
co.uk, Fax (0131) 220 3403 – ⇌, ☎ AE ① VISA JCB   DY
closed 1 week May-June, 1 week October, mid December-late January, Sunday and Monday
except during Edinburgh Festival and Saturday lunch – **Meals** (booking essential)
17.25/25.00 and a la carte 17.75/33.25 **t.** ⅃ 14.00.

XX **Hadrian's** (at Balmoral H.), 2 North Bridge, EH1 1TR, ℰ (0131) 557 5000,
Fax (0131) 557 3747 – ▤, ☎ AE ① VISA JCB   EY
Meals 10.50 and a la carte 15.70/23.95 **st.** ⅃ 24.00.

XX **Rhodes & Co.**, 3-15 Rose St (first floor), EH2 2YJ, ℰ (0131) 220 9190,
Fax (0131) 220 9199 – ▤, ☎ AE ① VISA JCB   DY
closed Sunday dinner – **Meals** a la carte 16.40/20.25 ⅃ 8.50.

XX **Rogue**, 67 Morrison St, EH3 8HH, ℰ (0131) 228 2700, info@rogues-uk.com,
Fax (0131) 228 3299 – ☎ AE VISA   CZ
closed Sunday dinner – **Meals** a la carte 12.50/32.50 **st.** ⅃ 12.15.

XX **Marque Central**, 30b Grindlay St, EH3 9AX, ℰ (0131) 229 9859, Fax (0131) 221 9515
– ☎ AE VISA   DZ
closed 25-26 December, 1-2 January and Sunday – **Meals** (booking essential Bank Holidays)
11.50/14.00 and a la carte 18.40/27.95 **t.** ⅃ 11.95.

XX **Yumi**, 2 West Coates, EH12 5JQ, ℰ (0131) 337 2173, Fax (0131) 337 2818 – ⇌ ℙ, ☎
① VISA JCB
closed 1 week September, 2 weeks Christmas-New Year and Sunday – **Meals** - Japanese
- (dinner only) 25.00/60.00 **t.** ⅃ 11.00.

XX **The Tower**, Museum of Scotland (fifth floor), EH1 1JF, ℰ (0131) 225 3003, mail@t
ower-restaurant.com, Fax (0131) 225 0978, 🌲 – ⇌ ▤, ☎ AE ① VISA JCB   EZ
Meals a la carte 20.40/33.40 **t.** ⅃ 12.00.

XX **Iggs**, 15 Jeffrey St, EH1 1DR, ℰ (0131) 557 8184, Fax (0131) 652 3774 – ☎ AE ①
JCB   EY
closed Sunday – **Meals** 16.00/29.50 (dinner) and a la carte 16.00/29.00 **st.** ⅃ 13.50.

XX **Haldanes** (at Albany H.), 39A Albany St, EH1 3QY, ℰ (0131) 556 8407, info@haldane
srestaurant.com, Fax (0131) 556 2662, 🌲 – ⇌, ☎ AE ① VISA JCB   EY
closed lunch Saturday and Sunday – **Meals** (lunch by arrangement) 13.25/16.95 lunch and
dinner a la carte 26.00/33.00 **t.** ⅃ 12.00.

Leith

🏠 **Malmaison**, 1 Tower Pl, EH6 7DB, ℰ (0131) 468 5000, edinburgh@malmaison.com,
Fax (0131) 468 5002, « Contemporary interior », 🛁 – 🛏 TV ⅏ ℙ – 🔬 55, ☎ AE ①
VISA, ⅏   by A 900   EY
Meals - Brasserie - 11.95/12.95 **t.** ⅃ 15.95 – ☑ 10.95 – **55 rm** 115.00/165.00 **t.**, 5 suites.

✗✗ **Martin Wishart,** 54 The Shore, Leith, EH6 6RA, 𝒫 (0131) 553 3557, info@martin-w
❀ ishart.co.uk, Fax (0131) 467 7091 – ⇔⇔. ◍◯ 𝗩𝗜𝗦𝗔   by A 900 EY
closed 2 weeks January, 1 week June, Christmas, New Year, Sunday and Monday – **Meals**
(booking essential) 13.50/16.50 *(lunch)* and dinner a la carte 30.00/34.00 **st.** ᐃ 12.00
Spec. Millefeuille of langoustine and foie gras with braised fennel. Pot-roasted pork cheek,
glazed vegetables, potato mousseline. Armagnac parfait with poached pear.

✗✗ **(fitz)Henry,** 19 Shore Pl, EH6 6SW, 𝒫 (0131) 555 6625, mail@fitzhenrys.com,
Fax (0131) 555 0025, « Part 17C warehouse » – ◍◯ 𝗔𝗘 𝗩𝗜𝗦𝗔 𝗝𝗖𝗕   by A 900 EY
closed 25-26 December, 1-16 January, Sunday and Saturday lunch – **Meals** 16.50/25.00
and a la carte 25.00/31.50 **t.** ᐃ 18.00.

✗✗ **The Rock,** 78 Commercial St, EH6 6LX, 𝒫 (0131) 555 2225, Fax (0131) 337 2153 – 🅿.
◍◯ 𝗔𝗘 𝗩𝗜𝗦𝗔 𝗝𝗖𝗕   by A 900 EY
closed lunch Sunday-Wednesday – **Meals** a la carte 22.95/48.65 **t.** ᐃ 13.90.

✗✗ **Vintners Rooms,** The Vaults, 87 Giles St, EH6 6BZ, 𝒫 (0131) 554 6767, thevintner
s@thevintnersrooms.demon.co.uk, Fax (0131) 467 7130 – ⇔⇔. ◍◯ 𝗔𝗘 𝗩𝗜𝗦𝗔
closed 2 weeks Christmas and Sunday – **Meals** 11.50/15.00 *(lunch)* and dinner a la carte
24.00/33.00 **t.** ᐃ 12.00.   by A 900 EY

t Bonnyrigg *(Midlothian) Southeast : 8 m. by A 7 on A 6094 EZ –* ✉ *Edinburgh :*

🏰 **Dalhousie Castle** ⌘, EH19 3JB, Southeast : 1 ¼ m. on B 704 𝒫 (01875) 820153,
res@dalhousiecastle.co.uk, Fax (01875) 821936, ≤, « Part 13C and 15C castle with Victorian additions », 🐎 ⇔⇔ 📺 ♿ 🅿 – 🛋 120. ◍◯ 𝗔𝗘 ◉ 𝗩𝗜𝗦𝗔 𝗝𝗖𝗕
closed 5-24 January – **Dungeon :** Meals *(booking essential to non-residents) (dinner only)*
29.50/34.50 **st.** – **The Orangery :** Meals a la carte 16.05/19.35 **st.** ᐃ 13.95 – **32 rm**
⊷ 115.00/275.00 **st.** – SB.

t Kirknewton *Southwest : 7 m. on A 71 CZ –* ✉ *Edinburgh*

🏯 **Marriott Dalmahoy H. & Country Club** ⌘, EH27 8EB, 𝒫 (0131) 333 1845, reservat
ions.dalmahoy@marriotthotels.co.uk, Fax (0131) 333 1433, ≤, « Part Georgian mansion »,
🛋, ⇔⇔, 🔲, 🐎, ≋, 🎾, ✗✗ – 🛗 rest, 📺 ✆ ♿ 🅿 – 🛋 350. ◍◯ 𝗔𝗘 ◉ 𝗩𝗜𝗦𝗔 ✄
Pentland : Meals *(closed Saturday lunch)* 18.00/27.50 **t.** ᐃ 14.95 – **The Long Weekend :**
Meals *(grill rest.)* a la carte 14.50/23.85 **t.** ᐃ 14.95 – ⊷ 12.50 – **212 rm** 175.00 **t.**, 3 suites
– SB.

t Edinburgh International Airport *West : 7 ½ m. by A 8 CZ –* ✉ *Edinburgh :*

🏨 **Hilton Edinburgh Airport,** EH28 8LL, 𝒫 (0131) 519 4400, Fax (0131) 519 4422, 🛋,
⇔⇔, 🔲 – 🛗 ⇔⇔ rm, 🛗 rest, 📺 ✆ ♿ 🅿 – 🛋 240. ◍◯ 𝗔𝗘 ◉ 𝗩𝗜𝗦𝗔 – **Meals** *(grill rest.)*
12.00/18.00 and a la carte 15.00/28.55 **st** ᐃ 14.00 – ⊷ 13.50 – **150 rm** 150.00 **st.** – SB.

t Ingliston *West : 7 ¾ m. on A 8 CZ –* ✉ *Edinburgh :*

🏨 **Norton House,** EH28 8LX, on A 8 𝒫 (0131) 333 1275, events.nhh@arcadianhotels.c
o.uk, Fax (0131) 333 5305, 🐎, 🎾 – ⇔⇔ rm, 📺 ✆ 🅿 – 🛋 200. ◍◯ 𝗔𝗘 ◉ 𝗩𝗜𝗦𝗔 ✄
Meals *(closed Saturday lunch)* 15.00/28.00 and a la carte 18.00/38.00 **st.** ᐃ 12.50 – **46 rm**
⊷ 135.00/155.00 **st.**, 1 suite – SB.

GLASGOW *Glasgow City* 🄁🄀🄁 🄁🄀🄁 *H 16 Scotland G. – pop. 662855.*

See : City★★★ – Cathedral★★★ (≤★) DZ – The Burrell Collection★★★ – Hunterian Art
Gallery★★ (Whistler Collection★★★ – Mackintosh Wing★★★ AC) CY **M4** – Museum of
Transport★★ (Scottish Built Cars★★★, The Clyde Room of Ship Models★★★) – Art Gallery and
Museum Kelvingrove★★ CY – Pollok House★ (The Paintings★★) – Tolbooth Steeple★ DZ **A** –
Hunterian Museum (Coin and Medal Collection★) CY **M1** – City Chambers★ DZ **C** – Glasgow
School of Art★ AC CY **B** – Necropolis (≤★ of Cathedral) DYZ – Gallery of Modern Art★.
Envir. : Paisley Museum and Art Gallery (Paisley Shawl Section★), W : 4 m. by M 8.
Exc. : The Trossachs★★★, N : 31 m. by A 879, A 81 and A 821 – Loch Lomond★★, NW :
19 m. by A 82 – New Lanark★★, SE : 20 m. by M 74 and A 72 BX.
🏌 Littlehill, Auchinairn Rd 𝒫 (0141) 772 1916 – 🏌 Rouken Glen, Stewarton Rd, Eastwood
𝒫 (0141) 638 7044 – 🏌 Linn Park, Simshill Rd 𝒫 (0141) 637 5871 – 🏌 Lethamhill, Cum-
bernauld Rd 𝒫 (0141) 770 6220 – 🏌 Alexandra Park, Dennistown 𝒫 (0141) 556 1294 –
🏌 King's Park, 150a Croftpark Av., Croftfoot 𝒫 (0141) 630 1597 – 🏌 Knightswood, Lincoln
Av. 𝒫 (0141) 959 6358 🏌 Ruchill, Brassey St. 𝒫 (0141) 946 7676.
Access to Oban by helicopter.
Erskine Bridge (toll).
✈ Glasgow Airport : 𝒫 (0141) 887 1111, W : 8 m. by M 8 – **Terminal :** Coach service
from Glasgow Central and Queen Street main line Railway Stations and from Anderston
Cross and Buchanan Bus Stations ✈ Prestwick International Airport : 𝒫 (01292) 479822
Terminal : Buchanan Bus Station – 🅭 11 George Sq. 𝒫 (0141) 204 4400 – Glasgow Airport,
Tourist Information Desk, Paisley 𝒫 (0141) 848 4440.
Edinburgh 46 – Manchester 221.

GLASGOW

BOTANIC GARDENS

A 82
A 81

0 — 300 m
0 — 300 yards

Great
116
128
Wilton
Street
Maryhill
Garscube
Road
Eldersl...

Western
Road
Raeberry
Street

B 808
HILLHEAD

Belmont
St.

North
Woodside
Hopehill
Road
Road

GLASGOW
M 2
Gibson
Bank
Street
KELVINBRIDGE
P
Great
Napiershall Street
Western
Road
George's
Road

UNIVERSITY
M 4
Park
St.
105
West
Rd
Prince's
Street
ST. GEORGE'S
CROSS

50
140
Saint

KELVINGROVE
MUSEUM AND
ART GALLERY

Park
Quadrant
Woodlands

Kelvin
KELVINGROVE
PARK
108

Way
107
34
143
U
35
M

Saint
17

Sauchiehall
47
Royal
Terrace
42
Argyle
Woodside Place
19
Sauchiehall
B
Stre...
95
Street
Street
Bath
St.

Kelvinhaugh
Street
P
Berkeley
Street
Kent
Road
North
Elmbank
POL
St.
West
V

Eldersli...
St.
Saint
Newton
Vincent
a
T
P
C

Stobcross
Road
e
Street
Street
West
Street

SCOTTISH
EXHIBITION
S
Pitt
Waterloo

f
CENTRE
P
P
Clydeside
Expressway
a
P
A 814

P
Finnieston
A 814
Lancefield Street
Lancefield
Street
Hydepark Street
18
Argyle
Street
York
St.
V

u
Lancefield
Quay
Anderston
Quay
M 8
Broomielaw
120

Z

Govan
CLYDE
85

Road

Govan
Road
Road
35
St.

A 814

2 2
93
West
Paisley
A 8
Admiral St.
Seaward
St.
D
20
Morrison
Street
Road
A 8
Kingston
Nelson Stre...

KINNING PARK
39
Milnpark
100
Street
West

A 8

C
M 8
(M 8)

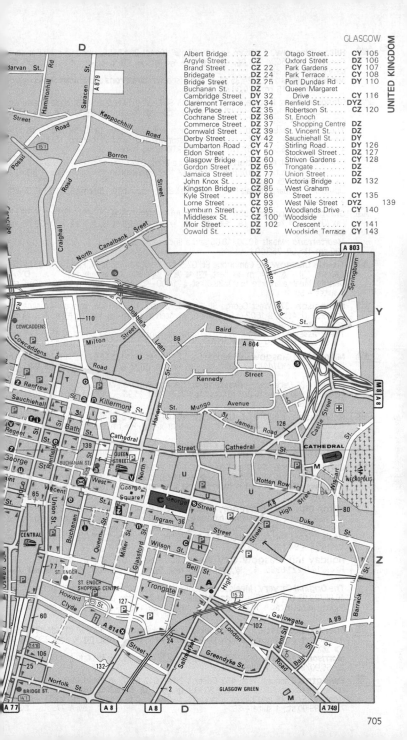

Hilton Glasgow, 1 William St, G3 8HT, ✆ (0141) 204 5555, glahitwgm@hilton.com
Fax (0141) 204 5004, ≤, ⅃₅, ⌚s, ⬚, – |≇|, ⇐ rm, ▤ ⅏ ✔ ⅙, ⇔ ℙ – ⬚ 1000.
AE ⓪ VISA JCB. ♨
CZ s
Minsky's : Meals 17.25/24.95 st. ⅃ 15.10 (see also *Camerons* and *Shimla Pinks* below)
– ⌚ 14.50 – **315 rm** 170.00 st., 4 suites.

Glasgow Moat House, Congress Rd, G3 8QT, ✆ (0141) 306 9988, cbgla@queensm
oat.co.uk, Fax (0141) 221 2022, ≤, ⅃₅, ⌚s, ⬚, – |≇|, ⇐ rm, ▤ ⅏ ✔ ⅙ ℙ – ⬚ 3000.
MⓈ AE ⓪ VISA JCB
CZ r
The Mariner : Meals (closed Sunday) (dinner only) a la carte 19.00/28.00 t. ⅃ 16.00 –
No 1 Dockside : Meals (closed lunch Saturday and Sunday) (buffet) 16.00/12.00 t.
⅃ 13.95 – ⌚ 13.50 – **267 rm** 170.00/199.00 t., 16 suites – SB.

One Devonshire Gardens, 1 Devonshire Gdns, G12 0UX, ✆ (0141) 339 2001, onea
evonshire@btconnect.com, Fax (0141) 337 1663, « Victorian town houses » – ⅏ ✔
⬚ 40. MⓈ AE ⓪ VISA
by A 82 CY
closed 6-11 January – Meals (see *Amaryllis* below) – ⌚ 14.50 – **38 rm** 165.00/345.00 st.,
3 suites.

Glasgow Marriott, 500 Argyle St, Anderston, G3 8RR, ✆ (0141) 226 5577,
Fax (0141) 221 7676, ≤, ⅃₅, ⌚s, ⬚, – |≇|, ⇐ rm, ▤ ⅏ ✔ ⅙ ℙ – ⬚ 700. MⓈ AE ⓪
VISA. ♨
CZ a
Mediterrano : Meals 10.00/18.00 and a la carte 17.00/33.00 t. ⅃ 15.00 – ⌚ 13.00 –
300 rm 135.00/250.00 t.

Thistle Glasgow, 36 Cambridge St, G2 3HN, ✆ (0870) 3339154, Fax (0870) 3339254,
⅃₅, ⌚s, ⬚, – |≇|, ⇐ rm, ▤ rest, ⅏ ✔ ℙ – ⬚ 1500. MⓈ AE ⓪ VISA
DY z
Gengis : Meals a la carte 16.00/28.00 st. ⅃ 14.00 – ⌚ 12.85 – **297 rm** 85.00/110.00 st.,
3 suites – SB.

Malmaison, 278 West George St, G2 4LL, ✆ (0141) 572 1000, glasgow@malmaison.
com, Fax (0141) 572 1002, « Contemporary interior », ⅃₅ – |≇|, ⇐ rm, ⅏ ✔ ⅙ – ⬚ 30.
MⓈ AE ⓪ VISA JCB. ♨
CY c
The Brasserie (✆ (0141) 572 1001) : Meals (closed Saturday lunch) 10.95/12.95 and
a la carte approx. 19.50 st. ⅃ 12.00 – ⌚ 10.95 – **64 rm** 120.00 st., 8 suites.

Millennium Glasgow, 40 George Sq, G2 1DS, ✆ (0141) 332 6711, sales.glasgow@m
ill-cop.com, Fax (0141) 332 4264, ⅃₅ – |≇|, ⇐ rm, ⅏ ✔ ⅙ – ⬚ 40. MⓈ AE ⓪ VISA JCB.
♨
DZ v
closed 25-26 December – *Brasserie on George Square :* Meals (closed Sunday lunch)
20.00 and a la carte 16.00/30.00 st. ⅃ 17.00 – ⌚ 13.95 – **112 rm** 190.00/250.00 st.,
5 suites – SB.

ArtHouse, 129 Bath St, G2 2SZ, ✆ (0141) 221 6789, info@arthousehotel.com,
Fax (0141) 221 6777, « Contemporary interior » – |≇|, ⇐ rm, ▤ rest, ⅏ ✔ ⅙ – ⬚ 30.
MⓈ AE ⓪ VISA
DY v
closed 25 December-1 January – *Grill :* Meals 11.50 (lunch) and a la carte 21.85/49.90 t.
⅃ 17.50 – ⌚ 9.25 – **65 rm** 90.00/140.00 st.

Carlton George, 44 West George St, G2 1DH, ✆ (0141) 353 6373, george@carlton
hotels.co.uk, Fax (0141) 353 6263 – |≇| ⇐ ▤ ⅏ ✔ ⅙ – ⬚ 35. MⓈ AE ⓪ VISA
DZ a
Windows : Meals 13.95 (lunch) and dinner a la carte 14.95/21.00 t. ⅃ 13.95 – ⌚ 12.95
– **64 rm** 150.00 t.

Hilton Glasgow Grosvenor, Grosvenor Terr, Great Western Rd, G12 0TA, ✆ (0141)
339 8811, res@glasgrosvenor.hilton.co.uk, Fax (0141) 334 0710, « Victorian terraced
town houses » – |≇|, ⇐ rm, ⅏ ℙ – ⬚ 450. MⓈ AE ⓪ VISA. ♨
CY s
Meals (closed Saturday lunch) 9.00/17.95 and a la carte 18.70/26.50 st. ⅃ 12.30 –
⌚ 14.25 – **94 rm** 120.00 st., 2 suites.

Holiday Inn Glasgow City West, Bothwell St, G2 7EN, ✆ (0870) 4009032,
Fax (0141) 221 8986, ≤ – |≇|, ⇐ rm, ▤ rest, ⅏ ✔ ℙ – ⬚ 1000. MⓈ AE ⓪ VISA JCB.
♨
CZ z
The Original Carvery : Meals (dinner only and Sunday lunch)/dinner 17.50 and a la carte
16.95/28.95 t. ⅃ 11.95 – *Jules :* Meals (closed Saturday lunch) (piano at dinner) 9.95
(lunch) and a la carte 14.95/28.95 t. ⅃ 11.95 – ⌚ 13.95 – **274 rm** 99.00 st., 1 suite –
SB.

Sherbrooke Castle, 11 Sherbrooke Ave, Pollokshields, G41 4PG, ✆ (0141) 427 4227,
mail@sherbrooke.co.uk, Fax (0141) 427 5685, ⌖ – ⇐, ▤ rest, ⅏ ℙ – ⬚ 250. MⓈ AE
⓪ VISA
Morrisons : Meals 16.00/25.00 and dinner a la carte 25.00/35.00 t. ⅃ 11.00 – **24 rm**
⌚ 65.00/85.00 t., 1 suite – SB.

Ewington, Balmoral Terr, 132 Queen's Drive, G42 8QW, ✆ (0141) 423 1152, info@c
ountryhotels.net, Fax (0141) 422 2030 – |≇| ⅏ – ⬚ 80. MⓈ AE ⓪ VISA JCB
Meals 9.95/16.95 and dinner a la carte 19.00/27.00 t. ⅃ 11.00 – ⌚ 10.95 – **42 rm**
79.00/99.00 st., 1 suite – SB.
by A 77 DZ

Langs, 2 Port Dundas Pl, G2 3LD, $\mathscr{C}$ (0141) 333 1500, *Fax (0141) 333 5700,* « Contemporary interior », $\mathit{L_6}$ – $|\mathsf{\$}|$, $\Leftrightarrow$ rm, $\equiv$ rest, $\overline{\text{TV}}$ $\mathscr{C}$ ξ. $\text{@}\text{⊙}$ AE ⓪ VISA JCB.
DY n
Las Brisas : **Meals** 13.95 (lunch) and a la carte 18.70/41.25 **st.** – *Oshi :* **Meals** - Asian specialities - a la carte 9.95/18.70 **st.** $\mathring{\mathbb{I}}$ 9.95 – $\rightleftharpoons$ 12.95 – **100 rm** 125.00 **st.** – SB.

City Inn, Finnieston Quay, G3 8HN, $\mathscr{C}$ (0141) 240 1002, *glasgow.reservations@cityin n.com, Fax (0141) 248 2754,* $\leqslant$, $\widehat{\mathbb{R}}$, $\mathit{L_6}$ – $|\mathsf{\$}|$, $\Leftrightarrow$ rm, $\equiv$ rest, $\overline{\text{TV}}$ $\mathscr{C}$ ξ. P – $\underline{\mathscr{A}}$ 50. $\text{@}\text{⊙}$ AE ⓪ VISA JCB
CZ u
closed 24-26 and 31 December – *City Café :* **Meals** 15.95 and a la carte 15.95/25.95 **st.** $\mathring{\mathbb{I}}$ 10.65 – $\rightleftharpoons$ 10.50 – **164 rm** 79.00 **t.** – SB.

Bewley's, 110 Bath St, G2 2EN, $\mathscr{C}$ (0141) 353 0800, *gla@bewleyshotels.com, Fax (0141) 353 0900* – $|\mathsf{\$}|$, $\Leftrightarrow$ rm, $\equiv$ rest, $\overline{\text{TV}}$ $\mathscr{C}$ ξ. $\text{@}\text{⊙}$ AE ⓪ VISA. $\mathscr{S}$
DY i
closed 24-26 December – *Loop :* **Meals** a la carte 15.40/23.40 **t.** $\mathring{\mathbb{I}}$ 10.50 – $\rightleftharpoons$ 6.50 – **98 rm** 59.00 **st.**, 5 suites.

Holiday Inn, Theatreland, 161 West Nile St, G1 2RL, $\mathscr{C}$ (0141) 352 8300, *info@higla sgow.com, Fax (0141) 332 7447,* $\mathit{L_6}$ – $|\mathsf{\$}|$ $\Leftrightarrow$, $\equiv$ rest, $\overline{\text{TV}}$ $\mathscr{C}$ ξ. – $\underline{\mathscr{A}}$ 130. $\text{@}\text{⊙}$ AE ⓪ VISA
DY a
closed 25-26 December and 1-2 January – *La Bonne Auberge Brasserie :* **Meals** 6.95/10.95 and a la carte 18.85/24.45 **st.** $\mathring{\mathbb{I}}$ 10.95 – $\rightleftharpoons$ 11.95 – **110 rm** 120.00/142.50 **st.**, 3 suites – SB.

Swallow Glasgow, 517 Paisley Road West, G51 1RW, $\mathscr{C}$ (0141) 427 3146, *glasgow. swallow@whitbread.com, Fax (0141) 427 4059,* $\mathit{L_6}$, $\widehat{\text{ES}}$, $\boxed{\text{S}}$ – $|\mathsf{\$}|$ $\Leftrightarrow$, $\equiv$ rest, $\overline{\text{TV}}$ P – $\underline{\mathscr{A}}$ 300. $\text{@}\text{⊙}$ AE ⓪ VISA
by A 8 CZ
Meals *(closed Saturday lunch)* (carving lunch) 9.50/21.00 and dinner a la carte 20.15/29.95 **st.** $\mathring{\mathbb{I}}$ 13.50 – **117 rm** $\rightleftharpoons$ 95.00/115.00 **st.** – SB.

Theatre without rest., 27 Elmbank St, G2 4PB, $\mathscr{C}$ (0141) 227 2772, *theatrehotel@cl ara.net, Fax (0141) 227 2774* – $\Leftrightarrow$ $\overline{\text{TV}}$ $\mathscr{C}$. $\text{@}\text{⊙}$ AE VISA JCB
CY a
58 rm 50.00/70.00 **st.**

Express by Holiday Inn without rest., Theatreland, 165 West Nile St, G1 2RL, $\mathscr{C}$ (0141) 331 6800, *hi@holidayinn.demon.co.uk, Fax (0141) 331 6828* – $|\mathsf{\$}|$ $\Leftrightarrow$ $\overline{\text{TV}}$ $\mathscr{C}$ ξ. $\text{@}\text{⊙}$ AE ⓪ VISA JCB. $\mathscr{S}$
DY o
88 rm 59.00 **st.**

Express by Holiday Inn without rest., Stockwell St, G1 4LT, $\mathscr{C}$ (0141) 548 5000, *managerglasgow@expressholidayinn.co.uk, Fax (0141) 548 5048* – $|\mathsf{\$}|$ $\Leftrightarrow$ $\overline{\text{TV}}$ $\mathscr{C}$ ξ. P – $\underline{\mathscr{A}}$ 35. $\text{@}\text{⊙}$ AE ⓪ VISA JCB
DZ x
128 rm 60.00.

Travel Inn Metro, Montrose House, 187 George St, G1 1YU, $\mathscr{C}$ (0141) 553 2700, *Fax (0141) 553 2719* – $|\mathsf{\$}|$ $\Leftrightarrow$, $\equiv$ rest, $\overline{\text{TV}}$ $\mathscr{C}$ ξ. P – $\underline{\mathscr{A}}$ 40. $\text{@}\text{⊙}$ AE ⓪ VISA. $\mathscr{S}$
DZ s
Meals (dinner only) – **254 rm** 49.95 **t.**

Travel Inn, Cambuslang Investment Park, Drumhead Pl, G32 8EY, Southeast : 5 m. by A 749 off A 74 $\mathscr{C}$ (0141) 764 2655, *Fax (0141) 778 1703* – $\Leftrightarrow$ rm, $\equiv$ rest, $\overline{\text{TV}}$ ξ. P. $\text{@}\text{⊙}$ AE ⓪ VISA. $\mathscr{S}$
Meals (grill rest.) – **40 rm** 41.95 **t.**

Travelodge, Hill St, G3 6PR, $\mathscr{C}$ (0141) 333 1515, *Fax (0141) 333 1221* – $|\mathsf{\$}|$ $\Leftrightarrow$, $\equiv$ rest, $\overline{\text{TV}}$ ξ. – $\underline{\mathscr{A}}$ 50. $\text{@}\text{⊙}$ AE ⓪ VISA. $\mathscr{S}$
DY c
Meals (cafe bar) (dinner only) – **95 rm** 49.95 **t.**

Travelodge, 251 Paisley Rd, G5 8RA, $\mathscr{C}$ (0141) 420 3882, *Fax (0141) 420 3884* – $\Leftrightarrow$ rm, $\equiv$ rest, $\overline{\text{TV}}$ $\mathscr{C}$ ξ. P. $\text{@}\text{⊙}$ AE ⓪ VISA JCB. $\mathscr{S}$
CZ n
Meals (grill rest.) – **75 rm** 49.95 **t.**

XXXX **Camerons** (at Hilton Glasgow H.), 1 William St, G3 8HT, $\mathscr{C}$ (0141) 204 5511, *Fax (0141) 204 5004* – $\equiv$ P. $\text{@}\text{⊙}$ AE ⓪ VISA JCB
CZ s
closed Sunday – **Meals** 21.50/28.50 **st.** $\mathring{\mathbb{I}}$ 18.00.

XXX **Amaryllis** (at One Devonshire Gardens), 1 Devonshire Gdns, G12 0UX, $\mathscr{C}$ (0141) $\mathbb{S}$ 337 3434, *info@amaryllis1.demon.co.uk, Fax (0141) 339 0047* – $\text{@}\text{⊙}$ AE ⓪ VISA
closed Saturday lunch – **Meals** (booking essential) 18.00/40.00 **st.** $\mathring{\mathbb{I}}$ 19.00
Spec. Ravioli of lobster and langoustine, pea purée. Roast duck, caramelised chicory and braised root vegetables. Cold chocolate fondant, honeycomb ice cream. by A 82 CY

XXX **Lux,** 1051 Great Western Rd, G12 0XP, $\mathscr{C}$ (0141) 576 7576, *Fax (0141) 576 0162* – $\Leftrightarrow$ $\equiv$ P. $\text{@}\text{⊙}$ AE ⓪ VISA
by A 82 CY
closed 25-26 December, 1-2 January, Sunday and Monday – **Meals** (dinner only) 28.50 **t.** $\mathring{\mathbb{I}}$ 15.00.

XXX **Eurasia,** 150 St Vincent St, G2 5NE, $\mathscr{C}$ (0141) 204 1150, *reservations@eurasia-resta urant.co.uk, Fax (0141) 204 1140* – $\equiv$. $\text{@}\text{⊙}$ AE ⓪ VISA
DZ u
closed 25 December, 1 January, Saturday lunch, Sunday and Bank Holidays – **Meals** 14.95/34.00 and dinner a la carte 17.95/34.00 **t.** $\mathring{\mathbb{I}}$ 14.95.

XXX **Rogano,** 11 Exchange Pl, G1 3AN, ✆ (0141) 248 4055, Fax (0141) 248 2608, « Art
Deco » – ▤. 🆗 🆑 ⓪ 🆅🆂🅰 DZ
Meals - Seafood - 16.50 (lunch) and a la carte 27.45/37.95 **t.** 🍷 12.00.

XXX **Buttery,** 652 Argyle St, G3 8UF, ✆ (0141) 221 8188, Fax (0141) 204 4639 – ✦✕ 🄿. 🆗
🆑 ⓪ 🆅🆂🅰 CZ
closed 25-26 December, 1-2 January, Sunday, Saturday lunch and Bank Holidays – **Meals**
17.50/19.50 (lunch) and a la carte 14.50/32.00 **t.** 🍷 10.50.

XXX **Yes,** 22 West Nile St, G1 2PW, ✆ (0141) 221 8044, Fax (0141) 248 9159 – ▤. 🆗 🅰
⓪ 🆅🆂🅰 DZ
closed 25-26 December, 1-2 January, Saturday lunch and Sunday – **Meals** 14.95/29.50
🍷 13.95.

XXX **Rococo,** 202 West George St, G2 2NR, ✆ (0141) 221 5004, res@rococoglasgow.com
Fax (0141) 221 5006 – ▤. 🆗 🆑 ⓪ 🆅🆂🅰 DYZ
closed 1 January – **Meals** 14.00/32.50 and a la carte 18.00/36.00 **t.** 🍷 16.00.

XX **Brian Maule at Chardon d'Or,** 176 West Regent St, G2 4RL, ✆ (0141) 248 3801
info@lechardondor.com, Fax (0141) 248 3901 – ✦✕ ▤. 🆗 🆅🆂🅰 CY
closed Saturday lunch, Sunday and Bank Holidays – **Meals** 15.00 (lunch) and a la carte
25.00/35.00 **st.** 🍷 13.00.

XX **Nairns,** 13 Woodside Cres, G3 7UL, ✆ (0141) 353 0707, info@nairns.co.uk
Fax (0141) 331 1684, « Contemporary interior » – ✦✕ rest,. 🆗 🆑 ⓪ 🆅🆂🅰. ✂ CY
closed Christmas, Sunday and Monday – **Meals** 9.00/29.50 **t.** 🍷 15.50.

XX **Puppet Theatre,** 11 Ruthven Lane, G12 9BG, off Byres Rd ✆ (0141) 339 8444, pupp
et@bigbeat.co.uk, Fax (0141) 339 7666 – ✦✕. 🆗 🆑 🆅🆂🅰 on B 808 CY
closed 1-2 January, Monday and Saturday lunch – **Meals** a la carte 20.00/32.00 **t.** 🍷 15.00

XX **The Restaurant at Corinthian,** 191 Ingram St, G1 1DA, ✆ (0141) 552 1101, info
@corinthian.com, Fax (0141) 559 6826, « Former Glasgow Ship Bank, fine Victorian
architecture » – 🆗 🆑 ⓪ 🆅🆂🅰 DZ
closed lunch Saturday and Sunday – **Meals** 9.95 (lunch) and dinner a la carte 18.50/23.50 **t**
🍷 10.25.

XX **Papingo,** 104 Bath St, G2 2EN, ✆ (0141) 332 6678, info@papingo.co.uk
Fax (0141) 332 6549 – 🆗 🆑 🆅🆂🅰 DY
closed 25-26 December, 1-2 January, Sunday lunch and Bank Holiday Mondays – **Meals**
10.95/19.95 and a la carte 17.00/28.00 **t.** 🍷 13.95.

XX **Farfelu,** 89 Candleriggs, G1 1NP, ✆ (0141) 552 5345, Fax (0141) 400 2141 – ▤. 🆗 🆑
🆅🆂🅰 DZ
closed 25 December, 1 January and Sunday – **Meals** 10.95/13.95 (lunch) and dinner a la
carte 25.85/31.25 **t.** 🍷 11.50.

XX **Ho Wong,** 82 York St, G2 8LE, ✆ (0141) 221 3550, Fax (0141) 248 5330 – ▤. 🆗 🆑
⓪ 🆅🆂🅰 CZ
closed 3 days Chinese New Year and Sunday lunch – **Meals** - Chinese (Peking) - 26.00 (dinner)
and a la carte approx. 20.40 **t.** 🍷 12.95.

XX **Amber Regent,** 50 West Regent St, G2 2QZ, ✆ (0141) 331 1655, Fax (0141) 353 3398
– ▤. 🆗 🆑 ⓪ 🆅🆂🅰 🅹🅲🅱 DY
closed Chinese New Year and Sunday – **Meals** - Chinese - 9.95/34.95 and a la carte
20.95/32.50 **t.** 🍷 12.95.

XX **Shish Mahal,** 66-68 Park Rd, G4 9JF, ✆ (0870) 0725771, reservations@shishmahal.c
o.uk, Fax (0141) 572 0800 – ✦✕. 🆗 🆑 🆅🆂🅰 🅹🅲🅱 CY
closed Sunday lunch – **Meals** - Indian - 5.25/6.50 (lunch) and a la carte 16.05/30.85 **t.**
🍷 8.90.

X **The Ubiquitous Chip,** 12 Ashton Lane, G12 8SJ, off Byres Rd ✆ (0141) 334 5007
mail@ubiquitouschip.co.uk, Fax (0141) 337 1302 – 🆗 🆑 ⓪ 🆅🆂🅰 by B 808 CY
closed 25 December and 1 January – **Meals** 19.95/33.95 and a la carte 9.75/24.85 **t.**
🍷 13.95.

X **No Sixteen,** 16 Byres Rd, G11 5JY, ✆ (0141) 339 2544 – 🆗 🆅🆂🅰 by B 808 CY
closed first 2 weeks December and Sunday – **Meals** 11.50 (lunch) and a la carte
19.25/25.00 **t.** 🍷 12.50.

X **Shimla Pinks,** 777 Pollokshaws Rd, G41 2AX, ✆ (0141) 423 4488, Fax (0141) 423 2434
– ▤. 🆗 🆑 ⓪ 🆅🆂🅰 by A 77 DZ
closed 1 January and lunch Saturday and Sunday – **Meals** - Indian - 6.95 (lunch) and a la
carte 11.10/21.85.

at Stepps (North Lanarkshire) Northeast : 5 ½ m. by M 8 DY on A 80 – ✉ Glasgow

🏠 **Garfield House,** Cumbernauld Rd, G33 6HW, ✆ (0141) 779 2111, rooms@garfieldho
tel.co.uk, Fax (0141) 779 9799 – ✦✕ 📺 🄿. – 🔒 100. 🆗 🆑 ⓪ 🆅🆂🅰
closed 1-2 January – **Meals** a la carte 9.95/21.50 🍷 10.50 – **46 rm** ⊑ 83.50/103.50 **t.**

at Glasgow Airport *(Renfrewshire)* West : 8 m. by M 8 CZ – ⊠ *Paisley*

🏨 **Holiday Inn Glasgow Airport,** Abbotsinch, PA3 2TR, ✆ (0870) 4009031, Fax (0141) 887 3738 – 🛗, 🛏 rm, 🔲 📺 ✆ 🅿 – 🏛 250. 🐵 🔿 AE ⓘ VISA 𝒮ℬ
The Junction : Meals *(closed Saturday lunch)* (carvery rest. Friday Sunday) 15.00/20.00 (lunch) and dinner a la carte 17.35/29.15 t. ⓪ 12.95 – ☞ 13.95 – **296 rm** 99.00 st., 2 suites – SB.

LEEDS W. Yorks. 🔢🔢🔢 P 22 *Great Britain G.* – pop. 424 194.

See : *City★ Royal Armouries Museum★★★* – *City Art Gallery★* AC GY **M.**
Envir. : *Kirkstall Abbey★* AC, NW : 3 m. by A 65 FY – *Templenewsam★ (decorative arts★)* AC, E : 5 m. by A 64 and A 63.
Exc. : *Harewood House★★ (The Gallery★)* AC, N : 8 m. by A 61.
🏌, 🏌 *Temple Newsam, Temple Newsam Rd, Halton* ✆ (0113) 264 5624 – 🏌 *Gotts Park, Armley Ridge Rd* ✆ (0113) 234 2019 – 🏌 *Middleton Park, Ring Rd, Beeston Park, Middleton* ✆ (0113) 270 9506 – 🏌, 🏌 *Moor Allerton, Coal Rd, Wike* ✆ (0113) 266 1154 – 🏌 *Howley Hall, Scotchman Lane, Morley* ✆ (01924) 472432 – 🏌 *Roundhay, Park Lane* ✆ (0113) 266 2695.
✈ *Leeds - Bradford Airport :* ✆ (0113) 250 9696, NW : 8 m. by A 65 and A 658
🚩 *The Arcade, City Station* ✆ (0113) 242 5242.
London 204 – Liverpool 75 – Manchester 43 – Newcastle upon Tyne 95 – Nottingham 74.

Plan on next page

🏨 **Devere Oulton Hall,** Rothwell Lane, Oulton, LS26 8HN, Southeast : 5 ½ m. by A 61 and A 639 on A 654 ✆ (0113) 282 1000, oulton.hall@devere-hotels.com, Fax (0113) 282 8066, ≼, « Part Victorian mansion », 🛁, ≋, 🔲, 🏌, 🏌, 🐎 – 🛗 🙌, 🔲 rest, 📺 🕭 👣 🅿 – 🏛 330. 🐵 🔿 AE ⓘ
Bronte : Meals *(closed Saturday lunch)* 13.50 (lunch) and a la carte 23.00/55.00 st. ⓪ 14.00 – **150 rm** ☞ 150.00/170.00 st., 2 suites.

🏨 **Leeds Marriott,** 4 Trevelyan Sq, Boar Lane, LS1 6ET, ✆ (0113) 236 6366, Fax (0113) 236 6367, 🛁, ≋, 🔲 – 🛗, 🛏 rm, 🔲 📺 ✆ 👣 – 🏛 280. 🐵 🔿 AE ⓘ VISA 𝒮ℬ
GZ x
John T's : Meals *(closed lunch Saturday and Sunday)* 24.00 and a la carte 18.25/32.00 t. ⓪ 12.25 – ☞ 13.00 – **243 rm** 114.00 st., 1 suite.

🏨 **Crowne Plaza Leeds,** Wellington St, LS1 4DL, ✆ (0113) 244 2200, Fax (0113) 244 0460, 🛁, ≋, 🔲 – 🛗, 🛏 rm, 🔲 📺 ✆ 👣 🅿 – 🏛 200. 🐵 🔿 AE ⓘ VISA
Meals 18.00 and a la carte 16.00/26.00 st. ⓪ 12.95 – ☞ 12.95 – **130 rm** 140.00 st., 2 suites – SB.
FZ r

🏨 **42 The Calls,** 42 The Calls, LS2 7EW, ✆ (0113) 244 0099, hotel@42thecalls.co.uk, Fax (0113) 234 4100, ≼, « Converted riverside grain mill » – 🛗 📺 ✆ 👣 🚗 – 🏛 85. 🐵 🔿 AE ⓘ VISA JCB
GZ z
closed Christmas – Meals (see *Pool Court at 42* below) (see also *Brasserie Forty Four* below) – ☞ 12.50 – **38 rm** 105.00/160.00 t., 3 suites.

🏨 **Le Meridien Queen's,** City Sq, LS1 1PL, ✆ (0113) 243 1323, queens.reservations@f orte-hotels.com, Fax (0113) 242 5154 – 🛗, 🛏 rm, 📺 👣 🚗 – 🏛 600. 🐵 🔿 AE ⓘ VISA JCB 𝒮ℬ
GZ u
No. 1 City Square : Meals (carvery lunch) 16.50 lunch and dinner a la carte 19.95/28.20 t. ⓪ 14.50 – ☞ 12.75 – **194 rm** 125.00/160.00 t., 5 suites – SB.

🏨 **Village H. and Leisure Club,** 186 Otley Rd, Headingley, LS16 5PR, Northwest : 3 ½ m. on A 660 ✆ (0113) 278 1000, village.l@cybase.co.uk, Fax (0113) 278 1111, 🛁, ≋, 🔲, squash – 🛗 🙌, 🔲 rest, 📺 ✆ 👣 🅿 – 🏛 220. 🐵 🔿 AE ⓘ VISA
Meals (grill rest.) a la carte approx. 21.00 st. ⓪ 8.50 – **94 rm** ☞ 98.00/129.00 st.

🏨 **Weetwood Hall,** Otley Rd, LS16 5PS, Northwest : 4 m. on A 660 ✆ (0113) 230 6000, sales@weetwood.co.uk, Fax (0113) 230 6095, 🛁, ≋, 🔲, 🐎 – 🛗 🙌 📺 👣 🅿 – 🏛 150. 🐵 🔿 AE ⓘ VISA
Meals (bar lunch Monday-Saturday)/dinner 16.25/30.00 st. ⓪ 11.95 – ☞ 10.75 – **108 rm** 96.00/167.00 st. – SB.

🏨 **Hilton Leeds City,** Neville St, LS1 4BX, ✆ (0113) 244 2000, leehnhngm@hilton.com, Fax (0113) 243 3577, ≼, 🛁, ≋, 🔲 – 🛗, 🛏 rm, 🔲 rm, 📺 ✆ 👣 🅿 – 🏛 400. 🐵 🔿 AE ⓘ VISA JCB
GZ r
Meals *(closed Saturday lunch and Sunday)* (bar lunch)/dinner 13.50/18.95 and dinner a la carte 19.85/25.65 t. ⓪ 12.30 – ☞ 12.95 – **186 rm** 135.00/145.00 st., 20 suites – SB.

🏨 **Malmaison,** Sovereign Quay, LS1 1DQ, ✆ (0113) 398 1000, leeds@malmaison.com, Fax (0113) 398 1002, « Riverside setting, contemporary interior », 🛁 – 🛗, 🛏 rm, 🔲 📺 ✆ 👣 – 🏛 40. 🐵 🔿 AE ⓘ VISA 𝒮ℬ
GZ n
Meals 11.95/12.95 and a la carte 22.40/24.40 st. ⓪ 13.95 – ☞ 10.75 – **99 rm** 95.00/120.00 st., 1 suite – SB.

Haley's, Shire Oak Rd, Headingley, LS6 2DE, Northwest : 2 m. by A 660 ℰ (0113) 278 4446, info@haleys.co.uk, Fax (0113) 275 3342 – ₴ TV ☎ 🄿 – 🕰 25. 🔞 AE ⓞ VISA JCB. ℠ closed 26-30 December – **Meals** (closed Sunday dinner to non-residents) (dinner only and Sunday lunch)/dinner 24.95 and a la carte 24.95/31.00 **st.** ↓ 13.95 – **29 rm** ⊇ 95.00/230.00 **st.** – SB.

Metropole, King St, LS1 2HQ, ℰ (0113) 245 0841, Fax (0113) 242 5156 – 🛗 ₴ TV ☎ ₭ 🄿 – 🕰 250. 🔞 AE ⓞ VISA. ℠
FZ e
Meals 18.00 (dinner) and a la carte approx. 26.00 **st.** ↓ 12.50 – ⊇ 12.95 – **117 rm** 105.00/125.00 **st.**, 1 suite – SB.

Merrion, Merrion Centre, 17 Wade Lane, LS2 8NH, ℰ (0113) 243 9191, info@merrio n-hotel-leeds.com, Fax (0113) 242 3527 – 🛗 ₴ rm, ⊟ TV 🄿 – 🕰 80. 🔞 AE ⓞ VISA JCB
GY e
Meals a la carte 19.45/24.40 **st.** ↓ 8.95 – ⊇ 11.75 – **109 rm** 99.00/170.00 **st.**

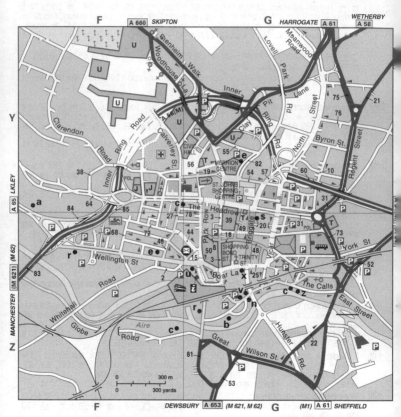

LEEDS

🏠 **Golden Lion,** 2 Lower Briggate, LS1 4AE, ℰ (0113) 243 6454, *info@goldenlion-hote l-leeds.com, Fax (0113) 242 9327* – 🛗, ⇔ rm, 📺 ℰ 🖳 – 🔬 120. 🚾 🎴 ⓪ 𝘝𝘐𝘚𝘈
Meals (bar lunch)/dinner a la carte 16.40/22.40 **st.** 🛭 9.25 – **89 rm** 🖙 99.00/120.00 **st.**
– SB.
GZ v

𝕏𝕏𝕏 **gueller,** 3 York Pl, LS1 2DR, ℰ (0113) 245 9922, *dine@guellers.com,*
✿ *Fax (0113) 245 9965* – 🗐. 🚾 🎴 𝘝𝘐𝘚𝘈
FZ e
closed Christmas, Sunday and Monday – **Meals** 16.50/24.50 **t.** 🛭 9.95
Spec. Roast scallops, celeriac purée, truffle vinaigrette. Braised pig's trotter stuffed
with ham hock and morels. Chocolate mousse with red berries.

𝕏𝕏𝕏 **Pool Court at 42** (at 42 The Calls H.), 44 The Calls, LS2 7EW, ℰ (0113) 244 4242,
✿ *poolcourt@onetel.net.uk, Fax (0113) 234 3332,* �────, « Riverside setting » – ⇔ 🗐. 🚾
🎴 ⓪ 𝘝𝘐𝘚𝘈
GZ z
closed Saturday lunch, Sunday and Bank Holidays – **Meals** 30.00/37.50 **t.** 🛭 17.50
Spec. Marinière of mussels and salted cod, artichoke, leeks and saffron. Fillet of beef, oxtail
risotto and parsnip crisps. Apricot and almond frangipane.

𝕏𝕏 **Rascasse,** Canal Wharf, Water Lane, LS11 5BB, ℰ (0113) 244 6611,
Fax (0113) 244 0736, ≤, « Converted grain warehouse, canalside setting » – 🗐. 🚾 🎴
⓪ 𝘝𝘐𝘚𝘈
FZ c
closed 25 December-3 January, Sunday, Saturday lunch and Bank Holiday Mondays – **Meals**
18.00 (lunch) and a la carte 22.00/32.50 **t.** 🛭 12.00.

𝕏𝕏 **Leodis,** Victoria Mill, Sovereign St, LS1 4BJ, ℰ (0113) 242 1010, Fax (0113) 243 0432,
🍽 �────, « Converted riverside warehouse » – 🚾 🎴 ⓪ 𝘝𝘐𝘚𝘈
GZ b
closed Sunday, lunch Saturday, 26 December and 1 January and Bank Holidays – Meals
a la carte 21.60/31.20 **t.** 🛭 13.95.

𝕏𝕏 **Brasserie Forty Four** (at 42 The Calls H.), 44 The Calls, LS2 7EW, ℰ (0113) 234 3232,
🍽 *brasserie44@onetel.net.uk, Fax (0113) 234 3332,* « Riverside setting » – 🗐. 🚾 🎴 ⓪
𝘝𝘐𝘚𝘈
GZ z
closed Sunday, Saturday lunch and Bank Holidays – **Meals** a la carte 20.35/26.40 **t.** 🛭 13.95.

𝕏𝕏 **Fourth Floor** (at Harvey Nichols), 107-111 Briggate, LS1 6AZ, ℰ (0113) 204 8000,
Fax (0113) 204 8080, �──── – 🗐. 🚾 🎴 ⓪ 𝘝𝘐𝘚𝘈 𝖩𝖢𝖡
GZ s
closed 25-26 December, 1 January, and dinner Sunday-Wednesday – **Meals** (lunch bookings
not accepted) 16.00 (lunch) and a la carte 27.00/31.00 **t.** 🛭 12.50.

𝕏𝕏 **Maxi's,** 6 Bingley St, LS3 1LX, off Kirkstall Rd ℰ (0113) 244 0552, *info@maxi-s.co.uk,*
Fax (0113) 234 3902, « Pagoda, ornate decor » – 🗐 🅿. 🚾 🎴 ⓪ 𝘝𝘐𝘚𝘈 𝖩𝖢𝖡
closed 25-26 December – **Meals** - Chinese (Canton, Peking) - 17.80/24.90 and a la carte
16.70/20.50 **t.** 🛭 9.90.
by Burley Rd FY a

𝕏 **The Calls Grill,** Calls Landing, 38 The Calls, LS2 7EW, ℰ (0113) 245 3870,
🍽 *Fax (0113) 245 9035,* « Converted riverside warehouse » – 🗐. 🚾 🎴 ⓪ 𝘝𝘐𝘚𝘈
GZ c
closed 22 December-3 January – **Meals** 11.95/17.50 and a la carte 16.70/26.25 **t.** 🛭 9.95.

𝕏 **Fishl,** 159 Headrow, LS1 3RG, ℰ (0113) 247 0177, Fax (0113) 245 3064 – 🗐. 🚾 🎴 ⓪
𝘝𝘐𝘚𝘈
FGY c
closed 25 December – **Meals** - Seafood - a la carte 18.05/30.15 **st.** 🛭 9.90.

at Garforth *East : 6 m. by A 64 GY and A 63 at junction with A 642 –* ✉ *Leeds :*

𝕏𝕏 **Aagrah,** Aberford Rd, LS25 1BA, on A 642 (Garforth rd) ℰ (0113) 287 6606 – 🗐 🅿.
🚾 🎴 𝘝𝘐𝘚𝘈 𝖩𝖢𝖡
closed 25 December – **Meals** - Indian (Kashmiri) - (booking essential) (dinner only) a la carte
13.30/17.25 **t.** 🛭 9.95.

at Pudsey *West : 5 ¾ m. by M 621 FZ and A 647 –* ✉ *Leeds :*

𝕏𝕏 **Aagrah,** 483 Bradford Rd, LS28 8ED, on A 647 ℰ (01274) 668818, *Fax (01274) 669803*
– 🗐 🅿. 🚾 🎴 𝘝𝘐𝘚𝘈 𝖩𝖢𝖡
closed 25 December – **Meals** - Indian (Kashmiri) - (booking essential) (dinner only) a la carte
13.30/17.25 **t.** 🛭 9.95.

at Horsforth *Northwest : 5 m. by A 65 FY off A 6120 –* ✉ *Leeds :*

𝕏 **Paris,** Calverley Bridge, Calverley Lane, Rodley, LS13 1NP, Southwest : 1 m. by A 6120
ℰ (0113) 258 1885, *Fax (0113) 239 0651* – 🗐 🅿. 🚾 🎴 ⓪ 𝘝𝘐𝘚𝘈 𝖩𝖢𝖡
closed 26-28 December, 1-3 January and Saturday lunch – **Meals** 13.95/15.95 and a la
carte 15.90/26.70 **t.** 🛭 10.95.

at Bramhope *Northwest : 8 m. on A 660 FY –* ✉ *Leeds :*

🏠 **Posthouse Leeds/Bradford,** Leeds Rd, LS16 9JJ, ℰ (0870) 400 9049, *gm1123@f orte-hotels.com, Fax (0113) 284 3451,* ≤, 🛌, 🚐, 🏊, �────, 🎱 – 🛗 ⇔ 📺 🖳 – 🔬 160.
🚾 🎴 ⓪ 𝘝𝘐𝘚𝘈
Meals 9.95/12.95 and a la carte 17.00/20.00 **t.** 🛭 12.95 – 🖙 12.50 – **130 rm** 99.00 **st.,**
1 suite – SB.

Winteringham North Lincolnshire **402** S 22 – pop. 4714 – ⊠ Scunthorpe. London 176 – Leeds 62.

XXXX 🏵🏵 **Winteringham Fields** (Schwab) with rm, Silver St, DN15 9PF, ℘ (01724) 73309■ wintfields@aol.com, Fax (01724) 733898, « Part 16C manor house » – 💱 📺 📞 📶 **L** **VISA**

closed last week March, first week August, last week October and 2 weeks Christma■ – **Meals** (closed Sunday-Monday) (booking essential to non-residents) 26.00/35.C and a la carte 56.00/67.00 **st.** ₰ 17.50 – � 10.00 – **8 rm** 75.00/165.00 **st.**, 2 suite■ **Spec.** Pan-fried langoustine, tuile of aubergine marmalade. Duo of squab with blac■ pudding and truffle potato purée. Rhubarb poached in rapsberry syrup with pu■ pastry.

Price | For full details of the prices quoted in this Guide, consult the introduction.

LIVERPOOL Mersey. **402 403** L 23 Great Britain G. – pop. 481786.

See : City★ - Walker Art Gallery★★ DY **M2** – Liverpool Cathedral★★ (Lady Chapel★) EZ Metropolitan Cathedral of Christ the King★★ EY – Albert Dock★ CZ (Merseyside Maritim■ Museum★ AC **M1** - Tate Gallery Liverpool★).

Exc. : Speke Hall★ AC, SE : 8 m. by A 561.

🏌 🏌 Allerton Municipal, Allerton Rd ℘ (0151) 428 1046 – 🏌 Liverpool Municipal, Ingo■ Lane, Kirby ℘ (0151) 546 5435 – 🏌 Bowring, Bowring Park, Roby Rd, Huyton ℘ (015■ 489 1901.

Mersey Tunnels (toll).

🛬 Liverpool Airport : ℘ (0151) 288 4000, SE : 6 m. by A 561 – **Terminal** : Pier Hea■ 🚢 to Isle of Man (Douglas) (Isle of Man Steam Packet Co. Ltd) 1-3 daily (2 h 30 mn/4■ 30 mn) – to Northern Ireland (Belfast) (Norse Irish Ferries Ltd) weekly (10 h 30 mn) daily 🚢 to Birkenhead and Wallasey (Mersey Ferries) frequent services daily.

🛈 Merseyside Welcome Centre, Clayton Square Shopping Centre ℘ (0151) 709 3631 Atlantic Pavilion, Albert Dock ℘ (0151) 708 8854.

London 219 – Birmingham 103 – Leeds 75 – Manchester 35.

Plans on following pages

🏛🏛 **Liverpool Marriott,** One Queen Sq, L1 1RH, ℘ (0151) 476 8000, Fax (0151) 474 500C■ 🖫, 🍴, 📼 – 🛗 💱 📺 ❤ 🔥 📞 – 🛎 250. 📶 🅰🅴 ⓞ **VISA**   DY **Oliviér's** : **Meals** (closed Saturday lunch and Bank Holidays) (buffet lunch)/dinner 24.0C and a la carte 16.70/24.00 **st.** ₰ 12.95 – ⊒ 14.45 – **143 rm** 109.00 **st.**, 3 suites – SE

🏛🏛 **Crowne Plaza Liverpool,** St Nicholas Pl, Princes Dock, Pier Head, L3 1QN, ℘ (015■ 243 8000, sales@crowneplaza-liverpool.co.uk, Fax (0151) 243 8111, ≤, 🖫, 🍴, 🖫 – 🛗 💱 rm, 🖥 📺 ❤ 🔥 📞 – 🛎 700. 📶 🅰🅴 ⓞ **VISA**. ⊛   CY ■ closed 24-26 December – **Meals** (closed lunch Saturday, Sunday and Bank Holidays■ 12.95/15.95 and a la carte ₰ 6.95 – ⊒ 12.95 – **155 rm** 125.00 **st.**, 4 suites – SB.

🏛🏛 **Holiday Inn,** Lime St, L1 1NQ, ℘ (0151) 709 7090, sales@holidayinn-liverpool.co.uk Fax (0151) 709 0137, 🖫, 🍴 – 🛗, 💱 rm, 🖥 📺 ❤ 🔥 – 🛎 500. 📶 🅰🅴 ⓞ **VISA** ⊛   DY z■ **Signals** : **Meals** (closed Saturday and Sunday lunch) 9.50/12.95 and a la carte 17.90/26.40 **t.** ₰ 10.95 – **138 rm** ⊒ 90.00/110.00 **t.**, 1 suite.

🏛🏛 **Liverpool Moat House,** Paradise St, L1 8GT, ℘ (0151) 471 9988, gmliv@queensm■ oathouse.co.uk, Fax (0151) 709 2706, 🖫, 🍴, 🖫 – 🛗, 💱 rm, 🖥 📺 📞 – 🛎 500. 📶 🅰🅴 ⓞ **VISA**   DZ n■ **Meals** 9.50/16.50 and dinner a la carte 18.15/27.05 **st.** ₰ 12.50 – ⊒ 11.50 – **261 rm** 120.00/140.00 **st.**, 2 suites – SB.

🏛🏛 **Thistle Liverpool,** 30 Chapel St, L3 9RE, ℘ (0151) 227 4444, liverpool@thistle.co.uk■ Fax (0151) 236 3973, ≤ – 🛗, 💱 rm, 🖥 📺 📞 – 🛎 100. 📶 🅰🅴 ⓞ **VISA** ⊛   CY r■ **Meals** (closed Bank Holidays) 14.00/19.00 and a la carte 14.90/25.90 **st.** – ⊒ 10.25 – **223 rm** 136.00/147.00 **st.**, 3 suites – SB.

🏛 **Devonshire House,** 293-297 Edge Lane, L7 9LD, East : 2 ¼ m. on A 5047 ℘ (015■ 264 6600, Fax (0151) 263 2109, ⚞ – 🛗, 💱 rm, 📺 ❤ 🔥 📞 – 🛎 300. 📶 🅰🅴 ⓞ **VISA** ⊛ **Meals** a la carte approx. 18.95 **st.** – **54 rm** ⊒ 75.00/85.00 **t.** – SB.

🏛 **Express by Holiday Inn** without rest., Britannia Pavilion, Albert Dock, L3 4AD, ℘ (0151) 709 1133, liverpool@premierhotels.co.uk, Fax (0151) 709 1144, ≤, « Victorian former cotton mill » – 🛗 💱 📺 ❤ 🔥 – 🛎 25. 📶 🅰🅴 ⓞ **VISA**. ⊛   CZ r■ closed 24-27 December and 31 December-2 January – **117 rm** 65.00 **t.**

🏨 **Travel Inn,** Northern Perimeter Rd, L30 7PT, North : 6 m. by A 59 on A 5036 ℰ (0151) 531 1497, Fax (0151) 520 1842 – ⚒⁀ rm, ▤ rest, 📺 ₺ 🄿 – 🛦 50. 🕼 🄰🄴 ⑩ 𝘷𝘪𝘴𝘢.
Meals (grill rest.) – **63 rm** 41.95 **t.**

🏨 **Travel Inn,** Queens Drive, West Derby, L13 0DL, East : 4 m. on A 5058 (Ringroad) ℰ (0151) 228 4724, Fax (0151) 220 7610 – ⚒⁀ rm, ▤ rest, 📺 ₺ 🄿. 🕼 🄰🄴 ⑩ 𝘷𝘪𝘴𝘢.
Meals (grill rest.) – **84 rm** 41.95 **t.** 					by A 5049	EY

🍴🍴 **60 Hope Street,** 60 Hope St, L1 9BZ, ℰ (0151) 707 6060, info@ 60hopestreet.com, Fax (0151) 707 6016 – ▤. 🕼 ⑩ 𝘷𝘪𝘴𝘢 							EZ x
closed 25-26 December, Saturday lunch, Sunday and Bank Holidays – **Meals** 10.95/13.95 (lunch) and a la carte 24.95/30.95 **t.** ⋔ 13.95.

🍴🍴 **Becher's Brook,** 29a Hope St, L1 9BQ, ℰ (0151) 707 0005, Fax (0151) 708 7011 – ⚒⁀.
🕼 🄰🄴 𝘷𝘪𝘴𝘢 							EZ a
closed 24 December-2 January, Sunday, Saturday lunch and Bank Holidays – **Meals** a la carte 12.90/50.00 **t.** ⋔ 12.95.

🍴 **Simply Heathcotes,** Beetham Plaza, 25 The Strand, L2 0XL, ℰ (0151) 236 3536, live rpool@ simplyheathcotes.co.uk, Fax (0151) 236 3534 – ▤. 🕼 🄰🄴 ⑩ 𝘷𝘪𝘴𝘢 		CY s
closed 25-26 December and Bank Holiday Mondays – **Meals** 15.50 (lunch) and a la carte 20.50/26.50 **t.** ⋔ 11.50.

🍴 **Ziba,** 15-19 Berry St, L1 9DF, ℰ (0151) 708 8870, Fax (0151) 707 9926 – 🕼 🄰🄴 𝘷𝘪𝘴𝘢
closed 25-26 and 31 December, 1 January, Sunday, lunch Saturday and Bank Holidays –
Meals 13.00/16.50 and a la carte 16.50/29.50 **t.** ⋔ 11.00. 				EZ s

🍴 **Mister M's,** 6 Atlantic Pavilion, Albert Dock, L3 4AA, ℰ (0151) 707 2202, mikemcdon ald@ misterms.freeserve.co.uk, Fax (0151) 708 8769, 🖵 – 🕼 🄰🄴 𝘷𝘪𝘴𝘢 𝘫𝘤𝘣 		CZ c
closed lunch Monday and Sunday, first 2 weeks January and 25 December – **Meals** - Seafood - 9.95/14.95 (lunch) and a la carte 25.85/53.90 **st.** ⋔ 9.95.

at Knowsley Industrial Park Northeast : 8 m. by A 59 DY and A 580 – ✉ Liverpool

🏨 **Suites H.,** Ribblers Lane, L34 9HA, ℰ (0151) 549 2222, enquiries@ suiteshotelgroup.com, Fax (0151) 549 1116, 🛦, �, 🔲 – 🗐, ⚒⁀ rm, ▤ 📺 ₭ ₺ 🄿 – 🛦 300. 🕼 🄰🄴 ⑩ 𝘷𝘪𝘴𝘢 ⌖
Meals (closed Saturday and Sunday lunch) a la carte 14.85/25.00 **st.** ⋔ 9.95 –, **80 suites** ⌑ 120.00/130.00 **st.**

🏨 **Howard Johnson** without rest., Ribblers Lane, Knowsley, L34 9HA, ℰ (0151) 549 2700, knowsley@ howardjohnson.co.uk, Fax (0151) 549 2800 – 🗐 ⚒⁀ 📺 ₭ ₺ 🄿 – 🛦 40. 🕼 🄰🄴 ⑩ 𝘷𝘪𝘴𝘢
86 rm ⌑ 49.95 **t.**

at Huyton East : 8 ¼ m. by A5047 EY and A 5080 on B 5199 – ✉ Liverpool :

🏨🏨 **Village H. and Leisure Club,** Fallows Way, L35 1RZ, Southeast . 3 ¼ m. by A 5080 off Whiston rd ℰ (0151) 449 2341, village.whiston@ village-hotels.com, Fax (0151) 449 3832, 🛦, �, 🔲, squash – 🗐, ⚒⁀ rm, 📺 ₭ ₺ 🄿 – 🛦 230. 🕼 🄰🄴 ⑩ 𝘷𝘪𝘴𝘢 𝘫𝘤𝘣. ⌖
Meals (closed Saturday lunch and Sunday dinner) a la carte 17.00/25.25 **st.** ⋔ 9.95 – **62 rm** ⌑ 95.00/108.00 **st.**

🏨 **Premier Lodge,** Roby Rd, L36 4HD, Southwest : 1 m. on A 5080 ℰ (0870) 7001426, Fax (0870) 7001427, 🖵 – ⚒⁀ rm, ▤ rest, 📺 ₭ ₺ 🄿 – 🛦 35. 🕼 🄰🄴 ⑩ 𝘷𝘪𝘴𝘢. ⌖
Meals (grill rest.) a la carte approx. 13.00 **t.** ⋔ 8.95 – **53 rm** 46.95 **t.**

🏨 **Travel Inn,** Wilson Rd, Tarbock, L36 6AD, Southeast : 2 ¼ m. on A 5080 ℰ (0151) 480 9614, Fax (0151) 480 9361 – ⚒⁀ rm, ▤ rest, 📺 ₺ 🄿. 🕼 🄰🄴 ⑩ 𝘷𝘪𝘴𝘢. ⌖
Meals (grill rest.) – **41 rm** 41.95 **t.**

at Grassendale Southeast : 4 ½ m. on A 561 EZ – ✉ Liverpool :

🍴🍴 **Gulshan,** 544-548 Aigburth Rd, L19 3QG, on A 561 ℰ (0151) 427 2273, Fax (0151) 427 2111 – ▤. 🕼 🄰🄴 ⑩ 𝘷𝘪𝘴𝘢
Meals - Indian - (dinner only) a la carte 19.05/23.45 **t.** ⋔ 8.95.

at Woolton Southeast : 6 m. by A 562 EZ, A 5058 and Woolton Rd – ✉ Liverpool :

🏨 **Woolton Redbourne,** Acrefield Rd, L25 5JN, ℰ (0151) 421 1500, wooltonredbourn e@ cwcom.net, Fax (0151) 421 1501, « Victorian house, antiques », 🖵 – ⚒⁀ rest, 📺 🄿.
🕼 🄰🄴 ⑩ 𝘷𝘪𝘴𝘢 𝘫𝘤𝘣
Meals (residents only) (dinner only) 25.50 ⋔ 11.95 – **18 rm** ⌑ 68.00/99.00 **t.**, 1 suite.

at Speke Southeast : 8 ¾ m. by A 561 EZ – ✉ Liverpool

🏨🏨 **Liverpool Marriott H. South,** Speke Aerodrome, Speke Rd, L24 8QD, West : 1 ¾ m. on A 561 ℰ (0151) 494 5000, reservations.liverpoolsouth@ marriotthotels.co.uk, Fax (0151) 494 5051, « Converted Art Deco former airport terminal building », 🛦, �, 🔲, 🏊, squash – 🗐 ⚒⁀ ▤ 📺 ₭ ₺ 🄿 – 🛦 250. 🕼 🄰🄴 ⑩ 𝘷𝘪𝘴𝘢. ⌖
Starways : **Meals** a la carte 17.40/25.95 **st.** ⋔ 12.95 – ⌑ 13.00 – **163 rm** 115.00 **st.**, 1 suite – SB.

LIVERPOOL
CENTRE

*Great Britain and Ireland
is now covered
by an Atlas at a scale of
1 inch to 4.75 miles.*

*Three easy to use versions:
Paperback, Spiralbound,
Hardback.*

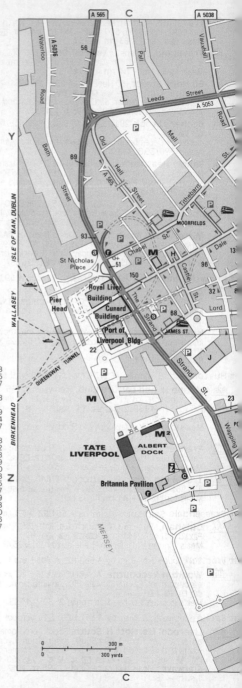

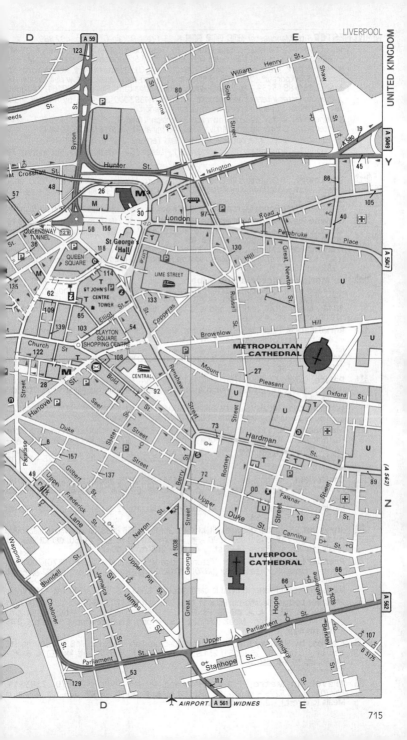

D A 59 E

123

eeds St.

Byron St. St.

U P

William Henry St.

Soho St.

Shaw St.

80

Anne St.

St.

Hunter St.

19

A 5049

A 580

Y

at Crosshall St.

Islington

45

57

48

26 M³

M

58

30 London Road

97

86

105

QUEENSWAY TUNNEL 129

36

156

Queen SQUARE

St George's Hall

Petrbroke

40

A 5047

St.

M

118 e

Lime St.

130 Hill

Great Newton St.

Place

135

114

62

ST JOHN'S CENTRE TOWER

Z

LIME STREET

St.

Russell St.

U

109

139

103

65

133

St.

Copperas

Hill

Elliot

54

Brownlow

Church St.

122

108

Clayton Square SHOPPING CENTRE

T

CENTRAL

Renshaw

Mount

METROPOLITAN CATHEDRAL

U

28

92

Pleasant

27

Oxford St.

T

Hanover

Bold St.

U

a

Paradise St.

6

Duke

Seel St.

Slater St.

Street

73 Hardman St.

Rodney

T

U

157

137

Gilbert St.

Berry

72

St.

P

89

A 562

N

49

Upper

Frederick

Park Lane

Nelson St.

Upper Duke St.

00 X

Falkner

10

Street

St.

Canning

St.

Wapping

Blundell St.

Jamaica St.

Upper Pitt St.

A 5038

Great George Street

LIVERPOOL CATHEDRAL

66

Cathcline

66

A 5039

A 562

Chaloner St.

James St.

St.

Hope St.

Parliament

Upper

Windsor St.

Bakley

107

B 5175

129

53

Parliament St.

Stanhope St.

117

D

AIRPORT A 561 WIDNES

E

MANCHESTER *Gtr. Manchester* **402 403 404** N 23 *Great Britain G.* – *pop. 402 889.*

See : *City★* – *Castlefield Heritage Park★ CZ* – *Town Hall★ CZ* – *City Art Gallery★ CZ* **M2**
– *Cathedral★ (Stalls and Canopies★)* CY *Museum of Science and Industry★* CZ **M**.

🛝 *Heaton Park, Prestwick* ℰ *(0161) 798 0295* – 🛝 *Houldsworth Park, Houldsworth St*
Reddish, Stockport ℰ *(0161) 881 3139* – 🛝 *Chorlton-cum-Hardy, Barlow Hall, Barlow Ha*
Rd ℰ *(0161) 881 3139* – 🛝 *William Wroe, Pennybridge Lane, Flixton* ℰ *(0161) 748 8680*
🛫 *Manchester International Airport :* ℰ *(0161) 489 3000, S : 10 m. by A 5103 and N*
56 – **Terminal** : *Coach service from Victoria Station.*

🛈 *Manchester Visitor Centre, Town Hall Extension, Lloyd St.* ℰ *(0161) 234 3157* – *Man*
chester Airport, International Arrivals Hall, Terminal T1 ℰ *(0161) 436 3344.*
Manchester Airport, International Arrivals Hall, Terminal 2 ℰ *(0161) 489 6412.*
London 202 – *Birmingham 86* – *Glasgow 221* – *Leeds 43* – *Liverpool 35* – *Nottingham 72*

Plan opposite

The Lowry, 50 Dearmans Pl, Chapel Wharf, Salford, M3 5LH, ℰ *(0161) 827 4000, enqu*
iries@thelowryhotel.com, Fax (0161) 827 4001, 🛁, ☎s – 🛗 ⇔ 🔲 📺 ✆ 🅿 – 🔬 400
🚫🅾 🆎 ⓪ *VISA*   CY r
Meals (see *River Room Marco Pierre White* below) – ☑ 15.50 – **157 rm** 185.00, 7 suites

Crowne Plaza Manchester-The Midland, Peter St, M60 2DS, ℰ *(0161) 236 3333*
sales@basshotels-uknorth.co.uk, Fax (0161) 932 4100, 🛁, ☎s, 🔲, squash – 🛗 ⇔ rm,
🔲 📺 ✆ 🅿 – 🔬 500. 🚫🅾 🆎 ⓪ *VISA*   CZ x
Trafford Room : Meals *(closed Monday and Tuesday dinner and Saturday lunch)* (carving
rest.) 16.95/26.95 **st.** 🍷 13.95 (see also **The French** and **Nico Central** below) – ☑ 14.50
– **289 rm** 160.00 **t.**, 14 suites.

Le Meridien Victoria and Albert, Water St, M3 4JQ, ℰ *(0161) 832 1188,*
gm1452@forte-hotels.com, Fax (0161) 834 2484, « *19C converted warehouse, television*
themed interior » – 🛗, ⇔ rm, 🔲 📺 ✆ 🅿 – 🔬 300. 🚫🅾 🆎 ⓪ *VISA*. ⚡
1844 : Meals 18.44 *(dinner)* and a la carte 16.70/35.00 **st.** – ☑ 15.00 – **154 rm**
170.00/190.00 **st.**, 4 suites.   by Quay St. CZ

Renaissance, Blackfriars St, Deansgate, M3 2EQ, ℰ *(0161) 835 2555, manchester.sa*
les@renaissancehotels.com, Fax (0161) 835 3077 – 🛗 ⇔ 🔲 📺 ✆ 🅿 – 🔬 400. 🚫🅾
🆎 ⓪ *VISA*. ⚡   CY v
Meals 12.50/15.50 and dinner a la carte 17.00/24.50 **st.** 🍷 14.00 – ☑ 12.50 – **196 rm**
110.00/145.00 **st.**, 4 suites – SB.

Palace, Oxford St, M60 7HA, ℰ *(0161) 288 1111, Fax (0161) 288 2222,* « *Victorian*
Gothic architecture, former Refuge Assurance building » – 🛗 ⇔ 📺 ✆ – 🔬 700. 🚫🅾
🆎 ⓪ *VISA*. ⚡   CZ s
Waterhouses : Meals *(carvery lunch)* 19.00/39.50 and dinner a la carte 19.00/39.00
🍷 13.50 – ☑ 13.50 – **241 rm** 154.00/174.00 **st.**, 11 suites – SB.

Malmaison, Piccadilly, M1 3AQ, ℰ *(0161) 278 1000, manchester@malmaison.com,*
Fax (0161) 278 1002, « *Contemporary interior* », 🛁, ☎s – 🛗, ⇔ rm, 🔲 📺 ✆ –
🔬 75. 🚫🅾 🆎 ⓪ *VISA* 🅹🅲🅱. ⚡   CZ u
Brasserie : Meals 11.95/12.95 and a la carte 21.35/26.80 **t.** 🍷 13.95 – ☑ 10.75 – **154 rm**
120.00 **s.**, 13 suites.

Castlefield, Liverpool Rd, M3 4JR, ℰ *(0161) 832 7073, info@castlefield-hotel.co.uk,*
Fax (0161) 837 3534, 🛁, ☎s, 🔲 – 🛗 ⇔, 🔲 rest, 📺 ✆ 🅿 – 🔬 60. 🚫🅾 🆎 ⓪ *VISA*
🅹🅲🅱. ⚡   by Quay St. CZ
Meals *(closed Sunday dinner)* (bar lunch)/dinner a la carte 12.35/21.00 **st.** 🍷 8.45 – **48 rm**
☑ 81.00/87.00 **st.** – SB.

Jurys Inn, 56 Great Bridgewater St, M1 5LE, ℰ *(0161) 953 8888, jurysinnmanchester@ju*
rysdoyle.com, Fax (0161) 953 9090 – 🛗, ⇔ rm, 🔲 📺 ✆ ♿ – 🔬 50. 🚫🅾 🆎 *VISA*. ⚡
Meals *(bar lunch)/dinner* 16.95 **st.** 🍷 10.00 – **265 rm** 67.00 **st.**   CZ p

Premier Lodge, North Tower, Victoria Bridge St, Salford, M3 5AS, ℰ *(0870) 7001488,*
mpremierlodge1@snr.co.uk, Fax (0870) 7001489 – 🛗, ⇔ rm, 🔲 rest, 📺 ✆ ♿ 🅿 🚫🅾
🆎 ⓪ *VISA*. ⚡   CY e
Meals (grill rest.) *(dinner only)* a la carte approx. 12.45 **t.** 🍷 8.45 – **170 rm** 49.95 **t.**

Premier Lodge, Gaythorne, River St, M15 5JF, ℰ *(0870) 7001490, Fax (0870) 7001491*
– 🛗, ⇔ rm, 📺 ✆ ♿ 🅿 🚫🅾 🆎 ⓪ *VISA*   by A 56 CZ
closed 24-29 December – Meals (grill rest.) *(dinner only)* a la carte approx. 12.45 **t.** 🍷 8.45
– **200 rm** 49.95 **t.**

Express by Holiday Inn without rest., Debdale Park, Hyde Rd, M18 7LJ, Southeast :
4 m. by A 6 off A 57 ℰ *(0161) 231 9900, Fax (0161) 220 8555* – 🛗 ⇔ 📺 ✆ ♿ 🅿 –
🔬 45. 🚫🅾 🆎 ⓪ *VISA* 🅹🅲🅱
97 rm 57.00 **st.**

Travel Inn Metro, 112-114 Portland St, M1 4WB, ℰ *(0870) 2383315,*
Fax (0161) 233 5299 – 🛗 ⇔, 🔲 rest, 📺 ✆ 🅿 🚫🅾 🆎 ⓪ *VISA* 🅹🅲🅱. ⚡   CZ d
Meals (grill rest.) – **226 rm** 49.95 **t.**

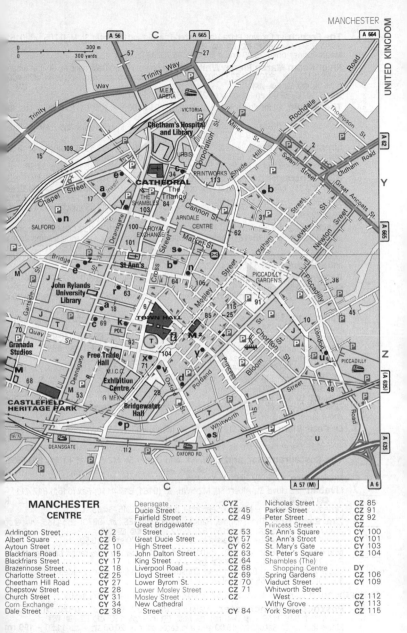

UNITED KINGDOM

A 62

A 665

A 635

A 6

MANCHESTER
CENTRE

🏨 **Travelodge,** Townbury House, Blackfriars St, Salford, M3 5AB, 🖊 (0161) 834 9476, *Fax (0161) 839 5181* – |📶|, ⇋ rm, ■ rest, 📺 ⚿ Ⓟ. ⓞ Ⓐⓔ ① *VISA*. ⌲⌲   CY **a**
Meals (cafe bar) – **181 rm** 49.95 **t.**

🏨 **Premier Lodge,** 7-11 Lower Mosley St, M2 3DW, 🖊 (0870) 7001476, *Fax (0870) 7001477* – |📶|, ⇋ rm, ■ rest, 📺 ✓ ⚿ – ⌲ 50. ⓞ Ⓐⓔ ① *VISA*   CZ **v**
Meals (grill rest.) – **147 rm** 49.95 **t.**

717

🕸🕸🕸 **The French** (at Crowne Plaza Manchester-The Midland H.), Peter St, M60 2DS, 𝒫 (016ʹ
236 3333 – 😅 ⚬ ☰ 🄿 ⦿ 🄰🄴 ⓞ 𝗩𝗜𝗦𝗔 CZ
Meals (dinner only) 29.00 and a la carte 34.70/48.85 **st.** ⚱ 13.95.

🕸🕸🕸 **River Room Marco Pierre White** (at The Lowry H.), 50 Dearmans Pl, Chapel Wharf,
Salford, M3 5LH, 𝒫 (0161) 827 4003, enquiries@thelowryhotel.com, Fax (0161) 827 400'
– ☰ 🄿 ⦿ 🄰🄴 ⓞ 𝗩𝗜𝗦𝗔 CY
Meals 12.00/22.00 and a la carte 23.50/35.50 **t.** ⚱ 10.50.

🕸🕸🕸 **The Lincoln,** 1 Lincoln Sq, M2 5LN, 𝒫 (0161) 834 9000, Fax (0161) 834 9555 – ☰. ⦿
🄰🄴 𝗩𝗜𝗦𝗔 𝗝𝗖𝗕 CZ
closed 1 week Christmas, Saturday lunch, Sunday dinner and Bank Holidays – **Meals** 16.5⁰
(lunch) and a la carte 19.40/28.85 **t.** ⚱ 11.00.

🕸🕸 **Simply Heathcotes,** Jackson Row, M2 5WD, 𝒫 (0161) 835 3536, manchester@sir
plyheathcotes.co.uk, Fax (0161) 835 3534 – 🔆 ☰. ⦿ 🄰🄴 ⓞ 𝗩𝗜𝗦𝗔 CZ
closed Bank Holidays – **Meals** 15.50 (lunch) and a la carte 23.50/31.00 **t.** ⚱ 11.50.

🕸🕸 **Nico Central** (at Crowne Plaza Manchester-The Midland H.), 2 Mount St, M60 2DS
𝒫 (0161) 236 6488, manchester@nicocentral.co.uk, Fax (0161) 236 8897 – ☰. ⦿ 🄰🄴 ⓞ
𝗩𝗜𝗦𝗔 𝗝𝗖𝗕 CZ
closed lunch Saturday and Sunday and Bank Holidays – **Meals** 12.95 (lunch) and a la carte
19.25/27.95 **t.** ⚱ 12.95.

🕸🕸 **Stock,** The Stock Exchange, 4 Norfolk St, M2 1DW, 𝒫 (0161) 839 6644, stockrestau
ant@aol.com, Fax (0161) 839 6655, « Edwardian, former stock exchange trading floor »
– ⦿ 🄰🄴 𝗩𝗜𝗦𝗔 CY
closed 25-26 December, first week January and Sunday – **Meals** - Italian - 12.50 (lunch)
and a la carte 17.45/31.00 **t.** ⚱ 12.50.

🕸🕸 **Reform,** King St, Spring Gdns, M2 4ST, 𝒫 (0161) 839 9966, Fax (0161) 839 0404 – ☰
⦿ 🄰🄴 𝗩𝗜𝗦𝗔 𝗝𝗖𝗕 CZ r
closed lunch Saturday and Sunday – **Meals** 16.95 (lunch) and a la carte 23.90/36.90 **t**
⚱ 16.00.

🕸🕸 **Yang Sing,** 34 Princess St, M1 4JY, 𝒫 (0161) 236 2200, info@yang.sing.com
Fax (0161) 236 5934 – ☰. ⦿ 🄰🄴 𝗩𝗜𝗦𝗔 CZ y
closed 25 December – **Meals** - Chinese - a la carte 14.70/21.80 **st.** ⚱ 10.95.

🕸🕸 **Koreana,** Kings House, 40a King St West, M3 2WY, 𝒫 (0161) 832 4330, 113036
1764@compuserve.com, Fax (0161) 832 2293 – ⦿ 🄰🄴 𝗩𝗜𝗦𝗔 CZ z
closed 25-26 December, 1 January, Sunday and lunch Saturday and Bank Holidays – **Meals**
- Korean - 12.40 and a la carte 12.50/27.00 **t.** ⚱ 7.95.

🕸 **Shimla Pinks,** Dolefield Crown Sq, M3 3EN, 𝒫 (0161) 839 7099, Fax (0161) 832 2202
⦿ 🄰🄴 𝗩𝗜𝗦𝗔 𝗝𝗖𝗕 CZ e
closed 25 December, 1 January, Sunday and Saturday lunch – **Meals** - Indian - 15.95/19.95
and a la carte **t.** ⚱ 10.50.

🕸 **Le Petit Blanc,** 55 King St, M2 4LQ, 𝒫 (0161) 832 1000, manchester@lepetitblanc.
co.uk, Fax (0161) 832 1001 – ☰. ⦿ 🄰🄴 ⓞ 𝗩𝗜𝗦𝗔 CZ b
closed 25 December – **Meals** 15.00 (lunch) and a la carte 19.45/29.00 **t.** ⚱ 11.00.

🕸 **The Restaurant Bar and Grill,** 14 John Dalton St, M2 6JR, 𝒫 (0161) 839 1999,
Fax (0161) 835 1886 – ☰. ⦿ 🄰🄴 𝗩𝗜𝗦𝗔 𝗝𝗖𝗕 CZ r
Meals a la carte 20.00/30.00 **t.** ⚱ 10.95.

🕸 **Livebait,** 22 Lloyd St, Albert Sq, M2 5WH, 𝒫 (0161) 817 4110, Fax (0161) 817 4111 –
☰. ⦿ 🄰🄴 𝗩𝗜𝗦𝗔 CZ k
closed 25 December – **Meals** - Seafood - a la carte 22.45/34.65 **st.**

🕸 **Zinc Bar & Grill,** The Triangle, Hanging Ditch, M4 3ES, 𝒫 (0870) 3334333, zinc@co
nran-restaurants.co.uk, Fax (0161) 827 4212, 🎋 – ⦿ 🄰🄴 𝗩𝗜𝗦𝗔 CY c
closed 25-26 December – **Meals** a la carte 17.00/35.00 **st.** ⚱ 10.50.

🕸 **Market,** 104 High St, M4 1HQ, 𝒫 (0161) 834 3743, marketrestaurant@btinternet.com,
Fax (0161) 834 3743 – ⦿ 🄰🄴 ⓞ 𝗩𝗜𝗦𝗔 𝗝𝗖𝗕 CY b
closed August, 1 week Easter, 1 week Christmas and Sunday-Tuesday – **Meals** (dinner only)
a la carte 19.15/26.35 **t.** ⚱ 9.95.

at Northenden South : 5 ¼ m. by A 57 (M) CZ and A 5103 – ✉ Manchester :

🏨 **Posthouse Manchester,** Palatine Rd, M22 4FH, 𝒫 (0870) 400 9056,
Fax (0161) 946 0139 – 📶, 🔆 rm, ☰ rest, 📺 🄿 – 🔥 150. ⦿ 🄰🄴 ⓞ 𝗩𝗜𝗦𝗔
Meals (bar lunch Saturday) 15.00 and a la carte approx. 20.00 **st.** – 😐 11.50 – **190 rm**
79.00 **st.** – SB.

at Didsbury South : 5 ½ m. by A 5103 CZ on A 5145 – ✉ Manchester

🏨 **Eleven Didsbury Park** without rest., 11 Didsbury Park, M20 5LH, 𝒫 (0161) 448 7711,
enquiries@elevendidsburypark.com, Fax (0161) 448 8282, « Contemporary interior », 🐾
– 🔆 📺 📞 🄿 ⦿ 🄰🄴 ⓞ 𝗩𝗜𝗦𝗔 𝗝𝗖𝗕. 🐾
😐 10.50 **14 rm** 99.50/125.50 **st.**

at **Manchester Airport** *South : 9 m. by Lower Mosley St.* CZ *and A 5103 off M 56 –* ⊠ *Manchester :*

🏨🏨🏨 **Radisson SAS Manchester Airport,** Chicago Ave, M90 3RA, ℰ (0161) 490 5000, *salesairport.manchestcr@radissonsas.com, Fax* (0161) 490 5100, ≼, **Ⅰ₅,** ⇌, 🔲 – ⧉, ⥺ rm, 🗏 🆃🆅 ✆ ₺ 🖭 – 🔏 350. 🕸 🖭 🆅🅸🆂🅰 🛇
Phileas Fogg : Meals (buffet lunch)/dinner a la carte 26.00/40.50 **t.** ₰ 18.00 – **Runway Café : Meals** a la carte 14.75/23.15 **t.** ₰ 18.00 – � 13.00 – **354 rm** 140.00/195.00 **st.,** 6 suites.

🏨🏨 **Hilton Manchester Airport,** Outwood Lane (Terminal One), M90 4WP, ℰ (0161) 435 3000, *manhitw@hilton.com, Fax* (0161) 435 3040, **Ⅰ₅,** ⇌, 🔲 – ⧉, ⥺ rm, 🗏 🆃🆅 ✆ ₺ 🖭 – 🔏 300. 🕸 🖭 🆅🅸🆂🅰
Meals 21.00 and a la carte ₰ 3.95 – **Portico : Meals** (closed Sunday) (dinner only) 22.50/35.00 **t.** ₰ 13.50 – **Lowry's : Meals** (closed Saturday lunch) 21.00/25.00 and dinner a la carte 20.70/29.85 **t.** ₰ 13.50 – ⊖ 16.50 – **224 rm** 150.00/185.00 **st.,** 1 suite – SB.

🏨🏨🏨 **Posthouse Manchester Airport,** Outwood Lane (Terminal One), M90 3NS, ℰ (0161) 437 5811, *Fax* (0161) 436 2340, **Ⅰ₅,** ⇌, 🔲 – ⧉, ⥺ rm, 🗏 🆃🆅 ₺ 🖭 – 🔏 30. 🕸 🖭 🅞 🆅🅸🆂🅰 🅹🅲🅱. 🛇
Meals (bar lunch Saturday) 15.00 and a la carte 22.85/27.95 **st.** ₰ 11.95 – **Sampans** (ℰ (0161) 448 4074) **: Meals** - South East Asian - (closed Sunday) (dinner only) 17.95/24.95 and a la carte approx. 25.00 **t.** ₰ 12.45 – ⊖ 13.95 – **295 rm** 109.00 **st.** – SB.

🏨🏨 **Etrop Grange,** Thorley Lane, M90 4EG, ℰ (0161) 499 0500, *etropgrange@corushot els.com, Fax* (0161) 499 0790 – ⥺ rm ✆ ₺ 🖭 – 🔏 40. 🕸 🖭 🅞 🆅🅸🆂🅰 🅹🅲🅱
Meals (closed Saturday lunch) 18.50/25.00 **st.** ₰ 14.00 – ⊖ 12.50 – **62 rm** 125.00/145.00 **st.,** 2 suites – SB.

🏨🏨 **Holiday Inn Garden Court,** Outwood Lane (Terminal One), M90 4HL, ℰ (0161) 498 0333, *reservations@mchap.co.uk, Fax* (0161) 498 0222 – ⧉, ⥺ rm, 🗏 rest, 🆃🆅 ✆ ₺ 🖭 – 🔏 90. 🕸 🖭 🅞 🆅🅸🆂🅰 🅹🅲🅱. 🛇
Meals (bar lunch)/dinner 15.95 and a la carte 15.70/29.70 **t.** ₰ 10.75 – ⊖ 9.95 – **226 rm** 72.50/99.00 **st.**

🏨 **Travel Inn,** Finney Lane, Heald Green, SK8 2QH, East : 2 m. by B 5166 ℰ (0161) 499 1944, *Fax* (0161) 437 4910 – ⥺ rm, 🗏 rest, 🆃🆅 ₺ 🖭 – 🔏 70. 🕸 🖭 🅞 🆅🅸🆂🅰. 🛇
Meals (grill rest.) – **60 rm** 41.95 **t.**

✕✕✕ **Moss Nook,** Ringway Rd, Moss Nook, M22 5WD, East : 1 ¼ m. on Cheadle rd ℰ (0161) 437 4778, *Fax* (0161) 498 8089 – 🖭. 🕸 🖭 🆅🅸🆂🅰
closed 2 weeks Christmas-New Year, Saturday lunch, Sunday and Monday – **Meals** 18.50/31.50 and a la carte 32.50/49.50 **t.** ₰ 12.00.

at **Trafford Park** *Southwest : 2 m. by A 56* CZ *- and A 5081 –* ⊠ *Manchester*

🏨🏨 **Golden Tulip,** Waters Reach, M17 1WS, ℰ (0161) 873 8899, *info@qualitymanchester.co.uk, Fax* (0161) 872 6556 – ⧉, ⥺ 🆃🆅 ✆ ₺ 🖭 – 🔏 250. 🕸 🖭 🅞 🆅🅸🆂🅰. 🛇
closed 24 December-1 January – **Meals** (see **Rhodes & Co.** below) – ⊖ 10.00 – **111 rm** 85.00/99.50 **st.**

🏨 **Old Trafford Lodge** without rest., Lancashire County Cricket Club, Talbot Rd, Old Trafford, M16 0PX, ℰ (0161) 874 3333, *lodge@lccc.co.uk,* ≼, « Within Lancashire County Cricket Club » ⧉ ⥺ 🆃🆅 ✆ 🖭. 🕸 🖭 🆅🅸🆂🅰 🛇
68 rm 59.00 **t.**

✕✕ **Rhodes & Co.,** Waters Reach, M17 1WS, ℰ (0161) 868 1900, *Fax* (0161) 868 1901 – 🗏 🖭. 🕸 🖭 🅞 🆅🅸🆂🅰
closed 1 week Christmas, Saturday, Sunday and lunch Bank Holidays – **Meals** 12.50 (lunch) and a la carte 18.70/30.15 **t.** ₰ 12.50.

at **Salford Quays** *Southwest : 2 ¼ m. by A 56* CZ *off A 5063 –* ⊠ *Manchester*

🏨🏨🏨 **Copthorne Manchester,** Clippers Quay, M5 2XP, ℰ (0161) 873 7321, *manchester@mill-cop.com, Fax* (0161) 873 7318, **Ⅰ₅,** ⇌ – ⧉, ⥺ rm, 🗏 rest, 🆃🆅 ✆ ₺ 🖭 – 🔏 150. 🕸 🖭 🅞 🆅🅸🆂🅰. 🛇   by A 56 CZ
Chandlers : Meals (dinner only) 31.50 **st.** ₰ 16.25 – **Clippers : Meals** (carving rest.) (bar lunch Saturday and Sunday) 21.00 **st.** ₰ 16.25 – ⊖ 13.95 – **166 rm** 150.00/185.00 **st.**

🏨 **Express by Holiday Inn** without rest., Waterfront Quay, M5 2XW, ℰ (0161) 868 1000, *Fax* (0161) 868 1068, ≼ – ⧉, ⥺ 🆃🆅 ✆ ₺ 🖭 – 🔏 25. 🕸 🖭 🅞 🆅🅸🆂🅰. 🛇
120 rm 65.00 **st.**

🏨 **Travel Inn,** Basin 8, The Quays, M5 4SQ, ℰ (0161) 872 4026, *Fax* (0161) 876 0094, ≼ – ⧉, ⥺ rm, 🗏 rest, 🆃🆅 ₺ 🖭 🕸 🖭 🅞 🆅🅸🆂🅰. 🛇
Meals (grill rest.) – **52 rm** 41.95 **t.**

✕✕ **The Lowry,** Pier 8, M5 2AZ, ℰ (0161) 876 2121, *Fax* (0161) 876 2021 – ⥺ 🗏. 🕸 🖭 🅞 🆅🅸🆂🅰
closed 25 December – **Meals** (booking essential Sunday and Monday dinner) a la carte 17.15/25.90 **t.** ₰ 11.95.

MANCHESTER

at Chorlton-Cum-Hardy Southwest : 5 m. by A 56 CZ and a 5103 on A 6010 – ⊠ Manchester

↑ **Abbey Lodge** without rest., 501 Wilbraham Rd, M21 0UJ, 𝒫 (0161) 862 9266, Fax (0161) 862 9266, 🚘 – 📺 🅿 🕸
⏴ 5.00 – **4 rm** 40.00/50.00.

at Trafford Centre Southeast : 6 ½ m. by A 34 CZ – ⊠ Manchester

🏢 **Travel Inn,** Wilderspool Wood, M17 8WW, 𝒫 (0161) 747 8850, Fax (0161) 747 4763 – 📶, ⥱ rm, 🍴 rest, 📺 📞 🕭 🅿 – 🔬 250. 🆖 🆎 ⓞ 𝘝𝘐𝘚𝘈 🕸
Meals (grill rest.) – **59 rm** 41.95 t.

at Eccles West : 4 m. by A 56 CZ, A 57 and M 602 – ⊠ Manchester

🏢 **Highbury** without rest., 113 Monton Rd, M30 9HQ, Northwest : 1 ¼ m. by A 576 on B 5229 𝒫 (0161) 787 8545, enquiries@highbury-hotel.co.uk, Fax (0161) 787 9023 – 📺 🅿 🆖 🆎 𝘝𝘐𝘚𝘈
16 rm ⏴ 38.00/49.50 st.

at Worsley West : 7 ¼ m. by A 6 CY, A 5063, M 602 and M 62 (eastbound) on A 572 – ⊠ Manchester :

🏨🏨 **Marriott Worsley Park Hotel & Country Club,** Worsley Park, M28 2QT, on A 575 𝒫 (0161) 975 2000, salesadmin.worsleypark@marriotthotels.co.uk, Fax (0161) 799 6341, 🚼, 𝑓₆, 🛋, 🔲, ⁅₈, 🎯 – 📶, ⥱ rm, 🍴 rest, 📺 📞 🕭 🅿 – 🔬 250. 🆖 🆎 ⓞ 𝘝𝘐𝘚𝘈 𝗝𝗖𝗕
Brindley's : Meals (closed Saturday lunch) 15.00/29.00 and dinner a la carte 24.00/31.00
🍷 13.50 – ⏴ 13.00 – **153 rm** 114.00, 5 suites.

🏨 **Novotel Manchester West,** Worsley Brow, M28 2YA, at junction 13 of M 60 𝒫 (0161) 799 3535, Fax (0161) 703 8207, 🛏 heated – 📶, ⥱ rm, 📺 📞 🕭 🅿 – 🔬 220. 🆖 🆎 ⓞ 𝘝𝘐𝘚𝘈 𝗝𝗖𝗕
Meals 13.00/17.00 and a la carte 17.15/22.00 t. 🍷 11.25 – ⏴ 9.50 – **119 rm** 72.00 t.

at Pendlebury Northwest : 4 m. by A 6 CY on A 666 – ⊠ Manchester :

🏢 **Premier Lodge,** 219 Bolton Rd, M27 8TG, 𝒫 (0870) 7001470, Fax (0870) 7001471 – ⥱ rm, 🍴 rest, 📺 🕭 🅿 🆖 🆎 ⓞ 𝘝𝘐𝘚𝘈 🕸
Meals (grill rest.) a la carte approx. 13.00 t. 🍷 8.95 – **31 rm** 46.95 t.

at Swinton Northwest : 4 m. by A 6 CY, A 580 and A 572 on B 5231 – ⊠ Manchester :

🏢 **Premier Lodge,** East Lancs Rd, M27 0AA, Southwest : ½ m. on A 580 𝒫 (0870) 7001472, Fax (0870) 7001473 – ⥱ rm, 🍴 rest, 📺 📞 🕭 🅿 🆖 🆎 ⓞ 𝘝𝘐𝘚𝘈 🕸
Meals (grill rest.) a la carte approx. 12.50 t. 🍷 7.80 – **27 rm** 46.95 t.

Calendar of main tradefairs and other international events in 2002

AUSTRIA

Vienna	Wiener Festwochen	10 May to 16 June
Salzburg	Salzburg Festival (Festspiele)	23 March 1 April
		27 July to 31 August

BENELUX

Amsterdam	Holland Festival	16 to 17 February
Bruges	The Holy Blood Procession	Ascension
Brussels	Guild Procession (Ommegang)	first Thursday of July and the previous Tuesday
	Holiday and Leisure Activities International Show	21 to 26 March
	Belgian Antique Dealers Fair	February
	Eurantica (Antiques Show)	Late March

CZECH REPUBLIC

Prague	Spring International Music Festival	12 May to 3 June
	International Book Fair	9 to 12 May

DENMARK

Copenhagen	Tivoli Gardens	19 April to 30 Sept.
	Jazz Festival	5 to 14 July
	International Ballet Festival	1 to 15 August
	Art Copenhagen	1 to 16 September
	Autumn Jazz Festival	7 to 10 Nov.
	Tivoli Christmas Market	mid Nov. to 23 Dec.

FINLAND

Helsinki	Finnish Boat Fair	February
	Helsinki Festival	23 August to 8 Sept.
	Helsinki International Horse Show	17 to 20 October

FRANCE

Paris	Paris Fair	26 April to 8 May
	International Tourism Show	14 to 17 March
	Book Fair	22 to 27 March
Cannes	International Film Festival	15 to 26 May
Lyons	Lyons Fair	15 to 25 March
Marseilles	Marseilles Christmas Fair	Last weekend November to 31 December
Monaco	Spring Art Festival	29 March to 28 April
Nice	Carnival	31 January to 17 February
Strasbourg	Christmas Market	End of November to Christmas
	European Fair	6 to 15 September

GERMANY

Berlin	Berlin Fair (Grüne Woche)	11 to 20 January
Frankfurt	International Fair	15 to 19 Feb. and 30 August to 3 September
	Frankfurt Book Fair	9 to 14 October
Hanover	Hanover Fair	13 to 20 March
Leipzig	International Book Fair	21 to 24 March
Munich	Beer Festival (Oktoberfest)	21 Sept. to 6 Oct.

GREECE

Athens	Athens Festival	June to Oct.

HUNGARY

Budapest	Spring Festival	16 March-1 April
	Motor Show	21 to 24 March
	Fashion Days	25 to 27 August
	10th International Wine and Champagne Festival	3 to 16 Sept.
	Motor Show	2 to 6 October
	Autumn Festival	19 Oct. to 4 Nov.
	Foodapest	26 to 29 Nov.

IRELAND

Dublin	St Patrick's Festival	1 to 31 March
	Dublin Film Festival	20 to 29 April
	Dublin Horse Show	7 to 11 August

ITALY

Milan	Bit (International Tourism Exchange)	20 to 24 February
	Fashion Fair (Moda Milano)	24 February to 5 March
	SMAU (International Exhibition of Information and Communication Technology)	24 to 28 October
Florence	Pitti Bimbo	28 to 30 June
	Fashion Fair (Pitti Immagine Uomo)	20 to 23 June
Turin	International Book Fair	16 to 20 May
Venice	International Film Festival	29 August to 8 September
	The Carnival	1 to 12 February

NORWAY

Oslo	World Cup Nordic Skiing and Ski Jumping	13 to 17 March
	International Jazz Festival	5 to 10 August
	Fashion Fair	last week August
	Horse Show	18 to 20 October
	International Film Festival	14 to 24 Nov.

POLAND

Warsaw	International Book Fair	Mid May
	Mozart Festival	Mid June to Late July
	Jazz Jamboree	Last weekend October

PORTUGAL

Lisbon	International Motor Show	30 May to 9 June

SPAIN

Madrid	Fitur	29 January to 2 February 2003
	Motor Show	24 May to 2 June
Barcelona	International Tourism Show in Catalonia	18 to 21 April
	International Book Trade Fair	2 to 5 October
Seville	April Fair	16 to 21 April
València	Fallas	15 to 19 March
	Automobile Trade Fair	30 November to 8 December

SWEDEN

Stockholm	International Dog Show	30 and 31 March
	Restaurant Days	30 May to 2 June
	Jubilee Week	1 to 6 June
	Jazz Festival	16 to 21 June
	International Antiques Fair	4 to 6 October
	International Film Festival	7 to 17 Nov.
	Nobel Prize Day	10 December
Gothenburg	Swedish International Travel &	21 to 24 March
	International Horse Show	4 to 7 April
	Ice Hockey World Championship	26 April to 11 May
	International Book Fair	19 to 22 Sept.
	International Consumer Goods Fair	26 to 30 September

SWITZERLAND

Bern	BEA : Exhibition for Handicraft, Agriculture, Trade and Industry	26 April to 5 May
Basle	European Watch, Clock and Jewellery Fair	4 to 11 April
Geneva	International Exhibition of inventions, new technologies and products	1 to 5 May
	International Motor Show	6 to 16 March 2003
Zürich	Züspa : Zurich Autumn Show for Home and Living, Sport and Fashion	19 to 29 September

UNITED KINGDOM

London	Book Fair	17 to 19 March
	Fine Art and Antiques Fair	7 to 17 June
	International Map Fair	9 June
	Internet World UK 2002	11 to 13 June
	International Film Festival	2 weeks November
Birmingham	Sportscar Show	25 and 26 May
	Antiques for Everyone	8 to 11 August
	British International Motor Show	22 Oct. to 3 Nov.
	International Classic Motor Show	6 to 10 Nov.
	International Motorcycle & Scooter Show	14 to 24 November
	Antiques for Everyone	28 Nov. to 1 Dec.
Edinburgh	Military Tattoo	2 to 24 August
	Fringe Festival	4 to 26 August
	International Book Festival	11 to 25 August
	International Film Festival	14 to 25 August
	International Festival	11 to 31 August
Glasgow	West End Festival	15 to 30 June
	International Jazz Festival	1 to 7 July
Leeds	International Film Festival	3 to 13 Oct.
Manchester	Commonwealth Games	25 July to 4 August

Note : when making an international call, do not dial the first "0" of the city codes (except for calls to Italy).

Indicatifs Téléphoniques Internationaux

Important : Pour les communications internationales, le zéro (0) initial de l'indicatif interurbain n'est pas à composer (excepté pour les appels vers l'Italie).

from \ to	A	B	CH	CZ	D	DK	E	FIN	F	GB	GR
A Austria		0032	0041	00420	0049	0045	0034	00358	0033	0044	0030
B Belgium	0043		0041	00420	0049	0045	0034	00358	0033	0044	0030
CH Switzerland	0043	0032		00420	0049	0045	0034	00358	0033	0044	0030
CZ Czech Republic	0043	0032	0041		0049	0045	0034	00358	0033	0044	0030
D Germany	0043	0032	0041	00420		0045	0034	00358	0133	0044	0030
DK Denmark	0043	0032	0041	00420	0049		0034	00358	0033	0044	0030
E Spain	0043	0032	0041	00420	0049	0045		00358	0033	0044	0030
FIN Finland	0043	0032	0041	00420	0049	0045	0034		0033	0044	0030
F France	0043	0032	0041	00420	0049	0045	0034	00358		0044	0030
GB United Kingdom	0043	0032	0041	00420	0049	0045	0034	00358	0033		0030
GR Greece	0043	0032	0041	00420	0049	0045	0034	00358	0033	0044	
H Hungary	0043	0032	0041	00420	0049	0045	0034	00358	0033	0044	0030
I Italy	0043	0032	0041	00420	0049	0045	0034	00358	0033	0044	0030
IRL Ireland	0043	0032	0041	00420	0049	0045	0034	00358	0033	0044	0030
J Japan	00143	00132	00141	001420	0149	00145	00134	001358	00133	00144	00130
L Luxembourg	0043	0032	0041	00420	0049	0045	0034	00358	0033	0044	0030
N Norway	0043	0032	0041	00420	0049	0045	0034	00358	0033	0044	0030
NL Netherlands	0043	0032	0041	00420	0049	0045	0034	00358	0033	0044	0030
PL Poland	0043	0032	0041	00420	0049	0045	0034	00358	0033	0044	0030
P Portugal	0043	0032	0041	00420	0049	0045	0034	00358	0033	0044	0030
RUS Russia	81043	81032	81041	810420	81049	81045	81034	810358	81033	81044	81030
S Sweden	0043	0032	0041	00420	0049	0045	0034	00358	0033	0044	0030
USA	01143	01132	01141	011420	01149	01145	01134	011358	01133	01144	01130

* Direct dialing not possible*   ** Pas de sélection automatique*

Internationale
Telefon-Vorwahlnummern

Wichtig : bei Auslandsgesprächen darf die Null (0) der Ortsnetzkennzahl nicht gewählt werden (ausser bei Gesprächen nach Italien).

国際電話国別番号

(H)	(I)	(IRL)	(J)	(L)	(N)	(NL)	(PL)	(P)	(RUS)	(S)	(USA)	
0036	0039	00353	0081	00352	0047	0031	0048	00351	007	0046	001	**Austria A**
0036	0039	00353	0081	00352	0047	0031	0048	00351	007	0046	001	**Belgium B**
0036	0039	00353	0081	00352	0047	0031	0048	00351	007	0046	001	**Switzerland CH**
0036	0039	00353	0081	00352	0047	0031	0048	00351	007	0046	001	**Czech CZ Republic**
0036	0039	00353	0081	00352	0047	0031	0048	00351	007	0046	001	**Germany D**
0036	0039	00353	0081	00352	0047	0031	0048	00351	007	0046	001	**Denmark DK**
0036	0039	00353	0081	00352	0047	0031	0048	00351	007	0046	001	**Spain E**
0036	0039	00353	0081	00352	0047	0031	0048	00351	007	0046	001	**Finland FIN**
0036	0039	00353	0081	00352	0047	0031	0048	00351	007	0046	001	**France F**
0036	0039	00353	0081	00352	0047	0031	0048	00351	007	0046	001	**United GB Kingdom**
0036	0039	00353	0081	00352	0047	0031	0048	00351	007	0046	001	**Greece GR**
	0039	00353	0081	00352	0047	0031	0048	00351	007	0046	001	**Hungary H**
0036		00353	0081	00352	0047	0031	0048	00351	*	0046	001	**Italy I**
0036	0039		0081	00352	0047	0031	0048	00351	007	0046	001	**Ireland IRL**
00136	00139	001353		001352	00147	00131	00148	001351	*	00146	0011	**Japan J**
0036	0039	00353	0081		0047	0031	0048	00351	007	0046	001	**Luxembourg L**
0036	0039	00353	0081	00352		0031	0048	00351	007	0046	001	**Norway N**
0036	0039	00353	0081	00352	0047		0048	00351	007	0046	001	**Netherlands NL**
0036	0039	00353	0081	00352	0047	0031		00351	007	0046	001	**Poland PL**
0036	0039	00353	0081	00352	0047	0031	0048		007	0046	001	**Portugal P**
81036	81039	810353	81081	810352	81047	81031	81048	810351		81046	8101	**Russia RUS**
0036	0039	00353	0081	00352	0047	0031	0048	00351	007		001	**Sweden S**
01136	01139	011353	01181	011352	01147	01131	01148	011351	*	01146		**USA**

* *Automatische Vorwahl nicht möglich*

Manufacture française des pneumatiques Michelin
Société en commandite par actions au capital de 304 000 000 EUR
Place des Carmes-Déchaux – 63 Clermont-Ferrand (France)
R.C.S. Clermont-Fd B 855 200 507

Michelin et Cie, propriétaires-éditeurs, 2002
Dépôt légal : mars 2002 – ISBN 2.06.100177-7

Printed in France : 03-2002/1

Compogravure : Maury imprimeur S.A., Malesherbes

Impression : Casterman, Tournai

Reliure : SIRC, Marigny-le-Châtel

Illustrations : Nathalie Benavides, Patricia Haubert, Cécile Imbert/MICHELIN
Narratif Systèmes/Genclo, Rodolphe Corbel.